Encyclopedia of Bilingualism and Bilingual Education

Colin Baker and Sylvia Prys Jones
School of Education
University of Wales, Bangor

Multilingual Matters

Cyflwyniad

Cyflwynir y Gwyddoniadur i'n plant, sydd yn rhan o ddyfodol dwyieithrwydd:
Sara, Rhodri ac Arwel Baker; Aled, Ifan a Trefor Jones.

Dedication

The Encyclopedia is dedicated to our children who are part of the future of bilingualism:
Sara, Rhodri and Arwel Baker; Aled, Ifan and Trefor Jones.

Library of Congress Cataloging in Publication Data

Encyclopedia of Bilingualism and Bilingual Education
Colin Baker and Sylvia Prys Jones
Includes bibliographical references and index
1. Education, Bilingual-Encyclopedias. 2. Bilingualism-Encyclopedias
I. Baker, Colin
LC3707.E53 1998
371.97'003-dc20 96-24015

Bntish Library Cataloguing in Publication Data

A CIP catalogue record for this book is available from the British Library.

ISBN 1-85359-362-1

Multilingual Matters Ltd

UK: Frankfurt Lodge, Clevedon Hall, Victoria Road, Clevedon BS21 7HH.
USA: 325 Chestnut Street, Philadelphia, PA 19106, USA.
Canada: OISE, 712 Gordon Baker Road, Toronto, Ontario, Canada M2H 3R7.
Australia: P.O. Box 586, Artamon, NSW, Australia.
South Africa: PO Box 1080, Northcliffe 2115, Johannesburg, South Africa.

Designed and typeset by B.J. Design.
Printed and bound in China by Imago.

Contents

Second Language Learning in Education

APPENDICES

Foreword

Bilingualism is a topic which must be treated on two levels at once – simultaneously as sociology and as psychology, just as learning a second language must be seen both as acquiring a culture and as embracing a new personal identity. Because of this bi-level character, bilingualism rarely gets treated in its full complexity within the covers of any single book, nor within any one lecture or course. There are books about bilingual societies and books about bilingual individuals, but how the latter fit into the former or the former generate the latter is hardly ever directly addressed. Now we know why – because it took an encyclopedia of 500,000 words to do justice to both topics and to their intersection.

Yet the intersection is precisely the intriguing and intractable aspect of bilingualism. The challenge of acquiring Spanish as a second language is entirely different for the Quechua speaker in Cuzco, the English speaker in Los Angeles, and the Catalan speaker in Girona. For learners in Cuzco and Girona, Spanish is the language of power, but power that works to promote loss of Quechua for good Spanish speakers in Peru and vibrant bilingualism for good Spanish speakers in Catalunya. For learners in Los Angeles, Spanish is the language of relative powerlessness; however much high school teachers invoke Cervantes and Garcia Marquez, Spanish in the US is likely to remain identified with poverty, the old ways, and oppression for many of its potential learners. Spanish is essentially the same linguistic system in Peru, the US, and Spain, but differences in its social function have a direct impact on its learnability and on whether its learners end up monolingual in their first or in their second language, or actually become bilingual.

Bilingualism is a field full of paradoxes as well, many of them engagingly exemplified by articles in this encyclopedia. Pope John Paul II and Sophia Loren manage important public functions in any of several different languages learned in adulthood and despite many other obligations, whereas the average foreign language student makes too little progress in several years of study to order a beer or make a hotel reservation using the second language. Children growing up in the third world function in two or three languages before they ever get to school, while children in Japan and the US remain stubbornly monolingual despite intensive (and expensive) foreign language education.

Probing these paradoxes requires having available lots of information about the distribution of languages and their status in the nations of the world, about the use of language in education and about language as a target of education, about learners and their characteristics. The *Encyclopedia of Bilingualism and Bilingual Education* provides readers with this information – with the facts and the concepts needed to understand what is happening when speakers select, use, learn, or avoid a language in the street, in the classroom, and in their own living rooms, across the differently constructed societies of almost 200 nations where more than 6000 different languages are spoken. The rampant bilingualism of today's world, and the pockets of monolingualism within it, are the product of billions of such choices, made throughout history and being made right now. At this moment, languages are dying and languages are being revived because of individual speakers' choices. Bilingualism is growing and bilingualism is receding because of such choices. To understand these processes, whether we wish to track them or to influence them, we need precisely the kinds of information made available through this encyclopedia, in its wealth, its breadth, and its accessibility.

It is a great read too. One can trace the history of Dutch, Russian, Portuguese and other languages during the times they filled the international role held today by English. One can read about how language data are collected through a census, and what the problems are using census data to trace bilingualism. There are language maps and school achievement data. There are anecdotes and analyses. The great unresolved issues are presented and discussed: Whole language or direct instruction in reading? Bilingual education or monolingual for language minority children? Grammar translation or direct methods in foreign language learning? Critical periods for second language learning or not? Language maintenance for tiny language communities or the practical acceptance of a language of wider communication?

I predict the *Encyclopedia of Bilingualism and Bilingual Education* will find its permanent place on the corner of many a scholar's desk – in part, of course, because it is too heavy to be continually lifted out of and back onto the bookshelf. It will be consulted for facts, for references, for definitions, and for purposes of procrastination, as a comprehensive, authoritative, and endlessly entertaining volume on the topic of bilingualism in society and in individuals.

CATHERINE E. SNOW
Cambridge, Massachusetts

Preface

The idea for an *Encyclopedia of Bilingual Education* derived from a meeting with a remarkably astute Pennsylvanian, Bob Rooney of Taylor and Francis, in November 1993 in Philadelphia. The first reaction was that his idea was exciting, enticing and an irresistible challenge. The initial ideas about the Encyclopedia took shape on a plane journey between New York and London. During eight long hours, many lofty ideas were dreamt and scribbled on scraps of paper. This could be an internationally significant event about a subject that is increasingly important.

Upon landing, the project seemed about as sensible as a flight in a lead balloon. How could there be complete coverage, for all manner of people, in all kinds of places, for all sorts of purposes? After all, around two-thirds of the world's population are bilingual. With the rise of the global village, bilingualism and multilingualism, language contact and language learning affect almost all of us. At the same time, the struggle of minority languages against the march of monolithic monolingualism is a battle that is played out in nearly every corner of the world. How could an Encyclopedia provide extensive or even representative coverage of all the world-wide manifestations of bilingualism? There would be a need to steer a careful course between complexity and superficiality, avoiding the opposing perils of over-emphasis and of omission, the academically abstruse and the patronizingly simple.

Loyalty and honor demand that rash promises are met. So, at the beginning of 1994, the commission was accepted and the long journey was commenced. It was clear early on that this should not be an A-to-Z Encyclopedia, nor a Companion or Compendium, nor a coffee-table book of colorful maps and pictures, nor a Dictionary of definitions and concepts. It had to be a bit of all of these, but essentially a resource for all manner of people, in a variety of places, for many different purposes.

The project was completed in three years in the institution that generously hosted and loyally supported the project, namely the School of Education, University of Wales, Bangor. There were day shifts and night shifts, weekends in a study and weekdays locked away in academic cloisters. Over 2000 references were studied, libraries were probed, and international databases searched. The team of three were expert on each new topic for about two weeks. Then we moved on with jet-like pace. There was writing, revising, deleting, editing and editing endlessly again, structuring, re-structuring, cleaning and polishing, integrating and cross-checking. Dealing with 500,000 words was about as easy as piloting an aircraft through a blizzard. The Apple Macs mastered all of this and saved at least another three years of work.

After three years in the writers' Flying Squad, it was on to reviewers: the eminent and the prominent, the perceptive and the helpfully pedantic. This magnificent International All Stars Team found the strengths, and advised constructively on the many weaknesses. The superb feedback provided the rich fuel to complete the remainder of the journey.

Aims

This Encyclopedia is based on a celebration of the colorful diversity of languages in the world. Our civilization has become aware of the need to preserve animals in danger of extinction and conserve forests, flora and fauna. We are in danger of failing to preserve the beauty of diverse languages and cultures. Languages are an important contribution to the richness and variety of our world, and unless conserved, many will decline and die. This Encyclopedia seeks to raise awareness about that language diversity, to help reduce the prejudice and stereotyping that surrounds language minorities, and to communicate the beauty of bilingualism. In doing this, we have aimed to be constructive and optimistic.

The overall aims of the Encyclopedia are twofold: firstly to promote the subject of bilingualism in an attractive, comprehensible and comprehensive manner; and secondly to be academically sound while being accessible to as wide an audience as possible. To achieve this, each topic assumes no previous knowledge and is presented in a clear and understandable style. Since the readership of the Encyclopedia will be international, the aim has been to write in a form of English that is clear, concise and comprehensible. We did not wish to be constrained by a purely academic style (e.g. as found in research reports and scholarly journal articles) and in this, we were profoundly influenced by the style and approach of David Crystal's *Cambridge Encyclopedia of Language* and his *Cambridge Encyclopedia of the English Language*.

Both Encyclopedias combine impressive scholarship with a technique of presentation that is widely intelligible, clear and concise, efficient and lively, popular and erudite. This Encyclopedia aims to follow in that tradition. It is not, by purpose or design, in the style of a work that is alphabetically ordered or written by a multitude of experts on specific topics.

The Encyclopedia contains four sections: (1) Individual Bilingualism; (2) Languages in Society; (3) Languages in Contact in the World: Language Maps of the World; (4) Bilingual Education. Each section contains a large number of topics. Each topic has some central text, often supplemented and illustrated by textboxes, graphics and photographs. To aid understanding, frequent examples are given both in the text and in textboxes. The textboxes are also designed to add interest and fascination to a topic. Photographs and other graphics are included to illustrate the topics, not just to decorate the text.

As in David Crystal's celebrated Encyclopedias, we have not permeated the text with references, in order to ensure a more vigorous and free-running text. However, where specific research has been mentioned, the references are provided. At the end of each topic, further reading is suggested for those who wish to pursue the topic in more detail.

While there is a definite order to the Encyclopedia, cross-referencing allows readers to move around the contents in a non-linear fashion. As far as possible (without too much repetition), each topic is a 'stand-alone', self-contained entity, allowing readers to study individual topics without specific reference to previous ones. The book could be read from cover to cover, but is primarily designed to be dipped into for shorter or longer periods.

No Encyclopedia is complete. This Encyclopedia could have been compiled in many different ways by different people – all worthwhile, all including something different. Each topic in this Encyclopedia has been the subject of many books and scholarly articles. Difficult choices have had to be made about: inclusion and exclusion; how much detail to include; the order of presentation; what to place earlier or later; what style of writing to use; what knowledge can be assumed of most readers and what needs a little more explanation. In any attempt to be comprehensive, it is easy to locate sins of omission and over-emphasis, superficiality and complexity. However, we have attempted to balance psychological, sociolinguistic, geolinguistic, educational, linguistic and cross-disciplinary perspectives, whilst making the contents interesting, lively and easily understood.

The goal has also been to share different perspectives. We have sought to represent the views of language minorities and language majorities faithfully, and to represent different political agendas. The technicalities of research studies and theoretical intricacies of the contributing disciplines (e.g. Linguistics, Sociology, Psychology) are often relayed in a relatively simple manner, and occasionally excluded, to maintain a more widely appealing text. For those who wish to dig deeper, a Bibliography of over 2000 entries is provided at the end of the Encyclopedia, in addition to the 'Further Reading' at the end of each topic.

Another thousand pages would not complete this Encyclopedia. Nor would another hundred years of writing. For the moment, as Samuel Johnson wryly remarked when making a defense against the triumph of destructive criticism, this is only a failure in an attempt to journey into the unknown.

Acknowledgements

The number of people who assisted us in this venture were multitudinous. We wish to express our great appreciation especially to the following:

Catherine Snow for writing the Foreword.

Those who acted as Consulting Editors for the Encyclopedia:
Don Cartwright, David Crystal, Manjula Datta, John Edwards, Viv Edwards, Ofelia García, François Grosjean, Charlotte Hoffmann, Nobuyuki Honna, Christer Laurén, John Maher, Casmir Rubagumya, Margaret Secombe, J.J. Smolicz, Richard Tucker and Colin Williams.

Those who gave of their expertise with particular topics, queries or requests:
The Agrawal family, Dr. Michelle Aldridge-Waddon, Rehana Ali, Professor Hugo Baetens Beardsmore, Michael Berthold, Evelyne Billey-Lichon, Bwrdd yr Iaith Gymraeg, Val Baker, Vanessa Birley, Camilla Haugen Cai, Professor Lawrence Carrin, Dr. Gitu Chakravarthy, CILT, Elizabeth Coelho, Christine Coker, James Crawford, Professor Jim Cummins, Maria Dias, Annette Davis, Dr. Bryn Lewis Davies, Professor Nancy Dorian, John Dorricott, Ambassador Norma Dumont, ECIS, Lord Dafydd Elis-Thomas, Rhian Ellis, Professor Rod Ellis, European Schools Organization, Canon Trefor and Mrs Chris Evans, Professor Joshua Fishman, Professor Ofelia García, Professor Robert Gardner, Peter Garrett, Professor Fred Genesee, Professor Howard Giles, Marjukka Grover, Mike Grover, Gwynedd Language and Speech Therapists, Ken Hall, Christine Helot, Professor Nancy Hornberger, Elisabeth Lundberg, Helen O Murchú, Dr. Ann Illsley, Dr. Paul Ghuman, Bob Jones, Dr. Geraint Wyn Jones, Glyn Tudwal Jones, Gwilym Trefor Jones, John Gwynedd Jones, John Walter Jones, Lesley Terfel Jones, Dr. Marion Giles Jones, Meirion Prys Jones, Myfanwy Bennett Jones, Dr. Prys Morgan Jones, Twm Prys Jones, Professor Stephen Krashen, Dr. Jim Kyle, Professor Christer Laurén, Professor Wallace Lambert, Linguaphone, Professor W.F. Mackay, Professor Ken MacKinnon, Dr. Seham Malallah, Professor Michael Marland, Stephen May, Professor Teresa McCarty, Heather McLeay, MEU Cymru, Dr. Delyth Morris, Helen Myers-Halling, Professor Hans Peter Nelde, North Wales Police, Dilys Parry, Andre Obadia, Professor Hideo Oka, Professor Denis O'Sullivan, Martin Owen, Professor Christina Bratt Paulston, Delyth Prys, Den and Ann Rees, Edward Thomas Roberts, Chief Superintendent Elfed Roberts, Professor Suzanne Romaine, Bob Rooney, Gwenllïan Rowlinson, Anne Sanderson, Barry Sanderson, Professor Elana Shohamy, Dr. Tove Skutnabb-Kangas, Professor J.J. Smolicz, Professor Bernard Spolsky, Surval Mont-Fleuri, Professor Merrill Swain, TERM-CAT, Alun Waddon, Professor Terry Wiley, Dr. Glyn Williams, Dr. Cen Williams, Professor Colin Williams, Professor Iolo Wyn Williams, Rhian Williams & Meithrhian, Philip Wilson, WJEC, and Ysgol Pendalar.

To all these, we offer our great appreciation and heartfelt thanks.

A special note of deep gratitude goes to Professor Iolo Wyn Williams who helped find the finance needed for this project, and to Anwen Baker who provided much needed assistance and support. We would also like to thank Professor Williams for contributing the evocative *englynion* which appear on the following page.

Encyclopedia Research Assistant

Non Heledd Ioan

The cartography, graphics and a substantial portion of the text of Section Three were contributed by Non Heledd Ioan, a Research Assistant in the School of Education, University of Wales, Bangor from 1995 to 1997.

Dwyieithrwydd / Bilingualism

These *englynion* were written by the Dean of the Faculty of Education at the University of Wales, Bangor, Professor Iolo Wyn Williams.

The *englyn* is a traditional Welsh four-line verse form, written in *cynghanedd,* composed according to strict rules and including a combination of alliteration, assonance and internal rhyme.

Ynys yw'r genedl uniaith – ynys bur,
Ynys bell, anghyfiaith;
Mwy croesawgar ei haraith
Ydyw un sydd â dwy iaith.

Hen alaw a chyfeiliant – a gafael
Ar gyfoeth mynegiant;
Trysor oes, heb loes, i blant
Yw allwedd dau ddiwylliant.

Mae lle sbâr i iaith arall – yn y cof,
Mae'r cof yn anniwall;
Nid mwy yw dwy i'w deall –
Oni all un hogi'r llall?

Iolo Wyn Williams

The country with one language is an island – a pure island,
A far, untranslatable island
The one which has two languages
Has a more welcoming speech.

An old melody and an accompaniment – and a grasp
Of the richness of expression.
The key to two cultures is
For children a lifelong treasure, without pain.

There is room for another language – in the memory.
The memory is insatiable.
Two are not harder to understand.
Can one not stimulate the other?

SECTION ONE

INDIVIDUAL BILINGUALISM

'We bring up children to be bilinguals,
not for the sake of language, but
for the sake of children.'

Adapted from Ioan Bowen Rees

Who is Bilingual?

1: Defining Bilingualism

Introduction

'Who is a bilingual?' 'How can a bilingual person be defined?' Most people would say that they know the answers to these questions. They would say that a bilingual is a person who can speak two languages.

However, defining who is and who is not bilingual is a more difficult task than first appears. There will be a lack of agreement about the answers to the following selection of questions.

- Is bilingualism measured by how fluent people are in two languages? Do bilinguals have to be as competent in each of their two languages as monolingual speakers?

Hispanic College Students in the US who speak Spanish at home and to Hispanic friends and relatives. However, their education and wider social contacts are often in English.

- If someone is considerably less fluent in one language than the other, should that person be classed as bilingual? Are bilinguals only those people who have more or less equal competence in both languages?

- Is ability in two languages the only criterion for assessing bilingualism, or should the use of two languages also be considered? For instance, a person who speaks a second language fluently but rarely uses it may be classed as a bilingual. What about the person who does not speak a second language fluently but makes regular use of it?

- Most people would define a bilingual as a person who can speak two languages. What about a person who can understand a second language perfectly but cannot speak it? What about a person who can speak a second language but is not literate in it? What about an individual who cannot speak or understand speech in a second language but can read and write it? Should these categories of people be considered bilingual?

- Is 'bilingual' a label people give themselves? Should self-perception and self-categorization be pre-eminent? Often people who do not speak a second language very fluently, or who are not literate in that language, lack the confidence to describe themselves as bilingual. Should a person's self-assessment be the yardstick?

- Is bilingualism a state that changes or varies over time and according to circumstances? Obviously a person can change from being a monolingual to being a bilingual by acquiring a second language. Can a person progress from bilingualism to monolingualism by forgetting a second language? Are there different degrees of bilingualism that can vary over time and with changing circumstances? Can a person be more or less bilingual.

Issues in Individual Bilingualism

The above questions indicate that there is no simple definition of bilingualism. Bilingualism involves a number of

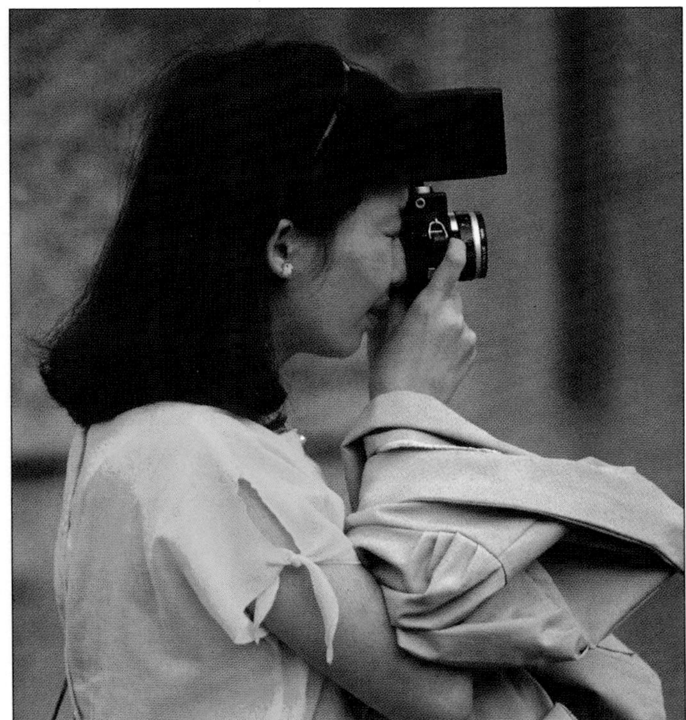

A young Japanese tourist in London. Can we class as a bilingual a tourist who is beginning to learn a foreign language?

dimensions. If we ask an individual about his or her bilingualism we are really raising not one issue but several.

First, there is a distinction between ability in language and use of language. A person may be able to speak two languages, but tends to speak only one language in practice. Alternatively, an individual may regularly speak two languages but has a halting fluency in one language. People's ability or proficiency in two languages may be separate from their use of two languages. This is sometimes referred to as the difference between degree (proficiency or competence in a language) and function (actual use of two languages).

Second, an individual's proficiency in a language may vary across the four language skills of speaking, listening, reading and writing. An individual may use one language for conversation and be fluent in speaking that language. However, he or she switches to another language for reading and writing. Another person may understand a second language very well, in its spoken and written form, but may not be able to speak or write it well, if at all. Such a person can be said to have a passive or receptive competence in a second language.

Third, few bilinguals are equally proficient in both languages, even though this is often thought to be the case. One language tends to be stronger and better developed than the other. This is described as the dominant language. It is not always the first or native language of the bilingual.

Fourth, few bilinguals possess the same competence as monolingual speakers in either of their languages.This is because bilinguals use their languages for different functions and purposes.

Fifth, a bilingual person's competence in a language may vary over time and according to changing circumstances. For instance, a person may learn a minority language as a child at home and then later acquire another, majority language in the community or at school. Over time, the second language may become the stronger or dominant language. If that person moves away from the neighborhood or area where the minority language is spoken, or loses contact with those who speak it, he or she may lose fluency in the minority language. (See page 99 for a discussion of majority and minority languages).

These five main issues show how difficult it would be to create any concise and all-inclusive definition of a bilingual person. They also show that many degrees of bilingualism may exist, sometimes varying in the same person over time. These issues will be discussed more fully in the remainder of this section.

Bilingualism in Society

Bilingualism exists as a possession of an individual. It is also possible to talk about bilingualism as a characteristic of a group or community of people. Bilinguals and multilinguals are most often located in groups, communities or in a particular region (e.g. Catalans in Spain). Some bilinguals live in smaller clusters (e.g. some of the Chinese who are scattered in many communities across the United States). In Britain, there is both scattering and communities, even among the same language group. For example, there are strong Gujarati communities in Brent (London), Panjabis in Bradford, and Bengalis in Tower Hamlets (London), as well as a considerable scattering across UK urban areas. Thus, there is no language without the existence of a language community. However, co-existing languages may be in a process of rapid change, living in harmony or one rapidly advancing at the cost of the other, or sometimes in conflict. Where many language minorities exist, there is often language shift (see page 150).

Thus an important distinction is between bilingualism as an individual possession and societal bilingualism. Some psychologists and educationists are particularly interested in bilingualism as it exists within an individual person. Geographers, political scientists, social psycho-

Leonard Bloomfield

Leonard Bloomfield (1887-1949) played a major role in establishing linguistics as an independent discipline in the United States. He was originally trained in Germanic philology, but spent many years analyzing and describing the Austronesian languages of New Guinea and Native American languages. His book *Language* (1933) analyzed language as a series of structures. He called for a reform in the teaching of modern languages, and outlined his beliefs in a book *An Outline Guide for the Practical Study of Foreign Languages* (1942). He himself was responsible for the preparation of materials for learning Dutch, German and Russian.

In Bloomfield's book *Language*, he gave the following definition of bilingualism, which has become famous. It is a severe and highly contentious definition, particularly in its concern with proficiency in monolingual 'native-like' terms.

> *In the extreme case of foreign language learning, the speaker becomes so proficient as to be indistinguishable from the native speakers round him. ...In the cases where this perfect foreign language learning is not accompanied by loss of the native language, it results in bilingualism, (the) native-like control of two languages.* (pages 55-56).

Hugo Baetens Beardsmore

Hugo Baetens Beardsmore lives and works in Brussels, Belgium. He is an internationally distinguished author, writing in English, French and German. His books and over 100 other publications encompass a wide field of study: bilingual education, English linguistics, the sociology of language, individual bilingualism, multilingual television and language planning to name but a few.

One of Hugo Baetens Beardsmore's most highly acclaimed publications was *Bilingualism: Basic Principles* (1982) which ran to a revised second edition in 1986. This was one of the first European publications that brought together a disparate mass of material on bilingualism and created a well organized and structured introduction to the subject. As the quotation below reveals, there was a gap in the literature. The book *Bilingualism: Basic Principles* (1982) filled that gap with great success.

Hugo Baetens Beardsmore received his higher education from the University of Wales and is now Professor of English and Bilingualism at the Vrije Universiteit in Brussels and Dean of the Faculty of Arts. He has been a visiting Professor in California, Singapore, Brunei and Hong Kong, and a consultant to many international bodies, including the European Commission (EEC) and the Council of Europe.

Hugo Baetens Beardsmore begins his 'Introduction' to *Bilingualism: Basic Principles* (1982) with the following:

> *As with so many introductory works the present book grew out of a pressing need. Although there is a plethora of titles in the field of bilingualism, as the bibliography at the end of this book attests, there is no single introductory work to the study of bilingualism that is readily accessible or easily digestible. When I was faced with teaching a course on the subject it proved impossible to find a suitable introductory guide in English that would lead into the more refined theory and experimentation currently developing with ever increasing momentum. Indeed, there are relatively few general works on the topic at all.* (page vii).

Father and son of an Italian in-migrant family outside their meat store in Little Italy, New York. Levels of bilingualism may vary within families. A common pattern in in-migrant families is that the parent's generation are more competent in their native tongue while the children, often born and educated in the new country, become more fluent in the majority language of that country.

logists, policy makers and sociolinguists are interested in bilingualism as it exists within societies. While the distinction is important, the interconnections between individual bilingualism and societal bilingualism are many. The attitudes of individuals towards a minority language, for example, may affect the maintenance, restoration, or demise of that language as it exists in a speech community.

The term bilingualism is usually reserved to describe two languages within an individual. When the focus is on two languages in society, the term 'diglossia' is often used. Hence the rest of this section concerns individual bilingualism. A separate section on languages in society is presented later (see page 96).

Further Reading

BAETENS BEARDSMORE, H., 1986, *Bilingualism: Basic Principles*. Clevedon: Multilingual Matters Ltd.

HOFFMANN, C., 1991, *An Introduction to Bilingualism*. London: Longman.

SKUTNABB-KANGAS, T., 1981, *Bilingualism or Not: The Education of Minorities*. Clevedon: Multilingual Matters Ltd.

Terms Used to Describe the Abilities of Individual Bilinguals

When talking about somebody's ability with a language, a range of different terms is used: language ability, language achievement, language competence, language performance, language proficiency and language skills. Do they all refer to the same idea, or are there subtle distinctions between these terms?

Language skills tend to refer to highly specific, observable, clearly definable components such as handwriting, spelling and grammar. In contrast, language competence is a broad and general term, used particularly to describe an inner, mental representation of language, something latent rather than overt. Such competence refers usually to an underlying system inferred from language performance. Language performance is the outward evidence (e.g. from language tests, conversations) for language competence. By observing general language comprehension and production, underlying language competence may be assumed.

Language ability and language proficiency tend to be used more as 'umbrella' terms and therefore used somewhat ambiguously. For some, the term 'language ability' represents a general, latent disposition, a determinant of eventual language success. Others use it to mean an outcome, similar but less specific than language skills, providing an indication of current language level. Similarly, the term 'language proficiency' is sometimes used synonymously with language competence; at other times to mean a specific, measurable outcome from language testing.

Both language proficiency and language ability are distinct from language achievement (attainment). Language achievement is normally seen as the outcome of formal instruction. Language proficiency and language ability are, in contrast, viewed as the products of a variety of mechanisms: formal learning, informal uncontrived language acquisition (e.g. at home, on the street) and of individual characteristics such as 'intelligence' and an 'aptitude for languages'

2: The Advantages and Disadvantages of Bilingualism

Current writing and research suggests that there are many advantages and few disadvantages in becoming bilingual. Eight overlapping and interacting benefits are often cited for a bilingual person, encompassing communicative, cognitive and cultural advantages.

Communication Advantages

Relationships with parents

Where parents have differing first languages, the advantage of children becoming bilingual is that they will be able to communicate in each parent's preferred language. This may enable a subtler, finer texture of relationship with the parent. Alternatively, they will be able to communicate with parents in one language and with their friends and within the community in a different language.

For many mothers and fathers, it is important for them to be able to speak to a child in their first language. Many parents can only communicate with full intimacy, naturally and expressively in their first (or preferred or dominant) language. A child who speaks to one parent in one language and to the other parent in another language may be enabling an optimally close relationship with the parents. At the same time, both parents are passing to that child part of their past, part of their heritage.

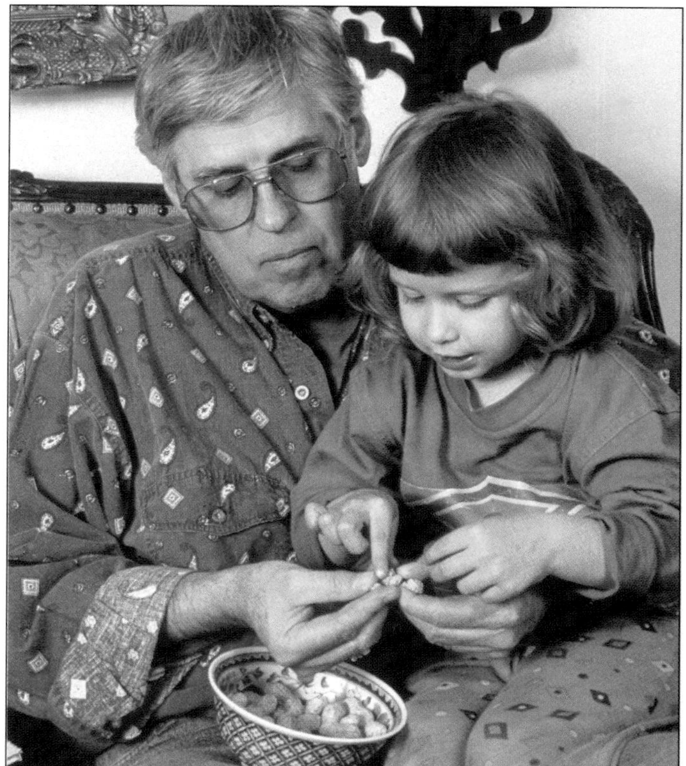

Bilingualism can create a bridge between generations.

Extended family relationships

Being a bilingual allows someone to bridge the generations. When grandparents, uncles, aunts and other relatives in another region speak a language that is different from the local language, the monolingual may be unable to communicate with them. The bilingual has the chance of bridging that generation gap, building closer relationships with relatives, and feeling a sense of belonging and rootedness within the extended family.

Children in families who speak a minority language (with the majority language being used outside the home), have the advantage of carrying forward the heritage language of the family and all the intimacy and rootedness involved. The monolingual without the heritage language of the family (sometimes also called the ancestral or native language) may feel a sense of alienation from relatives and from the past. Bilingualism often contributes to the sense of continuity of a family across generations.

Community relationships

A bilingual has the chance of communicating with a wider variety of people than a monolingual. Bilingual children will be able to communicate in the wider community and with school and neighborhood friends without problems.

When traveling within a country, in neighboring countries and internationally, bilinguals have the advantage that their languages may provide bridges to new relationships. While monolinguals are able to communicate with a variety of people in one language, they have more limited opportunities to build relationships with people of other nationalities and ethnic groups.

Transnational communication

One barrier between nations and ethnic groups tends to be language. Language is sometimes a barrier to communication and to creating friendly relationships of mutual respect. Bilinguals in the home, in the community and in society have the potential of lowering such barriers. Bilinguals can act as bridges within the nuclear and

Jeddah airport, Saudi Arabia. Competence in other languages is an aid in international travel.

extended family, within the community and across societies.

Language sensitivity

Being able to move between two languages may lead to more sensitivity in communication. Because bilinguals are constantly monitoring which language to use in different situations, they may be more attuned to the communicative needs of those with whom they talk. Research suggests that bilinguals may be more empathic with listeners' needs in communication. When meeting those who do not speak their language particularly well, bilinguals may be more patient listeners than monolinguals.

Cultural Advantages

Another advantage of being a bilingual is having two or more worlds of experience. Bilingualism provides the opportunity to experience two or more cultures. The monolingual may experience a variety of cultures – from different neighbors and communities, who use the same language but have different ways of life. The monolingual can also travel to neighboring countries and experience other cultures as a passive onlooker. But to penetrate different cultures requires the language of that culture. To participate and become involved in the core of a culture requires a knowledge of the language of that culture.

With each language go different systems of behavior, folk sayings, stories, histories, traditions, ways of meeting and greeting, rituals of birth, marriage and death, ways of conversing, different literatures, music, forms of entertainment, religious traditions, ways of understanding and interpreting the world, ideas and beliefs, ways of thinking and drinking, crying and loving, eating and caring, ways of joking and mourning. With two languages goes a wider cultural experience. The bilingual has an improved chance of actively penetrating the cultures expressed in both languages. However, to be bilingual is not automatically to be bicultural. Bilingualism provides the potential for, but not the guarantee of biculturalism.

There are potential economic advantages to being bilingual. A person with two languages may have a wider portfolio of jobs available. As economic trade barriers fall, as international relationships become closer, as unions and partnerships across nations become more widespread, an increasing number of jobs are likely to require a person to be bilingual or multilingual. Jobs in multinational companies, jobs selling and exporting, and employment prospects generated by the European Union make the future of employment more versatile for bilinguals than monolinguals.

In Britain and Catalonia, for example, knowledge of the minority language is required in particular geographical areas to obtain teaching and administrative posts, for translation work in law courts, and is of prime value in business and commerce. Bilingualism does not guarantee a meal ticket or future affluence. However, as the global village rises and international trade increases, bilinguals and multilinguals may be in a relatively strong position in the race for employment. For example, when India lifts its trade barriers, the language proficiencies of Indian minorities in Britain and North America could be used in business negotiations. Such proficiencies can

A Chinese-American girl in New York. A 'hyphenated identity' can be an enrichment.

provide entry into a market, help establish effective working relationships, and ensure swift and efficient communication. On a more personal level, there can be a sense of partnership derived from a shared language, common understandings and shared nuances of meaning.

Cognitive Advantages

Apart from social, cultural, economic, personal relationship and communication advantages, research has shown that bilinguals may have some advantages in thinking (see page 62). Possible advantages range from creative thinking, to faster progress in early cognitive development and greater sensitivity in communication. For example, bilinguals have two or more words for each object and idea. This means that the link between a word and its concept is usually looser. Sometimes corresponding words in different languages have different connotations. For example, having two (or more) words for folk dancing, one in English the other in, for example, Spanish or Swahili, Portuguese or Panjabi, will extend the range of meanings, associations and images.

When slightly different associations are attached to each word, the bilingual may be able to think more flexibly and creatively than a monolingual (see page 66). Therefore, a bilingual has the possibility of more awareness of language and more fluency, flexibility and elaboration in thinking than a monolingual.

The Disadvantages of Bilingualism

It would be false and misleading to suggest that there are never any disadvantages to bilingualism. Some problems, both individual and social, may be falsely attributed to bilingualism. When children exhibit language problems (e.g. delayed speech), or personality problems (e.g. low self-esteem, concerns about self-identity), bilingualism is sometimes blamed. Problems such as social unrest may unfairly be attributed to the presence of two languages in a community.

Educational failure may also be wrongly attributed to bilingualism. For instance, if a child lacks success at school, the parent or teacher of the monolingual child may lay the blame with the child's motivation, intelligence, personality, the standard of teaching, or the school itself. The parent of the bilingual child may think of all these causes, but add to them the child's bilingualism as another major potential cause. However, bilingualism of itself does not cause educational failure. These are examples of problems that are wrongly attributed to bilingualism. What are the real possible disadvantages?

There will be a temporary disadvantage if a child's two languages are both underdeveloped. One crucial definition of underdevelopment is that, for a short time, a child is unable to cope with the school curriculum in either language. When this occurs, it is the 'disadvantaged' social and educational context surrounding the bilingual that creates the problem, not bilingualism itself. Such underdevelopment infrequently occurs, but it is important that it should be remedied.

A potential problem or challenge is the amount of effort often required by some parents to raise bilingual children. For some parents, the route children take to full bilingualism is relatively straightforward and uncomplicated. This is usually the case in bilingual or multilingual communities where most children acquire two, three or even more languages quite naturally. For other parents, the task might be more of a challenge. This might be the case where monolingual parents are attempting to foster bilingualism in their children, or alternatively, where bilingual parents try to raise their children bilingually in largely monolingual communities. However, the individual, cognitive, social, cultural, intellectual and economic advantages given to the child via bilingualism make all the effort worthwhile.

A third problem area tends to be with the identity of a bilingual (although this is a problem about biculturalism rather than bilingualism). If children have both a French and an English parent and speak each language fluently, are they French, English or Anglo-French? If such children speak English and a minority language such as Welsh, are they Welsh, English, British, European, Anglo-Welsh or what? If parents regularly move (e.g. due to the nature of their employment), does the child find adaptation to a new culture and language difficult? Does the child have difficulties in identification with any specific reference group?

This raises the issue of multiple identities. We all have multiple identities. A woman may have the identities of mother, javelin thrower, church-goer, company executive, daughter and grand-daughter, expert on Chilean wines, wife and client in counseling. We all move in and out of a selection of roles in different contexts, with varied audiences and diverse supporting players. Having two or more languages can add to the number of sub-identities of a person (see page 24).

For many individuals, identity is not a problem. While speaking two languages they are resolutely identified with one ethnic or cultural group. For example, many bilinguals in Wales see themselves as Welsh first, possibly British next but not English. Being able to speak the English language is important. However, it is anathema to be considered 'English'.

At the other end of the spectrum are some in-migrants (see the Glossary page 698). Sometimes, the first or second generation in-migrants desperately want to identify with the majority language people and culture. They may actively want to lose the identity of their home or heritage language. For example, in the United States, Spanish speakers from Mexico, Cuba or Puerto Rico, sometimes want to assimilate and become monolingual English-speaking Americans. They want to lose the identity of their native country, and be as American as any monolingual, monocultural American.

Between the two extremes presented above, there are potential cases of identity crisis and conflict. There are some bilinguals who feel both English and French, Spanish and Catalan, Mexican and American. There are some people who feel quite happy being culturally hyphenated (e.g. Swedish-Finns, Anglo-French, Chinese-Malaysians, Italian-Americans). There will be others who feel uncomfortable moving between two identities. Bilinguals may ask: am I Asian, am I British or am I Asian-British? Am I Swedish, am I Finnish or am I Swedish-Finnish? Am I Chinese as if I came from China, like the Chinese scattered throughout the world, or a Malaysian-Chinese? Am I Italian, American or some integrated or uneasy combination of these? A danger is never feeling that one belongs fully to either one group or the other.

Identity crises and conflicts are never static. Identities change and evolve over time, with varying experience, interaction and collaboration within and outside a language group. An example is certain in-migrants into Britain who initially tended to identify themselves as Asians. Over time this has changed, and many identify themselves as British Asians.

Such identity conflicts are not inevitably the result of language. It is possible to own two languages and not have such identity conflicts (see page 26). However, languages are clearly a contributor. Languages enable a person to participate in two or more cultures, to think and act within two different ethnic groups, to identify with each group or neither group. Language is a vehicle through which an identity conflict may arise. Self-identity, cultural identity and ethnic identity can be a problem for some bilinguals.

Further Reading

BAKER, C., 1996, *Foundations of Bilingual Education and Bilingualism*. Clevedon: Multilingual Matters Ltd.

EDWARDS, J., 1994, *Multilingualism*. New York: Routledge.

GROSJEAN, F., 1982, *Life with Two Languages*. Cambridge, MA: Harvard University Press.

GROSJEAN, F., 1994, Individual Bilingualism. In R. E. ASHER & J. M. SIMPSON (eds), *The Encyclopedia of Language and Linguistics* (Volume 3). Oxford: Pergamon.

SKUTNABB-KANGAS T., 1981, *Bilingualism or Not: The Education of Minorities*. Clevedon: Multilingual Matters Ltd.

3: Two Views of Bilinguals: Two Halves or One Whole?

An argument advanced by François Grosjean (1985, 1994) is that there are two contrasting views of bilinguals. First, there is a fractional view of bilinguals, which evaluates the bilingual as 'two monolinguals in one person'. There is a second, holistic view which argues that the bilingual is not the sum of two complete or incomplete monolinguals, but has a unique linguistic profile. While these are not the only views of bilinguals that are possible, the contrast between them underlines some important points.

The Monolingual or Fractional View of Bilingualism

Many teachers, administrators, politicians and researchers look at the bilingual as two monolinguals in one person. For example, if English is a bilingual's second language, scores on an English reading or English attainment test will normally be compared against monolingual averages and norms. A bilingual's English language competence is measured against that of a native monolingual English speaker. Is this fair? Should a bilingual be expected to show the language fluency and proficiency of a monolingual?

One consequence is that the definition of a bilingual will be restricted to those who are equally fluent in their two languages, with proficiency comparable to that of a monolingual. If that competence or proficiency does not exist in both languages, especially in the majority language, then bilinguals may be denigrated and classed as inferior. In the United States, for example, children of

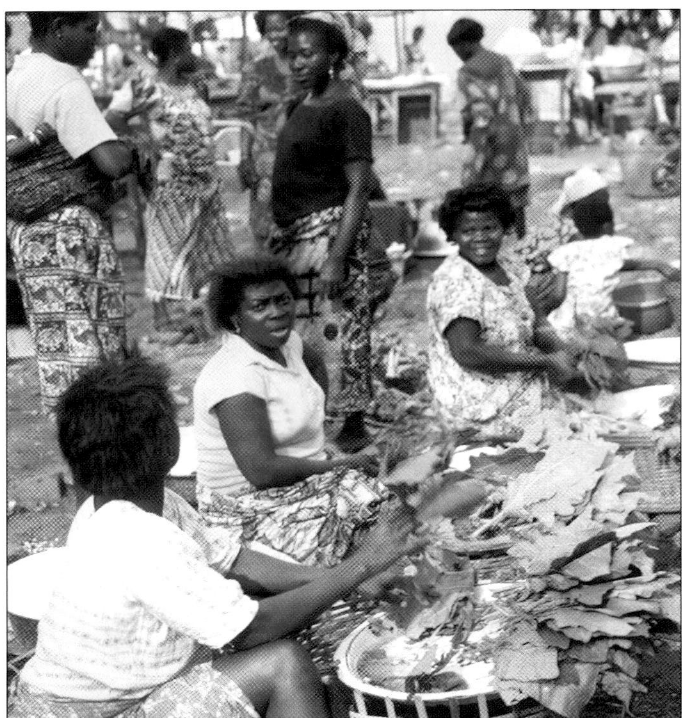

A market place in the African country of Ghana. In countries of Africa and Asia, bilingualism or multilingualism is often the norm. Forty-five indigenous languages are spoken in Ghana, as well as English, the official language. Many Ghanaians speak at least two or three languages; their own native language, one or more regional languages and English, mainly learnt through education.

in-migrant families, or of other language minority families, have sometimes officially been categorized as LEP (Limited English Proficient). Bilinguals who appear to exhibit a lack of proficiency in both languages may be described as 'semilingual'. When tests are used to compare bilinguals' proficiency in either of their languages with monolinguals, such tests don't take into account that bilinguals will often use their two languages in different situations and with different people.

While areas such as Africa, India and Asia see bilingualism as the norm, in countries such as the United States and England in particular, the dominant view of the world is monolingual. Although between a half and two-thirds of the world's population is bilingual to some degree, the monolingual is seen as normal in these two countries, and the bilingual as an exception, if not an oddity. This monolingual view of bilinguals often holds that there will be negative consequences in cognitive processing for bilinguals, because of the potential confusion between what monolinguals perceive as two underdeveloped languages.

Many bilinguals themselves feel they are not sufficiently competent in one or both of their languages compared with monolinguals, thus accepting and reinforcing the monolingual view of bilinguals. A bilingual may apologize to monolinguals for not speaking their language as well as do the monolinguals. Bilinguals may feel shy and embarrassed when using one of their languages in public among monolinguals in that language. Some bilinguals strive hard to reach monolingual standards in the majority language, even to the point of avoiding opportunities to use their minority language.

The Holistic View of Bilingualism

François Grosjean presents a more positive alternative view of bilinguals. Monolinguals should not be used as the point of reference as comparing bilinguals and monolinguals does not compare like with like. Grosjean uses an analogy from the world of athletics, and asks whether we can fairly judge a sprinter or a high jumper against a hurdler. The sprinter and high jumper concentrate on one event and may excel in it. The hurdler concentrates on two different skills, trying to combine a high standard in both. With only a few exceptions, the hurdler will be unable to sprint as fast as the sprinter or jump as high as the high jumper. This is not to say that the hurdler is a worse athlete than the other two. Any comparison of who is the best athlete makes little sense. This analogy suggests that comparing the language proficiency of a monolingual with a bilingual's dual language or multilingual proficiency is similarly unjust.

However, this raises the question, should bilinguals only be measured and compared by reference to other bilinguals? When for example, someone learns English as a second language, should that competency in English-only be measured against other bilinguals? This is obviously not a practical proposition. In countries like Wales for instance, where first language Welsh-speaking children will have to compete in a largely English language job market against monolingual English speakers, the only realistic view is that they should be given the same English assessments at school. However, Grosjean stresses that any assessment of a bilingual's language proficiency should ideally move away from the traditional language tests with their emphasis on form and correctness, and to an evaluation of the bilingual's general communicative competence. This appraisal would be based on a totality of the bilingual's language usage in all domains, whether this involves the choice of one language in a particular domain, or a mixing of the two languages.

There is sometimes a political reality that prevents a holistic view of the bilingual. In Australasia, most of Canada, the United States and Great Britain, the dominant English-speaking monolingual politicians and administrators will not accept a different approach or

François Grosjean

Professor François Grosjean is perhaps best known for his book *Life with Two Languages: An Introduction to Bilingualism,* first published in 1982. The book has become a 'classic', because of its comprehensive and perceptive study of bilingualism.

François Grosjean was born in 1946 in Paris, the son of a British mother and a French father. As a young child, he spoke only French, but at the age of seven he was sent to an English boarding school in Switzerland where he was immersed in English. The staff and other children at the school were friendly and supportive, and thus the experience was not at all traumatic.

At the age of 14, he was sent to a boarding school in England where he remained until he was 18. He found this change culturally difficult and could not adapt completely to a monocultural English environment. At 18, he returned to Paris to attend university, but, after 11 years spent in English language schooling, it took him a considerable time to adapt linguistically and especially culturally to life in France. This tension between the two languages and cultures is the reason why he could write about the bilingual situation with such personal insight and awareness several years later in the book *Life with Two Languages.*

At university, François Grosjean specialized in psycholinguistics and, in 1974, he moved to the United States with his French wife, Lysiane, and their baby son, Marc, to help establish a psycholinguistics laboratory at Northeastern University. They stayed for 12 years. Marc quickly picked up English and so did his little brother Eric, born in the United States. Although the parents always spoke French to one another, the monolingual English environment outside the home meant that the children grew up speaking only English, with a limited comprehension of French. When the family moved to Switzerland for a year, in 1982, the boys quickly picked up French and more or less forgot their English for a while. These experiences, which are retold using pseudonyms in *Life with Two Languages,* gave François Grosjean further insights into the realities of bilingualism. In 1986, the family left the United States when he was appointed Professor of Psycholinguistics at the University of Neuchâtel in Switzerland.

François Grosjean has devoted much research time to language processing in bilinguals, and has consistently advocated a holistic view of bilingualism, which maintains that the bilingual should not be evaluated or appraised as the sum of two complete or incomplete monolinguals within one person, but as an individual with a unique and specific linguistic configuration. The bilingual should be viewed or evaluated in terms of his or her total linguistic repertoire, which involves the totality of language use in all domains of life and for all purposes, whether one language or the other is used separately, or both together as in codemixing and codeswitching.

Life with Two Languages: An Introduction to Bilingualism

Professor Grosjean conceived the idea of writing this book when he was asked to teach a course on bilingualism in the United States and realized that there were no books that provided a general and comprehensive introduction to the subject. His aim was to write on bilingualism in a personal way and from a bilingual's point of view. Professor Einar Haugen, the renowned scholar of linguistics, bilingualism and Scandinavian languages, himself the bilingual son of Norwegian in-migrants to the US, provided support and editorial advice for the book. Professor Grosjean felt that Haugen was, of all the authors on bilingualism, the most 'human', in the sense that he was concerned with the individual bilingual, and Grosjean tried to follow his example in the book.

The book gives a valuable overview of bilingualism in various countries, from the official multilingualism of countries like Switzerland, where the vast majority of the population are monolingual in one of the official languages, to the practical multilingualism of many African and Eastern countries. The book discusses aspects of bilingualism in society generally, covering such topics as attitudes to language groups and to languages, diglossia, language domains and language choice. The latter part of the book deals with individual bilingualism, the development of bilingualism in childhood, language dominance and language processing by bilinguals, interlanguage, borrowing and codeswitching.

The book owes its success not only to its comprehensiveness and clarity, but also because it is written by a bilingual and is firmly rooted in authentic experiences. The text is augmented by numerous textboxes, describing bilingual situations in various countries, and also giving short, first-hand accounts of the personal experiences of bilingual and multilingual individuals.

standard of assessment (one for monolinguals, another for bilinguals). And if there is a double approach, will less be expected of bilinguals in their school achievement? Will bilinguals be expected to under-perform? This is discussed on page 570.

Yet the bilingual is a complete linguistic entity, an integrated whole. Bilinguals use their two languages with different people, in different contexts and for different purposes. Levels of proficiency in a language may depend on which contexts (e.g. street and home) and how often that language is used. Communicative competence in one of a bilingual's two languages may be stronger in some domains than in others. This is natural and to be expected. Any test of a bilingual's competence in two languages needs to be sensitive to such differences of when, where and with whom bilinguals use either of their languages.

Further Reading

GROSJEAN, F., 1985, The Bilingual as a Competent but Specific Speaker-Hearer. *Journal of Multilingual and Multicultural Development,* 6, 467-477.

GROSJEAN, F., 1994, Individual Bilingualism. In R. E. ASHER & J. M. SIMPSON (eds), *The Encyclopedia of Language and Linguistics* (Volume 3). Oxford: Pergamon.

4: Balanced Bilinguals

One of the myths of bilingualism is that a bilingual person has two, equally well developed languages. In reality, bilinguals will rarely have a balance between their two languages. Terms such as balanced bilinguals (or related terms such as equilingual or ambilingual) are idealized concepts that do not relate to the great majority of bilingual people throughout the world. Rarely will anyone be equally competent in speaking, reading or writing both languages across all different situations and domains. Nor do people's languages stay constant over time.

A Welsh-medium school. A bilingual may have oral competence in two languages but be literate in only one.

The literal interpretation of balanced bilinguals may include those who are less than proficient in both languages. However, most of the literature on the subject identifies a balanced bilingual as a person who possesses age-appropriate competence in two languages. In other words, that person would be as competent as a native speaker of the same age in both languages. One case is a student who understands the curriculum in school in either language. For example, a student in a Dual Language school or Immersion education program may be able to operate in classroom activity in either language. Such a person would tend to be called a balanced bilingual.

Research on bilingualism and intelligence (and bilingualism and thinking), tends to show that children who are balanced bilinguals (see page 88 for tests to identify balanced bilinguals) may have some cognitive advantages over those who are monolingual. For example, they appear to be more flexible in their thinking and more able to 'look inside' their language. This illustrates that the term 'balanced bilinguals', while an idealized concept, has been found of value in research. (Insufficient research has been done to show whether these advantages continue into adulthood). However, eight issues surrounding this concept can be listed:

1. Most bilinguals use their two languages for different purposes and functions. For example, some bilinguals use one language at home, in church and in the local community. They use another language at work and in meetings to do with their trade or profession. A person may be fluent in one language inside the mosque, temple or church, but cannot use that language fluently in the home or in school. For example, a young Muslim Panjabi might speak Panjabi in the family and with adults in the community, learn Urdu particularly for literacy purposes, learn Arabic to recite prayers and follow the Qur'ān, and learn English for school socialization and employment purposes. Thus dominance in languages varies according to the contexts where those languages are used.

2. In the majority of bilinguals one language is more dominant than the other. However, this dominance sometimes changes as age, education, work, area of residence, friends and motivation change. A child may be brought up in a Spanish-speaking family. Spanish is dominant in the early years, but if the school and neighborhood is predominantly English-speaking, the balance may gradually shift to English language dominance. Later in life, when working in a Spanish-speaking country, the dominance may revert to Spanish. If ever an approximate balance does exist, it is usually temporary and transitory.

3. If individuals are not particularly proficient in either of their two languages, are they still balanced bilinguals? Should the term balanced bilinguals be reserved for those who are relatively proficient in two languages? In the sense employed by many researchers on bilingualism, it is the latter case that is included and the former case excluded.

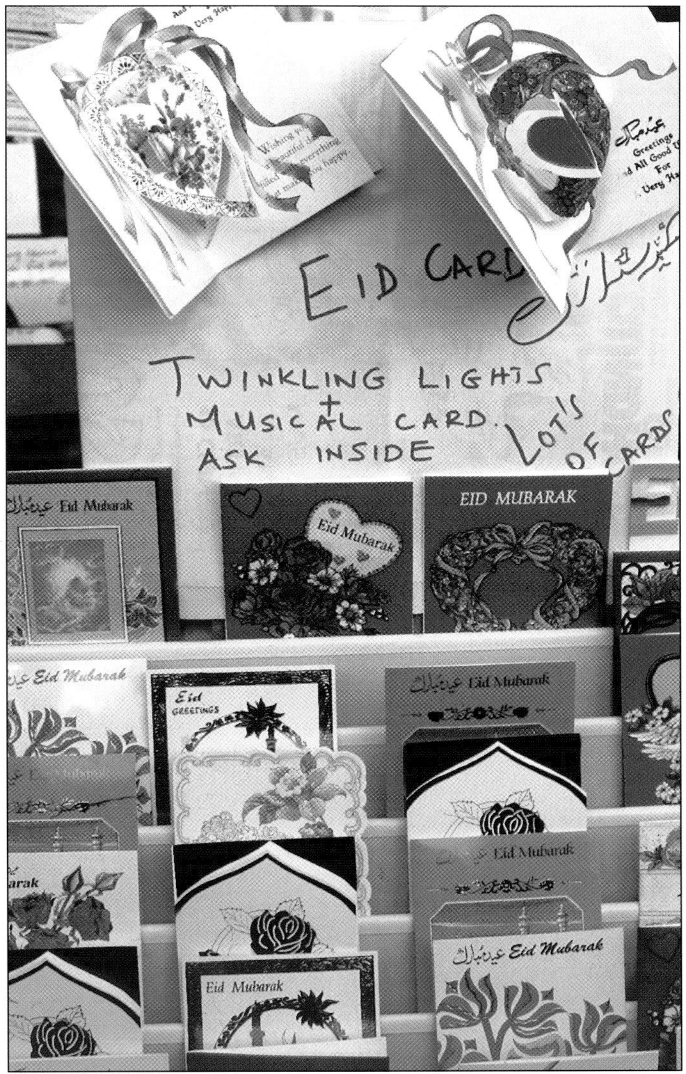

Bilingual Arabic-English cards on sale in London for the Muslim Eid festival, which celebrates the end of the fast of Ramadan. For some Muslims in the world, Arabic is a religious language only, and they do not use it in everyday life.

4. To expect someone to be exactly equal (and fluent) in two languages is a simplistic view of bilinguals. Bilinguals are sometimes expected to be two monolinguals inside one person. This viewpoint is unreal and mistaken.

5. While the term 'balanced bilingual' has research value, it is unclear who is included or who is excluded from this group. Must balanced bilinguals be biliterate or does inclusion in this category only take account of speaking and listening skills? What levels of proficiency are required in the different language skills (listening, speaking, reading and writing), to be called a balanced bilingual? Opinions may vary as to what constitutes age-appropriate proficiency or fluency in both languages.

6. One solution to locating balanced bilinguals has been to use tests of language proficiency to make such a classification. In research on bilingualism and thinking, balanced bilinguals have often been located by their scores on language proficiency tests. For example, students may be tested in Spanish and English, and their balance or dominance described in test scores. There is a problem in defining who is, and who is not, a balanced bilingual using language proficiency tests. This solution focuses narrowly on language ability rather than language usage. If someone has ability in two languages yet only uses one of their two languages in almost all domains, can that person be fairly categorized as balanced? Should a person use both their languages regularly, although for different functions, to be called a balanced bilingual?

7. The danger is that we classify too rigidly and make the term 'balanced bilingual' too elitist. 'Balanced bilinguals' tends to refer to a group of privileged people who have the choice and opportunity to use two languages, and who have the educational chances for both their languages to blossom.

8. Since bilinguals use their languages for different purposes, they are often not effective translators or interpreters. Such interpretation and translation entails close correspondence between vocabularies in both languages. Many bilinguals do not have equivalent vocabularies in each language, thus interpreting can be difficult (see also page 55 on child interpreters for their immigrant parents).

Further Reading

BAKER, C., 1996, *Foundations of Bilingual Education and Bilingualism.* Clevedon: Multilingual Matters Ltd.

EDWARDS, J. R., 1994, *Multilingualism.* New York: Routledge.

GROSJEAN, F., 1994, Individual Bilingualism. In R. E. ASHER & J. M. SIMPSON (eds), *The Encyclopedia of Language and Linguistics* (Volume 3). Oxford: Pergamon.

HOFFMANN, C., 1991, *An Introduction to Bilingualism.* London: Longman.

ROMAINE, S., 1995, *Bilingualism* (Second edition). Oxford: Blackwell.

SKUTNABB-KANGAS, T., 1981, *Bilingualism or Not: The Education of Minorities.* Clevedon: Multilingual Matters Ltd.

5: Double 'Semilingualism'

Bilinguals will tend to be dominant in one of their languages due to factors such as exposure, experience and use. This may vary with context and change over time. Dominance in one language may change over time with geographical or social mobility. For others, the dominance may be relatively stable across time and place. A few bilinguals may possess approximately equal competence in both their languages.

There is a category of bilinguals that has been proposed as distinct from balanced and dominant bilinguals. Sometimes termed pejoratively as 'semilinguals' or 'double semilinguals', the category is regarded as not having 'sufficient' competence in either language.

Hansegård (1975) described 'semilingualism' in terms of deficits in six language competencies:

- Size of vocabulary.
- Correctness of language.
- Subconscious processing of language (automatism).
- Language creation (neologization).
- Mastery of the functions of language (e.g. emotive, cognitive).
- Meanings and imagery.

Thus a 'semilingual' is seen as someone with deficiencies in both languages when compared with monolinguals. Such a person is considered to possess a small vocabulary and incorrect grammar, consciously thinks about language production, is stilted and uncreative with both languages, and finds it difficult to think and express emotions in either language.

The notion of semilingualism, or double semilingualism, has received much criticism (e.g. Skutnabb-Kangas, 1981). There are six major problems with this notion.

First, the term has taken on disparaging and belittling overtones, particularly in Scandinavia and with in-migrant groups in the US. Semilingualism may be used as a negative label which invokes expectations of failure and underachievement.

Second, if languages are relatively undeveloped, the origins may not be in bilingualism *per se*, but in the economic, political and social conditions that evoke underdevelopment. The danger of the term 'semilingualism' is that it locates the origins of underdevelopment in the individual rather than in external, societal factors that co-exist with bilingualism. Thus the term may be a political rather than a linguistic concept.

Third, many bilinguals use their two languages for different purposes and events. Language may be specific to a context. A person may be competent in one language in some contexts but not in others.

Fourth, the quantitative educational tests that are most often used to measure language proficiencies and differentiate between people are insensitive to the unquantifiable aspects of languages and to the great range of language competencies. Language tests may measure a small, unrepresentative sample of a person's total language behavior. A person may 'fail' on language tests but be a competent speaker in the street and home.

Fifth, there is a dispute regarding the frequency of double semilingualism, for example among Finnish-Swedish speakers (see Skutnabb-Kangas, 1981). How many or how few fit clearly into a semilingual category will be contentious and controversial. Establishing a cut-off point for who is, and is not a double semilingual will be arbitrary and value-laden. There is a lack of sound objective empirical evidence on such a categorization.

Sixth, the comparison with monolinguals may not be fair. It is important to distinguish if bilinguals are 'naturally' qualitatively and quantitatively different from monolinguals in their use of their two languages (as a function of being bilingual). An apparent deficiency may be due to unfair comparisons with monolinguals.

These criticisms raise considerable doubts about the value of the term 'semilingualism'. However, this does not detract from the fact that people do differ on many language abilities, with some people remaining at the earlier stages of development. Also, bilinguals sometimes worry about their language abilities. When monolinguals are near-by and of higher status, bilinguals can be concerned that their competence in the majority language is lower than a monolingual. Minority languages speakers, in-migrants and those who frequently move countries with their employment are often anxious that their ability in the prestige language of the locality makes them appear inferior. While bilinguals in such situations communicate in the local prestige language with ease, there is still the residual worry about less capability in that language than monolinguals.

Being at an early stage in language development may not be a result of being bilingual. Economic and social factors or educational provision may, for example, be the cause of underdevelopment in language (see page 486 on English language submersion nursery education). Rather than highlight the apparent 'deficit' in language development, the more positive approach is to emphasize that, when suitable conditions are provided, languages are easily capable of evolution beyond the 'semi' state.

Further Reading

EDELSKY, C. *et al.*, 1983, Semilingualism and Language Deficit. *Applied Linguistics*, 1983, 4 (1), 1-22.

MARTIN-JONES, M. & ROMAINE, S., 1986, Semilingualism: A Half Baked Theory of Communicative Competence. *Applied Linguistics*, 7 (1), 26-38.

SKUTNABB-KANGAS, T., 1981, *Bilingualism or Not: The Education of Minorities*. Clevedon: Multilingual Matters Ltd.

6: Prestigious Bilingualism

Prestigious bilinguals are typically (but not exclusively) those who own two high status languages. Prestigious bilinguals can also be those who are of high status in their society and are bilingual. Often those who are high status speak two or more high status languages. (A more restricted term is 'elite' bilinguals). For example, children who speak French and English fluently or Japanese and German will tend to be prestigious bilinguals. Such bilinguals often come from middle class and upper class families and thus prestigious bilingualism is often paralleled by social, cultural and economic prestige. Such families often regard bilingualism as a way of preserving family status and educational and employment advantage. High status bilingualism tends to exist at an individual or family level, but is not organized at a group or societal level.

Among prestigious bilinguals will be those who regularly travel or live abroad (e.g. diplomats and their children, bureaucrats in United Nations, UNESCO, the European Union and the Council of Europe). With an increase in schemes for students to travel abroad to take part (or most) of their studies in another country, prestigious bilingualism is sometimes reproduced by higher and tertiary education. For example, the ERASMUS program in Europe has allowed students to take one semester or a year or more of their studies in another European country. This has promoted the desirability of having second and third majority languages.

'Elite' bilinguals may be produced by having a nanny or governess who speaks a different language to the children. The 'finishing schools' in Switzerland (see page 16) also enable the daughters of the more affluent to polish their cultural and behavioral repertoire and become fluent in one or more prestigious European languages (especially French). Bilingualism in this sense is often planned and purposeful.

While bilingualism in two or more international languages defines a 'prestigious bilingual', the term is also occasionally used to include those whose first language is a prestigious majority language, but who learn a minority language to secure employment and economic

Saudi Arabians in Jeddah. English is an important language in Saudi Arabia. It is commonly used as a lingua franca by the large, multinational workforce and is widely spoken as a second language by educated Saudis.

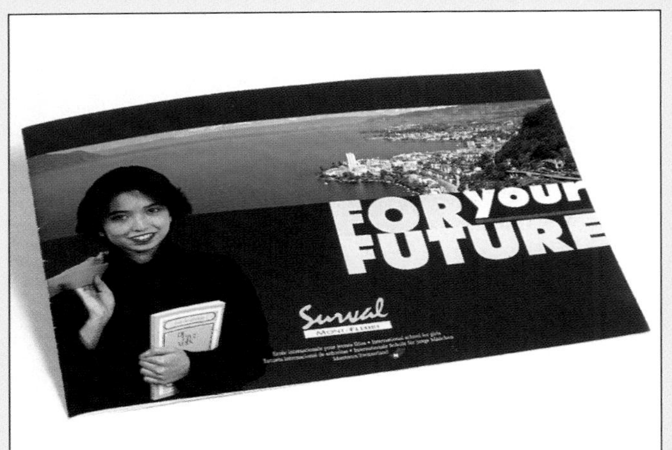

Surval Mont-Fleuri, a Swiss Finishing School

Surval Mont-Fleuri is an international language and finishing school for young women, overlooking Lake Geneva near Montreux in Switzerland. Every September up to 80 girls, aged 15 and over, go there to complete their secondary education, before beginning a career or going on to college.

Finishing schools have traditionally been private, fee-paying establishments where young women from relatively privileged backgrounds are 'refined ' or 'polished', before making their entry into society. The term 'finishing school' conjures up images of well-bred, polite young ladies learning cookery and flower-arranging. Certainly Surval Mont-Fleuri continues this tradition. As well as academic subjects and business courses, there are courses in 'etiquette', 'fashion design' and 'art', among others, which prepare the students for an elegant and cosmopolitan future lifestyle.

Swiss finishing schools also make a positive contribution to multilingualism, multiculturalism and a broader, international outlook. The 80 or so girls at Surval Mont-Fleuri represent as many as 20 nationalities and have a variety of home languages, including Spanish, Japanese, German, Dutch, Danish, English, Portuguese and Arabic. At the school, they learn to live together and to respect and appreciate one another's nationality and culture. The study of French and English to a high level represents a main element in the curriculum and can be combined with other courses. The presence of native- speaker teachers, a high teacher–student ratio, intensive teaching and excellent multimedia facilities mean that the students have every advantage in language learning.

In addition, French is the official language of the school, and after the first six weeks the girls are asked to speak only French until 4 p.m. each day. Thus the students have the opportunity to acquire the language in an advantageous 'total immersion' situation. German, Spanish and Italian are also taught, as optional subjects. The study of different cultures, international cookery, and travel are also part of the school program.

The educational objective is that their year at the school will prepare students, not just for life within a social elite, but for a future enriched by a broader understanding of other languages and cultures.

Such a school is very different from many language minority schools (as are considered in Section 4 – see page 508). Surval Mont-Fleuri contrasts sharply with the education of many bilinguals from language minorities. Yet such widely different educational, social and economic circumstances both relate to bilingualism and biculturalism. It is customary and popular to portray the contrasts and contradictions; there are also less noticed 'language outcome' resemblances in the production and celebration of bilingualism.

advantage. For example, in Wales, English in-migrants may purposefully learn the Welsh language as adults to secure prestigious jobs, and ensure readiness for promotion, thus reproducing economic and social advantages within their families.

Among prestigious bilinguals, there has historically not been a debate about the disadvantages and problems of bilinguals. During the 20th century, such bilinguals have recognized the economic, social and educational advantages of bilingualism. Prestigious bilinguals have continuously accepted that bilingualism causes no problems in thinking, academic achievement or cultural acceptance.

Further Reading

SKUTNABB-KANGAS, T., 1981, *Bilingualism or Not: The Education of Minorities*. Clevedon: Multilingual Matters Ltd.

TOSI, A., 1991, High-Status and Low-Status Bilingualism in Europe. *Journal of Education*, 173 (2), 21-37.

The Dumont Family

Norma Dumont and her husband Alberto are both ministers at the Argentine Embassy in London, England. With their two daughters, Natalia (ten years old) and Alejandra (eight years old), they have lived in London for the past five years.

Alberto Dumont is himself the son of a former Argentine Ambassador and, as such, lived in several countries during his childhood and had the opportunity to learn several languages. Norma Dumont grew up in Buenos Aires, Argentina and attended the Instituto Nacional Superior del Profesorado en Lenguas Vivas, a secondary school which specializes in the teaching of foreign languages. There she studied English. After graduating in law at the National University of Buenos Aires, she studied at the National Institute of Foreign Affairs, in preparation for a diplomatic career.

Candidates for the Argentine Diplomatic Service have to have high academic qualifications and are required to speak at least two foreign languages, (one of them English or French). During her time as a student Norma Dumont also studied French, Italian and Portuguese.

During her diplomatic career, Norma Dumont has been posted to Lagos, Nigeria, Geneva (where she married her husband) and Buenos Aires. She has also had the opportunity to make several missions to foreign countries, including the United States, France, Portugal, Spain, New Zealand, Uruguay, Brazil and Yugoslavia.

The home language of the family is Spanish, naturally. However, the children attend a local international school in London, and thus they speak English with classmates and friends and with one another. In order to maintain the children's Spanish, the parents make a point of always speaking in Spanish to them, even if they sometimes answer in English. The children's nanny, who comes from Paraguay, also speaks Spanish to them, and kind grandparents back in Argentina send Spanish videos. Embassy life allows plenty of contact with other Argentine families and a chance to celebrate special occasions and festivals in Argentine style. Norma Dumont believes that a secure and stable family life ensures that the children preserve their identity as Argentines.

The Dumonts are aware that the diplomatic life does involve some sacrifices. Being far away from relatives, friends and familiar places can be hard. However the opportunity to travel and adapt to different cultures and to live in a cosmopolitan city like London compensates for this. The children attend an international school in London where half the students are from other countries, and this has been a very good experience for them. Alberto Dumont's own experience as the son of a diplomat has made the Dumonts confident that the advantages for their children will far outweigh the disadvantages.

7: Multilingualism

The word 'bilingual', used of an individual, primarily describes the possession of two languages. However, it can also be taken to include the many people in the world who have varying degrees of proficiency in three, four or even more languages.

In many parts of Africa and Asia, several languages may co-exist and large sections of the population may speak two or more languages. In such countries, individual multilingualism is the result of a process of industrial development, political unification, modernization, urbanization and greater contact between different local communities. Many individuals in these countries may speak one or more local or ethnic languages, as well as another indigenous language that has become the medium of communication between different ethnic groups or speech communities. Such individuals may also speak a foreign language, such as English, French or Spanish, that has been imposed during the process of colonization. This latter language is often the language of education, bureaucracy and privilege.

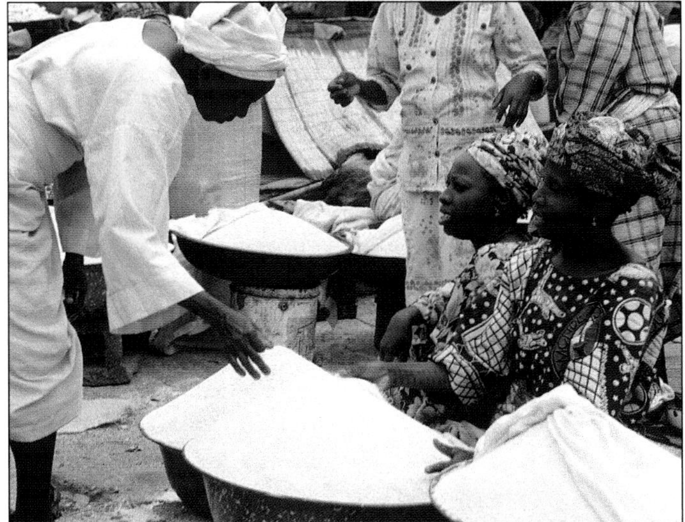

A market place in Nigeria. It is estimated that about 400 different languages or dialects are spoken in Nigeria. Several languages have developed as languages of wider communication, for use in trade and social contact, namely Yoruba, Hausa, Igbo and more recently Nigerian Pidgin English.

In Kenya, for instance, many people speak their own native language and also Swahili, the designated national language. Swahili has long been a medium for intergroup communication in parts of Africa and has risen in its status and prestige (see page 123). Many people also speak English. Although colonial rule in Kenya ended in 1963, English is still an official language.

In many Western countries, individual monolingualism rather than multilingualism is the norm. This has often been the result of a drive towards political and national unification which requires the establishment of an official language or languages to be used in education, work and public life. However, some in-migrant minorities may be multilingual. In Asian communities of Britain and Canada, many individuals are trilingual, in their native language or dialect, in another Asian language often associated with literacy (e.g. Urdu or Hindi) and in English. In addition, a Muslim child will learn Arabic – the language of the Qur'an and the Mosque. In Mills & Mills (1993), interviews by Sidhu and Mills were conducted with primary school teachers who spoke three or four languages from among Hindi, Urdu, Panjabi, English and Pushtu.

Multilingualism can also be the possession of individuals who do not live within a multilingual speech community. Families can be trilingual when the husband and wife each speak a different language as well as the majority language of the country of residence. A person who has sufficient social and educational advantages can learn a second, third or fourth language at school or university, at work or in leisure hours. The motives for language learning in such cases may include personal enrichment, travel, educational betterment and economic advantage.

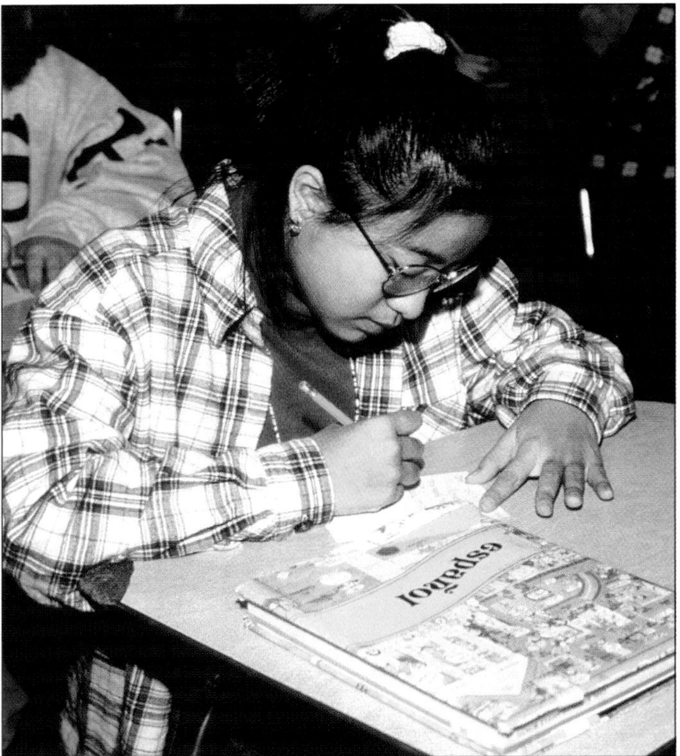

A young Asian girl in a US school is bilingual in her native language and English and is learning a third language, Spanish.

Well Known Multilinguals

In recent times, there have been well known figures who have been trilingual at least. Here are just a few.

ELIAS CANETTI (1905–1994) writer and native of Bulgaria: Spanish, Romanian, German, English.

MAHATMA GANDHI (1869–1948) nationalist leader of India: Gujarati, Hindi and English.

POPE JOHN PAUL II (1920–) head of the Roman Catholic church and native of Poland: Polish, Latin, Italian, English, Spanish, French, Russian and German.

INGRID BERGMAN (1915–1982) actress and native of Sweden: Swedish, English and Italian.

SOPHIA LOREN (1934–) actress and native of Italy: Italian, French and English.

ARTHUR RUBINSTEIN (1887–1982) US classical pianist and native of Poland: Polish, German, French and English.

Like 'prestigious bilingualism' (see page 15) this type of individual multilingualism is usually voluntary and planned, and brings economic, educational and social advantages. It is more widespread in countries where the native language is not an international, high prestige language. In such countries, the inhabitants see the economic, employment and travel value of being multilingual.

Many mainland European children learn two languages in school (e.g. English, German, French) as well as being fluent in their home language (e.g. Finnish, Swedish, Danish, Luxembourgish, Dutch). The Scandinavians

Jesus

It is likely that Jesus was trilingual at least. He was probably a native speaker of Aramaic, a language used widely in Palestine at the time. In his religious training, Jesus would have learnt Hebrew and later used it in talking to the Pharisees. He may also have known Greek and Latin. Latin was the language of the occupying Roman forces and was used in the Law Courts and in trading. Greek was used by the upper classes and sometimes by the Romans.

The town square in Chouen, Morocco. About 60 percent of Moroccans speak Moroccan Arabic as a native language. At school they learn Modern Standard Arabic and also French. Classical Arabic is used in Islamic worship. The Berber people, who comprise the remaining 40 percent, may know as many as four or five languages, their own variety of Berber, as well as Moroccan Arabic, Standard Arabic, French and Classical Arabic.

seem particularly experienced and successful in producing trilingual children. Language learning has relatively high status in Scandinavian countries. The economic, employment and travel value of being multilingual is one partial explanation of the Scandinavian accomplishment of multilingualism.

Some school systems encourage multilingualism. In the European Schools Movement (see page 527), many children become relatively fluent in three languages by the end of secondary education. In Canada, through schooling, children have become trilingual in Hebrew, English and French. In New York, there are children and adults who speak Yiddish, Hebrew and English.

The Reality of Multilingualism

As these examples from around the world indicate, individual multilingualism is possible, non-problematic and potentially valuable. Human beings have the brain capacity to learn and retain several languages. In many countries, it is not just the advantaged 'elite' who are multilingual, but the majority of the population, of all social classes. For example, in Calcutta, a rickshaw-wallah may speak a native language with family and close friends, speak Hindi to some customers and Bengali to others, as well as having a working knowledge of English.

However, it is important to recognize that a multilingual person mostly uses different languages for different purposes, and does not typically possess the same level or type of proficiency in each language. In Morocco, for instance, a native speaker of Berber may also be fluent in colloquial Moroccan Arabic, but not be literate in either of these languages. This Berber speaker will be educated in modern standard Arabic and use that language for writing and formal purposes. Classical Arabic is the language of the mosque, used for prayers and reading the Qur'an. Many Moroccans also have some knowledge of French, the former colonial language.

The Greatest Linguists

According to the Guinness Multimedia Disc of Records, the person able to speak the most languages in history was Dr Harold Williams of New Zealand (1876–1928). Dr Williams spoke 58 languages and many dialects. He attended the League of Nations (1920–46) in Geneva, Switzerland and was able to communicate with every delegate in that person's own language. A similar ability was shown by Alexander Schwartz who used 31 languages as a translator for the United Nations in New York between 1962 and 1986.

The Guinness Multimedia Disc of Records claims that the most multilingual living person is Derick Herning of Lerwick, Shetland Islands in Scotland. His ability in 22 languages earned him victory in the first 'Polyglot of Europe' contest held in Brussels in May 1990.

In addition, languages within an individual may grow and decay over time. One or two of them may become stronger, another may become weaker. This is even more true of multilinguals than of bilinguals. As opportunities for practice vary and motivations change, so may language dominance. Few multilinguals live in a situation that allows regular use of their three or more languages over a lifetime.

As friends, work and residence change, so will the balance of languages within an individual. The co-existence of three or more languages within an individual or within the family will shift according to religious, cultural, social, economic, political and community pressures. A person's languages may be surrounded by 'market forces', manipulation from without, motivations from within, honest advice and active hostility. Where trilingualism and multilingualism are seen as unnatural, unnecessary, in need of compensatory or remedial action, or as a deficiency rather than a proficiency, then reward structures in society (e.g. employment, preferment) may exert pressure in favor of a monolingual or bilingual norm.

Further Reading

COOK, V. J., 1992, Evidence for Multicompetence. *Language Learning*, 1992, 42 (4), 557-591.

EDWARDS, J. R., 1994, *Multilingualism*. New York: Routledge.

MILLS, R. W. & MILLS, J., 1993, *Bilingualism in the Primary School. A Handbook for Teachers*. London: Routledge.

Casmir Rubagumya

Casmir Rubagumya was born in Rwanda in 1946. His mother tongue is Kinyarwanda and he spoke only that language until he started primary school at the age of six. He then started learning French,which was used as the medium of instruction in the last two years of primary school.

In 1960, political disturbances in Rwanda forced Casmir Rubagumya and his family to move to Tanzania. At the age of 14, he started learning Swahili and English. He spent another two years in primary school in Tanzania so as to acclimatize to the new educational system. He completed his secondary and university education (first degree) in Tanzania through the medium of English. Like many Africans, being multilingual was typical rather than exceptional.

Throughout the school years, Swahili was the main language of communication outside the home, while Kinyarwanda remained the main language of the home. French was a passive language because there was no opportunity for using it. At university, Casmir Rubagumya tried to revive his French by taking it as a subject. He can now understand spoken French and read French texts.

He has also lived in England for periods, undertaking MA and PhD studies. During this time, his main language of communication was English. He is, at present, a Senior Lecturer in Linguistics at the University of Dar es Salaam, Tanzania, where his main working language is English. He also uses Swahili extensively outside the office and lecture room.

Casmir Rubagumya has researched and written in the areas of language policy in education, classroom discourse and English for Special Purposes. His recent publications include: *Language and Education in Africa: A Tanzanian Perspective* (1990) and *Teaching and Researching Language in African Classrooms* (edited, 1994). He is one of the foremost experts on multilingualism and multilingual education in Africa.

Rehana Ali

Rehana Ali is 15 years old. She lives in Rochdale (northern England) with her parents and her little sister Zarmina who is nearly two. Rehana is unusual in that she has inherited two different cultural traditions, one Celtic, the other Asian. Rehana's father, Farzand, is from the North West Frontier Province in Pakistan. His native language is Pushtu.

Various forms of Pushtu (also known as Pashto) are spoken by some 10 million people in Pakistan, as well as parts of Afghanistan. Pushtu has a written form and is widely used in education. Rehana's father was educated at school and later at medical school through the medium of Pushtu, (although he did some pre-medical training in English). The official language of Pakistan is Urdu, which is spoken as a mother tongue by 10 million of the country's inhabitants and as a second language by perhaps another 80 million. Rehana's father learnt Urdu at school, but does not consider that he speaks it very well. Rehana's mother, Ann, is from Anglesey, North Wales and her first language is Welsh, a language spoken by about 19 percent of the 2.8 million inhabitants of Wales. Like all Welsh speakers, she learnt English at school and speaks it fluently.

Rehana's parents met while working together in a hospital in Bangor, North Wales. They have always spoken English together, but when Rehana was born it seemed natural to speak their own native languages to her in the home. Welsh was the language Rehana spoke first, but English soon became stronger. When Rehana was very young, she would sometimes answer her parents in English when they asked her something in Welsh or Pushtu. She never refused to speak either of these two languages, however.

Rehana spent her first months of school in the Welsh-medium primary school at Bangor before the family moved to Rochdale in the North of England. There she attended the local primary school. There is a strong Asian community in Rochdale and 65 percent of the children at the school are Asian. When Rehana attended the school, there were no provisions for teaching any Asian language, but there was a language support teacher who helped the Asian children who did not speak fluent English. Rehana had no difficulty settling in at school.

Rehana describes her strongest language as English. This is quite natural, because it is the language of school, and, to a large extent, of the young Asian people in the neighborhood. The main Asian languages spoken in the area are Panjabi, Urdu and Bengali. Pushtu is not spoken by many people in Rehana's neighborhood, so the only opportunity she has to speak Pushtu is with her father, and on visits to Pakistan. A neighboring family also speak Pushtu in the home, but Rehana speaks to the children in English. She speaks Welsh to her mother and little sister and on visits to her family in North Wales.

Rehana has learnt to read and write Welsh well, through her mother helping her at home and has also learnt a little Urdu at school in extra lessons. She reads Urdu quite well, and understands more than she can speak. She can also read Arabic fairly well, and learns French in school. Rehana appreciates her two cultures but identifies more with Islamic-Asian culture because she is a Muslim.

One feature of Asian communities in Britain is that they are multilingual. Families from India or Pakistan may speak Panjabi, Gujarati, Bengali, Hindi, or a lesser known language such as Pushtu. Many Asians in Britain speak more than one Asian language. For instance, a small number of Asians in the UK speak Urdu as a mother tongue, but for many more it is a second language, and considered as the language of culture, religion and literacy. Bilingualism or trilingualism among Asians represents a valuable cognitive skill as well as a rich cultural heritage. It is not always recognized as such by monolingual people in Britain.

The variety of languages within Asian communities in Britain does mean that the transmission of languages to the next generation is more difficult. The influence of English on the younger generation is very strong. It is the language of their education, and the language they will need to succeed in the job market. However strong family, cultural and religious ties means that many Asian young people try to maintain their home languages.

John Paul II, a Multilingual Pope

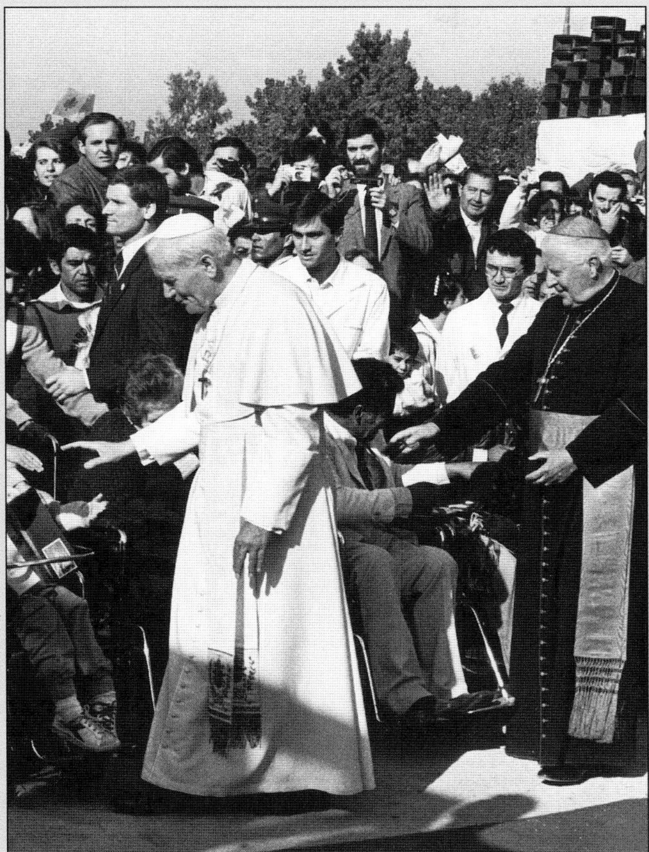

Pope John Paul II greets the crowds in Santiago on his tour of Chile in 1987.

A spiral of white smoke rose from the Sistine Chapel. For the crowds waiting in St Peter's Square, Rome, on October 16th, 1978, a long vigil was over. A new Pope had been elected.

When it was announced that the new Pope was not only a non-Italian, but also a Cardinal from the Communist world of Eastern Europe, they were amazed. The new Pope was Cardinal Karol Jozef Wojtyla from Poland. When the new Pope appeared on the balcony and began to address them in Italian, their concern turned to relief and enthusiasm. The new Pope had used his talent for communication and his linguistic ability to welcome the crowd gathered to greet him.

Karol Jozef Wojtyla was born on May 18th, 1920 in Wadowice, Poland. As a young boy he learnt German from his father. Later he studied Latin, Greek and German, and of course Polish, at the local Gymnasium or high school. When the Russians and Germans agreed on a joint occupation of Poland in 1939, he came into contact with German.

As a university student, still before the war, at the Jagiellonian University in Cracow, he studied the old Slav language, which, together with his native Polish, gave him the ability to understand and later to read texts in different Slav languages: Czech and Slovak (similar), Croatian and Serb (similar), Russian, Belorussian and Ukrainian. During the German occupation he took private lessons in French and English.

In 1946 he was ordained as a priest. Shortly afterwards, he was sent to study in Rome for two years. He lived at the Belgian college with French-speaking seminarians and thus had an opportunity to learn French as well as Italian. He wrote his doctoral thesis on a Spanish mystic, St John of the Cross, so he learned Spanish to be able to read the original works. The thesis and its final defense were in Latin.

During his 30 years of service in Poland, first as a parish priest, then as a university professor, bishop, archbishop and finally cardinal, he continued using the languages he had learnt. While Cardinal of Cracow, he traveled to Australia and to the United States. By 1962, when he served on the Second Vatican Council, he was fluent in French, German and Italian, as well as Latin, in which council business was conducted. In 1976, he gave a homily at the Eucharistic Congress in Philadelphia and lectured on philosophy at Harvard and other universities. To improve his English, he took a 15-minute lesson every day for a month.

The Pope uses his many languages on a regular basis. He always tries to address the people he is speaking with in their own language, if possible. On Wednesdays he holds a General Audience, with many thousands present. He regularly speaks at the General Audience in Italian, French, English, German, Spanish, Portuguese and Polish (all transmitted by radio). According to the groups that are present, he might also read from prepared texts in Japanese, Slovak, Czech, Hungarian, Croatian, Slovene, and sometimes Dutch, Swedish, Danish, Belorussian and Russian.

On other mornings, he gives private audiences to people of many nationalities. He is regularly visited by Catholic bishops from all continents, heads of state, ministers and ambassadors. He speaks to them in a variety of languages. At Christmas and Easter, the Pope greets the Christians of the world on radio in more than 50 languages.

During his years as Pope, he has traveled the world, visiting South America, Poland, Ireland, America, Turkey, France, Africa, Germany, the Philippines, Tanzania, Japan, to name only some countries. His love for people, and his desire to communicate with them, means that he works hard to improve and increase his repertoire of languages. For example, before his visit to Brazil, he learnt Portuguese from his secretary. In Tanzania, he celebrated the Holy Mass in Swahili.

In 1991 he learnt Japanese before his visit to Japan, and mastered it so well that he surprised some missionaries who had not managed to learn as much during many years in Japan. In 1993, he learnt Lithuanian, and mastered that language with its Baltic grammar (e.g. six case endings for nouns) to the point where he could correct his own mistakes.

He tries to find time to learn new languages by taking lessons during breakfast, and repeating the new material in short spare moments, from a handbook or liturgical text. In many cases, he reads his sermons and speeches in the language of the country he is visiting. In every country that he visits, he addresses a few words of greeting, says the Mass or at least begins and ends it in the vernacular. People appreciate his efforts as a courteous recognition of their national or ethnic identity.

There can be no doubt that John Paul II's knowledge of many languages and his ability to learn new ones has been invaluable to his ministry. The presence of a translator can detract from the quality of a personal encounter, hence the preference for the direct appeal of using a native language, even when pronounced in a foreign accent. Through the Pope's multilingualism, he has made a warm and personal contact with a wide panorama of humanity.

Sophia Loren

The famous actress Sophia Loren was born Sofia Scicolone in 1934. She grew up as an Italian speaker in Naples in a poor neighborhood. At the age of 14 her film career began when she traveled with her mother to Rome to find work as an extra in the film *Quo Vadis*.

She very soon realized the importance of languages in the film industry. She studied French, which had been her best subject at school. She also began to learn English with a tutor in Rome.

She first made films in Italian but soon American and British film directors were showing an interest in her work and her future husband and mentor, the film director Carlo Ponti, cabled her from America 'BRUSH UP YOUR ENGLISH. YOU'LL NEED IT SOON.'

By then Sophia was spending every spare moment studying English with an Irish woman called Sarah Spain. Sophia studied from 5 a.m. to 7 a.m. every morning, before beginning the day's filming, and also at odd moments during the day. Sarah Spain made Sophia read T. S. Eliot and Bernard Shaw aloud to improve her pronunciation.

Fortunately Sophia had a good ear for languages and learned quickly. Carlo Ponti encouraged her and gave her books to read: *Madame Bovary* in French, *Don Quixote* in Spanish and Eugene O'Neill's *The Emperor Jones* in English. She also read Chekhov and Tolstoy, Baudelaire and Stendhal, Shaw and Dickens. Her first film in English was *The Pride and the Passion* in 1957, starring opposite Cary Grant. Later she learnt colloquial Spanish while making films on location. She has made films in Italian, French, English and Spanish and does her own dubbing. Her practice has been to take a quick refresher course in the appropriate language before making a film that is not in Italian. She speaks some German and always checks the German dubbing of her films to make sure that the German voice sounds like her own.

Sophia Loren's two children were brought up to speak Italian and English with their parents and German with their Swiss-German nanny. They also learnt French while living and attending school in France.

8: Personality, Social Development, Identity and Bilingualism

Introduction

It is only recently that anything other than a negative view about the personality and social development of bilingual children has been expressed. For many decades, bilingualism was associated with (and even said to be the cause of) schizophrenia, mental confusion, identity crises, emotional problems, deficits in social attachment, conflicts of loyalty, conflicts of identity, low self-esteem and a poor self-concept. Problems as wide as stuttering and poor moral development were regarded as the likely consequences of being bilingual.

It will always be possible to locate some bilinguals who think of their bilingualism as a problem. But as Grosjean (1982) found, the majority of bilinguals and trilinguals find no inconvenience in speaking two or more languages. If we trawl for advantages, they will be found in bilinguals. The question is not 'are there bilinguals who show personality, identity or social problems?' Among bilinguals, as among monolinguals, there will always be some individuals with such problems. The issue is whether bilingualism is the cause of the problems. Take two examples.

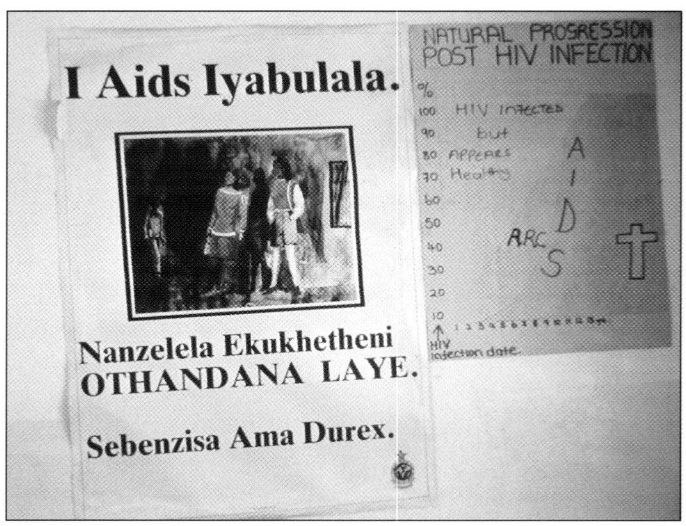

An Aids poster in the Ndebele language in Zimbabwe. As in most other countries of Africa, linguistic diversity is accepted as natural and normal. About 15 indigenous languages are spoken in Zimbabwe. Ndebele, spoken by about 10 percent of the population, and Shona, spoken by at least 75 percent, are the two main lingua francas of the country and are widely used in local trade and business, health education, vocational training and some early primary education. English, the mother tongue of only one percent, is the language of government, the media, the economy and much of the educational system.

1. A question about stuttering is not 'do bilinguals stutter'? Some bilinguals stutter, as do many monolinguals. Rather the important question is whether bilingualism, in and by itself, causes stuttering. Research tends to suggest that bilinguals are no more or less likely to stutter than other groups. Bilingualism does not seem to be the cause of stuttering.

2. One frequently voiced concern about bilinguals is that mixing two languages is cognitively and socially undesirable. Here bilingualism would seem to be more causally linked to potential 'problems'.However, in some societies (e.g. particular groups of Puerto Ricans in New York), switching between languages can be normal and accepted. Codeswitching can have advantages (e.g. giving a further explanation of an idea). (See Codeswitching, page 58).

Negative Viewpoints

One author, in particular, symbolizes a negative, prejudiced view about bilinguals' personality. Adler (1977) describes bilingual children as having split minds, as being 'neither here nor there', and as being marginal people. Adler (1977), using early research, wrote of the bilingual child: 'His standards are split, he becomes more inarticulate than one would expect of one who can express himself in two languages, his emotions are more instinctive, in short, bilingualism can lead to a split personality and, at worst, to schizophrenia' (page 40).

Much of what has been written about this topic is anecdotal, irrational and unscholarly. There is only a small amount of research in this whole area. For example, there are currently believed to be five main personality dimensions: extroversion-introversion; agreeableness; conscientiousness; neuroticism-stability; openness. Despite the considerable research on psychological personality traits, the personality of bilinguals has yet to figure as a line of inquiry. Personality tests such as the Myers-Briggs Type Indicator, Cattell's Sixteen Personality Factor Scale or Eysenck's Personality Tests have rarely been used in research on bilinguals.

When such formal tests of personality have been included in analyzing the characteristics of bilinguals, it is rare to find any difference between bilinguals and monolinguals on personality traits. Evidence of little or no difference in personality traits between bilinguals and monolinguals comes from Ekstrand (1989). One reason for such little connection (if any) is that the expression of personality in everyday behavior is filtered and changed by the context and situation of the moment. For example, an undertaker has little scope for extrovert behavior, even if so disposed. The individual's personality and the environment are inextricably linked and interdependent.

Another reason why personality traits may have little causal connection to bilingualism is expressed by Shakespeare in *Troilus and Cressida*:

'No man is the Lord of anything,
Til he communicates his parts to others;
Nor does he of himself know them for aught,
Til he behold them formed in th'applause'

(spoken by Ulysses in Act 3, Scene 3). This quote was centuries ahead of the recent social-constructivist argument of modern psychologists. We require our friends and others to help define and endorse the personal qualities that we seek to communicate to others. How we see ourselves is based on us (as the actor or actress), the audience, ourselves observing the interaction, other actors and actresses in our play, the scenery and props, the storyline, and the drama being enacted. We express our personality not just through our everyday behavior, but through the reactions (social meanings) others assign to our behavior. What we believe about our personalities reflects a negotiation and construction of meaning derived from our behavior. Seen in this light, bilinguals and monolinguals may have many similarities in most personality areas. A consideration of two areas (self-esteem and self-identity) will show how this consideration of personality connects with bilingualism.

Bilingualism and Self-esteem

One popular belief is that some bilingual children have lower self-esteem. Children of guest workers, recent or long-term in-migrants, and language minority children are sometimes thought to possess lower self-esteem. One argument against Submersion education or Transitional Bilingual education (see page 469) is said to be that it causes a lowering of a child's self-esteem. One major justification for the inclusion of an ethnic heritage language and culture in the curriculum is its positive effects on language minority children's self-esteem. Educating a child in the minority language (see page 508) is often believed to raise such children's self-esteem.

There is little research on this area. Generally, research finds no difference between the self-concept or self-esteem of bilingual compared with monolingual children. It is difficult to measure self-concept and self-esteem validly. Tests of self-concept and self-esteem tend instead to be measures of self-report. They measure what students are willing, or prefer to say about themselves, rather than giving a true, inner self-image. Also, specific language minority situations affect the relationship between personality and bilingualism. Bilinguals in impoverished, low status conditions can be expected to show a difference from elite bilinguals (e.g. diplomats). That is, bilingualism and sociopolitical conditions need distinguishing in their effect on the self-esteem of bilinguals.

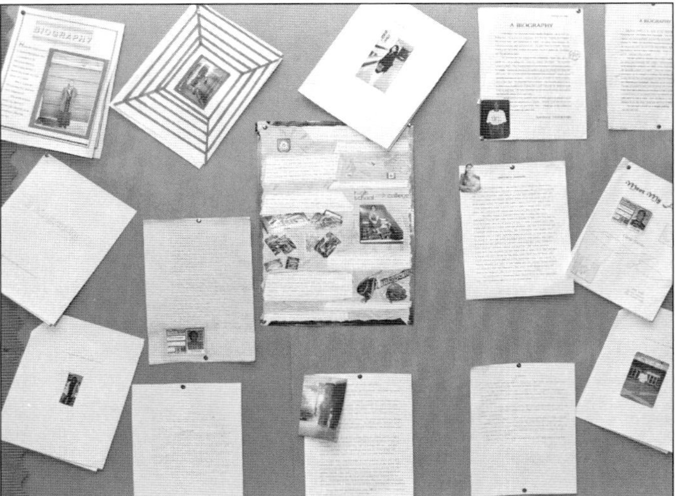

Minority language teaching and enculturation in both cultures in a school setting can enhance the self-esteem and self-image of minority language children.

Those who believe that self-esteem is lower among some language minority bilinguals disagree in their arguments for the remedy. Some argue that education in the minority language is essential. Only then will children appreciate their home language, home culture, gain security in their ethnic identity and raise their self-esteem. Others argue that low self-esteem among bilinguals exists because of their social isolation from mainstream, language majority society. The answer for some is that learning a majority language will improve self-esteem.

Alexander & Baker (1992) even suggest that being bilingual, or being in a bilingual education program, will result in negative labels allocated to a bilingual child which will, in turn, result in the lowering of self-esteem. Their argument is that being in a bilingual education program means separation from an English-speaking majority. The message is that segregation makes a child deviant or disadvantaged, with consequent damage to self-esteem. Such arguments include a preference by Alexander & Baker (1992) for assimilation of language minority groups, eradicating language and cultural variations, and producing a monolingual, mainstream society (as in the United States).

Bilingualism and Identity

Another popularly voiced worry about bilinguals is whether they are caught in between two languages and two cultures. Will a bilingual belong to neither language group, feel neither North American nor Spanish, neither English nor Irish, neither Japanese nor English? In learning another language and another culture, will a bilingual experience social alienation, a conflict of personal and ethnic identity, personal disorientation, social isolation and anxiety?

A potentially poignant example is in-migrants. Some in-migrants may feel bewilderment and frustration when expected to adapt to a new culture and a new language. A conflict of loyalties may arise. For example in the United States, such in-migrants may ask of themselves whether they are still Mexicans, or Puerto Ricans, or North Americans, or whether they are a mix of the host and the native culture, or have no or little identity.

Some United States in-migrants quickly switch to being North American in culture and lifestyle. Others, often for social and cultural reasons, try hard, or are influenced, to retain their native culture and language. Yet others manage to bridge the two. A few may have a sense of rootlessness. Some have the choice of a new identity, others have no choice, finding themselves unable to break out of the circle of economic, social and political oppression.

At its worst, shame and guilt, lawlessness or powerless resignation among in-migrants may set in. Others attempt to lose their language minority identity and, in the United States, show an open preference for North American cultural values and language. Cutting oneself off from the family unit may result. Some resign themselves to apathetic withdrawal; yet others strive hard to

Three generations of an in-migrant Asian family in England. In-migrants may experience bewilderment, anxiety and loss of self-esteem as they try to adjust to a new country, culture and language.

retain their heritage language and culture. Some reject the past and take on a new identity. In between rejection and acceptance are those with a temporary or permanent confusion of self and ethnic identity. Others assimilate more or less successfully, and some integrate whilst retaining the family's traditional culture and language.

Children of in-migrants, in particular, may find themselves in the middle of two language communities. The home culture supports the heritage language. The culture of the host nation requires a different set of values and behaviors. When a teenager is trying to find a core self-concept and an integrated self-image, (and when an adolescent identity crisis may be present), there is an extra layer of ambivalence. The teenager may have to move between two sets of values, two solitudes, two cultures. Some can switch cultures and identities as easily as they switch languages. Others may be disoriented. Conflicts of loyalties may arise as learning a language often involves acquiring the values, attitudes and behaviors of the target language community.

It is nevertheless possible to be accepted when bridging two languages and cultures. It is possible to hold different but integrated identities. A person could be a Yiddish-speaking Jew, an English-speaking Jew, a Yiddish-speaking North American and an English-speaking North American. A Yiddish- and English- speaking North American could thus be a combination of multiple identities. Cuban-Americans, Gaelic-Canadians, Chinese-Malays and German-Australians, are each examples where relatively few problems of identity exist. A hyphenated variety is possible in the cognitive and affective psyche of an individual.

The choice of 'withdrawing' or 'rejecting' is replaced by accepting that it is possible to live in two language groups. Given appropriate motivation and environmental support, confusion of identity is replaced by a unique integration of values and beliefs, allowing a person to bridge two language groups and mingle on either side. Unfortunately, not all bilinguals have the favorable circumstances or drive to enable biculturalism and bilingualism to live peacefully and creatively within the psyche.

The demands of a language community will be important in identity formation. If the language community criticizes bilinguals (or incipient bilinguals) for their accents, dual cultural norms or split loyalties, a dual identity may be more difficult. Speaking English and Arabic, being Western and Islamic, for example, may cause conflicts of identity and loyalty within the individual and within the language community. Cultural inappropriateness may be admonished. The relative status of languages and cultures may affect the accommodation of dual identity.

Identity and Mixed Language Marriages

Do children suffer or gain if their parents speak different languages to them and come from different language backgrounds? One piece of Canadian research investigated the effect on teenagers of mixed language marriages (Aellen & Lambert, 1969), testing them on their ethnic identification, identification with (or rejection of) one of their ethnic groups, their self-esteem and stability, perception of parents, peer relationships, and attitudes and values.

Analysis of the data showed that, in comparison with children from monolingual home backgrounds, bilingual teenagers had no problem in identifying with both their parents, nor suffered at all in self-esteem or stability. Such teenagers showed a positive attitude to both their parents' cultural groups. Children from monolingual homes tended to favor their own ethnic group.

Aellen & Lambert (1969) concluded that the characteristics of teenagers of mixed language background marriages were socially and emotionally healthy on each measured dimension. Such children showed no signs of personality disturbances, social disorientation or anxiety. Their self-concepts were positive and they saw their parents as giving them relatively more attention. The teenagers' values reflected the influence of both ethnic backgrounds. Rather than developing a divided allegiance or rejecting one of their dual language backgrounds, such teenagers had developed a dual allegiance. Mixed language background marriages did not produce division, only multiplication and integration of two languages and cultures. For the children of mixed language marriages, a double inheritance is much more likely than a division of loyalties.

This result concerns children from Canadian middle class backgrounds where both languages and both cultures have status and prestige. In in-migrant situations in England and the United States for example, a slightly less rosy picture may be obtained. Such positive outcomes are helped when there is a degree of cultural and language equilibrium in a society. Children who are brought up from birth to celebrate bilingualism and biculturalism do seem to share dual identity advantages.

When children come from language minority backgrounds, working towards an equilibrium between their two cultures and languages may require more accent on the minority language, particularly in the early years. To counterbalance the effect of the dominant majority language, there may need to be two objectives. First, ensuring the child feels secure and confident in the minority language and culture. Second, to ensure that the child is taught the advantages of biculturalism, the value of harmony between cultures and languages, and not taught that conflicting competition is the inevitable outcome of two languages and cultures in contact.

REFERENCE: AELLEN & LAMBERT, 1969

Three Reactions to Acculturation

Working with Italian in-migrants in Great Britain, Tosi (1984) described three reactions of the Italian British to acculturation.

1. Many Italian-Britons became apathetic because they could not cope with pressures from two different cultural experiences. Accepting British values while retaining their Italian background led to passive attitudes. Such apathy was a defense mechanism for resolving the conflict they found between the two cultures and the two languages.
2. Other British-Italians maintained a strong identity with their Italian community. Such people mostly stayed within the social boundaries of the Italian community.
3. A smaller group of young people made an effort to become bilingual and bicultural. They refused to identify solely with the heritage culture (Italian) nor became totally British. This suggests that rootlessness, social isolation and disorientation is not an inevitable part of being an in-migrant, particularly after the first generation. Yet to deny the existence of tension and conflict within in-migrants is to be unsympathetic and insensitive to the dislocation in moving from native to host culture, and being required to consider elements such as allegiance, heritage, rootedness, acceptance and socialization.

A fourth possible outcome would be an identification solely as 'British', which means rejecting an Italian identity, and finding security within a 'British-only' monoculturalism. When such a change is attempted, the reactions of 'significant others' is influential, and, at times, whether such 'significant others' allow entry to, and membership of a British peer or reference group.

Tosi (1984) found that first generation in-migrants tend to cling to their heritage language and culture. In the second generation, there is more pressure to attempt to become bilingual and bicultural. Some second generation in-migrants feel it necessary to choose between the conflicting values of two opposing cultures and environments. Some come to reject the heritage language and culture. By the third and fourth generation, a move from heritage language and culture to that of the host country may be complete, but is not irreversible.

REFERENCE: TOSI, 1984

Cultural Differences

- What seems logical, sensible, important and reasonable to a person in one culture may seem irrational, stupid, and unimportant to an outsider.
- Feelings of apprehension, loneliness, lack of confidence are common when visiting another culture.
- When people talk about other cultures, they tend to describe the differences and not the similarities.
- Differences between cultures are generally seen as threatening and described in negative terms.
- Understanding another culture is a continuous and not a discrete process.
- Stereotyping is probably inevitable in the absence of frequent contact or study.
- The feelings that people have for their own language are often not evident until they encounter another language.
- People often feel their own language is far superior to other languages.
- It is necessary to know the language of a foreign culture to understand a culture in depth.

ADAPTED FROM: HARRIS & MORAN, 1991

Problems of Identity Conflict

Baetens Beardsmore (1986) provides five pieces of advice to avoid or minimize potential problems of identity conflict and alienation.

1. Parents should provide support and encouragement for their children when becoming bilingual and bicultural. Parental attitudes need to be positive to both languages and both cultures.
2. Bilingual education should include bicultural awareness. Language awareness, enculturation in both cultures can be positively conveyed in a school setting.
3. Monolingual language and cultural norms/values should not be applied to measure or evaluate bilingual and bicultural matters.
4. Language problems and adjustment problems may be temporary rather than permanent. Like knots in a plank of wood, they can easily be planed smooth as time proceeds and as opportunities arise to use both languages (and engage in both cultures).
5. Bilingual teachers should become appropriate role models for their particular languages and cultures. They should have positive attitudes to both languages and cultures, providing a positive and harmonious view of biculturalism, and not imparting negative and conflicting views.

REFERENCE: BAETENS BEARDSMORE, 1986

Happy Korean-American children holding balloons and Korean flags watch the Korean Day Parade in New York. When language minority children grow older and try to integrate into majority language society, they may experience anxieties about acceptance and identity.

The identity of a bilingual is a particularly Western problem. In many African, Pacific Rim and Indian language communities, bilingualism (or multilingualism) is accepted as the norm. The oddity is the person who is monolingual and monocultural, who cannot switch between different cultures and language communities. In countries such as Malaysia, linguistic diversity within society, and within an individual, is accepted as natural, normal and desirable.

Cause and Effect

When bilingualism and biculturalism have a detrimental effect on personality, bilingualism is not likely to be the cause. That is, it is not language *per se* that causes personality or social problems. Rather, it is often the social, economic and political conditions surrounding the development of bilingualism that generate such problems. Where the bicultural community is stigmatized, seen as socially inferior, economically underprivileged, and where there is symbolic or physical violence towards the minority language community, personality problems within children may arise. It is not the ownership of bilingualism, but the condition in which that language community lives that may be the cause of the problem. Where language communities are oppressed and downtrodden, it is the prejudice, discrimination and hate by other communities, and not bilingualism, that may affect character and personality.

If there are problems of self-esteem and social and personal identity among bilinguals, they may be caused by an antagonistic pressure on an individual from the dominant, monolingual society. If a bicultural community is stigmatized as socially inferior, the bilingual may suffer in terms of self-esteem and identity. Thus, it is not bilingualism which is the cause, but the environmental circumstances in which bilinguals are located. Particular examples tend to be migrant workers, in-migrants into a dominant monolingual society, showing that color and creed, race and religion may be part of that discrimination.

The key variable may therefore be whether an individual is in a subtractive or additive bilingual and bicultural environment. Where bilingualism and biculturalism is additive, the chances of negative effects on children's personal adjustment may be minimal. Instead, there may be positive effects. In a society where learning a second language and culture is subtractive, where the first language is being depreciated and replaced, potential harmful effects on personality and adjustment may be increased. (See Additive and Subtractive Bilingualism, page 154).

Where bilinguals are encouraged to become monolinguals in the majority language, personality problems may arise. Such integration and assimilation may be demanded but difficult to achieve. The majority language community may be resistant to newcomers. Where race and skin color enter the equation, a bilingual may not be admitted into the host culture. There may be a bar on access to the better jobs, to educational opportunities and to achieving affluence.

The learning of English as a second language (e.g. in England and the United States) is often demanded. But it may increase discrimination and racist attitudes rather than dispel them. The more a teenager moves into English-cultural and English-speaking groups, the more problems of acceptance, identity and integrity of character may occur. In such a subtractive situation, a person may either strive hard to identify with mainstream, monolingual cultural and social values, or alternatively, come to reject everything about the majority language culture, and embrace the heritage language and culture more warmly.

Further Reading

BAETENS BEARDSMORE, H.,1986, *Bilingualism: Basic Principles*. Clevedon: Multilingual Matters Ltd.

HOFFMANN C.,1991, *An Introduction to Bilingualism*. London: Longman.

Bilingualism and the Family

1: Types of Bilingual Family

Introduction

It is very difficult to define simply what is meant by a bilingual family. It is a 'family term' which encompasses an almost infinite variety of situations. Each bilingual family is different, with its own patterns of language within the family and between the family and the local community.

A profile of a bilingual family involves a consideration of the following factors:

- The native language(s) of the parent or parents.
- The language(s) spoken by parents to one another.
- The language(s) spoken by the parent or parents to the children.
- The language(s) spoken by the children to the parent or parents.
- The language(s) spoken by the children to one another.
- The language(s) spoken (or understood) by the extended family (e.g. grandparents, aunts, uncles and cousins) living in the family home or nearby.
- The language(s) spoken (or understood) in the local community and /or by minority language groups.
- The language of the children's education.
- The language of the family's religious observance.
- The official or majority language(s) of the state or country.
- Whether the family is geographically stable or mobile with changing language needs.

This list of questions illustrates the number of factors that influence the nature and level of bilingualism within an individual family. They also show how difficult it is to place individual bilingual families into neat categories. However, the list raises important points for a discussion about bilingualism within families.

A family of Emberas Indians in Panama, Central America. The parents may be monolingual in Emberas, but the children may also learn Spanish through education.

Issues

Bilingualism is not always acquired within the home

The members of a bilingual (or multilingual) family may be able to speak more than one language but may use only one language at home (often a minority language) while they may acquire the dominant language of the community outside the home.

Not every individual in a 'bilingual' family is necessarily bilingual

One parent in a family may be bilingual and may decide to speak his or her native language to the children while the other parent may only be able to speak the dominant language of the local community (e.g. a family living in England with a French-speaking mother and an monolingual English-speaking father). In many in-migrant communities in Western Europe and North America, where local minority speech communities have formed, parents who stay at home may be monolingual or have limited command of English while their partners who work and children who attend school become bilingual outside the home.

Monolingual parents may have bilingual children, while bilingual parents may have monolingual children

Many first generation in-migrants may only develop a limited command of the majority language of the host country. Their children may learn the majority language at school and on the streets. To use a different example, parents who speak only the dominant, majority language of a country may decide to have their children educated in a second majority language or in a heritage minority language. In Canada, many monolingual English parents choose French Immersion education for their children so that they may benefit from bilingualism in the two majority languages of Canada. Similarly, in Wales, monolingual English parents sometimes choose Welsh language education for their children, so that their children may have the advantage of speaking not just English but also the heritage language of Wales.

Sometimes, the opposite can happen. Minority language parents may have negative attitudes towards their language and may opt to raise their children in the majority language. Many in-migrant families, for instance, progress from monolingualism (in the minority language) to bilingualism (minority/majority languages) and again to monolingualism (in the majority language) within two or three generations. This happened with many inmigrants to the United States in the nineteenth and early twentieth centuries, and continues to happen in many parts of the world today.

There may be different degrees of bilingualism within families

Bilingualism itself is not simple to define. Few individuals have equal competence in both languages in all domains of their lives. The majority of bilinguals are dominant in one language. This may not necessarily be their mother tongue, but rather the language they use most frequently. Within bilingual families language dominance and language competence may vary among members and over time. Where parents speak a minority language to their children, and where the language of the community and education is the dominant, majority language, the children may have only passive competence in the minority language. In in-migrant communities, parents may only have limited command of the majority language, while children may eventually become dominant in the majority language. A family move to another area or country, or a switch to a minority language (or majority language) school for the children, may mean a change in the language balance within a family.

Sometimes, where a strong, cohesive language minority community exists, a second, majority language does not play any significant role in the daily life of many individuals and families. In many areas of North and West Wales, for instance, the language of home, school, religion, community and even the workplace is Welsh for many people. English is acquired through the mass media and by contact with non-Welsh speakers inside and outside the community, and through education. Nearly all Welsh speakers, except for the very young and sometimes the very old, are functionally bilingual, but many are dominant in Welsh. Thus a Welsh-speaking family living in a predominantly Welsh-speaking area may have little occasion to use English, and have a much greater competence in Welsh.

Attitudes towards bilingualism determine the fate of bilingualism within the family and in the wider society

Grosjean (1982) makes a distinction between 'elite bilingualism' ('prestigious bilingualism' – see page 15) and

The Agrawal Family

The history of the Agrawal Family illustrates (1) how important is parents' awareness of the process of language shift; (2) the benefits of bilingualism to the maintenance of minority languages and (3) how these factors affect the bilingualism of a child.

Janardhan Prasad Agrawal and his wife Kalpana live in London, and share Hindi as their common mother tongue. They have two children, Kisalaya and Parul. Kisalaya graduated in International Relations, and then undertook a law conversion course. Kisalaya says his 'passive' knowledge of Hindi will be useful to communicate with Hindi-speaking clients. His sister Parul is a student in a local primary school. Janardhan Agrawal works as a primary school teacher, while Kalpana is a librarian. Apart from his regular job, he is also a translator, (e.g. translating stories in Hindi, and helping out Asians in British courts). He is also an active community member.

In this family, the main language spoken at home is and has always been Hindi supported by a strong social network of Hindi speakers in the community. Despite this, Kisalaya has grown up to be a passive bilingual, active in English rather than Hindi. His sister, Parul, is a fluent bilingual through participating in many Indian cultural events and her almost yearly visit to India. However when Parul started going to a British nursery school, she started showing signs of language shift. Parul had always enjoyed stories in Hindi, which she sometimes recounted in her play. In the nursery school, the stories were often told in English, which she enjoyed.

Mr. Agrawal noticed that, after being to the nursery school, Parul felt uncomfortable about stories told in Hindi, until one day she said 'English-only, not Hindi'. Being 'aware' of what was happening, Mr. Agrawal proposed that he would tell the story in Hindi as well as English. Parul's response was 'English first'. Not wanting to upset his daughter, he agreed to rotate between English and Hindi. After the initial language shock of school, Parul with the support, sensitivity, and awareness of her parents, was able to maintain her Hindi. The school has a significant number of Asian bilinguals, hence her attitude to Hindi and her self-concept are positive.

Janardhan Agrawal feels that being new in the UK, he was not aware of how much the majority language could replace a child's own tongue if parents did not remain very committed to language maintenance.

'folk bilingualism'. 'Prestigious bilingualism' occurs when competence in two languages (often prestigious majority languages) is developed and maintained. 'Prestigious bilingualism' within a family context can occasionally occur when bilingualism is cultivated and maintained within the home without outside support. This can occur when one or both parents speak a language which is not widely spoken outside the home and which they decide to transmit to their children, for a number of reasons. These reasons may include a desire to maintain family heritage, contact with monolingual family members, and the educational, social and economic advantages of bilingualism.

'Folk bilingualism' is much more common than 'elite bilingualism'. 'Folk bilingualism' occurs when individual family bilingualism or multilingualism is part of a natural societal pattern. In large areas of Africa and Asia, relatively stable multilingual communities exist, and this is reflected in the language habits of individual families. A diglossic or triglossic situation may exist, where a local or ethnic language may be spoken in the family and immediate neighborhood, an indigenous language of wider communication in the wider area, and a prestigious international language such as French or English or indigenous national language in education and official life. Thus, the bilingualism of the individual family is supported and maintained by the bilingualism or multilingualism of the wider community. A European example of this is the state of Luxembourg, where Luxembourgish (known by its speakers as Lëtzebuergesch) is the family and community language of the majority of the population of four million, but where French and German are used in education, business and official life.

In many parts of Western Europe and North America, bilingual communities exist as a result of immigration (e.g. Latino communities in the US). Also, bilingual communities occur where an indigenous language co-exists with a prestigious international language (e.g. Breton in Brittany, France). However, bilingualism in these communities tends to be less stable. Factors such as the political and economic dominance of majority language speakers, education through the majority language, increased population mobility, the mass media, mean that the minority language may be used less and less in the community. Speakers of the minority language may develop favorable attitudes towards the dominant majority language, seeing it as culturally fashionable and conducive to social and economic advancement. The minority language may be perceived as inferior, old-fashioned, worthless, and a hindrance to progress. Over time, the prestigious language may encroach upon the domains and functions of the minority language within the home. Eventually the minority language ceases to be reproduced within the family.

Fishman (1991) sees the intergenerational transmission of a language as crucial to its survival. Once a language ceases to be reproduced within the family, it is very difficult to reverse its decline. Thus the dwindling of bilingualism within families mirrors the attitudes of society to the minority language and the fate of bilingualism in the wider community.

Categories of Family Bilingualism

Many in-depth studies of the childhood development of bilingualism have been carried out in recent years. Researchers have attempted to place these within broad categories according to the language or languages spoken by the parents to the children and the language of the community. Harding & Riley (1986) and Romaine (1995) suggest the following categories based on language strategies adopted by parents in raising children bilingually.

One person – one language

The parents have different native languages, one of which is the dominant language of the community. The parents each speak their own language to the child from birth. This has been much exalted in the literature on child bilingualism as an effective path to bilingualism. The advantage is that the child keeps the two language separate, realizes that there are two different languages codes, and that it is desirable to use one or the other and not codeswitch (see page 58). Recently, this orthodoxy has been loosened (e.g. by de Houwer, 1995) on the basis that complete separation is an ideal rather than a reality, and that there are case histories of children to show that when both parents use both languages, the child still communicates effectively using both languages. By having discrete episodes in one language before using the other language, and by correction when there is unacceptable mixing of languages, separation of a child's languages can occur.

Non-dominant home language

The parents have different native languages, one of which is the dominant language of the community. Both parents speak the non-dominant language to the child, who learns the dominant language of the community outside the home, particularly through education.

Non-dominant home language without community support

The parents share the same native language, which is not the dominant language of the community. The parents speak their own language to the child.

The Davis Family – an English-Danish Family

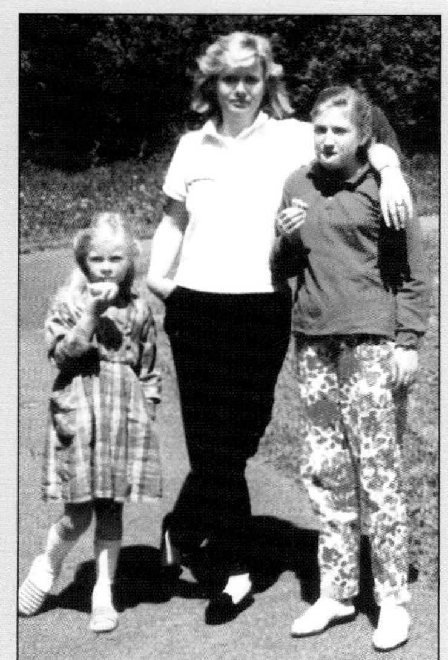

Annette Davis comes originally from Aarhus, one of the two largest cities in the Danish province of Jutland, and like many Danish children, she learnt English at school. Although German is the first foreign language in Danish schools, the incentive to learn English is greater as it is a major international language, and Danish children are exposed to a great deal of English in films and on television. Annette grew up in the 1960s, when many young people from all over the world were captivated by English 'pop' music and by the swinging London scene. Many Danish people have a good command of English and Annette herself found it an attractive language, and not difficult to learn.

Annette came to London at the age of 17, to work as an 'au pair' (family helper). She married an Englishman and has lived in England ever since. She and her husband Michael have two daughters, Suki and Camilla, now 19 and 15 respectively.

When Annette's elder daughter was born, Annette considered speaking Danish to her. However she decided to wait until Suki had mastered the basics of English. Once she had established a relationship in one language with her daughters, it was difficult to change. In the end she never made the transition from English to Danish.

Annette regrets now that she did not receive any advice or support for bringing up her children bilingually when they were little. At the time, she worried that Suki would confuse the two languages, and that she would not master either properly. Annette's husband speaks no Danish and she was concerned that Suki would not be able to communicate with him. Annette's English was, by that time, completely fluent, and she did not find it awkward or difficult to use English with her daughters, learning nursery rhymes and stories alongside them from books and television.

Annette's daughters have frequently expressed an interest in learning Danish and, from time to time, she has made efforts to speak to them in Danish. However, it has proved too difficult to change the habit of speaking one language.

Annette and her family visit relatives in Denmark about once a year, and Annette's mother comes to stay once or twice a year. This gives the girls the opportunity to hear Danish. Although they can only speak a few basic words and simple phrases in Danish, Annette is surprised at how much they understand of everyday conversations since they do not read or write the language. Annette's mother does not speak much English, but she and her granddaughters communicate well in a mixture of English and Danish. When the elder daughter, Suki, was five years old, she visited Denmark with her father for two or three weeks, and came back speaking quite a lot of Danish. Although Annette regrets that she did not speak Danish to her daughters, she acknowledges that it would have been difficult to maintain a language only spoken by one parent and only inside the home. She also feels that, were her daughters to visit Denmark for an extended stay, they would pick up the language quite easily, because of their basic knowledge of it.

The experience of the Davis family shows that bilingualism and biculturalism are not 'all-or-nothing' acquisitions, but can rather be measured on a sliding scale. A restricted measure of bilingualism and biculturalism can be valuable in enriching a child's personality and breadth of experience, helping them to be tolerant of other languages and cultures. This foundation could be built upon at any time in the child's life, to a attain a fuller measure of bilingualism and biculturalism.

Mireille and Joseph – a Haitian Family in New York

Mireille emigrated from Haiti to New York five years ago and her husband, Joseph, joined her two years ago. They both come originally from Port-au-Prince, the capital of Haiti, and their native language is Haitian Creole.

Most of the five million inhabitants of Haiti are the descendants of African slaves brought over by French colonists in the 17th and 18th centuries, to work on the sugar plantations. Haitian Creole is the native language of over 90 percent of the population. It is a French-based creole that also includes elements of Spanish and English. French is the official language of Haiti: it is used in government, in the press and is taught in schools.

Haiti is the one of the poorest countries in the Western hemisphere, with a high level of unemployment. Mireille and Joseph came to New York in search of a better life, but they are proud of their Haitian heritage and eager to maintain their language and culture.

When they arrived in the United States, they realized that they must learn English in order to survive and to gain employment. Mireille is employed as a home attendant and Joseph works in a bakery. Both of them must use English to communicate in their jobs, although some of Joseph's co-workers are Hispanics and speak Spanish among themselves. Mireille learnt English by attending night school in New York and now speaks it quite well. Joseph does not speak a lot of English yet, but he has learnt some by listening to tapes. The couple speak Creole together, and sometimes French (when they don't want their children to understand).

Mireille and Joseph speak mainly Creole to their two daughters, Murielle, eight years old, and her little sister, only a few months old. Murielle was born in Haiti and came to the US with her mother when she was three, so it has been natural for them to speak Creole to her. They are anxious for their children to maintain their Haitian heritage so, three years ago, they placed Murielle in a bilingual Haitian-English program, when she entered first grade. However, prior to that, she spent two years in English-only daycare, while Mireille was at work. Every day she was surrounded by English speakers and English became her dominant language.

Murielle tends to answer her parents in English, although they mainly speak to her in Creole. She also answers her teacher in English during Creole-medium lessons, although the teacher always addresses her in Creole. She tends to speak English to her peers in and out of school, except where the other child has recently moved from Haiti, and speaks only Creole.

Mireille and Joseph feel that the fact that Haiti and the Haitians are viewed in a negative way by the public and the media has not helped Murielle to feel pride in her language and culture. She is more eager to identify with the English language and with US culture. However, her parents are determined at least to give her the option of maintaining her native heritage.

Bilingualism in Changing Circumstances – Christine Helot and Her Children

Christine Helot is Professor of English Linguistics and Applied Linguistics at the University of Strasbourg in Alsace, France. She was born in France, and French was the language of her home, but she learnt fluent English at school in the United States and in Ireland. She learnt German while at school at the Goethe Institute in Germany and speaks it fairly well. The Alsace area is on the border between Germany and France, and many native Alsatians speak the German dialect of Alsatian, High German and French.

Christine Helot married an Irishman and lived for 17 years in Ireland, where their three children were born, Ciara in 1976, Aoife in 1981 and Fabrice in 1982. The children's father was an English teacher and a fluent French speaker, as well as having a working knowledge of Irish. The parents spoke both English and French together and when their elder daughter, Ciara, was born, they decided to try to maintain a strategy of speaking French within the home. When the children were small, this was fairly successful, and the children tended to speak to one another in French. As the children grew older, their exposure to English was greater, from school, friends and television. Both parents were working outside the home, and it was not possible to obtain a French-speaking home help.

The father tended to speak more English with the second and third children. However, Christine Helot continued to use as much French as possible with them, reading books in French, having contact with other French mothers and their children in Ireland, and going regularly to France to visit monolingual French relatives. Both girls continued to speak mainly French to their mother and switched easily and confidently between English and French. They learnt to read English at school, and taught themselves to read French without difficulty. Their brother was more reluctant to switch languages, preferring to use English in Ireland and French in France.

When the children were nine, five and four, the family spent a year in the South of France, living in a small village. During this period, the parents switched to using English in the home in order to maintain that language.

The elder daughter attended a local primary school where she learnt to write in French. The younger children attended the local nursery school. During the year French gradually became the children's dominant language, owing to the influence of school and community. After only a few weeks Fabrice, the four year old, had changed from preferring to speak English to showing a definite preference for French.

After the family's return to Ireland, Fabrice joined a playgroup and, for a week, didn't say a word either in French or English. On his second Monday there, he said something in English, with a very strong Southern French accent. Gradually, over a period of months, the accent disappeared and English became his dominant language again.

Christine and her husband separated in 1988, and she returned to live in France in 1990 with the children, then aged fourteen, nine and eight. All three were still bilingual, but to different degrees, with English being their dominant language. Christine's son had some initial difficulties at his French school. Since he understood French perfectly and spoke it without a foreign accent, it was hard for his monolingual teacher to accept that he came from a different culture and school system, and would need help to adapt, and to develop his reading and writing skills in French. He did not receive any recognition, either, for his fluency and literacy in English. The teacher's solution was to move him to sit with the other 'problem' children, who had no knowledge of French. In spite of this difficult beginning, Christine's son made excellent progress during the first year, catching up in literacy skills with his French peers, adapting to his new life and to a less flexible French school system, and becoming dominant in French. He then transferred to a private school where the teachers were more sensitive to his needs as a bilingual child who had changed the language of his education.

Christine was aware of the need to maintain the children's English after the move to France. However, the children needed a lot of help with their school work, and the stress of moving and a new job meant that Christine's time and energy were limited. However, she has continued to speak English, as well as French to the children. She tends to speak more English than French to the eldest daughter, roughly equal amounts of English and French to the second daughter, and more French than English to her son. Christine has obtained cable TV so that the children can watch British and American TV channels. She also buys them English language videos and books.

The children tend to speak French to her and to one another most of the time, but the family all switch to English in the presence of monolingual English speakers. Sometimes, the conversation turns quite naturally to English when the family are talking about Ireland.

When the family lived in Ireland, the children's English was stronger than their French. Naturally, this has changed since the family moved to France. Christine feels that the elder daughter, who was 14 when they moved to France, is still slightly dominant in English but has native speaker fluency in French. She also speaks fluent German. French is the younger daughter's dominant language, although she has native speaker fluency in English and also speaks good German. French is the son's stronger language. He speaks fluent English but is having to relearn how to write English in school. He is making progress in German.

The children are very happy to have dual cultural identity. The elder daughter feels equally Irish and French, the younger daughter is undecided, and the son feels more Irish than French. Christine makes an effort to maintain their awareness of their Irish identity by taking them to see Irish films, listening to Irish music, having books about Ireland and in the Irish language in the house, and talking to them about the changing political situation in Ireland. She feels that through their bilingualism and biculturalism the children have grown up to appreciate other cultures and nationalities and to be sensitive to prejudice and racism. Their knowledge of English has also helped them to master German.

The experience of Christine Helot's family is similar to that of many families who have to adapt to moves to different countries and to changes in personal circumstances. Her experience shows that, in spite of many practical difficulties, bilingualism can be maintained in changing situations.

Double non-dominant home language without community support

The parents have different native languages, neither of which is the dominant language of the community. The parents each speak their own language to the child from birth. This results in family trilingualism.

Non-native parents

The parents share the same native language, which is the dominant language of the community. One of the parents always addresses the child in a language which is not his/her native language.

Mixed language

The parents are bilingual and the family lives in a community which is at least partly bilingual. The parents speak both languages to the children, tending to codeswitch and mix (see page 58).

These categories are useful in that they enable researchers to classify and compare family situations. However, they only represent a typology of the research already undertaken. They are, of necessity, simplistic and by no means exhaustive. One main limitation is that most studies (apart from Type 6 and Type 3 studies of language minority children) are concerned with 'prestigious bilingualism', where there is a stable bilingual environment and a commitment to bilingualism in spite of changing family circumstances. As has been discussed in this section, in many families, bilingualism can be in a state of development or decline, and this often reflects the state of bilingualism in the wider speech community.

One-Parent Families and Bilingualism

Almost all case-studies of bilingual children have been based on two-parent families. Books dealing with raising children bilingually tend to assume the presence of two parents in the family home. By accident rather than design, this implies that a one-parent family has little or no chance of raising a child bilingually. This is not true for a number of reasons.

For instance, a second language is often acquired outside the home. In parts of Africa, children acquire one language at home or in the neighborhood and another language (or even two or three) at school, in inter-ethnic communication and in urban areas. Children of inmigrant Asian communities in Britain may acquire Panjabi, Urdu, Bengali, Hindi or another Asian language in the home and neighborhood, and learn English at school. A single parent who speaks French but resides in Britain may decide to make French the family language so that the children may have the opportunity of bilingualism. In cases like these, the absence of a parent does not necessarily hinder a child's bilingual development.

In some cases, the maintenance of a family's bilingualism may be challenged by the absence of a parent. In cases such as (1) above, where one parent speaks the dominant language of the community to the children, and the other parent uses a minority language with them, the death or departure of the second parent may mean that the family is in danger of becoming monolingual. However, if the remaining parent is committed to the maintenance of the family's bilingualism, it could be accomplished in various ways.

In cases of separation or divorce, frequent contact with the absent parent may ensure that the children maintain competence in the minority language. Where death has occurred, or where there is infrequent or no contact with the second parent, the remaining parent may occasionally choose to speak the minority language (rather than the majority language) to the children some or all of the time, to safeguard the lower status language. If this is not possible or desirable, the single parent may decide to send the children to a school where the minority language is the medium of education. Contact with friends and relations who speak the minority language, and trips to places it is spoken, are other ways to support children's bilingualism.

The disruption of a family by death or divorce is extremely traumatic for both parents and children. At times of great mental and emotional stress, when many practical difficulties and changes have to be faced, bilingualism may seem low on the list of priorities. However, single-parent families are often adept at meeting challenges and may look for ways of maintaining a child's bilingualism without causing further disruption to the child's life. In addition, where a child has undergone such stress, it may be wise, if possible, to avoid the added trauma of losing a language, a culture and an intrinsic part of the child's identity.

Further Reading

ARNBERG, L., 1987, *Raising Children Bilingually: The Pre-School Years.* Clevedon: Multilingual Matters Ltd.

BAKER, C., 1995, *A Parents' and Teachers' Guide to Bilingualism.* Clevedon: Multilingual Matters Ltd.

DÖPKE S., 1992, *One Parent One Language.* Amsterdam/Philadelphia: John Benjamins.

HARDING, E. & RILEY, P., 1986, *The Bilingual Family.* Cambridge, Cambridge University Press.

ROMAINE, S., 1995, *Bilingualism* (Second edition). Oxford: Blackwell.

SAUNDERS, G., 1988, *Bilingual Children: From Birth to Teens.* Clevedon: Multilingual Matters Ltd.

The Lundberg Family – Swedish at Home, English Outside

Elisabeth Mossler-Lundberg comes originally from Stockholm in Sweden and her husband Olof is from Gothenburg. The study of international languages, especially English, is considered to be very important in Scandinavian countries. The population of Sweden is only nine million and Swedish people are highly motivated to learn English, since it is so widely used internationally. Swedish children grow up hearing English in pop music, television programs and commercials. They are very aware that learning English will help them to communicate with people in other countries, and will be a great advantage for travel and in the job market. Children begin to learn English in primary school. Older people, who have not had the opportunity to learn foreign languages at school, or who learnt by old-fashioned grammar-based methods, often go to adult education classes or follow evening courses at the university. Many employers sponsor foreign language classes for their employees.

Both Olof and Elisabeth studied English, German and French at school. Olof's amateur radio hobby helped improve his English, and later, when he started working at Swedish Telecom, he participated in international committees. He also read widely in English. While still at school, Elisabeth had English-speaking penfriends, and went to the US for three months on a international educational program.She also made use of her English while traveling in Europe. She studied English and German at the University of Stockholm. The Lundbergs moved to England in 1980, when Olof was offered a job in an international organization. Elisabeth was trained as an economist but now works as an interpreter and translator, and as an organizer of study programs in Britain for Swedish professionals. She uses Swedish and English at work, and translates and interprets from English and German into Swedish.

Their elder daughter, Christina, was born in 1980, and Anna in 1982. Both parents were eager to bring them up to speak Swedish. In largely monolingual countries such as England, it is sometimes hard to obtain accurate information and support for bilingualism. Elisabeth found some literature on raising children bilingually, which gave her ideas and inspiration.

When Christina was born, it was natural for the parents to speak Swedish to her. For the first three years of her life, she heard little but Swedish, since the family had not had time to develop many outside contacts. Other people tried to persuade the parents to speak English to her, 'in case she was at a disadvantage', but they continued their policy of speaking Swedish. When Christina started playschool at three, she could only say 'bye-bye' in English. However, after the first few days she made a friend and settled in. She did not speak a word during the first term, but after a few months she suddenly began to speak English.

When Anna was little, she heard more English than Christina at the same age, because the family had more social contacts in English. However, she really did not learn much English until she went to playschool.

After playschool, the girls attended an English-medium school, and thus all their contacts outside the home were in English. Where a minority language is used only within the home, it often happens that the children understand the minority language, but tend to reply in the majority language. In other words, they become 'passive' or 'receptive' bilinguals. The Lundbergs had met several Swedish families in England where this was the case. They were determined that their children would become competent and active Swedish speakers. As well as always speaking Swedish within the home, they read Swedish books to the children, sang Swedish songs, obtained videos of Swedish television programs and Swedish language cassettes to play in the car. They were able to spend summer and Easter holidays in Sweden, and had many Swedish visitors to stay. They attended services at the Swedish church in London, where the girls met other Swedish-speaking children. Celebrating special festivals such as Christmas, Lucia and Midsummer helped the children to develop an awareness of their Swedish heritage.

The children have always spoken Swedish to their parents, and to one another. They are proud of their ability to speak two languages, and enjoy the advantage of having a 'secret' family code in which to communicate.

The girls feel that English is their stronger language because they have been educated solely through English, and most of their contacts outside the home are in that language. They speak fluent English without an accent and both have excellent grades for English in school, which shows that bilingualism has not been a handicap.

The girls also speak excellent Swedish with a natural Swedish accent. Once, while on a skiing holiday in Sweden, no-one believed them when they said that they lived in London. Olof and Elisabeth wanted the girls to be able to read and write in Swedish, but the girls were not interested in the reading books they had bought from a school shop in Sweden. However, Elisabeth subscribed to some comics in Swedish and, once the girls had learnt to read in English, they were eager to read these, and learnt to read independently in Swedish. From there they progressed to reading Swedish books. They gradually learnt to write Swedish, without any formal tuition, and get plenty of practice by corresponding with Swedish penfriends. They write as correctly as many of their peers in Sweden.

It is natural that the girls' competence in their two languages does not always match that of monolingual speakers, especially in vocabulary. This is generally true of bilinguals, as they tend to use their languages in different domains or contexts.

There is often transfer of vocabulary from English into Swedish, for instance, when the children are discussing school matters. This is quite natural, because the whole of their school life and other aspects of their life outside the home are lived through the medium of English. Their parents try to help them by repeating the term in Swedish. Whenever they spend a period of time in Sweden, immersed in the Swedish language, the English influence on their Swedish tends to disappear.

The girls are very proud of their ability to speak Swedish and of their Swedish heritage. Christina feels that she has a dual cultural identity, but Anna is aware that she is not familiar with the life of her contemporaries in Sweden, having never lived there. The girls are aware that possessing two languages and being a part of two cultures is an enriching experience.They have access to their Swedish roots and can communicate with grandparents and other monolingual relatives and friends in Sweden.

The Myers-Halling Family – Receptive Bilingualism is a Worthwhile Asset

Helen Myers-Halling comes originally from Cheshire, England. Her home language was English. She studied German and French at school, and then at University. She has lived in Meppen, Germany since 1974, and works as a language teacher, teaching English and some French. She still feels that English is her dominant language, but she speaks fluent German and feels comfortable and confident in both languages.

Bernd Halling comes originally from the Hanover area of Germany. He was brought up to speak German. He is a teacher of Art and CDT (Craft, Design and Technology) at a local secondary school. He studied English at school for nine years and has improved his command of the language by listening to his wife, and during visits to England. Sometimes he has an opportunity to use English at school when speaking to students on exchange visits.

Helen and Bernd speak German together, as her German is more fluent than his English. They have two children, Torsten (16 years old) and Sonja (14 years old). Before they were born, the parents discussed the idea of bringing up their children bilingually. They decided to do what seemed natural, each parent speaking their own native language to the children. From birth onwards, the children heard only German from Bernd and only English from Helen.

Living in a small town in Germany, there was little opportunity to meet other bilingual families. However Helen had met a family living in Germany with an English mother who had only spoken English to the children. When she visited them, the teenage sons always answered their mother in German, but were able to speak English to British guests or relatives. This was an encouragement for Helen.

When the children were very small, they spent some of the time alone with their mother, hearing only English, and they spoke English to her. After starting nursery school at about three, their exposure to German increased considerably, and they began to speak only German. For a while Helen tried to persuade them to speak English to her: they played English games, including one where the children had to pretend to be English relatives. This worked quite well until Sonja announced that she wanted to be a baby and could only say 'Da-da-da'! Eventually, Helen decided to continue to do what seemed natural, i.e. to speak English to the children, and not try to persuade them to reply in the language. Some years later, in 1987, Helen obtained literature about bilingualism which described families where the children were 'receptive' or 'passive' bilinguals (i.e. understanding but not speaking the second language). This emphasized that 'receptive bilingualism' did not represent failure, but was a worthwhile asset. The children have continued to speak German to Helen. They have always attended German schools and speak German to one another and to all their friends.

Bernd Halling has always spoken German to Helen, and to the children, but, since he understands English well, he is not left out when his wife speaks to the children in English. When visitors are present, Helen has tried to be consistent in speaking English to the children, even if this can be awkward at times. Only on rare occasions has she switched briefly to speaking German to them, for instance, when a young German friend is present, so that the friend does not feel excluded. (Now that the children's friends study English at school, this is not so necessary). When the children started number work at school, English numbers seemed to confuse them, so their mother switched to saying the numbers in German. When they had grasped the basics of Mathematics this was no longer necessary.

The family tries to reinforce the children's English by providing books and cassette tapes in English. They visit Britain once a year, and the children always speak English to their English relatives, although they are sometimes embarrassed when they don't know a word, or when an English person speaks quickly or indistinctly, with a strong accent or on an unfamiliar topic, so that they have trouble comprehending. Both children have learnt to read English, although, since the age of about 11, Torsten has not wanted to read any English books except for one about football which is not published in German. Sonja has continued to read English books about her favorite hobby, riding.

Since the age of 10 (Sonja) and 11 (Torsten) the children have studied English in school alongside their classmates. Initially, they found the English lessons rather boring, but as time went on they were pleased that they knew so much. They started learning French at the age of 12 (Sonja) and 13 (Torsten) and are aware that they know much more English than French. However they are sometimes daunted by the fact that the teachers expect so much more of them, knowing that they were brought up bilingually.

Both the children appreciate their partly British heritage. Torsten identifies more with Germany and the German people, but says that British culture is very familiar to him because of the family's yearly visits. Sonja is very fond of Britain: she says that she feels at home there, and that people are friendly and talkative. However, she would not like to bring up her children in Britain because of the longer school hours. (In Germany, children only attend school in the morning). She feels that, because British children spend longer hours in school, peer pressure is stronger and children are more vulnerable to problems such as drugs and bullying.

The experience of the Halling family indicates that 'receptive bilingualism' need not represent a failure to develop full bilingualism, but is a valuable asset in itself. The children have access to two cultures, and, at some future date, could easily build on this foundation to become fluent English speakers.

2: The Development of Bilingualism in Children

Introduction

The development of bilingualism in children can take place in various ways. Some children are exposed to two languages from birth and learn to speak them at the same time. This is often called simultaneous bilingualism. Other children hear one language in the home and come into contact with another later, in the neighborhood or wider community. This often happens through playgroup, nursery school and school. This has been variously called consecutive, sequential or successive bilingualism. Three years of age is generally regarded as an approximate borderline between simultaneous and consecutive bilingualism.

Young Asian children in England acquire English as a second language through the school system.

Any distinction between simultaneous bilingualism and sequential bilingualism will be artificial because each family and community situation is different. Children who hear both languages in the home rarely hear those languages for equal amounts of time. One parent may spend more time with the child, or one of the languages in the home may also be the dominant language of the community. Children who only hear one language at home may pick up a second language at a very early age from friends and neighbors, and sometimes from television.

Simultaneous Bilingualism

The way in which children acquire language has been the subject of much research. The language development of bilinguals has been compared to that of monolinguals in several studies. It has been shown that the language development of bilinguals follows the same basic steps as that of monolinguals (de Houwer, 1995). Until recently, it was thought that a three-stage model of early bilingual development in a child was accurate. This model, originating from Volterra & Taeschner (1978), portrays the young bilingual moving from mixing two languages to partial and then full separation. A thorough review by de Houwer (1995) of this area finds the three-stage model has little research basis, and children as young as two separate rather than mix their languages. Similarly, Paradis & Genesee (1996) have shown that the grammars of French and English of two and three year olds in Canada are acquired separately and autonomously. Although based on only one case, Quay (1994) found that translation equivalents in Spanish and English were produced from the beginnings of speech (around one year old). The child in this case had equivalent terms in both languages (e.g. for objects, events and processes) from the beginning of speech.

The Early Years

Language acquisition does not begin when children utter their first recognizable words at around the age of one. Language acquisition begins at birth or perhaps even before. Some experts believe that babies in the womb not only hear sounds, but learn to recognize them. Studies of children only a few hours old have shown that they can recognize and respond to their mother's voice, and after a few weeks can react to subtle differences in consonantal sounds. In their first year of life, children pass through several important stages in their language development. They engage in different types of vocal play, like cooing and babbling which helps them learn to co-ordinate their muscles and try out different sounds. They begin to comprehend language long before they can speak. They also begin to learn that language is a vehicle for interaction and communication.

At about one year, many children utter their first recognizable words and begin to build a vocabulary. This is mainly composed of naming words and some words for actions. At around eighteen months old, many children

Age	Language
First year	Babbling, cooing, laughing (dada, mama, gaga).
Around 1 year old	First understandable words.
During the second year	Two-word combinations, moving slowly to three- and four-word combinations. Three element sentences (e.g. *Daddy come now; That my book; Teddy gone bye-byes*). For bilinguals, the combinations may sometimes 'mix' two languages.
3 to 4 years	Simple but increasingly longer and complex sentences involving more than one clause start to develop. Conversations show turn taking, but not always respond ing to each other. Increasing fluency and accuracy but still many errors. Starting to join phrases with 'and' and 'but'.
4 years onwards	Increasingly complex sentences, structure and ordered conversation. Use of pronouns and auxiliary verbs.

begin to string two words together to make phrases. From then on, their utterances develop and become progressively more complex.

During this initial stage, children are defining the boundaries of words and trying to express themselves with the vocabulary available to them. Sometimes a child will over-extend the meaning of a word. For example, she might use the word 'dog' to refer to any four legged animal. A child can sometimes 'under-extend' the meaning (e.g. use the word 'dog' just to refer to the family's own dog).

Set out above is an average pattern of language development for monolingual children. Children in families where two languages are approximately equally developed will be similar in the sequence of development (Lyon, 1996). However, it must be stressed that many children, monolinguals and bilinguals, differ from these general averages and will show perfectly normal language development later in childhood.

Young children who are learning two languages simultaneously follow very much the same pattern as children learning one. First, they assemble a vocabulary composed of elements from both languages, but usually with only one 'label' for each object or action, taken from one of their languages. Later, they begin to separate their vocabularies, using equivalent terms in each language, but using a combination of the grammatical rules of both languages.

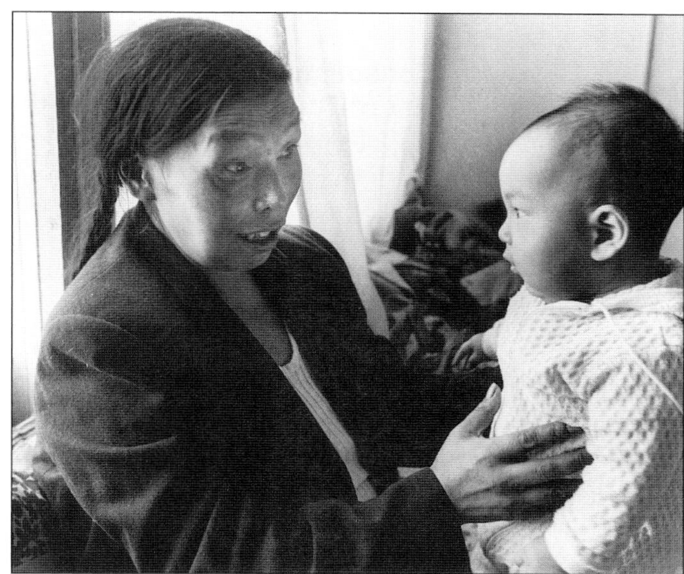

An Inuit (Eskimo) mother from Northern Canada speaks her native language, Inuktitut, to her child. Children begin to comprehend language long before they can speak it. The Inuit people of North America no longer live in isolation, and the existence of their native language and culture is threatened. The child will learn English in the community and at school, although Inuktitut-medium teaching in the early grades is becoming more common.

Codeswitching in Young Children

There is frequently a stage of 'mixing' two languages in children. Early research suggested that the child initially sees the two languages as a single unified system and only gradually distinguishes between them. However, some recent studies have suggested that the child can distinguish between the two systems from a very early stage and that the use of elements from both languages is an elementary form of 'codeswitching' (see page 58).

'Codeswitching' is the term used to describe the subtle and purposeful way in which bilinguals switch between their two languages. Bilinguals often codeswitch because they simply do not know a word or a phrase in one language or because they can express an idea more adequately or effectively in a second language. Thus, very young children, rather than confusing their two languages, may be codeswitching in a practical and purposeful way, attempting to express themselves with the vocabulary and grammar available to them. Just as the monolingual English child will over-extend the meaning of the word 'dog' to refer to any four-legged animal, so the bilingual Spanish-English child might 'over-extend' the use of the word *'perro'* to refer to a dog when speaking English. Codeswitching often occurs from the child's weaker language into the child's stronger or 'dominant' language. A child may also codeswitch when a word or phrase is simpler or easier to pronounce in the other language.

Stages in Consecutive Language Development of Young Bilingual Children

Tabors & Snow (1994) argue that children pass through four stages when sequentially learning a second language. That is, children aged over three who already have one relatively well developed language and who begin to learn a second language, develop through four stages.

Stage 1 When everyone around a child is speaking a different language, children will usually try to use their home language. This leads to increasing frustration as the child realizes that other children cannot understand this language. Eventually the child gives up trying to make others understand the home language.

Stage 2 Children may abandon any attempt to communicate with others in the classroom in their first language. They enter a period when they may not talk at all but use non-verbal actions to get adults and other children to help them. This may be a short or a relatively long phase. However, during this phase children begin to actively 'crack the code' of the second language. For example, children in this phase will rehearse the new language by repeating what other people say in a low voice and playing with the sounds of the new language.

Stage 3 At this stage, children are ready to 'have a go' publicly with the new language. The language will tend to be non-grammatical and telegraphic.They make very short utterances, using just enough words to convey meaning as in 'get book' to convey the meaning of 'I want to go and get a book from the shelf'. The child may also use simple formulas and repeat some phrases without understanding the full meaning.

Stage 4 The final stage is reached when the child moves beyond short utterances and understands the language that is being conveyed more appropriately and grammatically. The child has acquired the rules of the new language and is able to communicate relatively competently.

There are considerable individual differences at the rate at which children pass through these four stages. For example, the no-talking, non-verbal stage can last for a few weeks or for a year or more. More extrovert children may not even have a silent period.

REFERENCE: TABORS & SNOW, 1994

Children make use of their growing competence in two languages in other ways. Semantic transfer may occur from one language to another e.g. the Welsh verb '*gwneud*' and the French verb '*faire*' both mean 'do' and 'make'. Thus, a Welsh- or French-speaking child may announce, in English, that she is going to 'make her homework' or 'do a cake'.

Parents are often concerned when their bilingual children 'mix' their two languages and worry that they are mentally confused. This is not accurate. The bilingual child, like his or her monolingual counterpart, is learning at a tremendous rate, experimenting with language, defining and refining usage.

Codeswitching is also learned behavior. In many homes where more than one language is spoken, family members switch freely between two languages and thus the child imitates this behavior. (This also happens in relatively stable bilingual communities where codeswitching has become a norm). In families where the adults keep the languages separate, children tend to codeswitch much less. Some children in such families do not appear to codeswitch at all. By the age of about three, most bilingual children appear to be aware of the existence of two distinct languages and are beginning to use them in a separate and consistent way.

Language Development and Language Boundaries

The pace of the average bilingual child's language development is not significantly different from that of the average monolingual child. Bilingual children utter their first words at roughly the same age as monolingual children (approximately one year). During a bilingual child's early years, progress may be slower, because a child is learning two vocabularies and language systems instead of one. However, many bilingual children catch up with their monolingual counterparts in one of their languages by the age of four or five. (This usually happens when one of the languages spoken by the child is the language of the wider community). It is only when children approach formal schooling (and require sufficient language development in one of their languages to be able to understand the curriculum) that most developmental language concerns should begin. A separate topic deals with language-delayed children (see page 574).

A valuable feature of the bilingual child's development is the creation of language boundaries. The child learns to associate one language with certain individuals or with certain contexts or situations. In families where two languages are spoken, many parents try to help this process by maintaining a strategy of 'one-parent/one language'

The Case of Hildegard

One classic study of childhood bilingualism is by Werner Leopold. Born in Germany, he emigrated to the United States in 1925. Having initially taught Spanish at Marquette University in Milwaukee, he became a phonetics professor at Northwestern University in 1927. Leopold married one of the students on his Spanish course at Northwestern, and, on the 3rd July 1930, their first child, Hildegard Rose Leopold was born. She was to become the subject of one of the most intensive case studies of bilingual development in childhood.

Leopold's study of the bilingual language development of a child was not the first. Ronjat as early as 1913 had published his experience of raising his son Louis. Louis was spoken to in French by his father, and in German by his mother. The father's relatives spoke to Louis in French; the mother's relatives in German. Louis became fluent in both languages. Ronjat concluded that his son's intellectual development was not retarded in any way by his becoming bilingual.

Ronjat's study was innovative, but more anecdotal and less methodical than W. F. Leopold's classic study. Leopold's highly systematic observations were recorded in four volumes, published between 1939 and 1949 by the Northwestern University Press in Evanston, Illinois and entitled *Speech Development of a Bilingual Child. A Linguist's Record.* Running to 859 pages, the concern for accurate and detailed description is formidable and impressive.

Leopold spoke German to Hildegard (and to his wife, Marguerite, who was an American of German descent). Marguerite spoke English to Hildegard. As with Ronjat, the family adopted the 'one-parent/one language' approach to developing bilingualism in their child. When Hildegard was only eight weeks old, Leopold attempted to make as complete a record as possible of her initial sounds and speech in both English and German. This continued until Hildegard was age eight. From eight years onwards, Leopold recorded just the major and significant speech events in Hildegard's life.

Volume 1 records Hildegard's vocabulary development; Volume 2 the development of her sound system; Volume 3 the development through the first two years of bilingualism; and Volume 4 Leopold's diary notes from age two onwards, plus observations about Hildegard's younger sister, Karla.

In the first two years, Hildegard did not differentiate between English and German. Nor did she recognize that German should be spoken to her father, English to her mother. She initially mixed English and German as if it were one language. In her third year, Hildegard began to separate her two languages and became aware of speaking and listening to two languages. She also increasingly became able to translate between two languages and inspect those languages.

One theme in Leopold's study is shifts in dominance between Hildegard's two languages. At the start of her second year, Hildegard visited Germany for three months, and her German accelerated and became dominant. On their return to the United States, her father was the only source of German. English became dominant, reflecting the wider experience of English among friends, relatives and neighbors.

Around her fifth birthday, Hildegard visited Germany for seven months. German became her dominant language. On return to the United States, she understood English but could only produce brief, awkward sentences. Before playing with a friend called Mary Alice, Hildegard had to practice what to say to ask Mary Alice if she would like to play. When playing with Mary Alice, there were many silences as Hildegard had to relearn how to speak English. Within six days, Hildegard 'chatted incessantly in English'.

At age seven, Hildegard still spoke German with her father. However, the predominance of English in Hildegard's world led to the supremacy of English. By time she was 14, Hildegard's German was notably weaker than her English. The formal and informal aspects of English-only schooling were a major contributor to the imbalance. English was increasingly used with her father. Werner Leopold did not insist Hildegard spoke German to him. With touching humanity, particularly from someone who so intensely studied his daughter's two languages, he focuses on life's priorities:

> *'There is a danger that much of what has been built up laboriously over the years will be lost. But there are things in the life of a family which are even more important than the preservation of a linguistic skill.'*
> (Leopold, 1949, Volume 4, page 53)

Werner Leopold was a prophet ahead of his time. In a period when research had connected bilingualism to lower IQ, he suggested that bilingualism was advantageous for the child. It took two decades for research on IQ and bilingualism to confirm his suggestion. Leopold also indicated that Hildegard had an advantage in that she was able to separate word meaning from word sound. Since she had two or more words for each object or idea, she recognized earlier than monolinguals that words are arbitrary labels and do not, in themselves, contain meaning. *'I see in early bilingualism',* Leopold wrote, '*the advantage that it trains the child to think instead of merely speaking half mechanically.'* Three decades passed before research on cognition and bilingualism confirmed this suggestion. In the 1990s, this interest in the metalinguistic advantages of bilinguals has been prominent.

Leopold created a pioneering and visionary study. While there is much description in the four volumes, there is also vision. A finishing quotation illustrates:

> *'Ignorance and superstition make the decisions of life simple. Education does not make life easier, but better and richer. Few would condemn education for this reason. Bilingualism should be seen in the same light.'*
> (Leopold, 1949, Volume 3, page 188)

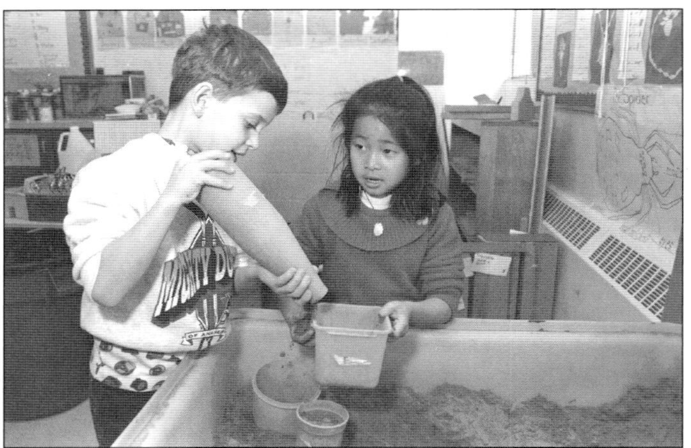

Younger children may learn a language more easily because they have more time, the language is simpler and more concrete.

Both parents may be able to speak both languages and may use one or both when speaking with one another. However, in their interaction with the child, each uses a separate language.

In homes where only one language is spoken, often a minority language, parents may seek to safeguard the development of that language by attempting to create a geographical boundary, and generally avoiding the use of the majority language in the home. As children grow older, this becomes more difficult. In a few families, time boundaries are used. Both parents speak both languages to the child but at different times of the week. For example, a family may speak English on weekdays and French at weekends. However, what needs avoiding is an arbitrary change of language that may confuse the child.

Children themselves often create their own language boundaries, to simplify the task of knowing which language to speak in each situation. Children sometimes generalize from specific situations, with amusing results. A child with a German-speaking father may attempt to address all men in German, and, when asked why, may explain 'All daddies speak German'. A child with a Swedish-speaking mother and older sister may believe that 'only ladies speak Swedish'.

In a bilingual community, geographical boundaries may become established in the child's mind: one language in the home, at Granny's house, in the church or mosque, at the local shop; another language in school, at the doctor's surgery and in the town center. The child may also assign boundaries of age. In situations where a minority language is in decline, for instance, the child may associate the language only with older people.

Small children often react with surprise, confusion or even embarrassment when these language boundaries are crossed. If a parent or grandparent, for instance, attempts to address a child in a different language from the one they use generally, the child may become upset or angry. If one language is usually spoken in a neighbor's house and the child encounters a speaker of the other language there, the child may refuse to speak. If a child is addressed by a young person in a language associated with older speakers, the child may become confused or insist on replying in the majority language.

Consecutive Bilingualism

There are a variety of routes to consecutive bilingualism. Some bilingual children learn one language first in the home and another in the community. Many children from minority language homes are exposed to the majority language for the first time when starting school. (See page 99 regarding minority and majority languages.) Some older children learn a second language at a later age after a move to a foreign country. If children learn

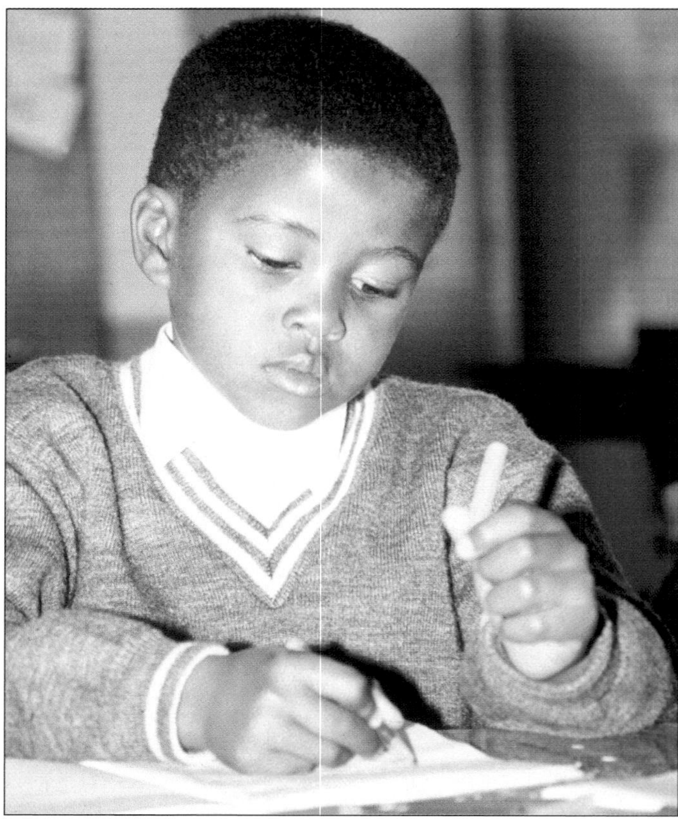

A seven-year-old boy learns to write in the first grade of an English-medium school in Gaborone, Botswana. The African country of Botswana was a British Protectorate until 1966 and English is still the official language and the main medium of education. However, 85 percent of the population speak Setswana as a first language. In many former colonial countries, the main medium of education is still the former colonial language (e.g. English or French). However, since the colonial language is usually not widely spoken as a mother tongue, children may find it hard to cope in the curriculum with an unfamiliar language. The development of both languages may suffer.

language in a 'natural' environment (as opposed to foreign language learning which is confined to the classroom), there are many similarities between the simultaneous acquisition of two languages and consecutive acquisition of two languages. Children tend to pick up single phrases and set phrases first, concentrate on simple grammatical constructions, over-extend vocabulary and grammar (e.g. using the present tense instead of the past tense). In the initial phases of second language acquisition, transference of vocabulary and grammatical structures from the first language tends to occur.

There is no critical age for second language learning (see page 660 on age and bilingualism). Studies have shown that older children, (and adults), can learn a language more quickly and efficiently than younger children, because their cognitive skills are more developed. (It appears that after a certain age, children have more difficulty in achieving native-like pronunciation, for reasons that are not yet fully understood.) However, it is sometimes simpler for younger children to learn a second language. They have fewer demands on their time, the level of language required is not so high and they have fewer inhibitions.

While children can learn a second language at any age, it is important that the acquisition of a second language does not detract from mastery of the first language. This can happen, for instance, when a child from a minority language home is placed in a majority language school where the minority language and culture are ignored. The young child may be in an alien environment, being taught in an unintelligible language, often having to compete with native speakers of the majority language. The child's first language skills, as well as the home environment and culture, may be devalued.

A Vietnamese in-migrant family to the US. Children born and educated in the new country may quickly acquire and prefer to speak the majority language. They may only develop a passive competence in their home language, understanding what is said to them, but replying in the majority language.

This type of situation can be defined as a subtractive bilingual situation (see page 154). Here, the introduction of a second language detracts from the child's developing skills in the first language. In this situation the first language skills fail to develop properly, yet the child struggles to attain the second language skills needed to cope in the classroom. An example is Tanzania, where the introduction of English-medium instruction at secondary school level detracts from the development of academic

Charlotte Hoffmann

Charlotte Hoffmann is a Professor at the Department of Modern Languages at the University of Salford in the North of England and Associate Director of the European Studies Research Institute. She was educated at the University of Heidelberg in Germany and the University of Reading in England. Her book entitled *An Introduction to Bilingualism* has been acknowledged as a comprehensive first introduction to the subject of bilingualism that incorporates a linguistic, psychological, sociolinguistic and political survey of research and theories. Focusing on bilingualism as an individual and societal phenomenon, the book has provided students of linguistics, sociolinguistics and psycholinguistics with a broad and balanced introduction to this subject.

Charlotte Hoffmann is also well-known for her innovative writing on trilingualism in children. Presenting an analysis of her experience in raising children in Spanish, German and English, she has shown the anxieties and advantages that will be encountered in raising trilingual children.

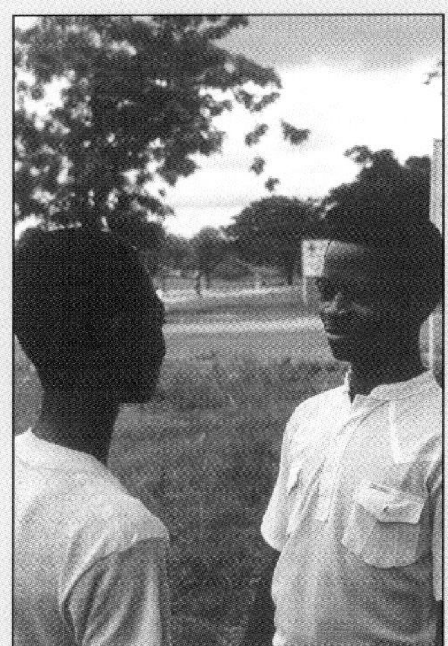

Teenage boys socialize in the African country of Zaire. Between 300 and 400 language varieties are spoken in Zaire. Children learn their own vernacular at home and then learn one of the regional languages such as Lingala or Kikongo in the wider community or at school. If they continue with their education, they also learn French, the official language.

Childhood Trilingualism

Since the larger part of the world's population is bilingual, the majority of children in the world grow up speaking two languages. Many children in the world acquire at least a passive competence in several languages. In multilingual communities in Africa and Asia, for instance, children may acquire one or more languages at home, and others in the local neighborhood, at school and in the wider community.

In North America and Europe, urbanization, centralization and the spread of education have meant that trilingualism and multilingualism are relatively uncommon. One documented route to trilingualism is parents speaking two different languages to their children at home. The children then take their education through a third language. The majority language of the community will influence the relative strengths of the three languages and relative proficiency in each of the three languages may also change over time. Stable trilingualism seems less likely than stable bilingualism. Establishing trilingualism early on is usually easier than successfully maintaining trilingualism over the teenage years. A school that is positive towards multilingualism and multiculturalism is needed to ensure that children's (and particularly teenagers') attitudes to their language ability is favorable.

Specific references are given below to case studies of raising trilingual children. One case study (Charlotte Hoffmann) concerns Spanish (acquired mostly from the father and au pairs), German (acquired mostly from the mother and visits), and English (acquired mostly among peers and in school). The one-parent/one language 'rule' was followed. English came to be dominant as school experience and peer relationships developed. Equal facility in all three languages is much less likely than less competence in one or two of the languages (e.g. in grammar, breadth of vocabulary).

One proviso about trilingualism is that at least one language needs to be developed fully. It is important for a child's cognitive development that at least one language develops at age-appropriate levels. For example, the child will need sufficient language competence to operate in the increasingly abstract nature of the school curriculum. A worry (that parents of trilingual children do usually avoid) is a low level of development in all three languages. This would impede the child's academic development. This need not happen, but it does require extra vigilance within the 'trilingual family'.

REFERENCES: HELOT, 1988; HOFFMANN, 1985

communication skills in Swahili, which is the medium of instruction at primary school level. The outcome is often that Swahili skills are not properly developed, and a student's level of English is insufficient to cope when used as the medium of instruction. The development of both languages can therefore suffer.

Some minority language children survive and succeed in this subtractive environment. For many others, the subtractive situation initiates a pattern of failure that continues throughout their school career. Current research suggests that minority language children succeed better when they are taught, at least initially, through their home language. In this situation, the child's language skills are valued and built upon. Later, when the majority language is gradually introduced, the child's academic skills and knowledge acquired initially through the first language will transfer easily to a second language.

For majority language children, the situation is different. Some parents, wishing their children to become bilingual, send them to 'immersion' schools where a second majority language is taught, or to a heritage language school where teaching is through the medium of a minority language. Research has shown that such majority language children usually cope well in the curriculum in a second language. Their home language and culture has status and prestige and will not be supplanted by a second language. This is an additive bilingual situation (see page 154). In most 'immersion' situations, all the children are learning the language from the same point of departure and do not have to compete with native speakers. The teachers may be specially trained in second language teaching skills. Research has shown that children in this situation not only learn another language, but that their proficiency in the first language approaches that of native speakers educated monolingually.

The Reality of Childhood Bilingualism

Parents are often concerned that their child will not be able to 'cope' with bilingualism. They worry that bilingualism will have an adverse effect on the child's general mental development. A popular assumption is that the brain can only cope with one language and that two languages will overload the brain. This is a common belief in countries where monolingualism is the norm. According to this view, the bilingual child will learn neither language properly and will become mentally confused. However, much research has shown that this is not the case, provided that the child does not acquire the second language in a totally subtractive situation. Studies have suggested that, where both languages are relatively well developed, a bilingual child may have slight thinking advantages over a monolingual. (See Bilingualism and Thinking, page 62.)

It is important, however, that parents of bilingual children do not have unrealistic expectations of their children's bilingual development. A bilingual is not two monolinguals inside a single person. Bilinguals rarely achieve the same level of proficiency in both their languages as monolinguals. Most adult bilinguals have one dominant language which can change according to circumstances (e.g. a move to another country).

Bilingual children often have a dominant language and this will not necessarily remain the same throughout their childhood. Unequal exposure to the languages may cause one to develop at a faster rate than the other, as when the minority language of home and neighborhood becomes secondary to the majority language of school and the wider community. Over time, the second language may become the child's dominant language.

Adult bilinguals may not achieve monolingual competence in either of their two languages. This does not indicate that bilinguals are inferior in ability or intelligence, but merely that they use their languages in different contexts and for different purposes. Similarly, a child may feel most comfortable discussing religion, special festivals or family relationships in the home language, but be most competent in the outside language when discussing computers, sports or a school project.

Although the bilingual child may not have as large a vocabulary in either language as the monolingual child (because of their use of different languages in different contexts), the bilingual child's total vocabulary will usually be considerably larger than that of the monolingual. (This is also true of adult bilinguals.)

A child's language development depends on many factors: the amount and quality of exposure to the language at home, in school, in the community, on the mass media, for example. If the child's contact with the language is minimal, or confined to the home, the child will not achieve the same level of competence as monolingual peers. The child may not progress much beyond understanding the language, what is termed passive or receptive bilingualism. However, it is important not to view bilingualism in terms of 'success' or 'failure', 'all' or 'nothing'. Any degree of bilingualism can be a valuable asset, and competence in a language may increase with greater exposure to a language.

Imagine, for example, a child who goes to school, who is always spoken to in English by one parent and in German by the other parent. The parents speak English together. The child speaks English with friends and neighbors and in all other social situations, The language of the school is English. The child's competence in German may lag far behind that of monolingual German speakers of the same age. He or she may not progress much beyond 'receptive' bilingualism.

However, if the child is given more opportunities for contact with the German language, prolonged visits from German-speaking friends and relatives, trips to the home country, German cassettes, books and videos, contact with other German-English families in the same area, the child's German will improve. If the family were to move to a German-speaking country the child would probably catch up quite quickly with monolingual peers.

Further Reading

BAKER, C., 1995, *A Parents' and Teachers' Guide to Bilingualism*. Clevedon: Multilingual Matters Ltd.

DE HOUWER, A., 1995, Bilingual Language Acquisition. In P. FLETCHER & B. MACWHINNEY (eds), *The Handbook of Child Language*. London: Blackwell.

DÖPKE, S., 1992, *One Parent One Language*. Philadelphia, USA: John Benjamins.

HARDING, E. & RILEY, P., 1986, *The Bilingual Family*. Cambridge: Cambridge University Press.

PARADIS, J. & GENESEE, F., 1996, Syntactic Acquisition in Bilingual Children: Autonomous or Interdependent? *Studies in Second Language Acquisition*, 18 (1), 1-25.

ROMAINE, S., 1995, *Bilingualism*. Oxford: Basil Blackwell.

SAUNDERS, G., 1988, *Bilingual Children: From Birth to Teens*. Clevedon: Multilingual Matters Ltd.

Tanya Datta – a Case of Passive Bilingualism

Tanya Datta is in her twenties and works as a journalist on a weekly UK newspaper targeted at British Asians. Tanya considers herself to be a British-Indian, being born and brought up in the UK. Both her parents are Bengali Hindus and come from Calcutta in India, with Bengali as their native language. Tanya's father, Satya Narayan, attended a Hindi medium school in Calcutta where he learned Hindi and English, although he always spoke Bengali with his family and friends. Tanya's mother, Manjula, spent her childhood in Nairobi, Kenya before moving to India in her early teenage years, and it was there that she became multilingual. She spoke Bengali with her family, learnt English and Hindi at school, spoke fluently in Panjabi with her school friends and could converse with others in simple Gujarati and Urdu. She also picked up a basic knowledge of Swahili.

After Satya Narayan and Manjula's arranged marriage in India, they spoke together almost exclusively in Bengali, reserving their English for those contexts where it was pertinent. But as the years passed and their daughter, Tanya, was admitted to school in the UK, the absence of a Bengali social network, and the adaptation necessary in a foreign country (UK) soon meant that English became the dominant language in the house, especially between Tanya and her parents.

Everyday conversation in the house was in Bengali. Culinary dishes, delicacies and foods common to India were given their Bengali names, conjuring up an image and aroma that did not belong to a traditional English table. Words with strong emotional ties to India continued to remain in force. Relatives were referred to by their Bengali 'addressee' names, as English simply doesn't have the words to express Indian 'extended family' terminology. This complexity is vital to Indian cultural identity as it comprises the principle of respect of elders-you cannot simply call an elder by his or her personal name.

Tanya had been brought up bilingually in English and Bengali. For example, her mother would read bedtime tales in English, then lull Tanya to sleep with a Bengali cradle song. When her parents discussed private matters in Bengali (hoping the child would not understand), she did comprehend, silently noting they were arguing in another language for her benefit. Hence, Bengali became a language symbolizing secret emotions.

When Tanya was eight, her parents became divorced. However, her interest and active participation in Indian culture continued, with her taking part in Indian cultural activities in the local community center. She acted in well known episodes from the Hindu epic *The Ramayana* and *The Mahabhharata*. A racist incident at the age of twelve also cemented her desire to deepen her attachment to India by reading both religious scripts and Indian literature such as the works of the poet and philosopher, Sir Rabindranath Tagore.

3: Bilingualism and Marriage

Introduction

Marriages between people from different ethnic groups, different 'clans' and different languages have been present since the beginnings of history. One major trend in the 20th century has been the increasing number of marriages (or partnerships) where bilingualism is present. More and more partners find themselves in the situation where two or more languages and cultures are in contact in the relationship. Sometimes both languages are retained, sometimes there is the gradual loss of one, and occasionally languages are revived within the partnership. Just as in society at large there is increasing inter language contact, sometimes language conflict, issues of language maintenance, shift, vitality and the revival of languages, so within a marriage (however widely defined), language can become an issue.

Some of the major changes in the 20th century have affected the place of languages within a marriage. For example, changes in transport (railways, aircraft, cars and sea travel), increasing mobility of labor (emigration, immigration, tourism and retirement), industrialization and urbanization, cultural change (e.g. the advent of the Information Society), increasing social and geographical mobility, have each increased the chances of marriages involving bilingualism.

Given the rise of inter-cultural and mixed language marriages, what factors influence the relative dominance of languages within a partnership?

Influencing Factors

The profile of language usage in a marriage will vary according to factors such as:

1. The language or languages spoken by each partner.
2. The strength and personal dominance of those languages (in ability and use).

An intercultural marriage between Hideo Oka (now Professor of English at the University of Tokyo) and his wife Waltraud, née Reisinger. Hideo was born in Shimane, Japan and his wife comes from Austria. They were married in her hometown of Schwanenstadt, Austria, in 1972. They now live in Tokyo, Japan. Their family life is trilingual: English between husband and wife; German between mother and the children, now adults: and Japanese between father and children as well as between the two children.

3. The relative status and prestige value of the languages.
4. The language used when the couple first met (and the subsequent history of language interaction).
5. The effect of living in a particular community with pressures and trends concerning language usage – or language avoidance.
6. The effect of the extended family (e.g. grandparents living in the same residence).
7. Family policy (latent or articulated) about children's language development.
8. The topic of the conversation.

The influence of such 'static' and 'dynamic' factors (that influence change) is illustrated in different patterns of language partnership in couples.

One type of bilingual marriage is when each partner has two or more languages which are the same (e.g. both partners are Spanish/English bilinguals). If both partners can speak both languages, the early pattern of communication will usually set a precedent that is followed throughout the relationship. The initial language of communication may become the home language of both (e.g. both partners come from a language minority background and prefer to speak in their heritage language).

Where the dominant language differs between the two partners, factors such as the language of initial conversations, relative power dominance inside the partnership, the language of the peer group where the partnership was created and forged, extended family and community may all have an effect on language choice. The decision to use one language rather than another may sometimes involve a desire to maintain and promote a language within a partnership, particularly where there are children e.g. a native French speaker and a native English speaker living in England may decide to use French exclusively at home, in order to maintain their proficiency in the language, and in order to transmit it to their children.

A second type of language partnership is when one language is a common denominator. One or both partners may be able to speak other languages, but those languages are not shared. However, such a relationship may provide an opportunity for one partner to learn another language, if there is sufficient motivation. For instance, where one partner is bilingual and the other partner is monolingual, there is the opportunity for the monolingual to become bilingual. Where it is advantageous for both partners to be bilingual (e.g. for acceptance in the community, for economic advantage in the labor market), the partnership provides plentiful, informal opportunities for language learning and bilingualism to succeed. If one partner desires to transmit a heritage language to children of the partnership, the other partner may learn that language in support.

Sometimes, both languages are used on a regular basis by both partners. In some bilingual communities, switching between two languages within conversations (often called codeswitching) occurs regularly. If a couple live in such a community, this will tend be part of their normal language practice, in public and private. Alternatively, different situations and 'audiences' may require a change of language by partners. For example, when guests in the house only speak one of the two languages, both partners may converse in that language both to their guests and, for social acceptability, to each other. When in a public place, in an office or school, parents may use a different language to each other (as they are on 'public show') compared with the home. The prestige of a language and conforming to the norms of language behavior 'in public' can change the languages used in public compared with private places.

Occasionally, both partners may make a conscious decision to make use of both languages, but at different times, to avoid mixing them. They may use different languages on different days (e.g. reserving French for the weekend).

The examples given so far suggest that the decisions in a partnership about which language to speak with whom and where may either be conscious or subconscious ones. A language policy inside the marriage is not always discussed. For example, in cross language marriages, the higher status language may sometimes become the language of the family – without discussion.

If children become a product of a partnership, there may be more focus on conscious language planning within the family. Parents may decide to separate their languages in speaking to the child. One parent may speak in one language, the other parent in a different language. Many alternatives are possible. Both parents may speak the same language to the child, or the mother may prefer to speak her native tongue (not used with her husband)- feeling it natural to speak to her child in that language.

One central question frequently asked about bilingual marriages is whether bilingualism causes a conflict in marriage? The first answer is that if there is conflict within a partnership, the cause is most often outside issues of language. Compatibility problems between partners are rarely due to the existence of two or more languages within a marriage. Problems of personality, attitudes, culture-specific beliefs, finance and sexual relationship will tend to be among the real causes. Nevertheless, language differences may still be blamed- usually unfairly. Language differences tend to be an excuse, not a cause of marriage conflict.

The biennial Highlands Show at Goroka, Papua New Guinea. Interethnic marriage is one way in which the great cultural and linguistic diversity of Papua New Guinea is gradually lessening.

In bilingual marriages, communication within the extended family can become complex, especially when one partner or the children are unable to communicate with relatives. When children are able to communicate with maternal and paternal extended families, relationships and family cultural continuity are aided. Otherwise, translation and interpretation, tolerance and imaginative means of communication will be needed.

Discussions are valuable, particularly when one partner is unable to understand one of the languages of the other partner. This produces a situation where, for example, one parent will be talking to the child; the other parent being unable to understand. What is natural in communication may be interpreted as exclusion. Ideally, a partnership needs to have a policy, and an understanding, about the use of a language the other partner cannot understand (and of the possibility of that partner becoming proficient in that language). If there are going to be occasions of conflict due to languages in the partnership, shared understanding is required as to why one partner needs to use the non-understood language in particular circumstances. This can allay the other partner's fear that he or she is being excluded, even being criticized when the conversation is not understood.

Where both partners are bilingual or when one partner is monolingual, a danger is that the minority language will not be reproduced. A personal cost-benefit analysis, at a subconscious level, may push or pull the partnership towards the majority language and away from the minority language. Inadvertently, minority languages may decay when consciously or subconsciously, a new partnership changes previous language patterns. Sometimes, mixed language marriages mean language shift. This indicates the highly important part played by families in the transmission of minority languages to succeeding generations.

In bilingual or multilingual societies, marriage can be a major factor for or against language maintenance. In most multilingual societies in the modern world, growing urbanization and industrialization have resulted in increased population mobility and consequently more contact between speakers of different languages. In Papua New Guinea in the western half of the Pacific island of New Guinea (see page 452), it is estimated that over 700 languages or dialects are still spoken. The mountainous terrain has contributed to the relative isolation of ethnic groups and so to continued language diversity. However, in recent years, there has been a trend for young men to leave isolated communities to seek work elsewhere, attracted by the prospect of economic advancement. These young men often marry wives from other ethnic groups and their children are usually raised to speak the wife's language or to speak a language of wider communication such as Tok Pisin or Hiri Motu.

Meanwhile, the young women left behind in the rural villages often move away to marry men from other communities who speak other languages. While their children may be bilingual in the mother's and father's languages, they often only transmit their father's language to the next generation. In Papua New Guinea, as in many multilingual countries in Africa and Asia, intermarriage has been a strong factor in the decline of minority languages (see also Mother Tongue in Lusaka, Zambia, page 49).

Thus marriage becomes an important life event in the history of languages within a society. Marriages may become a vehicle for the maintenance and growth, or decay and death of languages and bilingualism. When there is clear language planning within the partnership, bilingualism may become a valuable asset for the family. Minority languages may be reproduced in such bilingually active families.

Further Reading

BAKER, C., 1995, *A Parents' and Teachers' Guide to Bilingualism*. Clevedon: Multilingual Matters Ltd.

HARDING, E. & RILEY, P., 1986, *The Bilingual Family*. Cambridge: Cambridge University Press.

ROMAINE, S., 1995, *Bilingualism*. Oxford: Basil Blackwell.

4: Mother Tongue

The term mother tongue is often used in everyday conversation to refer to the original language of an individual. It is also used to talk about the heritage or native language of a group of people, especially a language minority within a language majority region. It is important to dissect the different meanings and implications in the usage of this term (Skutnabb-Kangas, 1988). Such a discussion not only focuses on the ambiguity of the term 'mother tongue' (e.g. language learned first; language known best; language used most; and identification with a language), it also demonstrates how a term can have negative connotations and be politically loaded.

On the surface, 'mother tongue' refers to the language that the mother speaks to a child, implying that such a language is embedded within the child. The concept of 'mother' can be problematic. Not all children are raised by their biological mothers. Many are raised by fathers, grandparents or other relatives. Some live with adoptive or foster parents. Others spend most of their time in a nursery from birth through to schooling. What is the mother tongue of such a child?

The term 'mother tongue' reflects the positive qualities of a mother caring, nurturing and protecting her child. As part of a loving maternal role, the mother is portrayed as nurturing the child's language. While in many countries (but not all), and in many families (but certainly not all), the mother is the regular and major language model for the child from the start, does use of 'mother tongue' understate the language role of the father? The importance of a father in language development is one recent theme in the psychology of child development. There are also increasing cases where the father is the primary caregiver and is the regular and enduring model for a child's language growth. There are many cases of one parent speaking one language to a child, the other parent speaking a different language. Thus the child learns one 'mother tongue' from the father.

One interpretation of mother tongue might be the language that a child learns first. Many bilinguals learn two languages simultaneously. If the mother tongue is defined as the language a child learns first, what is the implication if a child soon becomes dominant in the second language? If the children and parents become guest workers or in-migrants to a particular region and start switching to the majority language of that region, what is the mother tongue? The language learnt first or the language which becomes dominant in the family and particularly outside the home?

Competence in a language can change easily over time as circumstances change. The balance between two lan-

The Role of the Father in Childhood Bilingualism

Research in language development has shown the important contribution of the father. This implies that fathers need to be aware of the important role they play in child language development. Some fathers have relatively fewer hours of employment, or are unemployed. Leisure time has grown in the 20th century. In such situations, the role of the father in language development has become more important. Some fathers stay at home to raise the children while the mother goes out to work.

In many societies, mothers are often responsible for housekeeping and child-rearing. Research has shown that much of mothers' language interaction with their children is often about basic housekeeping functions (e.g. feeding, bathing, dressing, discipline). Fathers have opportunities to play with their children, allowing considerable language stimulation. Many fathers interact with their children in child-centered ways. Both fathers and mothers play an important role in the child's language development in terms of both the quantity and quality of language input and interaction.

In families where children are learning two languages (e.g. where one parent speaks one language, the other parent a different language or where both parents speak a minority language to the child), both parents can help promote bilingualism. In this situation, fathers can take pride in their conversations with the child, even at the babbling and cooing stage. As the baby grows to a young child, the father plays an important role in the quantity of language interaction.

Fathers also influence the attitudes of their children to languages. Whether the father is positive or negative about bilingualism will considerably affect the child. For example, if the father is skeptical about bilingualism, or doesn't like the mother using her 'own' language, the child will soon become aware of these negative attitudes and language behavior will be affected. On the other hand, if a father encourages his children's bilingualism, applauds them speaking to their mother in her 'own' language, the effect on the child's language confidence and attitudes will be substantial.

Research on the role of the father in deciding the language of the home

Research shows that the language(s) of the father are sometimes dominant in decision-making, sometimes creating monolingualism. In one of the early researches in this area, Harrison *et al.* (1981) found that monolingual fathers' influence 'is overwhelming: none had bilingual children. When they are for Welsh there is a good chance that their children will be bilingual' (page 63). When fathers are monolingual, there is the opportunity to develop some degree of fluency in a second language as the children are growing up in that language. When the mother is monolingual, the father may still use another language with the child, giving the mother some opportunity to learn the basics of that language. For both partners, there will sometimes be language classes available in the community for both to become bilingual.

More recent research (C. H. Williams, 1987) shows that the chances of children becoming bilingual depend heavily on different language constellations and language patterns within the home. If both parents were able to speak Welsh and English, 91 percent of children across Wales (in the National Census) became bilingual. The remaining nine percent could not speak Welsh. If the father spoke Welsh and the mother didn't, 36 percent of children were bilingual; the remaining 64 percent spoke English only. If the mother spoke Welsh and the father didn't, 42 percent of children became bilingual; the remaining 58 percent were monolingual English speakers. Similarly, Lewis (1975) found that monolingualism was the more probable outcome of a mixed language marriage. The important results from a more detailed study (Lyon, 1996) are given in a table below.

Jean Lyon (1996) found particular trends in the use of two languages in a family:

1. Welsh-speaking mothers were more likely to speak Welsh to their children in mixed language marriages than Welsh-speaking fathers. (See table below).
2. English-speaking mothers were more likely to try to learn and speak Welsh in the home and neighborhood than English-speaking fathers.
3. Welsh-speaking wives were more likely to speak English to neighbors than Welsh-speaking husbands. Thus women are more likely to adapt their language use than are men in mixed language families or neighborhoods.
4. A husband and wife do not have an equal influence on the language(s) of the home. The preferred language of the husband tends to dominate language use in the home. Women are more likely to change their language use to suit their partner.
5. More Welsh-speaking mothers than Welsh-speaking fathers wanted their children to be fully bilingual (i.e. encouraged the use of Welsh as well as English). Mothers influence the language of their children more than the language of their husbands and the home.
6. More Welsh-speaking mothers than Welsh-speaking fathers read to their children in the minority language (Welsh).

Dominant Language of Parents	Dominant Language Mother to Child	Dominant Language Father to Child
Both Parents Welsh-speaking	93% spoke Welsh	92% spoke Welsh
Welsh Mother/ English Father	72% spoke Welsh	17% spoke Welsh
English Mother/ Welsh Father	21% spoke Welsh	46% spoke Welsh
Parents used both languages	0% spoke Welsh	3% spoke Welsh

Adapted from Lyon (1996). Number in sample = 383 respondents

REFERENCE : LYON, 1996

Mother Tongue in Lusaka, Zambia

Siachitema (1994) researched into language use in three neighborhoods in the capital city of Zambia, Lusaka. Ninety-eight percent of the population of Zambia are of African descent and speak languages related to Bantu. Nearly 40 different ethnic languages are spoken in Zambia, of which the most important is Nyanja, spoken by almost a million people (11.7 percent of the population), both as a mother tongue and as a widely used lingua franca. Nyanja is the official language of the police and army. It is used in newspapers and radio and is recognized in education and administration. English is the official language of Zambia and is used in parliament and administration, and is the teaching medium in schools. It is the native language of very few Africans, but is used as a language of communication among educated folk.

Siachitema's study shows how the term 'mother tongue' can be ambivalent in meaning in a multilingual situation. In Lusaka (population one million) there is a shifting population, due to widespread emigration from rural areas, and also government policy. Since independence in 1964, it has been government policy to post civil servants away from their local areas, to other areas of the country, to weaken ethnic loyalties (which can be divisive), and to promote a new national consciousness.

This large-scale movement of population has had several consequences. Firstly, many people find it necessary to learn the main language of the area to which they move, in order to communicate with other people there. Thus married couples may speak their local language at home, and a lingua franca such as Nyanja. Their children may grow up speaking the lingua franca of the area where they live, in addition to, or even instead of the ethnic languages of their parents.

Inter-ethnic marriage has become common in most urban centers of Zambia, and, rather than couples learning one another's local, ethnic language, they often use the main language of the area in which they live to communicate with one another. Again, children of such marriages may grow up speaking the lingua franca as their first, main or only language. Since all indigenous languages in Zambia are related to Bantu, and have structural and lexical similarities, this means that it is relatively easy for the speaker of one language to learn another.

English may also be used in the home, but since proficiency in English depends on several years of formal education, the use of English tends to be confined to more affluent, educated families.
Boarding schools are also common in Zambia, and children often leave their native area to board in another area of the country. In boarding school children inevitably learn English, and sometimes other languages. Boarding schools have further facilitated intermarriage.

The extended family system means that when people move to another area of the country, they may take with them a relative other than the immediate family. Thus more members of the family learn other languages, and the chance of intermarriage is increased.

Siachitema (1994) researched into the use of English in the home, work and public life, in three socioeconomic neighborhoods of Lusaka: a shanty town, medium-cost housing and high-cost housing. Results showed that bilingualism and trilingualism within the home was a common phenomenon (more so in the more affluent neighborhoods than in the shanty town) with a local, ethnic language (the mother tongue of one or both of the parents), as well as Nyanja and/or English all being used. Codeswitching between two or three languages occurred according to the topic of conversation. Overall, the mother tongue tended to dominate in the home (including Nyanja in that capacity), but 18 percent of the sample claimed Nyanja (not as a mother tongue) as the most frequently used language, while 8 percent claimed English as the most frequently spoken language. (Where Nyanja or English dominated, this tended to be in more affluent neighborhoods).

The study showed that many people used the term mother tongue to describe the language they claimed to have spoken first as children. In most cases this was the language of the ethnic group to which they considered themselves to belong, and had great significance as a symbol of identity and belonging. However, for a number of households in the survey, the mother tongue was not the language used most frequently or habitually now, by parents or children. Thus, in this situation, mother tongue refers to the first language learnt by the respondents as children, rather than the language used most often now, or perhaps even spoken most fluently now. Siachitema's (1994) research shows the limitation of the definition of mother tongue in a changing multilingual situation.

Reference: SIACHITEMA, 1994

When a language creates – as it does – a community within the present, it does so only by courtesy of a community between the present and the past.

Chistopher Ricks, 20th-century British critic.

The Case of Tove Skutnabb-Kangas.

Tove Skutnabb-Kangas is an internationally renowned writer, thinker, advocate and researcher. Educated at the University of Helsinki, she spent a short time at Harvard University working with Professor Einar Haugen. After teaching in schools, she has lectured not only in Scandinavia but throughout the world. Currently affiliated to Roskilde University in Denmark and the University of Ostrobothnia in Finland, she has made a contribution in fields as wide-ranging as bilingualism, multilingualism, minority education, sociolinguistics, politics, language rights, gender and language, minority women and power, ethnic identity, assimilation and integration, racism, linguistic imperialism and multiculturalism. With a prolific output in over fourteen languages, Tove Skutnabb-Kangas is competent in Finnish, Swedish, English, Danish, Norwegian and German.

One of her most important contributions has been a book entitled *Bilingualism or Not: The Education of Minorities*. First published in 1981, it has been one of the most influential books on bilingualism and is internationally recognized as a classic. Still highly relevant, this book was one of the first to open up the subject of bilingualism and language minorities to an international audience. Few books have had such an important impact.

Having been active in many minority organizations, she has been a staunch advocate for language minority peoples wherever they exist, and is interested in how politics and education reproduce the precarious status of minorities. The life of Tove Skutnabb-Kangas raises interesting questions about mother tongue.

Tove Skutnabb-Kangas had bilingual parents who both spoke Swedish to her. However, Finnish was also regularly spoken to her (and by her) from birth onwards. In this respect, Skutnabb-Kangas has Finnish and Swedish as two mother tongues. She went to a Finnish school and has native competence in both languages. She identifies with both Finnish and Finland Swedish, belonging to both of these groups and cultures. However, in everyday life as an adult, Swedish and English are the languages used both privately and professionally. While not regarding herself as a native speaker of English or belonging to an English-speaking community, she nevertheless has high competence in English.

So is the mother tongue Finnish – as she was born in Finland and Finnish was a language spoken from birth? Is it Swedish which has a continuation from early childhood to the present? Is the mother tongue both Finnish and Swedish? Or because Tove has lived and worked in Denmark for many years, is the mother tongue Danish? Or do present circumstances make the current mother tongue Swedish and English?

guages may vary as family situations change, school and peer group norms become influential, and as employment and marriage create socioeconomic and geographical mobility. Identification with a language and use of a language may change according to different contexts and across time.

Skutnabb-Kangas (1981, 1988) and Skutnabb-Kangas & Phillipson (1989) have argued that the term 'mother tongue' when applied to different ethnic groups often reveals a bias and a prejudice. When Maori peoples in New Zealand, or Finns in Sweden, or Kurds from Turkey in Denmark, or Mexican Spanish speakers in the United States, or the different Asian language speakers in Canada and England are referred to in terms of their 'mother tongue', the expression may refer to minorities who are oppressed. The term has then taken on an evaluative meaning- symbolizing migrant workers, guest workers, oppressed indigenous peoples and language minorities. 'Mother tongue' tends to be used for language minorities and much less so for language majorities. The term therefore tends to be a symbol of separation of minority and majority, or those with less, as opposed to those with more, power and status.

Further Reading

SKUTNABB-KANGAS, T., 1981, *Bilingualism or Not: The Education of Minorities*. Clevedon: Multilingual Matters Ltd.

SKUTNABB-KANGAS, T., 1988. Multilingualism and the Education of Minority Children. In T. SKUTNABB-KANGAS & J. CUMMINS (eds.), *Minority Education: From Shame to Struggle*. Clevedon: Multilingual Matters Ltd.

SKUTNABB-KANGAS, T. & PHILLIPSON, R., 1989, 'Mother Tongue': The Theoretical and Sociopolitical Construction of a Concept. In U. AMMON (ed.), *Status and Function of Languages and Language Variety*. New York: W. de Gruyter.

The Everyday Language Use of Bilinguals

1: Language Choice

Introduction

When monolinguals talk, they often change their language to suit whom they are talking to and the context. For example, monolinguals may change their accent and speed of talking, or use different vocabulary when with people from their home region as opposed to their way of conversing with people from a different part of the country. The South Virginian in the United States and the Cockney in London have particular ways of talking when they are with kindred folk. Monolinguals can change the register or type of language they use depending on the situation or the people they are talking to. An English-speaking teenager in the United States may speak in a formal way to a teacher in school, in a less formal way to parents, and in an informal, slangy style with classmates and friends. Italians or Germans may use the standard form of their language with people from different parts of the country, but switch to a dialect with other locals. Bilinguals can change their register (as do monolinguals), in either language. They also have the ability to move between their two languages, and that is the focus of this topic.

Portraying a bilingual's linguistic abilities in two languages is insufficient to create a linguistic profile of that individual. Language ability is not the same as language use. Not all bilinguals have the opportunity to use both their languages on a regular basis. Where a bilingual lives in a largely monolingual community there may be little choice about language use from day-to-day. A person living in England may be bilingual in English and German, but may rarely have the opportunity to use German. However, in communities where two or more languages are widely spoken, bilinguals may use both their languages on a daily or frequent basis. Some bilinguals will not have mastery of both languages, yet still use both languages successfully for communication in varying circumstances.

When bilinguals use both their languages on a day-to-day basis, language use is not haphazard or arbitrary. Rather, bilinguals tend to use their different languages in different contexts or domains and with different people.

Functions and Uses of Language

To describe the language use of bilinguals, many factors have to be taken into account. To study the use a person makes of the two languages, it is helpful to ask these five questions.

1. Who is speaking?
2. Who is being spoken to? (Who is listener or co-participant in the conversation?)
3. What is the situation or context? (E.g. in the temple, mosque, church, factory, office, home, classroom.)
4. What is the topic of conversation? (E.g. the weather, food, sport, work, leisure, family, health.)
5. What is the purpose of the conversation? (What is the expected outcome, hidden agenda or intended effect of the conversation?)

These five questions help us see how language choice can vary along five dimensions: speaker, addressee, context or situation, topic and purpose.

Monitoring Language Choice

The choice of language in a given situation may not always be simple. Many subtle and overlapping factors may affect a bilingual's choice of language, particularly in a new and unrehearsed situation. Two major factors will now be considered, which may give some indication of the complex and subtle way in which a bilingual monitors language choice.

The other person in the conversation

If the other person is already known to the bilingual, as a family member, friend or colleague, a relationship has usually been established through one language. If both are bilingual they have the option of changing to the other language (e.g. to include others in the conversation).

If the other person is not known, a bilingual may quickly pick up clues as to which language to use. Clues such as dress, appearance, age, accent and command of a lan-

Language Use

The table illustrates some of the range of choice in the use of two or more languages. First, different language targets, specific groups or people are listed. A person may change language according to the others participating in the conversation. Second, different language domains or contexts will also affect which language a bilingual uses. A context or domain refers to a particular aspect, area or activity of a person's life and experience. A language domain or context may sometimes imply a specific place or location, e.g. the workplace or the shopping center, but it means more than location. For instance, an individual may use a specific language with colleagues at the workplace, but may also use that language when discussing work with colleagues over the phone at home. An individual may use one language when discussing and working with computers and information technology, whether at home, at work or elsewhere.

Examples of Language Targets	Examples of Language Contexts (Domains)
• Nuclear Family	• Shopping
• Extended Family	• Visual and Auditory Media (e.g. TV, Radio, Records, Cassettes, CDs, Video)
• Work Colleagues	• Printed Media (e.g. Newspapers, Books)
• Friends	• Cinema/Discos/Theater/ Concerts
• Neighbors	• Work
• Religious Leaders	• Correspondence/ Telephone/ Official Communication
• Teachers	• Clubs, Societies, Organizations, Sporting Activities
• Presidents, Principals, Other Leaders	• Leisure and Hobbies
• Bureaucrats	• Religious Meetings
• Local Community	• Information Technology (e.g. computers).

The concept of domain may include such notions as formality and informality. In a minority/majority language situation, the minority language may be used extensively in informal situations. In Paraguay, for example, where the majority of the population are bilingual in Spanish and Guaraní, most people in rural areas speak Guaraní as their first language and all activities are conducted in that language. In urban areas and in more formal situations, Spanish is more widely used (see page 459). A limitation in the use of the term 'domain' is that it does not engage differences of power and status that affect language use in different situations.

guage may suggest to the bilingual which language it would be appropriate to use. In parts of Africa, a well-dressed African would automatically be addressed in English. In bilingual areas of Canada and Wales, employees dealing with the general public may often glance at a person's name on their records to help them decide which language to use. A person called Pierre Rougeau or Bryn Jones might be addressed first in French or Welsh, rather than English.

Young children acquiring two languages soon learn which language to speak to which person and tend to adhere rigidly to this. However, even young children learn to base their choice of language on factors such as appearance, accent or age of the person they are addressing, as Stephanie Ryan's experience shows (see page 54). If addressed by another child or adult in the 'wrong' language, they may react with confusion, anxiety or embarrassment. (See Childhood Development of Bilingualism, page 36.)

Individual preference

An individual's own attitudes and preferences may influence the choice of language. In a minority/majority language situation, older people may prefer to speak the minority language. Younger folk (e.g. second-generation in-migrants) may reject the minority language in favor of the majority language because of its higher status and more fashionable image. In situations where the native language is perceived to be under threat, some bilinguals may avoid speaking the majority or dominant language to assert and reinforce the status of the other language. French-Canadians in Quebec sometimes refuse to speak English in shops and offices to underline the status of French.

Some minority languages are often confined to a private and domestic role. This happens when a minority language has historically been disparaged and deprived of status. In Western Brittany, for example, many Breton speakers only use their Breton in the family and with close friends. They are often offended if addressed by a stranger in Breton, believing that such a stranger is implying they are uneducated and cannot speak French.

An individual may also change languages, either deliberately or unconsciously, to accommodate the perceived preference of the other participant in the conversation. The perception of which language is regarded as more prestigious or as more accommodating may depend on the nature of the listener. To gain acceptance or status, a person may deliberately and consciously use the majority language. Alternatively, a person may use a minority language as a form of affiliation or belonging to a group.

At other times, bilinguals may mix and switch between languages. For example, they may deliberately explain an idea in one language and then switch to another language to reinforce or explain further the idea. Another example is in telling a story, where relating a conversation may authentically mirror the dual use of languages. The conversation may have occurred in English and therefore is relayed in English; comments about that conversation may be spoken in the minority language. (See Codeswitching, page 58.)

Multilingualism and Language Choice

When three or more languages are widely spoken in a community, the equation of language choice in a given situation can become even more complex. One example is the country of Morocco, in North Africa, where most inhabitants grow up understanding and speaking at least two languages. Most children in Morocco acquire as their first language either one of the indigenous Berber dialects or Moroccan Arabic. Children who learn Berber as their mother tongue usually pick up Moroccan Arabic outside the home. (Children who speak Moroccan Arabic at home do not usually learn Berber as they can communicate with Berber speakers through the medium of Moroccan Arabic). When children begin their education they are obliged to learn modern standard Arabic, and then French. (Students who proceed to higher education might also have the opportunity to learn foreign languages such as English and German.)

Berber children in a mountain village, Morocco. These children speak a Berber dialect in their village but learn Moroccan Arabic through contact with non-Berber Moroccans. They learn Modern Standard Arabic at school and some French. The language of Islamic worship is Classical Arabic.

Language Choice among the Chinese

An individual's own attitudes and preferences may influence the choice of language. In a minority/majority language situation, older people may prefer to speak the minority language. Younger folk (e.g. second generation in-migrants) may reject the minority language in favor of the majority language because of its higher status and more fashionable image. Li Wei, Milroy & Pon Sin Ching (1992), in a study of a Chinese community in northern England, indicate that the degree of contact with the majority language community can be a factor in language choice. Their research shows that Chinese speakers who were employed outside the Chinese community were more likely to choose to speak English with other Chinese speakers. In contrast, those Chinese in-migrants who worked in family businesses, mainly catering, and had less daily contact with English speakers, were more likely to use Chinese with other Chinese-English bilinguals.

In situations where the native language is perceived to be under threat, some bilinguals may avoid speaking the majority or dominant language to assert and reinforce the status of the other language. French-Canadians in Quebec sometimes refuse to speak English in shops and offices to underline the status of French.

REFERENCE: LI WEI, MILROY & PON SIN CHING, 1992

A Moroccan university lecturer describes his daily language use as follows: 'A Moroccan bilingual is constantly, though usually unconsciously, making choices as to which language to use in a particular situation. In many situations he also has the possibility of using what has been called Codeswitching, in which he switches back and forth between, say, Arabic and French in the course of a single conversation, often mixing the two within the same sentence. This variety too seems to have its own rules and its own function, being associated with a casual, relaxed kind of atmosphere. I myself, for instance, will find myself, in the course of a single day, using Moroccan Arabic when shopping, French when chatting to colleagues, a mixture of French and Arabic to my brothers, and English to my wife or my students. Similarly, during the day I may write a report in Classical Arabic and a letter to a friend in French, read newspapers in both these languages and watch a film in English. Such factors as the nature of one's addressee, the topic under discussion and the kind of setting or place one finds oneself in all seem to have an effect on which language is chosen.' (Bentahila, 1987).

Further Reading

APPEL, R. & MUYSKEN, P., 1987, *Language Contact and Bilingualism*. London: Edward Arnold

GROSJEAN, F., 1982, *Life with Two Languages*. Cambridge, MA: Harvard University Press.

ROMAINE, S., 1995, *Bilingualism*. Oxford: Basil Blackwell.

Appearance as a Factor in Language Choice in Japan

Stephanie Ryan is British and married to a Japanese. She speaks English to their two sons, Leo (Japanese 'Ryo') and John (Japanese 'Jun'). The couple speak mainly English to each other. In 1986, when the boys were four and two, she wrote an article for the *Bilingual Family Newsletter*, in which she commented on the importance of appearance as a factor in language choice. (At the time of writing, her Japanese was developing and her husband's English was very good).

Appearance as a factor in language choice – both by the child and the interlocutor – is very important in a country like Japan, as it is also for identification with the speech community. Mr. Saunders in his book, *Bilingual Children*, mentioned that his boys tended to use the language first used by an interlocutor in all subsequent contacts. With my son, Leo, this is subordinate to his classification of the interlocutor by race. If a friend of mine or the parent of one of his friends addresses him in what he believes to be the inappropriate language (English by a Japanese and Japanese by a non-Japanese) he will answer very abruptly in that language but change to the appropriate language subsequently. This pattern can continue for a whole conversation. If the person, usually a Japanese, is not a close friend, for example a doctor, he will reply in English and then be uncharacteristically quiet. I shall mention this type of encounter again when referring to the interlocutor's reasons for choice of language.

It seems clear that Leo assumes that all Orientals are Japanese and, in common with the majority of Japanese, that everyone else speaks English. He did, however, very quickly understand that the daughter of a Japanese-French couple does not speak English even though the French mother and I converse in English. It is clear that even though his English is, at present, better than his Japanese he still prefers to speak Japanese to Japanese although the topic just now is invariably his set of English *Mr. Men* books. He patiently relates the stories in Japanese to his baffled audiences.

The reaction of Japanese – both young and old – to him seems to depend on which adult he is with. If he is with me, the Japanese tend to assume he does not speak Japanese, even if I am speaking in Japanese to the person in question. If they have to address him they tend to use forms more suitable for a much younger child. This is also true if I am speaking in English to the Japanese, although there the person may use English to him, as noted above. Complete strangers often call out to us in an approximation of English, to which he makes no response; I am not sure whether he understands or not. If he is with his father or another Japanese, he is treated, as far as we can tell, the same as a 100 percent Japanese child, even in one case by the same person who speaks to him in simple Japanese if he is with me.

The reaction of British people to him does not seem to vary according to whom he is with, although we have not been able to observe this situation extensively. Family, friends and strangers seem to assume he will be bilingual, and do not seem greatly impressed with the situation. Japanese seem to find it hard to believe and unnatural, I think. If Leo is alone with me in the UK, strangers will comment on his appearance – especially his black eyes and may ask what nationality his father is. No one in Japan has ever asked such a question to my husband, despite Leo's light brown hair! In Japan, differences within the race are ignored where possible and similarities are stressed. On the other hand, when he is with me his Japanese features are ignored and he is treated as foreign. This need to classify inclusively and exclusively is fundamental to Japanese society.

Extracted with permission from: *The Bilingual Family Newsletter,* March 1986

2: Bilingualism and Sensitivity in Communication

Because bilinguals living in a bilingual environment often switch languages, they subconsciously develop a sensitivity or awareness to the communication needs of particular situations. They constantly need to monitor the language in which they should respond, or into which they should switch. For example, someone may start a telephone conversation in English, but the bilingual picks up (e.g. from the accent or style of talking) that Spanish may be that person's preferred language. The bilingual may then switch to Spanish so that a more intimate and friendly conversation takes place. In entering a shop for the first time, a bilingual may consciously or subconsciously monitor in which language the shopkeeper would prefer to converse. Or the shopkeeper who is bilingual may try to pick up clues and cues as to what language to speak to each customer.

Many (but not all) bilinguals seek to monitor and restrict mixing their two languages when speaking (and writing). They also tend to be continuously alert for hints and signals as to when to switch languages. This may give bilinguals increased sensitivity to the use of language. Bilinguals can also be more aware of the needs of their listeners. Bilinguals constantly monitor different situations and different people to establish the need to switch between their languages. Bilinguals may be more subconsciously aware that language contains different functions and purposes, so that using the appropriate language is important. Very young children (e.g. two and three year olds) have been found quite adept at being sensitive to the language preferences of the listener and the communicative context (de Houwer, 1995). Such children also do not usually mix languages when speaking to monolinguals.

Research by Ben-Zeev (1977b) found that bilinguals were more responsive to hints and clues in a social situation. Bilinguals seemed to be more sensitive in an experimental situation to the required form of language and to instructions, and they corrected their errors faster than monolinguals. This was one of the first research hints that bilinguals may have increased sensitivity in interpersonal communication.

Children as Interpreters

In language minority families, children often act as interpreters for their parents. For example, in first and second generation in-migrant families, parents may have a little or no competency in the majority language. Therefore, their children act as interpreters.

There are a variety of contexts where this may happen. When there are visitors to the house, such as sellers and traders, religious persuasionists and local officials, a parent may call a child to the door to help translate what is being said. The child interprets for both parties (e.g. the parent and the caller). Similarly, at hospital, the doctor's, dentist's, optician's, school and many other places parents visit, the child may be taken to help interpret. Interpretation is needed in more informal places: in the street, when a parent is watching the television or listening to the radio, reading a local newspaper or working on the computer.

Kaur & Mills (1993) found that children accustomed to acting as interpreters sometimes took the initiative. For example, a child may give the answer to a question rather than relaying the question to the parent. This puts children in a position of some power, even of language censorship. The comments of the teacher, in written or oral form, may be transformed by the child from something negative to something positive!

Pressure is placed on children in interpreting: linguistic, emotional, social and attitudinal pressure. First, children may find an exact translation difficult to achieve as their language is still developing. Second, children may be hearing information (e.g. medical troubles, financial problems, arguments and conflicts) that is the preserve of adults rather than children. Third, children may be expected to be adult-like when interpreting and child-like at all other times; to mix with adults when interpreting and 'be seen and not heard' with adults on other occasions. Fourth, seeing their parents in an inferior position may lead to children despising their minority language. Children may quickly realize when interpreting that the language of power, prestige and purse is the majority language. Negative attitudes to the minority language may result.

However, interpreting can also bring parental praise, reward and status within the family. The child learns adult information quickly and learns to act with some authority and trust. Early maturity has its own rewards in the teenage peer group.

When parents become dependent on their children for interpretation, it may make the family closer and more integrated. Such interpretation is a lifeline for the many parents who have to hand over much power to their children. Yet it may make parents aware of their own language inadequacies, feeling frustration and resentment, particularly in language minority cultures where children are expected to stay in a subordinate position for a long time.

The cognitive outcomes for child interpreters may be valuable. Children who are regular interpreters for their parents may quickly realize the problems and possibilities in translating words, figures of speech and ideas. For example, such children may learn early on that one language never fully parallels another. Sometimes, it is hard to translate exactly the inner meaning of words and metaphors. This may lead such children to be more introspective about their languages. This is termed metalinguistic awareness and is considered on page 71.

Another advantage for the child interpreter is possibly gaining more empathy. The children are negotiating between two different social and cultural worlds, trying to understand both, and providing bridges between them. This handling of dialogue may lead to increased maturity, astuteness, independence and higher self-esteem. Being expected to carry an adult role early in life may lead to a positive self-concept, an adult feeling of responsibility, and having a privileged position in the family. Through having language skills, a child may feel more responsible, more adult like and of more value in the family and community.

In Kaur & Mills (1993, page 119) one of the authors gives her own experience when interpreting on behalf of her mother as an adult.

> 'I sometimes make judgments about the way she is presenting herself and if I feel, for example, that she is being too humble, will not present this in my choice of words. I make judgments about the way she organises her language and what she wishes to convey to another person and I become frustrated by any perceived inadequacies. I often make judgments about her message clarity, about the appropriateness of what she is saying, about the manner in which she expresses it. When I interpret for her, it is in my power to modify both the medium and the message, and I do.'

A quote from a child called Nerinder in Kaur & Mills (1993, page 124):

> 'Some English people don't like it if you speak Punjabi. On a bus there were two English people sitting behind two Indian women who were speaking Punjabi. The English man was saying to his neighbour, "How dare they speak this? They could be speaking about me. It's rude. I wouldn't speak another language."
>
> I felt like telling him, "You are speaking another language. They can't understand".'

REFERENCE: KAUR & MILLS, 1993

An interesting experiment on sensitivity in communication was conducted by Genesee, Tucker & Lambert (1975). They compared children in bilingual and monolingual education on their performance in a game. In this game, students aged between five and eight were asked to explain a board and dice game to two listeners. One listener was blindfolded, the other not. The listeners were classmates and not allowed to ask any questions after the explanation. The listeners then attempted to play the game with a person giving the explanation. It was found that children in a total immersion bilingual education program (i.e. bilinguals) were more sensitive to the needs of listeners than the children in the monolingual education control group, and gave more information to the blindfolded children than to the sighted ones. The authors concluded that such bilingual children 'may have been better able than the control children to take the role of others experiencing communicational difficulties, to perceive their needs, and consequently to respond appropriately to these needs' (page 1013).

Communicative Sensitivity in Hospital Staff

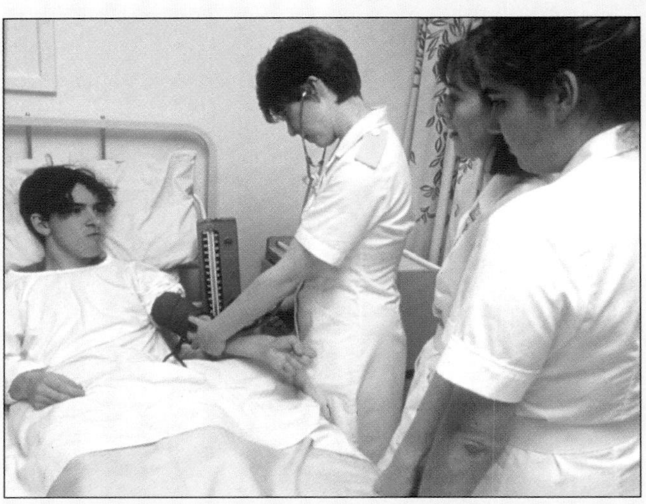

In regions where two languages are spoken, bilingual hospital staff can communicate with patients in their preferred language.

An essential part of nursing is the communication between nurse and patient, as well as the relationship built up over the period in hospital. When the patient is allowed to choose the language of communication and relationship, there may be positive outcomes for the quality of care provision. In a hospital ward where there may be anxiety and worry, some comfort and reassurance may be given when the patient is allowed to choose the language of interaction with nurses and doctors.

Where nurses and doctors cannot speak the language of the patient, or choose not to use that language, different problems for the patient may result. First, the patient may feel uncomfortable and incapable of expressing symptoms, worries and personal details in a weaker language. Second, the closeness of relationship may be reduced considerably when relating to someone in a second language. Third, in a psychiatric context, a patient may only be fully able to convey inner meanings, inner feelings and the depth of the soul, by explaining matters in the first language. For most bilinguals, one language is stronger than the other, especially in younger people and the aged. When patients are sick and vulnerable, and particularly when mentally ill, explaining medical matters coherently in the first language may be important.

Thus, bilingual nurses and doctors need to be sensitive towards the communication needs of speakers. The kinds of communicative sensitive competences that nurses and doctors require include (Roberts, 1994):

- Listening carefully to patients.
- Attending carefully to their needs and requests.
- Responding appropriately to patients.
- Being sympathetic and empathic with patients as revealed through language choice.
- Creating a positive and encouraging atmosphere in which recovery (or in some cases, a peaceful death) can occur.
- Clarity of expression in relaying medical diagnoses, explanations and prognosis.
- Giving information to the patient on a variety of medical, social, dietary and personal matters. This will include knowing which language and which register to use, and sometimes involve interpreting for doctors.

Three quotes from Roberts (1994) sum up the importance of language sensitivity with patients:

> *'Language choice and language switching may prove critical factors in maintaining the quality of the nurse/patient relationship.'* (page 60).
>
> *'Cultural misunderstandings between nurse and patient, often accompanied by language difficulties, present a barrier to effective communication. This, in itself, may have a detrimental effect on the nurse/patient relationship.'* (page 61).
>
> *'In general, bilingual patients on the ward claim that they feel more at ease using their first language and can express themselves better in their mother tongue.'* (page 64).

Roberts (1994, page 66) relates another side to communication in a hospital ward. Language switching by the nurse deliberately accents authority with a difficult patient. A male Welsh patient is rapidly proving unpopular with the ward nurses. He is ringing his call button continually, and, on one occasion, he rings it twice. A nurse approaches the patient, and says :

> *'Ganoch chi'r gloch DWY WAITH! Peidiwch byth â'i ganu e dwywaith – 'Emergency' ydy hynny. Dim ond UNWAITH sydd angen.* Only ring it ONCE!'
>
> [Translation from Welsh: You rang the bell TWICE! Don't ever ring it twice – that's an emergency. ONCE is enough. (In English) Only ring it ONCE!]

Reference: ROBERTS, 1994

The Attributes of an Effective Speaker and Listener

1. Listens attentively to the speaker and values their contributions.
2. Makes appropriate responses to the speaker.
3. Is willing to exchange experiences and provide continuity in the conversation.
4. Asks questions of the speaker to ensure continuity of dialogue and the exchange of each other's experiences.
5. Asks questions to clarify the contribution of the speaker and to make sense and meaning from the interaction.
6. Anticipates what is going to be said and reflects on and relates to what has gone before.
7. Is prepared to suspend judgement, modify opinions, correcting first impressions.
8. Uses exploratory talk to understand in more depth the thinking of the speaker.
9. Is aware of different ways of speaking and listening.
10. Is willing to try and understand unfamiliar speakers, in different and varying circumstances.
11. Appropriately uses and appropriately responds to non-verbal communication (e.g. head nods, smiles, physical proximity, eye contact).
12. Correctly interprets pauses and changes of style in conversation.
13. Can make decisions about who to talk to in order to fulfill current needs and purposes.
14. Is confident about communicating and making appropriate responses.
15. Reflects on own contribution to shape future utterances.
16. Is willing to be adventurous with language, creative and imaginative.
17. Can vary ways of talking and listening according to the demands of the audience, task or context.
18 Is aware of the needs of those who have difficulty in understanding the speaker (e.g. different dialect, hearing impaired or deaf person, language learner or a difference of culture).

REFERENCE: Adapted and extended from JOHNSON, 1990

This implies that bilingual children may be more sensitive than monolingual children in a social situation that requires careful communication. A bilingual child may be more aware of the needs of the listener, more sensitive to, and empathic with the listener. The possibility is that, for the listener, understanding of messages is enhanced due to the extra communicative sensitivity of the bilingual.

Much more research is needed to define precisely the characteristics and the extent of the sensitivity to communication that bilinguals may share. Research in this area is important because it connects bilingualism with interpersonal relationships. It moves from questions about skills of the bilingual mind to a bilingual's social skills.

There are currently more hypotheses and hunches than clear evidence in this area. Nevertheless, one interesting subject for future research on bilingualism is likely to focus on how being bilingual affects sensitivity in communication in interpersonal relationships. While there is relatively plentiful research showing that bilinguals tend to have advantages in thinking skills, there are only small pieces of evidence, needing much replication and extension, suggesting that bilinguals may have particular social skills compared with monolinguals.

Further Reading

BEN-ZEEV, S., 1977, The Effect of Bilingualism in Children from Spanish-English Low Economic Neighbourhoods on Cognitive Development and Cognitive Strategy. *Working Papers on Bilingualism*, 14, 83-122.

BIALYSTOK, E. (ed.), 1991, *Language Processing in Bilingual Children*. Cambridge: Cambridge University Press.

DE HOUWER, A., 1995, Bilingual Language Acquisition. In P. FLETCHER & B. MACWHINNEY (eds), *The Handbook of Child Language*. Oxford: Blackwell.

GENESEE, F., TUCKER, G. R. & LAMBERT, W. E., 1975, Communication Skills in Bilingual Children. *Child Development*, 46, 1010-1014.

3: Codeswitching

Codeswitching is a change of language within a conversation, most often when bilinguals are in the company of other bilinguals. When bilinguals converse together, they consciously or subconsciously select the language in which the conversation will take place. The factors governing this initial choice have been discussed in the previous topic. This selected language may be called the base language, recipient language or matrix language. Codeswitching occurs when items from another language are introduced into the base language. This second language may be called the donor language or embedded language. Codeswitching may occur in large blocks of speech, between sentences or within sentences. Codeswitching within sentences may involve single words or phrases. Codeswitching may occur between a base language and more than one donor language. While bilinguals do consciously codeswitch, usually the event is subconscious.

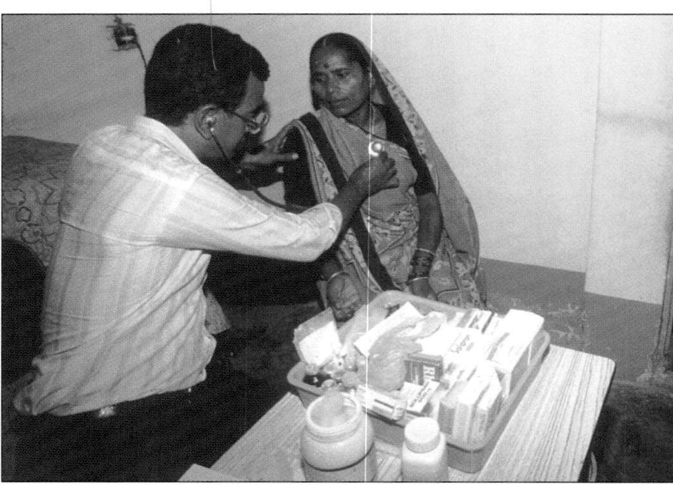

A health center in Bombay, India. The doctor, fluent in Hindi, English and his native language, switches languages to speak to different patients and other medical staff, or to discuss medical or personal matters.

Monolinguals who hear bilinguals codeswitch may have negative attitudes to codeswitching, believing that it shows a deficit, or a lack of mastery of both languages. Bilinguals themselves may be defensive or apologetic about their codeswitching and attribute it to laziness or sloppy language habits. However, studies have shown that codeswitching is a valuable linguistic strategy. It does not happen at random. There is usually considerable purpose and logic in changing languages.

The Monolingual Mode and the Bilingual Mode

The term 'codeswitching' is used to embrace a complex variety of phenomena. Very few bilinguals keep their two languages completely separate, and the ways in which they mix them are complex and varied. Grosjean (1992a) distinguishes between the 'monolingual mode' (when bilinguals use one of their languages with monolingual speakers of that language) and the 'bilingual mode' when bilinguals are in the company of other bilinguals and have the option of switching languages. Even in the 'monolingual mode', bilinguals occasionally mix their languages to some degree. Few bilinguals speak both their languages with native speaker fluency. One language may influence the other, and often the bilingual's dominant language influences his or her less dominant language. Such influence is sometimes called 'interference' although the term 'transfer' is also used because of the negative connotations of the term 'interference'.

Grosjean (1992a) distinguishes between 'static interference' and 'dynamic interference'. Static interference occurs when influence from one of the bilingual's languages is present relatively permanently in the other language. Accent, intonation and the pronunciation of individual sounds are three common areas where static interference may be present. A native German speaker may speak English with a German accent and intonation, and pronounce various sounds in a 'German' way, such as hardening soft consonants at the end of words ('haf' instead of 'have' and 'goot' instead of 'good'). Because few bilinguals who have learnt a second language after early childhood attain complete native speaker pronunciation, these kind of features tend to be permanent.

Dynamic interference occurs when features from one language are transferred temporarily into the other language. Interference can occur at any level of language (syntax, phonology, vocabulary) and in either written or spoken language. One example of dynamic interference would be a native English speaker who also has some competence in French using the word *librairie* to mean library whereas it means bookshop.

Because interference (or transfer) usually occurs from the dominant language into the less dominant language, it is often a feature of second language learning or acquisition, whether by children or adults. (See Interlanguage page 143.) 'Language interference' is a term often used when young children acquiring two languages mix their languages. When a child seems to have a temporary difficulty in separating out two languages, interference has often been the ascribed term. Many bilinguals regard this as being a negative and pejorative term, revealing a monolingual's perspective. For the child, switching between languages may be to convey thoughts and ideas in the most personally efficient manner. The child may also realize that the listener understands such switching. When such interference is temporary in a child's bilingual development, the more neutral term transfer is preferable. As children become older, there is less transfer between languages and more separation. (See page 36.)

Terminology

Various terms are used to describe switches between languages in bilingual conversation. The term 'codemixing' has sometimes been used to describe changes at the word level (e.g. when one word or a few words in a sentence change). A mixed language sentence such as '*Leo un magazine*' (I read a magazine) might be called codemixing. In contrast, 'Come to the table. *Bwyd yn barod*' (food is ready) might be called codeswitching. The first phrase is in English; the second in Welsh. However codeswitching is now the term generally used to describe any switch within the course of a single conversation, whether at word or sentence level or at the level of blocks of speech.

Language borrowing is the term used to indicate foreign loan words or phrases that have become an integral and permanent part of the recipient language. Examples are 'le weekend' from English into the French language and 'der computer' from English into the German language. All languages borrow words or phrases from other languages with which they come into contact (see page 164). Codeswitching may often be the first step in this process. Individuals codeswitch, using words or phrases from the donor language for a variety of purposes. As these words or phrases are widely used, they become accepted and perceived as an integral part of the recipient language. Some linguists have tried to distinguish between 'nonce borrowings' (one-time borrowings, as in codeswitching) and established borrowings. Myers-Scotton (1992) argues against trying to establish criteria to distinguish between codeswitches and loans. Codeswitches and loans are not two distinct and separate entities. Rather, they form a continuum.

How and Why do People Codeswitch?

Codeswitching is complex and subtle, capable of a linguistic description (see Hoffmann, 1991), but also understandable in social and psychological terms. It has not yet been possible to establish the presence of linguistic constraints upon codeswitching that would be universally applicable to any pair of languages. However, research has shown that such linguistic constraints do exist and that codeswitching does not reflect linguistic incompetence, but rather linguistic skill. (See 'The Grammar of Codeswitching', page 61.) Concerning the functions of codeswitching, some of the most common functions are listed on the following page. It can be seen that many instances of codeswitching are triggered by social and psychological factors, rather than linguistic factors.

Codeswitching as the Norm

Swigart (1992) distinguishes between 'marked' and 'unmarked' codeswitching. 'Marked' and 'unmarked' are terms commonly used in linguistics. 'Unmarked' generally means 'conventional, neutral, unremarkable' while 'marked' tends to mean 'positive, unconventional, out of the ordinary, remarkable'. Most research has concentrated on marked codeswitching, where codeswitching is used strategically or purposefully to achieve an aim.

However, in many bilingual situations throughout the world, codeswitching between two languages has become the norm. Among Wolof-French bilinguals in Dakar, the capital of Senegal, (the subject of Swigart's paper), there is continuous and acceptable mixing of the two languages. A similar pattern is found in India where there is sometimes a relatively stable use of codeswitching (e.g. between Hindi and English). In such cases, Swigart (1992) argues, codeswitching is unmarked and does not have the same stylistic or sociological significance as in marked codeswitching. Rather, it is a general marker of belonging to a mixed group with a multiple identity. From a linguistic and grammatical point of view, current thinking indicates that such stable codeswitching should not be analyzed in terms of the donor language or the recipient language, but rather on its own terms as a third code or language.

The Absence of Codeswitching

Terms such as Hinglish, Spanglish, Tex-Mex and Wenglish (respectively for Hindi-English, Spanish-English, Texan-Mexican and Welsh-English) are often used in derogatory fashion to describe what may have become standardized and accepted language borrowing within a particular community. However, in other bilingual communities, strict separation of languages may be the acceptable norm for political, social or cultural reasons. If a power conflict exists between different ethnic groups, then language may be perceived as a prime marker of a separate ethnic identity, and codeswitching may be unacceptable. Treffers-Daller (1992) illustrates

The Functions and Results of Codeswitching

Codeswitches have a variety of purposes and aims. Codeswitching will vary according to who is in the conversation, what the topic is, and in what kind of context the conversation occurs. The languages used may be negotiated between those conversing, and may change with the topic of conversation.

Codeswitches may be used to emphasize a particular point in a conversation. If one word needs stressing or is central in a sentence, a switch may be made.

If a person does not know a word or a phrase in a language, that person may substitute a word in another language. This often happens because bilinguals use different languages in different domains of their lives. A young person may, for instance, switch from the home language to the language used in school to talk about a subject such as mathematics or computers. Myers-Scotton (1972) describes how a Kikuyu university student in Nairobi, Kenya, switched constantly from Kikuyu to English to discuss Geometry with his younger brother.

> *'Atiriri angle niati* has *ina* degree eighty*; nayo* this one *ina mirongo itatu.'*

Similarly, an adult may codeswitch when talking about work, because the technical terms associated with work are only known in that language.

Words or phrases in two languages may not correspond exactly and the bilingual may switch to one language to express a concept that has no equivalent in the culture of the other language. For example, a French-English bilingual living in Britain may use words like 'pub', 'bingo hall' and 'underground', when speaking French, because there are no French equivalents for these words. (When such words or phrases from one language become established and in frequent use in the conversation of speakers of the other language, they are often called 'loans' or 'borrowings' (see page 164). However, there is no clear line of demarcation between a codeswitch and a borrowing.

Codeswitching may be used to reinforce a request. For example, a teacher may repeat a command to accent and underline it (e.g. *Taisez-vous les enfants!* Be quiet, children!). In a majority/minority language situation (see page 56), the majority language may be used to underline authority. In a study conducted at a hospital in Mid-Wales (Roberts, 1994), it was found that nurses repeat or amplify commands to patients in English in order to emphasize their authority (e.g. *Peidiwch a chanu'r gloch Mrs Jones* – don't ring the bell if you don't need anything! See page 56**)**. A Spanish-speaking mother in New York may use English with her children for short commands like 'Stop it! Don't do that!' and then switch back to Spanish.

Repetition of a phrase or passage in another language may also be used to clarify a point. Some teachers in classrooms explain a concept in one language, and then explain it again in another language, believing that repetition adds reinforcement and completeness of understanding.

Codeswitching may be used to communicate friendship or family bonding. For example, moving from the common majority language to the home language or minority language both the listener and speaker understand well, may communicate friendship and common identity. Similarly, a person may deliberately use codeswitching to indicate the need to be accepted by a peer group. Someone with a rudimentary knowledge of a language may inject words of that new language into sentences to indicate a desire to identify and affiliate. The use of the listener's stronger language in part of the conversation may indicate deference, wanting to belong or to be accepted.

In relating a conversation held previously, the person may report the conversation in the language or languages used. For example, two people may be speaking Spanish together. When one reports a previous conversation with an English monolingual, that conversation is reported authentically – for example, in English – as it occurred.

Codeswitching is sometimes used as a way of interjecting into a conversation. A person attempting to break into a conversation may introduce a different language. Interrupting a conversation may be signaled by changing language. The message to the speakers from the listener is that 'I would like to become involved in this conversation'.

Codeswitching may be used to ease tension and inject humor into a conversation. If discussions are becoming tense in a committee, the use of a second language may signal a change in the 'tune being played'. Just as in an orchestra, different instruments may be brought in during a composition to signal a change of mood and pace, so a switch in language may indicate a need to change mood within the conversation.

Codeswitching often relates to a change of attitude or relationship. For example, when two people meet, they may use the common majority language (e.g. Swahili or English in Kenya). As the conversation proceeds and roles, status and ethnic identity are revealed, a change to a regional language may indicate that boundaries are being broken down. A codeswitch signals there is less social distance, with expressions of solidarity and growing rapport indicated by the switch. A study of Italian in-migrants into the United States at the turn of the 20th century (Di Pietro, 1977) showed that the in-migrants would tell a joke in English and give the punch line in Italian, not only because it was better expressed in that language, but also to emphasize the shared values and experiences of the minority group. This is a common feature across many languages and cultures, East and West. Conversely, a change from a minority language or dialect to a majority language may indicate the speakers' wish to elevate their own status, create a distance between themselves and the listener, or establish a more formal, business relationship. Myers-Scotton & Ury (1977) describe a conversation between a Kenyan shop keeper and his sister, who had come in to buy some salt. After exchanging greetings in their own Luyia dialect, the brother switches to Swahili in front of the other customers. For the rest of the conversation, the brother speaks in Swahili and the sister in the Luyia dialect. The brother's codeswitch to Swahili, the business language of Kenya, indicates to his sister that, although they are closely related, he must maintain a business relationship with her. She should not expect any favors or to receive anything for free.

Codeswitching can also be used to exclude people from a conversation. For example, when traveling on the underground (subway, metro), two people speaking English may switch to their minority language to talk about private matters, thus excluding others from the conversation. Bilingual parents may use one language together to exclude their monolingual children from a private discussion. A doctor at a hospital may make a brief aside to a colleague in a language not understood by the patient.

In some bilingual situations, codeswitching occurs regularly when certain topics are introduced (e.g. money). Spanish-English bilinguals in the South West United States regularly switch to English to discuss money.

Familiarity, projected status, the ethos of the context and the perceived linguistic skills of the listeners affect the nature and process of codeswitching. This suggests that codeswitching is not just linguistic; it indicates important social and power relationships.

The Grammar of Codeswitching

Codeswitching is sometimes wrongly perceived as a haphazard process and a sign of linguistic incompetence. However, studies over the last 20 years have shown that codeswitching is a highly complex and sophisticated process governed by certain rules and constraints. When codeswitching occurs between blocks of speech or between separate sentences, there is no problem. A sentence or block of speech in either language follows the grammatical and structural rules for that language. However, when codeswitching occurs intrasententially, in other words, within sentences, the situation is more complex. Linguists have directed their efforts into trying to locate regular patterns that may be found in instances of intrasentential codeswitching between any two languages. It is clear that fluent codeswitchers do not codeswitch at random, but subconsciously follow certain rules and constraints, which do not violate the syntax of either language.

To give one example, in English the adjective always precedes the noun, whereas in French it almost always follows the noun. Thus the word order in English for a noun phrase would be Article (the/a/an)–Adjective–Noun whereas the French order would be Article–Noun–Adjective. An English speaker would say 'an American car' whereas a French speaker would say '*une voiture Americaine*'. It would be possible for a bilingual to codeswitch and say '*J'ai acheté* an American car' (I've bought an American car) but not '*j'ai acheté une American voiture*'. The latter would violate the French word order (Grosjean, 1982). Sankoff & Poplack (1981) defined this as the 'equivalence constraint'. The equivalence constraint predicts that codeswitches will tend to occur at points where the combination of elements from the two languages will not violate a syntactic rule of either language.

The other constraint proposed by Sankoff & Poplack (1981) was the 'free morpheme constraint', which predicts that a switch may not occur between a bound morpheme (i.e. a dependent grammatical element) and a lexical form (a word conveying lexical meaning, i.e. an item of vocabulary) unless the lexical form has been phonologically integrated into the language of the morpheme. To take an example from Spanish/English bilingual speech, '*flipeando*' – 'flipping' might be permissible, but '*catcheando*' – 'catching' might not, because catch has not been integrated into the phonology of Spanish, and therefore cannot take the Spanish progressive suffix '-ando.' Also, codeswitching does not usually occur between two words which are bound together in close association. For instance, it would not be acceptable to codeswitch between a subject pronoun and a verb in English/French. A bilingual speaker would not say '*Je* went to the park' or 'I *suis allé au parc*'.

Sankoff & Poplack's (1981) work generated much interest but was found not to be universally applicable to all instances of codeswitching, especially those occurring between languages of different origins and dissimilar grammars (e.g. between the English language and African ethnic community languages).

Myers-Scotton (1993) proposes a Matrix Language Frame Model. According to this model, the Matrix Language (ML) (base language or recipient language) sets the framework for all codeswitching. The language (or languages) from which words or phrases enter the matrix language is referred to as the Embedded Language (EL). Myers-Scotton (1993) distinguishes between three types of codeswitching categories. The first consists of ML 'islands', in other words, units of ML speech, such as clauses or phrases. These follow ML syntactical and grammatical rules. Conversely, the second category consists of EL 'islands' which follow EL syntactical and grammatical rules. The third category comprises constituents that include both EL and ML elements. In this third category, the EL material is always integrated into the syntax and often into the morphology of the ML. In other words, the EL elements adapt to the ML grammatical patterns and word order, and generally ML grammatical particles are used (e.g. verb inflections).

FURTHER READING: MYERS-SCOTTON, 1993

how in Brussels, the capital of Belgium, French-Flemish codeswitching was acceptable among the older generation of bilinguals, who identified with both French and Flemish ethnic groups. It has, however, become less acceptable among younger Belgians, because there has been a gradual polarization of the two main ethnic groups, Walloon and Flemish.

Similarly, French-English codeswitching is not acceptable among some Canadian francophone groups, because of the power and ethnic identity struggle with anglophones. The situation in the African country of Tanzania tends to show the reverse. English, the colonial language, was marginalized for many years after independence in 1964, while Swahili was promoted as the national language. Although older Tanzanians, who still associate English with colonialism, do not favor Swahili-English codeswitching, it has become more widespread and acceptable among young Tanzanians, as English has become the fashionable medium of Anglo-American culture.

Further Reading

HOFFMANN, C., 1991, *An Introduction to Bilingualism*. London: Longman.

MYERS-SCOTTON, C., 1992, Comparing Codeswitching and Borrowing. *Journal of Multilingual and Multicultural Development*, 13 (1&2), 19-39.

MYERS-SCOTTON, C., 1993, *Social Motivations for Codeswitching: Evidence from Africa*. Oxford: Clarendon Press.

MYERS-SCOTTON, C., 1996, Code-switching. In F. COULMAS (ed.), *The Handbook of Sociolinguistics*. Oxford: Blackwell.

Bilingualism and Thinking

1: Bilingualism and Intelligence

One vigorous theme in the history of bilingualism has explored the relationship between languages and thinking. Does bilingualism result in problems in thinking? Is having two languages in the brain a burden to thinking processes? Does the ownership of two languages result in mental confusion? Does speaking a minority language at home hinder the acquisition of a majority language?

In the 20th century, parents and teachers have sometimes been advised by well-meaning doctors, counselors, speech therapists and psychologists to use only one language with their children so there would be no mental confusion. Just as oil and water mixed together would cause an engine to dysfunction, so mixing two languages has been said to lead to the mental engine running more slowly, with coughs and splutters.

One intuitive belief during the 20th century has been that, if two languages reside inside an individual's thinking 'quarters', there is less room to store other areas of learning. Therefore, the ability to speak two languages will be at a cost to efficiency in thinking. Fortunately for bilinguals, such beliefs are now known to be naïve and incorrect. Throughout this section, we will explore the relationship between ownership of two languages and thinking. We start by focusing on a dominant concept in psychology (and in everyday language), that of intelligence. Are bilinguals less intelligent, as intelligent or more intelligent than monolinguals?

There are three overlapping and approximate periods in the 20th century reflecting a change in research findings regarding this question. These periods can be labeled: the period of negative effects; the period of neutral effects; and the period of positive effects. Each will be considered in turn.

The Period of Negative Effects

From the 19th century to approximately the 1960s, the belief among both the public and academics was that bilingualism had a negative effect on intelligence. Professor Laurie, when lecturing at Cambridge University in 1890, stated that intellectual growth would not be doubled by being bilingual. On the contrary, intelligence would be halved. If language is the soil in which intelligence grows, two languages produce a thin soil and monolingualism a much more rich and fertile soil.

Some of the earliest research on bilingualism compared monolinguals and bilinguals on intelligence (IQ) tests. Much of this early research came from Wales and the United States and compared the IQ scores of bilinguals and monolinguals, especially on verbal IQ tests (see textbox). The typical result was that monolinguals were found to have a higher IQ than bilinguals.

For example, an enterprising headteacher from Wales, D. J. Saer (1923), used 1400 children aged seven to 14 and compared bilinguals and monolinguals. He found a ten-point difference in IQ between these two groups in favor of monolingual English speakers. Saer's conclusion was that bilinguals were mentally confused and at a disadvantage in thinking compared with monolinguals.

In a later piece of research, this same author found that the same difference in IQ existed between university monolinguals and bilinguals. Saer concluded that bilinguals' mental disadvantage was of a permanent nature

The coastal town of Aberystwyth, in mid-Wales, where D.J. Saer lived.

since it existed from the age of seven through to university. If the IQ disadvantage existed among the most able in society (those at university), the problem of bilinguals being less intelligent would be as great, or greater, among people of lower IQ.

However, we now know that such early research had a series of flaws and limitations which cast doubt on these early individual studies and on all early studies taken cumulatively. For example, Saer did not compare like with like. Saer's bilinguals were mostly of lower socioeconomic status, with monolinguals coming from a higher social class. Hence the result, showing monolinguals to be ahead of bilinguals, may be due to differences between higher and lower social classes, rather than, or as well as, bilingualism.

A fair comparison requires monolinguals and bilinguals to be matched on all the other factors that might otherwise explain the result. It is necessary to match these two groups on variables such as sociocultural class, gender, age, type of school attended, and urban\rural as well as subtractive\additive environments.

A second problem in the early research was that bilinguals were often given an IQ test in their weaker language. Many verbal IQ tests were administered in English only. This tended to be to the disadvantage of bilinguals because they were tested in their second or weaker language. Had bilinguals been given the IQ test in their first or dominant language, different results may have been obtained.

A third issue concerns the proficiency in two languages of the bilinguals. There are not simply two categories: bilinguals and monolinguals. Rather, there exists a whole range of different language skills and proficiencies that may be used to classify bilinguals and monolinguals. Were all the basic language abilities (reading, writing, speaking and listening) used for classification? What was the degree of fluency in each language of the bilinguals? Were bilinguals classified by their use of languages or by their ability in languages? Were the bilinguals relatively balanced in their language proficiencies or were there considerable imbalances? Such classification criteria have been found to be crucial in making fair comparisons between bilingual and monolinguals.

Fourthly, there is a general problem in using IQ tests to measure 'intelligence'. The concept of intelligence is hotly debated and highly controversial in psychology and education. What is intelligence? What is intelligent behavior? Who is intelligent? A thief who cracks a bank vault? A famous football coach? Someone poor who becomes a rich billionaire? A chairperson who manipulates the members of a board? Is there social intelligence, musical intelligence, military intelligence, marketing intelligence, motoring intelligence, political intelligence, sporting intelligence, financial intelligence? Are all, or indeed any of these forms of intelligence measured by a simple pencil and paper IQ test that demands a single, acceptable and correct solution to every question?

What someone defines as intelligent behavior, or who is defined as an intelligent person, will differ from psychologist to psychologist, teacher to teacher, person to person. Defining intelligent behavior or an intelligent person requires a value judgment as to what kind of behavior and what kind of person are of more worth in a particular society. IQ tests tend to relate to a very narrow set of skills, to a middle class, 'white' and western view of academic intelligence. Such IQ tests (as used in this early bilingualism research) measure only a small sample of everyday intelligence. Whatever relationship is found between IQ tests and bilingualism refers only to 'pencil and paper' intelligence where only correct and not creative answers are demanded.

The Period of Neutral Effects

There are a series of researches on IQ and bilingualism that reported no difference between bilinguals and monolinguals. In the United States, when comparing Yiddish/English bilinguals with English monolinguals, no difference on IQ tests was found. In Wales, in the 1950s, research found that once the socioeconomic class of bilinguals and monolinguals was taken into account, there was no difference between these two groups on non-verbal IQ.

This period of neutral effects (approximately the late 1950s and early 1960s) was valuable because it highlighted the inadequacies and methodological mistakes of the earlier research. It showed that bilingualism was not necessarily a source of intellectual disadvantage. In the 1960s in Wales, such a conclusion was a boost to parents who wished to support bilingualism in the home and bilingual education in the school. As a short transitional period, it led to the questioning of a fashionable belief of bilingualism as cerebral confusion, and heralded in the current period: the period of positive effects.

The Period of Positive Effects

One of the most famous pieces of research on bilingualism was conducted by Peal & Lambert (1962) in Canada. This piece of research proved a turning point and a signpost for future research on bilingualism and cognitive functioning. The highly influential piece of research was valuable for four reasons.

The Research of Peal and Lambert

Peal & Lambert's (1962) sample of children comprised 164 ten year olds from six middle class French schools in Montreal with a gender ratio of six boys to every four girls. The original sample of 364 children was narrowed down to 164 children by four tests of bilingual proficiency. The authors then further reduced the sample to 110 children so that there would be equal numbers of 'matched' bilinguals and monolinguals in each of the seven socioeconomic classes. Only balanced bilinguals and monolinguals were included. Among the 46 variables on which data was gathered, 18 variables measured IQ.

Of the 18 variables measuring IQ, 15 variables showed bilinguals to have a statistically significant higher IQ than monolinguals. On only three variables was there no difference, these being the Space, Perception and Number components of the Primary Mental Abilities Test. The significant 15 variables included verbal and non-verbal aspects of IQ. Separate factor analyses of monolinguals and bilinguals revealed a difference in factor structure. The authors suggest that there is a difference in the structure of the intellect, with bilinguals having a more diversified intelligence.

The historical importance of this research lies in the authors' discussions of the findings. In an interpretation of the positive relationship of IQ to bilingualism, Peal & Lambert (1962) argued that bilingualism may give:

1. Greater mental flexibility.
2. The ability to think more abstractly, less concretely, more independently of words, resulting in superiority in concept formation.
3. A more enriched bicultural environment which benefits IQ.
4. Positive transfer between languages benefiting verbal IQ.

The research aroused debate. The controversy has not so much disputed that bilingualism can, under certain circumstances, be cognitively beneficial. Rather, debates centered on the methodological weakness of the research. Principally there are four limitations to the research.

Limitations

First, the results concern 110 children of 10 years of age and of middle class, Montreal extraction. This is not a sample that can be generalized to the population of bilinguals either in Canada or throughout the world. This is particularly so since the results concern 110 children selected from the original sample of 364. An unanswered question is how the other 254 children performed across the broad range of tests given by Peal & Lambert (1962).

Second, children in the bilingual group were 'balanced' bilinguals. While the term 'bilinguals' includes balanced bilinguals, there are many other groups of children 'less balanced'. We cannot assume that the results from this study apply to such less balanced bilinguals. Are balanced bilinguals a special group with their own characteristics in terms of their motivation, aptitude for languages, cognitive abilities and attitudes? Are balanced bilinguals a special group of children who have a higher IQ that is due not only to owning two languages, but due to other factors as well (e.g. parental values and expectations)?

The third problem with Peal & Lambert's (1962) research is the chicken and the egg problem – which comes first? What is the cause and what is the effect? Is it bilingualism that enhances IQ? Or does a higher IQ increase the chances of becoming bilingual? When research suggests that IQ and bilingualism are positively related, we cannot conclude the order of cause and effect. It may be that bilingualism enhances IQ. It may be that those with a higher IQ are more likely to become bilingual. The relationship may also be such that one is both the cause and the effect of the other.

The fourth problem concerns socioeconomic status. While Peal & Lambert (1962) tried to equate their bilingual and monolingual groups for socioeconomic class by exclusion of some children, there are residual problems. Equating socioeconomic class does not control for all the differences in a child's home environment. Socioeconomic class is only a rough, simple and very partial measure of a child's home and environmental background. This is true of monolingual children. It is even more so with children who are bilingual and bicultural where there may be an even more complicated sociocultural home and family background. Parental occupation of bilingual children is likely to summarize differences between children very inadequately.

In the following example, notice how the sociocultural element is very different, yet the socioeconomic class is the same. Take two Latino children of the same age and gender living in the same street in New York. Their fathers both have the same job – taxi drivers. One family regularly attends church services in Spanish and belongs to a Latino organization with cultural activities in Spanish. This taxi driver and his wife send their children to a Spanish-English dual language school. The child is bilingual. In the second family, the child speaks English only. There is no interest in sending their children to a Dual Language school. Neither does the family attend a church or another organization where Spanish is spoken and valued. The Latin-American roots are neither discussed nor appreciated. While the families are matched on socioeconomic status, the sociocultural differences between them are considerable. In this example, the first child is bilingual and the second child is monolingual, with the bilingual child having a higher IQ. The child's bilingualism may not be the only explanation of a higher IQ. Rather the alternative or additional explanation may be in the different social and cultural environment of these children. Thus, with Peal & Lambert's (1962) study, socioeconomic class may have been controlled, but not sociocultural class.

REFERENCE: PEAL & LAMBERT, 1962

Bilingualism and Intelligence

Early Quotes

A 19th-century quotation from a Professor Laurie of Cambridge University portrays the early deficit viewpoint: *'If it were possible for a child to live in two languages at once equally well, so much the worse. His intellectual and spiritual growth would not thereby be doubled, but halved. Unity of mind and character would have great difficulty in asserting itself in such circumstances'.* (Laurie, 1890, page 15).

Research by Saer, Smith & Hughes (1924) suggested that University student monolinguals were superior to bilinguals: *'the difference in mental ability as revealed by intelligence tests is of a permanent nature since it persists in students throughout their University career'* (page 53).

From a student child psychology textbook used in the United States in the 1950s : *'There can be no doubt that the child reared in a bilingual environment is handicapped in his language growth. One can debate the issue as to whether speech facility in two languages is worth the consequent retardation in the common language of the realm'.* (Thompson, 1952, page 367).

Recent Quotes

'Bilinguals performed significantly better than monolinguals on both verbal and non-verbal intelligence tests. Several explanations are suggested as to why bilinguals have this general intellectual advantage. It is argued that they have a language asset, are more facile at concept formation, and have a greater mental flexibility.' (Peal & Lambert, 1962, page 22).

'Take any group of bilinguals who are approximately equivalent in their L1 and L2 abilities and match them with a monolingual group for age, socioeconomic level, and whatever other variables you think might confound your results. Now, choose a measure of cognitive flexibility and administer it to both groups. The bilingual will do better.' (Hakuta, 1986, page 35).

First, it rectified many of the methodological weaknesses of the period of negative effects. Second, the research found that bilingualism need not have negative or neutral consequences. Rather, that there is a real possibility that bilinguals, or at least a specific group of balanced bilinguals, have cognitive advantages over monolinguals. Third, the findings of Peal & Lambert have been widely quoted to support bilingual policies in different educational contexts. In Canada, the political implication was that bilingualism (French/English) was not going to be a source of national intellectual inferiority. Rather, linguistic diversity in Canada could be a source of intellectual advantage. Fourth, the research, while using IQ tests, moved to a much broader look at the processes and products in cognition. Other areas of mental activity apart from the narrow idea of IQ stimulated continuing decades of research into bilingualism and cognitive functioning.

The main points of Peal & Lambert's (1962) research are outlined in the accompanying Textbox. In essence, the researchers found that balanced bilinguals scored significantly higher on 15 out of 18 variables measuring IQ. Their conclusion was that bilingualism provides: greater mental flexibility, the ability to think more abstractly, the ability to think independently of words, and superiority in concept formation. Their argument was that a more enriched bilingual and bicultural experience benefits the development of intelligence.

They also argued that there was a positive transfer between a bilingual's two languages (rather than interference between the two languages). While there were criticisms of the research, recent research using IQ tests tends to confirm the original findings.

One interesting issue is the chicken and the egg question – what comes first? Does bilingualism enhance IQ or does a higher IQ increase the chances of becoming bilingual? Is one both the cause and the effect of the other in a cyclical fashion? This question is discussed later in this section.

Further Reading

BAKER, C., 1996, *Foundations of Bilingual Education and Bilingualism*. Clevedon: Multilingual Matters Ltd.

DIAZ, R. M., & KLINGER, C., 1991, Towards an Explanatory Model of the Interaction between Bilingualism and Cognitive Development. In E. BIALYSTOK (ed.), *Language Processing in Bilingual Children*. Cambridge: Cambridge University Press.

HAKUTA, K., 1986b, *Mirror of Language. The Debate on Bilingualism*. New York: Basic Books.

HAKUTA, K., 1990, Language and Cognition in Bilingual Children, Bilingual Education. In A. M. PADILLA, H. H. FAIRCHILD & C. M. VALADEZ (eds), *Issues and Strategies in Bilingual Education*. London/New Delhi: Sage Publications.

HAKUTA, K. & DIAZ, R. M.,1985, The Relationship Between Degree of Bilingualism and Cognitive Ability: A Critical Discussion and Some New Longitudinal Data. In K. E. NELSON (ed.), *Children's Language*, Volume 5. Hillsdale, NJ and London: Erlbaum.

2: Bilingualism and Creative Thinking

Introduction

At the beginning of this subsection we examined a possible relationship between bilingualism and increased intelligence. Another question sometimes asked is whether bilinguals are any different from monolinguals in their styles or strategies of thinking. Does bilingualism affect a person's cognitive style i.e. methods of sorting information, remembering, transforming and using information? If a bilingual stores and processes two languages inside the thinking quarters, does that have any effects on the way bilinguals think in the classroom, in everyday conversations or in internal cerebral activity?

We will be looking at three aspects or dimensions of cognitive style i.e. creative thinking, field dependency or independency and language awareness.

Creative or Divergent Thinking

IQ tests require children to find the one correct answer to each question. This is often called convergent thinking. Children have to converge onto the sole acceptable answer. An alternative style of thinking is called divergent thinking or creative thinking. Some people seem to have a more free, open-ended, elastic, imaginative and creative form of thinking. Instead of finding the one correct answer, divergent thinkers prefer a variety of answers, all of which may be valid.

Measuring Creative and Divergent Thinking

To probe divergent thinking, simple and straightforward questions are used. For example, 'How many uses can you think of for a brick?' 'How many interesting and unusual uses can you think of for a cardboard box?' On this open-ended kind of question, a student has to diverge and think of imaginative answers – as many as possible.

A convergent thinker tends to produce a few, fundamental answers to the question. A converger may say that bricks can be used to build houses, build a wall, and build a barbecue. The diverger tends rapidly to produce a large number of different answers. Some may be quite unusual and original. A diverger may give 10, 15, 20 or more answers to such a question. Apart from the expect-

Measuring the Creative Thinking of Bilinguals and Monolinguals

Fluency, flexibility, originality and elaboration can be measured by Torrance's (1974a) Tests of Creative Thinking. For example, a person is asked to think of 'Unusual Uses of Tin Cans'. Imagine that in response to the 'Uses of Tin Cans' question a student gives six answers:

1. Animal bed.
2. Animal cage.
3. Insect house.
4. Hole for golf green.
5. Hair roller.
6. Tie together and put boards on top for a raft.

The answers would be scored on four dimensions. The student's fluency score will be 6. By reference to Torrance's (1974a) manual, it is possible to derive scores for the flexibility, originality and elaboration of the responses. For flexibility Torrance lists 28 different categories into which almost all responses fall. For example, listed categories include Animal Shelter, Art Use, Tools and Weapons. A person's flexibility score is the number of different categories into which answers can be placed. Thus animal bed, animal cage and insect house all fall into one category (Animal Shelter) and earn one point. Answers four, five and six above fall into three different categories.

For originality, reference to the Test Manual provides a score of 0, 1 or 2 for the originality of some 180 responses. A score of 1 on originality means that Torrance (1974a) found the answer to occur in less than 20 percent of the population. A score of 2 means that the answer is rare, occurring less than 5 percent of the time. 'Insect house' would be scored O on originality; hair roller and hole for golf green both score 2.

Elaboration refers to the extra detail which elaborates over and above that which is necessary to communicate a basic idea. Thus 'Animal house' has no elaboration and scores O; 'tie together and put board on top for a raft' elaborates twice on the 'raft' idea and obtains an elaboration score of 2 (Torrance, 1974a). The average 11 year old obtains a score of 20 on Fluency, 7 on Flexibility and 11 on originality (Torrance, 1974b).

ed answers, such as to build a wall and to build a house, the diverger may give some unusual answers: for propping up a wobbly table, as an ashtray, for use as a foot wiper, an abstract sculpture, as a plumb line, for breaking a window when there's a fire, for making a bird bath, to raise a car when mending a puncture.

In the British tradition, such divergent thinking tests also ask students to make up short sentences based on four letters (e.g. W__ C__ E__ N__). Examples of answers are: Woven Coats Established Newcastle; Wise Cats Eat Nougat). Also, figural (non-verbal) divergent tests can be employed. For example, a page of 40 empty squares or 40 empty circles is given to a sample of people. They are invited to make drawings from these squares or circles and place a label underneath.

In these tests, convergers provide a few straightforward and sensible answers. Divergers tend to produce many short sentences starting with W__ C__ E__ N__ and many drawings with labels. For example a diverger may not only make a window frame, a house and a clock out of the squares, but also make a robot, an advertisement on the subway, and a maze. Other imaginative responses include leaving the squares blank and putting a label underneath, such as a 'white cat in flour', 'a politician's promise' and 'my mind during an examination'.

In the North American tradition, it is more usual to talk about creative thinking than divergent thinking. The same kinds of tests are used (for example, unusual uses for a cardboard box). Such creativity tests are often scored by the fluency, flexibility, originality and elaboration of each of the answers given. The accompanying Textbox provides an example.

Bilingual Humour

A Mother's Experience

My (French/English bilingual) son was just over two and a half when I heard him chattering to himself in his bedroom, trying to put a picture on the wall. Here is what I heard:

'Ai besoin de Blue Tak. Où est mon Blue Tak?
(Need Blue Tak. Where's my Blue Tak?)

Dans le placard peut-être. .. Non. .. trouve pas...
(In the cupboard perhaps.. . No... can't find...)

Ai besoin d'un clou. ... un clou. ..'
(Need a nail. .. a nail. ...)

Two seconds of silence, then a loud and uncontrollable chuckle:

'I haven't got a clue!'

And me, next door, the flabbergasted but proud mother left to reflect on her son's linguistic awareness!

(Extracted with permission from the *Bilingual Family Newsletter,* Volume 2, No. 4, page 5, December 1985 from a submission by Mrs B. Harvey, Whittington, England).

Creative Thinking and Bilingualism

Researchers tend to find a link between creative thinking and bilingualism. It seems that the ownership of two or more languages may increase fluency, flexibility, originality and elaboration in thinking, at least when these are measured by psychological tests. Possibly because of their processing of two languages, bilinguals may have a slightly higher probability of fruitful divergent thinking. How does this occur? Bilinguals will have two or more words for a single object or an idea. They will have two or more ways of referring to the same content area, concept, idea or information. The central notion is that having two or more words for the same object or idea allows bilinguals more freedom and richness in their thinking.

Research on bilingualism and divergent or creative thinking has occurred in a truly international arena: Canada, Ireland, Mexico, Singapore and the United States, for example. Most research findings show that bilinguals are superior to monolinguals on their creative or divergent thinking. Such superiority is found particularly among bilinguals whose two languages are both reasonably well developed. Where there is proficiency to a reasonable level in both languages (so-called balanced bilingualism), fluency, flexibility, originality and elaboration in thinking appear to have a higher probability of occurring.

Further Reading

BAKER, C., 1996, *Foundations of Bilingual Education and Bilingualism.* Clevedon: Multilingual Matters Ltd.

BIALYSTOK, E. (ed.), 1991, *Language Processing in Bilingual Children.* Cambridge: Cambridge University Press.

Bilingual Associations

Here are some examples of where a bilingual has two (or more) labels for the same object or idea. This may give an extra dimension in thinking, more associations, and more elaborate concepts. This may also mean that the link between a word and its concept is looser.

A French/English bilingual has two words for kitchen (i.e. 'kitchen' in English and '*cuisine'* in French). Sometimes corresponding words in different languages have different connotations. For example, kitchen in English has traditionally been a place of hard work (as in the phrase 'tied to the kitchen sink'). '*Cuisine'* in French has different connotations – a place for creativity, a place where the family congregate, not only to eat, but also to socialize. In Swahili, the word '*jiko*' (kitchen) has a different connotation from kitchen and '*cuisine*'. In Swahili, '*kupata jiko*' (to get a kitchen) means to get married, when referring to a man. Since bachelors usually do not eat regularly at home, it is only when they get married that they are considered to have a proper kitchen.

Languages affect the way we perceive and categorize the world, because different languages have different ways of talking about concepts and cognition. Even simple everyday objects may have different connotations in different languages, so that the way the language represents that object may affect the way it is seen. To take one example. In English, the word 'handle' is widely used. We talk about the handle of a brush, a door handle, the handle of a cup or saucepan. In other words, that part of the object is defined according to its use: it is the part we grasp with the hand to move or manipulate the object. In other languages, the handles of those same objects might be differently defined, not according to their function but rather according to their appearance. In Welsh people talk about '*coes brwsh*' (the 'leg' of a brush) and in some areas about '*coes sosban*' (the 'leg' of a saucepan). People also talk about '*clust cwpan*' (the 'ear' of a cup). (This also used to be said in English which is why parents still mutter 'little pitchers have big ears' when their children are eavesdropping!) Some French speakers talk about '*la queue d'une casserole*' (the 'tail' of a saucepan) and '*la poignée d'une porte*' (the 'fistful' of a door i.e. door knob).

Languages reflect the culture, beliefs, values and ethnic identity of people who speak them. For this reason, languages sometimes possess words which have no exact equivalent in other languages. One example is words which describe personal qualities that are valued in the particular culture. The Finnish word '*sisu*', meaning 'grit, determination and moral courage' is a valued quality in Finland where people have traditionally had to struggle for survival against the elements. In France, it is a compliment to call someone '*fin*', which can be translated as 'subtle, perceptive, grasping ideas easily'. This reflects the French respect for philosophy, intellectual discussion and individual opinions.

A Finnish-made lorry, appropriately named 'Sisu'.

3: Field Dependency and Independency and Bilingualism

Another well-researched dimension of cognitive style along which people vary is field dependence-field independence (Witkin *et al.*, 1971). An example from one of their tests will help describe the dimension. In the Embedded Figures Test, a child has to draw in the left hand figure over the right hand figure. Can the child recognize the cuboid in the right hand figure?

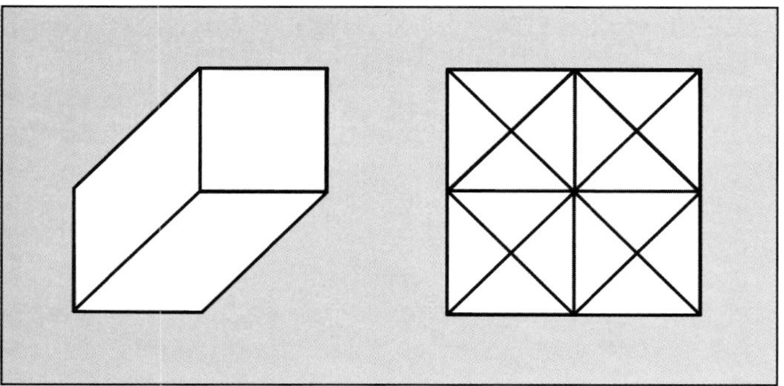

Children who are field independent will tend to be able to see the object separate from the other lines in the right hand figure. Those field dependent will tend not to be able to separate out the cuboid figure from the background. Simply stated, some people tend to see in wholes, others in parts. Witkin *et al.* (1962) found that as children grow to maturity they become more field independent. While field dependence-independence may appear as a perceptual ability, Witkin and his co-workers regard it as a general ability to be aware of visual contexts, which relates particularly to problem-solving ability and ease of cognitive restructuring. Field independent individuals tend to achieve higher academically than those who are field dependent.

One early study which examined whether bilinguals have a particular cognitive style compared with monolinguals was conducted in Switzerland by Balkan (1970). French-English balanced bilinguals aged 11 to 17 were matched with monolinguals on IQ and compared on an adaptation of the Embedded Figures Test. Balkan (1970) found that bilinguals were more field independent and that those who learnt their second language before the age of four tended to be more field independent than late learners (who had learnt their second language between four and eight years). In Canada students age 12 to 13 years in a bilingual education program were superior to the control groups on the Embedded Figures Test (Bruck, Lambert & Tucker, 1976). Although the comparison groups were different from Balkan (1970), the Canadian research provides confirmation of bilingualism being linked to greater field independence. Genesee & Hamayan (1980) found that those more field independent learnt a second language better. This highlights the cause-effect relationship. Does field independence cause bilingualism to occur more easily? Does bilingualism cause field independence? Or is one both the cause and the effect of the other?

Apart from the Swiss and Canadian research, one further confirmatory piece of evidence comes from English/Spanish bilinguals in the US (Duncan & De Avila, 1979). Using the Children's Embedded Figures Test, the descending order of scores on field independence was:

1. Proficient Bilinguals.
2. Partial Bilinguals, Monolinguals and Limited Bilinguals.
3. Late Language Learners.

The authors conclude that proficient bilinguals may have advantages in cognitive clarity and in analytical functioning.

Further Reading

DUNCAN, S. E. & DE AVILA, E. A., 1979, Bilingualism and Cognition: Some Recent Findings. *National Association for Bilingual Education Journal* (NABE), 4 (1), 15-50.

4: Piaget and Bilingualism

One of Piaget's tests. The child is required to sort the triangles into groups, taking into account size and color.

Jean Piaget has been a central figure during the 20th century in understanding how children think. A Swiss biologist and psychologist, Piaget attempted to identify how different types of childhood and teenage thinking developed. He proposed various stages of thinking from birth to the development of formal logic in late childhood. Piagetian cognitive tests have been used to compare bilinguals and monolinguals. These tests are used to indicate which stage of conceptual development (sensorimotor; pre-operational; concrete operational; formal operations) a child has reached. Do bilinguals show any differences from monolinguals on such cognitive tests?

Examples of the kinds of tests used to measure bilingual and monolingual children's conceptual development include:

1. A cardboard cup is crushed and placed next to a cup identical to the original non-crushed cup. The child is asked to select the object as it initially existed.

2. When a length of plasticine is changed from a ball to a worm, the child is asked if the mass has been conserved or has changed.

3. Children are asked to sort the shapes (see diagram) into correct groups. Account must be taken of shape, color and size. A child is asked to sort outside circles from outside squares, thus ignoring color and inside shape. Then red objects may be requested to be separated from yellow objects, thus ignoring a previous classification.

On these kinds of tests, bilinguals have been found to be ahead on concept formation. In acquiring the concept of conservation (e.g. that a ball of plasticine is the same when it is rolled into a worm of plasticine) and on the concept of measurement, bilinguals have been found to be more advanced.

One explanation has been that bilinguals have two worlds of language experience compared with the one world of language experience of monolinguals. Others have argued that the ability to analyze language accelerates concept formation.

One line of research using Piaget's tests of conceptual development has located differences between bilinguals according to their levels of language proficiency. Duncan & De Avila (1979) compared five different language groups on Piagetian tests of conservation of identity, number, length, substance and distance. The order of performance on these conservation tasks was as follows. Highest performance was by proficient bilinguals- that is

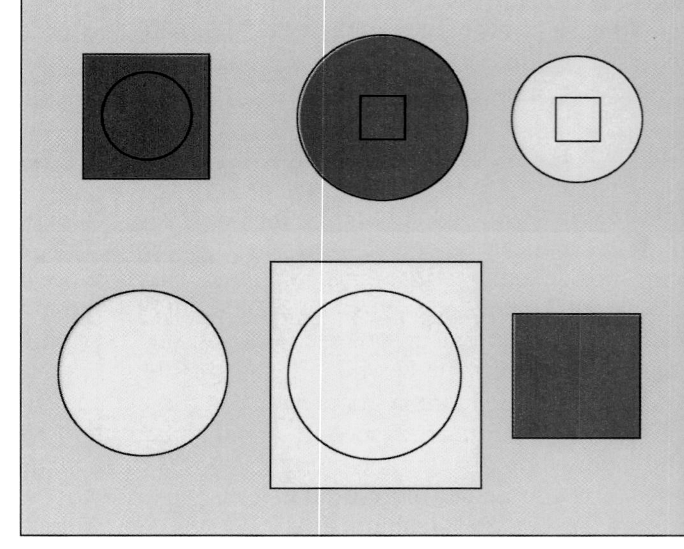

bilinguals with well-developed skills in both languages. The order after that was: monolinguals, 'limited bilinguals', 'partial bilinguals' and late language learners. This is one piece of evidence showing that the cognitive and conceptual advantages of bilingualism are not shared by all bilinguals. Rather, a child needs to attain a certain level of proficiency in both languages before such cognitive advantages are assured. This adds some credence to Cummins' Thresholds theory (see Thresholds Theory page 74).

Further Reading

BEN-ZEEV, S., 1977b, The Effect of Bilingualism in Children from Spanish-English Low Economic Neighborhoods on Cognitive Development and Cognitive Strategy. *Working Papers on Bilingualism*, 14, 83-122.

DUNCAN, S. E. & DE AVILA, E. A., 1979, Bilingualism and Cognition: Some Recent Findings. *NABE Journal*, 4 (1), 15-50.

5: Bilingualism and Metalinguistic Awareness

Young bilinguals sometimes have an enhanced ability compared with monolinguals to focus on the important content and meaning of language rather than the external structure or sound. For example, a bilingual child is taught a new nursery rhyme. Rather than merely learning the words, rote fashion and concentrating on the rhyme, some young bilingual children seem to focus more (compared with monolinguals) on the meaning and storyline of the nursery rhyme. Does this mean that bilingual children are less bound by the words, focusing more on meaning than the words themselves?

Take two illustrations. First, there is Leopold's famous case study of the German-English development of his daughter Hildegard (see page 39). Leopold (1939-1949) noticed that Hildegard accepted very early that a word itself and its meaning were loosely linked. There was nothing absolute or inevitable in the link between the word and its meaning. Words were just arbitrary labels given to an object or an idea. Word sound and word meaning were separate. The name of an object or an idea was separate from the object or the idea itself. Leopold found that his stories to Hildegard were not repeated with stereotyped wording. Plenty of substitutions and adjustments were made to relay the central points of the story.

The second illustration is how bilingual children sometimes have a greater propensity to alter the words in memorized songs and rhymes. The monolingual child is sometimes more likely to repeat a verse of a song with little or no alteration. Their focus is on repeating the verse accurately and getting the words right. The bilingual child tends to center more on the meaning than repeating the words parrot fashion. The following illustrates:

Imagine a kindergarten monolingual and bilingual child are taught the same nursery rhymes:

Jack and Jill went up the hill
To fetch a pail of water.
Jack fell down and broke his crown
And Jill came tumbling after.

Ring around the rosy,
A pocket full of posies.
Ashes, ashes,
We all fall down.

The bilingual may offer the following versions; the word substitutions suggesting that the nursery rhyme has been processed for meaning:

Jack and Jill climbed a hill
To get a bottle of water.
Jack fell down and hit his head
And Jill fell on top of him.

Rings and rings of roses,
And a big bunch of pansies.
Ashes, ashes,
We all fall dead.

One of the first to examine whether bilinguals and monolinguals are different in their attachments of word sounds and word meanings was a South African researcher, Ianco-Worrall (1972). In a delightfully simple experiment, she compared matched groups of monolinguals and bilinguals. To ensure other explanations could be ruled out, the two groups were matched on IQ, age, gender, school grade and socioeconomic class. Ianco

Ring around the rosy.

Worrall (1972) tested the sound and meaning separation idea on 30 Afrikaans-English bilinguals aged four to nine.

In the first experiment, a typical question was: 'I have three words: CAP, CAN and HAT. Which is more like CAP: CAN or HAT?' A child who says that CAN is more like CAP would appear to be making a choice determined by the sound of the word. That is, CAP and CAN have two out of three sounds in common. A child who chooses HAT would appear to be making a choice based on the meaning of the word. That is, HAT and CAP refer to similar objects.

Ianco-Worrall (1972) showed that, by seven years of age, there was no difference between bilinguals and monolinguals in their choices. Both groups chose HAT, their answer being governed by the meaning of the word. However, with four to six year olds, she found that bilinguals tended to respond to word meaning, monolinguals more to the sound of the word. This led Ianco-Worrall (1972) to conclude that bilinguals: 'reach a stage of semantic development, as measured by our test, some 2-3 years earlier than their monolingual peers'. (page 1398).

In a further experiment, Ianco-Worrall (1972) asked the following type of question: 'Suppose you were making up names for things, could you call a cow 'dog' and a dog 'cow'? Bilinguals mostly felt that names could be interchangeable. Monolinguals, in comparison, more often said that names for objects such as cow and dog could not be interchanged. For bilinguals, names and objects are separate. This seems to be a result of owning two languages, giving the bilingual child and adult awareness of the free, non-fixed relationship between objects and their labels.

Does Bilingualism Really Improve Intelligence and Thinking?

- The cause and effect relationship must be highlighted. What comes first? Most research in this area assumes that bilingualism comes first and causes cognitive benefits. It is not impossible that the causal link may run from cognitive abilities to enhanced language learning. Or it may be that language learning and cognitive development work hand in hand. One both promotes and stimulates the other. It is unlikely that a simple cause and effect pattern exists. A more likely situation is the continuous process of interaction between language and cognition. However Diaz (1985), using sophisticated statistical techniques, suggests that bilingualism is more likely to be the cause of increased cognitive abilities than the reverse.

- We must ask whether the positive benefits from bilingualism in terms of thinking are temporary or permanent? Most research studies tend to use children of school age. There is almost no research on the cognitive functioning of bilinguals and monolinguals after the age of 17. Does bilingualism accelerate cognitive growth in the early years of childhood with monolinguals catching up in later years? Are cognitive advantages predominant in younger rather than older children? Or are the advantages additive, cumulative and long-lasting? It is possible that certain advantages (e.g. sensitivity to language, separation of word sound from word meaning) may be temporary. Age and experience may eventually give bilinguals and monolinguals similar cognitive skills. However, cognitive style (such as field dependency/independency, divergent or creative thinking and also communicative sensitivity), may produce relatively more stable and lasting effects.

- A certain level of proficiency in both languages must be attained before the positive effects of bilingualism, cognitive style and language awareness can occur. This is examined by the Thresholds theory (see page 74).

Further Research

One of the strongest recent lines of research on the psychology of bilinguals has been on the apparent ability of bilinguals to think about and reflect upon the nature and functions of language. Simply stated, it appears that bilinguals tend to have a greater awareness of language than monolinguals. In much of the literature, this is called metalinguistic awareness.

Metalinguistic awareness is the ability to reflect upon and manipulate spoken and written language. Language is inspected, it is thought about (as different from simply being used) as a system to understand and produce conversations. Such language awareness may include reflection about the intended meaning, being sensitive to what is implied rather than stated, inner meanings and intentions and being analytical towards language.

In one experiment, Bialystok (1987a) researched on 120 children aged five to nine. Children were asked to judge sentences and correct them if they were grammatically wrong. These sentences tested the level of analysis by a child of the linguistic structure of the sentence. The research found that bilingual children consistently judged more accurately whether the sentences were grammatically right or wrong than did matched groups of monolingual children at all the ages.

In a separate piece of research, Bialystok (1987b) found bilinguals superior to monolinguals in a word test. For example, children were asked to determine how many words there were in different sentences. It can be surprisingly difficult for young children to count how many words there are in a sentence. Until children are learning to read (around the ages of six and seven), they do not seem to comprehend what constitutes a sentence. Being able to count the number of words in a sentence depends on two things: first a knowledge about the boundaries and separation between words; second, an understanding of how the meanings of words create a meaningful whole sentence. Around seven years of age, children learn that words have their own individual meanings and can be isolated from their sentences.

The research found that bilingual children were developmentally ahead of monolingual children in their ability to count the number of words in a sentence. They were more sure about what constituted a word and could better separate out words from meaningful sentences.

The possibility is that bilinguals, because they own and process two languages, may be better at analyzing their languages. They seem more able to look inwardly on each language and accumulate knowledge about the language itself. Because two languages are continuously processed inside the bilingual, they seem better able to regulate, manage and control their language processing.

One important outcome of the bilingual's greater language awareness at an early age is that this 'metalinguistic awareness' may facilitate earlier reading acquisition. The possibility is that bilinguals, because they daily process two languages, pick up reading readiness skills faster than monolingual children (see page 596f regarding literacy and biliteracy). If this occurs, then earlier reading may also relate to higher levels of academic achievement in various areas of the curriculum.

This is not to say that all bilinguals will have such language awareness or metalinguistic awareness advantages. Research by Galambos & Hakuta (1988) found that such awareness is most developed when a child's two languages are proficient at reasonably high levels. The effect of bilingualism on the processing of errors in Spanish sentences was found to vary depending on the level of bilingualism. The more bilingual the child, that is, where both languages were relatively well developed, the better the performance on the test items.

Further Reading

BIALYSTOK, E., 1987, Influences of Bilingualism on Metalinguistic Development. *Second Language Research*, 3 (2), 154-166.

BIALYSTOK, E., 1987, Words as Things: Development of Word Concept by Bilingual Children. *Studies in Second Language Learning*, 9, 133-140.

BIALYSTOK, E., 1988, Levels of Bilingualism and Levels of Linguistic Awareness. *Developmental Psychology*, 24 (4), 560-567.

BIALYSTOK, E. (ed.), 1991, *Language Processing in Bilingual Children*. Cambridge: Cambridge University Press.

CUMMINS, J., 1987a, Bilingualism, Language Proficiency, and Metalinguistic Development. In P. HOMEL, M. PALIJ & D. AARONSON (eds), *Childhood Bilingualism: Aspects of Linguistic Cognitive and Social Development*. New Jersey: Erlbaum.

GALAMBOS, S. J. & GOLDIN-MEADOW, S., 1990, The Effects of Learning Two Languages on Levels of Metalinguistic Awareness. *Cognition*, 34 (1), 1-56.

IANCO-WORRALL, A. D., 1972, Bilingualism and Cognitive Development. *Child Development*, 43, 1390-1400.

6: Thresholds Theory

One important theme in research on the thinking advantages resulting from bilingualism is that not all bilinguals obtain those advantages. The term 'bilingual' includes those who are highly proficient in both languages (across a variety of dimensions) to those whose dual language abilities are underdeveloped in both their languages. In-between are many variations and possibilities. Do all bilinguals share the thinking advantages of operating in two languages? Which bilinguals are advantaged and which are less advantaged?

The two key issues are:

1. Under what conditions does bilingualism have positive, neutral or negative effects on thinking?
2. How far does a bilingual need to be proficient in two languages to obtain thinking advantages from bilingualism?

One influential answer is contained in the Thresholds theory.

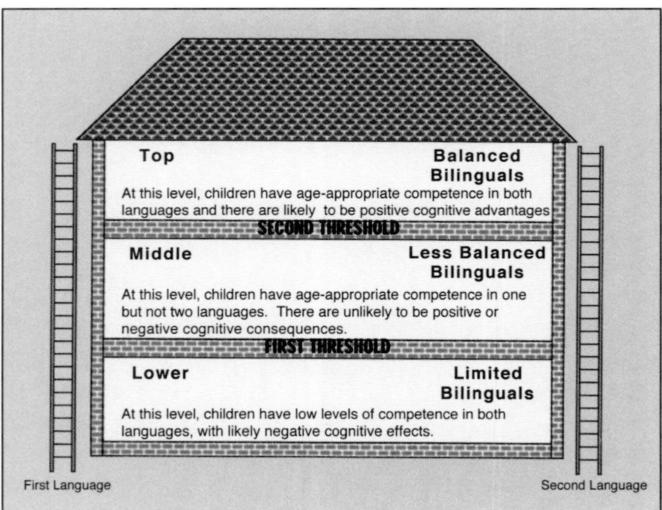

The Thresholds theory may be portrayed in terms of a house with three floors. Up the sides of the house are placed two language ladders, indicating that a bilingual child will usually be moving upward and is not stationary on a floor. On the bottom floor of the house will be those whose current competence in both their languages is insufficiently or relatively inadequately developed, compared with their age group. When there is a low level of competence in both languages, there may be negative or detrimental cognitive effects. For example, a child who is unable to cope in the classroom in either language may suffer when processing curriculum information.

At the middle level, the second floor of the house, will be those with age-appropriate competence in one of their languages but not in both. For example, children can operate in the classroom in one of their languages but not in the other. At this level, a bilingual child will be little different in cognition from the monolingual child and is unlikely to have any significant positive or negative cognitive differences compared with a monolingual.

At the top of the house, on the third floor, reside children who can be described as 'balanced' bilinguals. At this level, children will have age-appropriate competence in two or more languages. For example, they can cope with curriculum material in either of their languages. It is at this level that the positive cognitive advantages of bilingualism often appear. When children have age-appropriate ability in both their languages, they may have cognitive advantages over monolinguals.

Research on thinking and bilingualism thus suggests two thresholds. Each threshold is a level of language competence that must be attained (or surpassed) to reach the next level. The first threshold is a level a child must reach to avoid the negative cognitive consequences of bilingualism. To surpass this first threshold, for example, one language must at least be proficient enough to cope with the academic content of the classroom. The second threshold is when both languages are well developed to the point where a child may cope, for example, in the classroom in either language. Once past this second threshold, a bilingual child may have thinking advantages over monolinguals.

The Thresholds theory has important implications for bilingual education. In immersion bilingual education in Canada (see page 496), there is often a temporary lag in achievement while the early curriculum is taught through the second language. Once French is sufficiently well developed to cope with classroom tasks, Immersion education seems to enable children to reach the second and then the third floor of the house.

The Thresholds idea helps identify why minority language children taught through a second language sometimes fail in the system. An example is the case of immigrants into the United States who do not develop sufficient competency in their second language (e.g. English) to master school work. Their lower level of proficiency in English limits their ability to cope in the curriculum. This points to the importance of the strong development of the first language.

Limitations

One major problem with the Thresholds theory is in defining precisely what are the thresholds of language proficiency. What kind of speaking, listening, reading, or writing skills does the child have to attain in a language to cross the first threshold or the second threshold? Any specification of language proficiencies required to cross thresholds will depend on the context. For example, the relative complexity and variety of the academic activity in a classroom will affect specification of the language threshold. This suggests that in different classrooms, different subject areas and with different ages of children, the threshold will change.

While the idea of Thresholds is an important one, it does not specify what a child must attain in language proficiency to avoid the negative effects of bilingualism and to attain the positive advantages of bilingualism. The danger of the Thresholds theory is that artificial critical stages are constructed.

In reality, movement along many language dimensions continuously occurs. Development in bilingual proficiency is gradual and smooth rather than jumping from one floor to another. That is why the picture has two ladders up the sides of the house reflecting the idea of continuous development (and sometimes decline) of a language within an individual.

Children at the Police Public School, Peshawar, Pakistan. Most of these children speak Pashto as their mother tongue and receive their education in both Pashto and English. It is important that their proficiency in English is sufficiently developed to cope with the context-reduced environment of the classroom.

A second limitation is that children who are temporarily resident on the lowest floor (limited bilinguals) may be there, not because of lower cognitive abilities, but because they do not have the linguistic abilities to perform well on cognitive tests. For example, such children may not understand the instructions of the cognitive test or the content of the assessment questions. Thus such children's limited language understanding masks their level of cognitive ability.

The Thresholds theory can thus place children into a 'Catch 22' situation. The initial argument is that a low level of language competence will produce negative cognitive effects. However, these negative cognitive effects are themselves tested and located by means of the language in which the child has low competence. The relationship between language and cognition is thus confounded.

Refinements

The Thresholds theory has been developed and refined in recent years.

One development has tried to express the relationship between a bilingual's two languages. The two languages are not separate as in the idea of two language ladders; rather there is an interdependence. Cummins' (1978b) developmental interdependence hypothesis suggested that a child's second language competence is partly dependent on the level of competence already achieved in the first language. The more developed or proficient the first language, the easier it may be to develop the second language. When the first language is at a lower stage of evolution, the more difficult it will be to achieve proficiency in the second language.

The second development of the Thresholds theory was to add a distinction between the kind of conversational or surface fluency a child or adult may have in a language compared with the more advanced language competence required to learn in a formal classroom setting.

Simple communication skills (e.g. being able to hold a simple conversation with a shopkeeper), may hide a child's lack of proficiency or inexperience in a language that is necessary to meet the cognitive and academic demands of the classroom. The distinction is between Basic Interpersonal Communication Skills (BICS) and Cognitive/Academic Language Proficiency (CALP). This distinction is discussed in detail later (see page 93).

The distinction between BICS and CALP helps explain the relative failure within the educational system of many minority language children. For example, in the United States, Transitional Bilingual education programs aim to give students English language skills sufficient for them to be able to converse with peers and teachers in mainstream education and to operate in the curriculum. Having achieved basic English language communication skills, such students may be transferred to mainstream classrooms. The transfer occurs because children appear to have sufficient language competence (BICS) to cope in mainstream education. Cummins' (1984a) distinction between BICS and CALP explains why such children tend to fail when mainstreamed. Their Cognitive/Academic Language Proficiency is not developed enough to cope with the demands of the curriculum.

What Cummins (1984a) regards as essential in the bilingual education of language minority children is that the 'common underlying proficiency' is well developed (see page 81). That is, a child's fundamental, central language proficiency needs to be sufficiently well developed to cope with the curriculum processes of the classroom. This underlying ability could be developed through the first or the second language (and in both languages simultaneously).

A third development of the Thresholds theory tries to define the crucial dimensions of language communication particularly needed in school. Different classrooms, different curriculum areas in school, and different teaching styles use (and require of their students) different communication skills. Compare the language demands and expectations of science, humanities, art and craft, sports and religious education lessons. Each is different in content, style and complexity of language.

In some classrooms the teacher provides considerable support in the communication with students. For example, a teacher may use plenty of body language, pointing to objects, using eye contact, head nods, hand gestures, intonation and smiling to explain and motivate. Some teachers give plenty of clues and cues to help students understand what is being taught. This is referred to as context-embedded communication. In communicating curriculum content to children, some teachers don't rely solely on their words but use objects, demonstrations, concrete examples, illustrations, pictures and graphics to convey meaning.

Other teachers tend to rely on words alone. Or a child is given a work card or work book and expected to rely solely on the language of the work card or book to understand how to proceed. This is called context-reduced communication. There are very few cues and clues as to the meaning being transmitted. The words of the sentence, oral or written, exist alone in conveying the meaning. There may be a subtlety and precision of meaning in the vocabulary of the teacher which may elude the student.

The implication is that the type of communication that bilingual children receive needs adjusting to their level of proficiency. One crucial dimension in matching a child's level of proficiency with the material to be taught is providing the appropriate level of context-embedded or context-reduced communication. The lower a child's proficiency in language, the more context-embedded communication needs to take place. As a child's language proficiencies grow, the more context-reduced

Classroom Examples

The following examples attempt to illustrate the difference at classroom level between Basic Interpersonal Communication Skills (BICS) and Cognitive/Academic Language Proficiency (CALP). Children who are monolingual, as well as bilinguals, face these kind of language comprehension problems. Children learning through a second language may find such comprehension problems all the more difficult as their second language has yet to develop to understand such deeper, different or difficult meanings.

Example 1 A child is given a mathematical question such as: 'You have 10 dollars. You have 4 dollars more than me. How many dollars do I have?' At the higher CALP level, the child will conceptualize the problem correctly as 10 – 4 = 6. At the BICS level, the word 'more' may be taken to mean 'add-up' with the child getting the wrong answer of 14. The 'BICS child' may think of 'more' as used in basic conversation.

Example 2 A child is asked to draw a map in a Geography lesson and add a scale. At the higher CALP level, a child may correctly add on a scale (e.g. a line showing a scale of one centimeter to every 10 kilometers). At the BICS level, the word 'scale' may confusing (e.g. conceptualized as a musical scale or weighing scales).

Example 3 A second language student is required to use the term 'fuse' in Chemistry and Physics. At the BICS level, the student connects the meaning of 'fuse' with that used in everyday language (e.g. blown a fuse – to go wrong). In electricity contexts (i.e. a fuse in a plug, a fuse in an electrical circuit) the meaning is similar. If the current flow heats the metal strip above its melting point, the fuse blows. But the general concept of substances fusing together (e.g. melting together) is different – and may be at the CALP level.

Example 4 Where subtle differences exist in curriculum language, the BICS child may need extra language (and non-verbal communication) support. For example, the terms 'weather' and 'climate' have different meanings. A 'BICS child' may be more prone to use weather to mean climate. Another geographical example is the important difference between site and location. A 'BICS child' may need a careful explanation of the difference in terms as well as plenty of illustrations – the use of maps, 'systems' drawings (e.g. the water cycle), graphs.

communication can take place. On the lower floors of the house, more context-embedded communication is needed. As the child climbs the floors of the house and reaches past higher thresholds, more context-reduced communication may be possible.

A different dimension of communication in the classroom relates to the cognitive demands made of the child in communication. Sometimes the cognitive complexity level of mathematics and science, reading or writing may be highly demanding for the child. The level of performance required is ever challenging. A child needs to process very quickly the information being given. This is referred to as cognitively-demanding communication.

At the other end of the dimension is cognitively-undemanding communication. This is where language is sufficiently simple to enable understandable classroom exchanges and relatively easy understanding of the curriculum. If simple instructions are given, the processing of information by the child may be relatively simple and straightforward.

The two dimensions concerning the amount of cognitive demands and the degree of contextual support can now be illustrated diagrammatically.

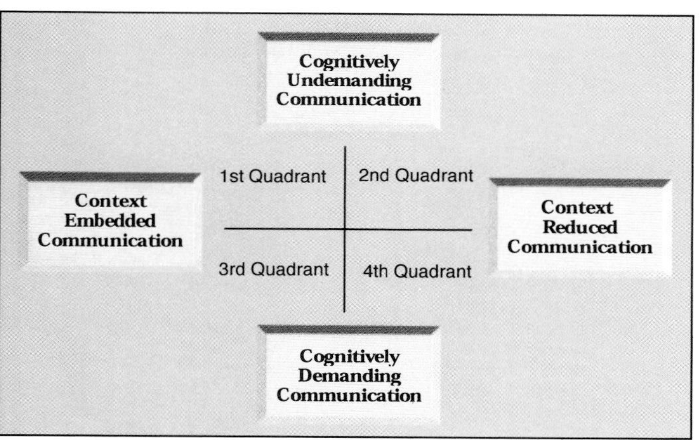

Adapted from Cummins, 1981b

There are four quadrants in the diagram. Basic interpersonal communication skills (BICS) is context-embedded, cognitively-undemanding use of a language. Language that is cognitively and academically more advanced (CALP) fits into the fourth quadrant. The idea is that second language competency in the first quadrant (surface fluency) develops relatively independently of first language surface fluency. In comparison, the ability to communicate, and to process communication in context-reduced, cognitively-demanding situations, can develop interdependently. It can be promoted through either language, or through both languages.

Context-embedded communication. Children do practical work in a multi-ethnic school in Canada. However, basic communicative skills may not be sufficient for more complex, cognitively-demanding activities.

Implications

What the theory suggests is that education often requires children to work in context-reduced, cognitively-demanding situations. Language proficiency needs to be sufficiently well developed to match those demands. It may take an elementary school child approximately two years to acquire context-embedded second language fluency. However, it may take the same child five to seven years or more to acquire context-reduced fluency in a language. Such time spans will vary with age and with the nature of the demands in different subjects.

Children with some conversational ability in their second language may falsely appear ready to be taught through their second language in a classroom. Cummins' (1981b) theory suggests that children operating at the context-embedded level in the language of the classroom may fail to understand the content of the curriculum and fail to engage in the higher order cognitive processes of the classroom, such as synthesis, discussion, analysis, evaluation and interpretation.

This two-dimensional model also helps explain various research findings:

1. In the United States, minority language children may be transferred from Transitional Bilingual programs into English-only schooling when their conversational ability in English seems sufficient. Such students frequently perform poorly in mainstream schooling. The theory suggests that this is due to their not having the developed ability in English to operate in an environment that is more cognitively and academically demanding.

2. Immersion students in Canada tend to lag behind their monolingual peers for a short period in academic

achievement. Once they acquire second language proficiency sufficient to operate in a cognitively-demanding and context-reduced environment, they normally catch up with their peers.

3. Experiments in the United States, Canada and Europe with language minority children who are allowed to use their minority language for part or much of their elementary schooling show that such children do not experience retardation in school achievement or in majority language proficiency. Through their minority language, they develop the ability to be relatively successful in the cognitively-demanding and context-reduced classroom environment. This ability then transfers to the majority language when that language is sufficiently well developed. Take learning to read as an example.

Children learning to read in their home language, be it Welsh, Gaelic, Irish, Spanish or Frisian, are not just developing home language skills. They are also developing higher order cognitive and linguistic skills that will help with the future development of reading in the majority language, as well as with general intellectual development. As Cummins (1984a) notes, 'transfer is much more likely to occur from minority to majority language because of the greater exposure to literacy in the majority language and the strong social pressure to learn it' (page 143).

Curriculum Relevance

What a child brings to the classroom in terms of previous learning is a crucial starting point for the teacher. A child's reservoir of knowledge, understanding and experience can provide a meaningful context from which the teacher can build. For example, there will be occasions when a child will learn more from a story read by the teacher than from listening to a language tape. When the teacher dramatizes a story by adding gestures, pictures, facial expressions and other acting skills, the story becomes more context-embedded than listening to it on a tape cassette. Getting a child to talk about something familiar will be cognitively less demanding than talking about something culturally or academically unfamiliar. This is illustrated in the diagram to the right.

The Cognitive Demands of the Classroom and Contextual Supports

The implication is that any curriculum task presented to the bilingual child needs analyzing for the following:

- What demands a classroom task makes of a child. What is the content of the task in terms of its cognitive demands?
- What the student brings to the task in terms of language proficiencies, skills, understandings, knowledge, learning style, cognitive strategies, interests and motivation. The student provides a personal context for the task.
- How the task should be presented to the child. The extent to which the task should be context-reduced or embedded.
- What is to be accepted as evidence of task success, of learning having occurred, or of a need to retry an adapted task to gain success.

An example of using the two dimensions to produce an appropriate teaching strategy is now presented (adapted from Frederickson & Cline, 1990).

A teacher wants a group to learn how to measure height and to understand the concept of height. Listed below are a few of the strategies for teaching about height. Following the list is a diagram placing the four strategies on the two dimensions:

- One-to-one, individual teaching using various objects to measure height (1).
- A demonstration from the front of the room by the teacher using various objects (2).

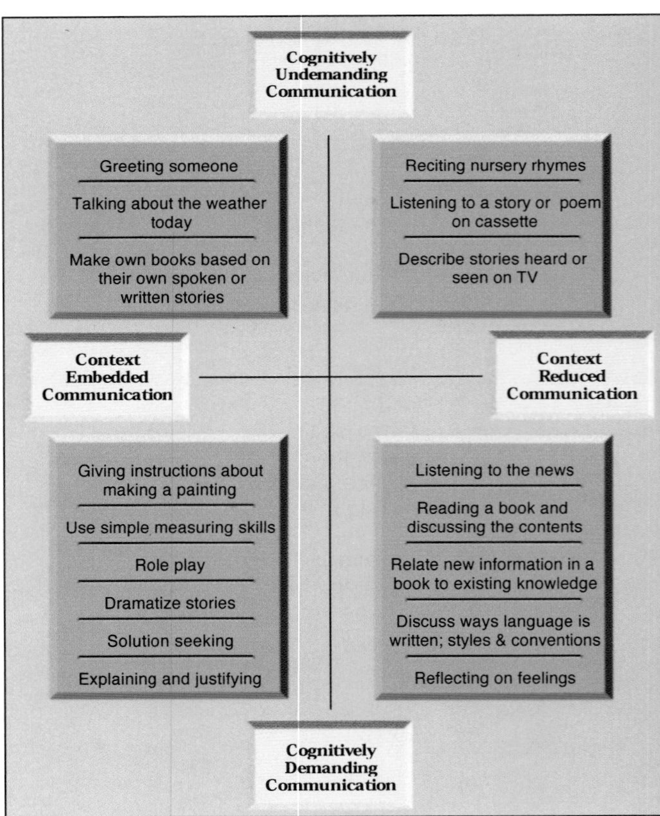

Research in Papua New Guinea

Clarkson & Galbraith (1992) researched on the Thresholds theory in five Community schools in Papua New Guinea. Their sample comprised 227 thirteen-year-old-students who were more or less bilingual in Tok Pisin and English. The sample were split into three groups: high language competence in Tok Pisin and English (i.e. above Cummins' second threshold); dominant in one language (i.e above Cummins' first threshold but below the second threshold); and low language competence in Tok Pisin and English (i.e. below Cummins' first threshold).

The students were given three mathematics tests.

1. A General Mathematics test
   e.g. What percentage of a kilogram is 250 grams?

2. A Mathematical Word Problem test
   e.g. Danny had some biscuits. He gave his friend four biscuits and kept the same number for himself. How many biscuits did Danny have at the start if there were none left over?

3. A Number Competence test
   e.g. 3.65 x 8 = ?

Results

Before the three groups were compared on the three maths tests, differences between the groups (other than language) were controlled statistically. That is, the groups were statistically equated on level of cognitive development, father's occupation, parental education, student's expectation of schooling and occupation, parental encouragement and quality of housing (i.e. socioeconomic and sociocultural variables).

The graphs show that the three language groups scored significantly differently on all three mathematics tests. More specifically:

1. The high/high bilinguals scored significantly higher on all three mathematics tests than the low/low group.

2. The 'one language dominant' group scored significantly higher on all three mathematics tests than the low/low group.

3. The high/high bilinguals scored significantly higher on the General Mathematics test than the 'one language dominant' group. No statistically significant difference was found between these two groups on the Word Problem or the Number Competence tests although the trends favored the high/high bilinguals.

4. Clarkson & Galbraith (1992) concluded that: 'The results give some support for the notion of thresholds. Cummins' lower threshold receives strong support. .. the support for the higher threshold is not so strong' (page 41).

REFERENCE: CLARKSON & GALBRAITH, 1992

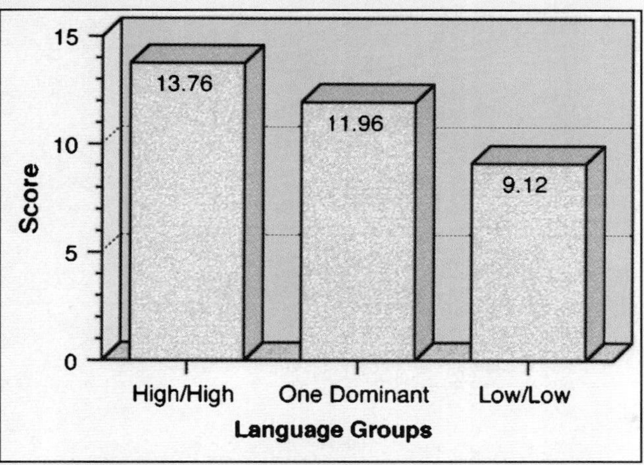

Average Score on General Mathematics

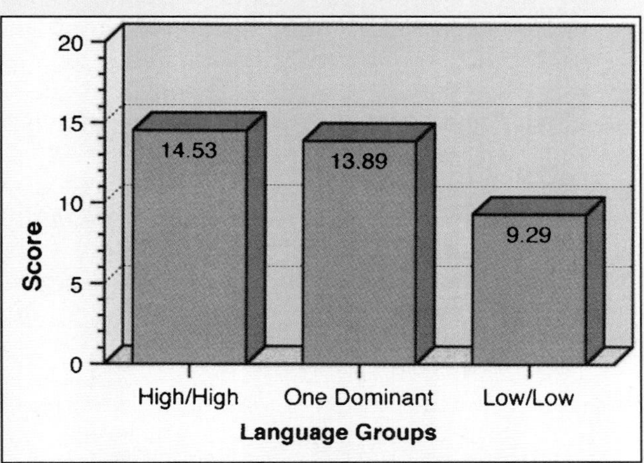

Average Score on Word Problem Test

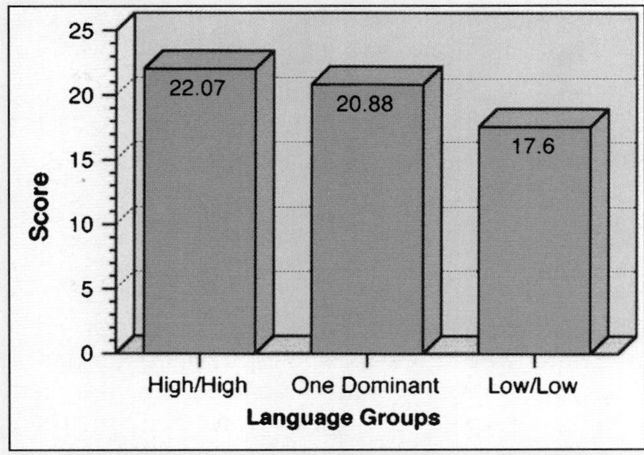

Average Score on Number Competence

- Teacher giving oral instructions without objects (3).
- Reading instructions from a work card without pictures (4).

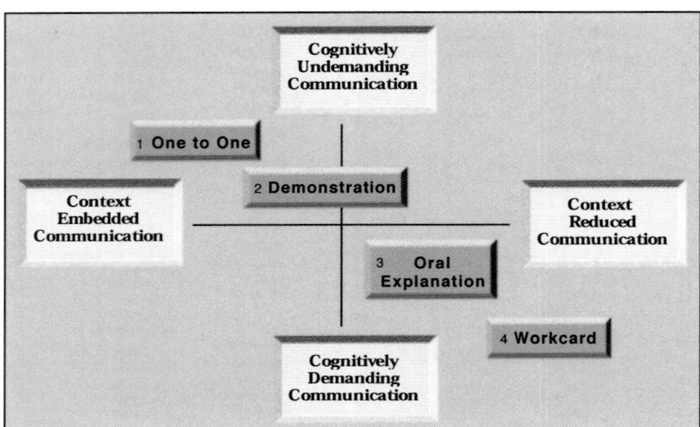

As the above diagram indicates, the example of teaching height can be analyzed in terms of the two dimensions. One-to-one individual teaching will fit somewhere in the context-embedded, cognitively-undemanding quadrant. Using work cards may be closer to the context-reduced, cognitively-demanding area. Demonstrations and oral explanations appear on the diagonal from 'top left' to 'bottom right', in-between individual teaching and work cards. The exact location of teaching approaches on the graph will vary according to teacher, topic, learner and lesson. The example illustrates that using the two dimensions can be a valuable way of examining teaching approaches with bilingual children.

The dimensions are also useful for analyzing appropriate methods of classroom assessment. The dimensions may help focus on task-related curriculum assessment that is more fair and appropriate to bilingual children than norm-referenced testing (comparing one child with another and against averages). A teacher wanting to check progress on measuring height has a choice. For example:

- Observing a child measure the height of a new object (1).
- Asking the child to give a commentary while measuring a new object (2).
- Asking the child to provide a write-up of the process (3).
- Discussing in an abstract way the concept of height (4).

In plotting these four methods of assessment, placement on the graph will vary with different kinds of tasks and testing procedures. All four quadrants can be 'filled' depending on the student, teacher, topic and test. There is also value in comparing the two graphs presented above. The teaching and learning approach taken may well influence the form of assessment. That is, if a context-embedded, cognitively-undemanding learning strategy is used with a child, assessment may be on similar lines (e.g. observation of child activity). Equally, a context-reduced, cognitively-demanding learning strategy suggests a 'matched' method of assessment (e.g. discussion).

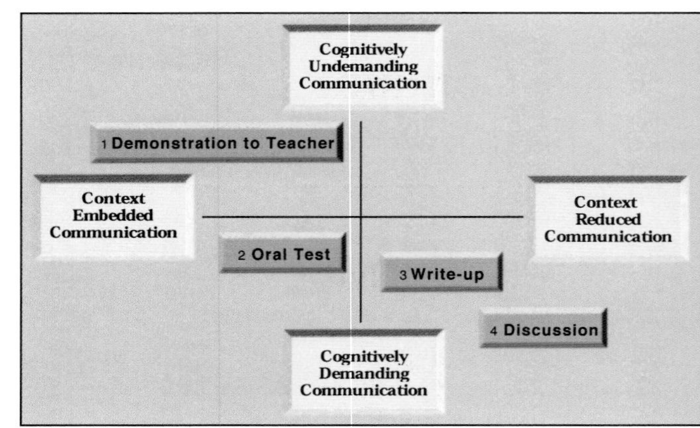

Further Reading

CLARKSON, P. C. & GALBRAITH, P., 1992, Bilingualism and Mathematics Learning: Another Perspective. *Journal for Research in Mathematics Education,* 23 (1), 34-44.

CLINE, T., 1993, Educational Assessment of Bilingual Pupils: Getting the Context Right. *Education and Child Psychology,* 10 (4), 59-68.

CLINE, T. & FREDERICKSON, N. (eds), 1996, *Curriculum Related Assessment. Cummins and Bilingual Children.* Clevedon: Multilingual Matters Ltd.

CUMMINS, J., 1981, The Role of Primary Language Development in Promoting Educational Success for Language Minority Students. In CALIFORNIA STATE DEPARTMENT OF EDUCATION (ed.), *Schooling and Language Minority Students. A Theoretical Framework.* Los Angeles: California State Department of Education.

CUMMINS, J., 1984, *Bilingualism and Special Education: Issues in Assessment and Pedagogy.* Clevedon: Multilingual Matters Ltd.

FREDERICKSON, N. & CLINE, T. (eds), 1990, *Curriculum Related Assessment with Bilingual Children. A Set of Working Papers.* London: University College, London.

7: Common Underlying Proficiency and Separate Underlying Proficiency

The Separate Underlying Proficiency (SUP) model

One erroneous idea of how two languages are represented within the mind of a bilingual is to consider the languages balanced on weighing scales. As one language increases on one side, the other language decreases proportionately on the other side. A second language increases at the expense of the first language. This is part of what is termed the Separate Underlying Proficiency (SUP) model of bilingualism (Cummins, 1984a).

A simple illustration of the Separate Underlying Proficiency (SUP) model is to conceive of language as existing in two balloons inside the head. This idea is also incorrect, but it is the kind of picture that many people assume to be true of bilinguals. The picture opposite portrays the monolingual as having one well-filled language balloon, with plenty of room inside the thinking quarters for that language to exist. A well-filled balloon, full of vocabulary, grammatical rules, associations between words, ideas and concepts may superficially appear as the most efficient language environment.

The worse-off bilingual is pictured as having two language balloons inside the head. Given the thinking room available, the bilingual is assumed to have two half-filled balloons. Two half-filled (or less full) balloons compared with the monolingual's larger language balloon implies less room to store vocabulary, grammatical structures, associations and ideas in either language. The Separate Underlying Proficiency (SUP) model assumes that there isn't enough room to fill the language balloons as full as the monolingual's. As the second language balloon increases, so the first language balloon is assumed to decrease proportionately. Unfortunately many parents, teachers, politicians and large sections of the public instinctively assume that this dual balloon picture represents bilingual cognitive functioning.

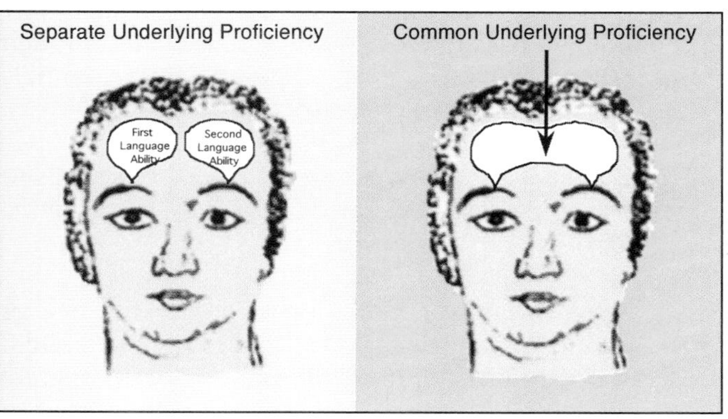

The assumption is also that the two balloons exist without inter-connection and that there is no transfer between the two balloons. The languages operate independently. This is one of those cases when common sense is common, but not sense. There is no research evidence to support this model.

The absurdity of this idea is revealed in the curious predicament a bilingual would meet when 'talking internally'. If a bilingual had to switch languages, he or she might have difficulty in explaining in the second language what they had heard or said in the first language. Everything learnt in one language would have to be relearnt in another language. Clearly that is not the case. A different model is therefore required – called the Common Underlying Proficiency model of bilingualism (Cummins, 1984a).

Common Underlying Proficiency (CUP) model

Research has shown that it is wrong to assume that the brain has only a limited amount of room for two languages. Firstly, evidence suggests that there are enough cerebral living quarters not only for two languages, but for other languages as well. The amount of room or thinking space available seems vast, even endless. Secondly, evidence suggests that there is easy and considerable transfer between the two language balloons. There is substantial interaction between the two languages, with language switching and cooperative sharing. To illustrate:

- When children are taught subtraction in one language, they do not have to relearn subtraction in the second language. Once the concept is understood, it can be applied in either language. Spanish-medium lessons do not feed the Spanish part of the brain, and English-medium lessons the English part of the brain. Ideas, concepts, attitudes, knowledge and skills transfer into either language.

- Children who have learned to use a dictionary, or are learning to use the computer, will be able to explain their understandings to other children in either language. A child does not have to be retaught in the second language. Given that language skills are sufficiently well developed to understand ideas and knowledge in the second language, what is learnt in the first language easily transfers.

This idea of a common underlying proficiency model is illustrated in the analogy of an iceberg. The picture of the two integrated icebergs (see below) suggests that above the surface, two icebergs are visible. In outward conversation, the two languages are often kept separate. Below the surface level, the internal processing and storage of a person's two languages occurs. Beneath the surface are storage, associations between concepts, and representations (e.g. in words and images) that belong specifically and separately to the two languages. There is also a common area where the two icebergs are fused. There is a central, unified processing system called Common Underlying Proficiency that both languages can contribute to, access and use.

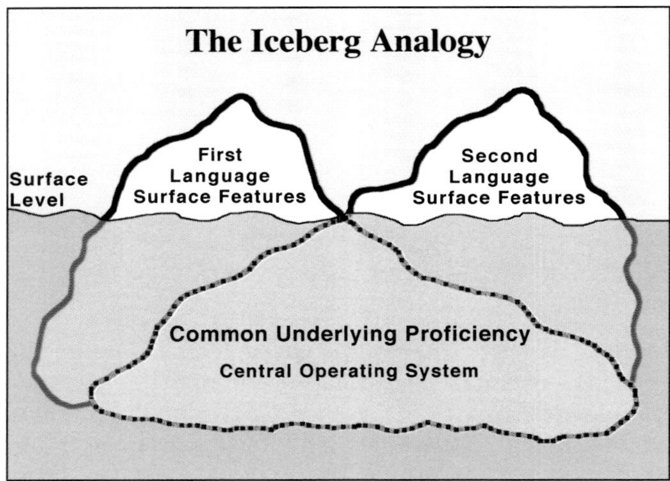

Let us return to the examples given above. When a child learns to use a library or a computer, it is this central processing system which is fed. The understandings, concepts and processing operate from 'common ground' between the languages. Six implications derive from this important iceberg analogy:

1. Irrespective of the language in which a person is operating, the thoughts that accompany talking, reading, writing and listening come from the same central 'engine'. When a person owns two or more languages, there is one integrated source of thought.

2. Bilingualism and multilingualism are possible because people have the capacity to store easily two or more languages. People can also function in two or more languages with relative ease.

3. Information-processing skills and educational attainment may be developed through two languages as well as through one language. Cognitive functioning and school achievement may be fed through one monolingual channel or equally successfully through two well-developed language channels. Both channels feed the same central processor.

4. The language the child uses in the classroom needs to be sufficiently well-developed to process the cognitive challenges of the classroom.

5. Speaking, listening, reading or writing in the first or the second language helps the whole cognitive system to develop. However, if children are made to operate in an insufficiently developed second language (e.g. in

Jim Cummins

Jim Cummins is a Professor at the Ontario Institute for Studies in Education, a Graduate School of the University of Toronto in Canada. Born in Dublin, he gained his Doctorate from the University of Alberta in Canada. After a short period in the Educational Research Centre in Dublin, Jim Cummins returned to Canada in 1976 and has carried out research and written many highly influential articles on areas such as: multiculturalism, minority language education, bilingual education, psycholinguistics, language and the school curriculum, critical pedagogy and linguistic diversity. As the Bibliography reveals, Jim Cummins' output on bilingualism and bilingual education is prolific. His writing has also been highly influential in both theoretical and applied areas. His most recent publications include *Brave New Schools: Challenging Cultural Illiteracy Through Global Learning Networks* (with Denis Sayers) published in 1995, and *Negotiating Identities: Education for Empowerment in a Diverse Society* published in 1996. He is acknowledged internationally as being one of the foremost authorities on all aspects of bilingualism and bilingual education as well as being a 'founding father' of many new ideas, concepts and theories in this area.

a 'submersion' classroom), the system will not function at its best, as the quality and quantity of what they learn from complex curriculum materials and produce in oral and written form may be relatively weak and impoverished. This has been the experience of some Finns in Swedish schools who were forced to operate in Swedish (Skutnabb-Kangas & Toukomaa, 1976). Such children tended to perform poorly in the curriculum in both Finnish and Swedish in Sweden because both languages were insufficiently developed to cope with given curriculum material.

6. When one or both languages are not functioning fully (e.g. because of an unfavorable attitude to learning through the second language, or pressure to replace the home language with the majority language) cognitive functioning and academic performance may be negatively affected.

Further Reading

CUMMINS, J., 1981, *Bilingualism and Minority Language Children.* Ontario: Ontario Institute for Studies in Education.

CUMMINS, J., 1984, *Bilingualism and Special Education: Issues in Assessment and Pedagogy.* Clevedon: Multilingual Matters Ltd.

CUMMINS, J. & SWAIN, M., 1986, *Bilingualism in Education.* New York: Longman.

8: Bilingualism and the Brain

We are at an early stage of understanding how a bilingual's two languages function inside the brain and thinking system, as exactly how they function independently and interdependently is far from fully comprehended. The cognitive system of a bilingual was assumed to contain two languages that are structurally separate and yet interconnected. Precisely how separation and inter-connection grow and are related to language output, is only beginning to be researched. Two theories are now examined, the Dual Coding Model and the Common Underlying Proficiency Model.

The Bilingual Dual Coding Model

One line of inquiry has examined how bilinguals store language in their memories. Does a bilingual, particularly someone who has learnt a second language later in life, have two functionally independent storage and retrieval memory systems? In the separate storage model, the two languages would interact only through translation. If, alternatively, there is one overall memory store for both languages, there is considerable interdependence in both input and output in language. This is called the shared store memory hypothesis.

Evidence exists both for independence of language storage and for interdependence (Grosjean, 1994). There currently appears an element of truth in both the idea of a separate storage and a shared storage of languages within the memory system. The most recent models emphasize both the separateness and connected aspects of a bilingual's mental representations. The following diagram shows the bilingual dual coding systems model of Paivio & Desrochers (1980) and Paivio (1986, 1991).

Bilingual Dual Coding Model

This model suggests that there are the following:

- Two separate verbal language systems, one for each of the bilingual's two languages.
- A separate non-verbal imagery system, independent from a bilingual's two language systems. Such an imagery system holds and generates the pictures and non-verbal associations that we hold as sensory information. The non-verbal imagery system functions as a shared conceptual system for the two languages.
- Between the first language and the second language systems, there are interconnections (e.g. in vocabulary). Around such interconnection are the associations that accompany language.
- An important part of the model is the strong, direct, interconnecting channels between the first and second language and between those languages and the non-verbal image system. The interconnections between the two languages comprise association and translation systems. Common images are also the mediators between the two languages.

Lateralization

A topic in the study of bilingualism and the brain has been lateralization. In the majority of right-handed adults, the left hemisphere of the brain is dominant for language processing. The question has arisen as to whether bilinguals are different from monolinguals in this left lateralization? Is the functioning of the brain different for bilinguals and monolinguals? Vaid & Hall (1991) reviewed this topic in terms of five hypotheses examined by research:

1. Balanced bilinguals will use the right hemisphere more than monolinguals for first and second language processing.
2. Second language acquisition will involve the right hemisphere in language processing more than first language acquisition.
3. As proficiency in a second language grows, right hemisphere involvement will decrease and left hemisphere involvement will increase This assumes that the right hemisphere is concerned with the more immediate, pragmatic and emotive aspects of language; the left hemisphere with the more analytic aspects of language (e.g. syntax). That is, the core aspects of language processing are assumed to reside in the left hemisphere.
4. Those who acquire a second language naturally (e.g. on the street) will use their right hemisphere more for language processing than those who learn a second language formally (e.g. in the language classroom). Learning rules about grammar, spelling and irregular verbs will result in more left hemisphere involvement in second language learning. Picking up a language in a natural manner and using it for straightforward communication will involve more right hemisphere involvement.

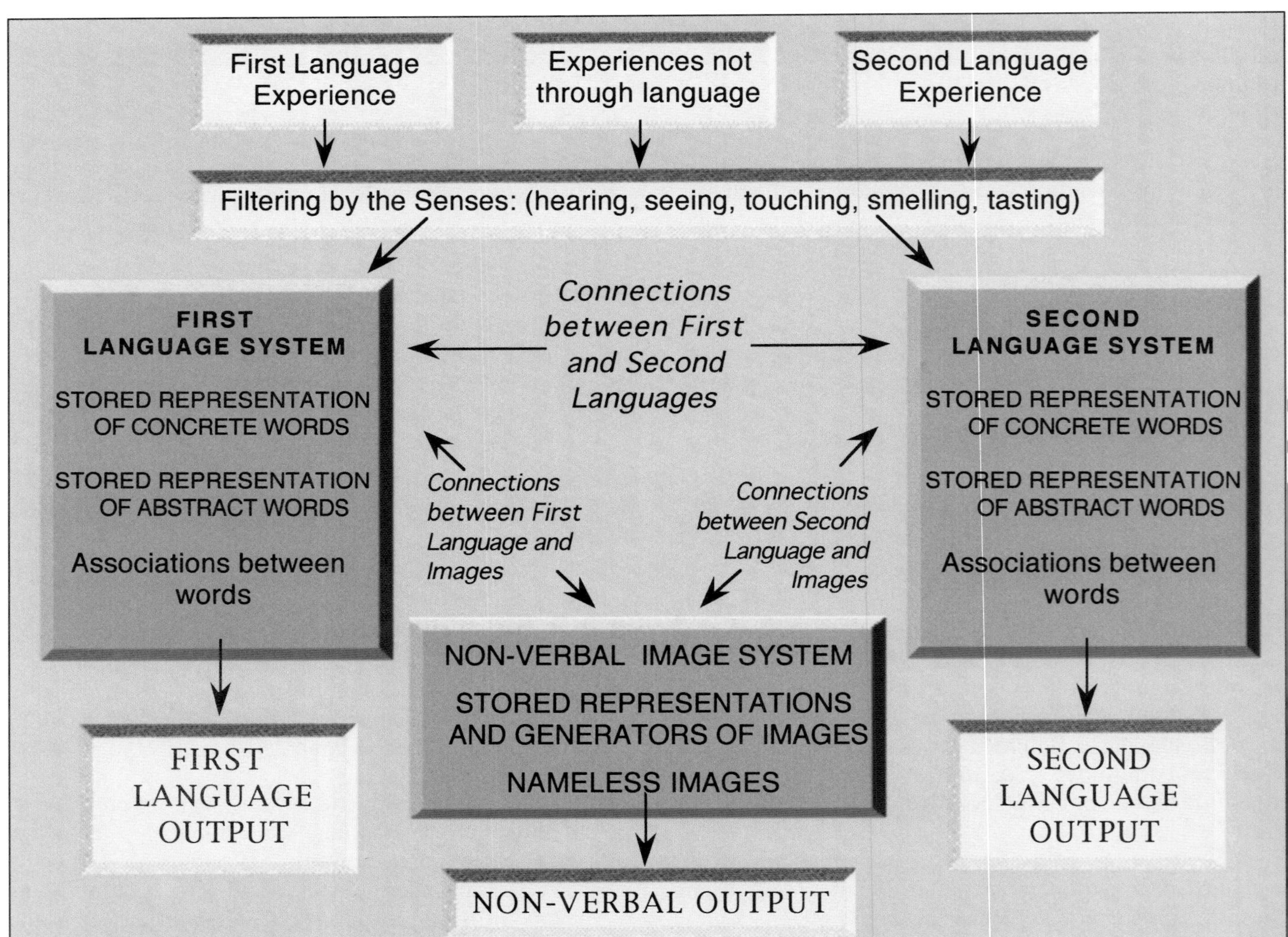

Adapted and simplified from Paivio & Desrochers, 1980,1991

5. Late bilinguals will be more likely to use the right hemisphere than early bilinguals. This proposition states that there might be a 'predominance of a left-hemisphere "semantic-type" strategy in early bilinguals and for a right hemisphere "acoustic-type" strategy in late bilinguals' (Vaid & Hall, 1991, page 90).

Using a quantitative procedure called meta-analysis to review previous research in this area, Vaid & Hall (1991) found that the left hemisphere strongly dominated language processing for both monolinguals and bilinguals. However, differences between monolinguals and bilinguals were the exception rather than the rule. Bilinguals did not seem to vary from monolinguals in neuropsychological processes; the lateralization of language of the two groups being relatively similar. 'The largely negative findings from the meta-analysis must be taken seriously as reflecting a general lack of support for the five hypotheses as they have been addressed in the literature to date' (Vaid & Hall, 1991, page 104).

Most researchers are of the opinion that: monolinguals and bilinguals do not differ in hemispheric involvement in language processing and that a bilingual's languages are not stored in two different locations (Paradis, 1992; Grosjean, 1994). For example, Klein *et al.* (1994, 1995) found that similar brain regions supported word repetition exercises in the first and second language, and that the first language is not differently represented in the brain compared with a second language learned later in life. The only difference is in the increased articulation demands on the brain in the production of the second language, which require additional processing.

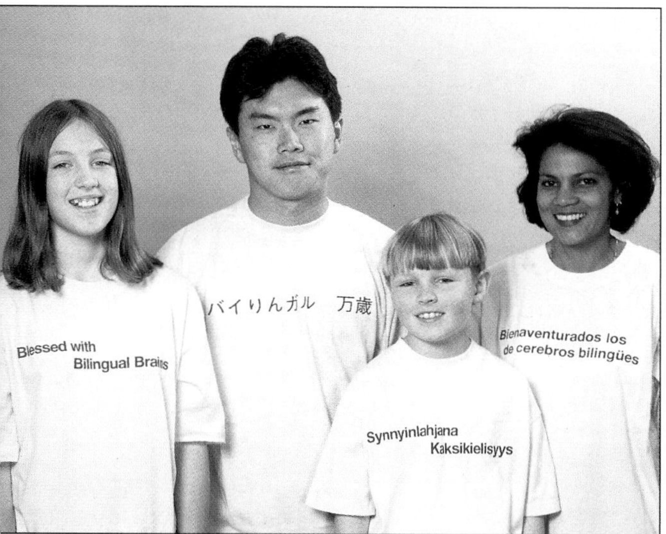

Four young people from four different areas of the world who have one thing in common – they are all bilingual. Their T shirts proclaim the message in (from left to right) English, Japanese, Finnish and Spanish, that bilingualism is an advantage, a privilege and a blessing, rather than a burden.

While the relationship between the brain and bilingualism is an interesting area, the present state of knowledge makes generalization unsafe, but an area where future research holds some promise.

Further Reading

GROSJEAN, F., 1994, Individual Bilingualism. In R. E. ASHER & J. M. SIMPSON (eds), *The Encyclopedia of Language and Linguistics* (Volume 3). Oxford: Pergamon.

KLEIN, D., MILNER, B., ZATORRE, R., MEYER, E. & EVANS, A. C., 1995, The Neural Substrates Underlying Word Generation: A Bilingual Functional-imaging Study. *Proceedings of the National Academy of Sciences of the United States of America*, 92 (7), 2899-2903.

KLEIN, D., ZATORRE, R. J., MILNER, B. & MEYER, E., 1994, Left Putaminal Activation When Speaking a Second Language: Evidence from PET. *Neuroreport*, 5 (17), 2295-2297.

PARADIS, M., 1990, Language Lateralization in Bilinguals: Enough Already! *Brain Lang (B5H)*, 39 (4), 576-86.

PARADIS, M., 1992, The Loch Ness Monster Approach to Bilingual Language Lateralization: A Response to Berquier and Ashton. *Brain Lang (B5H)*, 43 (3), 534-7.

PARADIS, M., 1995, Another Sighting of Differential Language Laterality in Multilinguals, This Time in Loch Tok Pisin: Comments on Wuillemin, Richardson, and Lynch. *Brain Lang (B5H)*, 49 (2), 173-186.

VAID, J. & HALL, D. G., 1991, Neuropsychological Perspectives on Bilingualism; Right, Left and Center. In A. G. REYNOLDS (ed.), *Bilingualism, Multiculturalism and Second Language Learning*. Hillsdale, NJ: Lawrence Erlbaum.

The Measurement of Bilingualism

1: Measuring Bilinguals

Bilinguals and bilingualism are often measured and assessed. Teachers and researchers, for example, may want to know the relative competence of a bilinguals in their two languages. Research on bilingual language development, performance of bilinguals in different types of bilingual education, the size of minority languages in particular regions, possible thinking advantages and disadvantages of being bilingual, the use of a person's two languages in different situations, and the balance between them, all require some kind of measurement of bilinguals. How is such measurement achieved? What are the different types of measurement of bilinguals? What are the specific purposes in measuring bilingual language competence? These questions are now examined by firstly considering three illustrative reasons for measurement.

Distribution

In many countries, there are census questions to estimate the size of a language minority and its distribution within a region (e.g. United States, Canada, United Kingdom, many countries in mainland Europe, Ireland, Malaysia). Geographers will be interested in mapping the proportion and location of language minority groups, for example, to see whether there have been changes over time.

Comparison

Bilinguals are often compared with monolinguals. In everyday conversation, in the committee rooms of administrators and politicians, in academic and research circles, bilinguals are often distinguished as a separate group and compared in their characteristics and performance with monolinguals. For example, an administrator may wish to know how different groups of bilinguals are faring in the school system compared with monolinguals. How do Spanish-speaking Cubans, Mexicans, Puerto Ricans and other language groups in the United States perform in the curriculum compared with English-speaking monolinguals? A psychologist may be interested in comparing balanced bilinguals with partial bilinguals and monolinguals in their performance on tests of creativity or processing of information. A school may measure bilinguals in order to allocate them to different classes, tracks (streams, sets) or groups based on their degree of bilingual proficiency or language background. In the United States, the English language ability of bilingual students is measured to see whether or not they should leave a Transitional Bilingual program and transfer to mainstream classrooms.

School Performance

Children may be measured in school during the course of the school year or at the end, to assess their current performance in one or both languages. A school may test a child's reading comprehension or reading vocabulary to ensure satisfactory progress during the year. A diagnostic test of a child's bilingual language development may be used to enable remedial or compensatory activity to occur. The assessment of bilinguals is covered as a separate topic (see page 575).

One area of increasing importance in measuring bilingual proficiency is naturalistic rather than purely linguistic measurement. While it may be important to measure somebody's size of vocabulary, grammatical accuracy and ability to write well in languages, natural performance in everyday, different language situations is also needed. For example, evidence may be sought about a person's ability to sustain conversations or ability to improvise with language when there is difficulty in communication. Qualitative evidence is needed as test scores would fail to give the richness of information about language competencies.

Language proficiency has linguistic components, sociolinguistic, discourse and strategic components. To be able to communicate in two languages isn't just about knowledge of those languages, or competence within those languages, it is about using that competence in different contexts with different kinds of people. The language used needs to be appropriate to the person listening, or the situation. There may be a different language or style of language in a board room, baseball game, bar or bedroom. Language is about communication and about negotiations in human relationships. Measurement of bilinguals and language abilities too often focuses on

Language Background Measurement

Whereas discussions on the uses and functions of bilingualism focus on direct involvement in language situations, language background refers also to non-participative experience of two languages in a person's world (e.g third party or bystander experience). Language background concerns the indirect experience of two languages, as well as 'direct' language interaction.

Language background scales are used in research on bilingualism. A language background measurement will attempt to profile how often individuals use their two languages with different people such as father, mother, friends and neighbors. The scale will also attempt to find out which language different people in a bilingual's world speak for how long to that bilingual. Also, a language background scale will measure which language a person uses when engaged in activities such as watching television, shopping, speaking on the telephone, working, leisure, religious observance and in relationships with local or regional government. It is difficult for such scales to be all-inclusive. The language used with members of the extended family, correspondence, social situations and travel, for example, may not be included. The number of domains included may be a sample of the total number of domains where the two languages are used.

What is important in such scales is to measure the frequency of usage in different contexts and not just to whom and where a person uses their two languages. The 'how often' question is important as the following illustration reveals:

> Imagine a young person who says that she speaks Spanish to her father who is mostly away at sea, Spanish to her grandparents whom are only seen once a year, and to her friends in the neighborhood except that she is socially withdrawn.She attends an English-medium school, reads Spanish books very occasionally, attends a Spanish service in church (such as a marriage or a funeral) about once every two years, but spends most of her time with her English-speaking mother.This person would tend to obtain a fairly high Spanish score because of the large number of different domains in which Spanish is occasionally used. Once the 'how often question' is brought in, this person would be seen to be more English- than Spanish-speaking, and a more valid profile obtained.

An illustration of a scale to assess child language background is given below.

Here are some questions about the **language** in which you talk to different people, and the **language** in which certain people speak to you. Please answer as honestly as possible.
There are no right or wrong answers. Leave an empty space if a question does not fit your position.

In which language do YOU speak to the following people? Choose one of these answers:

	ALWAYS IN SPANISH	IN SPANISH MORE OFTEN THAN ENGLISH	IN SPANISH AND ENGLISH EQUALLY	IN ENGLISH MORE OFTEN THAN SPANISH	ALWAYS IN ENGLISH
1. Father	☐	☐	☐	☐	☐
2. Mother	☐	☐	☐	☐	☐
3. Brothers/Sisters	☐	☐	☐	☐	☐
4. Friends in the Classroom	☐	☐	☐	☐	☐
5. Teachers	☐	☐	☐	☐	☐
6. Neighbors	☐	☐	☐	☐	☐
7. Grandparents	☐	☐	☐	☐	☐

In which language do the following people speak to you?

	ALWAYS IN SPANISH	IN SPANISH MORE OFTEN THAN ENGLISH	IN SPANISH AND ENGLISH EQUALLY	IN ENGLISH MORE OFTEN THAN SPANISH	ALWAYS IN ENGLISH
1. Father	☐	☐	☐	☐	☐
2. Mother	☐	☐	☐	☐	☐
3. Brothers/Sisters	☐	☐	☐	☐	☐
4. Friends in the Classroom	☐	☐	☐	☐	☐
5. Teachers	☐	☐	☐	☐	☐
6. Neighbors	☐	☐	☐	☐	☐
7. Grandparents	☐	☐	☐	☐	☐

Which language do YOU use with the following?

	ALWAYS IN SPANISH	IN SPANISH MORE OFTEN THAN ENGLISH	IN SPANISH AND ENGLISH EQUALLY	IN ENGLISH MORE OFTEN THAN SPANISH	ALWAYS IN ENGLISH
1. Watching TV/Videos	☐	☐	☐	☐	☐
2. Religion	☐	☐	☐	☐	☐
3. Newspapers/Comics/Magazines	☐	☐	☐	☐	☐
4. Records/Cassettes/CDs	☐	☐	☐	☐	☐
5. Shopping	☐	☐	☐	☐	☐
6. Telephone	☐	☐	☐	☐	☐
7. Reading books	☐	☐	☐	☐	☐

Critical Language Testing

Elana Shohamy (1997), a Professor in the School of Education, Tel Aviv University, defines Critical Language Testing as follows:

- Language testing is not a neutral activity. It relates to cultural, social, political, educational and ideological agendas that shape the lives of all students and teachers. Such language tests are deeply embedded, in cultural, educational and political debates where different ideologies are in contest.
- Critical language testing thus views test-takers as political subjects in a political context.
- Critical language testing asks questions about whose formal and hidden agendas tests relate to, and what sort of political and educational policies are delivered through tests.
- Critical language testing argues that language testers must ask themselves what sort of vision of society language tests create, and for what vision of society tests are used? For example, are language tests intended to fulfill pre-defined curricular or proficiency objectives or are there other rationales and aims?
- Critical language testing asks questions about whose knowledge the tests are based on? What is the intended or assumed status of that knowledge (e.g. 'truth' or something that can be negotiated and challenged)?
- Critical language testing considers the meaning of language test scores, and the degree to which they are prescriptive, final and absolute, or the extent to which they are open to discussion and interpretations.

Critical language testing thus widens the field of language testing by relating it to political and social debate. Such a debate should be about the forms and practices of language testing. "This debate is surrounded by the oles that tests play and have been assigned to play, about competing ideologies, the discourse that are constructed and the roles of language testers. This debate draws language testers towards areas of social processes and power struggles embedded in the discourses on learning and democracy." (Shohamy, 1997, page 4).

REFERENCE: SHOHAMY, 1997

Language Balance Measures

Various ingenious tests have been devised to gauge the relative dominance or balance of a bilingual's two languages. Five examples are given below:

Speed of reaction in a word association task
This seeks to measure whether a bilingual can give an association to stimulus words more quickly in one language than the other. No particular difference would seem to indicate a balanced bilingual. An example is presenting a word such as 'house', then measuring the time taken to produce an association (e.g. window). When a person is consistently quicker in giving associations in one language than another, the likelihood is that one language is dominant. However, dominance is different from competence. A person may be competent in two or more languages while being dominant in one. Similarly, there could be equal dominance and a low level of competence in both languages.

Quantity of reactions to a word association task
Bilinguals are measured for the number of associations given within one minute when a stimulus word (e.g. 'color') is presented. An approximately equal number of responses might indicate a balance between the two languages.

Detection of words using both languages
Words in both languages are to be extracted from a nonsense word such as DANSONODEND. The letters in the nonsense words must be representative of both languages. A German-French bilingual who extracted a majority of German words within an allotted time would be considered dominant in German. If another bilingual produced an approximately equal number of words in German and French, he or she would be regarded as a balanced bilingual.

Reading time
Time taken to read a set of words in the respondent's two languages.

The amount of mixing
The borrowing ('interference') and switching from one language to another (see page 58) in either a test situation or in ordinary conversation. A person who relatively infrequently mixes languages would (debatably) be considered a balanced bilingual.

The major problem with such balance and dominance tests lies in the representativeness of the measure of language proficiency and performance. In this respect, such tests would appear to tap only a small part of a much larger and more complex whole. The tests cover a small sample of language subskills that might be tested. What can be tested is also only a small sample of a wide definition of language attributes of individuals.

skills and specific proficiencies, and too little on the ability of bilinguals to make relationships and communicate information.

A Limitation in the Measurement of Bilinguals

The measurement of bilinguals often ascertains their language competences and achievement in one or more of their languages. In this case, language is the focus of assessment. An example is assessing bilinguals' relative dominance in their two languages. Bilinguals' language competences are also measured when the focus of research, for example, is on another entity (e.g. thinking style). For example, bilinguals may be measured and classified as 'balanced bilinguals' or otherwise (see page 88) and compared on their school achievement or ability on a test of creative thinking.

In this latter case, the measurement uses language (e.g. tests of creative thinking are based on the manipulation of language). This can produce a 'Catch 22' situation for some children. They are tested for their level of creative thinking, for example, and such tests are not purely cognitive but involve the use of language. Thus if a child performs poorly on such a test, what is the cause? Is it that they did not understand the language of the instructions? It may be that the creative thinking of the child is relatively high but that the language of the test obstructs a full display of cognitive abilities?

If a child appears to have cognitive problems, is the real problem not thinking competence but short-term language competence problems? Is the child's language insufficiently developed so that test performance is hindered by language rather than cognitive ability? Low scores on school or psychological tests may not reflect cognitive level, but a temporary linguistic inability to understand the nature of the test (both instructions and content). In the Bilingual Education Section, we return to this issue (and many other problems in the assessment of bilinguals (see page 575).

Further Reading

BACHMAN, L. F., 1990, *Fundamental Considerations in Language Testing*. Oxford: Oxford University Press.

BAKER, C. & HINDE J., 1984, Language Background Classification. *Journal of Multilingual and Multicultural Development*, Volume 5, No. 1, pages 43-56.

EUROPEAN COMMISSION, 1996, *Euromosaic: The Production and Reproduction of the Minority Language Groups in the European Union*. Luxembourg: Office for Official Publications of the European Communities.

RIVERA, C. (ed.), 1984, *Language Proficiency and Academic Achievement*. Clevedon: Multilingual Matters Ltd.

SKUTNABB-KANGAS, T., 1981, *Bilingualism or Not: The Education of Minorities*. Clevedon: Multilingual Matters Ltd.

SPOLSKY, B., 1995, *Measured Words: The Development of Objective Language Testing*. Oxford: Oxford University Press.

VALDÉS, G. & FIGUEROA, R. A., 1994, *Bilingualism and Testing: A Special Case of Bias*. Norwood, NJ: Ablex.

The United States Foreign Service Oral Interview

A test which attempts to approximate the conditions outlined by Skehan (1988) is the oral interview. An example is the US Foreign Service oral interview which is in four stages (Lowe, 1983; Shohamy, 1983). Following a warm-up period, there is a check on the level of language proficiency, a deeper probe of that level, finishing with a wind-down period. The interview takes about half an hour. The two middle stages check that a person can perform consistently at a level across varying themes and in various language functions. The session is jointly conducted by two interviewers.

By training, the interviewers avoid narrow, predetermined checklists and attempt to make the interview sensitive to the candidate. The interviewers judge and score using prescribed criteria. A person is assigned to a level ranging from 0 (No Competence) to 5 (Educated Native Speaker competence). This assumes a distinction between educated native speakers and other native speakers in their language competence. The levels 1 to 5 also have the possibility of a '+' rating, thus giving an eleven-point rating scale.

Such interview procedures may not reflect reality. Does genuine communication take place between strangers, in a contrived, artificial context? Is the language repertoire of a person truly elicited? Is 'interview language' representative of a person's everyday language functioning? Can we generalize from oral communicative tests based on a single type of test, given on a single occasion, based on a test interview which is not a typical event in real life? There are doubts as to whether such interview procedures can validly imitate and investigate real communicative competence. At the same time, such interview procedures are often a necessary compromise between artificial 'pencil and paper' tests and everyday communication in authentic circumstances. Such interviews are often a pragmatic arrangement given constraints of time, money and human resources.

Communicative Language Testing

In attempting to assess a bilingual's competence in two languages, there is a danger of using a simple paper and pencil test, believing the test will provide a faithful estimation of everyday language life. Multiple choice language tests, dictation, reading comprehension tests and spelling tests are all well worn paths in the testing of language skills. Reducing everyday language competence to tests of specific skills is like measuring Michelangelo's art solely by its range of colors. A radical alternative is seeing how bilinguals perform in both languages in a range of real communicative situations. Observing a bilingual in a shop, at home, at work and during leisure activity might seem the ideal way of measuring bilingual competence. This idea is impractical in terms of time, and may be biased by the presence of the tester. Such an observation situation is unnatural because of the presence of the tester and, being a 'test' situation, intrusive into individual privacy and unrepresentative across time and place. In short, real life observation is likely to be imperfect in terms of reliability and validity.

One particular current emphasis in language testing is on communicative skills. While tests of spelling, grammar, written comprehension and reading abound, the importance of using languages in realistic, everyday settings is reflected in current testing movements. The ideal is expressed by Skehan (1988).

> 'Genuine communication is interaction-based, with more than one participant; unpredictable and creative, i.e. genuine communication may take the participants in unforeseen directions; is situated in a context which is both linguistic/discoursal and also sociocultural; has a purpose, in that participants will be trying to achieve something by use of language, e.g. to persuade, to deceive, etc.; uses authentic stimulus materials, and avoids contrived, specially produced materials; is based on real psychological conditions, such as time pressure; and is outcome evaluated, in that successful performance is judged in terms of whether communicative purposes have been achieved.' (page 215)

A test of language proficiency which meets Skehan's (1988) criteria is probably impossible to achieve. A test which truly measures purposeful communication across sufficient contexts without tester effects is improbable. For some, the answer is simply not to test. For others, a best approximation is accepted. A test may therefore be used that measures the more limited notion of performance rather than the wider idea of competence.

2: Bilingual Proficiency

Bilingual proficiency refers to an individual's ability in their two languages. The extent to which such inner competence is measured by different tests of language proficiency will vary considerably. No test will perfectly measure proficiency in either language, however such proficiency is defined and classified.

There are four basic language abilities: listening, speaking, reading and writing. A profile of a person's bilingual proficiencies immediately takes on eight dimensions as the table below illustrates. The four language abilities form an approximate ladder of complexity. Listening would seem to be the easiest aspect to acquire, followed by speaking, reading and writing. However, some bilinguals will be exceptions to this as they are able to read, even write in a language without speaking it particularly well. (This may be because of a lack of speaking practice in that language.)

	1st LANGUAGE		2nd LANGUAGE	
	Oracy	**Literacy**	**Oracy**	**Literacy**
Receptive	Listening	Reading	Listening	Reading
Productive	Speaking	Writing	Speaking	Writing

Another danger of separating out listening, speaking, reading and writing is that they are not four separate skills. Rather growth in one relates to growth in another. Listening to a language enhances speaking; a wider spoken vocabulary and more accurate grammatical structure will facilitate writing skills. Listening and speaking enhance reading ability.

The table of the eight dimensions of bilingual proficiency warns against stereotyping who is and who is not bilingual. Some people speak a language but do not read or write in that language. Are they bilingual? Some people listen with understanding and read a language (passive bilingualism) but do not speak or write that language. Are they bilingual? Some understand a spoken language but do not, for one reason or another, speak that language. Are they bilingual? To classify people as either bilinguals or monolinguals is too simplistic. In between white and black are many shades of gray.

These basic language proficiencies of listening, speaking, reading and writing have many shades of color within them. For example, reading comprehension can range from being simple and basic to being fluent and very accomplished. Some people listen with understanding in one context (e.g. shops and simple conversation) but do not understand the same language in another context (e.g. in bureaucratic settings or in a public lecture). Their vocabulary, understanding and experience has yet to evolve to the level demanded of the context.

Within listening, speaking, reading and writing skills there are subskills. For example, when speaking, there are subskills of pronunciation, a repertoire and width of vocabulary, exactness of grammar, ability to convey different meanings, and styles of speaking. Reading can also be subdivided into increasingly microscopic parts.

If language proficiencies are multidimensional, simple classification concerning who is bilingual or not becomes impossible. To be sensitive to differences in individual proficiencies in two languages will require a detailed profile rather than a simple test score or judgmental categorization.

Classic definitions of bilingualism such as someone who has native-like control of two or more languages become too tough and severe. What is native-like proficiency? Who is the native reference group, for example, for Spanish speakers in the United States? Is the native reference group Spanish speakers in Spain, in Mexico, in Puerto Rico or Cuba, or in the US itself?

If Bloomfield's (1933) definition of bilingualism as 'the native-like control of two or more languages' is too extreme at one end, is the other extreme tenable as in 'incipient bilingualism'? The term 'incipient bilingualism', coined by Diebold (1964), allows people with minimal competence in a second language to squeeze into being called bilinguals. So students learning a language, tourists with a few phrases, business people with a few greetings in a second language could be included as incipient bilinguals. The danger of being too exclusive is not overcome by being too inclusive. Trawling with too wide a fishing net can make discussion about bilinguals too ambiguous and imprecise.

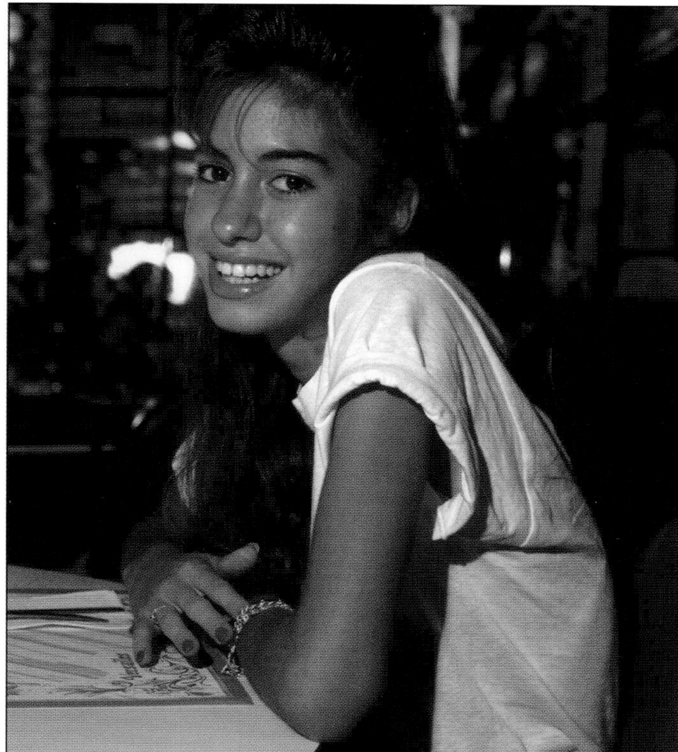

A teenager from a Cuban family in Miami, Florida. Young people whose parents came to the Miami area from Cuba after 1959 have been born and bred in the United States. Their relative proficiencies in Spanish and English will depend on such factors as the language of the home, neighborhood and education.

Who is categorized as a bilingual or not may depend on the purpose of the categorization. Sometimes governments wish to include or exclude language minorities for particular purposes. Where a small indigenous language exists (e.g. in Ireland) a government may wish to maximize its count of bilinguals. A high count of bilinguals may indicate government success in its language policy to preserve the indigenous language. In comparison, in a suppressive, assimilationist government regime, minority languages and bilinguals may be underestimated (e.g. in France).

Is there a middle ground in between maximal and minimal definitions of bilingual proficiency? The great danger is in making arbitrary cut-off points about who is bilingual or not along too few proficiency dimensions. Where possible, the avoidance of simplistic classification and categorization is preferred. Instead, a multicolored canvas profiling the proficiencies of an individual may be preferable.

If language abilities are multicolored, and if bilinguals have a wide range of colors in both of their languages, then positive terms may be preferable to portray that colorful variety. In suppressive, assimilationist regions, bilinguals are often given simple, negative, pejorative labels. In the United States, students in school who do not have proficiency in English comparable to monolingual English-speaking children are labeled Limited English Proficiency (LEP) students.

Such labels stress children's perceived deficiency rather than their multicolored language proficiencies. Children's perceived 'deprivation' rather than their accomplishments are portrayed. Such labels are based only on their measured proficiency in one of their languages and serve to reinforce their lower, marginalized, minority status rather than their bilingual potential. Such labels often unfairly stress lack of proficiency in the majority language, emphasizing past and present performance rather than the possibility of such children becoming full bilinguals.

The Structure of Bilingual Proficiency

The classic structure of a bilingual's language proficiencies is described in terms of their listening, speaking, reading and writing abilities in two languages. But since these skills can be broken down into subskills, the question arises as to the detailed structure of bilinguals' language abilities. Recent theories of the structure of intelligence has suggested there may be 150 different components to intelligence, many of which are language-related. Hernandez-Chavez *et al.* (1978) have suggested there are 64 separate components to language proficiency.

There are two important questions or issues here. The first issue is how many different components there are to language to provide the most sensitive profile of a bilingual's language structure. The second issue is about crucial distinctions between different levels of language skill that relate to judgments made by teachers, parents, administrators and politicians. These two issues will now be discussed.

At one end of the scale there are people such as Hernandez-Chavez *et al.* (1978) who provide a multicomponent structure of language. Basic skills such as listening, reading, writing as well as speaking can be broken down into the different linguistic components that make up these abilities. At the other end of the scale are those (e.g. Oller, 1982) who argue for just one, overall component in a language.

Supposing we give students a test to measure a variety of different language skills (e.g a spelling test, a reading test, an oral comprehension test), Oller's (1982) research suggested that there is sufficient overlap between the different language skills to argue for one overall component of language proficiency. This global factor of language ability was said to co-exist with specific factors which measure relatively minor language skills.

There is an important and related comparison with the structure of intelligence. Some authors have argued for multiple intelligences such as musical intelligence, interpersonal intelligence, political acumen, financial wizardry and criminal intelligence. Others have argued that there is something common among all these that can be labeled a general (g) factor of intelligence. A global language factor is based on the same ideas. If we give students pencil and paper tests in a variety of language skills, the students who do well on one test will tend to do well on another.

The idea of an underlying, global language factor is very contentious. It tends towards an elitist view of language skills. It doesn't allow for the reality that people do vary in their language abilities, some being stronger on communication skills, others on the receptive skills such as listening and reading rather than the productive skills of writing and speaking. Such a global language factor is insufficiently sensitive to the multicolored differences between people.

The concept of a global language factor is also contentious because it is based on pencil and paper tests of language proficiency, usually with right and wrong answers. When more qualitative approaches to measuring differences between people are explored (e.g. by an interview, a group activity exercise, observation of natural language in the street), the variety of differences between people becomes more obvious than an overall language ability.

Questions about how many subskills exist in a bilingual's language proficiency will relate to the purpose and uses of language. In an interview for a job which requires bilingual skills, the focus may be on aspects of communication skills using both languages. In the classroom the teacher may be concerned with the development of skills in speaking and particularly in reading and writing in both languages. A religious leader may be interested in language for reading religious texts and for public and private worship. A speech therapist will aim for a profile on the linguistic structure of language. The educational psychologist may refer to the psychology of language to profile a child's strengths and weaknesses in a language and to provide diagnostic information. The sociolinguist may focus on a person's actual language use in situations, such as the home, the workplace, in the community, preferring a more context-based structuring of language. These illustrations show a difference between a classroom, academic focus on language and a focus on language as used in everyday life. This leads us to an important distinction.

BICS and CALP

The basis of the distinction is that the language needed in the classroom, particularly as children go through schooling and into college, is different from the kind of conversational language required to communicate in the shop and street, when watching the screen, or relaxing with friends. On the one hand, there is conversational competence in languages; on the other hand, there is academically related language competence.

Another term for conversational competence is surface fluency in a language. Surface fluency refers to the ability to hold a simple conversation, for example, in the shop, with neighbors and to understand simple television programs in a language. Such surface fluency tends to be acquired fairly quickly, either informally in the home or in the community, or by second language learning and may be acquired in a matter of months or over several years.

To cope in the curriculum in school or college, surface fluency or conversational language competence may not be enough (Skutnabb-Kangas & Toukomaa, 1976). The language of the classroom becomes more formal, more technical (e.g. special terms are used in science, mathematics, social sciences and social studies), more abstract and more specialized.

This distinction is expressed by Cummins (1984b) in terms of BICS (which stands for Basic Interpersonal Communication Skills) and CALP (which refers to Cognitive/Academic Language Proficiency - see page 000). BICS is said to occur when there is much contextual support in the classroom, and particularly in the street and home. When chatting to other people, we often use non-verbal communication to help understanding. We gesture, use our eyes, give instant feedback by smiling and nodding our head, we gesticulate with our hands and whole body, we use cues and clues to support verbal language. Simple conversation is said to be context-embedded. There are plenty of aids in conversation to convey meaning and to help understanding.

In contrast, cognitive/academic language proficiency is needed in context-reduced, particularly academic situations. In discussing an historical issue, explaining algebra or trigonometry, analyzing a novel or explaining a scientific equation, the teacher may use few supports to the stream of words. Language, in and by itself, is almost the sole conveyor of meaning when more advanced thinking skills such as synthesis, analysis and evaluation are required in the curriculum. Hence, language is said to be disembedded from a more supportive and concrete situation. Where the language is disembedded and stands on its own to convey meaning, the situation is often referred to as context-reduced.

This distinction means that it is important not to make hasty judgments about the language competence of students in particular. In conversing with students, conversational competence must not be confused with being able to cope in the school curriculum. As children move through the grades in school, the language proficiency they require is much more than conversational fluency if they are to cope in their second language with a complex curriculum.

To take one example, an in-migrant child may be given English language lessons in withdrawal classes, in a special Center or in a Transitional Bilingual education program. After one or two or three years the child may seem able to hold a conversation in English with the teacher. That child may also be competent in using English in the shop, with friends in the playground and watching cartoons on television. The danger is that child would then be placed in an English language mainstream classroom alongside first language English-speaking peers, because he or she seems fluent in English. The level of English in the classroom is very different from the shop, screen and street. The child may not have the vocabulary, more advanced grammatical constructions, nor an understanding of subtleties of meaning to grasp what is being taught. The level of language is too deep and abstract, too context-reduced, and the child may begin to fail.

It is not impossible that a child's bilingualism may be blamed for being unable to cope in the classroom. Yet the

Bilingual children write in their second language, Welsh. Cognitive/Academic language proficiency is needed in context-reduced situations like a classroom.

fault may lie in the early exiting of the child from English language classes or Transitional Bilingual education. From being able to swim with a swimming support, the child is thrown into the deep end to sink or swim, to survive, splash helplessly or look around for support to avoid drowning.

This distinction between two different kinds of language has been influential. While academics have been critical, the distinction has intuitive appeal with explanatory power for many parents and teachers. While it may be simplistic and partial, it remains a crucial, popular distinction that sensitizes people to the dangers of too much reliance on judgments about a child's language proficiency based on listening to conversations.

While the distinction between BICS and CALP has had a positive influence on bilingual educators, there are limitations that need to be shared. First, the distinction paints a two stage idea. A child would seem to be in one category or another. Instead, children and adults move forward on multiple language dimensions with various sliding scales (e.g. listening, speaking, reading, writing) rather than in one big jump. Just as we can gradually increase the volume on a compact disc player or television, so language proficiencies gradually increase. A second danger is that labels are misused to stereotype students. The terms may oversimplify reality and the way students are labeled.

Further Reading

BACHMAN, L. F., 1990, *Fundamental Considerations in Language Testing*. Oxford: Oxford University Press.

CUMMINS, J., 1984, *Bilingualism and Special Education: Issues in Assessment and Pedagogy*. Clevedon: Multilingual Matters Ltd.

HARLEY, B. *et al.*, 1990, *The Development of Second Language Proficiency*. Cambridge: Cambridge University Press.

SKUTNABB-KANGAS, T., 1981, *Bilingualism or Not: The Education of Minorities*. Clevedon: Multilingual Matters Ltd.

SPOLSKY, B., 1995, *Measured Words: The Development of Objective Language Testing*. Oxford: Oxford University Press.

VALDÉS, G. & FIGUEROA, R. A., 1994, *Bilingualism and Testing: A Special Case of Bias*. Norwood, NJ: Ablex.

LANGUAGES IN SOCIETY

'Bilingualism is a singular noun for a plural experience.'

Bilingualism in Communities

1: Language Communities

Introduction

At its simplest, a language community is formed by those who use a given language for part, most or all of their daily existence. The term 'language community' is sometimes used by linguists to describe groups of majority language users, however large. Thus the 50 million people who use English as their daily language in Britain can be described as 'the English language community'. However, the term tends to be used more frequently to describe groups of minority language speakers. Thus it is possible to talk about a French language community in Louisiana or a Sámi community in Norway, or the Bengali language community in the East End of London. Other frequently used terms are 'speech community' and 'language group'. These terms are most often used to describe a localized group of people who speak the same (minority) language.

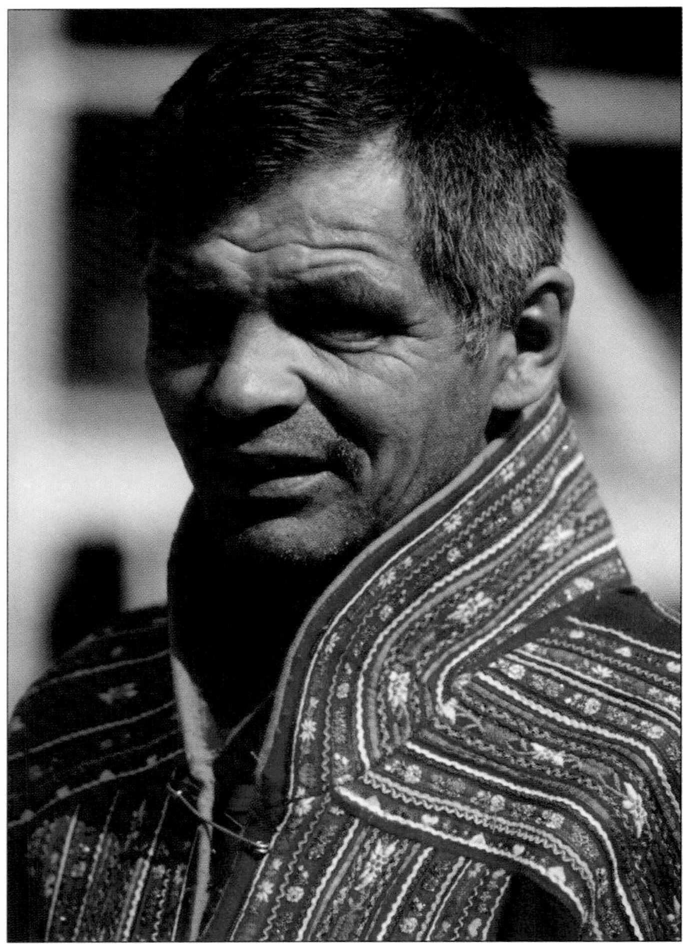

A Sámi man in Tromso, Norway.

Problems in Usage

There are many problems in using terms such as 'speech community', 'language community' and 'language group'.

Size

Size is not specified in the term 'language group'. In Sociology, terms such as 'small group', 'reference group', 'peer group', 'national group' and 'ethnic group' are used. Thus a group can consist of only two or three people or refer to an ethnic group of many millions. The use of the term 'language group' hence gives no indication of its size and vitality. Similarly, a 'language community' may consist of three or four households in a sparsely populated rural area, an extended family of nomads in the desert, or many thousands of minority language speakers in a region.

Geographical area

The idea of a speech community or a language community tends to imply, for some, geographical cohesiveness and integration. However, members of a language community may be linked over a wider geographical area by social, religious or educational institutions (e.g. churches, synagogues, Saturday schools) or even by business interests (e.g. Chinese restaurants). Schooling in the minority language or bilingual education may also become a focus for a language community. The term 'language communities', does not have an absolute geographical implication. Rather, the term 'language communities' tends to refer to those who are in communion with each other irrespective of this being a short or a long-distance away. While such a language community may have spatial as well as social connotations, (that is the language community is found in a distinct area of a city and in particular streets), it is the social form or organization of a language community that is more important

An insurance company in Chinatown, Manchester. Language communities may be bound together by geographical proximity, but other sources of cohesiveness are shared activities and institutions such as religion, education, trade and business.

than its geographical location. Such language communities tend to have a particular language as one important basis of their interaction and have shared values and meanings that are part of that language and its culture. There is solidarity based on a common tongue, and a common interest in maintaining and renewing heritage cultural forms.

The opposite may also be true. There may be a group of people who speak the same language and live close together, but who do not interact with each other. In this latter case, there is not the sense of cohesiveness or integration to merit the term 'language community' or 'speech community'. Some sociologists argue that communities are no longer found in modern societies and that they have been destroyed by mass communication, easy transport and a lessening of the power of institutions like the church. Such sociologists argue that there is little sense of unity, coherence, sense of shared purposes and bonding within a locality. A community in the modern sense can mean people living apart from each other rather than living together. In this sense, it is possible to have community as a geographical term but without an implication of there being an integrated local social system with relationships between people and close forms of human association. (This reflects the distinction between *Gesellschaft* and *Gemeinschaft* – see the Glossary.)

Non language links

A major problem with the terms 'speech community', 'language community' and 'language group' is that an individual's membership of a community or group does not depend on language alone. Communities are not formed solely by language. Language is just one marker in social organization. Relationships between groups of people are created along social, ethnic, economic, cultural, political and social class lines. Language may be one means of setting a boundary and the means of social interaction and communication. Language may be a way of distancing one group from another with different language patterns. But language is not by itself the sole determiner of social groupings. Age and gender, sociocultural and socioeconomic interests and common values will tend to play a part in the formation and continuation of groups. A problem with the related term 'speech community' is that it may give the impression that relationships between people are purely on an oral speech dimension. Interaction by writing, or other forms of literary engagement are not initially included in the term.

Multiple memberships

People do not usually belong to just one community or group. Each of us tends to have multiple membership of different groups and communities and for bilinguals, this may be even more so. Bilinguals may be members of particular groups through one language, and use a different language in other groups. In employment, religious affiliation, leisure activity and other cultural activities, there are different target communities. The use of language or languages within and across these groups tends to be varied and is not usually the principal determinant of any particular group.

Areas of conflict

The idea of a language community is that it is cohesive, integrated and stable. Yet contested politics and struggles for power often mean that there is conflict, tension, struggle and lack of equilibrium within the community and not just co-operation for the common good.

Language Networks

Generic problems with defining a speech community, language community and language group have led some to prefer the term 'language networks' or 'speech networks'. The concept of a 'language network' is that there are a set of people who all interact with each other and create a network of speakers of a particular language. Language networks can be verbal or diagrammatic representations of who interacts with whom, how often, where and when. Actual patterns of daily interaction may be described and explained in great detail and can be mapped in graphic format. When diagrams are used, they tend to suggest relatively stable if not static relationships.

A market place in Yogyakarta on the island of Java, Indonesia. Indonesia is one of the most multilingual countries in the world, with an estimated 700 languages spoken. The majority of the inhabitants of Java speak Javanese as their first language, and an increasing number are gaining competence in the official language, Bahasa Indonesia. Malay, closely related to Bahasa Indonesia, has also been widely spoken as a second language in Indonesia for centuries, mainly as a trade language.

However, interactions with others (along language and other lines) tend never to be static, with networks changing in their cohesiveness and integration. If language is used as a basis of graphically plotting a social network, it tends to have many of the problems listed above in defining speech and language communities. In addition, the term 'language networks' has the problem that it can ignore the 'why' question. Why are there relationships, cohesiveness and different patterns of integration or otherwise between individuals? The analysis of daily interaction at a deeper and more complex level can be absent if diagrams, in particular, are used.

Also what tends to occur when describing the social networks of bilinguals is that the wider contexts of relationships are absent. For example, it is possible to display patterns of relationship in rural communities. Yet rural communities are affected by more national or macro concerns. Patterns of relationship in a rural community may be affected by national politics, economic concerns and ideology as much as by local concerns.

Another problem with the concept of a language network, similar to a language community, is that it may suggest that relationships between people are relatively equal, stable and without conflict. In particular, the idea of a language network does not usually include different status relationships between people who interact. Dimensions of power and prestige in relationships are not necessarily included in a simple, purely linguistic, network analysis.

Language Community

The concept of 'language community', while not without criticism, has enjoyed some popular appeal. This may be partly due to:

- The positive associations of the term 'community' – as found in 'community schools, community radio, community representatives, community social work, community medicine' and 'community policing'.
- Talk about a diglossic country or region may fail to clarify that minority language speakers tend to be concentrated in particular communities, and that their use of the minority language may be restricted to these communities. Focusing on individual minority language communities may help us to become closer to the living and working reality of a minority language than talk of a language region.
- Isolated individuals speaking a minority language, who therefore rarely use that language, are unlikely to maintain or spread that language. Within the concept

John Edwards

Born in Southampton, England, with Canadian and British citizenship, John Edwards was educated at the University of Western Ontario and McGill University. As well as being a highly productive and prolific author, John Edwards has been editor since 1993 of the *Journal of Multilingual and Multicultural Development* as well as editor of a book series entitled *Multilingual Matters* (since 1995). He is currently Professor in the Department of Psychology at the St Francis Xavier University, Antigonish, Nova Scotia, Canada. Among his many books is one entitled *Multilingualism.* Published in 1994, this book provides an extensive and highly knowledgeable view of bilinguals and bilingualism. He is also well known for a book published in 1985 entitled *Language, Society and Identity*. Creative, versatile and provocative, John Edwards' contribution as an author and as an editor is remarkable in both its breadth and depth of scholarship.

of the community is the idea that language needs to have living and daily functions. Language communities are often seen as essential to the continued life of a language. Their vitality is central to the preservation of a language, much more than external legislation.

- Action for preservation and maintenance of a minority language often takes its inspiration and its justification from the visible presence of language communities. It is their local language life, whether in rural villages or geographically defined urban districts, that frequently provides supporters of the language with a tangible and cogent reason for its preservation.

Community Languages

The term 'community language' has recently become popular. Community languages has been a term particularly used in Britain to describe the newer, non-Celtic languages. For example, in large English cities such as London, Leeds, Birmingham, Bradford and Cardiff, there are language communities. Examples of such language communities are formed by Bengali, Sylleti, Panjabi, Urdu, Gujarati, Spanish, Greek and Turkish speakers. The language community may center on the local mosque, temple or a Saturday school system to teach the heritage language and culture. The community may also focus around local schools, shopping areas and recreational amenities.

The term 'language community' in Britain has become particularly important for those who cannot claim the territorial principle (see page 119). That is, those established in-migrants, recently arrived migrants and refugees, cannot claim (as do the Welsh, Irish and Gaelic speakers) that theirs is an indigenous language with territorial rights. Instead, they argue from the personality principle (see page 119), that their language and culture has unique features with a long and strong tradition that needs preservation. Where the language does not belong to the land, they can argue that it belongs to a community.

Conclusion

The aim of this topic has been to show that, unfortunately, there can be no preferred term that is capable of summing up all the complexity, dynamism and color of bilinguals existing in groups. Simple labels hide complex realities. What is needed is an awareness of the limitations of these simple terms, of the many dimensions underneath them, and those factors outside such terms that affect language groups.

Further Reading

COULMAS, F. (ed.), 1997, *The Handbook of Sociolinguistics.* Oxford: Blackwell.

EDWARDS, J. R., 1994, *Multilingualism.* London/New York: Routledge.

EDWARDS, V., 1984, *Language Policy in Multicultural Britain.* London: Academic Press.

GEACH, J., 1996, Community Languages. In E. HAWKINS (ed.), *30 Years of Language Teaching.* London: Centre for Information on Language Teaching and Research (CILT).

HUDSON, R. A., 1996, *Sociolinguistics* (Second edition). Cambridge: Cambridge University Press.

TOVEY, H., 1985, 'Local Community': In Defence of a Much-Criticized Concept. *Social Studies* (now called *Irish Journal of Sociology*), 8 (3 & 4), 149-163.

2: Types of Language Minority

While 'language minority' is a frequently used phrase, an exact definition of the term is difficult. The term 'language minority' may be used to describe many groups that differ in size, geographical distribution, status and origin. We begin with some particular groups of language minority people.

One type is composed of those people who are indigenous to an area. The Maori in New Zealand, the Aboriginals in Australia, many Native American groups in the United States, the Sámi in Norway, the Frisians in Germany and the Netherlands, the Walloons in Belgium, the Galicians in Spain, the Friulans and Ladins in Italy, and the Bretons and Occitans in France are just a few examples of indigenous (autochthonous) language minorities. Among such language minorities, there is a variation in the amount of official recognition and rights afforded them. Official recognition includes the right to use the language in official contexts e.g. in courts of law, when dealing with government officials, and also provision of services in the minority language including healthcare and education. (See Language Rights, page 276f.) For example, the Welsh language in Wales has (in theory if not always in practice) a considerable amount of official status. In Italy, by contrast, many small indigenous languages are not recognized by the Italian government in any official way. Some minority languages that are genetically related to the majority languages of the countries where they are spoken are not even recognized as separate languages. Occitan and Provençal in France are considered by many French people to be dialects of standard French. (See Dialects and Language Boundaries, page 135.)

Another grouping of language minorities are those who are recent in-migrants into a country. For example, in Canada the recent influx of Asian speakers has led to the development of different language communities and in Germany, the influx of guest workers since the 1960s has led to the creation of Turkish, Italian, Spanish, Greek, Portuguese and Yugoslav minority language communities. In Britain, there are large numbers of Asian language minorities, including Urdu, Panjabi, Hindi and Gujarati and there are many in-migrant Spanish speakers in the United States.

Two Asian women wait for a train in Bonn, Germany. Many in-migrant minority language communities exist in Germany because of the influx of guestworkers to the country.

The tendency is for in-migrant languages in Europe and North America to receive minimal recognition from governments. In the European Union, there is official recognition of indigenous minority languages, such as Welsh, Irish, Frisian, often labeled as the lesser used languages of Europe. However, the same recognition in the European Union is not given to in-migrant languages such as Turkish in Germany, various Asian languages in Britain, and, for example, Sign Languages and Romani in many countries. Therefore, there is clear, official differentiation between indigenous minority European languages and in-migrant minority languages. The speakers of indigenous languages are perceived to have rights because of their historical and territorial connection with a region. The rights of in-migrant language minorities are seemingly not so easily recognized. (See Territorial Principle and Personality Principle, page 119.)

Where a minority language has status within a region because it is a language of heritage and history, this can work against recent in-migrant languages such as Turkish in Germany and Asian languages in Canada. Thus, while minority languages see themselves as the poor relations of majority languages, in-migrant languages tend to be the poorest of the poor, the lowest status of those with low status.

In any grouping of language minorities it is important to recognize the status and perceived vitality that the language group accords itself. Thus, the Occitans and Corsicans in France tend to perceive themselves as having a separate identity even though the majority of monolingual French people do not see them in the same way.

The Definition of the Term 'Minority'

The term 'minority' is itself ambiguous. Does the term 'minority' refer to the numbers of people who speak the language? Is the comparison implied in 'minority' a comparison at the regional or state level? Is the total number of speakers taken into account or is the density of speakers within a region of importance?

In Spain, the Catalan language is spoken by a minority within the country. In the autonomous province of Catalonia, the majority of the people speak the Catalan language. So is Catalan a minority language? In Wales, Welsh is a minority language numerically in many areas. Yet in north-west Wales, there are many communities where the language is spoken by a clear majority of people. Thus the saturation of language minority speakers in an area may be different from their numerical representation in a nation.

Is German a minority language in Belgium? Although only one percent of the population of Belgium speak German, German is regarded as a majority language. In Ireland, the Irish language is recognized as a national language and given official status, yet it is spoken by a minority of people in the country. Is Irish therefore a minority language? Charlotte Hoffmann (1991, Chapter 11) provides many telling examples of the difficulty of deciding whether a language is a minority language or not.

The term 'minority' may be used to reflect less (or low) political status and power. Thus in Peru, Quechua has less power and status than Spanish, in France, Breton less status than French and in Malaysia, Tamil is less prestigious than the Malaysian language. This tends to be the preferred academic use of 'minority' – that is, not referring to numbers of people but to the relative power and status of a language within a country.

Categorizations of Language Minorities

Various dimensions, categorizations and typologies of language minorities have been proposed. For example, Haarmann (1986), in discussing language ecology, uses seven categories for the classification of language groups:

1. Demography (e.g. size of language group, concentration, urban-rural)
2. Sociology (e.g. gender, age, social stratification)
3. Politics (e.g. group-state relations, institutional status)
4. Culture (e.g. traditions, promotion of a distinctive ethnicity)
5. Psychology (e.g. identity, attitudes)
6. Interaction (e.g. language use in different domains)
7. Linguistics (e.g. language contact between dialects)

John Edwards (1994c) suggests a basic three-fold distinction between languages that are unique to a state, languages not unique to a state but which are still minority languages, and local-only minority languages. Such minorities can be adjoining or non-adjoining, and cohesive or non-cohesive. John Edwards (1994c) uses these dimensions to create a ten-fold categorization of language minorities. Some examples are given below:

1. Friulian, Sardinian and Welsh: Unique and cohesive indigenous language minorities.
2. Pennsylvania Dutch: Unique and cohesive in-migrant language minorities.
3. Basque (Spain/France) and Catalan (Spain/Andorra): Non-unique, adjoining and cohesive indigenous language minorities.
4. The Romanies in Europe: Non-unique, non-adjoining and non-cohesive.

In the United States, an oft-quoted typology derives from John Ogbu. Ogbu (1978, 1983) attempted to distinguish differences between different types of language minority. His research attempted to discover whether there were, indeed, significant differences between in-migrant and indigenous language minorities, or differences between different in-migrant minorities (e.g. the Chinese and the Mexican-Americans in the US). Were there important differences between their language orientation, their social and economic status in society, their success in assimilation or in maintaining their ethnic identity?

Ogbu (1978, 1983) makes a distinction between 'castelike', 'immigrant' and 'autonomous' minority groups. Autonomous minorities are not subordinate to the dominant majority group and have distinct separate identities. For example, some Jews in the US often have a distinct racial, ethnic, religious, linguistic or cultural identity and are generally not politically or economically subordinate. Such autonomous minorities are unlikely to be characterized by disproportionate or persistent failure in school.

Castelike minorities tend to fill the least well-paid jobs, are often given poor quality education, and are regarded as inferior by the dominant majority who sometimes negatively label them as 'culturally deprived', with 'limited English proficiency', with 'low innate intelligence' or pejoratively as 'bilinguals'. Ogbu (1978) classes African Americans, Puerto Ricans, Mexican Americans, Native Americans and many Hispanic groups in the US as castelike minorities. The 'outcastes' of India and some of the Caribbean in-migrants in England also share these characteristics. Such minorities may see themselves as relatively powerless, immobile in status and confined to subservience and domination. Most have been permanently and often involuntarily incorporated into the host society. Such a group experiences disproportionate failure at school, which confirms the low expectations they have of themselves and the negative attributions of majority groups. A sense of inferiority is joined by low levels of motivation to succeed in the wider society.

In the main, Ogbu's (1978) immigrant minorities have moved relatively willingly to the US and may be more motivated to succeed at school and seek prosperity. The Cubans, Filipinos, Japanese and Koreans were included in this group. Another example is the Chinese in-migrants who, as a generalization, are keen to succeed, positive about the opportunities in schooling and are fairly optimistic about improving their lot. Some immigrant language minority individuals may arrive having been educated in the home country, and are literate and motivated to achieve.

Immigrant minorities tend to lack power, status and will often be low down on the occupational ladder. However, they do not necessarily perceive themselves in the same way as their dominant hosts. 'As strangers, they can operate psychologically outside established definitions of social status and relations' (Ogbu, 1983, page 169). Such immigrant minorities may still suffer racial discrimination and hostility, yet are less intimidated and paralyzed by dominating majorities compared with castelike minorities. Parents may have relatively strong aspirations for the success of their children in school and also expect vocational and social mobility in their offspring. Pride in ethnic identity is not lost but preserved by the parents, who see their reference group as back in the homeland or in the in-migrant neighborhood.

Ogbu's (1978) distinction between autonomous, castelike and immigrant minorities does not allow easy classification of different language minorities into these three groups. The criteria for classification are not precise enough nor are they validated by research studies. There is also the danger of stereotyping different language groups when there is much variability within such groups; sometimes more than the variability between the groups. However, the differences between castelike and immigrant minorities help explain why equally disadvantaged groups facing discrimination from the dominant majority, perform differently at school. Poverty, poor quality schooling and powerlessness do not fully explain language minority failure in education. Beyond socioeconomic class and language differences, academic and economic success or failure may, in part, be due to cultural differences among language minorities. Castelike minorities seem locked into a system that perpetuates inequalities and discrimination. Other minorities attempt to escape the subtractive system which confines their participation in society and confirms their powerlessness. Immigrant and autonomous minorities may show less failure at school, partly explained by a more positive orientation to their language and culture, and an optimism about their likely success in the school system. Language minority education ('strong' forms of bilingual education) therefore becomes highly important for castelike minorities in the attempt to counteract both the discrimination of the dominant minority and the acceptance and internalization of that discrimination and economic deprivation.

The call for increased provision of 'strong' forms of bilingual education for castelike and immigrant minorities may not be welcomed by the dominant majority. Those with power and wealth may see such 'strong' forms of bilingual education as upsetting the status quo and usurping the power structure. The worry for the dominant majority may be that the castelike, the unemployed and those in poorly paid manual labor will be empowered by such education. The dominated may then begin to contest and threaten differences of rank, reward and rule. 'As the minority group is empowered through jobs, preferred status, professionalization, the majority becomes frightened. In an effort to regain control, it enforces monolingualism not only as an educational goal, but also as the most valuable educational approach' (O. García, 1991a, page 5). When there is prosperity and liberal politics (e.g. the Civil Rights era), some empowerment of language minorities may be granted through 'strong' forms of bilingual education.

When there is economic recession, less liberal politics and less language minority self-assertiveness, 'strong' forms of bilingual education may be less acceptable. Dominant majorities at such times may wish to control access to the more prestigious jobs, preserve their power and wealth. This may result in hostility to 'strong' forms of bilingual education which threaten to give language minorities an increased share of power, wealth and status.

REFERENCES: EDWARDS, 1994; OGBU, 1978, 1983

Native Americans

A Paiute mother and child (in a burden basket) in Havasu Canyon, Northern Arizona in 1898.

The origin of Native Americans (also called American Indians) can be traced to around 40,000 years ago. The first groups of Mongolians made their way into present day Alaska and settled in parts of Canada and the United States and elsewhere in South America. It is estimated that around five hundred separate languages and dialects were spoken by Native Americans before the Europeans arrived in the late 15th century. Such natives numbered approximately two million people living within the current boundaries of the United States.

Within a few decades, the European invaders had begun to appropriate native land (although they occasionally signed treaties with Native Americans for the acquisition of their land). Such negotiations and conflicts marked the beginning of language contact and language conflicts between European settlers and Native Americans.

Territorial rights, with reservations for Native Americans, did not necessarily preserve Native American languages and dialects. Once living on a reservation, a Native American group needed to meet and negotiate with agents of the government, and, when enduring periods of starvation (through the government ignoring treaties regarding food distribution), the relative power and value of native compared with 'the white man's' languages was much in contrast.

While Native American languages have survived until the present, the story of such languages is one of decline, desperation and often death. Assimilative forces, often represented in government agents and teachers, have made the maintenance of Native American languages difficult, leading to replacement rather than preservation. The economic poverty of Native Americans, the relatively poor quality of education provided for them, and problems of health and alcohol, each helped make assimilation into language majority society in the United States attractive and desirable. Only on the surface was there a choice of language, a choice of culture and a choice of lifestyle. Where economic deprivation existed, the pull and the push was both towards the majority language and its attendant culture.

There have been attempts to reverse the downward language shift in Native American languages. Following the Indian Reorganization Act of 1934, native languages were encouraged, and standards of education were improved. This program aimed to reverse the effects of continuous assimilation. The Act recognized the cultural and linguistic distinctiveness of Native Americans and wished to preserve their differences. In recent decades, the National Indian Youth Conference, the 1975 Self-Determination Act and various protests have raised not only an awareness of the native people's situation but also a conscience about it.

It is estimated that there are currently as many Native Americans in the United States as when Christopher Columbus landed in 1492 – approximately two million (see page 444). Due to cross-breeding, many of these may only have a small percentage of Native American blood. The number of languages that appear to have a future among Native Americans is few and, if these languages die, or become further weakened, the long ancestral history of those languages and their cultures in the United States will be impoverished.

REFERENCE: CANTONI, 1996

Native American girls sewing at a US Government school at Lac du Flambeau, Wisconsin, in about 1895. Native American children were often cruelly and forcibly separated from their families and taken to boarding schools far away from their homes where they underwent a process of compulsory assimilation, in dress, beliefs, lifestyle and language.

Iraqi Kurds bargain over the price of tobacco at a market in Irbil in Iraqi Kurdistan. Kurdish, a language related to Persian, is spoken by approximately 20 million Kurds in their home region of Kurdistan, an upland region in south-western Asia which covers areas of several countries, including Iran, Iraq and Turkey. The Kurdish people are a minority group in all these countries, although they have limited autonomy in Iran. There are Kurds, especially in Turkey, who no longer speak the language, but for most Kurds, their language is both a proof and a symbol of their ethnic identity.

'Minorities vary in size, geographical situation, social composition and economic strength, and the political status that they enjoy may range from almost full autonomy to total suppression' (Hoffmann, 1991, page 233). This quote suggests that a language minority may be defined not just in terms of size but, perhaps more importantly, by its status, political power and prestige within a country. In this sense, a language is a minority language when it has less power and status than a majority language. Thus German in Belgium can be perceived as a majority language because of its high status, particularly in Europe. Catalan can be perceived as a minority language in Spain, despite its six million or more speakers, because it has less status at a national level than Spanish.

Nevertheless, solely defining a majority language in terms of status and power runs into difficulties. For example, in Ireland where Irish is an official language of the state, it may be perceived as a minority language because in education, business and government, English tends to have much higher perceived status. While Spanish is a high status language in Spain and most countries of Latin America, it is a minority language in the United States because of its comparison with the all-powerful English language in that country.

When the term 'minority' is used, for example among sociologists, there can be an additional meaning to the word. A minority is often regarded as having the attributes of disadvantage, underprivilege, so that a minority becomes a euphemism for a group who are oppressed, exploited and discriminated against. Not all language minorities are relatively disadvantaged – but most are, or perceive themselves as such.

Conclusion

This discussion has revealed that an exact demarcation between language majority and language minority is imprecise and inexact. Also within the umbrella term of language minorities, there appears to be a variety of language groups: some with large numbers, some with small numbers; some with recently attained power and status (e.g. Catalan and Welsh), others with minimal recognition (e.g. Asian languages in England). In one sense, the use of the term minority evokes images of disadvantage, underprivilege, oppression, discrimination and exploitation. In a more negative sense, the term 'minority' carries with it a stereotype, a label or a prejudice that diversity and difference means less valuable, less worthwhile and with less of a future.

Breton men pack a cargo of artichokes for export at Kerishel, a town on the coast of Brittany in north-west France. Breton, a Celtic language related to Welsh, is spoken by between half a million and a million people in the north-west peninsula of France. Almost all Breton speakers also speak French, the official language of the whole of France.

Further Reading

EDWARDS, J. R., 1994, *Multilingualism.* London/New York: Routledge.

HOFFMANN, C., 1991, *An Introduction to Bilingualism.* London: Longman.

MCKAY, S. L. & WONG, S. C. (eds), 1988, *Language Diversity: Problem or Resource?* New York: Newbury House.

SKUTNABB-KANGAS, T., 1981, *Bilingualism or Not: The Education of Minorities.* Clevedon: Multilingual Matters Ltd.

Aboriginal Australians

An Aboriginal Australian elder.

Aboriginal Australians are the native people of Australia with a rich cultural heritage and a history which goes back to approximately 50,000 BC. Such natives were among the first artists, mariners and religious thinkers in the world.

In 1770, the sovereignty of around 250 different Aboriginal cultural and linguistic groups was contested by a British invader, Lieutenant James Cook, who claimed much of the eastern half of Australia for the British. Without negotiation or a lawful treaty, Cook took possession of the land and judged the Aboriginals to be primitive and economically unproductive. Colonialism in Australia was born, with vestiges of colonialism remaining today.

Since the 1770s, Aboriginal Australians have often been pressed into service, providing cheap labor, and subject to assimilation policies. For example, children were removed from Aboriginal families for so called neglect and placed in orphanages, training homes and 'white' family foster care. Other Aboriginals were confined to reserves, particularly in north and south-west Australia. Various Aboriginal Acts removed many of their civil rights, including freedom of movement, right to property, and freedom of marriage across racial groups. This restrictive and disparaging behavior by colonialists and their descendants meant that Aboriginal languages suffered, with downward language shift across many decades.

Aboriginal activism for self-sufficiency and protection of their languages and cultures began in the 1930s and has grown since the 1960s with the dismantling of discriminatory legislation. It was not until 1967 that Aboriginals were included in the Australian Census, and not until 1972 that a policy of self-determination by Aboriginals was introduced into government. The growing Australian political and economic difficulties of the 1980s tended to push Aboriginal concerns lower down the political agenda. However, those concerned with social welfare plus some crusading social scientists added to the pressure for Aboriginal peoples to receive positive discrimination and affirmative action from central and regional bureaucracy.

Aboriginal people currently form less than two percent of the Australian population and, despite recent anti-discrimination laws, still tend to be marginalised and disadvantaged. Majority group prejudice and racism still constitutes a threat to the Aboriginal people. Also the Aboriginal people often prefer social boundaries in order to retain their cultural and linguistic heritage. The aim has been for a full reconciliation between Aboriginal people and 'white people' in the year 2001. There is a new impetus among Aboriginal people to celebrate their traditional culture in rural areas and to reclaim it where Aboriginals live in urban areas.

REFERENCE: LO BIANCO, 1987

3: Immigration, Emigration and Language

Introduction

Emigration and immigration are present in almost every country of the world. While the United States has been the recipient of in-migrants from most countries of the world, and European countries have received in-migrants from many developing countries of the world, almost every country has been affected by either emigration or immigration or both. This topic focuses on the role and fate of language in such a process.

Take some well known examples: Spanish speakers entering the English-dominated United States, or Turkish in-migrants in Germany, the Asian populations in Britain and Canada, as well as the white settlers in Africa and India, Arabic countries and the Far East. All have a history of one language encountering another, sometimes leading to bilingualism, at other times to language decay and death. Whether emigration was due to religious or ethnic persecution, political oppression or economic hardship, the home language spoken (and sometimes written) was variously replaced or retained, forgotten or forbidden following immigration.

Most often, the language of in-migrants tends to be lost between the first and the third generations through the melting pot processes of employment, schooling, mass media, and many other assimilating influences. Most countries, as part of the basic philosophy of the melting pot, expect in-migrants to shed their language and culture in favor of the majority language and culture soon after settling in the new country.

When the headlines of host country newspapers talk about floods, waves or influxes of in-migrants who may overwhelm the country, the pressure on in-migrants is to lose their heritage language. Even when the host country actively calls for more immigration (e.g. Canada which between 1992 and 1995 wanted 250,000 in-migrants per year to adjust for an aging population and needed extra labor in its workforce), the pressure is still for in-migrants to lose their language. Assimilation is a common political demand, with language a visible sign of the extent of assimilation of an individual or ethnic group. When immigration occurs, language often takes on a symbolic value. Language is a highly visible mark of group identity.

Yet the language of the in-migrant is not essential to the maintenance of ethnic identity. Various groups of in-migrants in different countries have retained their ethnicity despite losing their language: Dutch in-migrants in Australia, Greeks and Turks in London, and various French communities in the United States. In the United States over the last few decades, there has been a revived interest and pride in ancestry, roots and the maintenance of ethnic identity, although the original native languages have been lost.

A shop in Chinatown, New York.

The Speed of Assimilation and Integration

There are various factors that influence whether an in-migrant will rapidly or slowly assimilate or integrate (see also page 150). Examples of such factors are:

1. Whether an in-migrant has chosen or been forced to move. When emigration is chosen, assimilation may be more expected and desired. When a person has been forced to move, then assimilation may be more resisted. For example, for employment or economic reasons, some people choose to emigrate: other in-migrants are refugees with little or no choice. However, even when people appear to have a choice, this is rarely a 'free choice' as the dice is heavily loaded (e.g. a choice between continued material poverty or emigration and potentially greater affluence.
2. The amount of preparation and support, both emotionally and financially, will affect the transition and integration. Refugees, for example, often have little preparation, and emotionally and financially may be very vulnerable.
3. The amount of family separation in the nuclear and extended family will have an effect on integration. In-migrant families often arrive in stages, with reunification difficult and often occurring after a long period of time. At a time of considerable stress in immigration, the support of the family is missing both on a short-term and often on a longer-term basis. In-migrants often feel isolated when they arrive, helpless and rootless.
4. Many in-migrants settle in large cities where it is difficult to adjust to a strange and new environment. For those who come from rural backgrounds where patterns of interaction with neighbors are very different, adjusting to a new culture, new living conditions and styles of relationship may be difficult.

A Scandinavian family reach New York, ca. 1920.

5. When newcomers cannot speak the language of the host country, there is often both linguistic and cultural isolation. Not knowing the host language may make it difficult to pick up the culture, rules of social interaction, cultural rituals, values and beliefs of the host country. Social and racial intgration can often be difficult, not only because of language barriers, but often through the hostile attitudes of certain members of the host country.

6. Many in-migrants experience a loss of status. Often unable to find immediate employment, or given a minimal salary, discriminated against in applications for employment, the self-esteem and positive self-identity of in-migrants may be affected. If in-migrant parents have to take jobs well below their standard of qualification, that are poorly paid and 'dead-ends', the children's view of their parents may be affected. Some children will then be more motivated to assimilate, to learn the language and culture of the country in order to improve their material conditions and identity.

When in-migrants are placed in conditions of poverty, deprivation and prejudice, then their children may be less successful in school, dropping out earlier, having low expectations of themselves and of their families.

In-migrants into the United States: The Statue of Liberty

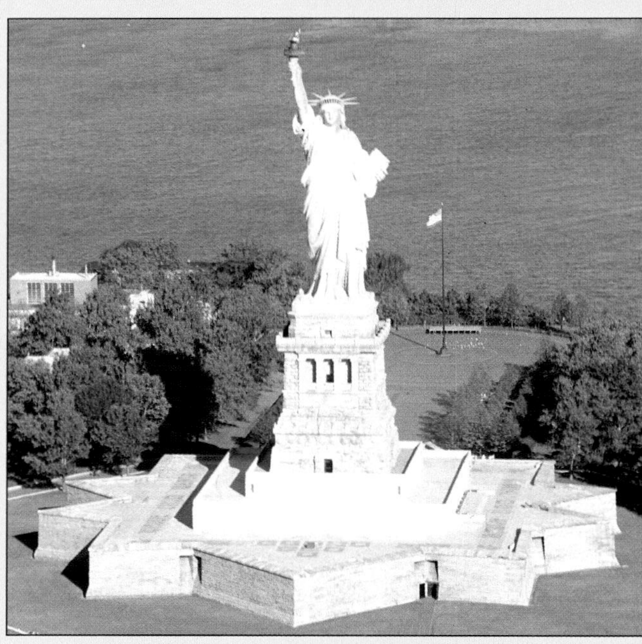

When approaching New York for the first time, the Statue of Liberty was one of the first buildings seen by in-migrants. Some thought it was the tomb of Christopher Columbus; for many it came to symbolize the dawn of life in a new country. Leaving behind religious persecution, political oppression or economic hardship, over 12 million people passed the Statue of Liberty and entered, one by one, the Immigration Center at Ellis Island.

> 'Give me your tired, your poor, your huddled masses
> yearning to breathe free,
> The wretched refuse of your teeming shore,
> Send these, the homeless, tempest tossed, to me:
> I lift my lamp beside the golden door.'

Emma Lazarus from her 1883 poem about the Statue of Liberty, *The New Colossus*. The poem was written to help raise money for the Statue pedestal.

The country of origin and the number of in-migrants who passed through Ellis Island between 1892 and 1931

Italy	2,502,310
Russia	1,893,542
Hungary (1905–1931)	859,557
Austria-Hungary (1892–1904)	648,163
Austria (1905–1931)	768,132
Germany	633,148
England	551,969
Ireland	520,904
Sweden	348,036
Greece	245,058
Norway	226,278
Ottoman Empire	212,825
Scotland	191,023
The West Indies	171,774
Poland	153,444
Portugal	120,725
France (including Corsica)	109,687
Denmark	99,414
Romania	79,092
Spain	72,636
Belgium	63,141
Czechoslovakia	48,140
Bulgaria	42,085
Wales	27,113
Yugoslavia	25,017
Finland	7,833
Switzerland	1,103

REFERENCE: AMERICAN PARK NETWORK, 1993

7. In-migrants often do not involve themselves in parent/teacher and school activities, thus not providing that valuable link between home and school. The home/school relationship is widely recognized as an important factor in the academic success of children. Parents who are unable to speak the language of the school, who work long evening hours, or have no tradition of interaction with children to help with their school work, may not create relationships with the school, despite the efforts of the school. Many parents are limited by the absence of proficiency in the host country language or a lack of fluency in that language.

   At other times, there is a cultural 'mismatch', even conflict between home and school. For example, when parents expect particular gender roles appropriate to their religious beliefs, or expect immediate respect for elders, or patterns of dating and heterosexual relationships that are all different from the host nation, and when school teachers have different cultural values, there may be problems for in-migrant children in particular. For example, Muslim families often find Western school culture alien and degenerate. When there are courses on sex education, drugs, Christianity and Women's Studies, the home-school relationship may become one of conflict and culture clash.

   In-migrant children therefore have to navigate between both cultures. Somehow, they have to be loyal both to their parents and to their school, to their heritage culture as well as to the culture of the host nation. If a middle path, however ambiguous and conflicting, is not steered, then there may be isolation either from the parents or from the school. Sometimes such isolation becomes a means of survival and security.

8. Those who are refugees often have experienced traumatic wars and witnessed brutal killing, including family murders and the death of close friends. The family therefore flee from the horrors of the home country. The experience of refugee camps and the waiting for immigration recognition is often a period of stress, anxiety and depression.

   When arriving in a new country, there is often a period of great elation and relief at having escaped finally from persecution, murder and the refugee camps. Sometimes, such refugees feel guilty about those who have been left behind, particularly close-family relatives and friends. They may then develop a phase of depression, realizing that there is little or no chance of returning to the home country. Exile will be permanent. Withdrawal, or sometimes aggression may result from such a realization and sense of desperation.

In-Migrant Adaptation

When in-migration occurs, there are different reactions from people concerned. Reactions vary across different people, different age groups, in different countries and across time. There are those who experience rootlessness or dislocation between two cultures.

For example, with older in-migrants, there is sometimes a passive reaction, isolation, numbness and loss of a rooted identity. In younger in-migrants, there is sometimes an aggressive reaction, due to having lost the identity of home and heritage, and the difficulty of penetrating the new host culture.

For some in-migrants, there may be a sense of rootlessness, confusion of identity, feeling neither one ethnic identity nor the other. This can lead to hopelessness, an ambiguity of cultural existence, or feeling lost in a cultural wilderness. Others adapt eagerly, easily and enthusiastically. Quickly settling, they overcome hurdles with relative confidence and ease.

Reactions among in-migrants include (sometimes in approximately this order):

- a brief honeymoon period when there is great optimism, a pleasure in the new surroundings and much hope for the future.
- a period of frustration, when optimism and hope are dashed and barriers to integration seem overwhelming.

Age and Adaption

Among in-migrants, ethnic identity begins around three to five years of age, and by seven or eight, is well established but continues to develop. In the teenage years, ethnic differences may become increasingly conscious and considered. Overt and covert racial discrimination, racial abuse and harassment, color, religion, dress and dietary differences surface to increasingly focus ethnic awareness, ethnic identity and ethnic inequity as age increases.

Two Case Histories of In-migrants to New York

Vladislav Gadelov – looking towards assimilation

The Gadelov family, the mother, father and two sons, now aged 21 and 14, moved to the United States from Uzbekistan, formerly part of the Union of Soviet Socialist Republics, two years ago. They moved to escape the ethnic violence and other hardships in their native land. The Gadelovs are Russians, and Russian is their native language. Upon arrival in New York they received a government grant of $5000 and $500 per child. A Russian organization also found them a two-bedroom apartment in Forest Hills, Queens, New York. They live in a multilingual and multiethnic community that includes many Russians, Chinese and Hispanics.

Mr Gadelov runs a fruit and vegetable store in Astoria, New York. He is 46 years old and has not succeeded in mastering English. Many of his customers are Russian-speaking and he employs an English-speaking assistant. Even so, his lack of English has made it difficult for him. Mrs Gadelov works as a hairdresser and has learnt enough English to communicate with her clients.

Mikkheal Gadelov is 21. He had finished school before leaving Uzbekistan and now attends Queens College, and hopes to enter medical school. Russian is still his strongest language, although he is coping well with English, and follows his studies entirely in English. He has several Russian friends with whom he speaks Russian.

Vladislav Gadelov is nearly 15. His schooling in Russia was disrupted after the fourth grade when his school burnt down. However, when he reached New York, the standard of his math and other subjects was high enough for him to be placed in the tenth grade. He follows an ESL class and his father has hired a tutor to help him with his studies.

Vladislav feels that he has already forgotten a lot of his Russian. He speaks a mixture of Russian and English to his older brother and mother, and Russian to his father and other monolingual Russian-speaking relatives. Several of his relatives have moved to New York from Russia in recent months, and they visit several times a week. He speaks English with his friends who are mainly Hispanic, and he feels that English is his stronger language. He failed his Russian class in high school because he cut so many classes and maintains that he didn't understand anything. Vladislav is quite happy to speak Russian but he already identifies strongly with American culture. He feels that in another three years he will have forgotten all his Russian, like so many Russian young people he knows who have been in the United States for a few years.

Vladislav's parents are anxious for him to maintain his Russian. His mother teaches him to write in Russian, and he corresponds with an uncle in Russia. His mother also buys newspapers and books in Russian and rents Russian videos. Vladislav also watches Russian films on TV. When he answers his mother in English she continues to speak Russian to him and is disappointed that he has forgotten so much. However she has encouraged him to learn English at school in order to cope in the new country.

The experience of the Gadelov family shows that a desire to maintain the home language and culture must be balanced against the need to adapt and succeed in the new country, An educated family such as the Gadelovs are ambitious for their children and recognize that they need to master English to gain qualifications and compete in the job market.

The children themselves are not necessarily hostile to their heritage culture, particularly if it is one that has a high status in society, such as Russian. However, they are often anxious to be accepted by their peer group and wish to assimilate as quickly as possible. If the in-migrant community is not large, then the pressure to adapt to the culture and language of the new country is greater.

Nani Rodriguez – support from a close-knit community

Nani Rodriguez comes from Santiago in the Dominican republic. Her native language is Spanish. She moved to New York two years ago with her three children, now aged 14, 10 and 7. Her experience illustrates how a strong in-migrant community can help ease the pain and practical difficulties of adaptation to a new culture, language and environment.

When Nani first arrived in America, shortly after the break up of her marriage, she was not eligible for welfare and was not informed of any official support schemes. However, several members of her family live nearby and they gave her a great deal of support, assisting her financially while she was looking for a job and giving her and her children accommodation while she found an apartment.

The local community comprises mainly in-migrants from the Dominican republic. At the beginning Nani was frightened to go out on her own, but as she got to know the neighborhood and people, her confidence increased. She does all her shopping and other errands in the locality so that she can use Spanish. Services such as the dentist and doctor's office are nearby and Spanish-speaking staff are available.

The presence of a strong Spanish-speaking community means that Nani has less motivation to learn English. Even after two years she speaks and understands very little English and is reluctant and embarrassed to practice it. Since she does not leave her neighborhood she can 'get by' using Spanish. Her lack of English meant that she had great difficulty finding a job. She now works as a waitress in an uptown restaurant where the clientele are mainly Spanish speakers. When she serves English-speaking customers they help her by pointing to the food they want on the menu.

Nani's two sons, age 14 and 10, attended a Transitional Bilingual class for a year after their arrival. They have now moved to an ESL class and are doing fairly well. They can speak enough English to carry on a conversation but they codeswitch frequently into Spanish like other local children. Nani's daughter has had learning difficulties, but is doing well in a private school sponsored by her uncles. All the children feel more comfortable speaking Spanish and use Spanish with one another.

Nani and her family still consider themselves to be Dominicans. They feel comfortable within the local community, with its familiar lifestyle, language and culture, but with the advantages of American life. Because most people in the locality are Dominican there are few ethnic tensions.

The experience of Nani and her children shows that the support of a strong, closely knit ethnic minority community can help maintain a minority language and culture, at the expense of assimilation in the majority language and culture. However, in-migrants must find a way to access the majority language and culture, in order to take part in public life and to compete in education and in the job market. Ideally, there should be avenues for them to achieve this without having to lose their minority language and culture.

- a period of anger, when the wrong decisions seem to have been made (internalized anger) or other people are preventing access to jobs, integration, friendships and success (externalized anger). Followed by:
- a period of isolation, when pessimism and gloom are dominant. The in-migrant may become a marginalized person. Or:
- rejection of the 'old' language and culture and wanting total assimilation and identification with a new language and culture. A person may suppress the home country, concentrating solely on being a true citizen of the new country. Or:
- integration which means retaining all that is best from the past and adding on all that is good in the new way of life. Or:
- conforming without conviction to the call for allegiance to a new language and culture.

Adjustment among in-migrants thus takes many different forms: happy integration, uncomfortable assimilation, isolation, rejection and anomie. Bilingualism is greatly affected by the outcomes of adjustment.

Further Reading

DICKER, S. J., 1996, *Languages in America. A Pluralist View*. Clevedon: Multilingual Matters Ltd.

PARRILLO, V. N., 1994, *Strangers to these Shores* (Fourth edition). New York: Macmillan.

PARRILLO, V. N., 1996, *Diversity in America*. Thousand Oaks, CA: Pine Forge Press.

SKUTNABB-KANGAS, T., 1981, *Bilingualism or Not: The Education of Minorities*. Clevedon: Multilingual Matters Ltd.

TAKAKI, R. (ed.) 1994, *From Different Shores: Perspectives on Race and Ethnicity in America* (Second edition). New York: Oxford University Press.

Quotes about In-migrants to the United States

1. From an exhibit on 'The Go-Betweens' at Ellis Island, New York

Immigrant children walked a fine line between two opposing cultures. On one side were their parents and centuries of ethnic traditions; on the other, new friends and public school teachers who frowned on foreign ways. Young enough to learn English quickly and adjust to American customs, immigrant children often served as their parents' translators and envoys to the new world. Jacob A. Riis called them 'go-betweens', shuttling back and forth like emissaries, carrying messages to doctors, landlords, or shopkeepers for their non-English-speaking parents.

2. From Maria Oogjen, a Russian in-migrant in 1923

'We had learned that there were other families who had emigrated and who were living in the vicinity. We formed a social club, where we could gather on Sundays. We rented a hall. We formed a dramatic group, and we presented plays in our own language and some of us were able to dance. So we sort of had our unity, and perpetuation of our culture. We knew we were not complete strangers.'

3. From Stoyan Christowe, a Bulgarian in-migrant written in 1919

'While I am not a whole American, neither am I what I was when I first landed here; that is a Bulgarian. Still retaining some inherited native traits, enough to bar me forever from complete assimilation. I have outwardly and inwardly deviated so much from a Bulgarian that when recently visiting in that country I felt like a foreigner and was so regarded.... In Bulgaria I am not wholly a Bulgarian; in the United States not wholly an American.'

4. From the US Commission on Immigration and Naturalization, 1953

'Our growth as a nation has been achieved, in large measure, through the genius and industry of immigrants of every race and from every quarter of the world. The story of their pursuit of happiness is the saga of America. Their brains and their brawn helped to settle our land, to advance our agriculture, to build our industries, to develop our commerce, to produce new inventions and, in general, to make us the leading nation that we now are.'

A Slovak girl arrives at Ellis Island, New York.

Irish Emigration

Close to half of all the people born in Ireland from 1820 to the present have emigrated. Many emigrated to the United States to try to find fame and fortune, yet the sadness of leaving home, family and friends is present in most accounts of emigration from Ireland, as it is from all other countries. As Jeremiah Murphy, an Irish in-migrant wrote about such sadness in 1925: 'If the tears of Irish emigrants could be collected in one spot, it would form a pool many feet wide and many feet deep and would float a good sized ship.'

Here is one Irish New York emigrant's bitter-sweet letter to his mother back home in Ireland. It is full of the mixed feelings surrounding emigration: of loving and longing, of sadness and sorrow, as well as hopes of future happiness.

Dear Mother, I take up my pen to write you these few lines,
Hoping for to find you well, and close on better times,
I send home a ten pound note to my brothers Mick and Joe,
And that's all I can afford till the champions grow.

So Mother keep the cabin untill I write to you again
Be sure to weed the garden and keep it very clean,
For they are not like the former seed we had some time ago
And we will be all together when the champions grow.

The last letter that you sent me it told a dismal tale,
That thousands they do cross the sea from poor old Grannale.
But Mother when they are landing, I hear their cries of woe,
They were sorry to leave old Ireland where the champions grow.

Now say how is my Father, and my uncles Tom and Ned,
Tell me if you'd rather send over Kate and Fred,
I'll pay their passage to New York when they are ready for to go,
But I advise them to stop in Ireland till the champions grow.

I would like to hear from Maggy Walsh, and Mary Donoghue,
And say how is Tom Malone, and Ellen Slater, too,
Don't forget poor Kate O'Brien, I was courting long ago,
For I intend to make her mine when the champions grow.

Post me a shirt and pair of socks, in the next letter that you send,
For I am digging gold upon the rocks along with many a friend,
And if you could send me a spud when over ground they show,
For I would like to see the champions that now in Ireland grow.

So Mother I am doing fine and hope to see you soon,
And remember when you're coming to fetch a tin can, fork, and spoon,
And don't forget the feather bed I slept in long ago,
But stay at home alanna, till the champions grow.

In Castle Gardens in New York, you first do put your foot,
And you will want a knife and fork the meat and bread to cut,
And don't forget the still upon the hill, where I made the mountain dew,
But hide it in the garden from the peeler's view.

Now to conclude my letter I have no more to say,
I think you would be much better to be in America,
Tell Kate O'Brien to stop her crying, for she's making me a show
And I will send her forty kisses when the champions grow.

Explanatory notes:

1. 'Champions' is a variety of potato – an historically crucial source of food for the Irish.
2. 'Grannale' a term of endearment for Ireland as in 'Mother Ireland'.
3. 'Spud' is a common term for potato.
4. 'Alanna' is a personal term of affection, as in 'love' and 'dear'.
5. 'Still' refers to apparatus for the distillation of whiskey.
6. 'Mountain dew' refers to illicit whiskey made at home.
7. A 'peeler' is a police officer.

REFERENCE: IRISH TOURIST BOARD, 1992, *The Irish Abroad.* Dublin: Irish Tourist Board.

German Settlers in Wisconsin

A German Singing Society in 19th century Wisconsin

Of all the nations of Western Europe, Germany contributed the most to the peopling of the United States. Even in Colonial times, Germans constituted the largest non-English-speaking group of settlers. Between 1820 and 1910, nearly five and a half million Germans crossed the Atlantic in search of a new life. Most of them came to settle in the North Central States, including Wisconsin. By 1900, out of Wisconsin's total population of a little over two million, 34 percent were of German background. Other nationalities included the Welsh and Irish, Swedes, Danes, Poles, Belgians, French, Dutch, Swiss, Finns and Icelanders

As they slowly established themselves in the new country, Germans continued to attract more of their countrymen to Wisconsin through letters and information sent to relatives and friends back home. Thus, much like other ethnic groups, Germans concentrated in settlements according to their home provinces and religious backgrounds. This process has been called 'chain migration': the ties between people in the homeland often determined where the newcomer would settle in the New World.

Until the latter part of the 19th century there was no such country as Germany. Rather, the land consisted of hundreds of small regions which had by 1815 been consolidated into some 30 different states. After reaching the New World, however, a common 'German' ethnic awareness began to evolve among the various German communities. This phenomenon was true of other in-migrant groups as well.

Ethnic institutions helped to create a communal Germanic consciousness in Wisconsin. There was a lively social and community life, centering on numerous musical, athletic, political, philosophical, cultural and religious societies. The tavern or beer hall was a meeting place for the whole community, and families would visit after church to have a glass of beer and a friendly conversation. This rich community life helped to alleviate homesickness and made it much easier for the new in-migrants and their families to settle in American society.

German settlers gave high priority to the maintenance of their native language. They raised money to establish and maintain private German language schools. Up until the middle of the 20th century, most German communities still had their own parochial schools where German was taught. In the words of one in-migrant, 'All would like to have their children read and write in German, and to receive religious instruction in that language'. Germans had a great respect for learning, and many in-migrants had achieved relatively high levels of education in their homeland. Up until the end of the 19th century many German language newspapers were published and preaching in German was very common.

German settlers were loyal to their Protestant denominations, and family life was inextricably bound up with religion. As their pioneer lives became more secure they were able to express their preferences in food, festivals and architecture.

German in-migrants, like other ethnic groups, tended to lose their language and become gradually assimilated into American society over a period of three or four generations. But, because of their numbers in Wisconsin, they developed an awareness of their common German identity at the same time as they became Americanized.

With the advent of the First World War, a wave of anti-German sentiment swept through the United States. Banks changed their names to escape a German title, the teaching of the German language was discontinued in many high schools, and the popularity of German classics declined at the University of Wisconsin. This accelerated the process of assimilation. During the Second World War there was another escalation of anti-German feeling.

The German influence in Wisconsin lives on today, in the names of villages, towns and streets and in the surnames of people. In downtown Milwaukee most supermarkets still stock German sausage, breads and pastries and many people of Germanic descent still speak English with a German lilt. Many German expressions have, until recently, survived in the English of Milwaukee. People 'stay to home'(*'zu hause'*) instead of 'stay at home'; instead of saying 'sit down', people often say 'set yourself down' which is a translation of the request *'setzen Sie sich nieder'* (literally 'perch yourself down there'); 'make my apron shut' is another literal translation from the German instead of the English expression 'tie my apron'.

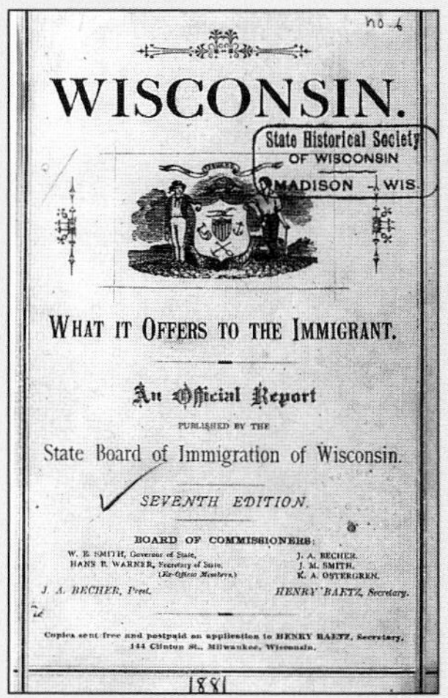

no 6

WISCONSIN.

State Historical Society OF WISCONSIN MADISON WIS.

WHAT IT OFFERS TO THE IMMIGRANT.

An Official Report

PUBLISHED BY THE

State Board of Immigration of Wisconsin.

SEVENTH EDITION.

BOARD OF COMMISSIONERS:

W. E. SMITH, Governor of State,
HANS B. WARNER, Secretary of State,
(Ex-Officio Members.)

J. A. BECHER.
J. M. SMITH.
K. A. OSTERGREN.

J. A. BECHER, Prest.

HENRY BAETZ, Secretary.

Copies sent free and postpaid on application to HENRY BAETZ, Secretary, 144 Clinton St., Milwaukee, Wisconsin.

1881

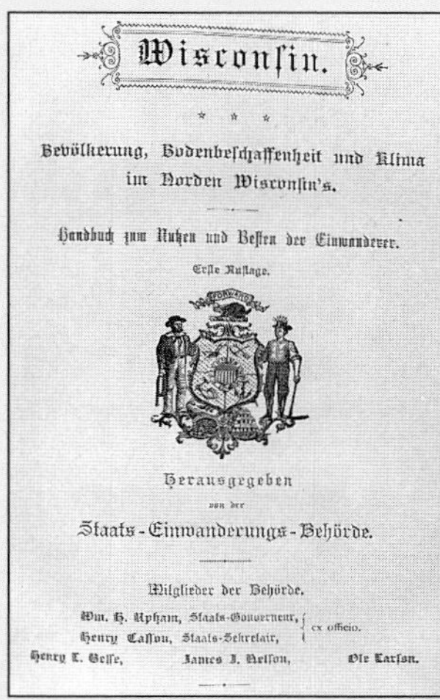

Wisconsin.

Bevölkerung, Bodenbeschaffenheit und Klima im Norden Wisconsin's.

Handbuch zum Nutzen und Besten der Einwanderer.

Erste Auflage.

Herausgegeben von der Staats-Einwanderungs-Behörde.

Mitglieder der Behörde.

Wm. H. Upham, Staats-Gouverneur, Henry Casson, Staats-Sekretair, } ex officio.

Henry C. Gesse, James J. Nelson, Ole Larson.

Title pages, in English and German, of 19th century pamphlets advertising opportunities for in-migrants to Wisconsin.

4: Ethnic Identity

Introduction

It is very contemporary to talk about ethnic groups. The Alsatians and the Aymara, the Mongolians and the Maori, the Somalians and the Sámi, the Walloons and the Welsh, each consider themselves to be distinct ethnic groups. Such ethnic groups seemingly have internally similar sociocultural patterns of behavior. Ethnic groups tend to live in defined communities (e.g. the Pennsylvania Amish), in regions such as Brittany, in nations such as the Welsh, or are distributed across neighboring countries such as Latinos and the Basques. Within an ethnic group, there may be differences in politics, social class, occupation, age and subculture. Yet there will usually be elements that bind the ethnic group together.

Defining ethnicity, ethnic identity or an ethnic group is difficult and problematic. One danger is to use only 'objective' criteria to describe an ethnic group. The dress, hair style, manners, eating habits, religious tradition, architecture, art, literature, music, patterns of trade, commerce and child rearing tend to be used as the observable symbols of an ethnic group. However, such attributes are often superficial and outward signs. They may change across generations, still leaving ethnic identity intact.

Ethnic identity is something that has continuity over time and lives across generations. Ethnicity is a term used to describe a group of people who have some kind of coherence and solidarity based on common origins, a common self-consciousness, and who may be united by shared understandings, meanings to life and experiences. Ethnic identity may be historically deep, collectively felt with a sense of rootedness and togetherness. There may be common ways of understanding ethnic group history, common values and life experiences, common meanings, common ways of organizing and viewing the world.

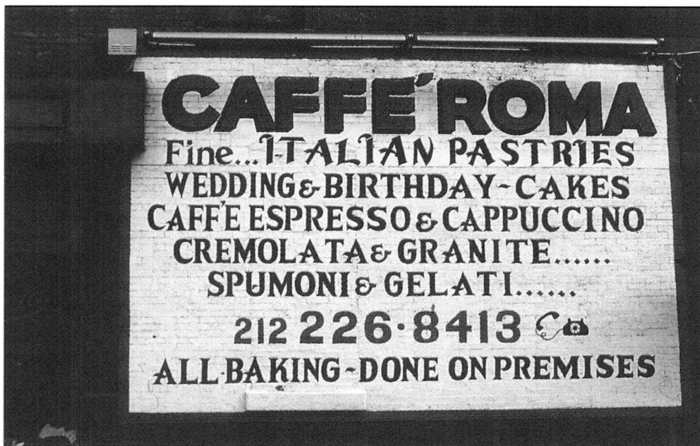

A cake shop in Soho, Little Italy, New York. Traditions, customs and lifestyles can outlast language as markers of ethnic identity.

Such an understanding of the ancestry and history of an ethnic group may be real or it may be mythical. It may be embedded in historical fact or it may be part of a legend. For ethnic identity, fact or fiction does not greatly matter. What is important is that there is a collective belief that roots are historically deep, and that a continuity of tradition has occurred across generations. At times, the emotive may be more potent than the rational in ethnic belonging.

One danger in talking about ethnic groups or ethnic identity is to presume that it refers to ethnic minorities only. It is rare to talk about 'white English-speaking Americans' as an ethnic group, French speakers in France, or English speakers in England as ethnic groups. Rather the term tends to be used for minority groups. For example, in the United States, it is not uncommon for 'white' English-speaking monolinguals to think of ethnicity as referring to Puerto Rican migrants, Cuban exiles or Mexican, Greek and Chinese in-migrants. In England, ethnic groups are often perceived as the Asians in inner-city areas, or the Turks, Greeks, Italians, Chinese or Vietnamese. English-speaking monolinguals in the United States or England are unlikely to think of themselves as an ethnic group. This is dangerous as it is wrong. An ethnic group is not just a minority group; majority groups are also ethnic groups. If the term is reserved only for minority groups, it will take on connotations of disadvantage, servility, of peoples who are despised and rejected.

Having 'ethnic identity' is essentially a self-perception (e.g. seeing oneself as Cuban, Chinese, Latino or Latvian). It depends on people attributing to themselves an identity with a group that collectively expresses historical rootedness and continuity of culture. It is belief that one belongs to an ethnic group. 'Genetic' ancestry need not create ethnic membership. For example, a Tamil may self-categorize, and prefer to be seen as a Malaysian.

It is a presumed common identity with others, common ways of understanding history, common values and understandings that defines ethnicity. Ethnic identity is thus essentially subjective in nature. Ask in-migrants into the United States are they Mexican, American, Mexican-American, Latino or Aztec? Or ask English in-migrants to Wales whether they are Welsh, English, British, or European? The answers from different people will reveal varied self-perceived ethnic identities – and increasingly multiple identities.

The labels for such groups tend to change over time as old labels take on negative connotations. Ethnic labels such as Coloreds, Blacks, African Americans and Native Americans are variously used, applauded, disputed and rejected. Other ethnic labels tend to be relatively less temporary (e.g. the Welsh, Bretons, Jews) although sometimes there are the same associations of inequality, discrimination and relative material deprivation.

However, the danger of the term ethnicity or ethnic group is that it becomes a 'deviance' concept. Ethnic groups in this normative sense refers to those who are deviant from what is normal, who are not part of the majority and who are not accepted as the norm in society. The power of the term 'ethnicity' is that it recognizes a variety of groups in society, and especially highlights those who, as an entity, feel relatively deprived, lack power, are of low status and are less valued.

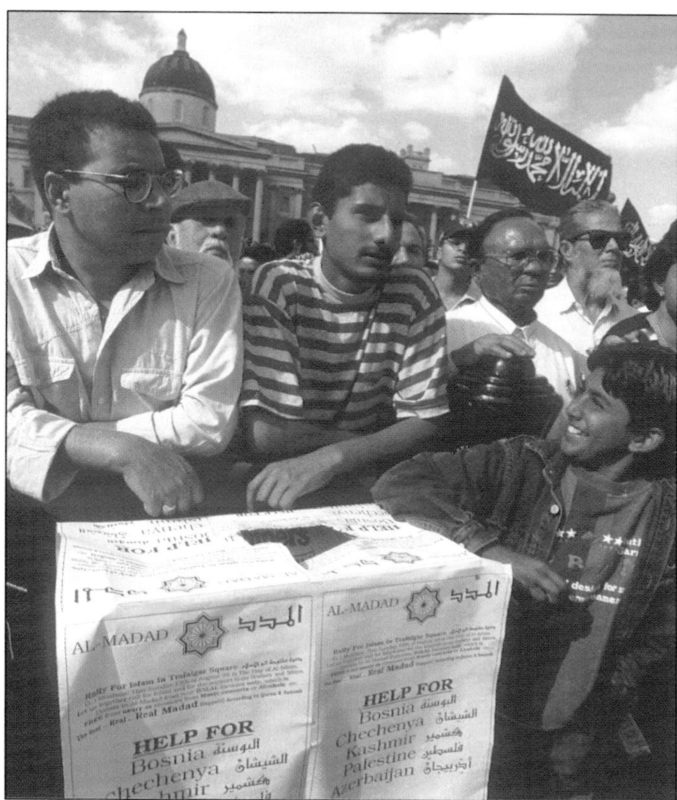

A Muslim rally in Trafalgar Square, London. Ethnic identity can be based on a shared language, history and religion and can transcend the borders of countries.

Language Boundaries

One important component of ethnicity is the boundaries that exist between ethnic groups (Barth, 1969). As the culture of an ethnic group evolves over time, boundaries (that may also change) are important in separating different ethnic identities. Boundaries (e.g. speaking a particular language) tend to be more continuous and long-standing, whereas cultures within an ethnic group may be more changeable. At the same time, it is the culture or cultures of the ethnic group that are often used to establish boundaries.

Boundaries create contrasts and sometimes conflicts between different ethnic identities. When boundaries (e.g. languages) between ethnic groups are endangered, heightened awareness of ethnic identity may occur. Sometimes unity from within is enhanced by opposition from without. Also, unity from within may sometimes elicit opposition from without.

Boundaries are created from a continuing sense of 'groupness', from a sense of group 'oneness'. Boundaries, in turn, become important in establishing ethnic identity. Boundaries are created from boundary 'markers'. Language is an important marker, but not the only marker. Language is not an essential marker for boundary-making as other markers (e.g. culture, religion) are available. However, there are also boundaries within ethnic groups. Different communities and regions of the same ethnic group may have boundaries, different social classes existing within the ethnic group, varied networks of interaction. Social and cultural boundaries may exist within the ethnic group and not just between ethnic groups.

A most important boundary for many ethnic groups is language. Language symbolically and behaviorally may establish a boundary between neighboring ethnic groups. Speaking Walloon in Belgium or Welsh in Wales establishes boundaries between such groups and the majority language speakers in those countries. Through language, ethnic identity may be expressed, enacted and symbolized.

Consider an example. Surveys of attitude to the Irish language show that Irish is seen as a symbol of ethnic or national identity. The population in Ireland tend to believe that the Irish language is necessary to their ethnic and cultural integrity. It is a symbol of a separate culture, heritage and identity. However, Irish is used daily

Fishman's Dimensions of Ethnicity

According to Fishman (1977), there are three dimensions in the derivation of ethnicity.

The first dimension is paternity. Ethnicity is said to derive from parents, the intergenerational experience that is handed to children, reflecting the values and traditions, beliefs and ideas of an ethnic group. Fishman regards paternity as the central cord around which other notions of ethnicity are tied. Paternity is the central experience where the essence of ethnicity, sensitivities and sensibilities are handed down from generation to generation.

The second dimension is patrimony. Ethnicity is not just a state of being as paternity implies, but also a set of behaviors or acts. Patterns of child rearing, music, art, religion, dress, sexual behavior, skills and trades are each part of patrimony.

The third dimension is phenomenology. This is the subjective interpretation or meaning that people attach to their paternity. This is where people interpret and reinterpret their perceived ethnic legacy, and includes the subjective attitudes of people towards their membership of a particular ethnic group.

REFERENCE: FISHMAN, 1977

Core Values

Smolicz (1981, 1984a) has argued that ethnic groups differ in the extent to which they emphasize the native tongue as part of their core values. Some Irish nationalists (in Northern Ireland, for example) may not be able to speak Irish, but nevertheless regard themselves as thoroughly Irish in identity. Being Irish for such a person concerns values, beliefs, meanings, understandings and forms of interaction that create an Irish identity, but not Irish language usage. There are many Jews (e.g. in the United States) who do not speak Hebrew or Yiddish, yet have a strongly developed sense of Jewish identity.

Other ethnic groups have emphasized language as being an integral and pivotal part of ethnic identity. For such groups, the ethnic language is the essential carrier of the ethnic culture. Smolicz (1984a) suggests that Polish and Greek inmigrants, and the French in Quebec, have relied on their heritage language as a defense mechanism against assimilation. Similarly the Chinese often take pride in their languages as symbols of ethnic identity. For example, Mandarin speakers often regard their language as civilizing, linked with the importance of retaining strong family bonds and integral to reproducing the 'heritage of the blood' (Smolicz, 1992b). Language for such groups becomes a marker of a boundary between, for example, an in-migrant group who wish to retain their ethnicity and the ruling majority.

When in-migrant groups (for whom language is an integral part of their ethnic identity) lose their language, the probability of losing their separate identity is greatly increased. Loss of the heritage language often means fragmentation of cultural life and eventual assimilation. Religious traditions (e.g. Roman Catholicism), preservation of folk-lore and cultural traditions (e.g. folk dancing, music) and in-group marriage may act as boundaries to slow down assimilation if the heritage language dies. However, when language is part of core values and the heritage language is lost, there may be difficulty in preserving a distinct and vibrant ethnic identity. 'The survival of such language-centered cultures depends largely on the preservation of the home language. In these circumstances, the language is more than a medium of communication, it is a symbol of ethnic identity and a defining value which is a prerequisite for "authentic" group membership' (Chiro & Smolicz, 1993, page 313).

An example of language being part of core values is that of the many Polish speakers in Australia. The Polish language is bound up with a rootedness in political independence, a sense of historical continuity and pride in a Polish cultural and literary legacy. Therefore, the Polish language in Australia has been more resistant than most to English language assimilation (see page 158). The essential nature of the Polish language, as a core part of ethnic identity, is revealed in the table below. The table is based on research by Smolicz and Secombe (1987, page 139) which investigated 73 young Polish-Australians' assessment of those aspects of culture that would aid the survival of a Polish tradition in Australia. The rank order puts 'Speaking Polish' in first place.

Rank Order	Aspect of Culture	Percentage Saying 'Vitally important'
1.	Speaking Polish	69
2.	Close Family Ties	46
3.	Reading and Writing Polish	45
4.	Love of Homeland	43
5.	Communication with Family and other Poles	41
6.	Having Polish Friends	41
7.	Polish Customs and Celebrations	40
8.	Contribution of Polish Culture	37
9.	Polish History	34
10.	Polish Songs and Music	30
11.	Polish Contribution to Multicultural Australia	28
12.	Church Liturgy	28
13.	Polish Literature	28
14.	Polish Dances	26
15.	Polish Arts and Crafts	23
16.	Geography of Poland	22
17.	Helping Fellow Ethnics	20
18.	Religious Doctrine	19
19.	Respect for Aged	17
20.	Sharing Language with other Groups	16
21.	Intra-group Marriage	14
22.	Religious Rules	12

by only a relatively small minority of Irish people. This highlights an important distinction between language as a communication device (e.g. a living use of a minority language) and language as a symbol.

Yet language is not essential to ethnic identity. For example, less than two percent of the Scottish nation speak Gaelic. English is the dominant language. Yet the Scottish people hold on fiercely to their Scottish identity. Speaking English with a Scottish accent is one symbol of that ethnic identity. Thus Scottish ethnicity can be about speaking Gaelic, but there are other markers of the boundary (e.g. accent, sporting identity, shared history and traditions) to create a Scottish ethnic identity.

For many ethnic groups, their heritage language is much more than a symbol of ethnic heritage. The minority language best expresses the heritage culture and its vocabulary, idioms, and metaphors are the ones that best explain and transmit heritage culture. The language and the culture of an ethnic group are intertwined, as are heart and mind in a flourishing body. The taste and fla-

Puerto Rico: Language as a Marker of Identity

Language in Puerto Rico is a history of conquest and controversy, change and challenge. Indigenous languages were spoken on the island before the Spanish conquest of 1493. After that, the Spanish community remained dominant, politically and numerically, until the United States gained sovereignty over the island in 1898. That initiated a long debate over the relative value and validity of Spanish and English in government and education. Language became a battleground – not in terms of a code – but as a symbol of power and dominance, a marker of political inclination and national identity. Instead of just being a tool of communication, language in Puerto Rico became an emblem of belonging, solidarity, groupness and affiliation.

Up to 1898, the residents of Puerto Rico were subjects of the Spanish crown but had developed a distinct identity as Puerto Ricans and not Spaniards. Following the Spanish-American War, the United States assumed control of Puerto Rico and through military governors, sought to Americanize Puerto Ricans. Assimilation into the American culture, customs and civilization meant the infusion of the English language. The means of anglicization was the installing of English as the principal language of the school system for over 50 years. Teachers and textbooks were imported from the United States to disseminate the English language and the American experience.

The exclusive use of English in the classroom, and the rejection of Spanish, caused opposition and resistance. The issue was soon allied to the demand for self-rule. Supporting English was a symbol of agreeing to the rule of the United States over Puerto Rico. Resisting English was a marker of a political pressure for self-government. Loyalty to the US meant supporting English. Loyalty to home rule meant supporting Spanish. Language became a badge of allegiance, an emblem of association. Those who favored Spanish were portrayed as separatists and disloyal to the United States. Those who favored English were regarded as assimilationists and imperialists, disloyal to Puerto Rico. Three events will illustrate the conflict.

- In 1913, the Puerto Rican Teachers' Association influenced the elected House of Delegates to make Spanish the medium of instruction to the eighth grade. The US-controlled Executive Council vetoed the decision.
- In 1925, an expert commission from Columbia University found the English program led to underachievement. They recommended that English classes should begin in the fourth grade. The Commissioner of Education rejected the advice. Apart from Spanish being the language of the home and the language reflecting the island's self-identity, Spanish was also the medium through which Puerto Rican children would learn more efficiently and effectively. Learning through English was like taking a long and difficult journey on an imported bike when a home-built, powerful motorbike was more easily available. Success in school was being hindered by children having to work through an undeveloped language.
- President Franklin Roosevelt wrote in 1937: 'It is an indispensable part of American policy that the coming generation of American citizens in Puerto Rico grow up with complete facility in the English tongue. It is the language of our Nation. Only through the acquisition of this language will Puerto Rican Americans secure a better understanding of American ideals and principles'.

In 1947, the island was given a measure of self-government. In 1949 Spanish was declared as the language medium of the school. The power for self-rule meant power to control the language of the classroom. Continued United States citizenship for Puerto Ricans, economic ties with the United States, and the ultimate sovereignty of the United States has maintained a lively language debate that continues (see Morris, 1996).

REFERENCE: MORRIS, 1996

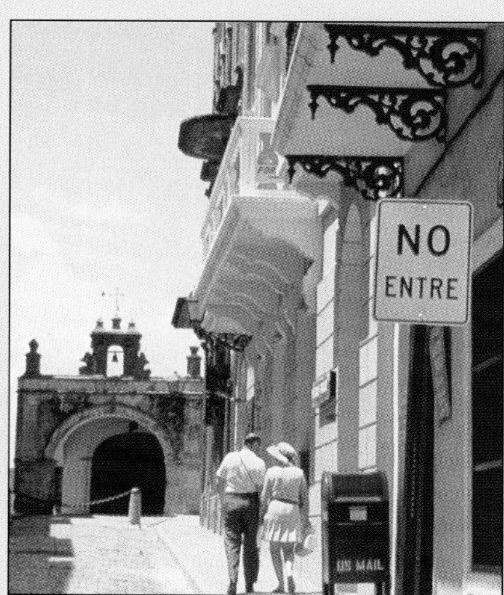

A street in San Juan, Puerto Rico, with signs in English and Spanish

A Ceilidh (evening of traditional Highland music and dance) on Mull in Scotland. The Gaelic language is spoken by just over one percent of the Scottish population, but history, traditions and music help to preserve Scottish ethnic identity.

vor of a culture are given through its language; its memories and traditions are most fully stored and expressed in its language.

Recently, ethnic identity has been related to ethnic conflict, but it is important to establish that the two are not directly related, especially when considering ethnic cleansing in Eastern Europe in the 1990s. Many ethnic groups live harmoniously with their neighbors throughout all continents of the world. In large cities, within regions and countries, on borders between countries, the majority of ethnic groups live peacefully and cooperatively. At the same time, ethnic identity may become part of religious, economic or political conflict. Just as water is essential for life, yet can cause drowning; just as electricity gives light yet can kill, so ethnic identity gives cultural light and life, yet may be linked to intergroup conflict, even killing.

There is no essential or direct link between ethnicity and conflict. It is only the extreme that results in conflict. Just as the extreme of religion is bigotry, of sexuality is sexism, of democracy is anarchy, so the extreme of ethnicity can be ethnocentrism and racism. Generally the extreme case (ethnocentrism) is rare, ethnic tolerance is more usual. The extremes win the glare of publicity; tolerance and civility are more regular but much less newsworthy.

Ethnicity and Racism

While ethnic identity celebrates the collective heritage of a sociocultural group, racism concentrates on the difference between ethnic groups. Implied in ethnicity is that all ethnic groups have an equal right to maintain their heritage; that cultural pluralism is valuable to individuals and groups. Racism makes judgments about what is better or worse, acceptable or unacceptable, even what should be obliterated. Inside racism, as different from ethnicity, is the concept of dominance and superiority of one ethnic group over another. Racism requires a belief in superior races, of the superiority of color of skin, ethnic origin or culture.

While ethnic groups may be more or less ethnocentric, racism occurs when there is active behavioral or psychological aggression against another ethnic group. While there is sometimes a thin line separating vigorous ethnic identity and racism, (and ethnicity and ethnocentrism), at its best, ethnicity celebrates a similarity among people that does not spill over into conflict. While there is often tension, dispute, political conflict, argument and debate (particularly between a minority ethnic group and a majority ethnic group), warfare is not inevitable. While polemic and protest may be an essential part of an ethnic group's life, only in relatively rare circumstances does this change into armed aggression.

The ethnicity of an individual will vary across time and with changing contexts. One of the increasing tendencies of the 20th century is for people to take on multiple loyalties, multiple identities and group memberships. It has become increasingly possible to be Welsh, British and European, or Cuban-American rather than Cuban or American.

Bilingualism is one enabler of multiple identities. As a modern world economy, global co-operation, internationalism and the Information Society have grown, the boundaries between ethnic groups may weaken. Paradoxically, such international changes appear to have encouraged multiple membership of groups.

There is no certainty that internationalism will make ethnic group identities wither and fade. Instead, it may push inhabitants of the global village to discover who they are and from whence they came. As the world becomes smaller and differences melt, the need for rootedness and security within a local identity may grow.

Further Reading

EDWARDS, J. R., 1985, *Language, Society and Identity*. Oxford: Basil Blackwell.

FISHMAN, J. A., 1997, *Language and Ethnicity: The View from Within*. In F. COULMAS (ed.), *The Handbook of Sociolinguistics*. Oxford: Blackwell.

TABOURET-KELLER, A., 1997, Language and Identity. In F. COULMAS (ed.), *The Handbook of Sociolinguistics*. Oxford: Blackwell.

Quotes from Paul Singh Ghuman about Asian Children living in Canada and the United Kingdom

1. 'Most youngsters support the idea of mixing with indigenous whites. They reject the "ghetto mentality" of sticking to their own respective ethnic group. But, a lot depends upon the attitudes of the indigenous white group (the dominant group – which in both countries is Celtic/Anglo-Saxon). If the majority opinions are racist and these are expressed both covertly and overtly, then the minority ethnic groups might (and do) revert to the security of their own enclave'. (page 71)

2. 'We teach girls to be independent and critical thinkers, but at home they are taught the virtues of collective responsibility and unquestioning respect to the elders in the family ... naturally this creates tension in the youngsters'. (page 86, a quote from a deputy headteacher of a school)

3. 'Asian languages are very much tied to the religious consciousness and are also an important tool for social intercourse and solidarity. For instance, Panjabi written in Gurmukhi script, is the language of *"Granth Sahib"* – the religious text of the Sikhs. Without the written knowledge of Panjabi, children would be unable to read the original text'. (page 105)

4. 'From my observations both in Canada and the UK, it seems that the weekend community schools are not very popular with the youngsters and are poorly attended. There are many reasons for this; the main one being the lack of proper facilities and resources. Schools are held in rundown, noisy, make-shift buildings and books and other illustrative materials are imported from India/China and these do not capture the hearts and minds of children. The related problem is that the youngsters do not perceive their community's language as of a high status that deserves their attention. It is not included in the school programs and its use is limited. Therefore, the schools should consider very seriously including the teaching of community languages in their curricula. Such language programs should be open to all students and "language" qualifications thereby gained in secondary/high schools should be recognized by the universities and other professional bodies. Otherwise there is a dark future in store for ethnic languages'. (page 107)

5. 'The settlement patterns of Asians, both in Britain and Canada, have been along the lines of religious, regional and caste affiliations. As a result, there have emerged "ethnic enclaves". Communities have re-created the primary institutions of their respective home societies. The foremost of such institutions are *Biraderi* (the extended family network), places of worship and community organizations which are often aligned to Mosques/Gurdwaras/temples. Their reception in Britain was mixed; they were welcomed by industry where there was a shortage of manpower, but met a cool, if not hostile, reception from neighbours and indigenous communities. Most first-generation migrants, both in Canada and Britain, were content to confine themselves to their own communities and had little interaction with the indigenous white people. Their aims were modest: to work hard and save as much as possible for the folks back home. Later on, most of them used their savings to buy a house and/or sponsor a relative to join them in their new country of domicile. Most retained their religion and family loyalties, spoke their mother tongue, kept their food habits and maintained their original social customs and practices'. (page 136)

6. 'The young people favour a degree of acculturation: they support inter-ethnic friendship, celebrate Christmas, they like European-style clothes, watch English films and listen to Western pop music. However, there was overwhelming support for the maintenance of the mother tongue, respect for parents, retention of family names and for aspects of family religion – suggesting adherence to home cultural values. The girls showed a higher degree of acculturation than boys'. (page 137)

REFERENCE: GHUMAN, 1994

5: Diglossia

ntroduction

'he term 'bilingualism' is typically used to describe the wo languages of an individual. When the focus changes o two language varieties co-existing in society, the term ften used is 'diglossia' (Ferguson, 1959; Fishman, 972, 1980a). In practice, a language community is nlikely to use both language varieties for the same puroses. A language community is more likely to use one ariety in certain situations and for certain functions, the other variety in different circumstances and for different functions. For example, a language community may use its heritage, minority language in the home, for religious purposes and in social activity. The majority language may be used at work, in education and in the mass media.

Ferguson (1959) first defined diglossia as the use of two very divergent varieties of the same language for different societal functions. Most languages have spoken, informal varieties which are used in different contexts from written, formal varieties. In a diglossic situation as defined by Ferguson (1959), the two varieties are markedly different and their functions tend to be separated. Ferguson (1959) distinguished between a high language variety (called H) and a low variety (called L). The low variety is generally used in informal, oral contexts and the high variety in formal, often written contexts. Well-known examples of diglossic situations exist in Arabic-speaking countries and the German-speaking part of Switzerland. Fishman (1972, 1980a) extended the idea of diglossia to two languages existing side by side within a geographical area. In both situations, different languages or varieties may be used for different purposes as the table below illustrates.

Context	Majority Language (H)	Minority Language (L)
1. The home and family		✔
2. Schooling	✔	
3. Mass media	✔	
4. Business and commerce	✔	
5. Social & cultural activity in the community		✔
6. Correspondence with relatives and friends		✔
7. Correspondence with government departments		✔
8. Religious activity	✔	

The example shows that languages may be used in different situations, with the low variety or minority language more likely to be used in informal, personal situations; the high or majority language being more used in formal, official communication contexts.

The table suggests that the different language contexts usually make one language more prestigious than the other. Many minority language situations are diglossic. Because the majority language is used for prestigious functions, it may sometimes be perceived as being superior, more elegant and more educative and may be seen as the door to both educational and economic success. On the other hand, the low variety is often restricted to interpersonal, domestic functions, and may be perceived as being inferior, inadequate and low-class.

The concept of diglossia can be usefully examined alongside the concept of bilingualism. Bilingualism refers to an individual's ability to use more than one language. Diglossia refers to society's use of two language varieties. Fishman (1980a) combines the terms 'bilingualism' and 'diglossia' to portray four language situations where bilingualism and diglossia may exist with or without each other. The following table, based on Fishman (1980a) portrays this relationship between bilingualism and diglossia.

	Diglossia	
Individual Bilingualism	1. Diglossia and Bilingualism together	3. Bilingualism without Diglossia
	2. Diglossia without Bilingualism	4. Neither Bilingualism nor Diglossia

The first situation is a language community containing both individual bilingualism and diglossia. In such a community, almost everyone will be able to use both the high language variety and the low language variety. The high language is used for one set of functions, the low language for a separate set of functions. Fishman (1972) cites Paraguay as the example. Guaraní and Spanish are spoken by almost all inhabitants. The former is the Low variety, Spanish is the High variety.

The second situation outlined by Fishman (1972, 1980a) is diglossia without bilingualism. In such a context there will be two languages within a particular geographical area. One group of inhabitants will speak one language, another group a different language. In some cases, the ruling power group will typically speak the high variety with the larger less powerful group speaking only the low variety. For example, in a colonial situation, English or French was spoken by the ruling elite, with the indigenous language spoken by the masses. Within this category, Fishman also includes examples of politically or governmentally arranged diglossia. One example is Switzerland where, to a large extent, different language groups (German, French, Italian, Romansch) are located in different areas. The official status of the different languages may be theoretically equal. Fluent bilingual speakers of both languages may be the exception rather than the rule (Andres, 1990).

The third situation is bilingualism without diglossia. In this situation, most people will be bilingual and will not restrict one language variety to a specific set of purposes. Either language may be used for almost any function. Fishman (1972, 1980a) regards such communities as unstable and in a state of change. Where bilingualism exists without diglossia, the expectation may be that one language will, in the future, become more powerful and have more purposes. The other language may decrease in its functions and decay in status and usage.

The fourth situation is where there is neither bilingualism nor diglossia. In some societies where there are few

Language Boundaries: The Territorial and Personality Principles

The Pennsylvania Amish at worship

The territorial principle can be defined as the granting of a measure of recognition, rights or official status to a language based on its use in a certain geographical area. Where the territorial principle exists (e.g. in Wales, Switzerland), geography is used to define language boundaries, with inhabitants of a region classified as a distinct language group. The argument for the survival, maintenance and spread of the language is based on its historic existence within a defined boundary. As the indigenous language of the region, language rights may be enshrined in law. Welsh speakers have certain language rights in Wales (e.g. using Welsh in courts of law) but not when they cross the border into England. The territorial principle benefits the Welsh but has unfortunate implications for other 'in-migrant' language minorities in Britain. The limitations of the territorial principle are revealed in a set of questions. If Welsh is the language of Wales, is English to be seen as the only rightful language of England? Do languages belong to regions and territories and not to the speakers of those languages or to groups of those languages wherever they may be found? Do Panjabi, Urdu, Bengali, Hindi, Greek and Turkish only belong in the home country? Do such languages have no home in Britain? Do the users of sign languages have any rights, since those languages cannot be connected with any geographical community?

Under the territorial principle, should language minorities either speak the majority, official language of the territory or return to the home country? The territorial principle thus has benefits for some (e.g. the Welsh). For others, it is unacceptable and unfair. In Europe, there are many indigenous (or autochthonous) languages that are seeking preservation status in the European Community. But what status is accorded the in-migrant languages of Europe (e.g. the various Asian languages such as Panjabi, Urdu, Bengali, Hindi and Gujarati)?

The term 'personality principle' is particularly helpful to describe minority groups who cannot claim a language territory principle. The 'personality' of each language is the sum of its more or less distinctive attributes (e.g. as revealed in its uses and functions, communication styles and literature, and also the customs and rituals, culture and meanings enshrined in it). One example of the use of the personality principle is the Pennsylvania Amish who decided to ensure the continuity of their heritage language by reserving an exclusive place for that language at home, and reserving English for school and for contacts with the outside secular world. One language is reserved for particular societal functions; another language for distinctly separate functions. This compartmentalization exists in a relatively stable arrangement. Such separation of identity for each language exists within the psyche of each group member. There cannot be diglossia without bilingualism if diglossia is based on the personality principle. In contrast, there can be diglossia without bilingualism where the territorial principle exists.

The personality principle can be an attribute of those claiming territorial principle. However, the personality principle is an especially supportive concept for in-migrant groups (e.g. Asian languages in Europe and the many in-migrant language minorities in Canada and the US). Those who cannot claim territorial rights for their language can assert that their heritage language has a 'personality' and is used for particular functions that need safeguarding and separating from uses of the majority language. Such language groups can argue that their right to use their minority language is fully portable across national borders and boundaries because it has its own 'personality' of uses.

Different to the territorial and personality principles when applied to language rights is the idea of the 'asymmetrical principle' or 'asymmetrical bilingualism' (Reid, 1993). Such principles (territorial, personality, asymmetrical) are one basis for a language minority claiming group rights to preserve and strengthen its language.

As conceived by its Canadian advocates (e.g. in Quebec), the asymmetrical principle gives full rights to minority language speakers and fewer rights to the speakers of a majority language. For example, in Quebec, the application of the asymmetrical principle might give French speakers certain preferential treatment in language rights over English speakers. Such preferential treatment might debatably be justified by the need to safeguard the French language. This is a form of positive discrimination, seeking to discriminate in favor of those who are usually discriminated against. Some of the functions of a minority language may be legislated for, so as to preserve that language in a proactive manner.

Diglossia and Civil Strife

There are countries with mainly one majority language among the population (e.g. Iceland) and countries where there are a wide variety of languages (e.g. India). These two situations are referred to as linguistic homogeneity and linguistic heterogeneity. Different questions can be asked about linguistically homogeneous and linguistically heterogeneous countries. We can ask, for example, what factors make for greater or lesser linguistic homogeneity and heterogeneity in a country? In countries where there are many languages, what effect do such languages have on politics, economics, social and religious functioning?

While the relationships are often very complex, Joshua Fishman (1989) provides an analysis of these kinds of questions. For example, he found that linguistically homogeneous countries (where there is one majority language) tend to have Christianity as the main religion, with a religiously and racially homogeneous people and high population density. Such countries also tend to be westernized, modernized, democratized and economically well developed. However, no cause-effect relationships can be implied from this analysis. A solitary language can not be regarded as a cause or an outcome of such factors.

Fishman (1989) also examines whether linguistic heterogeneity and linguistic homogeneity are related in any way to civil strife. Joshua Fishman concluded as follows: 'The widespread journalistic and popular political wisdom that linguistic heterogeneity *per se* is necessarily conducive to civil strife has been shown, by our analysis, to be more myth than reality' (page 622). The factors which do contribute independently to civil strife are not minority languages or diglossia but factors such as authoritarianism, material deprivation and modernization. Thus it was possible to conclude from an international analysis that the presence of one or more minority languages within a country is not a factor in civil disorder.

REFERENCE: FISHMAN, 1989

Triglossia in Africa

An example of triglossia is where indigenous, national and international languages co-exist (e.g. in areas of Africa). The example is loosely based around that given by Bloor and Tamrat (1996) for Ethiopia. Triglossia occurs where three languages exist in a relatively stable relationship, with different usage in varying domains.

Language Domain	Mother Tongue	National Language	International Language
1 INFORMAL			
Home	✔		
Neighbors	✔		
Work place	✔		
2 CULTURAL			
Religion	✔		
Literacy		✔	✔
3 COMMERCIAL			
Large Businesses		✔	✔
Small Businesses	✔		✔
Tourism			✔
4 EDUCATIONAL			
Primary school medium	✔	✔	
Secondary School medium		✔	✔
University medium			✔
Adult education medium	✔		

Language Domain	Mother Tongue	National Language	International Language
5 POLITICAL			
Parliament		✔	
Public meetings	✔		
6 ADMINISTRATION			
Village	✔		
District/Regional	✔		
National		✔	
7 JUDICIARY			
Primary court		✔	
District court		✔	
Higher/Appeal Court		✔	
8 MASS MEDIA			
Radio		✔	
Television		✔	✔
Daily Papers		✔	✔
9 INTERNATIONAL			
Diplomacy			✔
Trade			✔
Cultural exchange			✔
Information exchange			✔
Science and technology	✔		

3russels, the capital of Belgium. Belgium is an example of a country where liglossia exists without bilingualism. The country has three official lanquages, French, Flemish and German, but they predominate in different reas of the country and there are relatively low levels of bilingualism.

ndigenous language minorities and little recent in-migraion, monolingualism is the norm (e.g. Norway, Portugal). Another example is where a linguistically diverse society has been changed over time to a relativey monolingual society and monolingualism in the majorty language has been imposed by governmental policies. New Zealand is one example of a relatively monolingual, English-speaking country, where the indigenous Maori anguage has been seriously weakened by governmental policies. Cuba and the Dominican Republic are also nonolingual countries where the indigenous languages were eradicated and where there is little in-migration. A different example would be a small speech community using its minority language for all functions and insisting on having no relationship with the neighboring majority anguage.

Fishman (1980a) argues that diglossia with and without bilingualism tends to provide a relatively stable, enduring anguage arrangement. Yet such stability may be increasngly rare. The modern world is typified by increasing ease of travel and communication, increased social and vocational mobility, mass literacy and better educational opportunities, a more global economy and more urbanzation. In such a situation the high prestige language almost inevitably gains ground at the expense of the low variety. In the modern world, language shift tends to be nore typical than language stability.

Also, some contemporary language minorities do not want a diglossic situation. For a minority language to survive in the modern world, they argue, it must be equipped to take over the more prestigious functions traditionally occupied by the majority language. It must become the language of such fields as education, science, technology, politics, administration and computers. Only thus, they argue, will it gain prestige and the respect of its speakers, and survive in the modern technological, urban world.

The problem with diglossia and the idea of language domains is that the reasons for the distribution of two or more languages across domains are left unexplained. A full understanding of a diglossic situation requires an historical analysis of socioeconomic, sociocultural development within geographical areas. That is, by itself diglossia and the concept of the domains are in danger of providing descriptions rather than explanations; a static picture rather than an evolutionary explanation.

Further Reading

FERGUSON, C., 1959, Diglossia. *Word*, 15, 325-340.

FISHMAN, J. A., 1972, *The Sociology of Language*. Rowley, MA: Newbury House.

FISHMAN, J. A., 1980, Bilingualism and Biculturalism as Individual and as Societal Phenomena. *Journal of Multilingual and Multicultural Development*, 1, 3-15.

SCHIFFMAN, H. F., 1997, Diglossia as a Sociolinguistic Situation. In F. COULMAS (ed.), *The Handbook of Sociolinguistics*. Oxford: Blackwell.

A school for learning to read the Qur'ān at Nouakchot in Mauritania. The majority of the population of the country speak Hassinya Arabic as their first language. Modern Standard Arabic, the official language of the country, which is very different from the colloquial spoken variety, is used in formal and official contexts. Classical Arabic is studied as the language of the Qur'ān.

6: Languages of Wider Communication

In contexts where speakers of many different languages come into contact, one or more languages may serve as a medium of communication between them. For instance, in many African or Asian countries, where numerous different local languages may be spoken, one or more languages may have evolved as languages of wider communication, at a regional or national level. In the Central African Republic, about 50 indigenous languages are spoken, but about 90 percent of the population also speak Sango, an African language, either as a first or second language. Sango has become an official language alongside French and is increasingly used in education. This pattern has been replicated in other African countries where the former colonial language has been retained as the official language, but where it is not widely spoken among the general population.

In such cases, an indigenous language or languages such as Sango, which is widely spoken either as a first or second language, may gain official recognition. In Nigeria, where over 400 languages or language varieties are spoken, three indigenous languages of wider communication, Yoruba, Igbo and Hausa have (since 1979) gained a measure of official status. Governments may actively promote certain languages as languages of wider communication. In Ethiopia, where between 70 and 100 language varieties are spoken, Amharic, the official language, is spoken as a first or second language by about 70 percent of the population and is taught as a second language to all children in primary education.

Often languages of wider communication are restricted in function because they are only used for trade or other limited purposes. Pidgin languages may evolve for communication between different language groups. These pidgin languages start out as restricted codes for intergroup communication. However, as they become increasingly used, especially in urban areas, they may become expanded and elaborated and eventually become the first language of children of mixed marriages. (See Pidgins and Creoles page 142.) In Nigeria, Nigerian Pidgin English is increasingly spoken in the south and in northern cities. In Papua New Guinea, where about 700 indigenous languages are spoken, Tok Pisin, an English-based pidgin, evolved as a restricted code for intergroup communication and is now spoken by over one and a half million people, about half the population, as a first or second language. In the Republic of Chad, in North Africa, about half the population speak Arabic as a firs or second language, and a form of pidginized Arabic als exists as a trade language.

A language of wider communication is sometimes calle a lingua franca. This term originally applied to a mixe language, based on Italian and Occitan, used for militar purposes and trade in the Mediterranean in the Middl Ages. Lingua francas, or languages of wider communica tion, may be used across national borders. Swahil (Kiswahili) is the official language of Tanzania, and i spoken as a first or second language by 90 percent of th population but is also widely used in other East Africa countries. The Textbox shows how Swahili has evolve as a language of wider communication across Easter Africa.

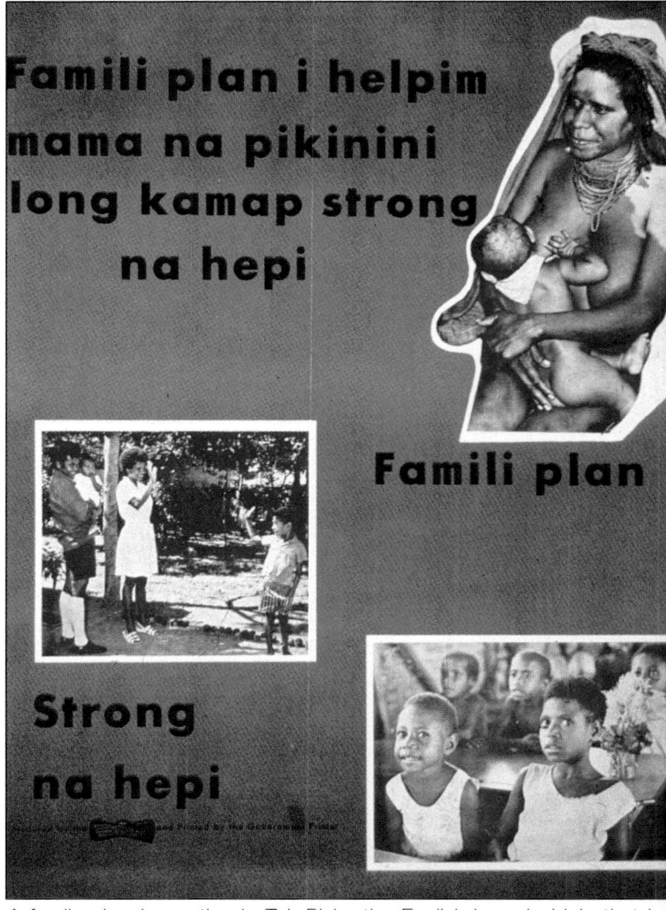

A family planning notice in Tok Pisin, the English-based pidgin that ha become an official language and lingua franca in Papua New Guinea.

A rural health worker in Malawi. Thirteen indigenous languages are spoken in Malawi. Chichewa is the native language of half the population and is widely used as a language of wider communication by native speakers of other languages.

Another term associated with the concept of a language of wider communication is *'koine'*. This term comes from the Greek *'koine dialektos'* or common usage and originally referred to a variety of Greek that was the lingua franca of the Eastern Mediterranean between the fourth century BC and the fourth century AD, spanning many dialects. One of its forms was the New Testament Greek. The word *'koine'* is thus used to mean a language variety that can be used as a common variety between people speaking different dialects of the same language. A *'koine'* can be the first step towards a standard language.

During the 20th century, the rise of the global village and the need for rapid exchange of information between countries has meant that certain languages have become languages of international communication. English has become the main international language of wider communication in fields such as science, technology and international diplomacy (see World Englishes, page 311.) There have been attempts to create artificial languages that could be used as languages of international communication but these attempts have not been very successful (see below).

Language use in Tanzania

	Language Domain	English	Kiswahili	Ethnic community languages
1.	Higher law courts	✔✔	✔	✕
2.	Lower and local law courts	✔	✔✔	❍
3.	Consultant hospitals	✔	✔✔	❍
4.	Local hospitals	❍	✔✔	❍
5.	Mosques and churches	❍	✔✔	❍
6.	Police and armed forces	✕	✔✔	✕
7.	Parliament	✕	✔✔	✕✕
8.	Local bureaucracy	✕	✔✔	❍
9.	Central and higher bureaucracy	❍	✔✔	✕
10.	Primary education/literacy	✕	✔✔	❍
11.	Higher education	✔✔	✔	✕
12.	Mass media	✔	✔✔	✕
13.	Literacy	❍	✔✔	✕
14.	Correspondence	❍	✔✔	✕
15.	Market trading	✕	✔✔	✔
16.	Travel in Tanzania	✕	✔✔	✕
17.	In the home	✕	✔	✔✔
18.	In the neighborhood.	✕	✔	✔

KEY: ✔✔ = almost always
✔ = frequently
❍ = sometimes
✕ = no

ADAPTED FROM: MEKACHA, 1993

The Swahili Language in Tanzania

Swahili, which belongs to the Bantu family of languages, is probably the most widely spoken language in Africa. The language is known by its speakers as Kiswahili, according to the custom of Bantu languages, which place a prefix ki- or chi- to denote a language.

Kiswahili has been spoken in coastal areas of East Africa since about the tenth century. Since that time it has been the first language of communities along the coast of East Africa from Mogadishu (Somali) in the north to Mozambique in the south, and in the off-shore islands, especially Zanzibar and Pemba. Throughout the centuries there was considerable contact and sometimes intermarriage between these communities and Arab traders. Thus many Arabic words have been borrowed into Kiswahili, especially in law and religion. Through trade inland, the language spread as a lingua franca as far east as Zaire and into Zambia in Central Africa. During the colonial period, Kiswahili was used as a language of administration and education in Tanzania. In Kenya, it was used in administration, while in Uganda it was the language of the security forces. During this period there was a considerable influx of English loan words.

It is estimated that Kiswahili is spoken by approximately 60 million people, mainly as a second language. It is spoken as a first or second language by almost all the 28.7 million population of Tanzania. It is also spoken by sizable populations in Kenya (around 16 million people), Uganda and Zaire (around six million speakers in each country), and in the north of Mozambique (around one million). It is also spoken by about 10 percent of the populations of Rwanda and Burundi.

As might be expected with a language that is spoken over such a wide area, Kiswahili has many regional dialects. At least 15 dialects are recognized. The most widely known are Kiunguja, the dialect of Zanzibar town, also widely spoken in mainland Tanzania, and Kimvita, the dialect of Mombasa. The British colonial administration in the 1930s helped to establish a standard form of the language for use in education, based on the Kiunguja variety. This standard or literary variety is widely used in East Africa as a literary medium.

When Tanzania became independent in 1961, Kiswahili became the national language. It was chosen over English to express and underline freedom from colonial domination. In contemporary Tanzania, Kiswahili is the state language, an ethnic language and also the strongly promoted common language of the country (a supra-ethnic language). Approximately 1 in 10 of the 26 million population of Tanzania speak Kiswahili as a mother tongue. The other 90 percent of the population almost all speak Kiswahili as a second language.

Following Independence in 1961, Kiswahili experienced rapid growth in usage and status. President Nyerere delivered an historic speech to parliament in 1962 in Kiswahili, and declared Kiswahili as the national language, a symbol of national unity and national identity.

English is also used in Tanzania, but has tended to be used decreasingly. Kiswahili has taken over many of the roles and domains of English since Independence. English symbolizes a colonialist past, colonial domination and cultural alienation. English is perceived as having divided society into English-speaking elites and lower status speakers of national, ethnic languages. English is currently used for medical purposes, in courts, at a high status level of bureaucracy, for some correspondence and some general literacy functions in adult society. There are also approximately 120 ethnic community languages in Tanzania (Mekacha, 1993; Batibo, 1995). Such ethnic languages are usually transmitted in the home.

From the start of primary schooling, Kiswahili is used in the classroom for learning. In the eighth grade, children begin to learn English. Thus Tanzanians who complete secondary schooling are likely to be trilingual in their ethnic language, Kiswahili and English. The language shift is towards bilingualism in Kiswahili and English, and against the maintenance of ethnic community languages. Tanzanian language policy tends to pay little attention to such ethnic community languages, fearing that emphasizing their value may encourage loyalty to divisive ethnic groups at the expense of national unity. Ethnic community languages tend to be disregarded as they appear to pose a danger to unity and an obstacle to easy communication throughout the country. Such ethnic community languages reflect a long indigenous history and culture, and are thus perceived by their owners as sacred, but by those in power as a threat.

Kiswahili has grown from being the language of about one in six of the population at the turn of the 20th century, to being the language of 50 percent of the population in the 1960s, to being spoken at the end of the 20th century by almost the entire population.

Kenya, which became independent in 1963, has chosen a different route from Tanzania. English and Kiswahili are both official languages, but English is the main language of education and administration. However, Kiswahili is widely used as a lingua franca, since it is spoken as a second language by about 70 percent of the Kenyan population.

Kiswahili is firmly established as a language of wider communication across a large area of eastern and central Africa. Its Bantu structure means that is relatively easy to learn by speakers of other Bantu languages. At the end of the colonial era, in the 1960s, Kiswahili had political appeal as an indigenous African language, symbolizing freedom and independence from colonialism. It is generally regarded (except perhaps in Uganda) as being a neutral language, which does not favor or threaten any ethnic group. At a time when greater mobility of population, urbanization and more widespread educational opportunities in many African countries mean the decline of minority languages, Kiswahili is gaining ground.

REFERENCES: BATIBO, 1995; MEKACHA, 1993; RAJABU & NGONNYANI, 1994; RUBAGUMYA, 1994

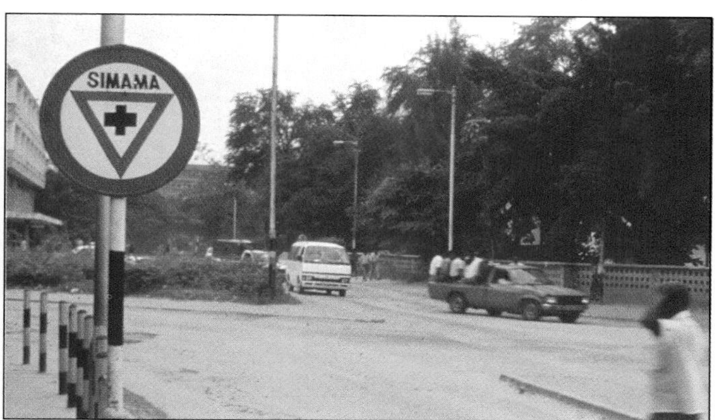

A traffic control sign in Dar es Salaam, Tanzania. Simama is Swahili for 'stop'.

Constructed Languages

One kind of lingua franca are artificial languages or constructed languages of which the best-known example is Esperanto. The basic idea of a constructed language is that it is seemingly neutral and could facilitate global communication. Advocates of Esperanto suggest that a universal use of this constructed language is preferable to choosing Arabic, English, French, German, Chinese, Japanese or Spanish as a universal lingua franca. A choice of Esperanto would not favor any political power or any language that is embedded in a long history, in colonialism and in traditional struggles about language status and prestige.

Esperanto was launched by Ludwig Zamenhof in 1887. A relatively simple language with 16 rules of grammar, Esperanto has straightforward rules about forming nouns, the definite article, gender, verb forms and stresses (always on the penultimate syllable). The founder, Zamenhof, originated in Poland and hoped that Esperanto would become a universal second language to people's mother tongues, and therefore contribute to global identity and global unity.

Between 1887 and the 1970s, there was a gradual rise in the number of people speaking Esperanto, particularly in Europe. By 1979, the Universal Esperanto Association based in Rotterdam had 30,000 members. In the 1970s, Esperanto was taught in some 600 schools around the world. Since the 1970s, Esperanto has not appeared to develop or strengthen its position.

One problem with a constructed language such as Esperanto is that it has no long and established history, no strong ingrained cultural traditions, and is not part of legends and folk tales and not part of a person's or group's rooted identity. Idealistic in nature, constructed languages such as Esperanto are often insufficiently connected with basic instrumental and integrative motives (see page176) for learning new languages. Recently, there has also been criticism that Esperanto is a sexist, male-oriented language, indicating that no language is neutral.

There are no historic or traditional communities of Esperanto speakers. Rather, there are groups of enthusiasts for whom language is sometimes an end rather than a means. Thus, the noblest of language intentions tends to flounder on a naïvete about language purposes, language planning and language prosperity.

The Manding of West Africa

Africa has considerable diversity of indigenous languages (see page 354f). Many indigenous languages have declined mostly due to the rapid spread of former colonial languages (e.g. English, French and Portuguese). However, indigenous language decline is not the only case in Africa. A converse of language decline is language spread. Language spread, language reversal or language expansion are always reflections of other types of spread, military expansion, expansion of trade or economy, social, cultural or religious expansion. Mansour (1993) gives an example of language spread in the history of the West African Manding people and their language.

The Mande group of languages consists of several small, closely related languages and a large dialect cluster. The Mande languages are spoken by between seven and ten million speakers throughout 15 countries of West Africa. A Mande variety, Bambara, is the main lingua franca of Mali, being spoken as a first or second language by about 80 percent of the population and having the status of a national language. Mande varieties are spoken as mother tongues or lingua francas by large groups in the Ivory Coast (Jula), Guinea (Maninka), Sierra Leone (Mende), Liberia (Kpelle, Vai and Mandingo), Burkina Faso (Jula), Senegal (Mandingo), Gambia (Mandinka) and Guinea Bissau (Maninke). Mande languages are found in isolated pockets in Mauritania, Benin, Togo, Niger, Nigeria and Ghana. The varied names for the Mande languages conceal their close relationship. The central dialects, Bambara, Jula, Maninka and Mandinka share 95 percent of a common vocabulary and thus have a high degree of mutual intelligibility.

Manding was the language of the medieval empire of Mali, which existed in the 9th century and which flourished between the 11th and 16th centuries. Mansour (1993) shows how non-linguistic factors contributed to the spread of the Manding language, both as a second language and as a first language. First, geographical conditions facilitated communication and the development of trade. Second, the Manding conquered new territories, and established trading centers in them. Manding was learnt by the speakers of other languages as a trade language and lingua franca. Manding speakers colonized these new territories and gradually assimilated members of other ethnolinguistic groups. Long-distance trade meant that there was constant contact between the center of the Mali empire and more distant territories, which contributed to language stability and unity and impeded the fragmentation of the language into disparate dialects.

Mansour (1993) also shows how sociolinguistic factors also contributed to the spread of the Manding language. She indicates that language cohesiveness and language awareness were important aspects of the Manding social structure. The Mandings perceived language as a tool to maintain social cohesion and preserve the structure of power. At the height of the Mali empire, all official exchanges were in the Manding language, using interpreters if necessary. The royal bard or *'jeli'*, who sang the praises of the king and his warriors, and whose other tasks included the transmission of history, tradition and law from generation to generation, had an important role to play in preserving the stability and unity of the language.

REFERENCE: MANSOUR, 1993

Bahasa Indonesia – Promoted as a Language of Wider Communication

Bahasa Indonesia is an example of a language that has been actively promoted as a language of wider communication. Bahasa Indonesia, the official language of the Republic of Indonesia, is a form of Malay. Varieties of the Malay language are widely spoken throughout Asia, in Indonesia, Malaysia, eastern Sumatra, southern Thailand, Singapore, Brunei, and coastal regions of Indonesian Borneo.

Indonesia has a large population of about 185 million people, speaking over 600 distinct languages or dialects. In any multilingual situation, languages of wider communication are essential for contact between language groups. Of all the lingua francas in the region, Malay has traditionally been the most important. For over one thousand years, Malay has been the main trade language of South East Asia. During the 17th and 18th centuries, the Dutch East India company used Malay to communicate with native employees. During Dutch colonial rule in Indonesia between 1800 and 1942, Dutch was the language of administration and the educated elite, but, since dialects of Malay were widely spoken, mainly as lingua francas, Malay became increasingly important as an administrative language and in education. Riau Malay, the dialect spoken in central Sumatra near Singapore, became the standard. In the early part of the 20th century, the Malay language became a symbol of the movement for Indonesian independence and in 1928 Indonesian nationalists renamed it Bahasa Indonesia. During the Japanese occupation (1942–1945), Dutch was banned and Bahasa Indonesia was promoted, and when the country became independent in 1945, Bahasa Indonesia became the national language.

At the time of independence, Bahasa Indonesia was spoken as a first language by only five percent of the population. Meanwhile, Javanese was spoken by almost half the population and Sundanese by fifteen percent. However, the status of Bahasa Indonesia as a symbol of independence, and its widespread usage throughout Asia, meant that it was an appropriate choice, and avoided any ethnic tension that might have arisen had either Javanese or Sundanese, for example, been chosen.

Since independence, the Indonesian government has strongly promoted Bahasa Indonesia as the official language of government, education and mass communication, while at the same time supporting the maintenance of 'regional languages', including regional Malay varieties. Regional languages are used for the first three years of primary education, gradually making the transition to Bahasa Indonesia. Bahasa Indonesia has great prestige as the means of socioeconomic improvement and the Indonesian government has strongly supported the development of the language as a medium of science and technology, with the preparation of specialist terminology

Although Bahasa Indonesia is now spoken with some degree of fluency by the majority of Indonesian citizens, on the whole it does not tend to supplant the great variety of regional and local languages, but rather exists in a stable diglossic situation with them. Many people use their native language for informal and private communication, while using Bahasa Indonesia in official and public contexts. However, there is a gradual shift from regional languages to Bahasa Indonesia as the primary language in some areas, particularly in the cities.

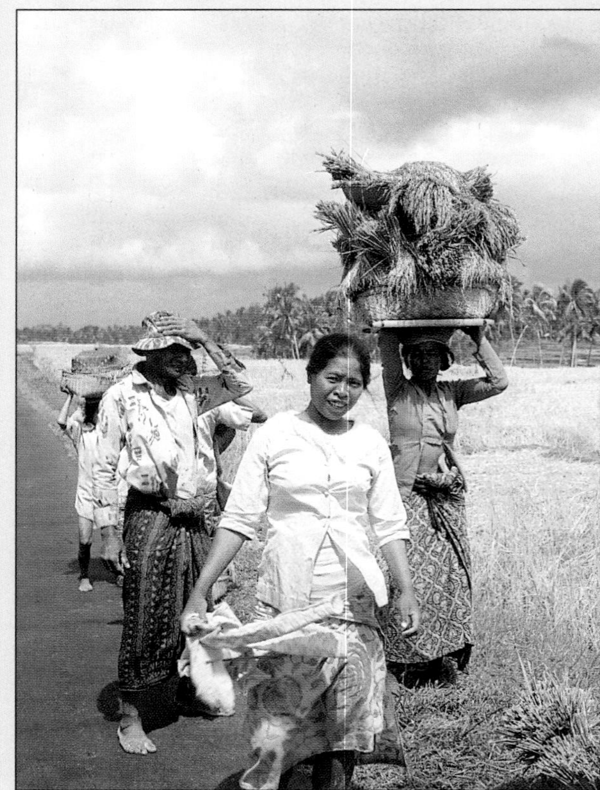

The rice harvest at Tegalalang on the island of Bali in Indonesia. Most inhabitants of Bali speak Balinese as their native language, and an increasing number also learn Bahasa Indonesia, mainly through education. Many Indonesians also speak Malay as a second language.

Language Change

1: The Origins of Language and Language Families

The Origins of Language

Speculation over the origins of language seems to have persisted since the dawn of history. How did language develop? How did people begin to speak? At what point in the evolution of humans did language emerge? What was the first language spoken in the world? These are questions that can never be answered because these events happened such a long time ago and no records exist. Many theories have been put forward, none of them very convincing. Some 19th century scholars suggested, for instance, that language first emerged with onomatopoeic sounds in imitation of the sounds of the world around (the 'bow wow' theory). Others have suggested that language had its beginning in instinctive sounds of pain and anger (the 'pooh pooh' theory).

More recently, experts have tried to reconstruct the possible size and shape of the brain, tongue, larynx and pharynx of early humans of different periods, using fragments of skull and jaw bone. From this reconstruction, they have attempted to estimate at what period primitive man would have had the articulatory capacity and the neurological capacity for speech. The evidence is too scanty and there is too much disagreement among experts to permit definite conclusions, but research has suggested that human speech had developed by 30,000 BC. It has been suggested that the development of speech was accompanied by gestures or sign language. Another theory is that speech developed at the same time as the ability to work with tools. Some kind of communication would have been necessary to share the skills needed for working with tools. Language learning and manual skills are located in the same area of the brain and their development might have been interrelated.

The study of language origins is still at a very early stage. Hopefully, developments in fields such as paleontology, microbiology, human ethology, neurobiology and formal linguistics will shed fresh light on the issues. Researchers need to understand how the human brain stores and processes language, and linguists must agree on what aspects of language should be directly represented in the brain. Only then can they begin to find answers to the questions: what were the changes in brain structure that allowed language to emerge, and what structural and ecological factors caused those factors to occur?

The First Language of the World

Throughout the centuries, many scholars have debated the mystery of the oldest language of the world. Some Judeo-Christian scholars were sure that Hebrew was the language spoken in the garden of Eden.

One theory is that all languages are descended from a single original language (monogenesis). A second theory is that different languages emerged more or less simultaneously in several places (polygenesis). A third possibility, given the vast timescale involved, is that all living languages are descended from a single language but that language was itself only one of several languages that have become extinct without leaving any trace.

Language Families

Just as brothers and sisters in human families are genetically related and show a family likeness, so languages can be related and show similarities to one another. If languages exhibit certain correspondences in vocabulary, syntax, inflections and other aspects, we can conclude that they are descended from a common 'parent' or 'ancestor'. In other words, a 'parent' language was spoken some time in the past in a certain region. Speakers of this language migrated to different areas and the language evolved in different ways, giving rise to more than one dialect and eventually separate languages.

One well-documented example of this is Latin, originally the language of Rome and the surrounding region. As the Roman Empire expanded and Roman armies occupied and colonized much of Western Europe, they took their Latin language with them. By the end of the Roman occupation, Latin was spoken widely throughout present day Italy, France, Spain and Portugal. Over the centuries, the language evolved in different ways in different areas, giving rise to the contemporary languages of Italian, French, Occitan, Catalan, Spanish, Portuguese, Romansch,

Friulian, Ladin, Galician and Romanian. We can say that Latin is the 'parent' language and that Italian and French, for instance, are 'sister' languages.

The analogy of a family has limitations when applied to languages. A new language is not 'born' overnight. Languages gradually change their shape and form over the years. A parent language does not 'give birth' to a daughter language and then 'die'. Rather, the parent language 'becomes' the daughter language over a period of years. We say that Latin is a dead language, but it has not died but evolved. It no longer exists in the form spoken and written by the Romans, but it lives on in the various Romance languages. Another useful analogy would be the idea of a river that diverges into several channels, just as languages diverge from an original source.

However, the analogy of a family is helpful, because it gives us the idea of genetic similarities. It also gives us the idea of a family tree. Just as we can chart relationships over time within a family by making a family tree, so we can show how a single language can give rise to a number of 'daughter' languages, and how these 'daughter' languages may themselves split up subsequently, each giving rise to a further number of languages, that are, in a sense, 'granddaughters' of the original language.

Comparative Linguistics

Where substantial records of a parent language still exist, as in the case of Latin, it is easy to follow the pattern of changes that have taken place. For instance, we can take the Latin words for 'mother' and 'father' and see what these have become in contemporary Romance languages.

Latin	Italian	Spanish	French	Catalan	Portuguese
pater	*padre*	*padre*	*père*	*pare*	*pai*
mater	*madre*	*madre*	*mère*	*mare*	*mai*

However, where few or no records of the parent language remain, it is possible to construct the form of the parent language by comparing the forms of the daughter languages. The science of philology or 'comparative linguistics' emerged at the end of the 18th century, when scholars began to examine languages in detail and to search for similarities and correspondences between them. By examining the contemporary forms of languages, and by working back as far as written records existed, it was possible to reconstruct with a fair degree of certainty the form of the parent language from which the languages derived. When languages have a common parent, they are said to be cognate.

These same methods were applied to larger groups of languages, and, by the beginning of the 19th century, scholars had assembled a convincing body of evidence to show that many languages of Europe and Asia had descended from a common ancestor, to which they gave the name 'Indo-European' or 'Proto-Indo-European'.

The Nature of Language Change

The historical study of languages exists because of language change. If the original Indo-European language had spread throughout Europe and continued down the centuries without changing, there would be relatively little to study. However, languages are always evolving and changing. They change, first of all, for internal reasons. Because the human beings that speak languages are creative and innovative, they are continually initiating changes in their speech, often unconsciously. Words gain new meanings and lose old ones, new words and expressions are invented, the pronunciation of different sounds gradually changes. To give one example, in medieval English, the *k* was pronounced in words such as 'knight, knave, knock, know, knell'. It is now silent. This indicates one very important aspect of sound changes. They tend to affect all words in a language, without exception. (If there is an exception, there is usually an explanation for it.) In modern English, *k* is never pronounced in the combination *kn*. Interestingly, medieval Welsh borrowed several words from English with the initial combination *kn* and in Welsh the initial consonant is still pronounced, e.g. *cnul* (knell), *cnaf* (knave), *cnoc* (knock).

Another main reason for language change is contact with other languages. Through language contact, a language may be influenced by the phonology, vocabulary and syntax of other languages. One example is South African English which has been influenced by Afrikaans and by indigenous African languages (see page 314).

If speakers of a language migrate to different regions and have little or no contact with one another, their speech will evolve in various directions, eventually giving rise to very different forms of the language. Their speech may be influenced by other languages in the area. Afrikaans, originally dialects of Dutch spoken by colonists in the Cape of Good Hope, has evolved differently from the Dutch still spoken in the Netherlands. Afrikaans has also borrowed extensively from indigenous African languages and from the English spoken by settlers of British descent.

Changes may occur over decades or over centuries within a language, gradually altering the language as it were beyond recognition. If a contemporary English speaker were to travel back in time to the 18th century, he or she would have no real difficulty in conversing with speakers

Classifying Languages

Instead of placing languages in families according to historical or 'genetic' relationships, it is possible to class languages according to the characteristics they possess. Languages may be categorized according to their phonology or sound system, for instance, how many vowels they have, whether they use clicks or tones to express meaning. Languages can also be classified according to the word order used, and whether it is fixed or free. The earliest topologies were in the field of morphology, or how a language constructs its words. Three main linguistic types have been defined, according to word construction.

Isolating, analytic or root languages

There are no word endings. Relationships between words are shown solely by word order. Chinese is an example of an analytic language.

Inflecting, synthetic or fusional languages

Grammatical relationships are expressed by changing the internal structure of words, usually by the use of inflectional endings. Latin, Greek and Arabic are example of inflecting languages.

Agglutinative languages

Words are constructed out of a long sequence of units, with each unit expressing a particular aspect of grammatical meaning. Turkish, Finnish, Japanese and Swahili form words in this way.

Many languages show all three types of morphology, but belong primarily to one group. English, for instance, is primarily an analytic language, using a fairly fixed word order to indicate meaning and grammatical relationships. For instance, 'the dog chased the cat' and 'the cat chased the dog' mean two different things. The same words are used but the word order is different. A language such as Latin, on the other hand, would be able to express the difference in meaning (i.e. which animal chased which) by the endings of the words, and could put the words in any order.

The Celtic Languages

The Celts first emerged as a separate people in central Europe (Switzerland and Austria) in the seventh century BC.Their language has been reconstructed by linguists and given the name Common Celtic. As the Celts migrated westwards the language diverged into several separate languages.The Celtic languages spoken on the continent were Celtiberian (in Northern Spain), Gaulish in Gaul and Galatian in Asia Minor. All are now extinct. The continental Celts had a purely oral culture, but evidence for their languages comes from inscriptions and coin legends (written in the alphabets of other languages), as well as personal and place names, items of vocabulary and brief quotations found in Greek and Latin authors.

The Celts also migrated to Britain and Ireland, about the sixth century BC. The two branches of insular Celtic are Goedelic (from which Scottish, Irish and Manx derive) and Brittonic (from which Welsh, Breton and Cornish derive). It is considered that the modern Celtic languages emerged in the fifth and sixth century AD, when a generalized accent shift gradually occurred, resulting in the dropping of the inflectional endings. The Goedelic language was first spoken in Ireland, and carried to Scotland and the Isle of Man by Irish colonists in the fifth century BC. Manx is now extinct but Irish and Scots Gaelic are still very similar. Dialects of Brittonic were spoken throughout most of Britain before the first century AD. The invasions of the Romans, then later the invasions of the Anglo-Saxons and Irish, drove the British Celts westward into Wales and Cornwall, and while some migrated to north-west France to present day Brittany.

The modern Celtic languages have been heavily influenced by contact with other languages throughout their history. Latin has left its mark on both the Goedelic and Brittonic languages, mostly in religious vocabulary. The Celtic languages of Britain have been heavily influenced by English, and Breton has had prolonged contact with French, and this has left its mark on the vocabulary, syntax and phonology of these languages.

Sir William Jones

Sir William Jones (1746–1794) was a lawyer, politician and an eminent scholar of languages, with a lifelong interest in Oriental languages. He is best known for a famous excerpt from his *'Third Anniversary Discourses'* read to the Bengal Asiatick Society in 1786.

'The Sanskrit language....is of a wonderful structure; more perfect than the Greek, more copious than the Latin, and more exquisitely refined than either, yet bearing to both of them a stronger affinity, both in the roots of verbs and in the forms of grammar, than could possibly have been produced by accident; so strong, indeed, that no philologist could examine them all three, without believing them to have sprung from some common source, which, perhaps, no longer exists'.

Prior to this time, scholars had already begun to recognize the correspondences between Sanskrit, Greek and Latin, but the tendency was to believe that Sanskrit was the parent language from which Greek and then Latin had derived. This famous statement is regarded to the earliest reference to the existence of a parent language from which Sanskrit, Greek and Latin had derived.

of a fairly standard or literary form of English. To go back to Shakespeare's English would be more of a problem, and 14th century English would be, initially, almost unintelligible.

Language is always changing. The question is when can a new language be said to have come into being? A new language is evidently not born in a day. Can we point to any period of time when a new language emerges? Is a 'new' language simply a new label on an old language, with scholars arbitrarily pinpointing a certain time in a continuous process of change? Although language change is a continuous process, at times the rate and nature of change is such that a new language can be said to come into being. This type of change often occurs during times of social upheaval e.g. migrations of population, breakdown of political structures. As the Roman Empire gradually crumbled during the fourth and fifth centuries AD, the *'lingua vulgaris'* or common Latin spoken widely in Western Europe, gradually evolved into the modern Romance languages. The main changes that took place between the fifth and ninth centuries AD were that the inflections at the ends of words that indicated grammatical relationships in Latin gradually became redundant: in the modern Romance languages the relationship between different elements in a sentence or utterance is expressed more by word order.

The Methods of Comparative Linguistics

The methods of comparative historical linguistics involve comparing words corresponding in meaning from a number of languages to establish whether or not they are related. If a relationship is found, then the form of the words can be examined in more detail to draw conclusions about their common ancestor. Comparative linguistics is founded on two basic assumptions. First, language is essentially arbitrary, in the sense that there is no connection between a linguistic symbol or word and the concept or object it represents. (The only exceptions are onomatopoeic words that imitate the sound of an object e.g. cock-a-doodle-doo.) If many words with the same or similar meaning have similar forms in two different languages, this suggests a connection or relationship between the two languages that cannot be due to chance. A single pair of words that correspond may just be coincidence (e.g. German has the word *'nass'* - 'wet' and so does Zuni, a language of New Mexico). However, if several words correspond, then the reason for this correspondence must be investigated.

The correspondence may be due to language contact, with one language having borrowed from the other. In order to distinguish language contact from a genetic relationship, it is important to look at the core vocabulary of a language, that is, such categories as kinship terms, local wildlife and plant life, numbers, colors, or inflectional endings, as languages tend not to borrow these items. It is also helpful to know the histories of both languages. If we look at the Maori words *'tiriti'* (treaty), *'niupapa'* (newspaper), *'motoka'* (motor car), we may conclude that Maori and English are related languages. However, if we look at the core vocabulary of Maori, words like *'rua'* (two), *'manu'* (bird), *'ike'* (fish), it appears that the two languages are not historically related. If we know something of the history of the Maori people, and the colonization of New Zealand by English speakers, then we realize that the Maori language has borrowed words from English for concepts that were foreign to their culture.

The second basic assumption underlying comparative linguistics is that sound changes are usually consistent or regular rather than haphazard. Thus, if we find consistent sound correspondences between words with similar meanings in different languages, this suggests that they may be historically related. For instance, English frequently has *f* where Latin has *p* in words with similar meaning, such as 'father: *pater*, foot: *pes*, fish: *piscis*.' There are other correspondences between Latin and English, for instance, *s: s* in 'six: *sex*, seven: *septem*, salt: *sel*, sun: *sol*.' Another correspondence is *t: d*, for instance 'two: *duo*, ten: *decem*, tooth: *dens*.' There are so many correspondences of this kind that the two languages are obviously connected. If we look at the history of the two languages, correspondences between items of core vocabulary are not due to borrowing, since they were an established part of the Anglo-Saxon vocabulary before the Anglo-Saxons had any contact with the Latin language. (English has borrowed from Latin throughout the ages. See World Englishes, page 311.) We can conclude that Latin and English are related languages.

If we widen our research to examine other languages related to English and Latin, we can start to draw some conclusions about the hypothetical form of the parent language. For instance, a number of Indo-European languages have *s* at the beginning of certain words, but Greek has an *h*.

English	six	seven	sun	salt	sow
Latin	*sex*	*septem*	*sol*	*sel*	*sus*
Greek	*hex*	*hepta*	*helios*	*hals*	*hus*

We conclude that the original sound in Indo-European was probably *s* and that in Greek the original *s* changed to *h*. From further studies we confirm that *s* to *h* is a fairly common development and that the reverse, *h* to *s* is unheard of. (Another basic principle of comparative linguistics is 'uniformitarianism', i.e. that types of changes that occurred in the past are the same as those occurring in the present.)

In reality, the situation is more complex than this simple example would suggest. Correspondences between languages are not always regular, for various reasons. To take one example, we know that *p* in Latin often corresponds to the lack of an initial consonant in Celtic (e.g. *'piscis - uisce'* (Irish), *'pater - athair'* (Irish)). However, the word for fish in Welsh is *'pysg'* (later *'pysgodyn'*). This inconsistency is explained by the fact that the Celtic Brittonic language (the parent language of Welsh) borrowed the word *'piscis'* from Latin. The original Brittonic word for fish is found in the Welsh river name *'Wysg'* (Usk in English). This shows that languages may be historically related but may also borrow from one another at some stage because of language contact. To take another example, English is a Germanic language, a sister language of German, Dutch and Flemish. The Germanic languages are Indo-European languages. French is also an Indo-European language, a daughter language of Latin. English and French are therefore related. However, during its history, English has borrowed extensively from French, spoken widely in England by the nobility for two centuries after the Norman invasion.

Another problem that may arise is when words gain new meanings and lose old meanings. French is a daughter language of Latin. The word for head in French is *'tête'* while the word for head in Latin is *caput*. What probably happened was that the Latin word for a pot, *'testa'* came to be used metaphorically for 'head' in certain Latin dialects (rather like 'nut' in English). The Latin *'caput'*, meanwhile, has given *'chef'* in modern French, meaning 'head' in the sense of 'chief'.

These examples indicate that language evolution is not a simple linear progression and language relationships are not clear-cut like relationships within a family. Languages evolve and change because of tendencies within themselves, but also because of contact with other languages. The science of comparative historical linguis-

The Indo-European Family of Languages

The original Indo-European language is believed to have been spoken by a semi-nomadic population living in the steppe region of Southern Russia around 4000 BC. They began to migrate into the Danube area of Europe and beyond from around 3500 BC, arriving in the Adriatic region before 2000 BC. During this period of migration, the language began to split up into different languages. The first written records appear between 2000 BC and 1000 BC, in the form of inscriptions, which attest to the well-established differences between the Greek, Anatolian and Indo-Iranian languages.

It has been possible to establish the relationships between the Indo-European languages and to reconstruct the form of the parent language with a high degree of certainty, because of the wealth of written evidence that exists, in the form of printed books, manuscripts, inscriptions, place names and personal names.

Numbers are part of the core vocabulary of a language and are not usually borrowed. A comparison of numbers up to ten in some languages of the Indo-European language family show the broad correspondences. One non-Indo-European language (Finnish) is included to show a very different pattern.

English	Latin	Spanish	German	Greek	Urdu	Irish	Finnish
one	*unus*	*uno*	*ein*	*ena*	*ek*	*aon*	*yksi*
two	*duo*	*dos*	*zwei*	*dhio*	*do*	*do*	*kaksi*
three	*tres*	*tres*	*drei*	*tria*	*teen*	*tri*	*kolme*
four	*quattuor*	*cuatro*	*vier*	*tessera*	*cha*	*ceathair*	*nelja*
five	*quinque*	*cinco*	*funf*	*pente*	*pauch*	*cuig*	*viisi*
six	*sex*	*seis*	*sechs*	*heksi*	*che*	*se*	*kuusi*
seven	*septem*	*siete*	*sieben*	*hepta*	*sat*	*seacht*	*seisteman*
eight	*octem*	*ocho*	*acht*	*okto*	*ot*	*ocht*	*kahdeksan*
nine	*novem*	*nueve*	*neun*	*enea*	*nav*	*naoi*	*yhdeksan*
ten	*decem*	*diez*	*zehn*	*dhalea*	*das*	*dach*	*kymmenen*

Native American languages appear to belong to many different language families.

tics involves painstaking detective work, studying contemporary language and historical written examples of the language, in books, manuscripts, glosses, inscriptions, coin legends and other sources. It also involves studying the history of the people who spoke the language, and patterns of contact with other languages.

How Accurate is Reconstruction?

A great wealth of research has been conducted on the Indo-European family of languages over the last two centuries. Because of the mass of written sources available, it has been possible to establish, with some degree of certainty, the form of the Proto-Indo-European. However, the reconstruction of an unrecorded parent language is at best a hypothesis with many unanswered questions. It is not necessarily a true reflection of historical reality. For instance, the pronunciation of the language cannot be reconstructed with any degree of certainty. Also, early records are scanty and do not give a clear picture of possible dialectal variations in a language. So far, scholars have concentrated their attention on the hypothetical reconstruction of individual words, but research has progressed on the possible syntax and word order of Proto-Indo-European. The picture can never be complete, however. Other branches of Indo-European may have existed and may have become extinct without leaving any written records. An inclusion of such languages in a reconstruction would have affected the outcome of that reconstruction.

Many languages in other language families only exist in oral form, or written records are scarce or do not go back very far. Thus, research can only draw very tentative conclusions about the relationship between languages in some language families, and even whether languages are related at all.

Sometimes, two languages appear to be historically and genetically related, whereas in fact one has borrowed extensively from the other and this has caused them to appear similar. Conversely, historically related languages may be influenced so greatly by other languages that the differences may be more apparent than the similarities. Some languages do not appear to belong to any other known group of languages (e.g. Basque, Japanese).

Other Language Families

Indo-European is only one of many language families in the world. Other main families have been identified: Uralic (including Finnish, Estonian, Sámi and Hungarian), Altaic (including Turkish, Azerbaijani and Turkmen), Caucasian, Dravidian (including Tamil, Telugu, Kannada and Malayalam), Austro-Asiatic (including Vietnamese), Tai, (including Thai), Sino-Tibetan (including Chinese, Burmese and Tibetan), Afro-Asiatic (also known as Hamito-Semitic and including Hebrew, Arabic and Berber languages), Austronesian, Indo-Pacific.

Some groups of languages spoken in certain areas (e.g. the North American Indian languages), appear to belong to many separate families. Other groups of indigenous languages, such as the Aboriginal languages of Australia, appear to be interrelated in some way. In cases where the relationship between languages appears unclear or distant, the grouping is referred to as a 'phylum'. The term 'macro-phylum' is used for an even more general and more distant grouping of languages.

Researchers in the fields of philology and comparative linguistics have tried to establish links between language families. Any hypotheses in this area must necessarily be tenuous and very contentious. However, it is not impossible that at least some of the language families descend from a common ancestor.

Further Reading

AITCHISON, J., 1991, *Language Change: Progress or Decay?* (Second edition). Cambridge: Cambridge University Press.

AITCHISON, J., 1996, *The Seeds of Speech*. Cambridge: Cambridge University Press.

CRYSTAL, D., 1987, *The Cambridge Encyclopedia of Language*. Cambridge: Cambridge University Press.

RUHLEN, M., 1991, *A Guide to the World's Languages, Volume 1, Classification*. London: Edward Arnold.

2: The Origins of Bilingualism

The history of bilingualism derives from the history of language contact and relationships between peoples of different languages. Contact between peoples speaking differing languages gives rise to the need, for example, for bilinguals as translators and bilinguals who can operate in both language groups. For example, when different people are at war, bilingual arbitrators may be needed. When one language group has a commodity another wants (e.g. cattle, corn, tools), there is a need for bilingual commerce. To market one's wares, selling in the language of the buyer has been important throughout history.

Language contact has historically developed from exploration and exploitation. Across many centuries, explorers, invaders, and missionaries have traveled to foreign lands, sometimes for trade, at other times to plunder, colonize and enslave, or to spread their religion. Such travelers took their language, often imposing it on the natives. Groups of people have migrated from their homelands in search of new territories, or to escape war, invasion or oppression. Emigration, economic trade and colonization have all led to language contact and bilingualism.

During the last one hundred years, the growth of mass communication has dramatically increased language contact. The development of transport systems (railways, cars, ocean liners and particularly airlines), has enabled an increasingly frequent contact between peoples of different language groups. The rise of vacations abroad, international business (see page 258), multinational companies, exchanges and visits, have each multiplied language contact.

Mass communication systems such television, radio, telephones, faxes, computers and telex have increased the language associations between peoples of different languages and hence the increased existence of bilinguals and multilinguals. Multilingual satellite transmissions and the Internet at home are becoming more frequent (see Mass Media, page 269), allowing the chances of bilingualism and multilingualism to increase.

Another modern source of language contact is the mobility of labor. The huge increase in in-migration since the Second World War (e.g. into the United States, Canada, Britain, Scandinavia, Germany) has led to the changing fortunes of bilingualism within receiving societies and in-migrant families (see page 104). While there is an initial increase in bilingualism in the host societies, this is usually followed by gradual linguistic assimilation to a monolingual norm. While many in-migrants lose their heritage language within three generations, other language groups become bilingual (e.g. Chinese in many countries). Intercultural marriage has increased the chances of bilingualism and biculturalism.

Bilingualism in recent decades has also resulted from the emergence of many bilingual education movements (e.g. the immersion bilingual education programs in Canada and Australia). The existence of ethnic schools and Dual

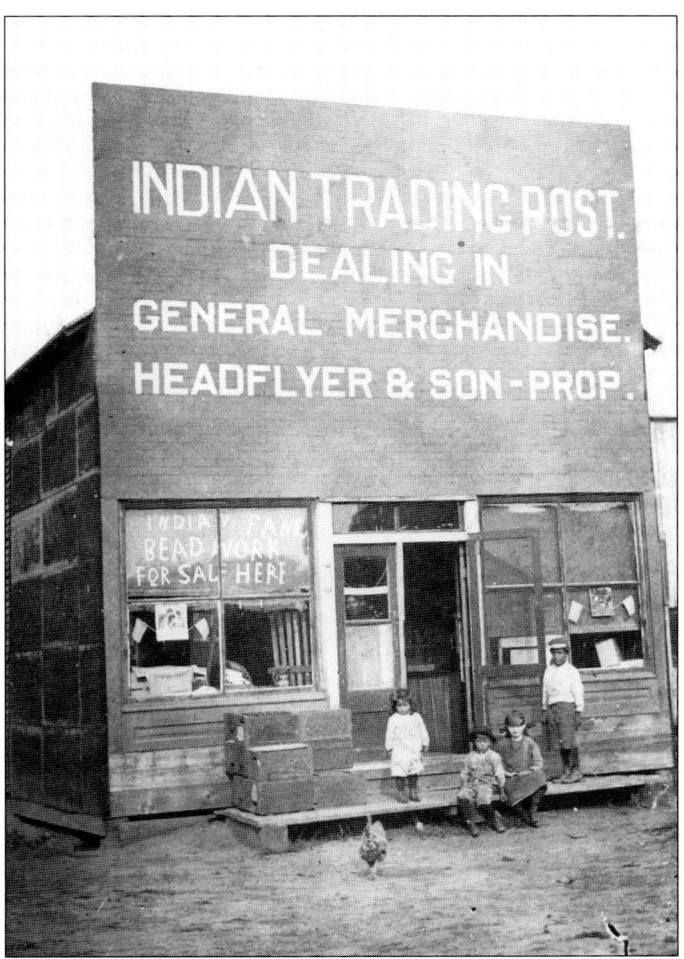

An Indian Trading Post at Lac du Flambeau between 1910 and 1915. Trade between people of different languages has been one reason for the spread of bilingualism.

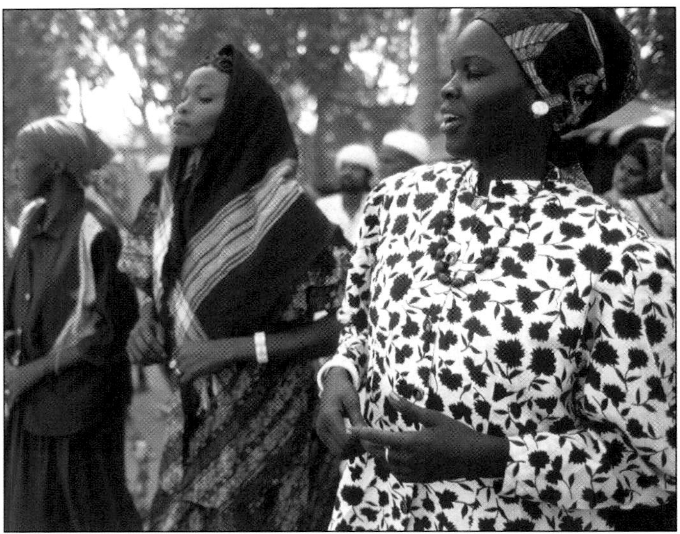

A Nubian dancer in the Sudan. Military conquest has been a reason for the emergence of bilingualism. Arabs conquered the region of Nubia in the 14th century, and it now forms part of southern Egypt and northern Sudan. Most Nubians speak Nubian, and also Arabic, the official language of Egypt and the Sudan.

Language schools in the United States are two different examples of the possibility of engendering bilingualism in children through education.

In today's world, it is estimated that between half and two-thirds of the world's population is bilingual. The majority of people live in situations where regular use of two or more languages is the norm, yet across the centuries there has been an ebb and flow between bilingualism and monolingualism. In many situations of language contact, certain individuals have initially become bilingual. Then widespread bilingualism has resulted (usually among the subordinate or minority language group). Finally, the wheel has turned full circle as the minority group are assimilated linguistically and become monolingual in the majority language. In North America and Europe, the trend in the last two hundred years has been for governments to encourage or enforce competence in the majority language. This has led initially to bilingualism in minority language speakers, and eventually to monolingualism in the majority language. Other language contact situations may result in relatively stable and enduring bilingualism. To take one example, in Paraguay the majority of the population are bilingual in Guaraní and Spanish, using the two languages in different situations. (See Diglossia, page 117.)

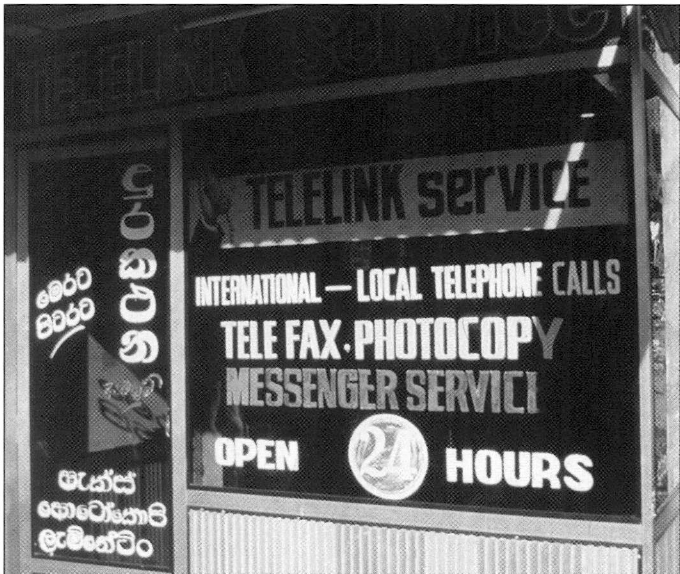

A shopfront in Kandy, Sri Lanka, advertises telephone and fax services in English and Sinhalese. Since the middle of the 20th century, mass communications have increasingly facilitated the spread of major languages.

The spread of mass communications has not only promoted bilingualism, but also monolingualism. Satellite transmissions, for instance, have given people access to programs in other languages, but have also promoted the spread of a few majority languages, notably English.

Thus, bilingualism has its origins in a variety of needs and motives, cultural changes (e.g. mass communications) and historical circumstances (e.g. war and trade). Sometimes the contexts are entrepreneurial, at other times about leisure; sometimes enforced, at others desired. Bilingualism may be stable and long-lasting, or short-lived and ephemeral. Language contact, and hence bilingualism, derive from a collage of individual economic need, societal and cultural change, and movements in political power.

Further Reading

AITCHISON, J, 1996, *The Seeds of Speech*. Cambridge, Cambridge University Press.

CRYSTAL, D., 1987, *The Cambridge Encyclopedia of Language*. Cambridge: Cambridge University Press.

CRYSTAL, D., 1995, *The Cambridge Encyclopedia of the English Language*. Cambridge: Cambridge University Press.

EDWARDS, J. R., 1994, *Multilingualism*. London/New York: Routledge

3: Dialects and Language Boundaries

Dialects and Bilingualism

Any discussion of bilingualism or multilingualism, in the individual or in society, implies that at least two different languages are involved. When we say that a person speaks two languages, or that three languages are spoken in a certain community, this raises an important question. How do we define a language? How do we separate one language from another? How do the speakers of languages themselves perceive the boundaries between languages? What is the difference between language X and language Y?

In many cases the answers to these questions seem obvious. To give one example, the two languages spoken in the Basque country, Spanish and Euskara (the Basque language), come from different language families. They have very different syntax and morphology, different lexicons (although Euskara has borrowed from Spanish) and different orthographies. A monolingual Spanish speaker would not be able to understand Euskara, and Spanish would be totally unintelligible to a monolingual speaker of Euskara, except for words that Euskara has borrowed from Spanish. Here the boundary between the two languages is very clear. It is more like a chasm.

To give a contrasting example: Catalan, French and Spanish are closely related languages of the Romance family. A monolingual Spanish or French speaker would be able to decipher a text in written Catalan without much difficulty. Spoken Catalan would be a little harder to understand, but a person fluent in French or Spanish would soon become attuned to the sound of the language and be able to follow conversations. Catalan is very similar to both French and Spanish in syntax and lexicon, although the form of words is slightly different. The three languages are closely related and the boundary between them is very narrow. Yet they are still classed as three separate languages.

To present another aspect of the problem, if we look at written Dutch and written German, or listen to these two languages as spoken on television or radio, or as used in schools and official and formal contexts, we can see that they are manifestly two separate languages. There are many similarities in syntax and lexicon, but a monolingual German speaker would not be able to understand Dutch and vice versa. However, people living in a rural community on the Dutch side of the Dutch-German border would say that they are speaking Dutch. Inhabitants of a rural community a few miles away on the German side of the border would say that they are speaking German. Yet the languages they speak are very similar, and mutually intelligible. They are more similar to one another than they are to the respective written languages. In this case, when we separate German and Dutch, what are we separating? Is there any linguistic foundation for boundaries between related languages or should we look at political and social considerations for an explanation? One way of explaining this situation is to say that the inhabitants of these border communities are speaking 'varieties' or 'dialects' of German and Dutch. These 'dialects' are different from a 'standard' form of the language, employed in writing or in formal spoken usage. To understand this, we need to look more closely at what constitutes a dialect.

What is a Dialect?

The word 'dialect' is frequently used in common speech. The term may be used to describe a low status form of language, often spoken in rural areas and by people with relatively little education. 'Dialect' is contrasted unfavorably with the 'standard' or 'correct' speech or writing used by educated people. The implication is that dialect

Older men, all speakers of Occitan, enjoy a game of cards at an open air café in the South of France. The Occitan language is a 'Romance language', most closely related to Catalan and French and spoken by an estimated eight million people in the South of France. It has no official status in France and is viewed by many as a collection of divergent dialects of French. However, a common written standard is generally accepted and many speakers of Occitan defend its status as a separate language. Young people are moving towards the use of Standard French mostly due to the influence of education and the mass media.

A trilingual sign (Urdu, Hindi and English) outside a mosque in Rajasthan, India. Hindi and Urdu both derive from the mixed speech of the region of Delhi, India, known as Khari Boli, and they are still sufficiently similar to be dialects of the same language. The main difference between them is in their religious traditions, their vocabularies and the way they are written. Hindi is spoken mainly by Hindus while Urdu is spoken predominantly by Muslims. Hindi is written in the Devanagari script while Urdu uses a Persian Arabic script. Hindi vocabulary has drawn on Sanskrit, while Urdu has borrowed many words from Persian and Arabic languages.

is inferior to the standard or literary language, more crude and primitive, and less able to express a wide range of meanings.

This common usage of the word 'dialect' is limited, and implies a negative value judgement. Linguists prefer to use the term in a more general, neutral sense, to describe any variety of language. According to this definition, every single individual speaks a dialect, or a slightly different variety of language from everyone else. No two people speak a language in an identical way. People differ in their accents, pronunciation, syntax and vocabulary. The speech of an individual is often called an 'ideolect'. A dialect is really a collection of ideolects, similar varieties of language with common features, spoken by a number of individuals. Linguists often call dialects 'speech varieties' to avoid the negative connotations and value judgments of the term 'dialect'.

A dialect may be a regional dialect, used in a certain geographical location. We can speak of Bavarian German or Parisian French. Alternatively, it may be an urban dialect that reflects a particular employment or social class. Every variety of a language can be described as a dialect, even the standard variety. No one variety of language is linguistically superior to others. The person who says 'I ain't done nothin' yet' is conveying meaning just as effectively as the person who says 'I haven't done anything yet'. Standards of correctness in language are arbitrary, and decided by social, political and cultural, rather than linguistic factors.

If a language is spoken over a wide geographical area, and by a substantial number of people, there are bound to be dialectal differences between different communities or networks of speakers. Dialects can be described as subdivisions of a language. Within the English spoken in the British Isles, we can talk about Yorkshire English, Somerset English, Cockney English, Cardiff English and standard spoken English. In the United States, because of immigration, westward expansion and general population mobility, dialectal variation is not as widespread or as clear cut as in Britain. However, there are broad regional variations, and there are obvious differences between the varieties of English spoken in, for instance, Texas and Pennsylvania, or Los Angeles and Washington. There are many urban English dialects in the United States, as in Britain, (e.g. the famous Brooklyn dialect of New York).

All these and other English dialects in the world come under the heading of English. We tend to talk about these dialects as if they were discrete and separate entities. We can describe the main features of these English dialects in general linguistic terms, drawing attention to the differences between them from the point of view of accent, pronunciation, vocabulary, grammar and verb forms.

However, dialects are not separate entities but merge into one another. We may notice the broad differences between, for instance, the German of the North Germany and the German spoken in the South. However, throughout Germany there is a geographical continuum of speech varieties, each one slightly different from its nearest neighbor. Natural boundaries such as forests, rivers and mountains may mark separation between neighboring dialects. The dialects farthest apart are obviously the most different from one another. Sometimes they may be mutually unintelligible. Urban dialects tend to differ not geographically but according to social class or employment.

What is a Language?

When people talk about dialects, they invariably define them in relation to a language (e.g. Parisian French is perceived as a dialect of French, Nurembergerisch is a dialect of German). However, when we try to define what a language is, as opposed to a dialect, and the relationship between dialects and language, we find that it is impossible to achieve a linguistic definition. We discover that the concept of separate languages has more to do with cultural, social, historical and political realities than with linguistic boundaries.

When people attempt to define the parameters of a language such as French, Spanish, Norwegian, German Japanese, one possible answer is 'A language is a collection of mutually intelligible dialects' (Chambers & Trudgill, 1980). However, this answer is not always accu-

The Germanic Dialects of Alsace

Not all language varieties are heteronomous to an autonomous norm, as in the example of the Alsatian dialects of the French province of Alsace. These are Germanic dialects, closely related to the dialects of German spoken on the other side of the border. The vast majority of the population still speak the Alsatian varieties, but most people also speak French, the official language of Alsace, and the language of education, administration and public life. Because of the Alsatian people's unwillingness to identify with Germany since their reunification with France in 1945, they do not regard standard German as the norm for their dialect. An interesting development is the recent introduction of optional bilingual elementary schooling in French and standard German. Publicity for this new initiative emphasizes the connection between the Alsatian dialects and standard German.

US Dialects of English

There exists a basic difference between the United Kingdom and the United States in the structure of dialect differentiation. Research has demonstrated that most of the dialect differences in the United States have their origin partly in regional varieties of British English which earlier settlers brought with them. There is linguistic evidence for a historical link between American speech of the north and west and that of northern England, and to some extent that of the American south and the pronunciation of southern English. These linguistic similarities correlate to the history of American colonization, the movement of settlers to the West and later immigration. Since settlers came from diverse areas and since the American population has always been more mobile socially and geographically, the local dialects of individual groups of settlers could not be maintained and developed as they would have been in Britain.

However, four major regional varieties of English have been identified in the United States, North, Coastal South, Midland and West. The Northern dialect area extends from New England and New York westward to Oregon and Washington. The Coastal South dialect area stretches through Virginia, the Carolinas and Georgia westwards into Texas. The North Midland dialect is found in Pennsylvania, Ohio, Indiana and Illinois, while the South Midland dialect extends into Kentucky, Tennessee, Missouri, Arkansas and the interior of the southern coastal states. The Western dialect of English includes California, New Mexico, Arizona, central Texas, Oregon and other western states. Patterns of in-migration and the speech patterns of different ethnic groups have affected the development of these regional varieties. Mexican Spanish has also influenced English speech in the west just as Black English has influenced southern speech.

Various in-migrant groups have developed their own style of English (e.g. Jewish English, the English of the Amish communities in Pennsylvania, Black English, the Cajun English of Louisiana, and the Native American English of Arizona and New Mexico).

rate. In Japan, the geographical nature of the country, with its scattered islands and high mountains, has meant that dialects have developed in isolation and many dialects of Japanese are mutually unintelligible. Many dialects of German are also mutually unintelligible.

The dialects spoken in the Scandinavian countries of Denmark, Norway, Sweden, and the Swedish-speaking areas of Finland represent a Scandinavian dialect continuum. They are all descended from a West Scandinavian group of dialects. The Scandinavian dialects show that mutual intelligibility may be a matter of degree. Danish speakers, for instance, tend to understand Norwegian speakers better than Norwegian speakers understand Danish. Even if two languages are mutually unintelligible, they may be so similar that speakers of one language may find it easy to learn the other language, or at least to understand it. Speakers of Castilian Spanish find it quite easy to 'tune into' Catalan and to achieve at least a passive competence in it. Thus degrees of mutual intelligibility or unintelligibility are not criteria for setting boundaries between languages.

As we look more closely at how boundaries between languages are established, we see that they are often the result of historical processes, and conscious decisions based on ethnicity and nationalism. This is shown in the history of the Norwegian language, discussed in more detail in the discussion of Language Standardization (see page 210). During the long union with Denmark, from 1380 to 1814, Norway was ruled by the Danish king and the Danish of the Copenhagen court was the official, written language of Norway. Most Norwegian speakers

A trilingual sign at Barcelona airport, Catalonia. The languages are Catalan, Spanish and English.

perceived their own dialects as dialects of Danish. After Norway regained its independence a movement for an independent standard language for Norway emerged, along with a new perception of the dialects of Norway as belonging to a separate Norwegian language.

The West Germanic dialect continuum is another example of how boundaries between languages may be decided by historical and political factors. The West Germanic continuum includes all dialects of the standard languages of German, Dutch and Flemish. It also includes the national language of Luxembourg, Luxembourgish (known by its speakers as Letzeburgesch/ Lëtzebuergesch), used mainly as a spoken language for daily communication, and the non-standard Alsatian dialects of Alsace in Western France. Lastly, it includes the dialects of Frisian, spoken in the Netherlands, Germany and formerly in Denmark. The majority of Frisian speakers (nearly half a million) live in the Dutch province of Friesland and their language has been standardized in an effort to preserve and promote it.

Another example is the Catalan language, spoken in Catalonia, Valencia, Andorra and the Balearic Isles. Catalan is one of the official languages of Catalonia, and has a standardized norm. Unfortunately, this norm is not accepted by Valencia, who want their language to be recognized as a separate language, and not a dialect of Catalan.

These examples show that the definition of what constitutes a language cannot be made on linguistic grounds, but is caused by social, cultural and political factors. For this reason, boundaries between languages may change over time, as the history of peoples changes.

Chambers & Trudgill (1980) propose a useful concept of dialects and languages as being 'heteronomous' or 'autonomous'. Heteronomy is the opposite of autonomy. Whereas autonomy means independence, heteronomy means dependence. We can say, for instance, that certain varieties on the Romance dialect continuum are dialects of French, others are dialects of Spanish and others are dialects of Italian. The French dialects are heteronomous in relation to standard French, the Spanish dialects are heteronomous in relation to standard Spanish. This means that speakers of French dialects consider that they are speaking French and that they regard standard French as the norm that corresponds to their own dialect variety. The dividing line between, for instance, French and Catalan is linguistically arbitrary, and politically and culturally determined.

The spread of education, mass literacy and the information revolution have meant that people in developed countries have much contact with the standard form of their language. They may not speak or even write the standard form, but they read it and hear it, and any changes in their dialects will often be in the direction of the standard form of the language.

The concepts of 'heteronomy' and 'autonomy' help us to understand the way the word 'language' is generally used and understood in the modern world. The modern concept of a language is of an autonomous variety with other varieties that are dependent on it. The modern concept of language is closely linked to the emergence of the modern nation in which political autonomy is linked with national solidarity, ethnic identity and cultural and linguistic unity (see Language and Nationalism, page 327). The autonomous variety has its own standard norms that have been established or have evolved as a result of social, political or cultural factors. The standard, autonomous variety represents the nation, and all the heteronomous varieties look towards it as a norm. Because language boundaries are often decided by non-linguistic factors, they may change. Varieties of language may move in the direction of autonomy or heteronomy.

Varieties of standard English have been established in many parts of the world where British people have emigrated or established colonies. These varieties originally looked towards British English as their standard norm in speech and writing, but the tendency is now for other varieties of English to establish their own standard norms. English in the United States has had its own standard written norms since the reforms of Noah Webster in the late 18th and early 19th centuries.

A further example is that of the Czech and Slovak languages. Until the 19th century, the various related dialects of Czechoslovakia were linked to a single, literary standard language. Then, during the 19th century, a separate Slovak literary language was established. The desire for a separate norm was connected with the wish for a separate ethnic and political identity for the Slovaks. This was eventually realized in 1993 when Czechoslovakia separated into two republics, the Czech Republic in the west and the Slovak Republic in the east. This indicates that the desire for a separate, autonomous standard language may be part of a desire for political self-determination and a more distinct ethnic identity (see page 210 on Language Standardization).

Some language varieties have not progressed from heteronomy to autonomy, where this might have been expected. Canadian French differs quite markedly from the French of France, but the latter is still the standard variety for French speakers in Canada. Some language varieties achieve semi-autonomy (i.e. some degree of recognition as a norm). One example of this is the national language of Luxembourg, Letzeburgesch, used as a daily spoken language by the majority of the inhabitants of the country, but rarely used in writing. Another example is the Swiss variety of German.

Some language varieties progress from autonomy to heteronomy. This has happened to varieties of the English dialect continuum spoken in Scotland. Lallans was formerly an autonomous variety, but has been regarded as a variety of English for the last two centuries.

The Establishment of Afrikaans as an Autonomous Standard Language

A bilingual English-Afrikaans sign in Knysna, Western Cape, South Africa.

Afrikaans and English are the two oldest official languages of South Africa. (Since 1993, nine African languages have been given the status of official languages.) Afrikaans is the descendent of the Dutch dialect varieties spoken by the settlers who arrived from Holland at the Cape of Good Hope in 1652. Afrikaans is spoken as a mother tongue by approximately six million people in South Africa and Namibia and by many others as a second language. Afrikaans has borrowed many words from indigenous African languages (Khosian, Bantu), from Malayo-Portuguese Creole, and from French, German and English. English has also influenced the idiom of Afrikaans, but the syntax, inflections (although simplified) and pronunciation are still similar to Dutch. The two languages, Afrikaans and Dutch, are still mutually intelligible to a large degree.

Until the mid–19th century, Afrikaans was a spoken language only, and was still considered to be a dialect of Dutch. Standard Dutch was used for writing. A movement then arose to make Afrikaans a standard literary language. It was no coincidence that this movement originated at about the time of the creation of autonomous republics in the interior of the country. These were established by Afrikaans speakers, partly to escape British rule.

Conflict between British and Afrikaaners continued, as the British tried to extend their dominion over the new trekker territories, following the discovery of diamond and gold deposits there. These clashes culminated in the South African war of 1899–1902, resulting in the loss of independence for Afrikaaner communities. However, in 1906, the British granted autonomy to the Afrikaaner republics, and in 1910, they united with the British-controlled areas, the Cape Colony and Natal, to form the Independent Union (later Republic) of South Africa.

Thus the movement for the creation of a standard Afrikaans was directly linked with the growth of Afrikaaner nationalism. The Afrikaaners wanted their language to be recognized as an indigenous African language, rather than a dialect of a colonial language. For them, Afrikaans was a marker of Afrikaaner identity and affirmed their right to be regarded as an indigenous South African people, present in the land for over two centuries, rather than as in-migrant settlers. Afrikaans was gradually used in more official and public functions. It replaced standard Dutch in newspapers, in Afrikaaner schools (1914) and in the Dutch Reformed Church (1919). Standard norms were established for the spelling, grammar and vocabulary of Afrikaans and in 1925 it officially replaced standard Dutch as an official language of the Union.

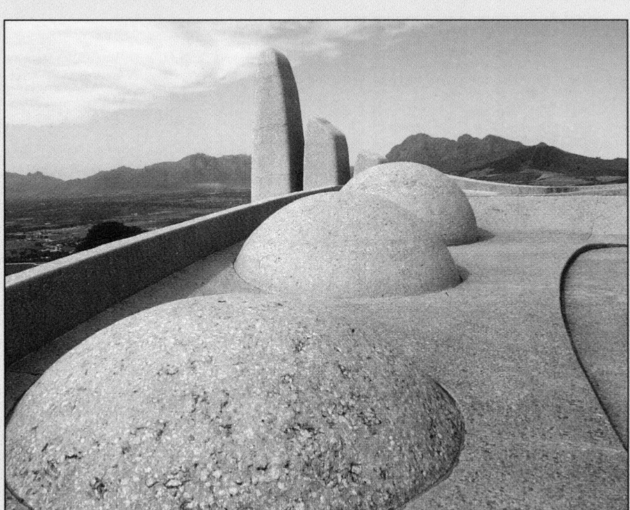

The Afrikaans language monument on the slope of Paarl mountain, designed by Jan van Wijk, celebrates the history, independence and vigor of the Afrikaans language. In the distance are three columns of unequal height, which represent the European languages and cultures out of which Afrikaans developed. In the foreground is a podium carrying three convex structures which symbolize Africa with its indigenous languages and cultures. Lines run from both these symbolic groupings to meet at the base of the ascending curve of the main column, which symbolizes Afrikaans reaching up into the free air.

Ebonics: 1

A controversy about the use of 'Ebonics' in Californian schools has highlighted the difference between how linguists define and evaluate different language varieties and how society generally perceives them. Ebonics is the recent name used to describe the varieties or dialects of English used by many contemporary African Americans, which are also known as BVE (Black Vernacular English), Pan-African Communication Behaviors, African Language Systems, and AAVE (African American Vernacular English).

This variety of American English has many distinctive features which distinguish it from other varieties. It is generally accepted that AAVE is a direct descendant of the Creole English which developed among the slaves forcibly transported from western Africa to the plantations of the southern states of the US between the early 17th and the mid-19th century. (See Pidgins and Creoles page 142.) According to many linguists, AAVE is a partially decreolized form of this English Creole, still spoken by the African American descendants of the slaves. The relative social isolation of African Americans within wider US society has meant that many creole features have persisted in AAVE, and elements of West African languages (such as Yoruba, Igbo and Ewe) can still be seen in its vocabulary and grammatical structure.

In the US, there are two opposing attitudes towards AAVE. The traditional attitude, which still prevails among large sections of the population, (including some African Americans), has been that AAVE is a low status dialect of English. This view maintains that AAVE is an incorrect, inferior, 'slang' form of English and that African American children, should, through education, be taught 'correct English' so that they can progress in the world. This view dates from the time when Black English was the language of slaves and was considered a rudimentary, inferior form of language, which reflected the supposed genetic inferiority of the slave population. As late as 1966, Karl Bereiter, in his study of four-year-old African American children, concluded that 'the children had no language...The language of culturally deprived children...is not merely an underdeveloped version of standard English, but it is a basically non-logical mode of expressive behavior'.

However, an opposite view has spread in recent years. As African Americans have fought against widespread oppression and racist discrimination, they have begun to take increasing pride in their history, culture and distinctive variety of language. The Black Arts Movement of the 1960s celebrated Black American culture and history and also language. Since the low status of AAVE is a reflection of the disadvantaged status of many African Americans in modern US society, some African Americans have desired to increase its prestige as a valid language variety and an expression and symbol of their unique heritage. Since the 1960s, many prominent linguists have defended AAVE and established that it is a rich, multifaceted, complete and comprehensive language variety. 1975 saw the publication of an important work, *Ebonics: The True Language of Black Folks* by Robert Williams. *The Journal of Black Studies* devoted an entire issue to Ebonics in 1979.

Ebonics or AAVE is categorized by some as a separate language or languages, using terms such as African Language Systems and Pan African Communication Behaviors to emphasize African roots and heritage. In education, this has led, first, to the teaching of African American history and culture in many schools. Second, since the 1960s, there have been attempts to make use of AAVE in schools to aid the transition to Standard American English for some African American students, mainly teaching reading with books in AAVE. However, these innovations were not generally accepted by teachers and parents.

In December 1996, the Oakland Unified School District Board of Education in California passed a resolution concerning the status and use of AAVE in district schools. Fifty three percent of students at Oakland schools are African American and the Board called for Ebonics to be recognized as the 'primary language' (i.e. home language) of many students, and to be studied in school as a rich means of communication and also as a means of enabling children to acquire standard US English more successfully. It was argued that this would then lead to greater achievement across the curriculum. The new plan of instruction proposed that AAVE should not be treated as a deviant or incorrect dialect by teachers but rather as a legitimate and valuable means of communication. Children would be helped to learn Standard American English by studying their own dialect and comparing it with the standard variety of English they need to learn.

However, the resolution caused a wide variety of reactions and intense debate throughout the United States. The debate was made more complex because people interpreted the wording of the resolution in different ways, and also because people interpreted the relationship between AAVE and Standard American English in different ways. However, from the resolution and the ensuing debate, various issues have become apparent.

1. The debate has no purely linguistic basis. From a linguistic point of view, AAVE is simply a distinctive language variety. Linguistically, it is as complete, expressive and satisfactory a means of communication as any other language variety spoken in the US, including Standard American English, other dialects of English and other languages. Thus, those who devalue AAVE on the basis that it is 'ungrammatical', 'bad', 'deviant', 'inferior', 'slang', are not arguing on linguistic grounds. However, attitudes towards language varieties are determined by non-linguistic factors, including historical, social, economic and political factors. Each society generally has a prestige variety, used in official and formal contexts and one or more low status varieties, which may be dialects of the high status variety and/or separate languages.

   Those who support the concept of independent African Language Systems with a separate history and separate influences do so on historical, political, social and cul-

Ebonics: 2

tural grounds rather than purely on linguistic grounds. As has already been shown, whether two related language varieties are categorized as dialects of the same language or as separate languages is a matter of social perception and is determined by social, political and historical factors. For AAVE to attain any kind of prestige or independent status, there would have to be widespread public support. This would seem to run against the tide of public opinion in the United States which still tends to favor linguistic assimilation to Standard American English and is against linguistic fragmentation which is seen to be socially and politically divisive and also disadvantageous for linguistic minorities.

Since the 1960s, when the dialect debate first began, and when pilot projects were run to teach AAVE speakers to read AAVE as a transition to reading Standard American English, many African American parents have opposed the use of AAVE in schools since they felt that it would further impede their children's educational and economic progress.

2. The Oakland Board of Education argued for the introduction of AAVE into schools on pedagogical grounds. They argued that AAVE should be recognized as the 'primary' or home language of many students entering Oakland schools. Whether AAVE is perceived as a separate language or as a dialect of English, it diverges markedly from Standard American English in both syntax and vocabulary to the extent that mutual intelligibility is often difficult and that speakers of AAVE have to learn Standard American English almost as a foreign language. Thus, students who speak AAVE as their home language can suffer the same disadvantages at school as other minority language students in that their home language is deprecated or ignored and they are forced to sink or swim in the curriculum in an unfamiliar language. The Board of Education maintain that the failure of many African American students to attain full competence in Standard American English leads to failure across the curriculum, in a pattern similar to that of many minority language students in US schools.

Much of the furor over the Oakland Board's original resolution was caused by different interpretations of what the resolution means by using AAVE in schools. Some ambiguities in the wording of the resolution fueled the debate. Does it mean that AAVE will be used as a main language of instruction, or as a supporting language? Will AAVE be studied in depth and actively promoted as a language, or used as a tool to aid the transition to Standard American English? Some prominent African Americans angrily opposed the resolution on the grounds that children would be further disadvantaged by the use of AAVE in schools. The Reverend Jesse Jackson was quoted as saying 'In Oakland some madness has erupted over making slang talk a second language...You don't go to school to learn to talk garbage'. The Oakland school board denied that they regarded AAVE as a separate language rather than a dialect of English and they also denied that they were attempting to classify AAVE as a separate language to gain funds earmarked for bilingual education.

A key question is, would AAVE students be helped or hindered by the use of AAVE in schools? If we look at the debate on bilingual education generally in the US, we see, on the one hand, those who argue that minority language children benefit from acquiring Standard American English as early as possible. On the other hand, there is the trend of current international research that indicates that minority language children benefit educationally, socially and psychologically from being taught initially in their home language, and that it does not adversely affect their eventual achievement in the majority language, but rather tends to enhance it, and also enhances their performance across the curriculum. The Oakland district board made reference to bilingual education in their resolution, and there is an implication that some kind of implementation of the principles of transitional or maintenance bilingual education might improve the educational opportunities of AAVE students, given the national statistics which show that African-American students tend to underachieve in schools.

In mid-1997, a new Oakland Board of Education document omitted use of the term 'Ebonics'. While the 1997 report retained the idea that teachers should be trained in African American linguistic pattern, it omitted a suggestion that teachers be trained to speak AAVE. Generally, the 1997 report moved away from the promotion of AAVE. However, the 1997 report maintains the origin intent, namely of improving the educational achievements of such students, arguing that this requires recognizing linguistic differences.

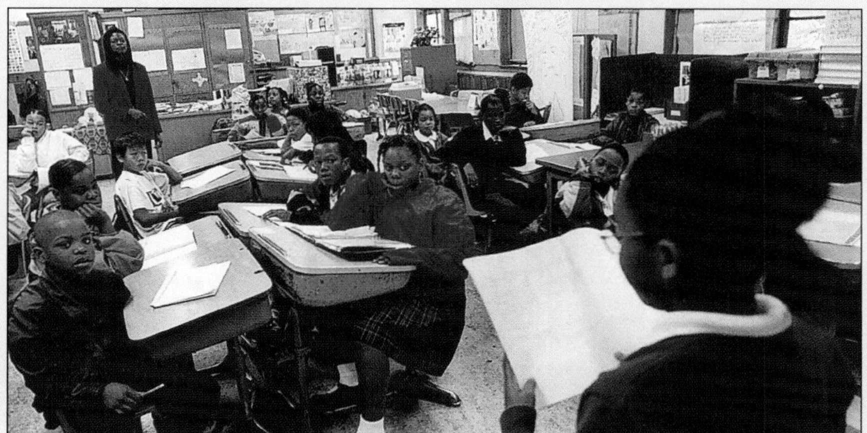

Tatiana Johnson reads to her fifth grade classmates at the Parker Elementary School in Oakland, California, November, 1996.

There may be dispute as to whether a language variety is heteronomous or autonomous. Reference has already been made to the Japanese language, that owing to geographical factors consists of many dialects that are often mutually unintelligible. The standard norm is based on the dialect of the capital, Tokyo. The southernmost islands of Japan are the Ryukyuan islands, that for centuries constituted an independent kingdom. The dialects of Ryukyuan are as similar to standard Japanese as German to English (see page 162). However, as has been explained earlier, mutual intelligibility is not a criterion for determining what dialects are dependent on what language. The Ryukyuan dialects are not all mutually intelligible but during the period of independence there existed a standard written norm based on the Shuri dialect.

The new nationalism of the Meiji Restoration called for Japanese national solidarity and unity, the assimilation of cultural and linguistic minorities, the promotion of a standard, national language and the eradication of local dialects. The dialects of Ryukyuan were deemed to be dialects of Japanese. This was a political rather than a linguistic decision. As in other developed countries, the promotion of a standard national language has provided a point of reference and identification for the dialects. Technological and industrial development in Japan in the 19th century necessitated mass literacy and increased the mobility of the population. A common language for use in schools and urban areas was required. People learnt this standard language as a second variety and it has influenced their native dialect variety. The Ryukyuan dialects are heavily influenced by standard Japanese, and younger people tend to speak more Japanese than dialect. There are supporters of Ryukyuan who would like to see the dialects recognized as distinct varieties. However, because of the political situation, this is currently unlikely to happen. (See page 162.)

Conclusion

The famous statement, 'A language is a dialect with an army and a navy' underlines the important idea that the boundaries between languages in the modern world are largely determined by political power and sovereign nations. The modern concept of a language is closely linked with the idea of an autonomous standard norm. The existence and form of such a standard is decided mainly by cultural, social and political factors rather than linguistic considerations. The process of language standardization is discussed later (see page 210).

Further Reading

CHAMBERS, J. K. & TRUDGILL, P., 1980, *Dialectology*. Cambridge: Cambridge University Press.

DILLARD, J. L., 1992, *A History of American English*. New York: Longman.

HUDSON, R. A., 1996, *Sociolinguistics* (Second edition). Cambridge: Cambridge University Press.

TRUDGILL, P., 1983, *On Dialect Social and Geographical Perspectives*. Oxford: Blackwell.

4: Pidgins and Creoles

Introduction

A pidgin is a system of communication that has developed between two or more groups of people who speak different languages, but who need to communicate with one another in a common language for a variety of specific reasons (e.g. trade). A pidgin is not spoken by any individual as a mother tongue. Pidgins typically have a limited vocabulary (reflecting their specific function) and a simplified grammatical structure. A creole is a pidgin language that has become the mother tongue of a community, that has been adopted as the native language in a region and is used by parents with their children and by many for their daily conversational needs. It tends to be more complex in grammar with a wider vocabulary than a pidgin language (e.g. French-based creoles in the Caribbean).

A market in a Nigerian town. Nigerian Pidgin English is spoken as a second language by at least 30 percent of Nigerians, although as yet it has no official status. It is becoming increasingly popular in towns and cities and on university campuses.

Slaves on a 19th century slave ship. Slaves of different ethnic groups were transported together so that they had no common language and could not conspire to rebel.

Pidgins have doubtless existed for thousands of years, wherever different language groups have come into contact. However, since they have been mainly oral languages, and since many have been short-lived, few records remain. Most documented pidgins evolved between the 16th and 19th centuries. This reflects the period when voyagers from Europe colonized many parts of Africa, South America, the Caribbean and Indonesia, establishing trade, plantations, and beginning the transportation of slaves. Pidgins generally have at least three 'parent' languages. One will typically be a European language (English, French, Spanish, Dutch or Portuguese): Much of the vocabulary of the pidgin is typically derived from this language, known as the 'superstrate' language. Two or more 'substrate' languages are also involved, typically indigenous languages of the colonized region.

Many non-European pidgins, of which no record remains, have undoubtedly existed in parts of the world where many different language groups came into contact. One well known non-European pidgin is Chinook Jargon, once the trading language of Native Americans in the north-west of the USA. It seems probable that a form of Chinook Jargon was used by speakers of Chinook and Nootka before French and English speakers adopted it to communicate with the Indians. Another trading pidgin is 'Bazaar Malay', used by travelers and traders in Indonesia and Malaysia for at least four centuries.

Until the 1950s, pidgins and creoles tended to be devalued and despised as corrupt 'mongrel' languages and deficient forms of communication. Many Europeans assumed arrogantly that European languages were too complex and sophisticated to be learnt by 'savages' and that pidgin languages represented an attempt by primitive natives to simplify these advanced languages down to their own level.

There were three main reasons for this. Firstly, the speakers of pidgin languages were usually low status servants or manual workers. Secondly, many had no written form, and were not used in education, official life or in literature. Thirdly, since many had European languages as their main source languages, they were perceived as corrupt or 'broken' versions of high prestige languages. This impression was reinforced by the tendency to use the orthographical conventions of the source language to represent the pidgin or creole.

More recently, however, pidgins and creoles have been studied more closely and recognized as efficient and creative adaptations of existing languages. A stable pidgin or creole is not the same as the imperfect utterances of a person who is in the process of acquiring a second language. A stable pidgin or creole has grammatical and structural norms, like any other language. It is possible to speak it more or less correctly, or more or less well.

Pidgins and creoles are also valued because they are sources of information about language change. Language change tends to happen so slowly that it is only possible to document it in retrospect. Because of the particular social circumstances surrounding the evolution of pidgins and creoles, change has occurred relatively rapidly. This has provided a valuable field of study for linguists who are trying to understand more about the process of language birth and language change.

Pidginization

The process of development of a pidgin is known as 'pidginization'. Pidgins typically evolve through several phases. Firstly, there is the phase of marginal contact where speakers of different languages pick up words and phrases from other groups. A rudimentary jargon, sometimes called a 'minimal' or 'makeshift pidgin' evolves, comprising a basic vocabulary but with no real grammatical structure.

If contact continues for some time between the speakers of different languages, the jargon develops into a more structured language, sometimes described as a 'stable pidgin', often used for a specific function (e.g. trading and bartering, in sea ports, between masters and servants or between members of a multilingual work force).

Recent studies of pidgin languages have compared the early stages of a developing pidgin to the 'interlanguage'

Languages in St. Lucia

St. Lucia is a relatively small and mountainous island of 233 square miles belonging to the Lesser Antilles group of the West Indies. St Lucia was variously occupied by the British and the French during the 17th and 18th centuries, but the majority of the permanent colonists were French, and the French language and culture predominated in the islands. The majority of the present day population are descendants of African slaves brought in by the French to work in the sugar cane plantations. The most widely spoken language in St. Lucia is Lesser Antillean French Creole, also called Kwéyòl (Kwiyrl) or Patwa. This creole first evolved as the language of the African plantation slaves who had no common language.

During the period prior to 1803, the entire population of the island could speak French Creole. The majority of slaves were monolingual in Creole, and the white population were bilingual in French and Creole. In 1814, the British gained possession of the islands and the use of French has declined since then. In 1971 Saint Lucia became fully independent, and English remains as the official language. However, Kwéyòl is the first language and mother tongue of a majority of the 156 thousand St. Lucians. Kwéyòl or Patwa uses mainly French or French-derived words with a small amount of English, Amerindian and African borrowings. West African languages have influenced other aspects such as Kwéyòl grammar and semantics.

A diglossic situation exists in the island in that most St. Lucians use more than one language for different purposes. English is favored for public, formal communication and French Creole (Kwiyrl or Kwéyòl) for private, informal communication. It is the language used for socialization into the community and the main language for the acquisition of local culture. It is estimated that at least 90 percent of St. Lucians have some degree of fluency in Kwéyòl. (Estimates are not exact as no language question was included in the 1960 or 1970 Census).

English in St. Lucia

Developments such as the increased opportunity for formal schooling, the increasing impact of radio and television, and the expansion of the road network providing greater means of communication, have all increased the pressure English has placed on Kwéyòl. This has resulted in a growing number of bilinguals speaking both English and Kwéyòl. It is estimated that about 80 percent of the population are bilingual in English and either a French- or English-based Creole.

English is the language used for formal and official purposes and has considerable social, economic and cultural prestige. It has traditionally been seen as a mark of intelligence, social status, culture and potential. Creole, on the other hand, has been perceived as a marker of lack of education and ignorance. Since English is the language of public and official life, many opportunities have been closed to St. Lucians whose competence in English was limited.

An example of the relative status of Creole and English is found among politicians who need to campaign for votes using Creole, yet are unable to use Creole in the House of Assembly. Those who do not speak English and are not literate in English are debarred from election to the House of Assembly or nomination to the Senate.

The majority of St. Lucians do not acquire English at home but are taught it at school. English is the language of formal education and no other St. Lucian language variety has been supported in the curriculum. While there can be a tolerance of Creole in the early stages of education, the curriculum system has operated through English.

The Promotion of Kwéyòl

Kwéyòl in St. Lucia has acquired negative attitudes inherited from colonial times. St. Lucians were forced through official policy and education practices to regard Kwéyòl as a barrier to learning and personal development. As a result, many denied their home language and passed on the same negative attitudes to their children.

Much effort has recently occurred to reverse those negative attitudes and to ensure that Kwéyòl develops alongside English as an important part of the culture of St. Lucia. The work of organizations such as the Folk Research Center, Mouvman Kwéyòl (MoKwéyòl) and the National Research and Development Foundation has helped to promote a significant positive change in attitudes among St. Lucians towards the Kwéyòl language and culture. There is also increasing pressure on government to include Kwéyòl in the education system both as a means to attain initial literacy, foster national pride and to ensure indigenous cultural development.

An important development in encouraging the use of Kwéyòl has been the establishment of an official orthography or writing system for Kwéyòl. This was the work of Caribbean linguists, cultural workers, teachers and speakers of the language. Since 1981, the orthography has been tested and is being taught in literacy programs around the island. A 621-page Dictionary of Kwéyòl by Jones Mondesir and Lawrence Carrington (published in New York by Mouton de Gruyter) was launched in 1992 with funding from the International Development Research Center of Canada.

French Creole in other countries

St. Lucian Kwéyòl overlaps with French Creoles spoken in some neighboring countries, to the extent that they are sometimes regarded as being the same language. Research has shown that St. Lucians and Martiniquans understand approximately 89 percent of each other's language, while St. Lucians and Dominicans can understand as much as 99 percent of each other's language. The five islands of St. Lucia, Dominica, Cayenne, Guadeloupe and Martinique share approximately three-quarters of their vocabularies. Other territories where similar languages are spoken include Mauritius, Seychelles, Réunion, Louisiana in the United States, and Haiti. Pockets of French-based Creole language can be found in the English-speaking Caribbean islands of Grenada, the Grenadines, and Trinidad. After Spanish, the second most widely spoken language among Caribbean people is French Creole.

Other languages

There has been an increasing popularity of English Creole especially in urban areas. There is a debate whether this English Creole represents a relexification of French Kwéyòl with English words, or whether it is a completely separate Creole language developing alongside Kwéyòl.

ısed by foreign language learners as they gradually ǀevelop competence in the target language. Studies of oreign language learning have shown that, if there is nsufficient contact with native speakers of the target language or, if learners do not integrate sufficiently with the arget language group of speakers, then they may not progress beyond this interlanguage or imperfect model of he language. Pidgins may have originally evolved as a kind of interlanguage. The difference between a pidgin and an interlanguage is that a stable pidgin has established 'norms' or rules of usage. It is not merely an imperfect model of the source language.

Another factor in the early development of pidgins has been identified as 'foreigner talk', the way in which native speakers of a language consciously or unconsciously simplify their syntax, pronunciation and vocabulary to communicate with those who speak their language imperfectly. This would have happened in situations where masters, employers or plantation owners had o speak to slaves or servants.

If the pidgin is used for a wider range of social contacts, he vocabulary will expand and the structure will tend to become more stable. The pidgin is then variously called an extended, expanded or elaborated pidgin. Some pidgins have a written form and are used in the media. The Bible has been translated into some pidgin and creole languages. Some have become the official languages of he countries where they are spoken (e.g. Tok Pisin in Papua New Guinea – see page 147). Other widely used and expanded pidgins are Krio (in Sierra Leone), Nigerian Pidgin English, and Bislama (in Vanuatu).

Slaves being sold at a 19th century market in the southern US.

The Origins of the Words 'Pidgin' and 'Creole'

The origin of the word 'pidgin' has been the subject of much discussion. Various derivations have been proposed, notably the Portuguese *'ocupaçao'* ('business'), or *'pequeno'* ('little' – suggesting baby talk), Hebrew *'pidjom '* ('barter'), and English *'pigeon'* (suggesting the carrying of simple messages). Recent research has established the Chinese Pidgin English pronunciation of the English word 'business' as its source. The word was used in a popular Chinese Pidgin English phrase book in Chinese characters in the early 1900s. The word, spelled 'pigeon' in the Western alphabet, was already used in 1807 for Chinese Pidgin English, and it was only many decades later that it became used as a general term for all pidgins. Until then, the term 'jargon' was commonly used to describe pidgins. North American pidgins are still called jargons but the term 'jargon' is now more often used to describe a rudimentary or incipient pidgin. Europeans also used the term 'lingua franca' as a generic term for pidgins. That term is now generally used to describe a language of wider communication, which may or may not be pidginized.

The word 'creole' derives ultimately from the Latin *'creare'* (to beget) and more immediately from the Portuguese *'crioulo'* (a person – often a slave – of European descent born in the New World) which gave the Spanish *'criollo'* and then the French *'creole'* or *'criole'*. The term was applied to Europeans who were born into the New World, then to Africans born there, to people of mixed race, to the forms of language spoken by people in the Americas and eventually to any pidgin that has become a mother tongue for a community.

Some pidgins have become 'nativized': in other words, they have become the mother tongues of some of their speakers. Where parents in a multilingual environment have no common language but the pidgin, the result is that their children often use the language as one of their mother tongues. This has happened widely amongst urban settlers in both Africa and Papua New Guinea.

When a pidgin becomes the first language of some of its speakers, it is said to have been 'creolized'. However, some academics make a distinction between nativized pidgins and creoles. This will be discussed below.

These are some of the main linguistic features of pidgins:

Morphology

Pidgin languages are usually more analytic than their source languages. In other words, they express meaning by using separate words, and by word order, rather than by inflections. (Inflections can include endings on words or changes within words to express plural forms, different tenses or persons of the verb etc.). Pidgins typically have short words and these words are usually morphologically simple. E.g.

Kamtok (Cameroon Pidgin English)	English
a go	I go
igo	he/she/it goes
wigo	we go
yu bin go	you went
wuna go go	you (pl.) will go
a go go?	shall I go?

Phonology

The sound system of pidgins is usually simpler than that of the source languages. Often they have a five or seven vowel system.

Vocabulary

Generally the lexicon comes from one source language, which is called the 'superstrate' or 'base' language. Words are often used for several functions. A single word, for instance, can be used as a noun, an adjective, an adverb or a verb. E.g.

In Kamtok *bad* (<bad) can be an adjective;
tu bad pikin (two bad children):

a noun;
wi no laik dis kain bad (we do not like this kind of badness):

an adverb, modifying an adjective-verb;
i gud bad (he's very good):

as an adjective-verb;
di pikin bad (the child is bad).

Words are often polysemous, i.e. they can express a variety of meanings.

In Kamtok *hia* (hear) means 'hear, sense, understand'.

In Tok Pisin (Papua New Guinea), the word *gras* (grass) is used in a variety of ways.

gras bilong het	hair (grass belonging to the head)
gras bilong fes	beard (grass belonging to the face)
gras bilong pisin	bird feathers (grass belonging to the pigeon)
gras bilong solwara	seaweed (grass belonging to salt water)

Abstractions are often expressed by compounds

E.g.

Kamtok

drai ei (<dry+ eye) = brave, bravery: brazen, brazenness

Tok Pisin

big maus (< big mouth) = conceit, conceited

drai bun (< dry + bone) = tough, toughness

Tense, mood and aspect

Tense, mood and aspect are usually indicated by the context or by an adverbial phrase or adjunct, or by a set of auxiliaries that occur in a fixed order. E.g.

Kamtok	English
Eni dei, eni dei, a mek chup.	Every single day, I cook.
Las nait, a mek chup.	Last night, I cooked.
Smul taim a go mek chup	In a little while, I'll cook

Word order

Because the language is usually more analytic than its source languages, and depends on word order to express meaning, the word order is rigid.

Emphasis

Emphasis is often indicated by reduplication. E.g.

Kamtok	Petit Negre (West African French-based pidgin).	English
big	*gran*	big
big big	*gran gran*	enormous
luk	*vwa*	see
luk luk	*vwa vwa*	stare at

Reanalysis

This is the process by which an existing form or sequence is reinterpreted, e.g. in Tok Pisin the English verb 'belong' has been changed to a preposition meaning 'of' (e.g. *Mama bilong mi.* – My mother.)

Negation

Usually expressed by placing a negator before the verb.

Kamtok	Tok Pisin	English
kam	*kam*	come
no kam	*no kam*	don't come
I no kam	*em i ni kam*	he isn't coming/hasn't come

The Origins of Pidgins and Creoles

Nearly all pidgins and creoles derive most of their vocabulary from a single language. Many documented pidgins derive their vocabularies from European voyagers who established trade and plantations in many parts of the world. In such cases the language of the socially dominant group became the lexical basis of the developing pidgin. Those pidgins that derive most of their vocabulary from English are called 'English-based' or are said to have English as their 'superstrate' or their 'lexical source' language. English-based pidgins derive as much as 90 percent of their lexicon from English. Examples of English-based pidgins are Tok Pisin (Papua New Guinea) and Krio (Sierra Leone, Africa).

A few pidgins have been formed from the mutual adaptation of two equal languages e.g. Chinook Jargon, or Russenorsk in northern Norway, spoken between Norwegian and Russian fisherman and traders. In such cases the vocabulary is derived in approximately equal proportions from both languages.

In studying the syntax and sound systems of pidgin languages, it is often harder to identify the 'substrate' languages from which these have evolved. Many pidgins from different parts of the worlds, including some that are lexically unrelated to European languages, share structural features.

Many theories have been proposed to explain the origin of pidgins and creoles but the three most comprehensive are monogenesis, polygenesis and linguistic universality.

Monogenesis

According to this theory, all pidgins related to European languages originate from a single Mediterranean trade language, based on Portuguese. This language may have been a form of Lingua Franca or Sabir, the medieval link language between Muslims and Christian crusaders. The Portuguese are thought to have used this pidgin during their explorations in Africa, Asia and the Americas. The pidgin may have been a nautical 'Sailor's Jargon' which would have been used on board ship, and in the ports. This theory proposes that, as other nations established colonies in these areas, the basic jargon was used in the ports and 'relexified' (i.e. different vocabulary was substituted) according to the dominant colonial language in the area. The structural similarities of pidgins and creoles related to Dutch, English, French, Portuguese and Spanish support this theory. Also, every English-based creole has a few Portuguese words, such as *'savi'* (know), *'pikin'* (child), and *'palava'* (trouble). In Saramaccan, an English-based creole of Suriname, 38 percent of the core vocabulary is from Portuguese. These languages also use nautical words. The weakness of this theory is that it does not explain the similarities with non-European pidgins, such as Euondo Populaire (Cameroon) and Hiri Motu (Papua New Guinea).

Polygenesis

According to this theory, all pidgins and creoles evolved independently but in a parallel fashion. The early European language based pidgins developed in situations where masters, overseers or plantation owners had to communicate with slaves or servants. They would have a used a simplified version of their language, a kind of 'foreigner talk' (see ' pidginization' above). Since the slaves had limited contact with native speakers of the language, this simplified version would have been used among them and would have become the norm. The structural similarities between these pidgins are accounted for by the fact that all the superstrate or lexifier languages are Indo-European and so are alike in many basic ways. Supporters of this theory suggest that all Atlantic pidgins and creoles share a common West African substrate and many of the Pacific varieties share a similar Pacific substrate.

These claims are supported by much empirical evidence, but they cannot explain the structural similarities found in pidgins from all over the world, including those with a non-European base language.

Universalist theory

According to this theory, pidgins and creoles have evolved independently but in parallel fashion for several reasons.

A poster in Tok Pisin condemning wife-beating.

Tok Pisin

In 1953, the pidgin English of Papua New Guinea was described as 'inferiority made half articulate' and its grammar was criticized as 'crude and incredibly tortuous'. By the end of the 20th century, the same language had been renamed Tok Pisin (talk pidgin). It is one of the country's official languages and is used in official speeches by important visitors from other countries. It is used in parliament, in newspapers and on the media. It is spoken as a mother tongue by over 20,000 people and as a second language by a further 1.5 million people. The change in the status of Tok Pisin reflects the change in attitude during the last 50 years towards pidgin and creole languages. Formerly they were considered as primitive and undeveloped jargons. They are now recognized as being complete and effective systems of communication.

- These languages evolved in similar social conditions, where people who did not speak a common language, often of different social status, needed to communicate quickly and efficiently.

- Foreign language learning processes are very similar, whatever the target language. The 'interlanguage' of learners of a variety of unrelated languages bears many similarities.

- People have innate linguistic skills which they can use to develop and elaborate a limited language system, according to basic rules which underlie all human languages.

- Studies of 'foreigner talk' and 'baby talk' have shown that speakers of all languages tend to simplify their languages in similar ways. It follows that, once a simplified, restricted system has been established, it must inevitably depend on word order to express basic syntactic relationships (e.g. between subject, object and verb). Consequently there are only a limited number of routes along which a language can evolve.

- People the world over are likely to need to express the same basic distinctions in language (e.g. the difference between past and present, and between singular and plural.)

This theory is attractive because it postulates an explanation for the similarities between all known pidgins and creoles, whatever their source languages. However, much research is still needed on the nature of inherent linguistic abilities, and the connections between the development of pidgins and interlanguage and foreigner talk.

Creoles

The term 'creolization' generally refers to the process by which a pidgin language becomes a mother tongue for a community. Creolization occurs when children growing up in a community or in a home where a pidgin language is spoken, acquire that language as their first language or as one of their first languages. This can happen in an urban environment, where an expanded pidgin is the main means of communication between different language groups. When intermarriage takes place, the children of that marriage will speak the pidgin as their native tongue. In such cases, the pidgin has already developed into a stable and elaborate language over a period of time, even when only spoken as a second language. Studies of Tok Pisin, the official language of Papua New Guinea, have not shown any difference between the language abilities of first language and second language speakers.

A pidgin that has become the mother tongue or first language of a community is often referred to as a creole. However, some researchers maintain that there is a difference between nativized pidgins and true creoles. They argue that only languages that develop suddenly and dramatically as a result of a major social upheaval, should be called creoles. Derek Bickerton (1981) of the University of Hawaii defines a creole as a language that arises from a pidgin that has not existed for more than a generation, in a population where at least 80 percent of the speakers are composed of diverse language groups.

Creoles emerged in plantations, where there was a mass influx of slaves of different language groups. They also evolved in situations where 'maroons' or escaped slaves formed communities. They also developed in the fortified trading posts of West Africa, where Europeans and Africans needed to communicate, and where children were born to European men and African women.

For instance, a high rate of in-migration of slaves of different language groups into a new plantation might have resulted in the emergence of a rudimentary or incipient pidgin. Men and women belonging to different language groups might marry and the evolving pidgin language would be their only means of communication. Children born on the plantation would grow up learning this rudimentary and restricted jargon as their mother tongue and perhaps their only language and would face the need to develop an adequate language system from this deficient system of communication.

Bickerton (1984) argues that children have an innate creative linguistic ability, which he calls a 'bioprogram', that they can use to expand and enrich the resources of a pidgin. Bickerton's theory has not been so far substantiated by sufficient evidence but has provoked much discussion.

Nativized pidgins and creoles share many features. These include:

- Creole speakers tend to speak much faster than pidgin speakers, so words are shortened. This process is known as phonological reduction.

- Vocabulary is increased, both by borrowing and by new word formations. Concepts are expressed in a simpler, shorter way e.g. Tok Pisin *wara bilong skin* ('water of skin' = 'sweat') has become *skinwara*. Also *man bilong pait* ('a man of fight' = 'an aggressive man') has become *paitman*. Polysemy (the use of a single word to express more than one meaning) is reduced.

- Unnecessary variety (expressing the same thing in different, overlapping ways) is eliminated.

- Sentence structures become more complex.
- Syntax is made less dependent upon context, i.e. the past tense would be expressed by verb forms rather than having to be inferred from the context or indicated by temporal adverbs.

After a few generations, a creole or nativized pidgin will usually have as wide and complete a range of expression and as stable a structure as any other full language.

Decreolization

When a creole is spoken in the same geographical area as its main source language, there is a tendency for the speech of individual creole speakers to approximate more closely to the norms of the source language, in pronunciation, vocabulary and syntax. This is likely to happen if the source language is a prestigious, official language, used in education and public life. This process is known as 'decreolization', and can be observed in places like Barbados, Cameroon, India, Nigeria, Papua New Guinea and Sierra Leone. A situation evolves where there is a continuum of language forms, ranging from the 'basilect', representing the original creole, a middle variety, the 'mesolect', and the 'acrolect', a variety fairly similar to the source language. Many scholars believe that African American Vernacular English was originally a creole which has been largely decreolized.

In communities where a creole is spoken alongside the lexifier language, many speakers possess more than one variety of the creole, and tend to use them in different domains. For instance, a speaker might use a variety fairly close to the source language in an urban environment, or at work, while a 'basilectal' or more extreme version might be used by the same speaker in the domain of home and family, or in rural areas. Alongside the movement towards the standard language for reasons of education, prestige, economy, social mobility and wider communication, there has been a corresponding shift back towards more extreme 'basilectal' creole forms, as people, consciously or unconsciously, seek to preserve their heritage and ethnic identity.

Thus in some cases, the creole gradually merges into the source language while in other cases, a certain degree of 'recreolization' occurs. This has happened recently in the speech of young disaffected people in urban communities, in England, the Caribbean and the US, whose speech shows more creole features than that of their parents and grandparents. The creole-like speech is an expression of their shared cultural and ethnic identity.

The Future of Pidgins and Creoles

It is estimated that forms of pidgin and creole languages are spoken in the late 20th century by some 100 million people. Cape Verde Crioule is spoken by over three million. Haitian Creole is spoken by over five million. Nigerian Pidgin English is spoken by over 20 million. Tok Pisin is spoken by over 1.5 million. (Afrikaans, regarded by some linguists as a Creolized Dutch, is spoken by over five million).

Pidgins are often, by their nature, short-lived. Sometimes they only exist for a few years, and rarely for more than a century. They often die out when the purpose for which they evolved disappears. Sometimes, language groups move apart, or a certain way of life comes to an end, or one language group becomes bilingual, learning the language of the other language group. The Pidgin English which appeared during the American Vietnam campaign virtually disappeared when the war ended. However, there are exceptions. 'Bazaar Malay', mentioned above,

Suzanne Romaine

Suzanne Romaine is the Merton Professor of English Language at the University of Oxford in England. A scholar of international repute and experience, she has conducted research in many countries of the world, including Papua New Guinea, Hawaii, Canada, England and the United States. Suzanne Romaine was educated at Bryn Mawr College in the United States, in Edinburgh (Scotland) and gained her PhD from Birmingham University.

Suzanne Romaine is internationally known for her books in the area of bilingualism and sociolinguistics. Following *Pidgin and Creole Languages* (1988), *Language in Australia* (1991) and a celebrated study of *Tok Pisin in Papua New Guinea* (1992), Suzanne Romaine published a text entitled *Bilingualism* in 1989 which ran to a second edition in 1995. This provides a wide-ranging, expert introduction to areas such as sociolinguistics, the bilingual brain, codeswitching, the bilingual child, bilingualism and education and attitudes towards bilingualism. A recent book is entitled *Language in Society: An Introduction to Sociolinguistics* which was published in 1994. Suzanne Romaine is noted for her intercontinental understanding of bilingualism and the clarity of her research and theoretical writing.

lasted for four centuries. If the pidgin becomes established as a widely spoken language, and gains official recognition, it will last longer. Creoles may co-exist in a stable diglossic situation with a more prestigious language, like Haitian Creole, which co-exists with French on the island of Haiti. In many instances, creoles are becoming reabsorbed into the prestigious source language.

Wherever languages come into contact, some kind of pidgin may evolve. However, this will probably not occur again on the same scale as in the past, because of the passing of colonialism and the social changes which gave rise to pidgin and creole languages. Also, more people in all parts of the world are able to learn high status languages of wider communication through education and the mass media.

Further Reading

AITCHISON, J., 1991, *Language Change: Progress or Decay?* (Second edition). Cambridge: Cambridge University Press.

ARENDS, J., MUYSKEN P. & SMITH N. (eds), 1995, *Pidgins and Creoles: An Introduction.* Amsterdam/Philadelphia: John Benjamins.

BICKERTON, D., 1980, Decreolisation and the Creole Continuum. In A. VALDMAN & A. HIGHFIELD (eds), *Theoretical Orientations in Creole Studies.* New York: Academic Press.

BICKERTON, D., 1981, *The Roots of Language.* Ann Arbor, MI: Keroma Publishing.

BICKERTON, D., 1984, The Language Bioprogram Hypothesis. *The Behavioral and Brain Sciences,* 7, 173-188.

RICKFORD J. R. & MCWHORTER, J., 1997, Language Contact and Language Generation: Pidgins and Creoles. In F. COULMAS (ed.), *The Handbook of Sociolinguistics.* Oxford: Blackwell.

ROMAINE, S., 1988, *Pidgin and Creole Languages.* New York: Longman.

ROMAINE, S., 1994, *Language in Society: An Introduction to Sociolinguistics.* Oxford: Oxford University Press.

5: Language Shift, Language Decline and Language Death

Introduction

Languages, like living creatures, sometimes become extinct. When we say that a species like the Dodo has become extinct, we mean that the last living member of that species has died and that no Dodos remain to breed and create a new generation. When we say that a language has become extinct, we mean that the last living speaker of the language has died. No speakers remain to maintain a language community.

The death of a language is not the same as when a language changes and evolves over a long period of time, perhaps acquiring a new name. No one speaks Latin anymore and we say that it is a 'dead' language. However, the common dialects of Latin spoken in many parts of Europe at the height of the Roman Empire have given rise to the Romance languages, which include French, Italian, Spanish, Catalan, Galician, Portuguese and Sardinian. (See The Origins of Language and Language Families, page 127.)

Language death means that the language totally disappears as a means of communication. Written records or even tape recordings of the language may remain, which may be studied by scholars, linguists and other interested people. However, the language no longer exists as the living language of a community, as a medium of work, social life, religious worship and home life. No speakers exist who can transmit the language to the next generation.

Language death does not happen because of some inherent weakness in the language itself. In the 19th century, Darwin's evolutionary theories influenced the way in which students of language viewed language decline and language death. Darwin's theory of the survival of the fittest in the natural world was applied to languages. It was widely believed that languages declined and died because they were intrinsically inferior to languages that survived. Darwin himself wrote of language 'the better, the shorter, the easier forms are constantly gaining the upper hand, and they owe their success to their inherent virtue'. The advances in language studies during the 19th and 20th centuries mean that we now know much more about many languages throughout the world, and this has underlined two important principles about languages.

First, all languages are equally adequate as modes of expression for the people who use them. All languages are perfectly adapted to express whatever their speakers need to say, whether it be about family life, work, religion or culture. All languages have the resources for innovations, as their speakers devise new words for new concepts. A language spoken by a technologically primitive people in some remote forest may not have words for 'airplane' or 'computer', but if these objects were introduced to the people, they would create words for them.

Second, no language is intrinsically more difficult than another language. Different languages appear to have different levels of complexity in different areas and this is often demonstrated by the age at which children who are native speakers of a language master different aspects of its syntax and morphology. When people claim that a language is 'difficult', they mean that they find it difficult to learn. This happens especially when two languages are unrelated or only distantly related to each other. Languages do not die out because they are 'complex' or 'difficult'.

Language Shift

Languages do not become extinct when they are the only means of communication available to a community. Speakers of a language do not suddenly stop talking to one another. Language decline and death always happen in a bilingual or multilingual situation. The process of language decline and death may begin when two language communities come into contact. Gradually more speakers of one language 'shift' to using the other language for an increasing number of functions. This is called language shift. Language shift represents an unstable situation. One language is in decline, both in its functions and also frequently in the number of its speakers and their fluency. If the decline is not arrested, the eventual result will be language death.

Here is one typical scenario. Speakers of language A come into contact with language B. Language B is spoken by a socially, economically and/or politically dominant group. Over time speakers of language A become bilingual in language B. Language B becomes the preferred means of communication for an increasing number of language functions. Gradually, younger speakers of language A lose fluency in their native language. Language B becomes the preferred language of the younger, child-bearing generation and most of them speak it to their children, although they may still speak language A to their parents. Eventually, no children are raised to speak language A. By this time only a few adult native speakers of language A are left. As these grow older and die, so language A dies out.

The Reasons for Language Shift

Language shift and language decline do not happen because one language is inherently weaker than another. Language is intrinsically linked with its speakers, their society, culture, religion, economic situation, status and

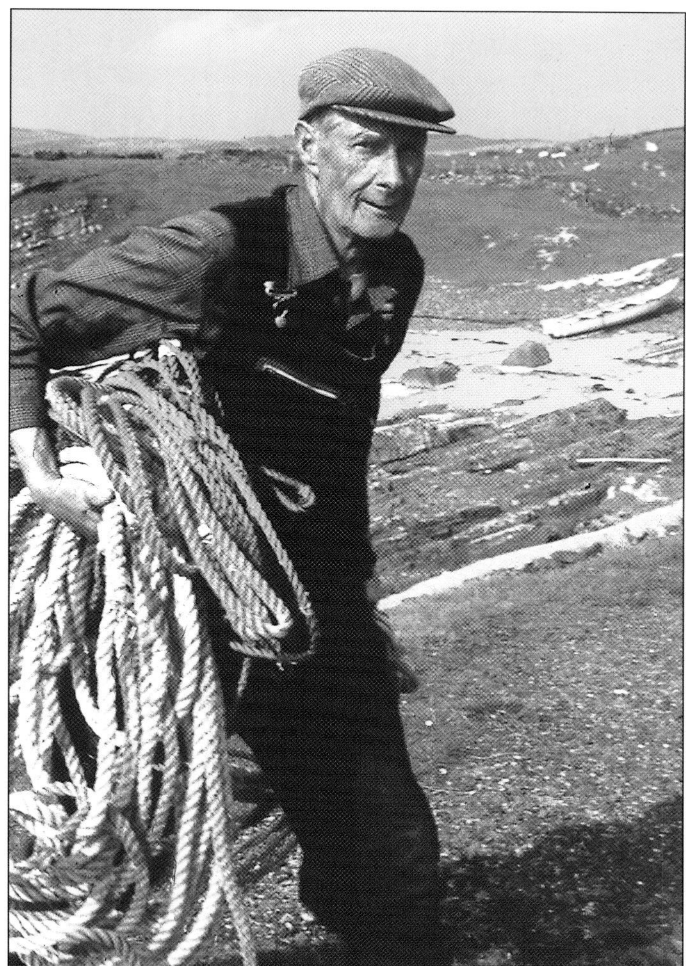

A fisherman at Clachtoll Beach in Wester Ross near Lochinver in Scotland. A decline in the traditional livelihoods of Gaelic-speaking communities, such as fishing, has led to the break up of those communities and a consequent decline in the Gaelic language.

political power. Language shift and language decline occur because the speakers of one language have more political power, privilege and social prestige than the speakers of the other language.

A variety of factors create language shift. For example, out-migration from a region may be vital to secure employment, a higher salary or promotion. In-migration can be forced (e.g. the capture of slaves) or may be more a matter of free will (e.g. guest workers). Sometimes there is also forced or voluntary movement of minority language groups within a particular geographical area. Within a country, intermarriage may also cause shifting bilingualism. For example, bilinguals from a minority language community may marry majority language monolinguals. The result may be majority language, monolingual children. Increasing industrialization and urbanization in the 20th century has led to increased movement of labor. The breakdown of traditional eco-

Language Shift in Peru

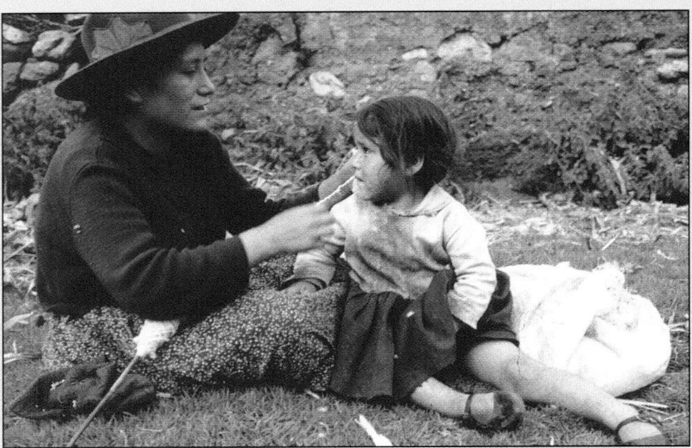

A Quechua speaker with her child, spinning wool in Chavin, Peru.

Quechua is the name given to varieties of a language family, widely spoken in the South American republics of Bolivia, Ecuador and Peru (see pages 456, 458 and 460). Quechua speakers represent about a quarter of the total population of these three countries. Small minorities of Quechua speakers are also found in Argentina, Brazil, Colombia and Chile. Sometimes known as the language of the Incas, there are over 10 million speakers of Quechua.

The Chinchay variety of Quechua became a language of supra-regional communication during the period of expansion of the Inca Empire in the 15th and 16th centuries. It was used for trade and administration, by civil servants and the local nobility.

In the early 16th century, the Spanish began to colonize the South American mainland. They soon defeated the Incas, and the other two main empires, the Aztecs and the Mayas, with their combination of superior technology and non-native diseases. During the period of Spanish colonization, the Castilian (Spanish) language was promoted by the agents of the Spanish crown. The use of native languages, including Quechua, was initially acknowledged and permitted in formal and official contexts, including Christian evangelization. The reason for this was that there was not sufficient knowledge of Spanish among the local population to make exclusive use of Spanish feasible in religion and administration. Clergy were brought over from Europe and required to learn the local languages (native clergy were not permitted), while religious tracts and Bible portions were carefully translated into the native languages. However during the 17th and 18th centuries, the teaching and use of Spanish became more strongly encouraged and was eventually enforced by Charles III. Together with the promotion of Spanish went the suppression of indigenous languages and cultures. However, the spread of Spanish was hindered by the low levels of literacy and scarcity of educational opportunities for the indigenous population.

After independence from Spain, gradual changes in the economy, the development of transport, the expansion of trade and advances in farming and mining methods, meant that the use of Spanish increased and encroached on domains in which Quechua was formerly used. Castilian became the language of modern trade, administration and education.

In Peru, according to the 1981 census, Quechua was the mother tongue of just over a quarter of the population, and over ten percent were monolingual in Quechua, mainly those living in isolated rural areas. In 1972, a general education reform act addressed the question of bilingual education. It was stipulated that the native Indian language (whether Quechua or another Indian language) was to be the major vehicle of education in all areas with dominant Indian populations, with Spanish relegated to second language status. In 1975, Quechua was given the status of a second official language alongside Spanish. In 1991 in Peru, regional laws were passed requiring compulsory instruction of and in Quechua together with Spanish at all educational levels. Also, Quechua was required in place names and official documents.

Most Quechua speakers are now bilingual in Spanish and there is a gradual shift towards Spanish (see below). However, there has been in recent decades a movement for the maintenance of Quechua and the extension of its use into new domains (e.g. education, literacy). Projects have included: bilingual education programs; the production of printed educational materials; Quechua second language courses for adults and adult literacy programs; the publication of reference grammars and dictionaries in the six major Quechua varieties and the establishment of standardized orthographies; and increased use of Quechua on the radio.

Research

Von Gleich & Wölck (1994) researched into changes in attitudes to and use of Quechua in Peru between 1969 and 1978. Comparison of the 1971 and 1981 censuses showed that there had been a slight shift towards Spanish during the 1970s, with an increase in the percentage of monolingual Spanish speakers and in the percentage of those bilingual in Spanish and Quechua. Von Gleich & Wölck (1994) showed that there was a slight shift towards the use of Spanish rather than Quechua in certain domains, and that the domains where only Quechua was used were becoming scarcer. There was also a slightly increased tendency for parents to speak only Spanish to their children. However, on the whole, there remained a fairly balanced and stable bilingual situation. Their research revealed that the elevation of Quechua to the status of co-official language meant that people were more aware of their linguistic rights as Quechua speakers and there was slightly more use of Quechua in some public and work situations.

Von Gleich & Wölck (1994) found that Quechua in Peru has undergone five stages of language shift, starting with monolingualism in Quechua and moving to monolingualism in Spanish. They argue that bilingualism in Quechua and Spanish is a mid-way stage in language shift. The five stages are as follows:

Stage 1: Monolingualism in Quechua.
Stage 2: Bilingualism in Quechua and Spanish, but with Quechua stronger than Spanish.
Stage 3: Bilingualism in Quechua and Spanish with both languages approximately equal in strength.
Stage 4: Bilingualism, with Spanish stronger than Quechua.
Stage 5: Monolingualism in Spanish.

This research shows the danger of bilingualism being a half-way house in between monolingualism in a minority language and monolingualism in a majority language.

REFERENCE: VON GLEICH & WÖLCK, 1994

nomic structures (e.g. traditional community livelihoods such as fishing, crofting, craftwork), has led to new work structures or emigration in search of employment. With the growth of mass communications, information technology, tourism, road, sea and air links, minority languages seem more at risk. Bilingual education, or its absence, will also be a factor in the ebb and flow of minority and majority languages. Language decline tends to happen at a time of social upheaval, when the infiltration of another language and culture is accompanied by the breakdown of traditional social and economic structures that safeguard the minority language.

Language shift and language decline usually occur because of pressures from without and within. A two-way process may occur. First, speakers of the high status language may wish low status language speakers to become more like them. Second, speakers of the low status language may wish to move towards the high status language. The dominant language may be enforced from without, as the language of politics, administration, the law, education and official life. The spread of compulsory education for all in the dominant language has been one of the main causes of language shift and decline in many bilingual situations in the 19th and 20th centuries. The dominant language may also be desired from within, by speakers of the subordinate language, as a condition of access to power and privilege and a marker of status and prestige. It is often the main language of the mass media and of fashionable culture.

Language shift and language decline may happen gradually over a period of decades. At the other extreme, it may happen within two or or three generations as in many 19th century in-migrant communities in the US (See page 104f). Some in-migrant communities held on to their language for longer. This tended to happen where in-migrant communities were large, socially, culturally and/or religiously cohesive with their own social structures such as schools, churches. e.g. the Pennsylvania German community. This is still the pattern in the United States today. Large in-migrant communities such as Chinese and Spanish tend to maintain their language for longer than small scattered groups of in-migrants.

Language shift may sometimes stabilize within a bilingual community and a stable diglossic situation may emerge. The dominant, prestigious language is used for some functions (e.g. official functions). The subordinate or minority language continues to be used for other functions (e.g. home and family life, socializing, sometimes work). (See Diglossia, page 117). This usually happens where there is economic and social stability within a community, and where the structure of the community is sufficiently strong to safeguard the continuing use of the minority language. However, this tends to be the exception rather than the norm in Western countries. Because of factors such as mass communications, ease of transport, the mobility of labor, widespread compulsory education in the dominant language, cultural change, industrialization and urbanization, many diglossic situations have become unstable, and a period of further language decline has ensued.

Language shift is particularly related to economic and social change, to politics and power, to the availability of local social networks of communication between minority language speakers and to the legislative and institutional support supplied for the conservation of a minority language. While such factors help clarify what affects language shift, the relative importance of factors is debated and unclear. Nor do they reveal the processes and mechanisms of language shift.

Social Change and Language Shift

Susan Gal (1979) studied in detail the replacement of Hungarian by German in the town of Oberwart in eastern Austria. After four hundred years of relatively stable Hungarian-German bilingualism, economic, social and family life became more German language based. Using an anthropological style, Gal (1979) studied the process of language decline. The issue was not the correlates of language shift, but the process. For example, while industrialization was related to language decline in Oberwart, the crucial question becomes:

> 'By what intervening processes does industrialization, or any other social change, effect changes in the uses to which speakers put their languages in everyday interactions?' (page 3)

Gal (1979) showed how social changes (e.g. through industrialization and urbanization) change social networks, relationships between people, and patterns in language use in communities. As new environments arise with new speakers, languages take on new forms, new meanings and create new patterns of social interaction.

Four Aspects of Language Decline

Language decline has four forerunners.

1. A decrease in the functions of a language and its use in different contexts. Often, the dominant language encroaches first on the official, public functions of the minority language. Then it ousts the minority language from an increasing range of social and interpersonal functions, and finally even supersedes the minority language as the language of the home.

In-migrant Communities and Language Shift

A frequent, if generalized, scenario for in-migrant language shift is given by Garcia and Diaz (1992):

'Most US immigrant groups have experienced a language shift to English as a consequence of assimilation into American life. The first generation immigrants sustain their native or first language while learning English. The second generation, intent upon assimilation into a largely English-speaking community, begin the shift towards English by using the native language with first generation speakers (parents, grandparents, others) and English in more formal settings. By slow degrees, English is used in contexts once reserved for the first language. Encroachment of English into the domain of the first language serves to destabilize the native language.

Eventually, third generation speakers discontinue the use of the native language entirely. The shift completes when most of the third generation are monolingual English speakers' (page 14).

However, a 'three generation shift' is not the only possible pattern. Paulston (1994) cites the Greeks in Pittsburgh as experiencing a four generation shift. She attributes this slower shift to: use of a standardized, prestigious written language; access to an institution teaching Greek language and literacy (i.e. Greek churches in Pittsburgh), and arranged marriages with one partner being a monolingual Greek speaker from Greece. In contrast, the three generation shift among Italians in Pittsburgh is attributed to their speaking a non-standard, non-written dialect of Italian with no prestige; no religious institutional support as they shared English language Roman Catholic services with, for example, Irish priests, nuns and laity, and marriage to Roman Catholics with religious compatibility more important than language compatibility.

Amongst Panjabi, Italian, Gaelic and Welsh communities in Britain, there are occasional 'fourth generation' individuals who sometimes wish to revive the language of their ethnic origins. For some, assimilation into the majority language and culture does not give self-fulfillment. Rather, such revivalists seek a return to their roots by recovering the language and culture of their ethnic heritage.

An early 20th century Swiss family in Wisconsin, US enjoy a a typical Swiss wurst roast. This family were descendants of a Swiss in-migrant who arrived in Wisconsin in 1857. Most Swiss who emigrated to Wisconsin in the 19th century were Swiss-German speakers, but families tended to shift to English within one or two generations as a result of social contacts, intermarriage and English-medium education.

Additive and Subtractive Bilingualism

An additive bilingual situation is where the addition of a second language and culture is unlikely to replace or displace the first language and culture. For example, English-speaking North Americans who learn a second language (e.g. French, Spanish) will not lose their English but gain another language and parts of its attendant culture.The 'value added' benefits may not only be linguistic and cultural, but social and economic as well. Positive attitudes to bilingualism may also result. In contrast, the learning of a majority second language may undermine a person's minority first language and culture, thus creating a subtractive situation. For example, immigrants may experience pressure to use the dominant language and feel embarrassment in using the home language. When the second language is prestigious and powerful, exclusively used in education and in the jobs market, and when the minority language is perceived as of low status and value, bilingualism may be threatened. Instead of addition, there is subtraction with the potential loss of the second language.

When a second language and culture have been acquired with little or no pressure to replace or reduce the first language, an additive form of bilingualism may occur. Positive self-concept is then a component of additive bilingualism. When the second language and culture are acquired (e.g. in-migrants) with pressure to replace or demote the first language, a subtractive form of bilingualism may occur. This may relate to a less positive self-concept, loss of cultural identity, with possible alienation and assimilation and also the danger of failure in education and work.

The terms 'additive and subtractive bilingualism' have been used in the context of both individuals and language communities. For example, additive bilingualism may be an attribute of a 'balanced' bilingual who has cognitive advantages from being bilingual. Subtractive bilingualism can, in contrast, be found in a person with negative effects from their bilingualism (e.g. where both languages are 'underdeveloped'). A second and more frequent use of the terms additive and subtractive bilingualism relates to the enrichment or loss of minority language, culture and ethnolinguistic identity at a community or societal level. In an additive language context, a language minority uses both languages in a relatively stable diglossic manner, with ethnolinguistic vitality in the language community. In a subtractive language context, a language minority uses both languages in a shifting, unstable way (e.g. both languages used for the same purpose, with a declining use of the minority language).

Reference: LAMBERT, 1980

2. A decrease in the number of speakers and the concentration of speakers within the community. As the minority language is used for fewer functions, there are increasing numbers of people who use it infrequently or not at all, especially among younger folk. As the minority language is ousted as the main language of the home, fewer and fewer children learn to speak it.

3. A decrease in the fluency of speakers, the presence of 'semi speakers' who understand the dying language but do not speak it, or sometimes cannot speak it. As the minority language is employed for fewer functions, and thus used more infrequently by its speakers, their fluency in the language decreases. There may be frequent codeswitching into the majority language. Younger speakers in a situation of language decline may not have the opportunity to learn the language well, and may speak an impoverished or simplified version of that language.
4. The presence of 'rememberers', those who in an early stage of their lives were native fluent speakers of a language, but through lack of use, have forgotten their early linguistic ability.

The Decline of Scots Gaelic

One celebrated study of the process of language decline is by Nancy Dorian (1981). Dorian carried out a detailed case study of the decline of Gaelic in east Sutherland, a region in the north-east Highlands of Scotland. In the history of the region, English and Gaelic co-existed with English generally being the ruling language and the 'civilized' language. Gaelic was regarded more as a 'savage' language of lower prestige. In this region of east Sutherland, the last two groups to speak Gaelic were the 'crofters' (farmers of a small amount of land) and the fishing community. Dorian (1981) studied the fishing community who had become a separate and distinct group of people in a small geographical area. Surrounded by English-speaking communities, these fisher-people originally spoke only Gaelic and later became bilingual in English and Gaelic. The fisher-folk thought of themselves, and were thought of by their neighbors, as of lower social status. They tended to marry within their own group. When the fishing industry began to decline, the Gaelic-speaking fishing-folk began to find other jobs. The boundaries between the Gaelic speakers and the English speakers began to crumble. Inter-marriage replaced in-group marriage, and 'outside' people migrated to the east Sutherland area. Over time, the community gave up its fisher identity and the Gaelic language tended to decline with it. 'Since Gaelic had become one of the behaviors which allowed the labeling of individuals as fishers there was a tendency to abandon Gaelic along with other "fisher" behaviors' (Dorian, 1981, page 67).

Across generations in the 20th century, Gaelic in east Sutherland declined. Whereas grandparents talked, and were talked to, only in Gaelic, parents would speak Gaelic to other people but use English with their children and expect their children to speak English in reply. The children were able to understand Gaelic from hearing their parents speak it, but were not used to speaking it themselves. Younger speakers had less fluency in Gaelic, making use of lexical borrowings and English constructions, and tending to simplify the system of mutations and inflections.

> 'The home is the last bastion of a subordinate language in competition with a dominant official language of wider currency... speakers have failed to transmit the language to their children so that no replacement generation is available when the parent generation dies away.' (Dorian, 1981, page 105.)

Nancy Dorian

Nancy Dorian is Professor of Linguistics in German and Anthropology at Bryn Mawr College in the United States. Educated at the Connecticut College for Women, the University of Bonn and the Free University of Berlin, Yale University and the University of Michigan, Nancy Dorian is renowned for her research on language death.

In 1981 she published a book entitled *Language Death: The Life Cycle of a Scottish Gaelic Dialect* which became an acknowledged classic and is still an influential study of language death.

In 1989 she edited a book called *Investigating Obsolescence: Studies in Language Contraction and Death.*

Dying Languages: Some Statistics

According to Michael Krauss (1992) of the Alaska Native Research Center, there are estimated to be 6000 languages on this planet (give or take 10 percent). Krauss (1992) claims that between 20 percent to 50 percent of the world's existing languages are likely to die or become perilously close to death in the next one hundred years. In the long term: 'It is a very realistic possibility that 90 percent of mankind's languages will become extinct or doomed to extinction' (Krauss, 1995, page 4). This disputed 90 percent death: 10 percent safe ratio is based on the following argument:

- Fifty percent of the world's languages are no longer being reproduced among children. Thus many of these 50 percent of languages could die in the next 100 years unless there are conservation measures.
- An additional 40 percent are threatened or endangered. Economic, social and political change is one such threat. For example, such a threat is found in countries where there are a large number of languages and where centralization, economic and social development for example, will take priority over language survival. Nine countries have more than two hundred languages: Australia, Brazil, Cameroon, India, Indonesia, Mexico, Nigeria, Papua New Guinea and Zaire. These nine countries account for about 3300 of the world's 6000 languages. Another dozen countries have more than one hundred languages each (e.g. Burma, Chad, Ethiopia). Many of these countries have relatively small numbers of speakers of the different languages. Assimilation, urbanization, centralization, uniformity and economic pressures will make future generations prefer majority languages.
- As few as six hundred languages (10 percent) may survive, although Krauss (1995, page 4) believes this is too optimistic and suggests that 'it does not seem unrealistic to guess on these bases that 300 languages may be deemed safe'.
- Officially, 7.5 percent of mammals and 2.7 percent of birds are listed as 'endangered' or 'threatened', although this may be an underestimate.There are consequently enthusiastic conservation measures. If 90 percent of the world's languages are threatened, conservation measures to maintain linguistic and cultural diversity are urgently required.

REFERENCES: KRAUSS, 1992, 1995

A Havasupai family in Havasu Canyon, a side canyon of the Grand Canyon in northwestern Arizona, 1898. The decline of indigenous languages in the US and Canada has reflected the subordinate status of their speakers as Europeans migrated to North America and appropriated their territory. Language shift is always linked to social and economic change, to politics and power.

Language Suicide and Language Murder

Some linguists have drawn a much debated distinction between language suicide and language murder. Aitchison (1991) defines language suicide as the process by which the language of the subordinate or minority group gradually borrows vocabulary, constructions and sounds from the more prestigious language. If the two languages are similar, then over time the subordinate language may be totally absorbed into the more prestigious language. Aitchison (1991) uses as an example the process by which a creole moves back towards the base language from which it is derived.

A creole is often situated geographically near to its parent language. Since the parent language often has more social prestige and is used in education and official life, there is a tendency for speakers of the creole to move closer to the norms of the more prestigious language. This process is known as 'decreolization' and is discussed in more detail in the topic on Pidgins and Creoles (see page 142). It is similar to the process by which speakers of a dialect move closer to the norms of a standard language, because of social pressures and the influence of education, for example.

Aitchison (1991) contrasts this process which she terms 'language suicide' with 'language murder'. She defines 'language murder' as the process of language shift already described, by which a socially prestigious language becomes used for more and more functions. Speakers of the less prestigious language use it less and less and thus lose fluency in it. Younger speakers tend to speak an impoverished version of the less prestigious language and more and more children are raised solely in the more prestigious language.

Aitchison's (1991) analysis of the situation makes a distinction that does not always exist. She herself admits 'there is not always a clear-cut line between the two types of death'. In most situations of language decline, there is a tendency to borrow from and codeswitch into the more prestigious language, to the extent that the two languages become intermingled. This may eventually result in a complete shift to the more prestigious language. Thus her use of the terms 'murder' and 'suicide' does not really help our understanding of the process of language decline and death.

A different and more controversial use of the terms 'language suicide' and 'language murder' is made by John Edwards (1985). When languages die, Edwards asks, are they murdered or do they commit suicide? In the histories of the Native American (Indian) languages of Canada and the United States, and particularly in the histories of the African languages of those who became slaves, the process of elimination of languages could be compared to murder. African slaves, for instance, were transported on ships and transferred to plantations in linguistically mixed groups to avoid the possibility of conspiracy and revolt. In histories of the Irish, Gaelic and Welsh languages, it is typically argued that the languages have been 'murdered' by the enforcement of English as the sole language of law, official life and education. Language 'suicide' on the other hand, describes a situation where speakers of a minority or subordinate language seemingly choose to speak the majority or prestigious language and thus acquiesce, whether consciously or unconsciously, in the process of language decline.

This use of the terms 'language murder' and 'language suicide' can be opposed for more than one reason. First, languages are not usually murdered, nor do they commit suicide. They decline and eventually die, because of non-linguistic factors such as changes in community structures, economy, and the social needs of their speakers. If governments do decide to eradicate regional or minority languages, it is invariably for non-linguistic reasons such as national solidarity, or the need for mass literacy and ease of communications (to be accomplished through the majority language). Equally, speakers of a language do not usually make conscious, individual decisions not to use their language. Over time, a variety of social and economic pressures may induce a gradual bias towards the majority or more prestigious language.

Second, it is difficult to make a distinction between choice or coercion in any given case of language shift. Elements of both may be present. A majority language may be enforced in education but may also be adopted by minority language speakers in social situations because of its prestige.

In the end, what is choice? Language shift often reflects a pragmatic desire for social and vocational mobility, and an improved standard of living. The answer to the environmentalist who wishes to preserve a garden of great beauty is that, when the priority is food in the stomach and clothes on the back, 'you can't eat the view'. Sometimes, there may be a gap between the rhetoric of language preservation and harsh reality. This is illustrated in a story from Bernard Spolsky (1989b). 'A Navajo student of mine once put the problem quite starkly: if I have to choose, she said, between living in a hogan a mile from the nearest water where my son will grow up speaking Navajo or moving to a house in the city with indoor plumbing where he will speak English with the neighbors, I'll pick English and a bathroom!' (page 451). One can argue that the student's 'choice' was more apparent than real. The need for a basic standard of living and for economic security must inevitably eclipse matters of language 'choice'. There is often no viable choice, or a very constrained choice, among minority language speakers.

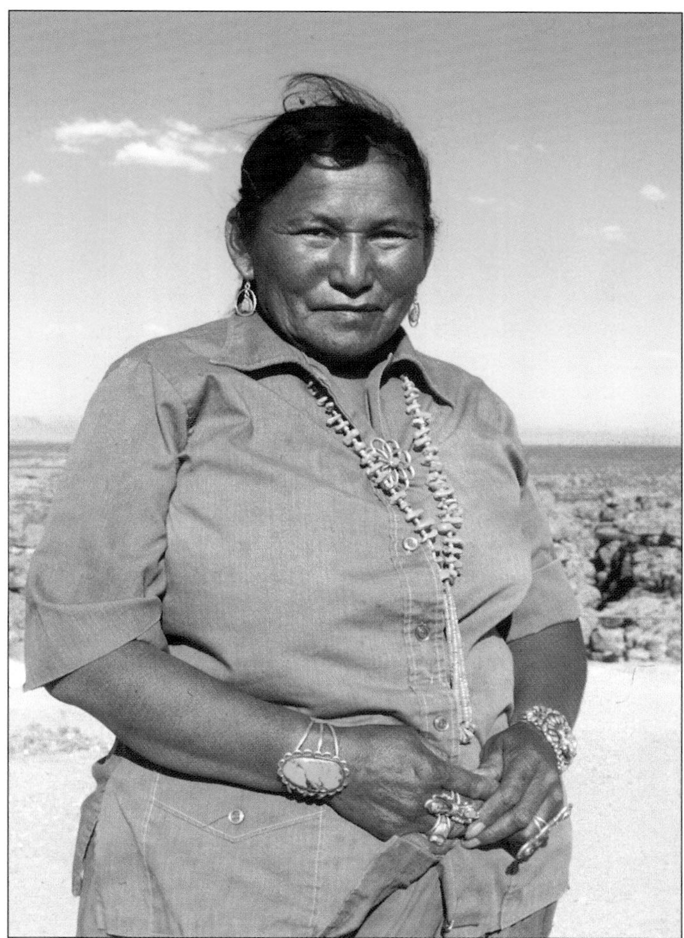

A Navajo woman wearing the traditional turquoise beads. Navajo, also spelt Navaho, is spoken by about 130,000 Native Americans in New Mexico, Arizona, Colorado, and South East Utah. It is used in education, the local media and in public life in the Navajo Reservation. However, social and economic forces can militate against the survival of a language such as Navajo.

Language Attrition in Australia

At the end of the Second World War, Australia was regarded as a predominantly English-speaking country. Since 1947, over four million people from more than one hundred different countries have emigrated to Australia. The 1991 Census in Australia revealed that 75.4 percent of the current population were born in Australia. The remaining 24.6 percent were in-migrants from Oceania (2.1 percent), Europe (13.6 percent), Asia (4.9 percent), Africa (0.8 percent), North America (0.5 percent) and South America (0.9 percent), (with 2.2 percent 'not stating' or classified as 'other' on the Census form; Smolicz, 1994b).

Clyne (1991b) and de Bot & Clyne (1994) have shown the rate of language shift and language attrition in Australia. For example, the Australian 1986 Census showed that there were 95,000 Dutch-born persons living in Australia. The Dutch have been considered model in-migrants 'quick to discard their language and culture and adapt to the dominant group' (de Bot and Clyne, 1994, page 18). The shift of the Dutch to English has been greater than any other group, as the following graph reveals:

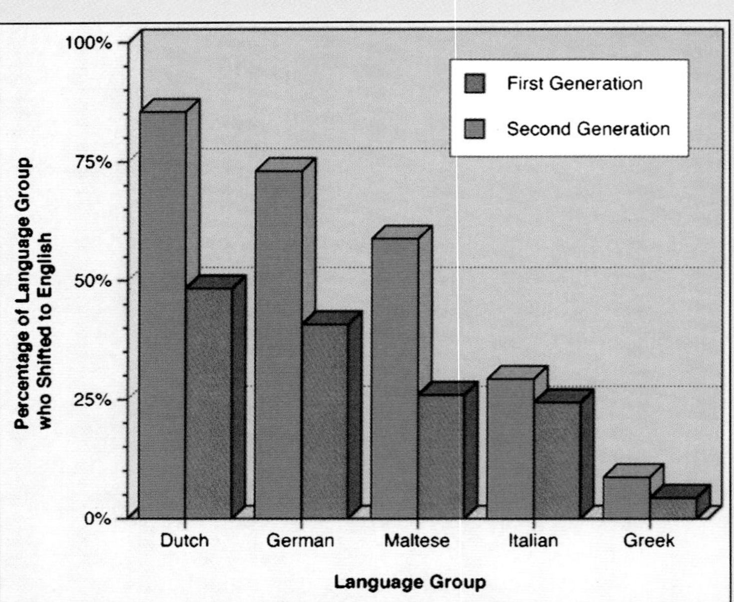

Language shift in Australia. (De Bot & Clyne, 1994)

Conclusion

In spite of the considerable social, political and economic pressures towards language shift, people are often determined to keep a language alive. Language activists, pressure groups, affirmative action and language conservationists may fight for the survival of the threatened language. In Puerto Rico, the government introduced English into schools to attempt bilingualization of the island. Over three-quarters of the population remain functionally monolingual in Spanish (see page 115). Resnick (1993) has shown that nationalism, political uncertainty and the relationship between language and identity have made many Puerto Ricans resistant to language change and the use of English.

Determination is not always enough. The most worthy of minority language causes can founder on the rocks of economic and political realities. Strong wills and affirmative action towards language survival can meet failure in a turbulent sea of personal priorities and political power. Yet language pessimism, even if tinged with realism, in itself constitutes a condition of language decay. Language pessimism can only foster the demise of multilingualism. Therefore, it is important to promote language optimism as it provides the needed psychological energy for multilingualism to struggle and attempt to survive.

Further Reading

AITCHISON, J., 1991, *Language Change: Progress or Decay?* Cambridge: Cambridge University Press.

BRENZINGER, M., 1997, Language Contact and Language Displacement. In F. COULMAS (ed.), *The Handbook of Sociolinguistics*. Oxford: Blackwell.

CRAIG, C. G., 1997, Language Contact and Language Degeneration. In F. COULMAS (ed.), *The Handbook of Sociolinguistics*. Oxford: Blackwell.

DORIAN, N. C., 1981, *Language Death: The Life Cycle of a Scottish Gaelic Dialect*. Philadelphia: University of Pennsylvania Press.

DORIAN, N. C. (ed.), 1989, *Investigating Obsolescence. Studies in Language Contraction and Death*. Cambridge: Cambridge University Press.

DORIAN, N. C., 1994, Choices and Values in Language Shift and Its Study. *International Journal of the Sociology of Language*, 110, 113-124.

EDWARDS, J. R., 1985, *Language, Society and Identity*. Oxford: Blackwell.

EDWARDS, J. R., 1994, *Multilingualism*. London: Routledge.

FISHMAN, J. A., 1989, *Language & Ethnicity in Minority Sociolinguistic Perspective*. Clevedon: Multilingual Matters Ltd.

PAULSTON, C. B., 1994, *Linguistic Minorities in Multilingual Settings*. Amsterdam/Philadelphia: John Benjamins.

PAULSTON, C. B. (ed.), 1988, *International Handbook of Bilingualism and Bilingual Education*. New York: Greenwood.

SKUTNABB-KANGAS, T., 1981, *Bilingualism or Not: The Education of Minorities*. Clevedon: Multilingual Matters Ltd.

The Mapping of Bolivian Language Shift

One of the most outstanding current language maps derives from the 1992 Census in Bolivia. Entitled *Lenguas en Bolivia* (Languages in Bolivia) it has the following features:

1. The map clearly represents not only Aymara, Quechua, Guaraní and Spanish, but also many minority languages (e.g. Chiquitano).

2. The map distinguishes between the indigenous minority languages and in-migrant languages (e.g. Portuguese, Japanese and Menonita – a mixture of German and English).

3. The map has single color areas to show where one language dominates (e.g. Spanish in the north-west) plus shaded areas where both languages are strong. For example, the Aymara language is in yellow and the Quechua language in brown in regions where each language dominates. Where both are found, the areas are shaded using both colors.

4. The presence of minority languages (e.g. in relatively urban areas) is shown clearly by a colored dot and a letter (e.g. a purple dot and the letter 'j' for the presence of the Japanese language).

5. The map uses arrows to show the geographical direction of language shift. For example, Portuguese is advancing in the extreme north-west of Bolivia. Spanish is generally advancing on Aymara, Quechua, Guaraní and the many smaller indigenous languages. A simplified version of the map is presented here.

The population of Bolivia in 1989 was estimated to be over seven million (see page 456), giving the country one of the lowest population densities in South America. There are three official languages, Spanish, Quechua, and Aymara. Guaraní is also recognized as a national language. Up until 1993, Spanish was the sole official language, but the government of President Gonzalo Sanchez de Lozada, elected in June 1993, also gave recognition to the native languages. Spanish is widely spoken in the cities and has traditionally been the language of the educated elite. Quechua and Aymara, together with other Amerindian languages, predominate in rural areas. The new government has also introduced the right of every child to read, write and learn in its mother tongue. The current reforms of education are introducing bilingual education. Approximately 65 percent of the population, or over four million speak one of the native languages, usually in addition to Spanish. There are 35 indigenous Amerindian languages in Bolivia, mostly concentrated in the eastern part of the country. None of the indigenous languages has more than 25 thousand speakers.

The two largest Indian groups are the Quechua and the Aymara. They constitute 37 percent and 25 percent of the population respectively. Mestizos, people of mixed American Indian and European descent, constitute about 25 percent to 30 percent of the population, while people of European ancestry, mainly Spanish, constitute between five percent and 15 percent of Bolivians.

Bilingualism is fairly common in Bolivia. Most of the native Aymara and Quechua speakers also speak Spanish, and an estimated 200 thousand are trilingual in these three languages. Other minority languages include Chiquitano and Guaraní. Both languages have around 20 thousand speakers and are located mainly in south-eastern Bolivia.

REFERENCE: CENSO, 1992

Languages and Language Shift in Bolivia

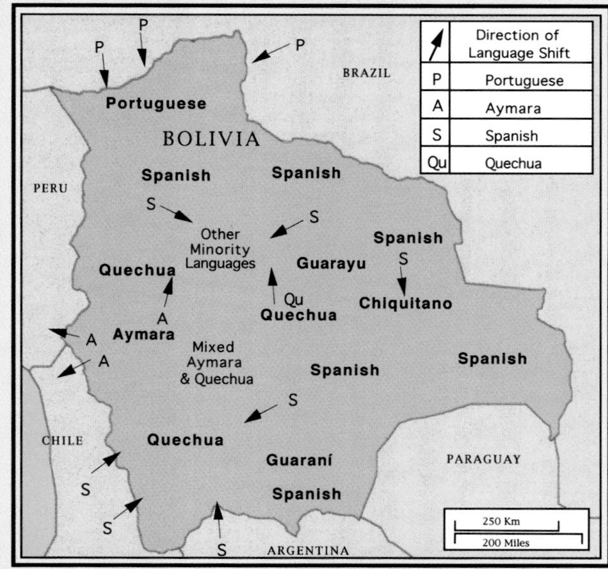

Source: CIPCA (Centro de Investigación y Promoción del Campesidado), 1995, *Bolivia Plurilingüe, Guia Para Planifecadores y Educadores,* UNICEF.

Language Shift among Norwegian In-migrants in the United States

Einar Haugen studied the language usage of Norwegian in-migrants in the United States from the beginnings of immigration from Norway in 1825 until the 1950s. Between 1825 and 1900, over half a million Norwegians emigrated to America, mainly to the rural Midwest, from Illinois to North Dakota. Most Norwegian in-migrants started out as farmers, although many gradually switched to other occupations. They spoke a variety of Norwegian dialects, while most had mastered the standard Dano-Norwegian language that was the current written norm in Norway and taught in schools.

There was a high degree of social and religious cohesion among the 19th century in-migrants. This was encouraged by the close-knit family structure and the relative isolation of Norwegian farms and settlements. Widespread literacy in the minority language was also a factor in its maintenance. The in-migrants quickly established their own cultural and religious institutions.These included a Norwegian language Lutheran church (split into rival synods), a Norwegian language press (consisting of two or three major papers and hundreds of minor journals), many secular organizations such as choral and temperance societies, and Norwegian-American language schools (from elementary to college level). The conservative Norwegian synod, organized in 1853, took a firm stand on the matter of the Norwegian language. As late as 1900, Norwegian only was used in their churches.

At the beginning of the 20th century, the language still seemed to be prospering in America. Newspapers were flourishing and many novels, essays, short stories and books of poetry were published. Norwegian choral societies and other special interest societies proliferated. Societies were formed to work for the preservation of Norwegian in America and to strengthen links with Norway. However, everyday use of Norwegian was diminishing. There were many reasons for this: contact with in-migrants from other nationalities and with English language institutions, intermarriage, change of residence, (moving away from the Norwegian community to seek work in areas where English was dominant), urbanization and improved communications. Over time, loss of contact with relatives and friends in the homeland also lessened peoples' sense of Norwegian identity. As the flood of immigration from Norway diminished, there were far fewer monolingual Norwegian new arrivals to reinforce the community language and ethnic identity.

Another major factor in language shift was the English language school system. The resources had never been available to establish a full-time Norwegian school system, and eventually the English language district schools played their part in Anglicizing Norwegian-American children. The Norwegian Lutheran church had remained resolutely Norwegian in language until 1900, but gradually its leaders were forced to acknowledge that times had changed and that many of its younger members lacked the fluency in Norwegian to follow services in that language. This is a common development in many minority language situations. Religion may initially be a powerful tool in minority language maintenance and minority group cohesion. However, once language shift begins to occur, religious leaders may be forced to assess their priorities and provide opportunities for worship, confession, Bible study and other religious observances in the majority language. Otherwise they may lose their followers.

The factors that influenced the shift from Norwegian to English were similar to those affecting other minority language in-migrant groups in the United States at the time. Notably, the virulent anti-German sentiments created by World War I affected not only German-speaking in-migrants, but other ethnic groups as well, including the Norwegian speakers. Public opinion turned against cultural and linguistic diversity and in favor of assimilation to the English-speaking majority.

The process of shift from Norwegian to English occurred in a similar way to the shift from other languages to English in the United States. It did not occur in all areas and all communities simultaneously. The shift occurred at different times within individual communities and indeed within individual families. First, the children and grandchildren of emigrants became fluent speakers of American English. Second, the borrowing of many words and expressions from English into Norwegian became acceptable.The English loans were fully integrated into the linguistic framework and phonology of Norwegian. So distant from the speech norms of the home country, this Anglicized form of Norwegian was considered normal and acceptable. Third, the functions of Norwegian gradually diminished. Even in the most conservative communities it became limited to family and neighborhood use. Outside the immediate neighborhood and with strangers, English was the automatic choice. Fourth, the use of the language diminished gradually over generations. By the second or third generation born on American soil, most children generally understood at least some Norwegian, but rarely spoke it.

REFERENCES: HAUGEN, 1966, 1967, 1969, 1976

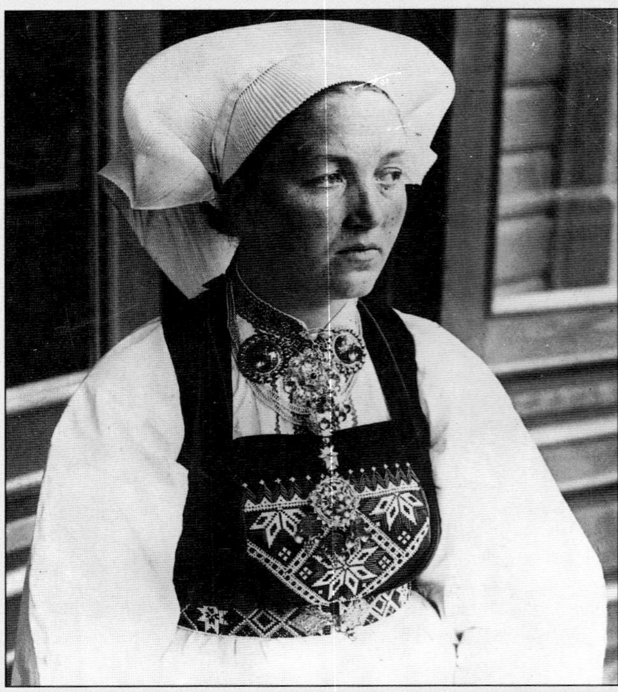

A 19th century Norwegian in-migrant to the US wearing traditional Norwegian costume.

Einar Haugen

Einar Haugen (1906 –1994) was born in Sioux City, Iowa, the son of Norwegian in-migrant parents. At the age of eight his parents took him back to Norway for a two year visit and began his lifelong interest in Scandinavian languages. He taught Scandinavian languages at the University of Wisconsin between 1931 and 1964, and during World War II he taught in the army specialized language training program.

In 1964 he was appointed professor of Scandinavian studies and Linguistics at Harvard University where he remained until his retirement in 1975. He also held visiting lectureships in universities in Sweden, Norway, Iceland, Tokyo, Hungary and the United States. He was recognized as a foremost authority on the Scandinavian languages, with many definitive publications, notably *The Scandinavian Languages: An Introduction to their History* (1976). He also wrote widely on linguistics and bilingualism and published dictionaries and biographies.

Because of his experience as a member of a minority language community in the United States, he had great understanding of the tensions between minority and majority languages and the process of linguistic assimilation. He was recognized as a leader in the development of the fields of bilingualism and language contact, sociolinguistics and language planning.

Among his most influential works were *The Norwegian Language in America* (1953), *Bilingualism in the Americas* (1956) and *Language Conflict and Language Planning: The Case of Modern Norwegian* (1966). Professor Haugen's work to promote the study and understanding of Scandinavian culture and language in the United States earned him the Order of St Olaf, First Class, the highest honor awarded by the Norwegian government.

Language Death

The terminology used to describe language death often borrows its terms from biology, but not without dangers in analogy: language ecology, language survival, language extinction, language death and threatened species. However, unlike animal and plant species, languages have no genes and thus no mechanism for natural selection. Their prospects for survival are determined not by biological mechanisms or the capacity for adaptation, but by social forces.

Thus one major argument for the survival of minority languages is the call for social justice as well as the call for maintenance of diversity of the language garden of the world.

The gravestone of Dolly Pentreath in the churchyard of St Pol-de-Léon in Cornwall, England. Dolly Pentreath, who died in 1777, was claimed to have been the last living speaker of Cornish, a Celtic language closely related to Breton and Welsh. However, others have argued that Cornish lived on as a daily language until the 19th century. There are current attempts to revive the Cornish language.

Language Decline in the Ryukyuan Languages of Japan

The state of Japan in East Asia is comprised of four large islands, Hokkaido, Honshu (the largest, called the mainland), Shikoku and Kyushu, as well as the islands of Ryukyu, to the south-west of Kyushu, and over a thousand adjacent islands. Almost the entire population of Japan (121 million in 1986) speaks dialect varieties of Japanese. (The Japanese language is also spoken by another two million Japanese people living in other parts of the world.)

Japan is reputed to be a relatively monolingual and monocultural country. This is not true. Beside sizable in-migrant populations of Korean and Chinese as well as other, smaller in-migrant groups, and a widespread knowledge of English, there are two indigenous minority language groups, the Ryukyuan and the Ainu.

The Ryukyuan languages

The group of languages spoken on the islands of Ryukyu are related to the dialects of other parts of Japan. There has been considerable discussion as to whether the Ryukyuan languages should be described as dialects of Japanese or as a separate group of languages. Certainly, a Japanese speaker from another part of Japan would not be able to understand the vernaculars of Ryukyu. However, it must be stressed that, because of the geographical nature of Japan, consisting of an archipelago of numerous mountainous islands, considerable dialectal variety exists between different areas. Many Japanese dialects are not intelligible to Japanese speakers from other parts of Japan. The dialects spoken in the Ryukyuan islands are not all mutually intelligible. However, this group of dialects do form a distinct variety.

It is not clear when the Ryukyuan language began to develop separately from Japanese, but some scholars have suggested that this happened about 1500 years ago. The question whether a speech form is a dialect or a separate language is often a political rather than a linguistic issue. (See Dialects and Language Boundaries, page 135.) Today Ryukyuan is as similar to Standard Japanese as English to German or French to Italian. Less similarity exists between it and Standard Japanese than many pairs of languages, e.g. Catalan and Spanish.

A national language for Japan

Since the Meiji Restoration in 1867, there has been a strong movement for national unity in Japan. This required the linguistic and cultural unification of the country and the assimilation of linguistic and ethnic minorities. The economic, educational and social development of Japan also led to the adoption of a common or standard language. From the late 19th century onwards, the government promoted the use of a standard form of Japanese, based on the dialect of the Tokyo area. This was called hyojun-go (standard language). Standard Japanese was taught in schools, and children were not allowed to use Ryukyuan. A child heard speaking Ryukyuan would be made to wear a wooden plate, the hoogen-huda. The child would wear the wooden plate until it could be passed on to another child caught using Ryukyuan. Students wearing the plate were punished. Use of the hoogen-huda, (reminiscent of punishment for speaking Welsh – the 'Welsh Not', or speaking Breton – the Symbole in Brittany), continued until after the Second World War. The banning of Ryukyuan from schools was a means of reinforcing the idea that dialects were inferior.

Descriptions of language decline, especially from the viewpoint of partisans and supporters of a minority language, often portray this process as one enforced from without, against the wishes of the minority group. However, the factors that create the conditions for language decline are myriad and complex, and often involve the acquiescence in some way of the minority group. This acquiescence can be caused by a variety of pressures, including social and economic pressures.

A major factor in the decline of Ryukyuan has been the economic development of Japan. Industrialization and centralization of government have meant the movement of people from rural to urban areas. Because of the dialectal variety existing in Japan, a single common language has been seen as desirable. The promotion of the standard language in Japan has provided a lingua franca for a more economically mobile population. Education has also encouraged the use of a common language. The decline of the local dialects in the Ryukyuan islands has happened very swiftly because this need has been perceived and agreed by many in the local population.

The desire to identify with Japanese nationalism has also led to the swift adoption of Standard Japanese among rural peoples. As stated earlier, the Ryukyuan islands formed an independent kingdom during the Middle Ages. In 1609 they were adopted as a Japanese protectorate and in 1879 were incorporated into Japan. After World War II, the islands were occupied by the US military until 1972, when they were officially returned to Japan. The history of the islands has made the islanders more eager to identify with and to assimilate with the rest of Japan. In the case of the Ryukyuan islands, the local government, the Okinawa prefecture, was one of the first prefectures in Japan to promote the use of Standard Japanese. The hoogen-huda was originally implemented voluntarily by junior high school students in Okinawa.

The future of the Ryukyuan dialects

In the Ryukyuan islands at the end of the 20th century there remain few monoglot speakers of local dialects. Most people over 50 are proficiently bilingual in a local dialect and Standard Japanese, and can switch from one to the other according to context. The younger generation of speakers are generally less fluent in their local dialects, and tend to codeswitch into Standard Japanese, and use many lexical borrowings from Standard Japanese. Their speech also shows less stylistic variation and a smaller repertoire of registers than that of older speakers. The local dialects are often no longer being transmitted from parents to children. Most parents of young children are themselves dominant in Standard Japanese and tend to use that language with their children.

The future of the Ryukyuan languages is uncertain. There are enthusiastic partisans of the local vernaculars who are concerned about their decline and are trying to promote the extension of their use. However, a variety of social and economic pressures are accelerating the shift to Standard Japanese and it may be difficult to reverse the tide and achieve a stable bilingual situation.

REFERENCES: MAHER & YASHIRO, 1995; MATSUMORI, 1995, SHIBATINI, 1994

The Ainu Language of Japan

The Ainu people are thought to have been the original inhabitants of Japan and to have been gradually driven north by invaders now known as the Japanese. Many anthropologists believe that the ancestors of the Ainu belonged to the Caucasoid race. However, because of intermarriage over many generations with the Japanese, the concept of a 'pure' Ainu ethnic group is no longer feasible. As with other ethnic groups throughout the world, to be Ainu is partly a matter of family heritage and partly a matter of self-identification. Some supporters of the Ainu language and culture are not Ainu by birth. Some people possessing an Ainu heritage have denied it, because of the risk of discrimination and stigmatization. The Ainu language was once spoken widely in Hokkaido, and in the Russian islands of Sakhalin and the Kuriles. Ainu is what is known as a 'language isolate'. In other words, it does not appear to be related to any other known language. Spoken Ainu has no standard form, but is a collection of dialects. However, the Ainu oral tradition that has been handed down is in an older, classical form of the language that has less dialectal variation.

The Japanese subjugated the northern island of Hokkaido, then called Yezogashima, at the end of the 18th century. When the Meiji government came to power at the end of the 19th century, with its emphasis on national unity and assimilation, the Japanese introduced an aggressive colonial policy. They took away the traditional freedoms of the Ainu people to hunt and fish, to use their language and practice their customs. The Ainu continued to exist as an underclass but gradually were assimilated almost completely by the Japanese. Occasionally, whole communities were relocated and this also destabilized traditional Ainu life. The fate of the Ainu people in Russian-occupied territories was similar. Over the years, most discriminatory legislation has been revoked, but the decline in the Ainu language, culture and lifestyle has been very marked and perhaps irreversible.

The current Ainu population of Japan, the majority of whom live in the northernmost island of Hokkaido, is estimated at about 24,000, although the true figure might be between 50,000 and 60,000. The Ainu language is now no longer used as a daily language of communication by any community. It is only generally spoken with any fluency by elderly people, who were brought up in Ainu-speaking communities. Some younger Ainu can remember their parents, grandparents and other people speaking the language, and have some basic competence in it. There are also many second language speakers of Ainu, who have learnt the language in organized courses. Several Ainu language schools have been established in Hokkaido, to teach young people the Ainu language, traditions and folklore.

A Japanese Aboriginal Ainu.

In recent years Ainu activists have campaigned for redress for the wrongs done to them and for the restitution of their linguistic and territorial rights. They have sought the help of the United Nations and other international bodies. The Japanese government refuses to acknowledge that the Ainu are a minority ethnic group with a separate ethnic, cultural and linguistic history. Despite the lack of government support, there has been a great increase in the publication of books and magazines, audio and video recordings of native speakers, and some radio and television broadcasts. There has been particular interest in audio recordings of the traditional *yukar* or epic verse and other types of verse, folktales and song performed by elderly native speakers. Ainu cultural festivals have become increasingly popular and the use of the language in traditional Ainu rituals has been revived. There has been an increased uptake of Ainu language courses in the community and at university. The Ainu language and culture have had a higher profile and greater support than ever.

The Ainu language will probably never again be a daily means of communication for any community. However, it appears that it may survive as the vehicle for the accessing and expression of traditional Ainu culture and ritual and an important marker of Ainu identity.

REFERENCES:
DECHICCHIS 1995; MAHER & YASHIRO, 1995; SHIBATINI, 1994

6: Language Borrowings

Introduction

When different languages come into contact, there is often transfer between languages. Words and phrases from one language may be adopted by speakers of the other language. This usually happens within a bilingual community, when both languages are used regularly by many members of the community, and where there is codeswitching and codemixing between languages. In such a situation, not only may words and phrases be borrowed, but idioms, expressions and syntactic structures of one language may be transferred in translation to the other language. Words and phrases may be borrowed from one language to another by individual speakers or temporarily by sections of the community. When words and phrases make their home permanently in the other language and are widely used, they are usually classed as loans or borrowings. The direction of the language transfer generally depends on the relative prestige, numerical strength and dominance of the languages within the community.

Language borrowing can also occur where widespread bilingualism and day-to-day language contact does not exist. Throughout the centuries, 'educated borrowing' has occurred from one written or literary language to another. Even after Latin ceased to be an everyday spoken language in Western Europe, it continued to be used in many countries as the language of the church, law, philosophy, science and government. Many words were borrowed from Latin by scribes, lawyers, politicians and scholars, and some became part of the everyday vocabulary of other languages. In the contemporary world, the advances in science and technology have meant that the borrowing of 'international' (usually Graeco-Roman) terminology has become commonplace. Another source of language borrowing in the modern world is the mass media. Television, advertising and popular music, in particular, have been a route for many English borrowings into other languages in all parts of the world, for instance, French and Japanese.

Reasons for Language Borrowings

Language transfer may happen for various reasons.

One language may possess words for which there are no equivalents in the other language. These may be words for objects, social, political and cultural institutions and events or abstract concepts which are not found in the culture of the other language. We can take some examples from the English language throughout the ages. English has borrowed words for types of houses (e.g. castle, mansion, teepee, wigwam, igloo, bungalow). It has borrowed words for cultural institutions (e.g. opera, ballet). It has borrowed words for political concepts (e.g. perestroika, glasnost, apartheid). It often happens that one culture borrows from the language of another culture words or phrases to express technological, social or cultural innovations.

A language may borrow a word for which it already has an adequate equivalent. In some cases, the borrowing may take the place of the indigenous equivalent. In other cases, both words may co-exist, often enriching the language by expressing different shades of meaning. French/Latin borrowings into English have often been used for more formal expressions than their Anglo-Saxon or Germanic equivalents. (See Textbox.)

With the rapid and constant advances in science and technology during the 20th century it has simply not been practical for speakers of different languages to create their own neologisms for every single one of the plethora of new scientific and technological terms that are constantly being spawned. There are three main reasons for this.

Firstly, languages form words in different ways. Not all languages have word formation processes that allow them to create equivalents for new terminology. Languages such as French and Japanese, for instance, tend to create rather roundabout expressions to correspond to a single term.

Secondly, creating new indigenous terminology takes time, expertise, and some method of publicizing and disseminating the new words. It is often simply more convenient to borrow an established 'international' term, if necessary adapting it to the phonology, orthography and pronunciation of the language.

Thirdly, within the fields of science and technology it is important to ensure accurate term-for-term equivalence between languages. Scientific and technological documents are constantly being translated into different languages. Scientists, computer experts, engineers, physi-

A Typology of Loan Words

Some of the terminology used to describe the form in which words or phrases can be transferred from one language to another is confusing. Appel & Muysken (1987), following Haugen (1950), have constructed the following simple typology of loans. They make an initial distinction between importation and substitution. Importation involves the introduction of an element from the source language into the target language. Substitution involves replacing an element from the source language with a native pattern. Loans may involve importation and/or substitution.

Appel & Muysken (1987) give the example of a Spanish speaker who says "Dáme un Wheesky' ('Give me a whiskey'). He has imported the English word 'whiskey' into Spanish but has substituted the Spanish sound 'ee' for English 'i'. Bearing in mind this initial distinction, Appel and Muysken (1987) define three main categories of loans.

Simple loan words, imported from the source language e.g. French *'chic'* borrowed into English. As the above example of 'whiskey' shows, often the word or phrase is adapted to some degree to the phonological system of the base (borrowing) language.The phonological system means the sounds used in a language and the way they are used. This includes both vowels and consonants, the distinctions made between them and the ways in which they can be combined. Not all languages use the same range of sounds. For instance, English has no equivalent vowel sound to the 'u' in French *'tu'* and no equivalent consonantal sound to the Welsh 'll' in Llangollen. For this reason, English speakers find these sounds difficult to pronounce. Languages do not make the same meaningful distinctions between sounds. In Chinese and Japanese, 'r' and 'l' are not distinguished as separate sounds which is why Chinese and Japanese speakers have difficulty distinguishing these sounds in English, and in English borrowings into Chinese or Japanese, the sound 'l' is often expressed as 'r', e.g. Japanese *erekutorinikkusu* for electronics.

When a word is borrowed into another language, it is usually first borrowed by bilinguals, who probably pronounce the source language fairly accurately. From there, however, it may be adopted into the speech of monolingual speakers of the borrowing language where it may undergo some form of phonological adaptation.

To give some examples of French-English borrowing, the words 'restaurant', 'savoir faire', 'hors d'oeuvres' have all been borrowed from French into English at a time when the French language had considerable prestige as a language of culture. They were first borrowed by an elite who pronounced them as they would be pronounced in French. Over the years they have become widely used by non-French speakers and thus have been adapted to the phonology or sound system of English. The 'r' at the beginning of the word 'restaurant' is pronounced like an English initial 'r', not rolled like a French 'r'. In British English the 'r's at the end of the two words 'savoir faire' are silent, like an British English 'r' in final position. In North American English the 'r's in final position are pronounced but not rolled as in French. In both British and North American English, the 's' at the end of hors d'oeuvres and the 't' at the end of restaurant are pronounced.

Similarly, the French have borrowed 'camping' from English (to mean campsite which they pronounce 'compeeng'. Parking borrowed into French from English to mean car park is pronounced with a rolled 'r' – 'parrkeeng'. Because the phonological systems of French and English are not very different, loan words tend to retain a fairly recognizable form. However, when words are transferred between two languages that have very divergent phonological systems, they may be transformed out of all recognition to speakers of the source language. One example is the growing number of English words that are being borrowed into Japanese. Japanese has quite a different phonological system from English, and so sounds that do not exist in Japanese may be converted to the nearest Japanese equivalent e.g. *rajio* radio, *takushi* taxi, *rabu* love, *basu* bus. Most final consonants are followed by a vowel and Japanese tends to break the clusters of consonants so often used in English. So Christmas becomes *kurisumasu* and project becomes *purojekuto.* Japanese tends to abbreviate many foreign words to adapt them to the Japanese system: most Japanese words are composed of only two, three or four *moras* (syllables). Thus in Japanese amateur has become *ama,* television has become *terebi* and illustration has become *irasuto.* Japanese has a tradition of abbreviating compound words, so department store has become *depaato*, word processor has become *wapuro* and mass communications has become *masukomi.*

Loan shifts, also called calques (literally 'copies') or loan translations, where only the meaning is imported. In a loan shift or calque, the components of a word or phrase in the source language are translated literally into the target language. To give one well-documented example, skyscraper in English has given *gratte-ciel* in French, *Wolkenkratzer* in German (literally 'cloud-scrape'), *wolkenkrabber* in Dutch and *rasca cielos* in Spanish.

Loan blend. A loan blend occurs when the meaning of a word is borrowed but only part of the form, e.g. Dutch 'software *huis'* from software house. Loan blends are quite common in Japanese where an English word is combined with a Japanese word, such as *ha-burashi* (toothbrush), and the now famous loan blend which has been borrowed into English and other languages from Japanese, *kara-oke* (literally 'empty orchestra').

REFERENCE: APPEL & MUYSKEN, 1987

Examples of Loan Words and Phrases Used in Speaking English

The following list contains a mixture of loan words. Some have been used for many years in spoken and written English (e.g. Latin words) and other words only recently used. Some words are regularly used and others are used by particular social groups and particular geographical areas. Some are seen by linguists as now part of the English language, other words as still 'foreign'. Thus dimensions of time and history, frequency of usage, sociocultural differences, standardization and geographical variation are present in this varied list.

adiós (Spanish) - goodbye
aficionado (Spanish) – fan, ardent follower
albino (Latin, Portuguese) – person or animal with white skin and hair, and pink irises
al fresco (Italian) – in the fresh, open air
amigo (Spanish) – a friend
anorak (Eskimo/Inuit) – a hooded outer jacket
bagel (Yiddish) – a hard bread roll in the shape of a ring
barrios (Spanish) – a neighborhood, community or district (often disadvantaged)
bête noire (French) – object of dislike
blitz (German) – a sudden, overwhelming attack, an air-raid
bon appetit (French) – good appetite, eat well
bungalow (Hindi) – a one-level house
c'est la vie (French) – it's life; that's life
chutzpah (Yiddish) – incredible nerve bordering on arrogance
cliché (French) – hackneyed phrase
connoisseur (French) – expert judge of taste
cul-de-sac (French) – a road closed at one end
curriculum (Latin) – a course of study, prescribed subjects
déjà vu (French) – the feeling that something happening has occurred before
doppelgänger (German) – a double, an apparition
élite (French) – high status, select
en suite (French) – connected, forming a unit, integral
esprit de corps (French) – team spirit, camaraderie
eureka (Greek) – I've found it, a discovery
ex officio (Latin) – by virtue of office
extempore (Latin) – without preparation, impromptu
faux pas (French) – false step, blunder, a mistake
fiesta (Spanish) – carnival, holiday, festivity
flak (German) – adverse criticism, disagreement
flotilla (Spanish) – a small fleet
gillie (Gaelic) – someone guiding or attending a hunter or a person fishing
gingham (Malay) – striped or checked material
glasnost (Russian) – a policy of openness and forthrightness; speaking belligerently
goulash (Hungarian) – a stew
guerrilla (Spanish) – harassment by small gangs
hasta la vista (Spanish) – farewell, until we meet again
hoi polloi (Greek) – the populace, the masses
junta (Spanish) – a meeting, council or cabal
kaput(t) (German) – ruined, broken, smashed
kiosk (Turkish) – a small pavilion or stall
kitsch (German) – art work that is inferior, pretentious, in bad taste
laissez faire (French) – allow matters to take their own course, non–interference
leprechaun (Irish) – small mischievous pixie or fairy
lieder (German) – a German song, especially from the Romantic period
machismo (Spanish) – a cult of male virility and masculine pride
mañana (Spanish) – tomorrow
marmalade (French and Portuguese) – a jam made from oranges
matinée (French) – afternoon performance
mavourneen (Irish) – my dear one
palaver (Portuguese) – wordy conferring
parka (Aleutian Eskimo/Inuit) – wind-proof shirt or coat
pas op (Afrikaans) – look out
patio (Spanish) – a courtyard, paved area adjoining a house
perestroika (Russian) – reconstructing society
persona non grata (Latin) – unacceptable person
plaza (Spanish) – market place or open square
pot-pourri (French) – a mixture of scented materials, tunes, writing or a stew
quid pro quo (Latin) – something given or taken in return for something else
raison d'être (French) – the reason for being
robot (Czech) – a mechanical, 'high tech' automaton
sabotage (French) – deliberate damage to property
salaam aleikum (Arabic) – peace be with you
sang-froid (French) – coolness, self-possession
sauna (Finnish) – a steam bath
savoir faire (French) – tact, diplomacy
savvy (Spanish) – to understand
señorita (Spanish) – a young lady (Miss)
shibboleth (Hebrew) – a test word, a catchword or password of a group (Book of Judges, 12, 5-6)
shish kebab (Turkish) – skewered meat and vegetables
sisu (Finnish) – determination, stubbornness, strength in character
sofa (Arabic) – a seat
spritzer (German) – a drink of white wine and soda water
tête-à-tête (French) – private, face-to-face conversation
thug (Hindi) – a violent person
torso (Italian) – trunk of a human body
tycoon (Japanese, old Chinese) – a business magnate
veranda (Hindi) – a roofed gallery or balcony
verbatim (Latin) – word-for-word
vice versa (Latin) – the reverse, the other way round
yashmak (Arabic) – a veil worn by some Muslim women in public
yen (Chinese) – a persistent desire
yeti (Tibetan) – the abominable snowman
yoghourt (Turkish) – milk fermented by bacteria
zeitgeist (German) – the spirit of the age

Foreign Words in the English Language

English is basically a Germanic language, first brought to Britain in the fifth and sixth centuries AD by a huge influx of invading immigrants from an area that is now Germany and Denmark. English has accepted borrowings from other languages freely and indiscriminately during its long history.

Old English was influenced by the Latin still spoken in Britain by the remnants of the Roman army and by merchants and romanized city dwellers with whom the earliest invaders came into contact. The invaders borrowed words for food, drink and household objects, for buildings and settlements, military and legal institutions, and commerce. However, the main source of Latin vocabulary was the Christian religion. Hundreds of Latin words pertaining mainly to religion and the church came into the English language via Christian missionaries. Borrowings from spoken Latin continued until the 11th century, and after that time, as Latin was still used as the language of scholarship, religion and law, many Latin borrowings were used in these and other technical fields.

The next big influence on English was the speech of the Viking invaders who raided Britain between the 8th and 10th centuries and settled in many north-eastern areas. Nearly a 1000 Norse words have survived in modern English, including again, anger, awkward, birth, bull, cake, crawl, die, dirt, egg, flat, fog, get, guess, happy, husband, ill, kid, knife, law, leg, loan, outlaw, race, reindeer, rid, root, scare, scowl, scrap, silver, sister, skill, skirt, sky, skin, take, Thursday, want, weak, window.

However, the main influence on English has been Norman French, following the invasion and accession to the throne of William the Conqueror in 1066. After William was established as king, French became the language of power and prestige. French-speaking barons took over the land, and French-speaking abbots and bishops were appointed. For over a century, French was used almost exclusively by the new aristocracy, while English was the language of the common people. After this time, contacts between English and French speakers, as well as widespread intermarriage, meant that bilingualism was on the increase. Eventually, English gained the upper hand. By the end of the 12th century, contemporary accounts suggest that some children of the nobility spoke English as a mother tongue and were educated in French. French continued to be used at the royal court and in government, law and administration and in the Church (often side by side with Latin).

At the beginning of the 13th century, England lost Normandy and the English aristocracy lost their estates in France. This led eventually to the Hundred Years War and to a rise in English nationalism and the status of English at the expense of French. However, the widespread bilingualism of the two previous centuries had meant a massive influx of French loan words into English, perhaps as many as 10,000. About three-quarters of these French loan words still survive in modern English. Some French words described new objects and concepts, others supplanted existing English words, while others co-existed with the English equivalent and often developed slightly different meanings e.g. doom (E) and judgement (F), house (E) and mansion (F).

Many words were loaned from French in the areas of administration, science and learning, law, religion and the military, reflecting the contexts in which they were used. Words were also borrowed from Latin for use in formal or literary contexts. The following table shows that English words of Anglo-Saxon provenance often have a more everyday, homely ring, while words borrowed from French or Latin have retained a more formal, literary flavor.

Anglo-Saxon	French/Latin
help	aid
begin	commence
hide	conceal
happiness	felicity
cut	incision
deep	profound
wish	desire

During the Middle English period, the estimated proportion of loan words in English rose from ten percent to 25 percent.

Throughout the history of the English language, English speakers have borrowed freely from other languages. The list below gives some idea of the variety of languages that have enriched English throughout the centuries. As the English language spread from England to the US, Australia, New Zealand, South Africa and many other countries throughout the world, it has borrowed from the indigenous languages of these areas, giving rise to regional varieties of English.

cists, medical experts and others involved in specialized technical fields need to communicate accurately with colleagues in other countries. Existing words in the indigenous languages or neologisms created from indigenous elements sometimes have the advantage that they are more 'transparent' to native speakers, but they may have more general meanings and may possibly be ambiguous. Borrowing from existing international terminology can ensure that the narrow, specialized, 'technical' meaning of a term is maintained.

Words and phrases can be borrowed simply because of their prestige value. If a language and culture are perceived to be prestigious, powerful, stylish or fashionable, then words and cultural expressions may readily be borrowed into other languages. One example is the way in which French words and expressions referring to fashionable or polite society have been borrowed into English over generations. Their use has declined over the last 20 years but one can still enter a high-class restaurant, open the 'menu', order a 'hors d'oeuvre' or an 'à la carte' meal, have a word with the 'chef' or ask for some wine from the 'cave de maison'. In recent years, French, together with many other languages, has borrowed extensively from English simply because the Anglo-American culture and language evokes connotations of power, prestige, authority and reliability, as well as being perceived as fashionable and fun.

Borrowing usually occurs from the stronger, majority language into the weaker, minority language. Borrowing is a normal phenomenon although language purists may oppose it for aesthetic, or nationalistic reasons. (See Linguistic Purism, page 217). Borrowing is a natural part of the evolution of a language. However, extensive lexical borrowing and widespread transfer of idioms and syntactic structures from a majority language into a minority language can be one aspect of language shift and language loss.

Further Reading

APPEL, R. & MUYSKEN, P., 1987, *Language Contact and Bilingualism.* London: Edward Arnold.

WEINREICH, U., 1968, *Languages in Contact: Findings and Problems.* The Hague: Mouton.

English Loan Words in Japanese: 1

An examination of the patterns of word borrowing in Japanese gives some insight into how the influence of one language on another can be positive and enriching. It also shows how linguistic and cultural constraints can affect the extent of foreign borrowing. Japanese, like English, has a relatively high proportion of loan words in its lexicon. Japan has traditionally borrowed from its more culturally advanced neighbor, China. It is generally believed that Chinese words first entered the Japanese language during the 1st century AD or perhaps even before that. Around 400 AD, there began a more widespread infiltration of Chinese words into Japanese, when Korean scholars brought Chinese books to Japan. For many centuries these remained as 'educated' borrowings by scribes and scholars for use mainly in official documents and literary and scholarly texts. By the 17th century, however, many Chinese words had penetrated into local Japanese dialects. It is estimated that over half the words in the Japanese lexicon are derived from Chinese. Words have also been borrowed from other neighboring languages, including Korean, Ainu, Thai and Indonesian.

However, the pattern of modern word borrowing in Japanese reflects the influence of more distant Western languages. The first Japanese contacts with the Western world were with Portuguese, Spanish and Dutch traders between the 16th and 19th centuries. The first Western loan words in Japanese came from these three languages. Later, French was also studied in Japan as an international language of culture and diplomacy, and German in the study of medical science. However, in the latter half of the 19th century, the focus gradually shifted to English as the main language of international communication.

With the spread of international trade and communications, geographical proximity is no longer a factor in word borrowing. English is the language of popular, prestigious, all-pervasive Anglo-American culture. It is also the medium through which many modern technological and scientific developments reach the world. It is the language of much international trade and business. It is perceived as representing status and authority. Many languages throughout the world borrow from English, even in countries like Japan where English is not widely used as a second or official language (see page 311 on World Englishes).

Foreign words, mostly English, constitute approximately ten percent of the lexicon of a standard Japanese dictionary. Thirteen percent of the words used in daily Japanese conversation are foreign words and 60–70 percent of new words coming into the Japanese language are from English. As we have seen, loan words are assimilated phonologically to Japanese, to the extent that they are often completely unintelligible to native speakers of the source languages.

There is concern about the growing influx of Western borrowings into Japanese, and linguistic purists are constantly advocating the use of indigenous Japanese words or the creation of neologisms from Japanese roots instead of borrowing foreign words. However, despite opposition on 'aesthetic' or 'nationalistic' grounds, the tendency to borrow from foreign words is unlikely to be reversed. There are several reasons for this.

1. Many loan words express new concepts which cannot easily or concisely be translated into Japanese (e.g. informed consent, terminal care.) Japanese equivalents for these and many other modern specialized terms tend to be unwieldy and circuitous, and it takes time to coin new terms. In many technical, scientific or other specialized fields, it has often been simpler to borrow from English or to use a recognized international term.

2. Japanese has earned the reputation, by those unfamiliar with it, of a 'vague' and 'imprecise' language. In fact, Japanese is no more imprecise than any other language. However, cultural values mean that Japanese people often prefer euphemisms and roundabout expressions to blunt and plain descriptions. Using a foreign word can provide a way of softening a harsh reality or giving something a better image. One example of this is the English borrowing, *loon* (= loan). Japan's development into a consumer economy in the 1950s depended on mass consumption and buying on credit. However, Japanese traditional ethics embraced thrift, frugality and living within one's means. The indigenous word for 'borrowing', *'shakkin'*, implied immorality, fecklessness and poverty. Using the neutral word '*loon*' meant that these unpleasant connotations could be avoided.

3. Loan words are used to express new experiences and concepts derived from the culture of the source language. Japanese has borrowed many English words describing aspects of modern Anglo-American culture e.g. soul food, ethnicity, homeless, drug, gun control.

4. A loan word can be used where a Japanese word already exists, to provide a different shade or texture of meaning. The indigenous Japanese word '*torikeshi*' means 'cancellation' and can refer to any type of cancellation, even the act of taking back one's words. The Sino-Japanese borrowing '*kaiyaku'* normally refers to the cancellation of contracts and other formal transactions. The English loan word '*kyanseru'* is only used for the cancellation of appointments or ticket reservations.

Foreign loan words in Japanese are thus often used in a narrower, more specific sense than their original meaning in the source language. The word '*sutekki*' (= stick) refers specifically to a walking stick. '*Hitto-end-run*' (= hit-and-run) refers specifically to a particular kind of play in baseball. '*Raisu*' (= rice) is cooked rice served in a Western-style restaurant or served on a plate as opposed to in a rice bowl.

Transfer or shift in meaning is also a fairly frequent occurrence. '*Manshon*' (= mansion) has come to mean a small condominium. The shift in meaning can sometimes be surprising. '*Abekku*' (= French *avec* = with)

English Loan Words in Japanese: 2

has come to mean a couple who are dating.

In general, native words have broader meanings than foreign borrowings. Borrowings from Chinese generally convey a more formal impression and are used for higher quality objects than their native equivalents. Many Japanese words for abstract and academic concepts are Chinese borrowings. Foreign loan words often give a modern, fashionable impression. The English loan word 'living room' has a more modern, contemporary feel than '*chanoma*' (tea room) or even '*ima*' (living room).

5. Foreign loan words, and especially English loan words, are popular because they are associated with high status Western culture and convey a stylish, fashionable, impression. English, particularly, is identified with prestigious Anglo-American culture and regarded as being 'trendy' and also having connotations of power, authority and status. This can be seen particularly in the area of commercial advertising. English borrowings in advertisement slogans and product names may not be fully understood by the general public. Nonetheless they convey an attractive impression. Entire phrases may consist of foreign loan words except for inflectional endings, particles and other minor function words. An advertisement for women's underwear reads: '*hippu o 3-senchi appu-suru*' (to up (raise) the hips 3 centimeters).

6. The structure of Japanese has made it easier for the language to accept foreign borrowings. The language does not mark gender, person or number on nouns, and thus a loan word may simply be inserted where a native noun would appear, without any morphological change. For borrowing verbal expressions, Japanese utilizes the verb suru which has the general meaning 'do'. It has been used with the English loan '*kopii*', for instance, '*kopii-suru*' means to copy.

7. A great influx of English loan words into Japanese occurred as Japan confronted Anglo-American language and culture at two particular periods. The first of these was the period following the Meiji restoration (1867) when Japan relaxed its ban on contact with foreigners, and the second was the period after the end of the Pacific war.

During the first of these two periods, there was a tendency to create Japanese equivalents for many English words that represented new concepts such as 'democracy' and 'liberty'. The meanings of these words were semantically transferred into Japanese using *kanji* characters. During the second period, the trend was to borrow English words. There was a particular reason for this. Japanese is written in two scripts. The *kanji* script, derived from Chinese characters, is mostly used to represent lexical items such as nouns and verb stems. Each item is represented by a single character. Elements of grammatical function such as prefixes, suffixes, and inflectional endings are usually represented by the phonetic *kana* script, where each syllable is represented by a separate symbol. There are two forms of the *kana* script: *Katakana* (partial *kana*) with an abbreviation of characters with a square shape; and *Hirakana* (plain *kana*) with a simplified style of writing characters with a more round shape.

A main disadvantage of the *kanji* script is that each character must be learnt separately. Children at school initially learn to read using the *kana* script and it takes many years for them to learn and master sufficient *kanji* characters even for everyday purposes such as reading a newspaper. There have been many campaigns to abolish the use of *kanji* in favor of *kana* script or *roomaji* (Roman script). Eventually, in 1946, the government decided upon a compromise, limiting the number of *kanji* characters to 1850 (revised in 1981 to 1945 characters). This basic list of Chinese characters represents those to be learnt during primary and secondary education. Most newspapers try to limit the use of characters to these 1945. If other characters are used, a reading of the word in *kana* script is printed alongside. Because of the restriction on the use of *kanji* script, and the increasing use of the *kana* script, it has been easier to borrow foreign words, adapting them to the phonology of Japanese and writing them in the *kana* script.

8. Since 1947, English has been a compulsory subject in Japanese high schools. The majority of people in Japan today have studied English as a foreign language for the statutory six years. However, this has not resulted in widespread competence in English, for two main reasons. First, English is not widely used in Japan as a language of general communication. Second, there has been an overemphasis on written examinations in English at the cost of emphasis on communicative English. The widespread teaching of English has meant, notwithstanding, that the majority of Japanese people are familiar with the English language, its sound, form and much basic vocabulary. This has facilitated the adoption of English loan words into Japanese.

Western, especially English, loan words, abound in modern Japanese. It has even been predicted that the vocabulary will be completely internationalized before long. A trend of relexification of Japanese, replacing Sino-Japanese borrowings by English borrowings, seems already to be happening. Thus '*nooto*' (= note) has superseded '*choomen*' (notebook). '*Depaato*' (= department store) is gradually replacing '*hyakkaten*'. Purists are alarmed at the tendency to use so many English words, especially since they are not always fully understood.

Despite protests, the trend of using English loan words is unlikely to abate, for the reasons outlined above. Word borrowing, together with other types of inter language influence, is a normal part of language evolution and is one way of enriching and strengthening a language.

REFERENCE: NOBUYUKI, 1995

7: Language Vitality

Introduction

The recent history of Hebrew and Welsh, of Catalan and Bahasa Melayu (the indigenous language of Malaysia) provide a more optimistic lyric than the lament of language decline and death. Just as rain forests and whales have become the subject of environmental protection, so languages may be protected and promoted to effect revival and reversal. This topic focuses on the possibilities of language maintenance and considers one major theoretical contribution to the question 'How is language vitality achieved?'

Language Shift and Vitality

In an attempt to create a model rather than a list of the many factors involved in language vitality, Giles, Bourhis & Taylor (1977) propose a three-factor model: status factors, demographic factors and institutional support factors, which combine to give more or less minority language vitality.

Status Factors

A key issue in language status is whether the language minority is in the ascendancy (superordinate) or is subordinate. The strong position of the Catalan language in the Spanish province of Catalonia reflects the province's economic vitality. Language minorities are very often in subordinate status to a language majority (e.g. Asian languages in Canada and England; Spanish in the US). However, a more refined analysis requires a breakdown into different types of language status.

The economic status of a minority language is likely to be a key element in language vitality. Where, for example, a minority language community experiences considerable unemployment or widespread low income, the pressure may be to shift towards the majority language. A minority language may be sacrificed on the altar of economic progress. A language of the poor and of the peasant is not the language of prosperity and power. Guest workers, in-migrants and refugees looking for social and vocational mobility may place a high value on education in the majority language. In 'Bilingualism and the Economy' (see page 250), the importance of an economic dimension to a minority language will be explored in detail as it is such a key element in language vitality and revival.

Young girls who are speakers of Karo Batak at Lingga in the Karo Highlands on the island of Sumatra in Indonesia. The Batak languages are spoken by an estimated 5.5 million people in Northern Sumatra. Over 700 languages are spoken in the country of Indonesia, and the national constitution declares that the state is obliged to support regional languages. Government educational policy in Indonesia permits primary education in the mother tongue with a gradual transition to Bahasa Indonesia, the national language, by the fourth grade. However, because Bahasa Indonesia is still the mother tongue of only a minority of Indonesians, regional languages continue to flourish.

The social status of a language – its prestige value – will be closely related to its economic status and is also a powerful factor in language vitality. When a majority language is seen as giving higher social status and more political power, a shift towards the majority language may occur. Where language minorities exist, there is often a preponderance of lower socioeconomic class families. Where a minority language is seen to co-exist with unemployment, poverty, social deprivation and few amenities, the social status of the language may be negatively affected.

A language's symbolic status is also important in language vitality. A heritage language may be an important symbol of ethnic identity, of roots in 'the glorious past'.

The symbolic importance of a language is exemplified in the Celtic countries. In Ireland, for example, the Irish language is sometimes regarded as a mark of nationhood, a symbol of cultural heritage and identity. There tend to exist positive public attitudes to Irish, Scottish Gaelic and Welsh, but private skepticism. There exists interest in the survival of the minority language, but not in personal involvement in that language. As a symbol of ethnic history, of heritage and national culture, the Celtic languages are sometimes valued by the public. As a tool of widespread personal communication, as a medium of mass education, the languages are less valued. When the personal balance sheet includes employment, educational and vocational success and interpersonal communication, the credit of positive attitudes towards language as a cultural and ethnic symbol is diminished by the costs of perceived prior needs and motives. Goodwill towards the language stops when the personal benefit is not great.

Is there a paradox beginning to emerge in the relationship between majority and minority languages? Majority languages such as English have high status as languages of international communication. At the same time, internationalism (e.g. the increasing Europeanization of the late 1990s) appears to awaken a basic need for rootedness, for an anchor in a local language and a local cultural community. Becoming European can revive and reawaken the need to belong to one's local heritage and historical groups. In becoming part of a larger whole, a local identity is essential and foundational. The push to become a member of the global village seems to lead to a strong pull towards primary roots.

Demographic Factors

The second of Giles, Bourhis & Taylor's (1977) factors concerns the geographical distribution of a language minority group. One part of this is the territorial principle; two languages having their own rights in different areas within a country. In Ireland, heartland areas have been designated where some protection and maintenance of the Irish language is encouraged (the Gaeltacht). A second part of this factor is the number of speakers of a certain language and their saturation within a particular area.

Research in Wales, using Census data, indicates that saturation of speakers within a particular area is important in language maintenance (Baker, 1985). For example, in communities where over 70 percent of people speak Welsh, there appears to be more chance of the language surviving. Also important in a language maintenance equation are the demographics of biliteracy. Analysis of the Welsh language Census data shows that where bilingualism exists without biliteracy, there is an increased likelihood of language decay. When someone can speak a minority language and not write in that language, the number of functions and uses of that language is diminished. Bilingualism without biliteracy also means a decrease in the status of that language, and less chances of a linguistically stable language. (See Biliteracy, page 607.)

At the same time, it is possible for a small language minority to survive and still maintain a lively language community, even when surrounded by the majority language, as the following three examples will illustrate. First, in a large city or in border areas, a small number of minority language speakers may be socially and culturally active in their minority language. Such speakers may interact regularly and create a strong language cell. The language of children in the home and street may be important for continuation over time. Second, when some language groups have strong religious or cultural beliefs, they may prefer not to interact with majority language speakers. Such is the case of the Old Order Amish, Pennsylvania Germans. They continued to speak Pennsylvania German at home and in the community. Such a minority has historically created strong boundaries in their language usage. Third, when minority language speakers can travel easily between the homeland and their current area of residence, the minority language may be invigorated and strengthened (e.g. Puerto Ricans in New York and Mexicans in Texas and California).

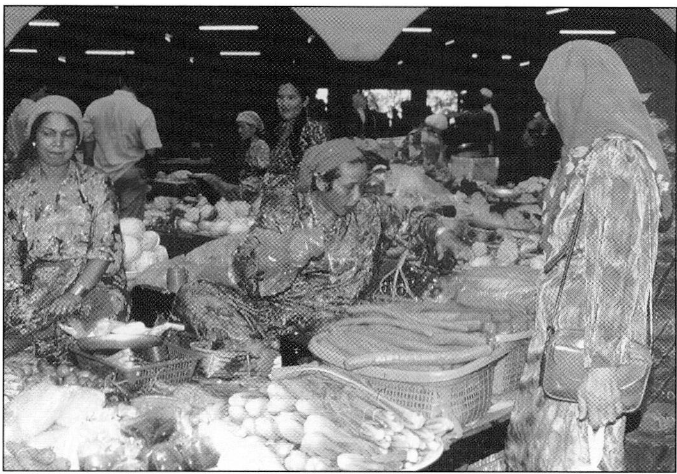

Khote Bharu market in North Peninsular Malaysia. The national and official language of Malaysia is Bahasa Melayu, but many other languages flourish in the country. Most Malaysians are bilingual or trilingual. Ethnic Malays speak Bahasa Melayu and often English, which has official status as a second language and is taught in schools. Members of other ethnic groups speak their own language as well as Bahasa Melayu and English. The educational system and the media supports the use of other languages, notably Mandarin Chinese and Tamil. Bazaar Malay, a Malay pidgin, and also a Chinese pidgin and a Tamil pidgin are all widely used as trade languages.

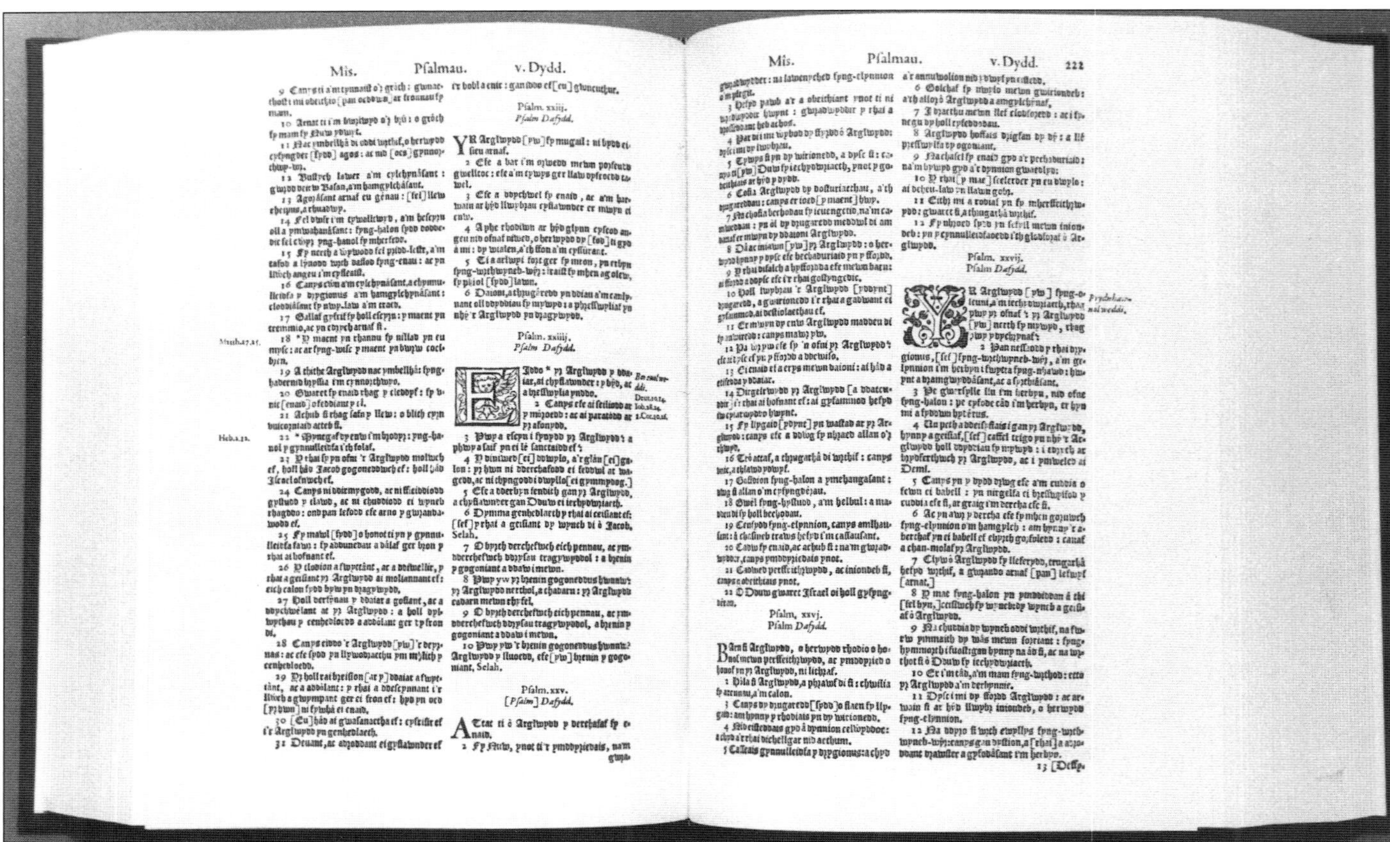
Mis. Pſalmau. v. Dydd.

Pſalm. xxiij.
Pſalm Dafydd.

Pſalm. xxiiij.
Pſalm Dafydd.

Pſalm. xxv.
[Pſalm] Dafydd.

Mis. Pſalmau. v. Dydd. 221

Pſalm. xxvj.
Pſalm Dafydd.

Pſalm. xxvij.
Pſalm Dafydd.

The Bible in Welsh. Bishop William Morgan's translation of the Bible into Welsh in 1588 was a key factor in facilitating literacy among Welsh speakers, and thus preserving the vitality of the language until the present day.

The idea of demographic factors relates to mixed, inter language marriages. In such marriages, the higher status language will usually have the best chance of survival as the home language. With inter language marriages specifically, and with language minority communities in general, there is likely to be a language shift across generations. For example, in-migrants may lose their heritage language by the second, third or fourth generation. This highlights the key importance of languages in the home as a major direct cause in the decline, revival or maintenance of a minority language. Language reproduction in the young is an important part of language vitality.

As a generalization, a minority language is more likely to be preserved in a rural than an urban area. Once migration of rural people to urban areas occurs, there is an increased chance of the minority language losing its work function. In the office and in the factory, the dominant language is likely to be the majority language with a minority language being depreciated. In rural areas, the language of work and of cultural activity is more likely to be the historical language of that area. The language of the farm or of the fishing boat, of religion and of rustic culture is more likely to be the minority language. There will be important exceptions (e.g. where an urban ethnic group generates its own industries, or is sited in a particular part of a city, or congregates regularly for religious purposes).

Institutional Support Factors

Language vitality is affected by the extent and nature of a minority language's use in a wide variety of institutions in a region. Such institutions will include national, regional and local government, religious and cultural organizations, mass media, commerce and industry, and not least education. The absence or presence of a minority language in the mass media (television, radio, newspapers, magazines, tapes and computer software) at the very least affects the prestige of a language. The use of a minority language in books and magazines, for example, is also important for biliteracy. Language may be given the status of a modern, 20th century language when it is used in the media. The perceived quality of television programs (compared to majority language programs) will be important (Baetens Beardsmore & van Beeck, 1984). However, it is possible to exaggerate the importance of television and radio in its effect on the communicative use of a minority language. Television and radio provide only a passive medium for language. Research from Wales (see Baker, 1985, 1992) suggests that it is majority language mass media that is the destroyer of a minority language and culture, rather than minority language television and radio being the salvation of the language. The glossy, high quality of TV English language programs provides fierce competition for minority languages. Media attractiveness has resulted in the invasion of Hollywood productions in countries where English is not prevalent. Active participation in a minority language is required for language survival; an event that mass media by its receptive nature does not provide.

Religion can be a strong and important vehicle for the maintenance of a majority and a minority language. The use of classical Arabic in Islam, Hebrew in Judaism, and German among the Protestant Old Order Amish in Pennsylvania each illustrates that religion has been a preserver of language. It is said in Wales that the language would not have survived into the 20th century had it not been for its dominant position in Welsh chapels and in Welsh religious life inside the home (e.g. the family reading the Bible in Welsh). Religion may help standardize a language. Through its holy books, tracts and pamphlets, traveling missionaries and teachers, a more standardized form of a language may evolve.

Providing administrative services in a minority language also serves to give status to that language. It also increases the usefulness of that minority language for communication. The use of languages within educational institutions is probably an essential but not sufficient condition for language maintenance. Where schooling in a minority language does not exist, the chances of the long-term survival of that language in a modern society may be severely diminished. Where the minority language is used in the school situation, the chances of survival are greatly increased but not guaranteed. Nancy Hornberger's (1988) acclaimed anthropological study of language planning, language shift and bilingual education in the Quechua-speaking highlands of southern Peru suggested that: 'Schools cannot be agents for language maintenance if their communities, for whatever reason, do not want them to be' (page 229).

Community support for bilingual education in the minority language and culture outside school is important. Education by itself cannot enable a minority language to survive. Other supports are essential, particularly regeneration of languages within the family and an economic basis for a language. The importance of the family in language maintenance is considered in 'Language Revival and Reversal' (see page 186).

Giles, Bourhis & Taylor's (1977) theory of language vitality has been extended (e.g. Landry, Allard & Henry, 1996) and criticized (e.g. Husband & Khan, 1982). First, Husband & Khan suggest that the dimensions and factors are not separate and independent of each other. In reality, these elements interact, interrelate and are often mutually dependent on each other. While presented as complete, comprehensive and wide-ranging, a critique is that the factors are 'something of an untheorized pot pourri' (page 195), relates to a consensus rather than a conflict perspective, with no means of 'sifting and weighing the many variables that are listed' (page 195). As this whole section reveals, there are multitudinous variables in language maintenance. This is a selection.

Second, different contexts have widely differing processes and recipes that lead to more or less language vitality. The historical, social, economic, cultural and political processes that operate in any language community vary considerably. We need a historical and sociological perspective, for example, to help explain patterns of interaction that relate to language vitality. Change and variability across time is seemingly not catered for in this theory. Third, the theory is not easy to operationalize in research. Many of the factors may not be easily or unambiguously measured. Thus the theory is difficult to test.

Further Reading

FISHMAN, J. A., 1991, *Reversing Language Shift*. Clevedon: Multilingual Matters Ltd.

GILES, H. & COUPLAND, N., 1991, *Language: Contexts and Consequences*. Milton Keynes: Open University Press.

LANDRY, R. & ALLARD, R. (eds), 1994, Ethnolinguistic Vitality. *International Journal of the Sociology of Language*, 108. Berlin: Mouton de Gruyter.

LANDRY, R., ALLARD, R. & HENRY, J., 1996, French in South Louisiana: Towards Language Loss. *Journal of Multilingual and Multicultural Development*, 17 (6), 442-468.

PAULSTON, C. B., 1994, *Linguistic Minorities in Multilingual Settings*. Philadelphia: John Benjamins.

8: Attitudes to Languages

The Importance of Attitudes

Attitudes are important in the thinking and behavior of both individuals and groups. For example, a positive attitude to sensible eating and exercise is regarded as important in increasing life expectancy. Learning a second language or losing the native language, language restoration within a geographical area or the death of that language may be considerably influenced by language attitudes. Attitudes to bilingual education may enable such a system to grow and prosper, or to decay and die.

Attitudes to languages are regarded as an important barometer, providing a measure of the climate of the language. Attitudes to Spanish in the United States or to French in Canada reveal the possibilities and problems of languages within those countries.

The Nature of Language Attitudes

Unlike height and weight, attitudes cannot be directly observed nor perfectly measured. Attitudes are a disposition to respond favorably or unfavorably to something like a language, a person, an institution or an event. An attitude represents internal thoughts, feelings and tendencies in behavior across a variety of contexts.

An attitude may be both a predisposing factor and also an outcome. As a predisposing factor, attitudes influence behavior. For example, if someone has a positive attitude to learning a second language, they may well succeed in becoming proficient in that language. Also, at the end of language learning, a desired outcome may be that students have a positive attitude towards that second language. Thus, attitudes are both an ingredient in language learning and also an important result.

Types of Language Attitudes

There are a variety of focuses of attitude to language. These may be listed as follows:

Attitude to a specific minority or majority language

Many studies of attitudes to specific languages have been conducted during the 20th century. Within particular regions, attitudes to Welsh, Gaelic in Scotland, Irish, French in Canada and England, attitudes to Frisian, Asian languages such as Bahasa Melayu, attitudes to Norwegian and attitudes to English have all been studied.

The focus of the research is usually on favorability or unfavorability towards that specific language. The extent of the goodwill towards the language, language policy and language planning may be portrayed. Such attitudes to individual languages also tend to highlight differences between particular groups of individuals. Differences according to gender, age, home language, type of school attended (e.g. bilingual or monolingual), youth cultural activities and socioeconomic class may each be examined.

Often the focus is on the attitudes of native speakers to their minority language. Such attitude surveys seek to portray the status and prestige of a language among its speakers. They provide an indication of the health of a language – a barometer of its present state and future prospects. Sometimes the focus is on second language speakers, or those learning the minority language. The aim of a 'learner' survey is similar to that of native speakers but with a spotlight on attitudes to the experience of learning that minority language.

Attitudes to language variation, dialect and speech style

One important theme in language attitudes examines attitudes to different language varieties. For example, what evaluations are made of speakers of minority languages such as Spanish, Italian and Navajo in the United States? What are the attitudes to different accents when speaking English with a Spanish accent, an Irish accent or a Japanese accent? The technique used to locate different attitudes to different language and accents is called the Matched Guise technique. The aim of this technique is to locate differences in the status of, and preference for different languages and accents.

In one 'classic' research using the Matched Guise technique (see Textbox), Edwards (1977) found varying evaluations of different regional Irish accents in Ireland, according to whether people came from Galway, Cork, Cavan, Dublin or Donegal (see map). A 230-word passage was tape recorded by a professional actor five times, using five different Irish regional accents. Fourteen Irish College students judged these recordings as valid samples of the five regional accents.

Using 178 Dublin Secondary school students, the accents were rated on the following scales which fit under three headings:

1. Competence
   - Industrious – Lazy
   - Intelligent – Unintelligent
   - Ambitious – Unambitious
   - Important – Unimportant

2. Social attractiveness
   - Friendly – Unfriendly
   - Sense of humor – Humorless

3. Personal Integrity
   - Trustworthy – Untrustworthy
   - Helpful – Unhelpful
   - Generous – Not generous

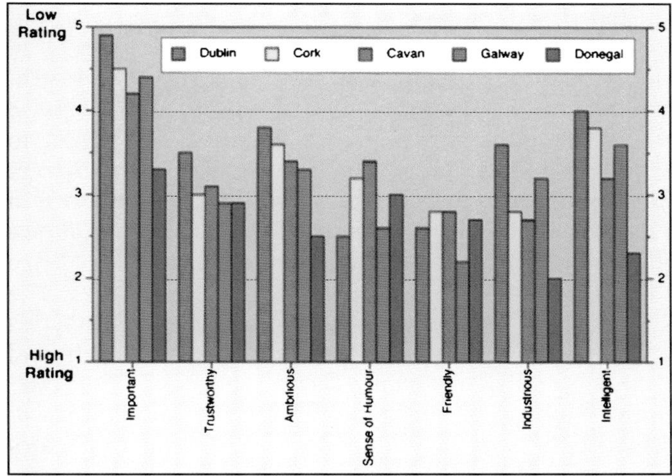

Attitudes to different Irish regional accents (Source: Edwards, 1977).

The results are presented in the graph, and may be summarized as follows. The Donegal accent was perceived most favorably on personality dimensions reflecting competence but not on social attractiveness or personal integrity. In contrast, the Dublin accent was rated relatively lower on competence but higher on social attractiveness. The Donegal accent tended to be regarded as the most 'standard' Irish accent, with other accents perceived as non-standard regional variations.

Attitude to language lessons

Students in school, college or university may be asked about their attitudes to different styles and strategies of language lessons. Students may be asked about their attitudes to the teaching of grammar, spelling, the functions of a language, the use of computer-assisted language learning (CALL), language laboratories, visits, use

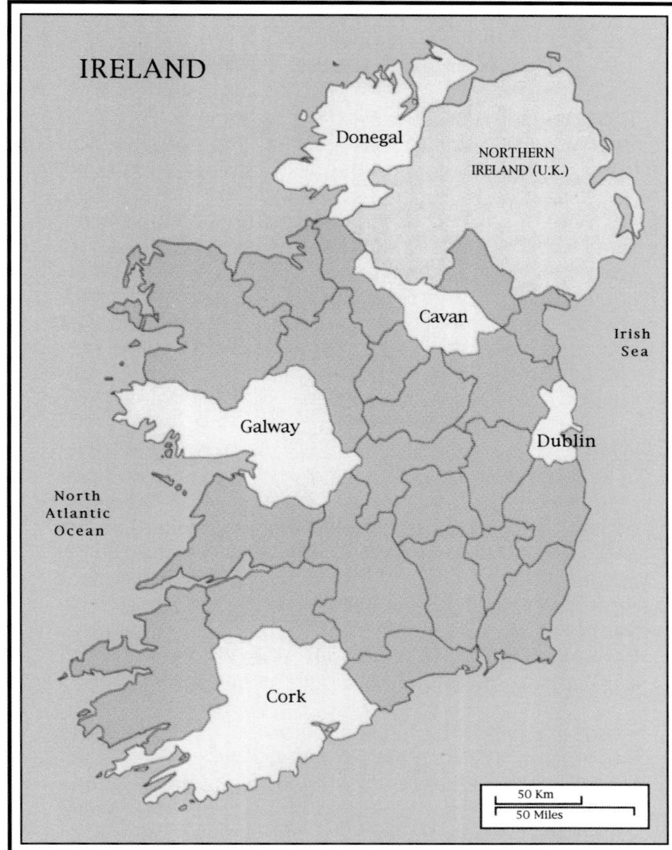

of second language newspapers, videos, and a preference for a communicative approach or the traditional grammar-translation approach Attitude questions may cover curriculum materials that are preferred, styles of teaching, types of teacher, different classroom environments (e.g. use of computers, audio visual aids), length of language lessons and attitudes to language assessment.

The wishes and needs, preferences and desires of students and teachers may be surveyed. Rather than techniques and strategies imposed by expert educationalists or by central dictate, attitudes of those learning a language may be elicited so as to improve the chances of second language learning success.

Attitude to learning a new language

Considerable international research has examined the motivations and reasons why students learn a new language. That some people learn a second language quicker and better than others may be partly due to their attitudes before and during the language learning process. In England and the United States, attitudes to learning a second language tend to be less favorable than in many parts of Asia, Africa, Latin America and mainland Europe where bilingualism and multilingualism are regarded as more typical, desirable and valuable. Research has found that only a third of students in England think learning French is of any use to them. Two-thirds of students regard English as all they need for employment, travel, friendships and acquiring knowledge in the future.

The Matched Guise Technique

The operation of the Matched Guise technique is as follows. A tape recording is made of one speaker who reads the same passage but uses different languages (e.g. French and English) or different regional accents. That the speaker is the same person under different 'guises' is not usually apparent to listeners. Listeners are asked to judge the speaker's personality with different languages or accents. Such judgments are considered to represent stereotyped attitudes to a particular language or variety of a language. Using the same person talking and a tape recorder standardizes the technique.

While this operation appears artificial, it has been found to reveal attitudes towards different languages and language varieties (e.g. French and English in Montreal; regional accents in Ireland and Wales; Broad, General and Cultivated Australian accents; different Spanish accents in the United States compared with 'standard American'; Black English in the United States; a comparison of 'Queen's English' (or Received Pronunciation) in England with regional accents such as Cockney, Yorkshire, Birmingham, Liverpool).

Research using the Matched Guise technique suggests that there are three main personality dimensions of listeners in their attitudes to language speakers. These dimensions are: a speaker's competence (e.g. intelligence and industriousness); personal integrity (e.g. helpfulness and trustworthiness); and social attractiveness (e.g. friendliness and sense of humor). Prestigious majority languages and standard accents tend to be associated with higher status and competence. Minority languages and regional accents tend to be connected with greater attractiveness and integrity, with solidarity and 'togetherness'.

One important line of research using the Matched Guise technique shows that teachers' judgments of students' intelligence and personality are affected by students' languages and accents. Social class, racial stereotypes and language prejudices are revealed in such studies. A prestigious majority language and standard accent tend to be associated with higher student ability and academic motivation. Minority languages and non-standard (e.g. working class, Black, Chicano) accents are often connected with lower estimates of ability and eagerness.

Such social judgments about language are powerful because they affect behavior (e.g. the expectations of different students held by the teacher). Listening to the language variety of a person evokes social stereotypes and expectations, coloring the behavior of the listener toward the speaker. While we are entitled to find certain accents and speech styles more or less pleasant, we are not necessarily entitled to make judgments about someone's personality, skills and ability from that accent. The Matched Guise technique shows how quickly and often we fall into that trap.

Integrative and Instrumental Attitudes

Two groups of attitudes are located in second language learning. One group concerns a wish to identify with, or join another language group. Learners may want to identify with a different language community, or join in with a second language group's cultural activities, or form new friendships. Other students with negative attitudes to language learning may reject the second language culture and its people. The more a student admires the second language people and its culture, wants to read its literature, visit a particular area on holiday or find employment that requires a second language, the more successful the student is likely to be in learning that language. This is termed an integrative language attitude.

The second type of language attitude is called an instrumental attitude. This refers to learning a second language for useful, utilitarian purposes. Learners may want to acquire a second language to find a job, further their career prospects, pass exams, help fulfill the demands of a job, or assist their children in a bilingual education program.

Research on instrumental and integrative attitudes tends to find that integrative attitudes have a greater likelihood of aiding proficiency in the second language. That integrative motivation may be a more powerful stimulus to persevere in learning a language is partly due to personal relationships being more long-lasting. On the other hand, instrumental motivation may be purely short-term and not sustained. When employment has been found, or money has been made, instrumental motivation may wane.

However, there will be occasions when instrumental motivation is more powerful than integrative motivation in fostering language learning. In India, it has been found that school students tend to give instrumental rather than integrative reasons for learning English. English has important value in education, employment and entrepreneurship. Hence, instrumental attitudes are seemingly dominant in the desire to learn English.

For many students, there is a subtle mix of instrumental and integrative attitudes behind second language learning. It is too simplistic to think of some students owning instrumental attitudes and others integrative attitudes. A more real equation is a mixture in different proportions between instrumental and integrative attitudes. While

Attitude to Bilingualism

To understand the meaning of 'Attitude to Bilingualism', it is helpful to make a comparison with an attitude to an individual language (e.g. attitude to Spanish). An attitude to a language will focus entirely on that language. For example, two contrasting attitudes to the Irish language might be: 'We should work hard to save the Irish language' and 'Irish has no place in the modern world'. Attitude statements about English include: 'English is the most important language in the world' and 'We should leave it to Anglos to speak English'. Each of these statements focuses upon one language without reference to another language.

Measurement

Language attitude surveys often contain the implicit assumption that a favorable attitude to one language excludes the possibility of a positive attitude to another language. The assumption is that languages cannot co-exist in a positive and mutually enriching relationship.

In some language attitude tests there are statements that include both languages. For example:

1. I should not like English to take over from the Spanish language.
2. English will take you further than Spanish.
3. English is easier to learn than Spanish.
4. Latinos ought to speak Spanish not a second-hand language like English.
5. The English language is killing the Spanish language.
6. English is more important than Spanish in the United States.

In the above examples, the contrasts between the languages are negative, as if one language is in competition and threatening the other. In each item, positive consequences for one language imply negative consequences for the other language. While there is more than a touch of reality about this, two languages need not exist in conflict (even in a majority-minority language situation). Even when there is a disparity of status between two languages (e.g. English and Spanish in the US), a complementary relationship is possible.

While there may be competition between languages within an individual and within society, a 'deficiency' model of bilingualism is not the only model. A 'conflict viewpoint' or a subtractive view of bilingualism, with one language increasing at the expense of the other is not the only view possible. While the 'conflict viewpoint' is a popular, important and real sociolinguistic notion, it does not present the whole story. The items below represent a complementary, holistic, positive, integrated and additive view of bilingualism.

1. French and English should be required in all Canadian schools.
2. It would be a good thing if all Welsh people could speak both English and Welsh.
3. All road signs should be printed in both English and Irish.
4. Speaking two languages is better than speaking one language.
5. Being bilingual helps people find employment.

The viewpoint of such attitude items is that two languages can co-exist within an individual in a positive, helpful, mutually reciprocating and beneficial manner. One language plus another language making more than two languages; the product being greater than the sum of the components. Such an additive view of bilingualism (rather than the subtractive view) is about partnership between two languages. Just as a tandem requires co-operation between two riders, so two languages within an individual or within society can be fused and synchronized.

REFERENCE: BAKER, 1992

Attitude to Bilingualism

Here are some statements about the English and the Spanish language. Please say whether you agree or disagree with these statements. There are no right or wrong answers. Please be as honest as possible. Answer with ONE of the following:

SA = **S**trongly **A**gree (circle **SA**) **A** = **A**gree (circle **A**) **NAND** = **N**either **A**gree **N**or **D**isagree (circle **NAND**)
D = **D**isagree (circle **D**) **SD** = **S**trongly **D**isagree (circle **SD**)

1. It is important to be able to speak English and Spanish . . . . SA A NAND D SD
2. To speak English is all that is needed . . . . SA A NAND D SD
3. Knowing Spanish and English makes people cleverer . . . . SA A NAND D SD
4. Children get confused when learning English *and* Spanish . . . . SA A NAND D SD
5. Speaking both Spanish and English helps to get a job. . . . . SA A NAND D SD
6. Being able to write in English and Spanish is important . . . . SA A NAND D SD
7. Schools should teach students to speak in two languages . . . . SA A NAND D SD
8. School wall displays should be in English and Spanish . . . . SA A NAND D SD
9. Speaking two languages is not difficult . . . . SA A NAND D SD
10. Knowing both Spanish and English gives people problems... . . . . SA A NAND D SD
11. I feel sorry for people who cannot speak both English and Spanish . . . . SA A NAND D SD
12. Children should learn to read in two languages . . . . SA A NAND D SD
13. People know more if they speak English and Spanish . . . . SA A NAND D SD
14. People who speak Spanish and English can have more friends than those who speak one language . . . . SA A NAND D SD
15. Speaking both English and Spanish is more for older than younger people . . . . SA A NAND D SD
16. Speaking both Spanish and English can help people get promotion in their job . . . . SA A NAND D SD
17. Young children learn to speak Spanish and English at the same time with ease . . . . SA A NAND D SD
18. Both English and Spanish should be important in the region where I live . . . . SA A NAND D SD
19. People can earn more money if they speak both Spanish and English . . . . SA A NAND D SD
20. I should not like the English language to be the only language in this area . . . . SA A NAND D SD
21. As an adult, I would like to be considered as a speaker of English and Spanish . . . . SA A NAND D SD
22. If I have children, I would want them to speak both English and Spanish . . . . SA A NAND D SD
23. Both the Spanish and English languages can live together in this region . . . . SA A NAND D SD
24. People only need to know one language . . . . SA A NAND D SD

> 'Any policy for language, especially in the system of education, has to take account of the attitude of those likely to be affected. In the long run, no policy will succeed which does not do one of three things: conform to the expressed attitudes of those involved; persuade those who express negative attitudes about the rightness of the policy; or seek to remove the causes of the disagreement.
>
> In any case knowledge about attitudes is fundamental to the formulation of a policy as well as to success in its implementation'
>
> (E. G. Lewis, 1981, page 262).

such attitudes may be stable, they are more likely to develop and change over time.

Changing Language Attitudes

Language attitudes are never static. Over time they change and are influenced by a variety of people, experiences and domains. There are many different theories of attitude change, parts of which have relevance to changing attitudes to a language. Some important concepts from attitude change theories are portrayed below, revealing how they relate to engendering more positive attitudes to languages.

Rewards

Attitudes may change when there is some reward. Acquisition of a language, using and maintaining a language, or acquiring a positive attitude to that language may depend on gaining reward and avoiding negative outcomes.

Rewards in school for speaking a language may be subtle: praise and encouragement from the teacher, more attention, more eye-contact, more interaction with the teacher. A language learnt in school needs encouragement and reinforcement outside the school gates. It is thus important to foster a wide range of popular and traditional cultural activities outside school to make second or minority language use more appealingand rewarding.

Having left school, adults need rewards to use a minority or second language. One example is employment which utilizes language usage. For language speech events to become more frequent, some tangible, social or individual reward system preferably needs to exist. Minority and majority language television, discos, pop music, novels, papers, concerts, for example, all provide the stage upon which the prestige and status of a language is viewed. Such status and prestige factors influence the perceived rewards and reinforcement for speaking a language.

Attitude change may be in a negative direction when 'punishment' is present for speaking a particular language. Such punishment may be latent and barely visible: the raising of a friend's eyebrows in speaking Irish in public; being given less attention in shops when speaking Spanish in the US; speaking Japanese when the disco music is in the English language.

Providing appropriate rewards for language activity depends on identifying what is perceived by the student or the employee as a reward. Praise for speaking a second language may work well with young children, but have the opposite effects to that intended if delivered by a teacher to an adolescent. What functions as reward and enticement changes over a person's life-span.

Boosting self-esteem

Self-esteem is essential to psychological health. People who hold attitudes which lead to insecurity, embarrassment and anxiety are likely to change their attitudes to achieve greater security and less anxiety. Speaking a minority language in a majority environment may lead to such anxiety. Being a peripheral member of a group, not sharing the common threads of identity of a group, lacking some of the attributes of a high status reference group may lead to attitude and behavioral change.

Majority group members sometimes defend their egos by denigrating a minority language. Fearing that minority language groups will be given privileges or receive positive discrimination, majority groups may hold negative attitudes towards such minorities to enhance their own self-worth and retain privileges and status. Attitude change strategies therefore need to ensure ego defense mechanisms are either enhanced (e.g. by adding to self-esteem) or are not threatened nor attacked.

The psychological notion of self-concept, the picture we hold of ourself, may be a powerful governor of attitude change. When, for example, self-concept in adolescence moves towards conformity with peer group identity, the peer group may become an important determinant of change towards, or away from, minority language and cultural identification. If comparisons are made between minority and majority cultural forms (e.g. 'regional' compared with Anglo-American pop culture), then self-concept and attitudes may change to gain higher personal prestige.

Imitation of others

Imitation of someone else (a model) may be a powerful source of attitude change. Human models are highly regarded, respected, admired and credible in what they say and do. Imitating the attitudes of the model becomes positively reinforcing. The imitator attempts to take on some of the attributes of the favored model, thus posi-

A Bilingual Sign with a Double Message

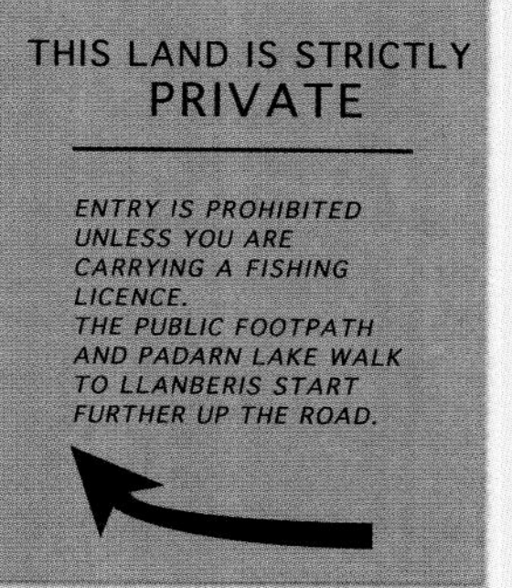

MAE'R TIR HWN YN
BREIFAT
DIM OND POBL LLEOL.
GYDA'R NOS YN UNIG,
A PHYSGOTWYR GYDA
THRWYDDED, GAIFF FYND
Y FFORDD HYN.
RHOWCH HELP I NI I GADW'R
YMWELWYR A THRESPASWYR
ODDI AR Y TIR HWN.
MAE'R LLWYBR CYHOEDDUS,
A DDEFNYDDIR YN YSTOD
Y DYDD YN DECHRAU'N UWCH
I FYNY'R FFORDD.
THIS LAND IS STRICTLY
PRIVATE
ENTRY IS PROHIBITED
UNLESS YOU ARE
CARRYING A FISHING
LICENCE.
THE PUBLIC FOOTPATH
AND PADARN LAKE WALK
TO LLANBERIS START
FURTHER UP THE ROAD.

This bilingual (Welsh/English) notice can be seen on a gate in Brynrefail, Gwynedd, North Wales. The sign is interesting because the English is not a direct translation of the Welsh. The English half of the notice announces, quite abruptly:

> 'This land is strictly private. Entry is prohibited unless you are carrying a fishing license. The public footpath and Padarn lake walk to Llanberis start further up the road.'

The Welsh half of the notice is rather longer and says:

> 'This land is private. Only local people, only in the evenings, and fishermen with a license, may go this way. Help us to keep tourists and trespassers off this land. The public footpath which is used during the day starts further up the road.'

The sign reflects the nature of part of the bilingual community in North West Wales. The overwhelming majority of the local people are Welsh-speaking. Monoglot English speakers are usually recent in-migrants to the area, or tourists. The sign, erected by a local farmer, reflects the somewhat wary attitude of some locals towards incomers and visitors. Local people, on the other hand, are considered to be responsible and trustworthy.

This notice exemplifies the fact that languages do not exist in a vacuum. Languages are spoken within communities, and in a bilingual situation, language use can reflect the attitudes of one speech community towards members of another speech community. Language can be used to include, or to exclude.

tively affecting feelings of status and worth. Models can range from parents, siblings, peers, teachers, to cultural, sporting and media figures.

Attitudes may change as a result of the content of a model's speech, conversation or message. Physical attractiveness, clothes and discourse, expertise, age, race, nationality are some of the variables affecting the persuasiveness of the communicator. Models need to be seen as having the appropriate status for their communication to effect attitude change. Where the 'ingroup' is a majority language group and the 'outgroup' a minority language group, finding a model to maintain favorable minority language attitude may be more difficult.

Being consistent and self-justification

An individual's attitudes need to be in harmony, but when discordant or cacophonous attitudes are present, attempts will be made to harmonize and seek congruence. When inconsistent attitudes are held, tension may result. There may follow a need to reduce tension by changing certain attitudes. Cognitive discomfort may require attitude change or attitude rationalization, especially when the integrity of the self-concept is at stake.

A piece of research by Bourhis & Giles (1977) showed how cognitive discomfort may work in speech style and identity. They formed two groups of people from South Wales: those who valued their Welsh identity and those who did not. When engaged in conversation with an English person, the Welsh people who valued their national identity emphasized their less prestigious Welsh accents when the English person derogated Wales. In contrast, Welsh people who did not value their Welsh identity responded to the English person's derogation by minimizing their Welsh accents. In each case, the two groups appeared to obtain cognitive consistency by changing their speech style. The first group did this by becoming more Welsh, thus maintaining harmony with their value of being Welsh. The second group achieved consistency by becoming less Welsh, identifying more with the English speaker and thus harmonizing with their lesser valuation of being Welsh.

Attitude change may be induced when an individual's attitudes are composed of different elements that may not be in harmony with one another. Attitude to a minority language may be positively engendered by the neighborhood, or negatively affected by Anglo pop culture or English language mass media. An individual, in striving for inner consistency, may have to reject one in favor of another. The Spanish-speaking church is spurned; English pop music and discos replace religion. A school where there are cliques of students with different language attitudes (e.g. anti-Spanish and anti-English), may pressurize a bilingual and bicultural student to develop a partisan attitude. Alternatively, reminding people of their indigenous cultural and language heritage may induce the inconsistency in attitudes which in turn spawns a change in attitude, becoming more favorable to a minority language.

Contexts

Ryan's (1979) research suggested that when children of bilingual parents observe the different contexts (domains) that accompany use of each language, such children form negative and positive attitudes towards each language. If the child perceives the contexts as having pleasant and enjoyable properties, favorable attitudes may develop towards that language. For instance, parents taking their children to an enjoyable Spanish-speaking church are conditioning attitudes to Spanish by the association of speaking Spanish with a pleasurable context.

One reason among many why positive attitudes to minority languages decline with age may be due to children perceiving that certain minority language speaking contexts are not pleasurable, or that majority language speaking contexts are more pleasurable. Discos, basketball, popular music and videos, CDs and the Internet provide potentially pleasurable contexts for adolescents and are often conducted in a majority rather than a minority language.

Community influence

In most minority language communities, there is an uneven balance of minority language speakers and non speakers. The crucial issue is often who is influencing whom? Where, for example, there are English-speaking monolingual in-migrants to a Welsh-speaking 'heartland' area, does the language attitude of the in-migrants change or that of the indigenous bilinguals? (T. P. Jones, 1990).

Research on racial integration provides some clues about the circumstances that may effect language attitude change when community relationships are considered. These ideas are listed below:

1. Change may occur when community integration and stabilization are sustained. Migrant workers who move from job to job and community to community, may be much less likely to change their attitudes to an indigenous language than those who settle in that community. A fast turn-around of in-migrants in a community may also effect a 'hardening' of attitudes to language survival in such communities. Attitude change may be enhanced when there is an integration among the settled and the settlers.

2. Change may occur when it is felt to be voluntary. Imposing conformity in an authoritarian, rule-bound manner is unlikely to change attitude. Informing and consulting, and giving freedom of choice, are paths more likely to lead to language attitude change. Convictions, unlike imposed conformity do not occur instantaneously. Coercion is rarely a long-term solution.

3. Change may occur when areas of similarity between different language groups are used to promote contact. Music, sport, a common goal, religion, hobbies and interests may promote contact, integration and change of attitude. For a minority language speaker, the danger is that common goals and interests will evoke attitude change that is less favorable to that language. Working through a common denominator language (e.g. English) may make minority language attitudes less favorable. However, as recent community movements in Celtic areas have shown, when indigenous language groups actively plan contact and events with in-migrants (e.g. choirs), such contact can be on 'minority language terms'.

4. Change may occur when relationships between monolingual and bilingual individuals in the community are warm and friendly. Passing sociability does not provide the mechanisms and motivation for attitude change. A 'bunker' attitude to monolinguals by minority language bilinguals often appears to monolinguals as a defense of the indigenous language. Being welcoming to the in-migrant majority language speaking monolingual may be the path to language death. Bunkers can be secure; they are, in the long term, unlikely to succeed. The global village of the 20th century ensures no long-term future for highly protected and introspective minority language communities. A marketing of the minority language seems a more likely route to language maintenance and restoration. Such a marketing would seem to suggest friendship and not separatism as a channel of language attitude change.

5. Change may occur when the social, economic, political and cultural environment is supportive of minority languages and bilingualism. Disparity in status or salary between a monolingual and a minority language bilingual, especially when in favor of the former, is tantamount to undermining community integration and the consequent halting of language attitude change.

Further Reading

BAKER, C., 1992, *Attitudes and Language*. Clevedon: Multilingual Matters Ltd.

GARDNER, R. C., 1985, *Social Psychology and Second Language Learning*. London: Edward Arnold.

GILES, H. & COUPLAND, N., 1991, *Language: Contexts and Consequences*. Milton Keynes, UK: Open University Press.

RYAN, E. B. & GILES, H., 1982 (eds), *Attitudes Towards Language Variation*. London: Edward Arnold.

Language Maintenance and Planning

1: Language Maintenance

Differing 'environmental' attitudes to the survival and spread of minority languages are well summed up by Colin Williams (1991a). First, the evolutionist will tend to follow Darwin's idea of the survival of the fittest. Those languages that are strong will survive. The weaker languages will either have to adapt themselves to their environment, or die. A different way of expressing this is in terms of a free, *laissez-faire* language economy. Languages must survive on their own merits without the support of language planning.

However, survival of the fittest is too simplistic a view of evolution. It only accents the negative side of evolution – killing, exploitation and suppression. A more positive view is interdependence rather than constant competition. Co-operation for mutually beneficial outcomes can be as possible as exploitation. An evolutionist argument about language shift also fails to realize that it is not a simple, spontaneous or impulsive process. Rather, the fate of languages is often related to the manipulated politics and power bases of different groups in society. Language shift (in terms of numbers of speakers and uses) occurs through deliberate decisions that directly or indirectly affect languages and reflects economic, political, cultural, social and technological change. It is therefore possible to analyze and determine what causes language shift rather than simply believing language shift occurs by accident. Thus, those who support an evolutionary perspective on languages may be supporting the spread of majority languages and the replacement of minority languages. Evolutionists who argue for an economic, cost-benefit approach to languages, with the domination of a few majority languages for international communication, hold a myopic view of the function of languages. Languages are not purely for economic communication, they are also concerned with human culture and human heritage.

The second approach to languages is that of conservationists (Williams, 1991a) who argue for the maintenance of language variety. For conservationists, language planning must care for and cherish minority languages. Just as certain animal species are now deliberately preserved within particular territorial areas, so conservationists will argue that threatened languages should receive special status in heartland regions of that language. Catalan in Spain, native Indian languages in North America, the Celtic languages in Britain and France, have invoked the conservationist argument and in Ireland, certain areas called Gaeltacht are officially designated for Irish conservation.

The third attitude to languages is that of preservationists (Williams, 1991a). Preservationists are different from conservationists by being more conservative and seeking to maintain the status quo rather than develop the language. Preservationists are concerned that any change, not just language change, will damage the chances of survival of their language. Such a group are therefore traditionalists, and anti-modern in outlook. Whereas conservationists may think global and act local, preservationists will tend to think local and act local.

Language Shift and Language Maintenance

No garden of flowers is stable and unchanging. With changes of season and weather comes growth and death, blossoming and weakening. Minority language communities are similarly in a constant state of change. Such language shift may be fast or slow, upwards or downwards, but shift is as likely as is garden growth.

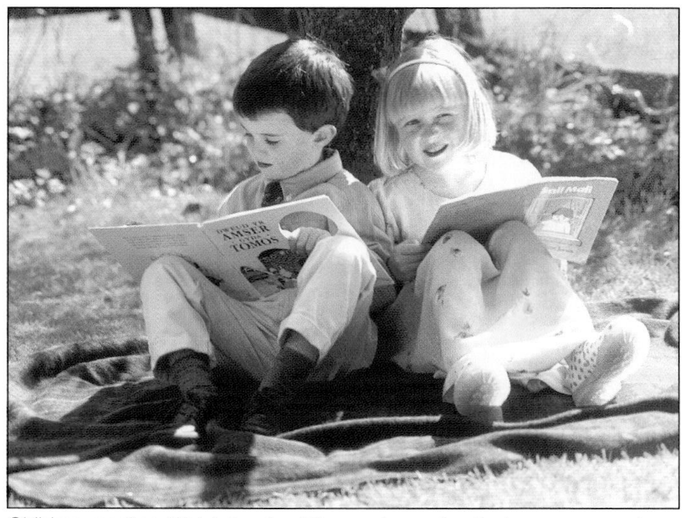

Children reading Welsh books. Literacy in a minority language can be a help in the maintenance of that language.

Political, Social and Demographic Factors Encouraging Language Maintenance	Political, Social and Demographic Factors Encouraging Language Loss
1. Large number of speakers living closely together.	Small number of speakers well dispersed.
2. Recent and/or continuing in-migration.	Long and stable residence.
3. Close proximity to the homeland and ease of travel to homeland.	Homeland remote or inaccessible.
4. Preference to return to homeland with many actually returning.	Low rate of return to homeland and/or little intention to return and/or impossible to return.
5. Homeland language community intact.	Homeland language community decaying in vitality.
6. Stability in occupation.	Occupational shift, especially from rural to urban areas.
7. Employment available where home language is spoken daily.	Employment requires use of the majority language.
8. Low social and economic mobility in main occupations.	High social and economic mobility in main occupations.
9. Low level of education to restrict social and economic mobility, but educated and articulate community leaders loyal to their language community.	High levels of education giving social and economic mobility. Potential community leaders are alienated from their language community by education.
10. Ethnic group identity rather than identity with majority language community via nativism, racism, isolation and ethnic discrimination.	Ethnic identity is denied to achieve social and vocational mobility; this is forced by nativism, racism, isolation and ethnic discrimination.

Cultural Factors Encouraging Language Maintenance	Cultural Factors Encouraging Language Loss
1. Mother tongue institutions (e.g. schools, community organizations, mass media, leisure activities).	Lack of mother tongue institutions.
2. Cultural and religious ceremonies in the home language.	Cultural and religious activity in the majority language.
3. Ethnic identity strongly tied to home language.	Ethnic identity defined by factors other than language.
4. Nationalistic aspirations as a language group.	Few nationalistic aspirations.
5. Mother tongue the homeland national language.	Mother tongue not the only homeland national language, or mother tongue spans several nations.
6. Emotional attachment to mother tongue giving self-identity and ethnicity.	Self-identity derived from factors other than shared home language.
7. Emphasis on family ties and community cohesion.	Low emphasis on family and community ties. High emphasis on individual achievement.
8. Emphasis on education in mother tongue schools to enhance ethnic awareness.	Emphasis on education in majority language.
9. Low emphasis on education if in majority language.	Acceptance of majority language education.
10. Culture unlike majority language culture.	Culture and religion similar to that of the majority language.

Linguistic Factors Encouraging Language Maintenance	Linguistic Factors Encouraging Language Loss
1. Mother tongue is standardized and exists in a written form.	Mother tongue is non-standard and/or not in written form.
2. Use of an alphabet which makes printing and literacy relatively easy.	Use of writing system that is expensive to reproduce and relatively difficult to learn.
3. Home language has international status.	Home language of little or no international importance.
4. Home language literacy used in community and with homeland.	Illiteracy (or aliteracy) in the home language.
5. Flexibility in the development of the home language (e.g. limited use of new terms from the majority language).	No tolerance of new terms from majority language; or too much tolerance of loan words leading to mixing and eventual loss.

(Adapted from Conklin & Lourie, 1983).

The Sámi

A group of Sámi in traditional dress in Karasjok, Norway.

The Sámi are an indigenous people who form an often vibrant ethnic minority in the northern regions of Norway, Sweden, Finland and on Russia's Kola peninsula. They are also known as Lapps, but prefer the name Sámi, because that is the name they call themselves and their language. The Sámi language consists of nine main dialects or closely related languages which belong to the Finno-Ugric family, the closest relatives being Finnish and Estonian.

The Sámi have inhabited their territories for at least four thousand years, living a nomadic life and subsisting on hunting and fishing. The size of the current Sámi population is estimated as between 60,000 and 100,000 with 70,000 to 80,000 as being a typical estimate. In Norway there are approximately 40,000 to 45,000 Sámi largely concentrated in the Finmark area. Sweden has around 17,000 Sámi, Finland around 6000 and Russia has approximately 2000 Sámi.

In Norway, the 1987 Act of Parliament relating to the Sámi (No. 56) defines a Sámi as a person who speaks Sámi as their first language, or whose parents or grandparents use Sámi as their first language, or perceive themselves as a Sámi by adopting Sámi culture and are recognized by Sámi people themselves as a Sámi; or whose parents satisfy the above conditions.

In the 19th century, the existence of the Sámi language and way of life was placed in jeopardy by an emphasis on the majority language of the state, and by a 'colonial' attitude which involved the exploitation of Sámi territories. For example, in Norway, teachers were instructed to restrict the use of the Sámi language in school and ensure Norwegian was spoken. Between the two World Wars, this process of Norwegianization was prosecuted aggressively. Land could not be sold to anyone who did not speak Norwegian.

After the Second World War, the policy towards the Sámi language became more liberal. The Nordic Sámi Council was established in 1956 to promote co-operation among the Sámi in Finland, Norway and Sweden. The Council has 12 members, 4 from each country. Both state authorities and the Nordic Council have recognized the Sámi Council as a valuable platform for the Sámi and have acceded to many of its demands. The1962-63 Norwegian Parliamentary Records note that:

> 'The policy of the national state must be to give to the Sámi speaking population the opportunity to preserve its language and other cultural customs on terms that accord with the expressed wishes of the Sámi themselves'.

Sámi people now have the right to preserve and develop their own culture particularly in Norway and Finland. The Sámi language is taught in schools, which is particularly important because far fewer people speak the Sámi language than perceive themselves to be ethnically Sámi. In Norway, it is estimated that about 20,000 people speak the Sámi language while in Finland around 3000 are Sámi-speaking. In Sweden, it is estimated that about 10,000 are Sámi speakers, and in Russia about 1000 speak Sámi. Sámi is taught in primary schools in several regions and there are Sámi high schools in Kautokeino and Karasjok in Norway. Sámi language and culture courses are held at several Nordic universities.

Apart from Sámi language in education, it is also represented in newspapers and magazines, on the radio and a little on television, in the theater and in literacy, and at universities and similar educational institutions (e.g. the Nordic Sámi Institute at Kautokeino which was established in 1974). This Institute is concerned with language and culture of the Sámi people, education and information, and Sámi economic activities and language rights. There is also a Sámi parliament in Karasjok.

The aims of the Sámi were presented in a political program adopted in 1980. It sets out the following principles:

1. We, the Sámi, are one people whose fellowship must not be divided by national boundaries.

2. We have our own history, traditions, culture and language. We have inherited from our forefathers a right to territories, water and our own economic activities.

3. We have an inalienable right to preserve and develop our own economic activities and our own communities, in accordance with our own circumstances and we will together safeguard our territories, natural resources and national heritage for future generations.

REFERENCE: CORSON, 1995

Bilingualism in Mozambique

Mozambique was invaded and colonized by Portuguese explorers in 1498. The Portuguese established coastal forts and conducted a thriving trade in gold, slaves, and ivory. Fixed colonial boundaries were drawn around Mozambique in the late 1800s, but little was done to develop the colony except to facilitate exploitation.

At the time of the Portuguese invasion, there were many existing indigenous languages. After the invasion, most indigenous Mozambicans were not given access to schooling. However a very small urban elite of Mozambicans were taught through the medium of Portuguese by Portuguese teachers. These few indigenous people were used to help and support the colonizing Portuguese. During the colonial period in Mozambique, the imposition of Portuguese was in order to strengthen the power and status, the political control and culture of the ruling elite, and marginalize those with indigenous language and cultures. By 1975 only ten percent of the population was literate, and even rudimentary bureaucratic and technical skills were rare.

Mozambique gained independence from Portugal in 1975. At the time, many indigenous languages were still spoken in Mozambique but none was regarded as appropriate as a national language. (This is an experience also found in India and parts of Africa.) A choice of an indigenous language may have implied that one ethnic group was preferred above others. No ethnic group or language was numerically dominant, nor were there enough teachers or books in such indigenous languages to make the choice of an indigenous language as the national language. Also, Mozambicans perceived that they needed an international language for economic development, for international trade and communications. Therefore, making Portuguese the official language of Mozambique was the solution to the official language problem. However, in 1975, in rural areas, less than five percent of the population knew Portuguese as compared with the cities, where the figure was approximately 40 percent. Thus Portuguese was still an imposed, non-indigenous language that did not necessarily promote a sense of national unity.

There still exists in Mozambique an imbalance between those who have access to the official language via birth and education and those who do not. This imbalance is reflected in different proportions of power, wealth and access to goods and services. For children in rural schools, Portuguese is a foreign language that is often imposed. The home language is subsequently often neglected and seemingly disparaged.

Given that not all Mozambican children attend school, and the necessity of sharing buildings means that children often attend school in rotation, not all children become fluent in Portuguese, nor become literate, nor achieve well in the curriculum. Trying to achieve literacy in the foreign language of Portuguese tends to result in illiteracy among many of the rural children. Parents may not be able to help their children as they also have little or no Portuguese. Many of the qualified teachers cannot teach fluently through Portuguese and do not feel confident in that language.

Since Portuguese has been promoted as the symbol of civilization, rural people in particular tend to regard their indigenous language as inferior, uncivilized and inadequate. Given that Portuguese has been a declining world language although still spoken in Portugal, Brazil and Angola for example, there are current doubts about the economic value of Portuguese in a world economy.

Thus language in Mozambique is a topic of debate. There are many indigenous languages that have an oral but not a written tradition. Over 30 indigenous languages exist in Mozambique, the largest language groups being Makua (around 7.5 million speakers), Tsonga (around 3.5 million), Sena (around 1.5 million) and Nyungwe (around one million). If local languages were to be promoted, questions about national unity and further political unrest might accelerate. The colonial language has been valued because it appears to give trade, economic and international advantages, yet the Portuguese language has declined in its trade, status and international value. Therefore, the political unrest and slow economic development in Mozambique are reflected in language uncertainties. Conflicting interests of national unity, preservation of the past, the unifying of different ethnic groups, and the need to secure greater economic development and international trade, produce a conflict of values and interests that are reflected in debates about the language of Mozambique for the future.

An election poster in Portuguese in Maputo, Mozambique. The poster's message reads 'Let us go together to vote for Mozambique'.

The Mont Keant Chinese school, Vancouver, British Columbia, Canada in 1951. In-migrant institutions can help maintain a minority language. Community schools can, for instance, teach minority language literacy as well as traditions and history and promote minority group cohesion.

Generally the term 'language shift' is used to refer to a downwards language movement. That is, there is a lessening of the number of speakers of a language, a decreasing saturation of language speakers in the population, a loss in language proficiency, or a decreasing use of that language in different domains. The last stages of language shift are called language death. Language maintenance usually refers to relative language stability in its number and distribution of speakers, its proficient usage in children and adults, and to retaining the use of the language in specific domains (e.g. home, school, religion). Language spread concerns the increase, numerically, geographically or functionally in language users, networks and use.

However, there is a danger in the ways these terms are used. First, the terms are ambiguous and may refer to the numerical size of the language minority, their saturation in a region, their proficiency in the language, or the use of the language in different domains. Second, these are predominantly sociolinguistic concepts. Linguists have their own use of these terms (e.g. referring to changes in grammar and vocabulary over time – see Aitchison, 1991; McMahon, 1994; Romaine, 1995). Third, languages do not lose or acquire speakers. Rather, speakers acquire or lose languages.

A relatively comprehensive list of factors that may create language maintenance and shift is given by Conklin and Lourie (1983) (see also Gaarder, 1977, page 141f). This list essentially refers to in-migrants rather than indigenous minorities, but many factors are common to both groups. What is missing from this list is the power dimension (such as being in subordinate status, e.g. the Puerto Ricans in New York City – see Zentella, 1988).

It has been shown that language maintenance or language shift is particularly related to factors such as economic and social change, politics and power, the availability of local social networks of communication between minority language speakers and the legislative and institutional support supplied for the conservation of a minority language. However, the relative importance of such factors is debated and unclear. There are various levels of establishing causes of language shift, such as the political, the economic, the psychological (e.g. at the individual or home level) and the sociolinguistic level. A list of the relative importance of these factors is simplistic because the factors interact and intermingle in a complicated equation. Such a list does not prioritize more or less important factors in language shift.

Further Reading

CONKLIN, N. & LOURIE, M., 1983, *A Host of Tongues*. New York: The Free Press.

EDWARDS, J. R., 1994, *Multilingualism*. London: Routledge.

FISHMAN, J. A., 1989, *Language & Ethnicity in Minority Sociolinguistic Perspective*. Clevedon: Multilingual Matters Ltd.

PAULSTON, C. B., 1994, *Linguistic Minorities in Multilingual Settings*. Amsterdam/Philadelphia: John Benjamins.

PAULSTON, C. B. (ed.), 1988, *International Handbook of Bilingualism and Bilingual Education*. New York: Greenwood.

SKUTNABB-KANGAS, T., 1981, *Bilingualism or Not: The Education of Minorities*. Clevedon: Multilingual Matters Ltd.

WILLIAMS, C. H., 1991, Language Planning and Social Change: Ecological Speculations. In D. F. MARSHALL (ed.), *Language Planning Volume III*. Philadelphia: John Benjamins.

2: Language Revival and Reversal

Introduction

This topic examines the factors and processes of language revival and the reversal of language shift with reference to the important contribution of Joshua Fishman (1991, 1993). Fishman (1991) notes a changing perspective in the topic of language shift. The premise has been that minority languages, like patients in a hospital or doctor's surgery, will ultimately die. Therefore all one can do is to understand the causes of death and illness, and attempt to overcome those causes for as long as possible. Instead, Fishman (1991) argues that language shift needs to take the jump of modern medicine by attempting 'not only to combat illness, but to cultivate "wellness" ' (page xii).

Fishman (1991) seeks to answer the question 'what are the priorities in planning language reversal?' For example, what is the point of pouring money into minority language mass media and bilingual bureaucracy when home, family, neighborhood and face-to-face community use of the minority language is lacking? It is like blowing air into a punctured balloon. Blowing minority language air in through the mass media and legislation doesn't make a usable balloon, because of the unmended hole.

Fishman (1991) provides a list of priorities to halt language decline and attempt to reverse language shift. His plan also shows why many efforts to reverse minority language situations have often resulted in failure rather than success. Before we examine the plan, Fishman (1991) provides a basic philosophy and set of assumptions that are required before establishing priorities in reversing language shift.

Assumptions of Reversing Language Shift

First, when a society or community is losing its language and culture, it is likely to feel pain. This hurt may be symptomatic of the social injustice towards that community. Although it may not be a cancer but more like a toothache, to those who experience it, there is real rather than imaginary suffering. Such suffering needs remedying. Second, the basis of reversing language shift is that a more global village, a world more unified by mass communication and speedy travel, a more integrated eastern and western Europe, does not bury the need for local language and local culture. Indeed, a more centrally organized and uniform world may increase rather than decrease the need for language and cultural identity at a local level. Having local cultural and linguistic roots may be a necessary precondition before integrating into a global village. Third, and most importantly for Fishman (1991), the political basis of the plan is to support cultural pluralism and cultural self-determination. The destruction of minority languages is the destruction of intimacy, family and community, often involving oppression of the weak by the strong, subjugating the unique and traditional by the uniform and central. Thus, Fishman (1991) argues for 'greater sociocultural self-sufficiency, self-help, self-regulation and initiative' (page 4) among linguistic communities.

Fourth, an ethnic or cultural group that has lost its language is different from that group with their minority language. Fishman (1991) cites the case of Jews who, not speaking Hebrew or Yiddish, tend to have a different daily life-pattern, a different kind of subculture. Language shift accompanies cultural change. This suggests that language shift is not just about language; it is about the attendant culture as well. The argument for language restoration and resurrection must therefore involve a call for cultural change and greater cultural self-determination. Fishman (1991) warns of the danger of language as the sole focus for shift.

A different warning is given to those who believe that reversing language shift is purely about the accumulation of power and money (e.g. as has been said about the use of Hebrew and Welsh). Believing that language minorities who are attempting language reversal and resurrection are concerned with achieving power and increasing wealth, is simplistic and misguided. Fishman (1991) argues that human values, feelings, loyalties and basic life-philosophies are present in the complex reasons for language change. Language activists often have ideals, commitments, even altruism that makes their motives more than just power and money. Minority languages and cultures, in their desire for a healthy existence, may be sometimes irrational or super-rational. This is similar to religion, love, art and music where there are personal elements that transcend conscious rationality and self-interest in power and money.

Fifth, to help understand language shift, Fishman (1991) clarifies the relationship between language and culture in terms of three links:

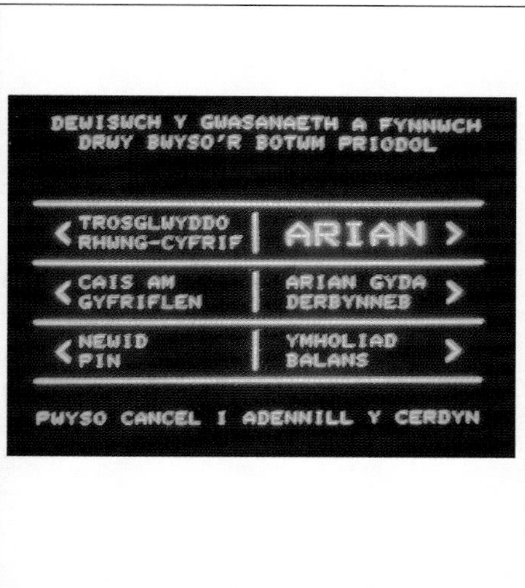

Widespread public and official use of Welsh has helped to raise its prestige.

1. A language indexes its culture. A language and its attendant culture will have grown up together over a long period of history, and be in harmony with each other. Thus the language that has grown up round a culture best expresses that culture. Its vocabulary, idioms, metaphors are the ones that best explain that culture at a cognitive and emotive level.
2. A language symbolizes its culture. To speak German in the US, during World War I and in France and Britain during World War II was not appropriate nor acceptable. Not that the allies were at war with the German language. Rather, the German language symbolized the enemy, therefore, that language was inappropriate in allied countries. A language tends to symbolize the status of that language. For example, to speak English in Kuwait following the victory against Saddam Hussein of Iraq was to be symbolically associated with status, power and victory. Speaking English often symbolizes money and modernity, affluence and achievement. English may also symbolize colonial subjugation. A language that is apparently dying may symbolize low status and low income. In certain parts of Ireland and Wales, the indigenous language is sometimes perceived as a symbol of the past rather than the present, of disadvantage rather than advantage.
3. Culture is partly created from its language. Much of a culture is enacted and transmitted verbally. The songs, hymns, prayers of a culture, its folk tales and shrewd sayings, its appropriate forms of greeting and leaving, its history, wisdom and ideals are all wrapped up in its language. The taste and flavor of a culture is given through its language; its memories and traditions are stored in its language. An example is a saying or a figure of speech in a minority language that requires a long explanation in another language. Even then that pithy saying may sacrifice some of its meaning and feeling in translation. At the same time, culture is derived from many more sources than language. For example, there are many different cultures which all use the Spanish language.

Sixth, Fishman (1991) makes an argument for language planning. Just as there is economic planning, educational planning and family planning, so there can and should be language planning. Such planning has as its base 're-establishing local options, local control, local hope, and local meaning to life. It reveals a humanistic and positive outlook regarding intergroup life, rather than a mechanistic and fatalistic one. It espouses the right and the ability of small cultures to live and to inform life for their own members as well as to contribute thereby to the enrichment of human kind as a whole' (page 35).

Language planning, also called language engineering, refers to 'deliberate efforts to influence the behavior of others with respect to the acquisition, structure, or functional allocation of their language codes' (Cooper, 1989, page 45). Such language planning involves status planning (raising the status of a language within society), corpus planning (concerning the vocabulary, spelling, grammar and standardization of the minority language) and acquisition planning (creating language spread by increasing the number of speakers and uses, by, for example, language teaching). (See Language Planning, page 203.)

Steps in Reversing Language Shift

Fishman's (1990, 1991, 1993) Graded Intergenerational Disruption Scale (GIDS) is an aid to language planning and attempted language reversal. Just as the Richter scale measures intensity of earthquakes, so Fishman's scale gives a guide to how far a minority language is threatened and disrupted. The higher the number on the scale, the more a language is threatened. The idea of stages is that there is little benefit in attempting later stages if earlier stages are not at least partly achieved. Various foundations are needed before building the upper levels. The value of the scale is not just in its eight sequenced steps or stages. Rather it provides a plan for action for reversing languages in decline and a set of priorities. The eight stages are briefly summarized, and then considered one by one.

Fishman's (1990, 1991) Graded Intergenerational Disruption Scale for Threatened Languages

Stage 8 Social isolation of the few remaining speakers of the minority language. Need to record the language for later possible reconstruction.

Stage 7 Minority language used by older and not younger generation. Need to multiply the language in the younger generation.

Stage 6 Minority language is passed on from generation to generation and used in the community. Need to support the family in intergenerational continuity (e.g. provision of minority language nursery schools).

Stage 5 Literacy in the minority language. Need to support literacy movements in the minority language, particularly when there is no government support.

Stage 4 Formal, compulsory education available in the minority language. May need to be financially supported by the minority language community.

Stage 3 Use of the minority language in less specialized work areas involving interaction with majority language speakers.

Stage 2 Lower government services and mass media available in the minority language.

Stage 1 Some use of minority language available in higher education, central government and national media.

Stage 8

Stage 8 represents the 'worst case' for a language. A few of the older generation will still be able to speak the language but probably not to each other because they are socially isolated. The few remaining speakers of a language are so scattered that minority language interaction is rarely possible. At this stage it is seen as important that folklorists and linguists collect as much information as they can from these few survivors of the language community. The folk-tales and sayings, grammar and vocabulary, need to be collected on tape and paper as a permanent record of that language. Since the language building is in ruins and the foundations have crumbled, can anything be done to save the language? The one ray of hope is that the records of the language can be used by a younger generation to revive the language. With Australian Aboriginal languages and Cornish in England, this has been attempted. Thus the remnants of the foundations can be reused to start to reconstruct the language.

Stage 7

A language in Stage 7 will be used on a daily communication basis, but by more mature-age speakers beyond child-bearing. A language used by the older rather than the younger generation is likely to die as that older generation disappears. The language is unlikely to be reproduced in the younger generation as parents speak the majority language with their children. While the aim of Stage 8 is to reassemble the language, the aim of Stage 7 is to spread the language amongst the young. Mothers and fathers are encouraged to bring up their children in the minority language as it is essential to reproduce the dying language in children who may later bring up their children in that language to ensure language continuity.

Fishman (1991) is clear about well-intentioned but, in the long term future of a language, less important events. The danger of Stage 7 includes positive attitudes towards the language without positive action: 'the road to societal language death is paved with the good intentions called "positive attitudes" ' (page 91). The danger also is in exaggerating the value of symbolic events in the minority language, on the stage and the written page, in the gathering of the clans and at ceremonies. These events are relatively unimportant in the long term salvation of the language compared with the raising of children in that minority language. However, this is not to argue that such language events are valueless. Their value ultimately lies in indirectly encouraging language life at the daily participative level.

When a language is passed on from generation to generation through child-rearing practices, then a language has some chance of long-term success. In child development and particularly in the teenage years, using rather than losing a minority language becomes crucial. When the popular majority language culture becomes attractive to teenagers, minority language youth activities with youth participating and interacting in their minority language becomes critical (Baker, 1992).

Joshua A. Fishman

Introduction

Joshua A. Fishman has been to sociolinguistics what Freud was to psychoanalysis and Skinner to behaviorism. Professor Fishman has made one of the most significant contributions to the study of bilingualism in the 20th century.

Joshua A. Fishman was born on July 18, 1926 in Philadelphia, Pennsylvania, in the United States. His father, a dental mechanic who had immigrated in 1910 from Bessarabia, had been a member of the Bund in Czarist Russia, and remained an ardent socialist in the US. Fishman's mother was born in the Ukraine. Both were dedicated Yiddish supporters. Yiddish was the language of the home, and the children grew up to speak the language and to support it actively. In this respect, they were quite an unusual family. The Fishmans lived in largely Jewish middle class neighborhoods, where many of the older generation were Yiddish-speaking in-migrants, but where the children and grandchildren spoke mainly English.

Joshua (nicknamed Shikl), and his sister, later a prize-winning Yiddish poet, were taught at an early age to read and write Yiddish. At the age of eight, he wrote his first Yiddish poetry, and at 14, he became the founding editor of a Yiddish youth journal (*Ilpik*, later known as *Yugntruf*). His parents organized Yiddish conferences, literary events and other activities, and were in contact with Yiddish activists, teachers and writers throughout the country. Joshua Fishman wrote in an autobiographical sketch:

'Many of the topics to which I have devoted several years of professional sociolinguistic attention, e.g. language maintenance and language shift, language and nationalism, bilingual education, the spread of English, language and ethnicity, language planning and reversing language shift, can be traced back to concrete concerns, topics, involvements and even specific discussions of my childhood and adolescence within the very unusual home and family which gave me my first perspective on language in society' (Fishman, 1991, page 107).

A keen childhood passion for stamp collecting inspired an early fascination with other countries, cultures and languages which has continued throughout Fishman's life.

Education

Fishman was educated at Philadelphia public schools and at Olney High School. This last school's rigorous academic standards and the emphasis on a thorough mastery of different disciplines helped Fishman to appreciate the value of a multifaceted, multidisciplinary approach. He was also educated at supplementary Yiddish schools. These schools, known as Workmen's Circle Schools, concentrated on the development of the students' mastery of Yiddish, and also taught Yiddish literature to a high level. Yiddish history was studied, and ideas and social issues were debated from a socialist viewpoint. Many children in these schools were from English-speaking homes, and learnt Yiddish through a process of total immersion in the language for all activities.

Fishman's experience in these schools inspired his vision of enrichment bilingual education, and a commitment to language teaching which used language as a medium of instruction rather than the target of instruction. It also shaped his firm adherence to a model of societal bilingualism where the two languages would have complementary roles.

Academic career

Fishman gained his BSc (majoring in History) and MSc (Psychology) degrees from the University of Pennsylvania. At the same time, he followed Yiddish courses at the YIVO Institute for Jewish Research. In 1951, he became an educational psychologist for the Jewish Education Committee of New York. In 1953, he gained his PhD in Education and Social Psychology from Columbia University. From 1955-58, Fishman directed research for the College Entrance Examination Board, and also taught the sociology of language (under the heading of Social Psychology) at the City College of New York.

In 1958, he was appointed Associate Professor of Human Relations and Psychology at the University of Pennsylvania, and Director of Research at the Albert Greenfield Center for Human Relations. In 1960, he became Professor of Psychology and Sociology at Yeshiva University, New York. From 1960-66, he was also Dean of the Graduate School of Education and then Dean of the Ferkauf Graduate School of Social Sciences and Humanities. In 1966, he became Distinguished University Research Professor of Social Sciences at Yeshiva University and from 1973-75, he served as Academic Vice-President. In 1988, he became Professor Emeritus at Yeshiva University.

He has also held visiting appointments and fellowships at several prestigious universities in the US and abroad. In 1970–1973, the family lived in Israel while Fishman participated in a Ford Foundation Study of Language Planning Processes in East Pakistan, India, Indonesia, Israel and Sweden. He has been a Fellow at the Institutes for Advanced Study in Stanford, Honolulu, Princeton, Wassenaar and Jerusalem.

Marriage

In 1951, Fishman married Gella Schweid, then a Yiddish teacher at a Sholem Aleichem day-school. Throughout the years, she has enthusiastically supported and strengthened the couple's commitment to Yiddish. They brought up their three sons to be trilingual in Yiddish, Hebrew and English, and they have supported and inspired many Yiddish loyalists and members of other language minorities. The family's commitment to Yiddish has been complemented by a commitment to Jewish ethnicity, expressed by modern orthodox Jewish traditions.

Contribution

Professor Fishman has had a lifelong interest in bilingual communities, and a warmhearted commitment to bilingual education, the maintenance of bilingualism and the support of linguistic minorities. His Yiddish background, as a member of a minority within the Jewish minority, has given him a perspective from the periphery, and an insight into the situation of marginal groups and struggling minorities. He has been one of the pioneers in the relatively recent field of the sociology of language, which encompasses the study of all facets of the relation between language and social organization. His publications include well over 700 items, including nearly 600 articles and over 60 books on such topics as multilingual communities, bilingual education and the education of language minorities, Yiddish, language planning, language maintenance and language shift, language and nationalism, language and ethnicity, and language revival and reversal. He has concentrated mainly on a wider historical and macrosociological perspective on these topics.

In 1994, the Special Collections Section of the Stanford University Libraries established the 'Joshua A. Fishman and Gella Schweid Fishman Family Archives', which include Professor Fishman's correspondence, manuscripts, course outlines, conference presentations (also in audio and videotape), research data and photobank, as parts of a unique family collection. It is, in large part, already open to researchers.

Recently Professor Fishman has been engaged in research on ethnolinguistic consciousness, language revival and the reversal of language shift. One of his recent books is thus entitled: *The Beloved Language: The Content of Positive Ethnolinguistic Consciousness* (1996). The main points of his book *Reversing Language Shift* (1991) are summarized on page 188.

References: FISHMAN, 1991; GARCÍA, 1991

The importance of ensuring that a minority language is passed from one generation to another is summed up by Fishman (1991): 'The road to societal death is paved by language activity that is not focused on intergenerational continuity, i.e. that is diverted into efforts that do not involve and influence the socialization behaviors of families of child-bearing age' (page 91). Performances and publications, ceremonies and cultural meetings need to be seen as a means to an end, and not as an end in themselves. Such formal language events, however carefully arranged, do not intrinsically lead to the passing of a language from generation to generation. Such events are valuable to the extent they foster the passing of a language across generations. Such events must not just be for the elite, the firm disciples or the converts, but have missionary aims to secure the language in the younger generation. Such events are important to the extent to which they encourage everyday activity, at family and community level, in that language. Major cultural events (e.g. the *eisteddfodau* – celebrations of poetry and music, dance and drama in Wales), may produce the feeling of a strong language and an emotional lift for the individual.

Fishman's (1991) argument is that unless such events link into usual, daily, family socialization, the language in the long term is not being promoted.

Stage 6

Stage 6 is seen as the crucial, pivotal stage for the survival of a language. In Stage 6, a language will be passed to the next generation. At this sixth stage, the minority language will be used between grandparents, parents and children. This is regarded as quintessential in the fate of a language. If the minority language is used in the family, it may also be used in the street, in shops, with neighbors and friends. The language will more probably be spoken in the neighborhood and in community life, in religious and cultural events, in leisure and local informal commercial activity. At Stage 6, there will be a language community of a greater or lesser proportion.

This stage essentially concerns the informal use of a language in the home and the community. As such, the language may be supported and encouraged, but it may be outside the realms of formal language planning. The focus of this stage is the family, and the family within its community. As an institution, the family creates and maintains boundaries from the outside that may prevent the majority language from over-intrusion. However, Fishman (1991) points out that the more urbanized 20th century family does not live in a strong enough castle to prevent considerable outside influence from other languages. With the increase in one-parent families and both parents going out to work, the idea of mother and father as sole transmitters of the minority language is less strong. The alternative is that agencies and institutions supporting the home also create a minority language and minority cultural environment (e.g. the availability of minority language nursery schools). What is crucial is that early childhood and teenage socialization is enacted in the minority language and culture. The danger is in believing that other institutions such as the school, the mass media, the economy and government legislation will reverse language shift in themselves. Rather, language reversal is pivotal on Stage 6. Fishman (1991) argues that Stage 6 cannot be dispensed with.

Unless a language is transmitted across the generations, other activity may have short-term success and long-term failure. 'If this stage is not satisfied, all else can amount to little more than biding time...Attaining stage 6 is a necessary, even if not a sufficient, desideratum of RLS [Reversing Language Shift]' (page 399).

Stage 5

Stage 5 occurs when a minority language in the home, school and community goes beyond oracy to literacy. First, literacy in the minority language is seen to be important because it facilitates alternative means of communication, especially across distance and time. Second, the image and status of a minority language is raised when it is present in print. Such status is not merely symbolic. Literacy in the minority language means that a person is not just subject to majority language print media. Majority language media will contain dominant and powerful viewpoints, the attitudes of the center, the values and the beliefs of the majority language. Minority language literacy allows the possibility of minority language culture, political and ideological viewpoints to be presented. Third, literacy ensures a much wider variety of functions for a language. Such literacy may open more doors to employment, increase the chance of social and vocational mobility. However, at stage five, literacy in the majority language or biliteracy may be more important than literacy purely in the minority language if such mobility is desired.

Where education is through the majority language, then literacy in the minority language may be achieved through local community effort. Via Saturday and Sunday schools, in evening classes and through religious institutions, a literacy program in the minority language may be established. While such local efforts may be costly in money, they have the advantage of giving control in such literacy education to the community rather than to the central majority language government. With such control, local institutions can determine the appropriate means of literacy and cultural acquisition. While creating a financial burden, such activities may give a language community a focus, a shared commitment and a further *raison d'être*. While self-sacrifice is often hard and unfair, it can result in vitality, commitment, enthusiasm and a sense of unifying purpose.

For Fishman (1991), Stages 8 to 5 constitute the minimum basis of reversing language shift. The activities at these stages rely solely on the efforts of the language community itself. Such stages reflect a diglossic situation where the minority language has separate functions from the majority language. Given that bilingualism rather than minority language monolingualism will exist, such a minority language group may not be disadvantaged. They will usually have access to mainstream education from elementary to university levels. The full range of government services also will be available, including educational and welfare services. After Stage 5 comes the attempt to capture the formal functions so far reserved for the majority language (e.g. mass media, compulsory education, political self-determination). It is at this point that the minority language may come out of its enclave and seek to challenge majority language castles.

Stage 4

One of the first approaches into the majority language castle may be through education. Schools may be created and supported by the minority language community itself, not funded by the central purse. Such private schools may be outside the budgets of many relatively poor minority language communities. Therefore, minority language medium education paid for by central government may be sought. Central government will often still require some control over the curricula of such schools. That is, minority language medium education may only partly be under the control of the local minority language community. Such schools may need to prove that they are as effective and as successful as neighboring majority language schools; those attending them not being at a disadvantage but an advantage.

Stage 3

In previous stages, some people will use their minority language in a place of work at the 'lower work' (local and less specialized work) level. In previous stages, a few such workers will function economically in a relatively isolated way in the local neighborhood or as a self-contained group. Few bridges will exist with the majority language community. At Stage 3, creating a wider economic base for the minority language becomes important.

Such economic activity will involve the establishment of minority language staffed enterprises and services, not just for the local market but for national and international markets as well. Such minority language enterprise will, at times, require communication in the majority language. However, the on-the-floor activity and in-house communication may all be through the minority language.

However, success by language minority enterprise in international and national economic activity may not be without danger to the minority language. The economic value of majority languages, and the arrival of in-migrants should there be economic success, are just two possible after-effects. As economic independence and self-regulation evolve, the temptation may be to increase profit by switching to international majority languages. Such minority language economic activity nevertheless opens doors to increasing affluence, vocational mobility and social status. Young minority language speakers may be more willing to stay in an area rather than migrate to majority language pastures when there is economic opportunity. When there are jobs and money in the local community, the minority language has firmer roots and resources.

Stage 2

The penultimate stage is extending lower government services and mass media into the minority language. Local government institutions may offer their services through the minority language; health and postal services, courts and the police service for example. Telephone and banking services, energy providing bodies and supermarkets may also become willing to use the minority language in their service and communication with the public.

Central government may wish to control its services to language minority regions to influence attitudes and opinions, information and ideology. The more the decision-making processes (educational, economic and political) are released to such regions, the more power that local language has to capture the minds of the minority. In Stage 2, national radio and television may be asked to broadcast a set number of hours in the minority language.

Alternatively, as in Wales, a particular channel may be mostly dedicated to minority language use. Not only does the use of minority language television and radio help to disseminate the attendant culture. It will also provide primary and secondary employment for minority language speakers.

The particular dangers of this stage may be in creaming off the most able and ambitious professionals into majority language positions. Minority language media also face severe viewing competition from Anglo-American, high budget programs. The mass media provide status for a minority language, a channel for the minority cultural message, but no salvation for the language in and by itself.

Stage 1

In this final stage, the pinnacle of achievement in language shift, the minority language will be used at university level and will be strongly represented in mass media output, governmental services and throughout occupations. Alongside some degree of economic autonomy will also be cultural autonomy. At this stage the language will be officially recognized in central government legislation or by a Language Act.

Throughout the four latter stages, Fishman (1991) is keen to point out that Stage 6 is still pre-eminent. When mass communications, economic rewards and vocational opportunities exist through the minority language, it is still the family, the neighborhood and community language life that is vital in the long term success of the language. All the trappings of language status (e.g. mass media), all the power of legislation, all the success in economic self-determination do not assure the future of a language. Important as are Stages 4 to 1, a language is ultimately lost and won inside the minds and hearts of individuals. While such individuals will doubtless be affected by economic, political and media factors, there is a personal cost-benefit analysis that ultimately determines whether one language is passed on to the next generation or not.

Limitations of Reversing Language Shift Theory

Fishman (1991) is careful to point out that, while one stage is not necessarily dependent on a previous stage, there are priorities. The more advanced stages cannot usually be secured unless more foundational stages are either first built or repaired. The danger increases in advancing on all fronts. Attempting to win individual battles without having a strategy for the whole war does not champion success. There is also a danger in working solely for tangible, newsworthy, easily recognized victories (Fishman, 1993). Changing the language of road signs, tax forms and gaining minority language presence on television are battles that have been fought and won in some minority language regions. It is more difficult, but more important, to support and encourage the minority language for communication in daily family and community life. For Fishman (1991, 1993), it is the informal and intimate spoken language reproduced across generations that is the ultimate pivot of language shift .Initial activity to reverse language shift will usually derive solely from the minority language community. The language community needs to be awoken and mobilized to support its language, especially at a family and community participative level. However, there may come a time when the majority language government will support that community's efforts to survive. Through the provision of bilingual education, government services and a minority language television service, the central government may come to support its minority languages.

Fishman (1991) is particularly guarded about how much bilingual education can achieve in reversing language shift. There is sometimes the belief that, where families do not transmit the minority language, the school is there to do it instead. Where parents do not bring up their children in the minority language, the school is expected to be the substitute minority language parent. The school may initiate second language acquisition in the minority language. But few rather than many may use the school-learnt language throughout life, particularly in parenting their children. Even when a child successfully learns minority language oracy and literacy skills in school, unless there is considerable support in the community and the economy outside school, that language may wither and die. A classroom-learnt second language may become a school-only language.

For that language to survive inside the individual, a person needs to become bonded in the language community while at school, and particularly after leaving school. There needs to be pre-school, out-of-school and after-school support and reward systems for using the minority language. The minority language needs to be embedded in the family-neighborhood-community experience and in the economics of the family. Unless this happens, it is unlikely that bilingually educated children will pass on the minority language to the next generation. Thus, for Fishman (1991, 1993), each stage needs examining for how it can be used to feed into Stage 6 – the intergenerational transmission of the minority language.

Fishman's (1991) eight stages must be seen as overlapping and interacting. In language revival, it is not the case of going one step or stage at a time. The myriad factors in language reversal link together in complex patterns. A language at Stage 2 may still be securing elements of previous stages. A language at Stage 6 may be engaged in long-term planning to secure higher stages. Also, different communities and different geographical areas may be at different stages within the same nation. One area may have secured bilingual education provision, a neighboring area may have undeveloped bilingual education provision. Minority language literacy may be strong in some communities, weak in others. The use of

Language Revival, Language Revitalization and Language Reversal

Paulston, Chen & Connerty (1993) offer a non-exclusive distinction between language revival, language revitalization and language reversal which can all be included under the term 'language regenesis'. Language revival is reserved for the giving of new life to a dead language (e.g. Hebrew, but see below). Maori and Welsh would not be included as there has been a continuous use of the language over many centuries.

Language revitalization is the imparting of new vigor to an existing language, often by increasing the domains where the language is used. Language reversal refers to the turning around of current (downward) trends in a language. For Paulston, Chen & Connerty (1993), language reversal often focuses on a more prominent use of a language vis-à-vis its relation to other state language(s). This may be in legal terms (e.g. the gaining of official status for Catalan in 1978); a renaissance in use (e.g. Maori); or a non-native language being accepted after a period of rejection for economic and international communication purposes (e.g. English in Singapore and Malaysia).

Other scholars do not distinguish between these terms, as they are all part of one process. Some would take issue with the definition of language revival as the giving of life to a dead language. For example, Hebrew has never been a 'dead' language, as for a period of nearly two thousand years it was used in religious, literary, academic and other communicative contexts. The revival of an extinct language for normal vernacular purposes (e.g. Cornish in the UK) has proved extremely difficult.

REFERENCE: PAULSTON, CHEN & CONNERTY, 1993

Colin Williams' Five Stages of Language Revival

Colin Williams (1994b) has suggested that there are five stages in revitalizing a minority language. These five stages focus on language minorities that are less threatened than those at Fishman's Stage 7 and 8. The stages should also be seen as overlapping and not mutually exclusive.

Stage 1: Idealism
It is important for language activist groups to construct a vision of language revival, to believe deeply that the language is threatened and dying and must be rehabilitated.

Stage 2: Protest
Language activists (who may be an elite) will mobilize people in the population to agitate for reform or revolution in the use and status of the minority language.

Stage 3: Legitimacy
Language rights will be attained for the minority language, and there will be a movement towards a more general acceptance among minority language (and possibly majority language) people for the survival and status of a minority language.

Stage 4: Institutionalization
The language is represented and grows in key strategic agencies of the state, for example the law, education, public administration, employment and commercial activity.

Stage 5: Parallelism
The minority language is extended into as many different social situations as possible (e.g. sport, media, entertainment, many public services, private industry). The aim is for the minority language to be as strong in use as the majority language.

REFERENCE: WILLIAMS, 1994

Colin Williams is currently Professor of Welsh at the University of Wales, Cardiff. With many important contributions to the understanding of the situation of the Welsh language, Colin Williams has also written authoritatively about international language contexts such as the rest of the United Kingdom, Ireland, Spain, Canada and many other parts of Europe. He is well-known for his work on ethnic relations and geolinguistics and has been active in the promotion of Europe's minority languages. He has taught and lectured in England, Canada, the United States and many European countries. As the Bibliography indicates, Colin Williams has a voluminous output which covers disciplines as wide as Geography, Politics, Education, Sociolinguistics and History.

Christina Bratt Paulston

Christina Bratt Paulston is Professor of Linguistics and Director of the English Language Institute at the University of Pittsburgh. With teaching experience in Sweden, Morocco, Peru and the United States, and with academic training at Carleton College, the University of Minnesota, and Teachers' College, Colombia University, she has published widely in the fields of language teaching, teacher training, language planning, sociolinguistics and bilingual education. She was President of TESOL in 1976 and has traveled and lectured extensively around the world.

There are two collections of her most seminal, provocative and influential contributions: *Sociolinguistic Perspectives on Bilingual Education* (1992) and *Linguistic and Communicative Competence: Topics in ESL* (1992). In 1994, she published a book entitled *Linguistic Minorities in Multilingual Settings* which provides a comprehensive and wide-ranging analysis of language behavior in social groups. The book makes an original and important contribution to the current international concern with language planning.

the minority language in business and the local economy may vary considerably from rural to urban areas, and according to closeness of access to airports, roads, railways and sea links. In some villages, language death may be close. In other villages within the same region, most community life may be in the minority language.

Glyn Williams (1992), in a critique of Fishman, has argued that the presupposition is that change is gradual, mechanical, evolutionary and cumulative. He suggests that the viewpoint of Fishman tends to be of a consensus nature, concerned with integration, equilibrium, order and cohesion. Williams (1992) regards the work of Fishman as politically conservative with a consequent limited discussion of deviance, power, struggle and conflict. The preference is to play down the conflict while ignoring power, thereby not expressing the anger, discrimination and frustration felt by language minority groups and their members. This theme is returned to in the section on Language Conflict (see page 333f).

The theories of Fishman may be isolated from the world as viewed by language minority actors and actresses themselves. Their explanations and discourse can provide an alternative basis for the explanation and understanding of language revival and reversal (a phenomenological perspective).

There is also a possible danger that the neatness of the eight stages of reversing language shift leads to a false belief that reversal is easy, plannable, deliverable and possible. Language situations are always highly complex, based on a long history with many interaction factors in any decision. The model may suggest there are simple solutions and easy decisions, when language planning involves many competing interests, values, ideologies and priorities. For example, if there is a budget for language planning, there are multitudinous pragmatic considerations, sensibilities and pressures that making working from a simple model impossible. At its worst, a simple model may deceive as to the complexity and difficulty of effecting reversal.

Yet typologies and graded scales are helpful in organizing thinking and in creating a general guide rather than a comprehensive map. They represent, in outline form, a consideration of a variety of phenomena. The GIDS scale is a valuable attempt at basic sequencing and prioritizing.

Further Reading

FISHMAN, J. A., 1990, What is Reversing Language Shift (RLS) and how can it Succeed? *Journal of Multilingual and Multicultural Development*, 11 (1&2), 5-34.

FISHMAN, J. A., 1991, *Reversing Language Shift*. Clevedon: Multilingual Matters Ltd.

FISHMAN, J. A., 1993, Reversing Language Shift: Successes, Failures, Doubts and Dilemmas. In E. H. JAHR (ed.), *Language Conflict and Language Planning*. Berlin/New York: Mouton de Gruyter.

WILLIAMS, G., 1992, *Sociolinguistics: A Sociological Critique*. London: Routledge.

3: Two Cases of Language Revival: Maori and Hebrew

The Maori Language and Culture in New Zealand

Settlement in New Zealand

The Maori people were the first settlers in New Zealand. They are a Polynesian people, and their migration from subtropical Pacific islands took place in successive waves over a long period. According to their folk legends, the migrations began in the tenth century, but archaeological evidence suggests the first settlers arrived long before that. The last and biggest influx of in-migrants arrived in the 14th century. They mostly settled in the warmer North Island and lived undisturbed for centuries.

In 1642, Abel Tasman, a Dutch sea captain, discovered the southern island and named it Nieuw Zeeland after a Dutch province. He did not stay long after being attacked by the Maori. In 1769, the English explorer Captain James Cook traveled round the islands and established friendly relations with the Maori. He was impressed by their martial skills, and also by their ability in arts and crafts. Cook returned on three more voyages, and published the diary of his travels, which was widely read, and translated into twelve languages. Many people in Western Europe became interested in the islands of Nieuw Zeeland, especially in Britain.

The first European settlers were whalers and sealers. In 1840, British sovereignty was officially declared, and widespread, organized migration from Europe began. At that time, the Treaty of Waitangi was signed between a representative of the British government and Maori chiefs. Under the terms of the treaty, the Maori ceded sovereignty to the British in return for protection and for possession of their lands, homes and all their *taonga* (treasured possessions). This treaty attempted to cement the relationships between the *pakeha* or white man and the Maori people, by defining the rights and responsibilities of both sides in the process of colonization. However, the treaty was soon laid aside and forgotten in the quest for land, and this created many conflicts between the British settlers and the Maori in the 19th century.

The situation of the Maori language in New Zealand

From a cultural and linguistic point of view, New Zealand is a relatively homogeneous nation. The overwhelming majority of the population are of British descent. Small in-migrant groups from other European countries, Dutch, Yugoslavs, Poles, Greeks, Hungarians, Italians and Scandinavians, were quickly assimilated by the majority English-speaking population, tending to shift to English by the second or at least third generation. Three percent of the population are recent Polynesian in-migrants and have also tended to shift to English. According to 1991 figures, English is now the first language of 95 percent of the population of 3.4 million, and the only language of 90 percent.

The largest minority group (12 percent) are the Maori. However, less than a quarter of Maori can speak the Maori language, (estimates range between 50,000 and 70,000) and the majority of these are middle aged and elderly. It is estimated that half as many again (about 35,000) have a passive understanding of the language. Gradually, over a period of a century and a half, the Maori language has yielded ground to English. In a pattern which has been replicated in many other countries in the world, the prestigious language of the powerful majority has ousted the language of the powerless indigenous minority. Like many other language minorities, the majority of speakers of Maori are concentrated in peripheral areas, in this case, in the northern and eastern areas of North Island.

The Maori language has been excluded from official life and actively suppressed in schools. The early mission schools taught through the medium of Maori but in 1847, the Education Ordinance made subsidies for mission schools dependent on the condition they taught in English. In 1867, the state established a system of village day schools in Maori rural communities. Initially the teachers were expected to use the Maori language to aid the teaching of English. However, by the turn of the century, the Maori language had been more or less banned from schools. The emphasis in Maori schools was on preparing the Maori people for work as manual laborers. They were believed to be unfit for 'mental labor'. This racist ideology explains to a large extent the comparative social, economic and educational deprivation of the Maori people today.

The loss of the language was initially quite slow. The Maori people provided strong resistance in the New Zealand land wars, and this helped them maintain their

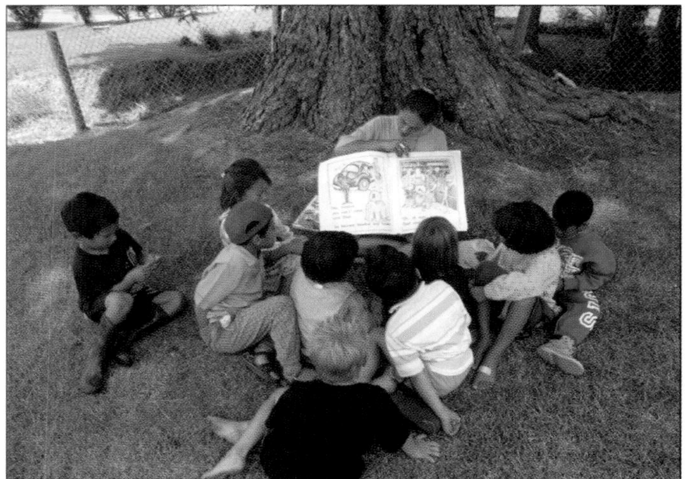
Maori children have an outdoor Maori language lesson at an elementary school outside the predominantly Maori village of Waima, North Island, New Zealand.

language, culture and separate identity. However, since the middle of the 20th century, the decline of the language has accelerated. Urbanization and industrialization have resulted in widespread emigration from rural areas to the cities, with Maori speakers being assimilated by the English-speaking majority. English-medium education and the all-pervasive influence of the mass media have also contributed to the rapid erosion of the Maori tongue. Another main reason for the decline of Maori has been its low status in the eyes of its speakers and in the eyes of the English-speaking majority. Even in isolated rural areas, Maori has been virtually replaced by English and few parents speak the language to their children. In 1930, a survey of children attending native schools estimated that over 96 percent spoke only Maori at home. By 1960, only 26 percent spoke Maori.

A sociolinguistic survey conducted by Richard Benton between 1973 and 1978 documented the process of Maori language loss. In Whangarei City, for instance, there was a fall off in the percentage of Maori able to speak their language as early as 1915. Only 40 percent of Maori born there 20 years later could speak Maori. Most born after 1955 speak only English. Even in rural areas, there was a switch to English during the 1930s: this happened more rapidly in some areas than others. By the early 1970s few Maori children knew the language. In less than eight percent of the households in Benton's survey could the children understand Maori: in only half of these could the children be described as fluent.

By the 1970s the language was widely spoken in only two communities, Ruatoki and Matawaia. There was a further decline in language use generally following the promotion of the use of English in the pre-school Play Centre movement. Maori mothers were encouraged to use only English with their children. The growing popularity of English-medium television was a further blow to the language.

The Maori language has been retained in some formal and ceremonial domains of Maori life. It is still used on the *marae* (plaza) in front of the meeting house for ceremonial speeches. It is also used in formal religious practices. However, as a living language of everyday communication, the Maori language is at a critical stage in its existence. Among those of Maori ancestry, only one in eight – 50,000 people in all – are first language speakers of Maori and the majority of these are middle aged or older.

The situation of the Maori people follows a pattern which is commonly found in ethnic minority groups, where the erosion of the language and culture is accompanied and exacerbated by poverty, political powerlessness and lack of status. Although there has been relatively little racial tension between the Maori and the *pakehas*, when compared with other countries, the Maori are still a comparatively disadvantaged minority group. For instance, according to 1995 figures, 37 percent of Maori students leave school without any qualifications, compared with about 12 percent of non-Maori students. More than 40 percent of Maori 15–19 year olds are unemployed compared with 25 percent of non-Maori. In 1991, 56 percent of Maori aged between 15 and 59 years were receiving some form of income support benefit.

Promotion of the Maori language

In recent years, a strong movement has arisen for the preservation and promotion of the Maori language and culture, together with a desire for the furtherance of the economic and social welfare of the Maori people. This has involved several aspects.

Revival of the language among young people

Firstly, there have been efforts to restore the knowledge and use of the language among children and young people. At the time of the last census in 1991, Maori represented 14 percent of the total population, but 21 percent of primary school students and 15 percent of secondary school students. The relative preponderance of young people in the total Maori population means that initiatives in education are an important part of the total strategy for Maori language revival and for improvement in the socioeconomic conditions of Maori people. Although education, as such, cannot create changes in social and economic conditions, it may create the potential for change in the young generation.

Since the 1960s, there has been a steady increase in the provision of tuition in the Maori language in New Zealand classrooms. Many non-Maori students have aken part in these relatively limited programs, and their nain effect has been to increase knowledge of and appreiation of Maori language and culture in New Zealand. n the late 1970s, bilingual primary school programs vere introduced and by 1991 there were 251 primary chools and 54 secondary schools offering some form of oilingual education to 13,000 primary and 2500 secondary students. This development has been encouragng, but these types of bilingual programs have not been ery successful in achieving and maintaining fluency in hildren. The approach has tended to be transitional, radually phasing out Maori in favor of English. Also the legree of teaching in the Maori language varies, with nany schools only offering four to five hours instruction week in Maori. This led to a knowledge of Maori rather han use of it outside school. It was felt that Maori-medium education should start even earlier and be more ntensive, so that the children might attain and maintain luency in Maori. Also there must be stronger links etween Maori-medium education and the community, o that the use of the language in the classroom might ead to its revitalization in the community. Spolsky 1989a) writes: 'An increasingly assertive Maori minoriy...requires much more from the schools than simply anguage teaching or language revival. Instead, it wishes he schools to assume a crucial role in the socialization of children, teaching them to be Maori as well as to peak Maori' (page 60).

n 1982 the first *kohanga reo* or 'Language Nest' (Maori anguage nursery school) was opened. Between 1982 nd 1993, more than 800 *kohanga reo* were established, nd by 1995, 13,000 pre-schoolers were enrolled. This epresents about a quarter of the total of Maori under ives. Most come to the *kohanga reo* from English-speakng homes. They learn Maori naturally through an mmersion process while playing, listening to stories, inging, taking part in games and other activities. lthough the *kohanga reo* has many similarities with immersion schooling in countries such as Canada and Wales, the idea was conceived entirely independently by a group of Maori parents. The fact that the *kohanga reo* sprang from a grass roots movement for the preservation of the language has been its main strength. It has meant that parents and other members of the local community have been able from the beginning to structure the schools in accordance with Maori social and cultural practices, and exercise a good deal of local control over their children's education. It has also meant that the schools have become a focal point for community life with a great deal of community involvement e.g. local Maori speaking teachers' assistants from the local communities. Also use of the Maori language and Maori cultural and social practices within the schools have reinforced their use in the community.

Vaitangi Day is an annual event in New Zealand, commemorating the hisoric Waitangi treaty. In 1995, Maori protests disrupted and finally forced ancellation of Waitangi day, causing a nationwide uproar.

At primary or elementary level, bilingual programs have existed since 1977. Immersion programs in state schools were initiated in the mid-1980s. A third option now exists. From *kohanga reo*, many children now have the option to progress to *kura kaupapa maori*, Maori immersion primary schools. These were originally privately funded, but are now state-funded. However, their strong links with the local community mean that parents exercise a good deal of control over the administration, curriculum and teaching methods of their local schools. Between 1990 and 1994, 28 *kura kaupapa* were set up, with more in the process of being launched. All subjects are taught through the medium of Maori and Maori culture, Maori knowledge and Maori spirituality permeate the whole of the curriculum. There are strong links between the school and the local Maori community, and children have the opportunity to study in different environments, the *marae*, the bush and the seaside.

English lessons are begun at the age of eight, and the children are taught to read and write English. By that age, they have already learnt to read and write Maori, a more phonetic language than English, and their literacy skills tend to transfer relatively easily to English. Every other subject continues to be taught in Maori.

Ongoing research needs to assess the effectiveness of *kura kaupapa*. Preliminary studies of the children's English skills, however, indicate that the results found in other types of maintenance education are being achieved (i.e. that early immersion in a second language does not adversely affect the students' attainment in the first, majority language). The proportion of Maori students attending these schools is small. By 1994, 1667 children were enrolled in these schools, representing just over one percent of the total school age Maori population. However, preliminary studies suggest that the *kura kaupapa* provide enormous benefits, not just for the students themselves but for their families and communities. The indication is that the students develop self-respect and pride in themselves and their ethnic identity, a more positive attitude to school and higher career aspirations. In most areas, the school represents the only place in the community where Maori is the first and dominant language. Thus, the Maori immersion school has a key role to play in promoting the Maori language, and has had beneficial influence on other types of Maori-medium education. Hopefully, the *kura kaupapa* will continue to grow and develop. In 1993/94 two *whare kura* (Maori-medium secondary schools) were established and two *whare wananga* (tertiary institutions) were formally recognized for funding purposes, with another waiting approval.

In addition to *kura kaupapa*, by 1995 335 other schools were offering some form of Maori-medium instruction, catering for 12.5 percent of Maori children. In one third of these schools, Maori was being used 80 percent of the time.

Currently, there is little provision for education through the Maori language at high school level. Some *kura kaupapa* have extended their provision to include the first year of high school (13 to 14 years old). Elsewhere, Maori language units are being set up within existing high schools so that graduates of *kura kaupapa* can continue their education through the medium of *Te Reo Maori* (the Maori language).

Promotion of Maori as an official language

Another aspect of the promotion of Maori is its greater prominence in public and official life. In 1974, an amendment to the Maori Affairs Act recognized Maori as 'the ancestral language of that portion of the population of New Zealand of Maori descent', but this had no force in law. At this time, the Treaty of Waitangi was reinvested with legal force. In 1975 The Waitangi Tribunal was set up, with limited powers to hear Maori grievances against the Treaty of Waitangi. In 1984 it was invested with the retrospective power to settle Maori claims against the Crown, dating back to 1840. Within months, any land claims had been lodged by *iwi* (ethnic groups). In 1986, the Waitangi Tribunal ruled that the Crown had failed to keep its promise made in the Treaty of Waitangi to protect the *taonga* (treasured possessions) of the Maori people and that the Maori language should be considered as one of these.

It recommended, among other things, that Maori be an official language and a medium of instruction in education, and that a Maori Language Commission should be set up to safeguard the interests of the language. In July 1987, the Maori Language Act was passed which accorded the Maori language the status of an official language in New Zealand. The Maori Language Commission was established, as a national agency with responsibility for promoting the use of the Maori language. It provides a forum where Maori language policy can be discussed, developed and promoted. The Commission offers a technical service by undertaking language research, including the creation and collection of new terms in the Maori language. It encourages the state sector to respond to the needs of Maori speakers particularly in providing information and publications in Maori and English and also in advertising using both languages. Since 1986, there has been a five minute daily news broadcast in Maori on the television. In 1995 the government approved the drawing up of a 15 year strategic plan to protect the Maori language.

Support for the Maori people

A third aspect of the Maori provision is the emphasis on the social welfare and cultural and economic development of the Maori people. January 1992 saw the establishment of *Te Puni Kokiri*, a government ministry which took the place of the former Department of Maori Affairs. The new ministry's task is no longer to deliver programs and enact policies but rather to advise the New Zealand Government on social, political, economic and cultural issues as they affect Maori people, and to ensure that a Maori perspective is incorporated into any new policies which might be developed. For instance, *Te Puni Kokiri* is involved in the promotion of Maori business ventures (e.g. fisheries and aquiculture projects), health programs, the management of Maori land, and forestry projects. *Te Puni Kokiri* has also developed distance learning technologies that will help isolated rural schools with large Maori rolls, including Maori-medium schools. The ministry has also published research on factors that influence Maori children to stay on at school after the age of 16.

There has been a new emphasis on respecting and maintaining traditional Maori customs and family and group structures. To mark the International Decade of the World's Indigenous Peoples (1994–2004), there has been a renewed interest in Maori culture, including dance, music, art and orally-transmitted history.

The future of the Maori language

Like many minority languages, it is not certain whether the Maori language will survive in the twenty-first century as a daily means of communication. When a language has reached the stage when it is no longer spoken by parents to their children, it becomes increasingly difficult to revive it. Despite the encouraging growth of Maori-medium education, the actual level of knowledge and use of the language is still quite low. Even within the Maori-medium nursery schools and schools, teachers are likely to be second language speakers of Maori, with a restricted command of the language. They themselves find it difficult to use Maori consistently with their families at home. Students in Maori-medium education tend to reply in English in class, and use English amongst themselves inside and outside the classroom, Most of them speak English with their parents, although more of them use Maori with their grandparents.

There are encouraging aspects of the revitalization of Maori. At the time of Benton's survey, only about 12 percent of adult Maori spoke the language. (This percentage was higher among older Maori – nearly half of those over 55 still spoke Maori). Now, about 12 percent of younger children are on their way to becoming relatively competent speakers of Maori.

Spolsky (1989) draws comparisons between the situation of the Maori language and the revitalization of Hebrew during the late 19th and 20th centuries. He points out how the development of Hebrew-medium education produced a generation of young Hebrew speakers who later were able to revitalize the language within the home, speaking the language to their children. Thus Hebrew-medium education was an important factor in the restoration of the intergenerational transmission of the Hebrew language. Spolsky implies that it is not impossible that this could happen in the case of Maori.

Another important factor bearing on the revitalization of Maori is the fact that the Maori people have to a large extent maintained their culture and ethnic identity. The Maori language will probably be retained as the language of certain social and religious ceremonies, and, as such, an important symbolic marker of ethnic identity for Maori people. Hopefully, the recent increase in Maori-medium education which has strong community links will help to restore the use of the language in Maori communities and revive its intergenerational transmission. The increasing governmental efforts to further the economic, social and cultural welfare of the Maori people can only help to increase their self-esteem and pride in their ethnic identity. This will no doubt encourage the learning and use of the Maori language as a central marker of the cultural and ethnic identity of the Maori people.

The Revitalization of Hebrew

Hebrew was the language of the people who, from the 11th century BC, were dominant politically and culturally in and around what is the modern State of Israel and who practised the Jewish religion. Members of this people stopped living in most of its ancient lands in any significant numbers following the Roman suppression of the

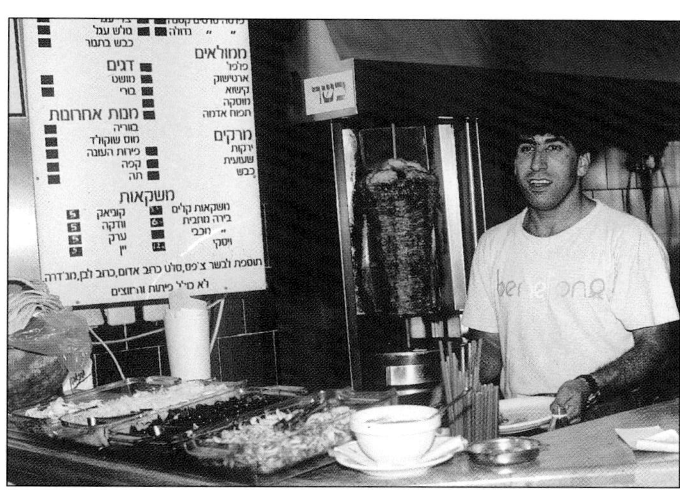

A Hebrew menu in a cafe in Tel Aviv, Israel. Hebrew can now be used in all areas of modern life.

Bar-Kochba revolt in AD 135. By AD 250 Hebrew had ceased to be spoken as a day-to-day language, giving way to Aramaic. After the Jewish people were scattered throughout the world in the Diaspora they adopted the languages of the countries in which they lived, and gradually modified versions of these languages evolved for use among many Jews. The most notable of these was Yiddish, which evolved between the 9th and 12th centuries among Jewish emigrants from Northern France who settled in a number of cities along the Rhine and adopted the German dialects of that area. Yiddish borrowed many words pertaining to religious life from Hebrew, and also adopted elements from Slavic languages, when Jews moved eastwards into Poland, Lithuania and Russia in the 14th and 15th centuries.

However, Hebrew continued to be used in synagogue worship and when reading religious texts. Most Jews lived in a triglossic situation, using the everyday language of the country in which they lived with non-Jews, using a Jewish vernacular such as Yiddish for daily community life, and using Hebrew for religious purposes. Hebrew was used as the medium of religious literature and also for philosophical and scientific topics. The degree of knowledge of Hebrew depended on factors such as social class, degree of orthodoxy and also gender (generally, only boys studied Hebrew). The language continued to evolve and by the 19th century, Hebrew was used as a medium for novels, poetry and journalism. It was also used for legal and commercial documents, and very occasionally as a lingua franca between Jews of different Diaspora languages.

When Jews began returning to their homeland in large numbers in the latter half of the 19th century, the question arose as to what language or languages should be used as the lingua franca between the settlers in the

A trilingual Hebrew-Arabic-English sign in Jerusalem.

homeland of Palestine. The Zionist movement was firmly rooted in modern nationalist ideology, which emphasized the importance of a shared history, culture and a single national language that would unify and express the soul of the nation. For many Zionists, especially those from Eastern Europe, the only language that could express the heart and soul of the reborn nation of Israel was Hebrew. However, there was much skepticism as to the possibility of this occurring and many thought that it would take a long time. The resurgence of Hebrew as a vernacular language was not an easy process. It involved the language being used for the first time in nearly two thousand years as an everyday spoken language. It also meant that the language must be modernized, with new words coined to express everyday and modern concepts, that it must be secularized and become a vehicle of expression for all domains of life.

The revitalization of Hebrew occurred because so many of the Zionist settlers possessed strong nationalist convictions and disciplined determination. Many settlers of the 'second *aliyah*', the second great wave of immigration that took place between 1905 and the First World War, came voluntarily to Palestine. They were deeply committed to Zionism and the revival of Hebrew. Some of them had begun to use Hebrew as an everyday spoken language even before arriving in Israel.

The revitalization of Hebrew first occurred in the rural Zionist settlements. The settlement schools established at the turn of the 20th century were largely responsible for the spread of fluency in Hebrew among children. The teachers were deeply committed and versed in the most recent methods of second language teaching. They used the 'natural' or 'direct' method to teach the language and also used it as a medium to teach all other subjects, thus predating modern immersion schools by over half a century. The teachers insisted on the use of Hebrew by children within schools and encouraged its use outside. It was not a school-only language for the young students, their parents and other community members were also

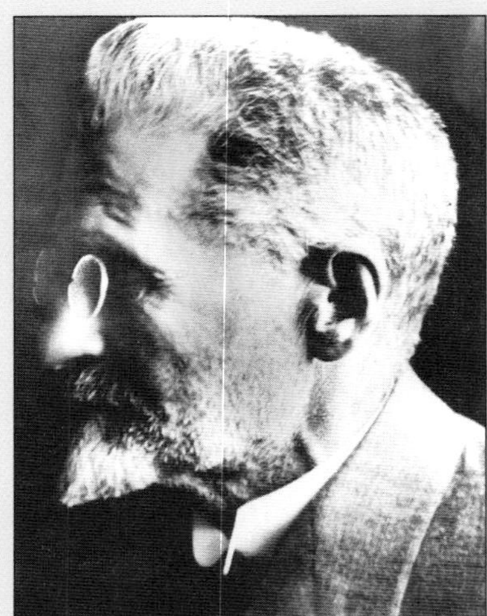

Eliezer Ben-Yehudah

Eliezer Ben-Yehudah (1858–1922) was a Lithuanian-born Zionist and linguist who has been credited with being the father of modern Hebrew. He was one of the first supporters of the idea that the Jewish people must have their own national and spiritual homeland that would serve as a symbol and a focal point for the Jews of the world. Ben-Yehudah advocated the revival of Hebrew as a spoken language in Palestine. He moved there in 1881, and he and his wife were among the first parents to speak Hebrew to their children at home. He founded the Hebrew Language Council, later called the Academy of Hebrew Language, and his most important work, the Complete Dictionary of Ancient and Modern Hebrew, was published between 1910 and 1959.

Ben-Yehudah did not single-handedly revitalize Hebrew, as is sometimes believed. However, his symbolic influence as a national figure on generations of Hebrew activists was very important.

actively engaged in learning Hebrew and using it to the best of their capabilities with their families and friends. Thus the revitalization of Hebrew did not occur solely through the schools, but as the result of the mutual reinforcement of the efforts of schools, families and the community.

By the early 1920s, the rural Zionist settlements were completely Hebrew-speaking. To change the language of the urban areas to Hebrew would be a more challenging task. One difficulty was the constant influx of new in-migrants, many of whom were not Zionists but were merely seeking asylum from persecution, anti-Semitism and social disadvantage in other countries. Jewish multilingualism in Palestine meant that a lingua franca was a pressing necessity. For those who did not ascribe to the Zionist vision, Hebrew was not the easiest option, as it was spoken by no one as a mother tongue. Another factor was the presence of large Jewish Orthodox communities in places like Jerusalem, who were implacably opposed to the use of Hebrew for anything but religious purposes. Many of these Orthodox communities used Yiddish as their daily language and educated their children in private Yiddish schools. Indeed, Yiddish was the first language of a large proportion of the Jewish in-migrants to Palestine.

Prior to World War II, Yiddish was the first language of approximately ten million Jews in Central and Eastern Europe. This represented about two-thirds of the world population of Jewish people. Thus Yiddish had a strong claim as a possible national language for the homeland, but it was not considered suitable by many Zionists because of its Germanic origins and its associations with the underprivileged and disadvantaged status of Jews in countries such as Germany. Other languages considered were German and English. However, no other language but Hebrew could, in the eyes of the Zionists, represent the heart and soul of the reborn Jewish nation.

Since the creation of the State of Israel in 1948, the official languages have been Hebrew, Arabic and English. Arabic is spoken by the Arab minority (13 percent of the total population). For the Jewish majority (82 percent of the population), Hebrew is the language of education, government and public and official life. The majority of

A 1950s collection of books about the new state of Israel shows the variety of languages spoken by in-migrants.

Jewish Israelis also speak Hebrew at home. However, the dream of the early Zionists of a monolingual Hebrew-speaking Israel has not become a reality.

Multilingualism in Modern Israel

Multilingualism is a fact of life in contemporary Israel. Waves of in-migrants learnt Hebrew informally and through *Ulpanim* (intensive language learning programs, see page 693). Yiddish is still widely spoken, especially among older in-migrants and in Orthodox communities, which tend to have a higher than average birthrate. Yiddish is learnt in school by around 3000 students. In addition, many other languages, apart from Hebrew and Yiddish are spoken: Arabic, Armenian, Assyrian, English, French, Ladino, Judeo-Aramaic, Hungarian, Romanian, Russian, German, Polish, Amharic, Domari and Tigrinya, for example. However, a remarkable feature of Israel is the spread of Hebrew since 1948 (Spolsky, 1996).

The flow of immigration into Israel became a flood after 1948, and *olim* (in-migrants) arrived from many other countries, including Europe and North America, Asia and North Africa, resulting in minority language communities that continue to use their native languages in the home and neighborhood. Strong facilities for learning Hebrew have been provided by the State. Residential and intensive courses have existed since 1949. New in-migrants generally have a high integrative and instrumental motivation to master Hebrew, but the native language is often retained and used at home, at least for one or two generations. The motivation of in-migrants to learn Hebrew is partly due to the effective institutionalization of Hebrew: for example, in communication with authorities and at the place of work; in the school curriculum; in study at university; in government publications; in the country's laws and legal system and on radio and television.

Recently, there seems to have occurred a softening in the traditional Hebrew-enforcement policy towards in-migrants. First, Hebrew is now a strong, established language, spoken as a native language by over half the population, and as a second language by nearly all the remainder. The dream of a Jewish homeland has been achieved and the Hebrew language, a main symbol of the revolutionary society, is firmly entrenched. Thus large groups of non-Hebrew-speaking in-migrants are not perceived as a threat. Second, the strong Zionist ideology of the early settlers is less widely embraced. When the battle is won, and goals have been achieved, there appears to be less need for a strong ideology.

Third, since late 1989, there has been a massive influx of Soviet Jews, mainly Russian-speaking, into Israel, forming the largest wave of immigration in Israeli history. Between 1989 and 1994, half a million Soviet in-migrants arrived in Israel, and more are still coming. Many of these in-migrants have less desire to assimilate linguistically and culturally, although they wish to adapt for instrumental reasons. Although the official government policy is still to absorb these in-migrants linguistically and culturally, the methods have changed. Traditional Israeli policy has been to assimilate in-migrants as rapidly as possible, by means of absorption centers, and mass exposure to the Hebrew language.

However, because of the scale of the Soviet immigration, the government has tolerated and even fostered education, culture and the diffusion of information in Russian. A daily radio service in Russian has been established, with news, information and knowledge about Israel. Ambitious plans for Russian-medium education were made in 1990, before a new government scrapped them. However, there is still some provision to help Russian-speaking students, with Russian-speaking link teachers available in schools, and some provision of Russian-medium courses at high school and college. (Most recent Soviet in-migrants are well-educated and their children are keen to succeed in school). Information pamphlets in Russian are widely distributed. The government's attitude to Russian in-migrants differs from that offered to another large in-migrant group recently arrived in Israel, the 60,000 Amharic speakers from Ethiopia. This latter group have been assimilated in a more traditional manner, with little official recognition of their own language and culture. There have been many complaints about the resources used to maintain Russian language provision for Soviet in-migrants. It has been argued that Soviet Israelis are being ghettoized, and that they need to be assimilated rapidly, with Russian language concessions only being made for one year after their arrival in Israel. However, it appears that, despite complaints, Russian is becoming an important fourth language in Israel, and is not likely to disappear for some time, if at all.

English is widely used as a second language, largely because of its status and usefulness as an international language. It competes with Hebrew in many prestigious and symbolic functions. Younger people are keen to learn English, and it is taught as a second language in schools.

The revitalization of Hebrew as a living daily language of the State of Israel has been successfully accomplished. The position of Hebrew now appears to be secure, because it is founded not only on daily use of the language but also on ideological convictions. However, the widespread use of other languages notably Yiddish and Russian (as community languages) and English (as a second language for public and official use) means that bilingualism is a reality of life in Israel.

Further Reading

BENTON R. A., 1986, Schools as Agents for Language Revival in Ireland and New Zealand in SPOLSKY, B. (ed.), *Language and Education in Multilingual Settings*. Clevedon: Multilingual Matters Ltd.

BENTON, R. A., 1988, The Maori Language in New Zealand Education. *Language, Culture and Curriculum*, 1 (2), 75-83.

BENTON, R. A., 1991, 'Tomorrow's Schools' and the Revitalization of Maori. In O. GARCÍA (ed.), *Bilingual Education: Focusschrift in Honor of Joshua A. Fishman*. Amsterdam/Philadelphia: John Benjamins.

FELLMAN, J., 1973, *The Revival of a Classical Tongue, Eliezer Ben Yehudah and the Modern Hebrew Language*. The Hague: Mouton.

MAY, S., 1994, School-based Language Policy Reform: A New Zealand example. In A. BLACKLEDGE (ed.), *Teaching Bilingual Children*. London: Trentham Press.

MAY, S., 1996, Indigenous Language Rights and Education. In C. MODGIL, S. MODGIL & J. LYNCH (eds), *Education and Development: Tradition and Innovation*. Volume 1. London: Cassell.

SCHUCHAT, T., 1990, *Ulpan: How to Learn Hebrew in a Hurry*. Jerusalem and Woodmere, NY: Gefen Books.

SPOLSKY, B., 1989, Maori Bilingual Education and Language Revitalization. *Journal of Multilingual and Multicultural Development*, 10 (2), 89-106.

SPOLSKY, B., 1995, Conditions for Language Revitalisation: A Comparison of the Cases of Hebrew and Maori. *Current Issues in Language and Society*, 2 (3), 177-201.

SPOLSKY, B., 1996, Prologomena to an Israeli Language Policy. In T. HICKEY & J. WILLIAMS (ed.), *Language, Education and Society in a Changing World*. Clevedon: Multilingual Matters Ltd.

4: Language Planning

Introduction

Two opposing views may be held regarding change and development in language. The first view holds that language is an organism that gradually changes over time. A language evolves gradually as its speakers make unplanned and usually unconscious innovations, such as changes in pronunciation and new uses of words. Language change may also be caused by external influences such as language contact where one language may borrow words and phrases from another. Unplanned and spontaneous language change is discussed under Origins of Language and Language Families (see page 127). Language borrowing is discussed under Linguistic Purism – see page 217).

A second view is that language is a social institution and that speakers of a language may wish to control and adapt their language for a variety of non-linguistic purposes: political, literary, economic, educational, religious, nationalistic, traditional or social purposes. Both these views of language are valid, but in this topic we will be looking at the second view of language and at the ways in which varieties or styles of language, or even separate languages, may be selected or adapted to be used as vehicles for literature, religious worship, mass media or education, or to further political or nationalistic goals.

Just as languages change over time, so their uses change. In Western Europe, for instance, Latin was the language of law and education for many centuries. It was gradu-

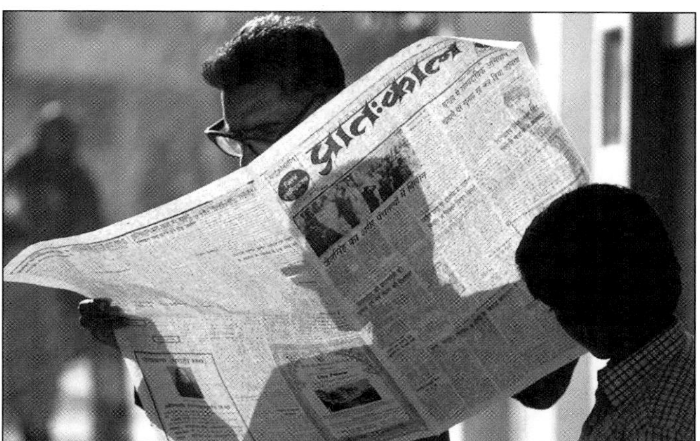

A man reads a Hindi newspaper in Rajasthan, India. Since independence in 1947, Hindi has been promoted as an official language, and its vocabulary has been modernized and expanded for use in areas such as science and technology.

Ofelia García

Ofelia García is Professor of Bilingual Education at the School of Education, City College of New York set in the Harlem area of New York. Ofelia García became an Cuban in-migrant to the US early in life, an experience that has given her much sensitivity to the destinies of in-migrants in the US.

Ofelia García has published widely in the areas of bilingual education, bilingualism and the sociology of language. She co-edited a reader entitled *Policy and Practice in Bilingual Education: Extending the Foundations* (1995) with Colin Baker and *The Multilingual Apple: Languages in New York City* (1997) with Joshua Fishman.

Ofelia García has a reputation as an outstanding teacher, original thinker, and an activist in support of Hispanics in the United States.

The idea of 'the language garden of the world' comes from Ofelia García, an analogy that generates a persuasive argument for the preservation and maintenance of languages in the world.

ally replaced by modern European languages. In Wales, Welsh was replaced by English as the language of the law courts in the 17th century. In Ireland, the 20th century has seen a large scale replacement of Irish by English as the language of the home and neighborhood. Many changes in the functional allocation of languages have happened spontaneously, as result of social, political and cultural factors. Some, however, are the outcome of deliberate planning.

Language planning, also called language engineering, refers to 'deliberate efforts to influence the behavior of others with respect to the acquisition, structure, or functional allocation of their language codes' (Cooper, 1989, page 45). Such language planning involves status planning (changing the status of a language within society by increasing or decreasing its functions), corpus planning (concerning the alteration or standardization of a language to fulfill new functions) and acquisition planning (creating language spread by increasing the number of speakers and uses by, for example, language teaching).

Status Planning

Cooper (1989) defines status planning as 'deliberate efforts to influence the allocation of functions among a community's languages' (page 99). He suggests that the status planning of a language can be targeted at the following:

- Official uses of language, for example as declared in legislation, declaration of official languages, status of languages in law and uses in political and government institutions.
- Planning at a regional (state, county, province) level, for example in Quebec in Canada, in Gaelic-speaking regions in Scotland, or Malayalam in the state of Kerala in India.
- Wider communication across regional and state borders (e.g. the adoption of Hindi across different states in India) and the adoption of Hebrew amongst a linguistically diverse Jewish population during this century.
- International, particularly referring to the spread and use of English as an official, international language in the world.
- The use of language in the national capital city for political power, social prestige and economic activity (e.g. in Brussels with the use of Dutch and French).
- The use of languages in a minority group (e.g. Bretons in France).
- The educational use of languages in nursery, primary, secondary, technical, vocational, further and higher education as well as in adult education.
- The use of languages in different curriculum areas.
- The literary use of languages not only amongst elites but also among the masses.
- The religious use of languages.

The Language Garden

Ofelia García (1992b) uses a powerful analogy to portray language planning. Her Language Garden Analogy commences with the idea that if we traveled through the countries of the world and found field after field, garden after garden of the same, one-color flower, how dull, boring and impoverished it would be.

Fortunately, there is a wide variety of flowers throughout the world of all shapes and sizes, all tints and textures, all hues and shades. A garden full of different colored flowers enhances the beauty of that garden and enriches our visual and aesthetic experience.

The same argument can be made about the language garden of the world. If only one of the majority languages of the world (e.g. English) existed in the garden, it would be easy to administer, easy to tend, but how dull and uninteresting our world would be. Rather, we have a language garden full of variety and color. For example, in London alone, there are said to be around 184 different languages being spoken. The initial conclusion is simply that language diversity in the garden of the world makes for a richer, more interesting and more colorful world.

However, language diversity makes the garden more difficult to tend. In a garden, some flowers and shrubs spread alarmingly quickly. Some majority languages, particularly English, have expanded considerably during this century. When the garden is neglected, one species of flower may take over, and small minority flowers may be in danger of extinction. Therefore some flowers need extra care and protection. This leads to the second part of García's (1992b) analogy. A free language economy allowing some flowers to dominate gardens is less preferable than careful language planning. When a gardener wishes to create a beautiful garden, there will be both careful planning and continued care and protection. Sometimes radical action may be taken to preserve and protect. The analogy suggests that language diversity requires planning and care. Four examples follow:

Adding flowers to the garden
The analogy suggests that, where the majority language is a person's first language, it may be enriching to add a second, even a third and fourth language. For example, in Canada, English speakers learning French may ensure that the colorful diversity of the Canadian multilingual situation is maintained. In mainland Europe, speakers of French, German, Spanish or Italian, for example, often learn a second or third language. In much of the United States, Oceania and Britain, a monochrome language garden seems more common.

Protecting rare flowers
In many countries throughout the world, the minority or indigenous language may be under threat from the quickly spreading majority languages. Just as environmentalists in the 20th century have awoken to the need to preserve the variety of flora and fauna, so in the language garden, it is environmentally friendly to protect rare language flowers. Through education and legislation, through pressure groups and planning, protection of language species in danger of extinction may be attempted.

Nurturing flowers in danger of extinction
Where a language species is in danger of extinction, stronger action may be needed than protection. Special efforts to revive a threatened language may be needed through intervention. For example, positive economic discrimination towards the Irish language in certain defined heartland areas has attempted to preserve the indigenous language in its traditional strongholds.

Controlling flowers that spread quickly and naturally
Flowers that spread rapidly and take the space of other flowers also need supervision and planning. While majority languages for international communication are an irreplaceable part of the Information Society, language planning may seek to allow spread without replacing and killing endangered species.

It is clear from using the language garden analogy that a *laissez-faire* situation is less desirable than deliberate, rational language planning. Gardeners are needed (e.g. teachers in schools) to plant, water, fertilize and reseed the different minority language flowers in the garden to ensure an enriching world language garden. While there are gardeners (e.g. teachers) tending the language garden, there are landscape engineers to plan and control the overall shape. The view of language landscape engineers (e.g. politicians, policy makers) is often to regard the language garden as just one part of a wider control of the environment. The dominant power groups who determine the social, economic and cultural environment may see language as just one element in an overall landscape design. For example, the type of bilingual education program that is allowed in a region (submersion, transitional, immersion or supportive of the minority community language) is but part of a design for the total landscape in which the languages are located.

A language landscape engineer who is concerned only for majority language flowers, will regard protecting rare flowers to be expensive and unnecessary, and will wish to limit the variety of languages in the country. A landscape engineer who wishes to protect rare flowers and increase flowers in danger of extinction may encourage the growth of such flowers alongside majority language flowers within bilingual education. In the US, for example, many politicians prefer monolingualism to bilingualism. The preference is for the assimilation of minority language flowers into a more standardized, monochrome garden. The dominant ruling group in US society is monolingual, with little perceived need to know or speak the minority languages existing in the country. Thus their view of bilingual education is determined by their wider ideology.

Reference: García, 1992

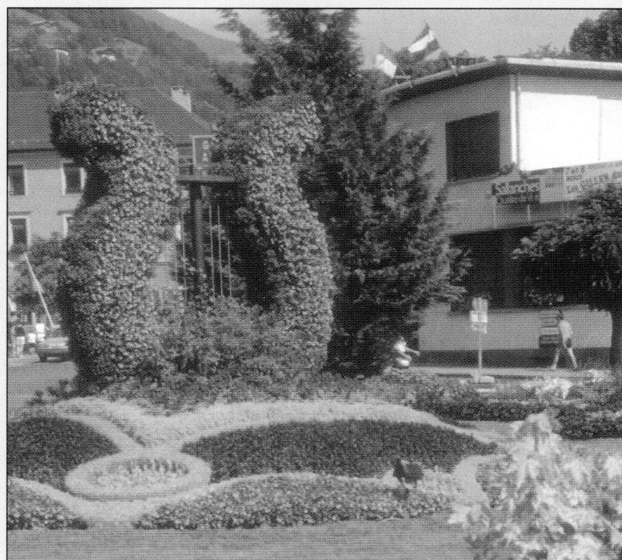

Colorful diversity is preferable to monochrome monotony.

Corpus Planning

If a language is used for new functions that it has not previously served, then the corpus or 'body' of that language may need to be adapted or elaborated to make it suitable for the new communicative functions. A prime example of this is the creation of new scientific and technological terminology. Another example is the development of suitable language styles for use in specialized fields such as computers and law.

Alternatively, the language may be modified to attain non-linguistic goals. A colloquial standard may be developed for use in mass literacy and education. A standard may be developed that is based on an archaic form of the language, to emphasize the shared history and worthy tradition of the speakers of the language. Attempts may be made to purify the syntax, vocabulary and even orthography of a language from foreign influence to emphasize the independence, dignity and distinctive character of its speakers.

Cooper (1989) identifies the following three aspects of corpus planning:

- Graphization – reduction to writing of a previously unwritten language or the reform of the system of writing.
- Standardization – the development of an overarching standard language that provides a norm for regional and social dialects. (See Language Standardization, page 210).
- Modernization – the development of styles of language and terminology in a range of topics of international relevance (e.g. science, medicine, technology), which can be easily transferred in translation to other languages.

Acquisition Planning

This refers to organized efforts to promote the learning or relearning of a language. These might include the learning of the language as a second or foreign language (e.g. anglophone children in immersion programs in Canada), and also the learning of a language by populations for whom it was once a vernacular (e.g. the learning of Maori by Maori children in *kohanga reo* and immersion schools, Welsh evening classes and intensive courses for local adults and Catalan language broadcasts for learners). It may also refer to the learning of a language for a wider range of functions (e.g. the reintroduction of written Chinese to Taiwan in 1945, when China regained Taiwan from the Japanese). In Cooper's (1989) definition of acquisition planning, he also includes language maintenance, because language maintenance safeguards the acquisition of the language by the next generation. Language maintenance includes initiatives such as the economic development of areas where a minority language is widely spoken, to lessen emigration and safeguard the minority language community.

A Scheme for Understanding Language Planning

Cooper (1989, page 98) provides a scheme for understanding language planning by asking a series of key questions: Which actors (e.g. elites, influential people, counter-elites, non-elite policy implementers):

- Attempt to influence which behaviors (e.g. the purposes or functions for which the language is to be used)?
- Of which people (e.g. of which individuals or organizations)?
- For what ends (e.g. overt (language-related behaviors) or latent (non language-related behaviors, the satisfaction of interests)?
- Under what conditions (e.g. political, economic, social, demographic, ecological, cultural)?
- By what means (e.g. authority, force, promotion, persuasion)?
- Through what decision-making processes and means?
- With what effect or outcome?

This relatively comprehensive set of questions makes some important points. First, language planning may be generated by different groups. For example, linguists, lexicographers, missionaries and soldiers, as well as administrators, legislators and politicians may become involved in language planning. The tendency is to present politicians, civil servants, government and the military as affecting language planning and language policy. However, both in terms of language as a code and language as social behavior, many other influential people and groups informally affect language planning. For example, influences on language have come from writers of books and film scripts, translators of major works, poets and priests, missionaries as well as the military, book publishers and journal editors, dictionary-makers and Internet providers. An historical instance is that of Martin Luther persuading the Protestants that God could understand languages other than Latin (Wiley, 1996).

Cooper (1989) argues, however, that language planning is more likely to succeed when it is embraced or promoted by elite groups or counter-elites. Such elites tend to work primarily from their own self-interests. Language planning is motivated by efforts to secure or reinforce the interests of particular people. However, language planning may positively affect the masses by adding to their

Language Planning in Estonia

When the Soviet Union occupied Estonia in 1940, the status of the Estonian language changed overnight. Hitherto, Estonian had been a majority language spoken by a majority of the population in the region. Russian had been spoken by a minority of the population and had been a minority language. With the Soviet Union occupation, Russian became the official language although it was only spoken by a minority in Estonia. After World War II, the Estonian language was replaced by Russian in many public domains since Estonia was subordinate to Moscow in matters such as banking, policing, transport, mining, energy and many other forms of production.

The Soviet Union's occupation of Estonia also affected the ethnic profile of the population. In the 1934 census in Estonia, 88 percent of the population were enumerated as Estonians, eight percent as Russians and the remainder were classified as Germans, Swedes and Jews. According to the 1989 census, 62.3 percent of the population of Estonia was ethnically Estonian, numbering almost a million people. However, following the movement of Russians into privileged positions and jobs in Estonia since the Second World War, the percentage of Russians in Estonia had risen to 30.7 percent. Much of the remainder of the population is composed of Ukrainians, Belorussians, Finns, Jews, Tatars, Latvians and Poles. A third of Estonians speak Russian and almost all Estonians speak the Estonian language. The half a million Russians have retained their mother tongue and 15 percent of Russians speak Estonian. Of the remaining ethnic groups, approximately two-thirds have Russian as their dominant language, but only seven percent speak Estonian. (These figures are based on the 1989 Census. Since 1991 there has been an exodus of Russians from Estonia to Russia and elsewhere.)

In the period of the Russian occupation, Estonian schools were required to teach Russian as a 'second native language'. The curriculum of these schools was Russian-based, containing little or no Estonian history or geography. During the post-war period, the Estonian language was publicly portrayed by the Russians as being a language with no future and hence was discriminated against in schools. In 1978, Russian was prioritized as a language over Estonian, and the Communist Party declared that Russian was the only means of active participation in social life. Teachers were advised to indoctrinate their students to love the Russian language. The salaries of Russian language teachers were raised to promote Russian as a means of assimilating and subjugating the Estonian peoples. Restrictions were placed on the use and teaching of the Estonian language so that, in school contexts, it was always below the status of Russian.

With the political and economic crises in the Soviet Union in the late 1980s, and the movement towards perestroika and glasnost, a new era for Estonia began. The regaining of national sovereignty of Estonia enabled the restoration of language rights and cultural rights for Estonians and other ethnic groups who had been discriminated against. In November 1988, the Supreme Soviet of the Estonian Republic proclaimed Estonian as the official state language in Estonia, and early in 1989, a 'law on language' was adopted. The language law requires the holders of certain jobs to have proficiency in both Estonian and Russian.

In 1990, democratic elections were held in Estonia and a national language board was established in the November. Courses to teach the Estonian language to non speakers have been planned for both children and adults. The Russian population of Estonia lost its linguistic privileges and thus became apprehensive of their future status.

The Language Law of Estonia came into force on February 1st, 1989. This restored the linguistic rights of Estonians and put an end to the official dominance of the Russian language that had lasted over the previous 50 years. While the official language of Estonia is Estonian, the Russian language is given a status and prominence above all other minority languages in Estonia, because of the large numbers of people in the country who speak it as a mother tongue and its value beyond the borders of Estonia.

The decision was to place the Estonian language in a category above the Russian language. If the two languages had been given equal status as official languages, it was reasoned that Estonian would thereby take a minor role as a state language. Nor would Russian-speaking employees have bothered to learn Estonian. Estonian would not have become a business language, an economic language or a major unifier in Estonia.

In terms of the 1989 Language Law of Estonia, the following applies:

1. All individuals have a right to conduct their affairs and communicate in Estonian with all forms of bureaucracy, institutions and organizations in Estonia.
2. The language of business management and communication between business and government shall be Estonian.
3. All laws and decrees shall be adopted and published in Estonian.
4. Financial documents and tax documents shall be in Estonian.
5. Education in Estonian is guaranteed so that everybody has the right to be taught in Estonian in all subjects of the curriculum, and in vocational, technical and higher education establishments in Estonia.
6. The use of Estonian in the mass media shall be guaranteed.
7. There should be a translation into Estonian of all non-Estonian films, videos and other audio visual material.
8. The text of signs, posters, notices and announcements in public places shall be in Estonian.
9. Goods for sale in Estonia shall be provided with an instruction sheet in Estonian.

These language laws are currently being implemented. For example, setting up language courses in Estonian for adults takes time and planning. However, there has been considerable pressure for all residents to learn Estonian. For example, trade and service workers were given three years to acquire Estonian to the level required by their jobs. Six different competence levels have been defined. An employer has the right not to make a contract with an employee whose linguistic competence does not meet the requirements of the job. For both applicants to jobs and employees in jobs, necessary linguistic competence is important. However, where the job does not require communication with customers or writing skills, competence in Estonian is not required. If an in-migrant wishes to become a citizen of Estonia, some knowledge of the Estonian language is required. Increasingly, the teaching of Estonian history, culture and language is becoming an integral part of the curriculum and in teacher training. This aims to ensure that Estonian enculturation occurs alongside language revival.

The Language Law also gives some rights to the use of Russian in institutions, and to a general education in Russian. However Estonian is present in all non-Estonian schools in the new independent Estonian Republic. The Language Law also guarantees that information on Estonia is given in Russian on the radio, television and in the press. Language minorities other than Russian can also set up their own schools, cultural establishments and organize out-of-school activities in their own language. However, the state itself cannot financially afford separate language schooling systems for each minority. Therefore, such language minorities have to organize and support their own language activities.

Minority rights in the Language Law allow such minorities to have local self-government if the community has at least three thousand members. Such local community government can be conducted in the minority language and respect is given to such language minority cultures.

REFERENCE: LAITIN, 1996

Language Planning: Romansch in Switzerland

Romansch is one of the four official languages of Switzerland. While the other three, German, French and Italian, have official status at federal level, Romansch only has official status in the canton of Graubünden in eastern Switzerland. Romansch is spoken by about 40,000 people who mainly live in Graubünden (see page 406).

A Swiss organization named *Lia Rumantscha* was founded in 1919 to maintain and promote the Rhaeto-Roman language and culture. From its office in Chur, it supports, promotes, and co-ordinates the diverse efforts of different organizations. *Lia Rumantscha* works for the conservation and cultivation of the Romansch language in the family, at school, in church, as well as in public life, and represents Rhaeto-Romania in Switzerland and abroad.

Lia Rumantscha has a clear focus in language planning, believing that Romansch will only survive and prosper if the following seven conditions are created:

- Romansch has a defined geographical area.
- Romansch has a solid economic foundation in this area.
- There is an overall presence of the language in all domains of everyday life.
- Romansch has a developed mass media.
- There is a standardized written language as a supra-regional channel of communication.
- There is a solid and well-balanced bilingualism, that allows Rhaeto-Romans to use their mother tongue for enrichment purposes.
- There is a harmonious co-existence with the other languages in Switzerland.

SOURCE: *Lia Rumantscha*, Via da la Plessur 47, CH-7000 Cuira, Switzerland.

self-identity, self-esteem, social connectedness and links with their heritage and future.

Language Planning and Political Planning

A consideration of language planning runs the danger of over-emphasizing its importance in overall political planning. First, there is often piecemeal pragmatism rather than planning. The revival of Hebrew is often quoted as one triumphant and successful example of language planning. Yet the rapid advance of Hebrew in Israel appears to have occurred by improvisation and diverse ventures rather than by carefully structured, systematic and sequenced language planning. Second, political and economic decisions usually govern language decisions. Language decisions are subsidiary and minor concerns of those in power, whose pervading interests are more frequently about power and purse. Language is usually an outcome from other decisions rather than a determinant of social, political or economic policies. Yet, as the European Commission has increasingly stressed, language minority issues and the need for bilingualism and multilingualism in a future Europe are relevant to European cultural and economic development. Bilingualism is one part of an interconnected whole in Europeanization.

Language Planning and Bilingualism

Language status and corpus planning often occurs in a bilingual situation, where a minority language group are attempting to maintain and elevate the status of their language. Such cases require full consideration of bilingualism and not just planning for the minority language. Where minority languages exist, there is usually the need to be bilingual if not multilingual. Minority language monolingualism is usually impracticable. To create blockades and barricades between languages is almost impossible in the 20th century. Cross-cultural communication is the reality; a bunker approach to a minority language and culture may be tantamount to language death (see page 161 where the concept of different functions for the minority and majority language is highlighted). Where different languages have different functions, then an additive rather than a subtractive bilingual situation may exist (see page 154).

When the second language is prestigious and powerful, exclusively used in education and in the jobs market, and when the minority language is perceived as of low status and value, stable diglossia and bilingualism may be threatened. Instead of addition, there is subtraction; division instead of multiplication.

Further Reading

COOPER, R. L., 1989, *Language Planning and Social Change*. Cambridge: Cambridge University Press.

EASTMAN, C. M., 1983, *Language Planning: An Introduction*. San Francisco: Chandler and Sharp.

HAUGEN, E., 1987, *Blessings of Babel: Bilingualism and Language Planning : Problems and Pleasures*. Berlin, New York: de Gruyter.

MARZUI, A. A., 1996, Language Planning and the Foundations of Democracy: An African Perspective. *International Journal of the Sociology of Education*, 118, 107-124.

WILEY, T. G., 1996, Language Planning and Policy. In S. L. MCKAY & N. H. HORNBERGER (eds), *Sociolinguistics and Language Teaching*. Cambridge: Cambridge University Press.

WILLIAMS, C. H., 1991, Language Planning and Social Change: Ecological Speculations. In D. F. MARSHALL (ed.), *Language Planning Volume III*. Philadelphia: John Benjamins.

Language Planning and Power

A major factor in language planning is 'who has the power to influence the behavior of others'? Thus the dominance of some languages and the dominated status of other languages is partly understandable if we examine who is in positions of power and influence, who belongs to elite groups that are in control of decision-making, and who are in subordinate groups, upon whom decisions are implemented. In a given language arrangement in society, there are those who have influence and privileges, those who benefit from any given arrangement of languages, and those who have relatively fewer privileges, and who may suffer from an inequitable distribution of power and privilege.

Arguments for the official status of English in the United States, Australia and England, for example, can be analyzed as a desire to retain power, privilege, dominance and advantage by those for whom English is their mother tongue. If minority languages are kept subordinate, more dominance and privilege, position and power are retained by the language majority. Thus an argument for majority language monolingualism and ascendancy can be seen as an argument that maintains the position of elites.

At other times, it may be a counter-elite that benefits from the promotion of a language. The restoration of Hebrew in Israel and the promotion of Hebrew in the Palestinian Jewish community can be seen as benefiting a counter-elite who wanted Jewish political autonomy and Zionist leadership in Palestine. The revival of Hebrew can be perceived as being partly about a claim to political power and influence by an elite. The same arguments have been made about Catalans, Basques and Welsh speakers whose apparent motive was language revitalization but whose ulterior reason or hidden agenda was the claiming (or reclaiming of power) for a hitherto language minority. According to this interpretation, political power and prestige, influence and authority over decision-making, as well as economic advantage and status can be high on the list of priorities of language minority activists. Such minority elites or counter-elites use their minority language and culture as a platform to gain political power and economic advantage for themselves.

In this analysis, debates, arguments and conflicts over the status of language and culture hide the real motives and values which are about acquiring wealth, power, advantage and control. Yet while ulterior motives may certainly be at play in language power struggles, those who argue from ethics or enlightenment, or from passion and ethnic pride, do not necessarily become those elites with high income and political power. Superficial analyses of motives in language movements tend to end in simplistic stereotyping, a lack of understanding of multiple motivation and a lack of appreciation of affective, emotional, areas of the individual psyche. A love of a language and culture can be real if unmeasurable and undefinable. Mixed motives are often present, combining different economic and cultural ambitions.

Political and economic motives in language planning are rarely far from the surface. Yet when language minority elites find power, all or most of the population of language minority speakers may benefit as well. For example, the rise of Hebrew to a position of power and status may have led to an increase in the self-esteem and more secure self-identity for many Jews who now speak Hebrew. It also opens doors for scholarly activity, for the mass media to expand its activities in the minority language, for agencies to promote language spread, and teachers to be trained for language minority schools. Not many of these people who benefit by the rise to power of a language minority are members of an elite. Indeed, the incorporation of this non-elite language minority group is important in gaining consensus in the struggle to assert power for the minority language and to maintain a language minority elite who are in power.

Once a counter-elite (e.g. in Israel, Catalonia, the Basque country, Estonia) have established themselves, there is a need to maintain power. Maintaining language power depends on using authority or a strong incentive system (sometimes force may be used). The use of authority and incentives tends to suggest that some kind of legitimacy is established. For example, new laws may be put into place governing use of the minority language. Incentives in employment may be created. The greatness and importance of retaining heritage language and culture may also be further emphasized to legitimize and normalize the spread of the minority language and culture. Concepts of a common destiny, the minority language as a symbol of ethnicity, a symbol of the glorious past and a better future may be evoked.

5: Language Standardization

What is a Standard Language?

Part of language planning is Corpus Planning (see page 206). A language may need to adapt or develop to become suitable for the present rather than the past (e.g. new information technology terminology). Relatively new disciplines (e.g. psychology and sociology) and new areas of interest (e.g. the Internet and space travel) develop new terminology. If a minority language wishes to maintain itself as a modern language, then it has to standardize its modern terms. A standard language needs developing for use in the mass media and education. Such standardization can occur with little intervention as when a language slowly evolves over time and there is borrowing from other languages. Standardization can also occur with deliberate intervention and planning.

Standardization refers to the development of a standard language that provides a norm for regional and social dialects. When a particular variety of language provides a standard or norm that will be capable of fulfilling certain functions in society, it can be called a standard language. Standard languages tend to be used for formal, prestigious functions, such as politics and administration, religion, law and education. Standardization of a language involves setting out norms for the orthography, spelling, grammar and vocabulary of the language. The standard norm tends to be more closely associated with the written form of the language, and may only be used in writing. In most cases, however, the standard norm influences speech, giving rise to a standard spoken norm.

Most western languages have standardized norms, incorporated in dictionaries and grammar books and taught in schools. Standard norms are usually appointed by the government, working in conjunction with institutions such as language academies, education boards and universities. Standard norms may allow variety and flexibility. Standard forms may be reviewed to take account of changes in the language over time. For instance, spelling may need to be revised to correspond to changes in the pronunciation of a language. Notions of grammatical correctness may need to be reviewed because styles of speech alter over decades.

Language standardization is sometimes part of formal language planning. Language planning may be divided into two main aspects, firstly, status planning, whereby a variety of language is selected to fulfill certain societal functions. The second aspect is corpus planning, which involves work on the language to adapt it for its functions. This may involve standardization of the language, as well as other aspects such as elaboration (i.e. creation of new terms).

Some languages have no standard form, and a standard must be created by language experts. In other cases, standard languages are the result of a process of natural evolution. This has occurred as speakers of local dialects have come under the domination of a political and economic center, and have adopted the speech of that center and particularly of the ruling elite. English is an example of a standard language that has gradually evolved over centuries, based on the dialects of south-east England. By whatever route a standard language comes into being, its existence depends on two factors, the creation or codification of the norm by an elite and second, the acceptance of the norm by a wider section of the population.

Reasons for Language Standardization

Standard languages have evolved or been established for a number of practical reasons.

1. The concept of standard languages emerged during the Renaissance in Europe, and was linked to the invention of printing. For the first time, books could be widely disseminated and the language used needed to be understood by a larger section of the population. A widely accepted language norm meant a larger market for publications.

2. The spread of education, industrialization and mass literacy, particularly during the 19th and 20th centuries, has necessitated the establishment of standard norms for text books, technical literature, government forms and official documents.

3. The increase in mass communications has been another factor in the proliferation of standard languages. When interaction between people was largely confined to the local community, and where communication in larger networks was carried out by an educated minority, there was little need for a standard language that

would be accessible to the whole population. With the rise of democracy, the need for swift and direct communication between central government and the wider population became vital. The development of the mass media has necessitated the establishment of standard norms for both the written and spoken language.

4. Standard languages tend to be the variety used by the ruling elite who control power. Thus the standard norm is identified with power and success, and is viewed as correct, prestigious and superior to other varieties. Those who control the standard norm may be regarded as superior, better educated and more powerful, and mastery of the standard norm may be a condition for access to power, privilege and economic success. Regional, colloquial or dialectal varieties that diverge markedly from the standard are viewed as inferior and uncouth and those people that use them may be regarded as uneducated, unintelligent, low status and powerless. Thus standard languages have another, more subtle function, that they reflect, reinforce and perpetuate the power and privilege of the ruling elite.

Language Standardization and Bilingualism

So far, language standardization has been discussed with reference to a monolingual situation where the standard language is in contrast to regional, non-standard varieties. However, language standardization, especially during the 20th century, is often the consequence of language contact or of a bilingual situation.This is not surprising. We have seen that language standardization is usually directed towards non-linguistic ends, and is closely linked with issues of power, prestige and inflence. In a monolingual situation, a standard language can reinforce the status and identity of the ruling elite. In situations where language conflict reflects a conflict or power struggle between ethnic groups or countries, language standardization may be one route to status, self-determination and a stronger self-identity for a country or ethnic group.

The rise of nationalist, independence and ethnic movements has given rise to the creation or establishment of numerous standard languages. If one country or political power has dominance over another country then the language of the controlling power will often be in a prestigious position in the dominated country. The dominant language may be used by the ruling elite in education, administration, the mass media, the judicial system and other prestigious functions, and will reflect the prestige and status of those functions. It will also be an expression of the culture and ethnic identity of the controlling power. Entry into the dominant group and access to power and economic success may depend on mastery of the dominant language. The dominant language is regarded by both members of the dominant and the subordinate groups as valuable, prestigious, correct and superior.

The language of the subordinate group, on the other hand, may only be used for a limited range of functions, in the home and local neighborhood. It may have no standard written form and consist of a range of dialects. The subordinate language may reflect the underprivileged and powerless status of the dominated country. If that country obtains independence or aspires to obtain independence, then standardization of the national language is one method of reinforcing the status, dignity and ethnic distinctiveness of the people. This occurred in Norway in the early 19th century as the country was emerging from centuries of Danish rule.

If the speakers of a non-standardized language are a minority group within a country, they may wish to gain power, status and a measure of cultural or political autonomy for the group. As part of their goal they may try to elevate the status and increase the use of the minority language, as an important marker of the group's identity and distinctive character, and so that it may be used in education, administration and other prestigious functions. This has been the goal of Breton language supporters in Brittany in the 19th and 20th centuries.

However, in this situation the task of standardization may be even more difficult. Since many of the speakers of the minority language may be bilingual or aspiring to be bilingual in the dominant language, that language may encroach upon many of the traditional functions of the minority language, even in informal, domestic contexts. The dominant language may also influence the minority language in vocabulary and syntax. The minority language may be viewed by both dominant and dominated as an inferior, valueless 'patois'. Many members of the minority group may wish to jettison the minority language as part of their desire for assimilation into the dominant group. There may not exist an influential elite which could establish or ratify a standard language nor a sufficient base of support for the language among its speakers for a standard norm to gain acceptance.

Ways of Establishing a Standard Norm

The kinds of difficulties involved in the creation and acceptance of a standard norm are common to both minority language groups in a bilingual situation and majority language groups. In both cases, the establishment of a standard norm is no easy task. It may be attempted in various ways.

The Unification of the Breton Language

The problems involved in the unification of the Breton language reflect the particular difficulties faced by a minority language in achieving a consensus of opinion for a standard form of the language.

The Breton language belongs to the Brythonic Celtic group of languages: it is closely related to Welsh and Cornish. Settlers from Wales and south-western Britain emigrated to the sparsely inhabited north-western peninsula of present day France in the fifth and sixth centuries to escape the invasions of the Anglo-Saxons and Irish. Brittany was an independent kingdom until 1532 and thereafter retained its independence as an autonomous province within the French kingdom until the eve of the French revolution. During this period Brittany also retained its cultural and linguistic independence, with Gallo dialects of French being spoken in the east of the country and Breton spoken in the west. In 1790 Brittany was carved up into five 'departements' and ceased to exist as an entity.

Breton women in Pont l'Abbé in their traditional coiffes. Pont l'Abbé is in the Kerne dialectal region, in south-western Brittany.

The Jacobin policy of centralization and assimilation was primarily directed against the regional languages, which were the vehicles of local culture, but also the main impediments to the flow of new ideas and to a sentiment of national solidarity. These regional languages included not only Breton, but also Alsatian, Flemish, Catalan, Corsican, Basque, as well as varieties closely related to literary French such as Provençal and Langue d'Oc. A common language i.e. French was the key to unifying the country and ensuring for every citizen the right to participate in government. In the 1880s the Jules Ferry laws introduced free, compulsory elementary schooling (in French). Industrialization, the railway and massive Breton emigration to seek work further weakened the Breton-speaking community, but Breton was still spoken by the overwhelming majority of the rural population of Lower (western) Brittany. In 1886 Paul-Yves Sebillot estimated the number of Breton speakers as 1, 300,000. In 1927 the Breton literary and nationalist magazine, *Gwalarn*, put the number of Breton speakers at 1,000,000. In 1927, the Minister of National Education of France, M. de Monzie, declared 'For the linguistic unity of France, the Breton language must disappear'. The belief on the part of the French government that cultural and linguistic diversity threatened national unity has persisted until the present day.

Modern Breton has four main groups of dialects, corresponding to the ancient kingdoms of Brittany, Kerne, Leon, Treger and Gwened. The Breton language has always been heavily influenced by the vocabulary and syntax of French. A unified tradition of writing had existed in Middle Breton, but this had begun to break down at the beginning of the 17th century, and from then on scribes wrote independently in their local dialects.

However, during the 19th century romanticism and nationalism were both vigorous ideologies in Europe. Nationalist movements sprang up that placed an importance on national history, and folk culture and on the national language, its literary tradition, purity and unity.

A small elite of Breton speaking intellectuals formed during the 19th century to work towards the evolution of a new literary standard for Breton that would fittingly represent the Breton nation. Their main targets were the purification of the language from the influence of French and the unification of the orthography. The puristic zeal of the early reformers was rather excessive. They tried to eradicate many French borrowings firmly established in the oral language, replacing them with Breton equivalents that sometimes represented an earlier stratum of French borrowings. Convenient terminology borrowed from French was often replaced with unwieldy Breton neologisms. Later language reformers tended to be more practical and less puristic.

In 1908 this elite of intellectuals signed an agreement ratifying a unified orthography for the three main dialects of Kerne, Leon and Treger. This standard form represented a compromise between the main dialectal divergences. (The fourth dialect, Gwenedeg, remained separate, because it diverged so markedly from the other three dialects.). However, the scholars had no structures (e.g. schools) through which they could popularize and disseminate their reforms, nor any wide base of support among ordinary people. The centralized French government remained hostile to any use of Breton in education and administration and the Breton language was derided as a vulgar patois.

In 1941 an orthographical unification of the four main Breton dialects was achieved, although it was never universally accepted. At the time of the German occupation of France the Breton language received a moderate amount of recognition from the Vichy government. The unification and standardization of the Breton language seemed to be matters of urgency, in view of the favorable climate for the Breton language and culture.

The debate on the standardization of Breton during the first half of the 20th century shows clearly that standardization of the language was not a linguistic matter but a political issue. The supporters of unified standard Breton were nationalists who dreamt of an independent Breton state with the Breton language as the chief marker of a separate ethnic and cultural identity. They wanted a Breton language that would be able to hold its own with the major languages of Europe in all areas of life, including science and modern technology.

Unfortunately, the nationalist movement has never enjoyed a wide base of support among ordinary Breton people. The goal of the French government since the late 18th century to eradicate regional languages and identities and to create a national French consciousness has had a profound effect on Breton perspectives on their language and identity. Attitudes of scorn, derision or condescension towards the 'quaint and rustic' language and lifestyle have created in many Bretons a negative self-identity. There has been a strong reaction on the part of many Bretons against their language, their regional culture, their songs, dances, costumes and folk tales, as symbols of backwardness and inferiority and reflections of their whole economically-deprived, rural lifestyle. They have wanted to become French more than the French have wanted to make them French.

The small progress made during World War II was completely wiped out at the end of the occupation. There was a backlash against Breton patriots and supporters of the Breton language, and many were imprisoned and some were even executed as German collaborators. After the war many families stopped speaking Breton to their children, thus seriously undermining the use of the language in the home. The main leaders of the Breton nationalist movement were imprisoned or exiled. The nationalist movement never fully recovered from this reverse of fortunes. The French government has continued its implacable hostility to the regional languages, although small concessions have gradually been won.

A 1987 radio survey reported that 61 percent of Bretons living in Lower Brittany could understand Breton and about 50 percent used it 'very often', 'fairly often' or 'sometimes'. The survey estimated that nearly quarter of a million Bretons still used Breton every day. However, the majority of Breton users are older people, and usage of the language is confined to domestic, everyday matters. There is wide support for the local Breton dialects, but the concept of a unified standard language capable of dealing with scientific, political or technological matters is foreign to the vast majority of Bretons. For them, French is the national, standard, urban language, whereas Breton is a marker of a local, rural identity, only suitable to be used for intra-group communication and oral traditions. Breton speakers tend to be proud of their colorful, local dialects, and many actively resist the idea of a more colorless, neutral standard language, viewing it as pointless and artificial. Standardization continues to be hindered by the lack of institutions (e.g. schools, government offices) to promulgate and ratify the standard norm.

The efforts to standardize the Breton language underline the fact that support for a standard language reflects political and cultural rather than linguistic ideologies. There is no certainty that the Breton language will survive as a living language until the end of the 21st century. The 20th century has seen a massive erosion of the Breton language in its stronghold in western Brittany. Most significantly, the Breton language is no longer transmitted by the majority of parents to their children. The question is no longer whether a standard language can be established but whether the Breton language will survive at all in any form. Hopefully a flexible acceptance of both the standard and dialectal forms in different contexts will provide a stronger united base for the maintenance and furtherance of the language.

REFERENCES: BROUDIG, 1995; MORGAN, 1979

The language may already possess a standard, literary, classical form, used in religion or literature. However, if this form is too far apart from the colloquial dialects spoken by ordinary people, it may prove too difficult for ordinary people to master it. Thus, instead of enhancing the prestige and functions of the language, it may prove a barrier to its use. (See page 217 on Sinhala standard language).

If no recognized standard form already exists, the speakers of the language have two alternatives. They may decide to select one regional variety for use as a standard form. A regional variety that has greater prestige than other varieties may already exist (e.g. the speech of a cultural, religious or economic center). This may prove acceptable to a wide section of the language population. Even so, there may be dissident elements among speakers of other regional dialects who feel that their own style of speech is being devalued, and in consequence that they themselves are being devalued.

Alternatively, a standard form may be created from an amalgamation of different dialects. This has been the case in Ireland, where a standard language has been established, based on the three main dialect areas of Ulster, Connacht and Munster. A standard language created in this way can have disadvantages. Since it depends on the subjective decisions of individuals who create the standard (e.g. which verb forms and vocabulary to use), it is likely to have many critics. Since a standard language created in this way is not the native variety of any individual, it is likely to sound strange and artificial to all native speakers of the language. This is one problem of standard Breton, based on a grammatical, lexicographical and orthographical compromise between the four main dialects.

In some cases a supra-local form may have already emerged where several dialects have come into contact and evolved common features (e.g. in an urban center where in-migration of different groups has meant a merger of dialects). This supra-local form may be generally acceptable as the basis for a new standard.

In both types of situation, there is the potential for dissension and for linguistic rivalry leading sometimes to the creation of rival standards. This can occur in a majority language situation (e.g. Norway, see page 214). However, it is even more difficult to create a standard language in a minority language situation because the language itself is in a weak position and speakers of the language may not value it highly or be strongly motivated to support it.

Another problem in a minority language situation is that official support for validating and promoting a standard norm may be deficient or absent. Central, majority language government may be hostile or at best indifferent to the maintenance of the minority language. The minority language group may not possess the institutions, (such as universities, schools, language academies, local government offices) or the recognized elite cultural group that might ratify and promote the new standard norm.

Different cultural factions may promote different norms, thus fragmenting an already weak base of support for the language. Dissemination and acceptance of a standard norm depend on literacy in the minority language and this may not be present. Educational opportunities in the minority language may be scarce or absent. Illiteracy in the minority language means that there is little market for any minority language publications, and thus little opportunity to promulgate the standard norm.

Many minority languages face considerable difficulties as they try to establish a standard norm. This is illustrated in the accompanying Textbox on the Breton standard language.

Standard Languages in the Post-colonial Era

During the latter half of the 20th century, many countries under colonial rule regained their independence. During the period of colonial rule, the colonial language (e.g. English, French, Spanish, Dutch) was used in the higher levels of administration and government. Following the colonial period, there was a fresh emphasis in many countries on the need for mass literacy and education. The need arose in these countries for an acceptable standard language that could be used in administration, government and education.

An important factor in the linguistic situation in most colonial countries (e.g in Africa and Asia) is that there is not just a simple bilingual or diglossic situation where a colonial language has been used side by side with an indigenous language. Rather a multilingual situation has tended to exist where the colonial language co-exists with numerous indigenous languages or dialects spoken by different ethnic groups. Many of these dialects have no literary or written form that could serve as a basis for a standard language.

In this situation the selection of a standard language from among these regional dialects or languages has proved problematic. Since language is a main marker of cultural, ethnic and sometimes religious identity, the elevation of one variety or language above others as a prestigious standard can be identified with the elevation of one regional or ethnic group above others. This opens up

The Norwegian Standard Languages

The Norwegian language is spoken as a native language by 95 percent of the population of approximately four million people in Norway. Norwegian is closely related to the other Scandinavian languages of Swedish, Danish, Icelandic and Faroese. All five derive from a West Scandinavian group of dialects. The languages of Denmark, Norway and Sweden are so similar that speakers can understand one another.

In 1380 Norway was joined to Denmark and remained under the rule of the Danish king for over four centuries, until 1814. During this period Norway lost its own written tradition (established before 1100) and literary Danish became the only written language of Norway. Because Danish and Norwegian are so closely related, they were regarded as a single language, 'Danish', and the spoken dialects of Norway were viewed as dialectal variations of Danish. Danish was generally spoken by the government officials and the educated classes, especially in the cities. This form of spoken Danish had a native Norwegian pronunciation and was influenced by Norwegian grammar, and also used many uniquely Norwegian words. Norwegian dialects continued in use in the country districts and among the working and middle classes of the towns.

In 1814, Norway regained its autonomy and initiatives were launched to replace written Danish with written Norwegian.These initiatives sprang from the nationalist and romantic ideas that were current in Europe at the time. These ideas emphasized the need for national self-determination, and a national identity based on a shared history and literary tradition, and a national and standard language. One strategy, proposed by Knud Knudsen in 1856, was based on the Danish-Norwegian speech of the educated urban dwellers. This Dano-Norwegian norm was first known as *Dansknorsk* or *Riksmål* (Language of the Kingdom), but has now been renamed *Bokmål* (Book Language).

However, a separate initiative was launched by those who wanted a written language that was native to Norway, and not based on a norm that was seen as foreign. In 1853 the self-taught linguist and dialectologist Ivar Aasen proposed a norm based on the rural dialects, especially the western ones which were closest to the old written Norwegian. Aasen's standard was known as *Landsmål* (Country Language) but has now been renamed *Nynorsk* (New Norwegian).

Since 1884 both these languages have been official standard languages in Norway, although *Bokmål* is in a stronger position than *Nynorsk*. *Bokmål* is the official language in over 80 percent of the country's schools, and even more adults regard *Bokmål* as their principal written language. It is the standard used in all cities, as well as the populous South Eastern part of the country, the dialects of which are more similar to Danish. *Nynorsk* dominates in the fjord country along the west coast and the mountain districts of central Norway. *Bokmål* is the language of choice of the major newspapers, the weekly magazines and paperback novels, and prevails in business and advertising.

By law all official documents, school textbooks, examination papers and similar publications should be in both standards, and all government employees should be able to use both *Bokmål* and *Nynorsk*. (This is not always achieved in practice).The inhabitants of local communities themselves decide which language is to be used as the language of instruction in the school attended by their children. All school students are tested in *Bokmål* and *Nynorsk*, with one as their primary written language. The law also states that 75 percent of all broadcasting should be in *Bokmål* and not less than 25 percent in *Nynorsk*.

The existence of two standard norms for a language like Norwegian, only spoken by four million people, creates a complex linguistic situation, but there is little tension or conflict. The reason for this is that there is a great deal of flexibility within both standards. A series of significant spelling reforms (1901, 1917 and 1938) have brought both standards closer together and both standards have incorporated features from one another as alternatives. A morphological feature or word may have two alternatives, one traditional form within the standard and another form parallel to that found within the other standard. Also local dialects have a privileged and respected position in Norway. In 1878 a law was passed which encouraged all school students to use their dialects in all oral contexts in school. Dialects are also widely used in broadcasting. Because of the existence of two flexible standards it is possible for Norwegian speakers to adopt a written language that is very close to their spoken language.

All the Nordic countries now have official bodies concerned with national languages. In Norway the official institution is called the Norwegian Language Council. It has 38 members, half from each of the two language camps.The Council's purpose is to foster mutual tolerance and respect between all Norwegian users, whatever their chosen standard, and to carry out practical language work- orthography, terminology, advisory functions, etc. According to the rules, questions that mainly concern one language can be resolved by the representatives for this language without interference from the other half.

The situation in Norway shows that the establishment of a standard language even in an independent country, is not free from controversy. It is also shows that a flexible norm and willingness to compromise can create a workable situation. English is the first foreign language in Norway and it is compulsory for every school child over the age of ten. Norwegians are highly motivated to learn English and many reach a good standard of competence, indicating that a fluid and flexible standard language does not create confusion or inhibit ability to learn foreign languages.

REFERENCES: HAUGEN, 1966, 1976

the possibility of inter-ethnic competition, conflict and social instability.

Different countries have approached this problem in different ways. Some countries (e.g. Kenya) have retained the colonial language as the official language for use in administration, politics and education. The advantage is that a colonial language already has standard norms for writing and speaking. Text books and other literature in the standard language are available for use in education and adult literacy projects.

Colonial languages are ethnically neutral and do not favor the interests of any one ethnic group over others. Colonial languages are usually international languages of major importance (e.g. English, French and Spanish). Education and administration through the medium of these languages facilitates contact with the international world, increasing educational and economic opportunities. The regional languages co-exist with the colonial language in a stable, diglossic or triglossic situation.

Other countries have chosen to elevate a major, regional language to the status of an official standard language. The position of Swahili (Kiswahili) in Tanzania is one example. Swahili is a Bantu language, the first language of communities living along the east coast of Africa. Even before independence, it had become widely used as a lingua franca in East Africa and a fairly standard form had evolved, used in administration and teaching (see page 123).

A third possibility is that the colonial language may continue to be used as an official standard language, but may co-exist with one or more major indigenous languages, which may be elevated to the status of national or official languages, as well as with numerous regional varieties or dialects. This is the situation in India, where English, the former colonial language, now co-exists with Hindi as associate official language. Fifteen other regional languages have been raised to the status of official regional languages, and used in education and administration in certain states.

Issues Affecting the Form of a Standard Language

The ultimate aim of language standardization or general language planning is to achieve non-linguistic goals. These may include a stronger and more distinctive cultural identity, political autonomy, a higher status for a minority group, widespread literacy in the language, stronger links with tradition and the past. These non-linguistic goals are certain to affect the form of the standard language.

Children across the harbor from Vardo, Norway.

The Lord's Prayer: *Fader vår*

The Lord's Prayer is presented below in both the standard Norwegian varieties, first in *Bokmål* and then in *Nynorsk.*

Bokmål

Fader vår, du som er i himmelen!
La ditt navn holdes hellig.
La ditt rike komme.
La din vilje skje på jorden
som i himmelen.
Gi oss i dag vårt daglige brød.
Forlat oss vår skyld,
som vi òg forlater våre skyldnere.
Led oss ikke inn i fristelse,
men frels oss fra det onde.
[For riket er ditt, og makten og æren
i evighet. Amen.]

Source: *Det nye testamente*, 1975, Oslo: Det Norske Bibelselskaps Forlag.

Nynorsk

Fader vår, du som er i himmelen!
Lat namnet ditt helgast.
Lat riket ditt koma.
Lat viljen din råda på jorda
som i himmelen.
Gjev oss i dag vårt daglege brød.
Forlat oss vår skuld,
som vi òg forlet våre skuldmenn.
Før oss ikkje ut i freisting,
men frels oss frå det vonde.
[For riket er ditt, og makta og æra
i all æve. Amen.]

Source: *Det nye testamentet,* 1975, Oslo: Det Norske Bibelselskaps Forlag.

For instance, if the aim of standardization is to strengthen links with historical tradition, then the standard language may be based on an older, classical form, and archaic constructions and vocabulary may be adopted in the standard language. In 19th century Greece, *Katharevousa* was established as a written standard, taking vocabulary and verb forms from Classical Greek.

If a distinctive cultural identity is the goal, and separation from a neighboring or related ethnic group, then the standard language may be differentiated in form and appearance. One example is the Catalan language, very closely related both to French and to Castilian Spanish. In order to distinguish Catalan in appearance from its close relations, certain distinctive orthographical conventions have been adopted.

Another way of emphasizing the distinctive character and worthy status of a language, and thus of the speakers of that language, is by 'purification' of that language, ridding the language of obvious foreign influence in syntax and especially vocabulary. (See Foreign Loans and Language Purism, pages 164 and 217.)

If a major goal is mass literacy in the language, or education through the medium of the language, then a norm that is easily accessible to ordinary people may be proposed. Orthography may be simplified, archaic forms may be abandoned, and colloquialisms and dialect forms may be deemed acceptable. The revision of modern Irish orthography that took place in 1948 was viewed by many traditionalists as an outrage and a sacrilege, but has made Irish much easier to read than its close relation, Scots Gaelic.

A standard language should be flexible and open to change and alteration. The standard norm is only one of a number of styles or registers available to educated speakers of a language. It is only deemed appropriate for certain functions. A lawyer, for instance, might use standard English in court and while writing reports, but would switch to a more regional or colloquial form while with friends or family. Since most people use several registers of language, there is continual cross-influence between different registers.

The rise of standard languages during the 20th century and their increased use in education and mass communications has meant that dialectal and regional varieties have tended to converge in the direction of the standard norm. However, regional varieties in their turn tend to influence and modify the standard. A grammar book may portray an 'absolute' standard of correctness, but in real life this is rarely achieved either in writing or speech. In real life situations, the standard language includes a range of forms that may be deemed acceptable for various functions. The standard may change gradually over time or may need to be revised to take account of a changing situation.

Standard languages vary as to the rigidity of their norms. Many minority languages that have had difficulty creating or maintaining a single standard language have found a more flexible standard to be acceptable and practical, one that embraces a wide range of regional differences. Modern Welsh has moved away from a literary standard based on the Bible to a very flexible standard that takes account of a wide range of dialectal variations. Similarly, the educational authorities in the Basque countries have given recognition to their major non-standard dialect (regarded by some supporters to be the basis of a separate, rival standard), and have published textbooks for the early, elementary school years in that variety.

Another reason for accepting a more flexible standard especially in a minority language situation is that minority language speakers tend to place a low value on their language and also lack confidence in their ability to speak it correctly. A rigid 'hypercorrect' standard is bound to devalue non-standard forms and further erode the confidence of native speakers and discourage them from using their language. The pragmatic emphasis must be on a standard that is fluid and wide-ranging, easily comprehensible and acceptable to all rather than a single, inflexible model of correctness.

Further Reading

BARTSCH, R., 1987, *Norms of Language*. London: Longman.

COOPER, R. L., 1989, *Language Planning and Social Change*. Cambridge: Cambridge University Press.

EASTMAN, C. M., 1983, *Language Planning: An Introduction*. San Francisco: Chandler and Sharp.

EDWARDS, J. R., 1985, *Language, Society and Identity*. Oxford: Blackwell.

HUDSON, R. A., 1996, *Sociolinguistics* (Second edition). Cambridge: Cambridge University Press.

MILROY, J. & MILROY, L., 1991, *Investigating Language: Prescription and Standardization*. London: Routledge.

The Sinhalese Language – A Standard Language in a Diglossic Situation

Sinhala (Sinhalese) is one of the two official, national languages of Sri Lanka. Sinhala is spoken by 11 million Sinhalese (74 percent of the population of the island). The other main ethnic group, the Tamils, speak Tamil, which is also the state language of Tamil Nadu in India. English, the official language of the country until 1957, is still widely used.

Since Sri Lanka gained its independence in 1948 there has been continuing conflict between the Sinhalese and the Tamils. There has been a strong Sinhalese-Buddhist nationalist movement whose goal has been to gain supremacy over the Tamils.

A diglossic situation (see page 117) exists in the Sinhalese community, where literary Sinhalese is the 'high' variety, since its structure is closer to the classical literary idiom. It is only used as a written language. It is used in all forms of non-fictional writing, including news bulletins (which are read), and in electronic media. The 'low', colloquial variety of Sinhala is used in all oral communication. Some genres of fiction use a mixture of both: literary Sinhala for narration and colloquial Sinhala for dialog.

The development and maintenance of literary Sinhala is directly related to the desire for a strong cultural identity and political autonomy among the Sinhalese people, following years of British colonial rule, and then the threat of Tamil unrest. Problems arise because the forms of the literary language are quite difficult to master for the average speaker. Sinhalese speakers do not usually have difficulty in reading and understanding the literary language, apart from certain vocabulary differences, but they find writing literary Sinhalese correctly a difficult task. Thus the Sinhalese written by students, government officials, for instance, tends to be a hybrid version between literary and colloquial Sinhala. Some progressive novelists have published work in a more colloquial variety of Sinhalese. In an effort to elevate the prestige of the language, forms from the literary language are also used in speech in formal contexts. Thus both varieties of language are influencing one another and producing new forms.

Another difficulty arises because the spoken language borrows freely from other languages, notably English: words borrowed are altered minimally to suit Sinhalese phonology and morphology. In the fields of science and technology a large number of such loan words are used in teaching, and thus, with a minimal command of English orthography, workers have been able to follow simple English technical handbooks.

However, literary Sinhalese does not allow borrowing of this nature. Sinhalese equivalents are found for foreign terminology by using calques or loan translations, or by resorting to Sanskrit. In this way Sinhalese has come to possess two sets of technical vocabularies, with adverse consequences especially in the fields of science and technology. The Government has decreed that the terminology used should be decided by the Official Language Department. This department generally supports the use of the puristic literary terms and it has been difficult for these terms to be accepted when Sinhalese speakers were already using more meaningful colloquial or non-Sanskrit equivalents.

The situation of literary Sinhalese shows the difficulty involved in maintaining a stable, standard norm when the standard, written language is very divergent from colloquial speech.

REFERENCE: HAAS, 1982

6: Linguistic Purism

Introduction

Linguistic purism aims to purify a language and eliminate what are perceived to be undesirable elements. These might include dialect forms, slang, vulgar speech and fashionable jargon. Foreign borrowings in a language, whether loan words, phrases, or translations of idioms and syntactic structures, are also frequent targets of linguistic purists. Purism is usually initiated by an intellectual elite who are aware of the ideological issues involved. Purist tendencies are strongest in the literary, standard, written, or formal languages.

We have seen that whenever languages are in contact, some degree of transfer from one language to another usually occurs, generally from the stronger, dominant language to the weaker or less dominant language. (See Foreign Borrowings, page 164.) This is part of the natural evolution of a language and may contribute to language vitality and efficient communication.

Purism has little to do with the pragmatic, instrumental aspect of language or with effective communication. People can communicate just as adequately in a community where codeswitching from one language to another is the norm, or when people's speech is peppered with foreign borrowings. When people borrow words from a neighboring language for new objects or concepts, or adopt foreign phrases or idioms that appear to have a particular communicative force, they are facilitating communication, not hindering it.

Linguistic Purism and Language Status

Linguistic purism is an attitude towards language that is usually part of a wider ideology. Linguistic purism can be linked with aesthetic considerations. A 'pure' language, free from dissonant foreign elements, may be perceived to be more beautiful to the ear and eye. Linguistic purism is often closely associated with nationalism. Nationalism seeks to emphasize the unique and unifying features of a group of people or a country and to differentiate it from other peoples or countries. Nationalism tends to flourish among ethnic groups and in countries that are in danger of being dominated by other ethnic groups or countries. It can be a response to the threat of foreign domination, whether political, cultural or religious. Nationalism aims to enhance the prestige and raise the status of a group of people, usually by giving them cultural and political autonomy.

Similarly, linguistic purism aims to give a language status and prestige, often for nationalistic reasons. Purism is often, but not always, a key element in language standardization (See Language Standardization, page 210.) In order to raise the status of a standard or national language, and to unify it, purists may wish to eradicate some dialectal features. Purists may also wish to emphasize the unique features of their language and distance it from other languages. This usually involves eliminating as many foreign elements as possible.

A language that is peppered with borrowings from a more prestigious language may be perceived as being inadequate in the eyes of its speakers, and in the estimation of the speakers of other languages. It may be classified as a 'pidgin' or a 'patois', a language unable to sustain itself without the 'help' of a more powerful language. Foreign borrowings may be a matter of style and fashion, a tacit recognition of the prestige and power of the source language. Purists may try to eradicate the use of such 'fashion' borrowings to raise the status of their own language.

Aspects of Linguistic Purism

Linguistic purism involves several aspects. First, an attempt may be made to eradicate obvious foreign elements already present in a language. Second, efforts may be made to prevent foreign words and phrases from entering a language. This second aspect is particularly prevalent nowadays, because of the plethora of terminology being coined almost daily to describe new concepts in science, technology, medicine and other specialized fields. Many languages have to face the dilemma of

Linguistic Purism in Orthography and Spelling

Occasionally the orthography of a language may reflect linguistic purism. Closely related languages may have differing orthographies which help to emphasize their unique character and to distance them from one other. One example is Catalan, since 1983 the official, majority language of the autonomous province of Catalonia in Spain. Catalan is so closely related to Castilian Spanish that most Castilian speakers can understand written Catalan without much difficulty, and find the spoken language easy to learn. Much of the vocabulary is similar or identical. However, certain orthographic conventions have been deliberately adopted in Catalan to make it look more different from Spanish. A similar example can be found in the two closely related Romance languages, Romanian and Moldavian. The fact that the former is written in Latin script and the latter in Cyrillic script serves to reinforce the differences between them.

In 1783 in the United States, the famous lexicographer Noah Webster (1758–1843) published his *Grammatical Institute of the English Language* which included *The American Spelling Book.* In that volume he tended to follow British usage in spelling. However, by the time his *American Dictionary of the English Language* was published in 1828, Webster had embarked upon a limited reform of spelling. Many of Webster's reforms became part of standard US spelling e.g. '-er' instead of '-re' at the end of words like 'theater, center'; '-or' instead of '-our' at the end of words like 'flavor, color, neighbor'; '-se' instead of '-ce' in words like 'defense, pretense'; '-k' for '-que' in words like 'check'; and a single 'l' before a suffix, depending on the stress ('traveling' but 'excelling').

The main purpose of this reform was ostensibly to regularize and rationalize American spelling. What is not so widely realized is that Webster also aimed to establish the independence and autonomy of American English as a separate variety of English spoken in a separate, independent nation. To accomplish this, he tried to distance American English usage as much as possible from the British usage set down in Samuel Johnson's *A Dictionary of the English Language,* published in 1755. Webster wrote 'Nothing can be more ridiculous, than a servile imitation of the manners, language and the vices of foreigners'.

Linguistic Purism and Yiddish

The difficulties facing linguistic purists can be illustrated by the situation of the Yiddish language. Yiddish evolved between the 9th and 12th centuries as the main means of communication of Ashkenazic Jews of Eastern and Central Europe. It consisted of an adaptation of German dialects of the Rhine area, together with Hebrew words pertaining to Jewish religious life. It was originally called Judisch-Deutsch (Jewish-German), later abbreviated to Yiddish.

When the majority of European Jews moved eastward into Slavic-speaking areas, there was some borrowing from Slavic languages. The vocabulary of the Yiddish spoken in Eastern Europe during the last century consisted of approximately 85 percent German, 10 percent Hebrew and 5 percent Slavic together with a few borrowings from Romanian, French and other European languages. Later, when Yiddish-speaking Jews settled in English-speaking countries, particularly the US, many English borrowings entered the language.

For many centuries Yiddish was considered a vulgar, common dialect of the poor. Hebrew was the language of teachers, scholars and writers. Gradually literature emerged in Yiddish, and by the 19th century it was used for novels, short stories, plays and poetry, as well as in scientific and educational texts. Yiddish was considered by some to be the first choice for the new language of the State of Israel, but it was eclipsed by Hebrew. Nevertheless, towards the end of the 19th century, a movement arose to create a single standard Yiddish language, and to bring the written and spoken languages closer together. At the time spoken Yiddish tended to avoid new borrowings from Standard German, while accepting both loan words and calques from Russian. At the same time the literary language, '*daytmerish*', or '*kongresdaytsh*', was highly influenced by contemporary Standard German. These forms of Yiddish were so close to Standard German that in Czarist Russia, where the public use of Yiddish was banned, theater companies were able to convince the authorities that their productions were in German, not Yiddish. Use of these heavily Germanized forms of Yiddish in literature, the press and by Jewish nationalist and socialist organizations was often a matter of prestige and convenience. Apologists for a standard, unified Yiddish sought to distance the language from modern German to enhance its uniqueness and its status. There was a concerted effort to remove some of the unnecessary, recent German loan words and to cultivate the non-German aspects of the language and this gradually gained widespread support. Nevertheless, the fact that Medieval German forms the very basis of Yiddish means that the two languages are closely linked and that there continues to be a tension between the need to move away from German and the Yiddish language's dependence on German.

Hasidic Jews in New York performing a traditional circle dance.

For Hasidic Jews and for some other Orthodox Jewish sects, the use of Yiddish in everyday life creates a line of demarcation between secular life and sacred worship (where only Hebrew is used) and also between the Jewish community and the outside world.

Linguistic Purism and the English Language

The English language has the reputation of being one of the languages least affected by puristic attitudes. This is not to say that English has avoided considerations of purity and standardization. John Edwards (1994c) has shown that, for example, 'Samuel Johnson and his dictionary of 1755.... was a one-man academy' (page 159). Noah Webster (1758–1843) was also a one-man language academy for the United States, aiming to: halt English language degeneration in the US; establish language independence for the US; remove vulgarisms and dialects, and halt foreign borrowings. Yet, relative to other languages, English has received less attention regarding standardization and purism. This gives rise to the question: why has linguistic purism rarely become a major issue in the development of English?

The answer lies in the issues discussed earlier in this article, namely, that linguistic purism is usually an attitude displayed by speakers of a language that is perceived to be under threat or, more generally, members of an ethnic group that is perceived to be in danger from foreign domination, whether religious, cultural, economic or political. The English language, from its arrival in the British Isles, has never been under serious threat from any other language or ethnic group. As a language spoken on an island, it has never had to compete with powerful neighboring languages. The Celtic peoples living in Britain, the Welsh, Cornish and Gaels, were never numerous enough or powerful enough to pose any threat to English, and it is their languages that have been eroded by English in recent times. Although Norman French, because of its powerful status, had a great influence on the development of English, its speakers were never numerous enough to pose any real threat to English. Some historians have estimated that following the Norman invasion, Norman French in England may have constituted as little as two percent of the population.

The history of English underlines the fact that linguistic purism is not a matter of language as a means of communication, but a matter of ideology.

whether to adopt the 'international' term or whether to create an equivalent from native elements.

The international term has the advantage that its meaning is precise and specific and that it provides a bridge for communication between speakers of different languages. (See Foreign Borrowings, page 164.) Against this, linguistic purists would argue that an over-abundance of international terms lowers the status of a language and ignores its existing lexical resources, creating what is instinctively felt by many native speakers to be to be an ugly hybrid. Many modern terminologists steer a middle way, using international terminology most widely for restricted and very specialized fields, while attempting to harness the lexical and word formation resources of the native language for more general use.

Linguistic purism may include an historical 'archaising' element. Just as the history of a people or nation is perceived as being important to their identity, so the history of a language buttresses its present existence. Linguistic purism may involve resurrecting obsolete native words to take the place of foreign borrowings.

Purism is not an exact science. It is essentially a subjective and relative process. Purists usually wish to eradicate the words they perceive to be of foreign derivation. They may not always identify foreign words correctly. Purism often seeks to eradicate recent and obvious foreign borrowings. To eliminate foreign words that have been in the language for centuries and have so adapted phonologically and morphologically that they are no longer recognizable as borrowings, is not usually an aim of purists. In modern Welsh, for instance, the educated elite seek to keep their speech free of contemporary English loan words. However, many English words have been in the Welsh language since medieval times, and are unrecognizable as English words except by consulting an etymological dictionary. Many Welsh words correspond to English words that are now obsolete, or echo the medieval pronunciation of the English word. Welsh has also borrowed quite widely from Norman French, and, before that, from Latin. To try to eradicate all the foreign borrowings from Welsh and leave only the Celtic stratum would be a futile and ridiculous exercise. (The Celtic languages no doubt borrowed from other languages before historical records began.)

A language may borrow from several other languages but linguistic purism may be directed at only one other language, the one perceived to be the most linguistically threatening, or the one connected with political or cultural dominance. Linguistic purism may be directed by the speakers of one language towards a closely related language in order to differentiate between the two. Conversely, linguistic purists may choose to borrow words from closely related languages to enrich the lexicon rather than turn to a language perceived as a threat and an enemy.

Linguistic Purism and Language Planning

A moderate degree of purism can have some benefits for a language. It can raise the status of the language in the eyes of its speakers and provide a unified standard form. Insistence on using native words or native word creations instead of foreign borrowings in certain cases can mean that the language is more intelligible to native speakers. Moderate purism is more likely to win support from the bulk of the population, especially if it is perceived to be symbolic of national prestige and status.

Extreme purism, on the other hand, would seem to be detrimental to a language. It can restrict the scope of a language, placing it in an artificial straitjacket. Extreme purism may sap the natural vitality of a language and make it a less efficient means of communication. By eradicating foreign borrowings, especially internationalisms, it may make a language more 'opaque' and inaccessible to speakers of other languages. The recommendations of extreme linguistic purists are unlikely to win widespread acceptance and their actions are likely to lead to a fragmentation in support for a language, and even to a fragmentation of the language itself.

In practical terms, linguistic purism usually forms part of a careful program of language planning and language standardization. Linguistic purism cannot be static but needs to evolve continuously. Those concerned with the issues involved in linguistic purism tend to be motivated by rational and pragmatic considerations such as the status and standardization of a language, the necessity for efficient communication, contact with other languages and respect for the resources of a language.

Further Reading

EASTMAN, C. M., 1983, *Language Planning: An Introduction*. San Francisco: Chandler and Sharp.

JERNUDD, B. & SHAPIRO, M., 1989, *Politics of Language Purism*. Berlin: de Gruyter.

THOMAS, G., 1991, *Linguistic Purism*. New York: Longman.

7: Language Marketing

Introduction

Marketing is a concept within most people's experience. But when we talk about marketing, it is often with reference to promoting products such as computers, toothpaste, insurance and televisions. Many people are aware of the vocabulary of marketing, for example, the product, customer needs, advertising and promotion, marketing outlets, loss leaders, soft and hard selling, competitive pricing and profit margins, marketing plans and performance indicators. But can social marketing theory and the ideas integral in its vocabulary be of value in marketing a language?

Language marketing derives from the concept of social marketing which has been defined as: 'the adaptation of commercial marketing technologies to programs designed to influence the voluntary behavior of target audiences to improve their social welfare and that of society' (Andreasen, 1994, page 110).

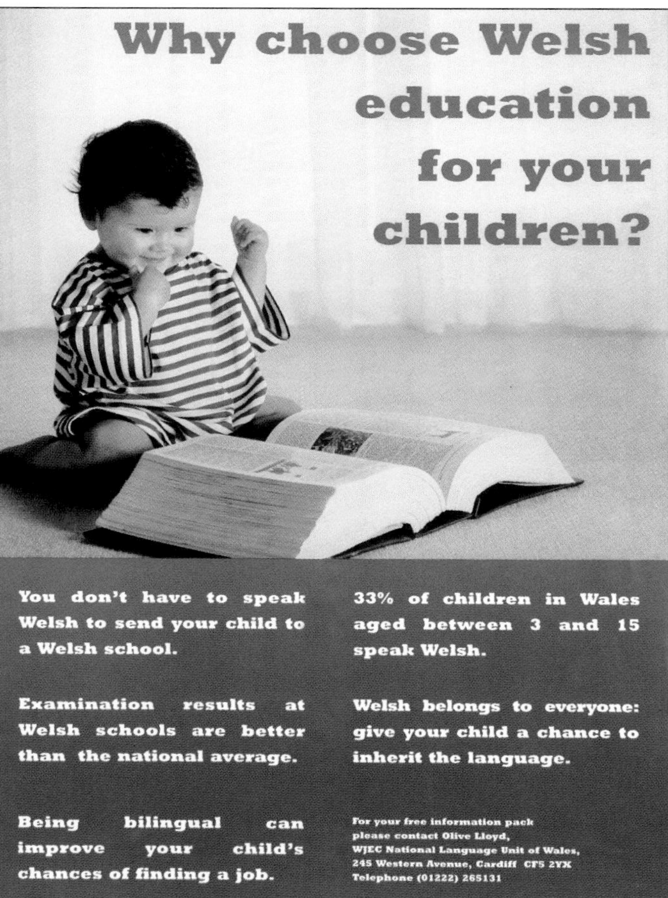

Why choose Welsh education for your children?
You don't have to speak Welsh to send your child to a Welsh school.
Examination results at Welsh schools are better than the national average.
Being bilingual can improve your child's chances of finding a job.
33% of children in Wales aged between 3 and 15 speak Welsh.
Welsh belongs to everyone: give your child a chance to inherit the language.
For your free information pack
please contact Olive Lloyd,
WJEC National Language Unit of Wales,
245 Western Avenue, Cardiff CF5 2YX
Telephone (01222) 265131

A poster promoting Welsh-medium education.

Little use has been made of marketing ideas in discussing language maintenance, reversing language shift or language planning. Language marketing is a relatively new concept with few references in the literature. There is perhaps the suspicion that marketing a language might degrade it, bringing that language into lower repute by commercialism. The concern among some people is that marketing language and its attendant culture is neither as simple nor as straightforward as promoting a brand of toothpaste, breakfast cereal or washing powder.

However, among the Catalan and Basque language planners in Spain, the promoters of Hebrew in Israel, and among the Welsh in Wales, some of the propositions of social marketing are being successfully adapted for the purpose of promoting the minority language as a desirable possession. While not all the concepts of marketing that deal with material products (e.g. washing powder) or social products (e.g. health campaigns) are usable in the marketing of a language, the following discussion will attempt to illustrate that the concepts of marketing are an important conceptualization in reversing language shift. This discussion tries to illustrate that language marketing can be a valuable component in language planning.

A Marketing Strategy for Languages

Ten stages of a marketing strategy for languages, particularly minority languages, will now be given. The following table provides an initial outline of this ten stage strat-

A Summary of the Ten Stages

Stage 1:	Defining the Product.
Stage 2:	Investigating Customer Needs.
Stage 3:	Defining the Market.
Stage 4:	Making the Product Attractive.
Stage 5:	Promoting the Product.
Stage 6:	Anticipating and Challenging Counter-Propaganda.
Stage 7:	Distributing the Product.
Stage 8:	Pricing and Yields.
Stage 9:	Evaluating the Product and the Marketing Strategy.
Stage 10:	Revising the Marketing Strategy and Implementing a Longer-Term Marketing Plan

egy. Many of the stages or levels both overlap and interact, and should not be seen as distinct or sequential but interrelated.

Stage 1: Defining the product

On the surface, it would seem simple (if contentious) to define a language as being a product to be marketed. The mere labeling of a language as Spanish, Irish, Arabic or Breton would seem to clarify the product. However, as entries in Section 1 reveal, a language has many dimensions and colors. It is therefore necessary to define what component of language is to be marketed. What is the particular competence or attribute of language that we are marketing as a valuable product?

- Is it language standardization – the preferred used of particular vocabulary, new technical words and preferred structures to the language?
- Is it everyday spoken language among those who already speak the language?
- Is it use of the language by non-speakers and learners?
- Is it the promotion of literacy in the minority language rather than oracy?
- Is the focus more on the culture or cultures attached to the language rather than the language itself?
- Is the focus more on identity attached to a language and its attendant culture rather than the language?

The above questions suggest that marketing a language is not just about language as a worthwhile possession. Language marketing is about influencing behavior through means of campaigns, different forms of communicating 'the message' and education.

Just as the Ford Motor company does not produce all forms of transport (e.g. bikes, motor cycles and racing cars), so the language product being marketed needs to be specifically defined and clarified. If one danger is in failing to focus, the opposite danger is focusing too myopically. Often a prioritization is needed in language marketing, while keeping the whole entity in mind.

Stage 2: Investigating customer needs

A most important part of marketing strategy is to ascertain the needs of potential customers and consumers. This also may include an investigation of their attitudes, even susceptibility to the selling of the product. The initial step is to identify the customers: non speakers, learners, those who are able to speak the language but don't, or illiterates in the language? What groups must be given priority for investigating needs and wants? Such questions are not about inclusion and exclusion in a target market, but about prioritization based on overall language planning goals and probabilities of success.

Having decided on a target sector of the consumer market, a set of questions need answering, for example:

- What are the opinions of the targeted group towards the language?
- What are their personal motivations about the language and other key factors (e.g. employment, leisure, education) that considerably affect their choice of language behavior?
- What are the differing needs of existing speakers of the language and non-speakers?
- Do different groups of non-speakers have different needs, motivations and attitudes?
- Does a profiling of different groups mean varying probabilities of likely marketing success of that language?

To sell a new model of automobile or breakfast food requires careful market research to establish current behavior patterns, preferences, likes and dislikes, and the likelihood of changing purchasing behavior. Such a consumer survey may also go deeper into reasons for choice. For example, it may look at emotional decisions made about the shape of the car or the colors on the breakfast food box.

In the same way, language surveys are needed that are directly and explicitly related to an overall marketing strategy. Such language surveys may seek to answer one or more of the following illustrative questions:

- Who speaks which language in what domains, and where are the weaknesses in a capture of language domains for the minority language?
- Which groups have a positive attitude to learning the minority language?
- Which groups of potential customers or clients are more susceptible to a soft sell?
- What are the needs and motivations of parents with regard to their children's education that relate to language marketing issues?
- What deeper and underlying factors affect whether parents decide to use the minority language with their newborn children (i.e. intergenerational transmission) that need marketing attention?

While there have been many language use surveys, attitude studies and censuses, few of these relate directly to a marketing strategy. Generally, language use questionnaires and language attitude surveys are created to provide up-to-date information about, for example, the size and density of active language speakers in a region, the use of language in different domains, intergenerational transmission and personal opinions about the status and value of the majority and minority languages.

In comparison, language surveys for language marketing purposes may need to be more specific, relating to the defined product and targeted markets. Such surveys should explicitly dovetail into the decision-making processes discussed in the remaining stages of languages marketing (given below). Such language surveys are an integral part of a language marketing framework.

Stage 3: Defining the market

Having investigated customer and consumer needs, it is important to define and target particular products for specific groups for marketing the language. There are usually limited human and material resources to market a language and create interventions (e.g. classes for learners, supporting mass media in the minority language). Therefore, targeting of particular products for particular groups (where there is likely to be a higher chance of success) becomes an important part of strategy.

Initial decisions may be about strengthening the language among existing speakers, or among those who have lapsed in using the language, or among non speakers, including recent in-migrants. Afterwards, a more refined targeting may occur. A consumer needs survey should reveal groups where there is an increased probability of success. For example, particular communities with 'vitality', particular areas or regions, particular employment groups or age groups, and particular constellations of needs and motivations may make the defined target groups either wide or narrow. There are never unlimited resources to target all groups, so that prioritization becomes essential.

Stage 4: Making the product attractive

In the world of marketing automobiles, lotteries and computers, it is important to make a product maximally attractive and appealing to as wide a defined market as possible. A parallel similar operation needs to occur in language marketing. For example, when language standardization is being marketed, the new technical terms or preferred vocabulary must be attractive and appealing to as many potential consumers as possible. When new technological terms for computing, information technology and telematics are introduced, they must be maximally appealing to the consumer.

Packaging an attractive language product means defining all the many and varied uses and values of a language. Packaging the language product means emphasizing customer needs that the product meets. No product will sell well unless it matches, and is attractive to customer needs.

Also, as part of its packaging, the language needs to be associated with major virtues and values. For example, a new perfume is marketed by being associated with beauty and romance. A charitable organization obtaining money for the poor of a region may emphasize relief from guilt and the raising of self-esteem among contributors if donations are given. An adult literacy campaign may associate itself with economic opportunity, greater affluence and more sophistication as a person.

Similarly, a minority language must be made as attractive and appealing as possible by being associated with major virtues such as liberty, freedom, social justice, enablement, empowerment and individual/group rights. As evidenced elsewhere in this Encyclopedia, speaking a minority language may be associated with cognitive or thinking advantages, with being able to enjoy two or more worlds of cultural experience, of greater achievement through bilingual education and raised self-esteem through celebrating heritage values and ethnic identity. Such positive benefits of speaking a language and enjoying its attendant culture may need advertising in no less an aggressive manner than advertizing automobiles or computer software.

Part of making a language attractive and appealing to as wide a market as possible means clarifying precisely what kind of language product will be attractive to which audience.

The marketing campaign may aim at raising awareness about the existence of the language, its history and heritage, its value and vitality. Such awareness-raising may be necessary before offering language learning. For example, among those who do not speak the language and have an ambivalent attitude towards the language, it is important 'not to sell them boot polish before they are willing to wear shoes'.

A different type of attractive and appealing product will be needed for those who have negative attitudes, who need more persuasion and where a longer-term reversal of attitudes needs attempting.

Another kind of language marketing is required to evoke as many positive associations with a minority language as possible. If it is thought that among both speakers and non-speakers there is a need to increase the attractiveness and appeal of the minority language, a more general, mass media-based marketing campaign may be commenced.

If the marketing strategy is directed at increasing the size and density of language uses within a defined area, a wide market that includes both language speakers and non-language speakers may be included, but this time, targeting institutional and infrastructural means of increasing language use (e.g. through bilingual education, nursery schooling, participative cultural use of the minority language).

A more specific product will be required when targeting increased proficiency among all current speakers of the language. When the focus is on those whose proficiency could be improved, the product may be concerned with more informal networks and relationships as well as with educative formal structures.

Another target may be extending the domains in which the minority language is used. For example, if the language is restricted to home and religious observance, there may be marketing to extend use of that language to mass media, education, literacy and/or employment.

If a major historical problem has been the lack of language reproduction in families and schools, and if marketing aims at producing a more stable language reproduction in the family and education system, then the marketing may target these two institutions. For example, means of encouraging mothers and fathers to use their minority language in raising their children need exploring. Ways of making bilingual education an attractive option for parents may also need a marketing strategy (e.g. the use of promotional videos, pamphlets, meetings).

Another target for marketing may be to secure the increased presence of state legislation and language rights for minorities. When law and litigation are included in language marketing, this can be a 'hard sell' in product marketing. At this point, marketing an attractive and appealing product moves towards conformity, even coercion.

While stipulating language rights and enforcing language normalization procedures (e.g. as in the Basque region and in Wales) are often seen as essential accompaniments to language marketing, conviction is stronger than conformity. Ultimately, conformity and coercion are temporary, with the consent of the governed being ultimately more powerful. Even in totalitarian and autocratic states, coercion is not a long-term solution. Through conflict or constitutional means, the consent of the governed is ultimately required in language planning enforcement.

Thus marketing an attractive and appealing language product becomes crucial, even if language legislation and litigation are available. In Race Relations and Equal Opportunity legislation, there has been a valuable stipulation of rights and freedoms. Yet the perpetuation of racial hostility and violence, and the continued existence of unequal opportunities, attest that legislation is never enough by itself. There has to be persuasion and promotion, and the marketing of an attractive and appealing product essential in language shift.

Stage 5: Promoting the product

We are all used to advertising on billboards, television and in newspapers and magazines; to slogans and mailings to promote particular products; to the soft sell and the hard sell; to gentle pressure and more persuasive coercion. Minority languages have generally failed to use the tricks and strategies of marketing material products to sell a language. (The Catalans are one of the few exceptions.)

As social psychologists reveal, advertising a product needs to be more than a one-off big bang. Rather advertising needs to be continuous and repetitive. The message needs to be frequently given to the consumer who increasingly

Media and Mobilization

Promoting a language does not only rest with language marketing and advertising. Promoting the language product can also come through political pressure, through individuals talking to their political representatives to persuade them to take political initiatives.

Writing letters to the editors of newspapers, campaigning for radio and television time to spread the message, working at the personal level to communicate the value of the minority language may each be powerful marketing processes.

Promoting a language may also mean getting legislation and achieving language rights and freedoms. It may also mean the mobilization of language activists to promote the language and its attendant culture.

associates a particular name with a product, and hopefully a quality product. The message needs continuous emphasis and re-emphasis so that it becomes a part of the consciousness and subconsciousness of the individual.

Advertising of a language can come in many forms. A language may be publicized on posters, through adverts in newspapers, magazines and television, videos and pictures, through cartoons and computer graphics, through balloons and plastic shopping bags, through badges and labels, and through signposts and speeches.

Slogans are an important part of marketing, especially when the effect is subliminal. Sometimes this will start by offering prizes to members of the general public producing the best slogans. The act of competition is a form of awareness-raising and of getting people to think in a positive way about a minority language. Thinking of a slogan for a language is a subtle form of attitude formation, even attitude change in the individual. The individual may come to believe their own propaganda.

Following the competition, the publicization of slogans becomes an important and valuable marketing activity. At a general level, television and radio, papers and magazines may broadcast the language slogan.Through postal literature and through marketing by the telephone, a more direct and targeted promotion may be attempted.

Stage 6: Anticipating and challenging counter-propaganda

When a minority language is promoted, it is often seen as upsetting balances of power, status, employment and earning power. Promoting a minority language often challenges existing power structures, privileges and dominant interests. Language marketing may challenge the status quo and appear to provoke political or social unrest. Therefore, opposition to marketing the minority language must be expected and anticipated. A campaign to present opposite and conflicting viewpoints must be assumed.

Preparation for this opposition is needed. As a football player once said, 'it is important to get your retaliation in first!' That is, it is important to anticipate what kind of counter-propaganda and counter-claims will be made. It is vital to work out in advance what kind of arguments against the minority language and its spread will be promulgated. It is also important to anticipate the marketing approach and strategy of such counter-propaganda.

When positively marketing the minority language, it is possible to implicitly counter-attack when promoting the language product and to build in lines of defense and arguments to attempt to defeat counter-propaganda when initially promoting the product. Also, there usually needs to be an explicit rebuttal of the counter-propaganda.

Stage 7: Distributing the product

When a new material product such as a computer or breakfast cereal is marketed, it is important to ensure there are plenty of appropriately sited outlets from which consumers can acquire the product. Part of marketing strategy is to target, for example, which shops to persuade to sell the product, appropriate advertisement and placement within the shop, and an efficient chain of distribution to ensure a plentiful supply.

In marketing a language, it is important to target the institutions and processes for acquiring the language product. For example, if the language is to be spread by bilingual education, a targeting of particular schools to promote bilingualism may be attempted. Or, if adult classes are to be provided for learners of the language, these must be sited in easily accessible, suitable, and well distributed buildings. Another example of distributing a product is in deciding which television and radio stations, what times of the day, and what kinds of attractive programs need to be presented on the media to increase proficiency and the numbers of language users. At a more informal level, sufficient participative cultural activities need to be provided to ensure an increased use of a language across domains, and to help foster strong local cells and networks of language users. For example, discos and dances, drinking and debating in the minority language need planning and provision.

Stage 8: Pricing and yields

In language promotion, money is never far removed from decision-making. For example, the cost of marketing and promotion or the cost of putting on language courses for new or existing speakers of the language need to be assessed and defended as cost-effective. An intensive crash course in the language for non-speakers needs to be costed against a more long-term and gradual course.

However, consumer needs (e.g. wanting to speak a language within a short time rather than slowly learning the language over a number of years) must be brought into account. The cost of such courses also needs to match what consumers, providers and sponsoring companies are willing to pay for language learning.

Another area concerned with finance is where there is a possibility of offering economic incentives for having learnt a language or being competent to use a language at work. For example, promotion within the job or an extra increment on a salary scale may be possible for having learnt a language.

Another element in this stage is to gauge the 'profit margin'. This will not be in monetary terms but, for example, in the increased proficiency of speakers who have been targeted, the extension of the minority language to other domains, an increase in the size and density of language speakers from one census survey to another, or the raising of awareness and positive attitudes towards the language in society.

Where new initiatives have been launched and existing schemes are examined for their profit margin, the concept of 'value-addedness' may be relevant. That is, what have initiatives and schemes of action delivered that is above a profit baseline or greater than customary delivery? This raises the question of what has been 'value added' when a language gets marketed. Is it the language or the people? Is the profit gauged in linguistic terms only, or is the spotlight more on the quality of life of individuals and communities?

Working out the language profit gained through interventions and the marketing of the language requires a baseline to be initially specified, and then improvements over and above that baseline to be measured at a later date. Some profits are not measurable. Indeed, some of the most important outcomes of language revival and maintenance are the least measurable (e.g. security in personal identity). However, this difficulty should not be an excuse for failing to set clear aims and objectives in language planning. Nor should it be an excuse for not monitoring and evaluating the successes and failures of language planning and marketing.

Stage 9: Evaluating the product and marketing strategy

Part of a marketing strategy is to monitor that strategy as it is being implemented, providing feedback to language planners and implementers as the product is distributed. Such evaluation is not purely in terms of profit, but takes on board questions such as:

- Was the product adequately defined before marketing?
- Were the markets well chosen?
- Was the product made as attractive and appealingas possible?
- Were customer needs fully and fairly investigated, and in sufficient depth?

Bilingualism and Spelling Slogans

The Bilingualism Alphabet

1. BiClingualism: Two languages grows on you.
2. BiFlingualism: A brief flirtation with second language learning.
3. BiKingualism: Prestigious or elite bilingualism.
4. BioLingualism: Is good for your health.
5. BiMingualism: Bilingualism helps you meet people.
6. BiRingualism: Networks of bilinguals.
7. BiSingualism: Musical bilinguals.
8. BiTingualism: Bilingualism gives you a thrill.
9. BiWingualism: The second language rising rapidly.
10. BiZingualism: Bilingual vitality.

The Lingualism Alphabet

1. CryLingualism: Lament over a lost language.
2. DieLingualism: Language loss.
3. MyLingualism: Language imperialism.
4. ShyLingualism: Reluctance to speak a minority language.
5. SighLingualism: Language learning is too much trouble.
6. SLingualism: Throwing away a heritage language.
7. SpyLingualism: Undiplomatic use of languages.
8. TieLingualism: Formal language learning.
9. TryLingualism: Trying to speak three languages.
10. WhyLingualism: Lack of language awareness.

- Was the product promoted in appropriate and effective ways?
- Was the promotion and distribution cost-effective?
- Was the anticipation of counter-propaganda well judged and effective in replying?
- Was the distribution of outlets to market the product adequate, effective and efficient?
- What are the performance indicators of success in marketing the language?

The evaluation of the marketing strategy needs to involve both an ongoing, formative evaluation of the process. At particular stages of development, there is also a need to audit in a more summative manner. Formative evaluation feeds back into the daily process of operating a language marketing strategy. Summative evaluation focuses on whether aims, goals and objectives have been attained. Such summative evaluation ensures accountability for past marketing plans and amount of progress achieved. It also feeds forward into Stage 10, a revised plan of action.

Stage 10: Revising the marketing strategy and implementing a longer-term marketing plan

Marketing a language is a continuous process. It is never a one-off event but rather will be incremental, with many developments that produce an upward spiral in the maintenance and spread of a minority language. Thus, the marketing strategy must be sustained rather than short-term, evolutionary and not momentary. The marketing strategy must be a cyclical activity. The evaluation of the past and the present must provide 'feed-forward'. Failures and unrealized ambitions need investigation, with an alternative marketing strategy put in place. Successes need sustaining and building on, in such a way that success breeds success.

The Limitations of a Language Marketing Strategy

As was indicated in the Introduction, some people are cautious, sceptical or even hostile to the idea of marketing language in a way that parallels marketing automobiles and washing-powder. So it is important to express the limitations and reservations about language marketing.

First, in language planning and language reversal, language marketing is one tool among many. Status language planning and corpus language planning already have a body of literature and a set of ideas and theories from sociology, linguistics, geography, social psychology and education to guide language reversal. Language marketing provides an extra perspective and an additional range of ideas. It is not a self-contained or stand-alone recipe for language restoration.

Second, language marketing is not an overall theory of reversing language shift (e.g. as attempted in Fishman's Reversing Language Shift Theory and his Graded Intergenerational Disruption Scale). It has neither the breadth of understanding of causes of language shift, nor a wide enough range of solutions for reversing language minority trends.

Third, the vocabulary of language marketing can trap the language planner within a narrow set of aims, goals and solutions. With the vocabulary of language marketing goes a particular perspective and culture. The language of the 'hard sell' does not always fit easily with the 'affective' language of heritage cultural transmission. For example, talk of capitalizing, profit-margins, persuasion and inducements is a world apart from preserving family language traditions, language community integration and self-identity. The very idea of language marketing thus may need marketing.

Further Reading

ANDREASEN, A. R., 1994, Social Marketing: Its Definition and Domain. *Journal of Public Policy and Marketing*, 13 (1), 108-114.

COOPER, R. L., 1989, *Language Planning and Social Change*. Cambridge: Cambridge University Press.

JONES, A. W., 1992, Marketing: A New Discipline for Language Planners. In DAFIS, Ll. (ed.), 1992, *The Lesser Used Languages – Assimilating Newcomers*. Proceedings of the Conference held at Carmarthen, 1991. Carmarthen, Dyfed, Wales: Joint Working Party on Bilingualism in Dyfed.

WELSH LANGUAGE BOARD, 1996, *A Guide to Bilingual Design*. Cardiff: Welsh Language Board.

Bilingualism in the Modern World

1: Information Technology and Bilingualism

Contemporary historians refer to the present era as the Information Age, the age of the computer revolution, and the age of the information super-highway. Since the 1980s, the explosion in the number of micro-computers, software on disks and CDs, cellular telephones, cable television, fax, voice communication by networked computers, multimedia, and the growth of the Internet system has reflected a period of rapid technological advance. Word-processors, databases, spreadsheets, graphics, computer games, electronic mail across the world, information servers, computerization of library catalogs and reference materials, and the rapid increase in the number of organizations providing information about themselves on the Internet have cumulatively created an information revolution.

Individuals can now gain instant access to world-wide information in written, graphic and sound forms. The Internet allows retrieval of information on almost every topic with a minimum of effort or technical ability. In the rise of internationally-networked computers and cordless communications, the role, status and functions of different languages are being transformed.

Thus the transformation has not only been in electronics, technology, software, communication between people and information exchange, but also in language, culture and styles of existence and employment. With the rapid spread of technology and networked information has gone the rapid spread of English. The inherent danger is that minority languages, heritage language cultures and therefore bilingualism come under threat. The information that transfers across the Internet highway tends mostly (but not exclusively) to be in English. The language of digitized encyclopedias on CDs and the multiplicity of software tends also to be in English as does the language of games software, word processors and spreadsheets. Linguistic diversity is threatened by the information revolution. Minority languages are potentially made even less stable by such technological growth.

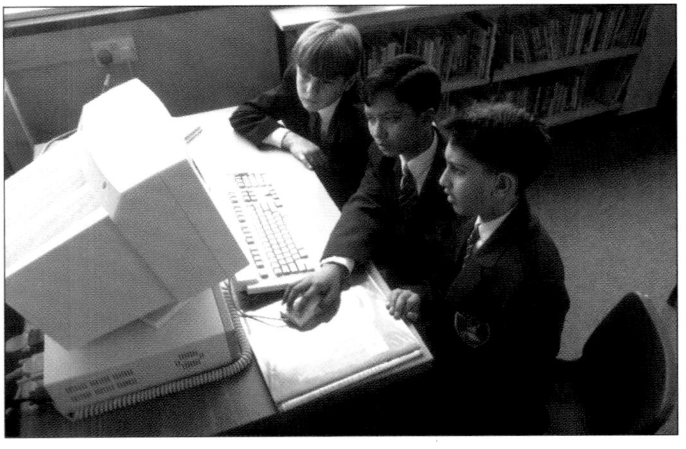

An advertisement for Apple Computers in Rostov, Russia. Information technology is available in a multitude of different languages, but, on the whole, English predominates.

The information technology revolution does not only present a threat to minority languages. Through its powerful forms of presentation and English-dominated medium of operation, it has become a major medium for transmitting majority anglophone culture. Just as mass media, communications and industrialization in the 20th century has threatened minority cultures and subcultures, so the information revolution is a current major threat to cultural diversity.

Minority languages may seem in comparison to be part of tradition, of heritage and history, and may fail to attain the status and prestige of modern, high-prestige and high profile international languages used by information technology. The danger lies in the identification of advanced technological society with the English language, and subequently minority languages being identified with home, eligion and history. The danger is that the information echnology revolution is another nail in the coffin of ninority languages. Unintentionally, the English lanuage has found another Trojan Horse to penetrate ninority language communities throughout the world. 'he danger is of a tiered information society: those who ave the linguistic abilities to access information; those vho cannot access new forms of communication and nformation as they are monolingual in a language not sed in the information society.

'et, on a more positive note, it is possible to harness the echnological horse to aid minority language education. 'or example, software can be displayed in or translated nto the heritage language, and electronic mail and infornation exchange can be in that minority language. It ecomes a challenge for the computer to be used in comnunication in minority languages and not just in majoriy, international languages.

utomatic translating facilities (machine-assisted transation) and electronic bilingual and multilingual dictioaries are available. Also, it is possible to transcribe comuter applications particularly for primary school level, nto the minority language. Thus in Wales, much of the requently used software in classrooms has an English nd a Welsh version. The user interface of a word proessing or database package can be in the minority lanuage. Computer-assisted learning (CAL) programs can e translated so that the language interface is in the ninority language and not just in English.

Vhat is also important in preserving minority languages n a technological age is to ensure that there is appropriite terminology in the minority language. It is important o extend minority language vocabulary to embrace technological and computer terms in languages other than English. In Wales and Catalonia for example, there has been the production of home-grown minority language software to complement the translation of high-quality majority language curriculum software to run in a minority language.

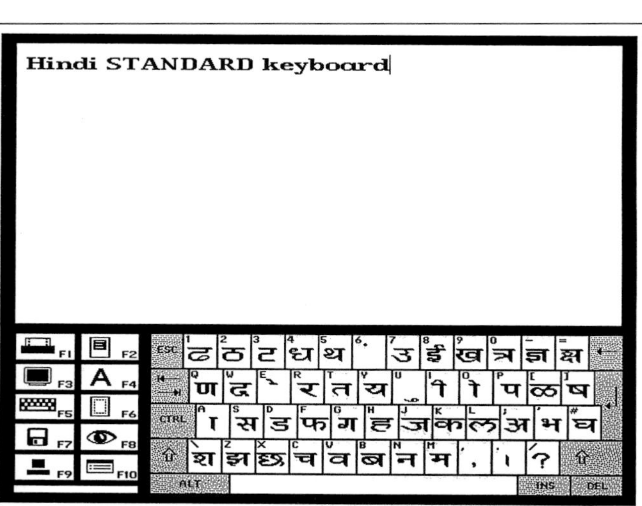

Hindi computer keyboard, produced by Allwrite

Computer Translation

Translation from one language to another is increasingly possible via computers. Translation software is increasingly able to translate from one language to another.

International telephone links in the future are likely to have an electronic 'operator' providing simultaneous interpretation for the users. In Japan, a major research undertaking has already demonstrated that it is possible to electronically translate a simple conversation between Japanese and English (see the topic on Translation and Interpretation, page 234).

REFERENCE: O'HAGAN, 1996

Minority language use of information technology can aid language survival and spread. Such a movement may help minority languages become more modernized in their terminology and technical functionality. Such modernization aids the symbolic status of the language, particularly among the impressionable young. This ensures that information technology is a supporter and not a destroyer of bilingualism in children.

Further Reading

CUMMINS, J. & SAYERS, D., 1996, Multicultural Education and Technology: Promise and Pitfalls. *Multicultural Education*, 3 (3), 4-10.

LAVER, J. & ROUKENS, J., 1996, The Global Information Society and Europe's Linguistic and Cultural Heritage. In C. HOFFMANN (ed.), *Language, Culture and Communication in Contemporary Europe*. Clevedon: Multilingual Matters Ltd.

PRICE, D. & BAKER, C., 1993, Bilingualism and Information Technology. In H. BAETENS BEARDSMORE (ed.), *European Models of Bilingual Education*. Clevedon: Multilingual Matters Ltd.

SAYERS, D., 1995, Educational Equity Issues in an Information Age. *Teachers College Record*, 96 (4), 767-774.

Multimedia Systems

One of the recent changes in information technology is the emergence of multimedia systems based on fast access, high capacity, compact disks, sound cards and speakers particularly suitable to help with learning a language. There are compact disks available to teach English, French, German, Italian, Spanish and other languages through a multimedia system. This allows text, still pictures, moving pictures, audible speech samples and the possibility of learner interaction to be combined on one CD. Authentic materials can be stored on the compact disk in great variety, with a multitude of still and moving pictorial representation of places, people and events to enhance exposure to the second language.

A Computer Teaching Network

ORILLAS is a computer-based collaborative teaching network between the Brooklyn College of the City University of New York and the University of Puerto Rico. A computer network is used to form long-distance, team-teaching partnerships between people in New York and Puerto Rico.

ORILLAS uses computer-based telecommunications for four purposes: first, to increase the mother tongue and English language proficiency of language minority students: secondly, to improve the self-esteem and academic achievement of these students; thirdly, to promote positive intergroup relations between majority and minority students; and fourthly, to promote the acquisition of foreign languages and cross-cultural knowledge.

ORILLAS is not a student-to-student communication but rather a class collaboration designed by partner teachers who are joined by their common teaching interests as well as their students' similar grade level. Typical projects in this computer collaboration are shared student newsletters and journals, joint surveys and investigations, science activities and geographical projects that have a comparative element, collections of oral histories, folklore, children's rhymes and riddles that are shared and compared.

According to Dennis Sayers (1994), there are over one hundred schools participating in the network, of which 30 are physically located in Puerto Rico. The computer link-up makes possible daily contact with students from the United States with students from the area from where their parents or grandparents once lived. As such, it helps to foster a stronger sense of bilingualism and biculturalism among language minority students in the United States.

REFERENCES: SAYERS, 1991; SAYERS & BROWN, 1987

La Clase Mágica (The Magical Class)

La Clase Mágica is a bilingual and bicultural educational innovation that seeks to raise the school performance of Spanish-speaking children in California. The aim is, via computers, to provide educational activities that raise standards of literacy in both Spanish and English for Latino children. The concept of *La Clase Mágica* is a make-believe world in which children negotiate their way through various tasks in a maze-like structure composed of 20 rooms, with each room containing two computer games. Some of the learning tasks are arcade-like games, but most tasks are from commercially available educational software. The computer usage increases the motivational features of play, fantasy and particularly of collaborative learning between students.

Teachers and tutors collaborate with the children to help find solutions to problems posed by the various tasks. Each activity in the computer-based environment promotes communication with the Wizard (a central teacher-controller) so that children can share their experiences, seek answers to their questions and aid their progress through the tasks. Such communication with the Wizard is an informal and latent way of helping the development of literacy and language skills. By communicating with the Wizard on average once a week via short letters or by live electronic conversation, children's literacy is raised in both Spanish and English.

The tasks are made as authentic, realistic and as intrinsically interesting as is possible. For example, traditional Mexican folk tales, family histories, and notable figures in Mexican history are used alongside the vocabulary of modern technology.

REFERENCE: VÁSQUEZ, 1993

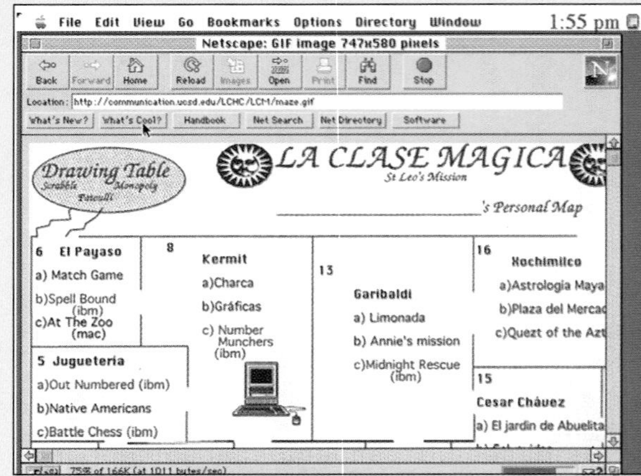

The maze as seen on a computer screen.

2: Bilingualism and the Internet

When students use communication technology, bilingual proficiency can be enhanced. Through the Internet, for example, authentic language practice is possible via purposeful and genuine activities (e.g. the use of electronic mail). There may be increased motivation to acquire a language via contact with real students in other countries and accessing authentic language sources to complete curriculum activity (e.g. a project on another country). Some examples follow.

The Internet is world-wide. A woman worker at the Union Bank of Colombo, Sri Lanka, accesses her company's home page on the Internet.

The Human Languages Page on the Internet (see later for the address) pulls together potentially useful language services like tutoring, audio samples of languages, on-line translation, dictionaries, resource banks and expert help. The Usenet news groups have sections on subjects such as the culture of Pakistan, Vietnam, the politics of China and Indian culture. There are also opportunities to communicate with native speakers of French, German, Spanish and Russian.

Electronic mail and electronic conferencing are already one of the major Internet activities for language students, giving the feeling of the global village where barriers to communication (such as cost and the time of travel) are removed. There are increasing numbers of foreign language servers on the Internet accessible via 'sensitive maps' of sites in each country. They provide useful, relevant and topical information which is in a different language. Linguistic competence develops as a by-product of interest in the information.

By its nature, the Internet brings people speaking different languages into closer contact. By exchanging information with students in other countries, students can build increasing independence in language use, vary their language according to audience, and use language for real purposes. Students can take part in conversations and conferences over the Internet with native speakers, using not only written text but increasingly video and audio conferencing as well. Exchange visits can be reinforced with preparatory and follow-up Internet links, and there are possibilities of virtual exchanges and 'telepresence' (it is already possible to visit 'digital Amsterdam' on the Internet). The Internet promises future automatic on-line translation of messages and other text, and students will need to spot nuances of meaning by referring to both original and translation. Digital radio on the Internet is set to expand, and decompression and file transfer will make receiving programs relatively straightforward.

The Internet provides teachers and learners with ready-to-use banks of multimedia resources: a wealth of video

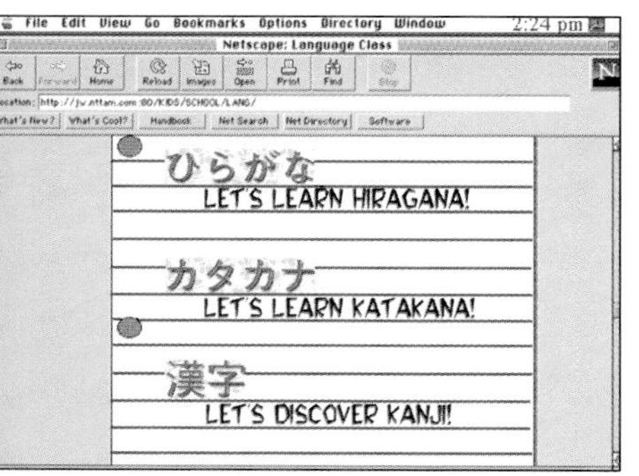

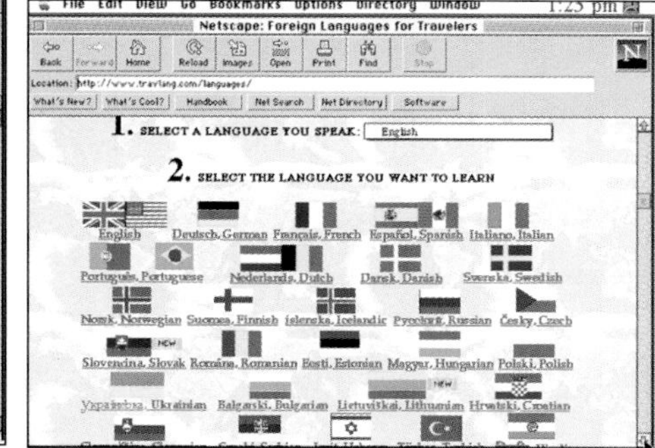

The Internet is dominated by English, but gradually access to a variety of languages is becoming available. These three Internet screens show Japanese language classes for children, a Spanish on-line newspaper from Colombia, and an on-line language learning program.

and audio recordings from all over the world, pictorial and written information, and activities generated by different language centers in different countries. Providers of information and training for language teachers can use the Internet to publicize events, courses, materials, services and a subscription-based, remote training, advice and information service.

Cyberspace has always been dominated by the English language, and a major anxiety of other majority languages and of minority languages is the extra emphasis, value and function given to English by the Internet. However, as more businesses begin to advertise using web pages, regional networks have developed using local languages on the Internet. It makes no sense advertizing a shop in Sweden if the main customers are local and not international. Also, as schools, colleges, universities, local government, libraries, record offices and local information agencies go on-line, their local pages are in the regional language.

Some World-Wide Web Sites for Bilinguals

1. **The Human Languages Page**
   http://www.hardlink.com/~chambers/HLP/
2. **WWW Sites for Languages**
   http://www.cortland.edu/www_root/flteach/flteach.html
3. **WWW Foreign Language Resources**
   http://www.itp.berkeley.edu/~thorne/HumanResources.html
4. **Virtual Media Lab**
   http://philae.sas.upenn.edu/
5. **Yahoo – Education – Languages**
   http:/www.yahoo.com/Education/Languages/
6. **Technical Translation**
   http://www.uni-frankfurt.de/~felix/eurodictautom.html
7. **Less Commonly Taught Languages**
   http://carla.acad.umn.edu/lctl/lctl.html
8. **CTI Center for Modern Languages**
   http://www.hull.ac.uk/cti
9. **Hobbes' Language World**
   http://info.isoc.org/guest/zakon/languages/
10. **Language and Linguistics on the World-Wide Web**
    http://eisv01.lancs.ac.uk/websites.htm
11. **Ethnologue Database**
    http://www.sil.org/ethnologue/ethnologue.html
12. **Center for Applied Linguistics (US)**
    http://www.cal.org/
13. **National Clearinghouse for Bilingual Education (US)**
    http://www.ncbe.gwu.edu/
14. **Office of Bilingual Education and Minority Languages (US)**
    http://www.ed.gov/offices/OBEMLA/
15. **US Race and Ethnicity Resources**
    http://www.contact.org/usrace.htm
16. **ERIC Clearinghouse on Languages and Linguistics**
    http://ericir.syr.edu/Projects/ericcll/
17. **Agora Language Marketplace**
    http://agoralang.com/agora/
18. **US Department of Education, Office of Civil Rights**
    http://www.ed.gov/offices/OCR/
19. **Central Bureau for Educational Visits and Exchanges (UK)**
    http://www.britcoun.org/cbeve/index.htm
20. **The MERCATOR Project (European Commission – Which Promotes the Interests of the Minority/ Regional Languages and Cultures Within the European Union).**
    http://www.troc.es/mercator/index.htm
21. **The Multilingual Information Society (MLIS) Programme (European Union)**
    http://www2.echo.lu/mlis/mlishome.html
22. **Welsh Language Board**
    http://www.netwales.co.uk/byig/
23. **Language Policy Research Center (Israel)**
    http://www.biu.ac.il:80/HU/lprc/
24. **ALIS Language Handling Technologies**
    http://babel.alis.com/
25. **James Crawford's Language Policy Web Site and Emporium**
    http://ourworld.compuserve.com/homepages/JWCRAWFORD/
26. **Office of the Commissioner of Official Languages (Canada)**
    http://ocol-clo.gc.ca/
27. **Multilingual Matters**
    http://www.multi.demon.co.uk
28. **Internet Resources for Language Teachers**
    http://www.hull.ac.uk/cti/langsite.htm

France and the Internet

For years the Internet had been seen in France as a anglophone intruder. The Internet initially appeared as an English language, American culture invader. The negative reaction was also understandable because of France's own telecom system. France already had its own electronic data transmission and information system in the Minitel system storing large amounts of information about all aspects of French life.

Available in more than seven million homes and offices across France, Minitel gives on-screen access to data on individuals, businesses, the arts, events, entertainment, finance, sport and much more. The system, which has been running for more than a decade, was among the first popular electronic information networks anywhere in the world. The French government did not encourage any interface between Minitel and the Internet, and no software was available to make Minitel accessible from personal computers. As computer-based communications (e.g. Electronic mail – e-mail) spread through many parts of the world, Minitel was left behind. Even more so, when the Internet flourished in the mid-1990s, France was seeming to be left behind. Many people in France felt that they were being pushed into the slow lane of the information revolution.

In June 1995, France Telecom, the state-run telecom monopoly, moved towards widespread access to the Internet. Some angry correspondence in *Libération*, the daily newspaper, denounced France Telecom for failing to develop its net culture, for producing isolationism and for not providing international access. France is now speeding along the fast lane of the *'infobahn'* (German for 'information highway').

Paris, Marseille and Nice have various cyber cafés. A French language net magazine – *PlaNete Internet* – is available and there are many French language sites. Cities such as Paris, Grenoble and Marseilles, and bodies such as the French Ministry of Culture have servers on the Internet providing multimedia information relevant to the curriculum (e.g. the environment, the local area, quality of life, shops and services, travel, culture and leisure). Some of these are listed below:

http://www.quelm.fr/Cybersphere.html http://www.itp.berkeley.edu/~thome/HumanResources.html
http://www.mmania.com/index.html http://www.campus.bt.com/CampusWorld/pub/FranceALC/

Some World-Wide Web Sites for Language Learners

1. **Spain and Spanish on the Net**
   http://gias720.dis.ulpgc.es/spain.html
2. **Arabic Language Course**
   http://i-cias.com/babel/arabic/index.htm
3. **German New**
   http://www.mathematik.uni-ulm.de/germnews/
   also: http://www.mathematik.uni-ulm.de/de-news/
4. **Lixl-Purcell's German WWW Trails**
   http://www.uncg.edu/~lixlpurc/german.html
5. **Der Spiegel**
   http://www.spiegel.de
6. **Bernadotteskolen, Denmark**
   http://www.algonet.se/~bernadot
7. **The Tecla Home Page**
   http://www.bbk.ac.uk/Departments/SpanishTecla
8. **Elementary Spanish**
   http://www.cyborganic.com/~lesliev/Curriculum/
9. **Digital Amsterdam**
   http://www.dds.nl/
10. **A Course in Learning Welsh**
    http://www.cs.brown.edu/fun/welsh/home.html
11. **Romance Languages Resource Page**
    http://humanities.uchicago.edu/romance/
12. **HENSA**
    http://micros.hensa.ac.uk/
13. **CILT (Centre for Information of Language Teaching and Research)**
    http://www.campus.bt.com/CampusWorld/pub/CILT/index.html

Some Useful World-Wide Web Sites for French Language Learners

1. **FranceNet**
   http://www.francenet.fr/
2. **W3 servers in France**
   http://www.urec.fr/cgi-bin/list
3. **Ministère de la culture et de la francophonie**
   http://www.culture.fr/
4. **France On Line**
   http://www.france.com
5. **Paris**
   http://www.paris.org//parisF.html
6. **Grenoble**
   http://www.grenet.fr/
7. **Web Museum, Paris**
   http://sunsite.unc.edu/wm/
8. **Frogmag**
   http://www.princeton.edu:80/Frogmag/
9. **ENS Lyon:Journal de Maths des Elèves**
   http://www.ens-lyon.fr/JME/JME.html
10. **American Association of Teachers of French**
    http://www.siu.edu/~aatf/missione.html

3: Translation and Interpretation

Introduction

Translation and interpretation have been a natural part of the multilingual world for thousands of years. Wherever people speaking different languages have come into contact, the need has arisen for translators and interpreters to transmit essential messages, ideas, culture, propaganda, religious beliefs and works of literature from one language to another.

The word 'translation' can be used generally to refer to both spoken and written translation from one language to another. However, the term 'translation' is generally used to refer to the written translation, and 'interpretation' to spoken translation. The language from which the translation occurs is often referred to as the 'source language' and the language into which the translation is made as the 'target language'.

Up until the 20th century, the majority of translated texts were religious, literary, scientific or philosophical. They were read mostly by an educated elite. However, during the latter half of the 20th century there has been an increased demand for translation. This has been caused by a number of factors.

Firstly, there was an increase in translation and interpreting during the Second World War, in the fields of Intelligence, radio monitoring and signal interpretation. After the war, the Allied Control Commissions (in Germany, Austria and France), and the Nuremberg War Crimes Trials, necessitated the employment of translators and interpreters. Later, the establishment and rapid growth of the United Nations meant that more translators and interpreters were needed.

Another factor has been the rise of democracy and an increased emphasis on the rights and empowerment of all individuals, including those in ethnic and linguistic minorities. There has also been an increase in literacy and public education in many countries of the world. This has led to a demand for the dissemination of information, for educational and reading material, for official documents, forms and government notices, in vernacular and minority languages. In many emerging third world countries, indigenous languages have been given national and official status alongside prestigious former colonial languages such as English and French. This has also led to an increase in the need for translation in state and government departments.

Other factors have been the rise of the global village, the increase in international trade, constant developments in science and technology that need to be disseminated worldwide, travel and tourism, popular culture, and the need for effective co-operation between countries. Political speeches need to be translated, as well as newspaper articles, scientific, legal and technical documents, creative literature and films. The worldwide use of English as a lingua franca, and the more restricted use of other major languages (e.g. Spanish, German and French) has simplified the situation to a certain extent. However, a language that is in regular, daily use in different parts of the world tends to develop different varieties. In the case of English, for instance, the evolution of distinctive varieties has meant that different versions of the same text have to be prepared. Also, simplified English texts have to be prepared in countries where English is the second official language.

As the demand for translation has increased, the number of translators and interpreters has grown, and the status and visibility of the profession has been raised. Professional bodies have been formed in many countries, and awards, fellowships and prizes for translation are given by many organizations. The International Federation of Translators was founded in 1953, under the joint patronage of UNESCO and the French government. The founding members were those countries in which professional bodies of translators already existed, the Federal Republic of Germany, Denmark, France, Italy, Norway and Turkey. Representatives from Canada, Hungary, Japan, Spain, Yugoslavia and the US also attended. International congresses have been held regularly and in 1970 the Federation achieved Category A status (i.e. full consultative status) with UNESCO.

In the US, the American Translators' Association was formed in 1959 and in the UK there exists the Translators' Guild of the (British) Institute of Linguists, founded in 1955. International Translation Banks have been formed, at the National Translation Center in Chicago, USA, and at the International Translations Center at Delft in the Netherlands.

The Work of Translators

Translators work in various capacities. International organizations employ translators to translate correspondence, working papers, reports and publicity literature. Multinational companies have in-house translators who deal with correspondence, reports and manuals, abstracts, specifications, advertising and publicity. Government departments employ translators to translate correspondence, official forms and information pamphlets, public signs and notices and educational material. The European Union has a large number of translators working in Brussels, translating official literature and reports from and into the eleven official languages of the European Union.

Many translators work freelance, translating academic and creative literature or working for companies who buy in their services. Some translators are well paid, but generally the job is still undervalued and underpaid, especially in the Western world. In the UK and the US, and to some extent in France, there is a lack of awareness of the importance of translation. This can be contrasted with the situation in places like India, China and Japan, for instance, where the art of translation, as well as individual translations, is a topic for serious discussion.

Many people believe that anyone with a fair knowledge of two languages can translate from one into the other. However, translation is a skill that requires an excellent, thorough and up-to-date knowledge of both the source language and the target language and their respective cultures. Moreover, it requires a sensitivity to language, and the ability to write correctly, economically and elegantly in a variety of styles and registers in the target language. For this reason, most professional translators usually only translate from one or perhaps two languages and only translate into one language. The target language will invariably be their 'language of habitual use', either their native language or the language they have spoken for a very long time.

It is important that the translator resides or makes frequent visits to the country where the target language is spoken, in order to keep his or her language skills in line with current developments. Words are coined or change their meaning or their connotations, idioms fall into disuse and others become popular, and cultural aspects of language evolve, such as ways of expressing politeness, and registers of language used in certain situations. It is essential that translators have at their fingertips the varieties of language currently in vogue in the target country, or their translations will sound outmoded, stilted or in some cases offensive. At the same time they must keep in touch with the current usage of language in the source language country, so that they are aware of nuances of meaning and cultural allusions in the texts they are required to translate.

Because translation requires such a high degree of skill, most translators are qualified linguists. They often go on to specialize in a certain field or topic. Some translators begin their careers as subject specialists in fields where an enormous amount of technical expertise is required. Translation involves transmitting technical or scientific information, and grasp of the subject is as crucial as linguistic ability.

Because of the increased relevance of translation in the modern world, there are now undergraduate and postgraduate courses available in translation and/or interpreting in many universities and other institutes of further education. These generally involve the study of two or three foreign languages and their cultures, linguistics and translation theory, consecutive and simultaneous interpreting, terminology, some politics, economics and law, and optional subjects such as science and technology. Plenty of translation practice is also given, both general and in specialist subjects. Undergraduate courses usually include a year abroad. Considerable emphasis is placed on good expression in the mother tongue or 'language of habitual use', as the medium into which the students translate. Most of these courses prepare students for a career in 'informative' (technical and scientific) translation. A few universities run courses in literary and creative translation.

Various national organizations run courses for translators and also offer examinations for recognized professional qualifications. Organizations that employ translators, such as the European Union, arrange in-service training for their staff.

What is Translation?

Effective translation concerns reproducing in the target language the closest possible equivalent of the source language message. The focus should first be on content and then on mirroring the style of language used. However, translation is not an easy concept to define, nor an easy skill to master. How does one measure a good or accurate translation?

Certainly, it is not difficult for the lay person to pinpoint a bad translation. It might include the following elements:

1. Mis-translation of words.

2. Grammatical errors.

Translating Skills and Purposes of Translation

Newmark (1993) identifies the specific skills of the translator

1. Sensitivity to language.
2. The ability to write neatly, plainly, nicely in a variety of registers in the target language, as well as having a good knowledge of its cultural background.
3. The ability to research topics, and master one specialism.
4. A good reading knowledge of two or more foreign languages, with their cultural backgrounds.

Newmark (1993) also defines five main purposes of translation.

1. To contribute to understanding and peace between nations, groups and individuals.
2. To transmit knowledge in plain,appropriate and accessible language, in particular in relation to technology transfer.
3. To explain and mediate between cultures, respecting their strengths, implicitly exposing their weaknesses.
4. To translate the world's great books.
5. To develop skills as part of the acquisition of a foreign language.

Translation Blunders

Marketing strategies need to take great care when translating slogans. While sales can be increased if advertisements are in the language of the locality, the translation must be accurate. The following tales illustrate that even multinational companies run into trouble:

1. A European vacuum manufacturer is alleged to have used the following in an American advertisement campaign: 'Nothing sucks like an [name of the machine].'
2. The name Coca-Cola in China was apparently first rendered as *Ke-kou-ke-la*. The company did not discover until many signs had been printed that the phrase means 'bite the wax tadpole' or 'female horse stuffed with wax' depending on the Chinese dialect. The company then researched 40,000 Chinese characters and found a close phonetic equivalent, *'ko-kou-ko-le,'* which can be loosely translated as 'happiness in the mouth.'
3. In Taiwan, the translation of the slogan 'Come alive with the Pepsi Generation' came out as 'Pepsi will bring your ancestors back from the dead.'
4. In Cantonese, a Fried Chicken slogan 'finger-lickin' good' was initially translated as 'eat your fingers off.'
5. When the Chevy Nova was first introduced into South America, marketing executives were apparently unaware that *'no va'* means 'it won't go.' After finding it wasn't selling many such cars, it was renamed (in its Spanish markets) as the Caribe.
6. In Brazil, a vehicle called the Pinto under-sold. It was found that Pinto was Brazilian slang for 'tiny male genitals'. The model was then called the Corcel instead.
7. When a ballpoint pen was marketed in Mexico, its advertisement was supposed to say 'It won't leak in your pocket and embarrass you.' However, the translator used the Spanish word *'embarazar'*, thinking it meant 'to embarrass'. In fact it means 'to get pregnant'. So the advertisement said that 'It won't leak in your pocket and make you pregnant.'
8. A US T-shirt maker printed shirts for the Spanish market to promote the Pope's visit. Instead of the intended 'I Saw the Pope' in Spanish, the shirts proclaimed 'I Saw the Potato.'
9. In Italy, a campaign by a major company to sell 'Tonic Water' translated the name as 'Toilet Water'.
10. A tourist agency in Japan was mystified when it entered English-speaking markets and began receiving requests for unusual sex tours. Upon finding out why, the owners of the Kinki Nippon Tourist Company changed the agency's name.

3. Awkward and unnatural syntax and sentence construction, often based on the syntax of the source language.

4. Lack of awareness of the registers of a language, a mixture of slang and very formal language.

Such obvious errors are caused by a lack of knowledge of the target language and also a lack of awareness of the complex process of translation, which must involve a consideration of the following issues.

Issues of Translation

Translation can never recreate a text that is totally equivalent to the original text in the source language. Languages are all different in form, structure, sound, accent, and lexical resources. Languages tend to perceive and categorize reality in different ways. Thus, a word or phrase in one language is not always exactly equivalent in meaning or does not produce the same effect on a reader as a corresponding word or phrase in another language. According to the Italian proverb *'traduttore traditore'* – the translator is a traitor. A translation may be an improvement on the original, if the latter is badly written. More often, something is lost in translation, either meaning or form.

Translation must involve contextual equivalence as well as, and sometimes instead of, word-for-word equivalence. Languages have words that are not translatable into other languages except by roundabout expressions. Languages have different ways of expressing concepts, especially abstract concepts like feelings. Different languages have different metaphors, and these cannot always be translated literally. Some languages are rich in figurative expressions: some languages belong to non-technological societies and draw much of their imagery from nature. The translator must consider not only the meaning of each individual word as the author intended, but the meaning of sentences, paragraphs, and the text as a whole.

Even where there is apparent one-to-one equivalence between words, the translator must be careful. The equivalent word in the target language may have different connotations or shades of meaning, or a wider semantic load. A similar or identical word in a closely related language may be a *'faux ami'*, not meaning exactly the same.

Rapid developments in science and technology during the latter half of the 20th century have led to the need to create appropriate terminology in these fields in many languages. In these areas, exact word-for-word equivalence between terms in different languages is crucial, and could, in some cases, be a matter of life and death. In education, translation of textbooks into many vernacular and minority languages has necessitated the creation of appropriate and unambiguous terminology in these languages. Other fields where accurate correspondence between terminology in various languages is important are international legislation and medicine. Terminology creation and standardization in Catalonia are discussed on page 243.

A good translation should not read like a translation, or, to use a common expression amongst translators, it should not be 'translationese'. The particular qualities or attributes of the target language should be respected and adhered to, such as word order, grammar and syntax, particular idioms, length of sentences, type of imagery. One example of this is between English and Welsh. In many places where English uses nouns, Welsh uses verb-nouns. Another example is that German tends to have longer sentences than in English, and these often have to be split up into shorter sentences in translation. This is achieved partly by the skill of the translator, and an excellent grasp of the target language. It is also achieved by checking and revising the translation, so any influence of the source language in syntax or expression may be detected.

Faux amis

French and English have many words derived from the same source (often Latin). Many of these words still appear very similar, but in fact their meanings are different.

It is important that a person translating from French into English or from English into French has a good enough grasp of both languages to translate these words correctly.

French	English	NOT
demander	ask	demand
sensible	sensitive	sensible
phrase	sentence	phrase
résumer	summarize	resume
contrôler	verify, check	control
affronter	to brave, confront	affront
dérider	to smooth, unwrinkle	deride
attirer	attract, draw towards	attire
achever	complete	achieve
fastidieux	boring, dull	fastidious

In translation there is a tension between the need to convey meaning accurately, and the need to convey the style and 'feel' of the source language text. Meaning has to take precedence over style. However, the extent to which this happens depends on the type of text being translated. Newmark (1993) divides material to be translated into three broad categories.

First, informative texts. Some types of translation involve the transmitting of factual information. These might include technical and scientific texts, instruction manuals, medical reports. Here the priority is to transmit the message accurately. The type of language used is not so important and may be paraphrased or condensed. The accent is on the correct terminology and the accurate conveyance of meaning.

Second, persuasive texts. These might include political speeches, advertising and publicity material. Here the emphasis is on either conveying the cultural and social background of the source text in a meaningful way in the translation, or on translating cultural and social allusions into their equivalents in the culture of the target language.

Third, creative/expressive texts e.g. creative literature. In poetry and creative prose, the medium is as important as the message, and is intertwined with the message.The translator must strike a balance between accurately transmitting what the author is saying, and conveying the style, aesthetic qualities and emotions of the source text. This is particularly important with poetry, where the translator will tend to keep to the same form as the original e.g. sonnet, *vers libre*, pentameter, and also maintain as far as possible any other stylistic features, such as alliteration, assonance, onomatopoeia and internal rhyme. This will inevitably be at the expense of a 'literal' translation.

In the case of prose translations, the translator may attempt to imitate the style of the source text. If a novel is written in a long-winded, complicated style, with lengthy, convoluted sentences, the translator may seek to imitate the style, instead of breaking the translation into shorter, simpler sentences that might convey meaning to the readers more directly. The translator may attempt to convey stylistic features such as puns and word play. If the source text is written in a certain dialect or register of language, the translator may try to translate into an equivalent type of dialect or a corresponding register in the target language.

In certain cases the translator of creative literature may translate in a more literal fashion, in order to convey the cultural 'feel' of the source text. The translator may translate metaphors and idioms literally, instead of searching for smooth equivalents in the target language. Aspects of the source language syntax may be maintained e.g. word order. This may be done deliberately to convey a feeling of 'foreignness', 'strangeness' or 'archaism'.

At other times, the translator may search for meaningful, contemporary equivalents in the target language. This may have the disadvantage of distancing the text from its cultural background: the advantage is that the meaning is more accessible to the average reader.

In popular translations of the Bible, for instance, modern translators have tended to sacrifice cultural allusions and Biblical metaphors and imagery for the sake of clarity and intelligibility.

Newmark (1993) makes a distinction between 'communicative' and 'semantic' translation. Briefly, communicative translation is freer, less literal, and attempts to produce the same effect on the target language readers as the readers of the source language. Semantic translation attempts, within the constraints of the target languages, to reproduce the precise contextual meaning of the author. Both types of translation may overlap in the same text.

The target audience must always be kept in mind. This will govern the choice of language, the presentation and the level at which the language is aimed. To give one example, many speakers of minority languages tend to speak in a simpler, more direct or concrete fashion than speakers of the major Western languages. They do not possess the formal, rather abstract registers of English used in many official documents. (Many people would think that this is a good thing!) A translator translating a public information pamphlet from English into a minority language may simplify or paraphrase the material in order to ensure that it is intelligible to the target audience. Sometimes the text may be pre-edited in English before being given to a translator. This happens in New Zealand, where official documents are translated into Maori and into other Polynesian languages. For example 'If citizenship is obtained by fraud, false representation, or the concealment of an important fact' becomes 'If a person obtains New Zealand citizenship by means of a trick, or by telling a lie, or by concealing an important fact'. This pre-editing method produces successful results in the final translation, whereas Polynesian translations from the original English texts are often almost unintelligible.

Sometimes, in an academic translation of a literary text, the translator may adhere closely to the style of the original and attempt as literal a rendering as possible. (This

Subtitling for Film and Television

A German language documentary program shown in France with French subtitles.

During recent years, television has become an increasingly important medium of entertainment, information and education. There is a growing choice of programs and an increasing flow of information as a result of developments in technology such as teletext, cable and satellite. These have also led to an international market for programs to fill broadcasting hours.

Language transfer by means of dubbing or subtitling means that films and television programs can be made accessible to audiences in other countries. It also means that programs produced in lesser used languages can reach a wider audience and thus increase their commercial viability.

Dubbing has traditionally been the more widely used means of language transfer in films because it is more 'naturalistic' and means that the audience does not have to listen to the unfamiliar sound of a foreign language. However, dubbing is an expensive and complex process, involving creative adaptation rather than translation of the script so that it synchronizes as closely as possible with the lip movements of the actors in the source language. Actors must then be used to interpret the target language script.

Subtitling has the advantage that it costs less than dubbing, and has become cheaper because of advances in technology. Luyken et al. (1991) estimated that subtitling only costs seven percent of the equivalent dubbing cost for one hour of language-transferred TV program.

Subtitling is more advantageous for acquiring other languages, because the viewer can hear the original language and may understand it to some extent with the help of subtitles and from contextual clues. The good command of English possessed by many Scandinavians is aided by the fact that so many English language television programs are shown with subtitles. Only small children's programs are routinely dubbed.

The technique of interlingual subtitling involves three separate processes. Information is transferred from one language to another, the text is adapted and abbreviated, and the spoken language is changed into written language. The source text must be considerably compressed for a number of reasons.

1. The space for text on the screen is limited.

2. Subtitles must be clear and big enough to be legible. In some countries like UK there are regulations governing the type of subtitles used, and the space allotted to them on the screen.

3. Sufficient time must be given for the subtitles to be read. Subtitles are usually presented at between 90 and 120 words per minute, whereas speech is generally delivered at between about 140 and 180 words per minute.

4. The subtitles must be synchronized with the camera shots.

These constraints mean that subtitling is a creative and often a very selective process. However, those who criticize the use of subtitles because they 'come between' the audience and the original artistic purpose of the film maker, ignore the fact that all translation involves a greater or lesser degree of subjective and individual interpretation on the part of the translator.

The advantage of subtitling over other forms of translation is that in films and television, communication occurs by both verbal and non-verbal routes. The actions, gestures and facial expressions of the actors, the context of the action, the music and sound effects, all contribute to the transfer of information. The dialogue in the source language, which may be understood to some degree, can reinforce the viewer's understanding. Even if the viewer has no comprehension of the source language, clues such as tone and pitch and emphasis of voice may add to the message of the subtitles.

The transfer from the spoken to the written language may cause some problems. Swear words and other 'taboo' words, some colloquial names, idioms and expressions may be acceptable in speech but can cause offense in the written language. The subtitler has to choose an acceptable equivalent in the target language. The subtitler also has to interpret cultural references, idioms, swear words and puns in a concise and meaningful manner.

There is no doubt that regular watching of subtitled foreign language programs can aid the acquisition of a second language. The viewer becomes accustomed to the sound of the language and may gradually improve his or her comprehension of the language with the aid of the subtitles and other visual and aural clues.

REFERENCES: LUYKEN *et al.,* 1991; ROFFE, 1995

may be called a linguistic translation). In a popular translation of the same text, the translator may paraphrase, modernize and sacrifice literal accuracy to produce a smoother, more easily intelligible version for a general readership.

The translator must be aware of the cultural context of the source language text, and be able to convey the meaning of this in the translation. This might include literary or cultural allusions (e.g. to be or not to be, the birds and the bees), or references to people and places and things, especially if little known or esoteric (e.g. The Iron Lady to describe Margaret Thatcher, Buck House instead of Buckingham Palace, the film title 'Britannia Mews' – referring to a London street but famously mistranslated and advertised in Belgium as *'La Grande Bretagne Miaule'* (Britain mews like a cat)). It might include ephemeral or recently coined expressions e.g. 'Cabinet Wets' (a British reference to Conservative Ministers during Margaret Thatcher's Premiership who did not subscribe to her hard-line views). It might include terms for governmental organizations, political parties and administrative units, for which there is no equivalent in the target language. The translator must be able to understand these allusions and explain them in the target language.

In some types of translation the translator may choose to convert the cultural context into an equivalent cultural context in the target language. This might be the case with a children's novel, where the storyline is important, and where an unfamiliar cultural context might come between the young reader and enjoyment of the plot. This is called a cultural translation and it is a kind of adaptation.

Similarly, companies who are trying to market a product in a foreign country will ask their translators to adapt the sales and publicity literature and the advertisement campaign to the context of the target culture. It is important that a product is not marketed in a way that might be culturally strange or offensive in the target country. One example is the French fizzy drink *Pschitt* – the name sounds very unappetizing to native speakers of English! Where a text is being translated for marketing or publicity purposes, a copy of the translation will be sent to the target country, for 'localization', i.e. to be checked by other native speakers that the cultural details would be acceptable and attractive to buyers or clients in the target country. (See Translation Blunders, page 236.)

Cultural allusions may often be an integral part of the localization or historicity of a text. Modern translators of the Bible, for instance, tend to change Biblical metaphor and imagery into forms that are meaningful for the target audience. This is essential, since the Bible is a religious text that should speak in a clear, unambiguous and relevant fashion to Christians in each generation and in each country of the world. To give one example, the Greek (and Biblical) expression 'to gird up the loins of one's mind' refers to the custom in the ancient world of hitching up one's tunic in preparation to do battle. This allusion is meaningless to most people in the modern world, so a simple translation such as 'to get ready in one's thinking: to prepare oneself mentally' is an appropriate alternative.

However, it would be incorrect to divorce the Bible from the specific historical context in which it is rooted. For instance, the description of Palm Sunday that occurs in Matthew 21:8 might be misunderstood in West Africa, where to cast branches in front of an approaching chief or ruler is a way of insulting him. However, the translator does not have the option of changing the concrete historical event, but must include a footnote or other translation to explain the allusion.

Other constraints may govern the translator's choice of language. A translation may be prepared for reading aloud, and the sound of words and possible aural ambiguities will be a major consideration. If the script of a film is being translated for dubbing or subtitling, a close translation will not be possible. In the case of dubbing, the script must be adapted to synchronize with the lip-movements of the characters. Where the process consists of subtitling, the script must generally be edited or reduced to fit the screen, and to be readable within the confines of a single shot (see following Textbox).

Where the original text is badly written, contains misprints or factual errors, or is an example of biased and bigoted writing, the translator must decide whether to alter and improve it, whether to include glosses or footnotes to draw readers' attention to the deficiencies of the original, or whether to leave it as it is. The translator's choice will depend largely on the nature of the text. If the message is more important than the style, the translator may attempt to improve and correct the original to make the message more accurate and easily intelligible to readers. If the style is intrinsic to the piece (e.g. a 19th century Gothic novel) the translator may attempt to convey its particular characteristics in translation while commenting on this in a footnote or preface. If the text to be translated shows bias, bigotry or factual inaccuracies e.g. a historical political speech, the translator will probably want to draw attention to this in a gloss or bracket.

These examples show that translation is not a mechanical process, or an equation, that can be right or wrong. It is a creative process, and the translator must make many

Idiomatic Usage in Language

One way in which the colorful variety and creativity of languages is reflected is in their use of idioms. Idioms are vivid expressions drawn usually from the everyday life and culture of the speakers of a language. Idioms include similes and metaphors, when a fact or a truth or an occurrence or the appearance of something is described in terms of something else. Idioms may be so widely used as to become almost meaningless to their speakers. For instance, when English speakers say 'I slept like a log' they are not usually thinking of a log lying motionless on its side. Nevertheless, every idiom, however, trite it has become, was once an original comment, and when we look at idiomatic usage in other languages from our own we can recapture the freshness and creativity of the expression. These examples from Italian, French, Spanish and Yiddish, together with the corresponding idioms in English, show how speakers of different languages use their own imaginations and draw from their own experiences to describe the world around them colorfully and memorably. The Italian example 'every death of a pope' to express the fact that something hardly ever happens is just one example of how cultural and religious life is reflected in language usage.

English	**Italian**
To eat like a pig.	To eat like a buffalo. *(Mangiare come un bufalo.)*
Don't bite off more than you can chew.	Don't take a step longer than your leg. *(Non fare il passo piu lungo della gamba.)*
Pride goes before a fall.	Pride rode out on horseback and came back on foot. *(La superbia andò a cavallo e tornò a piedi.)*
To go by fits and starts.	To go by hiccups. *(Andare a singhiozzo.)*
Once in a blue moon.	Every death of a pope. *(Ad ogni morte di papa.)*

English	**French**
Don't waste your breath!	Save your saliva! *(Epargne ta salive!)*
To turn up like a bad penny.	To arrive like a hair in the soup. *(Arriver comme un cheveu sur la soupe.)*
Let's get back to the subject.	Let's get back to our sheep. *(Revenons à nos moutons.)*
To pull a long face.	To make a funny nose. *(Faire un drôle de nez.)*
He laughs in your face.	He laughs in your nose. *(Il vous rit au nez.)*
To be knock-kneed.	To have your legs in an X. *(Avoir les jambes en X.)*
Put that in your pipe and smoke it!	Put this in your pocket with your handkerchief on top! *(Mets-le dans ta poche avec ton mouchoir dessus!)*
It's Greek to me!	It's Chinese! *(C'est du chinois!)*

English	**Spanish**
To hit the roof.	To scream at the sky. *(Poner el grito en el cielo.)*
Go fly a kite!	Go fry asparagus! *(Véte a freír esparragos!)*
There's always room for one more.	Where six can eat, seven can eat. *(Donde comen seis, comen siete.)*
To cut off your nose to spite your face.	To throw stones at your own roof. *(Tirar piedras contra su propio tejado.)*
To slam the door in your face.	To slam the door on your nostrils. *(Cerrarle la puerta en las narices.)*
Give him an inch, he'll take a mile.	Give him a hand and he takes a foot. *(Le da la mano y se toma el pie.)*
To be alive and kicking.	To be alive and wagging your tail. *(Estar vivo y coleando.)*
To swear like a trooper.	To toss out toads and snakes. *(Echar sapos y culebras.)*

English	**Yiddish**
Go jump in the lake!	Go whistle in the ocean! *(Gai feifen ahfenyam!)*
You can only do one thing at a time.	You can't dance at two weddings at the same time. *(Me ken nit tantzen auf tsvai chassenes mit ain mol.)*
He's as slow as molasses.	He creeps like a bedbug. *(Er kricht vi a vantz.)*
He repeats himself.	He grinds ground flour. *(Er molt gemolen mel.)*
Where there's smoke, there's fire.	When bells ring, it's usually a holiday. *(Az es klingt, iz misstomeh chogeh.)*
He makes a lot of trouble for me.	He makes my wedding black. *(Er macht mir a shvartzeh chasseneh.)*
Go fight City Hall.	Go fight with God. *(Shlog zich mit Got arum.)*
Thanks for nothing.	Many thanks in your belly button. *(A shainem dank dir ir pupik.)*

Various European languages use different idioms to describe children who are born to wealth and privilege. English people say 'they were born with a silver spoon in their mouths'. In Spanish, babies are born with 'bread under their feet', 'born on their feet' and even 'born with a flower in their bottoms'. The French say 'he was born with his hair nicely arranged'. This refers to the fact that some babies are born with part of the amniotic sac over their heads, which used to be considered a sign of good fortune. Similarly, the Greeks say 'born in a bag' while the Italians say 'born with a shirt on'.

In many languages there is a metaphorical use of color. English speakers say that someone goes green with envy, while in French you turn yellow. In English people can go red with anger, but the French turn blue, while Germans and Italians turn black. English tell blue jokes while Spanish speakers tell green jokes. Italians are green when they are short of cash, while Swedes are green when they are wealthy and English speakers are green when they are inexperienced!

Languages also use animals for terms of either endearment or abuse. In Japan, describing a woman as a crane compliments her beauty, while in France it means she is a prostitute. A cow in English means an unpleasant woman, while in Italy it means a prostitute. In Welsh, an unpleasant woman is often described a wood-pigeon. In English, calling someone a fox can indicate that they are crafty or sly, but in German it means that you smell. (SOURCE: *The European Magazine*.)

choices. For this reason, Newmark (1993) recommends that all translators should always write a preface to their translations, explaining the choices they have made and the reasons for these choices.

Since there is a strong subjective element in translation it is not easy to measure the accuracy of a translation. Apart from obvious examples of bad translation, mistranslation, and translationese, there is no one yardstick against which the effectiveness of a translation can be measured. One possible method of determining the standard of a translation is to translate back into the source language and compare the two source language versions. Another method is to test the accuracy of an information translation by asking speakers of the source language and of the target language factual questions about the text. These kinds of tests do not measure aspects of the translation such as style, succinctness and choice of vocabulary. Basically, the success of a translation depends on how effectively the translator has assessed the purpose of the translation, the relationship between content and style and the needs of the potential readers.

Interpreting

Although the term 'translation' can refer to both written and verbal translation, 'interpreting' is often used to describe the latter. Along with the increase in the demand for written translation in the modern world, there has been a corresponding increase in the need for interpreters, by international organizations, diplomats and ambassadors, politicians, mediators, the armed forces and international business.

Many translators either choose to specialize in written translation, or in interpretation, although in some situations e.g. minority languages, a translator may have to do both. It has been said that written translators tend to be introverts and interpreters tend to be extroverts!

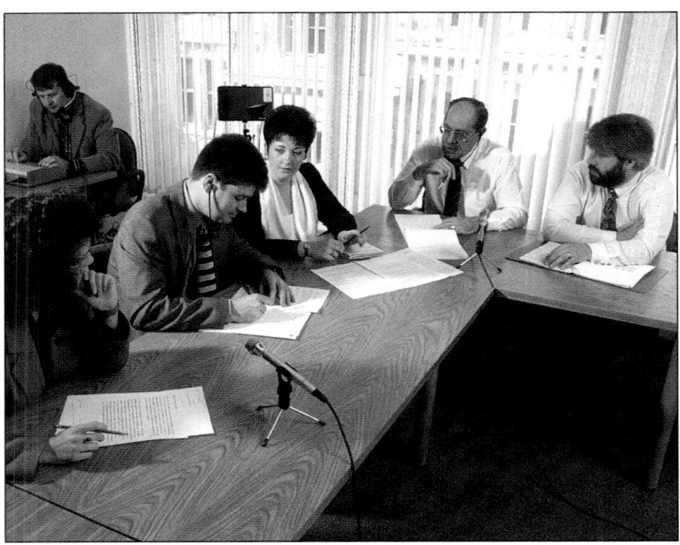

Simultaneous translation at a meeting.

There are two methods of oral interpretation. The first, consecutive interpretation, has always been used. Here, the interpreter translates after the speaker has finished speaking, either after each sentence or two or at the end of the speech. This type of interpretation tends to be very accurate, especially if the speaker makes allowances for the consecutive interpretation, speaking slowly and making frequent pauses.

The second, simultaneous interpretation, has now superseded consecutive interpretation to a large extent in formal situations and large meetings. Simultaneous interpretation has been made possible by the development of modern audiological equipment.

The simultaneous interpreter sits in a soundproof glass booth, screened from the audience but able to see the speaker. The speaker's microphone is wired to the translator's headphones. The translator listens to the speaker's words and begins to translate them into the target language into the microphone. The translation is relayed by transmitter to the individual headphones of those members of the audience who wish to follow the speaker in the target language. In international gatherings e.g. the European Parliament in Brussels, where translation is required into and from several languages, numerous translators will be present, each working in an individual booth.

Simultaneous translation is a remarkable feat that reveals the complexity and the linguistic capabilities of the human brain. The translator is required to listen to and comprehend the utterances of the speaker, while beginning to form a mental translation which will not be complete until the speaker completes the utterance. The translator then speaks the translation while at the same time listening to the next phrase or sentence, remembering it and mentally preparing an acceptable translation in the target language.

This becomes a particularly difficult task if the speaker's utterances are long and complex, because the complete utterance may have to listened to, remembered and analyzed before a translation can be attempted. Languages differ in their word order. In German the verb often comes at the end of a clause, in Welsh the verb nearly always precedes the subject, in Welsh, French and Spanish adjectives generally follow the noun. This can cause problems for the person translating from these languages into English. In many languages the whole structure and mode of expression may be radically different

TERMCAT: The Catalan Terminology Center

Modern terminology is constantly being, updated, revised and expanded, to cope with rapid changes in fields such as science, technology, medicine, law, politics, education, business and administration. Because the pace of change is so swift, traditional published dictionaries would be out of date almost before publication. For this reason modern terminology is often stored in computer databases known as term banks, where retrieval and updating of information is swift and convenient.

It is vitally important there should be clear word-for-word equivalences between specialized terminology in different languages, to ensure accurate and unambiguous translation.

In Catalonia, a province of Spain, the Catalan language enjoys equal official status with Spanish. After efforts were made to banish it during Franco's regime, it is now actively promoted in education and public life. In Barcelona, the capital city of the province, the Catalan Terminology Center, TERMCAT, was founded in 1985, under the auspices of the regional government's Department of Culture and the Institute of Catalan Studies.

TERMCAT has three main aims. Firstly, its staff engage in terminology creation, standardization and revision. Secondly, it is responsible for the storage of terminology on database. The data bank comprises Catalan terms with their concept definitions, along with equivalents in several other European languages, including French, Spanish, Italian and English. Thirdly, TERMCAT disseminates information about terminology in various ways. It publishes printed terminology lists and checks and revises those published by other bodies e.g. industry. It answers telephone enquiries about terminology. It revises technical texts and gives advice to authors. It advises on translation courses at universities, as the study of terminology is now an essential part of such courses. Its documentation center is much used. It also gives advice on the linguistic principles involved in terminology creation.

The Generalitat (regional government) is committed to the promotion of Catalan as the normal daily language of Catalonia, in education, public and official life. It is also committed to the maintenance of Castilian as the second official language of Catalonia. This bilingual policy means that translation is an important facet of life. TERMCAT provides the terminology required for technical, educational, scientific, industrial and administrative translation.

Some recent TERMCAT publications.

from English. It may be impossible to start translating in the middle of an utterance.

Studies have shown that an input speed of between 100 and 120 words per minute is a comfortable rate for interpreting, with an upper limit of 200 words per minute. When the input language is uncomplicated, the interpreter will be about two to three seconds behind the speaker. Where there is a complication, several seconds may elapse between hearing and speaking. This will affect the accuracy of the translation.

Interpreting, particularly simultaneous interpreting, is the art of the possible. It aims to convey the gist or essentials of what is being said, by paraphrasing, editing and condensing the speaker's words. Various methods can be used to help the interpreter. Speakers using prepared notes or a typescript may give the interpreter a copy in advance. Interpreters will read up about the topic they are translating and have a vocabulary list prepared. Speakers from the floor may wish to brief interpreters before a meeting concerning the topics they are likely to raise.

Successful simultaneous interpreting depends to an extent on the ability of the speakers in the source language to pace the delivery and adjust the complexity of what they say. More research needs to be done on ways of making simultaneous interpreting more effective.

Machine Translation

Machine Translation can be defined as automatic translation performed by a computer with or without human assistance. It must be distinguished from computerized terminology banks, word processors and other machine aids for translation (but where the actual translating is done by a person).

MT was first thought of in the 1930s, but in the years following World War II, the opportunity arose to turn the idea into reality. The rise of information theory, the success of advanced code-breaking techniques and the invention of the electronic computer, all made the concept of MT appear feasible. Several groups began research programs in the 1950s and there was great optimism that a high quality automatic translation would soon be possible.

The initial results were very disappointing, however. The limitations of the system soon became apparent. The type of material they could handle was limited. The translations produced were crude and full of errors. So much post-editing was required to make them comprehensible that it was more expensive than a translator doing the whole job. The problem was that the MT programs could not cope with the level of language analysis required to recognize and analyze the input in the source language and transform it into comprehensible output in the target language. They were little more than automatic bilingual dictionaries offering word-for-word equivalences. They were not able to deal with the different ways in which languages structure meaning, the different senses of words and idioms, and the different levels of syntactic organization.

In 1966, the Automatic Language Processing Advisory Committee published a report in which it declared that human translating was faster, cheaper and more accurate than MT, and that funding for the MT program should be withdrawn. Consequently, little MT research was carried out in the US and Europe until the 1970s (although research continued in the USSR). By the 1970s, however, developments in technology, computing and linguistic theory made MT once more a possibility. There were also more realistic expectations about the potential and limitations of MT. There was a realization that, rather than replacing human translators, MT would have to be used in collaboration with them.

Modern MT systems are often operated in conjunction with human pre-editing and/or post-editing. In pre-editing, the source text is altered before machine translation. Parts of speech may be marked, the boundaries of clauses or expressions may be indicated, ambiguities may be removed, sentences may be simplified. Although this may be a lengthy process, it may be cost-effective, especially if the text is to be translated into several languages. In post-editing, the raw machine translation is revised to make it acceptable and easily intelligible.

Sometimes there is little or no need for editing of the machine translation, if the text has been specially written according to clear guidelines and for a limited function. The MT system METEO (Canada) has translated Canada's weather forecasts into French since 1977, so successfully that over 80 percent of the output does not have to be post-edited.

Raw (unedited) machine translation may be used as an 'indicative' translation. An indicative translation need not conform to the target language grammar and need to not be of publication quality. It may be used by readers to get an idea of the content of the source text, before they decide whether to request a human translation. Indicative translations from Russian to English have been produced for years and are still used by the US Airforce.

As developments continue in the field of artificial intelligence, Machine Translation has become more refined and sophisticated and wider in scope. It has also become accessible to users of PCs. A wider range of programs are available, ranging from sophisticated, context-sensitive translation programs, for professional translators, to lexicons of stock phrases, expressions, idioms and words, which can be helpful, for instance, for the office secretary who wishes to translate business letters.

It is difficult to believe that MT could ever replace human translators. A computer could never match the versatility and ingenuity of human language, nor make the myriad of subtle and creative choices that the human translator makes when transforming a text from one language to another. However, a machine translation, even in collaboration with human editing, is much faster and cheaper than having a person do the whole task, and is adequate for a variety of technical texts. MT has proved that 'informative' translation' need not be perfect in style and syntax, providing the information (facts, figures, etc.) is accurate. There has been a greatly increased take up of raw machine translation in recent years, proving that 'elegance of translation' has to be weighed against speed, accessibility and economy.

Further Reading

NEWMARK, P., 1981, *Approaches to Translation*. Oxford: Pergamon Press.

NEWMARK, P., 1993, *About Translation*. Clevedon: Multilingual Matters Ltd.

O'HAGAN, M., 1996, *The Coming Industry of Teletranslation*. Clevedon Multilingual Matters Ltd.

PICKEN, C., 1983, *The Translator's Handbook*. London: Aslib.

SAMUELSSON-BROWN, G., 1993, *A Practical Guide for Translators*. Clevedon: Multilingual Matters Ltd.

4: Religion and Bilingualism

Sacred and Secular Languages

Religions such as Islam and Judaism have a sacred, historic language. Thus in Islam, the use of Arabic is sacred in praying and reading the Qur'an. It is considered important for Muslims to read the Qur'an in the original Arabic so that the original teachings do not become distorted by translation. Similarly, holy writings in Judaism and Hinduism stress that the language of the original text is sacred in itself. In contrast Buddhism and Christianity have often promoted the vernacular (as in the many translations of the Christian Bible).

In Judaism, Hebrew has traditionally been the sacred language of liturgy in the synagogue and praying. However, in both Islam and Judaism, there are exceptions to the prominence of Arabic and Hebrew as religious languages. For example, the Qur'ān is available in English so that new converts and potential converts in English-speaking countries can be aware of the wisdom of the Qur'ān. The Qur'ān is often used in mosques with a translation into the vernacular language (e.g. Gujarati, Pashto, Urdu), so that worshipers can follow the text. In Reformed synagogues, the vernacular language has often been promoted for public worship. Public readings of the scriptures continue to be carried out in Hebrew but with translations often accompanying or following that reading.

While the language of the mosque and the synagogue may be the sacred language, many people who attend may use a different language outside of their religion. Many of those who use Hebrew in the synagogue speak another language outside. Similarly, many Muslims use Arabic inside the mosque but speak one or more local languages outside. In Arabic-speaking Muslim countries, the classical Arabic of the mosque is different from the colloquial Arabic of daily life, and Modern Standard Arabic used in education, written communication and the mass media. For many such bilinguals, this is an example of relatively stable diglossia where the boundaries between the religious language and other language domains are kept stable and separate. Hence, the status and function of those languages is maintained. Such language compartmentalization (i.e. not allowing any other language than Hebrew inside a synagogue or Arabic inside a mosque) maintains the status and function of the sacred language, and provides some unity and continuity in religion.

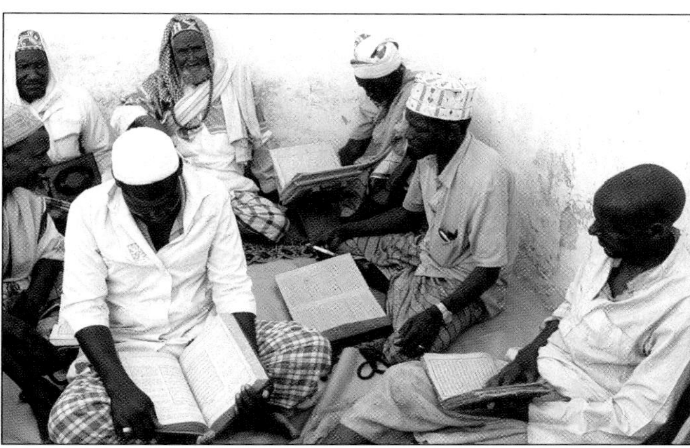

Men reading the Qur'ān in Mogadishu, Somalia. Most Somalis are Muslims and speak Somali as their native language but learn to read classical Arabic for religious purposes.

For some of those who use Hebrew in the synagogue and for some of those who use Arabic in the mosque, their understanding of those languages may be limited to religious domains. Such worshipers will not understand Hebrew or Arabic outside the confines of religious observance. Thus their bilingualism may be limited. For example, there are many Malaysians who are devout Muslims and use Arabic in the mosque. Yet their understanding of Arabic is limited.

In previous centuries, the language of religion was often the language of everyday existence. The Hebrew of the synagogue and the Arabic of the Mosque was little different from the language of daily communication. Over time, the language of religion tended to stay much the same, while daily languages shifted. For example, the Roman Catholic Church retained Latin as its language of worship until this century even though Latin has not been a language of everyday communication for over a thousand years, and has not been used in official life in Europe for several centuries.

Hinduism also has a sacred language. For Hindus, their scriptures are written in Sanskrit. The main body of classical Sanskrit literature consists of the *Vedas*, sacred Hindu writings from about 1400 to 1200 BC; the commentaries on the *Vedas* in the *'Brahmanas'*, the *'Aranyakas'*, and the *'Upanishads'* (1000 to 500 BC); the epic and wisdom literature (400 BC to AD 1000); and poetry in a style called *kavya* (AD 200 to 1200). Vedic

A Rabbi holds the Torah (sacred Hebrew scriptures). Throughout the centuries, Jews scattered throughout the world have spoken a variety of languages, but have continued to use classical Hebrew as the language of religious worship.

Sanskrit, the language used in the *Vedas,* is the earliest form of Sanskrit. A later variety of the language, classical Sanskrit (from about 500 BC), was a language of many literary texts. It is still studied in India and functions as a sacred and learned language. However, very few families use Sanskrit as a first language.

In Hinduism, Sanskrit is the language of ritualistic chants, litanies and mantras (prayers, words of power). For example, Hindus may start their ritual prayers at home in front of the altar by saying prescribed Sanskrit prayers alongside ritualistic observances (e.g. offering flowers to a specific deity at the altar). Near the end of this time of worship, Hindus may speak to God in their preferred language (e.g. Tamil, Bengali, Hindi, Malayalam). Hindus also have conversations with God (prayers) away from the temple or home altar (e.g. in a car). This will tend to be in the home language, except when repeating mantras or the name of the deity. Thus, formal and historic elements of prayer are often in Sanskrit; informal prayer may be in the home language.

In the Hindu temple, there is often a similar separation in use of languages. A priest and his helpers will clean the inner sanctum and statues of the temple. While doing this, they may talk to each other in the local language as will onlookers. When the service (*pooja*) begins, the priest will switch to Sanskrit to chant the prayers. Sanskrit will also be used for prayers (*archanei*) requested by individuals. Once the rituals are complete, the priest will converse with devotees in the local language(s).

Other religions also have important language traditions. The Ethiopian church uses Ge'ez for religious purposes. Ge'ez is an archaic form of the modern official language of Ethiopia, Amharic. In contrast, the Quakers have valued the inner language of silence, as do some meditational forms in Buddhism. Buddhist sacred literature is comprised of a vast body of texts that were transmitted both orally and in written form and have been preserved principally in four languages: Pali, Sanskrit, Chinese, and Tibetan. Pali, the language of the Buddhist canonical writings, is the oldest literary *Prakrit*. It remains in liturgical use in Sri Lanka, Burma and Thailand. The sacred teachings of Sikhism are recorded in Panjabi in the Gurmukhi script.

Zoroastrianism, an ancient monotheistic religion, has religious texts known as *Avesta* which were originally

Languages: Babel or Blessing?

In many religions, there are explanations for the multiplicity of languages in the world. For example, in the myth of the tower of Babel (similar to myths in other religions), the existence of so many languages in the world is ascribed to people's pride. God is seen to confound people's pride by dispersing them throughout the world and causing them to speak mutually unintelligible languages. Thus, the existence of language diversity is expressed as a result of sin.

In the Christian *New Testament*, there is a contrast to the myth of Babel. When Jesus was nailed to the cross, the inscription was written in Hebrew, Greek and Latin. 'Pilate also wrote a title and put it on the cross; it read, "Jesus of Nazareth, the King of the Jews". Many of the Jews read this title, for the place where Jesus was crucified was near the city; and it was written in Hebrew, in Latin and in Greek' (*Gospel of St. John*, Chapter 19, verses 19 & 20). Trilingualism was celebrated. Then, among the early Christians, one of the gifts of God, given at Pentecost, was the ability to speak in different languages.

documented in a form of ancient Persian. After the Parsis (descendants of the original Zoroastrians) fled from Iran in the 10th century and settled in India, the *Avesta* were translated into Sanskrit and parts are still extant. Thus, in present Zoroastrianism, the language of prayers, hymns and texts is Sanskrit. However, such Sanskrit is memorized and not often understood. The language of conversation for the many Zoroastrians living around Bombay is Gujarati.

The use of a sacred language creates a boundary between the sacred and profane. The language of religion sets apart the pious and the worldly. A separate language for religion may also help produce a holy, other-worldly atmosphere. Use of a sacred language and not the language of the street and screen may make religious liturgy and ceremony all the more evocative and ethereal. Yet at the same time, that sacred language may not be readily understandable, except through special classes for children and adults.

A similar contrast has been witnessed in the Roman Catholic church this century. With Latin traditionally the exalted liturgical language, there has been a general substitution of Latin by vernacular languages in public worship. What is lost in mystery, history and other worldliness may be gained by the homeliness, meaningfulness and modernity of the vernacular language.

Reading from Guru Granth Sahib, the sacred book of the Sikh religion, at a Sikh Gurdwara (temple) in London.

Missionary Work and Bilingualism

Christian missionaries and evangelists throughout the centuries have emphasized the importance of preaching to people in a language they can understand. This has often involved the missionaries learning local languages, and communicating religious truths and basic literacy and other skills to indigenous peoples in their own native tongue. Nineteenth century missionaries in New Zealand, for instance, established schools for Maori people where the instruction was mainly in Maori. In many situations, missionaries have translated religious texts into a vernacular literacy, so that the indigenous language was maintained.

However, just as often missionary work in the colonial period has meant the transmission of a colonizing language (e.g. English, French, Spanish), along with religion. Such missionaries shared the imperialist ideals of other colonizers. They viewed their own language as the language of a superior civilization, as opposed to the 'inferior', 'primitive' language and culture of the natives. They taught children of the local population the majority language and cultural practices as a means of not only converting them to a religion but also of civilizing them. In these situations, religion created bilingualism or increased multilingualism, but also reinforced the inequalities of power and status between the natives and the colonizers.

In the post-colonial era, missionary activity has tended to make use of indigenous languages and cultural practices. It has become standard for missionaries to learn the language of an area either before leaving their home country or as soon as possible after arriving in foreign lands. Part of missionary activity in the 20th century has been to translate the Bible into as many languages and dialects of the world as possible. Some Protestant sects, in hymns and sermons, deliberately use modern, colloquial language, partly to appeal to those preferring a less detached and more contemporary and relevant style of worship.

Russian Orthodox and Greek Orthodox churches have often retained a traditional service couched in an historic liturgical language. Yet, when wishing to convert others to their religion, they will switch to the vernacular. One example is St. Stefan of Perm, a 14th century Russian Orthodox bishop, and a native speaker of the Komi language. Instead of using Russian with the Komi people, he made extensive use of their language in his missionary activity. He preached in Komi, translated the Russian Orthodox liturgy into Komi, used Komi in church worship, and was so successful that the majority of the Komi were baptized into the Russian Orthodox faith. In contrast, the Anglican church in Ireland and Wales resisted using the native Irish and Welsh languages in their evangelizing and were relatively unsuccessful in winning converts.

Religion and the Maintenance of Minority Languages and Ethnic Identities

Religious practice can help maintain a separate ethnic or group identity, partly through use of the vernacular language. In Wales, for example, the translation of the

Jerusalem

There are few cities in the world that can compete with Jerusalem for a richness of history, culture and language. Many visitors to the city experience a fascinating living language mosaic, a rainbow of colors, cultures and languages. It is estimated that inhabitants of Jerusalem come from over a hundred countries of the world and speak more than 70 languages.

Within the city walls, it is possible to experience in quick succession Hebrew and Arabic, Armenian and Greek, Russian and Yiddish, English and Aramaic – the language of Jesus. Language is particularly bound up with religion in Jerusalem.The Hebrew prayers of the Jews at the Western Wall are contrasted with the Arabic prayers of the Muslims at the Dome of the Rock. In the Church of the Holy Sepulchre, the Russian and Greek language of the Orthodox traditions can be heard alongside English, French, German, Japanese, Spanish and many other languages of pilgrims visiting the traditional site of the Cross and the Tomb.

Along the Via Dolorosa, the Arabic of the street traders is contrasted with the multitude of languages of pilgrims moving between the Stations of the Cross. Street signs in Hebrew, Arabic and English are passed by groups of Italians and Irish, Swedes and Spaniards, Americans and Armenians, each using their native tongue for parley and prayer.

The multilingualism of Jerusalem is celebrated for Christians in the Pater Noster Church on the Mount of Olives. The Lord's Prayer is inscribed on the walls in the languages listed.

A selection of images from the walls of the Pater Noster church.

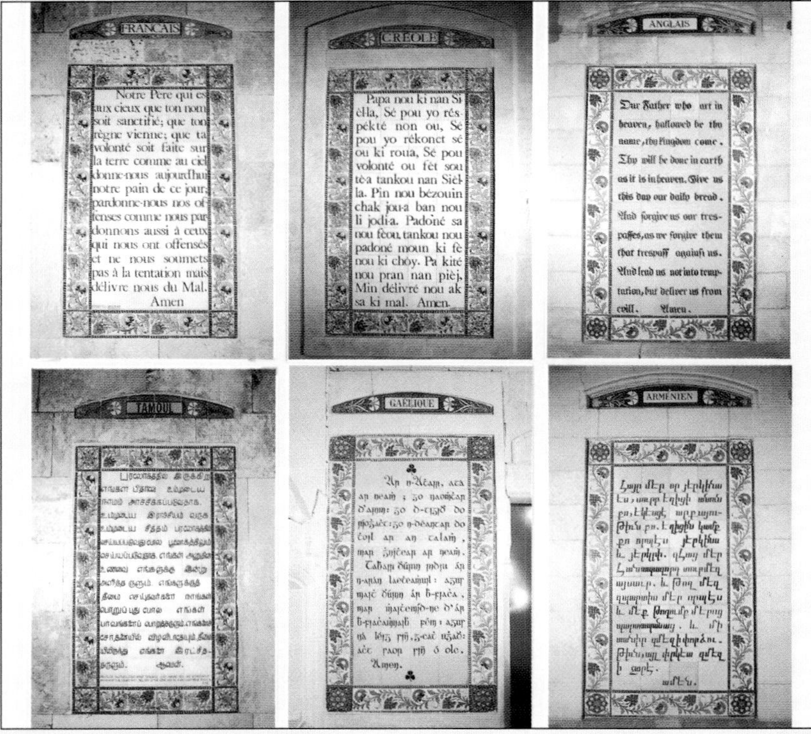

Afrikaans
Amharic
Arabic
Aramaic
Armenian
Asturian

Basque
Bahasa (Melayu)
Bohemian
Breton
Bulgarian

Catalan
Chaldean
Chamorro
Chinese
Coptic
Corsican
Cree
Creole
Croat
Czech

Danish
Dutch

English
Esperanto
Estonian

Fijian
Finnish
Flemish
French
Frisian
Friulian

Gaelic
Galician
Georgian
German
Greek
Gruyerian (dialect of Occitan)
Gujarati

Hebrew
Hungarian

Ilongo
Icelandic
Indonesian
Italian

Japanese

Kimamba
Kinyarwanda
Kirundi
Korean
Kurdish

Ladin
Latin
Latvian
Lingala (Zaire)
Lithuanian
Luganda

Maltese
Mallorquin

Nahuatl (Mexican Indian language)
Nicart (dialect of Provençal)
Norwegian

Occitan
Ojibwa (indigenous North American language)

Papuan
Pampanga (Philippines)
Polish
Portuguese
Provençal
Papiamento

Quechua

Romanian
Russian

Sinhalese
Samaritan
Samoan
Sanskrit
Serbian
Slavonic
Slovak
Slovenian
Sotho
Spanish
Swedish
Syriac

Tagalog
Tahitian
Tamil
Thai
Turkish

Ukrainian

Valencian
Vietnamese

Welsh

Yoruba

Christian Bible into Welsh in 1588 by Bishop William Morgan is said to have saved the Welsh language, which was thus preserved as the language of chapel and church, of prayers and Bible readings in the home. To read the Bible, children and adults needed to become literate in Welsh, adding status and function to the language. Later, in the 18th and 19th centuries, Welsh language Nonconformist denominations became an important marker of Welsh ethnic identity, and a boundary from the colonializing English.

Another example of religion maintaining ethnic identity is the existence of Saturday schools (and schools maintained and run by ethnic minorities) where Jewish or Muslim minorities, for example, teach their children to read and write Hebrew or Arabic, and to study religious texts. Muslims living in non-Muslim countries, for example, often set up extra schooling (and Muslim schools) to teach children Arabic, the Qur'an and Islamic beliefs. Such schooling helps preserve religious continuity and the language of religion and also maintains ethnic identity.

Other examples of religion maintaining a separate ethnic identity include: (1) Roman Catholicism in Quebec, which together with the French language has helped preserve a French Canadian identity; (2) 19th and early 20th century Brittany, where loyalty to Roman Catholicism maintained Breton identity in the face of French secularism.

In some situations of language shift, religion may eventually work against maintenance of the minority language. Christian denominations, especially Protestant denominations, have placed great emphasis on the importance of preaching and evangelizing in a language understood by the people. Once the process of language shift has begun, religious leaders may be forced to assess their priorities, and provide opportunities for worship confession, Bible study and other religious observances in the majority language.

In many historical situations, when a shift towards the majority language initially began, the church provided an institution where the minority language was used and respected. However, over time, as younger people tended to lose fluency in the minority language and became unable to understand sermons in it, the church made increasing use of the majority language. Eventually, the minority language was used seldom or not at all.

Further Reading

CRYSTAL, D., 1997, *The Cambridge Encyclopedia of Language* (Second edition). Cambridge: Cambridge University Press.

SMOLICZ, J. J., 1994, *Australian Diversity* (Second edition). University of Adelaide: Centre for Intercultural Studies and Multicultural Education.

Pennsylvania German and the Amish Community

One example of religion and language preservation working together is the historical survival of Pennsylvania German within the Amish community in the US. The Pennsylvania Germans, sometimes called the Pennsylvania Dutch, came from Germany in the early 18th century. They originally settled in farm communities in south-eastern and central Pennsylvania. Their language is a German dialect related to that spoken in the German Palatinate along the river Rhine. Distinctive in dress, these Protestant Old Order Amish and Old Order Mennonite sectarians still speak their German dialect at home and in the community. English is learnt at school since English is the language of instruction. English is also increasingly spoken as contact with other people and communities has increased. (Huffines, 1991).

Archaic forms of German are used in Protestant religious worship. The language of the community has thus been preserved within the established boundaries of that community. However, particularly among the non-sectarian Pennsylvania Germans, the language is dying (Huffines, 1991). As English replaces the High German used in religious worship, the *raison d'être* for the use of Pennsylvania German in the home and community disappears. Religion has preserved the language. As religious practices change, preservation changes to transformation.

REFERENCE: HUFFINES, 1991

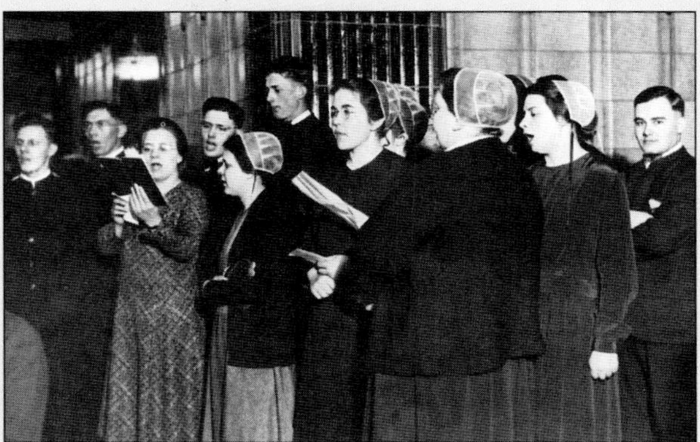

The Amish at worship. Religious practice can help maintain a separate group or ethnic identity.

5: Bilingualism and the Economy

Introduction

This topic explores a paradox among bilinguals. Among language minority groups, there is often unemployment, poverty and low pay. Yet bilinguals have linguistic capital. Bilinguals often have marketable language skills and intercultural knowledge. Bilinguals are often economically impoverished yet linguistically accomplished.

Bilingualism as an Economic Advantage

In an increasingly bilingual and multilingual world, with trade barriers being broken, with single markets in areas such as Europe growing, and with economic competition rapidly developing on a global scale, competence in languages is increasingly important. Those who have multilinguistic capital may be in a position to increase their economic capital.

This immediately raises the question of which languages may be useful for economic advancement? In many countries of the world, it is English as a second or foreign language that has visible economic value. As Coulmas (1992) suggests, 'no Japanese businessman ever tries to operate on the American market without a sufficient command of English, whereas the reverse case, of American business people who expect to be able to do business in Japan without being proficient in Japanese, is not at all rare. On the one hand, this is a reflection of the arrogance of power, but on the other hand, it testifies to the fact that the opportunities for realizing the functional potential of English on the Japanese market are far better than those of realizing the functional potential of Japanese on the American market' (pages 66 & 67). Nevertheless Japanese has increasingly become a desirable modern foreign language, as people realize that to sell to the Japanese requires a knowledge of the Japanese language and culture. As Helmut Schmidt, former chancellor of the old Federal Republic of Germany once said: 'If you wish to buy from us, you can talk any language you like, for we shall try to understand you. If you want to sell to us, then you must speak our language'.

Nomura Securities in Tokyo, Japan. English is widely used throughout the world in business and finance. However, there is a growing realization that success in business requires a knowledge of the customer's language.

Alongside the English language, the Japanese, German, French, Spanish and Portuguese languages have historically been regarded as important trading languages. However, in the future, this list of modern languages for marketing and trading purposes is likely to grow significantly. For example, Bahasa Melayu, Mandarin and Cantonese, Panjabi and Hindi, Arabic and Korean may each become increasingly valuable. This reflects the important half-truth of Coulmas (1992) who suggests that 'in spite of the non-economic values attached to language, what prevails in matters of language is often that which is profitable' (page 152). The other half of the truth is that language is also related to less tangible, measurable and affective characteristics such as the social, cultural and particularly religious value in some language communities for a particular language. The half-truth also hides the tension that can often exist between economic development and cultural reproduction. The economic value of a language may at times clash with preserving that language to reflect heritage, home values and historical traditions. Nevertheless, the economic value of language relates strongly to the prestige of that language and hence its chances of maintenance and reproduction.

If languages are increasingly important in international trading, are they equally important in small and medium-sized businesses as in multinational corporations? In large businesses, as García & Otheguy (1994) reveal, we should be cautious in assuming that a modern foreign language is needed in top executives and top managers. In multinational corporations, for example, the tendency may not be to send executives with modern language qualifications abroad. Rather there will be local nationals within a country, working for that corporation, who are bilingual in both the regional or national language and

A biscuit factory in Dhaka Bangladesh belonging to the multinational company Nabisco. Signs are in Bengali and English.

an international language such as English. United States corporations who run their operations abroad, and multinational organizations, may prefer locally based executives because of their native-like fluency in the national languages, their thorough understanding of the cultures of that region, and their ability to communicate with customers and the work force as well as with international colleagues. Local nationals are often paid a lower salary than executives sent from, for example, the United States.

This indicates that large corporations and multinational companies are increasingly aware that international business requires the use of regional and national languages. The imposition, for example of the English language, will not help to sell products abroad. To sell in Germany, Latin America, Japan, or the Pacific Basin, increasingly requires business people whose language and culture is congruent with that of the buyer. A congruent language is valuable for communication. Sometimes, there may be no other way to conduct trade (e.g. if the buyer does not speak English). Speaking the buyer's language also signals favorable attitudes to the buyer's ethnicity and culture. A competent understanding of the buyer's culture also signals respect for the buyer and their way of doing business.

García & Otheguy (1994) found in their research, that smaller and medium-sized businesses often require executives and managers who are capable of speaking in languages other than English or other majority languages. To have the edge over competitors, the language of business is important, and where it is congruent with the language of the area for business, a competitive edge is added. Those who insist that English should be the international medium of business may be selling themselves short, economically, socially and personally.

This reflects a paradox. While English is often accepted as the international language in multinational companies and international trade, the massive spread of English during this century has led to a reaction, rather like adjusting a balance, with national and regional groups wishing to assert their local identity through a retention of their heritage language and culture. This has occurred in France and England, for example, and in many other European countries. An increased accent on national and regional languages in the face of international trade, has led to buying from those who are willing to speak the language and culture of the region rather than imposing their own language on the buyer. Nevertheless, the competitive edge has often more to do with prices, lowest quotations, and the lowest bid rather than language preference.

Minority Languages

In suggesting that bilingualism has economic advantages, the only languages to be highlighted so far have been majority languages. English, German, French and Arabic, for example, are relatively prestigious majority languages. What is the place of minority languages in the economy? Will bilinguals from language minorities have no economic advantage, no valuable trading language in their minority language, no chance, due to their bilingualism, of getting out of the poverty trap that many experience?

In Europe, for example, the move from regional and state economies to a single European market policy, interlocking business structures in different European countries, encouraging mobility in businesses across European countries, may leave a distinction between core and periphery, between those in important urban business areas and those in rural peripheries (e.g. rural areas in Ireland, Wales and Scotland). Since many indigenous minority languages in Europe are found in regions that are relatively sparsely populated, economically underdeveloped, with poorer rural road and transport systems, there is a danger that there will be growing inequality between core and periphery.

In the economic restructuring that has occurred in the last 60 years, increased competition has led to the need for more efficiency to maintain profit. Industries and services have frequently had to 'automate, emigrate or evaporate'. Emigration of industries has been to countries such as Taiwan, Mexico, Brazil and Singapore, where wages, and therefore production costs, are relatively low. Such outside investment may sometimes offer work and wages to language minority members, but may also have negative consequences for language minorities. Such consequences now need to be discussed.

One negative consequence is that the investment may not reach a language minority. For example, where such minorities live in rural areas (e.g. Irish and Welsh speakers), economic growth may be in the urban 'core' rather than the rural periphery. Alternatively, the higher grade jobs may be in relatively affluent city areas, and the lower grade, poorly paid work in the more remote areas.

A different scenario is when a peripheral area attracts inward investment (e.g. factories are located in remoter areas). The tendency is for the local language minorities to provide relatively cheap workers, while the better paid (language majority) managers either operate from their faraway city headquarters or move into the periphery language community. In both cases (given below), the managers may have a negative effect on language maintenance:

1. By working from city headquarters, there is a geographical separation of majority language manager and minority language proletariat that represents a status, and a social, cultural, economic and power division. Such a division has prestige consequences for the majority and minority language. Each language is identified with greater or lesser affluence, higher and lower status, more or less power.

2. By living in the language minority community, a manager who does not learn the local language evokes a class distinction. The manager speaks the majority language; the workers the minority language. One is a higher socioeconomic class; the other a lower socioeconomic class. There is a social class division, and a separation or fracture within the social class structure of the community (Morris, 1992). Social tensions may result that lead to divisions along both social class and language dimensions. As Morris (1992) found in her research, one solution is language minority managers who are able to operate across social classes inside their language group. Being bilingual, such managers can also operate (e.g. for export purposes) in language majority and core regions.

For language minorities, it seems essential that, through entrepreneurial activity, enterprise and risk-taking, they develop networked small and medium-sized businesses. Such businesses, often located in rural areas, sometimes producing goods for export, sometimes using ease of communications (e.g. via computers) to deliver services, are essential for local languages to be preserved. Language minority businesses need to be networked where possible, within a region and increasingly internationally.

The absence of community-based, ethnically-based businesses, increases the risk of the emigration of more able, more skilled and more entrepreneurial people away from the area, hence leaving the language itself in peril. A language community without economic activity is in danger of starving the language of one essential support mechanism. An economically wealthy language has a higher probability of being a healthy language. An economically impoverished language is placed at risk.

While language communities are not necessarily internally integrated, (having their own inner power and status struggles, differences and divisions), such language communities need to generate their own local economies and to able to market their products and services beyond the region. In Gwynedd, North Wales, for example, there are two examples of economic language planning. First, new businesses located in language minority communities are initially subsidized, professionally advised and developed. Second, many jobs now demand bilingual applicants. The ability to use Welsh and English is regarded as essential for employment in teaching, many administrative jobs, local authority services, secretarial and clerical posts. Thus the Welsh language is given a vital economic foundation.

A Hispanic teenager sells tacos at a US fair. Bilingualism can help at the customer interface.

Some minority language businesses (e.g. local radio and television stations) create language-related economic activity that, in itself, spawns secondary economic activity to support such businesses (e.g. catering services, translation services, music and drama activities).

In many countries of the world, there are examples of language communities who are in-migrant rather than indigenous who, through fast food (e.g. the Chinese restaurants) and the clothes trade (e.g. various Asian groups) maintain their language via ethnic industries. The language is supported by businesses where factory workers, shop workers and managers work partly or mainly through their heritage language.

This raises an issue about those language minorities who are often located in inner-city, urban, in-migrant communities. As already expressed at the start of this section, such families and language communities are often surrounded by poverty, deprivation, unemployment and inequality of opportunity to acquire wealth. García & Otheguy (1994) provide an analysis of the economic possibilities of such urban language communities, particularly in the United States. The ability to speak a minority language can be crucial in gaining access to such an ethnic business. If everyone else in the organization speaks Spanish or Cantonese, to gain employment requires knowledge of that language.

A minority language may also be valuable at the customer interface. García & Otheguy (1994) relate an

The Language Abilities Used among Bilingual Administrative Support Personnel in the United States

Ability	Total Number of Corporations using Bilingual Staff
Telephone	752
Customer Contact & Relations	531
Translation & Interpretation	507
Word Processing	433
Correspondence	269
Machine Transcription	57
Shorthand	35
Spreadsheet	28
Desktop Publishing	27
Database	21
Other (unspecified)	232

ADAPTED FROM: WALDMAN, 1994

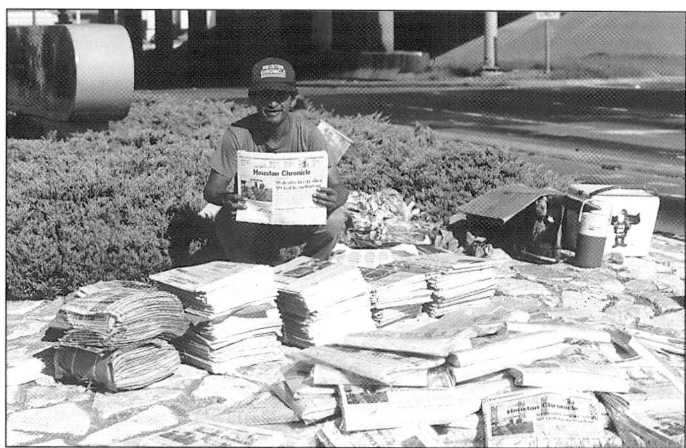

A Mexican immigrant sells newspapers in Houston, Texas. Many minority language speakers are in low status professions.

example. 'As the burgers and fries popped over the counter at the usual speed on the line with the Spanish-speaking employee, the line with the English-speaking employee was moving slowly, creating inefficiencies caused by her difficulty in communicating with the Spanish-speaking customers' (page 110).

The problem with many ethnic businesses is the level of status, salary and conditions that such businesses provide for their employees. Often the jobs available are of lower status with a lower salary, making advancement not always easy or possible. García & Otheguy (1994) found that in United States businesses, the demand for bilingual workers was not usually at the top executive levels. Rather, the need for bilinguals was for the lower and middle ranges of occupation. For example, US businesses required bilingual secretaries, clerks, shop floor assistants, rather than bilingual managers and executives. Waldman's (1994) US research found that the five most needed language abilities required were: telephone; customer contact or relations; translation and interpretation; word processing and correspondence. Spanish was the language most required by companies, followed by German, French and Japanese.

However, smaller companies indicated that language skills are of value in their higher positions. In small companies, the language of the whole workforce may be the minority language. Thus cohesion and an integrated purpose is attained when managers speak the same language as those whom they manage.

Bilingualism and Economic Inequality

In the economic recession years of the 1980s, divisions between the rich and the poor tended to increase. In the United States, for example, African Americans and Latinos tended to find that the quality of their employ-

An Australian Perspective from Joseph Lo Bianco

'In general terms, all Australians conducting business in non-English-speaking countries or who are involved in formal and informal arrangements between Australia and such countries will be greatly advantaged by having language skills and cultural knowledge appropriate to their task. There are many instances where this is indispensable.' (page 49)

'Other major English-speaking countries recognize that depending only on English in the world of business can be a major disadvantage. Australia's trade is mostly conducted with non-English-speaking countries, particularly Asian countries. The link between economics, trade and languages is not a simple or direct one, since languages are not only useful in negotiations – sometimes indispensable to avoid dependence – but also in getting to know markets, predicting demand for goods and services, ways of marketing and so on.' (page 192)

'There is substantial evidence that Australian economic activities, particularly in competitive situations requiring market penetration, would benefit from the skilled use of the host countries' languages and active knowledge and appreciation of cultural values and behaviours. This can be a determining factor in gaining a competitive advantage in trade. In situations of intense competition for markets and considering the particularly trade-dependent nature of Australia's economy, it is important to harmonise national economic strategies with the goals of languages policy. Australia's total trade with non-English-speaking countries greatly exceeds its trading volumes with English-speaking countries. This shift which has occurred over the last two decades has coincided with a general reduction in second-language learning and teaching in Australia. In addition the languages of the key trading partners are particularly poorly represented in Australia's schooling system.' (page 49)

REFERENCE: LO BIANCO, 1987

Languages for Foreign Trade: Two US Quotes

The importance of knowledge of languages other than English in economics and foreign trade is acknowledged by the United States in a report accompanying the formulation of the Foreign Language Assistance for National Security Act of 1983.

'It is precisely this combination of foreign language ability and business expertise ... that is now needed and will be required even more in the future by U.S. companies if they are to compete successfully in these (Asian, the Middle East, Eastern Europe) markets.'

(John McDougall, Executive Vice President of the Ford Motor Company).

'The United States can no longer afford to remain a monolinguist nation, expecting the rest of the world's people to adjust to our ways. Thus the need for Americans to learn foreign languages is more urgent than ever.'

(Richard Morrow, President of the Standard Oil Company)

REFERENCE: COMMITTEE ON EDUCATION AND LABOR, 1983

Family Poverty and Unemployment Rates in Latino Groups

Ethnic Group	% Families in Poverty (1987)
Puerto Ricans	37.9%
Mexicans	25.5%
Central and South Americans	18.9%
Cubans	13.8%
Other Hispanics	26.1%

Ethnic Group	% Unemployment (1991)
Average in US	6.7%
All Hispanics	9.4%
Puerto Ricans	11.8%
Mexicans	9.6%
Cubans	8.5%
Other Hispanics	8.2%

SOURCE: MORALES & BONILLA, 1993

ment, the chance of finding a job if unemployed, opportunities for upward mobility and the value of wages as against inflation were all made more difficult in the recession. Among Latinos, who showed a population growth in the 1980s and 1990s in the United States, the movement of jobs away from urban areas to suburban areas (for service-oriented and goods-producing industries) made the finding of jobs and moving above the poverty line increasingly difficult. As Morales and Bonilla (1993) suggest: 'Latinos entering the labor market in the last decade have encountered difficult conditions. For many, the outcome has been unstable employment, diminished job opportunities, and extreme impoverishment. Latinos in the United States display several distinct characteristics: high rates of immigration and reproduction, low levels of education, high rates of urbanization, concentration in low-paying jobs, and high levels of poverty' (page 11).

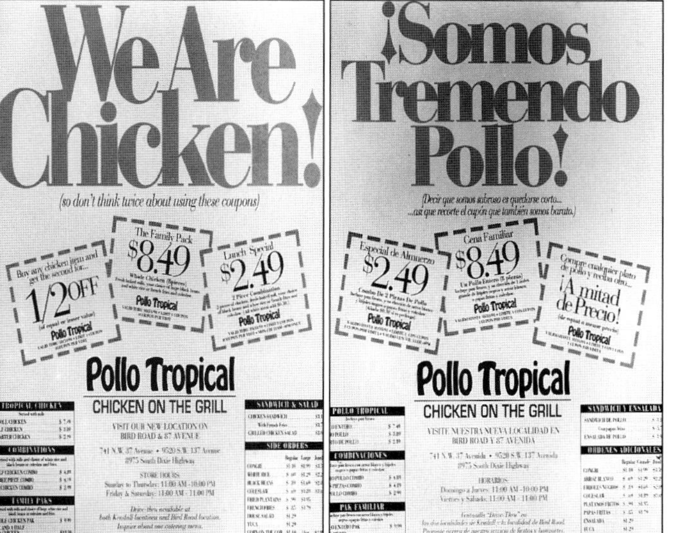

A Miami Herald advertising supplement promotes a restaurant in Spanish and English.

While there are ethnic group differences, the overall picture is of low wage employment among language minority members, relatively fewer opportunities for promotion and upward mobility, low vocational expectations and motivation, more economically disenfranchised communities and hence a possible economic poverty trap.

It is not an inevitable condition of language minorities that they are economically deprived, impoverished or that they lack entrepreneurial enterprise. In the United States, poverty and inequality are not equally shared by all Latinos. Morales & Bonilla (1993) suggest that Puerto Rican, Mexican and Dominican language groups in the US appear to share a greater burden of poverty. US Central and South Americans, and particularly US Cubans, exhibit less poverty than other Latinos.

A research study by García (1995) found that the salaries earned by different Latino groups in the US did not have a simple connection with their being bilingual or English monolinguals. While Mexican and Puerto Rican bilinguals in the US earned on average $4000 and $3200, respectively, less than those who were monolingual English speakers, the Cuban-American bilinguals showed a different pattern in earnings. Cuban Americans tended to earn almost $1000 more than the average English language monolingual. Because Cuban Americans may have reached a higher level of education, be regarded as political allies of Americans and enemies of Castro's Cuba, and because Cuban Americans in areas such as Dade County have created their own businesses to serve the local ethnic community and to trade in areas such as Latin America, Spanish-English speakers in this group have gained socioeconomic power. Ofelia García (1995) concludes that her findings 'demonstrate that speaking only English does not always make a difference in the achievement of economic prosperity, and that bilingualism, rather than monolingualism, is a useful commodity in some communities, including the Latino one' (page 157).

With the Spanish-speaking population of the United States rapidly growing, and with Spanish an important trading language in Latin America and elsewhere, there is a possibility that Spanish may be of increasing economic value inside the United States and for marketing abroad. Therefore, it seems economically valuable in the next century to be bilingual. For some individuals, this is to gain employment and try to avoid poverty. For others,

Barcud – A Welsh Language Business Success Story

The *'barcud'* or kite is a familiar sight in north-west Wales, gliding with wings outstretched over the hillsides of Snowdonia. It has also become a well-known symbol on the vans and studio of the Caernarfon television company, *Barcud*, founded in March, 1982.

Caernarfon is a small town situated on the banks of the Menai Straits, which lie between the North Wales mainland and the island of Anglesey. Caernarfon was originally a Roman fort. In 1283 the English king, Edward I, conquered the Welsh and built the castle which still dominates the town today. The town is in the largely Welsh-speaking county of Gwynedd. Of the population of 14,000, 70 percent can speak Welsh.

In recent years, Caernarfon and the surrounding areas have suffered high levels of unemployment. During the general economic depression of the 1980s and 1990s in Britain, local factories and businesses have closed. Because of the geographical remoteness of the area it has been difficult to attract suitable new business from the outside. However, new enterprise initiatives have arisen from amongst the local people.

One of the most remarkable developments in the area has the emergence of a flourishing Welsh language television industry that has provided employment for hundreds of people. Early in 1982, the British Government finally fulfilled its promise to provide a Welsh language television channel. It was announced that the new channel would be launched in October, 1982, broadcasting 25 hours a week of Welsh language programs, of which seven would be allocated to independent production companies. Many small companies were formed, of which several were in the largely Welsh-speaking Caernarfon area. During the years that S4C has been in existence, the independent companies have produced a great variety of original and creative programs, including comedy, thrillers, children's programs, light entertainment, documentaries and sports programs.

Barcud was formed in March, 1982, to provide permanent technical resources for the emerging independent companies in the Caernarfon area, and throughout Wales. It was felt that basing the company at Caernarfon would also reflect the fact that Welsh language television serves the Welsh-speaking community, which has its main heartlands in north-west and west Wales. *Barcud* now has several outside broadcast units, and two studios. The company also provides post-production resources, editing, sound and graphics. This full complement of resources means that *Barcud* is the only independent company in Wales that can take over the production process from start to finish. This enables it to compete effectively against other Welsh companies, and also to market its services in England.

By 1995 *Barcud* was employing 70 full-time staff, 62 in Caernarfon and eight in a permanent unit in Swansea, (the latter responsible for filming a Welsh language news and chat program each week-night). The staff include camera crew and sound crew, electricians and lighting crew, editors and dubbing editors, and administrative staff. In addition, the company employs local contractors to provide canteen, taxi and security services.

It has been company policy from the beginning to conduct all internal administration in Welsh, and to deal with public organizations, accountants and other outside contacts through the medium of Welsh. It has also been a policy to employ Welsh speakers. Of the 70 permanent staff in 1995, over 60 were fluent Welsh speakers. Ten of these were young people who were receiving technical training.

The directors of *Barcud* have not found that their Welsh language policy has been a hindrance. On the contrary, they have received much support from local people who have perceived *Barcud* as being a local venture, arising directly from the local language and culture, and benefiting the local economy. When the new studio was being built, at a cost of one and a half million pounds, many local people bought shares in the company to help the company reach the target of £600,000 of private money that was required. The company now has nearly 200 shareholders, the majority of them from the Caernarfon area.

The company's policy of employing Welsh-speaking technical staff has been an economic advantage. English has traditionally been the language of the technical side of television production in Wales, but *Barcud* can offer a complete service through the medium of Welsh. Producers in charge of Welsh language programs are usually happy that the technical and on-camera aspects of production can be co-ordinated through the medium of the same language.

Further afield, the company's use of the Welsh language has helped to give it a distinctive identity, both for those who use the outside broadcast units in other parts of Wales and in England, and also for those who visit Caernarfon to make use of the studio and editing facilities. The Welsh-speaking staff, the Welsh signs inside and outside the building, the use of Welsh quite naturally in all aspects of the work, tend to make a lasting impression.

The directors of *Barcud* modestly deny that their enterprise has had a more positive effect on the local economy than the sum total of the many smaller businesses in the area. However, there is no doubt that *Barcud,* because of its size and the scope of its operations, and because of its involvement in the high profile television industry, has received considerable publicity. It has been a focus for local support, and an example of a minority language business that has developed in response to a clear need, and in harmony with the minority language and culture.

Economic Restructuring in Bilingual Communities

There are various characteristics of regional development in minority language rural economies that can influence language shift. These characteristics are exemplified in the list below:

1. Inward investment with State support and subsidies.
2. Short-term projects, absence of sustained growth.
3. Tourism, agriculture, rural enterprises accented.
4. Manual, non-technical workforce skills and lower remuneration.
5. Management by people outside of language minority area.
6. Linguistic and cultural differences of outside managers and local workers; cultural and social divisions.
7. Education tends to relate to wider state rather than local needs.
8. Better educated migrate.
9. Lack of local entrepreneurial activity.
10. Lack of discussion of link between human capital and culture.

Instead, language minority communities may need to rethink their relationship to the local and international economy. Economic restructuring in language minority communities requires, for example:

1. A flexible and mobile labor force and workers.
2. Harnessing all human capital in all local communities.
3. A move from qualifications to skills (transferable skills).
4. Attitudinal change towards valuing the minority language in the workplace.
5. Understanding the need to compete internationally.
6. An integration of local economies.
7. The redress of inequalities in core and periphery economies.
8. Suitable training and re-training provision.

Some of the above derive from rurality (i.e. language minority communities in urban areas will be different), others from the peripheralism that occurs with being a language minority. However, the Information Superhighway makes residence in language minority rural areas more possible through improved speed and access in communications, and employment that allows people to work at home, using high speed computer links to receive and deliver services and products. Language minority communities have also recently found economic possibilities in mass media. Such mass media activity can use local human capital, generate economic activity (and secondary activity), give self confidence, and help rebuild the local social fabric. This is occurring in Wales, the Scottish Highlands and Islands, Galicia, the Basque Country and Catalonia.

REFERENCE: EUROPEAN COMMISSION, 1996

bilingualism may be of value to work locally for international and multinational corporations. For yet others, who wish to travel abroad to do their trade, languages also become increasingly important. The concept that speaking English is all one needs, whether in Europe or the United States, seems to only contain only a part of the truth.

There is no guarantee that those who become linguistically assimilated (e.g. speak English-only) in countries like the United States will gain employment. The evidence from García & Otheguy (1994) and Morales & Bonilla (1993) confirms that the ability to speak English does not give equal access to jobs and wealth. Linguistic assimilation does not mean incorporation into the economic structure of the country. If there is a growth of ethnic businesses (e.g. in urban areas), and a development of language minority businesses in peripheral, rural areas, then bilingualism rather than English monolingualism may become more economically valuable.

Further Reading

COULMAS, F., 1992, *Language and Economy*. Oxford: Blackwell.

GARCÍA, O., 1995, Spanish Language Loss as a Determinant of Income among Latinos in the United States: Implications for Language Policy in Schools. In J. W. TOLLEFSON (ed.), *Power and Inequality in Language Education*. Cambridge: Cambridge University Press.

GARCÍA, O. & OTHEGUY, R., 1994, The Value of Speaking a LOTE in US Business. *Annals of the American Academy of Political and Social Science*, 532, 99-122.

GRIN, F., 1990, The Economic Approach to Minority Languages. *Journal of Multilingual and Multicultural Development*, 11 (1&2), 153-171.

MORALES, R. & BONILLA, F., 1993, *Latinos in a Changing US Economy*. London: Sage.

MORRIS, D., 1992, The Effects of Economic Changes on Gwynedd Society. In L. DAFIS (ed.), *Lesser Used Languages – Assimilating Newcomers*. Carmarthen, Wales: Joint Working Party on Bilingualism in Dyfed.

MORRIS, D., 1995, Language and Class Functioning in a Peripheral Economy. *Journal of Multilingual and Multicultural Development*, 16 (5), 373-387.

SMOLICZ, J. J., 1991, Language Core Values in a Multicultural Setting: An Australian Experience. *International Review of Education*, 37, (1), 33-52.

6: Language Strategies for Business

Introduction

In recent years the world of trade and commerce has become more aware of the relevance of foreign language skills for success in the international market. Businesses have begun to recognize that lack of appropriate expertise in foreign languages can cost them clients, orders and trading opportunities in other countries. Co-operative projects, joint ventures and mergers between companies in different countries have underlined the importance of foreign language abilities. Foreign language competence is also important for buyers, as they search for goods and services at competitive prices.

Companies in English-speaking countries have been particularly slow to realize that they cannot rely on using only English in foreign business transactions. According to recent research, British companies still lag far behind the rest of Europe in their commitment to providing foreign language training for their staff.

The problem of how to develop appropriate foreign language skills is one that tends to affect smaller companies rather than large, multinational corporations. The latter tend to employ nationals in their local branches, and also have the resources to employ expert linguists for tasks that require competence in foreign languages. Employees of national companies, on the other hand, often have to develop a wide range of skills, including language skills. Since the primary aim of business is to market products or services, and since foreign language expertise is only one means to that end, it is important to develop cost-effective and time-effective strategies and clear objectives. Accurate assessment of the foreign language requirements of individual companies and businesses is needed, and advice on how to develop appropriate training.

European Initiatives

In 1992 the Council of Europe Lingua program (see page 626) funded the Flair project to research into the foreign language needs of small and medium-sized companies in seven European countries, England, France, Germany, Spain, Italy, the Netherlands and Denmark. The aim of the project was to provide data to set up a system of 'business language auditing' or assessment.

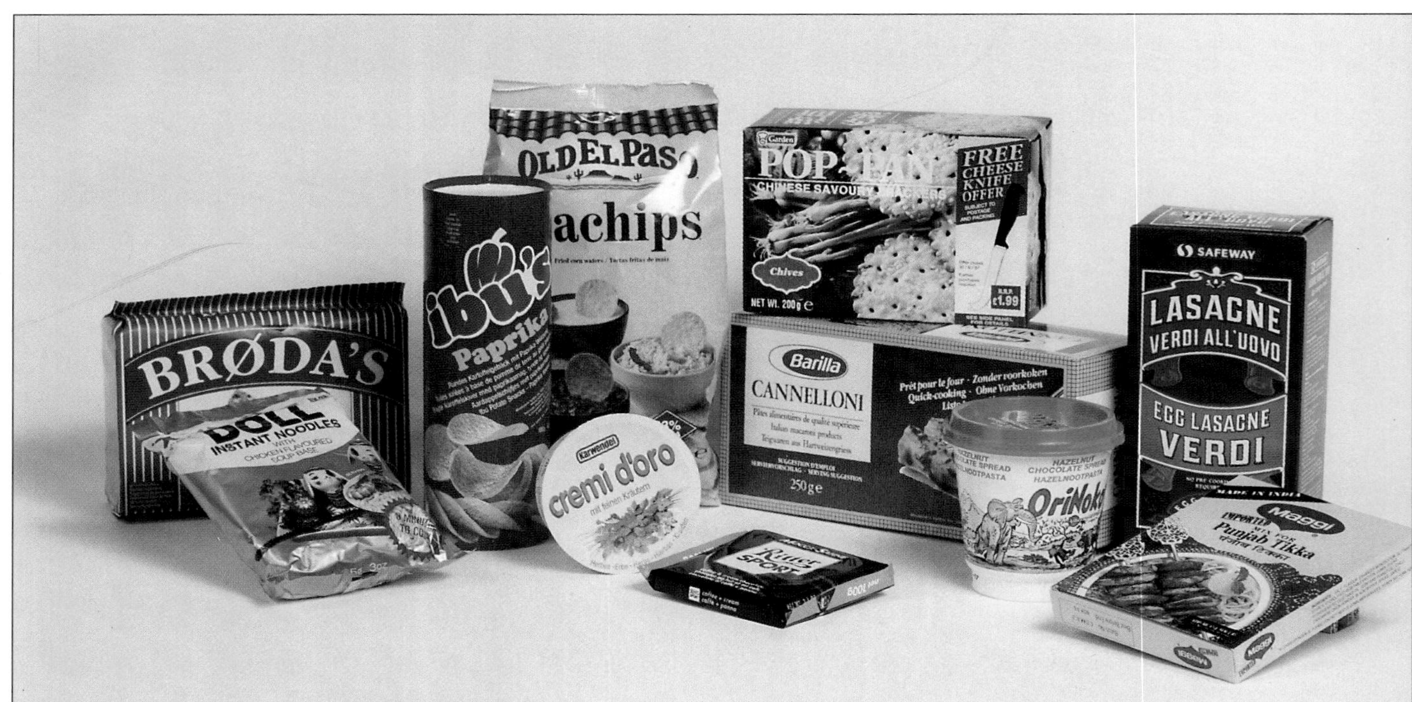

A selection of groceries from a UK supermarket show how world-wide trade has meant greater contact between languages.

The main conclusions of the report confirmed those of an earlier business language survey, carried out by the Council of Europe's Lingua program in 1990, and can be summarized as follows.

- English is still the predominant language in European business but French and German are also widely used. The use of German in business is growing: it is now the second business language of Europe. Italian and Spanish are defined as languages of 'intermediate usage', while other European languages, such as Portuguese, Greek, Swedish, Norwegian and Dutch are less widely used. Usage of languages varies according to geographical location. In some areas English is not the foreign language most used in business. The graph 'Usage of Languages in Businesses in Europe' provides further details.

- Knowledge of one foreign language alone is not enough. The minimum level of linguistic competence for a European company is the ability to perform in the three most widely used languages, English, German and French. A company should ideally possess competence in the five most widely used languages (including Italian and Spanish). Skills in the less widely used languages would give the opportunity to expand into other markets, particularly in Central and Eastern Europe. The demand in Europe for language learning for business usage is given in the pie chart 'Demand for Language Training in Europe'.

- Proficiency across all four language skills is not necessary for all tasks. Reading and writing skills are used more widely than oral and comprehension skills. There is often a need for employees to be proficient across more languages but in a narrower area (e.g. reading, comprehension), since most European companies trading with other countries have to use three or four foreign languages on a regular basis.

- A significant minority of companies are now officially bilingual, regularly using a second working language. This is usually the result of being owned by a foreign parent company or because of a partnership with a foreign company. Officially bilingual or multilingual companies are probably on the increase with the advent of the Single European Market.

Between 1992 and 1995, the Council of Europe Lingua program funded a project, 'Language Audit', to develop and disseminate techniques for the diagnosis and analysis of the linguistic training needs of the work force. During recent years, there has been a growth in agencies and consultancies throughout Europe with expertise in the analysis of companies' language requirements. Companies have been encouraged to seek the advice of experts who can formulate 'whole-company' strategies, rather than seeking piecemeal and amateur solutions to their language deficiencies.

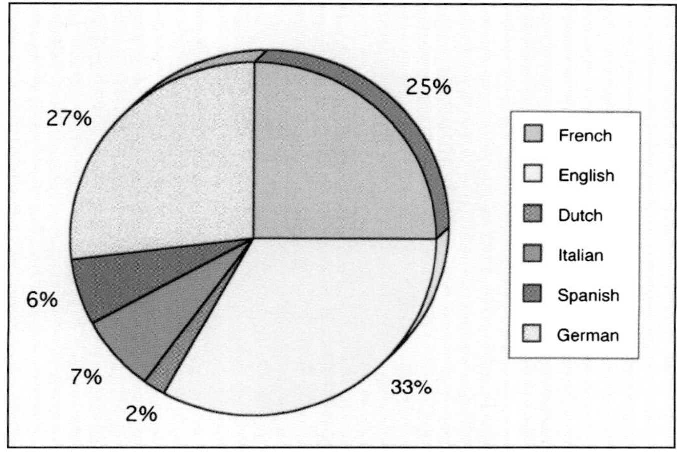

Demand for language training in Europe (Reference: Hagen, 1993).

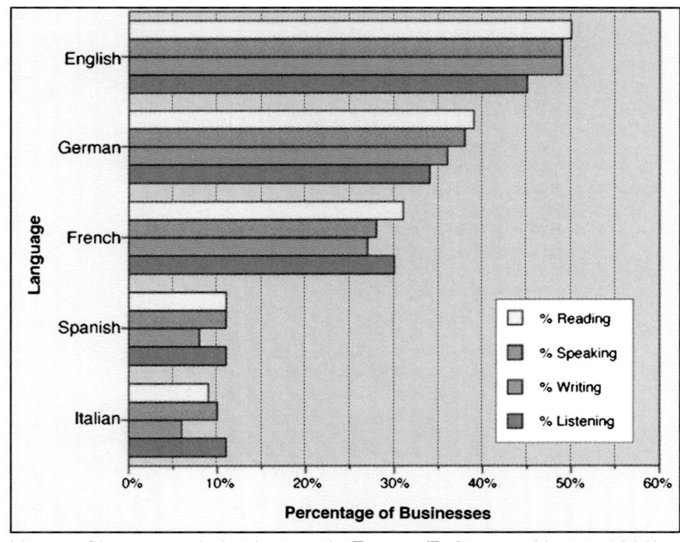

Usage of languages in businesses in Europe (Reference: Hagen, 1993).

Assessment of Foreign Language Needs

When assessing the foreign language needs of an individual company, the following questions would be asked by language consultants:

What languages need to be learned?

This will depend on the countries or regions with whom the company trades or hopes to trade.

Who needs to learn a foreign language?

Foreign language skills might need to be developed by

Trading Across Cultures

The story is told of a British business executive who visited a Japanese company in Tokyo. When he met the Japanese manager, the manager naturally presented his *meisha* or business card. The British visitor explained that he had only arrived the previous night and did not have any cards.

He then proceeded to tear in half the card he had just been given, scrawled his name and telephone number on one half, and handed it back to the manager. The manager was appalled at this exhibition of gross disrespect and the British visitor did not get the contract.

company directors, salespersons or travelers, receptionists or switchboard operators. Companies might need advice on testing their staff for language aptitude before beginning a training program.

For what purpose are the foreign languages to be learned?

The purpose will determine the level of language to be learned, and the language skills to be developed. A switchboard operator might need to develop basic listening and comprehension skills, and basic phrases in more than one foreign language. A secretary might need to be able to read and write a foreign language to understand letters and order forms, and to write letters, perhaps with the aid of a computer program. A salesperson might need a good degree of fluency to travel abroad and negotiate in a foreign language. A scientist might need to be able to read technical documents in a foreign language.

Sometimes the learning of a language is impossible for a variety of reasons. There may be no time before a scheduled business trip. The company concerned may trade with a number of different countries, where a great variety of languages are spoken. In such cases, business might have to be carried out in a major international language such as English, or by means of an interpreter. However, it would be possible for business executives visiting a country to learn a few basic phrases, as a mark of courtesy and respect.

By what methods are the foreign languages to be learned?

This would depend on the objectives involved, and the most convenient method for company staff. This might for example involve weekly sessions with a teacher, supported by several hours a week of self-study or distance learning, using computer technology. An intensive course might be the most appropriate method for business people about to visit the target country. In-house training, tailored to the company's needs, is often more cost-effective than sending staff on outside courses that may contain irrelevant material.

What if it is not possible or practical to learn the language of the client?

In this case, the medium of communication may be the home language of the trader or seller. Advice may be given on how to communicate with clients in a clear and intelligible manner. The use of simplified and unambiguous language to avoid misunderstanding is a key issue. Colloquialisms, idioms and complex sentence structures should be avoided.

A pamphlet published by the UK Department of Trade and Industry in 1994, 'Business Language Strategies', tells the story of the English chairman of an international project who asked a Dutchman to 'go away and think again'. The Englishman meant 'please drop the idea' but the Dutchman interpreted his words as 'go away and give it more thought.' A misunderstanding occurred because the English chairman had used an idiom that was not familiar to his Dutch colleague.

Teleconomy's Experiment

In 1990, a research experiment was conducted by Teleconomy, a UK training company, to find out how many large London companies could respond to sales enquiries in a variety of European languages. It was shown that most switchboard operators in the companies concerned were incapable of dealing with calls in foreign languages and often did not recognize the language in which the call was made. French, German and Spanish telephone callers, speaking in their own languages and in broken English, were unable to understand slurred responses such as 'S'ringin-fer-yer' (it's ringing for you) 'Putin-yerfru' (Putting you through) and 'Lines-bizi-ye-old?' (The lines are busy: will you hold?) One third of calls did not get past the switchboard, and callers reported reactions such as nervous laughter, long silences and replies in loud high voices.

Business and Culture

An important aspect of successful international trading is breaking down language and cultural barriers. To be able to use the language of the client is often essential. However, all languages are embedded in the culture of the countries where they are spoken. When traveling on business in a foreign country, it is not sufficient to learn the client's language, whether a few phrases or fluently. An understanding of, and a respect for the client's culture and way of life is essential to successful business transactions. It is important to understand how business affairs are conducted in different countries, how to behave in various social and work situations, how to communicate effectively, and what behavior is likely to cause offense. Many business deals have failed because business executives have been ignorant of, and insensitive to the cultural nuances of a situation.

Business culture training is now an important component of foreign language training. It can best be used as a complement to language training, or as a substitute, where language learning is impractical. It can prepare business people for visits to foreign countries, or for short or long residencies. It can help avoid offense and misunderstandings and gain business. It can also aid good working relationships between staff of different nationalities.

Business culture training tends to focus on two main areas.

General cultural awareness

People are taught to see their own culture not as an absolute from which other cultures deviate, but in relation to other cultures. They are helped to be sensitive to cultural differences, and to appreciate and respect them. This aspect of cultural training might be useful for a wide spectrum of staff in a company that deals with the foreign market.

Factual information on specific cultures, business etiquette and communication issues.

This latter area would be relevant to specific individuals within the company who have or will have regular contact with foreign clients. This aspect of culture training might cover the following issues.

Etiquette. This would cover greeting and leave-taking in the target culture and how to address representatives of the company. In some cultures, for instance, it is customary to shake hands with all the office staff upon arrival in the morning and upon leaving in the evening. In some cultures, it would be considered rude to address company staff by their first name unless invited to do so. Etiquette training would include advice on how to behave in specific situations, in the office, in meetings, in people's homes. It might cover issues such as whether to give gifts, or offer to pay for entertainment.

Business practice. In some countries, it would be considered strange or impolite to discuss business affairs outside office hours. In many Middle Eastern countries, business discussions will intermingle naturally with personal and family conversation. In some countries, a fast 'hard sell' approach might not be acceptable. Clients would prefer to chat in a leisurely fashion, to get to know you personally. Some business cultures are group-oriented, and consider trustworthiness and loyalty as very important. Other business cultures tend to be more individualistic and set great store by the individual's qualifications and achievements. In many Western cultures, only the written word is binding, and business people may be anxious to sign contracts and 'get it down on paper'. In Middle Eastern countries business is done largely through the spoken word, and it is important to develop trust in a business partner.

General cultural considerations. It is important to be aware of attitudes to such matters as religion. In Islamic countries, for instance, religion is a part of daily life to a much greater extent than in Britain. There may be times of prayer that must be respected, while dress must conform to local standards of propriety.

Issues of communication. This might include non-verbal communication, such as body language, eye-contact and tone of voice. In some cultures, for instance, to look someone straight in the eye indicates anger. Communication issues might involve the structuring and delivery of talks and presentations in a way that is sympathetic to the values and norms of the client's culture.

Translation and adaptation of printed matter. Publicity and sales literature, advertising and promotion, must be adapted in a way that respects the values and appreciates the nuances of the client's culture. Issues such as humor, male and female roles, the nature of community life, vary widely from culture to culture and need to be carefully considered in any adaptation or translation. Different cultures may have different preferences about the lay-out and typeface used in printing, and it is important to know what is currently fashionable in marketing.

Sir Peter Parker, chairman of the UK's National Languages for Export Campaign said, in the 1995 annual award ceremony:

> 'Communicating across cultural barriers means entering the mind-set, and even the heart, of other peoples – understanding their language, not only in a narrow sense of the language of the mind, but what makes them tick, how and why they react.
>
> And all the time the sparks are crossing the gap, not only from verbal messages but also from non-verbal skills. Not simply the voice, but the tone of the voice, the facial expressions, the behavior and the manner.'

UK Languages for Export Campaign

In the UK, the Department of Trade and Industry is seeking to give British exporters practical assistance through its Languages for Export Campaign, launched in 1994. The Languages in Export Advisory Scheme (Lexas) was established in 1995, to offer companies impartial and subsidized advice on their language and cultural needs in the export market. A consultant combining an understanding of business and export with language skills and international experience makes an initial half-day visit to companies to examine their foreign language usage, including written and spoken communication, translation, publicity, advertising, packaging and training needs. A further consultancy of up to three more days is available, to make a more in-depth assessment and produce a tailor-made language strategy for the company. This strategy is presented in the form of a written report, which includes the names of relevant language suppliers in the area.

The Council of Europe Lingua program is funding research into innovative techniques of language learning e.g. distance and computer-assisted learning, that will help companies to be able to buy in language services for a modest cost.

Should the language training contain a cultural component?

Language competence is not always adequate by itself for effective communication and good relationships between people of different cultures. Business people who travel abroad need to be well informed about the culture of their hosts, etiquette, social customs, and behavior that is likely to cause offense. An effective program of language training for executives traveling abroad will probably include a cultural component. This is discussed under 'Business and Culture' (see page 261).

What other language services does the company require?

These might include publicity literature in other languages, bilingual business cards, technical translations and interpretation facilities on foreign visits. It is important to hire the services of professional translators and interpreters, with an up-to-date knowledge of the language and culture. Professional interpreters may conduct complex negotiations on legal and contractual issues. Company members may need advice on how to brief interpreters and use them most effectively.

Professional translators will be able to translate documents such as contracts and technical literature accurately. They will be competent to adapt sales and publicity literature, advertising and promotion in a way that is sensitive and sympathetic to the values of the local culture.

Instead of training existing staff in foreign language skills, it may sometimes be more convenient and cost-effective to hire staff who are already multilingual. Companies may need advice on how to obtain secretaries and other key staff with foreign language qualifications.

Further Reading

HAGEN, S. (ed.), 1993, *Languages in European Business: A Regional Survey of Small and Medium-sized Companies*. London: Centre for Information on Language Teaching and Research (CILT).

NATIONAL LANGUAGES FOR EXPORT CAMPAIGN, 1994, *Business Language Strategies*. London: Department of Trade and Industry.

NATIONAL LANGUAGES FOR EXPORT CAMPAIGN, 1994, *Business Language Training: Guide 4*. London: Department of Trade and Industry.

NATIONAL LANGUAGES FOR EXPORT CAMPAIGN, 1994, *Trading Across Cultures*. London: Department of Trade and Industry.

VOGHT, G. M. & SCHAUB, R., 1992, *Foreign Languages and International Business*. An ERIC Digest. Washington, DC: ERIC Clearinghouse on Languages and Linguistics.

7: Bilingual Professions

The ownership of two languages has increasingly become seen as an asset as the 'communication world' gets smaller. As swift communication by phone and computer across great distances has become possible in recent decades, and as air travel has brought countries closer together, so the importance of bilingualism and multilingualism has been highlighted. As the world becomes more of a global village, the need for promoting bilingualism and multilingualism has become more obvious. As the amount of information available has dramatically increased, and the ease of delivering information round the world has quickened, so bilinguals, particularly those speaking a majority language such as English, may have become more important in the employment market.

There is often a marked contrast between bilingual professions that carry a high prestige, and professions where bilinguals are in jobs which symbolize the lower status of many language minority bilinguals. In this latter case, language minority members may speak two languages, yet be in jobs of lower status, and be marginalized in their employment prospects and chances of sharing wealth. We will first consider bilingual professions that are prestigious.

One example of the value of bilingualism is in marketing. Whether such marketing or business managers come from small, local businesses that are trying to sell their goods abroad, or from larger national corporations, or from transnational corporations (e.g. oil, computers, newspapers) the value of being bilingual may be directly connected with securing deals, making profit, expanding the market and selling well. To sell a product to the Japanese or Saudi Arabians, it may be a considerable advantage to speak Japanese or Arabic. The English monolingual walking in and expecting to sell to a language minority or different majority language organization, may find that communication is not only impeded, so also is personal acceptability. Building up rapport with a buyer will be considerably aided through the use of their native language.

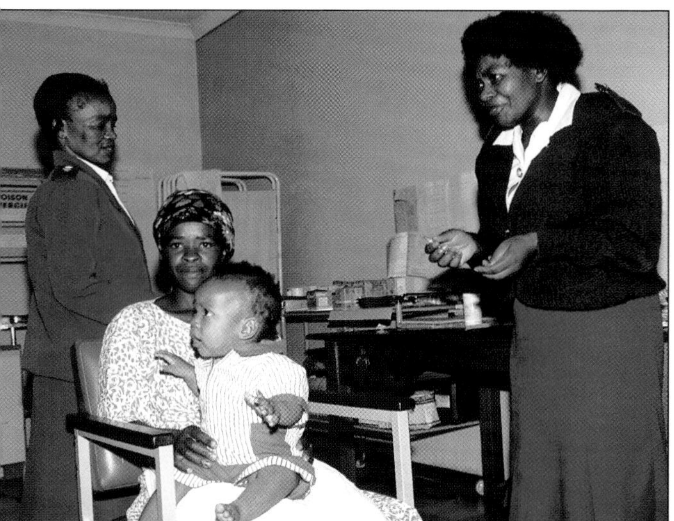

A Health Center in Welcomewood, South Africa. In an area where more than one language is spoken, bilingual skills may be essential for jobs that involve contact with the public, for instance, in the medical profession.

There is a growing realization that bilinguals and multilinguals will be important in increasingly competitive international trade. As Pacific Rim countries grow in economic power, in the rise of a more free market economy, and given the importance of international trade to developing nations, bilingualism is seen as opening doors to economic activity and advantage.

A second example of bilingual professions that are prestigious is the travel business. Air hostesses, instructors on ski slopes in mainland Europe, those who conduct safaris in Africa, those who cater for sun seekers in the Mediterranean all prosper when they are bilingual or multilingual. To communicate with clients, to inform those being instructed, to satisfy those seeking rest and excitement, the use of two or more languages enhances job performance.

For bilinguals and multilinguals who are skilled in two or more languages, being interpreters or translators is often a prestigious post. When politicians meet, (e.g. European Commission, United Nations, on foreign visits) interpreters form the essential bridge. For example, when a United States President meets the President of Russia, interpreters provide a smooth connection. Interpreting can also exist in a local language minority region.

In the highlands and islands of Scotland, translating facilities are available for those English-only speakers who need a translation when local government officials or elected community representatives are speaking Gaelic. Translating also can exist as a large scale enterprise (e.g. in the United Nations and the European Union) where many documents have to be translated

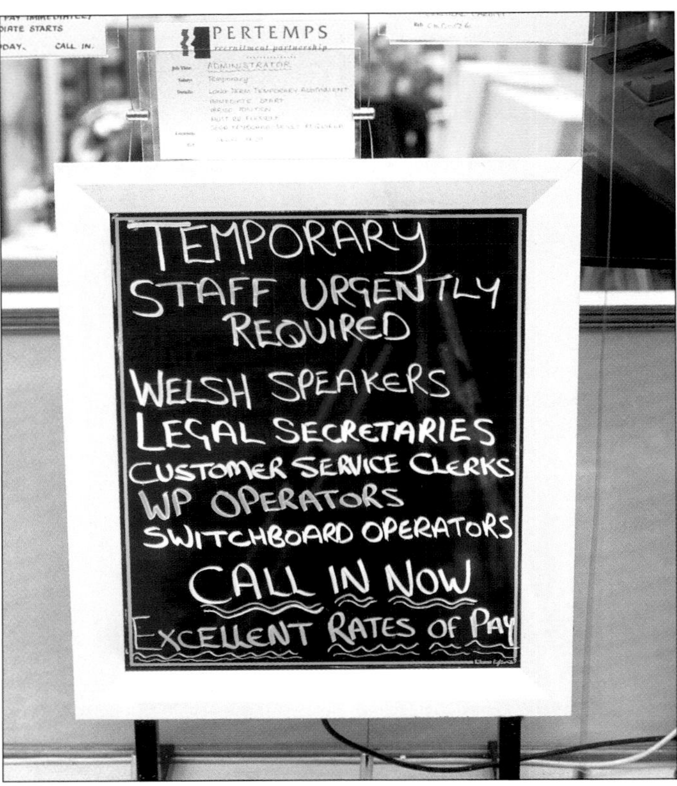

An employment agency underlines the importance of bilingual skills for many jobs in contemporary Wales.

into official languages. Translation may also occur in language minority communities where, for example, a book or an article may be translated to or from the minority language.

A third example of a relatively prestigious bilingual profession is that of local government officials who deal with their communities. When enquiries are made about health, social benefit or local taxes, it is often important and necessary to have people who can use the language(s) of the local people. In many language minority situations, bilinguals in local government may have to deal with superiors and paper work in the majority language, but deal orally or in writing in the minority language with some or many of the local population.

Another example is when a local government official in Africa or India visits an indigenous ethnic group in a relatively remote part of the country. That local government official may need to talk in the dialect or local language of the people as well as talking to colleagues back in the town or city in a more widely used common language.

In the caring professions (e.g. counselors, psychologists, doctors, nurses, religious leaders), one occasional issue of debate is the bilingual abilities of such professionals. Take for example the midwife. The midwife is present at that very special moment of a mother's experience. Communication with the midwife is not only important, it is also very emotional and precious. Is the midwife monolingual or bilingual? Can the midwife assist in the moment of pain and joy in the preferred language of the mother? If not, the mother will need to switch to using her second language.

When people visit a psychiatrist or counselor, it may be important for them to discuss and reveal the innermost depths of their being in the language of their choice. To switch to a second or third language because the professional is monolingual may not be satisfactory. In the temple, mosque or church, it is often highly important that a religious leader conducts prayer or a funeral service in the language of the people. People may find praying in a second language unnatural, even distasteful.

These questions highlight a tendency in language minority communities. Sometimes the more prestigious jobs are filled by monolinguals and less prestigious posts by bilinguals. This may send a signal. Monolingualism symbolically connects with higher status employment, and bilingualism with lower status employment.

There are many times when the more prestigious professional (e.g. the consultant surgeon) only speaks the majority language, while the relatively less prestigious professional (e.g. the nurse on the hospital ward) is bilingual. This raises the dilemma about whether it is more important to hire a monolingual who is very skilled at a profession, or a bilingual who is slightly less skilled? (Of course, there will be many cases when bilinguals are as skilled or more skilled than the monolingual applicant for a post).

This leads to the second part of this discussion about bilingual professions. In many minority language situations, those who are bilingual may be unemployed, or in the lower status jobs. A school is sometimes a good example. In a language minority community, many of the teachers may be monolingual in the majority language. Bilinguals are often in lower status jobs, for example, because they belong to underprivileged, marginalized ethnic minorities, sometimes underachieving in schools (e.g. United States). There is sometimes a vicious cycle of poverty, powerlessness, low expectations and lower motivation. Unemployment and lower status jobs become part of this cycle.

For example, in large cities in the United States, where there are large proportions of Spanish speakers, the teachers may be English language monolinguals. The cooks, cleaners, secretaries and janitors in the school may be the bilinguals. For students in the school, such a

Bryn and Lesley Terfel – The Harmony of Bilingualism

In October 1984, a well-motivated, highly efficient and hardworking student became an undergraduate at the University of Wales, Bangor. Three years later, Lesley graduated with two 'honors'. First, she was awarded a rare *'summa cum laude'* (literally, with the highest praise) degree. Lesley was the first undergraduate in the School of Education to gain a First Class Single Honors having taken her studies through the medium of Welsh. No one since has achieved that accolade in this Welsh-medium Single Honors degree course.

Second, she married the now famous international opera singer, Bryn Terfel. With Welsh as their first language, Lesley is trilingual and Bryn sings fluently in six languages. As this text will show, it is possible to speak a minority language (Welsh), identify passionately with that language minority, and use other majority languages (e.g. English, German) as well.

Bryn and Lesley were born and raised in small, rural communities in north-west Wales, around Penygroes in Gwynedd. The language of their homes, their schooling and play was almost entirely Welsh. Both musical from an early age, they participated in Welsh eisteddfodau (competitive Welsh cultural events, involving singing, folk dancing, recitations, poetry writing and many other activities). Such eisteddfodau have helped maintain the inspirationally high standards of Welsh music.

English was acquired during the primary school years. For Lesley, this was partly through having English-speaking friends. For both Lesley and Bryn, the mass media, English monolinguals in the village and school were also routes to bilingualism. In the secondary school, both were able to study the 'Advanced Level' curriculum through both the English and Welsh language. A thorough grounding in Welsh and the much later acquisition of English had no negative effects on their ability to receive the curriculum through either language. Lesley and Bryn's route through higher education demonstrates the same point.

After leaving school, Bryn went to the Guildhall School of Music and studied mainly through the medium of English. Lesley took her undergraduate courses mostly through the medium of Welsh. One of the authors (CB) taught her, and remembers her ability to produce outstanding work in both Welsh and English. Lesley then took a teacher training course in London, this time through the medium of English. For both Lesley and Bryn, working bilingually in higher education was not a problem, indeed it was an asset.

At the Guildhall School of Music, Bryn Terfel took singing classes that involved learning German, French and Italian (as well as continuing to sing in Welsh and English). With impeccable attention to meaning and pronunciation, Bryn has continued to strengthen his much praised command of 'singing languages'. He sings perfectly in German, Italian, French, Russian, Welsh and English. When Bryn Terfel sings Welsh hymns (according to the Welsh people, Welsh is the language of heaven), it is as if he is taking musical dictation from heaven itself.

Bryn Terfel

Bryn Terfel learns languages quickly, attributed by Lesley to his extrovert character, a great willingness to 'have a go' and a lack of anxiety about making mistakes. Lesley followed suit and learned conversational German by attending courses in London. With Bryn Terfel in great demand throughout the world's operatic houses, the couple have the chance to live for short periods in different countries, particularly in Germany and Austria. Both Lesley and Bryn are committed to using German when in those countries.

Lesley suggests that her and Bryn's competence in two languages has positive advantages for learning a third language. First, being bilingual gives confidence in learning another language. Knowing that it is easy to operate in two languages makes it seem entirely possible to learn a third (or fourth) language. Second, the different pronunciations used when speaking two languages may make it easier to learn the pronunciation of a third language. A bilingual may be more flexible and adaptable in language learning. For example, Lesley found German easier to learn because there are some similarities in sound between Welsh and German.

On July 1st 1994, Lesley and Bryn's lives were changed with the arrival of baby Tomos. Though living in London, Lesley and Bryn decided that Tomos was to be brought up Welsh-speaking. Both parents speak Welsh to Tomos and he will be educated in Welsh-medium schooling. While this 'opera family' is truly international, they are enthusiastic for Tomos to have strong roots in the Welsh language and culture. The international success has not changed their deep commitment to the Welsh language and culture.

Matching his wife's *'summa cum laude'* degree, Bryn Terfel's singing has gained the highest praise from critics in places such as New York, Salzberg, London and Tokyo. Apart from a voice of the rarest beauty, a captivating 6 foot 3 inch presence on stage and a remarkable sense of audience, Bryn Terfel has been acclaimed as having an exceptional facility when singing in different languages. More than one critic has attributed such language virtuosity and a love of the sound of words to his early bilingualism.

A Bilingual Spanish-English Receptionist in New York

Tiziana C. comes originally from Turin in North Italy. Her native language is Italian. She began to learn English in school and used it while traveling in Europe. When she came to the United States in the late 1980s she met her husband, a Hispanic who did not speak English. She learnt Spanish through attending courses and through practicing with her husband.

Tiziana lives in Brooklyn, New York, and for the last two years she has worked as a receptionist for a small company that markets textile machinery in South and Central America, as well as in other countries around the world, including Italy. The company deals frequently with clients in Mexico and Argentina, also Colombia, Ecuador and Bolivia.

The company advertised for a bilingual (Spanish-English) receptionist to deal with monolingual Spanish clients. Tiziana's work involves dealing over the phone with customers from South and Central America. She also meets customers who visit New York to see the machinery. She is present at discussions and negotiations and translates between management and clients. She writes follow-up letters in Spanish and deals with Spanish correspondence.

Tiziana has had to master a fair amount of technical knowledge about textile machinery, including specialist vocabulary in English and Spanish. Her job carries a good deal of responsibility since she has to interpret correctly during face-to-face negotiations and explain technical aspects of the machinery to clients. Her bilingual expertise is recognized as a necessity for her job but it is not rewarded as a skill. Her salary is quite low, smaller than that of her colleague in the sales department. Although he has considerable experience in the field, he is a monolingual English speaker.

Tiziana's experience reflects that many smaller businesses in Western countries now recognize that bilingual and multilingual skills are essential for expanding business markets. However, bilingual expertise is still not widely acknowledged or rewarded as a skill that might merit extra salary or status.

The Dallas Burn – a Soccer Team with a Bilingual Approach

1995 was a happy year for soccer fans in Dallas, Texas, when Major League Soccer announced that one of their ten new teams for the season would be based in Dallas, with their headquarters at the Cotton Bowl Stadium. Soccer is a relative newcomer to the ranks of the major professional sports in the US, and is still far behind football, baseball and basketball in popularity. However, it is rapidly gaining supporters, and has provided an interesting bilingual 'angle' in US sport.

Whereas soccer does not as yet attract wide interest on the North American continent, in most countries of South America, it is by far the most popular sport, and players and supporters at all levels are passionately committed. Many new soccer clubs in the US have signed South American players to strengthen their teams, and many of these are Spanish-speaking.

The difference with the new Dallas Burn club is that they have seen the specific marketing potential of Spanish-speaking players in an state which has a large Hispanic population. (Twenty percent of the population of Texas are Spanish-speaking.) Three of the first players to be signed by the team were 38-year-old Mexican international forward, Hugo Sanchez, who hopes to complete his playing career with the club, Uruguayan international midfielder Washington 'Secco' Rodriguez and Columbian international midfielder Leonel Alvarez. Argentine defender Diego Soñora and four Spanish-speaking US players, Rene Ortiz, Jorge Florez. Juanito Sastoque and Lawrence Lozzano were also signed. Most of the South American players are learning English.

With so many Spanish speakers within the team, and with a Spanish-speaking assistant coach, Carlos Cordoba, a former national star from Argentina, the language of training sessions and socializing between the players is often Spanish. The Dallas Burn club promotes this 'bilingual' angle, with the South American players saying on television that the strong Spanish presence in the club and in the locality has helped them and their families settle well. The club has signed contracts with local English and Spanish language radio so that all games will be broadcast in both languages. There has also been a contract with Spanish language network radio. The presence of so many Spanish-speaking players on the team has provided heroes and role models for many young Hispanic soccer fans, who the club hopes will provide a strong and growing base of support as the team moves through its inaugural year.

Bilingualism in Sport

In sports where there is a movement of players across countries, bilingual and multilingual sports stars are often found. One example is soccer (association football), a favorite sport in Europe and South America, and increasing in Asia and North America. Star players such as Pele (Brazil), Cruyff (Holland), Maradona (Argentina), Klinsmann (Germany), Donadoni (Italy), Sousa (Portugal), Kanchelskis (Russia), Stoichkov (Bulgaria), Hagi (Romania) and Laudrup (Denmark) are all bilingual or multilingual. In some cases, second language acquisition has occurred when such players transferred to famous clubs in foreign countries.

Another example of bilingualism in sport is when there are international events (e.g. Olympic Games, World Cup Finals in different sports). On such occasions, bilingual referees, umpires, judges and adjudicators are needed. For example, a basketball match between two countries may require officials who can speak to each team in their own language. The following list comprises referees in the 1996 European Football Championships. The people chosen were not only outstanding for their skills in refereeing football games, but also, most were bilingual or trilingual, and therefore able to communicate with many teams in their preferred language.

1996 European Football Cup: List of Referees

NAME OF REFEREE	COUNTRY	LANGUAGES SPOKEN
Marc Batta	France	French/English/Italian
Ahmet Cakar	Turkey	Turkish/English/German
Piero Ceccarini	Italy	Italian/English/French
Manuel Diaz Vega	Spain	Spanish/Portuguese/Italian
David Elleray	England	English
Anders Frisk	Sweden	Sweden/English/German
Dermot Gallagher	England	English
Guy Goethals	Belgium	Flemish/French/English/German
Gerd Grabher	Austria	German/English
Bernd Heynemann	Germany	German/English
Vaclav Krondl	Czech Republic	Czech/English/German/Russian
Hellmut Krug	Germany	German/English
Nikolai Levnikov	Russia	Russian/English
Antonio J L Nieto	Spain	Spanish/English/French
Peter Mikkelsen	Denmark	Danish/English/German/French
Leslie Mottram	Scotland	English/French
Serge Muhmenthaler	Switzerland	German/French/Italian
Kim Milton Nielsen	Denmark	Danish/English/German
Atanas Ouzounov	Bulgaria	Bulgarian/German
Pierluigi Pairetto	Italy	Italian/French/English
Sandor Puhl	Hungary	Hungarian/German
Leif Sundell	Sweden	Swedish/English/German
Mario van der Ende	Holland	Dutch/English/French/German
Vadim Zhuk	Belarus	Russian/English

differentiation between monolinguals and bilinguals in the roles they play may send out clear messages. There is a hidden curriculum in employment patterns within the school. The students may acquire the idea subconsciously that monolingual English speakers are prestigious, relatively well paid and in relatively secure jobs. Those who speak Spanish as their home language and can cope in English as a second language tend to be allocated the lower class, more menial jobs. The role models in the school convey the message that to be bilingual is to be associated with less status and more poverty and disadvantage, less power and more subservience.

This discussion of bilingual professions has revealed the dual nature in the link between bilingualism and employment. In the first case there are those who can use their bilingualism as an advantage: to sell, to satisfy clients' needs, to succeed in providing a service. Bilingualism has an economic potential; it is an asset used by an individual for advancement. Bilingualism can become a marketable ability to bridge languages and cultures, securing trade and delivery of services.

In the second case, there are those people whose bilingual nature tends to mark them for the lower status, more marginalized and precarious employment. Such bilinguals may be allocated the poorest paid jobs in schools and shops. Bilingualism is attached to low status jobs that symbolize the least powerful, the least affluent and least prestigious sections in a society.

Further Reading

GROSJEAN, F., 1982, *Life with Two Languages*. Cambridge, MA Harvard University Press.

A Bilingual Spanish-English Bank Employee in New York

Maria (not her real name) was born in Guatemala, South America, and her native language is Spanish. She currently lives in Manhattan, New York, and has worked at the same bank for nine years. Her job as a personal banker involves direct contact with the public. Some of her duties include dealing with business and personal accounts, processing credit card applications, dealing with enquiries, processing cheques, giving customers advice, and setting up mortgages, loans and investments.

When the job was advertised, the ability to speak two languages was not stated as a requirement. However, Maria makes constant use of both languages at work. In her experience, it would be very difficult to fulfill the demands of the job without using both languages, because so many clients speak only Spanish, or at least feel far more comfortable discussing financial transactions in their first language. There are other personal bankers at the branch where she works who perform the same job functions as she does, but are obviously not able to deal with customers who clearly prefer to speak Spanish.

In the past, management has not recognized or supported the need for bilingual skills in the workplace. An incident occurred in which Maria was asked by her superiors not to speak Spanish because English was the language of the workplace. Because of this dispute she stayed home from work for a period of time. In the meantime clients with five and six figure balances were withdrawing their funds since it was difficult for them to communicate in English. Regular consumer clients were doing the same, since there was no Spanish-speaking representative to help them. This incident helped management to recognize the need for bilingual staff, but bilingual skills are still not a requirement for jobs. A few months prior to the interview with Maria, branch managers had been encouraged to attend an intensive Spanish course, but there was no obligation on them to do so.

The organization is run through the medium of English, and management do not deal with employees in any other language. However, a new staff magazine is being sent to all staff members once a month, with information in English, Spanish, Greek, Chinese, Vietnamese, Polish and Japanese. Automated Teller Machines also operate in these seven languages. Literature is on offer in English and Spanish, and also in Chinese in Chinatown branches.

Maria's experience shows that, in relatively monolingual countries such as the US or England, there has traditionally been an expectation that members of the public can and should communicate in the dominant language of the country. The need for bilingual or multilingual skills in dealing with the public has only begun to be recognized recently. Many professions now ask for bilingual skills as a requirement for certain jobs e.g. health and social workers, and in certain cases these skills are financially rewarded. This needs to happen more widely.

8: Bilingualism and the Mass Media

Introduction

The 20th century has seen the rapid development of mass communications. There has been an explosion in the number and distribution of newspapers and magazines, but, more importantly, radio and television have become important vehicles of mass communication, in the form of news, information and entertainment. The majority of households in Western countries possess at least one television set, and to own a television is the ambition of many families in less economically advanced world countries.

The mass media has attracted both praise and censure for a radical change in our way of life over the last 50 years. At its best, television is innovative, creative and educative. Television has contributed to the creation of the global village – to the world-wide diffusion of important news, sport and culture. Television enabled many viewers to witness the historic South African elections of 1994. Television enables an international audience to watch the Olympic games. Through television, we can follow the best of music and the arts from all countries. Television enables viewers to cross cultures. The development of satellite and cable technology has facilitated the transmission of programs world-wide. Television can contribute to multiculturalism, and to an empathy and insight into other cultures and lifestyles.

The recent development of sophisticated methods of telecommunications have meant that radio and television programs can reach a world-wide audience.

Mass Media and Anglo-American Culture

However, there is another side of television. The largest television industry in the world is in North America. It churns out a mass of programs, mainly light entertainment. These programs transmit Anglo-American culture to other parts of the world. Anglo-American music, cultural practices and lifestyles may be seen as prestigious and important, and, by implication, the indigenous cultures of other countries may be disparaged as outmoded and backward.

The English language is also diffused throughout the world through the mass media. The wide use of subtitling (cheaper than dubbing) means that the English language is heard by audiences in many other countries and can be understood with the aid of the subtitles and the context. Since the advent of satellite television, more viewers have access to English language programs directly from North America and Britain.

The widespread diffusion of the English language has had some beneficial effects. It has contributed to the development of bilingualism. It has provided a means for speakers of other languages to develop competence in English, as a useful language of international communication. In Scandinavian countries for instance, many English language films and other programs have traditionally been broadcast with subtitles. Only children's programs are dubbed. Motivation to learn English is usually high in Scandinavian countries, and television is one aid to competence. This is an additive bilingual situation, where the second language does not displace the first.

A news broadcast in English on Ugandan television. The mass media, particularly television, often means the spread of majority or official languages, at the expense of minority or lower status languages.

However, at the same time, the English language has penetrated, via television, into many majority languages. French and Japanese are two languages heavily influenced by English via the mass media. This massive influx of borrowings from English has provoked anxiety among language purists in both Japan and France. The French government has taken steps to reduce the quantity of non-French language broadcasting on radio and television. (See page 271.)

One positive development caused by the proliferation of international satellite and cable channels is that there is an increasing international market for programs. This, and the increasing use of subtitling, 'voice-overs' and dubbing, means that programs and films can be made in many lesser used languages. The cost can then be recouped by selling them on the international market.

Majority Language Mass Media and Minority Languages

When majority language mass media (e.g. English) enter minority language homes, the effect may be a subtractive bilingual situation. Minority language children in Britain and North America are exposed to the English language and Anglo-American culture from an early age. (Surveys have indicated that the average child in the US watches up to 15-20 hours television a week.) Minority language groups tend to be concerned about the potentially harmful effect on speakers of their language, especially young people and children, of the daily diet of majority language and culture. They are concerned that it further weakens the prestige and status of their own language and culture, further widening the gap between English (or another majority language) as the language of power, prestige, modern technology, fashion and entertainment and their own language, as an old-fashioned, outdated, despised and backward language of yesterday. There is also concern that watching majority language television may affect children's acquisition of their native language, and hasten language shift to the majority language.

Popular opinion maintains that the mass media have considerable influence on people's attitudes and behavior, especially that of children and young people. Research does not support this belief. McGuire (1985) concluded that mass media do not have a great effect on public attitudes. It is commonly believed that television, radio, satellite broadcasts, films, magazines and records have a great effect on the language attitudes of teenagers in particular. However the research of E. P. Jones (1982) and Baker (1985, 1992), indicated that mass media effect on language attitudes was small.

The research examined the effects of watching majority language television on the attitudes of Welsh-speaking children between 10 and 13 towards the Welsh language. The conclusion was that the media seemed to have very little effect on attitudes and that other factors, such as home environment and involvement in Welsh cultural institutions, were much more important.

Research conducted in the US in the 1970s indicated that US minority groups were under-represented on television, both in terms of the number of minority group individuals seen on television (much less than their percentage in the population) and the portrayal of their lifestyles. Most drama and comedy series portrayed affluent, middle class, 'white' lifestyles. (Liebert, Sprafkin &

Youths in Lesotho, South Africa, listen to popular music on the radio English, the former colonial language, is still an official language in Lesotho but Sesotho is the native language of over 90 percent of the population and is increasingly used in government and the mass media. The radio being a relatively inexpensive medium, is a more likely vehicle than television for minority or indigenous languages.

The Influence of Television

'Increasingly, a nation is becoming what television says it is. People's perceptions of themselves are developed through these external influences rather than through personal or shared experiences.'

(Welsh Language Board, Letter to the Secretary of State for Wales, 7 March 1989.)

European Television and the Quota System

In 1995, the European Parliament enforced a highly controversial new quota system for mainstream television channels in all countries of the European Union. The quota requires that half the programming on channels should be of European origins. Supporters of the quota argue that it blocks the flood of cheap and poor quality Anglo-American programs into European television. 'Let us protect the soul of Europe' was the comment of Jack Lang, MEP for France, and France's former Minister of Culture. One argument against the quota is that it ignores the particular situation of countries such as Spain and Portugal, which import Portuguese and Spanish language programs from Latin America.

The French Language and Culture Protected on Radio

The French government has traditionally protected the French media from invasion by other languages and cultures, especially English and Anglo-American culture. In 1996, for instance, French culture minister Philippe Douste-Blazy decreed that 40 percent of music played on French radio must be by French artists, and that 20 percent must come from 'new talents'.

Some artists have welcomed the new quota system because it allows and encourages more French talent on the radio, which has tended to be dominated by British and American artists, singing in English. However, this had repercussions on singers and groups from ethnic minorities living in France. Some African artists living in France have recorded songs in Arabic or other African languages and these will be excluded from the quota of French music. For this reason, some stars are being pressurized by their recording companies to record more songs in French. Pressure is being place on the Minister of Culture to redefine French music to include music in other languages recorded by members of ethnic minority groups.

Davidson 1982). Where minority groups were seen, the portrayal was often stereotyped or unfavorable, showing blacks or other ethnic minorities as lawbreakers, poor, subservient or powerless. What has not been conclusively shown is the effect of such portrayal on the attitudes of majority group members and minority group members. Does television worsen racism and the disparagement of minority groups? Does television increase feelings of inferiority among minority group members? There is no clear evidence (Howitt, 1982). Research has indicated that television may reinforce existing attitudes, and that viewers tend to interpret television in a way that supports their own values and beliefs.

Nevertheless, during the last quarter of the 20th century, there has been a concerted effort by many minority language groups to gain access to radio and particularly television. Minority language activists have seen minority language radio and television as vitally important to the maintenance of their language for the following reasons.

- Minority language media adds to the prestige and status of a language in the eyes of its speakers.
- Minority language media can add to a sense of unity and identity among its speakers.
- Minority language media helps to keep minority language speakers, especially children and young people, from the influence of majority language and culture. It acquaints them with their own heritage and culture and gives them pride in it.
- Minority language media can help disseminate a standard form of the language and also promotes new and technical vocabulary. Mass media can help the standardization of a minority language across a variety of registers.
- Minority language media can help the fluency of minority language speakers and can also help learners master the language.
- Minority language media creates well paid, high prestige jobs for minority language speakers. The radio and television industry can help boost the economy of minority language regions.

The value of minority language media in the maintenance of minority languages and the reversal of language shift has been disputed by Fishman (1991). Fishman (1991) argues that radio and television should not be hailed as the saviors of a minority language. He maintains that many minority language groups spend valuable resources in the lengthy and expensive task of establishing and maintaining minority language media, at the cost of more basic and fundamental issues such as the intergenerational transmission of the minority language. Fishman argues that the impact of majority language television, particularly English language television in the UK and North America, is so immense, that it cannot be countered by the much lesser influence of minority language.

> '...local mass media...can make positive contributions to RLS (Reversing Language Shift) only to the extent that they are directly related to and connected to fundamental family-neighbourhood-community functioning. They may well extend the vocabulary and help foster the 'modernity' images of the languages associated with them, thereby improving the attitudes toward these languages among their speakers. But the impact of this attitudinal improvement is soon lost insofar as RLS is concerned, unless that impact is explicitly and quickly fed back to the establishment, functioning and protection of the families, neighborhoods and communities in which these languages can be intergenerationally transmitted as mother tongues' (Fishman, 1991, page 270).

Research in this area has been minimal but experience seems to attest to some benefits of minority language media in the prestige, maintenance and promotion of minority languages, cultures and economies. Siguan (1993) claims that Galician television has contributed greatly to the increase in social prestige of the language. In Catalonia, the two Catalan television channels, established in 1983 and 1989, are now watched by up to 40 percent of the population. In Wales, the establishment of a Welsh language television channel in 1982 led to the creation of many independent television companies in North Wales, which have boosted the economy of the area. Such minority language television is regarded as important in standardizing the language in a wide range of registers across the north and south of Wales. Welsh television has also been viewed as a major force in the creation and a maintenance of a sense of identity and unity among Welsh speakers. In Europe, there is also minority language television in Irish, Gaelic (Scotland), Catalan, Basque and Galician.

Further Reading

BAETENS BEARDSMORE, H. & VAN BEECK, H., 1984, Multilingual Television Supply and Language Shift in Brussels. *International Journal of the Sociology of Language*, 48, 65-79.

BERRY, G. L. & MITCHELL-KERNAN, C., 1982, *Television and the Socialization of the Minority Child*. New York: Academic Press.

CRYSTAL, D., 1997, *The Cambridge Encyclopedia of Language* (Second edition). Cambridge: Cambridge University Press.

9: Bilingualism and Tourism

Introduction

Tourism has been a growing industry throughout the world in the 20th century. Increasing ease of travel and communications, more leisure time, earlier retirement, longer life and a greater disposable income have meant that vacations in other countries are part of the lifestyle of an increasing proportion of the population of many developed countries.

People go on vacation for a variety of reasons. Many people simply want a rest and a change, a sunny beach or beautiful mountains. Others want to engage in a leisure activity such as fishing, skiing or sailing. Many are seemingly oblivious or indifferent to the indigenous language and culture of the region they are visiting especially if it is a minority language and culture. Of all the thousands of people who visited the 1992 Olympics in Barcelona, for instance, how many realized that Catalan, rather than Spanish, was the main language of the region?

Travel inevitably involves the contact of cultures and of languages. This can be a positive and enriching experience. Often, however, tourism is seen as the enemy of multiculturalism and multilingualism and especially of minority languages and cultures. It has been said that tourism pollutes the environment, by creating waste, by ruining unspoilt rural areas with hotels, blocks of flats and marinas. Tourism can also pollute the cultural and linguistic environment. Tourists can be unaware of, and insensitive to cultural and linguistic diversity, expecting the language, food and other customs to be the same as at home. Too often, tourists wear 'blinkers', seeing only sun, sand and scenery and not being aware of the language and culture of the local inhabitants.

Tourists can contribute to the decline of minority languages and cultures, by expecting the local people to conform to tourist expectations. English-speaking tourists, especially, have been guilty of insensitivity and arrogance to other languages and cultures, expecting people in other countries to speak English and provide the cultural surroundings of home. Café signs in the South of France and Spain, 'English spoken here', 'English afternoon tea served', 'Fish and Chips Served Here' bear witness to the narrow cultural and linguistic vision of some visitors.

Mass tourism has contributed to the spread of the English language and Anglo culture throughout the world, at a cost to other languages and cultures. Mass tourism can also weaken the cultural, linguistic and economic structure of a region by its tendency to provide casual, seasonal employment and also a mass influx of temporary workers from other regions. Because of all these negative implications, tourism is often viewed with suspicion and contempt, especially by minority groups.

Tourism, however, is a growth industry. In the UK, for instance, tourism is now one of the most important industries. In 1991 the tourist industry in Britain had an annual turnover of more than £22 billion, representing 3.8 percent of the national wealth. One and a half million people were employed in tourism. In 1980, 12.4 million people visited Britain from overseas. By 1990, this had risen to 18 million. By 1996, throughout the European Union, nine million people were directly employed in the tourist industry, and it represented five percent of the GDP. Tourism is becoming increasingly important to the economy of many countries. We must ask whether it is possible to develop tourism that is 'ecologically sound' from the point of view of language and culture as well as environment. Is it possible to develop positive strategies for tourism that also promote multiculturalism and multilingualism?

Tourism, Bilingualism and Biculturalism

Tourism can enhance awareness of bilingualism and biculturalism in two main ways. First, it gives those in the tourist industry the opportunity to introduce the local language(s) and culture(s) to visitors. This is especially important in minority language regions. Second, the tourist industry should cater for visitors from other countries by being aware of their language needs and providing appropriate multilingual services.

Raising the Profile of a Lesser Used Language and Culture

Tourist areas often coincide with minority language regions. If we compare a map of the minority languages of Europe, for instance, with a map of non-urban tourist areas, we see that the two have many correspondences. This is not accidental. Tourists often wish to visit unspoilt rural areas, that are not over-developed and over-industrialized. These areas tend to be on the periphery, far from

Tourist information pamphlets for London and New York in a variety of languages.

the urban centers of power and influence. Minority languages tend to be spoken in such areas. If we look at the regions where languages such as Welsh, Gaelic, Breton, Irish, Catalan, Basque and Frisian are spoken, we see that they correspond with areas of considerable tourist activity.

Ideally, tourism should raise the profile of minority languages and cultures. The reality is, however, that the imbalance in power and prestige between majority and minority languages and cultures is reflected in the tourist industry. The lack of status of many minority languages in everyday life means that they may be more or less 'invisible' to the average tourist. Shop signs, restaurant menus, hotel and banking services, are usually in the majority language only. Since the majority language of the country or region is more likely to be known and used by tourists, the tourist industry tends to operate in that language.

Also, the economic and power imbalance between minority and majority groups is often reflected in the fact that key positions in the tourist industry are often held by majority group members. Minority group members tend to be employed at the lower end of the scale, in jobs that are low status, not so well paid and often temporary or seasonal. In Wales, for instance, participation of Welsh speakers in tourism, especially at managerial level or above, is relatively low, and few Welsh speakers operate tourism enterprises. This means that the economic benefits of tourism are not reaped by the minority community. Also, tourism is not structured in such a way as to bring economic benefits to more remote communities and areas of high unemployment.

Since few minority group members tend to be involved in decisions about tourism, tourism in minority language regions does not reflect the reality of the life of the minority group. For instance, few tourist enterprises in Wales make use of the Welsh language and culture as a part of their strategy to attract visitors. Of the 1200 hotels registered by the Welsh Tourist Board, only a handful are owned and operated by Welsh speakers, and only one establishment makes creative use of the Welsh language and culture in its marketing and operations. Within the attractions sector there are only four commercially-owned enterprises which accord the Welsh language an appropriate and dignified position on site.

If use is made of minority languages and cultures in tourist enterprises, this tends to follow an 'ethnic additive' approach, focusing on traditions, customs and cultural artifacts in a way that may portray them as 'quaint', 'archaic' or 'strange'. Whether we are talking about Breton embroidered costumes, Scottish tartan, Welsh harp music, Amish traditional dress, Native American rituals or Maori war dances, they may be presented as spectacles for tourists rather than as part of real-life, contemporary living cultures.

This situation is worsened by the fact that many minority language cultural leaders and language activists shun the tourist industry, believing that it ignores, devalues and even destroys their language and culture, and further weakens the economy of their region. They concentrate on what they perceive as its harmful impact rather than on its potential opportunities. Thus, the very people who could make a difference opt out of involvement and enterprise.

Tourism need not militate against minority languages and cultures. Many visitors are interested in other languages and cultures and can be attracted by a more positive, distinctive and dignified image of a minority language and culture. However, to accomplish this, there is a need for a broad-based strategy. An important part of such a strategy would be the involvement of minority language speakers at a higher level in tourism. This could be accomplished by an attitude-building campaign, training in commerce and enterprise and financial incentives to set up new ventures. Another part of the strategy would be the central promotion by government and state tourist boards of minority language and culture in a positive and contemporary way. These types of strategies would ensure that minority language groups derive greater economic benefit from tourism, and that tourism itself is harnessed to promote and enhance the status of the minority language and culture, and reinforce its use in the community.

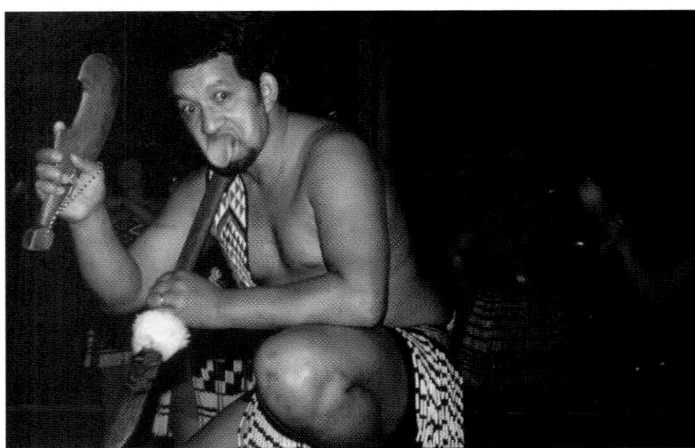

A man performs the haka, a traditional Maori war dance, for tourists in Rotorua, New Zealand. A danger of tourism is that aspects of local culture may become a quaint spectacle for visitors.

Tourism that actively promotes the host language and culture has been called 'cultural tourism'. With the growth of tourism throughout the world, more sophisticated and diverse strategies for boosting the tourist market have been devised. The importance of cultural tourism has been increasingly recognized.

In Europe, the European Union recently launched an action plan for cultural tourism. Fifty-three projects have already been launched throughout the community designed to foster long-term sustainable development and to benefit the host cultures.

Catering for the Language Needs of Tourists

When tourists visit a foreign country, they should ideally be aware of the differences in language and culture that exist. From a different perspective, those in the tourist industry should acknowledge, respect and cater for the different language backgrounds of their visitors. The quality of service is enhanced, and the visitors are made to feel more welcome, when information is given to them in a language they can understand. In countries where major international languages are spoken, particularly English, there may be a lack of awareness of the need to communicate with tourists in their own language. It may be assumed that all visitors have a basic knowledge of English but this is not necessarily true.

Also, the international status of English as a language of trade and enterprise is changing. The importance of using the customer's language is being increasingly perceived, and this, together with a growth in non-English-speaking markets, has caused an increase in the use of other languages in trading across nations. Similarly, in the tourist industry, there has been a growing recognition of the importance of using the customer's language to show respect and facilitate communication. In continental Europe, mastery of English and probably another foreign language would be seen as an integral part of all tourism training courses. Staff in contact with overseas visitors are expected to have at least basic foreign language skills. In

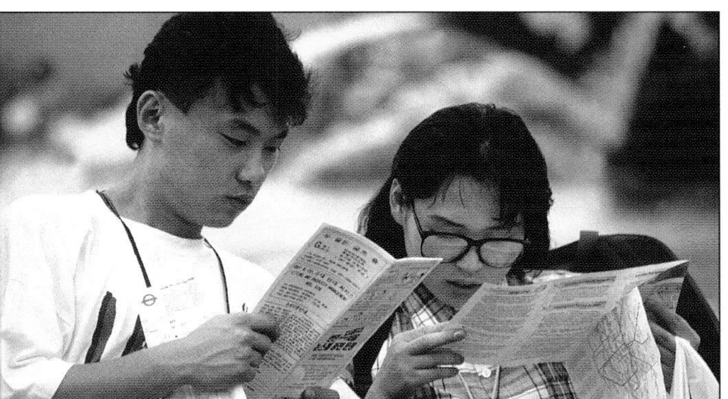

Japanese tourists in London study brochures and maps in Japanese. As the world wide tourism industry grows and as countries compete to attract tourists, it is becoming increasingly recognized that the industry must cater for a wide range of languages.

other parts of the world also, foreign language skills are perceived as a great asset for tourism employees.

The situation in the UK is improving. Pamphlets and guide books, notices, loudspeaker announcements and recorded tapes for use as visitor guides are now routinely provided in different languages in most major tourist centers. However, there is a need to train more bilingual staff in hotels, coach and taxi services, tourist information centers, travel agencies, restaurants, train stations and visitor attractions.

In 1990 and 1991, the British Tourist Authority published two reports entitled *Lost for Words* and *Winning Words*, urging the British tourist industry to focus on the need for foreign language competence among its employees. It emphasized the fact that nearly half the visitors from overseas do not speak English as a native language. It expressed the need for tailor-made courses to teach appropriate language skills to employees in different areas (e.g. basic comprehension and speaking skills for receptionists). It also underlined the need for financial rewards for foreign language skills in tourism. The report highlighted one problem, that companies with little or no language resources tended not to perceive opportunities for language use, while those with bilingual staff and positive language policies found demand increasing steadily. In Tourist Information Centers, for instance, it was discovered that the more languages were used, the greater the demand for language skills. Thus the centers were requiring greater language skills of new recruits in order to build up a body of expertise.

The British Tourist Authority publishes a wide range of statistics on incoming tourism to Britain. This enables companies to identify growth markets and plan their strategies. Companies are encouraged to conduct their own surveys. For instance, if a survey shows an increase in German visitors to a certain area, more German-speaking staff may need to be trained and appointed. Companies should not assume that only the most common European languages are needed. For example, Norwegian may be of far more use in the north-east of England than Italian or Spanish.

Gaelic Cultural Tourism

In 1993 the Scottish Highlands and Islands Enterprise published a report entitled *Gaelic Tourism Concepts*, making proposals for a tourist strategy based on marketing the Gaelic language and culture. Here are some of the recommendations.

The Gaelic language to be in a visible and high profile role. Gaelic or bilingual signage, including shop fronts, street signs, logos; tourist information in the form of booklets, brochures, pamphlets and videos; Gaelic written and audiovisual material in museums and visitor centers. These would bring the language to the attention of visitors and contribute to its reinforcement in the community.

A network of interpretive centers where the history and culture of the Gaelic-speaking areas would be explained through the medium of Gaelic but with interpretation in English and other languages.

The development of Gaelic-medium activities such as drama and music, and sports such as sailing or hill walking. Cultural tourist activities such as language courses, historical tours and genealogical study.

The development of the tourist potential of Gaelic cultural events such as the *National Mod, Feisean* (local non-competitive music festivals), *Blasad den Iar* (interpretive community-based tourist shows), Gaelic exhibitions and drama events.

The provision of Gaelic accommodation/pubs/restaurants with Gaelic speaking staff, Gaelic music, foods, customs. This would encourage a Gaelic atmosphere for the enjoyment of tourists and local people and would also contribute to the development of Gaelic at community level.

Bilingualism and Language Policies

1: Language as a Problem, a Right, and a Resource

Introduction

Bilingualism not only exists within individuals, within their cognitive systems, in the family and in the local community, it is also directly and indirectly interwoven into the politics of a nation. Bilingualism is not only studied linguistically, psychologically and sociologically. It is also studied in relationship to power structures, political systems and basic philosophies in society.

Bilingual education, for instance, does not just reflect educational preferences and curriculum decisions. Rather, bilingual education is surrounded and underpinned by basic beliefs about minority languages, minority cultures, in-migrants, equality of opportunity, empowerment, affirmative action, the rights of individuals and the rights of language minority groups, assimilation and integration, desegregation and discrimination, pluralism and multiculturalism, diversity and discord, equality of recognition for minority groups and social cohesion. Education has been conceived as part of the solution and part of the problem of achieving unity in diversity.

Bilingual Finnish-Swedish signs in Finland. In Finland, the Swedish-speaking minority residing in the south of the country have equal language rights with the Finnish-speaking majority.

It is important for students, teachers and educational policy makers to be aware of how their present and future activity not only concerns children in classrooms, but also fits into the overall language policy of a state or a nation.

Three Perspectives on Languages

In considering different assumptions and varying perspectives that are at the root of the politics of bilingualism, Ruiz (1984) suggests that there are three basic orientations or perspectives about language around which people and groups vary: language as a problem, language as a right and language as a resource. These three dispositions towards language planning are not necessarily at the conscious level. They may be embedded in the unconscious assumptions of planners and politicians. Such orientations are regarded as fundamental and related to a basic philosophy or ideology held by an individual.

Language as a Problem

Public discussion of bilingual education and languages in society often commences with the idea of language as causing complications and difficulties. This is well-illustrated in discussions about the supposed cognitive problems of operating in two languages. Perceived problems are not limited to thinking. Personality and social problems such as split identity, cultural dislocation, a poor self-image and anomie are also sometimes attributed to bilinguals. At a group rather than an individual level, bilingualism is sometimes connected with national or regional disunity and intergroup conflict. Language is thus also viewed as a political problem.

Part of the 'language-as-problem' orientation is that perpetuating language minorities and language diversity is perceived as causing less integration, less cohesiveness, more antagonism and more conflict in society. The perceived complication of minority languages is to be solved by assimilation into the majority language. Such an argument holds that the majority language (e.g. English) unifies the diversity. The ability of every citizen to communicate with ease in the nation's majority language is regarded as the common leveler. A strong nation is regarded as a unified nation. Unity within a nation is seen as synonymous with uniformity and similarity. The opposing argument is that it is possible to have national unity without uniformity. Diversity of languages and national unity can co-exist (e.g. Singapore, Luxembourg, Switzerland).

The co-existence of two or more languages is rarely a cause of tension, disunity, conflict or strife. The history of war suggests that economic, political and religious differences are prominent as causes. Language is seldom the cause of conflict. Religious Crusades and Jihads, rivalries between different religions, rivalries between different political parties and economic aggression tend to be the instigators of strife. Language, in and by itself, is rarely a cause of unrest (Otheguy, 1982). In a research study on causes of civil strife, Fishman (1989) found that language was not a cause. 'The widespread journalistic and popular political wisdom that linguistic heterogeneity *per se* is necessarily conducive to civil strife, has been shown, by our analysis, to be more myth than reality' (Fishman, 1989, page 622). Rather, the causes of strife were found to be deprivation, authoritarian regimes and modernization.

A minority language is often connected with the problems of poverty, underachievement in school, minimal social and vocational mobility and with a lack of integration with the majority culture. In this perspective, the minority language is perceived as a partial cause of social, economic and educational problems, rather than an outcome of such problems. This 'language is an obstacle' attitude is summed up in the phrase, 'If only they would speak English, their problems would be solved'. The minority language is thus seen as a handicap to be overcome by the school system. One resolution of the problem is regarded as the increased teaching of a majority language (e.g. English) at the expense of the home language. Developing bilingualism is seen as an irrelevant or a secondary and less important aim of schooling. Thus submersion and Transitional Bilingual education aim to develop competent English language skills in minority language children as quickly as possible so they are on par with English first language speakers in the mainstream classroom.

A language problem is sometimes perceived as caused by 'strong' forms of bilingual education. Such education, it is sometimes argued, will cause social unrest or disintegration in society. Fostering the minority language and ethnic differences might provoke group conflict and disharmony. The response is generally that 'strong' forms of bilingual education will lead to better integration, harmony and social peace. As Otheguy (1982, page 314) comments of the US: 'Critics of bilingual education with a concern for civil order and social disharmony should also concern themselves with issues of poverty, unemployment, and racial discrimination rather than concentrate on the use of Spanish in schools. In pledges of allegiance, it is liberty and justice – not English – for all that is to keep us indivisible'.

'Strong' forms of bilingual education should not be connected with the language problem orientation. Rather, the evidence suggests that developing bilingualism and biliteracy within a 'strong' bilingual education situation is educationally feasible and can lead to:

- higher achievement across the curriculum for minority language children;
- maintaining the home language and culture;
- fostering self-esteem, self-identity and a more positive attitude to schooling.

Such higher achievement may enable better usage of human resources in a country's economy and less wastage of talent. Higher self-esteem may also relate to increased social harmony and peace.

Within this 'problem' orientation, there not only exists the desire to remove differences between groups to achieve a common culture. There can be the desire for intervention to improve the position of language minorities. 'Whether the orientation is represented by malicious attitudes resolving to eradicate, invalidate, quarantine, or inoculate, or comparatively benign ones concerned with remediation and "improvement", the central activity remains that of problem-solving' (Ruiz, 1984, page 21).

Language as a Right

A different orientation to that of 'language as a problem' is thinking of language as a basic, human right. Just as there are individual rights in choice of religion, so it is argued, there should be an individual right to choice of language. Just as there are attempts to eradicate discrimination based on skin color and creed, so people within this orientation will argue that language prejudice and discrimination need to be eradicated in a democratic society (Skutnabb-Kangas & Phillipson, 1994).

The United Nations Building in New York.

Over time and with a gradual growth in public acceptance, matters such as religious persecution and the education of children develop a moral force and a collective will that enables religious rights and education rights to be embedded in society. Increasingly, arguments for language rights have become stronger, more widespread and accepted.

Such language rights may be derived from personal, legal and constitutional rights. Personal language rights will draw on the right to freedom of individual expression. It may also be argued that there are certain natural or moral language rights in group rather than individual terms. The rights of language groups may be expressed in terms of the importance of preservation of heritage language and culture communities, and expressed as 'rights to protection' and 'rights to participation'. This includes welfare rights and rights to liberty and self-determination.

A further level of language rights may be international, derived from pronouncements from organizations such as the United Nations, UNESCO, the Council of Europe and the European Community (see page 279). Each of these four organizations has declared that minority language groups have the right to maintain their language. In the European community, a directive (25th July 1977: 77/486/EEC) stated that Member States should promote the teaching of the mother tongue and the culture of the country of origin in the education of migrant workers' children. However, individual countries have generally ignored such international declarations. Particular international examples (e.g. Sámi in Norway, Kurds in Turkey and Gikuyu speakers in Kenya) are portrayed in Skutnabb-Kangas, Phillipson & Rannut (1994). The kind of rights, apart from language rights, that minority groups may claim include: protection, membership of their ethnic group and separate existence, non-discrimination and equal treatment, education and information in their ethnic language, freedom to worship, freedom of belief, freedom of movement, employment, peaceful assembly and association, political representation and involvement, and administrative autonomy.

In the US, the rights of the individual are a major part of democracy. As Trueba (1989, page 103) suggests, 'American democracy has traditionally attached a very high value to the right to disagree and debate, and to enjoy individual and group cultural and linguistic freedom without jeopardizing the right of others or our national unity'. In the United States, questions about language rights are not only discussed in college classrooms and language communities, and debated in government and federal legislatures. Language rights have a history of being tested in US courtrooms. This is significantly different from European experience where language rights have rarely been tried in courts. From the early 1920s to the present, there has been a continuous debate in US courts of law regarding the legal status of language minority rights. To gain short-term protection and a medium-term guarantee for minority languages, legal challenges have become an important part of the language rights movement in the United States. The legal battles are not just couched in minority language versus majority language contests. The test cases also concern children versus schools, parents versus school boards, state versus the federal authority (Ruiz, 1984). Whereas minority language activists among the Basques in Spain and the Welsh in Britain have been taken to court by the central government for their actions, US minority language activists have taken the central and regional government to court. One example will illustrate.

A landmark in United States' bilingual education was a lawsuit. A court-case was brought on behalf of Chinese students against the San Francisco School District in 1970. The case concerned whether or not non-English-speaking students received equal educational opportunity when instructed in a language they could not understand. The failure to provide bilingual education was alleged to violate both the equal protection clause of the 14th Amendment and Title VI of the Civil Rights Act of 1964. The case, known as *Lau versus Nichols*, was rejected by the federal district court and a court of appeals, but was accepted by the Supreme Court in 1974. The verdict outlawed English submersion programs and resulted in nationwide 'Lau remedies'. Such remedies reflected a broadening of the goals of bilingual education to include the possible maintenance of minority language and culture. The Lau remedies created some expansion in the use of minority languages in schools, although they rarely resulted in true heritage language, enrichment or maintenance programs. For the purposes of this topic, the Lau court case is symbolic of the dynamic and continuing contest to establish language rights in the US.

The 1992 United Nations Declaration of Rights

The United Nations 1992 Declaration on the Rights of Persons belonging to National or Ethnic, Religious and Linguistic Minorities includes the following articles:

Article 1

1. 'States shall protect the existence and the national or ethnic, cultural, religious and linguistic identity of minorities within their respective territories, and shall encourage conditions for the promotion of that identiy'.

2. 'States shall adopt appropriate legislative and other measures to achieve those ends'.

Article 2

1. 'Persons belonging to national or ethnic, religious and linguistic minorities (hereinafter referred to as persons belonging to minorities) have the right to enjoy their own culture, to profess and practice their own religion, and to use their own language, in private and in public, freely and without interference or any form of discrimination'.

2. 'Persons belonging to minorities have the right to participate effectively in cultural, religious social, economic and public life'.

3. 'Persons belonging to minorities have the right to participate effectively in decisions on the national and, where appropriate, regional level concerning the minority to which they belong or the regions in which they live, in a manner not incompatible with national legislation'.

4. 'Persons belonging to minorities have the right to establish and maintain their own associations'.

5. 'Persons belonging to minorities have the right to establish and maintain, without any discrimination, free and peaceful contacts with other members of their group and with persons belonging to other minorities, as well as contacts across frontiers with citizens of other States to whom they are related by national or ethnic, religious and linguistic ties'.

Article 3

1. 'Persons belonging to minorities may exercise their rights, including those set forth in this Declaration, individually as well as in community with other members of their group, without any discrimination'.

2. 'No disadvantage shall result for any person belonging to a minority as the consequence of the exercise or non-exercise of the rights set forth in this Declaration'.

Article 4

1. 'States shall take measures where required to ensure that persons belonging to minorities may exercise fully and effectively all their human rights and fundamental freedoms without any discrimination and in full equality before the law'.

2. 'States shall take measures to create favorable conditions to enable persons belonging to minorities to express their characteristics and to develop their culture, language, religion, traditions and customs, except where specific practices are in violation of national and contrary to international standards'.

3. 'States should take appropriate measures so that, wherever possible, persons belonging to minorities have adequate opportunities to learn their mother tongue or to have instruction in their mother tongue'.

4. 'States should, where appropriate, take measures in the field of education, in order to encourage knowledge of the history, traditions, language and culture of the minorities existing within their territory. Persons belonging to minorities should have adequate opportunities to gain knowledge of the society as a whole'.

5. 'States should consider appropriate measures so that persons belonging to minorities may participate fully in the economic progress and development in their country'.

Article 5

1. 'National policies and programs shall be planned and implemented with due regard for the legitimate interests of persons belonging to minorities'.

2. 'Programs of co-operation and assistance among States should be planned and implemented with due regard for the legitimate interests of persons belonging to minorities'.

Article 6

'States should co-operate on questions relating to persons belonging to minorities, including exchange of information and experiences, in order to promote mutual understanding and confidence'.

Article 7

'States should co-operate in order to promote respect for the rights set forth in this Declaration'.

Article 8

1. 'Nothing in this Declaration shall prevent the fulfillment of international obligations of States in relation to persons belonging to minorities. In particular, States shall fulfill in good faith the obligations and commitments they have assumed under international treaties and agreements to which they are parties'.

2. 'The exercise of the rights set forth in this Declaration shall not prejudice the enjoyment by all persons of universally recognized human rights and fundamental freedoms'.

3. 'Measures taken by States to ensure the effective enjoyment of the rights set forth in this Declaration shall not prima facie be considered contrary to the principle of equality contained in the Universal Declaration of Human Rights'.

4. 'Nothing in this declaration may be construed as permitting any activity contrary to the purposes and principles of the United Nations, including sovereign equality, territorial integrity and political independence of States'.

Article 9

'The specialized agencies and other organizations of the United Nations system shall contribute to the full realization of the rights and principles set forth in this Declaration, within their respective fields of competence'.

particularly through testing the law in the courtroom (Casanova, 1991; Hakuta, 1986b; Lyons, 1990).

Language rights are not only expressed in legal confrontations with the chance of being established in law. Language rights are often expressed at the grass roots level by protests and pressure groups, by local action and argument. For example, the *kohanga reo* (language nests) movement in New Zealand provides a grass roots instituted immersion pre-school experience for the Maori people (see pages 489 and 515). Beginning in 1982, these 'language nests' offer a 'pre-school all-Maori language and culture environment for children from birth to school age, aimed at fostering complete development and growth within a context where only the Maori language is spoken and heard' (Corson, 1990a, page 154).

Another example of grass roots expression of 'language as a right' is the recent Celtic (Ireland, Scotland, Wales and Brittany) experience. In these countries, 'grass roots' created pre-school playgroups, 'mother and toddler' groups and adult language learning classes have been established so that the heritage languages can be preserved in both adult social interaction and especially in the young. Stronger activism and more insistent demands have led to the establishment of heritage language elementary schools, particularly in urban, mostly English-speaking (or French-speaking) areas. Not without struggle, opposition and antagonistic bureaucracy, parents have obtained the right for education in the indigenous tongue. Such pressure groups have contained parents who speak the indigenous language, and those who speak only English (or French in Brittany), yet wish their children to be taught in the heritage language of the area.

A specific case is the growth of designated bilingual schools in Wales (UK). The growth in such state-funded bilingual schools owes much to parents insisting on the right to have their children educated in the home language. Through the activity of 'Parents for Welsh-medium Education' and through informal networks of local parents and language activists, Local Education Authorities (often as a reaction to sustained pressure and persuasion) have responded to market preferences. Such parental groups have naturally contained Welsh-speaking parents who wish the language to be reproduced in their children with the essential help of formal education. However, the pressure for bilingual schooling has also come from non-Welsh-speaking parents.

In North American and British society, no formal recognition is usually made in politics or the legal system of categories or groups of people based on their culture, language or race. Rather the focus is on individual rights.

Declarations of Language Rights

In the attempt to gain individual and group language rights, a variety of international and national bodies have proposed a series of human rights, political rights and minority rights. For example, there is the United Nations Universal Declaration of the Rights of a Child established in 1989. In the attempt to provide freedom, liberty and justice for minority and oppressed groups in the world, there has been a series of declarations, charters, covenants, conventions, resolutions, documents, proposals, and submissions.

However, as Skutnabb-Kangas, Phillipson & Rannut (1994) have shown, there has been a lack of consideration not only of human linguistic rights, but of their coordination, and their establishment in international law so that those who are oppressed have recourse to greater linguistic justice through national and particularly international courts. Examples by these authors include the Sámi in Norway, Finnish in-migrants in Sweden and the Kurds in mainland Europe. The kind of linguistic rights that appear to be denied in these cases include: the freedom to speak the native language in school, to deal with bureaucracy and officialdom (e.g. the police, local government) in the language of one's choice, for a regional language to have programs on television, and to use the language of one's community with a nurse or doctor.

The accent is on individual equality of opportunity, individual rewards based on individual merit. Policies of non-discrimination, for example, tend to be based on individual rather than group rights. Language minority groups will nevertheless argue for rewards and justice based on their existence as a definable group in society. Sometimes based on territorial rights, often based on ethnic identity, such groups may argue for rewards in proportion to their representation in society. Group-based rights are often regarded as a way of redressing injustices to language minorities. This may be a temporary step on the way to full individual rights. Alternatively, language minorities may claim the right to some independent power, some measure of decision-making and some guarantee of self-determination.

A note of caution about language rights needs sounding. Liberal words about individual rights can hide preferences for coercion and conformity (Skutnabb-Kangas, 1991). Stubbs (1991) talks of the experience in England with language minorities where government reports 'use a rhetoric of language entitlement and language rights, and of freedom and democracy...[which] makes the correct moral noises, but it has no legislative basis, and is therefore empty. There is talk of entitlement, but not of the discrimination which many children face; and talk of equality of opportunity, but not of equality of outcome' (pages 220-221).

Dimensions of Language Rights

One aim in expressing language rights in different Charters, Declarations, Covenants and Conventions is that language rights are made overt rather than covert, are formally stated rather than implied. Another dimension of language rights (illustrated below) moves from assimilation to maintenance orientation. At the assimilation-oriented end of the dimension is the prohibition of language rights for minority language speakers. Moving further along this dimension comes toleration of language minorities, followed by non-discrimination, by permission, and at the end of the scale (at the maintenance-oriented end) comes promotion of language minorities.

ASSIMILATION ORIENTATION → **MAINTENANCE ORIENTATION**

Prohibition of Language Rights — Toleration — Non-discrimination — Permission — Promotion of Language Rights

REFERENCE: SKUTNABB-KANGAS & PHILLIPSON, 1994

Documents that Mention Language Rights

Some major illustrative quotations from important documents that mention language rights are given below.

The 1945 Charter of the United Nations:
Article 55

'Universal respect for, and observance of, human rights and fundamental freedoms for all without distinction as to race, sex, language, or religion'.

The 1948 Universal Declaration of Human Rights by the United Nations:
Article 2

'Everyone is entitled to all the rights and freedoms set forth in this Declaration, without distinction of any kind, such as race, color, sex, language, religion, political or other opinion, national or social origin, property, birth or other status'.

The United Nations' Convention on the Rights of the Child, (1989):
Article 29

'The development of respect for the child's parents, his or her own cultural identity, language and values, for the national values of the country in which the child is living, the country from which he or she may originate and for civilizations different from his or her own'.

Article 30

'In those States in which ethnic, religious or linguistic minorities or persons of indigenous origin exist, a child belonging to such a minority or who is indigenous shall not be denied the right, in community with other members of his or her group, to enjoy his or her own culture, to profess and practice his or her own religion, or to use his or her own language'.

Language Rights in Kenya: Ngugi wa Thiong'o

Ngugi wa Thiong'o was born into a large peasant family in Kenya in 1938, became a lecturer at the University of Nairobi, was imprisoned without trial by the Kenyatta regime in the 1970s, and became a celebrated Kenyan novelist. Ngugi's first two novels, *Weep Not, Child* (1964) and *The River Between* (1965), portray the impact of colonialism on the East African peoples. His third and most successful work is about the Mau Mau rebellion, *A Grain of Wheat* (1967). His criticism of the Kenyan government in a later novel, *Petals of Blood* (1977), led to his detention (1978-79) under a charge of sedition.

Part of his writing portrays the struggle of African people to liberate their economy, politics, culture and languages from a European colonialist attitude and Americanization. For Ngugi wa Thiong'o, African language rights concern self-regulation and self-determination. 'English (like French and Portuguese) was assumed to be the natural language of literary and even political mediation between African people in the same nation and between African and other nations. In some instances these European languages were seen as having a capacity to unite African peoples against divisive tendencies inherent in the multiplicity of African languages within the same geographical state' (Ngugi wa Thiong'o, 1985, page 111).

Ngugi wa Thiong'o spoke Gikuyu as a child, in the fields, in the home, and in the community. Gikuyu is a Bantu language, spoken by about four million people or 20 percent of the population of Kenya. The use of Gikuyu in these different contexts produced a spiritual unity and a sense of belonging. Evenings of story-telling around a fire gave him a love of the suggestive power and music of the Gikuyu language. However, he was sent to a colonial school that taught solely through the medium of English. The harmony was broken. The language of education was at variance with the language of his culture. Gikuyu was suppressed, as he vividly recalls: 'In Kenya, English became much more than a language: it was *the* language, and all others had to bow before it in deference. Thus one of the most humiliating experiences was to be caught speaking Gikuyu in the vicinity of the school. The culprit was given corporal punishment – three to five strokes of the cane on bare buttocks – or was made to carry a metal plate around the neck with the inscription: I AM STUPID or I AM A DONKEY. Sometimes the culprits were fined money they could hardly afford' (Ngugi wa Thiong'o, 1985, pages 114-115).

A child was given a button at the start of the school day. If a peer was caught speaking Gikuyu, the button was passed to him or her. Whoever had the button at the end of the day was punished. Children were made language 'witch-hunters' and learnt to be traitors to their friends.

In contrast, achievement in English oracy and literacy was rewarded with prizes, prestige and applause. English was the passport to fame and success, the measure of ability and potential, and the main determinant of progress up the educational ladder. Nobody could pass an exam unless they passed English, no matter how brilliant in science or arts. Ngugi wa Thiong'o argues that children were mentally colonized by the imposition of English and the rejection of their home language.

REFERENCE: WA THIONG'O, 1985

Language Rights in Romania

A census was conducted in Romania on January 7th, 1992. This census revealed a population of 22.76 million residents of whom 89.3 percent (20,324,892) were registered as Romanians, with 7.1 percent (1,619,368) classified as Magyars (Hungarians) and 1.8 percent of the population (409,723) as Romanies (see also page 415). There are other ethnic groups in Romania: German, Serbian, Ukrainian, Slovak, Czech, Bulgarian, Croatian, Turkish and Tatar, Russian-Lippovan, Polish, Armenian, Greek and Italian minorities. Such language diversity has led to language rights being an important issue in Romania.

The Romanians pride themselves on their democratic approach to such a variety of ethnic groups and different languages in Romania. All children in school are expected to learn the Romanian language as it is the official language, and it is compulsory for all Romanian citizens to know the language irrespective of their nationality or ethnic origins. However, Article 118 of the new Education Law, passed by Parliament on July 25, 1995, states that 'Persons belonging to national minorities have the right to study and receive instruction in their mother tongue at all levels and all forms of education in accordance with the present Law.'

The following article, Article 119, states that if there is sufficient local need, then language classes or schools can be set up to teach through the language of national minorities. Thus, ethnic minority schools have been instituted to teach through the language of national minorities. Since 1994, Hungarian language education has been developed at all education levels, pre-school, primary, secondary and university level. With Hungarians forming 7.1 percent of the population, there are over a thousand pre-school units or sections teaching Hungarian as the mother tongue at the pre-school level. A similar provision is found at the primary school level. Over 130 high schools teach Hungarian as a mother tongue. German is also taught as a mother tongue in over 160 pre-school units, over 120 primary schools and in 14 high schools.

Language rights are also mirrored in multilingualism at institutional level. Romania is noted for its multilingualism in the mass media and culture. For example, there are Hungarian theaters and folk ensembles, choirs which operate in Yiddish, Ukrainian, Lippovan, Bulgarian and Greek. There are also publishers who produce work in Hungarian, German, Yiddish and Serbian plus newspapers in Hungarian and German.

Programs on radio and TV are available in Hungarian and German, while radio programs in Greek, Turkish and Armenian are broadcast for half an hour weekly.

Trueba (1991, page 44) sounds a further caution: 'Language rights of ethnolinguistic minorities are not detachable from their basic human rights, their right to their culture and their civil rights'. Social, economic and political participation rights should not be jeopardized at the expense of retaining language cultural differences. To win language and cultural rights at the expense of rights to free passage, full political participation and equal economic access would be little or no victory for the people, nor in the long term, the language and culture itself.

The implementation of language rights depends upon public education, the development of a consciousness and a collective will. The danger of language rights is that conformity rather than conviction is sought. While rights provide a valuable part of the official sanctioning of a minority language, in themselves, rights do not automatically mean increased language life. Language rights may seek to extend the potential range of functions for a language, but people cannot be legally compelled to retain a language or use a learnt language. Language rights have to be joined by fostering positive attitudes to a language, winning hearts and minds. At worst, language rights may compel. At best, such rights become part of the legitimization and institutionalization of a minority language. Rights may seek to empower a language. Empowerment at a personal level requires many other supports and rewards.

Language as a Resource

An alternative orientation to 'language as a problem' and 'language as a right', is the idea of language as a personal and national resource. The recent movement in Britain and North America for increased second and foreign language fluency (e.g. in French) fits into this orientation. Under the general heading of language as a resource also comes a view of minority and lesser used languages as a cultural and social resource. While languages may be viewed in terms of their economic bridge-building potential, languages may also be supported for their ability to build social bridges across different groups, bridges for cross-fertilization between cultures.

The recent trend in Europe and North America, for example, has been to expand foreign language education. Second language study is increasingly viewed as an essential resource to promote foreign trade and world influence. Thus, the paradox is that while bilingual education to support minority languages has tended to be depreciated in the United States, the current trend is to appreciate English speakers who learn a second language to ensure a continued major role for the US in world politics and the world economy. There is a tendency to value the acquisition of languages while devaluing the language minorities who have them. While integration and assimilation is still the dominant ideology in US internal politics, external politics increasingly demand bilingual citizens (Kjolseth, 1983). Ovando (1990) describes US language policy as schizophrenic. 'On the one hand we encourage and promote the study of foreign languages for English monolinguals, at great cost and with great inefficiency. At the same time we destroy the linguistic gifts that children from non-English language backgrounds bring to our schools' (Ovando, 1990, page 354).

In the United States, the idea of language as a resource not only refers to the development of a second language in monolingual speakers. It also refers to the preservation of languages other than English. For example, children whose home language is Spanish or German, Italian or Chinese, Greek or Japanese, Portuguese or French have a home language that can be utilized as a resource. One case is that of the Spanish speakers in the US who together make the US the fourth largest Spanish-speaking country in the world. Just as water in the reservoir and oil in the oil fields are preserved as basic resources and commodities, so a language such as Spanish, despite being difficult to measure and define as a resource, may be preserved for the common economic, social and cultural good. Suppression of language minorities, particularly by the school system, may be seen as economic, social and cultural wastage. Instead, such languages are a natural resource that can be exploited for cultural, spiritual and educational growth as well as for economic, commercial and political gain.

Within the 'language as a resource' orientation, lies the assumption that linguistic diversity does not cause separation nor less integration in society. Rather, it is possible that national unity and linguistic diversity can co-exist. Unity and diversity are not necessarily incompatible. Tolerance and co-operation between groups may be as possible with linguistic diversity as they would be unlikely when such linguistic diversity is repressed.

A frequent debate concerns which languages are a resource? The favored languages tend to be those that are both international and particularly valuable in international trade. A lower place is given in the status ranking to minority languages that are small, regional and of less perceived value in the international marketplace. For example, in England, French has traditionally been placed in schools at the top of the first division. German, Spanish, Danish, Dutch, Modern Greek, Italian and Portuguese are the major European languages placed in the second division. Despite large numbers of mother tongue Bengali, Panjabi, Urdu, Gujarati, Hindi and Turkish speakers, the politics of English education rele-

Linguistic Diversity and Minority Language Rights in Spain: 1

Introduction

Spain is a country of great cultural and linguistic diversity. The Spanish State is composed of several regions that have their own traditions, cultures and sometimes languages. Castilian (Spanish) is the majority language, spoken by over 70 percent of the population as a mother tongue. The other main languages are Catalan, spoken by seven million people in Catalonia, Valencia and the Balearic Islands. Catalan is a Romance language closely related to Spanish. Galician, a Romance language similar to Portuguese is spoken by about 2.5 million people in the Galician region. Basque (Euskara), a language seemingly unrelated to any other known language in the world, is spoken by half a million people in the Basque Country and also in Navarra. Catalan and Basque are also spoken in border areas of France.

During the rule of General Franco (1939-1975), a repressive policy towards regional languages was adopted. The emphasis was on uniting the country and eradicating regional identities and any movement for regional autonomy. Castilian Spanish was to be the unifying common language of all Spanish citizens. Regional languages were banned from schools and even churches and only Castilian was used in the government, the press, broadcasting and in public generally. Only towards the end of the dictatorship were these measures liberalized. Franco's harsh measures created a generalized opposition to the regime in territories with their own language and traditions of autonomy, and there was also sympathy for minority cultures among other Spaniards who were opposed to General Franco.

After Franco died in 1975, Spain began a period of transition from a dictatorship to a democracy, and towards increasing industrialization. This gave the various minority groups the freedom to assert their separateness, and all those who had been in opposition to Franco united in their support for these 'historical nationalities'. The new Spanish Constitution (1978) established the right to autonomy of the different regions of Spain. The country was divided into 17 Autonomous Communities, and each passed its own Statute of Autonomy. Not all communities have the same degree of self-government nor the same authority. Only seven, (Andalusia, the Basque Country, the Canary Islands, Catalonia, Galicia, Navarra and Valencia) have full authority over educational matters.

The 1978 Spanish Constitution declared its intent to *'protect all Spaniards and Spanish territories in the exercise of human rights, their cultures and traditions, languages and institutions.'* Article 3 of this Constitution declared that Castilian was the official language of the State and that all Spanish citizens should know it and have the right to use it in any part of Spain. It also granted the minority languages of Spain official status and declared that *'this language diversity should enjoy special respect and protection by institutions and citizens alike'.*

In the 1980s the governments of the regions where minority languages were spoken passed laws of 'linguistic normalization'. These laws were passed to ensure that the minority languages in question would become the 'norm' in their respective communities, in education and official life. The aim was also to ensure that all citizens living in these communities would be able to communicate in both languages, Castilian and the regional language.

Basque

The Basque country is situated both in France and Spain and has a population of approximately three million people. Basque (known by its speakers as Euskara) is spoken by about half a million people in Spain, and by about 80,000 over the border in France. Thus, for almost one in four of the inhabitants of the Basque country, Basque is their first language. The Spanish constitution of 1978 gave autonomy to the provinces of Alava, Guipúzcoa and Viscaya which make up the Basque Autonomous Community. Then, in 1982, the province of Navarra achieved its Statute of Autonomy. Thus the community of Basque speakers was divided into three different political and administrative units. One was in France within the Atlantic-Pyrenees Department, and two in Spain: the Basque Autonomous Community and the Community of Navarra.

Four out of five of all Basque speakers in Spain live in the Basque Autonomous Community. The 1986 Census revealed that of the 2.1 million resident in the Basque Autonomous Community, 24 percent spoke Basque. However, the language appears to be on the upturn due to language planning policies that will now be considered.

The Basque Autonomous Community has the power to organize itself through its own provincial parliament. This gives the Basques some independence in education, policing, local politics and particularly language planning. All the inhabitants of this community have the right to know and use both Basque and Spanish. This gives children the right to receive education in both of the official languages, and, for example, for Basque to be present in newspapers and magazines, radio and television, in employment and political activities, and the right to speak Basque during any meeting. Since 1983, both Basque and Castilian have been compulsory subjects in schools, although students can opt for Basque or Castilian as the main medium of their education. Training programs exist to equip teachers with the necessary oral or literacy skills for teaching through the medium of Basque.

Basque is used in administration, and different levels of competence in the language are becoming necessary for different types of employment. One recent movement within the Basque Autonomous Community is to define a language profile for different jobs. Once it has been established which jobs have an obligatory language profile, a target date is given to each job, by which the person occupying that post must have reached the language profile required. Five different language profiles are allocated to different jobs. These are given below.

Language Profile 1: Passive bilingualism; elementary competence in speaking and writing Basque. This profile often corresponds to jobs with a high manual work content with limited linguistic input.

Language Profile 2: The employee needs good written and spoken comprehension of the Basque language as the job requires much oral interaction. Thus competence in reading and writing Basque is not so important as oral competence.

Language Profile 3: The person should be the equivalent of a native Basque language speaker with competence in all four language abilities.

Language Profile 4: High abilities in all four linguistic skills at the level of a Basque speaker with a university level of education.

Language Profile 5: Specialist skills in the Basque language such as are needed for translating and language teaching.

At the beginning of each planning cycle, the secretariat for language policy sends to all public organizations in the Basque Autonomous Community a report analyzing their language profile and making proposals about the language profiles required in different posts within the organization. After receiving feedback from the organization, the secretariat for language policy writes a mandatory report for that organization. The report details the aims for organizational language planning, stating which posts have to achieve a particular language profile in a given period of time. That is, language targets for each job are set and expected to be reached. Each post is given a language profile and a date when such a language profile becomes obligatory for that job. This becomes a condition for the job and employment.

The exemptions are for people aged over 45, for those who lack the necessary skills to learn a language, and for those who suffer a form of physical or psychological disability making it impossible or difficult for them to learn the Basque language.

Part of the idea of language planning with respect to employment is that it will have a

Linguistic Diversity and Minority Language Rights in Spain: 2

positive effect on education and language reproduction in the family. If school children know that they have to be fluent and literate in Basque to gain employment, greater external motivation may be present for learning the indigenous language. If families (when rearing their children and sending them to nursery schools) are aware of the importance of Basque in gaining employment and gaining promotion, there may be more encouragement for their children to learn Basque from a very early age. In this sense, the economic status of the Basque language is seen to drive other language policies- in education and the family, for example.

However, the policy of requiring workers to learn the Basque language to a level required for particular employment has recently met some degree of opposition and failure. For example, in the summer of 1994, a total of 1014 workers failed to show that they had reached an elementary level in the Basque language, and, according to current legislation, could be removed from their work position at any time. Out of these 1014 workers, 588 decided not to take the language test, while 58 failed and 368 passed. In January and February 1995, 54 percent of workers failed in the language tests that were set. The mass media publicized these results as evidence of the failure of the Basquization plan. Many of the workers who failed or opted out of the test regard themselves as being Basque without having to speak the Basque language.

Other Basque workers are not prepared to exert the effort to learn the Basque language, finding it does not have sufficient pay-back value. Some workers regard the Basque language as segregationist, a barrier to understanding among Basque people, and divisive of the Spanish nation.

Another explanation of why many Basque workers fail to learn Basque is that the Basque plan may focus too much on instrumental rather than integrative motivation. The policy urges the workers to develop proficiency in Basque for economic and employment purposes. For some, this may be forcing them to do the right thing for the wrong reason. The language has to be learnt for jobs and money, with a love of the language and its attendant culture necessarily implied. Such compulsion and conformity can result in a backlash.

This leads to an argument that integrative motivation needs to be generated, and not just an instrumental and utilitarian driven pressure from outside a person. Integrative motivation may relate to more deep-rooted needs and desires. Integrative motivation may provide more long-lasting and less pressured incentives to learn the Basque language. Language policies, in turn, may need to accommodate both instrumental and integrative motivation (see page 651).

Catalan
Over 10 million people reside in Catalonia, Valencia and the Balearic Islands. Catalan is understood by nearly 90 percent of the population of the three regions and is spoken by nearly 60 percent. Literacy rates are much lower. In 1983 the Law of Linguistic Normalization was passed. The aim of the law was to normalize the use of Catalan in all domains of public and official life.

The position of Catalan is much stronger than that of Basque and Galician. First, it is a majority language within the Province of Catalonia. Second, it has traditionally enjoyed prestige as the language of the middle and upper-middle classes, as opposed to Castilian, which in Catalonia has tended to be the language of working class people from other parts of Spain who moved to the region, mainly in the 1950s and 1960s, to search for work in industry. The strong position of Catalan is reflected in the measures passed by the autonomous government, especially in education.

Catalan is the language of the autonomous government in Catalonia and of most local authorities in the region. All official documents are published bilingually and all government workers must be able to deal with the public in both languages. Catalan is used increasingly in the media. By 1992, 12 percent of daily and weekly newspapers were in Catalan, and, after the creation of two new Catalan channels, there was daily Catalan television coverage from midday to midnight. On radio, 100 local radio stations, as well as the regional Radio Catalunya, ensure a high profile for Catalan. The position of Catalan in the law courts and Central State Administration is still weak. It has also proved difficult to increase the use of the language in industry and the private business sector.

The aim of Catalonian educational policy is that Catalan should be the normal language of instruction in schools, with students also becoming proficient in Castilian by the end of their school career. There has been an increase in Catalan-medium education, with 90 percent of primary school students receiving their education either in Catalan or bilingually by 1989-1990. From 1993, education through the medium of Catalan was made compulsory for all children up to seven years of age, regardless of their cultural or language background. Parents whose native language is Castilian and who wish their children to be initially taught in that language can opt for special provision to be made, through a combination of withdrawal classes and in-class support. However, few parents have applied for this option. After age seven, all students taught in Castilian must study Catalan as a subject, and also study one or two other subjects through the medium of Catalan. A similar situation exists in the Balearic Islands.

In Valencia, the situation of Catalan has not traditionally been so strong, although educational policy aims to produce bilingual children. The situation in Valencia has been complicated by the fact that the variety of Catalan spoken there, Valencian, has been established as a separate official language in the Law of Linguistic Normalization passed in 1986. This means that instead of co-operation and unity, with the Valencian language benefiting from the strong position of Catalan and the resources available to it, there has been opposition and fragmentation.

Galician
Galician is a Romance language closely related to Portuguese. It is spoken in the Autonomous Community of Galicia, in north-west Spain, and in neighboring regions. Galician is spoken by 80-85 percent of the 3 million inhabitants of Galicia. The main obstacles to the normalization of the language were the fact that it has traditionally had little social prestige. Also, there have been disputes concerning the standard form of the language.

The increasing prestige of Galician is reflected in the fact that in the early days of the Autonomous Galician Parliament, most speeches were made in Castilian. Nowadays, most speeches are made in Galician.

The Autonomous Administration publishes all documents in both Galician and Castilian, and all citizens have the right to deal with the Administration in either language. The tendency is still for Castilian to be used for official and written communication, because many citizens still regard it as the language of prestige. Also few people are used to writing in Galician.

In Galicia, the law states that children up to eight years of age are to be educated in their first language, Castilian or Galician. From eight to 14, apart from Galician as a subject, one area of studies, Humanities, is to be delivered in Galician. From 14 to 18 years, two curriculum subjects, apart from Galician are to be taught in Galician. There are also training courses to improve teachers' competence in Galician. Since 1978 the social prestige of the language has increased. Most people now consider the teaching of Galician and teaching in Galician to be normal, whereas there was considerable hostility to it at first. All daily papers are edited in Castilian, but insert texts in Galician. There is a radio station that broadcasts entirely in Galician, and a television station which broadcasts almost entirely in Galician.

REFERENCES:
LEPRETRE, 1992; MACCLANCY, 1993; MARTÍNEZ-ARBELAIZ, 1996; SIGUAN 1993

gates these languages to a very low position in the school curriculum. In the British National Curriculum, the listed languages (Arabic, Bengali, Chinese (Cantonese or Mandarin), Gujarati, Modern Hebrew, Hindi, Japanese, Panjabi, Russian, Turkish and Urdu) were initially only allowed in secondary schools (for 11 to 18 year olds) if a higher division language (e.g. French) is first taught. Thus a caste system of languages is created in England. The caste system is Eurocentric, culturally discriminatory and economically shortsighted, 'allowing languages already spoken in the home and community to be eroded, whilst starting from scratch to teach other languages in schools and colleges' (Stubbs, 1991, page 225).

To conclude: while the three orientations have differences, they also share certain common aims: national unity, the individual's rights, fluency in the majority language (e.g. English) as being important to economic opportunities. The basic difference tends to be whether monolingualism in the majority language or full bilingualism should be encouraged as a means of achieving those ends. All three orientations connect language with politics, economics, society and culture. Each orientation recognizes that language is not simply a means of communication but is also connected with socialization into the local and wider society, as well as a powerful symbol of heritage and identity. The differences between the three orientations lie in the socialization and identity to be fostered: assimilation or pluralism, integration or separatism, monoculturalism or multiculturalism.

Further Reading

CAZDEN, C. B. & SNOW, C. E. (eds), 1990, English Plus: Issues in Bilingual Education. *The Annals of the American Academy of Political and Social Science* (Volume 508: March 1990). London: Sage.

CRAWFORD, J., 1992, *Hold your Tongue: Bilingualism and the Politics of 'English-only'*. Reading, MA: Addison-Wesley.

CRAWFORD, J. (ed.), 1992, *Language Loyalties: A Source Book on the Official English Controversy*. Chicago: University of Chicago Press.

RUIZ, R., 1984, Orientations in Language Planning. *NABE Journal*, 8, 2, 15-34.

SKUTNABB-KANGAS, T., PHILLIPSON, R. & RANNUT, M. (eds), 1994, *Linguistic Human Rights*. New York: Mouton de Gruyter.

Periods of Linguistic Rights

Skutnabb-Kangas & Phillipson (1994) suggest that linguistic human rights have moved through five approximate periods.

First period: Before 1815. In this period, language rights were not, as a rule, covered by international treaties. While religious minorities are mentioned in agreements between countries, language minorities are not. Generally, this period glorified civilizing languages and stigmatized local, vernacular languages and dialects.

Second period: 1815–1914. The Final Act of the Congress of Vienna in 1815 contained clauses safeguarding national minorities as well as religious minorities. Many national minorities were also linguistic minorities. While most 19th century Acts and Treaties contained no mention of linguistic minorities, this was the period of small beginnings.

Third period: 1914–1945. Between the First and Second World Wars, there were peace treaties and international conventions (often assisted by the League of Nations), that gave some protection to minorities. Also, some national constitutions gave rights to linguistic minorities. For example, the peace treaties that came with the ending of the First World War gave some rights to linguistic minorities in central and eastern Europe. While Britain and the United States agreed to minority rights in other countries, neither Britain, France nor the United States offered equivalent rights to language minorities within their own countries. This period saw the beginnings of the possibilities of the right of complaint to the League of Nations and the International Court of Justice about language discrimination.

Fourth period: 1945–1970s. After the Second World War, there was a desire to prevent the abuse of human rights that had been witnessed in fascist regimes. A major new movement towards the protection of human rights was undertaken by the United Nations. Universal Declarations by the United Nations were created with a clear emphasis on the protection of the individual. The emphasis on individual rights tended to mean that the group rights of language minorities were given little attention. It was considered that human rights allocated to the individual gave rights to everybody, so that rights for groups were little needed.

Fifth period: 1970s – to the present. In this period, there has been a growing interest in the rights of language groups, ethnic minorities and the protection of a variety of minority peoples as groups and not just as individuals. The strongest protection is currently given in national constitutions rather than in international and universal agreements.

Language has not figured prominently as a major issue of rights in this period. There tends to be some concern for indigenous ethnic minorities but less concern for in-migrant ethnic minorities. Often language is bracketed with religious and other ethnic rights, rather than being given separate treatment. Where there are migrant workers, refugees, aliens and other non-nationals, the rights, and particularly the language rights, of these people are too rarely considered.

REFERENCE: SKUTNABB-KANGAS & PHILLIPSON, 1994.

2: The Assimilation of Language Minorities

Introduction

The social and political questions surrounding bilingualism and bilingual education tend to revolve around two contrasting ideological positions. 'At one extreme is assimilation, the belief that cultural groups should give up their 'heritage' cultures and take on the host society's way of life. At the opposite pole is multiculturalism, the view that these groups should maintain their heritage cultures as much as possible' (Taylor, 1991, page 1). Between these two extremes, there are many different 'middle ground' viewpoints (e.g. pluralistic integration, participationist pluralism, modified pluralism, liberal pluralism, multivariate assimilation, social accommodation, integrationist – see Edwards, 1994c). Also these two extremes hide many different dimensions (e.g. racism, inter-culturalism, different conceptions of citizenship, identity, individualism, collectivity – see below and the multicultural education section, page 614).

The assimilationist viewpoint is pictured in the idea of a melting pot. Zangwill's play *The Melting-Pot* (1908) introduced the idea of diverse in-migrant elements being merged to make a new homogenized whole (see Textbox). The idea of the melting pot immediately throws up two different perspectives.

First, there is the idea that the final product, for example the US American, is made up by a contribution of all the cultural groups that enter the pot. The cultural groups melt together until the final product is a unique combination. No one ingredient dominates. Each cultural group makes its own contribution to the final taste. However, this is not the usual view associated with the melting pot. So second, the melting pot often means cultural groups giving up their heritage culture and adopting that of the host culture. In this second melting pot picture, cultural groups are expected to conform to the dominant national culture.

Norwegian in-migrants arriving at Ellis Island.

The rationale for this assimilationist perspective is that equality of opportunity, meritocracy and the individual having a chance of economic prosperity due to personal effort are each incompatible with the separate existence of different racial and cultural groups. When the emphasis is on individuality in terms of rights, freedom, effort and affluence, the argument for assimilation is that language groups should not have separate privileges and rights from the rest of society. Advantage and disadvantage associated with language minority groups is to be avoided so individual equality of opportunity can reign.

Assimilationist ideology is an umbrella term under which a variety of types of assimilation may occur: cultural, structural, marital, identificational, attitudinal, behavioral, social and civic (Gordon, 1964). An important distinction is between economic-structural assimilation and cultural assimilation (Skutnabb-Kangas, 1977). Some in-migrant and minority group members may wish to assimilate culturally into the mainstream society. Cultural assimilation refers to giving up a distinct cultural identity, adopting mainstream language and culture. Other language minorities may wish to avoid such cultural assimilation. However, economic-structural assimilation may be sought by language minorities. Such assimilation refers to equality of access, opportunities and treatment (Paulston, 1992b). For example, equal access to jobs, goods and services, equality in voting rights and privileges, equal opportunities and treatment in education, health care and social security, law and protection, may be desired by language minorities. Therefore, structural incorporation tends to be more desired and cultural assimilation more resisted (Schermerhorn, 1970; Paulston, 1992b).

Assimilation may be explicit, implied or concealed (Tosi, 1988). For example, explicit assimilation occurs when

James Crawford and the Status of English in the United States

A major contribution in the understanding of the 'Official English' controversy is by James Crawford. His two books *Language Loyalties: A Source book on the Official English Controversy* (1992) and *Hold Your Tongue: Bilingualism and the Politics of 'English-only'* (1992) have become important reading to understand the English-Only movement in the United States.

James Crawford graduated from Harvard University and has combined a career in journalism with the freelance lecturing and major academic publications. Once a Congressional Editor of the *Federal Times,* he joined *Education Week* as a staff writer and then as Washington Editor. In 1993, James Crawford served as writer-consultant to the Stanford Working Group on Federal Programs for LEP students. His two books on the Official English controversy in the United States combine a journalistic flair for communication with a perceptive portrayal of this ongoing controversy.

Hold Your Tongue is a careful and detailed account of the English-Only Movement, while *Language Loyalties* is an innovative and sagacious compilation of sources on the Official English controversy. The latter book contains an enterprising and discerning sequence of material from people as diverse as Benjamin Franklin, Noah Webster, Theodore Roosevelt, Senator Hayakawa, Joshua Fishman, the *Palm Beach Post*, the *Native American Language Act* and many relevant court cases.

James Crawford has also written a key text entitled *Bilingual Education: History, Politics, Theory and Practice.* The book grew out of a special supplement for Education Week in 1987 and was first published as a book in 1989, reaching its third edition in 1995. James Crawford has a Language Policy Web Site and Emporium on the Internet. The address is:http://ourworld.compuserve.com/homepages/JWCRAWFORD/

William J. Bennett and the Place of English in Schools

William J. Bennett served as US Secretary of Education from 1985 to 1988 and took a particular position on the issue of Official English. This position is revealed in the following two quotes from part of a speech, delivered in New York on September 26, 1985, that led to pressure against a 'strong' form of bilingual education:

'Our origins are diverse. Yet we live together as fellow citizens, in harmony. In America, and perhaps especially in New York, we can say, *E pluribus unum*; out of many we have become one. We cherish our particularities, and we respect our differences. Each of us is justly proud of his own ethnic heritage. But we share this pride, in common, as Americans, as American citizens. To be a citizen is to share in some thing common – common principles, common memories, and a common language in which to discuss our common affairs. Our common language is, of course, English. And our common task is to ensure that our non-English-speaking children learn this common language.

As fellow citizens, we need a common language. In the United States that language is English. Our common history is written in English. Our common forefathers speak to us, through the ages, in English. This is not contradicted by the fact that it is an enduring glory of this nation to have welcomed with open arms immigrants from other lands, speaking other languages; nor by the fact that it is a feature of our free society that these languages can continue to find a place here, in the United States. But beneath the wonderful mosaic of cultures here, beyond the remarkable variety of languages, we are one people.

We are one people not by virtue of a common blood, or race, or origin. We are one people, above all, because we hold these truths to be self-evident: that all men are created equal, that they are endowed by their Creator with certain unalienable rights, and that therefore just government is by consent of the governed. And government by consent means government by discussion, by debate, by discourse, by argument. Such a common enterprise requires a common language. We should not be bashful about proclaiming fluency in this language as our educational goal. And we should not be timid in reforming our policies so as to secure it. For with this goal comes the reward of full participation in this remarkable nation of ours – "not merely a nation but a teeming nation of nations," Walt Whitman said – but still, at the end of the day, beneath all the differences of politics and color and creed, one nation, one people.'

The Words of Einar Haugen

There is no final word on the debate over the place of English in the United States. The debate is about different philosophies, different policies and different politics. The tension between diversity and unity, pluralism and singularity is deeply embedded in hopes and fears, ambitions and anxieties. However, the view of one United States in-migrant, a compassionate and learned scholar, provides an insightful, historical perspective.

Einar Haugen was Professor of Scandinavian Languages and Linguistics at Harvard University. The two quotations are from a 1973 paper entitled 'The Curse of Babel' in *Daedalus,* Volume 102, pages 47-57.

'In their efforts to remove God's curse, men have resorted to various policies, ranging from neighborly tolerance to rigid isolation, from eager acceptance of a new language to brutal suppression of its speakers. Out of this crucible of language contact has come a class of speakers who can manage more than one language, the multilinguals or polyglots. To simplify our expression we shall call them all "bilinguals" and define them as "users of more than one language."

Those of us who love languages and have devoted our lives to learning and teaching them, and who find in language a source of novel delights and subtle experience, find it hard to put ourselves in the right frame of mind to understand the conception of language diversity as a curse'.

language minority children are required to take monolingual education solely in the majority language (e.g. Submersion education in the US). Implied assimilation is when such children are diagnosed as having 'special needs' and are offered compensatory forms of education (e.g. Sheltered English and Transitional Bilingual education in the US). Concealed assimilation may be found, for example, in some types of multicultural education programs where language minorities may be instructed in racial harmony, national unity, and individual achievement, using majority language criteria to gauge success. Such programs are designed to achieve hegemony and ethnic harmony.

Since there are a variety of forms of assimilation, measuring the extent to which assimilation has occurred is going to be difficult. Is assimilation measured by segregation and integration, in terms of housing of in-migrants, for example, by their positions within the economic order, by the extent of intermarriage between different cultural groups or by the attitudes they exhibit? Assimilation is thus multidimensional and complex. Assimilation is neither easily defined nor easily quantified. Assimilationists may have mildly differing views. One example will illustrate.

A few assimilationists may accept that school students should maintain their home language and culture. However, they would argue that this is the responsibility of the home and not the school (Porter, 1990). Most assimilationists will argue that, if economic resources are scarce and school budgets are stretched, bilingual programs should not be supported, particularly if the costs are greater than regular mainstream programs (Secada, 1993).

With the increased accent on ethnicity since the 1960s, the assumptions of assimilation were challenged and the 'new ethnicity' born. Ideologies that surround the terms 'integration', 'ethnic diversity', 'pluralism' and 'multiculturalism' challenged the assimilationist philosophy.

More recently, the debate over assimilation and pluralism has sharpened. A re-emphasis on personal endeavor, individual striving for success, a lessening of reliance on welfare and collectives (e.g. positive discrimination for ethnic groups) has been joined by ethnic conflicts (e.g. in Bosnia, Croatia, Serbia and Russia). This has led to increased arguments and disputes about the merits of assimilation and pluralism (Takaki, 1993).

Assimilation and In-Migrants

The expectation was that in-migrants into the US, Canada and England, for example, would be pleased to

In-migrant women learn English at a public night school in New York in the early 1900s, and are also taught to respect the flag.

have escaped political oppression or economic disadvantage and be jubilant to embrace equality of opportunity and personal freedom. The hope was that individuals would be pleased to give up their past identity and make a commitment to a new national identity. Yet heritage culture and cultural identity have persisted, resisted and insisted. Assimilation has often not occurred. Is this deliberate or difficult, desired or not desired?

Assimilation may be sought by in-migrants. Many wish to assimilate, but come to reside in segregated neighborhoods and segregated schools. Thus assimilation can be prevented by social and economic factors outside of the wishes of the in-migrants. Some groups of in-migrants may wish to be classed as US citizens, but are categorized and treated by mainstream society as different, separate and non-US. The conditions under which in-migrants live may create the negative labels and social barriers that enforce non-integration. As Otheguy (1982, page 312) remarks of the US: 'Because of their experience with racism in this country, many Hispanics have long ago given up hope of disappearing as a distinct group'. The result may be the prevention of assimilation and integration with a consequent need to embrace some form of multiculturalism for survival, security, status and self-enhancement.

Maintaining Ethnic Identity

A different situation is where a language minority prefers not to assimilate culturally. Where an ethnic group wishes to maintain its cultural identity and a degree of enclosure (Schermerhorn, 1970), boundaries between it and the dominant majority may be essential to continued ethnic identity (Barth, 1966 – see page 113). Boundaries between the language minority group and the dominant group will aid the preservation of ethnic identity and help

The United States English-Only Movement: 1

Introduction

Despite a widespread assumption to the contrary, English has no national official status in the US. For over two centuries, however, it has been the *de facto* national language which the vast majority of non-English-speaking immigrants have sought to adopt. An English Language Amendment to the constitution of the US has been proposed that would make English the official language of the country. The aim of the proponents of the English Language Amendment is to ensure that English maintains its leading role in US society, especially in the face of perceived or potential competition from Spanish.

In 1981, Senator Samuel Hayakawa, an American of Japanese origins, introduced a constitutional amendment to make English the official language of the US. The English Language Amendment was introduced in Congress but not voted on. While Senator Hayakawa did not succeed in his aim, others reintroduced the proposal. There have been bills in Congress since 1981 to mandate English as the official, national language of the US. In the 1990s, Bills were introduced into the US legislature to ensure that all government business be conducted in English and all public documents be in English with exceptions for public health and safety services and some judicial proceedings. Other proposed bills aimed to ban bilingual education and bilingual ballots.

In 1983, following lack of action on his original measure, Senator Hayakawa founded with John Tanton an organization called 'US English' to support and promote his cause. This grew to a nationwide organization promoting English as a common bond. In its publicity, 'US English' sometimes refers to official French/English bilingualism in Canada as a source of disharmony that the US should seek to avoid. Imoff (1990) describes the 'US English' movement as a public interest organization whose principles are that the 'government should foster the similarities that unite us rather than the differences that separate us... The study of foreign languages should be strongly encouraged, both as an academic discipline and for practical, economic and foreign-policy considerations.... All candidates for US citizenship should be required to demonstrate the ability to understand, speak, read and write simple English and demonstrate basic understanding of our system of Government'. (page 49)

There are many different and complex shades of opinion within the 'US English' movement, with some rejecting (and others seemingly courting) linguistic chauvinism, nativism and xenophobia, and on the other hand, foreign language study, and individual and private rights to use and maintain languages other than English. 'English First' is a separate organization, smaller and generally more extreme than 'US English'.

A major reason given by 'US English' for its existence is that, in the past, none of the many in-migrant languages had the capacity to threaten 'melting pot' English. With the influx of Spanish-speaking in-migrants, especially in such areas as southern Florida, the Southwest, and such large cities as New York, 'US English' members feel English is threatened in its dominant position. Such members prefer either Submersion education (see page 476) or bilingual education that is transitional (English replaces the mother tongue) and often reject maintenance bilingual education (in which a language like Spanish is retained alongside English). One such view was expressed by Senator Robert Dole, who is quoted as saying the following: 'Alternative language education should stop and English should be acknowledged once and for all as the official language of the United States... Schools should provide the language classes our immigrants and their families need, as long as their purpose is the teaching of English ... But we must stop the practice of multilingual education as a means of instilling ethnic pride or as therapy for low self-esteem or out of elitist guilt over a culture built on the traditions of the West.'

There is much popular and political support for Official English and the 'US English' movement as three examples reveal. (1) A 'sense of the Senate' measure declaring English as the official US language was passed three times before 1997 as an attachment to immigration legislation. Such declarations do not, however, have the force of law. (2) Public-opinion polls across the US have also shown considerable support for English. Many have been conducted by newspapers, radio, and television, and others have been taken by national survey organizations. (3) Various states have made English their official language: Alabama, Arizona (law ruled unconstitutional in 1995), Arkansas, California, Colorado, Florida, Georgia, Hawaii which in 1978 made both English and Hawaiian official, Illinois (law repealed in 1991), Indiana, Kentucky, Mississippi, Montana, Nebraska, New Hampshire, North Carolina, North Dakota, South Carolina, South Dakota, Tennessee and Virginia. In 1996, legislation was pending or planned in various other states.

At state level, 'English-Only' laws vary. Some states simply declare English as the 'official' language of the state. Other state and local laws limit or bar the provision of non-English language assistance and services. For example, some restrict bilingual education programs, prohibit multilingual ballots, or forbid non-English government services in general, including such services as courtroom translation or multilingual emergency police lines. Some laws prohibit state and local governments from providing bilingual services to residents not yet proficient in English. Others prohibit state legislatures from passing laws which ignore the role of English.

Some versions of the proposed English Language Amendment would void almost all state and federal laws that require the government to provide services in languages other than English. The services affected would include: health, education and social welfare services; job training and translation assistance to crime victims and witnesses in court and administrative proceedings; voting assistance and ballots; drivers' licensing exams, and AIDS prevention education.

Where basic human needs are met by bilingual or multilingual services, the consequences of eliminating those services could be tragic. For example, the Washington Times reported in 1987 that a 911 emergency dispatcher was able to save the life of a Salvadorian woman's baby son, who had stopped breathing, by coaching the mother in Spanish over the telephone to adminis-

The United States English-Only Movement: 2

ter mouth-to-mouth and cardiopulmonary resuscitation until the paramedics arrived.

Some lawyers argue that 'English-Only' laws are inconsistent with the Equal Protection Clause of the Fourteenth Amendment. For example, laws that have the effect of eliminating courtroom translation can jeopardize the ability of people on trial to follow and comprehend the proceedings. 'English-Only' laws may interfere with the right to vote by banning bilingual ballots, or with a child's right to education by restricting bilingual instruction. Such laws also may interfere with the right of workers to be free of discrimination in workplaces where employers have imposed 'speak English-only' rules.

Opposition

The English-Only movements have met considerable opposition. Many academics and ethnic leaders have seen 'US English', for example, as a nativist organization that: (1) ignores the civil rights tradition in the US; (2) fails to promote the integration of language minority citizens into the American mainstream; (3) neglects the need for American business people to communicate with foreign markets; (4) restricts the government's ability to reach all citizens; (5) is an attempt to disenfranchise minority citizens; (6) promotes divisiveness and hostility toward those whose first language is not English.

US education organizations that have either criticized or opposed the 'Official English' movements include the National Education Association (a teachers' union), the National Council of Teachers of English, Teachers of English to Speakers of Other Languages (TESOL), the Linguistic Society of America, and the Modern Language Association. Many critics see 'Official English' movements as promoting an English-only policy rather than simply Official English, despite claims to the contrary. Reaction has led to the 'English Plus' pressure group (formed in 1987), which encourages bilingualism (English plus one or more other languages). Supporters of 'English Plus' have proposed a constitutional amendment of their own: the Cultural Rights Amendment, which would give legal backing to the preservation and promotion of cultural and linguistic diversity.

The 'US Official English' movement believes that maintaining a language such as Spanish stops people from learning English. However, the tendency is that US in-migrants tend to lose their heritage language within two or three generations. The majority of Asian and Latino in-migrants acquire English proficiency if given supportive education and wish to integrate as did earlier generations of Italian, Russian and German in-migrants. In-migrants are usually well motivated to learn English to gain some equality of opportunity. Such evidence of language shift does not, however, impress English monolinguals who often feel threatened by the presence of an alternative language and culture, and are often against further immigration to the US.

The 'English-Only' movement and the 'English Plus' movement (the latter in favor of bilingual education) are in broad agreement about one main goal of education. Both movements believe that children should become fluent in English. Both groups appear to acknowledge that full English proficiency is important in opening doors to higher education, business, commerce and the occupational market. Full proficiency in the majority language will usually be equated with equality of educational and vocational opportunity. The difference between the two groups is in the route to attainment of English proficiency. The 'English-Only' group maintain that English language skills are best acquired through English monolingual education. The 'English Plus' group believe that skills in the English language can be successfully fostered through 'strong' forms of bilingual education (see page 486).

As the section on Bilingual Education shows, the evidence exists for support of 'strong' versions of bilingual education and hence for the 'English Plus' position. Such evidence supports the use of the home minority language in the classroom at least until the end of elementary education and probably further. Achievement across the curriculum, achievement in subjects as diverse as science and history, mathematics and geography, would not seem to suffer but be enhanced by 'strong' forms of bilingual education. Such achievement includes English (second) language competence. Research on the cognitive effects of bilingualism seems to support the ownership of two languages to enhance rather than impoverish intellectual functioning.

REFERENCES:
CRAWFORD, 1992; DICKER, 1996

Quotations from the Press

'The English First Movement is a reminder of prejudice towards speakers of foreign tongues. Many American Indians were prohibited from speaking their own languages. The Louisiana Legislature banned the use of Cajun French in Public Schools in 1912, but instead of abandoning their culture, many Cajuns dropped out of school and never learned English. The French language was finally allowed back in the schools in the 1960s. As recently as 1971, it was illegal to speak Spanish in a public school building in Texas, and until 1923 it was against the law to teach foreign languages to elementary school students in Nebraska. At Ellis Island, psychologists tested thousands of non-English-speaking in-migrants exclusively in English and pronounced them retarded. People ask me if I'm embarrassed I speak Spanish. I told them I'd be embarrassed if I spoke only one language' *(Martha Quintanilla Hollowell, a Dallas County (Texas) District Attorney).*

'In a global economy, it's the monolingual English speakers who are falling behind. Along with computer skills, a neat appearance and a work ethic, Americans more and more are finding that a second language is useful in getting a good job'.

'A judge in Amarillo, Texas claimed a mother in a custody case was committing "child abuse" by speaking Spanish to her child at home. Another Texas judge denied probation to a drunk driver because he couldn't benefit from the all-English Alcoholics Anonymous program.'

maintain the vitality of the heritage language. Establishing boundaries and ethnic identity rest on several criteria (Allardt, 1979; Allardt & Starck, 1981) :

1. Self-categorization as a distinct ethnic group.
2. Common descent and ancestry, be it real or imagined.
3. Owning specific cultural traits or exhibiting distinctive cultural patterns, of which language may be the strongest example.
4. Well-established social organization patterns for interacting within the group and separately with 'outsiders'.

Some of the members of an ethnic group will fulfill all these criteria; every member must fulfill at least one of the four criteria to be a member of that ethnic group. These criteria highlight the difference between self-categorization and categorization by others, particularly categorization by the dominant group. Barth (1966) argued that such categorizations essentially define an ethnic group. 'The existence of an ethnic group always presupposes categorization, either self-categorization or categorization by others' (Allardt, 1979, page 30).

Such categorizations are rarely stable and tend to change over time. Allardt (1979) argued that: 'Previously, it was majorities who mainly performed the categorization and labeling of minorities. The principal aim of categorization was exclusion: majorities acted in order to safeguard their material privileges or else to persecute minorities. The results were often severe patterns of discrimination. Of course, minorities also often defended themselves by defining their own criteria for inclusion and belonging. There has occurred a definite change in the present ethnic revival. It is now mainly the minority who categorizes...The problems in the fields of ethnic relations have, as it were, changed from problems of discrimination to problems of recognition' (page 68).

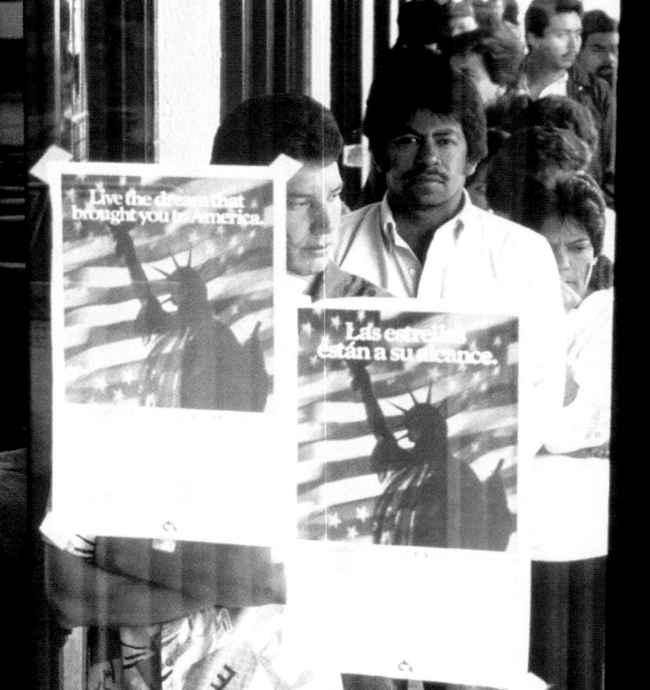

The US Department of Immigration Office at Hunington, California. A poster on the entrance declares in English and Spanish 'Live the Dream that Brought You to America'. But for many in-migrants to the US and other countries, their dream of social and economic integration is not realized.

Categorization by others will often use cultural and geographical criteria. Some categorizations are imposed upon a language minority (e.g. as having 'limited language proficiency') and at other times attributed less openly to that minority. Such categorizations from outside the group include negative remarks about non-assimilation and non-integration. Self-categorization

Israel Zangwill and *The Melting-Pot*

The author Israel Zangwill was born in London in 1864, of Russian-Jewish origin. He wrote a number of novels on Jewish themes but perhaps he is most famous for his play *The Melting-Pot*, published in 1908. *The Melting-Pot* tells the story of a young Russian-Jewish composer in New York, David Quixano, who believes deeply in the ideal of a new harmonious American nation, created from the interweaving of many different peoples. His musical ambition is to write a symphony celebrating this theme, while his personal dream is to overcome barriers of race and prejudice and marry Vera, a beautiful Christian girl. David says 'America is God's crucible, the great Melting-Pot where all the races of Europe are melting and reforming!...... God is making the American'. Zangwill's idealistic play captured the imaginations and enthusiasm of audiences throughout America.

Zangwill was married to a Christian girl and he was also a prominent Zionist, campaigning for the establishment of a Jewish homeland, although originally he supported the idea of a homeland in Uganda. He never emigrated himself, and died in Southampton in 1926.

A Response from Lily Wong Fillmore

The next quotation is from 'Against our Best Interests: The Attempt to Sabotage Bilingual Education' in James Crawford's (1992) book *Language Loyalties: A Source Book on the Official English Controversy.*

'Because bilingual education recognizes the educational validity of languages other than English and cultures other than "American", it is regarded with suspicion and treated accordingly. Only when we have eliminated this prejudice- that to be united, Americans must give up the very things that make them interesting – only then will the good bilingual programs outnumber the bad.'

may re-phrase outsider remarks as self-identity, ethnic awareness and self-recognition.

Ethnic identity can thus be created by imposed categorization from without, or by invoked categorization from within. Self-categorization can be achieved through promoting ethnic social institutions (e.g. law, mass media, religious units, entertainment, sport and cultural associations working in the heritage language). Ethnic community schools (heritage language education) plus the careful planning of the ethnic language in the curriculum may be major components in self-categorization. Mobilizing ethnic group members to agitate for language legitimacy and reform, and working towards a defined idealized vision of the status of the language may also aid self-categorization.

Further Reading

ALLARDT, E., 1979, Implications of the Ethnic Revival in Modern, Industrialized Society. A Comparative Study of the Linguistic Minorities in Western Europe. *Commentationes Scientiarum Socialium* 12. Helsinki: Societas Scientiarum Fennica.

BARTH, F., 1966, *Models of Social Organization. Occasional Paper No.23.* London: Royal Anthropological Institute.

CRAWFORD, J., 1992, *Hold Your Tongue. Bilingualism and the Politics of 'English-only'.* Reading, MA: Addison-Wesley.

CRAWFORD, J. (ed.), 1992, *Language Loyalties. A Source Book on the Official English Controversy.* Chicago: University of Chicago Press.

DICKER, S. J., 1996, *Languages in America. A Pluralist View.* Clevedon: Multilingual Matters Ltd.

EDWARDS, J. R., 1994, *Multilingualism.* London/New York: Routledge.

PAULSTON, C. B., 1994, *Linguistic Minorities in Multilingual Settings.* Amsterdam/Philadelphia: John Benjamins.

SKUTNABB-KANGAS, T., 1977, Language in the Process of Cultural Assimilation and Structural Incorporation of Linguistic Minorities. In C. C. ELERT *et al.* (eds), *Dialectology and Sociolinguistics.* UMEA: UMEA Studies in the Humanities.

TAKAKI, R., 1993, Multiculturalism: Battleground or Meeting Ground? *Annals of the American Academy of Political and Social Science,* 530, 109-121.

The Melting Pot

The goal of many US politicians and leaders has assimilation of in-migrants into the United States just like a melting pot that amalgamates and unifies. The dream has been a United States with shared social, political and economic ideals. Quotes from two US Presidents illustrate this 'melting pot' attitude. Roosevelt in 1917 urged all in-migrants to adopt the English language:

'It would be not merely a misfortune but a crime to perpetuate differences of language in this country... We should provide for every immigrant by day schools for the young, and night schools for the adult, the chance to learn English; and if after say five years he has not learned English, he should be sent back to the land from whence he came' (quoted in Gonzalez, 1979).

President Reagan's views in the late 1980s were that it is 'absolutely wrong and against American concepts to have a bilingual education program that is now openly, admittedly dedicated to preserving their native language and never getting them adequate in English so they can go out into the job market and participate' (quoted in Crawford, 1989; from Democrat Chronicle, Rochester, March 3, 1981, page 2a).

A different view is expressed by three academics who see cultural and linguistic diversity as part of the history, character and greatness of the United States

'Cultural and linguistic differences have been a source of strength and controversy in the United States since its founding. Indeed, this country's founding and much subsequent US history can be seen as a continuing search for unity in diversity, for *e pluribus unum'...*

This rich diversity is found among 'the New York Dutch, the Pennsylvania German, and the Virginia English; the Massachusetts Puritan, the Pennsylvania Quaker, the Maryland Catholic, and the Virginia Anglican; the Yankee trader, the northern farmer, and the southern plantation owner... its Norwegian, Irish, Russian, Italian, Polish, and Jewish immigrants... disenfranchised and economically marginalized African-American, Chinese, Japanese, Native American, and Latino minorities?' (Bull, Fruehling & Chattergy, 1992, page 1).

Ronald Reagan in 1986.

Russia and the Assimilation of Ethnic Minorities: 1

The history of the Russian Empire and subsequently the history of the Union of Soviet Socialist Republics is the history of, on the one hand, respect and encouragement for multilingualism and multiculturalism and, on the other hand, the attempted assimilation of numerous ethnolinguistic groups. During the 18th and 19th centuries, under the Czars, Russia expanded westwards and southwards, acquiring the territories of many linguistic minorities, the Ukrainians, Poles, Crimean Tatars, Estonians, Latvians, Lithuanians and Baltic Germans. By the mid 19th century, the imperial conquests also included the Central Asian Muslim peoples, Kazakhs, Kirgizh, Uzbeks and Turkmens. The purpose of conquest was colonization and economic exploitation: Russian settlers migrated to these areas and took their language and culture with them. Initially, there was a British-type colonial structure, with the native elite continuing to rule the provinces, with no attempt to assimilate the local peasantry. Provided that the common people paid their taxes, they were allowed their traditional institutions, religions and language, while the Russian nobility ignored the multiethnic nature of their empire. However, by the mid 19th century, a more aggressive Russian nationalism had developed. One result was the imposition of a more oppressive Russian administration in the provinces and a consistent policy of Russification. Ethnic minorities were discriminated against socially and economically and any nationalist movements were severely repressed. Also, the mass migration of Russian settlers to these areas resulted in ethnic conflict: millions of ethnic minority peasants were killed or fled to other countries.

When the Bolsheviks seized power in 1917, some national minorities took advantage of the situation to declare independence. Some, like Poland and Finland, were successful, others were reincorporated into the new Soviet Union. The Bolsheviks, led by Lenin, believed in the unity of the working class that transcended national and ethnic boundaries. Lenin believed in the economic rationality of belonging to a large political unit such as the Czarist empire. The Bolsheviks were confident that integration and assimilation of ethnolinguistic minorities would eventually take place, but that this could not be forced. Lenin believed that, if oppression of national minorities was removed, they would recognize for themselves their true identity as members of the working class. In the 1919 Communist Party Program, Lenin stated his commitment to the equal rights of nationalities whatever their size, the equal status of languages and to their development. Lenin, personally, strongly opposed using the Cyrillic script for non-Russian languages, calling this autocratic, oppressive and chauvinistic. Based on this commitment, the Czarist empire was reorganized in 1922 into the Union of Soviet Socialist Republics, on the basis of ethnic nationality in which language was the basic criterion. Lenin believed that eventually all Soviet citizens would adopt one or a few major languages as common languages. The ultimate aim from the beginning was the fusion of all the nationalities into a Soviet 'melting pot'. However, Lenin believed strongly in the recognition of the equal status of ethnic groups and their languages as a prerequisite for this development. Also, he believed that unity could be achieved without the disappearance of the mother tongues of ethnic groups.

The Stock Exchange at Kyyiv (Kiev), the capital of the Ukraine. The notices on the board are in Russian. Ukraine has been an independent republic since 1991 and Ukrainian, a language closely related to Russian, is now the sole official language of the country. However, Russian is still widely spoken and used in official life and in the economy.

The federal system of the Soviet Union was a four-tier system, organized as follows. There were 15 Union Republics, each named after the majority population, with a considerable measure of autonomy. The majority languages of the republics had wide functions. They were used at all levels of education and in all aspects of public life. Nationalities other than the majority group, which occupied a defined territory within a Union Republic, were constituted either as Autonomous Republics, Autonomous Regions, or National Districts. Each had some measure of administrative and linguistic autonomy.

The enlightened and pluralist Soviet policy towards ethnic minorities was not maintained, however. Lenin died in 1924, and by 1929 Stalin held undisputed power. Under Stalin, the USSR moved towards a greater centralized control. All attempts by the autonomous republics to gain genuine administrative autonomy were stamped out. The Russian language was promoted at the expense of minority languages. In the mid-1930s

Russia and the Assimilation of Ethnic Minorities: 2

the Cyrillic alphabet was enforced for all Soviet languages. In 1938 a decree made Russian a compulsory subject in all non-Russian schools. By the 1940s teaching in some of the small Siberian languages had stopped, and the use of the languages below the status of major Union Republic languages was restricted.

Two Stalinist policies had particularly harsh repercussions for Soviet ethnic minorities. First, in the 1930s Stalin imposed a policy of 'collectivization'. Individual peasant farms were replaced with collective farms. Millions of members of various language minority groups were killed in the conflict, or fled into exile. The result was that, in many of the Soviet Union countries, the indigenous ethnolinguistic group came to represent a smaller proportion of the total population than before.

Second, towards the end of World War II, Stalin decided that some Soviet nationalities had collaborated with the Germans, so he deported whole ethnic groups such as the Crimean Tatars out of their homeland to other parts of Russia. Another ethnolinguistic minority who were increasingly persecuted and discriminated against were the Jews. During the Soviet period, the official policy of Russification continued. Russian nationals were often placed in top administrative positions in Union Republics, and the use of Russian was frequently enforced in the workplace. Russian nationals living in other republics also had the opportunity of having their children educated solely in their mother tongue, Russian, while this was denied to other ethnolinguistic groups.

In 1958/9 Kruschev's education law gave non-Russian parents the option of educating their children in their mother tongue or in Russian. Many parents opted for education in Russian, in the hope of giving their children greater social and economic advantages. The Russian language was widely used in administration and public life. In 1961, at the 22nd Communist Party Congress, Russian was proclaimed as the 'Soviet language of inter-nationality'. Subsequently there was a rapid expansion in the promotion and teaching of Russian, while the use of other languages in administration was restricted. After the Tashkent Conference in 1979, a further step in the policy of Russification was taken. The teaching of Russian to pre-school children was introduced and parents and teachers were instructed in the methods of introducing Russian at home and in out-of-school activities.

By the last years of the USSR, the policy of Russification had been very effective. According to the 1989 census, more than three-quarters of the Soviet population spoke Russian very well. Millions of non-Russians had adopted Russian as their home language. Linguistic assimilation was most successful among other Slavic groups (Ukrainians and Belorussians), whose languages mostly closely resemble Russian, as well as among small and scattered minorities such as the Jews. Millions more spoke Russian as a second language. Russian was the main lingua franca throughout the Soviet Union, in all business, government, administration and education. Only 4.1 percent of ethnic Russians spoke another Soviet language but many non-Russians spoke their own language and also Russian. However, on the whole, the Soviet Union had not succeeded in fully assimilating the large number of ethnolinguistic minorities within its borders. According to the 1989 census, 114 languages were still spoken in the Soviet Union. Other ethnolinguistic groups, especially those living in Central Asia and Northern Siberia, tended to use Russian much less.

One major force behind the collapse of the USSR was the resurgence of nationalism among the minority groups. In September, 1990, the three Baltic Republics, Estonia, Latvia and Lithuania, achieved full independence. In December, 11 out of the remaining 12 republics (excluding Georgia), reconstituted themselves as the Commonwealth of Independent States. Since independence, countries such as Kazakhstan and Kirgizhstan have pursued a policy of de-Russification. During the last years of the USSR, Russians began leaving the autonomous republics and returning to Russia or seeking refuge elsewhere. In Russia itself, more than 100 languages are still spoken, and many ethnic groups have autonomy within their territories and make use of their own languages in official life.

References: ALLARDYCE, 1987; GUBOGLO, 1986; MARSHALL, 1996

During the Soviet era, schoolgirls in Dzhambul, Kazakhstan stand in front of a Russian language motto which declares 'Lenin is our knowledge, our strength and our weapon'. Only 42 percent of the population of Kazakhstan are ethnic Kazakhs and speak Kazakh as their mother tongue, while 85 percent can speak Russian as their first or second language. Until recently, ethnic Russians outnumbered ethnic Kazakhs. Kazakh is now the official language and is gaining status at the expense of Russian.

3: Integration and Language Minorities

It is valuable to distinguish between assimilation and integration with respect to language minorities. As the middle of the word assimilation suggests, assimilation is about becoming similar or the same. In this sense, a language minority speaker who undergoes assimilation will, via socialization practices of institutions such as education and the mass media, become similar to language majority speakers.

There is also an important distinction between cultural assimilation and structural integration. In-migrant groups are often expected to acquire a cultural similarity to language majority residents, but are often not allowed structural (e.g. economic, social) integration because of divisive factors such as racism, inequality of opportunity, and the reproduction of advantages by privileged groups in society.

In contrast to assimilation, integration refers to the situation where an ethnic group is able to maintain its uniqueness and maintain boundaries between it and the majority language, while having relatively equal access to jobs, employment, affluence, power and self-promotion. In integration, an ethnic group is able to maintain its differences and separate vitality while having equal opportunity in the political, economic, social and educational systems. Such integration allows a language minority person to become as empowered, employed and as effective a member of society as majority language members speakers.

The favorite metaphor for assimilation is the 'melting pot'. Individuals from different ethnic groups and language groups are 'melted down' by the socialization process to produce a people who all basically have the same characteristics. One metaphor for integration is the salad bowl where each ingredient, separate and distinguishable, is no less valuable than another ingredient. The final taste is more than a simple sum of the individual parts. A different metaphor for integration is used in Canada. The Canadian concept of an ethnic mosaic is the idea of different pieces of society (e.g. Quebecois, native Indian language communities, English speakers, and the newer in-migrant languages) being joined together in one overall political and economic arrangement.

Assimilation is a process that aims to shape everyone into the same characteristics. Integration is the affirmation of the value of diversity in society, with equal opportunity available in an atmosphere of mutual tolerance and respect. Assimilation is about absorption of one culture and language by another. Integration entails retaining ethnic, cultural and linguistic differences and celebrating variety for an overall common good.

A Japanese-American family who run a flower-growing business at Salinas, California. Some in-migrant families have found it possible to maintain their identity and sometimes language, while at the same time integrating successfully both socially and economically.

Integration tends to be an aim and an ideal, with the reality falling below that ideal. Integration implies cultural pluralism and equality of different cultures and languages within a society. The ideal is cohesion between different language minority groups. The reality tends to be competition and occasionally conflict. A mutual respect for ethnic, cultural and linguistic differences is important in a concept of integration, an aim that is often strived for, but rarely achieved in a stable way in society. Such integration is often said to be exemplified in Belgium, Canada and Switzerland where cultural differences are protected and some equality in distribution of resources is attempted.

Integration at one level can imply peaceful co-existence. At a higher level it implies an active participation of different language minority groups with the language majority group inside a stable framework that fairly allocates power, privileges, rights, goods and services.

Further Reading

CRAWFORD, J., 1992, *Hold Your Tongue. Bilingualism and the Politics of 'English-only'*. Reading, MA: Addison-Wesley.

CRAWFORD, J. (ed.), 1992, *Language Loyalties. A Source Book on the Official English Controversy*. Chicago: University of Chicago Press.

DICKER, S. J., 1996, *Languages in America. A Pluralist View*. Clevedon: Multilingual Matters Ltd.

GHUMAN, P. A. S., 1994, *Coping With Two Cultures: British Asian and Indo-Canadian Adolescents*. Clevedon: Multilingual Matters Ltd.

GHUMAN, P. A. S., 1995, Acculturation, Ethnic Identity and Community Languages: A Study of Indo-Canadian Adolescents. In B. M. JONES & P. A. S. GHUMAN (eds), Bilingualism, *Education and Identity. Essays in Honour of Jac L. Williams*. Cardiff: University of Wales Press.

Eight Strategies for Linguistic and Cultural Diversity

David Tyack (1995) suggests that there are eight strategies or solutions used to cope with ethnic, cultural or linguistic diversity in a country. They are based on a historical analysis of cultural diversity in the United States.

Discrimination. For example, the segregation into separate schools and the denial of schooling to Chinese and Japanese in-migrant children in California illustrate the most negative of reactions to linguistic and cultural diversity, and that is deliberate discrimination.

Separation. Another form of segregation is to separate different language and cultural groups, sometimes with benign intent. For example, different provision is made for those of different linguistic and cultural origins. The aim is to provide appropriate education for different groups.

Assimilation. The third strategy is to try and eradicate linguistic and cultural differences by assimilating in-migrants into the same common characteristics. Or in the case of colonialization, to assimilate indigenous minority groups into the colonizer's language and culture. Attacks on bilingual education and a multicultural curriculum are often based on a fear that assimilation will not occur (or be resisted) through bilingual education.

Desegregation. Desegregation attempts to secure full citizenship and educational rights for minority language and cultural groups. Equality of opportunity and equality of provision (e.g. in education) is attempted.

Ignore differences. Some believe that schools should act 'naturally' with regard to language and cultural minorities. As well as being color-blind, social class-blind, gender-blind, schools should also be blind to linguistic and cultural differences among children. With the idealistic aim of treating everyone equally and without presuppositions, such neutrality is difficult to achieve and tends to ignore the differences in power, wealth and status between different language and cultural groups.

Compensation. Another reaction to diversity is to give special help to ethnic, linguistic and cultural minorities. Compensatory education, remedial education, special tracks or streams and special reception centers for in-migrants, may each aim to give children a beneficial start, correct faulty socialization which children supposedly have received at home, or provide a fast transition into mainstream education.

Celebration. Another strategy, particularly found in intercultural and multicultural education, is to celebrate ethnic, linguistic and cultural diversity. The differences between groups are appreciated, proclaimed and celebrated.

Preservation. Another strategy is to maintain differences between the groups, believing that linguistic and cultural differences should be preserved in a positive way by detachment. Behind this idea is the concept of group as well as individual rights. The notion is that all groups have equal rights and such rights are best fostered by separate but equal treatment, preserving and not breaking down boundaries between groups.

There are not eight separate political or educational strategies. Rather, there is overlap and intermingling between the eight ideas. Nevertheless, they do suggest a variety of responses, a variety of motives, different perspectives and different wanted outcomes. For example, among the eight different responses there is a tension between:

- celebrating individual differences and celebrating group differences;
- a preference for individualism and personal freedoms and a preference for development that occurs through strong group membership;
- a desire for 'the common good' and universal equality of treatment for all people and a desire for local rights, local empowerment and minority group allegiance;
- solidarity at a national level, and solidarity in terms of an ethnic or linguistic group;
- social justice by equality of provision and social justice through diversity being celebrated and not eradicated.

REFERENCE: TYACK, 1995

The Ghuman Acculturation Scale

Paul Singh Ghuman has internationally researched the quest for personal identity and self-concept among children and teenagers of Asian origin. There are great differences within Asian communities, in different countries, of children from different social classes. However, Paul Ghuman valuably pinpoints some of the difficulties that are faced by Asian in-migrants in synthesizing influences from two or more cultures. Some of the potential dilemmas faced by some, but not all Asian children and teenagers include:

1. Strong parental authority compared with the quest for personal identity.
2. The difference in expectations of boys and girls in many Asian households, with boys tending to be given more freedom in their behavior than girls.
3. The need to maintain the family's honor (*Izzat*) yet retain individual autonomy; the precedence of the family's interests over those of the individual.
4. School developing personal autonomy, critical thinking and a questioning attitude whereas parents prefer to emphasize conforming to, and accepting parental values and beliefs.
5. Inter-generational conflict over teenage matters such as relationships with the opposite sex, time of coming home at night and going to bed, choice of clothes, music and videos.
6. For Asians who are Muslims, there can be a clash with the secular ethos of many schools. Schools may teach Christianity or multi-faiths or moral education. Asian parents may believe that such a regime undermines their children's faith in Islam.
7. The kind of activities that occur in drama, dance, sex education and swimming lessons in school may produce a conflict with traditional family culture and preferences.

Paul Ghuman investigated the extent of differences between different groups of Asians, for example in Britain and Canada, and investigated the dilemmas that such Asian children and teenagers feel, their concerns and anxieties, their integration of cultures or their cultural confusion, and sometimes their alienation from both home and school. Ghuman (1995a) defines acculturation as 'the degree to which the migrant communities take up the norms, values, customs and social practices of the host society' (Ghuman 1995a, page 215).

Ghuman has used his Acculturation Scale from the 1970s to the present to reveal such anxieties, dilemmas, interests and values among Asian young people. The scale consists of 30 items, (15 items examine opinions on Asian culture and 15 items relate to, in the example given, Canadian culture). The following scale is reproduced, with permission, as used with a sample of Vancouver, Canada Asian teenagers.

1.	Girls and boys should be treated the same	SA	A	U	D	SD
*2.	Schools should accept our traditional clothes	SA	A	U	D	SD
*3.	We should attend our places of worship (e.g. *Gurdwaras*, temple)	SA	A	U	D	SD
4.	I have no wish to go back to live in the country my parents came from	SA	A	U	D	SD
5.	I would like to see boys and girls from our community going out with white Canadian boys and girls	SA	A	U	D	SD
*6.	I would rather eat our own food all the time	SA	A	U	D	SD
*7.	We should always try to fulfill our parents' wishes	SA	A	U	D	SD
8.	We should celebrate Christmas as we celebrate our own religious festivals	SA	A	U	D	SD
*9.	We are better off living with people from our own countries	SA	A	U	D	SD
10.	Parents and children should live on their own and not with grandparents and uncles	SA	A	U	D	SD
*11.	A woman's place is in the house	SA	A	U	D	SD
*12.	Only our own doctors can understand our illnesses	SA	A	U	D	SD
13.	We should learn something about Christianity	SA	A	U	D	SD
*14.	We should learn to speak and write our own language	SA	A	U	D	SD
15.	Sometimes we should cook Canadian food in our own homes	SA	A	U	D	SD
16.	We should alter our names so that our teachers can say them easily	SA	A	U	D	SD
*17.	I would only like to make friends with my countrymen	SA	A	U	D	SD
18.	Boys and girls should be allowed to meet each other in youth clubs	SA	A	U	D	SD
*19.	I would prefer to live in an area where there are families from our own community	SA	A	U	D	SD
20.	We should visit the homes of our white Canadian friends	SA	A	U	D	SD
*21.	Our films are more entertaining than English language films	SA	A	U	D	SD
22.	We should ignore our own language if we want to get on in this country	SA	A	U	D	SD
*23.	I feel very uneasy with white Canadians	SA	A	U	D	SD
24.	There should be more marriages between our people and white Canadians	SA	A	U	D	SD
*25.	Men should make all the decisions about the affairs of the family	SA	A	U	D	SD
*26.	I would not like our women to behave like white Canadian women	SA	A	U	D	SD
27.	We should be allowed to choose our own clothes	SA	A	U	D	SD
28.	We should visit English language cinemas and playhouses	SA	A	U	D	SD
*29.	Marriages should be arranged by the family	SA	A	U	D	SD
30.	Our women should wear Canadian (European-style) clothes	SA	A	U	D	SD

Key: SA = Strongly Agree; A = Agree; U = Uncertain; D = Disagree; SD = Strongly Disagree; * indicates reverse scoring)

REFERENCE: GHUMAN, 1995

4: Multiculturalism

Introduction

At the heart of the assimilationist ideology is the belief that an effective, harmonious, society can only be achieved if minority groups are absorbed into mainstream society. Harmony and equal opportunity depend on a shared language and culture. At the other end of the spectrum is multiculturalism. Multiculturalism embraces the ideal of equal, harmonious, mutually tolerant existence of different and diverse languages, and of religious, cultural and ethnic groups in a pluralist society. A multicultural viewpoint is partly based on the idea that an individual can successfully hold two or more cultural identities. It is possible to be Ukrainian and Canadian, Chinese and Malaysian, Cuban or Puerto Rican or Mexican and North American. In a different sense, it is possible to be a Ukrainian-Canadian, a Chinese-Malaysian or a Cuban-North American. In this sense, identities are merged; the parts become a new whole. A redefined ethnicity creates a person who is not a replica of a Cuban in Cuba, Puerto Rican in Puerto Rico, Mexican in Mexico, nor a stereotypical 'white' North American. Rather that person becomes a more or less integrated combination of parts of both.

The Nature of Multiculturalism

The term multiculturalism tends to be used in a broad and sometimes vague manner. It needs to be defined. The basic beliefs of multiculturalists include the following.

- Two languages and two cultures enable a person to have dual or multiple perspectives on society.
- Those who speak more than one language and own more than one culture are more sensitive and sympathetic, more likely to build bridges than barricades and boundaries.
- Whereas assimilation produces a subtractive situation, multiculturalism is an additive process.
- Ideally, a person who is multicultural has more respect for other people and other cultures than the monocultural person who is stereotypically more insular and more culturally introspective.
- Assimilation leads ethnic minorities to adopt a positive attitude to the majority culture and a negative attitude to their own heritage culture.
- Pluralism and multiculturalism may lead to a positive attitude, not only to the host and heritage culture, but to the equal validity of all cultures.
- Multiculturalism promotes empathy and sensitivity, and helps eradicate prejudice and racism.

Multiculturalism vs. Assimilation

In England and the United States, movements towards multiculturalism have not tended to receive an official blessing nor encouragement. Rather, the assimilationist viewpoint has continued. In contrast, in parts of Canada, Scandinavia and New Zealand for example, a more multicultural approach has been taken, but with much dispute and debate.

The difference between assimilationists and multiculturalists is rooted in basic human needs and motives. The movement towards assimilation or heritage cultural maintenance is likely to be affected by the economic

The Mardi Gras festival in New Orleans, USA, reflects the continuing Cajun tradition of Louisiana. In 1755, several thousand French speakers were expelled from Acadia (Canada) for refusing to swear allegiance to the British Crown. About 4000 of them eventually settled in Louisiana. About half a million of their descendants still speak Cajun French, which is an archaic French dialect mixed with words taken from the Spanish, English, German, Black English and Indian languages. Cajun music, food and festivals are still an important part of Louisiana life.

reward system. Both assimilation and heritage cultural maintenance can be promoted by the need to earn a living and the desire to acquire or increase affluence. Assimilation may be chosen to secure a job, to be vocationally successful and to achieve affluence. The minority language and culture may be left behind in order to prosper in the majority language community. At the same time, language planning can be used to ensure that there are jobs and promotion within the minority language community.

The dominant group in society may at times prefer heritage cultural maintenance to assimilation. Minority groups may not be permitted to assimilate, thus keeping their members in poorly paid employment. Such a minority group is then exploited by the dominant group. The economic interests of the majority group can be served by internal colonialism rather than assimilation. Economic motives and decisions may occur without reference to heritage language and culture.

Often, being fluent in the majority language is an economic necessity, and this can promote assimilation. To obtain employment and compete with members of the majority group, a person has to function in the majority language. Bilinguals may also perceive that they can

Advert for the 1990 Carnaval Miami, Florida, USA. In the Miami area where a high proportion of the population is Hispanic, primarily of Cuban origin, many Caribbean and South American traditions are preserved.

function economically both in their minority group and with the dominant group. That is, they have the ability to be economically viable in either language community and form a bridge between those two communities. However, as the discussion on Bilingualism and the Economy reveals (see page 250), becoming bilingual by learning the majority language is no guarantee of economic improvement. Otheguy (1982, page 306) provides a salutary warning from the US experience. 'English monolingualism has meant little in terms of economic advantages to most blacks and to the masses of poor descendants of poor European immigrants. Hispanics who now speak only English can often be found in as poor a state as when they first came. English monolingualism among immigrants tends to follow economic integration rather than cause it'.

Between the two opposing views of assimilation and multiculturalism, intermediate positions are tenable. It is possible to participate in mainstream society and maintain one's heritage language and culture. For many individuals, there will be both a degree of assimilation and a degree of preservation of one's heritage. Total assimilation and total isolation are less likely than some accommodation of the majority ideology within an overall ideology of pluralism; cultural maintenance within partial assimilation. Within multiculturalism and pluralism, an

The Development of a Pluralist Identity

Lynch (1992) suggests that there has been an historical development of identity from (1) the family or ethnic group, through (2) the age of the city-state and single-state nationalism to (3) the present age of global rights and responsibilities and the internationalization of the lives of all inhabitants of this planet. He argues that 'we do not have to choose between local and ethnic loyalties, national citizenship and global community... and we are well on the way to recognizing three major levels of group affiliation: local community membership, by which is meant familial, ethnic, community or other cultural and social local groupings, including language, religion and ethnicity but not necessarily linked in the same geographic place at the same time; national citizenship, determined by birth or choice, but which may not be an exclusive membership; and international citizenship, which draws on the overlapping constellations which members of the world community have in common, regardless of the other two levels' (pages 16-17). The concept of international citizenship is part of the aims of multicultural education. (See Multicultural Education, page 614).

REFERENCE: LYNCH, 1992

Public Support for Multiculturalism in the US

Research by Donald Taylor and his associates has found in both the United States and in Canada that different public groups support multiculturalism more than assimilation. For example, the research of Lambert & Taylor (1990) showed that nine different US groups all preferred multiculturalism to assimilation. The basic research question poses two alternatives:

Alternative A: Cultural and racial minority groups should give up their traditional ways of life and take on the American way of life (Assimilationist).

Alternative B: Cultural and racial minority groups should maintain their ways of life as much as possible when they come to America (Multiculturalist).

The debate is more complex than these two statements, with other alternatives and compromise positions being possible. (There is also the insensitive use of the word 'American'. Meant to imply US, it may be denigrating to those from South and Central America.) Respondents are invited to respond by marking one number on the following 7 point scale:

1 _____2_______3_______4_______5_______6_______7

Agree Strongly with A — Neutral — Agree Strongly with B

Support for multiculturalism is generally high among Arabs, Puerto Ricans, Blacks, Mexicans, Albanians and Polish US citizens as the following graph reveals. Both 'white working class' and 'white middle class' US citizens favor multiculturalism more than assimilation, though less so than most other groups.

Thus Taylor (1991) is able to conclude over a series of studies that 'there is a strong endorsement for multiculturalism and an apparent rejection of assimilation' (page 8). However, we need to ask whether such endorsement is a latent attitude or whether it results in positive action and behavior? Is the population saying it permits multiculturalism without being committed to it? Are there positive public attitudes but private skepticism? Is there interest in multiculturalism so long as it doesn't lead to involvement? Are such attitudes dormant as cognitive representations but not related to personal action? We must also ask along which dimensions people's attitude to multiculturalism and assimilation differ? Is there a difference between nostalgic allegiance to heritage culture compared with regarding the heritage culture as something of instrumental value?

A note of caution is also sounded by Huddy and Sears (1990). A large scale US public survey found a majority in favor of bilingual education. However, the authors found that 'opposition is greater among the well informed, suggesting that opposition may increase further as the issue attains greater national visibility. Opposition is also likely to increase if bilingual education is presented as promoting linguistic and cultural maintenance among language-minority students rather than as a mechanism for teaching English' (Huddy & Sears, 1990, page 119).

aggressive, militant pluralism may be seen as a threat to the social harmony of society. Instead, a more liberal pluralistic viewpoint may allow both belonging to the wider community and an identification with the heritage cultural community.

Research is unlikely to solve debates over assimilation and multiculturalism. While research may inform and refine opinions, the two positions of assimilation and pluralism differ in such fundamental, ideological ways, that simple solutions and resolutions are impossible. When evidence for the maintenance of heritage languages and cultures is produced, assimilationists are likely to argue that attitudes and behavior are still in the change process. That is, assimilationists will argue that, over time, people will move away from heritage cultural maintenance and prefer majority language and culture. Assimilationists tend to believe that bilingualism and biculturalism are temporary and transient, and lead to a preferable unifying monolingualism. When evidence favors assimilation having taken place in society (e.g. by the second or third generation after in-migration), multiculturalists will tend to argue in two different ways. First, that the change towards assimilation has only occurred on certain dimensions (e.g. language rather than economic assimilation). Second, that sometimes the wheel turns full circle. Revival and resurrection in future generations may occur in response to repression and renouncement by previous generations.

Further Reading

DELGADO-GAITAN, C. & TRUEBA, H., 1991, *Crossing Cultural Borders: Education for Immigrant Families in America.* New York: Falmer.

DICKER, S. J., 1996, *Languages in America. A Pluralist View.* Clevedon: Multilingual Matters Ltd.

MAY, S., 1994, *Making Multicultural Education Work.* Clevedon: Multilingual Matters Ltd.

McKAY, S. L. & WONG, S. C. (eds), 1988, *Language Diversity: Problem or Resource?* New York: Newbury House.

NIETO, S., 1996, *Affirming Diversity: The Sociopolitical Context of Multicultural Education* (Second edition). New York: Longman.

5: Major World Languages

Introduction

English is often regarded as the main international language of the world, but several other languages have traversed the boundaries of the regions or countries where they were originally spoken, and are used internationally, either as first or second languages. A brief introduction to the major international languages of the world shows clearly that language spread and language status is always accompanied by political, religious or economic dominance.

German throughout the World

Throughout western and central Europe there are some 100 million people whose mother tongue is German. In Austria there are 7.5 million German speakers, in Switzerland and Liechtenstein 4.3 million, and in Luxembourg 330,000. German is an officially recognized language in seven countries, which, compared to the other languages of the world, places it in fifth position along with Portuguese. The four countries who hold a higher position are Arabic, an official language in 22 countries, Spanish in 23 countries, French in 34 countries, and English, which is an official language in 63 countries.

German is one of the most frequently learnt foreign languages in the world. According to the Federal Press and Information Office in Germany, in Europe there are an estimated 15 million people currently learning the language. World-wide this figure is closer to 20 million. As a foreign language, the numbers studying German in the European Union now ranks third after French and English, and in parts of Central and Eastern Europe it has become first choice, overtaking Russian. In Poland and the Czech Republic up to half the children in each grade choose German as their first foreign language. In countries such as Ireland, Sweden and Britain there is a strong trend towards learning German. The number of students studying German in Britain had increased from about 99,000 in 1992 to over 108,000 in 1993. The German Academic Exchange Service reports a steadily growing interest in German language and culture, which has expanded vastly in the past 15 years. There are a number of reasons for this increased interest.

- The reunification of Germany
- The enlargement of the European Union and the European single market, which spurs cross -frontier business.
- The change-over to free market democratic regimes in eastern Europe.
- Mass migration in Europe, largely towards Germany.

Dutch throughout the World

Dutch is the first language of over 21 million people world-wide. In the Netherlands, the majority of the population of over 15 million speak Dutch as a first or second language. There are over five million Dutch speakers in Belgium, where the language is known as Flemish, and has official status. About 90,000 Dutch speakers reside in north-west France.

In the 17th century, Dutch traders and colonists arrived in the Caribbean. Dutch is an official language in the South American country of Suriname, and also in the Caribbean islands of Netherlands Antilles and Aruba. The language is used mainly as the language of government and education. The Dutch East India Company, founded in 1602, brought many Dutch settlers into South East Asia. Most of present day Indonesia was governed by the Netherlands until 1945, but little Dutch influence remains there and the language has no official status.

In South Africa, 17th century Dutch settlers brought their language with them. Throughout the next three centuries, the Dutch dialects spoken by the Boers of South Africa evolved separately from the Dutch of the Netherlands, but the latter was still used as the standard, literary language. It was not until 1925 that Afrikaans attained the status of a separate language, and is still mutually intelligible with Dutch. Minority groups of Dutch speakers are also found in the US, Canada and Australia.

Portuguese throughout the World

An estimated 168 million people speak Portuguese, making it the fifth most widely spoken language in the world. Portuguese, a Romance language, is the official language of Portugal, and the native language of nearly all its 9.9 million inhabitants. Galician, the language of northern Portugal, is regarded in Portugal as a dialect of

Portuguese, but has autonomous status as an official language in the neighboring Spanish province of Galicia.

Between the 14th and 16th centuries, Portuguese seafarers and traders established an overseas empire, and the Portuguese language was heard in Asia, Africa and the Americas. A pidgin language developed among seafarers in medieval times, Sabir, based on Portuguese, and one theory is that this pidgin formed the basis for at least some other pidgin languages (see page 142). In South America, Portuguese seafarers colonized present day Brazil. Portuguese is the official language of the great country of Brazil and the native language of the vast majority of its 151 million inhabitants. In Africa, Portuguese is still the official language of Angola, Mozambique, Guinea-Bissau and Cape Verde. In Angola, 60 percent of the population speak Portuguese as their mother tongue, but in the other three countries, only small minorities are native speakers of Portuguese. The remainder either speak Portuguese Creoles, or African languages. Portuguese-based creoles are also spoken in Senegal and Equatorial Guinea, and the inhabitants of the island republic of São Tomé and Príncipe speak Portuguese dialects. Papiamento, a Portuguese-based creole, is spoken on some Caribbean islands. It is the majority language and one of the official languages on the Leeward Islands (part of the Netherlands Antilles). It is also the main language of the inhabitants of Aruba, also a Netherlands possession.

Portuguese was spoken extensively in the ports of India and South East Asia during the 16th and 17th centuries. Currently, Portuguese dialects and Portuguese-based creoles are still spoken by small, isolated minorities in Macao, Goa, Indonesia, Sri Lanka and India.

The Portuguese language varies throughout the world, in pronunciation, grammar and vocabulary. The Portuguese spoken in Africa has been influenced by African languages and in many cases a continuum exists between the Portuguese-based creoles and Portuguese. In Brazil, Portuguese has inherited some vocabulary from indigenous Amerindian languages and from the languages of other European in-migrant groups. Brazilian Portuguese also differs from the Portuguese of Portugal in that the latter was influenced by French in the 18th century. Independent creation of separate technical and scientific terminology have further widened the gap between these two main varieties of Portuguese.

In 1936, the Instituto de Alta Cultura was established in Portugal. Its work included the dissemination worldwide of Portuguese language and culture. (In 1976 its name was changed to the Instituto de Cultura e Lingua Portuguesa). In 1986 a National Portuguese Language

A bank in Manau, Amazonas, Brazil with signs in Portuguese.

Commission was created, with one of its main concerns being to unify the orthography of Portuguese. In 1989, the International Institute of the Portuguese Language was inaugurated by the seven countries in which Portuguese is the official language, its main aim being to consolidate and standardize the Portuguese language, and to encourage cultural relations between the member countries. In 1990, an orthographic agreement was signed by representatives of these seven countries, but there is still dissension over the necessity for a worldwide unified standard for the language. Those in favor argue that unity is necessary for the status and prestige of Portuguese. Those who oppose the agreement argue on the grounds that it is impractical to implement in such areas as education, science and technology. Also, in 1994, a community of Portuguese-speaking countries was created, to encourage the establishment of a uniform Portuguese standard and to facilitate cultural exchanges between the member countries.

Spanish throughout the World

Spanish, with an estimated 300 million speakers, is the fourth most widely spoken language in the world. It is the official language of the whole of Spain, and the native language of over 70 percent of the population of 39 million. The Spanish used in Spain is called Castilian, to distinguish it from the other main languages of the country, Catalan, Basque and Galician, which all have regional official status (see page 405).

Spanish explorers and traders traveled westwards from the 15th century onwards and gradually colonized most of South and Central America, and many Caribbean islands. Spanish is the sole official language of the following South American countries, Ecuador, Colombia,

Venezuela, Uruguay, Argentina and Chile, and is the first language of the majority of the population in each country. It is a joint official language with indigenous Amerindian languages in Bolivia, Paraguay and Peru. In Central America, Spanish is the official language and the majority language in Mexico, Guatemala, El Salvador, Nicaragua, Costa Rica and Panama. It is the official language in Cuba and the Dominican Republic, and the main language of the population of these two Caribbean islands. The Caribbean island of Puerto Rico has been under United States control since 1898, and Spanish and English have been the two official languages (see page 115).

Santiago, Cuba,1987. A revolutionary slogan in Spanish (above a mural depicting Che Guevara and economic recovery in Cuba) declares 'The 29th year of the revolution. On the right path'.

During the last 30 years, the Hispanic population of the United States has been on the increase. After Fidel Castro came to power in Cuba in 1959, many Cubans fled to the United States and the majority settled in the Dade County region of Florida. There has been a constant flow of migration to and from Puerto Rico, with the majority of Puerto Ricans settling in the New York area. There has also been some migration from the Dominican Republic and Columbia. Many Mexicans have migrated to the United States, mainly to the Southern states. In 1991, Spanish speakers numbered over 17 million and by 1995, close to one in ten of the population of the United States were of Hispanic origin. (See page 440.)

The standard Spanish used in North and South America is not very different from the Castilian Spanish of Spain. There are some variations in vocabulary and pronunciation but the two standards are very similar, and are likely to remain so, given the influence of the mass media and global communications.

In 1990, the Instituto Cervantes was established in Spain, to oversee and promote the use of the Castilian language and Spanish culture. The Instituto was established in response to the increasingly prominent status of Spanish as a world language, reflected in the growing number of Spanish speakers in the US, and the trade markets of South American countries. The Instituto has members representing the Spanish-speaking South American countries as well as Spain itself.

In Africa, Spanish is the official language of Equatorial New Guinea and is also spoken in Morocco, in small enclaves which were formerly part of Spanish Western Sahara. There is also a small and decreasing Spanish-speaking minority in the Philippines, from the time when those islands were under Spanish rule (between the 17th and 19th centuries). Spanish is the official language and the native language of the million inhabitants of the Canary Islands, off the North Coast of Africa.

Spanish is one of the six official languages of the United Nations, together with English, French, Chinese, Russian and Arabic and one of the three official languages of the Association of Olympic Committees, along with French and English.

French throughout the World

The French language is spoken as a first language by an estimated 120 million people throughout the world and as a second language by many more. It is the official language of 34 countries and one of the six official languages of the United Nations, together with Spanish, English, Arabic, Chinese and Russian. French, Spanish and English are the three official languages of the Association of Olympic Committees. French is the official language of the Republic of France and its overseas territories and the native language of the majority of the 60 million French citizens. French is also an official language in four other countries bordering France. It is one of the official languages of Belgium and the first language of five million Belgian citizens, a third of the total population. French is also one of the three official languages of Switzerland, spoken by two million Swiss, and also spoken over the border in the Val D'Aosta region of Italy. French is the official language of the small republic of Monaco and also one of the three official languages of Luxembourg.

French is widely spoken throughout the world, mainly as a result of colonies established by settlers and traders from France and Belgium. French is one of the two official languages of Canada, and the native language of about six million Canadian citizens. In the early 17th century, French colonists began to establish permanent settlements in north-east America. Although by 1763 the British had gained control of the whole of present day

A truck carrying bananas on the way to Yammasoukro, Côte d'Ivoire (Ivory Coast), Africa. Côte d'Ivoire was formerly a French colony and French has been retained as the only official language, and almost the only language used in education, the media and official life. About a quarter of the population speak French, mainly those people with high school education, and some 40 percent speak 'Ivory Coast French', a French-based pidgin. The signs in French on the back of the truck mean 'Thanks to God' and 'Good Luck'.

Canada, the French-speaking community have retained sufficient numerical and political strength to ensure the rights of their language, culture and traditions (see page 431). The French speakers live mainly in the province of Quebec. Canadian spoken French differs from that of France in pronunciation and vocabulary. (Many words now obsolete in the French of France have been retained and many Americanisms have been borrowed). A dialect of French, Cajun French, is also spoken in the state of Louisiana in the United States by about half a million descendants of 18th-century French settlers ejected from what is now Eastern Canada for refusing to submit to British rule.

In the first half of the 19th century, France began to make inroads into Africa, with the conquest of the territories of Algeria and Senegal. Throughout the second half of the 19th century, large areas of north and central Africa were occupied by France and Belgium. French is still an official language in 18 African countries. French is also widely used in education and public life in several other African countries, notably Mauritania, Tunisia, Algeria, Morocco, Ethiopia and Togo. However, in most of these countries, French is only spoken by a small proportion of the population.

Areas of Asia were also occupied by France in the 19th century. Laos, Vietnam and Cambodia were all French colonies until the mid-20th century, but French no longer has any official status in these countries, and its use has decreased considerably. In South America, French is an official language in French Guiana, and in Haiti. French is also the official language of four states in the Pacific, Vanuatu, French Polynesia, New Caledonia and Wallis and Futuna.

Many French-based creoles evolved in French colonies throughout the world. French-based Creoles are widely spoken in the Caribbean. Haitian Creole French is one of the official languages of Haiti, and the native language of the majority of the population. French-based creoles are also widely spoken in St Lucia, and Dominica. In the Seychelles Islands, off the east coast of Africa, Seychelles Creole French has replaced English and French as the official language and Creole French is also spoken in the Island of Réunion, an overseas territory of France, east of Madagascar, and in the Ivory Coast.

Arabic throughout the World

Arabic is the sole or joint official language of some 21 independent middle Eastern and African states, and is the native language of approximately 183 million people. Since January, 1974, it has been an official language of the United Nations, together with English, French, Spanish, Russian and Chinese. The spread of Arabic has been closely linked with the Islamic religion. Classical Arabic is the language of the Qur'ān, the holy book of Islam, the language of divine revelation, and the liturgical language of Muslims throughout the world. It is estimated that there are about one billion Muslims in the world today, living in more than 60 countries. This represents 20 percent of the world's population.

During the 7th and 8th century AD, Islamic armies emerged from Arabia to occupy territories in North Africa, Egypt and Spain. Arabic gradually supplanted the indigenous languages in these areas, such as Berber, Aramaic, Greek and Coptic. Language shift occurred first in urban areas, then spread out into rural regions. The shift to Arabic occurred because that language was the medium of religious and political dominance.

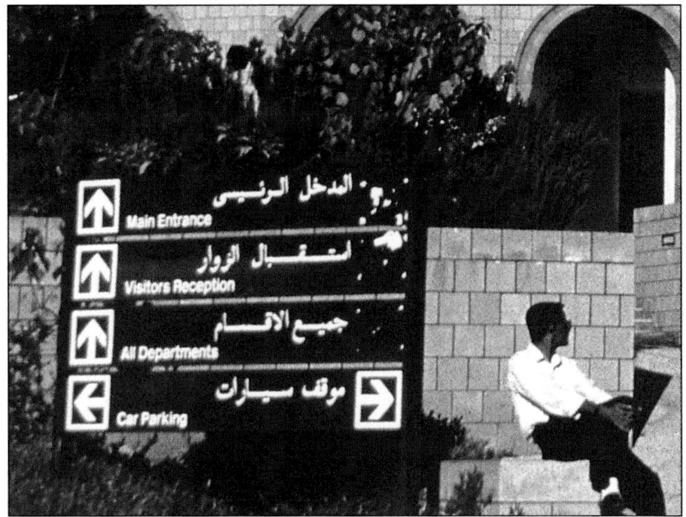

Signs in English and Arabic at the Faculty of Medicine at Sana'a University, Yemen.

Numerous Arabic vernaculars are spoken throughout North Africa and South West Asia, many of which are mutually unintelligible. However, throughout the centuries, Classical Arabic, as embodied in the Qur'ān, has provided a literary and written standard and a unifying force throughout the Arabic-speaking world. Its descendant, Modern Standard Arabic, is used as an official language in all Arabic-speaking countries and provides a lingua franca between them. A triglossic situation exists in all countries where Arabic is the majority and official language. Native speakers of Arabic use their own dialect at home and for informal purposes, while Modern Standard Arabic is the medium of education, administration and all written and official functions. Classical Arabic is used only for religious purposes.

Russian throughout the World

The Russian language is spoken by an estimated 160 million people world-wide and is one of the six official languages of the United Nations. According to the 1989 census, Russian was the native language of about 134 million citizens of the Soviet Union, out of a total population of approximately 286 million. It had official status and high prestige in all the countries of the Soviet Union and was widely spoken as a second language by other ethnic groups. Since the break-up of the Soviet Union in 1991 and the decline of Communism, the Russian language has decreased in status in most former Soviet or Communist countries, and the size of the Russian-speaking population in many of those countries has decreased as ethnic Russians have migrated to Russia or to other countries. Russian is now an important language in Israel, since the massive influx of Soviet Jews beginning in 1989. Over half a million Russian speakers now reside in Israel (see page 202).

In the Autonomous Republic of Dagestan in the Russian Federation, over 30 languages are spoken by different ethnic groups. Just over 10 percent of the population are ethnic Russians, but Russian is an important official language. In the village of Akhti on the Azerbaijan border, a poster from the Soviet era shows Russian language slogans.

Chinese throughout the World

The Chinese language has the most mother tongue speakers of any language in the world. Well over a billion people are estimated to speak Chinese, approximately one fifth of the world's entire population. Chinese is one of the six official languages of the United Nations. Approximately 92 percent of the 1.2 billion inhabitants (1995 estimate) of the People's Republic of China speak varieties of Chinese. Almost the entire population of Taiwan (21.5 million) speak varieties of Chinese. The Chinese form around 78 percent of Singapore's 2.9 million population and Chinese is one of the four official languages. Almost the entire population of Hong Kong (5.5 million) are Chinese speakers. Chinese is also the native language of large minority groups in other countries of South East Asia, as well as by in-migrant groups in most parts of the world. Chinese consists of five main groups of varieties, many of which are mutually unintelligible and disparate.

Chinese has a unified literary and written tradition. The classical written language represents linguistic units or morphemes by characters. Thus, the same written language can represent differing pronunciations and different vocabularies. This, together with a strong sentiment of historical unity among Chinese people, means that speakers of the various Chinese varieties regard them as dialects of a single language.

During the 20th century, varieties of a unified standard language called Modern Standard Chinese (or Mandarin Chinese) have been increasingly used in China, Taiwan and Singapore.

Chinese school children in Tiananmen Square, Beijing, below a clock showing the days until Hong Kong reverted to China.

Further Reading

COMRIE, B. (ed.), 1991, *The World's Major Languages*. London and New York: Routledge.

CRYSTAL, D., 1987, *The Cambridge Encyclopedia of Language*. Cambridge: Cambridge University Press.

DA SILVA, F. G. & GUNNEWIEK L. K., 1992, Portuguese and Brazilian Efforts to Spread Portuguese. *International Journal of the Sociology of Language*, 95, 71-92.

SANCHEZ, A., 1992, Política de Difusión del Español. *International Journal of the Sociology of Language*, 95, 51-69.

UNESCO, 1992, *Number of Speakers of the World's Principal Languages in 1989*. (Summary Prepared by the Section of Statistics on Culture and Communication, Division of Statistics). Paris: UNESCO.

6: Hispanics in the United States

In the United States, the terms 'Latino' and 'Hispanic' are both umbrella terms which refer to the many people of Spanish-speaking origin who come from Latin America and from the Iberian peninsula. Both terms are sometimes used more or less interchangeably. Latinos in the United States come particularly (but not exclusively) from countries such as Mexico, Cuba, Puerto Rico and recently from Central and South America. In the United States, 'Latino' is currently used to describe people who may have lost (or retained) the language of their ancestors but who are permanent in the United States. The term is often regarded as more inclusive of the African and indigenous heritage of these groups (and not only the Spanish heritage). Hispanic is often the official term used (e.g. in US Census). There are currently over 25 million Latinos in the United States and projections from census data suggests that, by the year 2020, Latinos will form the largest ethnic minority in the United States with close to 50 million members.

One topic of interest in the United States is the extent to which different Latino groups wish to retain their different national origins or wish to become aggregated into an overall Latino group which numerically, at least, will have potential power. While there are differences between these groups in terms of the percentage of their members who are native and foreign-born, who are more or less educated, who already have some power base and affluence or are disempowered and impoverished, who have US citizenship (e.g. Puerto Ricans) or are classified as refugees, permanent resident aliens or who are illegal in-migrants, this rapidly growing group of people have established Latinos as an important focus of study in present US society.

Who are the Latinos in US society? Approximately two-thirds of all US Latinos are of Mexican origin, and are found predominantly in the south-western region of the United States, but also in some regions such as Washington DC. Since the 1960s, the Chicano movement has developed a socially and politically more active stance with interests in more community control and Hispanic cultural maintenance (e.g. *Voz Fronteriza*). The Puerto Rican communities tend to exist mostly in the north-eastern United States, particularly in and around New York. Recently, issues of community control, acquiring a positive cultural self-image, attacking discrimination and unequal access to economic and political opportunities have become predominant in some Puerto Rican communities.

Cubans primarily migrated from Cuba to southern Florida. Cubans have generally been more welcomed into United States society than most other Latino groups. This is due to different factors favoring the Cubans such as: recognized political refugee status, government aid, many middle class Cubans migrating to the United States, trade embargos against Cuba, and US efforts against Communist regimes. Latinos from the Dominican Republic are particularly found around New York (e.g. in Washington Heights and the Lower East Side of New York). Joined by a desire for increased economic success, Dominicans in the United States include both working-class and middle-class sectors of society.

One concern among many Latino groups is the education of their Spanish-speaking children. The issue of bilingual education and equal resources and opportunities for Latinos in the schooling system is an issue that is part of a growing interest among Latinos in the United States.

The average performance of Latinos in the United States school system tends to reflect underachievement. However, Latinos are generally united in believing that educational attainment is important for improving social and vocational mobility, economic reward and increasing political power. The tendency among many Latino groups to experience relatively greater unemployment, lower

The Distribution of Hispanics in the United States

The graph, map and table present information about Hispanics based on the United States 1990 Census (see also US languages maps, page 438f). Such Hispanics may be of any race and country of origin. Those classed as Hispanics in the US do not all speak Spanish. Thus the following data and analyses refer to a grouping of which language is only one identificational feature. Section Three (see page 440) deals specifically with Spanish speakers in the United States.

At the time of the 1990 US Census, the total population numbered 248,709,873 of which 22,354,059 were counted as of Hispanic origin (nine percent). The graph shows the country or region of origin of such Hispanics. Of all Hispanics in the 1990 Census, 61 percent came from Mexico, 12 percent crossed from Puerto Rico, and almost five percent came from Cuba.

The following table provides the total number of Hispanics in the different States. Thus California heads the list with over 7.5 million Hispanics, followed by Texas with over four million, New York with over two million and Florida with over 1.5 million. The States with the fewest Hispanics were: Vermont, North Dakota, South Dakota, Maine and West Virginia.

STATE	NUMBER OF HISPANICS	STATE	NUMBER OF HISPANICS
California	7,557,550	Hawaii	78,742
Texas	4,294,120	North Carolina	69,020
New York	2,151,743	Missouri	60,429
Florida	1,555,031	Idaho	51,679
Illinois	878,682	Minnesota	49,664
New Jersey	720,344	Rhode Island	43,932
Arizona	680,628	Nebraska	35,093
New Mexico	576,709	Columbia	31,358
Colorado	419,332	Tennessee	31,075
Massachusetts	275,859	Iowa	30,642
Pennsylvania	220,479	South Carolina	28,334
Washington	206,018	Wyoming	24,976
Connecticut	203,511	Alabama	23,579
Michigan	189,915	Kentucky	20,363
Virginia	155,353	Arkansas	19,586
Ohio	131,982	Alaska	17,904
Nevada	121,346	Delaware	15,151
Maryland	119,984	Mississippi	14,745
Oregon	110,606	Montana	12,167
Georgia	101,379	New Hampshire	11,558
Indiana	95,363	West Virginia	7,892
Louisiana	90,609	Maine	7,069
Kansas	90,289	South Dakota	5,428
Wisconsin	87,609	North Dakota	4,658
Oklahoma	83,654	Vermont	3,862
Utah	83,097		

Percentage of Hispanics by State

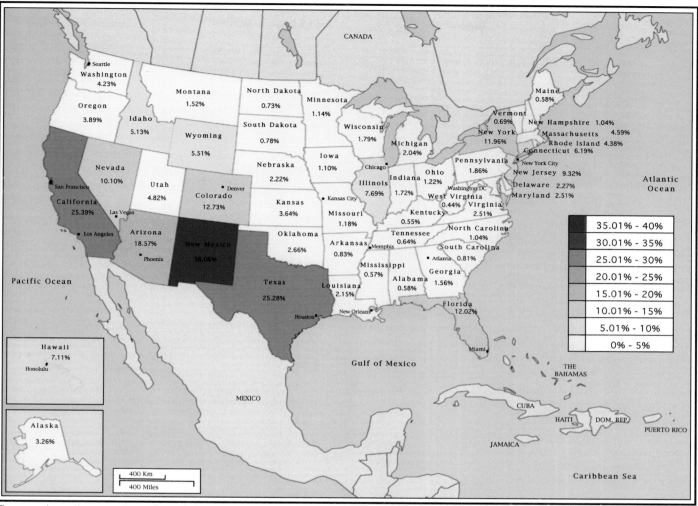

The map shows the percentage of population of each State which is of Hispanic origin according to 1990 census figures. In New Mexico, for example, 38 percent of the population is Hispanic, with 25 percent in California and Texas, 19 percent in Arizona and 12 percent in Florida and New York.

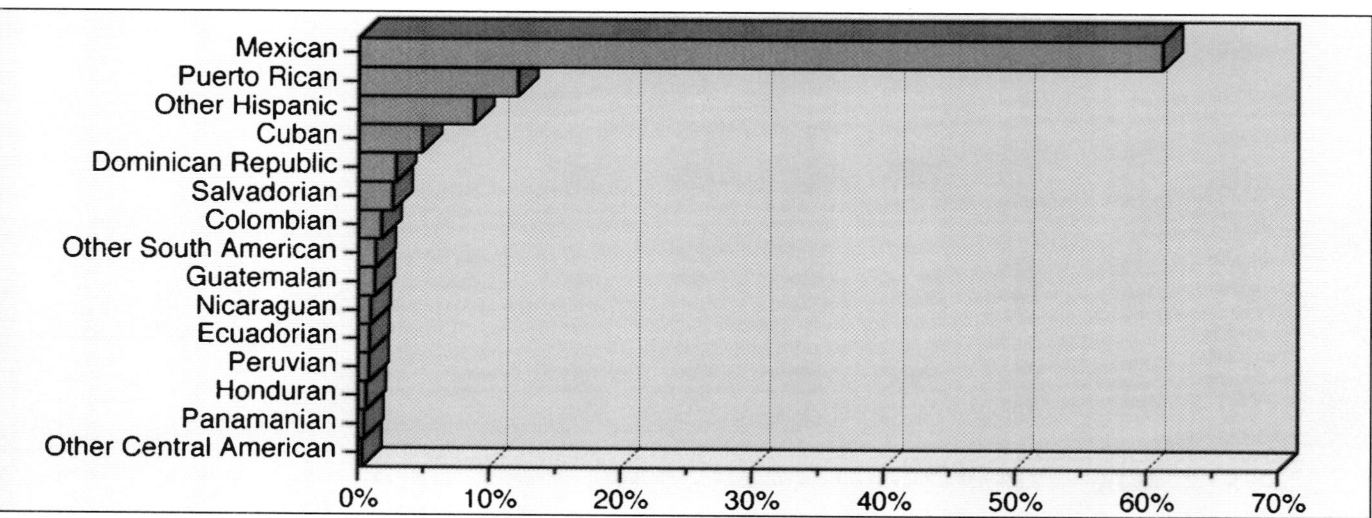

Origins of Hispanics in the United States census.

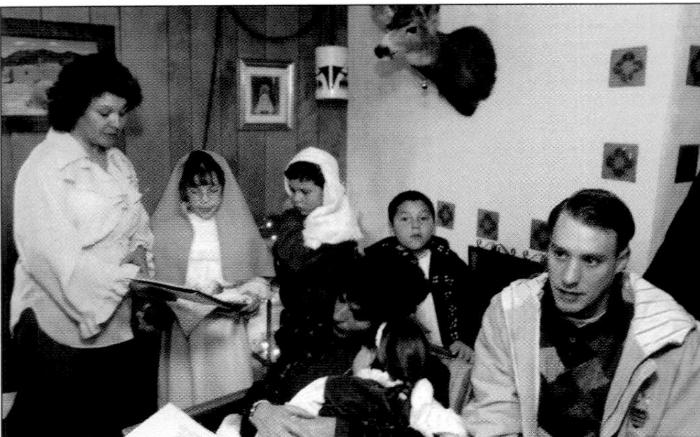

The Armijo family celebrate Christmas at their home on Christmas eve. The Armijos are a large and traditional Hispanic family that have resided in Santa Fe for many generations.

earnings and more discrimination when applying for employment, on occasions unites Latinos in the struggle for more equality of access and opportunity.

The growth of the Latino community in the US is also a source of central debate and controversy which can lead to a challenging political position. There are political arguments about illegal in-migration, and depressed wages due to inexpensive in-migrant labor, and this places Latinos on the defensive when immigration and economic reforms are discussed.

A related issue is a significant population of Latinos, especially Mexican-born, who are not legally naturalized United States citizens and therefore do not have voting rights. Because of this, efforts have been made in Latino circles to encourage Latinos to become naturalized citizens of the United States, and to become politically more participative and active. Yet, when Latinos do have the vote, evidence suggest that they are less likely to register as voter and less likely to turn out in elections than 'majority' populations, although Cubans are often an exception.

A group of Puerto Rican women and children with Puerto Rican flags during a parade in Wilmington Delaware in 1993. Because of the constant stream of two-way migration between Puerto Rico and the US, many Puerto Ricans have maintained their identity and language.

Nevertheless, there is a growing awareness among man Latinos of their origins, their ethnic identity and powe in numbers. The number of Latinos in the United State House of Representatives and Congress has steadil risen, although proportionally it is still small. Amon many Latinos, there is still an awareness of the value o retaining the home and heritage language. Whethe political ambitions, the desire for equality of access an opportunity of employment and avoiding poverty work against the preservation of the heritage language, is major issue still being fought over and unlikely to b quickly resolved in United States Latino society.

Irrespective of perceived ethnic group or original countr of origin, Latinos are joined by their common language - Spanish. Generally, Puerto Ricans, Dominicans, Cuban and Mexicans and those from Central and Sout America can interact and communicate with each othe in Spanish. Carrasquillo (1991, page 60) suggests tha 'the principle characteristic that is widely shared b Hispanics is the Spanish language: it is the single mos unifying element of Hispanics in the United States. Th retention of Spanish is the most obvious and visible sig of retained Hispanic cultural characteristics.'

It is estimated that approximately four-fifths of a Hispanic households speak Spanish, with newer in-migrants being more likely to speak Spanish than secon and third generations. In many cities in the Unite States, there are large and relatively integrated communities of Spanish speakers (e.g. the Puerto Ricans in Ne York, Mexican communities in California). Spanish radi stations, television stations, Spanish language newspapers have risen in numbers steadily since 1970, aiding consciousness of ethnicity. In contrast, the United State school system has generally worked very much agains the preservation of the Spanish language in Latinos. As i discussed in the entries on Transitional Bilingual education and Submersion education, the government ideology in United States education is to replace the Spanis language of Latino children by English.

Further Reading

CARRASQUILLO, A., 1991, *Hispanic Children and Youth in the Unite States: A Resource Guide.* New York: Garland Publishing.

MORALES, R. & BONILLA, F., 1993, *Latinos in a Changing U Economy.* London: Sage.

UNITED STATES BUREAU OF THE CENSUS, 1992, *Populatio Projections of the United States, by Age, Sex, Race and Hispanic Origi 1992 to 2050.* Washington, DC: US Government Printing Office.

7: World Englishes

Introduction

Several centuries ago, English consisted of a collection of dialects spoken by monolinguals within a small country on an island. Towards the end of the 16th century, there were probably between five and seven million native speakers of English, most of them living in the British Isles. By the middle of the 20th century, English was used by about 250 million people, the majority living outside the British Isles. Since the middle of the 20th century to the present, there has been around a 40 percent increase in the number of fluent speakers of English.

At the threshold of the 21st century, English is used either as a first or second language by millions of people and is one of the main or official languages in more than 60 countries in every continent of the world. It is estimated that English is spoken as a first language by about 400 million people, as a second language by a further 350 million people, and is also spoken fluently as a foreign language by over a further 100 million (Crystal, 1997b). It has been estimated by the British Council that, in the year 2000, there could be a billion people learning English. One current growth area is China where it is estimated that over 100 million people watched the BBC TV English language learning Series *Follow Me*. Estimates of the number of English speakers in the world that include speakers with a lower level of fluency range around 1.4 billion people. (The variations are due to guesses or estimates being required in many countries, and to the difficulty in deciding what degree of fluency counts as native-like English competence and what counts as using the English language – see Crystal, 1995; Crystal, 1997a &1997b).

The place of English in the US and much of the world is strong and becoming stronger. English was spread by British colonization, conquest and trade between the 16th and 20th centuries. English was particularly promoted by the emergence of the United States after World War II, as a world leader in military, political, economic and technical spheres.

The numbers of speakers is less important than the prestigious domains and functions that English dominates. English is considered to be the main language of international communication in many fields. 'English has a dominant position in science, technology, medicine, and computers; in research, books, periodicals, and software; in transnational business, trade, shipping, and aviation; in diplomacy and international organizations; in mass media entertainment, news agencies, and journalism; in youth culture and sport; in education systems, as the most widely learnt foreign language' (Phillipson, 1992, page 6). Crystal (1997b) indicates that: 'Over two-thirds of the world's scientists write in English. Three-quarters of the world's mail is written in English. Of all the information in the world's electronic retrieval systems, 80% is stored in English. People communicate on the Internet largely in English. English radio programmes are received by over 150 million in 120 countries. Over 50 million children study English as an additional language at primary level; over 80 million study it at secondary level (these figures exclude China).' Such a widespread use of English means that Anglo culture, Anglo institutions, and Anglo ways of thinking and communicating are spreading. English then tends to displace the functions of other languages and even displace the languages themselves.

The spread of English throughout the world is also reflected in English words being borrowed by other languages. For example, with computing terms and other technological terminology, an English word is often added to another language and eventually becomes accepted as part of the vocabulary of that language. (See Language Borrowing, page 164)

The Spread of English

The spread of English, like that of other prestigious languages throughout time, has come about in a variety of ways, including political domination, trade, colonization and emigration, education, religion and the mass media.

Political domination

Political domination by military conquest or by colonization has often meant the spread of English. In the British Isles, to take one example, England gradually conquered Wales, Scotland and Ireland. Political domination led to economic denomination. English became the language of the ruling classes, of power, status and prestige. It became the language of the legal and administrative system, in some cases of religion, and eventually, with the introduction of education for all in the 19th century, of the educational system. English has now become the majority language of all parts of the British Isles, while

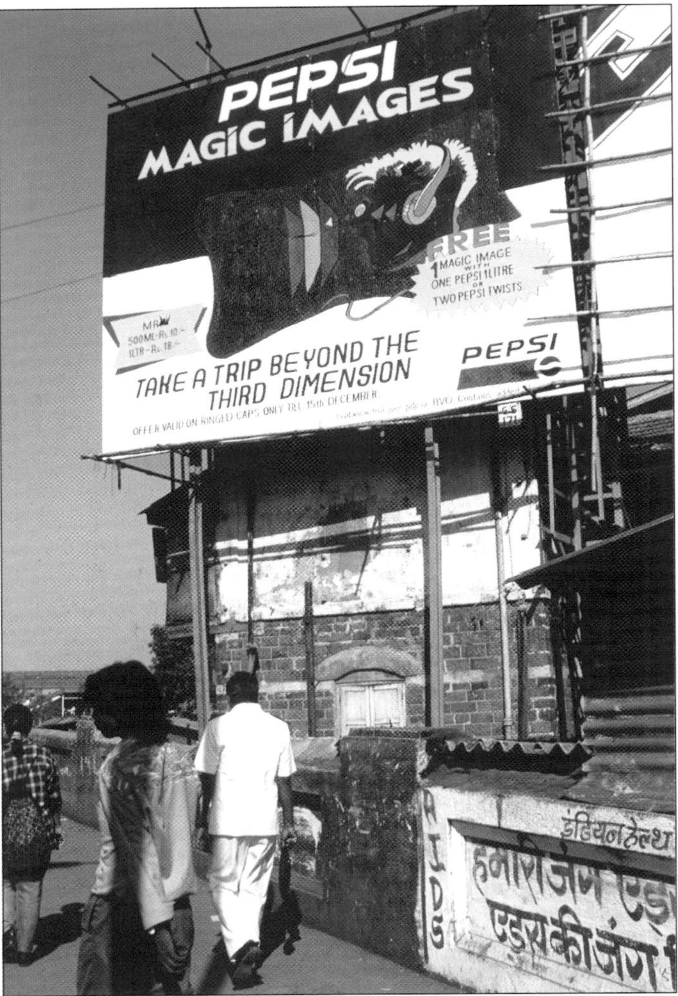

This Pepsi advertisement in Bombay, India, shows how the English language and Anglo culture has spread world wide.

the Celtic languages of Welsh, Scottish Gaelic and Irish are fighting for survival.

Trade and business

The voyages of English-speaking traders between the 16th and the 19th centuries, the transportation of slaves and the establishment of plantations in places like Africa, America, the Caribbean and South Asia, led to the use of English in these places and to the development of English-based pidgins and creoles (see Pidgins and Creoles, page 142). These English-based languages of wider communication have, in many cases, made it easier for indigenous peoples to learn a standard variety of English.

More recently, the emergence of the US as the dominant economic power in the 20th century has made English the main language of big business. Countries that wish to compete in the international market may have to ensure that they can communicate effectively in English.

Colonization and emigration

Colonization and emigration can occur for various reasons, for economic and trade reasons, or as an escape from religious or political persecution.

In-migrants from England began to colonize the east coast of North America at the beginning of the 17th century, some of them religious dissidents, some seeking economic betterment. Australia was first colonized towards the end of the 18th century by convicts from Britain. The colonization of New Zealand by English speakers from Britain began at the turn of the 19th century and gained momentum in the second half of that century. In all these countries, the colonists brought their language, together with their culture and way of life. Wherever they came into conflict with indigenous peoples they overcame them by military conquest, or by apportioning their land.

The colonists set up their own parliamentary, economic and judicial system, their schools and churches, all through the medium of English. In-migrants from other parts of Europe also colonized these countries, bringing with them their languages and customs. However, English was already established as the dominant language and, in most cases, the in-migrants from other European countries followed a common pattern of language shift towards English. The first generation in-migrants would generally remain monolingual in their mother tongue, the second generation would be bilingual in the mother tongue and English, and the third generation would often be monolingual in English. In some cases, the shift to monolingualism in English did not happen so quickly, for example, when there was a strong mother tongue community, reinforced by new arrivals from the homeland, or where the community tended to keep separate, often for religious reasons.

The establishment of British colonies in India, Africa and other places in the 19th and early 20th centuries meant that English became the language of the administration and the language of the politically and economically dominant elite. (See Colonialism and Languages, page 324.)

Religion

The preaching of Christianity by English-speaking missionaries has contributed to the spread of English in many areas of the world.

Education

The implementation of English-medium education in many former colonies has accelerated the spread of English to a wider section of the population. Where English-based pidgins or creoles are already widely spoken among the population, this makes it easier to learn a standard variety of English.

Anglo-American culture

The spread of English has been accelerated by the influence of popular Anglo-American culture disseminated by the mass media. Television, radio, the cinema, popular music and information via computers, mean that the English language has penetrated to the furthest reaches of the globe.

The prestige of English

The international prestige of English and English-speaking nations and the popularity of Anglo-American culture has given the English language associations of status, power and affluence. It is fashionable to speak English, and English words and expressions are extensively used, even in other prestigious languages such as French and German. Throughout the world English is taught as a foreign language and is widely used in advertizing to suggest power, status, authority and reliability.

Recently, many people on all continents have been willing to learn and accept English as a universal utilitarian language. Such learners have been willing to embrace English, not for Anglo-American enculturation, but as an international language that facilitates trade and commerce, and international and multinational communication. Communication in English is regarded by such learners as a means of communication to an economic or political (rather than a cultural or social) end. For example, when Japanese speak English to Singaporeans, United States or British culture is absent. The English spoken, and the behavior in the interaction, is Asian. In such situations, the stigma of a colonializing English is being replaced by a positive attitude about the multinational functionality of English.

English in the United States

At the federal level, there is no reference to language in either the 1776 Declaration of Independence or the 1789 United States Constitution, the two founding documents of the United States. Many founding fathers believed that language laws would run contrary to the guarantee of freedom of speech. However, in the last 25 years in the United States, there have been proposals to add amendments to the Constitution that would name English as the official language. Called Official English or English-only legislation, considerable debate has been provoked (see page 290f).

Among the 50 states in the United States, certain states make reference to language in their Constitutions: New Mexico where English and Spanish are official languages; Hawaii where English and native Hawaiian are official languages; Colorado, Florida and Nebraska where English has been named as the official language.

In 1988 Arizona passed an Amendment making English the official language. In 1990, this was invalidated as an infringement of the rights to free speech under the First Amendment of the Constitution.

By 1996, many states had Resolutions or legislation declaring English as the official language. These include: Alabama, Arizona, Arkansas, California, Georgia, Illinois, Indiana, Kansas, Kentucky, Louisiana, Mississippi, Montana, New Hampshire, North Carolina, North Dakota, South Carolina, South Dakota, Tennessee, Virginia and Wyoming. By 1996, three states had passed Resolutions in favor of English Plus, namely New Mexico, Oregon and Washington.

The Situation of English throughout the World

The situation of English is not uniform throughout the world but varies according to a multitude of factors, including the political situation, other languages spoken in the country, inter-ethnic relations and cultural attitudes. The situation of English can be divided into three broad categories: countries where English is the first language of the majority of the population; countries where English is spoken widely as a second language and enjoys official status; countries where English has no official status but is used. These three categories will now be considered in turn.

English as main language

In many countries, English is the first language and often the only language of the majority of the population. In Australia, Canada, England, Ireland, New Zealand, Scotland, the US and Wales, the majority of the population are monolingual English speakers. This has not always been the case. Historically, the spread of English in the wake of political and economic expansion has led to the decline and sometimes death of indigenous languages in all these countries. In Ireland, the English language gradually superseded Irish in the 19th century, and although the Irish language is still the official language of Ireland and has great symbolic significance for the majority of Irish, it is only spoken by a minority of the population. In the US, the indigenous Native American languages and other ethnic languages spoken by inmigrants from Europe yielded to English, which has become a symbol of national cohesion. This has led to conflict, and today, minority groups in many of these countries, (such as the Maori in New Zealand and Welsh

The International Adaptation of English

Where English has traveled to other parts of the world, it has borrowed many words from other languages to express concepts or to label objects belonging to the new country or the local culture. Some of them have only been used in the local variety of English, while others have become part of what might be called an international vocabulary of English.

South African English is one example of a distinctive regional variety of English. The Dutch first settled the Cape in 1652, and by the time the British took it over at the end of the 18th century, there was a strong Dutch community, speaking both standard Dutch and local variants which later became the basis of the standard language of Afrikaans. Since that time, there has been close contact between the English-speaking and Dutch-speaking communities, and widespread bilingualism in these two languages has resulted in the considerable influence of Dutch/Afrikaans on South African English. South African English has been influenced to a lesser extent by local African languages.

English is now the first language of about ten percent of the total population of the Republic of South Africa. English is spoken fluently by many Afrikaaners and is used as a lingua franca by many millions of South Africans. About half of the distinctively regional vocabulary of South African English comes from Afrikaans, about 30 percent are English neologisms and of the remaining 20 percent, half are from African languages and half from other languages. Some of this regional vocabulary has gained world-wide coinage (e.g. 'Afrikaaner, trek, apartheid, veld' – all Afrikaans words) and 'concentration camp', an expression coined by the British during the second Anglo-Boer war.

Other vocabulary has tended to be restricted to use in South Africa, such as: words for animals like eland (Dutch), impala (Zulu); words for food such as boerewors (Afrikaans: boer sausage), sosaties (probably Malay: curried kebabs); vocabulary associated with apartheid such as 'group area' (an area set apart for a particular ethnic group) and 'resettlement' (the often forcible relocation of people to such areas). The syntax of South African English shows some influence of Afrikaans: one notable example is the response 'is it?' (Afrikaans 'is dit?'): 'She had a baby last week. — Is it?' Within South African English there are many varieties (e.g. Anglikaans, a codemixing of English and Afrikaans), and South African Indian English. In the province of Natal, where the majority of ethnic Indians live, South African Indian English is the first language of most ethnic Indians under the age of 40. South African Indian English shows the influence of Indian languages such as Gujarati, Hindi, Tamil, Telugu and Urdu in its syntax, pronunciation and vocabulary. The English spoken by many people in South Africa, mainly as a second language, shows the influence of African languages.

Where English is spoken as a second language, there can be transfer of vocabulary, syntactic structures, intonation, idioms and other linguistic features from the mother tongue(s) and from local English-based pidgins and creoles. The transmission of the English language to learners by teachers, who themselves speak English as a second language, has facilitated the incorporation of local features into English. As in countries where English is spoken as a first language, many different non-standard dialects may exist at different distances from a standardized variety of the language. Linguists sometimes call this a 'continuum', although this is not an adequate description because every form of speech does not fit tidily onto a certain point on the continuum.

It is possible to generalize however, and place the standard variety of the language, which is not very different from standard British or US English, at one end of the continuum. Various non-standard varieties can be placed at different points on the continuum, according to how much they diverge from the standard variety. At the other end of the continuum would be dialects that are heavily influenced by the mother tongues of the speakers, or English-based pidgins or creoles. However, it is becoming accepted practice that, as these local varieties of English gradually diverge further from Standard British or Standard US norms, so such local standard norms are themselves revised and re-thought to incorporate local features, instead of such local differences being perceived as errors or substandard speech.

REFERENCE: MCARTHUR, 1992

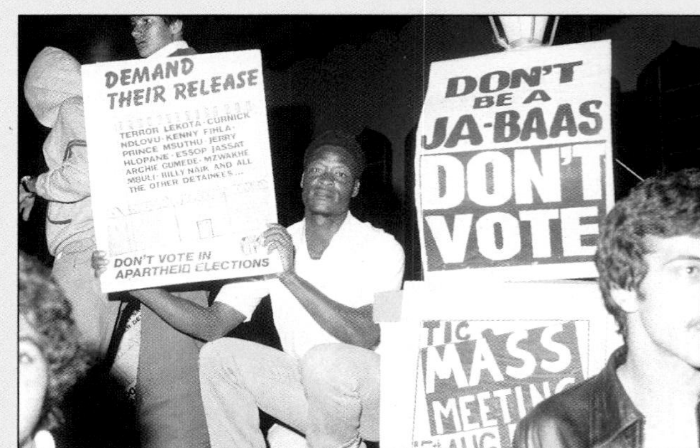

In this picture taken during the 1985 elections in South Africa, one protester holds up a placard saying 'don't be a Ja-baas, don't vote'. 'Ja-Baas' is an Afrikaans expression meaning literally 'Yes, Boss', thus coming to mean a servile person.

speakers in Wales), are struggling to preserve their national languages in the face of English domination.

English in a multilingual situation

In many countries of the world, English co-exists with other languages in a bilingual or multilingual situation. In former British colonies, English has often remained the official language or one of the official languages, and is still used widely in official contexts and education. English is not spoken as a first or home language by the majority of the population. It may only be spoken by an exclusive social elite. It may only be used in certain contexts (e.g. official and formal contexts) and its speakers may only be competent to use it in certain communicative situations. Many interconnected factors govern the extent of its use and the domains in which it is used. These factors will now be discussed.

The other languages spoken in the country. In countries where only one indigenous language is spoken by the majority of the population, the vernacular can be used widely as a medium of communication. English is often restricted to an official or administrative role. This is the case in Lesotho, Swaziland and Botswana, three countries of Southern Africa where the three national languages are Sesotho, Seswati and Tswana respectively. The use of English marks someone as a stranger or a foreigner.

Countries where a number of different languages are spoken. In this case English is often used more widely as a vehicle for intergroup communication. This happens in Zambia, Zimbabwe and Malawi. In each of these countries, a variety of local languages are spoken, some more widely than others. Language policy has favored English as a compromise, to avoid possible conflict between local language groups. English is used in a great number of domains, both official and non-official. If no common language exists between two speakers, they may switch to English. In Zimbabwe, where Shona and Ndebele are the principal regional languages, speakers of Shona may choose to speak Ndebele to a Ndebele speaker when in the Ndebele region. More often, however, they will speak in English. In the educational systems of these three countries, English is introduced as the sole language from the earliest grades.

Governmental decisions regarding language planning. In the post-colonial era, newly independent nations had to make decisions concerning the extent to which English would be used in parliamentary business, the legal system, administration and in education. Some nations have decided to continue the colonial pattern of using English in these areas, because of its value as an international language. Other nations have opted for an indigenous language that better expresses their independence and nationhood.

Inter-ethnic relations. If there is inter-ethnic tension, English may be preferred as a neutral and non-threatening vehicle of communication that does not elevate the status of one ethnic group over another. In South Africa, the two official languages were Afrikaans and English until 1993 (when nine African languages gained official status). English is in many respects a minority language. Afrikaans is the first language of the majority of the 'whites', and an important symbol of identity for those of Afrikaaner background. It is also the first language of the majority of the colored population. However most blacks, coloreds and Indians conduct their political activities in English, and would prefer to send their children to English-medium schools. For historical reasons, Afrikaans represents for 'non-whites' the language of authority and oppression, whereas English is the voice of protest and autonomy. (See also the accompanying Textbox on India.)

Attitudes towards English. In many former colonies, English is still considered to be the language of power and prestige, the chosen means of communication by the social elite. In other countries, a change in attitude may occur, favoring an indigenous national language or languages. The use of English may decline in non-official domains, and to speak English may be the marker of belonging to an outgroup. English may even be discarded as an official language, in favor of an indigenous lingua franca, which may be used in education and politics and administration.

It is difficult for Westerners living in largely monolingual societies to imagine the reality of life in a multilingual

English in the European Media

In 1995 the Dutch-based research group, Interview, conducted a European Media and Marketing Survey, in which they studied the media consumption of the wealthiest people in Europe, those earning at least double the average income in 17 countries. They discovered that English was the widely understood media language in Europe. Seventy percent of those surveyed said that they could understand English well enough to read a newspaper or follow the news on television. Forty-three percent of respondents could understand French language media, and 40 percent could understand newspapers and television in German. The introduction of pan-European and international channels on cable and satellite has made a wider choice of channels available to viewers in various countries.

English in India

The English language has existed in India for some 400 years, since the British East India Company was formed in 1600. It has achieved a special place in the country. During the period of British sovereignty, between 1765 and 1947, English became the medium of administration and education throughout India. In 1835, the principle of an English-medium educational system in India was accepted. In 1857, the Universities of Bombay, Calcutta and Madras were established, and English became the main medium of instruction. Some four percent of the people (30 million in 1994) now make regular use of English. The Indian Constitution recognizes 15 national languages, with Hindi as the official language and English as the associate official language.

When the Constitution was framed, the directive was given that English was to be replaced by Hindi over a period of 15 years. However, this has not happened. Hindi has not succeeded in rivaling English for the status of a pan-Indian language, for a number of reasons. Firstly, in post-colonial India, English still has tremendous prestige. It is used by members of the elite community. Its worth as an international language is recognized. It is the official language of four states (Manipur, Meghalaya, Nagaland, Tripura) and eight Union Territories.

Secondly, Hindi is the mother tongue of the largest group in India, spread over a wide geographical area. Other groups are reluctant to allow Hindi to be the main official language because they feel at a disadvantage, professionally, politically and socially. After Independence, there were violent and bitter conflicts between supporters of English, Hindi and regional languages. This led in the 1960s to the 'three language formula' in which English was introduced as the chief alternative to the local state language (typically Hindi in the North and a regional language in the South). English is a neutral language which does not threaten any group's ethnic identity. Research has shown, for instance, that middle and upper class Bengali and Tamil speakers in the largely Hindi-speaking city of Delhi choose to communicate in many informal situations in English rather than Hindi.

English is used in many important domains in India, including science and modern technology, education, administration and the mass media. It possesses appropriate and stable registers in these areas. Hindi, on the other hand, is still in the process of codifying and standardizing specific registers. Supporters of Hindi may have done some harm to their cause by identifying the use of Hindi with national integration, and advocating a pure, 'Sanskritized' variety of Hindi, which is difficult for many educated native speakers to understand.

Indian English has gradually been 'nativized', through transfer from local languages, and also by the different communicative needs caused by a different environment. Many older speakers, who were educated in private English schools in the tradition of the British Raj, still consciously try to emulate British English. Younger speakers, however, are more ready to recognize and accept Indian English as a distinct variety of English, and they are developing a positive attitude towards it as part of the cultural identity of India. There is a tension between the acceptance of the evolution of Indian English as a distinct variety and the need for a standard that is internationally intelligible and suitable for use as a teaching model in education.

So far, English has not replaced indigenous languages in India, but rather co-exists with them. It is used in an increasing number of contexts, both formal and informal, but, in the family domain, the mother tongue still predominates.

A bilingual English-Hindi sign in Jaipur, Rajasthan, India.

society, where English may be just one mode of expression in a complex repertoire of codes. In Kenya, for instance, different languages may represent different aspects of a person's identity. The mother tongue may express identification and solidarity with the local group; Swahili (Kiswahili) in its national variety may represent one's national identity. The use of English indicates a good level of education, modernity and Westernization.

Cultural constraints. English is widely regarded as conveying prestige and authority. Its use may not be appropriate in certain situations (e.g. when a younger person is addressing an older person). Even when English has penetrated into the domains of home and family, the indigenous language may still be used for cultural and religious ceremonies.

English with no official status

In many countries of the world, English has no official status, and may not be spoken at all by the vast majority of the population. Even in these countries, however, English is acknowledged to be an important and prestigious language, with people exposed to it in many domains. There may be considerable emphasis on the teaching of English as a foreign language in schools and on its use in business and industry. English language films may be shown with subtitles on television and in the cinema, and English pop songs heard on the radio. Many English words may have been borrowed into the indigenous language, and English may be used widely in advertising to suggest power, popularity and prestige.

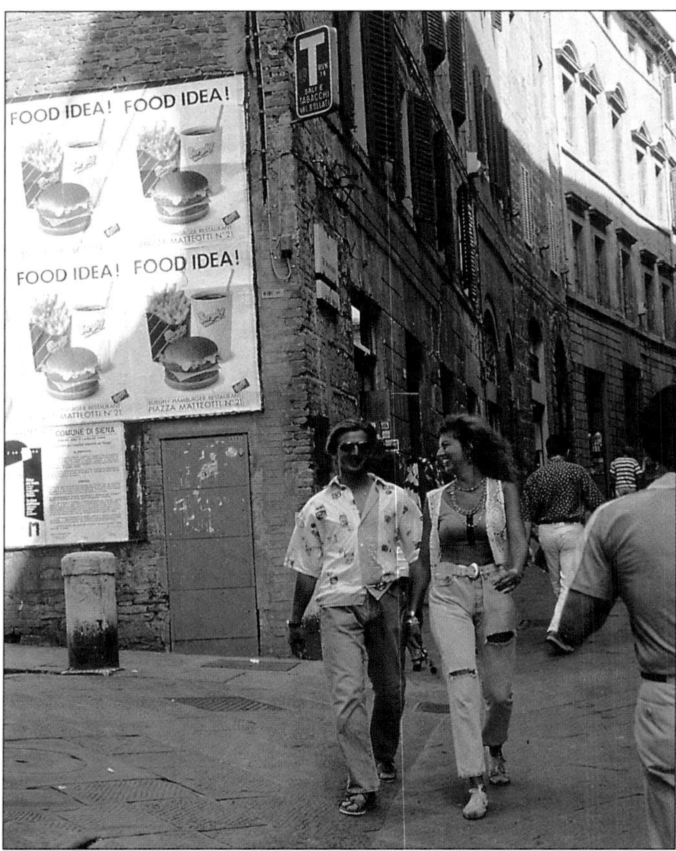

A fast-food advertisement in Siena, Italy. English may be used in advertising even in countries where it is not widely understood, to convey fashion, glamour and popularity.

Advantages of the Use of English

In situations where many languages co-exist and where there could be inter-ethnic tension, English may be a preferred means of communication between ethnic groups, as a means of avoiding the predominance of one ethnic group over another. It may be perceived as non-threatening and therefore a means of avoiding language conflict.

English is an international language of high prestige. It is used throughout the world in many different contexts, in trade and business, international diplomacy, science and education. Higher education in English may lead to the chance to study and gain skills in other, more developed countries. A developing country that encourages the learning and use of English in trade and business may widen its economic opportunities. A country that uses English in politics and official life may be able to participate more effectively in the international arena.

The English language possesses two very similar and stable standard versions, namely US English and British English. It has a wide repertoire and can be used for a range of different functions. Some indigenous languages may still be undergoing a process of standardization and codification. A standard form for use in writing, in official and technical contexts and in education may not have been agreed upon in some indigenous languages. The language may not have developed the necessary vocabulary to deal with many scientific and technical topics. The English language provides a ready-made tool in this regard.

Disadvantages of the Use of English

The spread of English has been connected to the decline and death of many indigenous languages. The dissemination of Anglo-American culture has caused the weakening and eradication of local, indigenous cultures. Besides having a large number of speakers, English dominates many prestigious domains and functions. Such a widespread use of English means that Anglo culture, Anglo institutions, and Anglo ways of thinking and communicating are spread. English then tends to displace the functions of other languages and even displace the languages themselves. In technology, communications and

entertainment, English has become the dominant language. It can take over some of the internal functions of other languages in a country (e.g. in business, mass media) and become the means of the external link in, for example, politics, commerce, science, tourism and entertainment. (See Language Imperialism, page 319.)

As English has spread throughout the world, many varieties have evolved. This will be discussed more fully below. This has made it harder for individual countries to decide on a standard variety for use in education and international communication.

Varieties of English

A language is never static. In England the English language has changed and evolved over a period of centuries. One has only to compare the 14th-century English of Chaucer with modern day English to see the difference. In parts of the world where English is spoken, either as a first or second language, many different varieties have evolved, with individual differences in accent, vocabulary, phonology and syntax.

The evolution of English can happen gradually in a largely monolingual environment, as has occurred in England. However, changes often happen when a language comes into contact with other languages. Where a group of speakers of one language has prolonged contact with other language groups, words and even idioms and syntactic structures may be borrowed. The evolution of local varieties of English has also been caused by non-linguistic factors (e.g. that English is spoken in different cultural settings and that people have different communicative needs).

The tendency has been until recently to accept Standard British English or US English as the norm, and to use these in text books and in the media. Also, many of the influential ruling elite of former colonial countries received an English-medium education and were taught by British or American teachers during colonial times. They still tend to adhere to these norms.

Until recently, regional varieties of English have only been examined in terms of British or US English standards, and described according to these norms. There has been a tendency to ascribe the existence of local features to learner errors. Only recently have the distinctive characteristics of local varieties been recognized as legitimate, stable features. Local varieties have begun to be described as autonomous systems. Recently, there has been an increase in confidence on the part of speakers of regional varieties of English and less of a desire to maintain British and American norms. The regional variety, with its particular grammar, vocabulary, pronunciation, idioms, orthography and conventions of use, is seen to represent a distinctive national and ethnic identity. This has long been true of countries where English is the first language of the majority of the population, such as Australia, New Zealand and Canada. It is becoming true of countries where English exists mainly as a second language in a multilingual setting, but is becoming valued as one aspect of a unique national identity (e.g. India and some African countries).

However, this may give rise to some problems in international communication and intelligibility. A tension exists between a desire to accept and codify regional varieties of English, and the need to agree on a standard version which can give access to international communication, and which will be acceptable in education. Some countries still use the British and American standards as their norms. Others advocate a degree of linguistic engineering to produce a World Standard English. Other countries are arguing for a flexible or polymodal model of standardization. The individual, regional variety of English could be used for internal communication. Difficulties of mutual intelligibility on a wider level could be overcome by strategies such as talking more slowly and simplifying expressions.

Further Reading

CRYSTAL, D., 1995, *The Cambridge Encyclopedia of the English Language*. Cambridge: Cambridge University Press.

CRYSTAL, D., 1997, *English as a Global Language*. Cambridge: Cambridge University Press.

CRYSTAL, D., 1997, *The Cambridge Encyclopedia of Language* (Second edition). Cambridge: Cambridge University Press.

DILLARD, J. L., 1992, *A History of American English*. New York: Longman.

GARCIA, O. & OTHEGUY, R. (eds), 1989, *English Across Cultures. Cultures Across English*. Berlin: Mouton de Gruyter.

KAPLAN, R. B., 1993, The Hegemony of English in Science and Technology. *Journal of Multilingual and Multicultural Development*, 14 (1 & 2), 151-172.

PLATT, J., WEBER, H., & HO, M. L., 1984, *The New Englishes*. London: Routledge.

TRUDGILL, P. & HANNAH, J., 1982, *International English*. London: Edward Arnold.

English in Nigeria

Nigeria has a population of over 90 million (but estimates vary), and about 400 languages are spoken in the country. It is probable that pidgin languages have existed in the country since ancient times, and have developed because of the need for communication and trade between language groups. Nigerian Pidgin English may have been used as a trade language as early as the 18th century and it has been suggested that it could be the descendant of a pidginized Nigerian language which was spoken along the coast before the coming of European traders. The vocabulary was gradually replaced by words of European origin. A British colony was founded at Lagos in 1861. In the late 19th century Western, English-medium education was introduced by missionaries and this was strongly supported by the colonial government. Nigeria received independence in 1960 and English continued to be the official language. The subsequent generalization of English-medium education helped the spread of English. However, the illiteracy rate in Nigeria amongst youths and adults is still very high and this has impeded the acquisition and use of English. Despite its wide use in education, administration, trade and the media, it remains a minority language. Nigerian Pidgin, on the other hand, is spoken by approximately 35 million people, and is the main link language in Nigeria. Varieties of pidgin form a continuum between an extreme, or 'basilectal' pidgin, strongly influenced by the speaker's mother tongue, and what is called WAVE, the standard West African Variety of English, with both ends of the continuum exerting an influence on one another.

A Nigerian news-stand selling English language magazines and newspapers.

8: Language Imperialism

The Oxford English Dictionary defines 'imperialism' as 'a policy of acquiring dependent territories or extending a country's influence over less powerful or less developed countries through trade, diplomacy, etc.' One main agent of imperialism throughout the centuries has been language. When a dominant or colonizing power promotes or enforces its language on conquered territories, it facilitates the spread of its own culture and political, social and sometimes religious ideologies.

As the item on World Englishes (see page 311) demonstrates, the 20th century has seen the emergence of English as a major world language. English has not always been dominant. In the 16th century, English was one of the lesser-spoken languages of the world. In four centuries, it spread throughout the world through British colonization, conquest and trade, and then through the emergence of the US as a dominant world power after World War II. British and later US economic and military expansion has meant the spread, and sometimes enforcement of English as the language of government, administration, education, science and technology, industry, business and commerce in many countries.

English is spoken as a first or second language by hundreds of millions of people. It is learnt as a second or foreign language by millions of people. It tends to dominate science and technology, information technology and medicine, computer software, the Internet, books, learned journal articles and telecommunications. English is ever-present in communication across the airways, in international business, in news agencies, television pro-

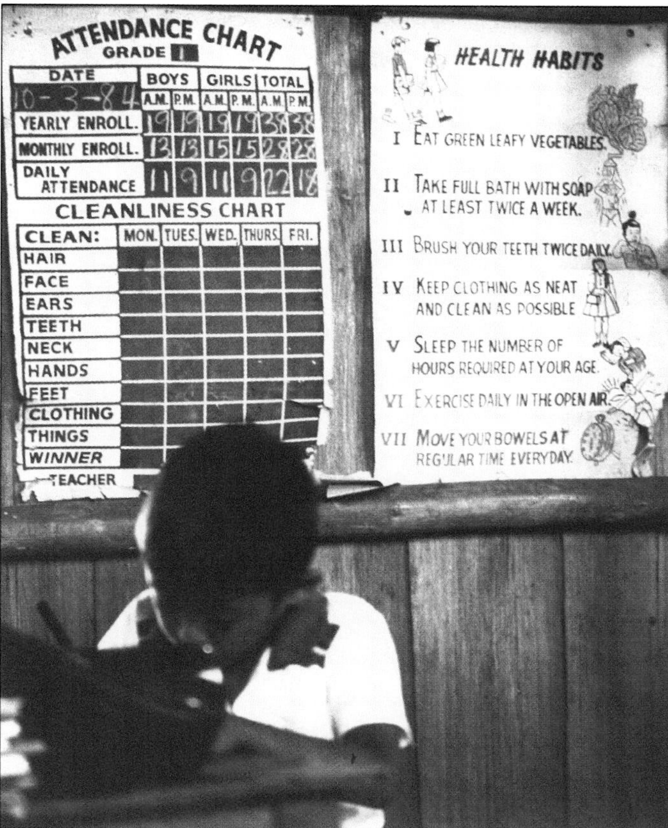

A tribal Filipino school in Mindanao, the Philippines. The Philippines was governed by the US between 1898 and 1946, and the two countries have maintained close links. English is an important second language in the Philippines, and is used widely in government and business. Learning English is considered necessary for social and economic advancement.

grams, international sports such as the Olympic Games, pop music and other forms of youth culture.

With the spread of English has gone the spread of ideas, ideology, culture, meanings and understandings. With English go associations of a popular modern language, a scientific and technologically advanced language, the language of affluence and power, the language of economic and social success.

To take one example, when the United States introduced English into the Philippines, the Filipinos were required to learn a new language, the North American culture and US forms of meaning and understanding. The Filipinos not only took on a foreign language but with it a foreign consciousness, foreign values and foreign interests. With US economic policy in the Philippines went also a cultural policy that included a mission to civilize, Americanize and capitalize.

Part of such language imperialism thus concerns the teaching of English to natives. Often, a belief in English language teaching to natives has been that English is best taught early. Also, the more English is taught, the better the level of competence that is achieved. If other languages are used in the curriculum, standards of English performance will fall.

In the post-colonial era, the imposition of English as an official language has become rarer. However, the momentum generated by the world-wide use of English has grown steadily, with the spread of Anglo culture, Anglo values and ideologies continuing unabated. However, imperialism is an insufficient explanation of the spread of English around the globe. As has been indicated above, there are too many other social, economic and political influences in the rise of English to make an 'imperialism' view simplistic by itself.

The history of the 20th century with respect to English is its replacement and displacement of other languages in the world. Where English has rapidly spread, the danger is that it does not encourage bilingualism but rather a shift towards English as the preferred language. Specifically, English tends to take over domains of usage in a developing and cumulative manner. With the technological revolution, computers and their software often make English the language of technology. English has frequently become an official language or a national language (e.g. Singapore, India, Kenya) and local vernaculars are viewed as substandard languages, languages of the socially or politically dominated, and languages with much lower status and prestige. Advanced schooling, for example in Kenya, often requires English to be the principal medium of language in the classroom. The use of vernaculars in the classroom will then be seen as of lower status, for the poor or less socially and economically mobile peoples.

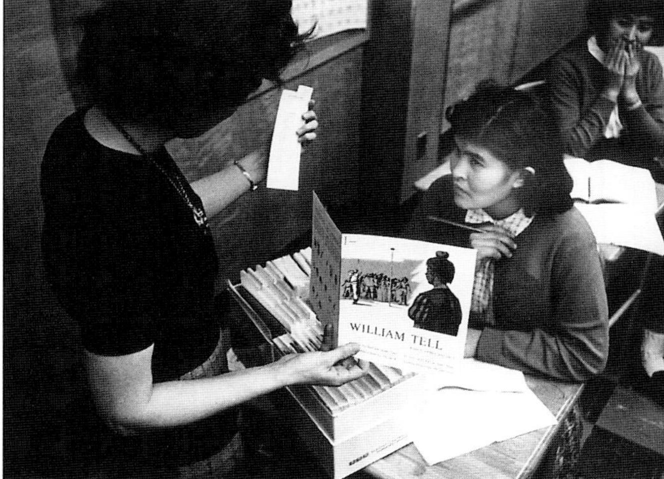

Imperialism involves imposing the dominant language and its attendant culture and world view on the dominated peoples. In 1959, in a school in the North West Territories in Canada, a Slavi Indian girl is taught English using a reading kit depicting the story of William Tell.

The Place of English in Africa

The following three quotes are from Casmir Rubagumya (1994a).

'The spread of English helps to maintain the existing unequal power relations between the rich and poor countries of the world. This is because in order to get access to scientific and technological information available in English, "developing" countries depend on developed countries for support institutions and facilities such as research centers and computer hardware and software. This "aid" is on many occasions used for ideological purposes by the rich countries to influence events in the poor countries' (page 156).

'The use of English in "developing" countries creates conditions that help to maintain inequality within those countries. The elitist school system ensures that English is available to a minority. This minority wields considerable political and economic power. For the majority English is a gatekeeping mechanism which holds them back socially, politically and economically, thus maintaining the privileged position of the elite. This is, by and large, the function of English in "Anglophone Africa" (page 156).

'Africans do not need to reject English or French altogether if they choose to resist the present language policies and practices. Rather, they should seek to reassess the values associated with both "international languages" and indigenous African languages. This should be done within the overall development strategy which takes into consideration all the African people, not only the elite' (page 157).

Reference: RUBAGUMYA, 1994

A British overseer supervises native workers at a brick kiln at Sapele, Nigeria ca. 1910.

French Linguistic Imperialism

It is not only the English language that spread rapidly in periods of colonization. The use of Spanish and Portuguese in South America, the use of French in Algeria and Morocco and in parts of Africa bear witness that languages other than English have been part of the colonizing experience. However, the overall goals of different colonial powers varied. For example, the French laid emphasis on an integrated union with the homeland, France. The British were more concerned with ruling from afar. The French were particularly concerned with civilizing the natives they conquered as part of the idea that the French language ensured access to reason and enlightened thinking. The British were often concerned with civilizing by the spread of Christianity.

However, languages in colonial situations have much in common: the retained low status of vernacular, native languages; a very small proportion of the native population allowed to take formal education; local traditions and educational practice being ignored; and a belief that the natives need to be civilized by the infusion of the colonizing language and culture.

At Abidjan, in Côte d'Ivoire (Ivory Coast), French-style balconied apartments and a French shop sign show the abiding influence of the French language and culture. Côte d'Ivoire is a country where French influence is deeply rooted. French is the sole official language, and two-thirds of the population speak French or pidgin French.

The Violence of English

Alaistair Pennycook (1994) quotes the case of television crews entering a scene of war and conflict. When there was ethnic conflict in Zaire and Zagreb, it was possible to hear phrases from television reporters leading their camera crew and technicians like commanders into hostile territory and shouting 'Has anyone here been raped and speaks English?'

Reference: PENNYCOOK, 1994

Gandhi and Opposition to Language Imperialism

There have been voices raised in protest against linguistic imperialism. For example, Gandhi (1927) accused English in India of being an intoxicating language, denationalizing the country, and bringing mental slavery. English changed the culture, mode of thinking, meanings and understandings of indigenous Indian people. He argued that the considerable amount of time spent in learning English in the classroom made performance in other subjects pitifully inadequate. English also served to promote and reproduce a small elite who spoke English fluently, and who dominated the masses through their linguistic imperialism. Those in charge of the nation owned the language of prestige. The remainder were ethnic groups with dialects and vernaculars.

Gandhi argued that English imposes linguistic uniformity that is culturally, intellectually, spiritually and emotionally restricting. Other languages are then portrayed as confining, ethnocentric, divisive, and alienating. Yet it is not the language that is dominating but the people who use it. A language is not intrinsically dominating. No language is more suited to oppression or domination than another. It is the speakers of that language who are the oppressors, dominators and imperialists.

Gandhi in 1939, eating his last meal before embarking on his fast.

Languages in India

The following quote concerns language uniformity and multilingualism in India and derives from Pattanayak (1986, page 22):

'From a predominantly monolingual point of view, many languages are a nuisance, as their acquisition is considered a burden. They are uneconomic and politically untenable. Even translation services are computed to be more economical than use of an additional language. In the case of multilingual countries, the reverse is the case. For them restrictions in the choice of languages is a nuisance, and one language is not only uneconomic, but it is politically untenable and socially absurd.

The amount of resources spent to produce the four percent of English-knowing persons in India over the past two hundred years proves the absurdity of efforts to replace many languages by one under democratic planning. The cultural deprivation and sociopolitical inequality introduced by the approach of monolingual control of a multilingual policy make nonsense of any talk of economic benefit.'

REFERENCE: PATTANAYAK, 1986

Dominant Languages or People?

The phrase 'dominant language' is a misnomer. Rather than domination by languages the dominance is by people.

People with power dominate people without power. Languages, in and by themselves, are not dominating. Phrases like dominant language are metaphors where the focus is transferred from people to language, thereby hiding the agents of domination.

One language is not more suited to oppression than any other. No language is more suited to be dominated by another language.

Any language can carry messages from the dominant power group.

Mickey Mao's' Hard Rock café in Yangshuo, near the city of Guilin in the province of Guangxi in China. Anglo American culture has spread to all corners of the earth.

In India, English has often functioned as a lingua franca, particularly among elite groups (although Hindi has also become a common language of India). English is often used as the link between countries, particularly between hitherto developing countries and North America and Great Britain. The link in politics, trade, science, technology, tourism and military alliances is often conducted through English.

English has not been the only imperialistic language in the world. At various times in history, French, Portuguese Spanish, German and Arabic have been languages associated with conquest, occupation and colonization. The difference with English is that it has continued after the end of invasions and conquests to become a colonizing and imperialistic language through more peaceful means such as trade, international communications, mass media and the information revolution.

There are exceptions to the imperialistic growth of English in countries of the world. Where a country has a 'great tradition', the place of English may be restricted to particular modern and separate functions. For example, in Arabic and Islamic countries, and in some oriental countries such as Malaysia, the strong promotion of religion or nationalism may help restrain English from infiltrating a variety of domains. Yet in other countries such as Singapore and India, English has been adopted as a unifier between different regions and as a common language. In India, there are 15 languages that have constitutionally guaranteed status, with English and Hindi being the main languages of intercommunication between different regions (see page 338).

When there are reactions against English as a colonizing language, the arguments tend to take on different dimensions: that English is anti-nationalism and likely to destroy native cultures; that English will introduce materialism and values that may destroy the religion of the people (e.g. Islam, Hinduism, Buddhism); that a people learning English will be rootless, in a state of flux and transition; that decadent western values such as sexual permissiveness, drugs and lack of respect for elders will be transmitted by the language; that English will bring divisions both in the country, in the community and in families, separating those who speak the native languages and those who prefer to move towards English; that there will be alienation from traditional culture, heritage values and beliefs, plus a lack of individual and unique identity.

Further Reading

DAVIES, A., 1996, Ironising the Myth of Linguicism. *Journal of Multilingual and Multicultural Development*, 17 (6), 485-496.

PATTANAYAK, D. P., 1986, Language, Politics, Region Formation and Regional Planning. In E. ANNAMALAI, B. JERNUDD & J. RUBIN (eds), *Language Planning. Proceedings of an Institute*. Mysore: Central Institute of Indian Languages.

PHILLIPSON, R., 1992, *Linguistic Imperialism*. Oxford: Oxford University Press.

TOLLEFSON, J. W., 1991, *Planning Language, Planning Inequality*. London: Longman.

WEBB, V., 1996, Language Planning and Politics in South Africa. *International Journal of the Sociology of Education*, 118, 139-162.

9: Colonialism and Languages

To understand the relative status and prestige of both indigenous language minorities and in-migrant language minorities, it is important to understand the history of colonialism. For example, the fate of Aboriginal people in Australia, the Maori in New Zealand, the Welsh in Wales, and Native Americans in the United States requires an understanding of the ways these language groups have been conquered and exploited. Also, the movement of native people from their home countries to more prosperous countries following colonization often demonstrates the effects of colonialism (e.g. Asians in Canada & UK).

Colonialism involves the domination of one group over another. An ethnic, linguistic or cultural group becomes subordinate to the ruling invaders. Following conquests, new forms of agricultural and industrial production, power and authority are imposed on native peoples.

During the conquest of the Aztec peoples of Mexico by the Spanish in the 15th century, thousands of indigenous Indians were killed. Indians continued to be the majority in the population and were exploited and used as slave labor by their Spanish rulers, as this mural by the Mexican artist Diego Rivera shows. Today, nearly two centuries after independence, one-third of Mexicans are Indians and nearly two-thirds are of mixed European and Indian descent.

Africans carry an English colonist on a chair in the Cameroon, 1929.

Inequality and discrimination results, often along lines of language, racial and cultural group differences. Quickly established at the beginning of colonialism, such patterns of inequality tend to persist and are reproduced across many generations. The wealth extracted by colonialists from their conquered territories is not shared. Rather conquered peoples often become the servants, even slaves, of their conquering masters, experiencing relative poverty and deprivation.

As part of the belief system of the conquering people, they perceive the colonized (e.g. language minorities) as inferior, primitive, heathen, even subhuman. Beliefs about racial superiority are used to justify the exploitation and the imposition of the majority language over native languages. The language of the conquerors (e.g. French and English) is regarded as a more civilized language, and native languages as a mark of an impoverished culture.

From the 16th century, the great imperial and colonizing powers of Spain, Portugal, England and France (and sometimes the Netherlands and Denmark) strove to colonize South and Central America, North America, India, Africa, and parts of Asia and Oceania. Also, an estimated 15 million Africans were forcibly exported to the Americas in the 19th century (mostly from West Africa, but also from East Africa), to provide cheap labor and slaves.

After the turn of the 20th century, the Europeanization of much of the world was complete, with colonial rule by

To rescue from oblivion even a fragment of a language which men have used and which is in danger of being lost – that is to say, one of the elements, whether good or bad, which have shaped and complicated civilization – is to extend the scope of social observation and to serve civilization.

Victor Hugo, French poet, dramatist, novelist (1802-1885).

Internal Colonialism and Languages

The term 'internal colonialism' has been particularly used in contemporary United States and Europe to describe in-migrant groups in those countries (e.g. Africans in the United States) and minority native groups (e.g. Native American language groups in the United States) who have been subjugated, conquered and depreciated inside the country. In the United States, it is sometimes suggested that North American Indians and Mexicans have been forced into a subordinate, inferior and internally colonized status by ruling majority groups. African Americans who have been residents in the United States for many generations have become enslaved in their own country.

Internally colonized groups exist in a society that does not display the characteristics of their ethnic and language group. Their social, vocational, educational and economic mobility is restricted by power relations which are controlled by majority language groups. Similarly, their political involvement is restricted and their distinctive culture is depreciated, sometimes criticized. Attempts may even be made to eradicate the internally colonized group's culture. The internally colonized group becomes trapped as an underclass in society, and may begin to perceive itself as inferior, of less worth and value, sometimes with protest, more often with passive resignation.

*One does not inhabit a country;
one inhabits a language.
That is our country,
our fatherland – and no other.*

E. M. Cioran, Rumanian-born French philosopher.

Affirmative Action

Affirmative Action for language minorities involves aiding those who are discriminated against, overcoming forms of discrimination, and reversing historical trends in racism. In education and employment, for example, forms of discrimination can be made illegal, equality of individual opportunity made more transparent, and preferential treatment given to those in disadvantaged positions. In this sense, there is positive discrimination towards those who are discriminated against.

In the United States, the 1964 Civil Rights Act is often regarded as the initial basis for Affirmative Action, especially regarding minority group employment. This Act forbade employment discrimination on the basis of race, sex, religion and national origin.

The concept of Affirmative Action has been fiercely debated in the United States in recent decades. For example, where there has been positive discrimination for minorities that has worked against those with better qualifications (e.g. for a place at college or university or employment), there is often controversy. Controversy has also been created by accusations that advantages are given to the best qualified minority members and that little is done to help the less qualified, poorer, underprivileged and most disadvantaged groups in society. Taking positive action, however, is still regarded by many as essential to reverse discrimination against language minorities where there is a co-existence of poverty, unemployment, low status, low power and little prestige with a minority language.

REFERENCE: DICKER, 1996

Dr Martin Luther King, (1929–1968) became the leader of the Civil Rights movement in the 1960s which led to the 1964 Civil Rights Act.

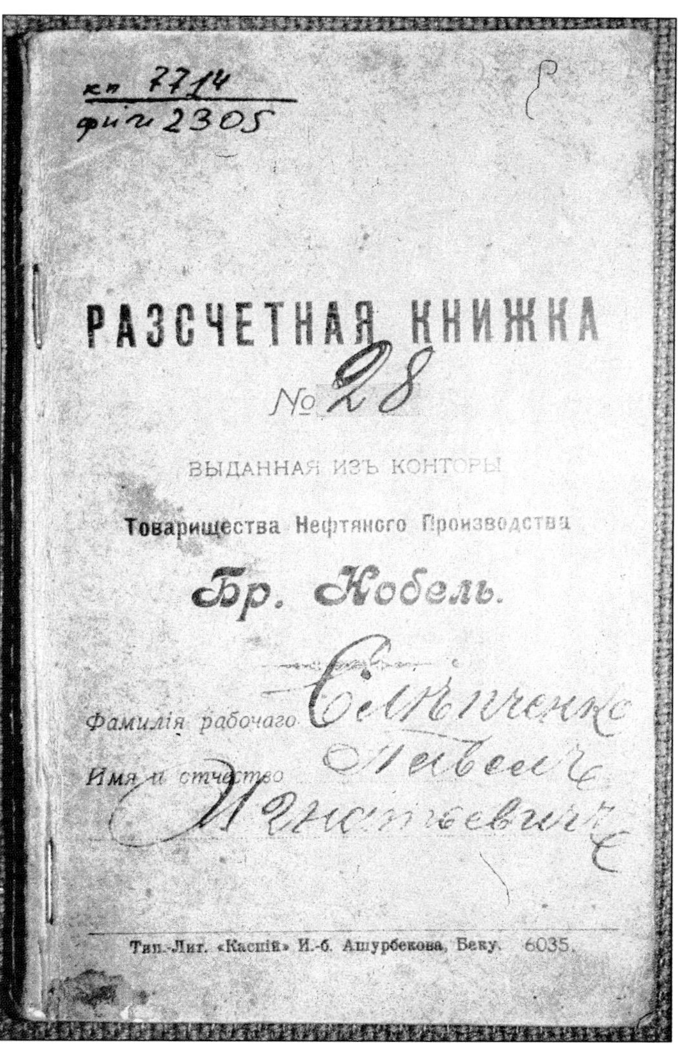

A 19th-century worker's pay book issued by the Nobel Oil Company in Azerbaijan. The wording on the book is in Russian. During the 18th and 19th centuries, Czarist Russia colonized many neighboring territories and Russian became a colonial language, used in government, education and business.

different European countries extending over most of the globe. Only Japan, Nepal, Thailand, Ethiopia, Liberia, Haiti (and to a certain extent Turkey and China) were without European political direction. Such European domination was established by military might and also by the power of proselytizing missionaries.

Alongside the sword and the gun went the threat of hell and damnation and the chance of Christian salvation. The concept of Christian salvation encouraged colonized peoples to accept political, economic, cultural and linguistic domination (and their continued existence in a state of poverty and deprivation) in the hope of avoiding Hell and of going to Heaven. This created a passive acceptance of domination and cultural and linguistic superiority, and helped quell rebellion and violent reaction. While missionaries were acting out of conviction and not conspiracy, the civilizing missionary became the unwitting supporter and agent of colonization.

Only after the Second World War did colonization begin to fade with the granting of independence to colonized countries. While this heralded in a new era of concern for ethnic minorities and for the preservation of colonized languages and cultures, many heritage languages and cultures had either been lost or had been irretrievably changed by contact and conflict with majority languages and cultures.

The basic assumption of human inequality that underlies colonialism has survived in the popular imagination and has become embedded in the style of thinking of some language minorities The idea of a 'colonial mentality' has often led to language minorities believing in their own inferiority, of their language being less modern, less valuable and less civilized than majority languages.

Further Reading

AMMON, U. (ed.), 1992, Language Spread Policy. Languages of Former Colonial Powers and Former Colonies. *International Journal of the Sociology of Language*, 107. Berlin: de Gruyter.

PENNYCOOK, A., 1994, *The Cultural Politics of English as an International Language*. New York: Longman.

PHILLIPSON, R., 1992, *Linguistic Imperialism*. Oxford: Oxford University Press.

In many former colonial territories in Africa, the colonial language has been retained as the official language and access to power and influence depends on competence in that language. In Borghou East in the country of Benin, sign boards for the veterinary drug center are in the official language, French and in two West African languages.

10: Language and Nationalism

Introduction

It is not easy to trace the origins of modern day nationalism. If we define nationalism very broadly as the consciousness of belonging to a separate people, located in a defined territory, bound by a common culture and history and common institutions, and desiring to achieve or maintain political autonomy, then we can see manifestations of nationalism throughout history. However, the modern ideology of nationalism is customarily said to have emerged after the French Revolution and became a major determinant of political policy and change throughout much of the 19th and 20th century. The ideology of nationalism was not created by the French Revolution, but this major event was a catalyst for major manifestations of nationalism during the 19th and 20th centuries.

Before the French Revolution in 1789, Europe consisted mainly of monarchies and governments with absolute control over their subjects. The boundaries of countries altered as territories changed hands between kings, princes and other nobility and the language of the royal court was acknowledged as the language of the kingdom. The common people had little or no control over the processes of government and the cultures and minority languages or dialects of individual communities or ethnic groups were not affected by the language and culture of the ruling elite.

The French Revolution marks a turning point in the emergence of democracy and the equal participation of all citizens in the process of government. Democracy evoked the need for national unity and a common language that would transcend regional or ethnic differences. In France, the necessity for a country *'une et indivisible'* led to the disparagement and attempted eradication of regional languages and cultures. Thus the French revolution marked the emergence of the modern nation, with its emphasis on assimilation and supra-ethnic unity for political reasons. However, at this time, minority ethnic groups became concerned about their particular identity. This led to a desire to maintain their languages and cultures and to achieve a measure of political self-determination. Romanticism in the late 18th and early 19th centuries inspired an interest in national history and literary traditions and hence national identity.

The basis of nationalism is first, that a defined population of people should organize its own institutions and institute its own laws so as to determine its own future. Second, nationalism maintains that a defined population has an unique set of characteristics that identify it as a separate nation from other surrounding nations. Third, the ideology of nationalism holds that it is pragmatically useful and 'natural' for the world to be divided up into a relatively stable number of well defined and distinct nations. Such nations were thought to create an organized and functional basis for global relations. The concept of 'ethnic identity' overlaps with the idea of nationalism. If there is a major difference, it is that nationalism concerns political autonomy and self-government and is essentially a political concept. Ethnicity does not necessarily have these political connotations (see Ethnic Identity, page 112).

As decolonization increased in the 20th century, the process of nationalism has been extended worldwide. Industrialism, modernization, the growth of capitalism and political mobilization have all influenced the growth of nationalism. The redrawing of political boundaries after two World Wars also affected the spread of nationalism.

This topic considers how language interacts with nationalism, the part that language plays in creating consciousness about national origins, and language as a marker of boundaries between people of different national identities. However, it is initially important to distinguish between a nation and nationalism. Then, it is necessary to explore how nationalism means different things to different people and is a rather ambiguous and multifaceted concept. Following that discussion, the relationship between nationalism and language is explored.

Nations

A nation is the term often used to describe a political unit with a defined territory. A nation has an autonomy, a defined political system and geographical boundaries marking it from other nations.

A nation may have more than one ethnic group or nationality within it, but the ruling group may wish to create and maintain a consciousness of national unity that transcends and even eradicates ethnic differences

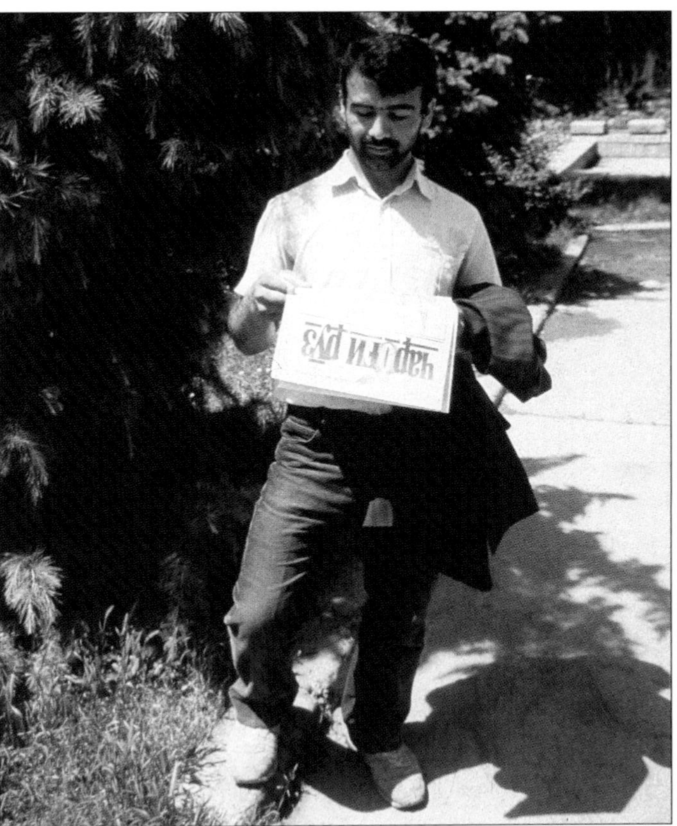

A young man in Dushanbe, Tajikistan, reads a newspaper in Tajik, a Persian language which is the official language of the country. About 65 percent of the population are ethnic Tajiks, speaking Tajik. Tajikistan was formerly a Soviet Socialist Republic until independence in 1991. During the Soviet era, Russian had become increasingly dominant, but since independence, like other former Soviet republics, Tajikistan has asserted its heritage language as a part of its nationalist identity.

and endorses the political boundaries. The languages and cultures of minority groups have sometimes been considered irrelevant and even injurious to the unity of the nation, and this has led to governmental attempts to disparage and even eradicate them. Minority languages represent important markers of ethnic identity and the maintenance of regional ethnic identities has been seen as contrary to the unity of the nation. Conversely, the majority language of the ruling elite is the medium of communication of centralist ideas and ideologies, and knowledge of the majority language is seen as vital for citizens for participation in democracy. Thus, attempts have been made by the governments to eradicate minority languages and establish the majority language in their place, by means of education and compulsory use of the majority language in public and official life.

Majority language nationalism tends to argue for the national majority language as an assimilative force. Within a state, people of different ethnic origins, cultures and creeds can be unified, it is argued, by a common language. Assimilative groups maintain that a sense of nationhood is achieved through everyone being competent in the majority language. Further, the majority language has greater relevance, worth and economic value than a minority language. For example, in the United Kingdom, Scotland and Wales have traditionally claimed their own nationality. However, their separate identities have tended to be disparaged and ignored in favor of the concept of 'Britishness'. During the 19th and first half of the 20th century, the Welsh and Gaelic languages were exiled from education and public life and this has led to their decline.

In Britain, some of those on the right wing of British politics often call for 'correct' English to be thoroughly taught in schools. Part of a British nationalistic philosophy is that all children, whether Welsh or Scottish, Asian or mainland European in origin, should learn to communicate effectively in 'correct' English at as early an age as possible. Part of British nationalist aspirations are often that all children should speak standard English, having correct grammar and a standard pronunciation so that children from different regions in the UK are fully integrated into a whole nation.

In the United States, the 'US English' and 'English First' movements often contain a covert nationalistic argument. English is the common denominator language, the language that will civilize and provide a common culture, it is argued. In the United States and in Britain, nationalism has accented the importance of monolingualism in English. Given the high in-migration into both of these countries, a melting pot, assimilationist policy has dominated. Such a policy suggests that American nationalism and British nationalism can be best engendered among in-migrants by their becoming monolingual in English rather than bilingual. For Asians, Turks and Greeks in England, for Latinos, Chinese and many other language minority groups in the United States, bilingualism is seen as a threat to loyalty to the nation, to national cohesion and political coherence. In these countries, bilingualism is seen as an attempt to preserve a different nationhood. For example, Spanish-speaking Mexicans are viewed as potentially expressing loyalty to Mexico rather than to the United States. In England, those Panjabi, Bengali and Turkish speakers, for example, who wish to preserve their heritage language, are seen as wanting to remain loyal to, and identify with their original nations.

The concept of a supra-ethnic nation state has been perceived as a necessity in many African and Asian countries in the post-colonial era. For countries such as Kenya, Tanzania and Nigeria, for instance, which consist of many local ethnic groups, maintenance of supra-ethnic unity is regarded as vital for economic and technological development. However, the imposition of a nation

state structure on diverse ethnic groups is at the root of many internal conflicts within modern African nations. One practical outcome of this is the need for a majority language for international relations, official life and education. A stable diglossic or triglossic situation exists in many third world countries, with an international and/or major indigenous language being used for public functions, and local vernaculars being used in the home and neighborhood. This shows that the concept of a nation does not inevitably mean cultural assimilation and the eradication of local languages.

Ethnic or Minority Group Nationalism

Another important facet of nationalism that emerged during the 19th and 20th centuries was the awakening of a desire for political recognition and self-determination among minority groups and oppressed peoples, often as a reaction to the political domination and assimilative, majority language policies of centralist governments. Thus modern Irish, Welsh and Breton nationalism arose in response to the political and cultural domination of the governments of London and Paris. Ethnic nationalism can also transcend national boundaries where there is a shared history and common culture and language.

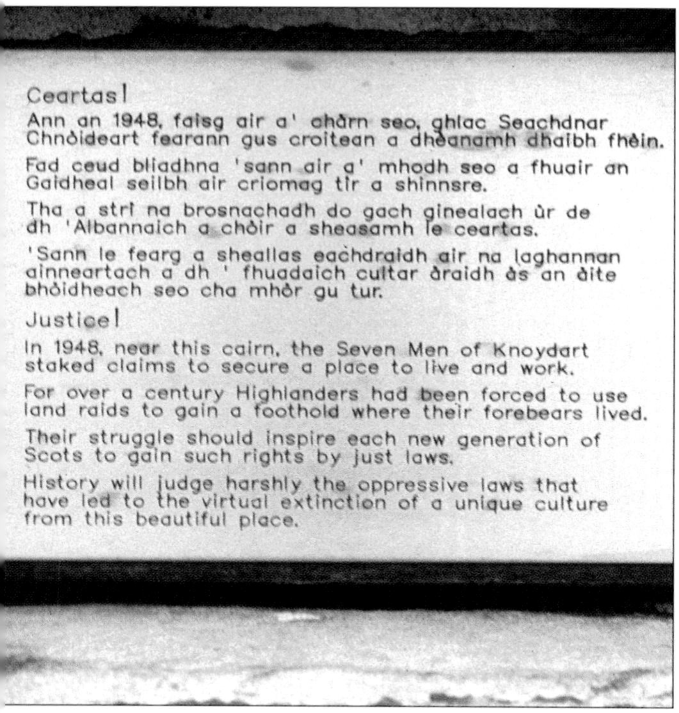

Ceartas!
Ann an 1948, faisg air a' chàrn seo, ghlac Seachdnar Chnòideart fearann gus croitean a dhèanamh dhaibh fhèin.
Fad ceud bliadhna 'sann air a' mhodh seo a fhuair an Gaidheal seilbh air criomag tìr a shinnsre.
Tha a strì na brosnachadh do gach ginealach ùr de dh 'Albannaich a chòir a sheasamh le ceartas.
'Sann le fearg a sheallas eachdraidh air na laghannan ainneartach a dh ' fhuadaich cultar àraidh às an àite bhòidheach seo cha mhòr gu tur.
Justice!
In 1948, near this cairn, the Seven Men of Knoydart staked claims to secure a place to live and work.
For over a century Highlanders had been forced to use land raids to gain a foothold where their forebears lived.
Their struggle should inspire each new generation of Scots to gain such rights by just laws.
History will judge harshly the oppressive laws that have led to the virtual extinction of a unique culture from this beautiful place.

A memorial in Gaelic and English at Inverie, near Loch Nevis in north-west Scotland. Scottish nationalism has its roots in a consciousness of a shared history, territory and culture, including language. In the 19th century, land clearances of the Highlands of Scotland, whereby large numbers of rural Gaelic-speaking crofters were harshly evicted by landowners, was one factor in the decline of the Gaelic language and culture. In 1853, the Laird of Knoydart in Scotland, a Lady MacDonald, evicted many crofters who then emigrated to Nova Scotia. In 1947, seven descendants of the evicted crofters arrived at Knoydart from Nova Scotia and 'settled' on ground which they claimed had belonged to their ancestors. The following year the then Laird took the case to court and the seven settlers were evicted like their ancestors.

Defining the Characteristics of Nationalism

The characteristics of nationalism are not easy to define and do not necessarily include language. They differ with each individual situation. This can be illustrated by some examples. For the Irish, nationalism is about membership of the Irish nation which has a definite territorial dimension. Irish nationhood is based on centuries of inhabitation of the homeland. Compare this with Arab nationalism, which does not always relate to territory but in a more general sense to people who have a shared history, shared ideals, shared aspirations (with Islam also being a major common cement). African nationalism contains an element that is different from Arab nationalism. African nationalism has a strong political dimension. Part of such nationalism is a negative feeling about European colonization, being against European rules and values, and in favor of African self-determination and African values and culture. Nationalism has also been found in liberation movements, and in left wing movements in Africa and South East Asia. In the United States in the 1960s, African American resistance to racism has sometimes been expressed in terms of 'Black nationalism'.

For many people, nationalism has negative connotations to it. It is associated with 20th century fascism in Germany, Italy and Spain. One danger of extreme and bigoted nationalistic views is that they overlap with some form of racism. Far from an ideology that embraces the equality of nations and the right of all nations to flourish independently, racist nationalism maintains that some 'races' are superior to others. Afrikaaner nationalism in South Africa was traditionally based on the myth of the white man's superiority. The racist ideology of Nazis and neo-Nazis represents an extreme form of nationalism based on the myth of racial purity (e.g. the Third Reich in Germany and neo-Fascism). This is also evident in contemporary British (English) nationalism where, for example, extreme right wing groups express their nationalism with an implicit and sometimes explicit use of racism as part of their main doctrines.

A difference is sometimes, and debatedly, made between nationalism and patriotism. Patriotism is regarded as a love of one's own people and country; nationalism (as an extreme) can be a love of one's own country but also hatred of other people and other countries. However, one person's patriotism is seen as another person's nationalism. This raises one negative face of nationalism, particularly found in majority ruling groups where nationalism

can emphasize majority group rights and de-emphasize individual rights, freedoms, liberties and interests. Although only extremist nationalist ideologies may exhibit overt racism, nationalism can often mask a belief in the superiority of one's own people and nation, with an accompanying prejudice towards minority groups. When minority groups come to power and gain self-determination, there is occasionally a danger that today's underdog will be tomorrow's bulldog.

Having noted the differences between Irish nationalism, Arab nationalism, African nationalism and Nazi-type nationalism, and before trying to work out the common ground, the basis of United States nationalism will be explored. Unlike the Irish, it cannot be based on historical territory given the massive immigration into the United States. Unlike the Arabs, there is no long shared history, and no overall religious dimension such as Islam that unites people into nationhood. While political feeling, for example against Communism, has been used as a means of creating nationalist sentiment in the United States, the US nationalist dimension has different values attached to it than African nationalism. United States nationalism is instead based around dimensions such as political freedom, emancipation, social and economic mobility, individual freedoms and liberties, individual enterprise, economic advantage and military advantage, and the superiority of US political and economic power in the world. United States nationalism is thus based in modernity rather than history, on a shared economic and political aspiration rather than on long ownership of territory, and is based on self-determination and patriotism. Such a basis for US nationalism has definite implications for language policy in the US.

A discussion of different kinds of nationalism among different peoples suggests that a loose constellation of attributes of nationalism may be possible. Nationalism, like ethnicity, appears to concern self-consciousness among a people, a primary loyalty, an attitude of belonging, a sense of group cohesion based on things held in common, such as a shared history, culture, religion, language and shared values. Nationalism differs from ethnicity in that it is invariably linked with a defined territory and involves a desire for self-determination and political independence. Where a group does not have political autonomy, there may be protests against oppression led by middle-class elite groups (e.g. Breton speakers in Brittany).

Language

We can now move on to discuss the role of language in such loyalty, self-determination and group cohesion. Language is clearly a badge of loyalty. For some, it is the

Language Minority Nationalism

As Colin Williams (1994) has argued, there can be language minority nationalism. In Catalonia, Wales, Ireland, Australia, and the Basque region in Spain, where there are indigenous language minority groups, there can be minority nationalism. As part of a separatist movement, as in Quebec, the Basque region, Catalonia and aboriginal areas in Australia, language minority nationalism may be exalted. The difference between language majority nationalism and language minority nationalism is that the latter is more likely to argue for a bilingual nation (in the majority and minority language) rather than a linguistically homogeneous nation as is the ideal in language majorities.

Colin Williams (1994) provides some of the characteristics of language minority nationalism:

1. A defense of an unique territory and the homeland.
2. A defense and promotion of a separate culture and identity, a separate language and social existence.
3. A resistance to centralist trends and the relative powerlessness of the periphery.
4. A perception that the language minority has been exploited and undeveloped and discriminated against.
5. A resistance to in-migrants, colonizers and outsiders.
6. A fear of loss of local power, dominance and influence witnessed in cultural change.
7. Non-violent movements of protest and sometimes expressions of ethnic dissent, discord and much use of protest.
8. An interpretation of history that supports a unique ethnic group, plus despises colonization, and reacts against persistent inequalities and repression.
9. A movement against the status quo, political action which is anti-state and intended to bring about new forms of political control by the language minority.
10. Defining current relationships, conflicts and problems between the language minority and the state in a manner to produce reforms, concessions, political accommodation, and moving towards a degree of self-determination for the minority.

Reference: Williams, 1994

pre-eminent badge that expresses a sense of belonging to a national group (e.g. speaking Catalan in Catalonia). Language becomes a symbol of independence of a separate nation and of a separate people. Language becomes important to gain and sustain group cohesion. The Basques as a national group define their boundaries and separatism by who speaks, and who does not speak, the Basque language. Language comes to represent an attitude to independence and separation. Thus the Quebecois in Canada make French a symbol of their continued drive for more independence from Canada.

When discussing the relationship between nationalism and language, it becomes clear that language helps mark a different people with either a different tradition and/or a different set of values and aspirations. Thus language is not just a tool for communication creating cohesion, shared meanings and understandings within a national group. Language is an important symbol of heritage and continuity with the past. It can also be the symbol of modern aspirations, ideals and values.

Nevertheless, language is not essential to either nationalism or ethnicity. Concerns about loyalty, self-determination and political independence do not necessarily require a separate language. While Irish nationalism uses the Irish language as a symbol, Irish nationalism is much more about territory, a shared history and a shared culture. These factors exist, for many, outside of the Irish language. In Wales, only one in five people speak Welsh, but the majority of non-Welsh speakers still see themselves as Welsh nationals and Welsh as a separate nation in the United Kingdom. Similarly, African nationalism is not based on language. Given the many different languages and dialects in Africa, language is clearly not a common denominator in African self-determination, membership and loyalty, nor in the desire for self-determination and political independence from Europe. In countries such as Pakistan, it is religion that tends to be the cement and symbol of loyalty rather than language. Thus language is a valuable but not an essential condition for nationalism to survive and thrive.

Bilingualism has been seen as an obstacle to nationalism (and not as an advantage) by both majority and minority language groups. This brings into play the important distinction between majority language and minority language nationalism. For the Basques and Catalans to express a sense of separate nationhood, it has become important to emphasize the Basque and Catalan language and, at times, to protest about Spanish. Given that a minority language is always in danger of being swamped by a majority language, bilingualism can be seen as an unstable state, a halfway house for people who are moving from the minority language to the major-

Quebecois Separatism

An example of minority language nationalism is found in Quebec with the movement towards greater or total separatism. The linguistic basis of Quebecois nationalism is revealed in a quote from Camille Laurin, the Minister of State for Cultural Affairs in Quebec in 1977.

'The Quebec we wish to build will be essentially French. The fact that the majority of its population is French will be clearly visible – at work, in communications and in the countryside. It will also be a country in which the traditional balance of power will be altered, especially in regard to the economy; the use of French will not merely be universalized to hide the predominance of foreign powers from the French-speaking population; this will accompany, symbolize and support a re-conquest by the French-speaking majority in Quebec of that control over the economy which it ought to have. To sum up, the Quebec whose speeches are sketched in the charter (of the French language) is a French language society.'

REFERENCE: LAURIN, 1977

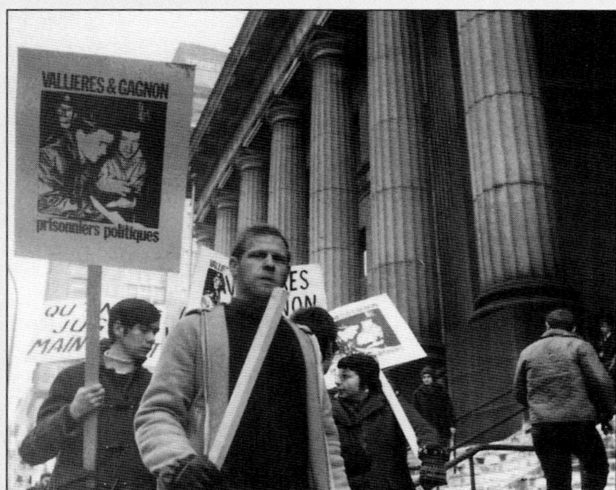

Quebecois Separatists demonstrate at the Montreal Court House in 1968. During the 1960s in Quebec, an awareness of a separate cultural and ethnic identity among Quebec francophones gradually evolved into a desire among many for political and economic independence. This culminated in the creation of Le Parti Quebecois, calling for autonomy for Quebec. However, despite the growing politicization of the situation, the French language and culture remained as the lynchpin of a separate Quebecois identity. In 1968, a conflict erupted in Montreal when the Catholic School Board of the St Léonard District of the city, an area heavily populated by Italian in-migrants, voted unanimously to enforce French as the sole language of schooling. There were angry clashes between French Canadians and Italian in-migrants in the streets. During the following years legislation began to be introduced to protect and promote French as the primary language of Quebec and one of the two official languages of Canada.

ity language. Thus, in Spain and in Wales, there has been a drive towards nationalism that emphasizes the minority language rather than bilingualism.

Since language is a badge of national loyalty, expressing independence, self-determination, and is a cohesive element amongst speakers, there are some minority language nationalists in Spain (e.g. the Catalans and Basques) and Wales, for example, who, on principle, minimize use of the Spanish or English language, believing that bilingualism is connected with a politically ambivalent and nationally anomalous state of mind. While pragmatically such activists use the majority and minority language, their nationalism may not support bilingualism as a first principle.

This is not the only possible view about the connection between bilingualism and nationalism. Bilingualism can be supported by nationalism, particularly in areas where there are a variety of ethnic groups, and where a group is in a numerical minority but uses a majority language as its mother tongue.

Political changes throughout the world are changing the concept of nationhood. For example, in Europe, with the growth of the European Union and the multimillion dollar drive towards Europeanization, a sense of more global identity rather than a purely national identity has begun, (although not without protests and anxieties). In the world of the Internet, the global economy and ease of transport between countries, the growth of economic and political interdependence in the world, new forms of loyalty and identity are beginning to occur. Thus supranationalism is beginning to have effects on language. The political dominance of English as a world language has meant more pressure towards being bilingual or multilingual in English and other languages. In Europe, having German and/or English as a second or third language has increasingly become important in recent years for economic and employment reasons. In countries such as Brunei and Malaysia, the value of English for access to information and the world-wide trade has led to the rise of English bilinguals in both countries. The movement towards a global economy has also led to more people learning Japanese and Chinese. In the future, Arabic as an additional language for both trade and religious reasons may be advantageous.

This does not mean that bilingualism in majority languages is the only likely situation among nations in the future. In Europe, for example, there is a major concern about ensuring that peripheral areas and not just core economic areas share the advantages of a global economy. Thus a fresh interest is being taken in local economies and their relationship to a macro economy. Via subsidies, seed-corn funding, initiatives and through the ease of computer communications, local communities may be protected and drawn into a more global economy. At its best, this means that those in the community can use their minority language in the workplace. Bilingualism in a majority and a minority language becomes viable and valuable.

There is also another reason why the move towards supra-nationalism may have a positive effect on bilingualism. The drive to share a wider identity (e.g. to be European or part of the global village) may lead to a reaction among individuals. To belong to a supranational group may initially require local loyalty, a rootedness in local group cohesion, a sense of belonging to a community first of all before being able psychologically to identify with large supranational groups. Thus bilingualism in the majority and the minority language may become important in gaining a feeling of rootedness in the locality, as well as belonging to an increasingly larger identity.

Further Reading

BARBOUR, S., 1991, Language and Nationalism in the German-Speaking Countries. In P. MEARA & A. RYAN (eds), *Language and Nation*. London: Center for Information on Language Teaching and Research (CILT).

EDWARDS, J. R., 1985, *Language, Society and Identity*. Oxford: Basil Blackwell.

EDWARDS, J. R., 1995, *Multilingualism*. New York: Routledge.

HOFFMANN, C., 1991, *An Introduction to Bilingualism*. London: Longman.

PAULSTON, C. B., 1994, *Linguistic Minorities in Multilingual Settings: Implications for Language Policies*. Philadelphia: John Benjamins Publishing Company.

PHILLIPSON, R., 1992, *Linguistic Imperialism*. Oxford: Oxford University Press.

WILLIAMS, C. H., 1994, *Called Unto Liberty! On Language and Nationalism*. Clevedon: Multilingual Matters Ltd.

11: Conflict and Equilibrium

Introduction

A fundamental debate exists concerning the route by which language rights are achieved and ethnic identity is maintained. On the one hand, there are those who believe that the rights of ethnic minorities can be achieved and safeguarded by means of development, co-operation and consensus. There are others that believe that struggle, conflict and strife are intrinsic to the process of defending the rights of language minorities.

Can minority language groups always be in a cooperative functional relationship with the majority language? Does non-violent conflict sometimes need to be present to achieve rights for a language community? The achievements of the Basques and the Welsh would both seem to suggest that conflict with the majority is one means of achieving language rights. Such a conflict viewpoint will place more emphasis on group rights than on individual rights. To be Basque may conflict with being Spanish. To be Welsh can conflict with being British. To be Quebecois may conflict with being Canadian. In these circumstances, cultural pluralism may not always lead to order and the maintenance of majority language rules in society. Should language minority groups pursue equilibrium or conflict?

The Equilibrium Paradigm

Christina Bratt Paulston (1980, 1992b) presents two major paradigms to theoretically interpret an important aspect of societal bilingualism, namely bilingual education. In the equilibrium paradigm, the different wheels that create the clockwork mechanism of society, the school, the economic order, social mobility and social processes interlock and work relatively harmoniously together. Change in society occurs by gradual, slow and smooth evolution. Conflict and disharmony are to be avoided because they lead to a breakdown in the clockwork mechanism. Radically new components will cause the system to stop functioning smoothly. Individual components in the mechanism are relatively unimportant in themselves. It is the overall clockwork mechanism that is important.

When the clock goes wrong, the fault is not within the system itself. One or more components must be a problem and will need to be adjusted. With language minority groups and bilingual education, any apparent failure will not be due to the system as a whole, but will be due to those components themselves. That is, the problems lie with the minority language groups and within the form of bilingual education system. Any failure in language minority students may be put down to their poor English proficiency rather than to the overall educational system. Individuals will be blamed, not the system. Since the system works through English language instruction, more English language is required by the language minorities. In turn, any disadvantage or poverty that exists in such groups can be solved by improving their achievement at school via greater competence in the majority language. Since the oil of the clockwork mechanism is English language proficiency, once this is in place, language minority students will have equality of opportunity in the educational and economic systems. Bilingual education must maintain equilibrium in society.

Genesee (1987) analyzes the Canadian bilingual education immersion programs from this equilibrium perspective. According to this viewpoint, such immersion programs may be regarded as giving the majority group in society – the English-speaking Canadian children – the bilingual proficiency to maintain their socioeconomic dominance in Canada. Set against the protests from French Quebec about the status of the French language in Canada, Immersion education may be seen as aiding the stability of the bilingual situation in Canada. More French-English bilinguals created by the immersion schools would, according to this perspective, be an answer to some of the protests of the Quebec people. (This is not necessarily the view of Quebec people who sometimes believe that their right to French-speaking jobs is threatened by such immersion students.) Thus Canadian immersion programs are perceived as producing equilibrium in the Canadian language situation.

A different viewpoint to the 'clockwork mechanism' equilibrium perspective is the conflict paradigm (Paulston, 1980, 1992b). Such a paradigm holds that conflict is a natural and expected part of the relationship between unequal power groups in a complex society. Given differences in culture, values, the unequal allocation of resources and variations in power within society, then conflict, radical views and disruption can be expected. Such a viewpoint often argues that real change occurs more by conflict, protest, non-violent and sometimes violent action, and less through the mending of minor problems within a system.

Language Conflict

Contact between ethnic groups does not always occur in a peaceful and harmonious fashion. There are sometimes tensions, differences of opinion, rivalries and disputes. Such disputes do not always lead to conflict, although, as in the case of Ethiopia, Rwanda, Bosnia and Serbia, ethnic conflicts can develop. More usually, as different groups compete for scarce resources, ascendancy in power, privileges and autonomous rights, there can be wars of words. When a minority language group is in conflict with the language majority group, the struggle may be at the level of debate and discussion. Yet, as an extreme, there can be 'linguistic cleansing'. When there is extreme interethnic conflict and civil war, an attempt to enforce the language of the ascendant group may be attempted.

As one instrument of social control, languages can at times be part of social conflict. For example, a monolingual and centralized bureaucracy may believe that multilingualism is like Babel: when there is linguistic diversity, there is a state of chaos, with resulting effects on law and order, economy and efficiency. Monolingualism is seen as a stable condition, multilingualism as linguistic imperfection leading to problems and conflicts.

When languages (e.g. official, national, ethnic, indigenous, in-migrant languages) enter such conflicts between groups, language tends to become a marker or a symbol of the conflict, rather than the real source of the conflict – racial, ethnic, religious, economic or cultural. When there are struggles for power and dominance between groups in society, language is often the surface feature or focal point of the deeper-seated conflicts underneath.

A Sinhalese soldier checks the identity of a Tamil civilian in November, 1996. Conflict continues between the Sinhalese majority and the Tamil minority in Sri Lanka. Their respective languages are an important part of the ethnic identity of the two groups.

For example, in the United States there are conflicts about the place of English and in-migrant languages. Often arguments about whether English should be the official language of the United States, and conflicts about the place accorded to in-migrant languages such as in bilingual education, hide deeper concerns about political dominance, status, defense of economic and social position, as well as concerns about cultural integration, nationalism and an American identity. Thus language minorities can appear as a threat to national unity, with language acting as a symbol of the threat.

Underneath, the conflict is more about economic and political advantage, political power and ethnic or national solidarity and identity. The real source of the conflict is often rooted in political power struggles, economic tensions and issues about rights and privileges. Social and economic disadvantages often tend to underlie language conflicts. Language is usually a secondary sign of primary or fundamental causes of conflict. Nevertheless, politicians and administrators often seize upon language as if it were the cause, and sometimes as if it were the needed remedy. Underlying causes are thus ignored or avoided.

Where a group is numerically weak or psychologically uninterested in friction, it will tend towards assimilation. Where groups are more activist and can assemble resistance, then some form of conflict may be offered. Another example is Canada, where English language groups dominate, leaving the francophone population more economically and politically marginalized. Therefore, language activism, as in Quebec, may be more about political and economic power than language and culture.

However, where one language is given preferential treatment by a government, there can be conflict about language itself. This especially occurs where language is joined by religious, socioeconomic class or cultural preferential treatment from a Government. Where a group is disadvantaged, whether there are impediments to social and economical mobility, then language can become an area which is contested alongside other markers or symbols of such disadvantage or suppression.

When there is language conflict, language may also become a mobilizing factor around which other economic, social or political issues are pursued by a group. If there is minimal or non-existent language conflict within a state, if a language policy is harmonious and effective, it may release people to strive for collective goals other than language. However, if a language policy within a country is imposed in an authoritarian way, or is divisive, unfair and unjust, it can lead to alienation, pressure for regional separatism, conflict and disruption.

In essence, conflicts cannot occur between languages, they only occur between the speakers of those languages. Thus, the idea of language conflict is a misnomer.

REFERENCE: NELDE, 1997

An Armenian martyr's grave in the Nagorno-Karabakh Enclave in Azerbaijan. The country of Armenia in South West Asia is populated by a majority of ethnic Armenians, who speak an Indo-European language, Armenian. The population of neighboring Azerbaijan are mainly ethnic Azeris who speak Azeri, a language closely related to Turkish. Since the late 1980s, there has been conflict between the country of Armenia in South West Asia and its neighbor Azerbaijan concerning sovereignty over the Nagorno-Karabakh Enclave, a portion of territory within Azerbaijan, but populated mainly by Armenians. Conflict between countries or ethnic groups rarely centers on language, but on issues of power, status and territory.

The picture of a clockwork mechanism is replaced by a picture of an operation on an unhealthy body. The removal of an organ, a painful injection, the replacement or addition of tissue by grafting or plastic surgery may be radical and initially disruptive, but perceived as important if the health of the whole body is to improve. Minority language groups may be allotted too little power, too few rewards, and be disadvantaged in resources and rights. Schools may perpetuate that disadvantage and subordinate power position, reproducing the dominance of the ruling elite over the masses, perpetuating economic, social and political inequalities, inequality of opportunity and inequality of outcome in society. Such linguistic, cultural and educational discrimination will need radical surgery.

'Weak' forms of bilingual education tend to perpetuate inequalities experienced by language minorities. In consequence, within the conflict perspective, bilingual education should attempt to right such inequality and injustice by positive discrimination. Bilingual education should be interventionist, even conflicting with dominant viewpoints. Bilingual education can serve to encourage social, economic and educational change and cultural pluralism (Rippberger, 1993). 'Strong' bilingual education can aid the status of minority languages and cultures, reduce the pulls and pushes towards assimilation, and aid the empowerment of minorities.

The Canadian bilingual education immersion programs, a 'strong' form of bilingual education, have been analyzed from a conflict perspective and not just through the equilibrium approach (e.g. Heller, 1994). There are many language tensions and conflicts in Canada. For example, many French first language speakers feel threatened by those bilinguals for whom French is a second language. Bilingual anglophones are seen to be accessing power, prestige and privilege that have hitherto been the preserve of bilingual francophones (e.g. by gaining positions in high status professions). With immersion schools, anglophones can gain the linguistic and cultural capital for increased social and economic mobility and for political power. 'Education is currently a major site of the struggle waged between anglophones and francophones, and within each group as well, over whether or not bilingualism should be valuable; and if so, whose property it should be. As such, it represents a struggle over the distribution of wealth and power' (Heller, 1994, page 7). Bilingual education is thus not about unity or integration, in this perspective, nor is it neutral. Bilingual education is about gaining advantages, cultural, linguistic and social wealth, and dominance in Canadian society. As such, it produces conflict with the minority francophone community (e.g. in Ontario).

In the conflict paradigm, the problems exist within society as a whole, not simply in terms of 'individual deficiency' or 'educational provision'. The causes and determinants of minority language problems are within society, and not simply due to the characteristics of minority language children. Radical surgery is sometimes defended for the survival and stability of a healthy body. Long-term health sometimes requires short-term pain.

Teachers and education administrators, researchers and college professors may sometimes be faced with a choice: whether to oil the wheels of the system or be radical and attempt to change the system. Often, compromises are made by professionals: seeking evolution within relative stability; development within dominant perspectives. Within an overall desire for equilibrium, small conflicts about policy and provision among school staff, for example, may regularly occur. Thus there can be a pattern of minor conflict which does not upset or challenge the overall equilibrium.

There is also another combination: those for whom conflict is, and must be, perpetual. For particular types of language activists (e.g. in Wales and the Basque region), conflict becomes the norm. One form of conflict politics may be minority language militancy (Schermerhorn, 1970). Language militants may attempt to gain control over the dominant majority and gain some form of ascendancy.

How can schools contribute to oiling and developing the clockwork machine, or changing the sick body by interventions into the core curriculum? The role to be played by schools comes partly through cultural and language awareness courses and mostly in attempts to introduce multiculturalism and anti-racism into a part of or throughout the curriculum.

Further Reading

HELLER, M., 1994, *Crosswords: Language Education and Ethnicity in French Ontario.* Berlin & New York: Mouton de Gruyter.

PAULSTON C. B., 1980, *Bilingual Education: Theories & Issues.* Rowley, MA: Newbury House.

PAULSTON, C. B., 1986, Social Factors in Language Maintenance and Language Shift: The Fergusonian Impact. In J. A. FISHMAN, A. TABOURET-KELLER, M. CLYNE, B. H. KRISHNAMURTI & M. ABDULAZIZ, *Sociolinguistics and the Sociology of Language. Volume 2.* New York: Mouton de Gruyter.

PAULSTON, C. B., 1992, *Sociolinguistic Perspectives on Bilingual Education.* Clevedon: Multilingual Matters Ltd.

PAULSTON, C. B., 1994, *Linguistic Minorities in Multilingual Settings.* Amsterdam/Philadelphia: John Benjamins.

12: Language Activism

Introduction

Contact between groups of speakers of different languages often involves an unequal relationship, with one group being dominant politically, socially, economically, culturally and linguistically. This unequal relationship may involve the minority group accepting its subordinate position or attempting to gain power and status by adapting culturally and linguistically to the majority group. Individuals within the minority group may attempt to preserve their language and culture at a personal or family level. However, awareness of their disadvantaged status may lead minority group members to joint action to change the situation. (See Affirmative Action, page 325.)

Group action thus involves an awareness of the unity and identity of the group, based on language, culture, religion or other factors. Before there is group action, there must also be a collective awareness of, and an agreement as to the nature of the threat to the group (e.g. lack of rights for the minority language, leading to its decline, the undermining of cultural practices, economic deprivation or lack of social privileges, racial or religious prejudice on the part of the majority group). There must also be a consensus of opinion as to the direction and goal of any actions. Minority group action requires a certain strength and cohesion in the minority group.

Minority group action may involve working within the established order and respecting the status quo. Members of a minority group may set up minority language nursery schools, or independent schools where minority religious or cultural practices are respected.

Language Activism in the Basque Country

During the Spanish Civil War (1936–39), an Autonomous Basque State was established by the Republican Government of Spain, but the victory of the Nationalists under General Francisco Franco ended this regime. Basque, like other regional languages of Spain, was banned from public life for over 20 years. It was forbidden to teach or speak Basque in schools, or use it in church, in the media or in public or official contexts. It was no longer permitted to give children Basque names in baptism and Basque language books were publicly burnt.

Prior to the Civil War, the Basque language was regarded, even by its speakers, as the language of the hearth and home, with Castilian Spanish being used in public and official contexts. However, the emergence of Basque nationalism merged with a renewed interest in the language, and a recognition that it was an important marker of the separate Basque identity. The outlawing of the language made it an even more important symbol of the fight for Basque independence and of opposition to the Fascist regime.

By the 1960s, restrictions against the use of Basque had been relaxed and it was taught in primary schools, and used in churches and the media. The campaign for Basque autonomy gathered strength and grew dramatically in the 1970s. The extremist organization, ETA, was formed to fight for Basque independence by means of a terrorist campaign of bombs, arson, kidnappings and murder. The Spanish constitution of 1978 granted the Basque Country a measure of autonomy, with its own elected parliament and internal control over matters such as education. Since then, the terrorist campaign of ETA has diminished but it is still active in pursuit of full independence for the Basque Country. ETA is an organization formed to fight for political freedom rather than language rights, but it uses the Basque language and promotes it as a central symbol of Basque nationhood.

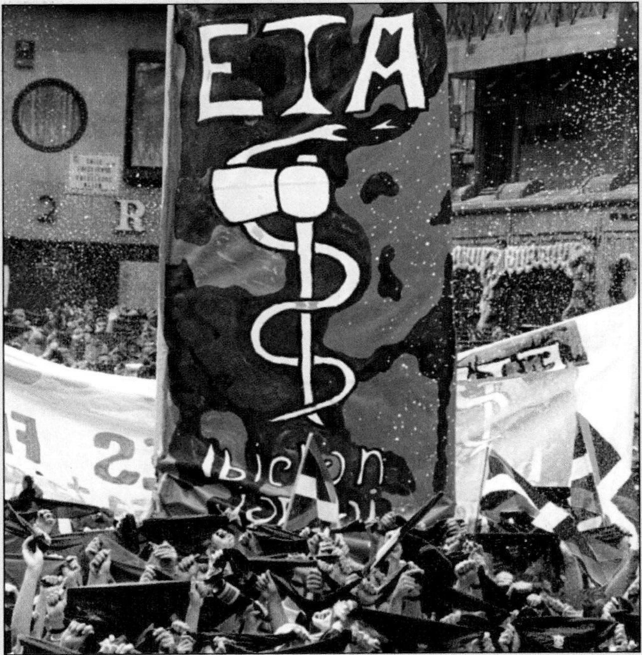

A banner supporting ETA is raised at a Basque cultural festival.

Language Activism in Wales

One example of language activism is the 13-year fight for a Welsh television channel, spearheaded by *Cymdeithas yr Iaith Gymraeg* (The Welsh Language Society). *Cymdeithas yr Iaith Gymraeg* was formed in 1962 to campaign for rights for the Welsh language. During its existence it has campaigned for bilingual road signs, the use of Welsh in the Post Office and other organizations dealing with the public, Welsh-medium education, and against the sale of houses in largely Welsh-speaking rural areas as holiday homes and permanent dwellings for people from outside Wales. The Society's methods have their roots in the tradition of non-violent protest and symbolic civil disobedience of the American Civil Rights movement. (This in its turn was inspired by the principle of non-violent persuasion established by Gandhi in India, and called *satyagraha.*)

The Society's membership has never been more than several hundred, and its members have often been condemned as vandals and criminals, even by members of the Welsh-speaking community, for some of its actions (e.g. limited destruction of public property, daubing slogans, symbolic lawbreaking). However, many of its campaigns have been successful because it has succeeded in raising public awareness of issues and mobilizing public opinion.

The campaign for a Welsh language television channel began in 1968. At that time, and up until 1983, when *Sianel 4 Cymru* was launched, Welsh language programs were scattered haphazardly and infrequently on English language channels. Welsh language programs were rarely shown at peak periods and the transmission of programs in Welsh instead of the English language programs shown in other areas of the UK often angered non-Welsh-speaking viewers. When the establishment of a independent fourth television channel in the UK became a possibility, it was suggested that the channel in Wales should be allocated to the Welsh language.

In 1974, the Crawford Report concluded that the fourth television channel in Wales should be devoted to Welsh-medium broadcasting, and that this would begin in 1976. However, there was a long and frustrating wait, while the campaign in Wales continued, and eventually, in September 1979, it was announced that there would be no Welsh-medium channel and that Welsh language programs would be divided between BBC 2 and ITV 2.

The reactions of many Welsh speakers ranged from anxiety to anger. The decision was viewed by many as representing a blow for the future of the Welsh language and culture. The event became symbolic of the struggle for the preservation of a minority language. The campaign culminated in an announcement on May 6th by a well known politician, Dr. Gwynfor Evans, that he would begin fasting to death on October 6th, unless the Government kept its promise to establish a Welsh language fourth channel, Dr. Evans was a revered member of the Welsh establishment, the President of the Welsh Nationalist Party (*Plaid Cymru*), respected and honored by many sections of the Welsh-speaking community. His announcement rekindled the campaign and caused a furor in Wales. Eventually the government, fearing mass social disturbances and the creation of a new martyr if Dr. Evans fasted to death, capitulated. On September 17th, 1980, the government reversed its decision once more and allocated 22 hours of Welsh language broadcasting to the fourth channel.

The long and eventually successful campaign for the establishment of a fourth television channel for the Welsh language, spearheaded by *Cymdeithas yr Iaith*, included the following aspects.

- Activities designed to involve a wider cross-section of Welsh speakers and gain public and media attention: protest marches, pamphlets and posters, hunger strikes, petitions, public rallies.
- A hard core of language activists involved in serious law breaking activities. These included taking over and damaging television studios, climbing transmitters and damaging them, to interrupt the broadcasting of English language programs in Wales. Many members received heavy fines and some went to prison.
- The involvement of a wider section of the community in civil disobedience, (e.g. the non-payment of the television license fee). Towards the climax of the campaign, there were 2000 households refusing to pay. Some individuals were imprisoned, including elderly people.
- The support of organizations such as the University of Wales Court, several religious denominations, some local councils, youth organizations and *Plaid Cymru.*
- The support of esteemed public figures and members of the British establishment. In 1979, three university professors were arrested for conspiring to damage a television transmitter. The support of public figures culminating in Dr. Gwynfor Evans' announcement that he was willing to fast to death in support of a Welsh television channel.

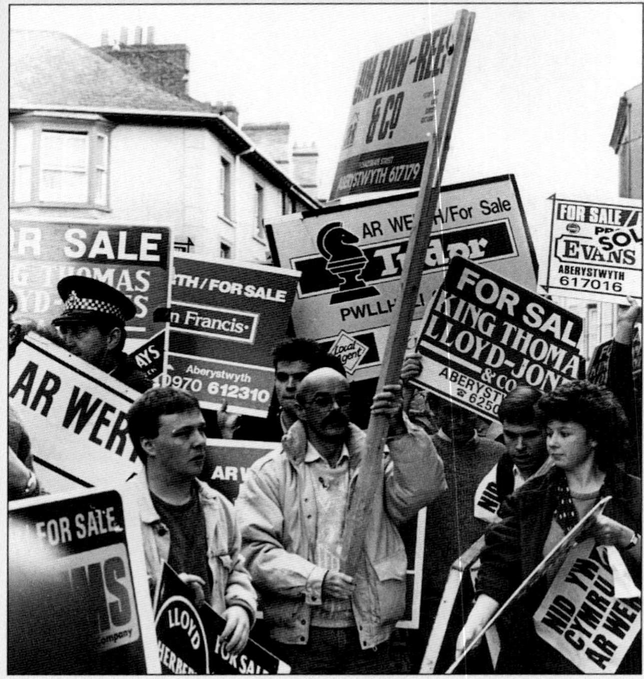

Members of Cymdeithas yr Iaith Gymraeg (The Welsh Language Society) protest against the widespread sale of houses in Wales to in-migrants or people looking for holiday homes, thus weakening the fabric of Welsh-speaking society. They argue for a Property Act which would place limits on the sale of property to people outside Wales.

Language Activism in India

India is a multilingual country. According to varying estimates, between 1000 and 1600 languages or dialects are spoken in the country. The major languages are regarded with pride as markers of the identity of the different ethnic groups who make up the country. When India became an independent republic in 1947, Hindi, the majority language, currently spoken by almost a third of the population of over 850 million, was chosen as the official language. This provoked an angry reaction from non-Hindi speakers, who felt that the establishment of Hindi as the official language made them second class citizens and discriminated against them in education and employment.

There were angry protests and some violent riots, especially in the south. Southern India is the home of 150 million speakers of Dravidian languages, the main languages being Tamil, Telugu, Kannada and Malayalam. Soon after Independence, Dravidian language militants began to campaign for a political structure which would give their languages official recognition and status. In 1948, the Linguistic Provinces Commission supported the status of Hindi as an official language and a means of national integration. It opposed official status for other languages, mainly on the grounds that such a move would reinforce regional or subnational identity and hinder the development of a national consciousness in the new India.

A second Committee of Enquiry reached the same conclusion, but announced that it would reconsider the matter if the demand continued. From 1949, the campaign became more intense, especially among Telugu speakers in Madras. The climax came in December, 1952, with the death of Potti Sriramulu, who had fasted to death in protest at the lack of official status for Telugu. Prime Minister Nehru conceded, and in October 1953, the state of Andhra Pradesh was established, based on the Telugu-speaking region. Three years later, the whole of Southern India was reorganized on the basis of linguistic regions.

Language protests continued against Hindi. Some people wanted English to be reinstated as the official language of India, since it was a neutral language and did not favor one ethnic group over others. In 1963, English was given the status of associate official language with Hindi, originally for a 15-year period. This provoked riots and protests by those who viewed English as a symbol of foreign oppression. Protesters demonstrated outside the Indian parliament in New Delhi, carrying placards and banners reading 'Death to English' and 'Long Live the Mother Tongue'.

The pattern that has emerged in many states of India since the 1960s is a three language system, with Hindi, English and the regional language all having official status. The Indian Constitution now recognizes 15 state languages, used in schools and official transactions.

The language conflicts in India underline the fact that language activism is not merely about language. Language never stands alone, but is also always associated with ethnic and sometimes religious identity, and civil and economic rights.

A 1965 rally in New Delhi, in support of Hindi/Urdu as the recently introduced official language of India, and protesting against the retention of English as an official language. Supporters of Hindi and Urdu carry placards in those languages while one man holds a tin of tar and brushes, ready to daub signboards printed in English. This was a counter demonstration following anti-Hindi language riots in Madras which resulted in more than 60 deaths.

Minority language newspapers may be established. Minority group business people may establish their own networks or organizations providing support and economic advice. Minority groups may depend upon gradual and peaceful processes to effect an improvement in their situation.

Often, however, collective minority group action may result in a clash with the majority language establishment. The rights or conditions sought by the minority group may be in conflict with majority group interests or perceived national unity and stability. The majority group may deny the requests of the minority group. The minority group may feel that their demands will not be met by a gradual process of change and that they must take more militant and aggressive action.

The American Heritage Dictionary defines 'activism' as a 'theory or practice based on militant action to achieve a social or political end'. Minority language activism involves actions by members of the minority group that bring them into conflict with the majority group. These actions may involve breaking the law and even violence.

Minority language activism is usually spearheaded by a hardcore of committed militants, but depends for its success on its ability to awake and mobilize popular opinion and gain support from a wider section of the community.

Further Reading

BOURHIS, R. Y., 1984, *Conflict and Language Planning in Quebec*. Clevedon: Multilingual Matters Ltd.

CLARK, R. P., 1984, *The Basque Insurgents: ETA 1952–1980*. Madison, Wis.: University of Wisconsin Press.

THOMAS, N., 1991, *The Welsh Extremist* (Second edition). Talybont, Wales: Y Lolfa.

WILLIAMS, C. H. (ed.), 1982, *National Separatism*. Cardiff: University of Wales Press.

13: The Question of Languages in the European Union

Introduction

The original official languages of the European Union, as agreed in the initial Treaty of Rome, were German, Dutch, French and Italian. In the mid-1990s, the European Union used eleven official, working languages (that is the majority languages of the current member states). The use of nine official working languages has meant 36 possible pairs of languages when interpretation of meetings and translation of administrative documents was needed. Such translation and interpreting accounted for approximately 40 percent of all administration costs of the European Union. Such multilingualism tended to produce delays in translation of important documents. So that there would be no barrier to comprehension by different contributing nations nor misunderstandings, translation and interpretation became a vital part of the European Union.

Multilingualism in the European Union has provided a dilemma for its members. Should there be a lingua franca such as French, German or English? Should all official languages have official status and use? As the European Union has expanded, should the language of new member countries be added to the official list of languages? What kind of place does this give to minority languages within member countries?

The principal objective of the European Community since the beginning has been the harmonious development of co-ordinated economic activities. A measure of economic unity was achieved with the advent of the Single European Market in January 1993. Yet the vision of Jean Monnet, the founder of the European Community, was of a social, political and economic integration. The concept of European Citizenship has provided fierce debate, with a European passport and European flag being the first symbols of European Citizenship already in place. A single European currency, due to be launched by 1999, will be another strong unifying force in Europe.

In comparison with other international bodies, the European Union has accepted a multilingual situation with the need for equality of majority languages of member countries as a first principle. In contrast, the United Nations works with six languages, the Council of Europe with two languages and NATO with two languages. Such organizations tend to go for a different principle, the need for ease of communication between partners from different countries. Thus, one part of the dilemma for the European Union is between the equality of majority languages of its member states and a cost-effective, easily manageable lingua franca or small subset of languages to ensure an efficient and effective organization.

The Equality of Official Languages

The principle of equality of languages rests on the image of the Nation State of 19th century nationalists. This image is that language provides identity, and that having one majority language, as in France, provides unity in diversity, one integrated people with a common purpose, unified and unanimous in orientation. Thus any argument for a lingua franca or a subset of languages for the European Union will immediately be criticized for ignoring national sovereignty and national identity which are symbolized in national languages. If the equality of national languages is maintained within the European Union, then all national majority languages will receive parity of status, producing a multilingual and multicultural Europe. Such a policy accents European diversity rather than unity, highlighting the paradox of a unified Europe created from a linguistic and cultural diversity of member states.

A Lingua Franca for Europe

A different argument advanced in Europe has been for the choice of a lingua franca. To aid bureaucratic effectiveness and efficiency, one argument has been to choose one language for European Union activities that is accepted by all countries. This would not be to deny the value and use of other languages within Europe. Rather a diglossic situation is contemplated, with different functions for the lingua franca and national languages.

One major problem with this is the choice of one language as a lingua franca. The main contenders are English, French and German. However, this would immediately seem to exalt and empower one nation over the others. Within Europe, there are many different language phobias and anxieties. The history books read by children and students are full of invasions, wars and struggles between current members of the European

European Identity

In the 1990s, political barriers between western and eastern Europe began to collapse. Not without considerable tension and anxiety, the 1990s also witnessed the increased economic and political union within the European community. Following many centuries of war and dispute between European countries, a new era of European identity has begun with some arguing that Europeanization has the potential for radically reshaping its peoples' identities. A new class of supranational Europeans is suggested. Others believe that local, community, regional, ethnic and national identities are so strong that a European identity is a mirage. In between, there are those who argue that European identity will be at an economic and political level, and not at a linguistic, cultural or social level.

However, even the trappings of limited political and economic European identity, such as a single flag, a single currency, a single Parliament and a single market, attract much debate and conflict. Notions of 'us and them' ensure that there can be no clear division between economic/political union and social, cultural and linguistic identity. Issues of allegiance cannot be simply placed into separate economic, political, social, cultural and linguistic categories. At the same time, identities develop and evolve over time. Europeanization is seen by some as a process that has begun, with a long journey ahead, but with European identity as a long-term outcome.

One theme in writings on European identity is the implicit assumption that local, ethnic and minority identities are good and healthy phenomena. The obverse of this is that larger identities such as a European identity are suspect, for the elite few, and a symptom of false consciousness that aims to promote Europeanization.

It is also easy to fall into the trap of romanticizing language minority identity, creating a rather quaint, museum-like concept of such identity. This can become a fantasy, where the economic and political powerlessness and injustice of local language minorities is ignored in favor of celebrating their distinctiveness, heritage and diversity. Instead, language minorities in Europe may require appreciation of their economic well-being and their political interests as well as to their distinct cultural and language needs.

The European Bureau for Lesser Used Languages

The European community has increasingly recognized the value and validity of lesser used autochthonous (see the Glossary) languages in Europe. Such languages include Irish, Frisian, Breton, Catalan, Occitan, Friulan, Ladin, Lëtzebuergesch (Luxembourgish), Basque, Welsh, Scots Gaelic and Cornish.

Established in 1982, the European Bureau for Lesser Used Languages has worked effectively to conserve and promote these language minorities of Europe. It has sought to conserve and promote the lesser used autochthonous languages of the European Union, together with their associated cultures. It has worked in close co-operation with the European Commission and the European Parliament, member state institutions, the Council of Europe and other bodies in the furtherance of its aims.

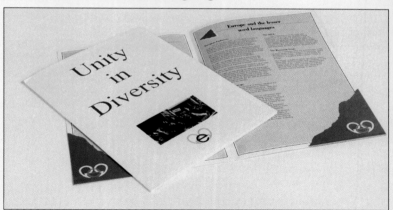

Literature published by EBLUL

With its main office in Dublin, (Ireland), it had four major aims:

1. To seek legal and political support for users of lesser used languages at the European, state and regional level.
2. To facilitate an exchange of information and experiences among activists who promote the lesser used languages of Europe. It publishes a letter three times a year in English, French, German and Italian. It organizes study visits which allow speakers of lesser used languages to visit other similar regions in the European Union.
3. To seek financial assistance from the European Union for projects that benefit lesser used language communities.
4. To provide an infrastructure to support lesser used language communities, databases of information, promotion of children's books in lesser used languages and Euroskol, a biennial gathering of primary school children from different parts of Europe who are receiving their education through the medium of a lesser used language.

It has apparently not been politically viable to support the non-indigenous minority languages of Europe. Thus in-migrant populations such as the Turks in Germany, the many different Asian groups in Britain, the Romani people scattered throughout Europe and the Jewish language communities (e.g. Yiddish) have not been included in many language discussions at pan-European level.

This tends to reflect the European three-tiered language system: the majority, official, working languages of the European community such as English, French, German, Italian and Spanish; the lesser used indigenous languages of Europe such as Welsh, Breton, Basque and Frisian; and the non-territorial, in-migrant and therefore lower status languages of Europe such as Panjabi, Bengali, Hindi and Urdu.

The European Parliament in Strasbourg, France.

Union. Suspicions and strong emotions about neighboring countries and their languages and cultures are still present. English is seen as a Trojan horse for a further invasion of Anglo-American culture and language. English is connected with economic and cultural imperialism and colonialism. English is the language of the member state (UK) whose commitment to the European ideal has been in question, with the British being reluctant to accept monetary, social, cultural and political union. Such a lack of commitment by the British to the European Union becomes a psychological barrier for the adoption of English as a lingua franca.

There is a strong lobby for French to be adopted as the lingua franca. However, French is not the language of the scientific community, the world of trade and international business communication, and is presented often as a foreign language rather than a second language, for example in language learning in school.

German is another contender, particularly with the growth of investment and co-operation between Germany and the former Communist countries in Eastern Europe. However, some member countries of the European Union were occupied by Nazi Germany in the Second World War, and still view the German language as being a symbol of invasion, power and dominance.

Since there is no easy or obvious choice for a lingua franca for the European Union, the recognition and use of all majority languages of member states may seem the easy option. However, the European Union has increasingly given recognition to small nations and to minority ethnic and language groups in Central and Eastern Europe. The Maastricht Treaty provides recognition of the cultural and linguistic diversity of the European Union. The regional language minorities have looked towards the European Union as a way of achieving language rights,

Options for Linguistic Minorities in Europe

Most European countries are multilingual to some degree. Iceland is perhaps the closest to a monolingual country in the sense of an absence of minority languages. France, for instance, has several indigenous language minorities (notably Basque, Breton, Alsatian and Catalan), while Norway only has one indigenous language minority, the Sámi, and small in-migrant groups. Wright & Ager (1995) assess the situation of minority languages in Europe and the options open to them. They comment that throughout the history of Europe, the membership of the dominant language group has been one means, often covert, to guard access to privilege.

Wright & Ager (1995) define four basic choices that are open to minority language groups in Europe. The first is to assent to linguistic assimilation, the solution favored by the dominant majority language groups of most Western European nations (e.g. France). Assimilation means the loss of the minority language but can mean profit by gaining access to prestige and power. The second choice is to fight for full or partial autonomy. In Catalonia, a measure of political autonomy has been gained in addition to linguistic rights for Catalan. In Wales, linguistic rights have been gained, but so far political autonomy has not been achieved.

A third option lies midway between acceptance of linguistic assimilation and the fight for recognition of linguistic rights. A minority group may decide to maintain its language but may acknowledge that it will not be able to win official recognition from the dominant majority group, so that the minority language might be used in official life. This is the difficult position faced by many in-migrant minority language groups. Their recent arrival, the fact that they are in scattered communities and their lack of political influence means that they are unlikely to demand basic linguistic rights. Some linguistic minorities may not even be offered the alternative option of assimilation. To take one example, no effort was made to assimilate the *Gastarbeiter* or 'guest workers' in Germany who were expected to return eventually to their native countries.

A fourth option, for the state, is to organize different language communities according to a 'federation' model, as in Switzerland and Belgium. In Switzerland, the numerically dominant German-speaking region, the French-speaking region, the Italian-speaking region and the small Romansch-speaking region all have equal linguistic rights. In practical terms this means widespread individual monolingualism, rather than bilingualism, with a number of bilingual or multilingual individuals assuring communication across group boundaries.

REFERENCE: WRIGHT & AGER, 1995

Language Use Surveys

The language background of an individual or language group needs to examine many different contextual dimensions. For example, in the Euromosaic research (see page 344) on the relatively indigenous languages of Europe by the European Commission (1996), the production and reproduction of European minority languages was initially analyzed in terms of many of the dimensions listed below.

1. Preferred categorization of the language (e.g. minority, lesser used, community, heritage, indigenous, autochthonous, see the Glossary, page 698).
2. Recent history of the language; major changes in the last decade.
3. Geographical (areal) extent of the language.
4. Number of users (e.g. from a census).
5. Legal status of language. Existence and effect of any language legislation. Use of language in courts.
6. Dominant language(s) of the territory.
7. Recent migration (in and out) affecting the language.
8. Relations with neighboring language groups and with the dominant language.
9. (*a*) Use of language in education in primary and secondary education.
    (i) As a medium of instruction.
    (ii) As a subject itself.
    (iii) The history and culture surrounding the language.
    (iv) Provision of teachers, schools and curriculum materials.
   (b) Use of language in Further, Vocational, Technical, Adult, Continuing and Higher Education.
10. Literacy and biliteracy of the language group.
11. Provision of language learning classes for in-migrants.
12. Effect of retirement patterns on the language.
13. Use of language in media (e.g. TV, radio, books, newspapers, periodicals, magazines, telephone, satellite).
14. Subsidization
15. Unemployment in the language group. Types of employment among language group (e.g. socio-economic status, industrialization, technologization). Whether language is a requirement or advantage in finding a job.
16. Use of the language in bureaucracy, forms, with regional and local authorities, with services (e.g. water, electricity, post office, railways, buses, police).
17. Effect of travel on language group (e.g. road access, train systems, air travel, shipping).
18. Effect of tourism on language group.
19. Effect of local and central government on the language. Attitude of government to the language.
20. Amount of language activism among the language group.
21. Cultural vitality of the language group; institutions dedicated to supporting the language and culture; cultural festivals.
22. Effect of urbanization and suburbanization on the language.
23. Use of language in computing (e.g. in schools, adapted keyboards and fonts).
24. Use of language in music: traditional, pop and rock, folk, classical.
25. Use of language in theater, cinema.
26. Use of translation, dubbing, subtitling of foreign language media.
27. Promotion of translation, terminological research, standardization of language.
28. Use of the language in advertizing on TV, radio, in the press.
29. Use of language in public speech and literacy events.
30. Use of the language on goods labels and instructions.
31. Use of the language in financial transactions (e.g. bills, banking).
32. Use of the language on signposts (e.g. streets, major roads, in hospitals, schools, religious buildings, government offices).
33. Use of the language in hospitals, care of elderly, homes and hostels.
34. Use of the language by parents with their children.
35. Use of the language in new and existing marriages.
36. Use of the language in religious events and among religious leaders.
37. Gender differences in the use of the language.
38. Social status of the language and language speakers.
39. Attitudes of speakers and non speakers to the language. Optimism or pessimism surrounding the language.
40. Promotion of research activity on the language .

Bilingualism and Higher Education in Europe

Strategies to increase bilingualism among undergraduates in European higher education include:

- teaching part of a courses through a foreign language;
- using foreign language textbooks to help teach a subject in the mother tongue;
- appointing foreign nationals to academic posts.
- developing language centers;
- providing optional language learning opportunities for students;
- using open and distance education and self-instruction 'packages';
- incorporating language studies into certain degree and diploma courses;
- strengthening language departments;
- establishing 'languages for all' policies at institutional level.

Languages in Europe

On the benefits and challenges of linguistic diversity in Europe

'The ability to communicate in several European languages is the key to mobility and access to foreign cultures, as well as to participation in the 'European skills market'. The cultural diversity of Europe, which is most evident in its languages, cannot adapt to one common language, however widespread the use of English has become in practice' (page 17).

[We] 'recommend trilingualism and expect students to have started a foreign language when entering higher education and be fluent in it when they finish their studies' (page 17).

On the central importance of language

Languages are seen as a 'prerequisite for co-operation and mobility in the new Europe, as well as a valuable source of cultural enrichment' (page 52).

With regard to language targets, it is recommended 'that all Community citizens should have the opportunity to acquire communicative competence in at least one Community language in addition to their mother tongue and that substantial portions of the population should be expected to acquire a knowledge of two Community foreign languages' (page 52).

It is also recommended that 'a knowledge of a foreign language as desirable for entry to higher education, but mandatory at the point of exit from it' (page 52).

REFERENCE: COMMISSION OF EUROPEAN COMMUNITIES, 1993

language status and a measure of autonomy for themselves. Increasingly, the European Union has recognized that relatively 'peripheral' regions need economic support.

The paradox of this is that such regional language minorities have tended to receive more recognition and support from the European Union than they have from their own nations. This has made for an increasingly complex linguistic situation in Europe with the formal recognition of many indigenous minority languages throughout Europe. However, this complexity may increase the drive for a lingua franca in Europe. If more and more majority and minority languages are officially recognized in Europe, the greater the need for a common language.

For individual countries, such European recognition of regional minority languages can also throw national language policies into question. The ideology that supports a single national language and encourages language assimilation begins to crumble with the European recognition of regional language minorities.

The new dilemma for member countries of the European Union is that they have argued for the importance of their majority language to have equality of rights within a multilingual European Union. At the same time, they have tended to refuse to give linguistic rights to language minorities within their state boundaries. Such inconsistency in arguing for multilingualism for Europe but monolingualism within the state, may create a tolerance for the diversity of languages within Europe.

A resolution of the dilemma may be by establishing a diglossic situation both for regional language minorities and within the European Union. A stable diglossic situation for regional language minorities could be paralleled, in principle and in practice, by a diglossic situation within the European Union. Regional language minorities would retain functions for their languages that are safeguarded and maintained by member countries. Nation states would have their national language safeguarded by retaining specific language functions within a European Union that has a lingua franca or a very small subset of working languages.

Further Reading

AMMON, U., 1991, The Status of German and Other Languages in the European Community. In F. COULMAS (ed.), *A Language Policy for the European Community*. Berlin/New York: Mouton de Gruyter.

COULMAS, F. (ed.), 1991, *A Language Policy for the European Community*. Berlin/New York: Mouton de Gruyter.

FREIBEL, W. *et al.* (ed.), 1996, *Education for European Citizenship: Theoretical and Practical Approaches*. Freiburg: Konzeption.

GRADDOL, D. & THOMAS, S., 1995, *Language in a Changing Europe*. Clevedon: Multilingual Matters Ltd.

HOFFMANN, C. (ed.),1996, *Language, Culture and Communication in Contemporary Europe*. Clevedon: Multilingual Matters Ltd.

HUGHES, M., 1993, *Citizenship 2000. The Lesser Used European Languages. The European Dimension in Education and Teacher Training, Citizenship 2000 Expert Group*. Cardiff: University of Wales.

MACDONALD, S. (ed.), 1993, *Inside European Identities*. Oxford: Berg.

WRIGHT, S. & AGER, D., 1995, 'Major' and 'Minor' Languages in Europe: The Evolution of Practice and Policy in the European Union. *The European Journal of Intercultural Studies* 5 (3), 44-53.

The Euromosaic Project

The European Union has taken an increasing interest in autochthonous language communities in Europe. The term 'autochthonous languages' describes indigenous languages, or languages resident relatively early in a territory or a region. This interest is witnessed in the funding by DGXXII (Education, Training and Youth) of the European Commission of a major Western Europe research project on the potential of language minority groups to produce (e.g. via second language learning in education) and reproduce (e.g. by families) their language. The research, called the Euromosaic project, was directed by Glyn Williams (Bangor, North Wales), Peter Nelde (Brussels) and Miquel Strubell (Barcelona). Based on theoretically innovative research on 48 language minorities in Western Europe, the *Euromosaic Report* (1996) provides one of the first comprehensive and comparative studies of the chances of language survival and reproduction of such language minorities.

Using a combination of questionnaires, detailed reports from 'key language witnesses' and eight detailed language surveys, the data was reduced to scores on scales representing the key variables in a pioneering, economically determined, theoretical model of language production and reproduction. Seven variables were used to produce a categorization of the 48 languages into five groups of 'chances of language survival' (see graph). These seven central variables were: Language Reproduction in the Family, Language Production and Reproduction in the Community, Language Production and Reproduction through Education, the Value of Language for Social Mobility, Relevance of Language in Cultural Reproduction, Legitimization (e.g. legal status, language rights) and Institutionalization (the 'taken-for-grantedness' of a language).

The graphs illustrate some of the patterns found in the Euromosaic research. Only 23 of the 48 language groups are profiled in these graphs. Generally, the language group chosen is where the language is stronger (e.g. Catalan in Catalonia is included; Catalan in Valencia and France is excluded). Also, languages that are in a minority within a country, but are in the majority in another country (e.g. German in Belgium, French in Italy) are also excluded from these graphs.

REFERENCE: EUROPEAN COMMISSION, 1996

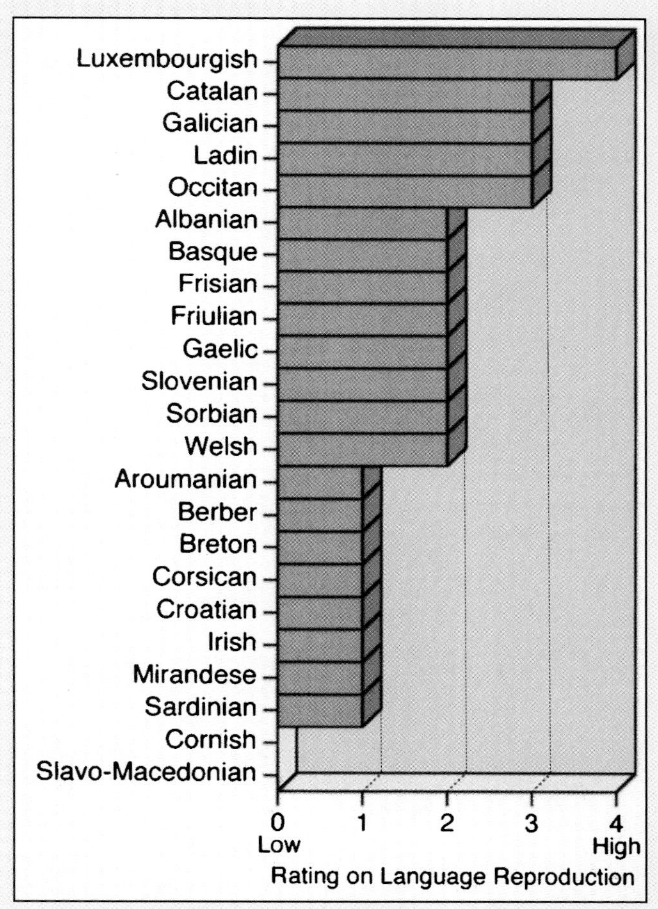

Reproduction of language in the community.

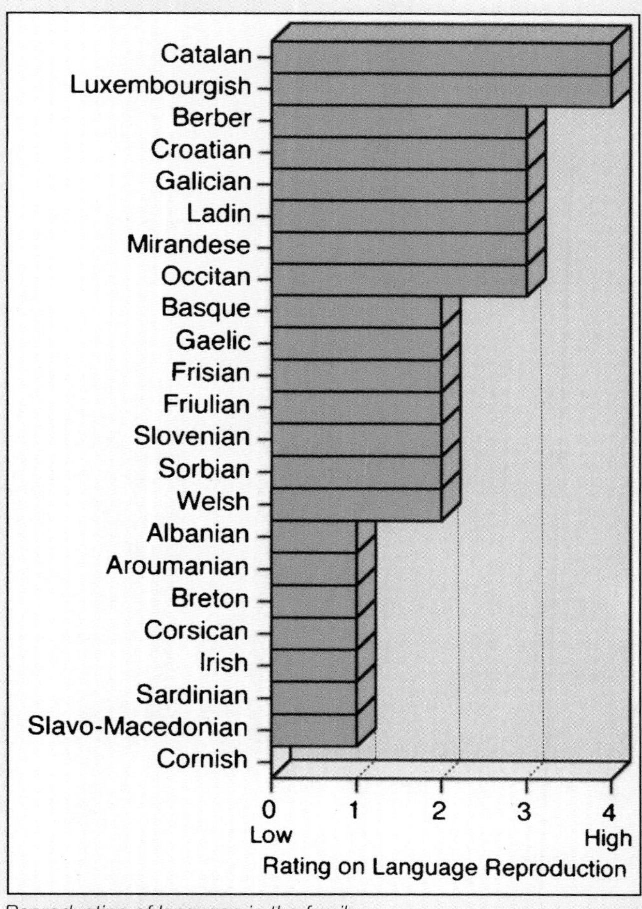

Reproduction of language in the family.

LANGUAGES IN CONTACT IN THE WORLD

'I am always sorry when any language is lost, because languages are the pedigree of nations.'

Samuel Johnson, English author and lexicographer (1709–1784).

Introduction

This section provides a pictorial and textual representation of languages in contact throughout the world. Some introductory remarks are necessary to explain the aim, design and nature of this section. In particular, the introduction explains some of the important issues involved in portraying languages in contact.

Issues

It is impossible to record every existing language even though there are language atlases that provide highly detailed information about languages in all regions of the world. The reasons for such an impossibility are varied and are now considered.

There is no agreement as to the number of languages in the world. Estimates vary at between 3000 and 7000. This wide variation is due to the difficulty in defining a language, and problems of gathering reliable, valid and comprehensive information about languages in large expanses such as Africa, South America and parts of Asia. These difficulties will now be explained.

Languages and Dialects

One major problem in mapping the languages of the world is in defining what is a language and what is a dialect. There are many debates about whether different speech communities speak dialects of the same language, or whether they speak separate languages. In African countries such as Nigeria or Cameroon, for instance, several hundred different speech varieties may represent a much smaller number of dialect clusters. Research in many multilingual situations is scanty or incomplete, and the fact that many dialects of the same language may have different names can be misleading. Also, the way the speakers of a language, or national governments, perceive and categorize the speech of different communities plays an important part in trying to distinguish between languages (and not just linguistic criteria).

One major difficulty is to locate data that are recent, comprehensive, reliable and valid. The initial problem is locating recent data. For example, census data from the 1960s or 1970s may hide considerable population change and language shift that has occurred in recent decades. Next, the data need to be comprehensive and cover the whole of a country and all language groups within a country. While a full geographical representation is often attempted in a national census, it is rare for language questions (if present at all) to cover many or all of the language groups present. In lowland South America (e.g. Brazil, Columbia, Venezuela, Ecuador, Bolivia and Peru), there are some remote groups of indigenous peoples whose languages are not yet fully recorded. Occasionally, hitherto unknown languages are located in South America, Africa or Asia.

The terms 'reliable' and 'valid' highlight the importance of gathering language data that are relatively accurate, stable across independent measurements, unbiased and that mirrors everyday behavior. However reliable or recent language data may be, the fact remains that the language situation in a country or area is constantly changing, sometimes slowly and at other times rapidly. Languages decline or die or acquire new speakers; language groups migrate to new areas; language varieties grow closer together or to a standard norm, or occasionally become further apart; pidgins evolve and may

How Many Languages in the World?

Barbara F. Grimes (edited) *Ethnologue: Languages of the World* lists 6,703 living languages in the world, while W. F. Mackey (1991) suggests that there are 6170 such living languages. Another scholarly source (C. Moseley and R.E. Asher (eds), 1994, *Atlas of the World's Languages*) specifies close to 5900 discrete languages, while Bright (1992) lists 6604 languages, but this includes around 300 extinct languages.

Such living languages are found in under 200 sovereign states. Around 120 states have adopted English, French, Spanish or Arabic as their official language. Another 50 states have their own indigenous official language. Mackey (1991) suggests that there are around 45 regional languages with official status in the world. If we add together these international and 'official' languages, they only account for around 1.5 percent of the total languages in the world. Or more dramatically, 98.5 percent of the languages of the world have no formal recognition. Williams (1996b) suggests that 'only 1 percent of the world's languages have more than half a million speakers and only 10 percent have more than 100,000. Hundreds of languages have no adolescent speakers' (page 47).

become creolized. Providing a totally accurate up-to-date snapshot of a language situation is not possible.

Language Censuses

In an increasing number of countries of the world, there are regular censuses, for example, every ten years. Such censuses are often perceived as providing relatively accurate measures of the number of language speakers. Thus, in Venezuela, Bolivia, Canada, United States, Britain, Australia and many other countries considered later in this section, a language question is included among the many other census questions.

Such language census data contain a set of limitations, even when there is a long tradition of census compilation, expertise and experience.

1. Census questions about home language, mother tongue and first language are often ambiguous. Sometimes the questions do not distinguish between language use and language ability (see page 3). Thus a question, 'Do you speak English?' does not specify whether the question is about everyday use of language, ability to speak the language irrespective of regular use, or both use and ability.

2. Questions on census forms sometimes do not include the four language abilities: understanding a language, speaking, reading and writing. Thus oracy may be evaluated and not literacy. Also, there are not usually specific questions about contexts or domains of language use.

3. Census data may rapidly become out of date when factors such as migration, social upheaval, war or a high birthrate mean that the language situation is rapidly changing.

4. Not all censuses include questions on language. Some censuses ask about ethnic groups, which may not correspond to language groups. In the former Soviet state of Georgia, for instance, 70 percent of the population were recorded on the last census as being ethnic 'Georgians'. However, this group includes not only first language speakers of Georgian, but also first language speakers of two closely related languages, most of whom also speak Georgian. A question about ethnic groups is sometimes wrongly used to estimate the size of a language groups.

5. Conversely, a language question in a census may be treated by respondents as if it refers to ethnic identification. For example, in Ireland, a non-Irish speaker may wish to be seen as ethnically Irish and therefore answer the Irish language question affirmatively.

6. Official government figures may inflate the numbers of majority language speakers and deflate the numbers of minority language speakers, for political reasons.

7. A census language question may be interpreted as an attitude question. For example, people from a particular ethnic group may feel they ought to say that they speak the indigenous or heritage language even if they do not. It may be regarded as socially desirable to say one speaks a language, and speaks it well. The opposite may also occur. If a minority language is disparaged and of low status, a speaker of that language may claim not to speak the language. Answers to questions about language on a census form may thus reflect 'posing', a socially desirable answer and not everyday behavior.

8. What constitutes the ability to speak a language, or what constitutes use of a language, is essentially arbitrary, without any clear cut-off points along with the dimension from 'full use' to 'no use', from high ability to no competence. (See page 3). Sometimes, a scale is provided (e.g. both the 1980 and 1990 US Census asked 'How well does this person speak English? Very well / Well / Not well / Not at all'). This helpfully allows some differentiation.

9. Censuses do not usually cover all of the population of a country despite considerable efforts to be inclusive. Some of the population may refuse to respond through the mail system, or to answer census personnel calling at their house. Other people are out of reach or difficult to track down. Itinerants, illegal inmigrants and the homeless, for example, may be missed by the census. In the US 1990 Census, it is known that minority language groups were not fully accessed for the reasons mentioned above.

10. In some countries, there is a short questionnaire which everybody completes and a longer questionnaire that a small sample (e.g. 17 percent) complete. Often the language questions are on the longer questionnaire. Thus inferences have to be made from the sample of people given the larger questionnaire. Therefore, the exact accuracy of the language figures can be questioned as there is a margin of error in the sampling and in the generalization of results from a sample to the total population.

11. Very often, if there is a language question, it is not inclusive of all languages. For example, in the 1991 British Census, there was no question about speak-

Language Mapping and GIS (Geographical Information Systems)

Throughout the major cities of the world such as New York, London, Brussels, Paris, Tokyo, Kuala Lumpur and Toronto, many diverse languages are spoken by in-migrants, community language groups and indigenous peoples. Thus it is often difficult to map the variety of languages, language contact and language shift in urban areas. In a recent study of language contact and social networks in Cape Town (Williams & van der Merwe, 1996), GIS (Geographical Information System) Technology was used to map 28 languages over 264 neighborhood subdivisions with arrows to indicate language change between 1980 and 1991. This is being extended in the work of the Logosphere Program that is to create multilayered ethnolinguistic maps on CD-ROM (School of Oriental and African Studies, 1993).

Collaborative research between the Observatoire Linguistique, the Centre des Industries de la Langue et du Développement (CILDA: University of Paris-Nanterre) and the School of Oriental and African Studies (The University of London) in the Logosphere Program aims to 'map and classify all the world's languages and dialects, using a unified and standardized system of reference, and to set up an international database for the storage, comparison and diffusion of all kinds of linguistic, demographic, ethnic and cultural information. Such information will be of vital importance for educational and linguistic planning as well as for the conservation of minority languages and the protection of the rights of those who speak them.' (School of Oriental and African Studies, 1993, page 1.)

The GIS can produce multilayered maps with three-dimensional views of languages in contact. Thus, in a multilingual area, where both official and non-official languages are used, more or less detail can be presented by zooming in and out of the map. The visual database can be integrated with selected sound recordings of different languages.

The United States Census of 1990

On the 1st April 1990, a Census of the population was taken throughout the United States. The decennial Census in 1990 cost more than $2.5 billion dollars and counted more than 98 percent of the population. However, some of the population were hard to reach or track down. It is estimated that nearly 5 million people were omitted from the 1990 census. They were disproportionately from minority racial and ethnic groups.

Two questionnaires were used. A short questionnaire was sent to every household in the US, requesting information on individuals (e.g. gender, race, Hispanic origin and age). A longer questionnaire was sent to one in six (17 percent) of all US households, and included questions about languages spoken at home, citizenship and year of in-migration, occupation and educational attainment. Some key language and ethnicity results are portrayed in the section on the United States (see page 438f).

Question 15a on the 1990 Census form was phrased as follows:

15a. Does this person speak a language other than English at home?

❍ Yes ❍ No — Skip to 16

b. What is this language?

[ ]

For example: Chinese, Italian, Spanish, Vietnamese.

c. How well does this person speak English?

❍ Very well ❍ Not well
❍ Well ❍ Not at all

This question is more comprehensive than the 1910 language question. It asks about the use of a minority language in the home irrespective of command of English. It also asks a more searching question about the level of ability in English.

Language Censuses in Belgium

The first language census in Belgium occurred in 1846. This was one of the first language questions to be asked in any country's census. Other countries were soon to follow Belgium's lead in the remainder of the 19th century. Language census questions commenced in Switzerland in 1850, Ireland in 1851, Hungary in 1857, Italy in 1861, Canada in 1871, Austria and Finland in 1880, India and Scotland in 1881, the United States in 1890, Wales in 1891 and Russia in 1897 (O Gliasáin, 1996).

In the 1846 Belgium census, the language question was restricted to asking what language was usually spoken by respondents. Soon after, language censuses in Belgium began asking questions about knowledge of the official languages of Belgium. Since there were a mixture of official and unofficial (autochthonous) languages in use in Belgium, the restriction of such questions to official languages provoked argument and debate. In such Belgium language census questionnaires, all those over 14 years of age had to complete and sign the questionnaire. This also provoked contention and controversy. The outcome was that, in 1961, the majority of parliamentarians in Belgium decided to suspend the language censuses in Belgium to avoid further dispute.

Languages in the United States Census

The United States Census was instituted at the beginning of the United States political system in Article 1 Section 2 which stated that political representation in the House of Representatives was to be based on a population census. The census has been taken every ten years since 1790, when Secretary of State, Thomas Jefferson, supervised the first census. Information from the US Census is used by many public and private interests. A few examples include: economic planning, housing, public school systems, community health planning, state and local highway construction, and to determine senior citizen needs. More and more, census data is used to help states and localities 'benchmark' and measure progress in meeting their objectives and legislatively mandated targets.

Two examples are given below of census questions on language from two different US censuses, the first from 1910 and the second from 1990. These examples illustrate how census questions are constructed in a way that does not always give accurate and comprehensive information about use of languages, and also reveals implicit official attitudes towards the use and maintenance of minority languages.

The United States Census of 1910

In the 1910 United States Census, advice was given to enumerators when asking respondents about the mother tongue of members of the household. Three extracts are given below illustrating notions from a bygone era. The following points should be noted.

1. The question of mother tongue excluded those born in the United States. This indicates an assumption that all those born in the United States would be able to speak English, and that the maintenance of minority languages or bilingualism in English and a minority language was not considered.
2. The language of the under 10 year olds was ignored.
3. A person's ability in languages other than English was ignored if they were able to speak English.
4. Ability in a heritage language was counted only if a person was unable to speak English.
5. The list of 'European' languages to be used for entry of 'mother tongue' gives an idea of the diversity of languages spoken in the US in the early 20th century.

Advice to Enumerators in the United States 1910 Census

'127. The question of mother tongue should not be asked of any person born in the United States'

'133. Column 17. Whether able to speak English; or, if not, give language spoken. This question applies to all persons age 10 and over. If such a person is able to speak English, write English [on the form]. If he is not able to speak English – and in such cases only – write the language which he does speak, as French, German, Italian.'

'134. The following is a list of principal foreign languages spoken in the United States ... With the exception of certain languages of eastern Russia, the list gives a name for every European language in the proper sense of the word.

Albanian
Armenia
Basque
Breton
Bulgarian
Chinese
Danish
Dutch
Finnish
Flemish
French
German
Greek
Gypsy
Irish
Italian
Japanese
Lappish
Lettish
Little Russian
Lithuanian
Magyar
Moravian
Norwegian
Polish
Portuguese
Rhaeto-Romansh *(including Ladin and Friulian)*
Romanian
Russian
Ruthenian
Scotch
Serbian or Croatian
Slovak
Slovenian
Spanish
Swedish
Syrian
Turkish
Welsh
Wendish
Yiddish

ing mainland European Asian languages in Britain. In the US 1990 Census, this problem was partly overcome with an open-ended question, inviting respondents to name their home language.

Sources other than Censuses

In many countries of the world, there is either no population census or else the census does not ask a language question. When there is no census, or no census language question, then an estimation of the number of language speakers within an area depends on other sources of information, often less recent, less comprehensive, less reliable, less valid and accurate than a population census. Sources will include locally provided information by missionaries, local scholars, students, teachers, visiting researchers and travelers. Such sources will rarely be able to give an accurate count of language speakers within a region and will tend to have information only about selected geographical areas.

As in census data, local sources of information, or visiting researchers, may believe that there is a one-to-one correspondence between members of an ethnic group and the number of speakers of a particular language within an area. While such an inference is all that may be possible, it typically results in over-estimation.

Another source of difficulty in providing accurate information about language contact in the world is the lack of information about in-migrant languages. For example, in Europe indigenous minority languages are often counted and mapped, while in-migrant languages (e.g. Asian languages) are ignored. The accuracy and comprehensive nature of language maps that ignore in-migrant languages is thus put into doubt. Census data from the United States is generally in advance of Europe, for example, in this respect.

Another language group that is omitted from language atlases are deaf people, for example, those who use sign languages and may be bilingual in a sign language and a spoken language. This is rectified in this book (see page 563f).

Mapping Bilinguals

Few censuses or local sources tend to gather data on those who use two or more languages. Usually the target is first language or home language usage. Those who are bilingual or trilingual are rarely asked to profile their use of different languages. (For exceptions, see the articles on India and Hong Kong, where census data on second language usage is discussed). For the purposes of this Encyclopedia, there is very little data available either in census or in other sources about bilinguals and multilinguals. Where there is information that is reasonably reliable on first and second language speakers, on bilinguals and trilinguals, this is shared in the following pages. However, languages in contact and bilingualism often has to be inferred from the co-existence of majority languages and minority languages in an area. The presence of several language groups in a country does not always indicate a high level of individual bilingualism (e.g. Switzerland). Possible or recorded patterns of bilingualism are usually indicated in the text accompanying the maps.

Levels of bilingualism or multilingualism may vary from region to region within a country, and between rural and urban areas. A common pattern in African countries, for instance, is that monolingualism is usually found in sparsely populated, rural areas where language groups may live in relative isolation. Bilingualism is common in areas where there is frequent language contact between language groups through, for example, geographical proximity or trade. Trilingualism or multilingualism is generally more frequent in urban areas because so many diverse language groups live in close proximity, and where there is much commercial contact, social contact and intermarriage.

In the following pages of this section, what is impossible to portray on maps is briefly considered in the accompanying text.

Language Mapping Issues

The following maps and texts do not list every language within a country or a region. Readers interested in such highly detailed consideration should refer, for example, to Moseley & Asher's (1994) *Atlas of the World's Languages*. This provides a relatively extensive geographical representation of the many different languages within particular countries. The other sources listed in the references will also be useful for the researcher seeking detailed and comprehensive information about individual countries.

The style of the following section is to provide introductory and basic details of the major, official languages within particular regions and countries, and give information about sizable minority languages within particular areas. Information not included on the maps is given in the textboxes. Considerations of space necessarily restrict examination of the many minority languages within particular countries (e.g. China, India, Africa, Australia). Pragmatic decisions had to be made about the type and level of information to include in each case, based on what might be

Ethnologue

One well known source for languages throughout the world is Barbara F. Grimes (edited) *Ethnologue: Languages of the World.*

The 13th edition, published in 1996, contains information on over 6700 languages spoken in the world, indicating the names of the languages, alternative names, approximate numbers of speakers, location, dialects, linguistic affiliation and other sociolinguistic and demographic data. The book details languages in 228 countries with a listing of over 39,000 language names in language families. This publication is also available on the Internet at:

http://www.sil.org/ethnologue/ethnologue.html

The Internet connection allows searching of the database by country, language family tree, language or dialect names.

The book categorizes the continental distribution of languages as follows:

	Number of Living Languages	Percentage
Africa	2011	30.0%
The Americas	1000	14.9%
Asia	2165	32.3%
Europe	225	3.4%
The Pacific region	1302	19.4%
Total	**6703**	**100%**

The *Ethnologue* contributors have tried to identify all the linguistically distinct societies of the world. While this is a valuable source of detailed information, like other sources, it should not be regarded as giving totally accurate coverage especially of remote and undeveloped areas and multilingual regions.

Some information in the *Ethnologue* is dated (e.g. Welsh figures date from 1971 whereas 1991 Census figures are available), and some contributors have provided inaccurate information. Thus classification of languages depends on sources, some of which may be less reliable than others, and on the self-categorization of speakers of the language.

The 1992 Census of the Wayuu Ethnic Group in Venezuela

The South American country of Venezuela has a population of about 20 million. The official and majority language of the country is Spanish. Just over 1.5 percent of the population are pure American Indians, and about 37 indigenous languages are spoken. Bilingualism and multilingualism are common among the American Indians. Most speak Spanish as well as their own mother tongue and some speak more than one indigenous language. About half the American Indian population belong to the Wayuu ethnic group. The following questions from the 1992 Venezuelan Census aim to give a comprehensive picture of an individual's use of languages. The following points should be noted.

1. The census asks about competence in more than one indigenous language, as well as competence in a non-indigenous language.
2. The census distinguishes between language ability and language use.
3. The census distinguishes between oracy and literacy in both indigenous languages and Spanish.

Solo Para Personas de 5 Años o Mas
For People over 5 Years Old

20. Habla algun idioma indigena?
Do you speak any indigenous language?
Si *Yes* ☐ No ☐
¿Cuálo cuáles?..

21. ¿Habla algun idioma no indigena? (Puedi mar car más de una respuesta)
Do you speak any non-indigenous language? (you may choose more than one answer)
Si *Yes* ☐ No ☐
Castellano *Spanish*...............................
Portugués *Portuguese*.........................
Inglés *English*...............................

22. ¿En que idioma se comunica usualmente con los demas habitantes de la comunidad?
Which language do you normally use to communicate with other members of the community?...

23. Save escriber en:
(Pueda marcar más de una respuesta)
Can you write in:
(You may choose more than one answer)
Castellano *Spanish*
Si *Yes* ☐ No ☐
Idioma indigena *Indigenous language*
Si *Yes* ☐ No ☐

24. Sabe leer en: *Can you read in:*
Castellano *Spanish*
Si *Yes* ☐ No ☐
Idoma indigena *Indigenous language*
Si *Yes* ☐ No ☐

relevant and interesting to a non-specialist reader. Such decisions also sometimes revolve around the perceived accuracy (and non-accuracy) of available data. This helps explain why maps do not convey similar levels of information across different countries and continents.

The maps, graphs and text should be read in conjunction to engage fully the theme of languages in contact. However, since there is very little data on the nature and extent of bilingualism in various countries, the maps, graphs and text vary in their comprehensiveness of 'language contact' coverage. In some parts of Eastern Europe, for example, where there have been changes in borders, new units of government and ethnic disputes, it has been particularly difficult to locate up-to-date, accurate and reliable information.

One expectation about language maps is that there will be coloring or shading to represent the geographical spread of languages in a country. Unfortunately, handsome looking maps are often deceptive and inaccurate, tending to give the impression of boundaries between one language group and another. The boundaries are sometimes 'guesswork' and do not allow overlap in language distribution. Neatness tends to be in advance of reality.

One example of inaccuracy in coloring and shading is found on maps of language minorities in Europe where boundary representations are misleading. For example, in Ireland and Wales, some maps indicate that these Celtic languages are spoken across the whole country. This is misleading as there are wide variations from village to village, county to county. Some areas may not have minority language speakers. Other maps show the indigenous languages as only spoken in heartland areas (e.g. *Gaeltacht* in Ireland). Simple shading and coloring often fails to represent a complex and varied reality. The recent mapping of the languages of Bolivia represents one of the best examples of color maps which are both clear and detailed, cover language contact in a dynamic manner (i.e. indicating areas of language spread and language shift) and are comprehensive. (See pages 159 and 456.)

The following maps and texts aim to provide basic details of major languages within particular areas, and where possible, numbers or percentages of speakers of minority languages. A problem in such mapping is classification. What is a majority and what is a minority language (see page 99)? Should the maps discriminate between indigenous and in-migrant languages? What is the relationship between official or officially designated languages of a country and majority languages? What is the relationship between lingua francas and other languages within a region?

William Francis Mackey

William Francis Mackey was born in Canada in 1918. From age five to 14, he was educated in French residential schools in St. Boniface, a suburb of Winnipeg, Manitoba where he was born. Both his parents came from Ireland and spoke only English to him, although his mother had some knowledge of the Irish language. Thus the home language was English and the language of schooling was French. He was further educated at the University of Manitoba, University of Laval, University of Columbia, Harvard University and Geneva University.

One of the foremost authorities this century on bilingualism, W. F. Mackey is multilingual himself, speaking French, English, German and Spanish with some Italian as well. His first academic post was at the University of Laval in 1941, rising through the ranks until being made Research Professor in 1974. Apart from teaching in Canada, he has also taught in London, Cambridge, Los Angeles, Nice and visited many countries of the world. He has been Director of different organizations, particularly the International Centre for Research on Bilingualism and the Centre International de Recherche en Aménagement Linguistique.

While W. F. Mackey was on leave from the University of London, he directed a month-long experiment on a chartered vessel sailing to Australia. The experiment involved language teaching to some 200 European immigrants allocated to 15 language groups. On board this vessel, he met Ilonka Schmidt who, because of her skill in 12 of the languages, became the Liaison Officer with the different language groups. When the ship docked near Sydney, he married Ilonka Schmidt. They returned to London in October 1949 where he continued to teach at the University of London Institute of Education until 1950.

Shortly after returning to Canada, his mother in law joined them and, as a result, five languages were in daily use in the house. Their two daughters were brought up in three languages, French, English and German. These two daughters, one a research neurologist and the other a translation administrator, are still fully competent in all three languages.

W. F. Mackey's research covers a wide area of linguistics, sociolinguistics, geolinguistics and education. His publications output is voluminous with 28 books, over 200 articles and countless conference presentations and consultancies. Among his most famous publications are *Language Teaching Analysis* (1965), which was published in English, French, Russian, Japanese and Chinese; and the *International Bibliography on Bilingualism* (1972) which ran to 757 pages with over 11,000 titles in the first edition, and to over 19,000 entries in the second edition (1982).

Sometimes official designations of languages and figures are political in orientation. An official language can be a minority language, depending on a definition of minority (see page 99). There are disputes about what are majority languages and what are minority languages. Such disputes are based on who is making the judgement (e.g. government, scholar), from what perspective (e.g. political, statistical) and from where (e.g. inside a region, international). A mapping of languages in contact is neither a value-free nor a neutral activity.

Maps of languages in contact reveal a spatial dimension to language, inevitably ignoring the historic, social, economic, temporal, political and linguistic dimensions of language that underlie such maps. While languages can be represented in space on maps, that 'space' requires further analysis to uncover the language action that occurs within the 'space'. A map of languages in contact may superficially suggest that languages are passive, static or fixed within their 'space'. On the contrary, languages in contact generate continuous shift and development.

Official and National Languages

The official language or languages for each country are indicated on the maps and in the text. The official language is generally the language used in government, administration and education. Many countries have a legally designated official language. In countries where the overwhelming majority of the population speak one language, the official language may never have been ratified by law. This has traditionally been the case of English in the UK and the US. However, where minority language groups have begun to demand recognition for their languages, the status of English has in some cases been reviewed and ratified by law (e.g. in Wales and in some US states). In countries where there are two or more official languages, they may have complementary functions. In former colonial countries, for instance, English or another former colonial language, may be used in international communication, and the higher levels of government and education. A vernacular language may be used in lower levels of administration and education. These functions may change over time.

It is not always easy to establish what are the official language or languages of a country. A vernacular language may gain official status or a former colonial language may lose official status, but still be widely used in official contexts. In multilingual countries where levels of education and literacy are low, or where primary education is conducted in the vernacular, the official language may only be known by a small minority of the population.

In some multilingual or former colonial countries, certain indigenous languages have been elevated to the status of national languages. Where the official language is a former colonial language, the elevation of an indigenous language or languages to the status of a national language may only have a symbolic significance, indicating a desire to enhance national pride and unity (e.g. in the Cameroon, where all languages have the status of national languages.) However, in some countries, certain widely spoken lingua francas have been designated as national languages and an effort is being made to promote their teaching and use. National languages may be used in primary education, adult literacy, the mass media, administration and in parliament.

In some multilingual countries, languages may be designated as regional official languages in regions where they are majority languages or lingua francas. (This is the case in India.) Because of reasons of space, it has not been possible to indicate national languages and regional official languages on the maps, but they are listed in the text.

Ethnicity and Language

The term 'ethnic group' is frequently used in this section. It has already been stressed in this introduction that membership of a particular ethnic group does not necessarily correlate with the ability to speak a particular language. Different ethnic groups may speak closely related languages or dialects, while members of the same ethnic group may speak different languages (sometimes as a result of language shift). However, official and/or census figures about ethnic rather than language groups may be the only information available. Also, the term 'ethnic' is used to distinguish between ethnic group and membership of a nation state. For instance, in the former Soviet state of Kazakhstan, less than half of the citizens are ethnic Kazakhs.

Sources of Information

The sources of the information used to create the maps include: existing language atlases, scholarly books and articles, published census material (available on paper or electronically), plus information from many research centers, universities, governments, embassies and consulates throughout the world. Wherever possible, sources have been compared and critically evaluated. For example, scholarly articles can provide incongruent information, atlases disagree about the names and sizes of language groups, government figures are at variance with information from research centers. Often, simple maps hide complex and difficult decisions about the information available.

Africa

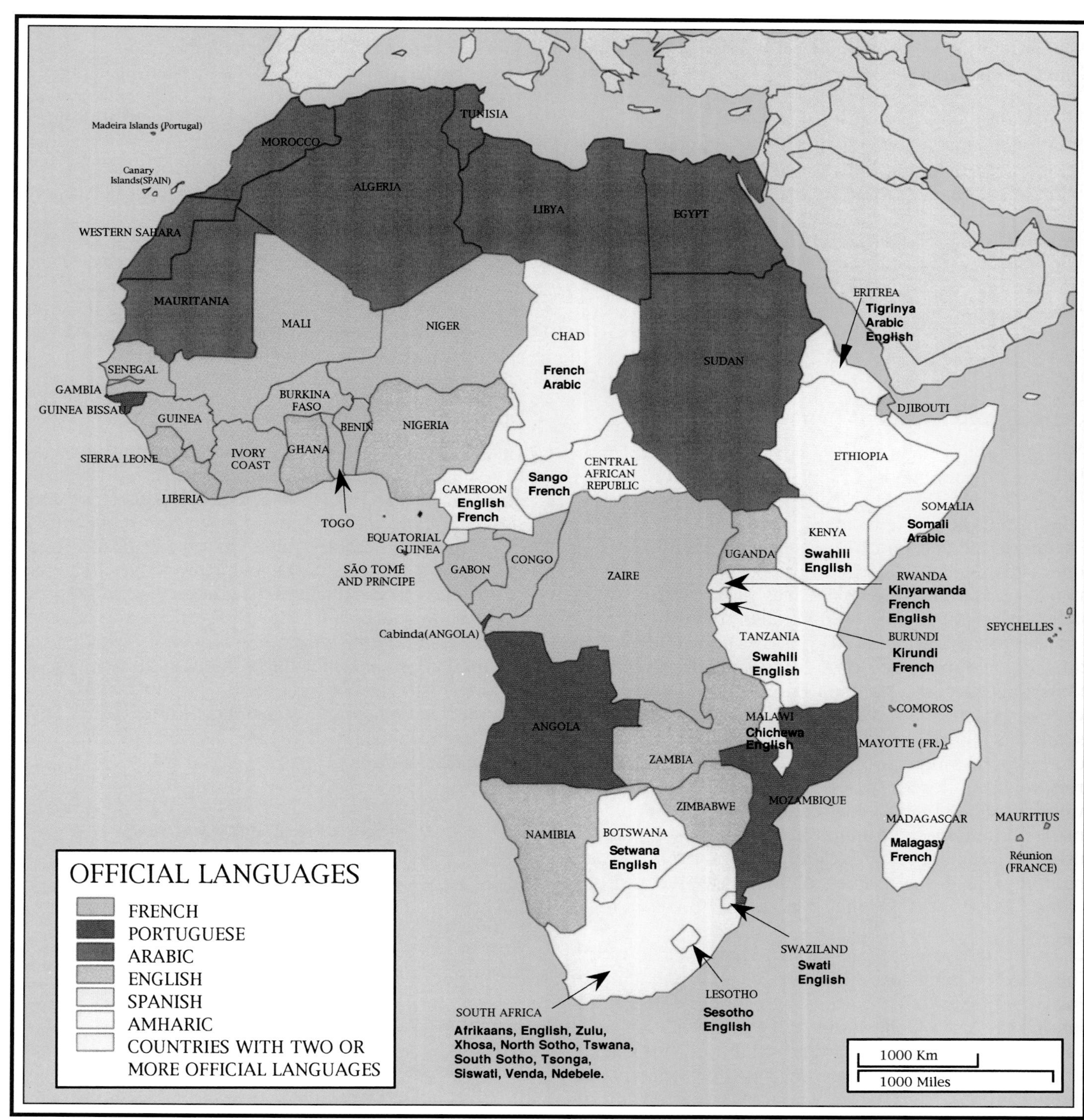

Official Languages of Africa

Algeria

The Democratic and Popular Republic of Algeria, formerly a French colony, gained independence in 1962, following the war against France. The population of 28.5 million (1995 estimate) is of Arab, Berber or mixed Arab–Berber ancestry. After 1962, the majority of the one million Europeans resident in Algeria left the country, and now less than one percent of the population is of European origin. A diglossic situation exists in Algeria, as in other Arabic-speaking countries. Modern Standard Arabic is the official language, used in public, official, formal and written contexts, while colloquial dialects of Arabic are spoken as a mother tongue and used in informal contexts by the majority of the population. (Classical Arabic is the language of Islamic worship.) Most of the remainder of the population speak dialects of Berber, the original indigenous language of a large part of North Africa. There are no accurate figures for the numbers of Berber speakers, since the language has no official status. Estimates for the number of speakers range at between 13 percent and 42 percent of the total population. Almost all Berber speakers also speak Arabic and thus are classed as Arabic speakers. Since 1988, Berber has received some government support. Two newspapers in Berber exist and there is news in Berber on television twice a day. Also, cultural societies and centers have been established to promote the teaching and popularization of Berber language and culture.

French still enjoys a high status in Algeria. It is a major foreign language and is still widely read and spoken by many educated Algerians. National radio has a French station. The only TV channel is in Arabic with some French material. The majority of newspapers and magazines are in French, and French is widely used in higher education. Scientific material in school and university text books is almost exclusively in French, while Arabic is the medium of primary education. A law to Arabize local administration, business, politics and the media from July, 1992 was postponed indefinitely, because it was felt that the necessary conditions for adequate implementation of the law did not yet exist. English is also a recognized foreign language in Algeria and is gaining in prestige.

Angola

The People's Republic of Angola was formerly part of Portuguese West Africa. The country gained independence from Portugal in 1975 after 14 years of guerrilla warfare and a brutal civil war. The population in 1995 was estimated at 10 million. Because of the devastation and social unrest caused by sporadic warfare since independence, it is not easy to assess the language situation in Angola. It is estimated that there are more than 90 ethnic groups in Angola, and numerous local languages are spoken. Over 90 percent of the population speak Bantu languages. There are three major ethnolinguistic groups, the Ovimbundu (37 percent) in the central and southern regions, the Kimbundu (25 percent) in Luanda and the east, and the Kikongo (13 percent) in the north.

Portuguese is the official language of the country, used in the media, government and education, and spoken by younger people and educated people especially in the larger towns of the coastal area. Prolonged contact with African languages has given rise to two-way language borrowing. Local varieties of Portuguese have evolved, heavily influenced by indigenous languages, and the local African languages have borrowed from Portuguese.

Most Portuguese left the country after independence and less than 80,000 remain. In addition, there are about 180,000 mesticos (people of mixed Portuguese–African ancestry). Six African languages have the status of national languages, and are used in adult literacy programs, radio and television. These are Kikongo, Kimbundu, Chokwe, Umbundu, Mbunda-Ngangela and Kwanyama.

Benin

The Republic of Benin is a former French colony, with a population of 5.5 million (1995 estimate). Over 50 language varieties are spoken, some of them closely related with a high degree of mutual intelligibility, and all having equal status as non-official national languages. The four main indigenous languages are Yoruba, Fon, Gen and Bariba. The official language is French, used in government, administration, education and the media. Some television programs are shown in the four main indigenous languages. There are rural radio broadcasts in 18 national languages. Increasing use is being made of national languages in education.

Botswana

The Republic of Botswana has a population of 1.4 million (1995 estimate). A former British Protectorate, it gained its independence in 1966. Twenty five African languages are spoken in Botswana, but the majority language, Setswana, a Bantu language, is the mother tongue of some 85 percent of the population and is spoken as a second language by a further nine percent. Kalanga is spoken by a small minority group (120,000). English and Setswana are the official languages and both are used in the media. Setswana is the medium of instruction in the first years of primary schooling, while English is used thereafter.

Burkina Faso

Burkina Faso, formerly the French colony of Upper Volta, achieved independence in 1960. Burkina Faso has a population of 10.4 million (1995 estimate) and is a country of great ethnic and linguistic diversity. It is estimated that approximately 60 languages are spoken in the country, and 18 have been designated as national languages. Thirteen languages are used on radio together with French, the official language. The three most important languages are Moore (Mossi), spoken as a first or second language by over half the population, mainly in the center of the country; Jula (a Mande variety), spoken in the west; and Fufulde (a variety of Fula), spoken in the east. These three languages are used over a wide area as lingua francas. Inhabitants of large towns tend to be multilingual, while bilingualism in the mother tongue and one of the main lingua francas is common. French, the language of education, government and administration, is only spoken competently by about ten percent of the population.

Burundi

Burundi, formerly administered by Belgium as part of Rwanda-Urundi (see Rwanda), became an independent monarchy in 1962. It has a population of 6.26 million (1995 estimate). French and Rundi (Kirundi) are the two official languages. Rundi is the same language as Rwanda (Kinyarwanda). Rwanda-Rundi is the Bantu language with the greatest number of first language speakers. Rundi is the mother tongue of over 99 percent of the population in Burundi. It is the first language of the Hutu (85 percent), Tutsi (14 percent) and Twa (less than one percent). Only one other recorded language variety exists as a mother tongue in Burundi, namely Hima, spoken by a few thousand speakers. Swahili is spoken as a second language by an estimated ten percent of the population. French is the language of education.

Cameroon

The Republic of Cameroon consists of the former French Cameroons (East Cameroon) and British Cameroons (West Cameroon) which gained independence in 1960 and 1961 respectively. East Cameroon and West Cameroon were joined in 1972. Cameroon, with a population of 13.5 million (1995 estimate), is a multilingual and multiethnic society. It is estimated that there are about 140–150 ethnic groups in Cameroon, speaking numerous languages and dialects, possibly as many as 300. English and French are the official languages, used in government and education, but French predominates, with the use of English being confined to the smaller Western region.

Because of the complex linguistic situation in Cameroon, bilingualism or multilingualism is the norm for the population. No one indigenous language predominates, although three are widely spoken. Fula or Fufulde, spoken in the northern part of the country, has over half a million first language speakers, and is used as a second language by up to four million others. Ewondo, the language of the capital, Yaounde, has over half a million first language speakers, the largest number of native speakers of any Cameroonian language, and is the lingua franca of the central region. Duala has less than 100,000 first language speakers but is widely used as a second language in the western region. However, the main lingua franca of the country is Cameroon Pidgin English. It is spoken predominantly as a second language by approximately two million people in the south-west and north-west provinces, but it is widely used in other areas, particularly major cities. Linguists have identified six major subvarieties of Cameroon Pidgin. Other Cameroonian languages have pidginized versions as second languages, for instance, Ewondo Populaire, a pidginized form of Ewondo spoken around Yaounde.

The fact that the territory of the Cameroon was formerly controlled by Britain and France means that there are varying attitudes towards use of indigenous languages in education. Following the tradition of the French, the government has given little importance to the use of indigenous languages in education. However, in the area of the former British colony, many private schools (usually mission schools) educate children in the local language for at least the first years of primary schooling.

Canary Islands

The Canary Islands comprise seven main islands and several smaller islands, most of which are uninhabited. The islands have been in Spanish possession since 1479 and are now divided into two autonomous provinces. The official language and main language of the population of approximately one million is Spanish. The indigenous Berber language has long been extinct.

Cape Verde Islands

The Republic of Cape Verde comprises the Cape Verde Islands, located in the North Atlantic ocean, west of Senegal (not shown on map). The former Portuguese colony gained independence in 1975 and has a total population of about 435,000 (1995 estimate). The majority of the population are of mixed African and European descent and are known as Creoles or mesticos. The official language is Portuguese, but the first language of 70 percent of the population and the main lingua franca is Crioulo, a Portuguese-based Creole. The remainder of

the population speak indigenous African languages, Balanta or Manjaku.

Central African Republic

Prior to independence in 1960, the Central African Republic was a French colony. It is estimated that about 50 indigenous languages are spoken. About 90 percent of the population of over 3.2 million (1995 estimate) also speak Sango, an Ubangi language that spread throughout the country during the colonial era. Sango is spoken as a first language by much of the urban population and a second language by almost the entire rural population. Sango became a national language in 1964 and an official language in 1991. French has been the official language of the Central African Republic since 1959. French is the medium of education in school and an important subject, but few people attain a high level of competence in it. French is used exclusively in written administration, but Sango is being increasingly used for official oral communication. Both French and Sango are used on radio and television but Sango predominates on radio and French on television. Official newspapers are in French. Since 1992, there has been an official policy of state bilingualism, encouraging the increasing use of Sango, particularly written Sango, in a variety of public spheres, including education.

Chad

The Republic of Chad was formerly a French colony which became independent in 1960. The population (1995 estimate) is 5.6 million. The country is home to numerous ethnic groups speaking over a hundred languages and dialects. Most of these are African languages, but dialects of Arabic are widely spoken in Chad. About half the population speak Arabic as a first or second language. A form of pidginized Arabic is used as a trade language.

Until 1979, French was the only official language, used in education and government. Since 1979, French and Arabic have been joint official languages, but in practice, French continues to be used as the language of administration, the media and the medium of instruction at all levels of education. Some Arabic medium primary schools and institutions of higher education exist, particularly in major urban centers. Chad national radio broadcasts in French, Arabic and eight African languages. All the languages of Chad have equal status as national languages and are used in local administration, regional agricultural training centers and health clinics.

Comoros

The Federal Islamic Republic of the Comoros gained its independence in 1975. It was formerly under the joint control of France and Madagascar. The Republic consists of three main islands, Njazidja, Nzwani and Mwali. A fourth island, Mayotte (Mahore), chose to remain under French administration. The Comorian people are of mixed Black African, Malagasy and Arab descent, reflecting the diverse waves of settlers. The official languages are Arabic and French, but the native language of the majority of the population is Comorian or Shafi Islam, a blend of Swahili and Arabic. Comorian is closely related to the Swahili of mainland Africa, but mutual intelligibility between the two is limited. Education at primary and secondary level is through the medium of French. The population is 549,000 (1995 estimate).

Congo

The Republic of Congo was a French colony until 1960. The population of 2.5 million consists of numerous ethnic groups, speaking a great variety of languages and dialects. The Kongo peoples constitute about half the population. Other major ethnic groups include the Teke and Sanga. French is the official language, but approximately 60 vernaculars have been recorded.

Nearly all Congolese are at least bilingual, and many are multilingual. Several languages are used as lingua francas and trade languages between ethnic groups. Lingala is widely used in the center and north, and Munukutuba (a Kongo-based creole) is the main lingua franca of the south. Both are widely used on radio and television and also in trade, small businesses and adult literacy programs. Several of the most important indigenous languages possess considerable bodies of literature, including religious literature. French is currently the medium of education at all levels but several indigenous languages are promoted in education.

Djibouti

Djibouti was formerly known as the French Territory of the Afars and the Issas. It became independent in 1977. This small country had an estimated population of 421,000 in 1995. The two principal ethnolinguistic groups are the Afar in the north (about 35 percent of the population) and the Issa in the south (about 45 percent). The latter are closely related to the people of Somalia, and speak a Somali variety which belongs to the northern cluster on which Standard Somali is based. French is the official language of the country, but both Afar and Somali are used on radio and both have the status of written languages. Arabic is spoken by 12 percent of the population, chiefly by traders from Yemen.

Egypt

The Arab Republic of Egypt has a population of over 62 million (1995 estimate). Most Egyptians are of mixed ancestry, having descended from Arab settlers and the indigenous pre-Arab population. A diglossic situation exists in Egypt, as in other Arabic-speaking countries. Modern Standard Arabic is the official language, used in public, official, formal and written contexts, while colloquial dialects of Arabic are spoken as a mother tongue and used in informal contexts by almost the entire population. (Classical Arabic, the language of the Qur'an, is used in Islamic worship). The Egyptian Copts, a Christian minority, represent five percent of the population. The Coptic language, the direct descendant of the ancient Egyptian language, has ceased to be used as a daily language, and the Copts speak Arabic as their mother tongue. Coptic is still used as a liturgical language in Coptic churches, but Arabic is used for sermons and Bible readings. The Nubians, living south of the Aswan, speak the Nubian language, which is also spoken in the Sudan. There are no official figures but it has been estimated that there may be as many as 250,000 Nubians living in Egypt. Small minorities of Italians, Greeks and Armenians live in the major cities. The 15,000 inhabitants of the Siwa Oasis, near the Libyan border, speak a dialect with a Libyan Berber component.

Egypt counts itself a francophone country, so French is the language of choice, when, for instance, diplomatic invitations are issued. But in practice, English is the dominant second language in the media and education. One prestigious university in Egypt, the American University in Cairo, teaches in English.

Equatorial Guinea

The Republic of Equatorial Guinea, a former Spanish colony, gained its independence in 1968. It consists of a mainland region, Mbini, and five offshore islands. The small country has a population of only 420,000 (1995 estimate) but the linguistic situation is complex and multilingualism is common. Spanish is the official language, used in administration, education and broadcasting. It is also used increasingly as a lingua franca. Six Bantu languages are spoken, and several creoles, notably Pidgin English (Weskos), which is spoken in major towns. French has become increasingly used, because of the influence of neighboring countries.

Eritrea

Eritrea was an Italian colony between 1890 and 1941. It was under British mandate between 1941 and 1951. It was forcibly annexed by Ethiopia in 1962, but regained its independence in 1993. The population in 1995 was estimated at 3.5 million, including one million refugees. The majority are speakers of the Semitic language Tigrinya. The official languages are Tigrinya, Arabic and English.

Ethiopia

The Ethiopian government estimated the population of the country at 53.2 million inhabitants in 1993. Two factors in the 1990s contributed to slight population changes in Ethiopia. Due to drought and war, over half a million refugees fled from Sudan and Somalia into Ethiopia by 1990 and as many as 1.5 million Ethiopian refugees had moved to Sudan and Somalia. Also, in 1993, the province of Eritrea gained its independence.

Between 70 and 100 languages are spoken in Ethiopia, with the most linguistic variety in the South West. The main languages are Amharic, Oromo, Tigrinya and Somali, with Amharic as the lingua franca being spoken as a first language by approximately 28 percent of the population and as a second language by a further 40 percent. Amharic is the language of the original inhabitants of Ethiopia, and its predecessor, Ge'ez (sometimes spelt Giiz), is still used as a liturgical language of the Ethiopian Orthodox Church, to which just over half the population belong. A third of Ethiopians are Muslims, using Arabic in their worship.

Ethiopia was relatively untouched by European colonialism, being the only African country that was not colonized by Europeans in the 19th century. This factor, plus the presence of the Ethiopian Orthodox (Coptic) Christian tradition, has affected the linguistic history of the country.

Only a minority of Ethiopians attend formal education (approximately 20 percent attend primary school and 12 percent attend secondary school). Thus languages are often transmitted informally in the community, and in relationships across communities, with many people becoming bilingual or multilingual without formal education. Bilingualism and multilingualism are the norm in Ethiopia.

Until 1974, Amharic was the sole national and official language, with English also being officially recognized. Amharic tends to be the language of government, the legal code and courts, and is dominant in the mass media. However, since 1974, official policy has acknowledged the equality of all the country's languages and recognized 15 regional languages: Afar, Amharic, Gurage, Hadiyya, Kambatta, Kefa-Mocha, Kunama, Oromo

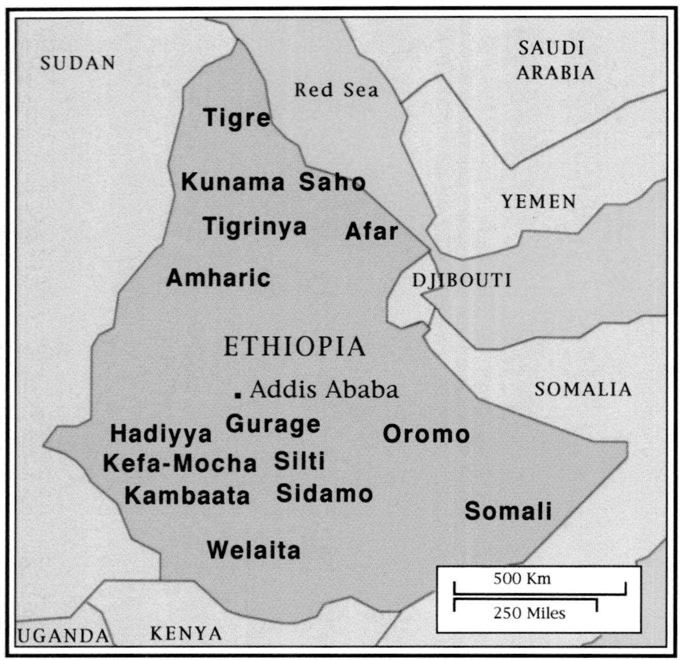

Some Indigenous Languages of Ethiopia

Saho, Sidamo, Silti, Somali, Tigre, Tigrinya, and Welaita. Since 1976, there have been mass literacy campaigns in rural areas, using these 15 regional languages. English appears on currency and postage stamps alongside Amharic, but is spoken by only a small educated minority of people.

The use of Amharic has increased during the 20th century, both as a first and second language, and in multilingual urban areas there has been a shift to Amharic as a mother tongue. The main reasons for the spread of Amharic have been urbanization, the media and education.

Mother Tongue Speakers in Ethiopia

Language	Estimated Percentage of Population	Estimated Size in Millions
Oromo	29.1	15.48
Amharic	28.3	15.06
Tigrinya	9.7	5.16
Gurage	4.5	2.39
Somali	3.8	2.02
Sidamo	3.0	1.60
Welaita	2.6	1.38
Others	19.0	10.11
Total	100	53.2

REFERENCE: National Office of Population, 1993

The 1994 Ethiopian Language Policy

Following internal wars and struggles in Ethiopia, a new language policy was adopted in 1994, attempting to create an ethnically fairer language policy. The new language policy stipulates the role of Amharic and English as well as other indigenous languages in the school curriculum. The new language policy directed that: (1) the language of primary education would be the language of a region. Thus, to a certain extent, mother tongues are allowed in primary education; (2) Amharic would be taught as the lingua franca for communication across Ethiopia; and (3) English would be the medium for secondary and higher education.

This potentially raises the status of local, indigenous mother tongues. The policy also allows such vernaculars to develop writing systems using the Roman Alphabet. Thus, the status of the Ethiopic writing system with its 275 symbols (which is used by most Ethiopians who are literate) has been challenged. The status of mother tongue language and literacy is being raised to try to bring about an accommodation of different ethnic and cultural identities (while also hoping that there will be national cohesiveness and a national identity through the lingua franca).

Since there are between 70 and 100 different languages in Ethiopia, it is not possible to accommodate all minority languages within the primary school system. Many of the minority languages that are used in the primary school initially lack educational materials in mother tongues, and also lack a sufficient number of teachers who can teach in and through these minority languages. Such a multilingual policy, while politically more appropriate, is pragmatically challenging.

The new Ethiopian language policy sees mother tongues having local usage, Amharic being the national language and English the international language. The outcome appears to give English a much greater place in the school system at the expense of Amharic. It may be easier to attain high standards of Amharic oracy and literacy than gaining competence and literacy in English as Amharic has wider usage and more communicative value in Ethiopia. Promoting English in the school system may also produce an English-speaking elite, with a social distance between those who are educated in English and the remainder.

A move away from a centralized nation towards regionalism includes trying to give equal treatment for regional languages. However, the multilingual situation of Ethiopia makes for a complexity that makes language planning difficult and constantly disputed.

Gabon

The Gabonese Republic, formerly part of French Equatorial Africa, gained its independence in 1960. The population of 1.1 million (1995 estimate) consists of approximately 40 ethnic groups, speaking over 50 languages or dialects, almost all of the Bantu family. The official language is French, used in government, administration and education. Because no widely spoken lingua francas exist, and because the school attendance rate is high, most individuals have at least some French, and French is increasingly used as a language of wider communication in the country.

Gambia

The Republic of the Gambia has a population of nearly a million (1995 estimate) and is one of Africa's smallest nations. The Gambia was a British colony until 1965. Numerous languages are spoken in the Gambia. The main indigenous language is Mandinka (a Mande language), spoken by about 40 percent of the population, living mainly in rural areas. The Fula are the second largest ethnic group in the Gambia, constituting about 12.5 percent of the population. Fula, like Mandinka, is spoken mainly in the rural areas of the interior.

Bilingualism in Mandinka and Fula is common in these rural areas. Another important language is Wolof. Although the Wolof ethnic group constitute only 12 percent of the population, they are a powerful and prestigious group, living mainly in urban areas on the coast, including Banjul the capital. Jola is the fourth most widely spoken language in the Gambia (6.5 percent). The Jola are almost always bilingual, also speaking Mandinka. Many urban Jola have adapted to other cultures, especially Wolof and Mandinka, and ceased to use their own language. A small, but economically powerful group are the Aku speakers. Aku is an English-based creole, the language of the freed slaves who settled in Banjul in the 19th century.

English is the official language of the Gambia, and the only language used in schools. Radio Gambia broadcasts news and cultural programs regularly in the main local languages.

Ghana

Ghana, formerly the British Colony of the Gold Coast, became independent in 1957. There are about 75 different ethnic groups in Ghana, and each group speaks a different language or dialect. Much of the population of 17.7 million (1995 estimate) are bilingual or multilingual, especially in urban centers. Most people living in the area where their first language is indigenous speak two or sometimes three languages, while people living outside their 'home' area typically speak three or more. The most important indigenous language is Akan, spoken by almost half the population as a first language, and widely used as a lingua franca.

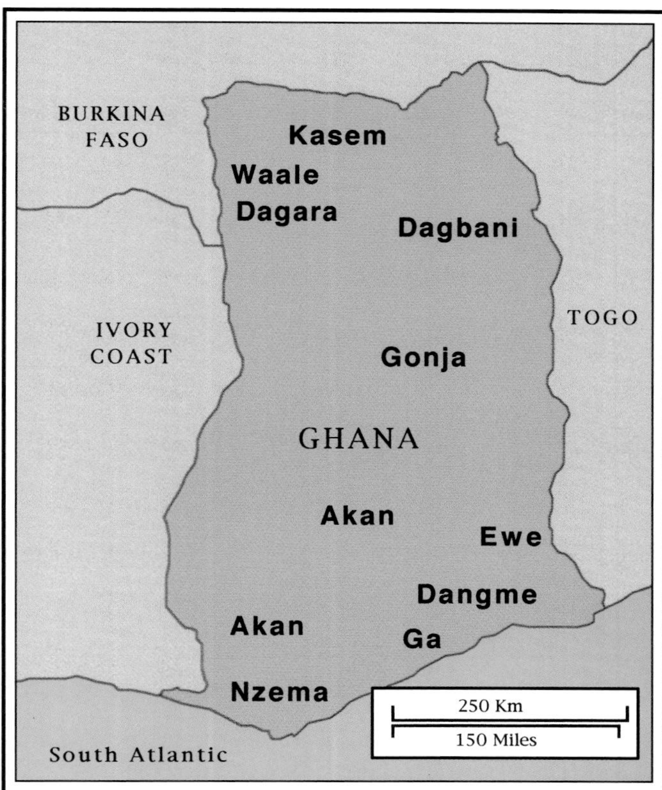

Some Indigenous Languages of Ghana

English is the official language. It is used in government, the media, large scale commerce and in education. For the first three years of primary school, indigenous languages are used to convey the curriculum, with English being used thereafter. Twelve major indigenous languages or dialects are officially recognized for use in schools: Akan (Asante, Akuapem, and Fante dialects), Ewe, Ga, Dangme, Nzema, Gonja, Dagbani, Dagara, Waale and Kasem. There are some radio and television broadcasts in the major indigenous languages but the majority of broadcasts are in English.

Guinea

The Republic of Guinea was formerly a French colony and became independent in 1958. About 25 different languages are spoken by various ethnic groups in the population of approximately 7.7 million (1995 estimate). The main indigenous language is Futa Jallon, a variety of Pulaar, spoken by about 40 percent of the population in

he central plateau. Maninke (a Mande variety) is spoken by 25 percent in the east. Susu is spoken by nearly 20 percent in the coastal areas. The main languages used as lingua francas are Maninke and Futa Jallon. French is the official language, used in education, the media and in government and administration. There are eight national languages: Maninke, Susu, Futa Jallon, Kissi, Basari, Loma, Koniagi, Kpelle (also a Mande language).

Guinea-Bissau

The Republic of Guinea-Bissau was formerly a Portuguese colony, but gained its independence in 1974. It consists of the mainland and numerous small offshore islands, most of them part of the Bijagos Archipelago. The population is just over 1.1 million (1995 estimate), and about two dozen vernacular languages are spoken. The three major vernaculars are Balante (the first language of 32 percent of the population, living mainly in the center), Fula (spoken natively by 22 percent, mainly in the north-east) and Mandinka (a Mande variety, mother tongue of 14.5 percent of the population, living mainly in the north-east). The official language of Guinea-Bissau is Portuguese, used in government, the media and education, but Crioulo, a Portuguese-based Creole, is spoken as a lingua franca by most of the population, and as a first language by many children of ethnically mixed marriages. When the country became independent in 1974 there were plans to develop Crioulo as the national language, but there were also fears that it would restrict access to the rest of the world. Bilingualism is common in the mother tongue and one main indigenous language, or in the mother tongue and Crioulo.

Ivory Coast (*Côte D'Ivoire*)

The Ivory Coast, a former French colony, became independent in 1960. It has a population of 14.8 million (1995 estimate), including about three million in-migrant workers and their families. There are more than 60 ethnic groups, speaking many indigenous languages or dialects.

French is the official language of the Ivory Coast, and the urban areas have been greatly influenced by French culture. In 1990, there were 3.5 million French speakers, nearly one quarter of the population. It is estimated that more than 60 percent of the population have some competence in French. A higher percentage can speak Popular Ivory Coast French, a kind of pidginized French.

In addition to French, two indigenous languages or language clusters are widely used as lingua francas, Jula (a Mande variety) and Anyin-Baoulé. Jula is the lingua franca of the Mande region where it is spoken by at least 60 percent of the population as a first or second language. Anyin-Baoulé is spoken in the south-east. It consists of a block of two closely related language varieties.

Kenya

The Republic of Kenya gained independence from Britain in 1963. The country had an estimated population of 28.8 million in 1995. About 54 language varieties are spoken in Kenya, some closely related. The five largest groups, with more than a million speakers each, are Kikuyu (20 percent), Luo (14 percent), Luyia (13 percent), Kamba (11 percent) and Kalenjin (6 percent). English and Swahili are the official languages of Kenya. About 16 percent of the population have some competence in English. Swahili is spoken as a first language mainly in coastal areas, but is spoken as a second language by almost 70 percent of Kenyans. Bilingualism and multilingualism are most common in urban areas where there is more language contact. Official educational policy is to encourage use of the mother tongue for the first years of primary schooling, thereafter making the transition to English.

Lesotho

Lesotho, formerly Basuto Land, was administered by Britain from 1868 until 1966, when it gained its independence. Nearly all the two million inhabitants of the country (1995 estimate) are ethnic Basothos, and speak Sesotho, a Bantu language. Other Bantu languages such as Zulu and Xhosa are spoken by small minority groups, but speakers of these languages typically speak Sesotho as well.

Sesotho is the medium of education for the first four years of primary school, then English takes over. Since many Basotho have only basic primary education, they remain monolingual in Sesotho. Only a few attain any degree of competence in English. English and Sesotho are the two official languages. English is used in government and administration, but Sesotho is increasingly used in areas such as religion, politics and broadcasting.

Liberia

The Republic of Liberia has its origins in the establishment of settlements in the 1820s by the American Colonization Society for the repatriation of freed African American slaves to Africa. In 1841, Liberia became an independent republic. It comprised the freed slave settlements and neighboring territory inhabited by indigenous African ethnic groups. The population was estimated at three million in 1995.

The linguistic situation in Liberia is diverse. At least 27 language varieties have been identified, grouped as 16 separate languages or clusters of closely related languages. The largest groups are Kpelle (a Mande variety), spoken by 20 percent of the population as a first language, and Bassa, spoken by 14 percent. None of the other languages is spoken as a mother tongue by more than eight percent of the population. Five percent of the population are descendants of the emancipated slaves, and speak an English-based creole called Americo-Liberian. Americo-Liberian is widely used as a lingua franca but has no official status. Two other languages used as lingua francas are Vai and Mandingo (both Mande varieties). Because of the linguistic diversity of the country, multilingualism is common. Typically a person may speak up to four languages, for example, English (if educated), Americo-Liberian, Vai or Mandingo and the mother tongue.

The official language of Liberia is English, used in the media, government, administration and education. Approximately 20 percent of the population are able to speak English. The indigenous languages are used on radio and in local administration. A program is underway to make use of all indigenous languages as media of instruction in early primary education.

Libya

The Socialist People's Libyan Arab Jamahiriyah comprises the former Italian colonies of Tripolitania, Cyrenaic and Fezzan. The country became an independent republic in 1951. The indigenous population is of mixed Berber and Arab ancestry. Arabic is the sole official language, and the native language of the vast majority of the 5.2 million citizens (1995 estimate). An estimated four percent of the population speak dialects of Berber, mainly in the few Berber-speaking villages in the south and west. Berber was the original indigenous language before the arrival of the Arabic-speaking peoples. Fifteen to twenty percent of the population consists of foreign workers and their families.

A diglossic situation exists in Libya, as in many other Arabic-speaking countries. Modern Standard Arabic is used as the official language, in government, public life, the media and education. Colloquial Arabic dialects are used in spoken, informal contexts. (Classical Arabic, the language of the Qur'an, is used in Islamic worship).

In Libya, English has become a most important foreign language. It is used as a means of instruction in science at college and university level. Both English and Italian are used in trade, and are widely understood in major cities, but the period of Italian colonization made little linguistic impact on the population as a whole.

Madagascar

The Democratic Republic of Madagascar comprises the main island of Madagascar and several small islands. I was a French colony until 1960. The vast majority of the population of approximately 13.8 million (1995 estimate are of mixed Malayo-Indonesian, African and Arabic descent. There are 18 main ethnic groups, comprising 98 percent of the population, but they all speak the same language, Malagasy, a Malayo-Polynesian language, tha has been influenced by Bantu languages and by Arabic and French. There are four main minority groups which together number less than 100,000: French, Cormorians South Asians (most of whom speak Gujarati) and Chinese. Malagasy and French are the official languages Since independence, the official use of Malagasy has increased. Both Malagasy and French are used as media of instruction in schools and at university. Governmen publications appear in Malagasy and French, and both languages are used in broadcasting.

Malawi

Malawi (formerly Nyasaland) was under British colonia rule until 1964, when it gained its independence. It is estimated that 13 indigenous languages are spoken in Malawi, The 1966 population census indicated tha Chichewa was the majority language, spoken as a native language by 50.2 percent of the population and as a second language by a further 25 percent. The present population is estimated at over 9.6 million (1995), not including refugees.

In 1968, Chichewa and English became official languages of Malawi, while minority languages were still encouraged. Chichewa is the medium of instruction for the first four years of primary education, and is then replaced by English. Chichewa continues to be taught as a compulsory subject. Parliamentary sessions are held in English only. Radio broadcasts are in English and Chichewa. Chichewa is used widely as a lingua franca between people of different ethnic groups, and is gaining ground at the expense of other indigenous languages Bilingualism is common in Malawi, as speakers of different languages learn Chichewa at school or work, and also use a mother tongue. Chichewa is the language o adult literacy classes. Chichewa has not yet supersede other indigenous minority languages in the home, bu this may happen as inter-ethnic marriages become more common. Trilingualism (English, Chichewa and a minority language) is also common among educated people.

Small British and Indian minorities also live in Malawi The recent civil war in neighboring Mozambique resulted in the influx of nearly a million Mozambican refugees

into Malawi by 1990, speaking indigenous Mozambican languages.

Mali

Mali was a French colony until 1960 and has a population of nearly 9.4 million people (1995). About 20 languages or dialects are spoken in the country. French is the sole official language in Mali, although it is only spoken by about five percent of the population. It is the main language of government and administration, of television and of education. Since the 1980s, four national languages, Fufulde, Songhai, Tamasheq, and Bambara, have been introduced in the first three years of primary education. Bambara, a Mande variety, is the majority language of Mali, and is spoken as a first or second language by 80 percent of Malians. It is gaining ground as a lingua franca and also as a home language at the expense of some other indigenous languages. Both French and Bambara are used on the radio.

Mauritania

The Islamic Republic of Mauritania has a population of 2.26 million (1995 estimate), including an estimated 224,000 Bedouin nomads. Mauritania, formerly part of French West Africa, became independent in 1960. About 80 percent of the population are Moors, of mixed Arab and Berber descent, and speak Hassaniya Arabic, a variety of Arabic which is not easily intelligible to speakers of other colloquial Arabic varieties. The remainder of the population are Black Africans, who mainly speak indigenous African languages. French is widely spoken by educated Black Africans. After independence, there was a long dispute between Moors and Black Africans about whether French should be retained as an official language, but in 1991, Arabic became the sole official language. Three other languages were granted the status of national languages: Soninke, (a Mande variety, spoken by about 30,000), Toucouleur (Pulaar) (spoken by about 250,000) and Wolof (spoken by about 120,000). The Berber dialect, Zenaga, is spoken among the Bedouins. Since 1988, Arabic has been the medium of instruction in all schools, although this measure was opposed by the French-speaking south. The state radio service broadcasts in Arabic, French and the other national languages. In Mauritania, like other Arabic-speaking countries, a diglossic situation exists, with Modern Standard Arabic being used in official life and education, and Hassaniya Arabic in informal and family contexts.

Mauritius

The population of the island state of Mauritius (just over a million in 1995) consists of the descendants of Arabs, Asians, Africans, and Europeans who settled in the island over centuries. The island was most recently a British colony, gaining its independence in 1968, and English has been the official language since 1810. French is spoken as a first language by almost ten percent of the population and also used in many official contexts. The main lingua franca is Mauritian Creole, spoken as a first language by 25 percent of the population, and in daily use by over half the population. About 20 other languages are spoken by small minority groups, including European and Asian languages.

Mayotte (Mahore)

Mayotte (Mahore) is one of the four islands of the Comoro archipelago. It is a French overseas territory and the official language is French. Mayotte has a population of about 97,000 (1995 estimate), mainly of mixed Arab, Black African and Swahili descent. Over two-thirds of the population speak Swahili as a first language. Most of the remainder speak Mahorian, a variety of Comorian, a blend of Arabic and Swahili also spoken on the other Comorian islands. A small minority speak a Malagasy dialect.

Morocco

In contemporary Morocco, the majority of the population are of mixed Berber and Arab descent. About 65 percent speak colloquial Moroccan Arabic as a first language. The remaining third are native speakers of Berber dialects living mainly in the mountains. There are three main varieties of Berber which are not always mutually intelligible, Tarifit (north), Tamazight (central areas) and Taselhit (south-west). The majority of Berber speakers also speak Arabic.

The official language of Morocco is Arabic. A diglossic situation exists in the country. Modern Standard Arabic is used in administration, education, mass media, some governmental offices and as a language of wider communication with other Arab countries. Moroccan Arabic is used in informal, oral situations. (As in other Islamic countries, classical Arabic is used in liturgical worship.)

Morocco was administered by France between 1912 and 1956 and French is still widely used in government, commerce and administration. It is studied and used as a teaching medium for over 50 percent of secondary school graduates, and it is the language most used by educated people. Some 15 to 20 percent of the population are estimated to be literate in French, but English, taught in schools as a foreign language, is beginning to gain ground at the expense of French.

Daily newspapers are published in Arabic and French. Part of Morocco, the north and part of the Sahara, was formerly under Spanish control and Spanish is still spoken in these areas.

Mozambique

Mozambique, a former Portuguese colony, gained independence in 1975. Portuguese remains the official language. Mozambique has a population of just over 18 million (1995 estimate). Numerous indigenous African languages exist in Mozambique belonging to the Bantu family. Eighteen Bantu languages have been identified, the

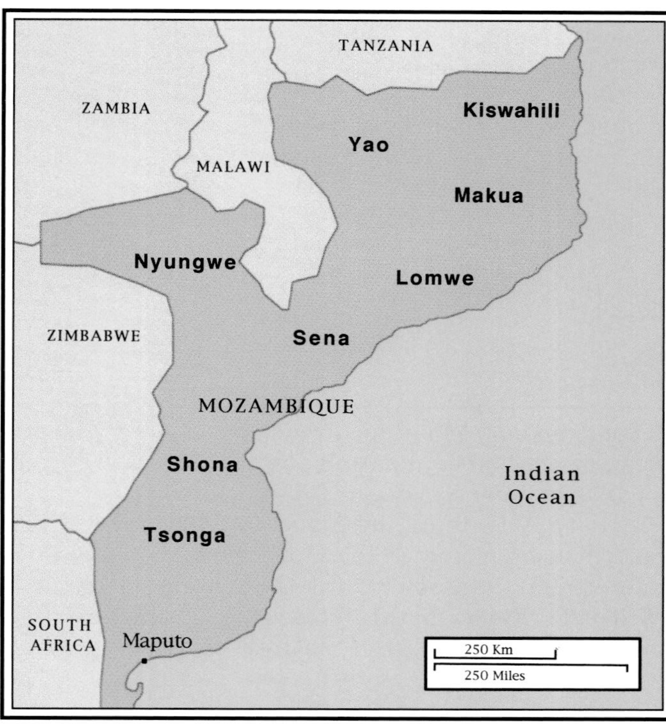

Some Indigenous Languages of Mozambique

largest language groups being Makua (around 7.5 million speakers), Tsonga (around 3.5 million), Sena (around 1.5 million) and Nyungwe (around one million). Only about one percent of the population speak Portuguese as a first language but almost a quarter of Mozambicans are bilingual in Portuguese and an African language. Some Mozambicans speak more than one indigenous Mozambican language. Portuguese is the language of prestige, the language of education, government and administration. Mozambican languages have no official status. Small minority groups speaking Asian languages also exist.

Namibia

Namibia (formerly South West Africa) gained independence from South Africa in 1990. Before independence English and Afrikaans were the official languages, while German had semi-official status within the administration of whites. Since independence, English has been the sole official language.

In 1995, the estimated population of Namibia was 1.6 million. Several African languages are spoken, and also English, Afrikaans, German and some Portuguese. The chief lingua franca of the central and southern areas is Afrikaans. In the Caprivi area, the main lingua franca is Lozi, a language also spoken in Zambia. Oshivambo is the first language of over half the population.

Before independence, the educational system made use of students' mother tongue as a medium of instruction in the first three years of school, subsequently transferring to English or Afrikaans. Since independence, English has been promoted as a language of national unity and of wider communication, and is the only medium of instruction in schools, with the major indigenous languages being studied as subjects until the end of the primary school phase.

Niger

The Republic of Niger, which gained independence from France in 1960, had an estimated population of 9.28 million in 1995. Ten indigenous languages are spoken in Niger, and they all have the status of national languages. The majority language and the main lingua franca is Hausa, spoken as a first language by about 53 percent of the population, and as a second language by about a further 30 percent. Other widely spoken languages are Songhai-Zerma, spoken by 21 percent, Tamashiqt, the Berber variety of the Tuareg nomads, spoken by 11 percent, Fufulde (a variety of Fula), spoken by ten percent and Kanuri, spoken by about five percent. Niger was administered by France until 1960 and French is still the official language, the language of government and administration, and all levels of education. However, less than ten percent of the population speaks, reads and writes French. Most inhabitants of Niger are bilingual in their mother tongue and another national language. The main national languages are used in adult literacy projects, radio transmissions and are taught in some primary schools.

Nigeria

The Federal Republic of Nigeria was administered by Britain until independence in 1960. The 1991 census indicated that the population of Nigeria was 88.5 million but other estimates have placed it at least 100 million. The ethnic and linguistic situation in Nigeria is very var-

ied. It is estimated that there are about 374 ethnic groups, speaking a total of over 440 languages. The largest groups are the Hausa and Fulani peoples of the north, the Yoruba of the south-west and the Igbo of the south-east. Hausa is spoken as a first language by about 20 percent of the population, and as a second language by a further estimated 20 percent. Yoruba is spoken as a first language by 25 percent and Igbo by 20 percent.

The 1979 constitution recognizes the three major indigenous languages (Hausa, Yoruba and Igbo) and stipulates that they may be used, alongside English, in the National and State assemblies. English is the official language of Nigeria, but is only spoken with some fluency by an estimated 10 to 30 percent of the population. While Hausa is the main lingua franca of the north, Nigerian Pidgin English is used as a second language by about 30 percent of population, mostly in the south, but increasingly in northern urban areas. Nigerian Pidgin English has been considered a low status form of English, but its increasing use means that it may eventually receive some kind of official recognition. Both English and African languages are used in the media. Educational policy is that the mother tongue or community language should be used in pre-primary and the first years of primary education, subsequently transferring to English. However, the great variety of languages and the fact that few of them have a written form means that this policy is difficult to implement. Many Nigerians would like to see an indigenous language as the official language of the country, but English has an advantage that it is neutral and does not exacerbate ethnic tension.

Réunion

The island of Réunion is an overseas territory of France, to the south-east of Madagascar. It was colonized by the French in the 17th century, who brought slaves from Africa to work the sugar plantations. The population of 666,000 (1995 estimate) is mainly of mixed African, Asian and French descent. There are also minority groups of Chinese, Pakistanis and Indians. French is the official language and the language of education, but a French-based Creole (called Réunion Creole French) is the most widely spoken language and is gaining in status.

Rwanda

The republic of Rwanda, formerly administered by Belgium as part of Rwanda-Urundi (see Burundi), became independent in 1962. The population of Rwanda consists of three main ethnic groups, the Hutu, constituting 90 percent of the population of 8.6 million (1995), the Tutsi (nine percent) and the Twa, a pygmy people (one percent). (These figures were calculated before the massive dislocation of population caused by the bitter ethnic conflicts of the mid-1990s.) Rwanda is unusual among African nations in that almost the entire population has the same native language, Kinyarwanda. Kinyarwanda is the same language as Rundi , the majority language of Burundi. It is the Bantu language with the greatest number of speakers. A small minority in Rwanda (about four thousand) speak Hima. French, English and Kinyarwanda are the official languages, the latter being used in the first years of primary education. Swahili is used by about ten percent of the population as a lingua franca.

São Tomé and Príncipe

The Democratic Republic of São Tomé and Príncipe consists of two main islands with a total population of 140,000 (1995 estimate). The uninhabited islands were discovered by the Portuguese in the late 15th century. They remained under Portuguese control until independence in 1975. The population of the islands is composed of descendants of African slaves brought to the island, in-migrants from Cape Verde islands and a few Europeans. Almost all the Portuguese left the islands after independence.

The official language and the medium of education is Portuguese. Varieties of a Portuguese-based Creole are widely used by about half of the population: Santomese and Angolar are spoken on São Tomé and Principense is spoken on Príncipe.

Senegal

Senegal, a former part of French West Africa, gained its independence in 1960. Numerous languages and dialects are spoken in the country. The dominant ethnic group are the Wolof, who constitute nearly half of the population of nine million (1995 estimate). The official language of the country is French, but the six most important indigenous languages have been elevated to the status of national languages. These are Wolof, Serer, Pulaar, Joola, Mandingo and Soninke. (The last two are varieties of Mande, a closely related group of languages widely spoken in West Africa.)

The language of administration and education (at all levels) is French, although Wolof is used in state-run nursery schools. Wolof is the main lingua franca of the country. Over 70 percent of the population can use or at least understand Wolof. In spoken contexts, Wolof can normally be used instead of French. Wolof is used as well as French in parliamentary deliberations. All six national languages and French are used in the media.

Seychelles

The Republic of the Seychelles consists of an archipelago of 92 islands and islets. The islands were under the control of France and then Britain from the 18th century, but gained their independence in 1976. Most of the population of around 73,000 are of mixed European, Asian and African descent. At least 95 percent of the population speak a French-based creole, known as Seychelles Creole French, which replaced English and French as the official language in 1981. Creole, English and French are all used in the National Assembly, in newspapers, radio and television. English is the main language used in schools, but Creole has been increasingly used as a medium of instruction since the 1980s. Also, the Catholic church has tended to make increasing use of Creole instead of French.

Sierra Leone

The Republic of Sierra Leone became independent from Britain in 1961. Eighteen languages are spoken in the country. Three main indigenous languages are spoken as first and second languages. Speakers of Mende (a Mande variety) in the south and east number about 30 percent of the total population of 4.75 million (1995 estimate). Temne is spoken by the other major ethnic group in the West. Krio, an English-based Creole, is spoken by the descendants of freed Black African slaves. In 1787, opponents of the slave trade founded a colony for freed slaves, Freetown, now the country's capital. By 1850, more than 50,000 former slaves had settled there. Krio is spoken as a first language by only two percent of the country's population, but is widely used in Sierra Leone as a lingua franca and trade language. The official language is English, used in government, business, administration, broadcasting, journalism and education. Attempts to use the main indigenous languages in education failed because of lack of printed curriculum materials, including dictionaries and grammars.

Because of social mobility and density of population, there is considerable language contact in Sierra Leone, resulting in widespread bilingualism and multilingualism. Many speakers of minority languages are bilingual in the mother tongue and one of the major indigenous languages, Krio, Temne or Mende. Many educated people also speak English. Arabic is used as a religious language by Muslims and also for some business and trade.

Somalia

The Somali Democratic Republic was formerly under both British and Italian colonial rule, but gained its independence in 1960. Ethnic Somalis constitute 98 percent of the country's population of 7.3 million (1995 estimate) and more or less the entire population speaks Somali. Some minority languages are spoken by small groups, but these languages have no official status and their speakers typically speak Somali as well.

In 1972, the government made Somali the official language of the country. A standard form was recognized, based on the northern dialect group and a written convention was established, using the Roman alphabet.

Arabic is the national language of the country. The majority of the population of Somalia are Muslims, and the country maintains close links with the Arab world. Somali is the language of the media and of education. Arabic is the most important second language in schools, while English and Italian are also taught.

South Africa

The Republic of South Africa has a total population of about 45 million (1995 estimate). According to 1995 estimates, the majority of the population (75 percent) were black African, 13.6 percent were white, 2.6 percent were Indian and 8.6 were of mixed race. Over half the white population are Afrikaners, descendants of Dutch settlers with a strong French and German element. According to 1993 official estimates, Afrikaans was the first language of 14.5 percent of the population, comprising almost all Afrikaners and many of those of mixed ethnic origin. English was the first language of 8.4 percent, comprising most other whites, and also some Asian, mixed race and black South Africans. Seventy-three percent spoke one of the nine official African languages as their mother tongues. Four percent spoke a variety of other languages, including Indian languages (such as Gujarati), Chinese, and European languages such as Portuguese.

Until 1993, English and Afrikaans were the only two official languages of South Africa. In 1993, the new constitution designated the nine most prominent African languages as joint official languages, although the use of English and Afrikaans still tends to predominate. The table below shows the nine official African languages and the number of their first language speakers as percentages of the total population. The nine African languages are all majority languages in different regions, and the new language policy allows for a regional or territorial bias in their official status and usage. However, the policy may be revised and refined to take account of the more complex, multilingual situation in the major urban areas.

Because of the multilingual nature of South Africa, bilingualism and multilingualism are commonplace, especial-

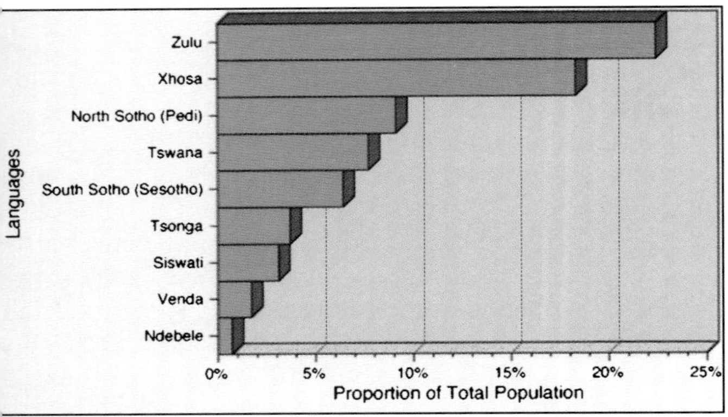

The official African languages of South Africa. (Source: Sidiropolous et al., 1995).

y among non-Whites. Afrikaans or English are the main languages of education, so first language speakers of these two languages receive their education in their mother tongue. Black African children are generally educated in their home language or one of the official African languages for the first four years of primary education, switching to English afterwards.

English and Afrikaans still predominate as the main languages of government but provision has been made for using the official African languages.

Sudan

The Republic of the Sudan is the largest country in Africa. Between 1898 and 1956 it was under joint British and Egyptian control. The country became an independent republic in 1956 and has a population of just over 30 million (1995 estimate). The inhabitants of the northern two-thirds of the country are mainly Muslims of mixed Arab and African ancestry. Other ethnic groups in Northern Sudan include the Beja, Jamala and Nubian people. About 60 languages are spoken in the northern areas, but most people also speak Arabic, the official language of the country. (About 50 percent of the total population of Sudan speak Arabic as a first language.) As in many other Arabic countries, a complex diglossic situation exists. Classical Arabic is used mainly for Islamic liturgical purposes. Modern Standard Arabic is used as the official written language and for formal spoken contexts, in government, schools, and for wider communication with other Arab nations. Sudanese Colloquial Arabic is the spoken form used orally at home and in informal contexts. An Arabic-based pidgin is also widely used in inter-ethnic communication.

The population of the Southern areas are mainly Black Africans, and about 50 minority languages are spoken in these areas. There has been considerable conflict between the Arab North and the African South. In 1972, the Addis Ababa Accord gave the three provinces of the Southern Region autonomy on most internal matters and established English as the working language of the region. Arabic is the official language of schools in the country, except in the Southern Region where English is used in many schools at all levels. The Southern Africans of the Sudan have a great loyalty to English and resist the encroachment of the Arabic language.

The Sudan government is encouraging the Arabization of the country, but has a policy of maintaining minority languages. The Addis Ababa Accord designated nine of the most important minority languages for priority in development. Multilingualism is common in the Sudan, especially in urban areas. Urban dwellers in the south might typically speak the mother tongue, another vernacular, Sudanese Pidgin Arabic and English.

Swaziland

The Kingdom of Swaziland became independent of Britain in 1968, and has a population of 967,000 (1995 estimate). More than 90 percent of the population are ethnic Swazi and speak Swati, a Bantu language. The official languages are English and Swati. English is the official medium of instruction in schools from the third year of primary schooling, with Swati being taught as a subject from then onwards. Both languages are used in government, administration and religion. Minority languages spoken include Tsonga and Zulu.

Tanzania

Tanzania became independent in 1961 and comprises the union of the two former British-administered countries of Tanganyika and Zanzibar. About 120 indigenous languages are spoken in Tanzania, almost all members of the Bantu language family.

In Tanzania, both Swahili and English are official languages. However, since independence, Swahili has been strongly promoted as the national language, and increasingly used instead of English (see page 124). Less than ten percent of the 28.7 million population of Tanzania (1995 estimate) speak Swahili as a mother tongue. However, almost all the remaining 90 percent now speak Swahili as a second language.

Swahili is used as the medium of primary education. In the eighth grade, children begin to learn English. Thus Tanzanians who complete secondary schooling are likely to be trilingual in their ethnic language, Swahili and English. The language shift is towards bilingualism in Swahili and English, and against the maintenance of ethnic community languages. There are 13 other main

ethnic languages. Sukuma is spoken as a first language by about 13 percent of the population, to the south-east of Lake Victoria. It is closely related to Nyamwezi, spoken in much of the east of the country by another five percent. Eleven other major Bantu languages are spoken by between three to six percent of the population.

Togo

The Republic of Togo was formerly administered by France, and became independent in 1960. The population of approximately 4.4 million (1995 estimate) comprises some 35 ethnic groups, speaking over 40 languages and dialects.

French is the official language of Togo, used in government, administration, education and commerce, but is spoken by only 30 percent of the population. Two indigenous languages, Ewe and Kabye, have the status of national languages and are used alongside French in the schools. Most Togolese are bilingual or multilingual, typically speaking their own native language or dialect, at least one language of wider communication, and also French if learnt at school. The Mina dialect of Ewe is the main lingua franca of Togo and is spoken as a first or second language by over 60 percent of the population. Kabye and Dagomba are widely spoken in the north. Four languages are used in adult literacy: Ewe, Tem, Kabye and Ben (a Mande variety). Hausa and Tem, used by nomads, can also be classed as lingua francas. Local Togolese languages are used in kindergartens.

Tunisia

The Republic of Tunisia gained its independence from France in 1956. The Tunisians are of mixed Arab and Berber descent, although only two percent of the population of almost 8.9 million (1995 estimate) speak Berber dialects. (Most Berber speakers also speak Arabic.) A diglossic situation exists in Tunisia, as in other Arabic-speaking countries. Modern Standard Arabic is the official language, used in formal, public and written contexts. Colloquial varieties of Arabic are spoken as a first language and in informal contexts by almost 98 percent of the population. French is still widely spoken, mainly by educated people. French is taught from the second year of primary school and is used as a teaching medium for most scientific subjects in higher education. Italian is increasingly spoken and understood through the media, and more people are learning English, because of its importance as a world language.

Uganda

The Republic of Uganda, a former British colony, gainec independence in 1962. Over 40 African languages ar spoken by a population of 19.5 million (1995 estimate) Luganda is the most prominent African language spoke in Uganda. It is spoken as a first language by about third of the population, and as a second language b another third. It is the main lingua franca of the south English, the official language, is spoken as a second lan guage by over 30 percent of Ugandans, and is the firs language of some educated urban dwellers. Swahili, th main trade language, is spoken as a second language b over 20 percent of Ugandans. Many other Ugandan have some minimal competence in either English o Swahili or both. Swahili is the language of the securit forces and has been promoted as a possible national lan guage. The use of local languages is supported by th government. The official policy is to use local language as media of instruction in primary education, but in practice, English or one of the regional languages is more often used.

Zaire

The Republic of Zaire, formerly the Belgian Congo gained its independence from Belgium in 1960. It is estimated that the population of 44 million (1995 estimate) consists of more than 200 ethnic groups, speaking more than 400 language varieties. (The majority ar Bantu languages, and many are closely related, makin it difficult to distinguish between dialects and separate languages.)

French is the official language of Zaire, used in government, education and business. Four African languages are widely spoken both as first languages and as lingua francas: Swahili in the east and south, Kikongo (Kituba) in the west, Tshiluba in Kasai, and Lingala along the

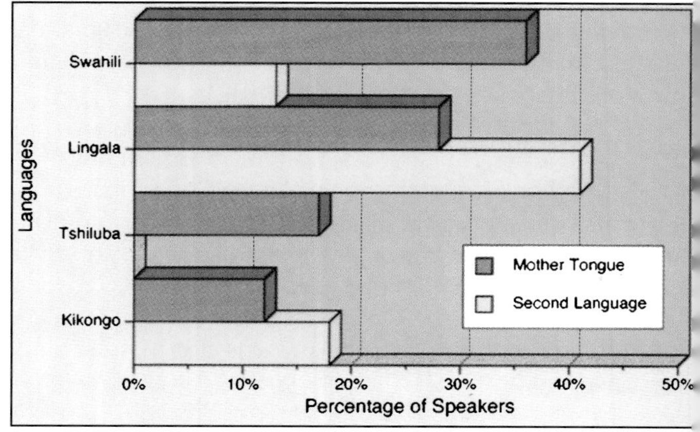

Main languages of Zaire.

Congo river. The World Bank (1987) provided estimated percentages of the total population using these four languages as mother tongues and second languages, and this is presented in a graph.

Lingala enjoys prestige as the language of the capital city, the army and national radio, and its use seems to be spreading. The regional languages are used as the media of education for the first two years of primary school, with a subsequent transition to French.

Zambia

The Republic of Zambia, formerly Northern Rhodesia, was under British control until independence in 1964. The population of 9.4 million (1995 estimate) comprises more than 70 ethnic groups, and about 25 to 30 Bantu language varieties are spoken. These have been classed into 16 separate languages or language clusters. English is the official language of Zambia. It is the language of government, business, and education. English is spoken as a first language by less than one percent of the population, and as a second language by only 30 percent, chiefly an educated elite. Seven African languages also have official status in the country: Bemba, Lozi, Tonga, Luvale, Nyanja, Kaonde and Lunda. Bilingualism in the mother tongue and a regional lingua franca is common in rural Zambia. In urban areas, the ability to speak three languages is common (the mother tongue, a lingua franca, and sometimes English). Bemba is the most widely used and understood Zambian language. It is spoken as a first language by 19 percent, and as a second language by 60 percent. Nyanja (also called Chewa or Chichewa) is spoken as a first language by 12 percent and as a second language by 40 percent. Nyanja is spoken by a total of ten million speakers in countries of Southern Central Africa, including Malawi, Zimbabwe and Mozambique.

Zimbabwe

Zimbabwe, formerly the British colony of Southern Rhodesia, became independent in 1965. English is the official language but is the mother tongue of no more than one percent of the estimated population of 11.1 million (1995). About 15 indigenous African languages are spoken. Shona, a Bantu language, is the first language of approximately 75 percent of the total population. Another Bantu language, Ndebele, is spoken by over ten percent. The country also has small minorities of Europeans, Asians, and persons of mixed race.

Asia

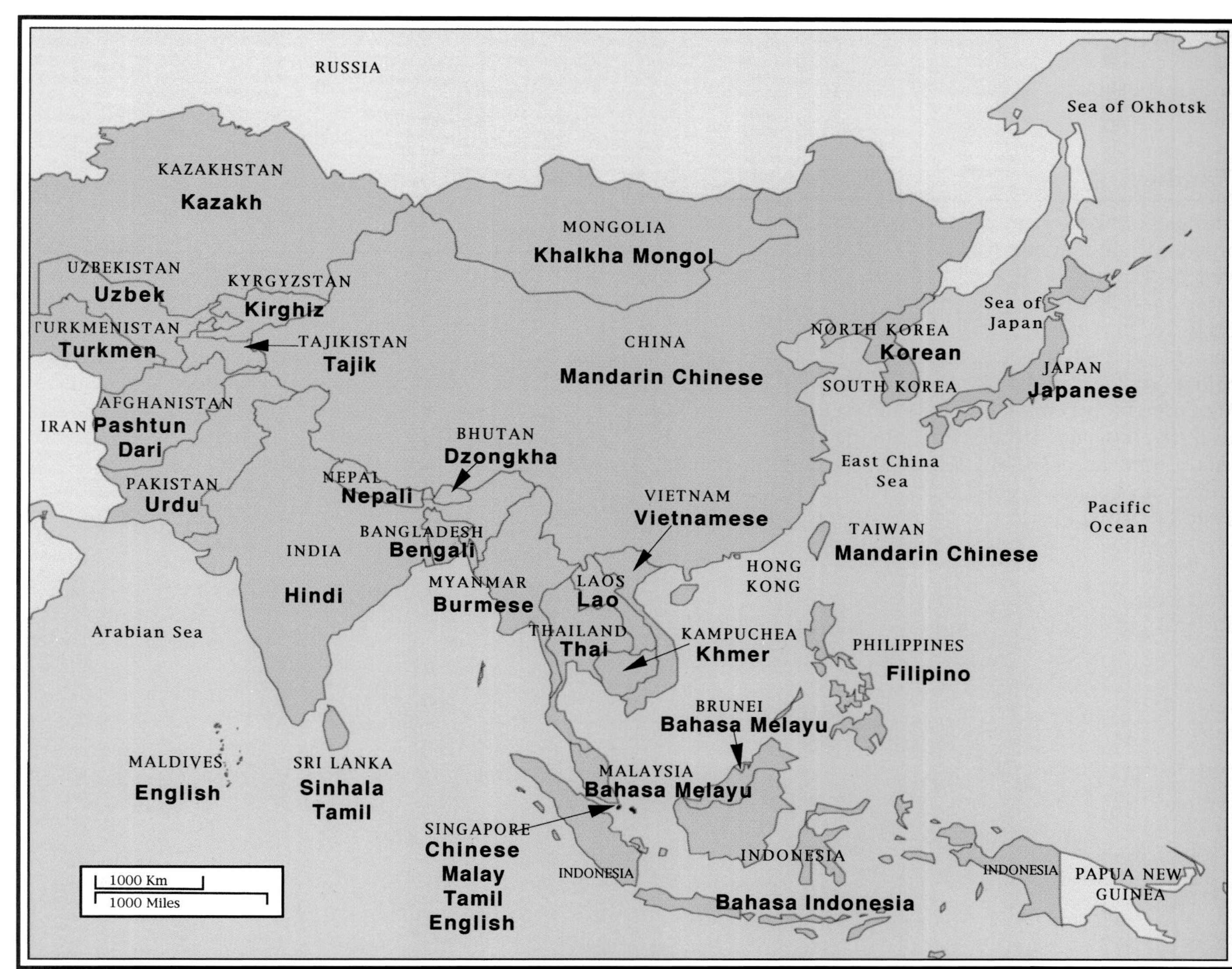

Official Languages of Central and East Asia

Afghanistan

Since 1964, Pashtun and Dari (a variety of Persian) have been the official languages of the Islamic State of Afghanistan. Pashtun is the language of the Pathan people, who account for just over half of the population of 21.25 million (July 1995). It is also called Pashto or Pushtu and is the majority language of the neighboring North West Frontier Province in Pakistan. The Pathan people are the economically and politically dominant group. They are to be found throughout Afghanistan, but are concentrated mainly in the east and south. Dari is the language of the Tajik communities, the second largest ethnic group, who account for 20 to 25 percent of the population. Dari is closely related both to Farsi, the majority language of Iran, and Tajik, the majority language of Tajikistan.

Together, Pashtun and Dari are spoken by an overwhelming majority of the population, and are the lan-

guages taught in schools. The provinces of Afghanistan are classified into two groups by the Ministry of Education. The first group comprise the provinces where Pashtun is the mother tongue and medium of education, with Dari taught as a second language. The second group is where Dari is the mother tongue, with Pashtun the second language. There appears to be a high degree of bilingualism in these two languages in Afghanistan. Although Pashtun has an extensive literature, Dari is used for cultural expression and for commercial and government business.

Some 11 percent of the population speak Turkic languages. Most of these live in the northern plains of the country. Uzbek is spoken by around nine percent, most of whom also understand Dari (Persian) or Pashtun as well. Turkmen is also spoken by a small minority.

There are around 50 minority languages in Afghanistan. Those with over 100,000 speakers are listed on the chart below. A great variety of languages are spoken in Afghanistan, belonging to a number of different language families, following centuries of migration throughout this region of Asia. Smaller language communities include Baluchi, which is spoken in the south and south-west of the country, and belongs to the same language family as Persian.

The Soviet occupation of Afghanistan (1979–1989) and the ensuing civil conflict have resulted in considerable social upheaval. One-third of the population have left the country to take refuge in neighboring countries such as Iran and Pakistan, some temporarily, some permanently.

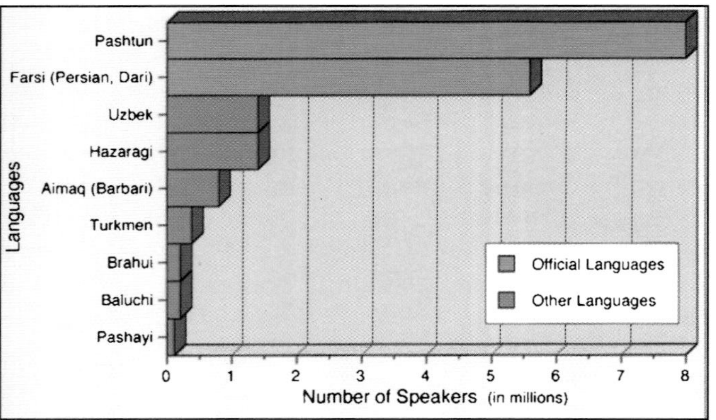

Languages spoken in Afghanistan.

Bangladesh

Bangladesh, formerly East Pakistan, became an independent nation in 1971. The name 'Bangladesh' means 'Bengal nation', and 98 percent of the population of 128 million (1995 estimate) are ethnic Bengalis and speak the Bengali language, an Indo-Aryan language. Bengali is also spoken by about 90 million people in the neighboring Indian state of West Bengal, and by sizable minority groups in other parts of India. There are over 200,000 Bengalis in the UK, about 150,000 in the US and over half a million Bengali workers in parts of Central Asia. It is predicted that the total number of Bengali speakers in the world will exceed 200 million by the end of the 20th century.

Bengali is the official language of Bangladesh and its use is obligatory in all spheres of public life. English is used as a second official language. Both Bengali and English are used as media of instruction in schools, colleges and universities and in the media. Educated Bengalis are bilingual in Bengali and English. A number of minority languages are spoken in Bangladesh, mostly by small groups resident in hilly regions. These minority languages do not belong to the Indo-Aryan family. Most minority language speakers, except for those living in remote regions, learn Bengali through schooling and from contact with Bengali speakers.

Bhutan

Bhutan is a relatively small country with a total population of 1.78 million (1995 estimate). The majority of the population are closely related to the people of Tibet in language, customs and religion.

About a dozen languages are spoken in Bhutan, all belonging to the Tibeto-Burman family, except for Nepali, which is Indo-Aryan. The national language of Bhutan is Dzongkha, a version of the principal language of Western Bhutan, and a descendant of classical Tibetan. Dzongkha is known throughout the country by members of the educated elite, and by those who have contact with dzongs (forts) or with large Tibetan Buddhist monasteries. The most important regional languages are Nepali, spoken by about 25 percent of the population, living mainly in the south-western foothills, Sharchop in the east, and Bumthang in central Bhutan.

Because of the linguistic diversity among the small population of Bhutan, English is the main language of the educational system from primary grades onwards. Dzongkha is taught for an hour a day in all schools. The Bhutanese Broadcasting Service broadcasts in English, Dzongkha, Sharchop and Nepali.

Classical Tibetan is also used as a liturgical language and the country's laws are written in this language.

Brunei

Brunei Darussalam is a small state on the north-west coast of the Island of Borneo. In 1995, the estimated population numbered around 292,000 people.

The official language of Brunei is Bahasa Melayu, or Standard Malay. It is the language spoken by the majority of the population, with about 69 percent of Brunei's inhabitants being ethnic Malays. The largest minority ethnic group in Brunei are the Chinese, who constitute 18 percent of the population. Other minority groups in Brunei include Indians, and various indigenous peoples, with 14,000 Dyaks, Ibans, and Lun Bawang living in the country. There are also around 20,000 expatriate workers from Europe and Asia.

The English language is also widely used in Brunei. It is one of the languages used in both primary and secondary schools, along with Bahasa Melayu and Chinese. Bahasa Melayu is closely related to Bahasa Indonesia.

In 1981, 22 percent of the population spoke Malay as their first language, with the largest bilingual group being those speaking Malay and English. Over 14 percent of people in Brunei were bilingual in these two languages in 1981.

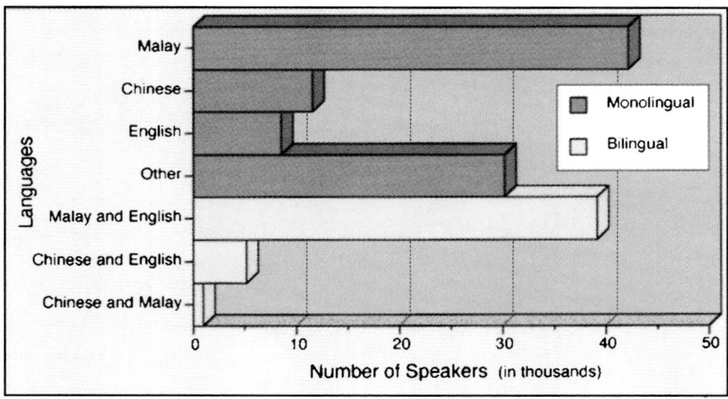

Languages spoken in Brunei. (Source: US Bureau of Census, International Database).

Cambodia

Cambodia, also known as Kampuchea, has a population of approximately 10.5 million (1995 estimate). Nearly 90 percent are ethnic Cambodians, known as Khmer. Their language, Khmer, is the sole official language of Cambodia. Cambodia was a French Protectorate between 1863 and 1953, and French was still widely used as an official language until recently. The present government, however, discourages its use. The remaining population includes Vietnamese (five percent), Chinese (one percent), and also small minorities of Laotians, Thai and Chaim-Malays.

China

It is estimated that more than a billion people, approximately one-fifth of the world's population, are speakers of some form of Chinese. Chinese belongs to the Sino-Tibetan family of languages. Within the Chinese branch, there are five main groups of dialects, Mandarin, Wu, Min, Yue and Hakka. Among these five major groups there are substantial differences in vocabulary and structure and many varieties of Chinese are thus mutually unintelligible. For this reason, some linguists prefer to view them as separate languages. However, the unified written tradition of Chinese and the strong sentiment of national unity and solidarity among Chinese people means that the Chinese themselves have always regarded their various vernaculars as dialects of a single language.

Approximately 92 percent of the 1.2 billion inhabitants (1995 estimate) of the People's Republic of China speak varieties of Chinese. Dialects of the Mandarin variety of Chinese are spoken in Northern China by about 70 percent of the total population. The dialects of this group are quite closely related, being mutually intelligible in varying degrees. This is the major dialect group in China, both in terms of political importance and in terms of number of speakers. The term 'Mandarin' is an English translation of the old Beijing expression *guan-hua* 'official language', which was for many centuries the dialect of Beijing.

The other four main groups of dialects are spoken by about a quarter of the total population of China, living in the south and south-east. They are much more disparate from the Mandarin dialects spoken in the north and are, for the most part, mutually unintelligible. The Yue dialects are spoken primarily in the southern province of Guangdong. There has been much emigration from this area to other countries and the Yue dialects are spoken in many expatriate Chinese communities in the United States, Europe and South East Asia. One well known Yue dialect is Cantonese, the language of Guangzhou (Canton), and many Chinese words borrowed into English, such as 'kumquat' and 'chop suey', are from the Cantonese dialect.

The Hakka dialects are spoken in small agricultural communities throughout southern China. These dialects are not well known outside China because there has been relatively little emigration among the Hakka people.

The Min dialects are spoken in the Fujian province in the south-east, on Hainan Island off the coast of Southern China, and in Taiwan. Most of the people of Taiwan and Singapore are descendants of Min speakers who emi-

rated from the coastal regions of Fujian province. For his reason, 85 percent of the people in Taiwan and most f the Chinese speakers in Singapore are native speakers f a Min dialect.

he Wu dialects are spoken in South East China, in the oastal provinces of Jiangsu, Zhjiang and Anhui, which nclude the major cities of Shanghai, Suzhou and Venzhou.

he classical written language, Wén-Yán, has been a neans of unifying the widely disparate spoken dialects of hinese. It is a logographic writing system, where charcters represent linguistic units or morphemes. Thus, the ame written language can represent widely differing prounciations and even different vocabularies. During the 0th century, the complex Wén-Yán has been largely uperseded by Bái-huà, a simplified written language ased on the contemporary spoken dialects.

)uring the 20th century, there has been a strong movenent for the promotion of a single standard, spoken lanuage, based on the Mandarin dialects and the pronuniation of Beijing. This language has been the official lanuage of China since the establishment of the People's epublic in 1949. In China, this language is called utonghua (common language) while in the West it is nown as Mandarin. However, since Mandarin can also efer to a wide variety of dialects, to avoid confusion, the tandard language is often referred to as Modern tandard Chinese. Putonghua is similar to the pre-1949 tandard, Guoyu ('national language'). It was officially efined in 1955 and adopted in 1956. Since then it has een the medium of instruction in schools and is increasngly gaining ground in public life and the media. lthough the aim of education is to increase knowledge f, and literacy in, Modern Standard Chinese, speakers f other forms of Chinese have not generally abandoned heir own dialects, and use the standard language as a econd language.

nother aspect of official language policy has been to acilitate the writing of Chinese. In the 1950s and 1960s, ver 2000 characters were officially simplified. Also, in 958, a Roman alphabet-based orthography called Ianyu Pinyin was officially launched. It is used with hildren starting school to help them learn Modern tandard Chinese.

ince the 1950s, because of political and geographical oundaries, the official language of China, Putonghua nd the official language of Taiwan, still called Guoyu national language', have come to differ from each other lightly in both vocabulary and grammar. One of the four fficial languages of Singapore, Huayu, is also based on the Beijing dialect. Again, it is somewhat different from both Putonghua and Guoyu.

An aim in language education in China is to increase knowledge of, and literacy in, the standard language. On starting school, children speaking the various Chinese dialects are first taught to write Pinyin, which is then used to help them master Modern Standard Chinese.

About eight percent of the Chinese population speak languages other than Chinese. There are currently about 55 minority ethnic groups in China, speaking a much larger number of distinct languages. Although minority language speakers only represent about seven percent of the population, over a quarter of the ethnolinguistic groups comprise over a million people each, and some of the minority languages are spoken over large areas of the country. In Northern China, the main minority language groups are Mongolian (four million), Tingus (4.5 million), Turkic (seven million), Korean (1.8 million). In Southern China, the major groups of non-Chinese languages are Tibeto-Burman (about 12 million), Thai (19 million) and Miao-Yao (about seven million).

Official language policies have been generally in support of minority languages. Minority language children are educated through the medium of their native language for the first three years of education. Alphabetic writing systems (mostly based on Pinyin) have been devised for some minority languages. There is also broadcasting and publishing in minority languages.

Cocos Islands

The Cocos Islands, (not shown on map) also known as the Keeling Islands, are a territory of Australia, consisting of 27 small coral islands in the Eastern Indian Ocean, only two of which are inhabited. The official language is English and the population of about 600 (1995 estimate) consists of both Europeans and Cocos Malays. Two-thirds of the population speak Cocos Malay, a local variety of Malay which is one of the most widely spoken languages in Southern Asia. Cocos Malay is used in broadcasting alongside English.

Hong Kong

Hong Kong is located at the south-eastern tip of China. It consists of a small area of only 1070 square kilometres, comprising Hong Kong Island, Kowloon and the New Territories, including the tip of the mainland and 235 outlying islands. Hong Kong Island was claimed by the British in 1841 and the rest of the territory became a British Crown Colony in 1897. Hong Kong reverted to China on July 1st, 1997.

According to 1995 estimates, the population of Hong Kong was 5.5 million, almost 98 percent of whom were Chinese. Cantonese is the most widely used Chinese dialect, spoken as a first language by over 88 percent of the population and as a second language by another 7.3 percent. There is widespread bilingualism in Chinese and English. English is spoken as a first language by over 100,000 people, but is more widely spoken as a second language by over a million people. Potonghua or Mandarin Chinese is spoken as a first language by only about one percent of the population, and as a second language by about 17 percent. Other varieties of Chinese are spoken, and in addition there are small minorities of Japanese and Filipino speakers.

Chinese and English are the official languages of Hong Kong, but English has been perceived as being more prestigious than Chinese. It has been the language of higher government administration and business, the medium of instruction in most secondary and tertiary educational institutions and the language of the law courts. However, there is currently a movement towards the greater use of Chinese in official contexts. Chinese was accorded the status of an official language in 1974 although the variety of Chinese to be used was not specified.

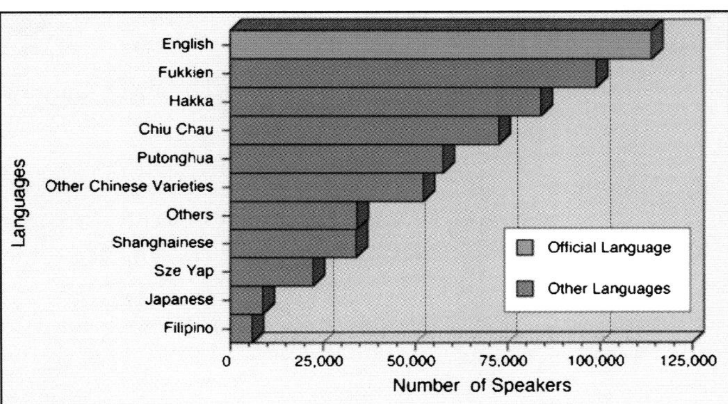

Languages spoken in Hong Kong. The official language, Cantonese, not shown on the chart, had 4.5 million speakers in the 1991 census. (Source: Hong Kong 1991 Population Census).

Usual Language and Second Language

First Language	Second Language			No Second
	Cantonese	English	Putonghua	Language
Cantonese	—	1,249,442	365,168	2,393,444
English	18,121	—	2,853	29,563
Putonghua	31,919	5,611	—	9,746
Chiu Chau	55,527	1,163	3,678	10,948
Hakka	63,019	871	4,016	14,419
Fukien	68,952	1,432	15,974	10,859
Sze Yap	14,096	287	378	7,453
Shanghainese	21,953	1,581	5,223	4,952
Other Chinese Dialects	36,481	573	4,439	9,169
Filipino	224	5,363	21	248
Japanese	668	5,699	206	2,234
Others	7,337	16,088	2,856	6,322
Total	318,297	12,88,110	404,812	2,499,357

Source: Hong Kong 1991 Population Census.

India

India is a country of great linguistic diversity. In the 1981 census, the population of 936.5 million (1995 estimate) were recorded as speaking 1600 separate languages or dialects. Two hundred distinct language varieties have been identified and 24 of these are spoken by more than a million people each.

Language politics play an important part in the recent history of India. During the struggle for Indian independence from Britain during the first half of the 20th century, Hindi and the closely related variety, Urdu, were promoted as symbols of national identity. When independence was attained in 1947, and when India and Pakistan were partitioned as two separate states, Hindi became the official language of India and Urdu of Pakistan. The non-Hindi speakers opposed Hindi as the official language, claiming that this gave Hindi speakers a superior status and an unfair advantage in employment and public life. The anti-Hindi movement was particularly strong in the 1950s in South India, with many riots and violent protests.

Many people supported the reintroduction of English as an official language, because of its neutral status, not favoring one ethnic group over another. As a compromise, English was given the status of an associate official language to Hindi for an indefinite period. Also the boundaries of the states were redrawn to correspond more closely to the boundaries of linguistic groups. The Three Language Formula was established, giving official status to Hindi, English and different regional languages in specified states. Most states have one predominant language, which is used as the official language of the state, plus several minority language groups (which comprise between four percent and 30 percent of the state's population).

In addition to Hindi and English, 15 languages have regional official status in various states. These are Assamese, Bengali, Gujarati, Hindi, Kannada (Kanarese), Kashmiri, Malayalam, Marathi, Oriya, Panjabi, Sanskrit , Sindhi, Tamil, Telugu and Urdu. These languages are used in schools and administration

English, although spoken by only about three percent of the population as a first or foreign language, remains important in government, education and science, a reminder of the British colonial influence. English is understood by many 'educated' persons and is used, for example, for correspondence between Hindi-speaking and non-Hindi-speaking states. It is also a language shared by the Dravidian-speaking south and the Hindi-speaking north. Hindi is spoken by an estimated 39 percent of the population, and is understood by a large number of other inhabitants. It is predominant in the northern and central regions.

Hindi and the other Indo-Aryan languages (including Assamese, Bengali, Gujarati, Kashmiri, Marathi, Oriya, Panjabi, and Urdu) are spoken mainly in the northern part of the country. The Dravidian languages (including Tamil, Telugu, Malayalam, and Kannada) are spoken in the four southern states. Sino-Tibetan and Austro-Asiatic languages generally survive only in small and isolated regions.

Multilingualism is quite common in India. According to the 1981 census, 13.3 percent of the population spoke a second language. Of these, 26 percent spoke English and 22 percent Hindi. A common pattern of multilingualism is that speakers of minority languages also speak English or Hindi, usually acquired through schooling. In accordance with the Three Language Formula, schools teach Hindi, English and another Indian language (usually the majority language of the state if that is not Hindi).

Indonesia

The Indonesian Republic, located in South East Asia, consists of over 13,000 islands, only half of which are inhabited. The larger islands include Sumatra, Java, Timor, Celebs and Moluccs. Indonesia also shares the governance of two islands. The Island of Borneo is shared with both Malaysia and Brunei, and the Indonesian region of Irian Jaya occupies the western half of the island of New Guinea.

Indonesia, with an estimated population of over 200 million, is one of the most densely populated countries in the world. Linguistically, Indonesia is a highly diverse country, with over 600 languages. The official language and the most widely spoken language is Bahasa

Languages in India at the 1981 Census

Language	Number of Speakers	State(s) where Languages are Located
Hindi	264,189,057	Uttar Pradesh/Madhya Pradesh/Bihar/Rajasthan
Telugu	54,226,227	Andhra Pradesh
Bengali	51,503,085	West Bengal
Marathi	49,624,847	Maharashtra
Tamil	44,730,389	Tamil Nadu
Urdu	35,323,282	Uttar Pradesh
Gujarati	33,189,039	Gujarat
Kannada	26,887,837	Karnataka
Malayalam	25,952,966	Kerala
Oriya	22,881,053	Orissa
Panjabi	18,588,400	Panjab
Assamese	10,000,000 (est.)	Assam
Bhili/Bhilodi	4,450,771	Madhya Pradesh/Rajasthall/Gujarat
Santali	4,208,304	Bihar/West Bengal
Kashmiri	3,174,684	Jammu and Kashmir
Gondi	1,954,693	Madhya Pradesh/Maharashtra
Sindhi	1,946,278	Gujarat
Konkani	1,584,063	Karnataka /Goa /Dadra/Nagar Haveli
Dogri	1,520,889	Jammu and Kashmir
Tulu	1,376,306	Karnataka
Kurukh/Oraon	1,264,590	Bihar/Madhya Pradesh/West Bengal
Gorkhali/Nepali	1,252,444	West Bengal/Sikkim
Khandeshi	1,186,921	Maharashtra
Manipuri/Meithei	904,353	Manipur
Ho	802,434	Bihar/Orissa
Mundari	752,683	Bihar
Khasi	632,443	Meghalalaya
Halabi	524,758	Madhya Pradesh/Maharashtra
Kui	507,639	Orissa

(Source: Asher, R.E. (ed.), 1994, South Asia. In C. Moseley and R.E. Asher (eds), Atlas of the World's Languages, Routledge.)

Indonesia. It is closely related to Bahasa Melayu, the official language of Brunei and Malaysia, but also includes elements borrowed from other indigenous languages of Indonesia, particularly from Javanese. Bahasa Indonesia was made the official language in 1945, when it was the mother tongue of only five percent of the population. Although this figure was relatively low, Bahasa Indonesia was chosen as it was the language associated with independence and nationalism. Since independence, the government has been active in developing, promoting and standardizing the Indonesian language, and extending its technical and scientific vocabulary.

The distribution of Indonesia's many languages is not even throughout the islands. In some regions, especially in western Indonesia, local languages have high numbers of speakers. There are over 70 million Javanese speakers, concentrated mainly on the island of Java. Languages in eastern Indonesia and Irian Jaya also have local importance, although the relative number of speakers are low, numbering in thousands rather than millions. The official language, Bahasa Indonesia, functions as the lingua franca throughout the islands.

In Indonesia, the state makes provisions for the development and support of some regional languages. The Ministry of Education and Culture ensures that many children are educated in their mother tongue at primary level, with Bahasa Indonesia taught as a second language. From the fourth primary grade onwards, the language of instruction is Bahasa Indonesia.

Main Languages of Indonesia

	Number of Speakers	Islands
Bahasa Indonesia *(Official Language)*	125,000,000	
Javanese	75,200,000	Java and Bali
Sunda	27,000,000	Java and Bali
Madura	10,000,000	Java and Bali
Minangkabau	6,500,000	Sumatra
Bali	3,000,000	Java and Bali
Aceh	3,000,000	Sumatra
Banjar	2,100,000	Borneo (Kalimantan)
Sasak	2,100,000	Lombok (Nusa Tenggara)
Batak Toba	2,000,000	Sumatra
Lampang	1,500,000	Sumatra

Japan

Japan is located in East Asia. It consists of four large islands, Hokkaido, Honshu, Shikoku and Kyushu, as well as the islands of Ryukyu, to the south-west of Kyushu, and over a thousand other islands. Almost the entire population of Japan (an estimated 125.5 million in 1995) speak varieties of Japanese, the official language. Because of the geographical nature of Japan, consisting of numerous mountainous islands, there is great dialectal variety, and many of the dialects are mutually unintelligible. The dialects spoken on the islands of Ryukyu constitute a distinct variety, and some linguists have preferred to view them as dialects of a separate language. (See page 162.)

Since the Meiji Restoration in 1867, there has been a strong movement for national unity in Japan. This has involved the promotion of a standard language, hyojungo, and the decline of local dialects. The use of the Ryukyuan dialects and other local Japanese dialects has declined because of the use of the standard language in schools and other public domains (e.g. the mass media).

The other indigenous minority language of Japan is Ainu, now almost extinct (see page 163). There are also small minorities of Chinese and Koreans. English has great prestige in Japan, but is not widely spoken, although students study it for six years in school.

Kazakhstan

Kazakhstan was formerly the Kazakh Soviet Socialist Republic and formed part of the USSR. It gained its independence in 1991 as part of the Commonwealth of Independent States.

Kazakhstan has been under Russian domination since 1866. Until recently, Russians outnumbered the indigenous Kazakh people. One reason was the large scale inmigration of Russians and other Slavic peoples since the 18th century. Also, the number of Kazakhs decreased as a result of attacks by Russian settlers and the forced collectivization of farms. Hundreds of thousands of Kazakhs were killed or emigrated to China. In recent years, the population of Kazakhs has increased and they now constitute about 42 percent of a population of almost 17.4 million, slightly more than the Russian minority (37 percent). There are also small minorities of Germans (4.7 percent) and Ukrainians (5.2 percent). The remainder of the population consists of smaller numbers of other Asian and European groups.

The official language is Kazakh, a Turkic language, but it is only spoken by the ethnic Kazakhs (i.e. 42 percent of the population). Eighty five percent of the population are recorded as being able to speak Russian, indicating that most members of other language groups are also bilingual in Russian. This reflects the high status of Russian as the main language of administration, business and education during the Soviet era.

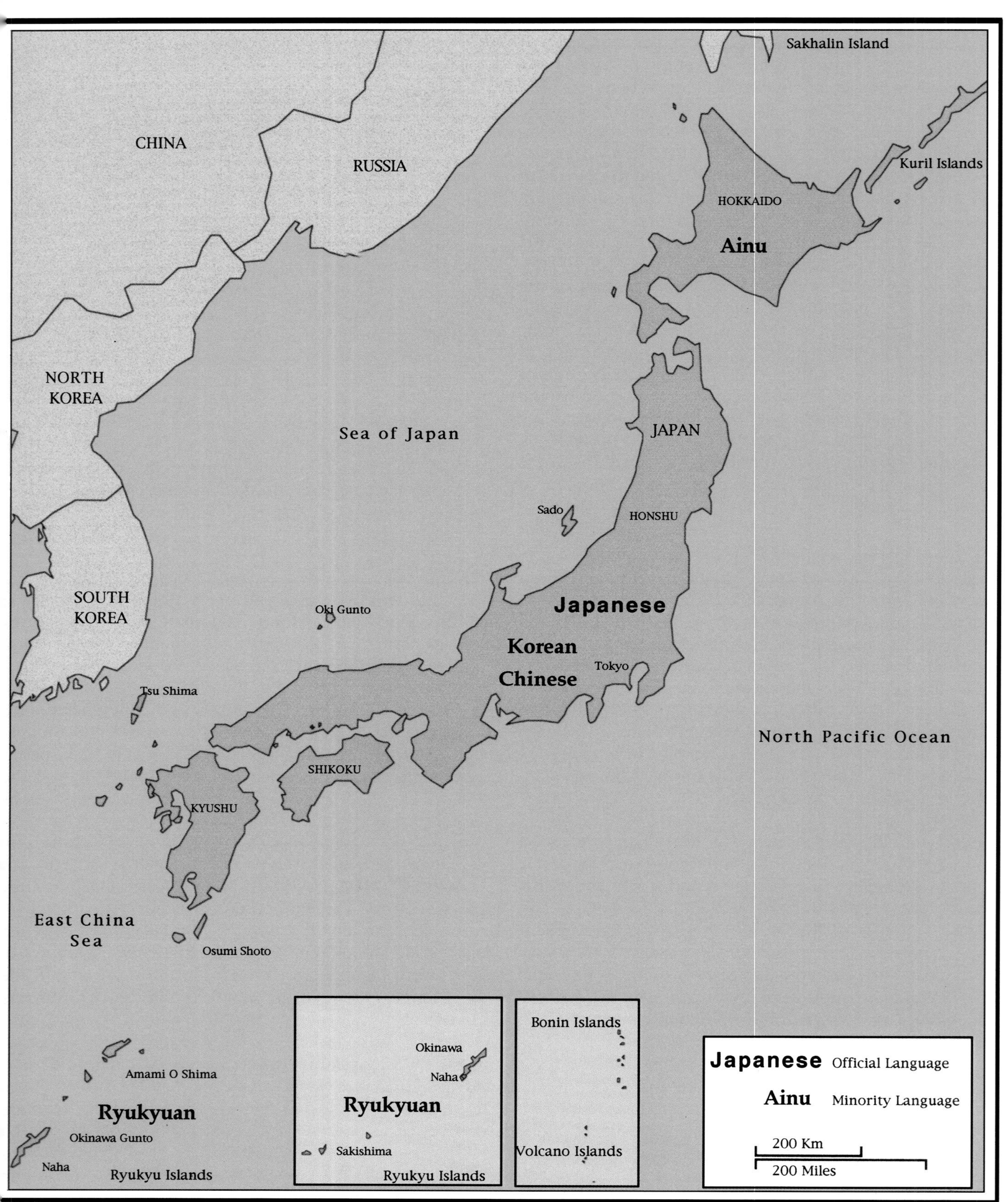
Sakhalin Island
CHINA
RUSSIA
Kuril Islands
HOKKAIDO
Ainu
NORTH
KOREA
JAPAN
Sea of Japan
Sado
HONSHU
SOUTH
KOREA
Oki Gunto
Japanese
Korean
Chinese
Tokyo
Tsu Shima
North Pacific Ocean
SHIKOKU
KYUSHU
East China
Sea
Osumi Shoto
Bonin Islands
Okinawa
Naha
Amami O Shima
Ryukyuan
Okinawa Gunto
Naha
Ryukyu Islands
Ryukyuan
Sakishima
Ryukyu Islands
Volcano Islands
Japanese Official Language
Ainu Minority Language
200 Km
200 Miles

Languages of Japan

Kyrgyzstan

Kyrgyzstan was formerly a republic of the USSR. Kirghiz territory was gradually annexed by Russia between 1855 and 1876, and many Russian settlers moved in. The Soviet imposition of a policy of collectivization during the 1930s had disastrous results. The Kirghiz resisted, and millions were killed, imprisoned or fled to China. For this reason, until recently the Kirghiz constituted less than half the population of Kyrgyzstan. The country gained its independence upon the dissolution of the USSR in 1991. The country has a population of 4.7 million (July 1995 estimate). The main ethnic groups are the Kirghiz (52.4 percent), Russians (21.5 percent) and Uzbeks (12.9 percent). The ethnic Kirghiz speak a Turkic language. Since independence, the government has pursued a policy of Kirghizization and de-Russification of the country. However, there has been a recognition of the need for ethnic tolerance, in view of the long-standing tensions between the Kirghiz and the Russian and Uzbek minorities. Kirghiz is the official language, but Russian is still widely used, and many people are bilingual in Kirghiz and Russia.

Laos

Laos, officially the Lao People's Democratic Republic, has a estimated population of approximately 4.8 million (1995). Laos is a country of great ethnic and linguistic diversity. Over 90 languages or dialects are spoken by different groups. The dominant ethnic group are the Lao, comprising 48 percent of the population. They live mainly in the lowlands and speak dialects of Lao, a language closely related to Thai. Lao is the official language of Laos, and the Vientiaine dialect is the basis for the standard form of the language.

Under colonial rule, French was the official language, and after independence in 1949, it continued to be the dominant language of government and higher education, until the Communist victory in 1975. Lao is now the sole official language of the country, and the only language used in government, education and mass communications. Lao is used as a lingua franca by many speakers of other languages. After decades of civil war in Laos, the government is trying to unite the country and create a sense of national identity. However, it is not an easy task to unite a country composed of so many ethnolinguistic groups, some of which transcend the country's borders. The government is conducting a campaign for mass literacy in the Lao language, and linguists are working on the creation of a technical, scientific and pedagogical vocabulary in Lao.

As well as the nearly two million speakers of Lao, there are approximately one million speakers of other Thai languages in Laos. Over 50 languages of the Mon-Khmer family are spoken by a total of 600,000 people. There are also 300,000 speakers of languages of the Miaow-Yao family living in high mountainous regions. Sixty thousand speakers of Tibeto-Burman languages live at lower altitudes. There are also small Chinese and Vietnamese minorities living in towns.

Dialects of the Lao language are spoken by more people outside Laos than inside. There are 15 million Lao speakers in Northeast Thailand, while sizable overseas Lao communities exist in both France and the US. The Lao language is similar to Thai, and in Thailand Lao is regarded as a dialect of Thai. Because of Thailand's cultural and economic dominance, most Lao people readily understand standard Thai. Thai radio and television is popular in Laos, and many educated people can read Thai. Through the mass media, Thai has influenced the Lao language, with many words and phrases being borrowed. Thai speakers usually have difficulty understanding Lao, because they do not have much exposure to it and because it is viewed as a low prestige variety of Thai.

Macau

Macau, an overseas territory of Portugal, consists of three islands off the south-east coast of China. It is the oldest permanent European settlement in the Far East, dating from the 16th century. Over 95 percent of the population of almost half a million (1995 estimate) are ethnic Chinese, speaking Cantonese. Only three percent are native speakers of Portuguese. Portuguese and Chinese are both official languages, and used in the media. Cantonese predominates in the education system.

Malaysia

Malaysia is divided into two main regions, Western and Eastern Malaysia. Western Malaysia lies on the peninsula south of Thailand where over half the population are ethnic Malay. In 1993, the population of the peninsula was 15.2 million, and out of this population, 56 percent were Malays and other indigenous peoples. Thirty four percent were ethnic Chinese and ten percent were Indians.

Eastern Malaysia includes the regions of Sabah and Sarawak on the island of Borneo. It is estimated that between a half and two-thirds of the population belong to one of the numerous indigenous groups which inhabit Borneo. The largest groups include Sea Dayaks (Ibans) Land Dayaks (Bidayuhs), Kadazans, Kenyahs, Melanaus and Muruts (who are known as Bumiputras). There are also ethnic Chinese, Indians and Europeans living

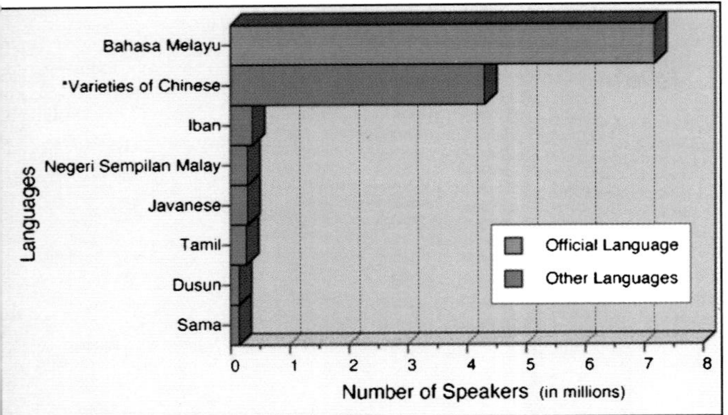

Languages spoken in Malaysia. Chinese varieties include Hakka, Mandarin, Min Nan, Mei Pin and Yue.

throughout Malaysia. The total population of Malaysia was estimated to be over 19.5 million in 1995.

The official language of Malaysia is Bahasa Melayu. It is spoken by most Malaysians as a first or second language and is the most important lingua franca. Bahasa Melayu is also the official language of Brunei on the north-west coast of Borneo, and is closely related to Bahasa Indonesia, the official language of the Indonesian Republic. Many other languages and dialects are spoken in Malaysia, including varieties of Chinese, as well as Tamil and English. Chinese varieties are spoken by around 30 percent of the total population, concentrated mainly in the Sarawak region. All the dialects have their own speech communities. The most populous is the Hokkien group, which numbers about a million speakers, followed by Yue (Cantonese) and Teochew.

Indian languages commonly spoken in Malaysia include Tamil, Telegu, Malayalam, Panjabi, Hindi, Gujarati and Urdu. English was the official language before Bahasa Melayu in 1957. It is widely used in law and medicine, the financial sector, trade and business and higher education. A Malay pidgin known as 'Bazaar Malay' and also a pidgin Chinese and a pidgin Tamil are all used as trade languages.

Maldives

The Republic of Maldives in Southern Asia consists of a group of atolls in the Indian Ocean, and has a population of 261,000 (1995 estimate). It gained its independence from Britain in 1965. The main ethnic groups are Sinhalese, Dravidian (from southern India), Arab and African. English is the official language, and the language spoken by most government officials, but the main language of the general population is Divehi, a language closely related to Sinhala, the language of the Sinhalese people in Sri Lanka.

Mongolia

The Republic of Mongolia, formerly known as the Mongolian People's Republic or Outer Mongolia, is situated in Central Asia. According to 1995 estimates, the population is almost 2.5 million. Ninety percent of the population are ethnic Mongols and speak Mongolian languages. The official language of the Republic is Khalkha Mongol (also known as Halh), spoken by 78.8 percent. Another 10.7 percent speak closely related Mongolian languages, some of which are regarded as dialects of Khalka. Kazakh, a Turkic language, is spoken by 5.9 percent of the population in the north-west. Uvin (Uriankhai), another Turkic language, is spoken by one percent in the north and west. Two other small minority language groups have been recorded, Evenki and Hoton (Northern Chinese), each with approximately 2000 speakers.

The Republic of Mongolia has had close links with the USSR from the beginning of the 20th century. Since the breakup of the former Soviet Union, the Republic has gained a greater measure of independence, but maintains close ties with Russia. A few thousand Russian speakers are permanent residents, and Russian is the most widely taught foreign language. Several thousand students go to study every year in Russia and other Eastern European countries.

Myanmar

Until 1989, Myanmar was known as Burma. Myanmar was under British colonial rule from the 19th century until 1948, and formed part of British India between 1885 and 1937. Over 100 distinct languages are spoken in Myanmar among the population of 45.1 million (1995 estimate). The majority and official language is Burmese, the language of the Burman ethnic group. This group comprises 68 percent of the population, living mainly in the more prosperous lowlands, and forms the dominant social and economic group. The Burmese language is the medium of trade, communications and education. Burmese belongs to the Tibeto-Burman family of languages and is distantly related to Chinese.

The largest ethnic minorities include the Karens and Kyahs (ten percent), the Shans (eight percent), the Chins and Kachns (four percent), the Chinese (three percent) and the Indians (two percent). Most of the minority groups live in the hilly regions and are relatively poor. Most minority language speakers also speak Burmese.

While the country was still under British colonial rule in the 1920s and 1930s, an upsurge in nationalistic sentiment led to the increasing use of Burmese instead of

English in education and public life. However, by the 1980s there had been a shift back to the use of English. English is widely used as a teaching medium in schools and is the only language used at university level. The single state run Burmese newspaper is published in both Burmese and English editions.

Nepal

The mountainous Kingdom of Nepal has a population of 21.5 million (1995 estimate). The official language of the country is Nepali, spoken as a first language by over half of the country's population, and as a second language by many more. Eighteen main languages were identified in the 1981 census, but it is likely that at least 35 languages are still spoken in Nepal. Nepali is strongly promoted as the 'language of the nation'; it is the sole language of education, administration, government and the law. English is also taught in schools. Until recently, Radio Nepali and Nepal TV only broadcast in Nepali and English, but from 1990, limited use has been made of Newari and Hindi. Many speakers of minority languages also speak Nepali. The other languages of Nepal have recently been given some official recognition.

Nepali is used throughout Nepal, especially in the east of the country, but in Tarari, in the south of Nepal, bordering India, Hindi is more commonly used as the lingua franca. In this region, there are calls to make Hindi a second national language. Tibetan dialects are spoken along the northern border of the country, identified as 'Bhote Sherpa' in the 1981 census.

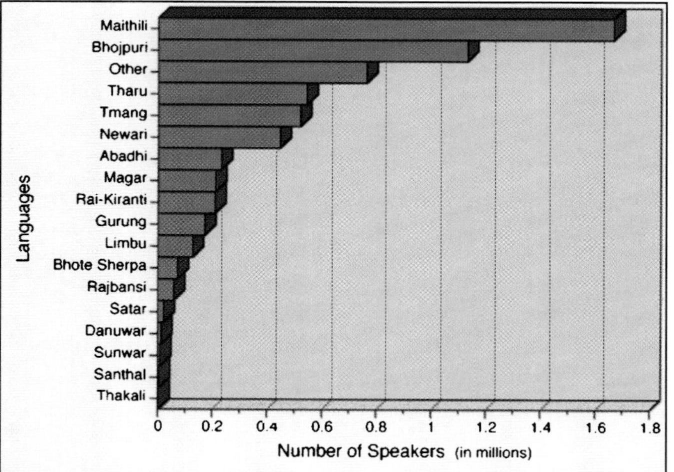

Languages spoken in Nepal, from the 1981 Census. The official language, Nepali (not shown on chart), had 8.76 million speakers in the 1981 Census. (Source: Bureau of Statistics, Kathmandu, 1981).

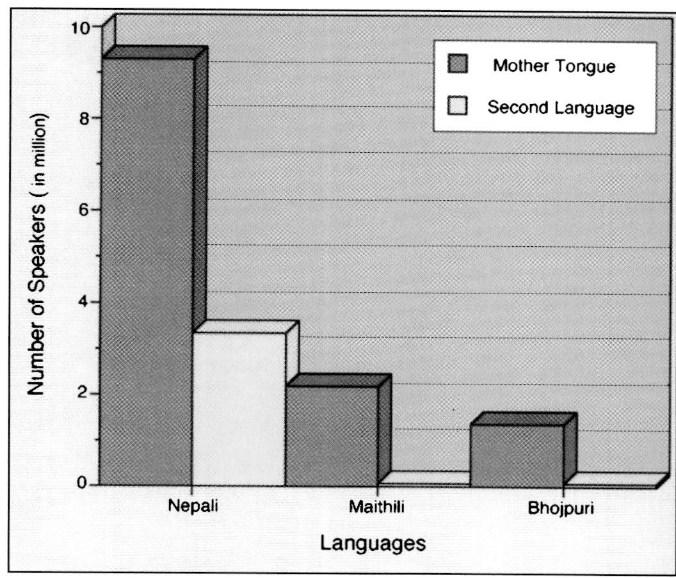

Number of mother-tongue and second-language speakers of Nepal's largest language groups. (Source: Bureau of Statistics, Kathmandu, 1981).

North Korea

In 1945, the peninsula of Korea was partitioned between the occupying forces of the US (in the south) and the USSR in the north. The Democratic People's Republic of Korea (North Korea) was established in 1948. According to a 1995 estimate, the population of North Korea was nearly 23.5 million. Almost the entire population speaks Korean, the official language, a member of the Ural-Altaic family of languages. There is also a small Chinese-speaking minority.

Pakistan

The Islamic State of Pakistan was created on August 14th, 1947, as a homeland for the Muslims of South Asia, by a partition of British India. The idea of partitioning India into separate Hindu and Muslim areas had originated in the 1930s. Pakistan originally consisted of two separate areas located about a thousand miles apart to the east and west of India. The two areas had no common linguistic or cultural heritage, but were united by Islam. Eventually, the eastern portion seceded in 1971, and became the independent nation of Bangladesh.

1995 estimates give the population of Pakistan as 131.5 million. The country is composed of many diverse ethnic and linguistic groups, following centuries of invasion and settlement. The Panjabis are the largest ethnic and linguistic group, comprising 64 percent of the population. (This figure includes about ten percent who are speakers of Siraiki, until recently regarded as a dialect of Panjabi).

The largest ethnolinguistic minorities are the Sindhis (12 percent) who represent the majority of the population in the province of Sind, and the Pashto or Pashtuns (13 percent) who are in the majority in the North West Frontier Province and have strong ties with Afghanistan. There are also the Baluchi (two percent) in the province of Baluchistan, and the Brahuis, a small Dravidian minority. The mountainous Northern Territories are home to a variety of diverse minor languages including Dardic (Shina, Khowar), Tibetan (Balti), and the isolated Burushaski. During the Soviet occupation of Afghanistan (1979-1989) and in the troubled years following, more than three million Afghan refugees fled to North West Pakistan and settled there. About half of these still remain in Pakistan.

The official language of Pakistan is Urdu. Urdu is spoken as a mother tongue by 6.7 percent of the population, the community of Mujahirs, or Muslim refugees from India who came to Pakistan in 1947. However, Urdu and the closely related variety Hindi, were prestigious literary languages in India for centuries and became symbols of nationalism and the desire for independence during the decades before 1947. Gandhi attempted to unify Hindi and Urdu as Hindustani, but because of the conflicts between Hindus and Muslims, this did not succeed.

Urdu is the medium of central government, administration, religion and broadcasting and is also used in education. It is widely spoken and understood as a lingua franca. English continues to be a high status language and is widely used in Pakistan, as in India, chiefly in government and business and by an educated elite. English-medium schools, colleges and universities continue to enjoy greater prestige than the officially encouraged Urdu-medium system.

Bilingualism and trilingualism are common in Pakistan. Although much of the rural population is monolingual, there are notable local patterns of bilingualism which include those between Sindhi and Siraiki in Sind, Baluchi and Brahui in Baluchistan, and Pashto and Hindko in the North West Frontier Province. Many people are bilingual in a local language and Urdu, and the urban elite are typically trilingual in English, Urdu and a local language.

No three language policy exists in Pakistan as in India, but the strongest provincial languages (e.g. Sindhi, Pashto, Panjabi), are used widely in the media and education, and there have been demands for increased official recognition for these regional languages alongside Urdu. The following table, based on data from the 1981 census, shows that Panjabi, Sindhi and Pashto are majority languages in their own regions.

Pakistan: Language Percentages by Household (taken from the 1981 Census)

Pakistan	% of Speakers
Urdu	7.6
Panjabi	48.2
Siraiki	9.8
Hindko	2.4
Sindhi	11.8
Baluchi	3.0
Brahui	1.2
Pashto	13.2

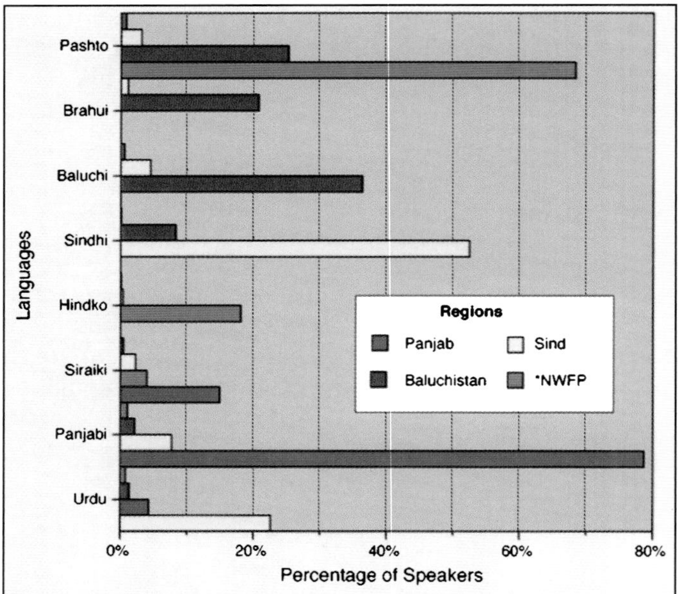

*Pakistan: Language percentages by region, taken from the 1981 Census. Note: *NWFP = North West Frontier Province. (Source: Shackle, 1994).*

Philippines

The Philippine Islands are situated at the northern end of the Malay Archipelago in the Western Pacific Ocean. The Independent Republic of the Philippines comprises approximately 7100 islands, most of which are tiny and uninhabited. The majority of the population of 73.2 million (1995 estimate) live on the 11 largest islands.

About 80 languages and dialects are spoken in the Philippines. The majority of Filipinos are of Malayan descent. Ten languages belong to the Malayo-Polynesian language family, and are of regional importance. The main Malayo-Polynesian languages are Bisayan, Talagog and Ilokano.

The Philippines were ruled by Spain from the late 16th century until 1898. Spanish is still spoken by a dwindling minority of Filipinos of Spanish descent. There is also a small Chinese-speaking minority, composed of in-migrants from China. There are two Muslim minority groups, the Moro and the Samel.

The official language of the Philippines is Filipino, based on the Tagalog language. Primary education is free and compulsory in the Philippines, and Filipino is the medium of education in all the state primary schools. However, English is also an important second language in the Philippines. Between 1898 and 1946, the Philippines was under US control and since the country gained independence in 1946, it has maintained close links with the US, which has military bases on the islands. English is widely spoken as a second language by the educated elite and is commonly used for government and commercial purposes and in the media. It is also widely taught in schools and used as a medium of teaching, especially at the higher levels of education.

Singapore

The Republic of Singapore comprises one large island and more than 50 small islets. It lies to the south of Malaysia, and is separated by a narrow strait, the Johor Strait. The island is one of the most densely populated countries in the world, and the majority of the population live in the south of the island. In 1995, there was an estimated population of almost 2.9 million.

Singapore has four official languages: Chinese, Malay, Tamil and English. The use of four official languages shows the diverse nature of Singapore's population and, within each language group, there are many people speaking various dialects of the languages. The Chinese form around 78 percent of the population of Singapore. The official variety of Chinese promoted by the government is a version of Modern Standard Chinese known as Huayu. Like the standard language of the People's Republic of China, Putonghua, Huayu is based on the Beijing dialect of Mandarin, but the two versions differ slightly in both vocabulary and grammar. Although Huayu is the official variety of Chinese in Singapore, a great number of Chinese speak other varieties of Chinese, as is shown on the chart.

The ethnic Malays form 14 percent of the population, from both Malaysia and Indonesia. There are about 396,000 speakers of Malay. Tamil is spoken around by 90,000 people, and ethnic Indians count for seven percent of the Singapore population. English has become a favored second or third language partly due to its value in Singapore's trade and commerce. It is the language of administration and is taught in most schools as a second language.

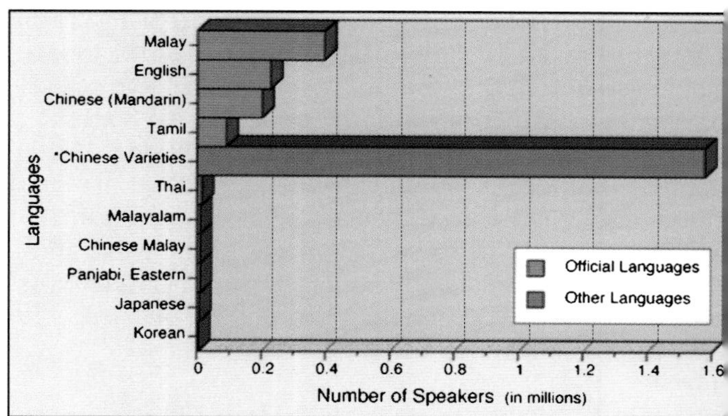

Languages spoken in Singapore. Chinese varieties include Hakka, Min Nan, Min Pei and Yue. Thai has 15,000 speakers, Malaysian and Chinese Malay have 10,000 speakers, Panjabi has 9500 speakers, Japanese has 7500 speakers and Korean has 5200 speakers. (Source: Singapore Department of Statistics, 1990).

South Korea

Following the post-World War Two partitioning of Korea between US and USSR forces, the Republic of Korea (South Korea) was established in 1948. Like North Korea, South Korea is one of the most linguistically and ethnically homogeneous countries in the world. There are no recorded linguistic or ethnic minorities and the entire population of nearly 45.5 million (1995 estimate) speaks Korean, the official language.

Korean is written in a phonetic script, called hangul. North Korea uses hangul exclusively, while, in the South, borrowed Chinese characters are used to supplement hangul. This practice is tolerated, but not encouraged.

The political and ideological separation between North and South Korea has accentuated linguistic differences between the two regions. The eventual reunification of the country is still an aim.

Sri Lanka

Sri Lanka, a former British colony, gained full independence in 1948. Seventy four percent of the population of 18.3 million (1995 estimate) are ethnic Sinhalese and speak Sinhala as their first language. Eighteen percent are ethnic Tamils, descendants of in-migrants from India, living mainly in the north and east, and speak Tamil as their mother tongue. Another seven percent are Muslims of Arabic descent and also speak Tamil as their first language. There are three tiny minority groups speaking Burgher (a pidgin based on Portuguese, Dutch, Sinhala

and Tamil), Malay or Veddah, an Aboriginal language. Together, these three groups comprise about one percent of the population.

English was the official language of the country until 1957 and is still widely used in government and administration. It is estimated that about ten percent of the population speak English as a second language, including many people in public and private sector administration. Sinhala and Tamil are both official languages and children may be educated in either language. English is widely taught as a second/foreign language in schools. Sinhala is used for all administrative purposes in all provinces except the North East province, where Tamil is used. Official documents are published in Sinhala, Tamil and English and these three languages are used in the media. Many educated Muslims are trilingual. They speak Tamil at home, are educated through Sinhala or Tamil, and conduct their business in English, Tamil or Sinhala.

Bilingualism in religion is common in Sri Lanka. In Buddhist worship, Sinhala and Pali are used; in Hindu worship both Sanskrit and Tamil are used; while Muslims use both Arabic and Tamil in worship and study of the Qur´ān in Arabic.

During recent years there has been ethnic conflict between Tamils and Sinhalese in Sri Lanka. While the Sinhalese have promoted Sinhala over English as a major marker of their ethnic and national identity, the Tamils have perceived the superior status of Sinhala as a sign of their own disadvantaged status.

Taiwan

After being under Japanese occupation for half a century, Taiwan was reclaimed by China in 1945. In 1947, the island was proclaimed a province of the People's Republic of China, but the Taiwanese people were not willing to recognize the Communist Chinese government. A rival Chinese government, the government of the Republic of China, was established in Taiwan and still exists. Long-term plans for a process of reunification with China are currently underway.

Eighty-five percent of the population of 21.5 million (1995 estimate) are ethnic Taiwanese. The Taiwanese are descendants of people who migrated from the coastal areas of South East China, and speak as their mother tongue, Taiwanese, a form of the Southern Min dialect of Chinese. About 14 percent of the population consist of mainland Chinese who have moved to Taiwan since the end of the Second World War. The mainland Chinese speak a variety of dialects of Chinese, including a version of Modern Standard Chinese, called Guoyu. Guoyu is the official language of Taiwan, the language of administration, education and most broadcasting, and its use as a first and second language is spreading. Guoyu was the official language of the whole of China until 1949. It is based on the Beijing Mandarin dialect. The official language of mainland China is now Putonghua, a redefined version of Guoyu, and because of the political and geographical separation, Putonghua and Taiwanese Guoyu are slightly different in vocabulary and grammar.

Ten percent of the population of Taiwan speak dialects of a variety of Chinese termed Hakka or Kejia. There are small minorities of speakers of other varieties of Chinese. About two percent of the population are Aboriginal peoples, perhaps related to people of the Philippines or Indonesia and speaking dialects of the Malay-Polynesian language group. Many older people retain a knowledge of Japanese acquired during the period of Japanese rule. There is much bilingualism and multilingualism in Taiwan, and this has increased with the spread of Guoyu.

Tajikistan

The Republic of Tajikistan (Tadzhikistan) was formerly the Tajikistan Soviet Socialist Republic. It gained its independence on the dissolution of the USSR in 1991. The population is 6.1 million (1995 census). The Tajiks, an Iranian Muslim people, comprise about 65 percent of the population. Their language, Tajik, is a Persian language, closely related to Farsi, the majority language of Iran, and Dari, the majority language of Afghanistan.

Tajikistan was part of Uzbekistan for some years in the 1920s, and both countries have sizable minority groups within one another's borders. Almost 24 percent of the population of Tajikistan are Uzbeks. Russians form 3.5 percent of the population. There has been ethnic tension and conflict over the years, and during the internal conflicts of the 1990s, Uzbeks and Russians left the country in large numbers, thus increasing the proportion of Tajiks. Other minorities include Kyrgyz, Ukrainians, Germans, Turkmen and Koreans. Tajik is now the official language, but Russian is still widely used in government and business. Most Tajiks speak Russian as a second language.

Thailand

The Kingdom of Thailand (formerly Siam) has a population of over 60 million (1995 census). Thailand has been a monarchy since 1350 and has never been colonized.

Eighty percent of the population are ethnic Thais and speak the Thai language. There are four main Thai dialects: Central Thai, on which the official language is based, Northern Thai, Southern Thai, and North Eastern Thai. North Eastern Thai is also called Lao and is the official language of the neighboring Republic of Laos. In Thailand, however, Lao is perceived as a low status dialect which speakers of Standard Thai find difficult to understand.

The largest ethnic minority in Thailand are the Chinese (12 percent). Over 50 other languages from various language families are spoken by small ethnic minority groups in Thailand. Other sizable minority groups are the Malay-speaking Muslims in the South, in the Northern hills, and Cambodian and Vietnamese refugees in the East. The governmental language policy is to promote only standard Thai as the official language, and to draw together all the diverse ethnic groups into a unified nation. About 97 percent of the population of Thailand can speak Thai. This indicates that bilingualism in Thai and a minority language is common. The main trade languages are Thai, Chinese and English. Japanese is frequently used in business circles. English is widely spoken by an educated elite.

Turkmenistan

Until independence in 1991, Turkmenistan (or Turkmenia) was the Turkmen Soviet Socialist Republic. The Turkmen people comprise about 73 percent of the population of just over four million (1995 estimate) and speak Turkmen, a Turkic language, which is the official language. The largest minorities are Russians and Uzbeks (about nine percent each). Other ethnic groups are the Kazakhs, Tatars, Ukrainians, Asians and Armenians.

Uzbekistan

Uzbekistan was formerly the Uzbek Soviet Socialist Republic. It became independent upon the dissolution of the USSR in 1991. Of the population of 23 million (1995), 71.4 percent are Uzbeks, and speak Uzbek, a Turkic language. Uzbek is the official language of the country. Russians comprise 8.3 percent of the population, living primarily in urban areas. There has been ethnic conflict in Uzbekistan, as in some other former Soviet countries, and the size of the Russian minority has decreased as Russians have emigrated to Russia and elsewhere. Tajiks, speakers of Tajik, a Persian language, comprise 4.5 percent of the population, living primarily in the cities. Other minorities include the Tatars, Karakalpaks, Koreans, Kirghiz, Ukrainians, Turkmens and Turks.

Vietnam

The Socialist Republic of Vietnam is situated in South East Asia. Nearly 90 percent of the population of almost 74.4 million (1995 estimate) are ethnic Vietnamese and speak the Vietnamese language. This includes over a million Vietnamese living in other countries. Vietnamese is the official language of Vietnam, and the majority language in all areas of the country. Over 50 minority languages are also spoken in Vietnam. A variety of languages are spoken by the 'montagnards', three million people of various ethnic groups living in the central highlands and mountains of the North. Khmer (Cambodian) is spoken by half a million people and Cham by 50,000 people. Most speakers of minority languages also speak Vietnamese. The official language policy of Vietnam has been to maintain and promote minority languages and protect and develop the rights of their speakers.

Vietnam was ruled by China for eleven centuries, between the 1st century BC and the 10th century AD. The Chinese language had a great influence on Vietnamese. Over half the words in the Vietnamese lexicon are borrowed from Chinese. Many Chinese migrated to Vietnam during the 17th and 18th centuries and settled mainly in urban areas, becoming involved in commerce, manufacturing, fishing and coal mining. During pre-colonial and colonial periods, the Chinese were placed under a separate administration. Recent governments, however, have attempted to assimilate them. Thousands of ethnic Chinese left the country after the reunification of Vietnam in 1976 because of a government decision to nationalize commerce and industry in the south. It is estimated that two million still live in Vietnam, representing about three percent of the total population.

French was spoken widely in Vietnam as a second language during the period of French colonization (1880–1945), and was still used in South Vietnam during the period of partition (1954–1976). Its use has now decreased. Vietnamese replaced French as the language of education in 1945. During the period of French colonial administration, French was widely spoken in urban areas, and many older city dwellers are bilingual in French and Vietnamese. French has had relatively less influence than Chinese on the Vietnamese language, but a large number of loan words from French are used in the speech of urban areas. French remains the official language in diplomatic and international political contacts.

Australia and New Zealand

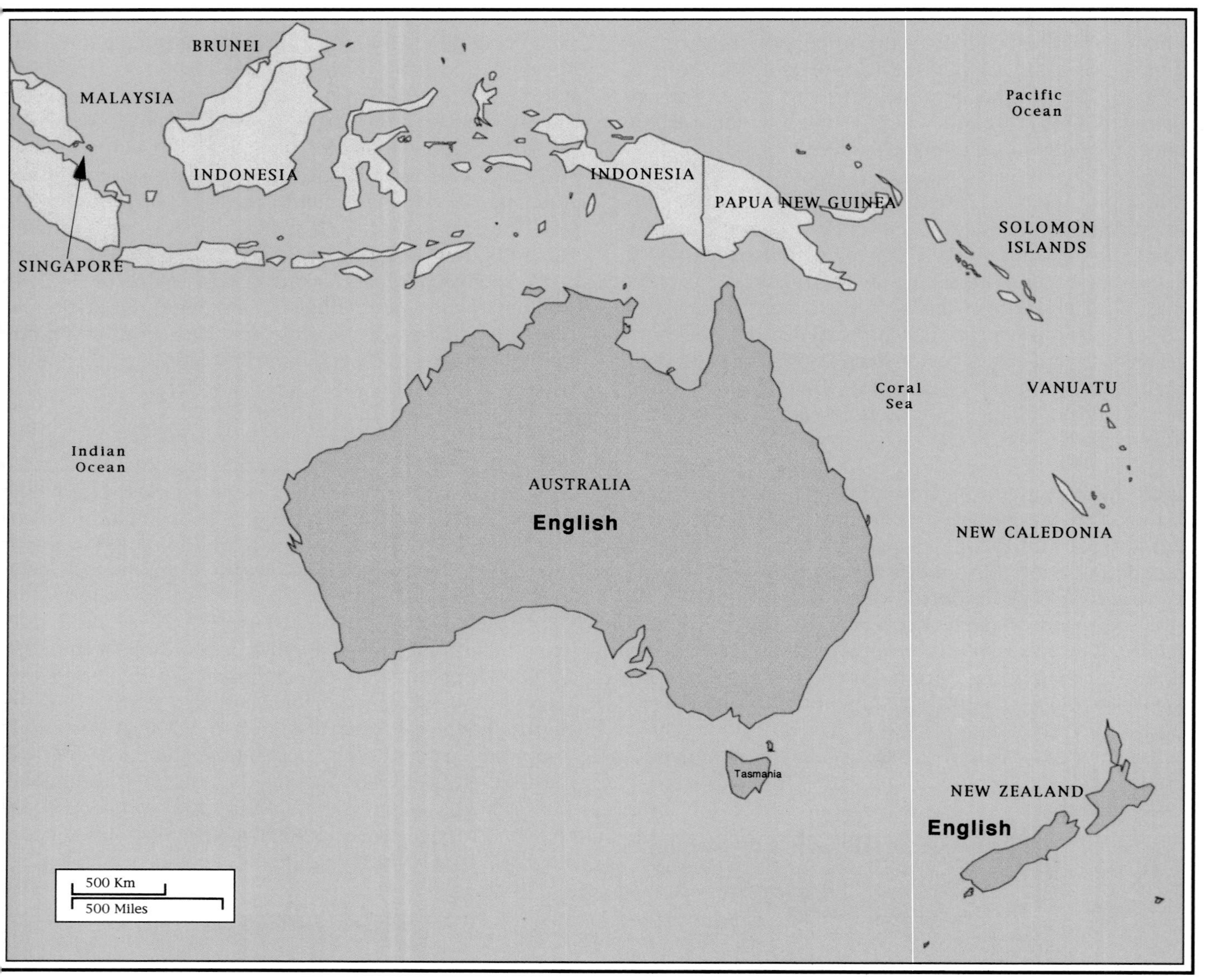

Official Languages of Australia and New Zealand

Australia

Australia, the sixth largest country in the world, had an estimated population of almost 17 million in the 1991 Census. Ninety percent of the population are of European descent, mainly British. The remaining ten percent include the indigenous Aboriginal peoples, who constitute 1.5 percent, and in-migrants from other parts of the world, notably Asia. The current Australian population, according to the 1991 Census, were born in the following areas:

Australia	75.4%	Rest of Oceania	2.1%
Europe	13.6%	North and South America	0.9%
Asia	4.9%	Africa	0.8%
Other	2.2%		

The official language of Australia is English, which is spoken by 82.6 percent of the population as their first language. Almost all of the remaining population speak a variety of different in-migrant languages, reflecting the vast migration to Australia from European countries, especially after the Second World War. In the 1991 Census, 17.4 percent (2,710,136) of the population of Australians claimed to use a language other than English at home. The most widely used European in-migrant languages are Italian, German, Greek, Macedonian, Maltese, Polish and Spanish. Among the Asian in-migrant people, Chinese, Filipino and Vietnamese languages form the largest language groups.

In total, about 100 community languages are in daily use in Australia. However, the tendency among minority language groups in Australia is for language shift to English to occur within one or two generations. (See page 158.) Official government policy until the 1970s was to help in-migrants to learn English as quickly as possible, by means of extensive 'English as a second language' teaching programs for children and adults. There was no official provision for minority language maintenance.

Since the 1970s, the government has moved from an assimilationist policy to a policy that shows some concern for community languages. Currently, there is widespread educational provision for community languages at primary and secondary level, and some successful bilingual programs have been run. However, the level of provision varies between regions. (Immersion education is also gaining in popularity, in languages such as German, French, Indonesian and Japanese – see page 496f.) Bilingual programs are found mostly in inner-city areas where the majority of in-migrants have settled.

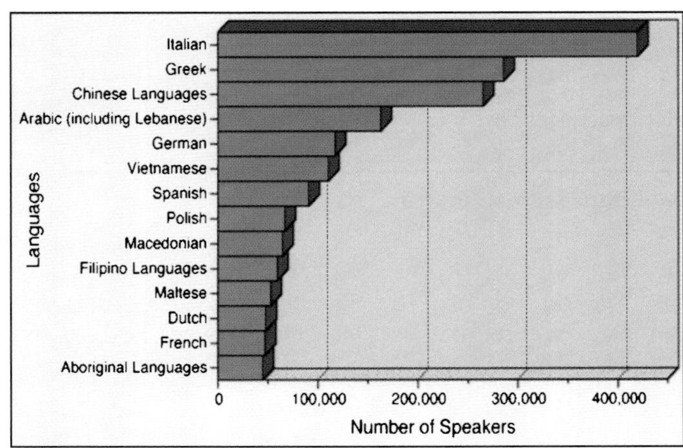

Languages used by the Australian population in the 1991 Census. The official language, English, not shown on the chart, has 14 million first language speakers. (Source: Smolicz, 1994).

The original inhabitants, the Australian Aborigines, constitute 1.6 percent (265,378) of the population based on the 1991 Census. (See page 104). Since the Europeans colonized Australia in the 18th century, the Aboriginal languages have been in decline and many have become extinct. It is estimated that there were over 260 Aboriginal languages spoken, comprising between 500 and 600 dialect varieties. None of the 150 Aboriginal languages still living is spoken by more than three thousand speakers and many have very few speakers, numbering between a few hundred and half a dozen. One of the largest Aboriginal languages is Kala Lagaw Ya, which has three thousand speakers in the Queensland area of Australia. Western and Eastern Aranda is spoken by two thousand Aborigines, mainly in areas surrounding the city of Alice Springs. Pitjantjatjara, spoken in northwest Australia, and Anindilyakwa, both have around a thousand speakers. Most Aborigines are bilingual in their mother tongue and English. Bilingual education in Aboriginal languages, mainly for Aboriginal communities, is increasing, especially in the Northern Territories. (See page 509.)

New Zealand

New Zealand comprises two large islands, North and South Island, and several smaller ones, including Cook Island, Niue and Tokelau. The total population is almost three and a half million people, three-quarters of whom live on North Island.

The official language is English. According to the 1986 Census, approximately 82 percent of New Zealanders are Pakeha, the Maori word for European settlers. Most of these settlers are of British descent. The Maoris form about nine percent of the population, some 300,000 people. Use of the Maori language has declined throughout the 20th century. Only about a third of Maoris now speak the Maori language, and all Maori speakers also speak English. The other two-thirds speak only English.

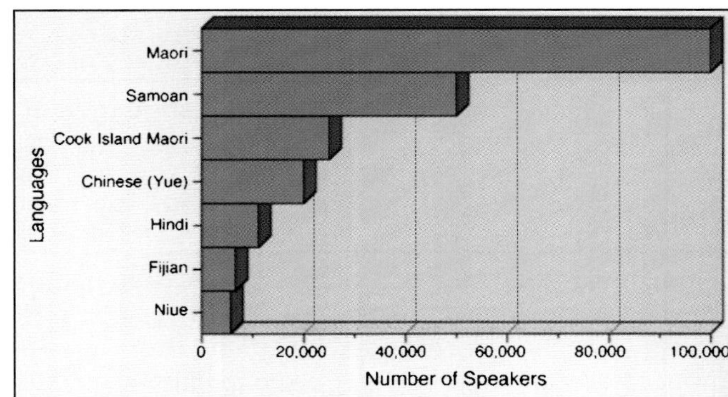

Languages spoken in New Zealand. The official language, English, not shown on chart, has 3.21 million speakers.

although most still strongly identify themselves as Maori. Efforts are being made to reverse the decline of the Maori language, through bilingual education and community involvement. (See pages 195 and 515.)

Maori is the largest minority language in New Zealand, but there are several other minority groups. These include migrant workers from other Pacific Islands, and people of Chinese and Indian descent.

Caribbean

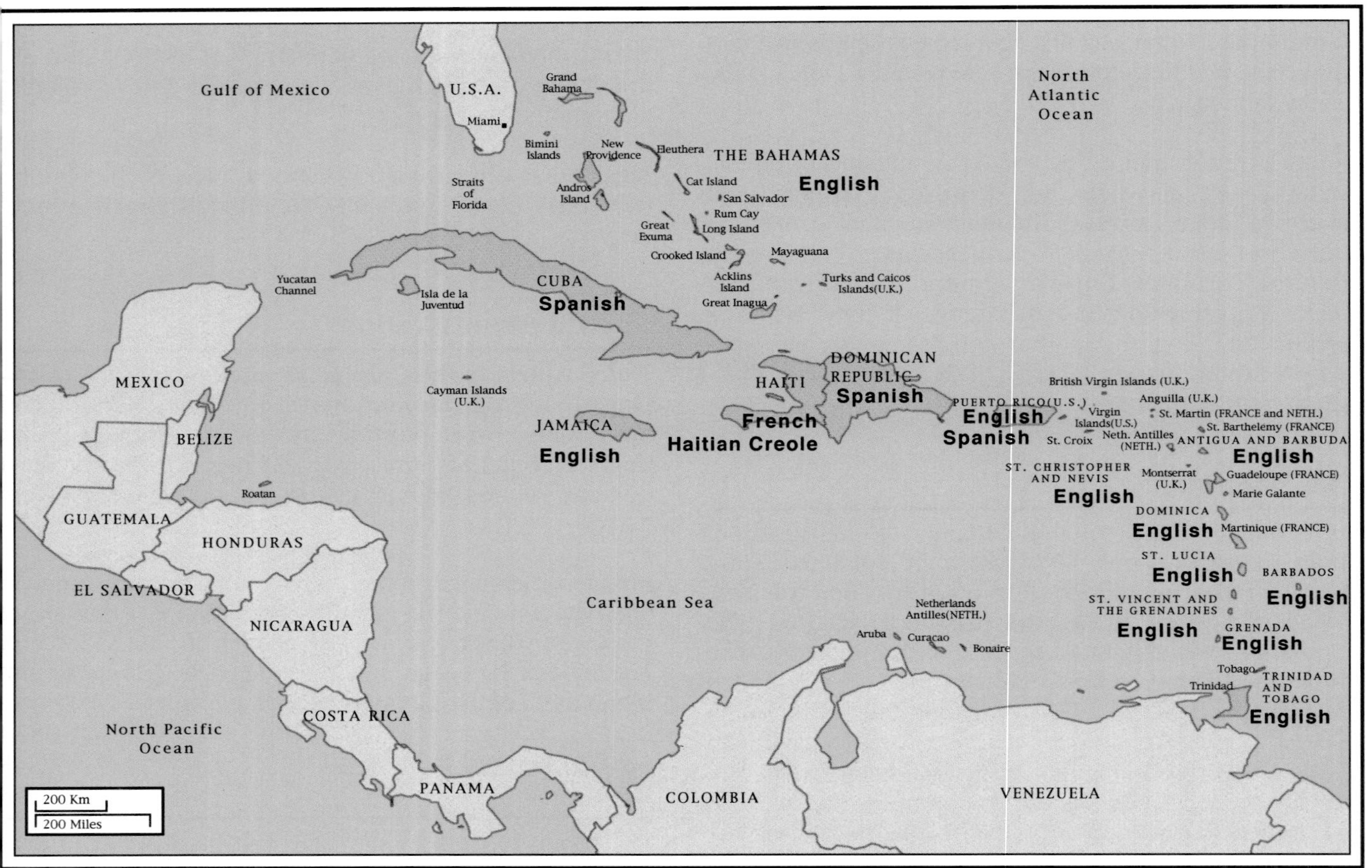

Official Languages of the Caribbean

Anguilla

The British dependency of Anguilla is located at the northern end of the Leeward Islands in the Caribbean sea. Anguilla was first colonized by the British in the 17th century, who brought Black African slaves to the island. Today, most of the 7000 inhabitants (1995 estimate), are descendants of Black African slaves.

English is the official language of Anguilla, but most of the population speak Lesser Antillean Creole English as their first language. This English-based creole is close to the creoles of neighboring Caribbean islands, such as Montserrat and Antigua. It has some degree of mutual intelligibility with the English-based creoles spoken in Jamaica and the Bahamas.

Antigua and Barbuda

The Caribbean country of Antigua and Barbuda is located to the south-east of Puerto Rico, in the Caribbean Sea. It

is made up of three islands, Antigua, Barbuda and Redonda (which is uninhabited). This former colony gained its independence from the United Kingdom in 1981 and the official language is English. However, the most widely spoken language is Lesser Antillean Creole English, which is spoken by most of the 65,000 inhabitants.

Aruba

Aruba, which lies off the Venezuelan coast, was formerly a part of the Netherlands Antilles, which is still an overseas territory of the Kingdom of the Netherlands. It separated in 1986, and became an autonomous region of the Netherlands. Aruba was first claimed by the Spanish, but was seized by the Dutch in the 17th century. Dutch is the official language.

In 1995, Aruba had an estimated population of almost 66,000, most of whom are of mixed European and American Indian descent. The main language spoken on Aruba is Papiamento, a Portuguese-based creole, with mixtures of Dutch, English, Arawak and African languages. Papiamento is the main language used in primary education. English, Spanish and Sranan are also spoken on Aruba. Sranan is an English-based creole, originating from Suriname.

The Bahamas

The Commonwealth of the Bahamas is composed of about 700 islands, only 40 of which are inhabited. More than half the population live on the island of New Providence, where the capital Nassau is situated. The population was estimated to be 256,000 in 1995. The Bahamas became a British colony in 1717 and gained their independence in 1973. More than 80 percent of the present population are descendants of Black African slaves. The official language of the Bahamas is English, which is widely understood by Bahamians and used in government, education and the media. However, the majority of the population, 86.5 percent, speak Bahamas Creole English as their mother tongue. Numerous varieties on a continuum between creole and Standard English are spoken and are known as Bahamian English.

Barbados

Barbados was a former British colony, and is a small island, the most eastern of the West Indies. It had an estimated population of 256,000 in 1995, making it one of the most densely populated islands in the world. Ninety percent of the island's population is Black African, and are descendants of slaves brought to the country from Africa to work on the sugar plantations. The remainder of the population is composed of Whites and people of mixed race. English is the official language of Barbados. The language spoken by the majority of Barbadians is Bajan, which is considered to be a dialect of English rather than a creole.

The British Virgin Islands

Four main islands and over 32 islets make up the British Virgin Islands, a possession of the United Kingdom. The four main islands are Anegada, Jost Van Dyke, Tortola and Virgin Gorda. They are located to the east of Puerto Rico in the Caribbean Sea. In 1995, the British Virgin Islands had an estimated population of 13,000. Most are the descendants of slaves who worked on the colonial plantations.

The official language is English, but most of the population speak Lesser Antillean Creole English as their main language.

The Cayman Islands

The Cayman Islands are a dependent territory of the United Kingdom, located about 160 km south of Cuba, in the Caribbean Sea. Grand Cayman, Little Cayman and Cayman Brac are the three islands which form the Cayman Islands, with an estimated population (1995) of 33,000.

British settlers from Jamaica first colonized the islands in the 18th century. The island's population is a mixture of European, Black African and people of mixed descent. The official language and the language spoken by the inhabitants of the Cayman Islands is English.

Cuba

The Island of Cuba is the largest in the Caribbean Sea, and is located south of the United States, separated by the Straits of Florida. The estimated population of Cuba in 1995 was 10.9 million. About two-thirds of the population are White, mainly of Spanish descent. Black Africans and people of mixed ancestry make up the remainder. Many of the Black Africans are descendants of slaves who were imported to the islands to work on the sugar plantations. The original population of the islands were American Indians. Their population declined as large numbers of Spanish people migrated to Cuba. None of the original Amerindian languages are spoken in Cuba.

Spanish is the official language, and the mother tongue of almost all of Cuba's population. English is widely spo-

ken in Cuba as a foreign language. English has been important as a language of trade throughout this century, although its use was discouraged after the Cuban revolution in 1959, when Cuba became a communist state. The importance of English in trade and industry is recognized and the language is taught in many schools. Russian was also taught to military students until the late 1980s, as Cuba and Russia had close ties as trade and defense partners. Other foreign languages taught include German, French, Portuguese, Italian and Arabic.

Dominica

The Commonwealth of Dominica, with an estimated population of 82,000 in 1995, is one of the smallest countries in the Western Hemisphere. The population is predominantly Black, with a small number of Carib Indians. The official language of Dominica is English. The French originally colonized the island in the 17th century but, in 1763, it came under British rule, until its independence in 1978.

Although English is the official language, at least 95 percent of the population speak Lesser Antillean Creole French, and 70 percent are monolingual in Creole. This French-based creole is also known as Patwa or Patois. About ten percent of Creole French speakers understand Standard French.

The language of those who do not speak Creole French is Dominican English, a local variety of English. The small minority of ethnic Carib Indians no longer speak their native language, Island Carib. This language died out in Dominica in the 1920s, and most of the Carib Indians now speak Creole French.

The Dominican Republic

The Dominican Republic occupies the eastern two-thirds of the Caribbean island of Hispaniola, with Haiti occupying the remaining third. The estimated population of The Dominican Republic was over 7.5 million in 1995, most of whom speak Spanish, the official language. The original Arawakan Indians who inhabited the land became extinct as the Spanish colonized the islands. French explorers also visited the land and colonized the area now known as Haiti. The largest minority language group in the country comprises those speaking Haitian Creole French. There are 159,000 speakers of Creole French, two percent of the population. (Creole French is the majority language of Haiti.)

There are also a small number of speakers of Samaná, an English-based creole. This is the main language spoken in the Samaná Bay area of the country. The inhabitants of this region are mainly descendants of freed slaves from the United States, who settled in the Dominican Republic in the 19th century. There are around 8000 speakers of Samaná English. English is the main foreign language taught in schools, with some Portuguese also taught.

Grenada

The State of Grenada is an independent island nation located 150 Km north of the South American Coast in the Caribbean Sea. In addition to the main island, Grenada, there are several smaller islands, including Carriacaou and Petit Martinique. In 1995 the islands had an estimated population of 94,000, most of whom are of Black African descent. Many of the Black Africans were brought from Africa to work on the sugar plantations during the 18th century. The official language of the country is English.

Most of the Grenadians speak English as their first language. The dialect they use is different from Standard English, and is known as Grenadian English. Two main minority languages are spoken in Grenada. A substantial minority of 43,000 people speak Lesser Antillean Creole English. The second minority language is Lesser Antillean Creole French. There are only a few speakers of this language, mainly older people, found in small scattered pockets of the country, generally in rural areas.

Guadeloupe

The French overseas department of Guadeloupe consists of a group of eight islands located to the north of the Windward Islands. The French first colonized Guadeloupe in the early 17th century, and conquered the original Carib Indians who lived on the islands. Today, the majority of the population are Black Africans, descendants of slaves brought to work on the sugar plantations. Black Africans and people of mixed African and European descent constitute 90 percent of the population, with small minorities of Europeans, East Indians and Chinese. The estimated population in 1995 was 402,000.

The official language of Guadeloupe is French. However, most of the population speak Lesser Antillean Creole French, also known as Patwa. The variety spoken on Guadeloupe is close to that spoken on the island of Martinique.

Haiti

Haiti comprises the western third of the Caribbean island of Hispaniola, bordered by the Dominican Republic in the east. The population of Haiti was estimated to be over 6.5 million in 1995, making it one of the most densely populated countries in the world. Haiti was ceded to France by Spain in 1697. Up to 95 percent of Haitians are of Black African origin, descendants of slaves brought by French colonists to work on the plantations. There are a small minority of Europeans and people of mixed descent. The original Arawakan Indian inhabitants became extinct as the Spanish and French colonized the island. The Spanish colonized the east of the island, now known as The Dominican Republic. (See page 389.)

The two official languages are French and Haitian Creole. Haitian Creole, a French-based creole, is the mother tongue and only language of over 90 percent of the population. In 1961, Creole was granted legal and education status in Haiti, but is not as widely used in education as French. Creole is regarded as being of lower social status than French. French is the second language of around 400,000 Haitians.

Jamaica

The Island of Jamaica, formerly a British colony, is the third largest island in the Caribbean sea and is located south of Cuba. The estimated population in 1995 was over 2.5 million. The population of Jamaica consists mainly of descendants of Black African slaves, with descendants also of South Asians, Europeans and Chinese.

The official language of Jamaica is English, and this is the language used in education. However, most of the population, especially in rural areas, speak a Creole dialect. Western Caribbean Creole English is the language used by 94 percent of the population. Western Caribbean Creole English is also known as Patwa, Bongo Talk and Quashie talk.

Martinique

Martinique is an overseas department of France, located in the eastern Caribbean sea. The island, first discovered by Columbus in the early 16th century, was colonized by France, and the official language of the island is French. The majority of the population are of Black African descent, whose ancestors were brought from Africa as slaves to work on the sugar plantations. In 1995, the estimated population was 394,000.

The language spoken by most of the inhabitants of Martinique is Lesser Antillean Creole French, also known as Patwa. Varieties of this creole are spoken on several of the Caribbean islands and the variety spoken on Martinique is close to the variety spoken on Guadeloupe.

Montserrat

The Caribbean island of Montserrat is a dependency of the United Kingdom, situated to the south-east of Puerto Rico. The islands were first discovered by Columbus in the 15th century, and have since been colonized by the Irish, the British and the French. In 1995, the island had an estimated population of almost 13,000, most of whom are descendants of Black African slaves brought to the Caribbean islands to work on the sugar plantations. The official language and the native language of the population is English.

The Netherlands Antilles

The Netherlands Antilles are an overseas territory of the Netherlands, made up of two groups of islands lying some 800 Km apart. The two largest and most populated islands are Curaçao and Bonaire, known as the Leeward Islands, which lie off the Venezuelan coast. Saint Martin, Saba and Saint Eustatius are smaller islands, collectively known as the Windward Islands. These islands are located to the north of Antigua and Barbuda. The Netherlands Antilles had an estimated population of 203,000 in 1995.

The original Arawak and Carib Indians were conquered by the Spanish and Dutch colonists. The population of the islands are descendants of American Indians, Dutch, Portuguese and Black African slaves.

The official languages on the Leeward Islands are Dutch and Papiamento. Papiamento is the language spoken by most of the population, with Dutch decreasing in importance. Papiamento is a Portuguese-based creole, with mixtures of Dutch, English, Arawak and African languages. The main language of instruction in the schools on Leeward islands is Dutch, with Papiamento used at primary level.

Inhabitants of the Windward Islands speak English, which is their official language. Spanish is also widely spoken. The main language of instruction in schools is English.

Puerto Rico

Puerto Rico is a Caribbean island, south of Hispaniola. It has been a freely associated commonwealth of the United States since 1952 (see page 115) and has an

estimated population of 3.8 million. Both Spanish and English are official languages. Puerto Rico used to be a colony of Spain up until 1898, when control passed to the United States. Almost all of the population are of Spanish descent. The vast majority of the population speak Spanish as their native language and Spanish is the language of everyday life in homes, shops and streets. In the 1990 Census, 52 percent of Puerto Ricans reported that they were monolingual Spanish speakers; another 24 percent as dominant in Spanish with some fluency in English. English is the mother tongue of some 107,000 Puerto Ricans. It is also the language used by the small minority of foreign-born residents, mostly from the United States. There are also a few speakers of French, German and Italian living in Puerto Rico. Approximately one-third of the Puerto Rican population have migrated to the United States. (See page 115.)

Three Creole languages are spoken in Puerto Rico, but only by a small percentage of the population. Haitian Creole French is spoken by approximately 400 people, Papiamento, a Portuguese-based creole, by around 200 people, and Dutch Creole has only a few speakers remaining.

Saint Christopher and Nevis

The islands of Saint Christopher and Nevis make up the Federation of Saint Kitts and Nevis. They are located in the eastern Caribbean Sea and were a colony of the United Kingdom until 1983. The estimated population of the islands is 41,000, most of whom live on Saint Kitts. The islands were originally inhabited by Carib Indians until British colonists arrived in the 17th century.

The official language is English. However, most of the inhabitants speak Lesser Antillean Creole English, known also as Kittitian Creole.

Saint Vincent and the Grenadines

Saint Vincent and the Grenadines are Caribbean islands, located to the north of Trinidad and Tobago. This former British colony gained its independence in 1979. The islands have an estimated population of 117,000, mainly of Black African descent. The original inhabitants of the islands were Arawak and Carib Indians. The official language of Saint Vincent and the Grenadines is English. Lesser Antillean Creole English is the most widely spoken language, and is the mother tongue of a majority of the population.

St Lucia

The island of St Lucia was claimed by both Britain and France during the 17th and 18th centuries, but was under British control from 1814 until it gained independence in 1979. About 90 percent of the island's population of 156,000 (1995 estimate) are descended from Black African slaves, imported by the French to work in the sugar-cane plantations. The official language is English but the most widely spoken language is a French-based creole called Kwéyòl (Kwiyrl) or Patwa, the creole which developed among the plantation slaves. Kwéyòl is still the first language and mother tongue of the majority of St Lucians, and it is estimated that at least 90 percent of St Lucians have some degree of fluency in Kwéyòl (see page 144). However, in recent years, more widespread educational opportunities, the mass media and better communication have increased the number of bilinguals speaking both English and Kwéyòl. It has been estimated that over 80 percent of St Lucians are bilingual in English and a Creole.

A diglossic situation exists in St Lucia: English is favored for public, formal communication and French Creole (Kwiyrl or Kwéyòl) for private, informal communication. French Creole is closely related to other creole varieties spoken in neighboring islands. An English-based creole is also used in Saint Lucia, particularly in urban areas.

English continues to be the language of prestige and official life. Recently there has been an effort to increase the status and raise the public profile of French Creole. A standard orthography has been established and there is also pressure on government to include Kwéyòl in the education system. There has recently been a greater use of Kwéyòl in the mass media. (See Pidgins and Creoles, page 142.)

Trinidad and Tobago

Trinidad and Tobago is an independent nation in the Caribbean Sea, seven miles to the north of the South American country of Venezuela. These two islands have a population of one and quarter million, of both Asian and African ancestry. The original Arawaka and Carib Indian inhabitants became extinct as the Spanish colonized the islands. Black African slaves were brought to work on the plantations, and when slavery was abolished in 1833, the British brought in Muslim and Hindu Indians to replace plantation slaves.

The official language is English, which is also the first language of the majority of the population, especially on Trinidad.

The largest minority language group in Trinidad and Tobago are those speaking Caribbean Hindi, or Hindustani. Thirty six percent of the population are of Asian descent, and ten percent of these, or 45,000, speak Caribbean Hindi as a native language. Most speakers of Caribbean Hindi also speak English. The rest of the Asian population speak English as their mother tongue. The use of Caribbean Hindi is slowly decreasing as the younger generations shift to English.

The second largest minority language spoken is Lesser Antillean Creole English. This language is spoken by about 36,000 people, who all live on the island of Tobago. Trinidad Creole French is spoken in some of the northern villages in Trinidad.

The Turks and Caicos Islands

The Turks and Caicos Islands are part of the British West Indies, and are a dependent territory of the United Kingdom. There are around 30 islands, located to the south-east of the Bahamas, only eight of which are inhabited. In 1995, the estimated population was 13,000.

The islands were first colonized by the British, who brought African people as slaves to work on the plantations. By today, the majority of the population are descendants of Black Africans, and their main language is English, the official language.

A small minority of people on the Turks and Caicos islands speak Haitian Creole French, mainly in-migrants from Haiti.

The Virgin Islands of the United States

The Virgin Islands are located east of Puerto Rico in the Caribbean Sea. There are over 90 islets and a group of seven main islands. Three main islands, Saint Thomas, Saint Croix and Saint John, and about 50 islets were acquired by the United States from Denmark in 1917, and have an estimated population of 97,000. The remainder are possessions of the United Kingdom. Most Virgin Islanders are descendants of slaves who worked on the colonial plantations. The official language of the US Virgin Islands is English.

A fairly high percentage of the current population have migrated to the Virgin Islands. Thirteen percent of the population were born in the United States. Most of these speak English as their main language. The West Indians of the island form 74 percent of the population, of whom 29 percent were born elsewhere in the West Indies. The West Indians speak Lesser Antillean Creole English.

There are about 200 speakers of Papiamento, a Portuguese-based creole, and also a few dozen speakers of a Dutch-based creole, called Negerhollands. Spanish is also spoken on the Virgin Islands by some 4000 people, mainly in-migrants from Puerto Rico.

Central America

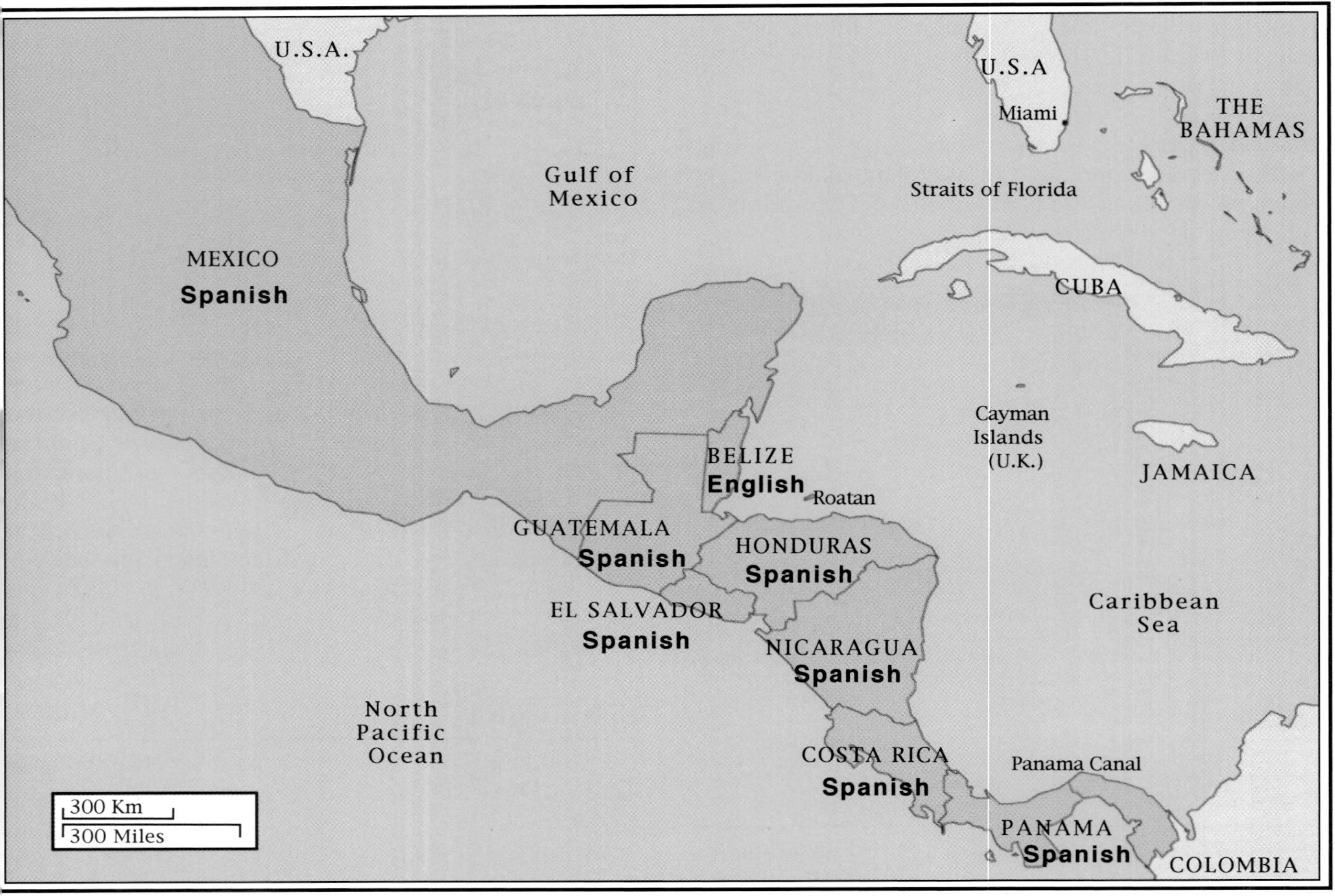

Official Languages of Central America

Belize

Belize is one of the smallest countries in Central America, with an estimated population of 214,000 in 1995, but linguistically and culturally, it is also one of the most diverse. Belize, formerly known as British Honduras, is a former British colony, which gained full independence in 1981. The official language of Belize is English. English is used by the government and the media and is also the main medium used in education, and English literacy rates are high.

English is widely spoken as a second language, but few people speak it as their native language. Amerindian languages and Belizean Creole are the languages commonly used at home. Spanish is spoken by some 33 percent of the population, concentrated mainly in the north of the country.

Belizean Creole, an English-based creole, is the mother tongue of 61 percent of Belize's population. It is also known as Creola. Most of its speakers live in urban areas. Second language speakers are mainly rural, increasing the percentage of those able to speak the language to 75 percent of Belizeans. Creola is a variant of West Caribbean Creole English.

Three main Amerindian languages are spoken in Belize, all belonging to the Maya group. These are Kekchí, Mopán and Yucatec. Mopán and Kekchí, (also known as Q'eqchi), are spoken mainly in the district of Toledo. Bilingualism is common, and Kekchí is the region's lingua franca. It is estimated that Mopán or Kekchí are the mother tongues of 64 percent of this region's inhabitants. The third Mayan language, Yucatec, is spoken by almost 6000 people, living mainly in the north of Belize.

Speakers of the Arawakan language, Garifuná, also known as Black Carib, live along the southern coast. Communities of Garifuná speakers are to be found in many Central American countries, and most of these communities are bilingual or multilingual. The Garifuná speakers of Belize are no exception. It is common for them to speak English, Belizean Creole or Spanish as well.

Plautdietsch, an archaic variety of German, is spoken by five thousand Mennonites. It is spoken mainly in the home, as are other small numbers of European and Asian languages spoken in Belize.

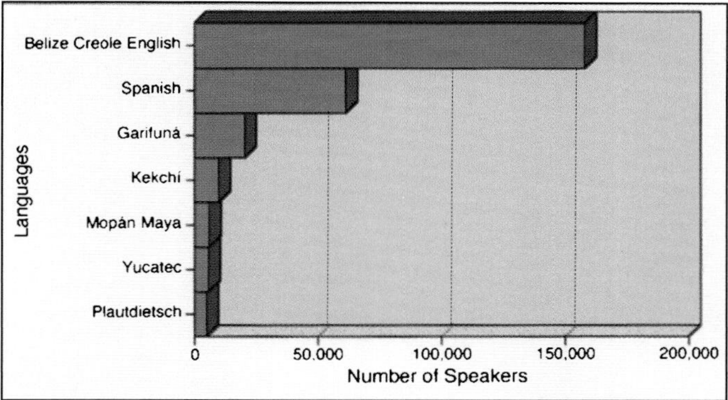

Languages spoken in Belize. The official language, English, not shown on chart, is widely spoken as a second language.

Costa Rica

The Republic of Costa Rica is bordered by Panama in the south and by Nicaragua in the north. In 1995, the estimated population of the country was 3.4 million. In Central America, Costa Rica probably has the highest percentage of people of European descent, around 96 percent of the population, mainly Spanish. The official language of Costa Rica is Spanish, the mother tongue of two-thirds of the population, used in education and government.

Most of the original American Indian population have been absorbed among the in-migrant population. However, Amerindian languages are still spoken by small groups. Two of the main indigenous languages spoken in Costa Rica are Bribri, also known as Talamanca, and Cabécar, which is also known by the name of one of its dialects, Chirripó. There are five thousand Bribri, who use the language mainly in the home. About half of them also speak Spanish. In areas with a high concentration of Bribri speakers, bilingual Spanish and Bribri schools are provided. Cabécar is spoken by some three thousand people in Costa Rica.

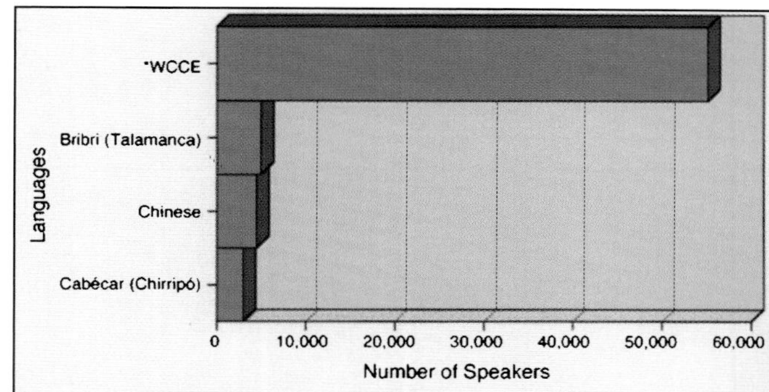

*Languages spoken in Costa Rica. The official language, Spanish, not shown on chart, has 2.15 million speakers. Note: *WCCE = Western Caribbean Creole English.*

Western Caribbean Creole English is spoken by an estimated two percent of the population, mainly descendants of African slaves who migrated to the country from Jamaica, and who live mainly along the Caribbean coast. Speakers of Creole English may not speak Standard English, but are likely to be bilingual in Creole and Spanish. There are a considerable number of people who speak Standard English, mainly US citizens resident in Costa Rica. The four and a half thousand Chinese living in Costa Rica speak Cantonese, Mandarin or Hakka varieties of Chinese.

El Salvador

The Republic of El Salvador is located on the Pacific Coast of Central America between Guatemala and Honduras. In 1995, an estimated 5.8 million people were living in El Salvador making it the most densely populated country in Central America. The majority of the population are mestizos, of mixed Spanish and American Indian ancestry, with around ten percent being American Indian. The official language and the native language of the majority of the population is Spanish.

El Salvador is different from other South and Central American countries in that most of the American Indian population no longer speak their indigenous language. The ethnic Lenca population numbers around 50,000, nearly all of whom speak Spanish as their mother tongue. Of almost 200,000 in the Pipil ethnic group, only about 20 older people are fluent speakers of the Aztecan language, Pipil. There is little or no effort to reverse such language shift by either the ethnic groups or by the El Salvador government.

A third American Indian language spoken in El Salvador is Kekchí, or Q'eqchi'. There are over 12,000 speakers, most of whom are in-migrants from Guatemala, where the language is widely spoken. The majority of the men

learn Spanish at work, while the Kekchí women are mostly monolingual.

In El Salvador, there is a small non-Hispanic foreign population, most of whom use Spanish. In the larger cities, English is also spoken.

Languages of El Salvador

	Number of Speakers
Spanish (official language)	5,670,000
Kekchí	12,286
Pipil	20
Lenca	nearly extinct

Guatemala

Guatemala has a population of 11 million people, making it the most populous country in Central America. The official language is Spanish, used by the government, media, and as the primary medium of education, and also used as a lingua franca by most Guatemalans. However, unlike other central American countries, a high percentage of the population still speak American Indian languages. Some 50 percent of Guatemala's population are Maya Indians, most of whom speak at least one Mayan language. This represents the largest existing Mayan community in the world, with smaller communities to be found in neighboring Honduras, El Salvador and Mexico. Twenty two Mayan languages are spoken in Guatemala, 16 of which have over 10,000 speakers each.

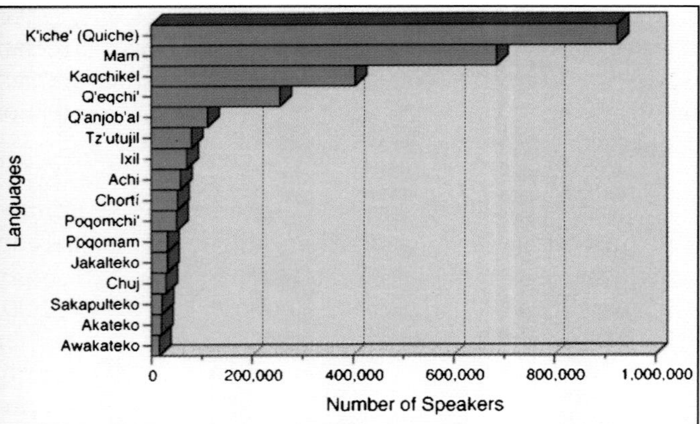

Mayan language population in Guatemala. Languages with more than 10,000 speakers. The official language, Spanish, not shown on chart, has 4.3 million speakers.

Although Spanish is the official and majority language, there is support for minority languages at local level. In areas with a high concentration of Mayan people, the government has introduced Mayan languages as the main languages of instruction in local schools. The four main languages, K'iche, Kaqchikel, Mam and Q'eqchi', are already used in schools, and work is underway to introduce other Mayan languages to schools. The degree of Spanish and Mayan bilingualism differs from one community to another. Mayan speakers living in urban areas are more likely to speak Spanish as well.

In addition to the Mayan language communities, Guatemala has a small population speaking the Arawak language, Black Carib, or Garifuná. There are around 4000 Garifuná speakers, living mainly along the Caribbean coast, and in the city of Livingston. Most of this language community are bilingual in Spanish and Garifuná, with many of the men also able to speak English and Western Caribbean Creole English. This is due to the fact that they travel to find work, often to other Caribbean and Central American countries.

Honduras

The Central American Republic of Honduras had an estimated population of 5.4 million in 1995. Most of this population are mestizos (of mixed Spanish and Amerindian descent), with only seven percent being American Indians. The official language is Spanish, which is the first language of about two-thirds of the population, but several Amerindian languages are also spoken in Honduras. These include Mískito, Tol and Sumo. In recent years, the Sumo and Mískito populations in Honduras have increased considerably as refugees have fled from Contra fighting in Nicaragua. It is estimated that migration quadrupled the pre-war population of Mískito living in Honduras.

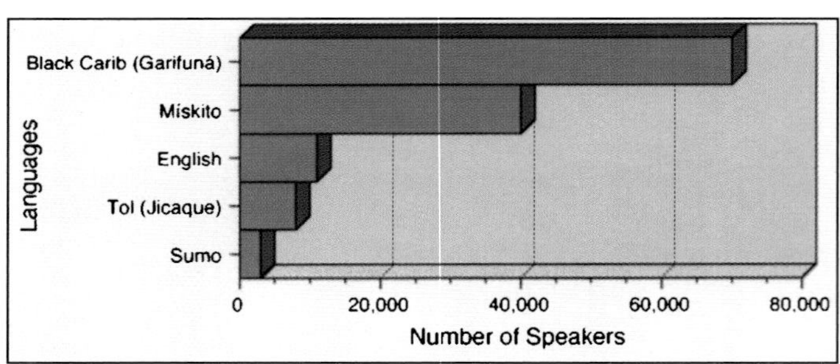

Languages spoken in Honduras. The official language, Spanish, not shown on chart, has an estimated 5.2 million speakers.

Off the northern coast of Honduras lie several small islands, such as the Bay Islands and Roatan. These are home to 70,000 Garifuná speakers. This Arawak language is also known as Black Carib. Garifuná is also spoken by small communities on the northern coast of Honduras. The Bay Islands are home to 11,000 first language English speakers, mainly descendants of pirate

traders. Many of the men from the Garifuná community speak English or Spanish as a second language, as they travel from the islands to find work.

Mexico

Mexico is bordered by the South American countries of Belize and Guatemala, and by the United States in the North. In 1995, Mexico had an estimated population of 93.9 million. The 1990 census showed that 91 percent, or some 85.5 million, of Mexico's population speak the official language, Spanish, as their first language, making Mexico the largest Spanish-speaking country in the world.

Over a hundred indigenous languages are also spoken in Mexico. The five largest are Náhuatl, Maya, Mixteco, Zapoteco and Otomí. The largest minority language, Náhuatl, has around 1,197,000 speakers, which constitutes about 27 percent of the total of minority language speakers. Náhuatl is also known as Mexicano. This was the official language of the Aztec empire. Speakers of Mexicano and other minority languages are concentrated mainly in the states of Oaxaca and Yucatan, in the east of Mexico. In both of these states, minority languages are spoken by over 40 percent of the population. In some parts of Mexico, almost no indigenous languages are spoken. The northern part of the country, for example, is almost entirely Spanish-speaking.

The levels of bilingualism among minority language groups in Mexico are fairly high, with over 75 percent of minority language speakers also fluent in Spanish. Spanish is the language used in the media and publishing. It is also the medium of education at all levels. (See page 513).

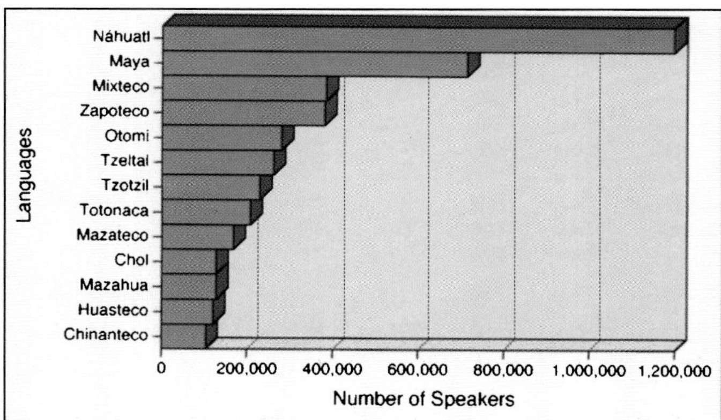

Minority languages in Mexico, which have more that 100,000 speakers. The official language, Spanish, not shown on chart, has 85.5 million speakers.

Nicaragua

The Republic of Nicaragua is bordered in the north by Honduras, and in the south by Costa Rica, and is the largest country in Central America. The estimated population in 1995 was 4.2 million. The official language is Spanish, the language of government and education, the first language of half the population and the lingua franca used throughout the country. Around 77 percent of Nicaragua's population are mestizos, of mixed European and American Indian ancestry. Another ten percent are of European descent, nine percent of Black African descent, and about four percent are Asian.

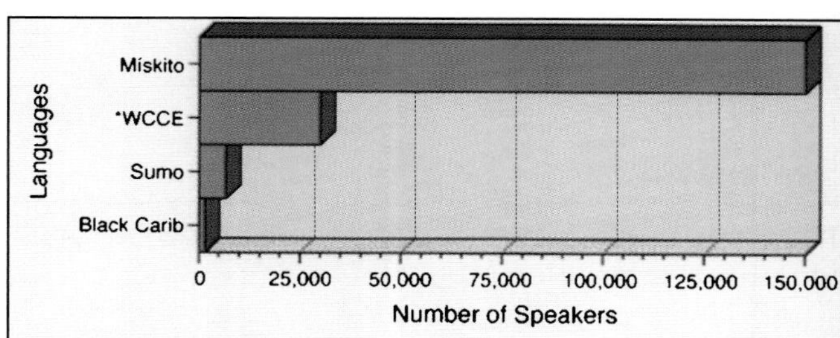

*Languages spoken in Nicaragua. The official language, Spanish, not shown on chart, has over 2 million speakers. Note: * WCCE = Western Caribbean Creole English.*

The African and American Indian populations are concentrated mainly along the Caribbean coast, and Mískito and English are the main languages spoken in this area. Mískito-speaking Nicaraguans number between 70,000 and 150,000, and Western Caribbean Creole English is spoken by 30,000, mainly by in-migrants from other Caribbean countries. The use of these and other minority languages such as Sumo is encouraged by the government. Minority languages are actively promoted, and the right of all citizens to use their local language is recognized by the government. Dictionaries and other literacy materials have been provided in Mískito. Most Mískito speakers are bilingual in Spanish.

In central Nicaragua, Sumo is spoken by 5000 people. The speakers of this Amerindian language are likely to know some Spanish or English, and occasionally Mískito.

Panama

The Republic of Panama lies on the stretch of land which joins North and South America. The country has an estimated population of 2.6 million, and the official language is Spanish. Spanish is the language used in education and by the government, and is spoken by 90 percent of Panamanians. English is also widely used in Panama especially in Panama City and in the Canal zone because

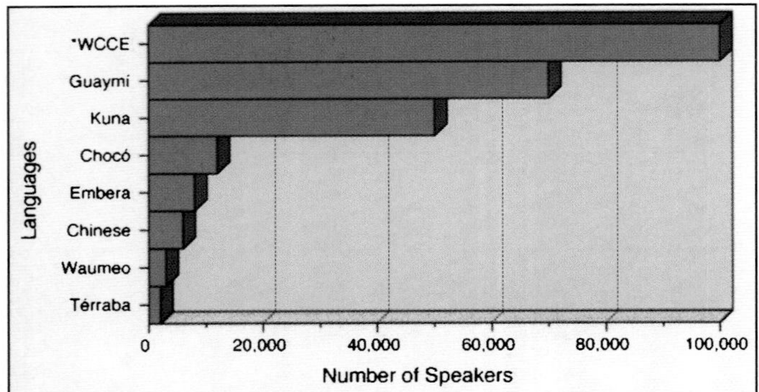

*Languages spoken in Panama. The official language, Spanish, not shown on chart, has over 1.3 million speakers. In addition, English is also widely spoken in Panama. Note: * WCCE = Western Caribbean Creole English.*

of the historical connection with the United States. English is the administrative language of this area, and bilingualism in Spanish and English is common. Many workers were brought into the country from Jamaica and Barbados to help build the Panama Canal. They constitute around 14 percent of the population and speak mainly English and West Caribbean Creole English rather than Spanish. Ten percent of the population are of European (usually Spanish) descent, the rest being mestizos, people of mixed Spanish and American Indian ancestry.

A number of Amerindian languages are spoken in Panama, and in recent years autonomous territories called *comarcas* have been developed to ensure their future. Two large *comarcas* have been allocated to speakers of Kuna and Chocó. Both these languages are concentrated in the east of the country. Ninety percent of those who speak Kuna live in the Kuna Yala *comarca*, which is situated near the coast in the San Blas region. Most Kuna speakers have some knowledge of Spanish. The Chocó *comarca*, Embera Drua, is in the province of Darién, and is home to 60 percent of the Chocó language group. About half of the Embera Dura's population speak some Spanish. There have also been proposals to develop *comarcas* for two other language groups, the Guaymí and Térraba.

Europe

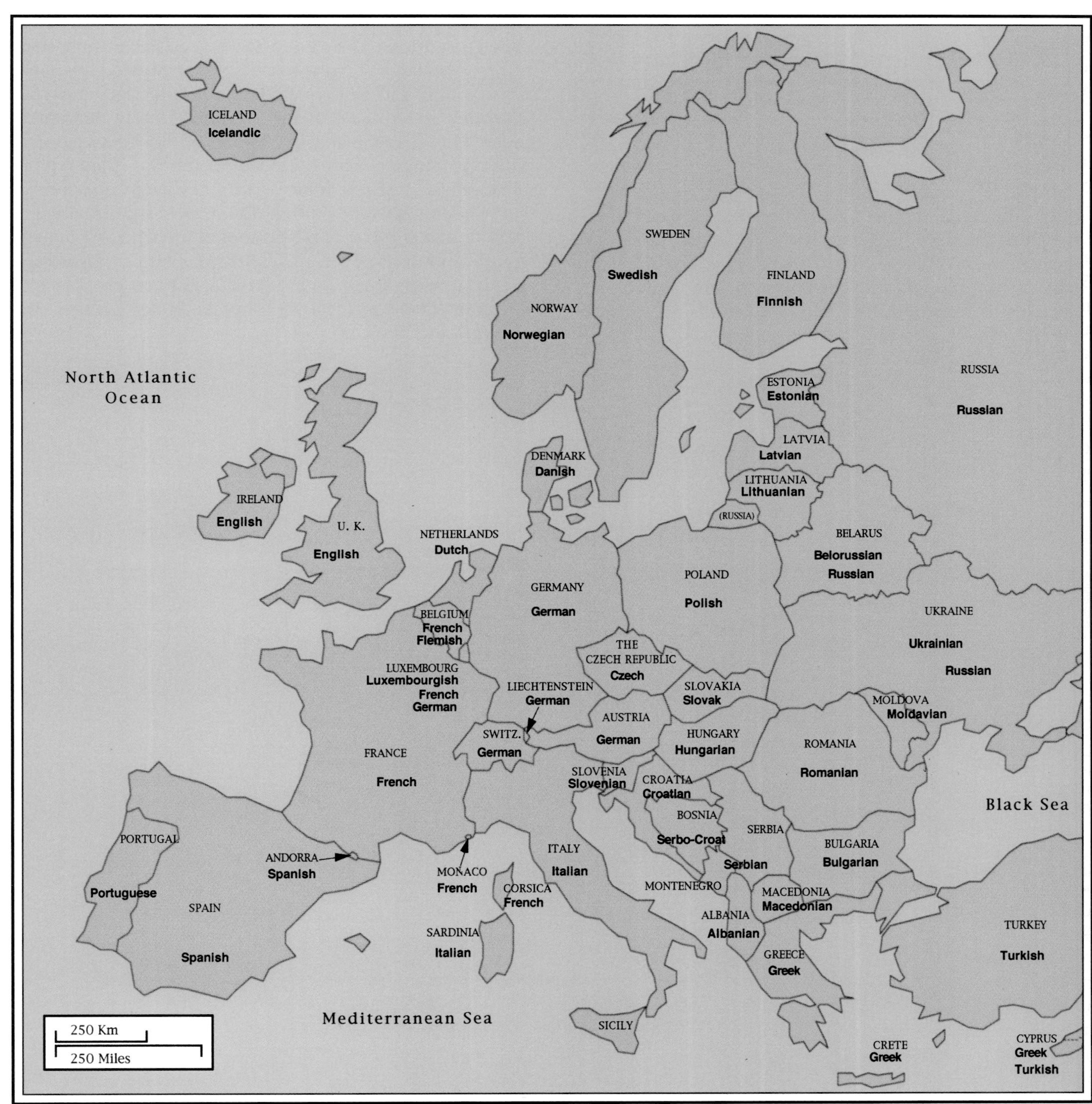

The Majority Languages of Europe

Western Europe

ustria

ustria has a population of just under eight million (1995 stimate) and its official language is Standard German. bout 98 percent of the population speak dialects of erman as their mother tongue. Minority language groups ount for a very small percentage of the population.

he minority languages include Croatian, Slovenian and Iungarian. These languages have some official recogni- ion, and are taught alongside German in some bilingual chools. This is the case in areas with a large proportion f speakers, for example in Burgenland, a state in the ast of Austria which borders Hungary. There are about 5,000 Croats, and 15,000 Hungarians living throughout he country. Slovenian is spoken mainly in the south of ustria and is an official language in the province of arinthia. There are an estimated 35,000 Slovenes living n Austria.

here are small groups of Czechs and Slovaks as well as omanian, Serb, Turkish and Italian speakers, who ogether count for less than 0.1 percent of the population.

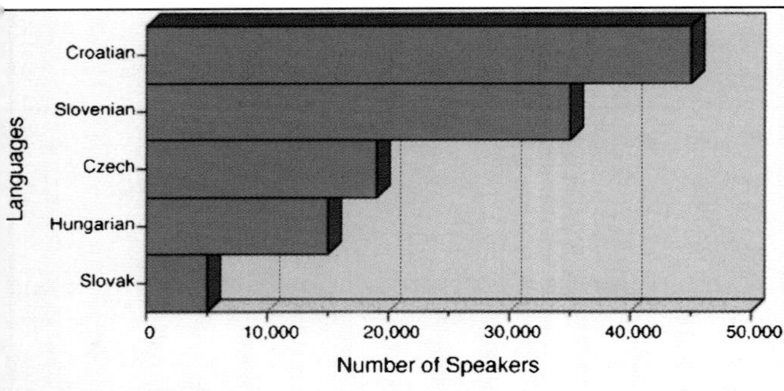

anguages spoken in Austria. The official language, German, not shown n chart, has over 7.5 million speakers. (Source: Smolle & Breathnach, 995).

elgium

elgium had an estimated population of 10 million in 995, and has three official languages, French, Flemish nd German. German is the least spoken, used by only ne percent of the Belgian population in the cantons of upen, Malmédy and St Vith. These cantons lie in the ast of the Wallon Region and have been part of Belgium ince 1918, when they were awarded to the country in he Treaty of Versailles.

rench, also known as Wallon, is spoken by 33 percent f the population and most Belgians have some knowl-

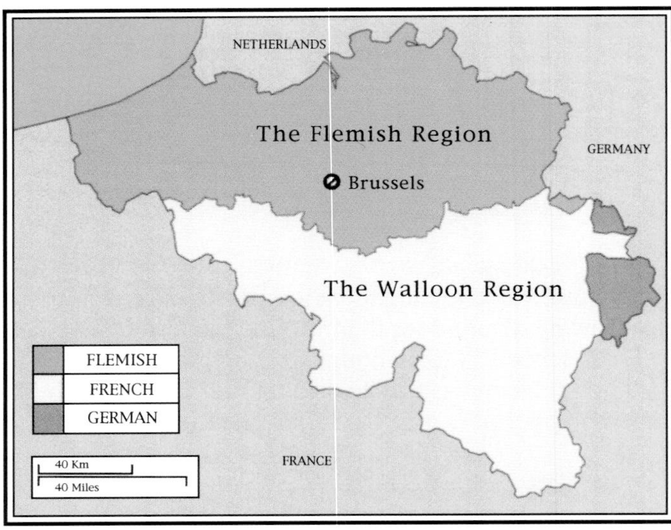

Language Communities in Belgium

edge of French. The capital, Brussels, is situated within the Flemish Region of the country and the city has two official languages, Flemish and French. The majority of the population of Brussels speak French.

The largest language community is that of the Flemish speakers. Flemings now constitute around 60 percent of the Belgian people, and the status of this language has risen continuously since 1932. Most of the Flemings are concentrated in the northern half of Belgium in the Flemish Region of the country. Flemish is also known as Dutch, which is the official language of The Netherlands. Dutch and Flemish share the same standard language.

Although Belgium has three official languages, there is a relatively low level of bilingualism, although speakers of the two main languages learn one another's languages in schools. Traditional social and economic tensions feature among the reasons for this.

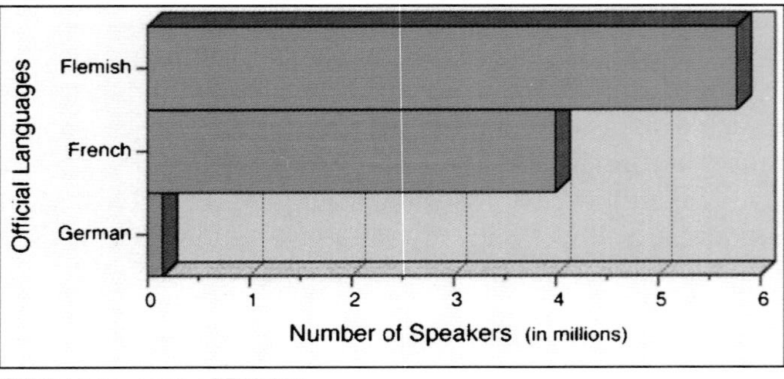

Official languages of Belgium.

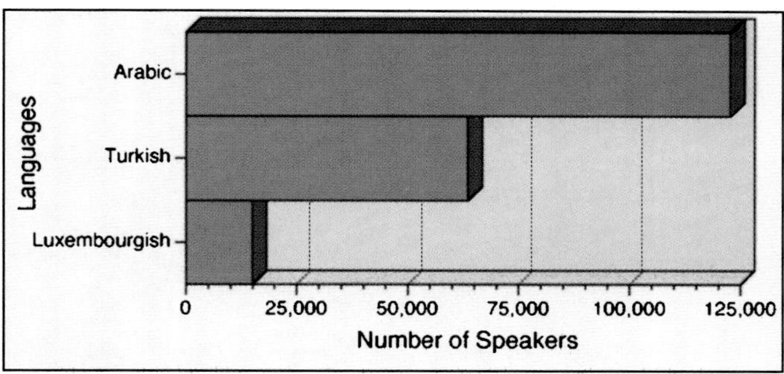

Main minority languages spoken in Belgium.

About 15,000 speakers of Luxembourgish live in regions of Belgium which are adjacent to Luxembourg, and there is a growing demand for the introduction of the language in local schools. Luxembourgish (or Lëtzebuergesch) is the national language in the neighboring Grand Duchy of Luxembourg, but is given no official status in Belgium.

Belgium has a large in-migrant population, amounting to about a tenth of the total population. Large non-native language groups include Italians, Spanish, Greek, Arabic and Turkish speakers. Most of the in-migrant population acquire a Belgian language, usually French.

The Czech Republic and the Slovak Republic

On January 1st 1993 Czechoslovakia separated into two republics. Bohemia, Moravia and parts of Silesia formed the new Czech Republic, with Slovakia in the east becoming The Slovak Republic. In the Czech Republic, the official language is Czech, and in The Slovak Republic, the official language is Slovak. Czech and Slovak are closely related languages, and are mutually intelligible to a large degree. Until the 19th century, there was a single literary language, but then a separate Slovak literary language was established, based on the speech of rural Slovaks.

The Czech Republic

1995 estimates number the population at 10.43 million, almost 95 percent of whom speak Czech. Within the Czech Republic, Standard Czech is the language of education, government and the media, but throughout the country, various dialects are spoken which differ from the standard form. There are 308,000 Slovaks living in the Czech Republic. The remaining two percent of the population comprises several small minority groups, chiefly ethnic Germans, Hungarians, Romanies and Poles. Most members of these minority language groups retain their mother tongue, but are also bilingual in Czech.

The Slovak Republic

In 1995, the population of the Slovak Republic was estimated at 5.4 million. Eighty five percent are ethnic Slovaks, speaking dialects of Slovak as their first language. Slovakia has a greater proportion of minority language groups than the Czech Republic, most living in the south of the country. The largest minority group are the Hungarians, who comprise over ten percent of the population. There are also small minorities of Romanies, Czech, Ukrainian, German and Polish. As most of the minority groups are concentrated in the Slovak Republic, more Slovaks than Czechs are bilingual in the majority language and a minority language.

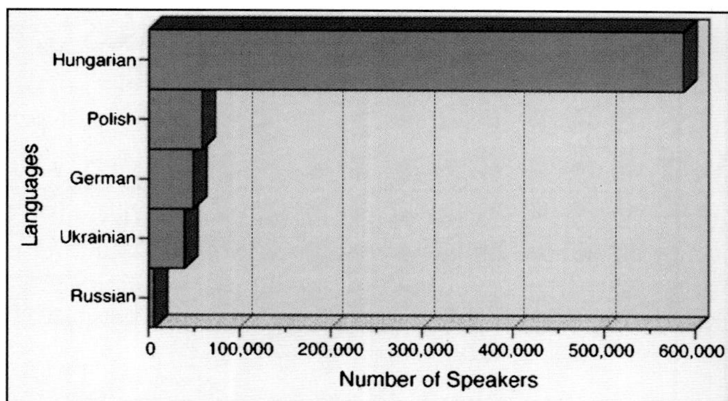

Main languages spoken in the Czech and Slovak Republics. Czech, the official language of the Czech Republic, not shown on chart, has approximately 10 million speakers. Slovak, the official language of the Slovak Republic, not shown on chart, has approximately 5 million speakers.

Denmark

The total population of Denmark in 1995 was estimated to be 5.2 million. The majority are native speakers of Danish, the official language.

Two main minority languages are spoken on the mainland, German and Greenlandic. German is spoken in the Nord-Schleswig region of Denmark, bordering on Germany, and is recognized as an official regional language. There are approximately 23,000 German speakers in this region, over nine percent of the region's population. German is taught as a second language in all Danish schools of the region, and there are some schools where German is the language of instruction.

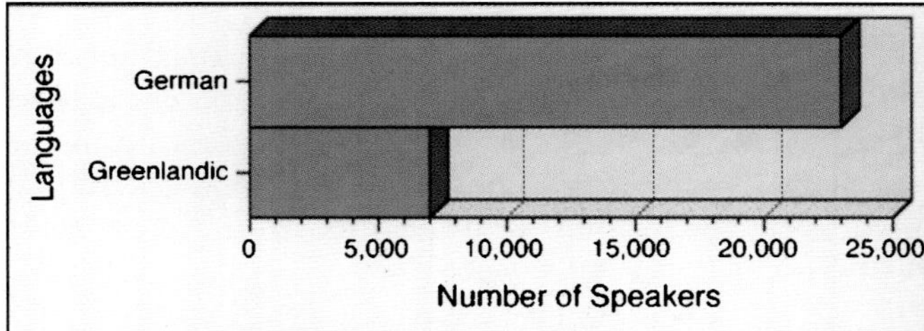

Languages spoken in mainland Denmark. The official language, Danish, not shown on chart, has over 5.2 million speakers.

Main Minority Languages of Europe

Greenlandic, an Inuit (Eskimo) language with some Danish borrowings, is spoken by about seven thousand people on the Danish mainland.

English is the first foreign language in Danish schools, and because of the international importance of English and the influence of Anglo-American culture, many Danes, especially among the younger generation, have some competence in English.

The Faroe Islands

These islands have been ruled by either Norway or Denmark since the 14th century, but today they constitute an autonomous region within Denmark.

The population of the Faroe Islands, which numbers around 49,000 (1995 estimate), still speak a form of the old Norse called Faroese, which is the official language of

the Islands. Danish is the second official language. All school students are educated bilingually, in Faroese and Danish.

France

The official language of France is French, spoken as a first language by the majority of the population of 58 million (1995 estimate). Outside France, there are about 60 million French speakers (first or second language – see page 304). French is spoken in Belgium, and in the former French colonies in Africa and Asia. There are over six million French speakers in Canada.

Many minority languages are also spoken in communities throughout France. There are 1.5 million speakers of German dialects, most living in Eastern France, in the Alsace-Lorraine and the Moselle provinces. Between 80 and 90 percent of these speak French as well. French is the official language and the only language of education in these two regions, although recently bilingual education in French and Standard German has been introduced.

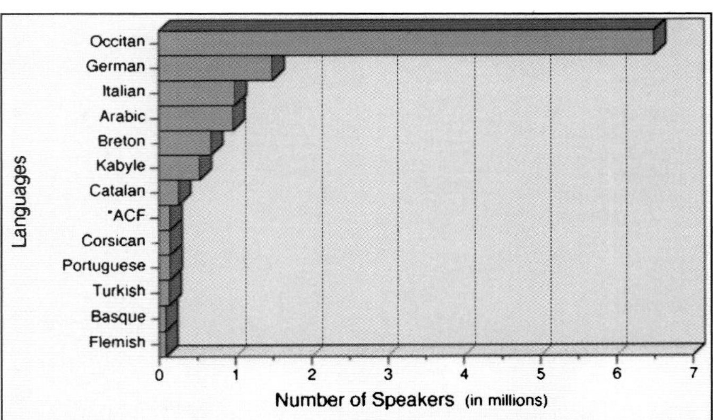

*Languages spoken in France. The official language, French, not shown on chart, has over 51 million first language speakers. Note: * ACF = Antillean Creole French.*

Basque (a language 'isolate', with no known genetic relationship to any other known language) is spoken along the French–Spanish border, and the number of speakers in France is estimated at about 80,000. Dialects of Catalan (a Romance language, closely related to French and Spanish) are also spoken in the South of France in the Pyrenean Mountain region (Pyrénées-Orientales) by about 260,000 speakers. Breton (a Celtic language, closely related to Welsh) is spoken in the north-west of France, and although there are no official figures, it is estimated that about 700,000 speak Breton. These three languages have no official status and are in decline. Attempts are being made to maintain them and increase their usage by language activists, but with little or no government support. (Basque and Catalan have official status in Spain.)

Flemish, or Dutch, is found mainly in the north-east of France, and is spoken by around 90,000 people. Near the Italian border, about one million Italian speakers reside, the majority of whom are bilingual in French and Italian.

Recent in-migrant languages in France include substantial numbers of Turkish, Arabic, Antillean Creole French and Kabyle speakers. Speakers of Arabic, mainly from North Africa, number about one million, the third largest minority language group in France. Kabyle is a Berber variety, spoken by in-migrants from Algeria. Antillean Creole French is spoken by in-migrants from former colonies of France in the Caribbean.

In the South of France, Occitan dialects of French are spoken, which are divergent from the Northern French varieties and from Standard French. In medieval times, Occitan had autonomous status as a literary language and many of its speakers argue that it should once more be given the status of a separate language. Of the 13 million inhabitants of the area where Occitan is spoken (comprising 31 *départements*), it is estimated that about half have a knowledge of one of the Occitan varieties. Occitan has no official status, but is taught in certain schools and at university level. Some speakers maintain that Occitan itself comprises more than one language.

Corsica

The island of Corsica, in the Mediterranean, has been part of France since the 18th century, and has close cultural ties with Italy. The Corsican language, closely related to the Tuscan dialect of Italian, is still spoken by about 200,000 people, many resident in mainland France or in other countries. Most of its speakers also speak French. There is a movement in Corsica for bilingual education in Corsican and French.

Germany

German is the official language of Germany, and the native language of almost all its citizens. In 1995 the estimated population of Germany was 81 million and over 95 percent speak German as their first language.

There are a number of long-established minority language groups within Germany. The Sorbian language is spoken by communities in the east of Germany, such as in the administrative districts of Brandenburg and Saxony-Anhalt. There are approximately 80,000 Sorbian

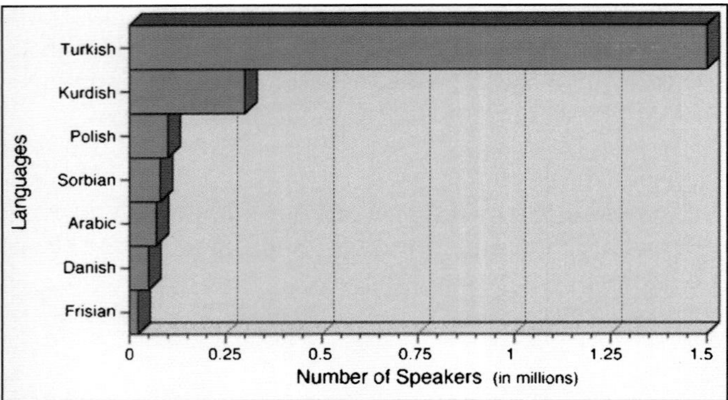

Languages spoken in Germany. The official language, German, not shown on chart, has over 78 million speakers.

speakers living in Germany and they form a majority of the population in a small number of villages.

Frisian, a Germanic language, is another minority language in Germany. In the Middle Ages, Frisian was spoken in an area between the Rhine estuary and the Weser. There are two main varieties, West Frisian and North Frisian. Although there are differences between the two dialects, the figures for Frisian have been combined on the chart. There are an estimated 10,000 Frisian speakers living in Germany, and most speak German as well. Many Frisians are trilingual, also speaking a variety of Danish. Frisian is spoken by an estimated 350,000 people in the Netherlands in the province of Friesland. The support given to Frisian in Germany depends on the districts in which it is found. The districts of Schleswig-Holstein in the north give some recognition to the rights of both Frisian and Danish communities. On the other hand, Niedersachsen, which is also in the north of Germany, offers little protection to its minority languages. Danish is spoken in areas of Germany which border Denmark with an estimated 50,000 speakers. These long-established minority language groups are relatively small in number, and nearly all their speakers also speak German.

Migrant Workers in Germany

Since the 1960s, over four million people have entered Germany as 'guestworkers' or *gastarbeiter.* Such migrant workers were needed by Germany as factory workers (for example, when the German economy expanded in the 1960s). Between 1955 and 1968, Germany signed agreements with other European countries to organize the recruitment of unskilled labor. Such recruits came from Italy, Spain, Greece, Turkey, Portugal and Yugoslavia. Rather than just becoming temporary guestworkers, many in-migrants brought their families to join them, planning to stay in Germany for a long period.

In the 1990s, the second generation in-migrant population has tended to reproduce at a faster rate than indigenous Germans. Such in-migrant or guestworkers mostly live in urban areas where there is heavy industry and a high density of population. Cities such as Frankfurt, Offenbach, Stuttgart, Munich and Berlin have large communities of guestworkers. Some live in ghetto-like accommodation.

The low status, relative poverty and marginalization of these guestworkers has tended to make integration into German society difficult. However, it is a sense of cohesiveness born out of relative material deprivation that has helped the maintenance of the languages of these in-migrants. For example, the Turkish in-migrants have tended to retain their sense of Turkish identity and culture.

For these in-migrants to access medical, bureaucratic and educational services, it is often necessary for one or more members of the family to know German. Generally, such in-migrants wish to learn the language of the host country, regarding it as a handicap if they are ignorant of the German language.

Greenland

Greenland, one of the world's largest islands, has been self-governing since 1979. The official languages of Greenland are Danish and Greenlandic Inuit (an Eskimo language). The majority of the population are Greenlanders, of mixed Danish and Inuit descent. The population is estimated to be over 57,000 (1995 estimate), and nearly all of the population live on the southwest coast of Greenland.

All children in Greenland are educated bilingually, in Greenlandic Inuit and Danish. The more widely used language of the two is Inuit, spoken by around 50,000.

Italy

Italian is the official language of Italy, and the mother tongue of an overwhelming majority of the population of nearly 58.3 million (1995 estimate). There are over 54 million native Italian speakers. The standard Italian language is based on the dialect of Tuscany. Italian has many diverse dialects, some of which are mutually unintelligible. Some of these are claimed by linguists to be separate languages (e.g. Friulian, Ladin, Sardinian). It is estimated that about half of the Italian population still speak a dialect as their mother tongue. However, because of the influence of education and the mass media, many of these dialects are becoming closer to the

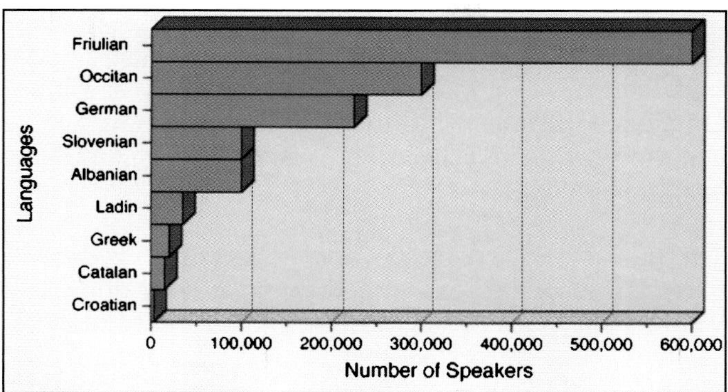

Languages spoken in Italy. The official language, Italian, not shown on chart, has 54 million speakers.

standard form of the language, and most Italian speakers can use and understand the standard language.

The largest minority language on the chart, Friulian, which has between 550,000 and 600,000 speakers, is considered by many to be a separate language from Italian, and more closely related to Provençal French than to standard Italian. Friulian is spoken mainly in the north-east of Italy and the majority of its speakers also know standard Italian.

Other minority languages in the north of Italy include Ladin (also related closely to Italian, but considered by many to be a separate language), Slovenian (a Slavic language), Provençal French and German. German is spoken mainly near the Austrian border by a very small percentage of the whole population. However, within some regions (such as the Trentino-Alto Adige), the 1981 census showed the number of speakers to be as high as 64 percent of the region's population. In the Trentino-Alto Adige region, equal status is given to German and Italian.

Albanian, Croatian and Greek are spoken in the south and on the east coast. The speakers of these languages are descendants from refugees and mercenaries from past centuries.

Most of Italy's minority language speakers are bilingual, speaking both a minority language and standard Italian. However, some of the minority language groups also speak other minority languages. For example, most of the Slovenians living in Italy near the Slovenian border speak Friulian as a second or third language, as do the Germans living in the area.

Sardinia
The island of Sardinia (population estimated at 1.6 million in 1988) is a part of Italy and the majority (over one million) are native speakers of Sardinian. Sardinian is regarded as being a separate language from Italian, but is not widely used in education or public life. Most of its speakers also speak Italian. Other minority languages spoken in this area include Catalan and Corsican.

Sicily
The Island of Sicily has 4.5 million inhabitants. Sicilian differs markedly from Standard Italian, but does not have the status of a separate language.

Liechtenstein

The Principality of Liechtenstein, situated between Austria and Switzerland, is one of the smallest independent states in the world. The official language is German, but the majority of the population of 30,000 speak a Germanic dialect known as Alemannish as their home language.

Luxembourg

Luxembourg is a small country in western Europe, situated between France and Germany. It has a population of around 400,000. A triglossic situation exists in Luxembourg. Both French and German are official languages and are used in official, formal and written contexts. German is widely used in written documents, notices and newspapers. French is used in government and official communication. The mother tongue and daily spoken language of the majority of the population is Luxembourgish (Letzeburgesch), a language closely related to German. Luxembourgish has the status of a national language.

The medium of kindergarten education is Luxembourgish. German is the main language of instruction at primary level, and French at secondary level.

A number of other languages are spoken in Luxembourg, mainly because of foreign workers and their families resident in the country. These include workers from Portugal, Italy, Belgium and Germany. Most foreign workers have no knowledge of Luxembourgish, but can learn to communicate with native Luxembourgers in French or German. However, young in-migrant children are encouraged to attend kindergarten to learn Luxembourgish.

Monaco

The small independent state of Monaco, situated in an enclave in south-east France, has 30,000 inhabitants, of whom 58 percent are speakers of the official language,

'rench. Seventeen percent speak the Ligurian dialect of talian, and 15 percent speak the Monégasque dialect of)ccitan. English is widely used. Internal radio broad-'asts are in French, Italian, Arabic and English.

The Netherlands

'he official language of The Netherlands is Dutch, and it s the language used by the majority of the population of 5.4 million (1995 estimate).

)utch is also a second language for many foreign nation-ls living in the Netherlands, such as Moroccans, Turks nd Spanish. Their children learn Dutch at school, but in nany cases, they are also given the opportunity of being aught in their mother tongue. In The Netherlands, and n Scandinavian countries, there is a relatively greater notivation to learn major European languages, especial-y English.

n the province of Friesland, in the north of the Vetherlands, a high percentage of the population, about 50,000, speak Frisian as their first language. It is recog-iized as the official language of this province besides)utch, and is also spoken elsewhere in the Netherlands. A study in 1984 showed that 94 percent of the popula-ion in Friesland understood the Frisian language. Seventy three percent speak Frisian, but only ten percent re literate in the language. Efforts are being made to ncrease the status of Frisian, and it is a compulsory sub-ect in primary schools in the province.

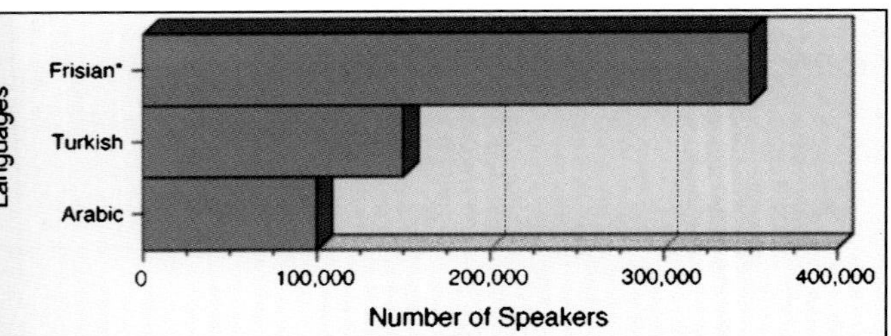

*anguages spoken in The Netherlands. The official language, Dutch, not hown on chart, has 13.4 million speakers. Note: * = number of Frisian peakers in Friesland.*

Portugal

'he official language of Portugal is Portuguese. It is the anguage of the vast majority of the population, which in 995 was estimated to be 10.5 million. Portugal is one of he most linguistically and ethnically homogeneous ountries in the world. The dialects of Portuguese are nutually intelligible.

The Galician variety of Portuguese is spoken in the north of Portugal. Galician has official status as an autonomous language in the neighboring autonomous province of Galicia in Spain, but is regarded as a dialect of Portuguese in Portugal. (Some Spanish Galicians would like Galician and Portuguese dialects to share a single standard language.) There are also some 5000 speakers of Romany. Due to the fact that Portuguese is the language of almost the entire population, there is not a high degree of bilingualism in Portugal. However, the influx of migrant workers from the north of Europe and the development of tourism has brought increasing numbers of people speaking other languages into permanent residence in Portugal.

San Marino

The Republic of San Marino, the smallest independent state in Europe, is situated in an enclave in Northern Italy. Italian is the official language and the native language of the 24,000 inhabitants.

Spain

The population of Spain in the 1986 Census was almost 39 million, and over 28 million (72.8 percent) of the population were first language Spanish speakers. By 1995, the population estimate was 39.4 million. Spanish is the official language of the entire country. However, the language is often called Castilian, to distinguish it from other widely spoken languages, Galician, Basque and Catalan, that have regional official status in Spain. The term 'Castilian Spanish' is also used to distinguish the Spanish spoken in Spain from Spanish as spoken in the US, Mexico and South America, for example.

Galicia is situated in the north-west corner of Spain, where Galician is recognized as the official regional language together with Castilian. Eighty two percent (1986)

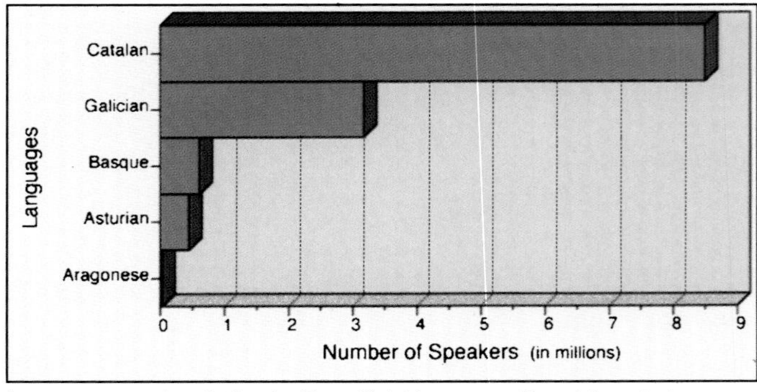

Languages spoken in Spain. The official language, Spanish, not shown on chart, has over 28 million first language speakers.

of the population of the region speak Galician, and 91 percent understand it. Galician is closely related to dialects of Portuguese, and some Galician speakers support the idea of a common standard language for Galician and Portuguese.

The provinces of Vizcaya, Guipúzcoa and Alava make up the Autonomous Basque Community. These provinces lie in the north of Spain, next to the coast and the French border. Castilian Spanish and Basque are both official languages. The 1986 Spanish Census showed that about 25 percent of the community spoke Basque.

In Catalonia in northwest Spain, Catalan and Castilian Spanish are co-official languages. There are around nine million speakers of Catalan and the 1986 census showed that 90 percent of Catalonia's population understand the language. About 64 percent speak Catalan. Catalan is also widely spoken in Valencia (where the local variant is known as Valencian) and in the Balearic Islands.

Aragonese is spoken mainly in the Pyrenean valleys, and there are an estimated 30,000 speakers. Asturian is spoken in the Asturias, in northern Spain. Neither of these languages is recognized as an official language.

Switzerland

Switzerland is a land-locked state in the mountainous center of Western Europe. It is bordered by Germany, France, Italy, Austria and the Principality of Liechtenstein. It is thus not surprising that the population of Switzerland comprises several different language groups. Structurally, Switzerland has evolved as a federal state with 26 member states, known as cantons and half-cantons, which enjoy a high degree of autonomy.

Switzerland has four official national languages: German, French, Italian and Romansh. Only the first three have official status at federal level. Romansh has official status at a local level. It is one of the three official languages, along with German and Italian, in the canton of Graubünden, in the east of Switzerland. The three cantons of Berne, Fribourg and Valais each have two official languages, German and French. The remaining cantons only have one official language each. The administration and educational system of each canton is conducted through the medium of the official language or languages.

In the 1990 Census, Switzerland had a population of over 6.8 million, 63.6 percent of whom spoke German as their first language. German is spoken throughout most of Switzerland, especially in cantons adjacent to Germany and Austria. Of all the German-speaking persons, 93.3 percent speak a Swiss German dialect on an everyday basis and 66.4 percent claimed that they spoke only Swiss German, and not Standard German. Standard German is the variety taught in schools, and used in most written communications.

French and Italian are spoken in the cantons which border France and Italy respectively. French speakers constitute 19.2 percent of the population and Italian 7.6 percent. Italian is the predominant language in the southern canton of Ticino.

Romansh, which is the main language of 39,600 speakers, or 0.6 percent of the population, is spoken mainly in the canton of Graubünden, in the east of Switzerland. It is not uncommon for those from this area to be fluent in Romansh, German, French and Italian. However, in Switzerland as a whole, bilingualism is not universal, because of the territorial boundaries between languages, and the fact that most cantons conduct administration and education through the medium of only one language. Schools promote Swiss solidarity over and above language barriers by requiring that every child learn the basics of a second national language. English is also taught in schools as a foreign language.

Many in-migrant workers reside in Switzerland, mainly from Italy, Spain and France. At the time of the 1990 census there were over 1.2 million in-migrant workers in the country, or 18.1 percent of the population. Many of these people speak a language other than one of Switzerland's national languages. Those declaring a language other than German, French, Italian or Romansh as their main language numbered 43.3 percent of all foreigners, and 1.3 percent of all Swiss. Such non-national languages, spoken by 8.9 percent of the population, were more common than Italian. These include Slavic languages at 1.9 percent, Spanish 1.7 percent, Portuguese 1.4 percent, and Turkish and English both constituting 0.9 percent of the languages spoken.

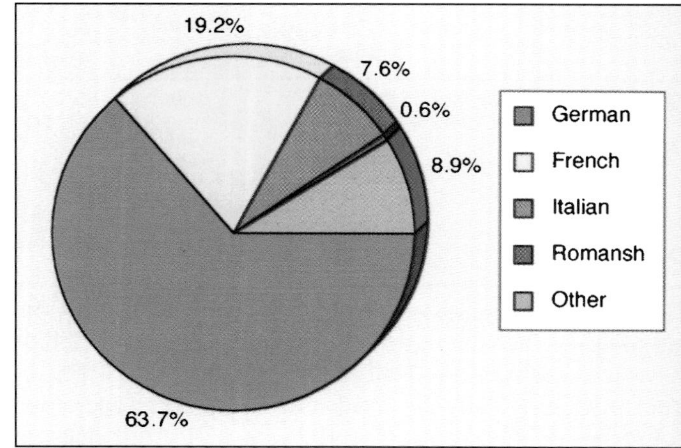

Languages spoken in Switzerland, 1990.

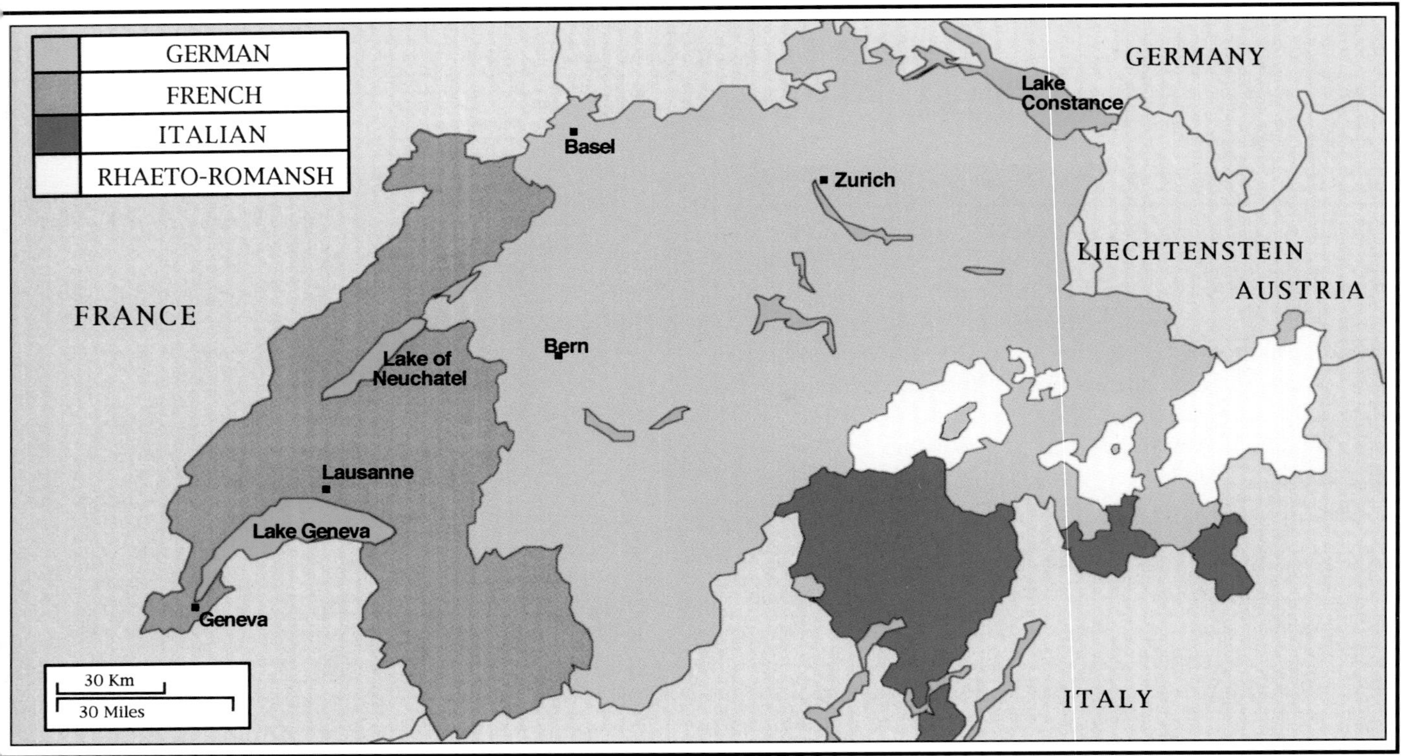

Language Zones in Switzerland

Main Languages of Switzerland's Five Largest Cities, 1991

The Five Cities	Total	German	French	Italian	Romansh	Other Language
Zurich	365,043	281,317	7,953	24,948	1,257	49,568
Basle	178,428	137,369	4,997	12,482	257	23,323
Geneva	171,042	9,610	112,419	9,786	139	39,078
Berne	136,338	110,279	5,236	7,134	224	13,465
Lausanne	128,112	6,799	95,455	6,755	79	19,024

CHARTS AND TABLE – SOURCE: SFSO , 1994, *The 1990 Population Census,* Switzerland in Profile. Swiss Federal Statistical Office, Berne, Switzerland.

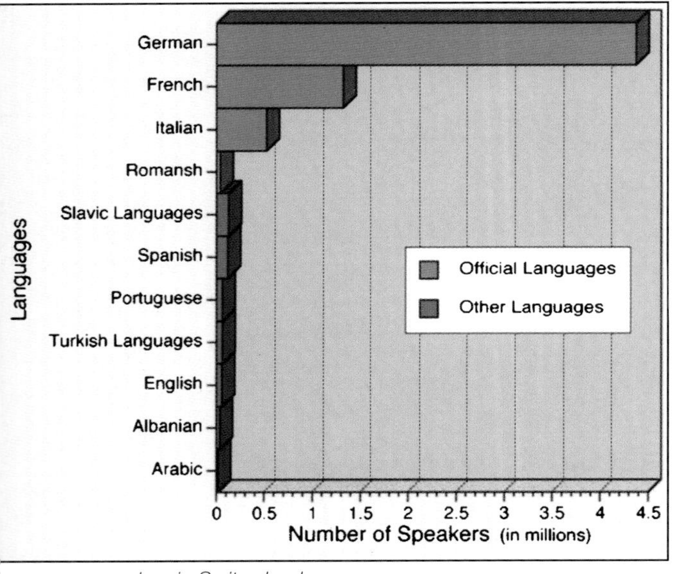

Languages spoken in Switzerland.

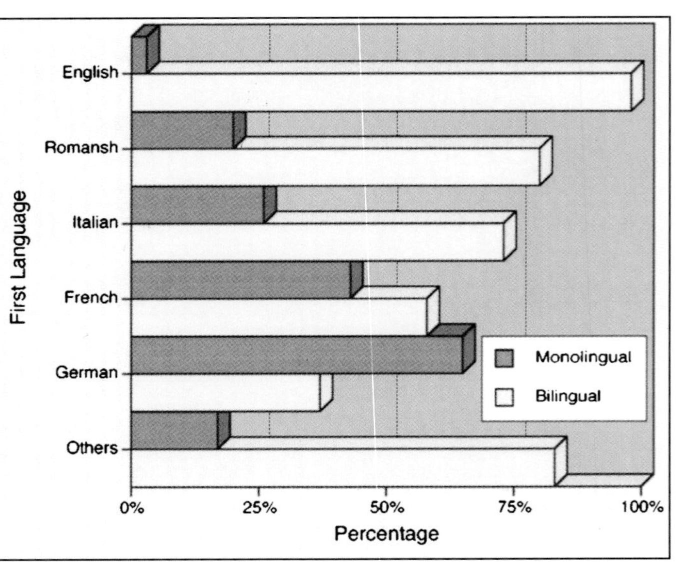

Monolingual and bilingual population of Switzerland, 1990. (Source: SFCO, 1994).

North East Europe

Belarus

Belarus was formerly a constituent republic of the USSR, but in August 1991 it achieved independence. It is estimated that three-quarters of the population are ethnic Belorussians, and the majority speak Belorussian as a native language. During the Soviet era, Russian was the official language of the country, and predominated in business, administration and education. Since 1990, Belorussian has had official status and its use has increased. In 1995, the population of Belarus was estimated to be over 10.4 million.

The Belorussians are related closely to Russians and Ukrainians, both culturally and linguistically, and most Belorussians also speak one of these languages. Another name for Belorussian is White Russian. Russians and Ukrainians form the largest minority language groups in Belarus. Russians count for 13 percent of the population, living mostly in the urbanized, industrial areas of the country. The Belorussians have tended to live in rural areas.

The figures used for the minority language graph, as for other former USSR republics, are from the 1979 USSR census. According to these figures, there were 100,000 Ukrainian speakers living in Belarus, 31,000 Polish speakers, and 15,000 Yiddish speakers. Figures for 1995 on the ethnic composition of Belarus suggest that Poles now account for 4.1 percent of the population, and Ukrainians for 2.9 percent.

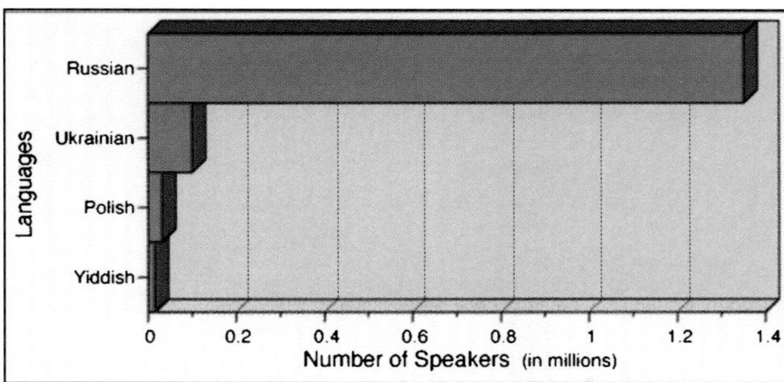

Languages spoken in Belarus. The official language, Belorussian, not shown on chart, has about 7.8 million speakers.

Estonia

On the January 6th, 1991, Estonia was recognized as an independent republic by the former USSR. The country

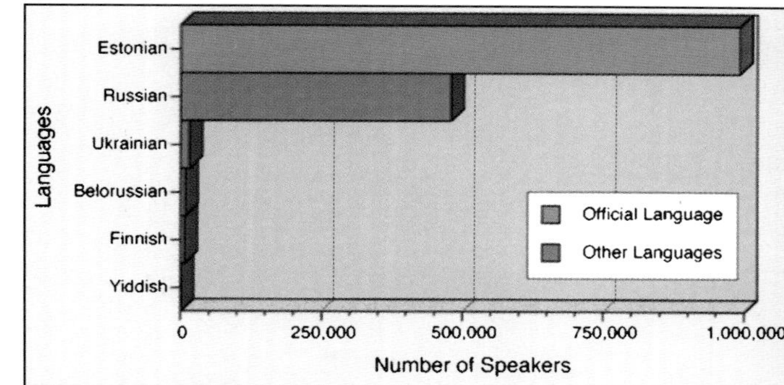

Languages spoken in Estonia.

has an estimated population of 1.6 million (1995). During the Soviet era, Russian was the predominant language of business, administration and education, but now the sole official language is Estonian, and the use of Russian has decreased. Estonian is spoken by 62 percent of Estonian citizens. At the beginning of Soviet rule in 1940, the percentage was much higher, closer to 89 percent, but the in-migration of Russians to the country reduced this figure dramatically.

Russians still form a large part of the Estonian population. They count for almost 30 percent of the population, making them the largest minority group in Estonia. Most of the Russian speakers live in urban, industrialized areas. In the city of Narva, in the north-eastern area of the country, the inhabitants are almost exclusively Russian. On the other hand, over half the ethnic Estonians live in rural areas of the country.

Other minority languages in Estonia include Ukrainian, Belorussian, Finnish and Yiddish. The figures used in the minority language graph are based on the 1979 USSR Census. However, recent estimates indicate that Ukrainians count for 3.17 percent of the population, Belorussians count for 1.8 percent, and the Finns for just over one percent. Many of the Finnish speakers also speak Russian. In these estimates, another 2.13 percent was ascribed to 'other' language groups. These other minority groups include Jews, Latvians and Swedish speakers.

Finland

Finland has an estimated population of five million (1995), and 93.5 percent speak Finnish as their mother tongue. Finnish and Swedish are both official languages.

Finland is usually described as being a Scandinavian country, but Finnish is not related to Swedish or to the other Scandinavian languages, Norwegian, Danish, Icelandic, Greenlandic and Faroese. There are about 296,000 Swedish speakers in Finland, about six percent of the total population. Most Swedish speakers live along the south-eastern coast in the province of Ahvenanmaa, and on the coast of Ostrobothnia. Most are bilingual in Swedish and Finnish. There are Swedish language newspapers, a radio station and TV programs in Finland.

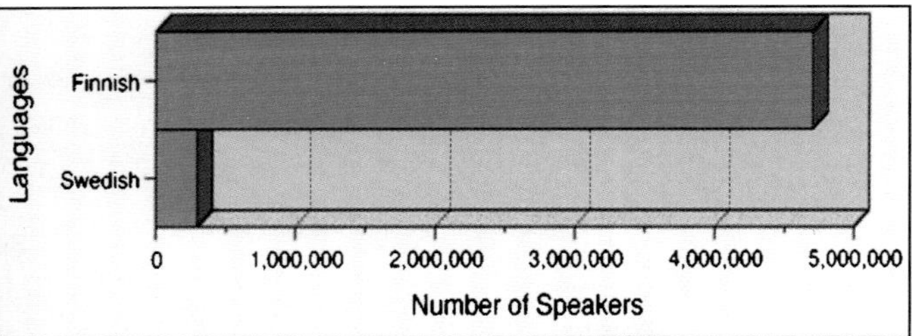

Official languages spoken in Finland.

A minority language in Finland, and other areas of Scandinavia (see map page 410) is that of the Sámi people. Sámi is spoken by an estimated 2,000 people in the north of Finland. It is difficult to specify the exact number of Sámi speakers due to their nomadic lifestyle. Most of the Sámi living in Finland are bilingual in Sámi and Finnish. Throughout Finland, Norway, Sweden and the Kola Peninsula in Russia, there are estimated to be between 70,000 and 80,000 Sámi people.

Although the numbers of foreign residents living in Finland has been fairly low in the past, the figure is now growing. In 1990, there were 26,200 foreign residents, a figure which had more than doubled since 1980 when foreign residents numbered 12,800. In-migrants have moved to Finland from Sweden, Germany, America and the former Soviet Union. According to 1993 statistics, the number of foreigners in Finland has gone up to 50,000, with Russians as the largest group.

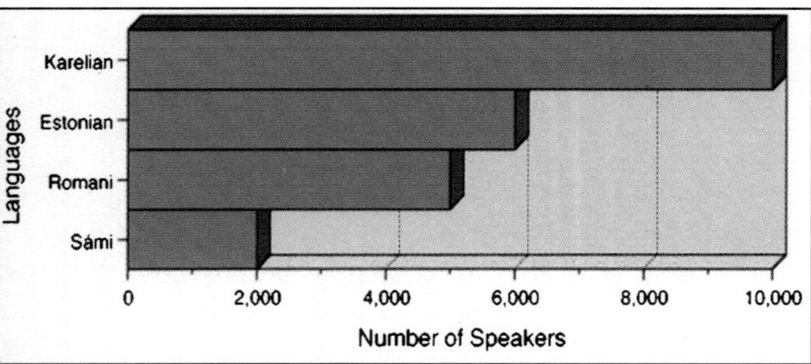

Main minority languages spoken in Finland.

Latvia

Both Latvia and Lithuania declared their independence from the USSR on September 6th, 1991. The official language of Latvia is Latvian, a Baltic language closely related to Lithuanian. It is the language used by the majority of ethnic Latvians.

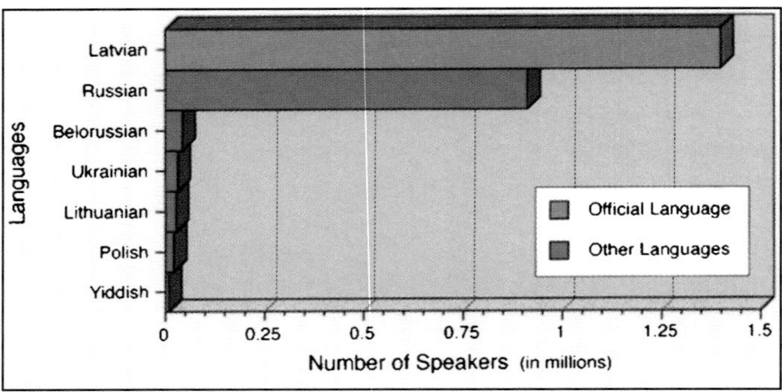

Languages spoken in Latvia.

Ethnic Latvians, or Letts, form 52 percent of the population, estimated at 2.7 million in 1995. This percentage was considerably higher before Latvia became part of the USSR in 1940. Letts formed 75 percent of the population in 1923. Russian in-migration into Latvia increased the proportion of Russian speakers to 33.8 percent of the Republic's population. The majority of the Russians live in urban, industrialized areas.

Minority language groups in Latvia include Belorussian, Ukrainian, Polish and Yiddish speakers. Each group is relatively small. Belorussians make up 4.5 percent, Ukrainians 3.4 percent, and Poles 2.3 percent of the population.

Lithuania

Lithuania declared its independence from the USSR on September 6th, 1991. The official language is Lithuanian, a Baltic language closely related to Latvian. The population was estimated to be 3.8 million in 1995, and over 80

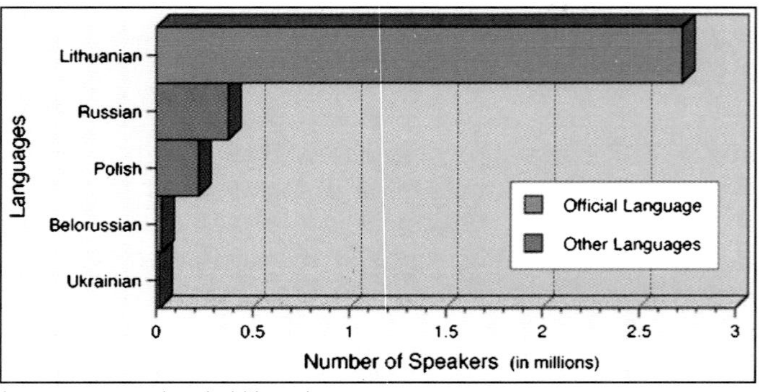

Languages spoken in Lithuania.

percent are ethnic Lithuanians, who speak Lithuanian as a first language.

The figures represented on the graph are those from the 1979 USSR Census, listing Polish, Belorussian, Ukrainian and Yiddish as minority languages in Lithuania. Russian is also spoken in Lithuania by a small percentage of the population. According to recent estimates, Russian speakers count for 8.6 percent of the population, while Polish speakers constitute 7.7 percent and are concentrated mainly in the south of the country. Belorussians make up 1.5 percent of the population and other groups form 2.1 percent.

Norway

The estimated population of Norway in 1995 was 4.3 million, 99.5 percent of whom speak the official language, Norwegian. Norwegian is closely related to both Danish and Swedish. The languages of these three neighboring Nordic countries are so similar that their speakers can understand each other to varying degrees.

There are two official written varieties of Norwegian, Bokmål (Book Norwegian) and Nynorsk (New Norwegian). Both have equal status. Bokmål is mainly used in cities and in the thickly populated area of east Norway surrounding Oslo. Nynorsk is the main language used along the western coast and the mountain districts of central Norway.

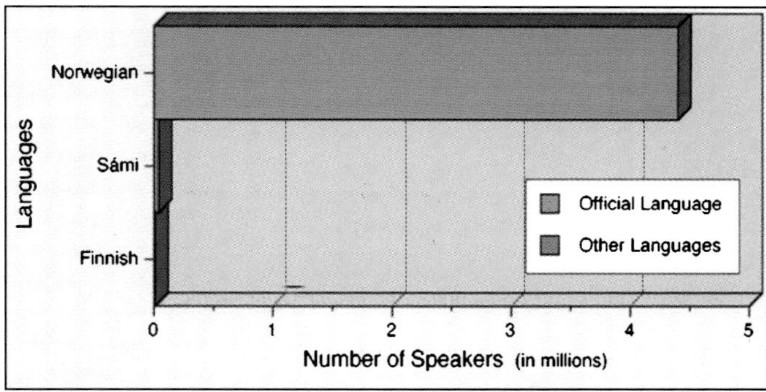

Languages spoken in Norway. (Source: Helander, 1992).

The media, schools and administration use both languages, but Bokmål predominates. The majority of books and magazines are published in Bokmål, and it is also the language used in business, advertising and industrial training. The language used in the schools varies from region to region depending on the choice of the local communities. Over 80 percent of schoolchildren use Bokmål, and between 16 and 17 percent use Nynorsk. (See page 215.)

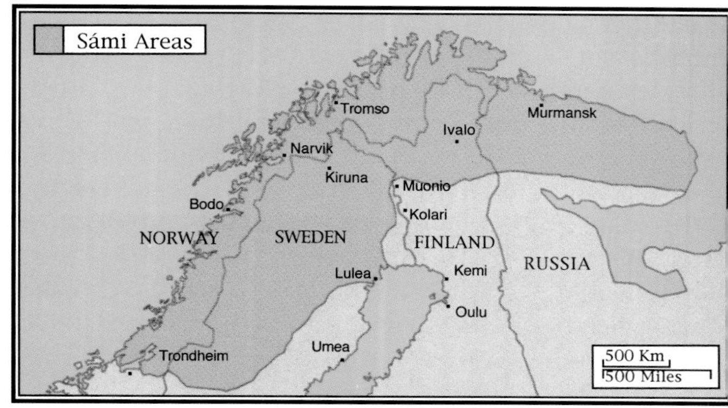

Sámi Areas

There are various minority language groups living in Norway. Around 10,000 Finnish speakers live in Norway, mainly in Finnmark in the North of the country. They constitute just over 0.2 percent of the population.

Another minority language within Norway is Sámi, which belongs to the same language family as Finnish. The Sámi live in the subarctic regions of Norway, Sweden, Finland and Russia. The total Sámi population throughout these four countries is estimated at 70,000 to 80,000. In Norway, it is estimated that the Sámi population numbers 40,000. Most of the Sámi also speak the main language of the country in which they live.

Poland

Most of the 38.7 million inhabitants of Poland speak Polish, the official language of the country. Ethnic Poles make up 98 percent of the country's population. Minority language groups count for two percent of the population.

Before the Second World War, minority languages formed a much more substantial 35 percent of the population. Poland not only had a large number of Germans, Ukrainians and Belorussians but also a Yiddish-speaking Jewish minority. Many Polish Jews did not survive the Holocaust, and, after the Second World War, large numbers of Germans, Ukrainians and Belorussians were expelled from the country. The boundaries of Poland were also changed: it lost its eastern territories and gained land to the west. Poland became far more homogeneous, both ethnically and linguistically.

Currently, the largest minority groups in Poland are the Germans, Ukrainians and the Belorussians. German communities are found mainly in the Opole region and Silesia, and, since 1991, some primary schools in these regions have offered education through the medium of German. The Ukrainians are found throughout Poland, and the Belorussians are concentrated mainly in the

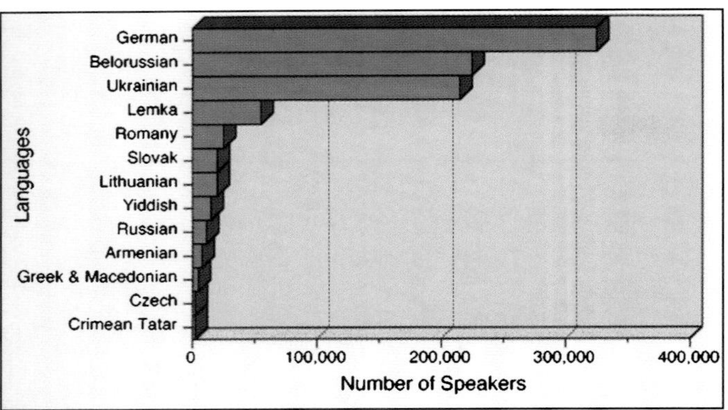

Languages spoken in Poland. The official language, Polish, not shown on chart, has 36 million speakers. (Source: Bulletin from the Office for Ethnic Minorities, Poland, 1993).

north-east. Smaller minority groups include Lithuanians, Slovaks, Greeks, Jews, and Tatars. Most of these groups speak both a minority language and Polish.

Russia

Russia is one of the largest countries in the world. It is home to over 100 nationalities and has an estimated population of almost 150 million (1995). Russian is the official language. Over 81 percent of the population are ethnic Russians. These Russian speakers are unlikely to speak a minority language. Only 4.1 percent of Russians in the former USSR could speak a language other than Russian. However most of the minority ethnic groups are bilingual in their minority language and Russian. Because of the difficulty in trying to represent over 100 languages on the minority language chart, only the languages with more than 500,000 speakers have been included. The data derive from the 1979 USSR census.

The largest minority ethnic and language group is the Tatars, who constitute 3.8 percent of the country's population. Tatar is the mother tongue of 85.9 percent of this ethnic group. Ukrainians make up 2.9 percent of the Russian population, and Chuvash 1.2 percent.

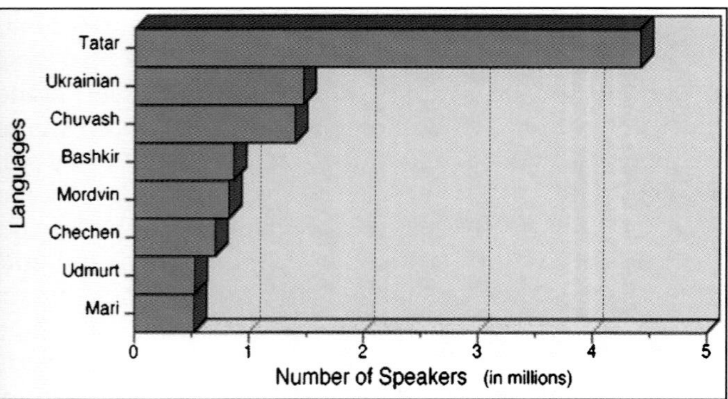

Languages spoken in Russia (with more than 500,000 speakers). The official language, Russian, not shown on chart, has over 121 million speakers.

Other ethnic groups with relatively large populations are the Bashkir, Mordvin, Chechens, Udmurt and Mari. Both the Mordvinians and Udmurts live along the border with Finland, in the Volga or Urals area. Although most of the minority languages count for less that one percent of the total Russian population, within certain regions, they form a relatively high percentage. For example the Karelian language has only 75,000 speakers and counts for only 0.05 percent of the country's population. However, within the region of Karelia, its speakers form 11 percent of the population.

Most minority language speakers also speak Russian, which is widely used throughout the country as a language of business, commerce and official life. During the 76 years of the Soviet Union, official policy gradually moved away from the equality of all Soviet languages to the promotion of Russian (see page 294). Russian is a compulsory subject in all schools and many minority language children are educated in the Russian language. Contemporary Russia has 21 ethnically based republics, one autonomous region and ten autonomous national areas, where minority languages have varying degrees of official status. Thus the languages of the larger ethnic groups have been maintained. The smaller minority groups, tending to live in scattered communities, have been more likely to shift to Russian.

Sweden

Most of the 8.8 million inhabitants of Sweden (1995 estimate) are native speakers of Swedish, the official language of the country. In 1986, 93 percent of the population were native Swedish speakers.

Finnish and Sámi are the main minority languages in Sweden. There are about 300,000 Finnish speakers forming three percent of the population. Most live on the

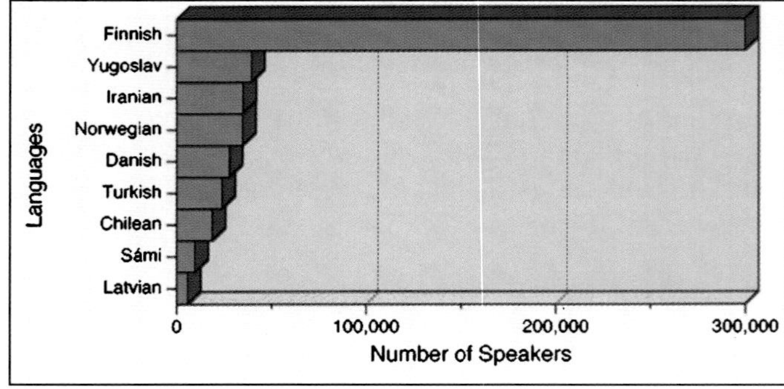

Languages spoken in Sweden. The official language, Swedish, not shown on chart, has 8.1 million speakers.

north-east coast of the country. The majority of the Sámi live in the north. It is estimated that there are about 10,000 Sámi speakers.

There are also small numbers of Danes, Germans and Norwegians, plus an estimated six thousand Latvians living in Sweden. After the Second World War, Sweden received a large number of refugees from the Baltic states. The in-migrants included Latvians, Serbo-Croat and Turkish people. It is the policy of the Swedish government to encourage minority language speakers to learn Swedish, while making some educational provision for the maintenance of minority languages.

Svalbard

Svalbard (formerly Spitzbergen) consists of an archipelago in the Arctic Ocean, and is a Norwegian territory.

The population of just under 3000 (1995 estimate) consists of 35 percent Norwegians and 64 percent Russians. Both Norwegian and Russian are spoken.

Eastern Europe

Albania

Albania is one of the smallest countries in Europe, and it is also one of the most linguistically homogeneous. Almost 98 percent of the 3.4 million inhabitants (1995 estimate) are ethnic Albanians, and Albanian is the official language of the county.

Two main dialects of Albanian are spoken, Tosk and Gheg. Tosk is spoken in the south of Albania, and the official language is based on this dialect. Gheg is spoken in northern Albania, and most Gheg speakers also speak standard Albanian. The speakers of both dialects can generally understand one another.

Minority languages in Albania include 60,000 speakers of both Greek and Romany, and small groups of Bulgarians and Serbs.

Bosnia and Herzegovina

Bosnia and Herzegovina, commonly called Bosnia, were formerly part of the now defunct Socialist Federal Republic of Yugoslavia. The country declared its independence in March 1992. However, the Bosnian Serbs took up arms to resist this, and to create Serb-controlled areas within Bosnia.

Before the war, Muslims constituted the largest ethnic group in Bosnia and Herzegovina, representing 44 percent of the population. Muslims are descendants of Turks and Slavs who converted to Islam during the period when the region was part of the Turkish Ottoman Empire. Serbs constituted 31 percent and Croats made up 17 percent of the population. These figures are not a reliable guide to the present situation, since there has been considerable dislocation of population since 1992 due to military action and 'ethnic cleansing'. The estimated population in 1995 was 3.2 million.

All three main ethnic groups speak varieties of a south Slavic language, which is called different names by different groups. The language has generally been known as Serbo-Croat, or Serbian and Croatian, reflecting the fact that the two main ethnic groups, Serbs and Croats, have developed two separate literary or standard languages, Serbian and Croatian. By establishing separate autonomous standards during the 19th century, and by maximizing the differences between the two standard languages, both Serbs and Croats have sought to reinforce their distinct ethnic identity. One main difference is in the orthography. Croatian uses the Roman alphabet, while Serbian uses the Cyrillic script. (Muslims also tend to use the Roman script.) There are also lexical differences between the different languages, and differences in the way they have expanded their lexical resources, Serbian tending to accept foreign borrowings, while Croatian is more puristic. Since the start of the war in 1992, Serbians and Croatians have increasingly attempted to distance their two languages from one another.

In Bosnia and Herzegovina, where one ethnic group does not predominate, the official usage has tended to draw on both Serbian and Croatian, using forms from both languages interchangeably.

Bulgaria

There are approximately 8.7 million people living in Bulgaria (1995 estimate), and an estimated 85 percent are speakers of Bulgarian, the official language. Bulgarian is closely related to the Macedonian language, and there is a small minority of Macedonian speakers in the country, approximately 2.5 percent of the population. However, in Bulgaria, Macedonian is not recognized as a separate language, but as a dialect of Bulgarian.

The minority language graph is based on the 1965 linguistic census figures available for Bulgaria. More recent figures classify the population along the lines of ethnic divisions, but the number of minority language speakers corresponds fairly closely to ethnic breakdown.

The largest minority are Turks, the descendants of Turks who moved to the country when it was a part of the Ottoman Empire. They make up approximately nine percent of the population. Other smaller minority groups included on the following chart are Romany, Gagauz, Tatar and Albanian. For example, in 1990, it was estimated that there were six thousand Tatars. Most of the 12,000 Gagauz live along the coast of Bulgaria. Both of these languages are closely related to Turkish.

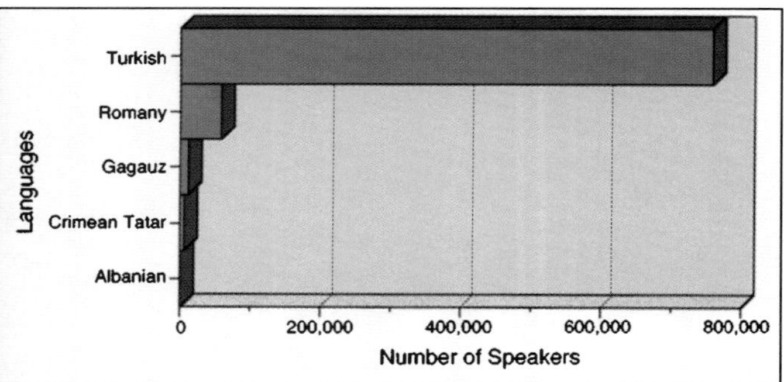

Languages spoken in Bulgaria. The official language, Bulgarian, not shown on chart, has 7.3 million speakers.

Croatia

Croatia was formerly one of the six constituent republics of the Socialist Federal Republic of Yugoslavia which now no longer exists. Croatia declared its independence in June, 1991 and the estimated population in 1995 was 4.6 million. However, it is not easy to make an accurate estimate of the population, because since the commencement of the war in 1992, large numbers of Croatian and Serbian refugees have crossed the border from Bosnia. Over two-thirds of the population are ethnic Croats, speaking Croatian, a south Slavic language.

There are five south Slavic languages, Bulgarian, Macedonian, Croatian, Serbian and Slovenian. Croatian and Serbian are so closely related that they have been regarded by some as the same language, and have traditionally been called by the collective term Serbo-Croat. Variants of this language are spoken by the three main ethnic groups in the territory of the former Yugoslavia: the Serbs, Croats and Muslims. However, the two most prominent ethnic groups, the Serbs and the Croats, have sought to maximize their own ethnic identities and the differences between them, including linguistic differences.

Since the 19th century, the two ethnic groups have developed their own autonomous literary standards. The most obvious difference between the Serbian and Croatian standard languages is that the former is written in the Cyrillic script, like most other Slavic languages (e.g. Russian), while Croatian employs the Roman alphabet. There are also differences in vocabulary and methods of creating new words. Both ethnic groups have jealously guarded the distinctiveness and autonomy of their own literary standards. In the 1960s, the production of a joint Serbo-Croat dictionary in the two scripts was stopped because the Croats felt that distinctive Croat usage was not sufficiently acknowledged. Since independence, the Croatians have sought further to increase the distance between Croatian and Serbian by resurrecting some archaic Croatian words and phrases.

According to the 1991 census, 78.1 percent of the population of Croatia were ethnic Croats. Ethnic Serbs are the largest minority in Croatia. In 1991, they represented 12 percent of the population. In 1996, Croatian Serb separatists still controlled about a third of Croatian territory. Other small minority groups include Muslims (0.9 percent), Slovenians (0.5 percent), Hungarians (0.5 percent) and Italians.

Cyprus

Cyprus, the third largest island in the Mediterranean, has an estimated population of 736,000 (1995). The population of the island is divided into two main ethnic groups, the Turks, about 12.9 percent of the population, and the Greeks, about 84.1 percent of the total. The remaining three percent of the population are foreigners residing in Cyprus. Both Greek and Turkish are official languages in Cyprus.

The language of the Greek Cypriot community is Greek, and much of the community adheres to the Greek Orthodox Church of Cyprus. In 1983, the north of Cyprus, where the majority of the Cypriot Turks live,

declared its independence, forming the Turkish Republic of Northern Cyprus. The Turkish Cypriot community generally adheres to Islam. The independence of the region is recognized only by Turkey.

The two main minority languages spoken on Cyprus are Armenian and Arabic. It is estimated that there are around 20,000 speakers of both these languages. Most speakers of Armenian and Arabic also speak Greek.

Greece

Greek is the official language of Greece, and is spoken by an overwhelming majority of the population. There are 10.6 million people living in Greece (1995 estimate), and the native language of 98 percent of the population is Greek.

Minority languages in Greece include Macedonian, Albanian, Turkish, Macedo-Romanian, Bulgarian and Armenian. The largest minority group in Greece are the Macedonians, who count for 1.8 percent of the population. Albanian is spoken by small communities in central and southern Greece. Turkish is found mainly in the Aegean regions of Greece, and their Muslim communities have some limited protection and rights. Some subjects in Muslim schools are taught through the medium of Turkish, and the rest through Greek.

Macedo-Romanian, or Arumanian, is spoken by around 50,000 people in Greece, mainly in the northern regions of the country. Armenian and Bulgarian are the smallest minority language groups. The Armenians constitute 0.2 percent of the population, and the Bulgarians around 0.3 percent. However, in the region of Kastoria on the border with Albania, the percentage of Bulgarian speakers is higher than Greek. None of these minority languages has official status.

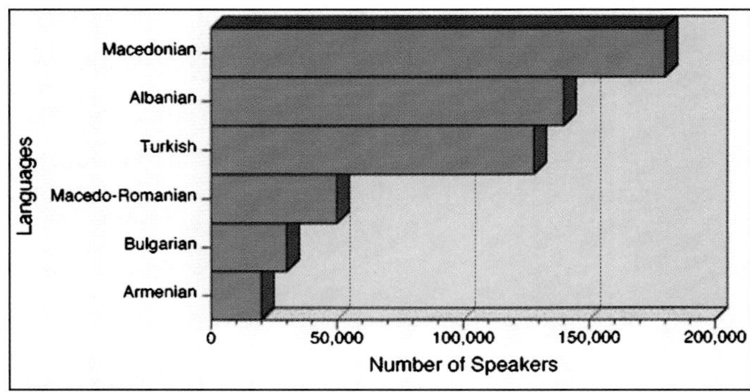

Languages spoken in Greece. The official language, Greek, not shown on chart, has 10.3 million speakers.

Hungary

Hungary has a population of over 10.3 million (1995 estimate), and about 98 percent speak Hungarian, the official language, as their mother tongue. Although Hungary is a fairly homogeneous country linguistically, this has not always been the case. Before the First World War, Hungarians constituted a minority in the country, but, as a part of the Treaty of Trianon, the country was reduced in size and the population reduced by about two-thirds. The land and people which remained in Hungarian control were the areas with the highest concentration of Hungarians.

There are some small minority groups within Hungary: Romanies, Germans, Slovaks, Romanians, Croatians, Serbs and Slovenes. There are also a number of Bulgarians, Greeks, Poles and Armenians. These ethnic minorities live throughout Hungary, but the number of people in the different ethnic groups is much higher in some cases than the number who speak the relevant minority languages. None of the minority languages have been given official status, with Hungarian recognized as the language of education and government. However, the Constitution does guarantee equal rights and freedom to all the national minorities to speak their own language.

On October 23rd, 1989, Hungary became a democratic republic after four decades of Russian domination and one-party rule. During the period 1948–1989, the Russian language was widely used in official life and was a compulsory subject in school, although few Hungarians learnt to speak fluent Russian. Since independence, the Russian language has been less used and there has been a fresh emphasis on the rights of minority language groups within Hungary. In 1990, the Office for National and Ethnic Minorities was set up by the government to ensure the enforcement of minority rights, and in 1993, parliament passed a law which embodied the rights of national and ethnic minorities.

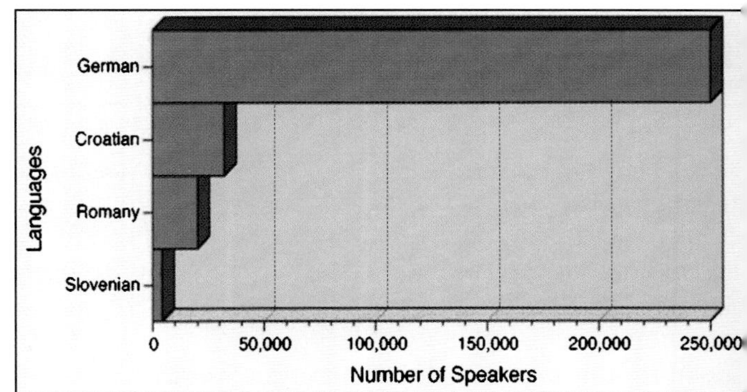

Minority languages of Hungary. The official language, Hungarian, not shown on chart, has about 10 million first language speakers.

Since 1989, there has been a growing movement for bilingual education, with Hungarian as the national language along with either a foreign or a minority language present in Hungary.

The Former Yugoslav Republic of Macedonia

Macedonia was formerly part of the Socialist Federal Republic of Yugoslavia, which came to an end in 1992, after four out of the six constituent republics seceded. Macedonia declared its independence in September 1991, and has temporarily adopted the name, The Former Yugoslav Republic of Macedonia, pending the settlement of a dispute with Greece, which objected to the use of the name 'Macedonia'. The majority of the population (67 percent) are ethnic Macedonians, and speak Macedonian, a Slavic language closely related to Serbian, Croatian and Bulgarian. Macedonian is similar to Bulgarian and is sometimes been regarded as a variety of that language.

Macedonian is spoken by about 200,000 people in Bulgaria, where it is viewed as a dialect of Bulgarian, and also in the province of Macedonia in northern Greece, where the language is called Slavika. However, in the Republic of Macedonia, a separate Macedonian literary language has been in existence since 1944, and most scholars now accept Macedonian as a separate language. The Macedonian standard language is based on a different group of dialects from the Bulgarian, and it is also written in a different version of the Cyrillic script.

Albanian Muslims are the largest minority language group, making up about 20 percent of the population according to the 1991 census. (Albanian politicians claim that the figure is much higher.) They speak Albanian, the official language of Albania, also spoken in southern Greece and parts of Italy. Turks constitute four percent of the population, Serbs two percent, Romany two percent and other ethnic groups five percent. Serbian and Croatian is commonly spoken. In 1995, the estimated population was 2.15 million. (An 1994 official government census gave the population as 1.94 million, but minority groups may have been under-represented).

Moldova

Moldova was formerly a member of the USSR, gaining its independence in 1991. The official language of the country is Moldavian. Moldavian and Romanian are often regarded as the same language, although there are regional differences. Also, Romanian uses the Roman alphabet while Moldavian uses the Cyrillic alphabet.

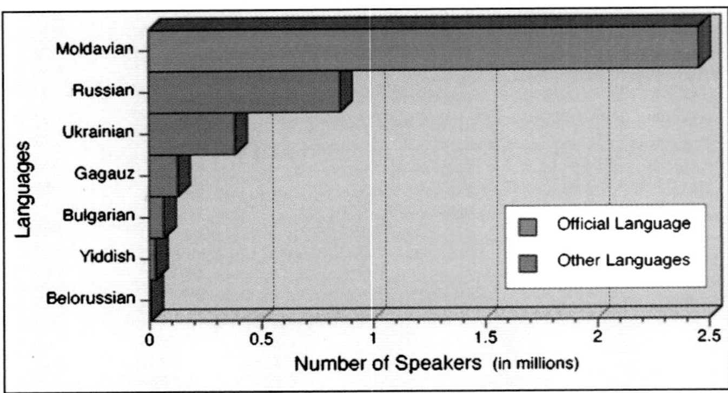

Languages spoken in Moldova.

The figures represented on the minority language chart are from the 1979 USSR census. No figures were available on language minority groups since independence.

There are approximately 4.5 million people living in Moldova (1995 estimate), and around 64 percent of these are ethnic Moldavians. Russians and Ukrainians form the two largest minority groups, each comprising 13 percent of the total population. The census figures for the former USSR show that the Russian group used to be considerably larger before independence, constituting 22 percent of the population. The majority of Ukrainians and Russians are concentrated in the Dnestr region, in the east of the country.

Other ethnic groups include Bulgarians and Gagauz. Gagauz numbered over 126,000 speakers in the 1979 USSR census, and is a language closely related to Turkish. The speakers of this language are concentrated mainly in the south-west of Moldova.

Romania

Romanian is the official language of Romania. The country has an estimated population of over 23 million (1995), and Romanian speakers constitute approximately 89 percent of this population.

Other languages spoken include Hungarian, German, Turkish, Romany, Bulgarian and Tatar. The Hungarian population are an important minority within Romania. They count for about seven percent of the population and live mainly in central Romania, in Transylvania. This part of the country has, at various periods through history, been a part of Hungary. Hungary's claim on the area is based on the large numbers of Hungarians, or Magyars, living there. It is estimated that between two and a half and three million Hungarian speakers live in the region. They perceive themselves as Hungarians rather than Romanians, and there has been considerable

ethnic tension. The region was last in Hungarian possession during the Second World War, but was subsequently returned to Romania.

The Transylvanian area of Romania is also home to many German speakers. They make up around 1.5 percent of the country's population. The other smaller minority groups are located throughout Romania, but count for only a very small percentage of the country's population.

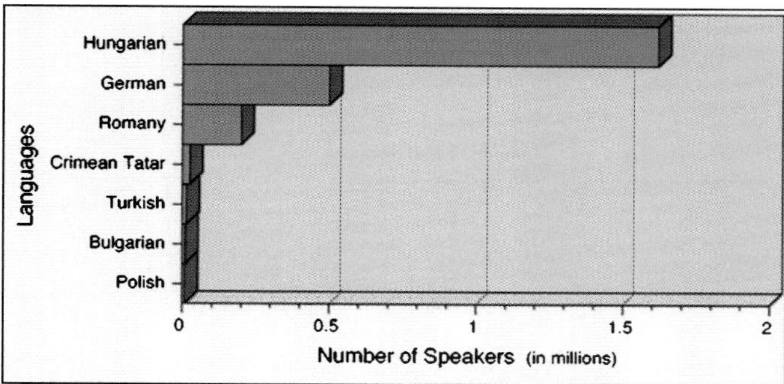

Languages spoken in Romania. The official language, Romanian, not shown on chart, has 19.5 million speakers.

Serbia and Montenegro

The two republics of Serbia and Montenegro, together with the autonomous provinces of Vojvodina and Kosovo, have, since 1992, constituted the Federal Republic of Yugoslavia, a country that was not internationally recognized in 1996. The former Socialist Federal Republic of Yugoslavia became defunct in 1992, after four of its six constituent republics, Bosnia and Herzegovina, Croatia, Macedonia and Slovenia, declared their independence. The former territory of Yugoslavia is inhabited by three main ethnic groups, and power conflicts between these groups provided the impetus for the break up of the former Yugoslavia, and for the subsequent conflicts.

The three groups, Serbs, Croats and Muslims, all speak varieties of the same south Slavic language, that has often been internationally known as Serbo-Croat. However, Serbian and Croatian have developed two different literary standard languages since the 19th century, reflecting the desire for recognition and maintenance of a separate ethnic identity on the part of the Serb and Croat groups. Serbians write the language in the Cyrillic script, like other Slavic languages, including Russian, while Croats and Muslims write the language in the Roman alphabet. There are some regional differences, and these have been emphasized and extended since the beginning of the conflict. The majority group in the new Yugoslavia are the Serbs, who comprise 63 percent of the population (75 percent in the republic of Serbia). Serbian is the official language, and the language spoken by the Serbs and Montenegrins. The latter constitute about six percent of the population, living primarily in Montenegro. Albanian Muslims comprise about 14 percent of the population of the new Yugoslavia. Hungarians, who live primarily in the autonomous province of Vojvodina in the north, constitute four percent. There are also a small group of Romanies. These figures are from the 1991 census. The estimated population of Serbia and Montenegro in 1995 was just over 11 million.

Slovenia

Slovenia was formerly part of the Socialist Federal Republic of Yugoslavia, which ceased to exist in 1992, after four out of the six constituent republics seceded. Slovenia declared its independence in June 1991, and the estimated population of the country in 1995 was two million. Ethnic Slovenes constitute more than 90 percent of the country's population and speak Slovenian, the official language. Slovenian is a south Slavic language closely related to Serbian and Croatian. It is written in the Roman alphabet, like Croatian and unlike Serbian and most other Slavic languages which use the Cyrillic script. Ethnic Serbs (about two percent), Croats (about three percent), Muslims (about one percent) and various other ethnic groups (about four percent) constitute the remainder of Slovenia's population. Serbian and Croatian, and also German, are widely spoken in Slovenia.

Turkey

Turkey's estimated population in 1995 was 63 million. The vast majority are Turks, and Turkish is spoken as a first language by 90 percent of the population. Turkish is the official language.

There are a number of minority language groups within Turkey. The 1965 census was the last to include a question on language, and the minority language chart is based on these figures.

Two minority languages which have not been included on the chart are Kurdish and Arabic. These are relatively large groups, compared to the other minority languages. There were 2.3 million Kurdish speakers in the last census, and it is currently estimated that there are 3.9 million first language Kurdish speakers, mostly living in the eastern provinces of Turkey. Most of the Kurdish population are bilingual in Kurdish and Turkish, and many Turks speak Kurdish as a second language.

Arabic was spoken by 365,000 at the time of the last census. It is estimated that their current number lies

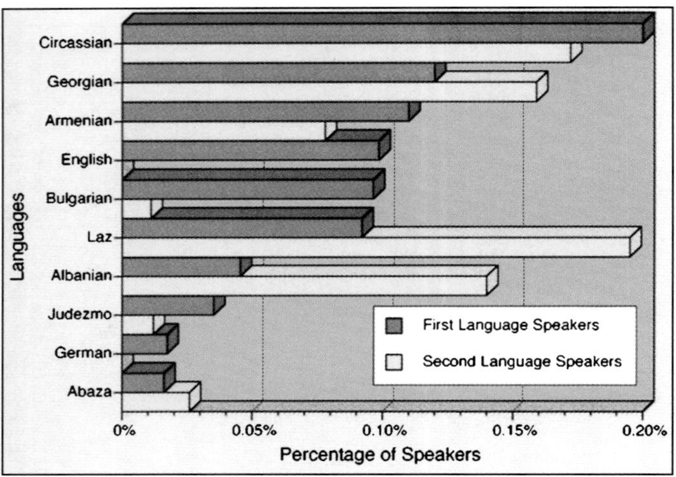

Minority languages spoken in Turkey (excluding Arabic, Kurdish and Greek). The official language, Turkish, not shown on chart, has an estimated 56.7 million speakers. Kurdish has an estimated 3.9 million speakers, Arabic between 600 and 800 thousand, and Greek between 5 and 8 thousand.

between 600,000 and 800,000. Most live in the southeast in enclaves adjacent to Syria and are bilingual in Arabic and Turkish.

Circassian is the largest minority language shown on the chart, spoken by over 58,000. Circassian communities are to be found throughout the whole of Turkey. Most of the Greeks, Armenians and Judezmo speakers live in the cities of Istanbul and Ankara. (Judezmo is a Romance language spoken by Jews). The number of Greeks living in Turkey has declined in recent decades, and a recent estimate numbers their population at between five and eight thousand.

Other minority languages in Turkey include Georgian, English, Bulgarian, Laz, Albanian, German and Abaza. A high percentage in all the different minority language communities also speak Turkish and there is also bilingualism in two minority languages.

Ukraine

Ukraine became an independent republic in 1991, as did many other Soviet republics. Both Ukrainian and Russian are official languages in the country. The Ukrainian language is closely related to Russian, and Ukrainians are also known as Little Russians. The Ukraine has a population of nearly 52 million (1995 estimate), of which 72 percent are native speakers of Ukrainian. Russians constitute 22 percent of the population, and live mainly in urban areas. Many of the larger cities are predominantly Russian-speaking.

The figures for the other minority language groups derive from the 1979 USSR census. These include Romanian, Bulgarian, Hungarian, Belorussian, Yiddish, Tatar, Polish and Greek. Romanian, the largest minority language listed, has nearly 300,000 speakers, counting for less than 0.6 percent of the population.

The distribution of these ethnic groups within the Ukraine varies from region to region. Western Ukraine is predominantly Ukrainian, with most minority groups living throughout the rest of the country.

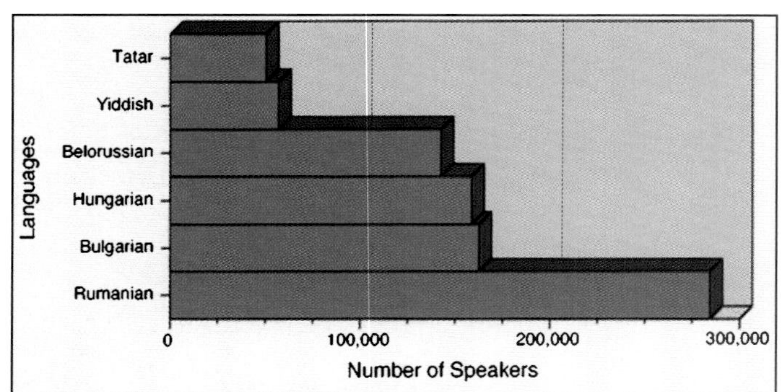

Languages spoken in the Ukraine. Russian, not shown on chart, is spoken by 11.4 million people. The official language, Ukranian, not shown on chart, is spoken by 37.4 million.

United Kingdom and Ireland

United Kingdom

The majority of the population of the United Kingdom (which includes England, Scotland, Wales and Northern Ireland) are monolingual English speakers. It is estimated that between 95 percent and 98 percent of the United Kingdom are monolingual in English. Thus, ipso facto, English is the all-powerful and dominant language of the United Kingdom, not needing official or legal ratification. Compared, for example, with the United States or Canada, the United Kingdom is a relatively monolingual country. However, there is linguistic diversity within the UK.

The linguistic diversity of the United Kingdom has various elements. In Northern Ireland, Scotland and Wales

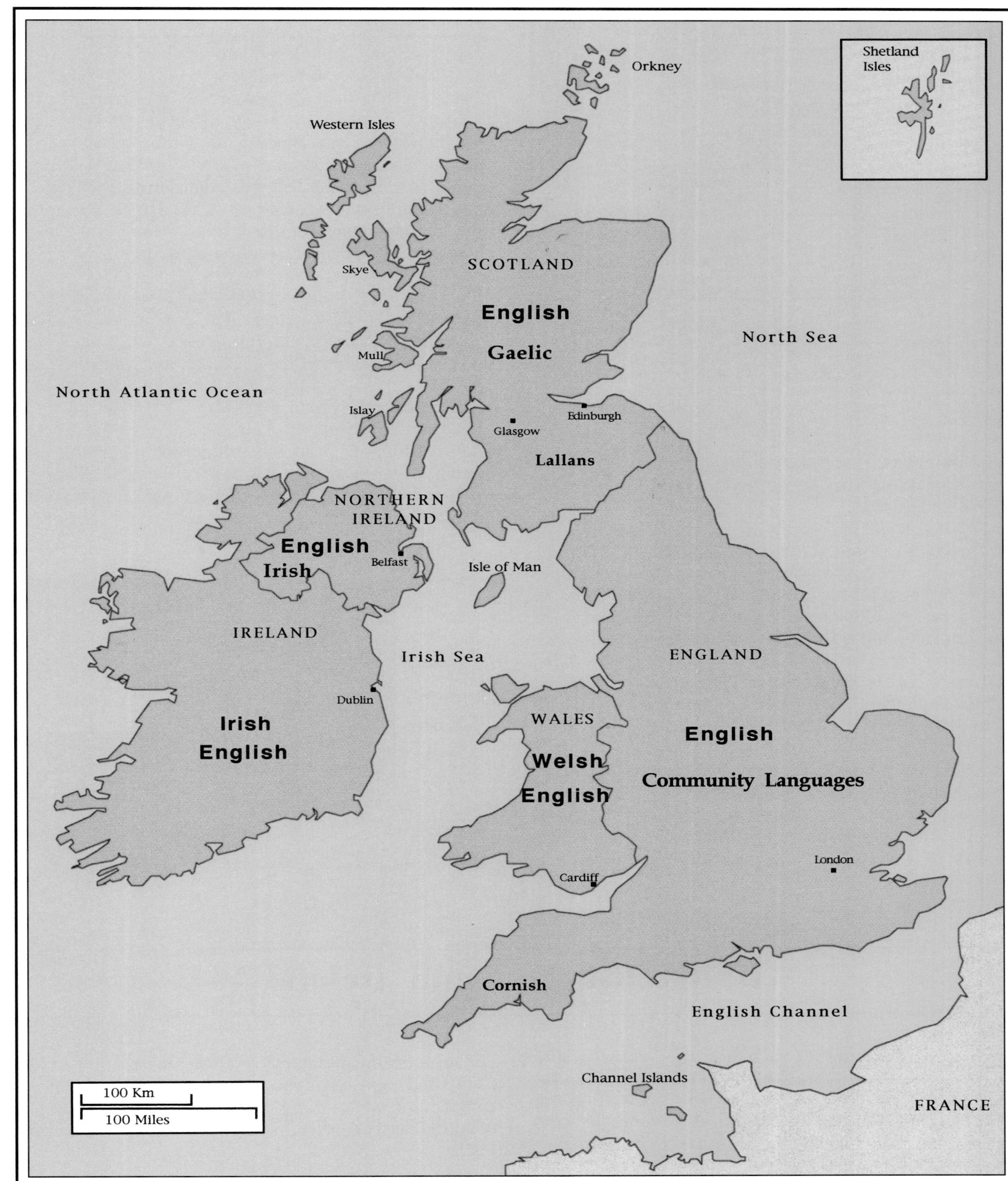

Languages in the United Kingdom and Ireland

there are different Celtic languages. In Northern Ireland, 6.6 percent are bilingual in Irish Gaelic and English (see the entry under Ireland, page 421); in Scotland, 1.4 percent are bilingual in Scottish Gaelic and English; and in Wales, 18.7 percent are bilingual in Welsh and English. However only the Welsh language has been given official status (within the borders of Wales).

Another element in the linguistic diversity of the United Kingdom comes with recent in-migrant languages, sometimes called 'Community Languages' or 'those for whom English is an additional language'. Such Community Languages include Bengali, Panjabi, Hindi, Gujarati, Cantonese, Italian, Polish, Greek and Turkish speakers. These groups will be considered next. Entries for the Celtic regions appear later.

Community Languages in the United Kingdom

The 1991 United Kingdom Census indicated that three million of the total population were from an ethnic minority group. This was the first census to include a question on ethnicity and it identified eight main ethnic minority groups in the United Kingdom. (Ethnic minority in the terminology of the United Kingdom Census refers to in-migrant minorities rather than indigenous minorities such as Welsh and Gaelic speakers, who are discussed below.)

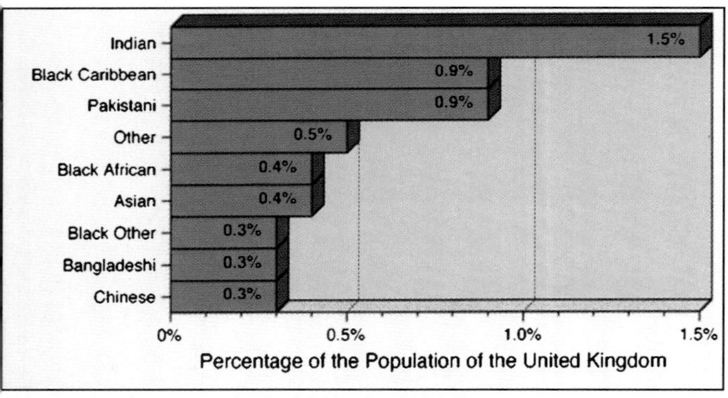

Ethnic minority groups in the UK in the 1991 Census.

Ethnic minorities account for 5.5 percent of the population. The largest ethnic minority are the South Asians (originating from India, Pakistan, Bangladesh) who represent 2.7 percent of the British population. Census data shows that the ethnic minorities are largely concentrated in the more populated and industrial areas. More than half the ethnic minority population of the United Kingdom live in south-east England and the Greater London area alone contains almost 45 percent of the total ethnic minority population. Community languages are not only found in England, but throughout the United Kingdom (e.g. in Glasgow, Cardiff and Belfast).

The Census did not include a question on the language of these ethnic groups. As the different ethnic communities have developed in the United Kingdom, a shift towards the use of English over generations has been witnessed. However, a Language Survey conducted by the Inner London Education Authority in 1987 found that a quarter of London's children had a mother tongue other than English. The largest language groups were Bengali, Urdu, Gujarati, Panjabi, Turkish, Greek and Chinese. In all, 131 languages were located in Inner London among school children.

Cornish

Cornish is a Celtic language closely related to Welsh and was once spoken in the most south-western part of England. The last native speaker of the Cornish language died in the 19th century. There have been attempts to revive the language during this century with around a hundred people at present being able to converse reasonably fluently in the language. The language has no official status, and is rarely taught in schools. Supporters of Cornish tend to learn the language through evening classes and correspondence courses.

British Sign Language

A common misconception about sign languages is that they consist of rudimentary gestures. A second misconception is that all signs are direct visual representations of objects and concepts, and thus all sign languages are mutually intelligible. On the contrary, there are numerous different sign languages in the world which all have their own structures and conventional signs. Someone using American Sign Language, for example, would not be able to communicate with someone who uses French Sign Language. Examples of other sign languages in the world include: Chinese Sign Language, Swedish Sign Language, Russian Sign Language, German Sign Language, Japanese Sign Language, Malaysian Sign Language, Mexican Sign Language, Spanish Sign Language and Kenyan Sign Language.

British Sign Language is a language of Britain (Alladina & Edwards, 1991). A linguistic analysis of British Sign Language (as with other Sign Languages of the world) shows that it is as complex and able to fulfill as wide a range of communicative functions as other languages (see page 566). British Sign Language was used in deaf education in the 19th century but until recently has been regarded as a language that would not allow the integration of deaf children and adults into mainstream society. Parents have often been urged to use speech and not sign language with their deaf children. However, as Ladd (1991) has shown, British Sign Language has a history traceable to the 1500s and developed in deaf schools and

deaf clubs in the Industrial Revolution of the 19th century. The British Sign Language community is estimated as between 50,000 and 100,000 strong. British Sign Language is used in deaf homes, as well as in clubs for deaf people and local community organizations. Parents of deaf children are now often encouraged to teach their children British Sign Language as their first language, and English as their second language. British Sign Language has regional variations and also has no written form.

Scotland

Gaelic

Scottish Gaelic (often just called Gaelic) and Irish Gaelic (often just called Irish) are closely related and have a degree of mutual intelligibility.

The 1991 Census found that of a Scottish population of approximately 5 million, 1.4 percent, (about 66,000 people), could speak Gaelic. Although there are Gaelic speakers through most of Scotland, with communities in the cities such as Edinburgh, Aberdeen and Glasgow, the highest concentration of speakers is to be found in the Western Isles.

In Scotland, Gaelic does not have national official status. However, in local government (e.g. the Western Isles Island Council), there is official regional status. Gaelic is used in local government meetings, economic initiatives, bilingual education and the media (e.g. programs on television). Gaelic also has institutional strength in bodies such as a Gaelic-medium business college and a Gaelic Playgroup Association, and cultural strength in music, dance and informal networks of Gaelic speakers.

The remoteness and inaccessibility of the Western Isles, where Gaelic is relatively strong, has meant that they have resisted Anglicization more successfully than the rest of Scotland. While the population of Gaelic speakers in the Western Isles, as in the rest of Scotland, has decreased, there is a strong revivalist approach in language planning.

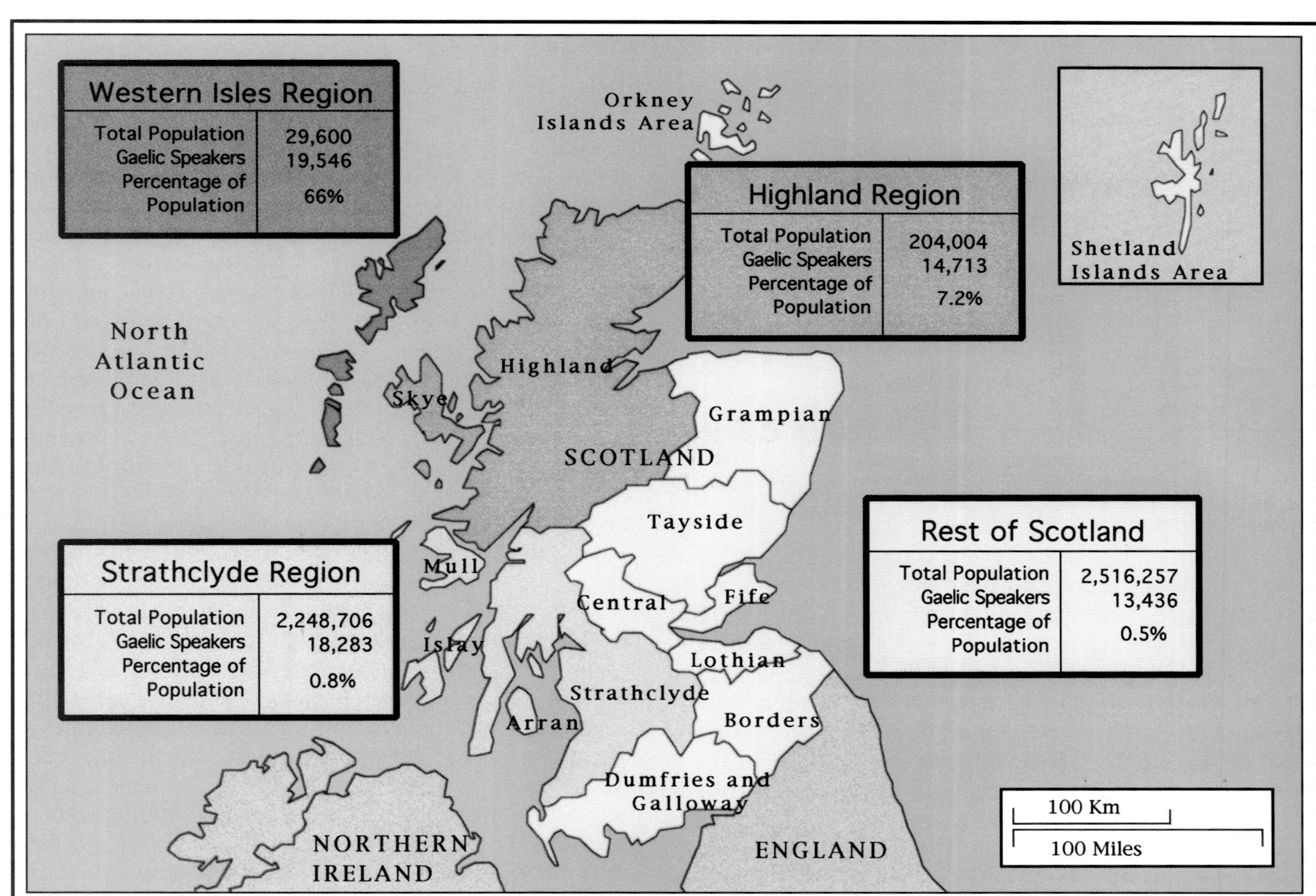

The Distribution of Gaelic Speakers in Scotland, 1991 Census

Lallans

Lallans, sometimes called Scots or Scottish, is found in areas south and east of the Scottish Highlands. There is no census or estimate of the number of speakers of Lallans. Lallans has descended from varieties of English spoken in the Lowlands of Scotland, and was made famous by the poetry of Robbie Burns (18th century). Its speakers do not generally perceive it as being a dialect of English, and recently there have been demands by some Lallans speakers to restore it to the status of an autonomous language. A visitor to Lowlands Scotland will tend to notice its differences rather than its resemblance to the English language. While the Lallans tongue has no legal status and no formal use in public administration, it is used in spoken communication. In 1985, the New Testament was translated into Lallans. There is no formal use in schools of the language but it is studied in Scottish universities and is included in the Scottish National Dictionary.

The Orkney and Shetland Islands

In the Northern Isles of Scotland (Orkney and Shetland), there has not been a Celtic tradition. The people of the Northern Isles were Norse in origin. Indeed, Orkney and Shetland were part of the Kingdom of Norway until the 16th century when they were turned over to Scotland in settlement of a debt. The people of the Northern Isles are still conscious of their separate identity and are reluctant to be called Scots. However, the Norse dialects have died out and been replaced by English. The funding of North Sea oil meant prosperity for the Northern Isles, but led to increased in-migration and Anglicization.

Wales

In the 1991 Census of the United Kingdom, the population in Wales was counted as 2.8 million of whom 18.7 percent could speak Welsh. Welsh speakers are to be found through the whole of Wales. However, the percentage of Welsh speakers in the industrial valleys and cities of South Wales tends to be quite low. In the heartlands of the language in the north and west of the country, the percentage is much higher, and in many communities, Welsh speakers are in a majority.

The number of Welsh speakers seems to be holding steady and has decreased by only 0.3 percent since the last Census in 1981. The highest percentage of speakers are between the ages of 3 and 15.

Welsh-medium education is available from primary school through to higher education, and the 1988 Education Reform Act ensured that Welsh is taught in almost all Welsh schools either as a first or second language. Welsh has official status in Wales, and there is a Welsh language television channel. (See page 337). Welsh is used in business, administration, courts, universities and colleges, playgroups and many other community activities (e.g. eisteddfodau – cultural events solely in Welsh).

The Isle of Man

The Isle of Man, in the North Sea, has at various times been ruled by the Norse, Scots and English but its Celtic population spoke a language called Manx closely related to Irish and Scots Gaelic. Around the 1700s, English was not understood by about two-thirds of the islanders. With the advent of public schooling, English became the dominant language, so that by the mid 19th century, Manx was rarely used in the law courts and was ignored by the schools. Manx became extinct with the death of the last native speaker of the language in December 1974. However, there are current revivalist attempts.

The Channel Islands

The Channel Islands are situated in the English Channel between England and France. Although geographically closer to France, they are affiliated to the British Crown. The process of Anglicization has led to English being the main language of the Islands. However Norman-French dialects are still spoken in some parts of Guernsey and Jersey, and French and English bilingualism is not uncommon.

Ireland

The Irish Republic

Since the Constitution of Ireland in 1937, the Irish language has been recognized as the first official language of the Republic. Irish is promoted through the education system and taught as a second language to many children.

The revival of Irish has had an important place within official state orthodoxy. The Irish language is enshrined in the constitution as the first of the state's two official languages, the second being English. The Republic of Ireland invested significantly, although not always effectively, in a wide variety of economic, social, cultural and educational initiatives to promote Irish. Since the founding of the Irish Free State, the Irish language received considerable state support and state sponsorship. One problem was that the Irish language became state-led rather than owned by local communities.

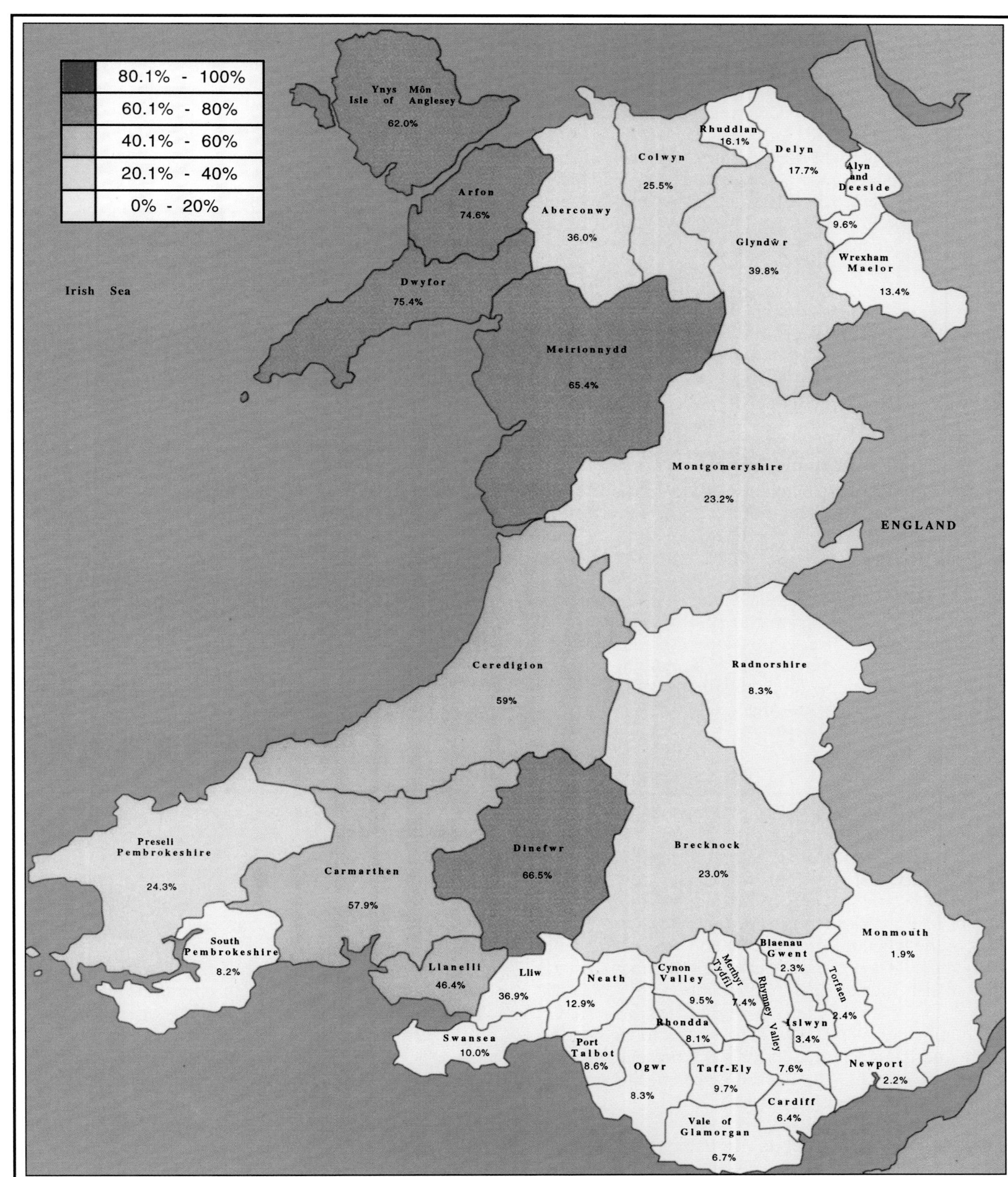

The Distribution of the Welsh Language in Wales by District, 1991 Census

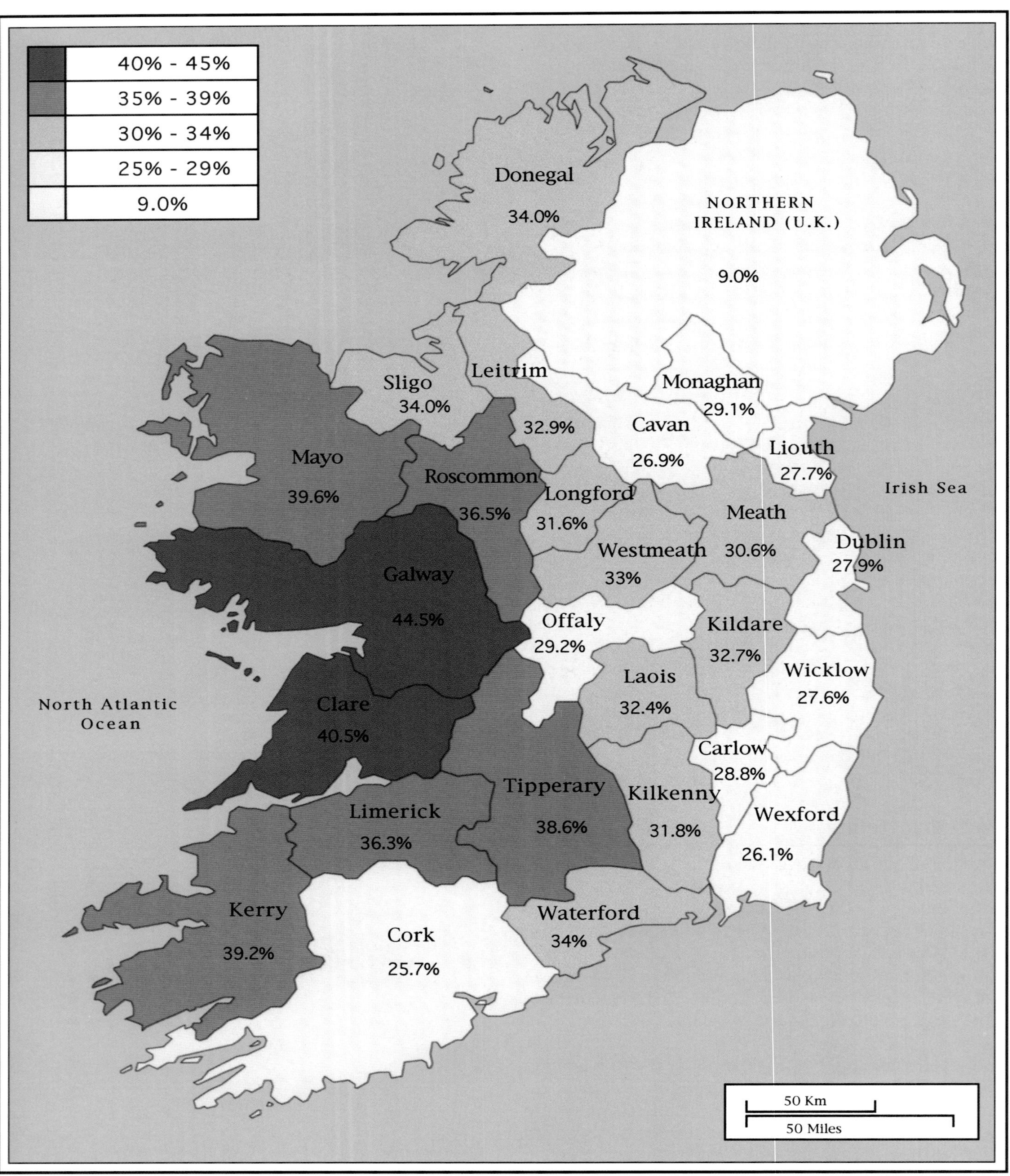

The Percentage of Irish Speakers in Ireland's Counties, including Northern Ireland (UK)

The 1986 Census found that 31.1 percent of the population of 3.5 million were able to speak Irish with varying degrees of ability, although it is estimated that only four to five percent use the language regularly. Irish can be found through the whole of the Republic, but the majority of speakers are to be found along the western coast in designated Irish language areas called the Gaeltacht.

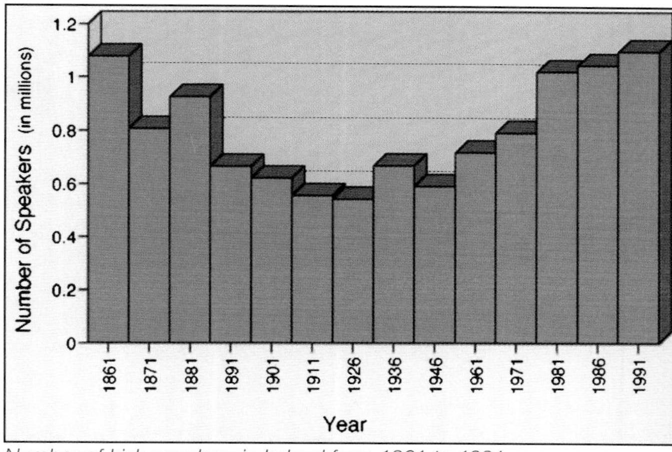

Number of Irish speakers in Ireland from 1861 to 1991.

The Gaeltacht

The Gaeltacht are officially designated Irish language areas. These areas were first set out in the 1956 Gaeltacht Area Order, and are mainly located along the Western coast of Ireland in counties Donegal, Mayo, Cork, Kerry, Galway, Waterford and Meath.

The Government's aim in establishing the Gaeltacht was to promote the use of the Irish language in strong heartland areas that would naturally reproduce the language. This was to be achieved through improving the social conditions of the Gaeltacht, providing a better infrastructure, providing Irish language schools, and encouraging economic development. Irish speakers could then hope to find employment in the Gaeltacht areas and enjoy a reasonable standard of living. 2.3 percent of the Irish Republic's population live in the Gaeltacht, although the numbers of Irish speakers in these rural areas are decreasing, as in the rest of Ireland. Many native speakers of Irish in the Gaeltacht have increasingly chosen English as a means of communication in their community, and sometimes with their children. Speaking Irish as the dominant language of communication in the Gaeltacht has therefore lately become a matter of conscious choice rather than of instinct or need.

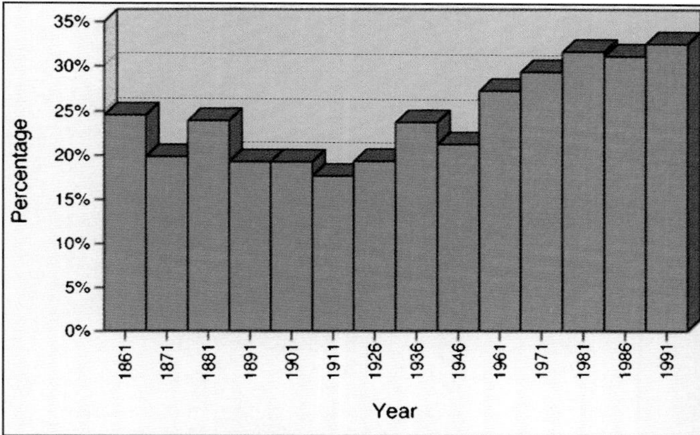

Percentage of Irish speakers in Ireland from 1861 to 1991.

Northern Ireland

The United Kingdom government does not give official status to the Irish language in Northern Ireland, and the 1991 Census was the first Census since 1911 to include a question on people's ability to understand and speak Irish. This Census found that Irish is spoken by 9.2 percent of the Northern Ireland population in communities scattered throughout its six counties. 6.6 percent have some degree of literacy in the language.

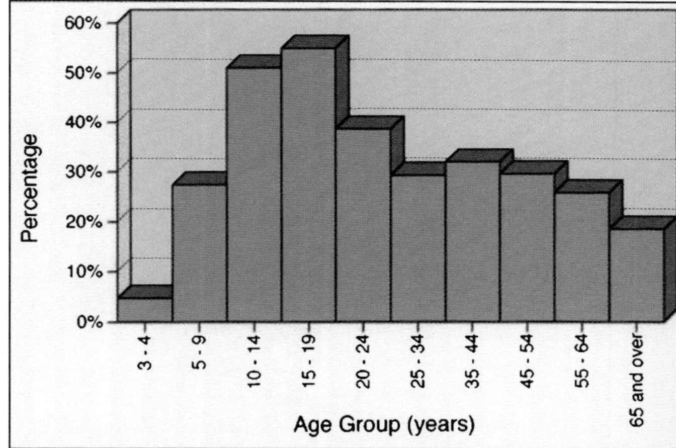

Percentage of Irish speakers by age, 1991. (Source: Central Statistics Office, 1996). (Note: These charts refer only to areas within the current Irish Republic).

In Northern Ireland, by the time of the Irish Free State, Irish-speaking communities had virtually disappeared. However, new generations of Irish speakers, wanting to revive the Irish language in Northern Ireland, have continued to emerge from the 1920s to the present. Thus, in contrast with the Republic of Ireland, there has been a people-led and not a state-led revival. The ruling forces of Northern Ireland (in London) have sometimes been hostile, and at best indifferent, to the Irish language in Northern Ireland. Language activists in Northern Ireland therefore have faced frustration in dealing with official indifference to the language. However, this has

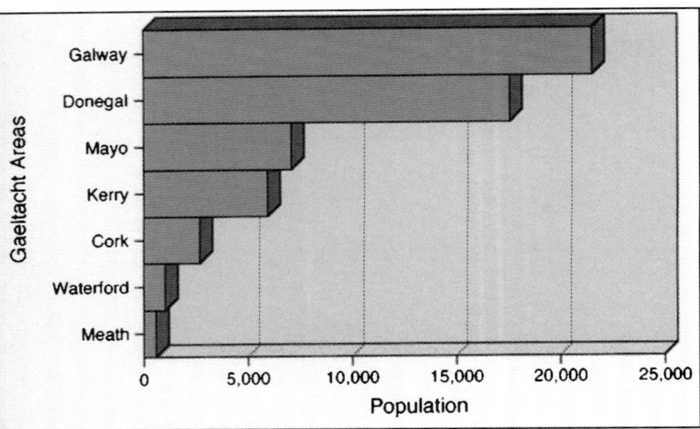

Population of Gaeltach areas in the 1991 Census. (Source: Central Statistics Office, 1996).

given their language activism a mission, a focus and an energy.

1991 Census analyses indicate that a knowledge of Irish is largely confined to the Roman Catholic population, although over 5000 non-Catholics also state that they speak Irish. Such Irish speakers are supported by a Belfast-based Irish language social club, a cultural center, an Irish language newspaper, a book shop, a radio station, art center and a theater. In the 1970s, Irish-medium education was begun in Northern Ireland, but outside the public system. Currently, there are around 1000 children attending Irish-medium schooling in Northern Ireland, a mixture of private and public schooling.

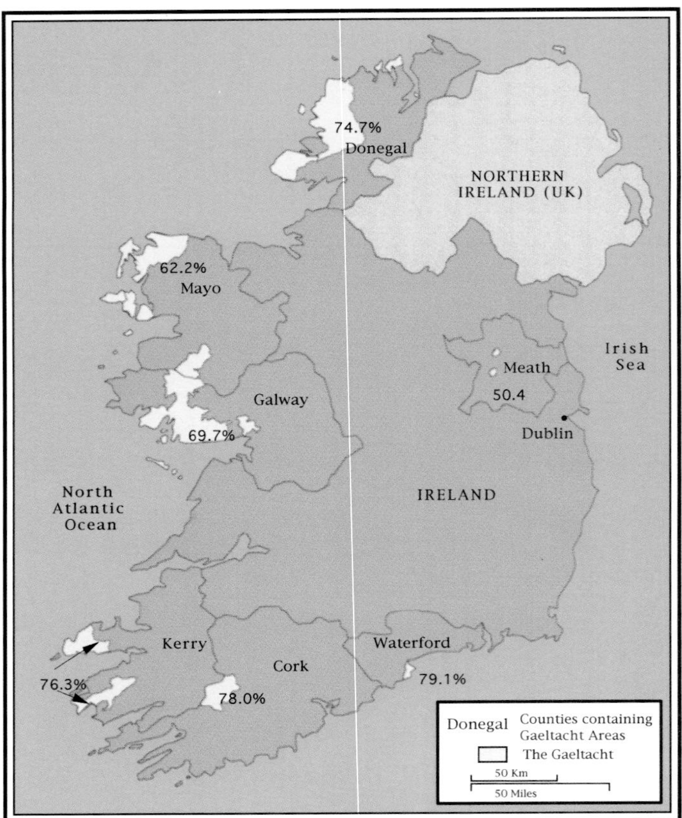

Percentage of Irish speakers in the Gaeltach: Designated Irish language areas. Figures represent numbers of Irish speakers as a percentage of the total population of each Gaeltach area. (Source: Central Statistics Office, 1996).

Middle East

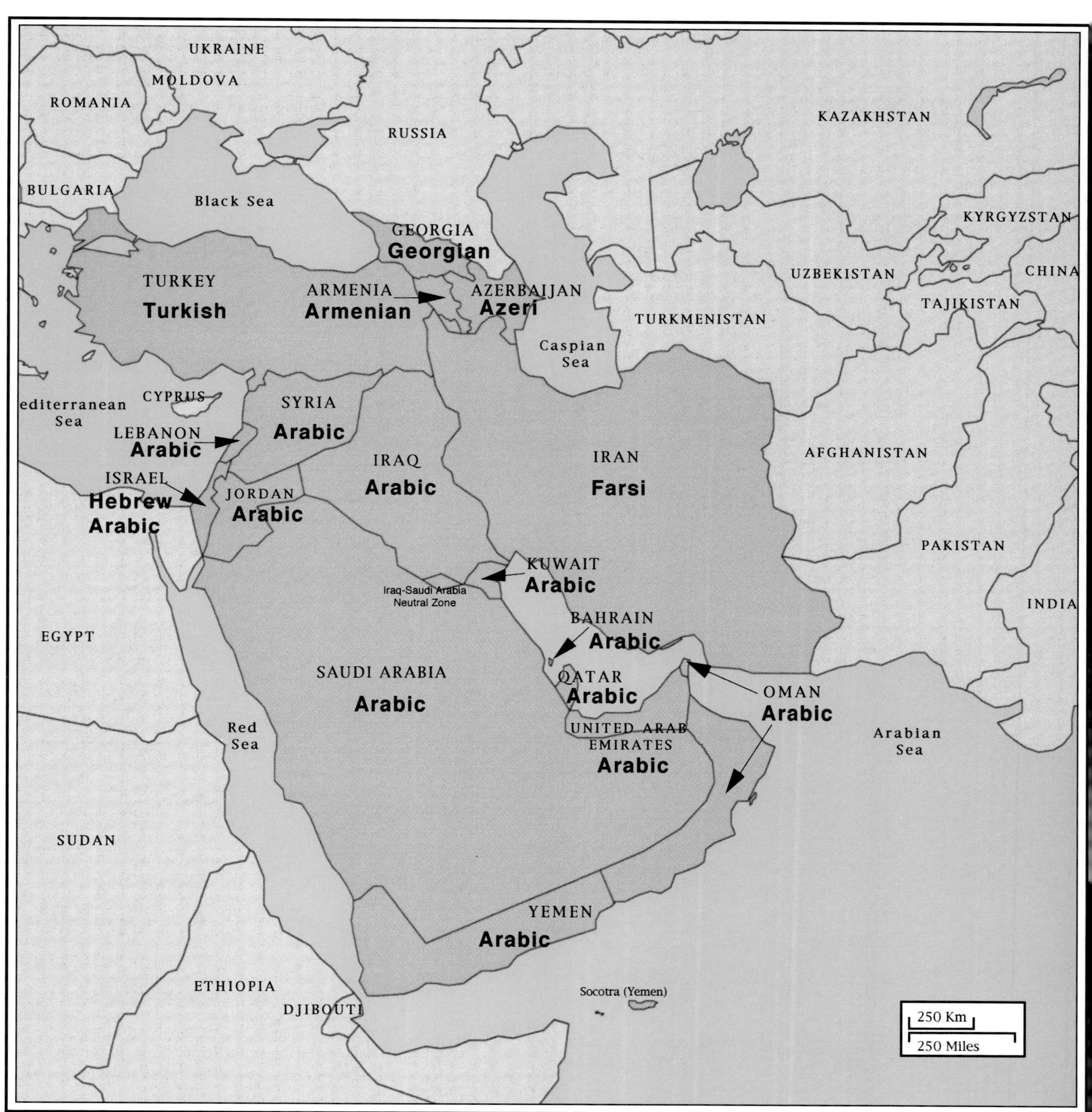

Official Languages of the Middle East

Armenia

The Republic of Armenia was formerly part of the USSR, but gained its independence in 1991. Armenia has a population of over 3.5 million (1995 estimate). Speakers of Armenian, an Indo-European language, comprise over 90 percent of the population. This proportion has increased considerably over recent years owing to the conflict with Azerbaijan over sovereignty of the Nagorno-Karabakh Enclave, which is officially part of Azerbaijan but is surrounded by Armenian territory. Many Azeris have left Armenia to return to Azerbaijan and only about three percent of the population are Azeris. Conversely, ethnic Armenians have left Azerbaijan to seek refuge in Armenia. The only Armenians left in Azerbaijan are those residing in the Nagorno-Karabakh enclave where they are in the majority. Russians comprise two percent of the population. Armenian is the official language but Russian is also commonly spoken. In 1989, nearly half of the Armenian population had a command of Russian. The Armenian people have faced waves of persecution over the centuries, most recently from the Ottoman Turks at the turn of the 20th century, and many have fled to form communities in other countries, throughout the Middle East, the US and other parts of the world.

Azerbaijan

The Republic of Azerbaijan was formerly part of the USSR, and became independent in 1991. Azeris now form about 90 percent of the population of almost 7.8 million (1995 estimate). They speak Azeri, a language closely related to Turkish. Azeri is the official language of the country. Azerbaijan is in conflict with its neighbor Armenia, over the Nagorno-Karabakh Enclave, a portion of land officially part of Azerbaijan, but surrounded by Armenian territory, and populated by a majority of Armenians. The percentage of Azeris in the country has increased in recent years, since the return of many Azeris from Armenia. Conversely the Armenian minority in Azerbaijan has decreased to only about two percent, almost all living in the Nagorno-Karabkh enclave. Other language minorities include the Russians (three percent), as well as small groups of speakers of Lezgian dialects, Kurds, Talysh, Tatars, Georgians, Ukrainians and Avars. Russian is still spoken, but its use is declining. Most speakers of minority languages also speak Azeri, and often use it as a written language, since most are not literate in their mother tongues.

Azeri is spoken by minority groups of Azerbaijanis living in neighboring countries, notably in Iran. According to official Iranian sources, there were nearly nine million Azeri speakers in Iran in 1986.

Bahrain

The independent Emirate of Bahrain consists of an archipelago of islands in the Southern Persian Gulf. The population of Bahrain is 575,000 and the official language is Arabic. Dialects of Arabic are the mother tongue of about three-quarters of the population. About eight percent of the population are of Iranian origin and mainly speak Farsi (Persian) as well as Arabic. Ten percent of the population are of Asian origin, and Urdu is widely spoken as well as other Asian languages. In recent decades, English has been spoken and understood as a second language by many Bahrainis, mainly in commercial and business contexts. This occurred because of British control of Bahrain's external affairs until 1971, and because of the country's subsequent development as an international commerce and banking center.

Georgia

The Republic of Georgia became independent upon the dissolution of the USSR in 1991. The population of 5.7 million (1995 estimate) comprises over 100 ethnic groups. The majority language and the official language is Georgian. Over 70 percent of the population are classed as 'ethnic Georgians', but this includes significant numbers or speakers of closely related languages such as Svan, Mingrelian and Laz. Most of these are bilingual in their mother tongue and Georgian. The main minority language groups are the Armenians (eight percent), the Russians (six percent), Azeris (5.7 percent), Ossetians (three percent) and Abkhazians (three percent).

Bilingualism is common in the Republic, with Georgian and Russian being spoken by many people as second languages. Almost ten percent of the population know Russian. The Republic contains three autonomous areas, based on ethnic groups, the Abkhaz Autonomous Republic, the Ossetian Autonomous Republic and the Adzhar Autonomous Republic. (The Adzhars are Turkicized Georgians.) The Abkhaz and Ossetian minorities have been in conflict with the Georgian government over demands for increased autonomy. These conflicts have been exacerbated since the Georgian supreme Soviet passed a law establishing the superior status of the Georgian language in 1989, making it obligatory in all schools, including minority language schools.

Iran

The Islamic Republic of Iran has a population of 64.6 million (1995 estimate). About 60 percent of the population are Persians and speak dialects of modern Persian (Farsi), which is the official language. Farsi is spoken in

all the major cities and in the north-east. There are several minority language groups, most of which have a strong ethnic identity. About seven to nine percent of the population are Kurds, living in the semi-autonomous province of Kurdistan. Baluchi is spoken in the south-east. Both Baluchi and Kurdish are Iranian languages, related to Persian. About 20 percent of the population speak Turkic languages, notably Azeri and Turkish, and also Uzbek. Other minority language groups include Armenian, Georgian and Syrian. Arabic is widely spoken in the oil region of the south-west. Since classical Arabic is the liturgical language of Islam, and since Iran has links with other Muslim countries, Arabic has high prestige in Iran, and Farsi borrows many words from Arabic.

Farsi is the main medium of instruction in schools and is the language of the media and the administration. However, it is not spoken or understood in all areas of the country.

Iraq

The Republic of Iraq has a population of over 20.6 million (1995 estimate). About 75 percent of the population are Arabs and speak various dialects of Arabic. Modern Standard Arabic is the official language. The largest ethnic and language minority are the Kurds, who inhabit the northern highlands, and who constitute about 15–20 percent of the population. Since 1980, the Kurds have been given some autonomy in their home region, and the Kurdish language has official status there. Other language minorities include the Turkomans. Dialects of Persian are spoken along the Iran border, and there are small Armenian communities in the larger cities. There are also some speakers of neo-Aramaic dialects. Most speakers of minority languages also speak Arabic.

Israel

The State of Israel, established in 1948 as the Jewish homeland, is a country of considerable linguistic diversity. Eighty two percent of the population of over 5.4 million (1995 estimate) are Jewish. Half of these were born in Israel, but their parents or grandparents migrated to Israel from over 100 different countries and spoke about 85 major languages or dialects. Hebrew and Arabic are the official languages of the country. Most Jews speak Hebrew, but, for some of them at least, it is a second language acquired in school or in intensive courses for new in-migrants (see page 693). Many Jews continue to speak their first languages at home rather than Hebrew.

The Israeli government has maintained a policy of linguistic assimilation for new in-migrants, but bilingualism continues to be widespread. Yiddish is still widely spoken, especially in Orthodox Jewish communities. A substantial number of Amharic speakers have recently migrated to Israel from Ethiopia and there has been a massive influx of Russian Jews since 1989. Because of the great numbers of Russian speakers, who have not yet been fully assimilated, the Israeli government has made language concessions, including some educational provision in Russian. English is widely used as a second or third language, and has some official recognition. (See also page 195.)

About 18 percent of the population of Israel are non-Jewish, mainly Arabs. Arabic is used in schools, in legal affairs and in the legislature. Many Arabs know some Hebrew, as Hebrew is taught in Arab schools. Also, some Jews are fluent in Arabic. Conflicts between Jews and Arabs in Israel is rarely caused by language differences. (See Language Conflict on page 333.)

Jordan

The Hashemite kingdom of Jordan had an estimated population of 4.1 million in 1995. Jordan gained independence from the British mandate in 1946. The population is almost entirely Arab, including many thousands of Palestinian refugees. There are small minorities of Circassians and Armenians, numbering less than 50,000 each. Arabic is the official language, and is used in schools. However, English is widely understood among the upper and middle classes. English is the main foreign language taught in schools. At university level, medicine and science are taught mainly in English. The second foreign language is French, mainly taught at elite private schools.

Kuwait

Prior to the Iraqi invasion of 1991, native Kuwaitis formed less than 40 percent of the population of Kuwait, and less than 20 percent of the labor force. The remainder comprised in-migrant workers, mainly Palestinians, South Asians, Sudanese, Yemenis and Egyptians. After the conclusion of the Gulf War, the population of Kuwait was less than half the pre-war total and the government planned to limit the number of foreign workers to less than 50 percent. The population of Kuwait is currently 1.8 million (1995 estimate) of which 45 percent are Kuwaitis and 35 percent come from other Arab countries. Thus 80 percent of the population speak various colloquial dialects of Arabic and the official language of the country is Modern Standard Arabic, used in government, administration and education. The main language minorities are nine percent South Asian (mainly from Pakistan and India) and four percent from Iran. There

are radio broadcasts in Arabic, Persian, English and Urdu. English is quite widely understood and spoken, and is used to teach science and medicine at tertiary level. Both before and particularly after the Gulf War, English has been accorded relatively high status.

Lebanon

Lebanon is an independent republic. According to 1995 estimates, the population was almost 3.7 million. The majority of Lebanese speak Arabic as their mother tongue and Arabic is the official language. There is a small community of Armenian speakers, about six percent of the population. Between 1920 and 1946, Lebanon was under a French mandate. French and English are widely used and understood in official life, business and commerce. Spanish is also understood by some Lebanese. A high literacy rate and a relatively high standard of education among the Lebanese means that many people are familiar with these three Western languages. Also, since the turn of the century, there have been large Lebanese expatriate communities in France, the US and South America which have maintained strong links with the mother country.

Foreign newspapers and magazines are available in Lebanon and the local press publishes in English, French and Armenian, as well as Arabic. French appears to be losing ground to English as a language of wider communication, although French is still the medium of education in some high schools.

Oman

The Sultanate of Oman had an estimated population of just over 2.1 million in 1995, the majority of whom were Arabs. Minority groups of expatriate workers, mostly South Asians (Indians, Pakistanis, Sri Lankans, Bangladeshis) are found in the principal ports, as are many East Africans. These expatriate workers, working mainly in the petroleum industry, constitute about half the salaried labor force. Arabic is the official language, spoken by virtually all Omani nationals as a first or second language. Bilingualism in Arabic and a minority language is widespread. There are minority groups of speakers of modern South Arabian languages, related to Arabic. Swahili is widely spoken in large coastal towns, being the native language of many Omanis who returned to Oman from the former Omani colony of Zanzibar in the mid-60s. Baluchi, Urdu and other Asian languages are spoken by workers from South Asia. English is widely used and understood in coastal areas, especially by Omanis who have returned from East Africa.

Qatar

The State of Qatar, a former British protectorate, became independent in 1971. Arabic is the official language, but only 40 percent of the population of 533,000 (1995 estimate) are Arabs. Many foreign workers reside in Qatar. Eighteen percent of the population are Pakistanis, and ten percent are Iranian. English is commonly used as a second language in government and commerce.

Saudi Arabia

Saudi Arabia had an estimated population of just over 18.7 million in 1995. According to the 1992 census, over a quarter of the population were expatriate workers, from the Middle East, Africa or Asia. About 90 percent of the population are Arabs, either Saudi citizens or workers from other Arab countries, and Arabic is the official language. The other ten percent speak English or Asian languages. English is often used as a language of wider communication among the multilingual workforce. Arabic is the language of government, commerce and education, but English is commonly used at tertiary level to teach science and medicine.

Syria

The Syrian Arab Republic had an estimated population of 15.45 million in 1995 (not including about 30,000 in the Israeli-occupied Golan heights). About 90 percent of the population are Arabs, and Arabic is the official language. The largest non-Arab minorities are Kurds who live along the Turkish border, and Armenians, who live chiefly in the larger cities. Syria was under a French mandate between 1919 and 1943 and French was once widely used in official life. Its use has now decreased considerably. Arabic is the language of education and administration. Syria has a very positive pro-Arabic stance, and requires the use of Arabic to teach medicine and science at tertiary level. In most other Arab countries, these subjects tend to be taught in English at this level.

United Arab Emirates

The United Arab Emirates consists of a confederation of seven small independent states, Abu Dhabi, Ajman, Dubayy al-Fujayrah, Ras al-Khaymah, ash-Shariqah, Umm al-Qaywayn. The official language is Arabic, but less than half of the population of 2.9 million (1995 estimate) are ethnically Arabs. 1982 figures recorded that only 19 percent were Emirian nationals and 23 percent were workers from other Arab countries. There has been a great influx of foreigners working in the petroleum industry. Half the current population are from South Asia, and nearly ten percent are from other parts of the

world, including western countries, East Asia and Iran. However, Arabic is spoken by the majority of population as a first or second language. English, Persian, Gujarati, Panjabi, Bengali, Malayalam, Tamil, Hindi and Urdu are all commonly spoken languages. English functions as a lingua franca to some extent in the multilingual coastal towns. Arabic is the language of government, official life and education, but English is used to teach science and medicine in some tertiary institutions.

The West Bank

The West Bank, an area of about 2280 square miles west of the Jordan river, was formerly part of Jordan, but was occupied by Israel in 1967. The Israeli–Palestinian interim agreement of September 1995 granted the area a broader measure of self-government, by means of an elected self-governing authority, the Palestinian Council.

Over 80 percent of the population of 1.3 million (1995 estimate) are Arabic-speaking Palestinians. The remainder are Jewish settlers, most of whom speak Hebrew. English is also understood by some inhabitants of this area.

The Gaza Strip

The city and seaport of Gaza on the eastern Mediterranean Sea and the surrounding area were formerly part of Egypt and were occupied by Israel in 1967. Over 99 percent of the population of 813,000 are Arabic-speaking Palestinians, while 0.6 percent are Hebrew-speaking Jewish settlers (1995 estimates). The Israeli–Palestinian interim agreement of September 1995 granted the area a broader measure of Palestinian self-government by means of an elected self-governing authority, the Palestinian Council. English is understood by some of the dwellers in this area.

Yemen

The Republic of Yemen was formed when the Yemen Arab Republic (Northern Yemen) united with the People's Democratic Republic of Yemen (Southern Yemen) in 1990. The population of 14.7 million (1995 estimate) is composed mainly of Yemenis, either of Arab descent or of mixed Arab and African descent who live in the coastal areas. Arabic is the official language, and the native language of the majority of the population, including 3–4 million expatriate Yemenis who have returned home since the 1991 Gulf War. South Arabian languages, Mahri and Sokotri, are spoken by indigenous groups, but they are in decline owing to depopulation from the Mahra and Sokotra areas, and the spread of Arabic. There are small minority language groups, mainly in Southern Yemen. These include expatriate workers from Pakistan, Malaysia, the US, the UK, the Philippines and Germany for example. There are a number of Somali refugees and a sizable Eritrean community.

Since the unification of the country, English has become the most important second language and tends to be used as a lingua franca between non-Arab groups. Arabic is the language of government, media, religion and education. However, English is the medium of teaching in the faculties of medicine, science and architecture at the University of Sanaa. As in many other Arab countries, a diglossic situation exists between Modern Standard Arabic, the official, written language and the colloquial Arabic dialects used in informal oral contexts.

North America

Canada

Canada is a federated state in North America which occupies the whole of the territory north of the United States, except for the state of Alaska (belonging to the US), Greenland (a self-governing territory of Denmark) and the two small islands of Saint Pierre and Miquelon, located south of Newfoundland, which are overseas territories of France.

In 1995, the estimated population of Canada was 28.4 million. The original inhabitants of the territory now known as Canada were the American Indians and Inuit (Eskimo) peoples, close relatives of the American Indians of the US. Their ancestors were Mongoloid peoples, from Asia who entered North America across the Bering Land Bridge sometime between 25,000 BC and 12,000 BC. By the beginning of the 17th century, about 250,000 of their descendants inhabited the territory now known as Canada.

The modern state of Canada has its origins in the arrival of French and British settlers in the 17th century. In the early 17th century, the first permanent French settlements were established in what is now New Brunswick, Nova Scotia, Quebec city and Prince Edward Island. By 1763, the British had gained control over the French colonies in Canada, including New France (the present day Quebec). However a law was passed in 1774 (the Quebec Act), guaranteeing the maintenance of the French language, French civil law and the Roman Catholic faith in the French-speaking region. In 1867, the Dominion of Canada came into existence, with the unification of Nova Scotia, New Brunswick, Quebec and Ontario. During the 19th century, Canada expanded westwards, adding new territories.

In-migration to Canada

Settlers of British origin came to Canada mainly after the completion of the British conquest of French territory in 1763. After the 13 seaboard colonies of North America declared their independence from Britain in 1776, thousands of British 'Loyalists' fled to Canada, increasing the number of English speakers. The large scale migration of English, Scots and Irish to Canada during the 19th century further swelled the ranks of the English-speaking population. In the late 19th century and 20th century, there has been considerable migration from other European countries.

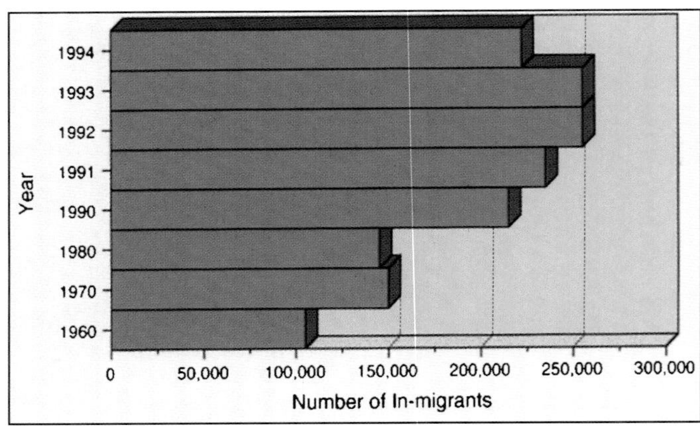

In-migration into Canada 1960–1994.

Of the population of 27 million (1991), 28 percent were of British-only origin and 23 percent of French-only origin. Another four percent of the population reported a combination of British and French backgrounds, with 14 percent having partly French and/or English backgrounds. The remainder were mainly German, Italian, Ukrainian, Dutch, Scandinavian, Polish, Jewish, Hungarian and Greek. The 1991 Census revealed that 16 percent of the Canadian population (or 4.3 million people) were in-migrants (defined as 'not Canadian by birth').

Due to a combination of a relatively low birth rate and in order to support economic growth, Canada embarked on a strategic policy of in-migration in the late 1980s. The chart shows the increase in in-migration in the 1990s. In 1960, there were just over 100,000 in-migrants, rising to just below 150,000 in-migrants in 1970 and 1980. In the 1990s, over 200,000 in-migrants per year have entered Canada.

In 1996, the quota for new in-migrants was set at around 200,000 in-migrants and refugees (with refugees comprising close to one in eight new in-migrants). In the 1970s to the 1990s, many in-migrants came from Asia and the West Indies.

Official Languages in Canada

During the 18th and 19th centuries, some politicians urged that the status of French in Quebec should be removed and that the French-speaking population should be anglicized. However, French speakers have been sufficiently numerous and sufficiently powerful to defend their linguistic, cultural and social rights.

English and French are both official languages in Canada. The Official Languages Act adopted in 1969 gave these languages equal status, rights and privileges in matters of federal jurisdiction. Citizens can demand services in either of the official languages from agencies or ministries of the federal government. In Canada, the official status of French and English applies at the federal level. Only one provincial government, New Brunswick, has declared the two as official languages. In 1977, the government of Quebec legislated that French should be the only official language of that province.

The 1991 Canadian Census showed that close to 17 in every 20 people spoke either French or English as their first language. Francophones are mainly found in Quebec, with anglophones representing 1 in 10 of the population of Quebec. In other parts of Canada, francophones are a minority, approximately 1 in 20 of the

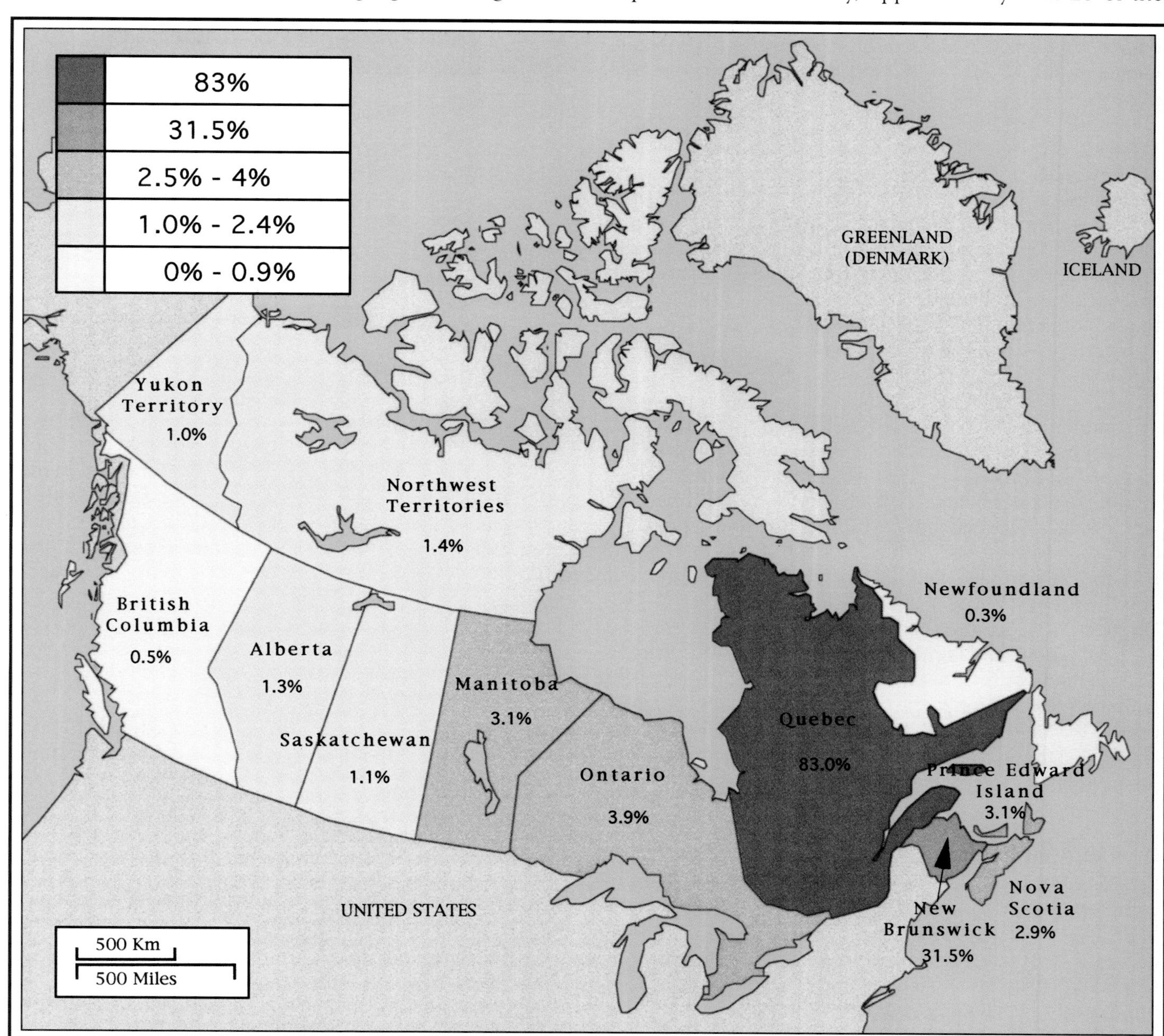

Percentage with French as their Home Language in Canada

population. However, in the province of New Brunswick, francophones represent about a third of the population.

English–French Bilingualism in Canada

According to the 1991 Census in Canada, 4.4 million people (16 percent of the population) were bilingual in English and French. As the accompanying map shows, the largest number of bilingual people is found in Quebec, New Brunswick and Ontario. In 1991, these three provinces contained 86 percent of all bilingual people in Canada.

There is a strong tendency for bilingual individuals to come from English and French linguistic minorities. That is, outside Quebec, francophones are more often bilingual than anglophones, whereas in Quebec, anglophones are more likely to be bilingual than francophones. Thus, bilingualism in Canada is particularly associated with language minorities in majority language areas. Twenty two and a half million Canadians (83 percent of the total population) can speak English. Of this group, 16.3 million indicated in the 1991 Census that English was their mother tongue.

Generally, over the past 40 years, the overall percentage of anglophones in Canada has remained stable. Of the

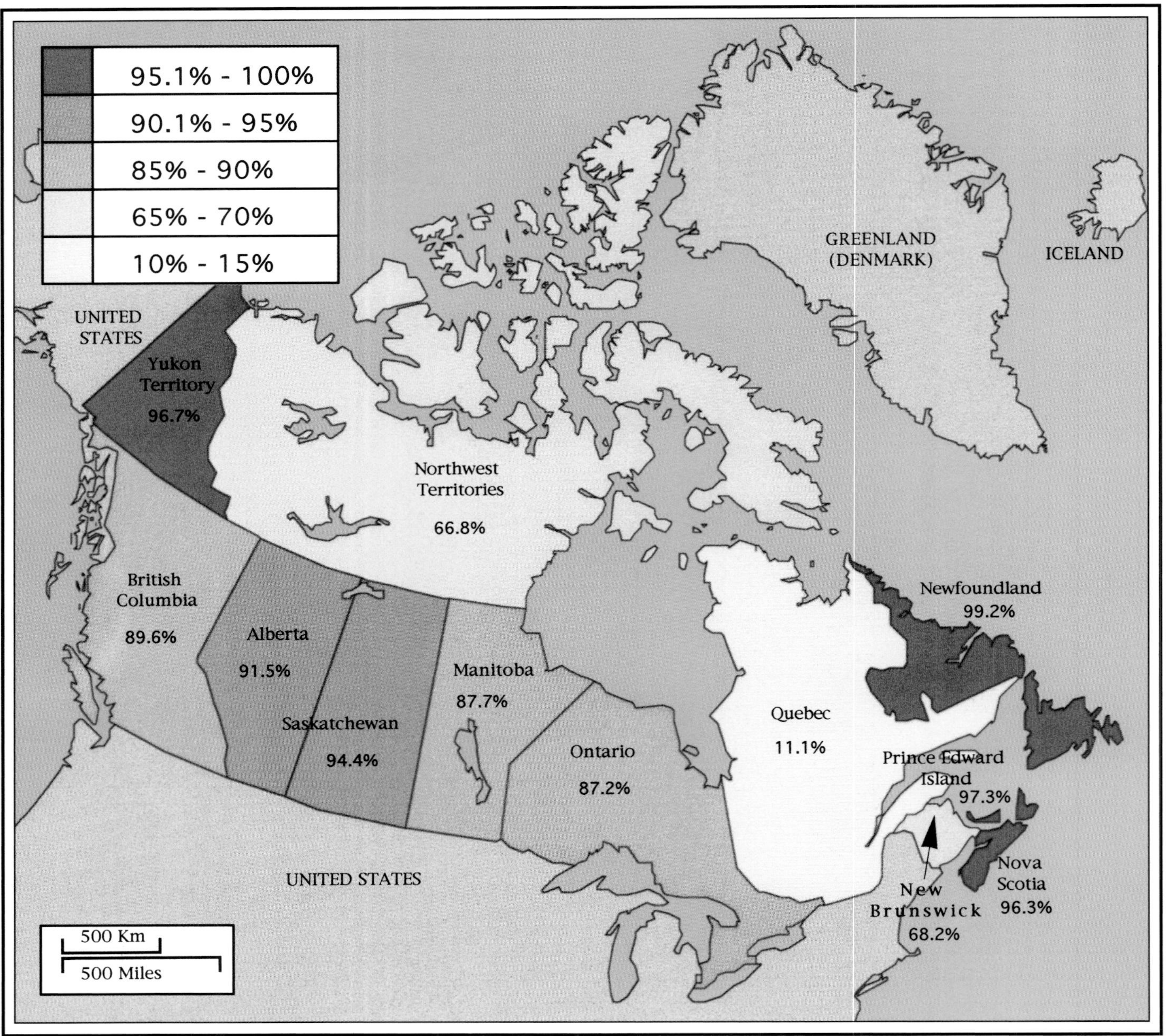

Percentage with English as their Home Language in Canada

8.5 million Canadians who speak French according to the 1991 Census, 6.6 million declared French at their mother tongue. In percentage terms, the proportion of francophones in Canada (in the total population) has decreased from 29 percent in 1951 to 24 percent in 1991. This is partly explained by the large number of in-migrants in recent years who have a mother tongue other than French. Francophones are particularly found in southern Quebec, while in northern Quebec there are large numbers of people who speak Aboriginal languages.

Non-official Languages in Canada

Other languages in Canada are often termed non-official languages. The accompanying charts and tables provide specific details about the size of these different language groups that make up the linguistic mosaic of Canada. Non-official languages have no special legal status, although the Official Languages Act (1969) encouraged the idea of multiculturalism throughout the nation. This included support for French culture outside Quebec, and also the maintenance of non-official languages,

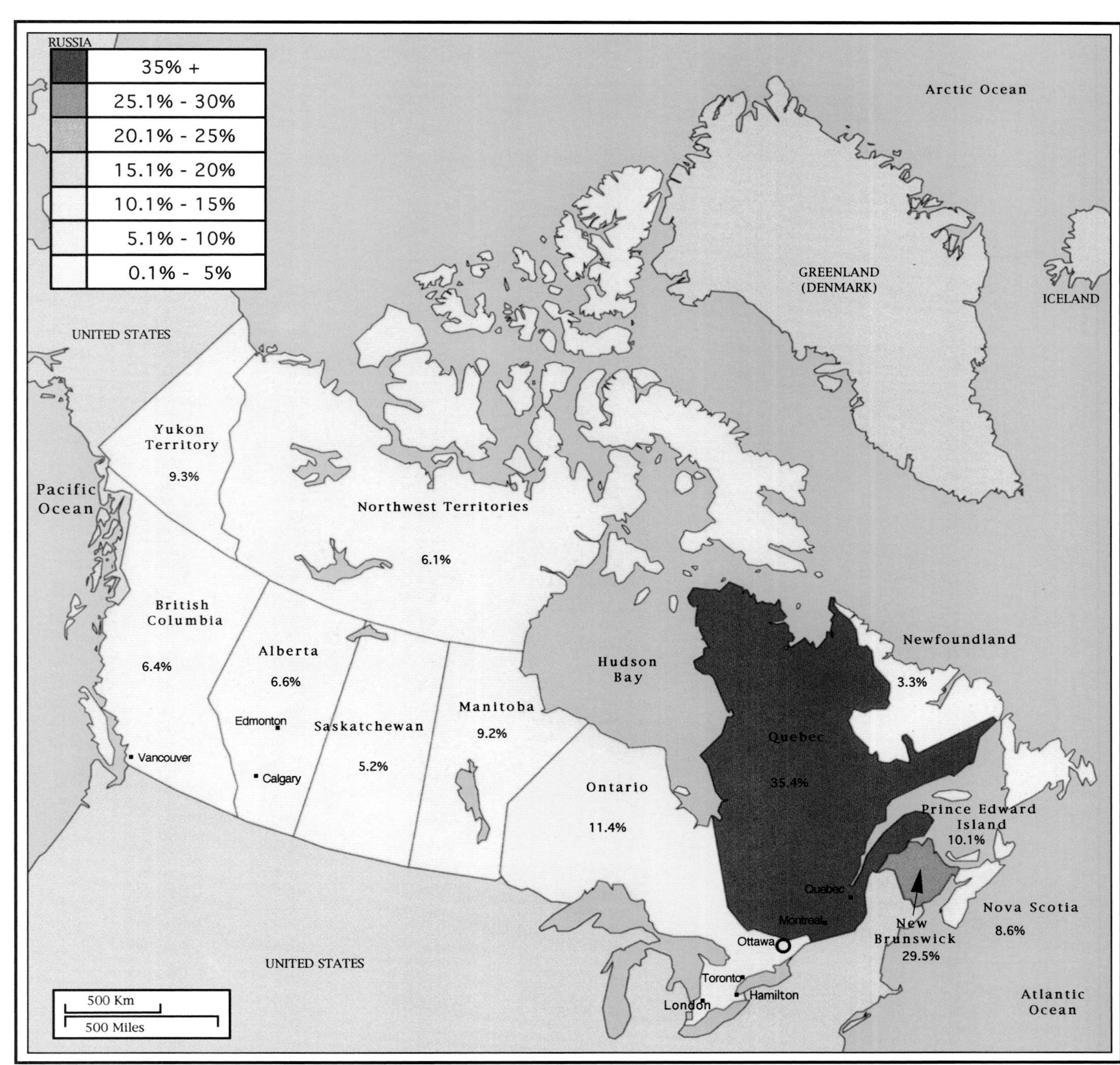

Percentage of French–English Bilingualism in Canada

both in-migrant and indigenous. There is some government subsidization of language schools, language festivals and local newspapers in such non-official languages. To distinguish such heritage language speakers from anglophones and francophones, some Canadians use the term 'allophones' to refer to Canadians whose mother tongue is any language other than French and English (but sometimes excluding Aboriginal groups). In 1991, some five million Canadians spoke a language other than French or English, and 4.1 million of these had a non-official language as their mother tongue. This is a result of the large in-migration that has occurred in the last 40 years.

In Canada, allophones tend to live in urban areas (approximately four out of five allophones live in large city areas). Almost half can be found in Ontario. Some two million allophones, approximately one Ontarian out of five, had a mother tongue other than English or French. The most popular destinations of in-migrants are Toronto, Montreal and Vancouver.

Canadians with a non-official language as a mother tongue represented 15 percent of the population in 1991. This is a rise of 12 percent since 1951 when three percent of the population had a non-official language. In 1951, Ukrainian and German were the most frequently reported non-official languages. In 1991, Italian, Chinese and German were the most represented non-official languages in Canada with about half a million speakers each. Heritage languages, both in-migrant and indigenous, are sometimes used in the media.

Language shift to English over two or three generations has been a feature of most in-migrant minorities in Canada. The majority of new in-migrants prefer to learn English rather than French and to enroll their children in schools where the language of instruction is English.

Aboriginal Language Groups

One important heritage language group in Canada is the Aboriginal peoples, the indigenous residents before the French and British arrived. The history of the indigenous peoples in Canada is similar to that of the indigenous peoples of the United States. Over a period of two centuries they were gradually subjugated, disempowered and their territories confiscated. Aboriginal peoples make up less than one percent of the population of Canada but form a majority of the population in the Northwest Territories and a significant percentage of the population in Yukon. More than 50 Aboriginal languages are spoken, but most are threatened or on the verge of extinction. The following table shows the regional distribution of eight of the most reported Aboriginal languages and gives the numbers of speakers in the 1991 Census.

Aboriginal Language	Size of Language Group	Main Area where the Language is Spoken
Cree	82,070	Manitoba and Saskatchewan (57%)[1]
Ojibway	25,245	Ontario and Manitoba (89%)
Inuktitut	24,980	Northwest Territories/Quebec (95%)
Montagnais-Naskapi	7,575	Quebec (84%)
Micmac	6,260	Nova Scotia & New Brunswick (68%)
Dakota	4,110	Alberta (71%)
Blackfoot	4,000	Alberta (97%)
South Slave	3,520	Northwest Territories/Alberta (94%)
Other	32,410	
TOTAL:	190,170	

Note 1: The percentage refers to the proportion of all speakers of an Aboriginal Language (e.g. 57 percent of Cree speakers live in Manitoba and Saskatchewan). Source: Harrison & Marmen, 1994

Saint Pierre and Miquelon

Saint Pierre and Miquelon, a French territorial collectivity, comprises two small groups of islands off the south coast of Newfoundland. French is the official language and the language spoken by the majority of the 6000 population (estimate 1995), most of whom are descendants of French settlers.

The Mother Tongue of Canadian Residents, 1991 Census

	Number	Percentage
English	16,169,880	59.9%
French	6,502,860	24.1%
Italian	510,990	1.9%
Chinese	498,845	1.8%
German	466,240	1.7%
Portuguese	212,090	0.8%
Polish	189,815	0.7%
Ukrainian	187,015	0.7%
Spanish	177,425	0.7%
Dutch	139,035	0.5%
Other	1,939,855	7.2%

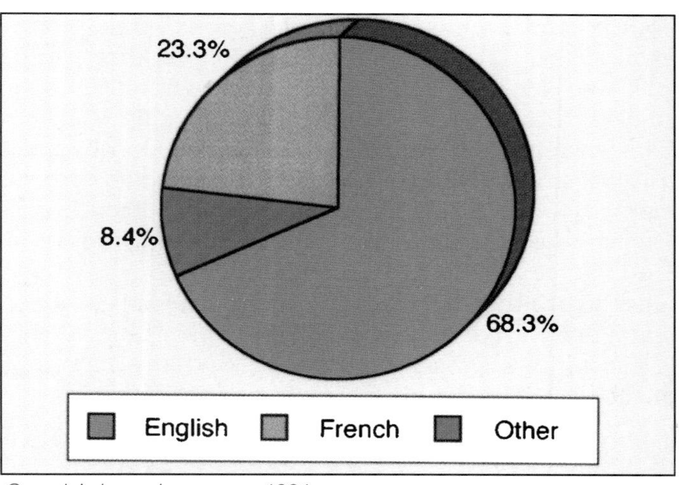

Canada's home languages, 1991 census.

Distribution of the ethnic origins of Canada's population, 1991 census.

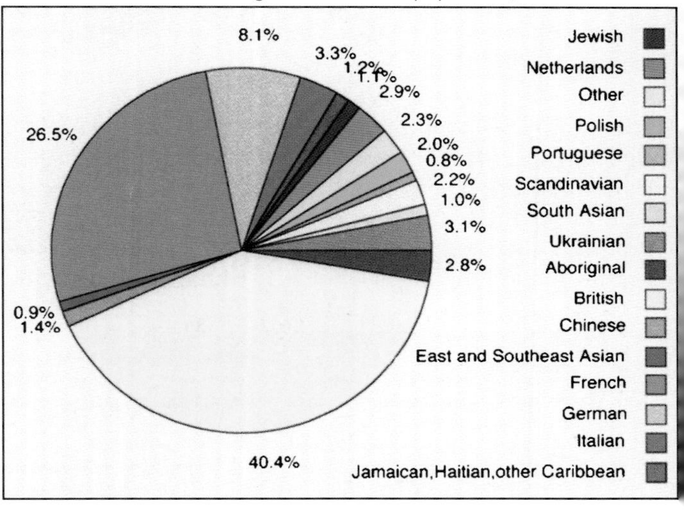

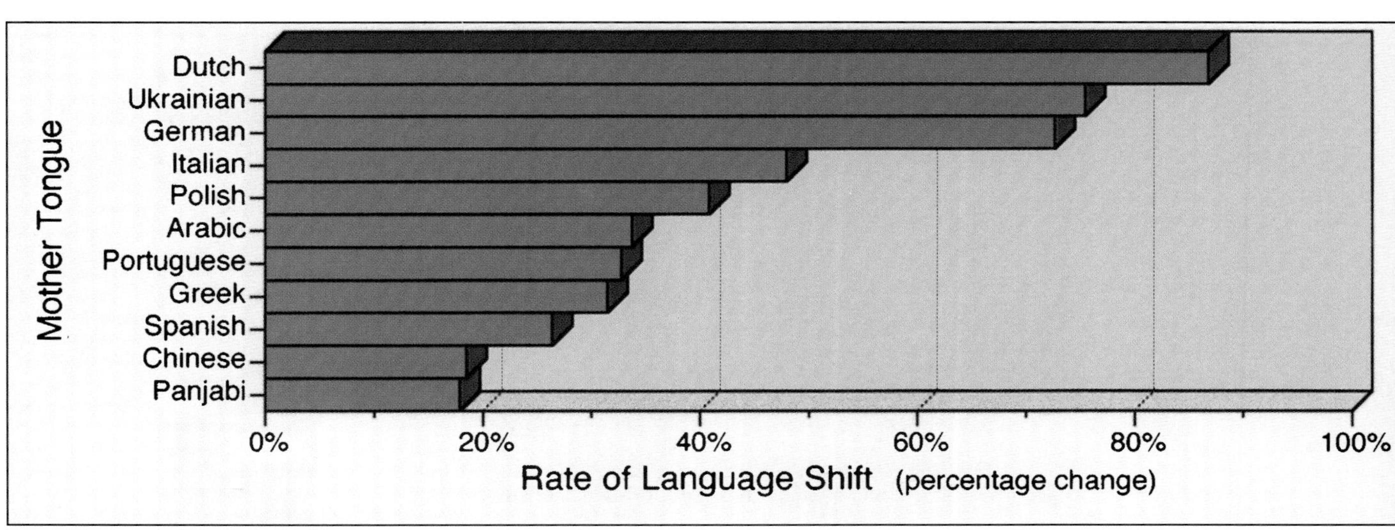

Rate of language shift of principal language groups with a mother tongue other than English or French. Canadian census, 1991. Note that a higher percentage indicates a greater movement away from the mother tongue to English. A lower percentage indicates greater retention of the mother tongue.

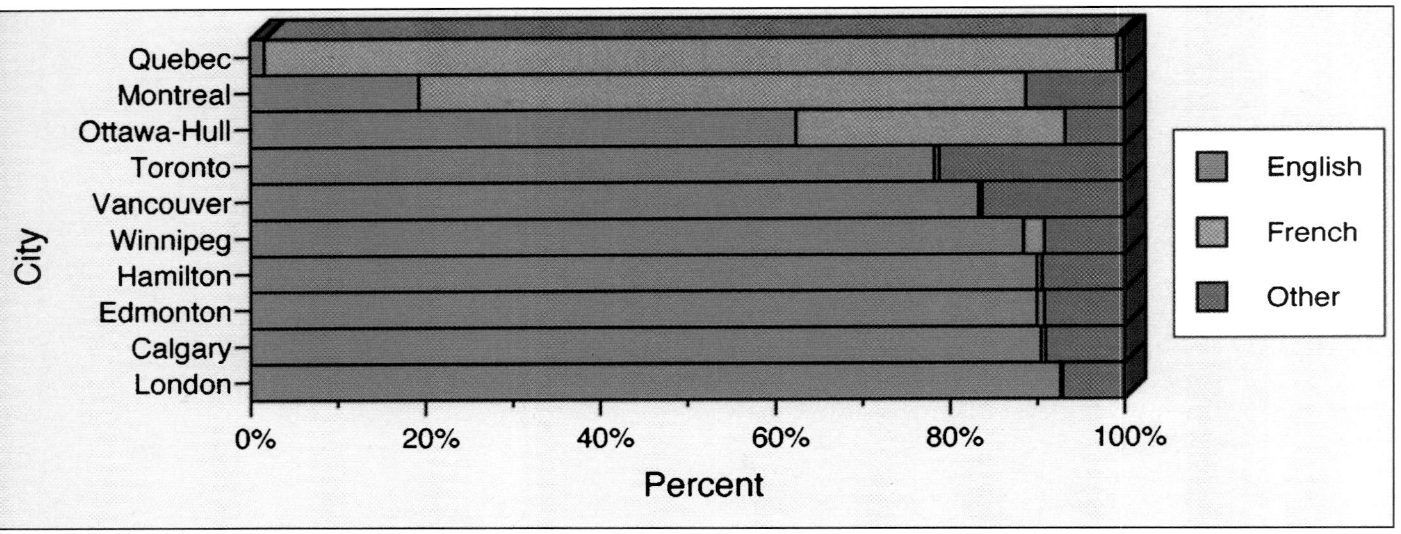

Home languages in Canada's ten largest cities, 1991 census.

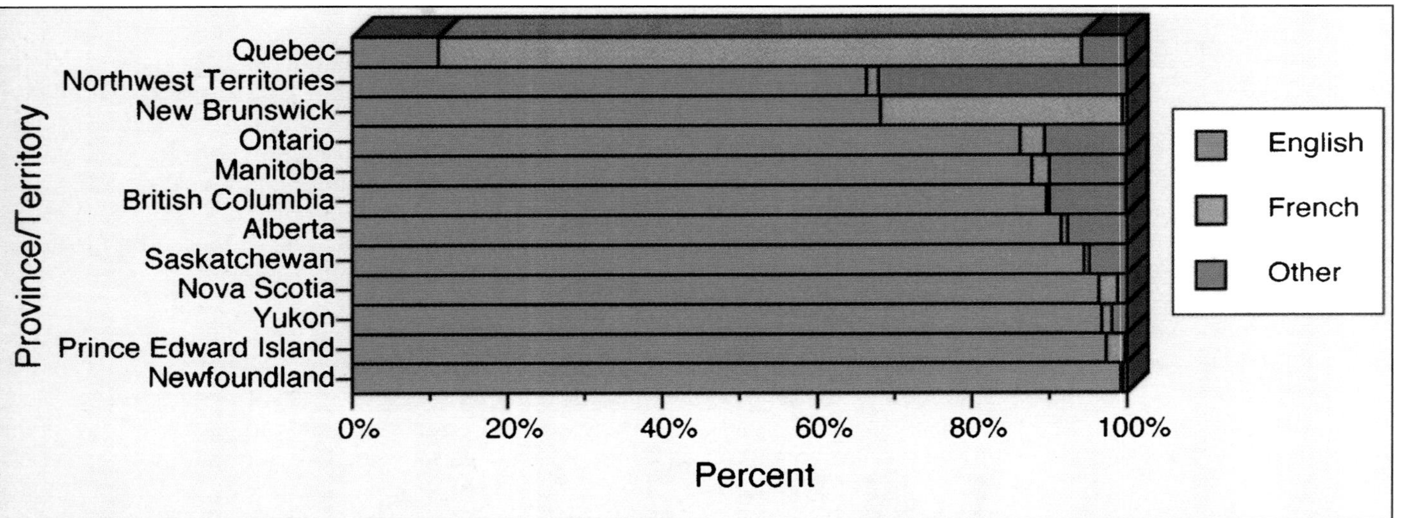

Home language in the 1991 Canadian census.

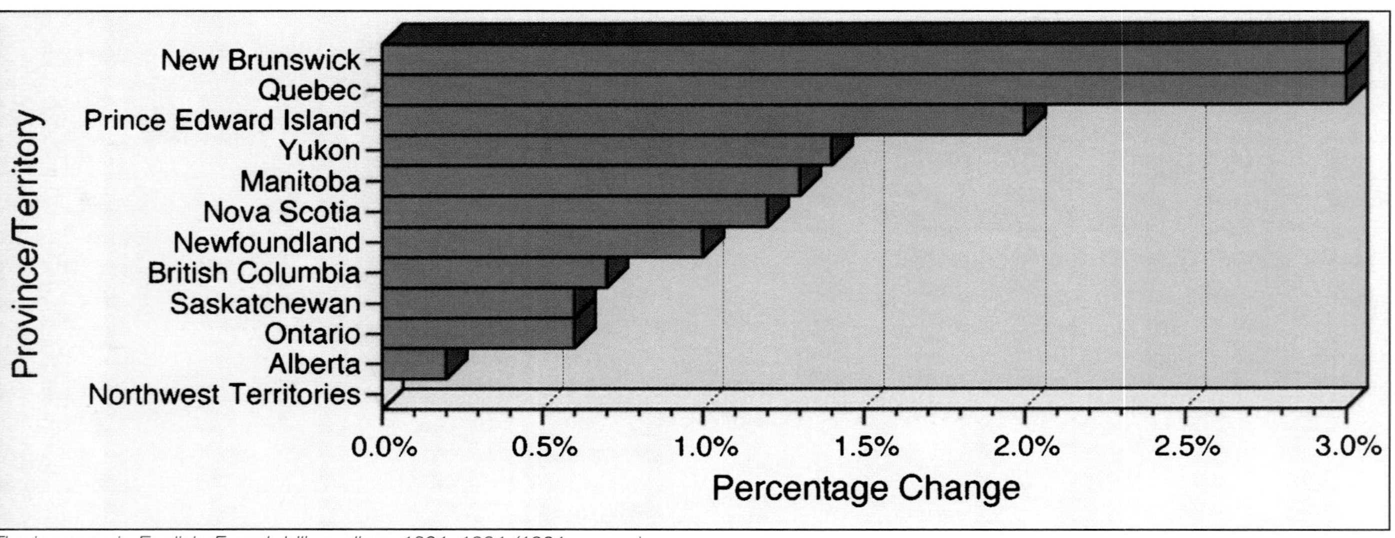

The increase in English–French bilingualism, 1891–1991 (1991 census).

United States

United States

The United States of America is the fourth largest country in the world, after the Russian Federation, China and Canada, and the third most populous, after China and India. In 1995, the estimated population of the US was 263,835,000. The territory of the United States consists of 48 contiguous states, in the center of the North American Continent, and two other states, Alaska, north-west of Canada and Hawaii, a group of Pacific islands about 2000 miles south-west of San Francisco. The US also has a number of overseas territories, Puerto Rico and the US Virgin Islands in the Caribbean, the Panama Canal Zone in Central America (scheduled for return to Panama by the year 2000) and American Samoa, Guam and Palau in the Pacific. The language situation in these overseas territories is discussed on pages 448, 450 and 452.

The Language Situation in the United States

The majority language of the United States is English. English is the language of government, international relations and the main language of the media, education and public life. The United States' Constitution does not specify English as the official language, but in recent years, some states have passed laws designating English as their sole official language, mainly in response to a perceived threat from minority language groups (see pages 290 and 313). The standard English used in the US differs in minor respects from that used in Britain but has long had the status of an autonomous variety. In the State of Hawaii, Hawaiian, a Polynesian language, is spoken by 2000 out of an estimated population of 200,000, but has official status in Hawaii.

English is the first and only language of the majority of the population. However, there is great ethnic and linguistic variety within the United States which reflects four centuries of in-migration and settlement from many parts of the world.

The History of In-migration to the United States

The original inhabitants of the North American continent were the American Indians, also known as Native Americans. The origin of Native Americans can be traced to around 40,000 years ago. The first groups of Mongolians made their way into present day Alaska and settled in parts of Canada, the United States and South America.

The first permanent European settlement in the United States was established by the British in Jamestown in 1607. From then on, throughout the 17th and 18th centuries, the Eastern seaboard was gradually colonized by the British and these colonies formed the nucleus of the future United States. The colonies gained their independence from Britain in 1783, and for over a century, the history of the United States became a history of westward expansion, including the acquisition of territories from the French and Spanish, and of in-migration, as people from many parts of the world arrived in search of the US dream of freedom, liberty, opportunity and prosperity.

Between 1790 and 1860, the population of the United States rose from four million to 32 million. By 1890 it had doubled again to 64 million, with 10 million in-migrants arriving during that 30 year period. In the first great wave of in-migration, between 1820 and 1860, more than five million new Americans arrived, of which 90 percent were from Britain, Ireland and Germany. Between 1860 and 1920, around 29 million in-migrants arrived, mostly from eastern and southern Europe, including Russia, Poland, the Balkans and Italy. During the same period, increasing numbers of Asians, especially Chinese and Japanese, migrated to the Pacific Coast and Hawaii.

Mass in-migration meant great ethnic and linguistic diversity, and this was often perpetuated over several generations, as in-migrants settled near relatives or compatriots, and created their own religious and social institutions in which their own languages were maintained. Over a period of two or three generations, however, descendants of in-migrants were usually assimilated to the English-speaking majority, although their distinctive lifestyles and ethnic customs often continued for longer. This depended on such factors as the number and distribution of in-migrants. Chinese and other Asian minorities tended to maintain their languages for longer because they formed distinct enclaves, usually in urban areas.

In-migration during the latter half of the 20th century has been mostly of Latinos (Hispanics), Pacific Islanders and Asians. The Hispanics entered mainly from Mexico, Cuba and Puerto Rico. Thousands of Mexicans (Chicanos) enter the US every year, many illegally, because of relative poverty and overpopulation in Mexico, and perceived greater opportunities in the US. Many Cubans fled to America after 1959 as refugees from the regime of Fidel Castro. They are concentrated mainly in Miami, Florida. Every year, several million Puerto Ricans travel between Puerto Rico and the US. Hispanics also come from Central American

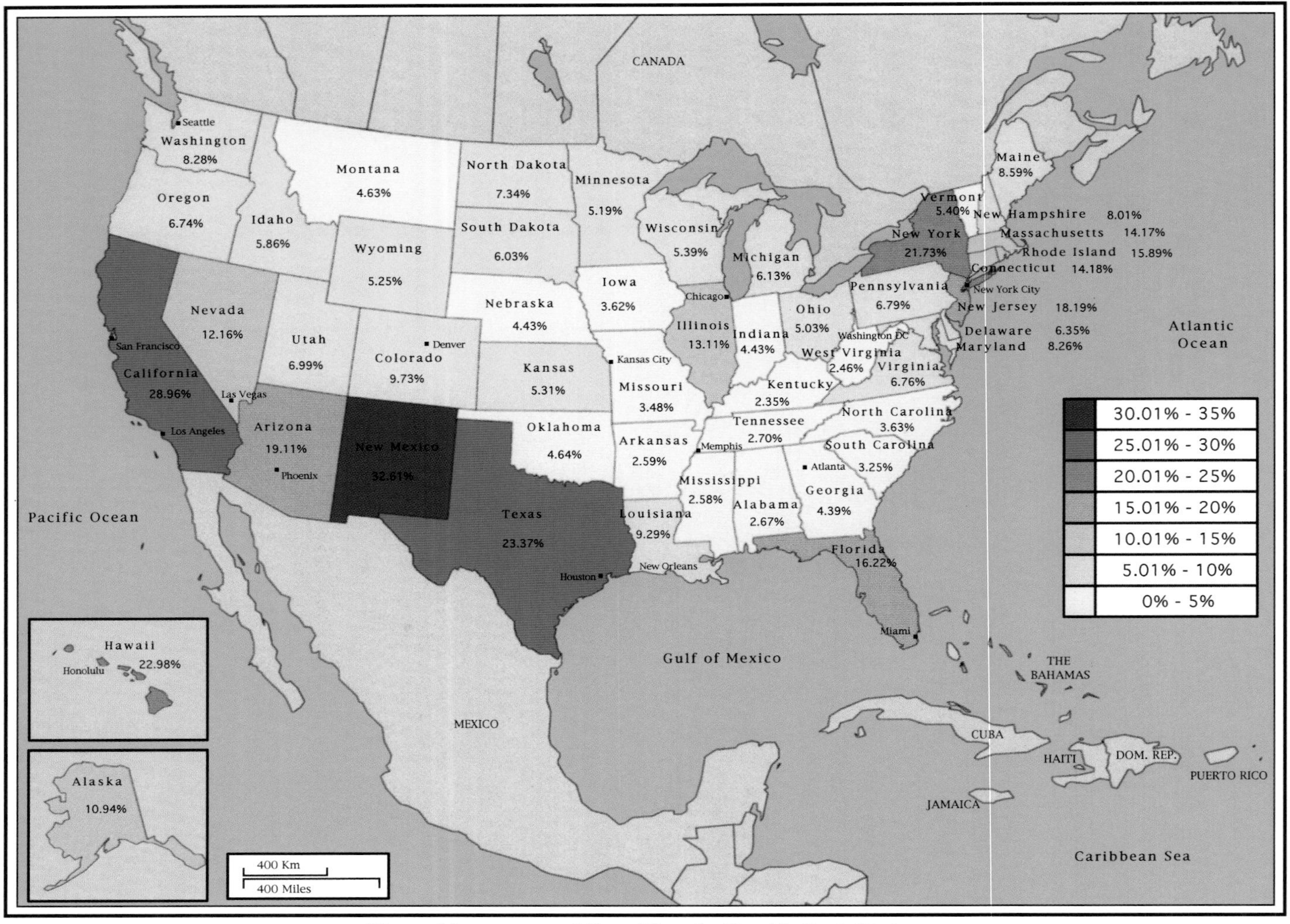

Size of Language Minorities in the United States

This map indicates all language minorities designated as such in the US 1990 census.

and Caribbean countries such as Columbia and the Dominican Republic. Pacific Islanders include many in-migrants from American Samoa, while the largest groups of Asian Americans are the Chinese, Filipinos, Japanese, Asian Indians, Koreans and Vietnamese. There are also communities of Haitians, speaking Haitian Creole.

An important in-migrant group in the history of the US are those originally from Africa. In 1990, the Black population of the United States was nearly 30 million. The majority are descendants of Black Africans captured and forcibly transported to North America to work as slaves on the plantations from the 17th century onwards. The slave traders deliberately separated slaves who spoke the same language to lessen the risk of conspiracy and rebellion. The slaves developed varieties of pidgin English as contact languages on the plantations. These became creolized (see page 142), and became the only languages of children born to slaves on the plantations. These English-based creoles no longer exist, but creole features are found in contemporary Black English.

Another of interest from the history of US in-migration are the Cajuns. Cajuns is the name given to descendants of French-Canadians expelled by the British from eastern Canada in 1755. They live mainly in southern Louisiana. Their language, which is in decline, is an archaic dialect of French with a mixture of words taken from Spanish, English, German, African and Indian peoples.

Maps

The accompanying maps portray the language profile of the United States at the 1990 Census. The first map (above) indicates the presence of language minorities in different States by percentage of total population. For example, 23.37 percent of the Texan population speak a language other than English as their home language.

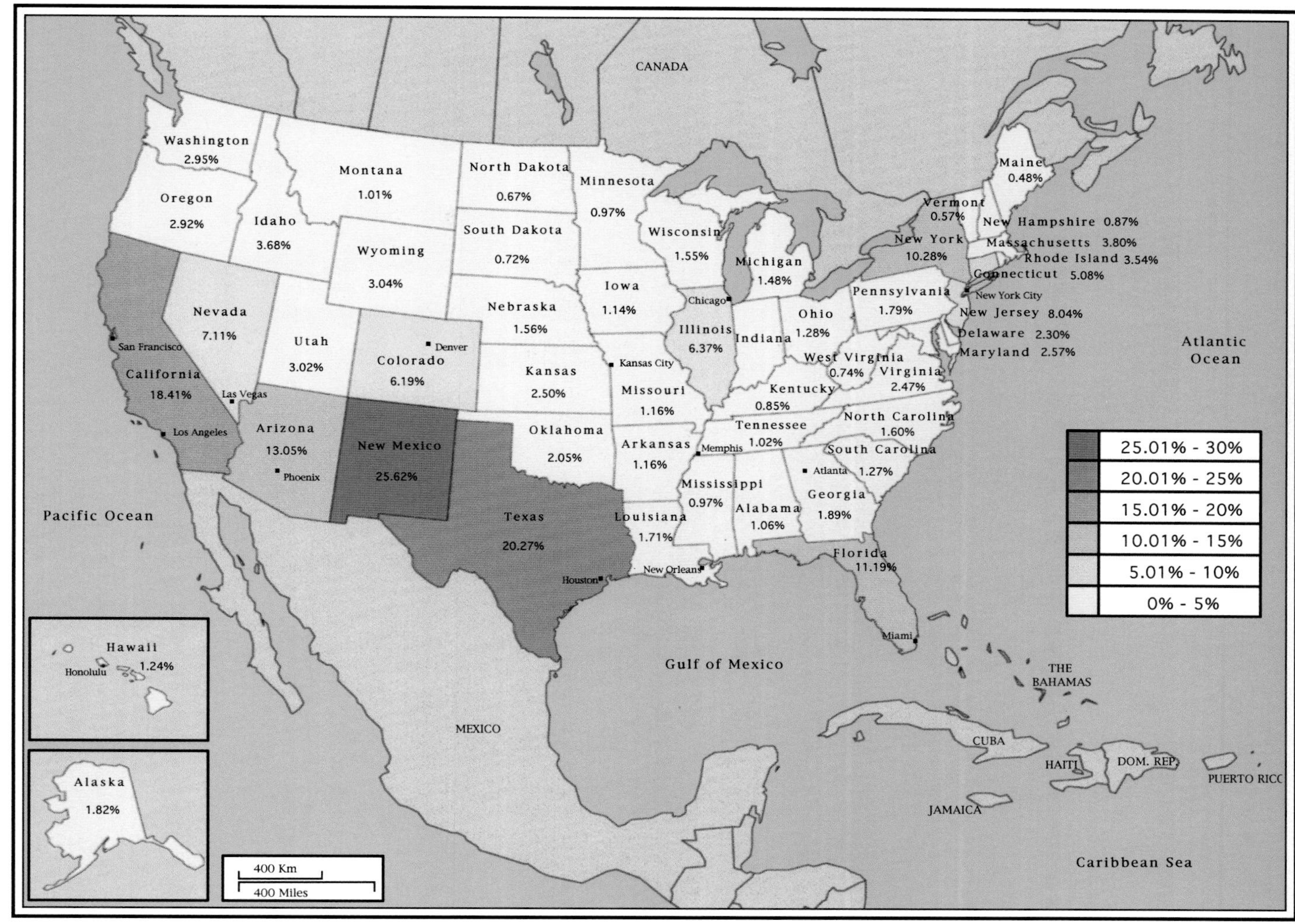

Distribution of Spanish Speakers in the United States

The figures represent the numbers of Spanish speakers in each state as a percentage of the total population of that state.

Relatively high percentages of language minority speakers are found in the States of New Mexico, California, Texas, Hawaii, New York, Arizona, New Jersey and Florida which all have over 15 percent of their population in this category.

A separate table provides details of the size of the language minority in each State. For example, there are 8.6 million Californians, four million Texans and 3.9 million in the State of New York enumerated as language minority members. There are also over two million language minority people in Florida, and over a million such inhabitants in the States of Illinois and New Jersey.

The second map (above) shows the distribution of Spanish speakers across States in the US according to the 1990 Census data. For example, in New Mexico, 25.62 percent of that State's population were enumerated as Spanish-speaking, followed by Texas with 20.27 percent, California with 18.41 percent, Arizona with 13.05 percent, Florida with 11.19 percent and New York with 10.28 percent. Four States are then portrayed in more detail: California, Texas, Arizona and New York. (See the map on page 441.)

For completeness, a fourth map (page 442) indicates the distribution, according to the 1990 Census, of those who are monolingual in English. The states of West Virginia, Kentucky, Tennessee, Alabama and Arkansas reveal the highest percentages of monolingual English speakers.

The fifth map (page 443) uses 1990 Census data and provides a map of bilingualism in the United States. Bilinguals are those who reported speaking a language other than English at home, and who also speak English 'well' or 'very well'. Thus, the map displays those States where bilinguals are more and less present. For example, 28.9 percent of New Mexicans spoke English 'well' or

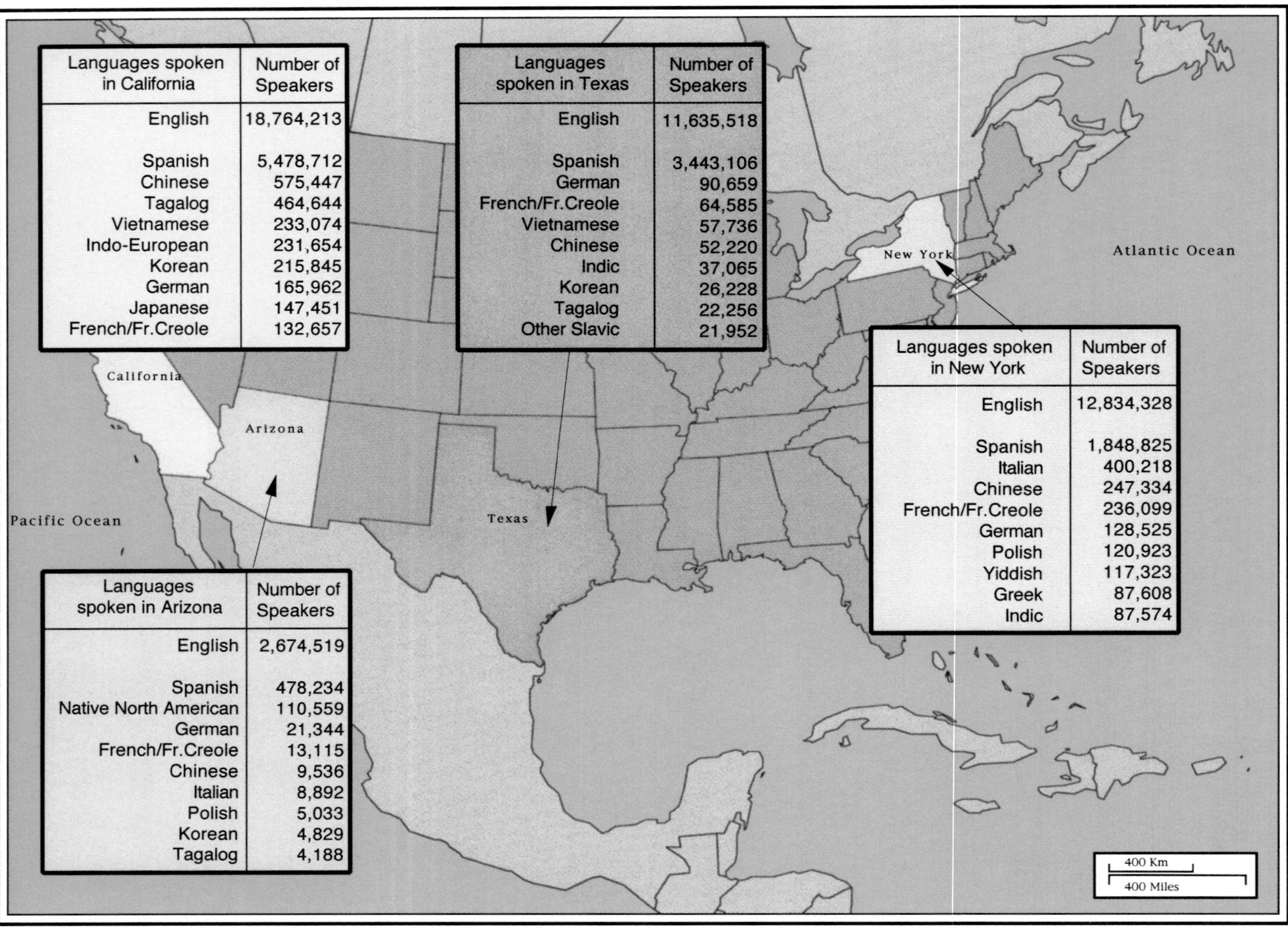

Languages spoken in California	Number of Speakers
English	18,764,213
Spanish	5,478,712
Chinese	575,447
Tagalog	464,644
Vietnamese	233,074
Indo-European	231,654
Korean	215,845
German	165,962
Japanese	147,451
French/Fr.Creole	132,657

Languages spoken in Texas	Number of Speakers
English	11,635,518
Spanish	3,443,106
German	90,659
French/Fr.Creole	64,585
Vietnamese	57,736
Chinese	52,220
Indic	37,065
Korean	26,228
Tagalog	22,256
Other Slavic	21,952

Languages spoken in New York	Number of Speakers
English	12,834,328
Spanish	1,848,825
Italian	400,218
Chinese	247,334
French/Fr.Creole	236,099
German	128,525
Polish	120,923
Yiddish	117,323
Greek	87,608
Indic	87,574

Languages spoken in Arizona	Number of Speakers
English	2,674,519
Spanish	478,234
Native North American	110,559
German	21,344
French/Fr.Creole	13,115
Chinese	9,536
Italian	8,892
Polish	5,033
Korean	4,829
Tagalog	4,188

The Top Ten Languages of Four States in the United States

Size of Language Minorities in the United States

State	Size of Language Minority	Percentage of State Population	State	Size of Language Minority	Percentage of State Population	State	Size of Language Minority	Percentage of State Population
California	8,619,334	28.96%	Colorado	320,631	9.73%	Maine	105,441	8.59%
Texas	3,970,304	23.37%	Georgia	284,546	4.39%	Iowa	100,391	3.62%
New York	3,908,720	21.73%	Wisconsin	263,638	5.39%	New Hampshire	88,796	8.01%
Florida	2,098,315	16.22%	Hawaii	254,724	22.98%	Kentucky	86,482	2.35%
Illinois	1,499,112	13.11%	Indiana	245,826	4.43%	Columbia	71,348	11.76%
New Jersey	1,406,148	18.19%	North Carolina	240,866	3.63%	Nebraska	69,872	4.43%
Massachusetts	852,228	14.17%	Minnesota	227,161	5.19%	Mississippi	66,516	2.58%
Pennsylvania	806,876	6.79%	Oregon	191,710	6.74%	Arkansas	60,781	2.59%
Arizona	700,287	19.11%	Missouri	178,210	3.48%	Alaska	60,165	10.94%
Michigan	569,807	6.13%	Rhode Island	159,492	15.89%	Idaho	58,995	5.86%
Ohio	546,148	5.03%	Nevada	146,152	12.16%	North Dakota	46,897	7.34%
New Mexico	493,999	32.61%	Oklahoma	145,798	4.64%	West Virginia	44,203	2.46%
Connecticut	446,175	14.18%	Kansas	131,604	5.31%	Delaware	42,327	6.35%
Virginia	418,521	6.76%	Tennessee	131,550	2.70%	South Dakota	41,994	6.03%
Washington	403,173	8.28%	Utah	120,404	6.99%	Montana	37,020	4.63%
Maryland	395,051	8.26%	South Carolina	113,163	3.25%	Vermont	30,409	5.40%
Louisiana	391,994	9.29%	Alabama	107,866	2.67%	Wyoming	23,809	5.25%

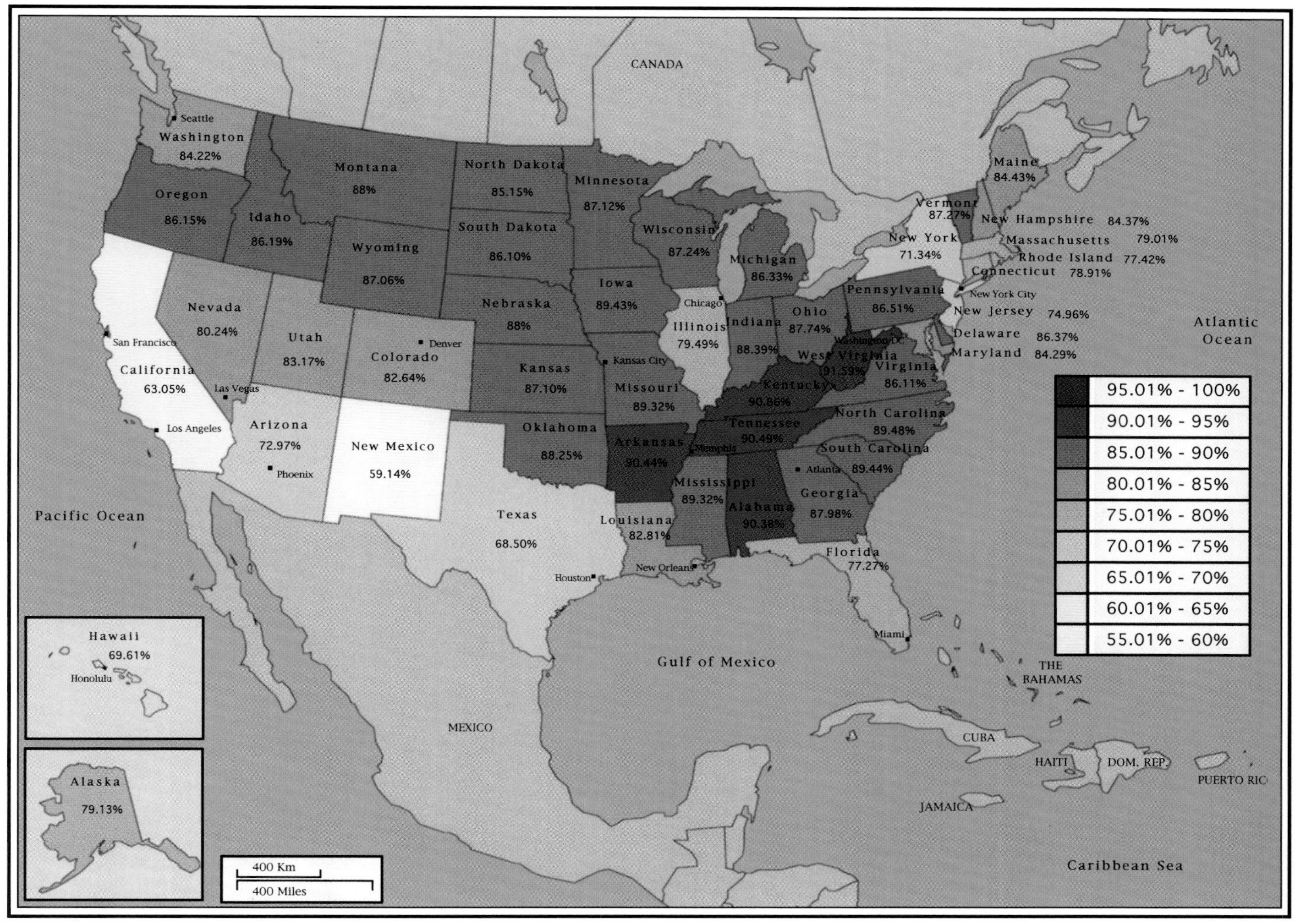

Distribution of Monolingual English Speakers in the United States.

The figures represent the numbers of monolingual English speakers in each State as a percentage of the total population of that State.

'very well' and another language. Other States with relatively high proportions of bilinguals are: Arizona, California, Hawaii, New York and Texas. At the opposite end of the dimension is Kentucky with 2.03 percent as 'bilinguals'. Low proportions of bilinguals are also found in Alabama, Arkansas, Mississippi, South Carolina, Tennessee and West Virginia.

Native Americans

The history of the Native American people is a history of plunder and exploitation, one outcome being language decline and death. It is estimated that around five hundred separate languages and dialects were spoken by Native Americans before the Europeans arrived in the late fifteenth century. Such natives numbered approximately two million people living within the current boundaries of the United States.

Within a few decades, the European invaders had begun

Languages (other than English) Spoken at Home: 1980 and 1990 United States Census

Language	1980	1990
Spanish	11,116,000	17,345,000
French/French Creole	*1,609,000	1,930,000
German	1,587,000	1,548,000
Chinese	631,000	1,319,000
Italian	1,618,000	1,309,000
Tagalog (Filipino)	*452,000	843,000
Polish	821,000	723,000
Korean	266,000	626,000
Vietnamese	195,000	507,000
Portuguese	352,000	431,000
Japanese	336,000	428,000
Greek	401,000	388,000
Arabic	217,000	355,000
Hindi (Urdu)	*130,000	331,000
Russian	173,000	242,000

*3 years and over; all other figures, 5 years and over

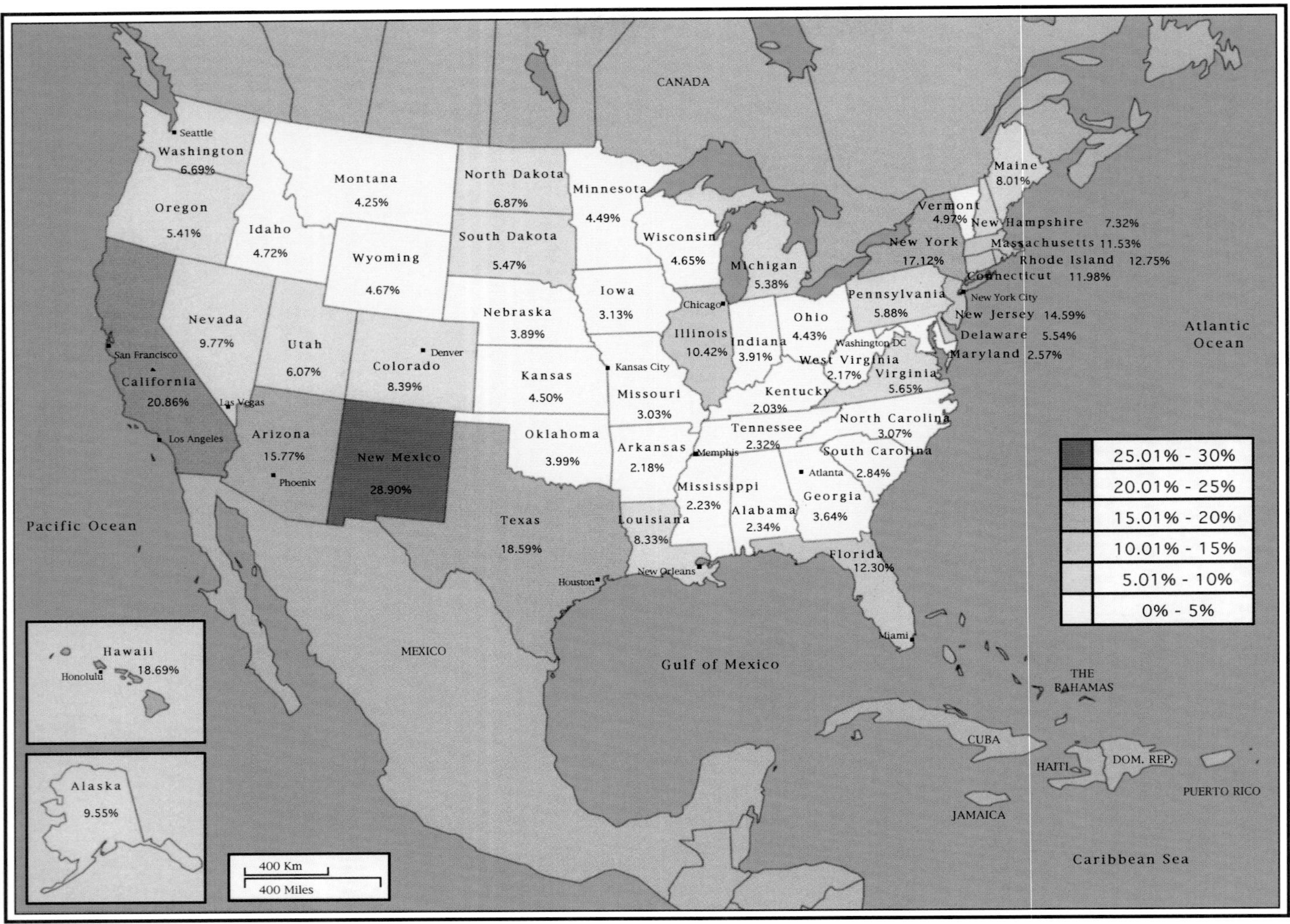

Percentage of the US Population Who Were Bilingual at the 1990 Census

The figures represent the numbers of bilinguals in each State as a percentage of the total population of that State.

to appropriate native land (although they occasionally signed treaties with Native Americans for the acquisition of their land). Such negotiations and conflicts marked the beginning of language contact and language conflicts between European settlers and Native Americans.

Territorial rights, with reservations for Native Americans, did not necessarily preserve Native American languages and dialects. Once living on a reservation, a Native American indigenous group needed to meet and negotiate with agents of the government. When enduring periods of starvation (through the government ignoring treaties regarding food distribution), the relative power and value of native compared with settlers' languages was much in contrast.

While some Native American languages have survived until the present, the story of such languages is one of decline, desperation and often death. Assimilative forces, often represented in government agents and teachers, have made the maintenance of Native American languages difficult, leading to replacement rather than preservation. The economic poverty of Native Americans, the relatively poor quality of education provided for them, and problems of health and alcohol, each helped make assimilation into language majority society in the United States appear attractive and desirable. Only on the surface was there a choice of language, a choice of culture and a choice of lifestyle. Where economic deprivation existed, the pull and the push was both towards the majority language and its attendant culture.

There have been attempts to reverse the downward language shift in Native American languages. Following the Indian Reorganization Act of 1934, native languages were encouraged, and standards of education were improved. This program aimed to reverse the effects of continuous assimilation. The Act recognized the cultural

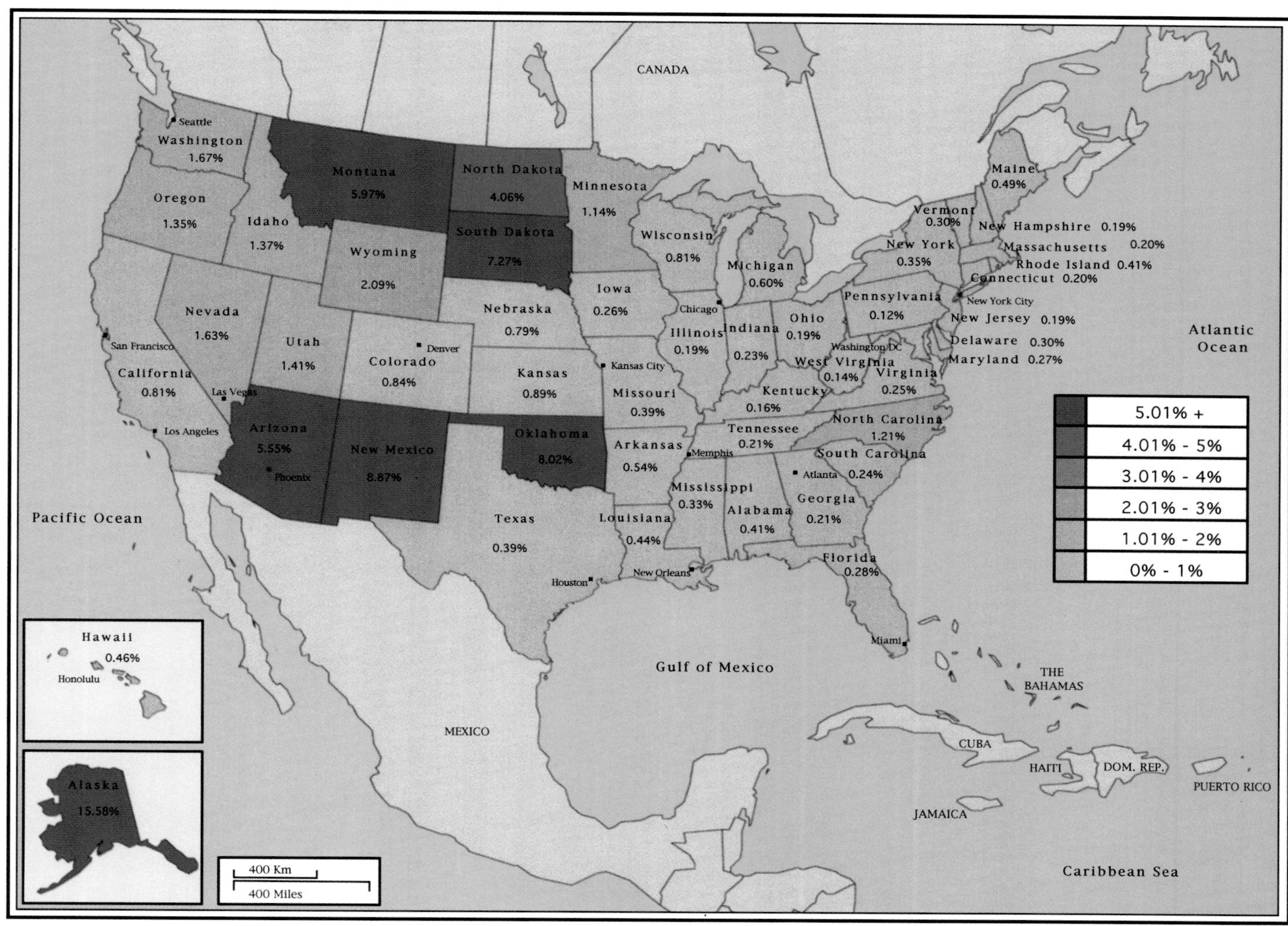

Distribution of Native Americans in the United States (includes: American Indians, Eskimos or Aleut)

The figures represent the numbers of Native Americans in each State as a percentage of the total population of that State.

and linguistic distinctiveness of Native Americans and wished to preserve their differences. In recent decades, the national Indian Youth Conference, the 1975 Self-Determination Act and various protests have raised not only an awareness of the native people's situation, but also a conscience about it.

It is estimated that there are currently as many Native Americans in the United States as when Christopher Columbus landed in 1492 (approximately two million). Many of these, due to intermarriage, may only have a small percentage of Native American blood. The number of languages that appear to have a future among Native Americans is few. If these languages die, or become further weakened, the long ancestral history of languages and their cultures in the United States will be impoverished.

Indigenous Ethnic Groups in the United States

Of a total US population of nearly 264 million, 0.7 percent were classed in the 1990 US Census as American Indian, Eskimo or Aleut; 3.4 percent as Asian and Pacific Islanders, 10.4 percent as Hispanics, and 73.5 percent as Whites (excluding Hispanics). The accompanying map (above) indicates the location of the American Indian, Eskimo or Aleut.

Those classed as American Indian, Eskimo or Aleut were

State	Total Numbers of American Indian, Eskimo or Aleut People	Percentage of the Population of the State
Alaska	85,689	15.58
Arizona	203,527	5.55
California	242,164	0.81
Montana	47,679	5.97
New Mexico	134,355	8.87
North Dakota	25,917	4.06
Oklahoma	252,420	8.02
South Dakota	50,575	7.27

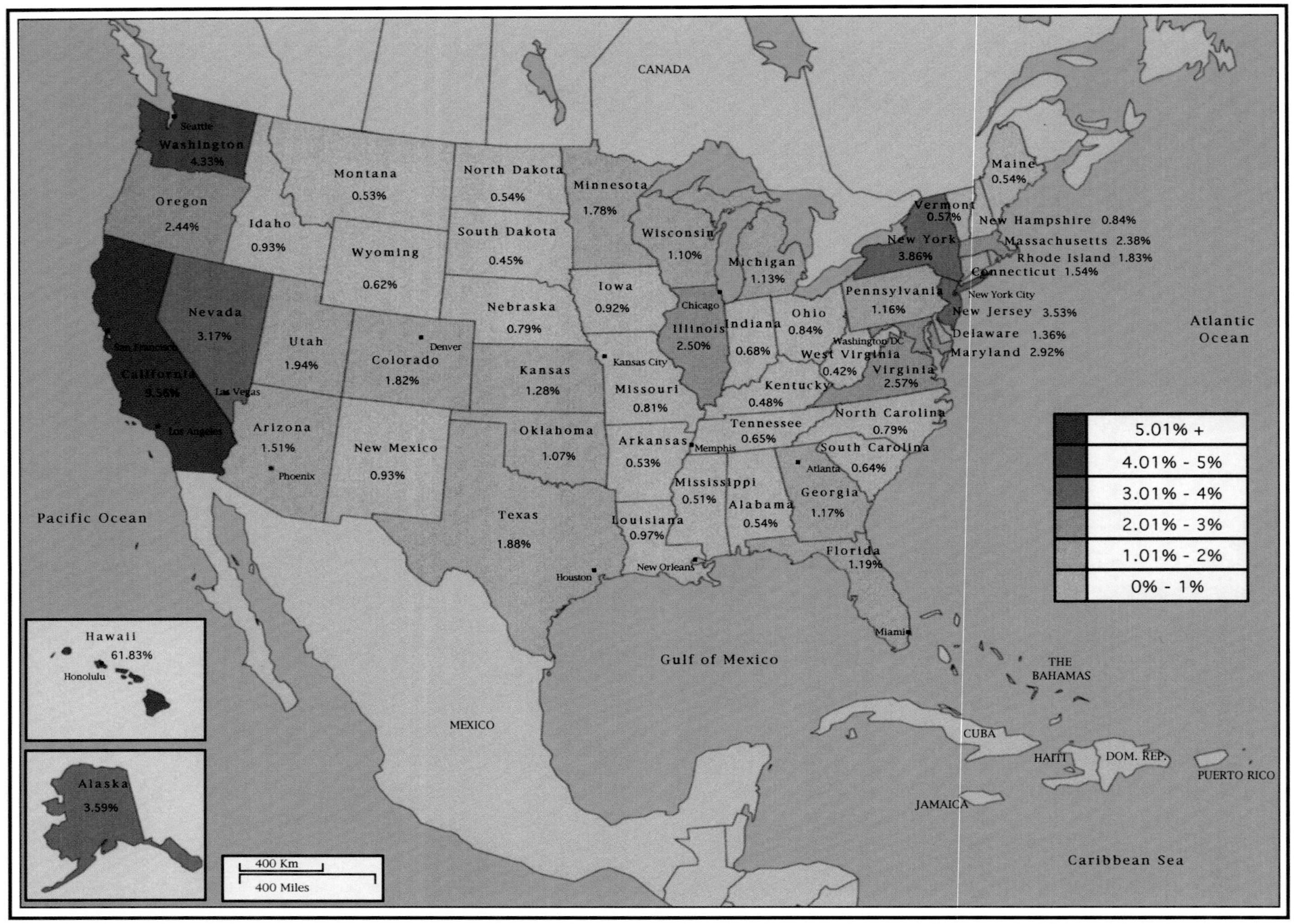

Percentage of Asians and Pacific Islanders in the United States

The figures represent the numbers of Asians and Pacific Islanders in each State as a percentage of the total population of that State.

particularly located in the States that are listed in the table opposite. As can be seen, some States have large numbers of American Indian, Eskimo or Aleut people (e.g. California), other States have smaller numbers but larger percentages of the total State population (e.g. South Dakota).

Asians and Pacific Islanders in the United States

The seventh map (above) shows the distribution of those classed as Asian and Pacific Islanders. In 1995, 3.4 percent of the population were Pacific Islanders. Asians and Pacific Islanders include: Chinese, Filipino, Japanese, Asian Indian, Korean, Vietnamese, Hawaiian, Samoan, Guamarian. Cambodian, Hmong, Laotian, Thai, Bangladeshi, Burmese, Indonesian, Malayan, Okinawan, Pakistani, Sri Lankan, Tongan, Tahitian, Northern Mariana Islander, Palauan and Fijian. The table indicates that California heads the list with close to three million Asian and Pacific Islanders. New York and Hawaii have close to 700,000 residents of Asian and Pacific Islander heritage. Apart from Hawaii (62 percent of the population), the States of California (9.6 percent) and Washington (4.3 percent) have relatively higher percentage densities of Asian and Pacific Islanders.

State	Total Numbers of Asian and Pacific Islanders	Percentage of the Population of the State
Alaska	19,728	3.59
California	2,845,659	9.56
Hawaii	685,236	61.83
Illinois	285,311	2.50
New Jersey	272,521	3.53
New York	693,760	3.86
Texas	319,459	1.88
Washington	210,958	4.33

Data from the US Census Bureau

Some findings from the 1990 Census

- In 1990, 31.8 million US residents (14 percent of the population) age five and over reported speaking a language other than English at home. In 1980, the figure was 23.1 million residents (11 percent of the population).
- After English, Spanish was the language most often spoken at home. More than half (54 percent or 17.3 million) of those who spoke a language other than English at home reported they spoke Spanish.
- Spanish was nine times more frequently a home language than French (including French Creole), which was the second most common non-English language spoken at home and was used by 1.9 million persons. Then followed German, with 1.5 million speakers, and Chinese and Italian, each with 1.3 million. In total, 4.5 million persons spoke an Asian or Pacific Island language.
- In all four regions of the US (Northeast, Midwest, South, West). Spanish was the language with the highest number of speakers (other than English). The next most widely used language, however, was different. In the Northeast, Italian was second; in the Midwest, German; in the South, French; and in the West, Chinese.
- In 39 States and the District of Columbia, Spanish was the most frequently spoken non-English home language. The most frequent non-English language for the remaining States varied. French (including French Creole) was the most common in Louisiana, Maine, New Hampshire, and Vermont. German was most used in Minnesota, Montana, and North and South Dakota. Portuguese was the most prevalent in Rhode Island, Yupik in Alaska, and Japanese in Hawaii.
- Between 1980 and 1990, the languages with the sharpest decline in the numbers of speakers included Italian (down 19 percent), Polish (down 12 percent), Greek (down three percent) and German (down two percent).
- In the same period (1980 to 1990), Vietnamese speakers had risen by 161 percent, Hindi (Urdu) by 155 percent, Korean by 135 percent and Chinese by 109 percent.

Census Updates

The US Census Bureau produces updates on population patterns in between Censuses. For example:

- Close to one in ten of the population were of Hispanic origin in 1995.
- In 1995, approximately nine out of every ten residents were born in the US. Eleven out of every 20 Hispanics were born in the US.
- In 1994, in-migration accounted for 30 percent of the increase in the US population that year.
- In 1994, the increase in population varied according to group. Asian and Pacific Islanders along with Hispanics increased in their total numbers by over three percent (respectively 3.8 percent and 3.5 percent), while the Black American and the American Indian, Eskimo and Aleut populations increased by 1.5 percent, and the white non-Hispanic population by 0.8 percent.

Future trends

The United States Census Bureau produces estimates of future population trends. Such trends show differences between ethnic groups. The pie charts show the predicted changes in the relative size of ethnic groups in the United States by comparing 1995 figures with projected year 2050 figures. They show that the White (excluding Hispanics) population may decline from 73.5 percent of the total population to 52.5 percent. In contrast, the Asian and Pacific Islanders and Hispanics will grow significantly. The Asian and Pacific Islanders are predicted to quadruple their numbers and the Hispanics to treble their population. Thus, the ethnic diversity of the United States will continue to grow, with possibilities also of increased cultural and linguistic diversity. This is portrayed in the accompanying table and pie charts.

	US Population December 1st 1995		Estimated US Population July 1st 2050	
	Number	%	Number	%
Total Population	263,835,000	100.0	392,031,000	100.0
White (excluding Hispanics)	193,881,000	73.5	205,849,000	52.5
Black (excluding Hispanics)	31,770,000	12.0	56,346,000	14.4
American Indian, Eskimo & Aleut	1,942,000	0.7	3,701,000	0.9
Asian and Pacific Islander	8,852,000	3.4	38,064,000	9.7
Hispanics	27,390,000	10.4	88,071,000	22.5

(Estimated statistics are based on United States Bureau of Census figures,1992).

Puerto Ricans in the United States

Puerto Rico is a Caribbean island approximately a thousand miles south-east of Florida. Originally colonized by the Spaniards, the dominant cultural influence remains Hispanic. After the Spanish-American War, Puerto Rico was given to the United States in the Treaty of Paris of 1898. The island was given a measure of local government until 1917 when Puerto Ricans were declared as citizens of the United States. Since 1952, the island has been a freely associated commonwealth of the United States. (See page 115.) During the 20th century, many Puerto Ricans have migrated to the United States in search of improved economic, health, educational and political conditions.

Approximately one-third of the total Puerto Rican population live in the United States, particularly in New York City. Almost a million Puerto Ricans live in or around New York. An area of East Harlem called El Barrio (the neighborhood) is a particular focal point for many Puerto Ricans.

Like many other in-migrant communities in the United States, Puerto Ricans tend to have inadequate housing conditions, relatively poorer health, are more likely to be unemployed or exploited at work, and face racial prejudice in mainstream society. Such problems tend to bind the people together, so that many Puerto Ricans have maintained a vigorous ethnicity in their New York communities.

Where modern Puerto Ricans are trying to advance their economic and educational success, this may be at the expense of traditional family solidarity, Puerto Rican ethnicity and loss of the Spanish language. While speaking Spanish provides social cohesion for the Puerto Ricans in New York, for those who wish to become socially and economically upwardly mobile, the perception is also that they need to increase English language competence often at cost to their Spanish language skills.

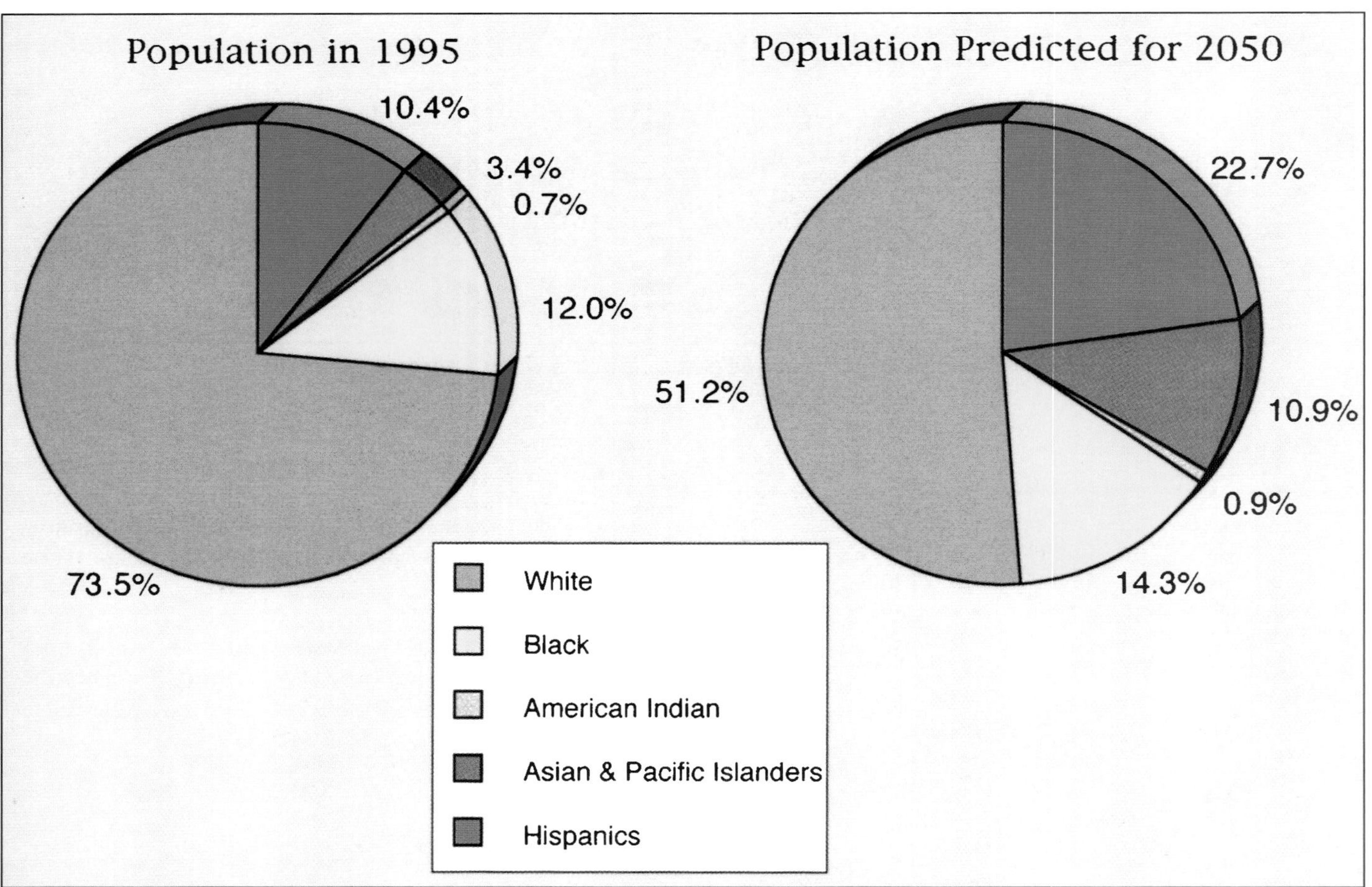

Predicted changes in the United States population. The groups in the pie charts are defined by US Census Bureau as: (1) White population excluding Hispanics. (2) Black population excluding Hispanics. (3) American Indian, Eskimo and Aleut population excluding Hispanics. (4) Asian and Pacific Islanders excluding Hispanics. (5) Hispanics from a variety of origins.

Oceania

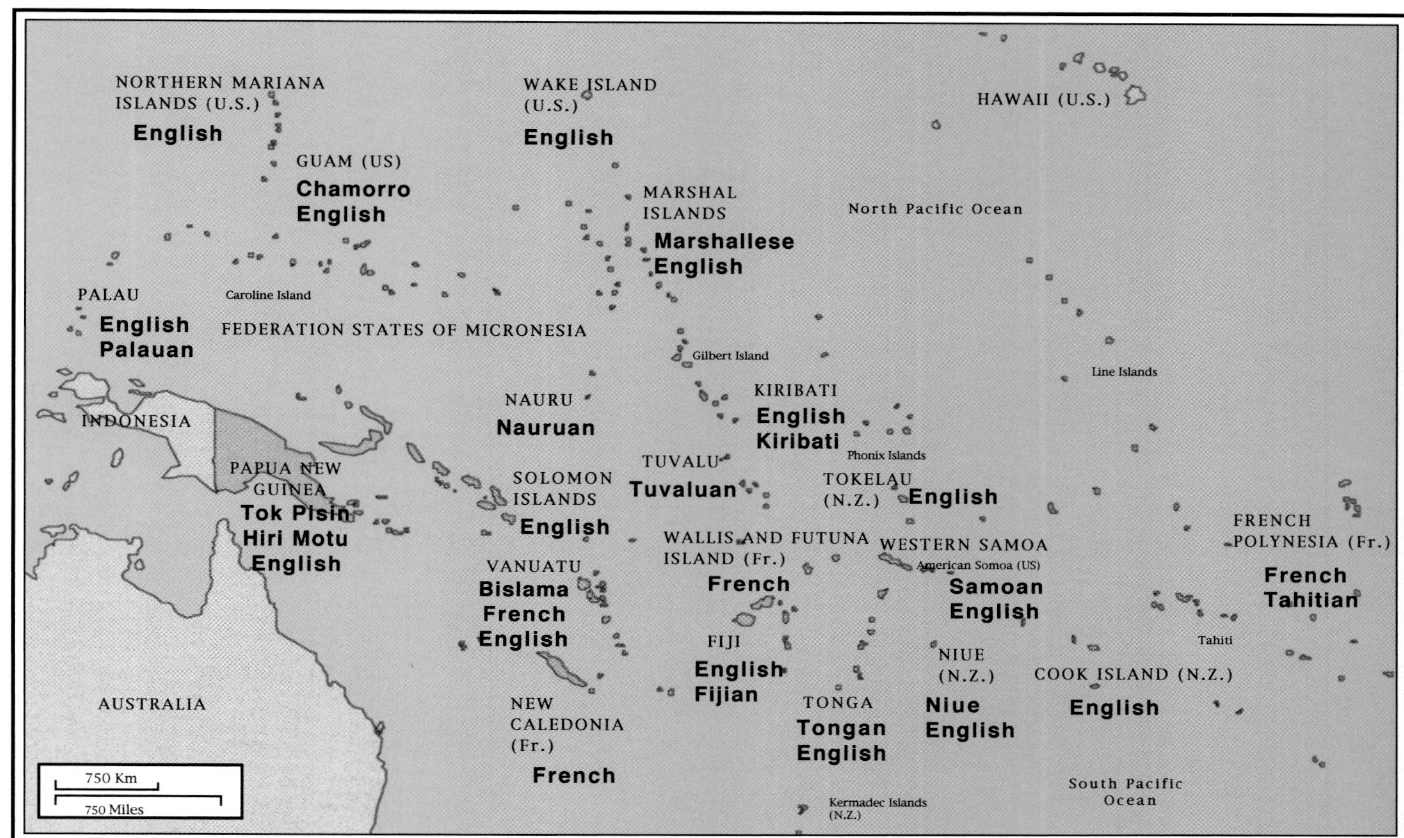

Official Languages of the Islands of Oceania

American Samoa

American Samoa comprises seven islands in the South Pacific Ocean, between Hawaii and New Zealand. In 1995 the estimated population of the islands was 57,000. The two official languages are English and Samoan. The islands are an unincorporated territory of the US, and have been under US control since the beginning of the 20th century. The largest island is Tutuila, the site of a US naval base.

English is the mother tongue of around 1200 people, most of whom are foreign-born. It is also a second language for 75 percent of native-born American Samoans. Although Samoan is the first language of the indigenous population, English is widely used as a lingua franca between Samoans, Americans and other migrants to the islands. Both languages are used in government, media and education. Bilingualism is widespread, and many of the younger Samoans use English instead of Samoan. Ninety percent of the population speak Samoan as their first language.

Two minority language groups in American Samoa speak Tongan and Tokelauan. There are around one hundred Tokelauan speakers, and approximately 500 Tongan speakers. Most have migrated to American Samoa from other Pacific islands.

Cook Islands

The Cook Islands are located in the south-east Pacific Ocean, midway between Hawaii and New Zealand. The 15 islands are dependencies of New Zealand. In the

1986 Census, the population was 17,610, but by 1995 the estimated population was over 19,000. Cook Island Maori and English are the official languages of the Cook Islands. Cook Island Maori is also known as Rarotongan and is an Eastern Polynesian language, related to New Zealand Maori. English is spoken by a small number of Cook Islanders, and 2.4 percent of the population are European.

A number of Polynesian languages are spoken on the islands. Cook Island Maori is the most widely spoken language, with some 17,000 native speakers. It is also the second language of many minority language speakers. It consists of several mutually intelligible varieties. There are approximately 600 speakers of Penrhyn, another Polynesian language not closely related to Cook Island Maori, living mainly on the island of Tongareva. Pukapuka, a language related to Samoan, is spoken by around 800 Cook Islanders on the island of Pukapuka. These are the two largest minority language groups. Smaller groups include speakers of Niue, of which there are around 20 speakers in the Cook Islands.

Fiji

Fiji is located in the South Pacific Ocean and comprises over 300 islands and islets, only a hundred of which are inhabited. Fiji was a British colony for nearly a century, but became independent in 1970. The population in 1995 was estimated at 772,000, 80 percent of whom live on the largest island, Viti Levu. Fiji has two official languages, Fijian and English.

The population of Fiji is divided into two main ethnic groups, which together constitute about 95 percent of the population. Before independence in 1970, the Indian population was by far the largest, and most of this population are descendants of Indian field workers brought to Fiji by the British during their time as colonial rulers. However, since independence, the Indian population has been declining, and it is currently estimated that the ethnic Fijians are the slightly larger group.

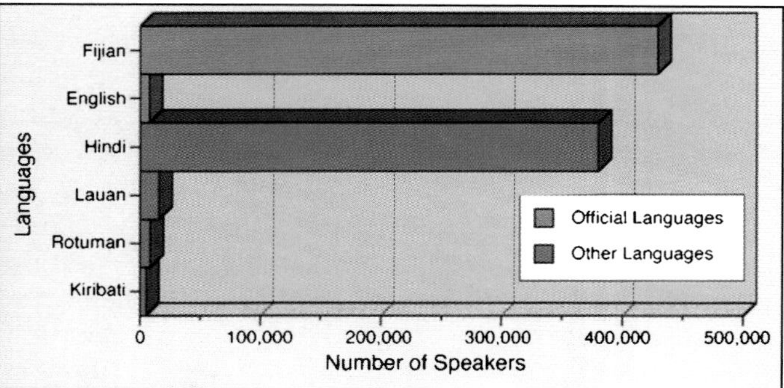

Main languages spoken in Fiji.

Fijian is spoken by about 430,000 people. Fijian comprises two main dialect groups, Western Fijian and Eastern Fijian. Western Fijian is spoken in the western half of the island of Viti Levu and on neighboring smaller islands. Eastern Fijian dialects are spoke in the eastern half of Viti Levu, on the other major island of Vuana Levu, and on the small islands to the south. Eastern Fijian forms the largest language group, numbering 330,000. Standard Fijian, based on the Eastern Fijian dialect, is used as a lingua franca between the two dialect groups.

The principal language of the Indian ethnic group is Hindi, spoken by around 80 percent of Indians. Other languages spoken include Tamil, Gujarati, Bengali, and Urdu. Most of the Indian population are bilingual in their mother tongue and English. English is the principal language of inter-ethnic communication, but two pidgins are also used, Pidgin Fijian and Pidgin Hindustani. Both these pidgins developed as contact languages on the plantations. Fijian, Hindi and Urdu are used as teaching media during the first years of primary education. In the mass media, English, Fijian, Hindi and Urdu are all used. English is spoken as a first language by about 20,000 citizens of European origin as well as some urban dwellers of non-European origin.

Other languages are also spoken in Fiji. These include Kiribati, Rotuman and Lauan. Rotuman is a language closely related to Fijian, and is spoken on Rotuma, a small island about 300 miles from Fiji. There are about nine thousand speakers. Lauan is spoken by 16,000, and Kiribati by over five thousand people. Several varieties of Chinese are spoken by the few thousand ethnic Chinese.

French Polynesia

French Polynesia has been an overseas territory of France since 1946, and is situated in the South Pacific Ocean, between South America and Australia. It comprises over 130 islands, including the island of Tahiti and the Society islands. In the 1988 Census, there was a total population of 188,814. By 1995, this figure was estimated to be 219,000. The two official languages of French Polynesia are French and Tahitian.

French is spoken by some 15,000 people in French Polynesia. Most of these are foreign-born. French, along with Tahitian, is the language of government, broadcasting and education. Tahitian is the principal language of the islands and is spoken as a mother tongue by over 70 percent of the population. Over half of the population live on the island of Tahiti. Tahitian is widely used by most of the population as a first or second language, for trade and general communication.

As well as Tahitian, four other indigenous Polynesian languages are spoken in French Polynesia, Tuamotuan, Marquesan, Mangarevan and Rapan. Most of the speakers of these languages are located on different islands. Speakers of Mangarevan are found mainly on the Gambier islands, with Marquesan spoken on the Marquesas Islands. On these islands, Marquesan is used in schools alongside French and Tahitian. Two percent of the population speak Hakka Chinese, although this figure is decreasing as many are shifting to Tahitian.

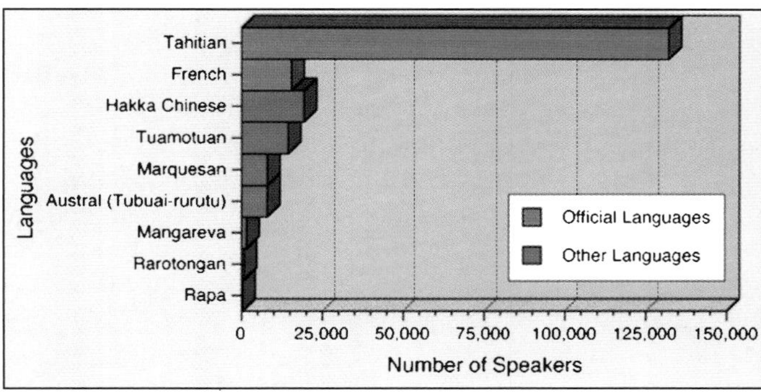

Languages spoken in French Polynesia.

Guam

The United States territory of Guam is a part of the Northern Mariana chain of islands. However, it is not considered a part of the Mariana group as it has long been governed separately. Guam is the largest and most populous of the Mariana Islands, and has an estimated population of 153,000 (1995 estimate). The official languages are Chamorro and English.

Speakers of English number around 29,000. Around nine percent of the total population are United States military personnel. The language of the majority of the population is the second official language, Chamorro. Over 50 percent speak Chamorro as their mother tongue. A total of over a 100,000 people speak Chamorro including second language speakers.

Tagalog (also the official language of the Philippines) is spoken by approximately 24,000 speakers, and Palauan by around 15,000 speakers. Chamorro, Tagalog and Palauan are all Western Malayo-Polynesian languages. Chamorro, English and Tagalog are used in the media.

Kiribati

The Republic of Kiribati, formerly known as the Gilbert Islands, is located on the equator in the Pacific Ocean. Kiribati gained independence from British control in 1979. Kiribati is a group of 33 islands, which include Line Islands and Phoenix Islands. The estimated population in 1995 was 97,000.

The official languages of Kiribati are English and Kiribati, a Micronesian language, known also as Gilbertese. Ninety seven percent of the population speak Kiribati as their first language, and most are literate in the language. Both English and Kiribati are used in the mass media. In the 1979 Census, 338 inhabitants spoke English as their first language, and there are small numbers of speakers of Polynesian languages.

Marshall Islands

The Republic of the Marshall Islands is located in the North Pacific Ocean. The republic includes the islands of Bikini, Eniwetak and Kwajalein, and has an estimated population of 56,000. The Marshall Islands were under US control between 1947 and 1991, when they gained full independence. The two official languages of the islands are English and Marshallese.

The majority of the population speak Marshallese, a Micronesian language which is also known as Ebon. There are two main dialects which are mutually intelligible. English is spoken by most of the population, and some people are able to speak Japanese.

Federated States of Micronesia

The Federated States of Micronesia, situated in the Western Pacific Ocean, consists of numerous islands and atolls, and includes the states of Kosrae, Pohnpei, Truk and Yap. Formerly a UN Trust Territory of the Pacific Islands, the Federated States of Micronesia has been independent since 1990. Fifteen Polynesian or Micronesian languages are spoken on the islands. The official languages of the four states and the main lingua francas of their inhabitants are Kosraean, Pohnpeian, Chuukese and Yapese. English is a second official language in each state and is used as a lingua franca throughout the nation. Children are educated in their native language for the first few years of primary school, gradually making the transition to English.

Nauru

Nauru is a small island republic in the south-western Pacific Ocean, in between Hawaii and Australia. It was most recently administered by Australia, until independence in 1968. In the 1983 census of Nauru, the population was enumerated as 8042. By 1995, the estimated population had risen to around ten thousand. Over half the population are indigenous Nauruans, and the remainder consists of smaller groups of Asians, Pacific

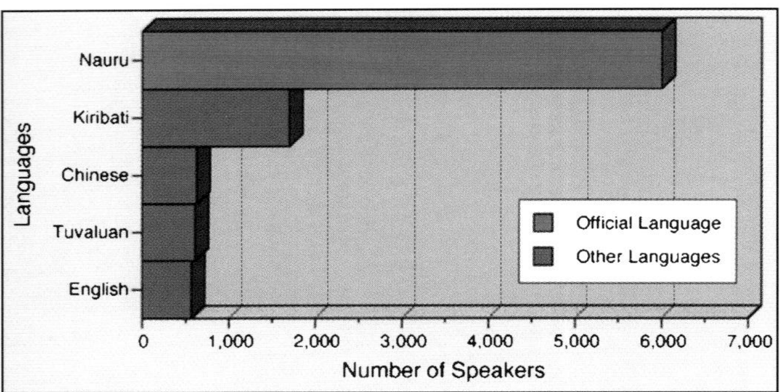

Main languages spoken in Nauru.

islanders, Australians and New Zealanders. The official language of Nauru and the mother tongue of the ethnic Nauruans is Nauruan, a Micronesian language. Nauruan is also spoken as a second language by other groups.

English is widely understood by most language groups in Nauru. Although it is the mother tongue of only a few hundred people, there are around seven thousand second language English speakers. While Nauruan is the official language, in practice, English is the language used for most government and commercial purposes, and as a lingua franca.

There are five minority languages spoken in Nauru. Of the Pacific Islanders, approximately 1700 speak Kiribati and about 600 speak Tuvaluan. There are a small number of speakers of two other Micronesian languages, Marshallese, also known as Ebon, and Kosraen. The speakers of these two languages are generally bilingual with Nauruan as their other language.

Chinese make up 15 percent of the Nauruan population. Some eight percent of the population speak either Mandarin or Cantonese.

New Caledonia and Dependencies

New Caledonia, together with the Loyalty Islands, has been a French overseas territory since the mid-19th century. In 1995, the population was estimated at about 184,000. The official language is French, and there are some 53,000 first language French speakers, mainly in-migrants from France. Twenty eight Melanesian-Polynesian language varieties are spoken on the islands by the indigenous inhabitants who represent about half the population. There has traditionally been a high level of bilingualism and trilingualism among the inhabitants of the islands, due to language contact and intermarriage. Many of the indigenous languages are not in decline, but there is a tendency for the younger generation to use French, which is the medium of primary and secondary education. The remaining half of the population is comprised of Europeans, mainly French, and other in-migrants, often from Vietnam, Indonesia and nearby islands such as Vanuatu, French Polynesia and Wallis and Futuna.

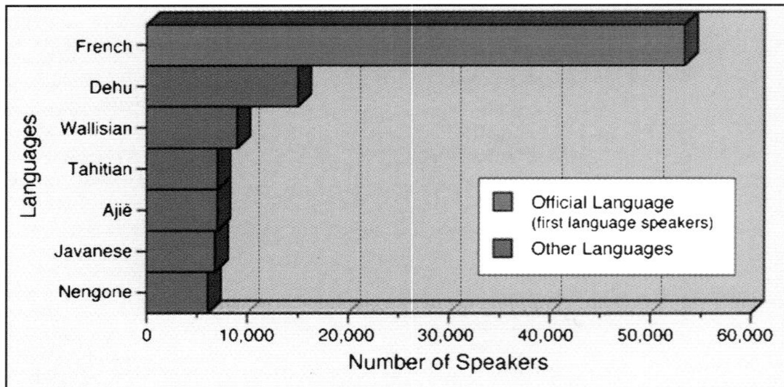

Main languages spoken in New Caledonia and Dependencies.

Niue

Niue Island, once called Savage Island, is located in the south-western Pacific Ocean. The island is a self-governing territory of New Zealand, and has a population of 2200. The official languages are English and Niue, a Polynesian language closely related to Tongan.

Niue is the mother tongue of 97 percent of the population, and is very much the language of everyday life. Niue is the language used in schools for the first three years of education, after which there is a transition to English. Niue is the language of government, while English tends to predominate in the media. Levels of Niue and English bilingualism are high.

Many Niueans have migrated to New Zealand. About 13,000 Niueans live in New Zealand, retaining their indigenous language while also being competent in English.

Norfolk Island

Norfolk Island is an overseas territory of Australia, located to the north of New Zealand (not shown on the map). The population of 2756 (1995 estimate) consists of descendants from Bounty mutineers relocated in 1856 from Pitcairn Island, and also in-migrants from Australia and New Zealand. English is the official language, and the native language of three-quarters of the population. About a quarter of the population speak the Norfolk dialect of Pitcairn-Norfolk, a language which has evolved from a mixture of 18th century British English and Tahitian. Some scholars consider Pitcairn-Norfolk to be a creole.

Northern Mariana Islands

The Northern Mariana Islands is the name given to a group of 14 islands located in the Western Pacific Ocean. They are also known as the Commonwealth of the Northern Mariana Islands, and are a commonwealth of the United States, like Puerto Rico. Only six of the islands are inhabited, including Saipan, Tinian and Rota. The official language is English. The Mariana Islands have a population of 51,000 (1995 estimate), the majority of whom speak Chamorro, a Micronesian language. Most of the speakers are concentrated on the island of Saipan where Chamorro is used as a trade language. Some Chamorro speakers are bilingual in English and Chamorro.

A second Micronesian language spoken in the Mariana Islands is Carolinian. This language is spoken mainly in the home, but is taught alongside Chamorro in schools.

Palau

Palau is an independent republic in the Western Pacific. Palau was formerly a part of the United States Trust Territory of the Pacific islands. Also known as Belau, the republic consists of over 200 islands, only eight of which are inhabited. In 1995 the estimated population of Palau was 16,600. The official languages of the republic are English and Palauan.

Palau is divided up into 16 states. English is official in all 16 states, but in three states, languages other than Palauan are second official languages. In the state of Sonsoral, Sonsorolese is the official language, as are Anguar and Japanese in Anguar, and Tobi in the state of Tobi. Most of Palau's population speak Palauan as either a first or second language.

Papua New Guinea

Papua New Guinea is made up of the eastern half of the island of New Guinea and smaller surrounding islands. The estimated population was almost 4.3 million in 1995. The first Europeans to claim Papua New Guinea were the Spanish in the 16th century. By the 19th century, the country had been take over by Great Britain, who transferred rule to Australia. Papua New Guinea gained independence in 1975.

Over 800 indigenous language varieties are spoken in Papua New Guinea, making it the most multilingual country in the world. Geographical extremes, such as high rugged mountains, have contributed to the isolation of different ethnic groups, and consequently to linguistic diversity. However, there is considerable language contact and much of the population is bilingual or multilingual.

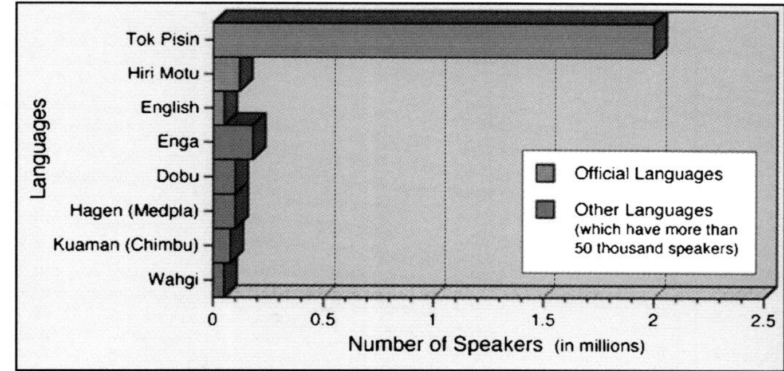

Main languages spoken in Papua New Guinea.

There are three official languages in Papua New Guinea. English has been an official language since the country was a British colony in the 19th century. The graph shows that the language has 50,000 speakers, although there may be as many as 200,000 first and second language speakers of English in Papua New Guinea. English has been the main language of state education at both primary and secondary level since the 1950s, but recent policy changes in the late 1980s mean that vernacular languages are being used in the first years of primary education with a gradual transition to English.

Two languages more recently given the status of official languages are Hiri Motu and Tok Pisin. They are used alongside English in government and the media and in some private primary schools. These languages are used by over half the country's population. The most important lingua franca is Tok Pisin, or New Guinea Pidgin, which has between one and a half and two million second language speakers. It is an English-based pidgin which developed during the late 19th century as a means of communication between European overseers and indigenous workers. Gradually it has become the main means of communication within the country. It has also become the first language of between about 20,000 and 50,000 people, living mainly in urban areas. Hiri Motu is a pidginization of the Austronesian language of Motu, or True Motu, spoken by about 200,000 people as a second language. Hiri Motu developed as a trade language around the capital, Port Moresby, before the colonial period and its use has spread rapidly during the 20th century, partly because it became the lingua franca of the multilingual police force.

Some of the indigenous languages have regional status and are used, though often only orally, in local government.

Pitcairn Island

Pitcairn Island is a dependent territory of the United Kingdom, located to the east of French Polynesia (not shown on the map). There are around 70 inhabitants who are the descendants of mutineers from the British ship HMS Bounty and Tahitians who settled in the uninhabited island in 1790. English is the official language but the inhabitants speak the Pitcairn-English dialect of Pitcairn-Norfolk, a language variety that has evolved from a mixture of 18th century British English and Tahitian. Some scholars consider that Pitcairn-Norfolk is a creole.

The Solomon Islands

The Solomon Islands are made up of 30 mountainous and volcanic islands, located between Papua New Guinea and Vanuatu, and have a population of around 400,000. English is the official language, although it is spoken by only 1.2 percent of the population. Ninety three percent of the population are Melanesians. Some 80 local languages are also used. Solomon Pijin, based on English, is one lingua franca widely used throughout the islands. Solomon Pijin is closely related to Bislama, one of the official languages of Vanuatu. Regional lingua francas in the Solomon Islands include Kwara'ae, Babatang, To'abaita and Gari.

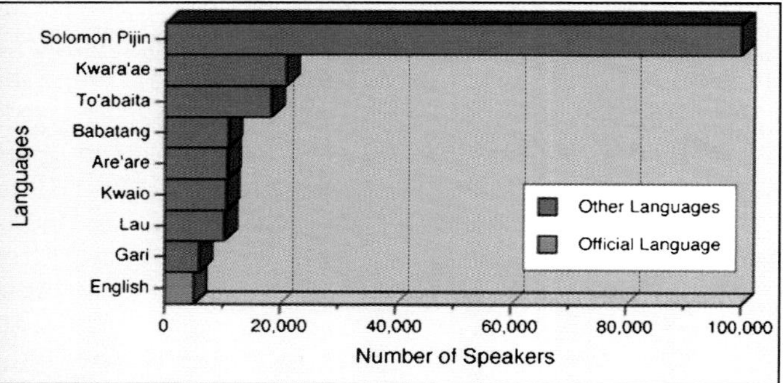

Languages spoken in the Solomon Islands.

Tokelau

Tokelau is a dependent territory of New Zealand, and consists of three small atolls, Atufu, Fakaofo and Nukunono. These islands are located in the South Central Pacific ocean, and are administered from a base in Western Samoa. In the 1986 Census, a total population of 1690 was recorded, but by 1995, the population was estimated to have decreased to around 1500. The official language of Tokelau is English.

Tokelauan, a Polynesian language, is the native tongue of 99 percent of the population. There are a few dozen native Samoan speakers. However, most of the population are bilingual in Tokelauan and Samoan, and English is also quite widely spoken. All three languages are used in schools.

Tonga

Tonga constitutes 150 small islands in the South Pacific Ocean. A former British Protectorate, it gained independence in 1970. It has an estimated population of 105,000 (1995 estimate), 98 percent of whom speak Tongan, the official language, a Polynesian language-related to Samoan. English is the second official language.

A small number of Tongans speak English as a first language, mainly expatriates, plus Tongans born and raised overseas. English is used alongside Tongan in government and education. French and Japanese are also taught as foreign languages in some Tongan schools.

The remaining two percent of the population mainly speak the language of the Niua Fo'ou island. This language, called Niua Fo'ou, is considered by some to be a dialect of Tongan.

Tuvalu

Tuvalu is made up of a group of nine islands, and was formerly known as the Ellice Islands. The islands became independent from the UK in 1978. These islands lie in the Western Pacific Ocean, south of Kiribati. In 1995, Tuvalu had an estimated population of 9500. The official language is Tuvaluan, a Polynesian language, the mother tongue of some 8500 of the population. The rest of the population speak Kiribati, a Micronesian language, or English as their first language. In 1987, there were 870 speakers of Kiribati in Tuvalu, constituting one percent of the population. English is not widely spoken as a language in Tuvalu, but is used in the media alongside Tuvaluan.

Vanuatu

Vanuatu is a small country consisting of 12 Pacific islands. The islands, formerly known as New Hebrides, were jointly administered by the British and French until independence in 1980. Melanasians account for 94 percent of the population.

Vanuatu is a country of great linguistic variety. Over a hundred indigenous languages and dialects are spoken

by the population of around 180,000. French, English and Bislama are all official languages, but Bislama, a Melanesian pidgin language based on English, is the lingua franca. Bislama is closely related to Solomon Pijin, spoken on the Solomon Islands, and less closely related to Tok Pisin, one of the official languages of Papua New Guinea. There are thought to be more than 100,000 speakers of Bislama (mainly second language) in Vanuatu. French and English are spoken by approximately four percent of the population. Although Bislama is the language of wider communication, both education and law are conducted through the medium of French and English.

A Census was conducted by the Statistics Office of Vanuatu in May 1989. The percentage of residents over the age of six who could speak particular languages is shown below, revealing that nine out of every ten residents are bilingual or multilingual.

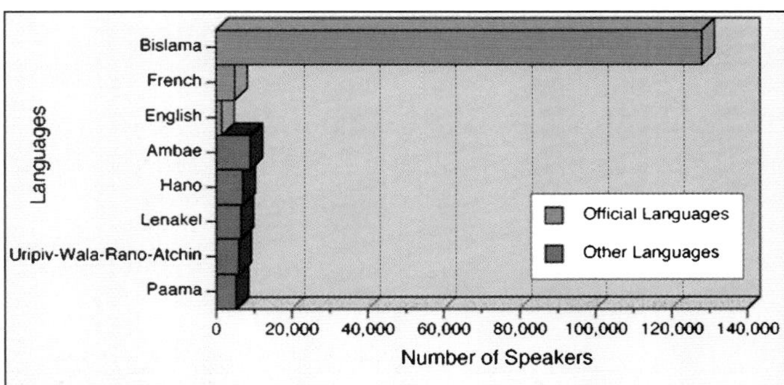

Languages spoken in Vanuatu.

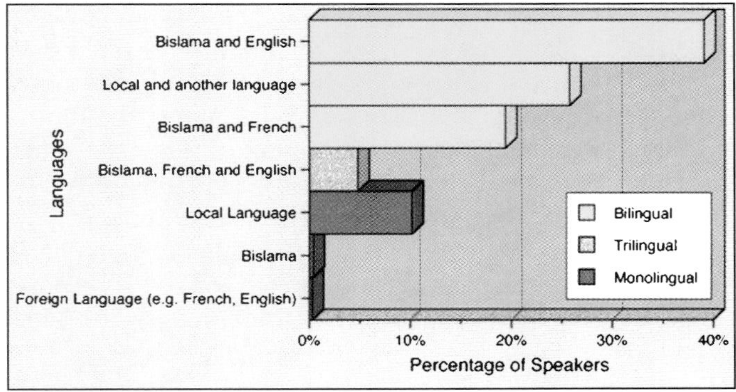

Percentage of bilingual and monolingual speakers in Vanuatu. (Source: Crowley, 1994).

Wake Island

Wake Island is located in the Central Pacific Ocean, and consists of three small coral islets. These islets were uninhabited until their discovery by the Spanish in 1568, and are currently administered by the United States. The islets are populated by US Air Force personnel who speak English. There are also a small number of workers from countries such as Thailand, who are bilingual in their native language and English.

Wallis and Futuna

The self governing French territory of Wallis and Futuna consists of two groups of islands in the south-west Pacific ocean. The Wallis Islands are comprised of over 20 islands, the largest being Uvea. Futuna, known also as Îles de Hooru, consists of the two islands of Alofi and Futuna. The estimated population of the territory in 1995 was 14,500. The official language is French.

The two main languages spoken on the islands are Wallisian (also known as East Uvean) and East Futuna. These two languages are related Malayo-Polynesian languages, but are not mutually intelligible. In 1987, there were about 3600 speakers of East Futuna living mainly on the Futuna Islands. They form 31 percent of the population, and most speak French as their second language.

Wallisian is spoken by about 7500 people, mainly on the Wallis group of islands. French, Futuna and Wallisian are all used in broadcasting and education.

Western Samoa

Western Samoa consists of a group of volcanic islands in the South Pacific Ocean. There are two main islands, Upolu and Savaii, and seven smaller islands. In 1995, the estimated population was 209,000. Western Samoa has two official languages, English and Samoan. The islands were formerly under the control of New Zealand, but gained independence in 1962.

Samoan is the mother tongue of the overwhelming majority of the population and is often given priority over English. In the parliament, all speeches are given in Samoan with English translations. In education, all children are taught through the medium of Samoan for the first three years of their education. They are then taught bilingually in Samoan and English. Although English is widely understood, it is used mainly as a lingua franca between Samoans and expatriates.

South America

Official Languages of South America

Argentina

In 1995, Argentina had an estimated population of over 34 million. Spanish is the official language, and the first language of the majority of Argentines.

Most Argentines are descendants of Spanish settlers. The mestizos, people of mixed European and American Indian ancestry, were once a majority in the country. Most have now been absorbed into the general population, and only about 30,000 still exist as distinct ethnic groups. The White population has increased greatly in the last two centuries. This is due to the many in-migrants arriving from Europe. These include French, Germans, Italians and British (e.g. the Welsh who emigrated to Patagonia in the 1860s), as well as Spaniards. The presence of these European in-migrants has led to languages such as French, German, English and Italian being taught in schools as a foreign language. Many in-migrants and their descendants still speak their own languages, but there is a shift to using Spanish as their main language (for example the use of Welsh in Patagonia is declining).

A number of Amerindian languages are also spoken in Argentina. Araucanian, or Mapudungun, is spoken by some 40,000 people in areas bordering on Chile. Also, along the Bolivian border, and in areas close to Peru, Quechua and Guaraní are spoken. In Argentina, Guaraní is known as Chiriguano.

The largest Quechuan variety is South Bolivian Quechua. Other varieties, such as Northwest Jujuy, are intelligible to speakers of the South Bolivian variety. Many members of the Quechua language group are temporary laborers in Argentina, with the highest concentration of speakers living in the capital, Buenos Aires. Most Quechua speakers also speak Spanish.

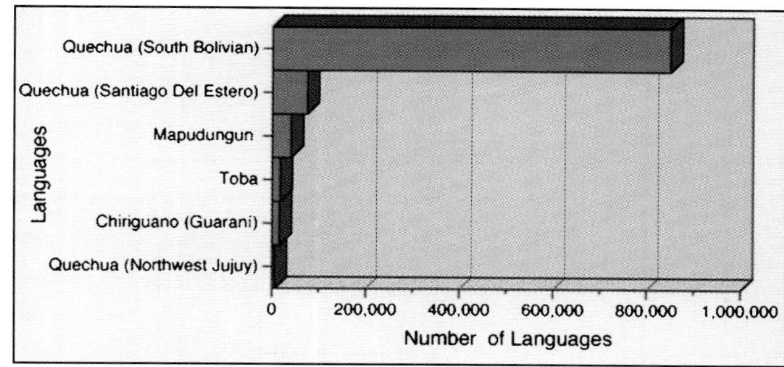

Languages spoken in Argentina. The official language, Spanish, not shown on chart, has over 25 million speakers.

Bolivia

The population of Bolivia in 1989 was estimated to be over seven million, giving the country one of the lowest population densities in South America. The majority of the population are American Indians. The two largest Indian groups are the Quechua and the Aymara. They constitute 37 percent and 25 percent of the population respectively. Mestizos, people of mixed American Indian and European descent, constitute about 25 percent to 30 percent of the population, while people of European ancestry, mainly Spanish, constitute between five percent and 15 percent of Bolivians.

Bolivia has three official languages, Spanish, Quechua, and Aymara. Guaraní (another Amerindian language) is also recognized as a national language. Up until 1993, Spanish was the sole official language, but the government of President Gonzalo Sanchez de Lozada, elected in June 1993, also gave recognition to the native languages. There are 35 Amerindian languages in Bolivia, mostly concentrated in the eastern part of the country and in rural areas. Apart from Quechua and Aymara, none of the indigenous languages have more than 70,000 speakers. Guaraní has around 66,000 speakers and Chiquitano has 20,000 speakers. Both languages are located mainly in south-eastern Bolivia. Spanish is widely spoken in the cities and has traditionally been the language of the educated elite. The new government has also introduced the right of every child to read, write and learn in its mother tongue.

Bilingualism is fairly common in Bolivia and the current reforms of education are introducing bilingual education. Approximately 65 percent of the population, or over four million, speak one of the native languages, usually in

Monolingual and Bilingual Language Groups in Bolivia, from the 1992 Census

Monolingual Speakers	Percentage
Spanish	41.7%
Quechua	8.1%
Aymara	3.2%
Other indigenous language	0.2%
Non-indigenous language	0.3%
Bilingual Speakers	
Spanish/Quechua	26.2%
Spanish/Aymara	19.8%
Other (e.g. indigenous languages, other non-indigenous languages such as Japanese)	0.8%

SOURCE: CIPCA, 1995

addition to Spanish. Most of the native Aymara and Quechua speakers also speak Spanish, and an estimated 200,000 are also trilingual in these three languages.

Number of Indigenous Language Speakers in Bolivia, 1992 Census

Language	Number of Speakers Enumerated in 1992 Census (age 6+)	Estimated Total*
Quechua	1,805,843	2,413,509
Aymara	1,237,658	1,654,129
Guaraní	49,618	66,315
Other Indigenous Languages	29,582	43,490

* Allowing for 10% of people not enumerated in Census and those under 6 years old.

SOURCE: CIPCA, 1995

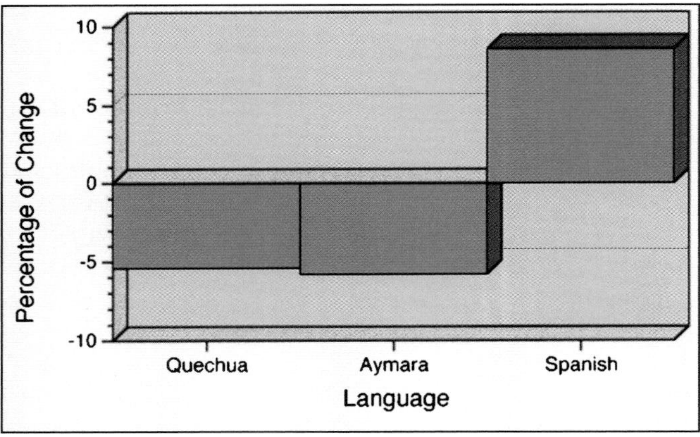

Percentage of change in the number of official language speakers in Bolivia, between 1976 and 1992. (Source: CIPCA, 1995).

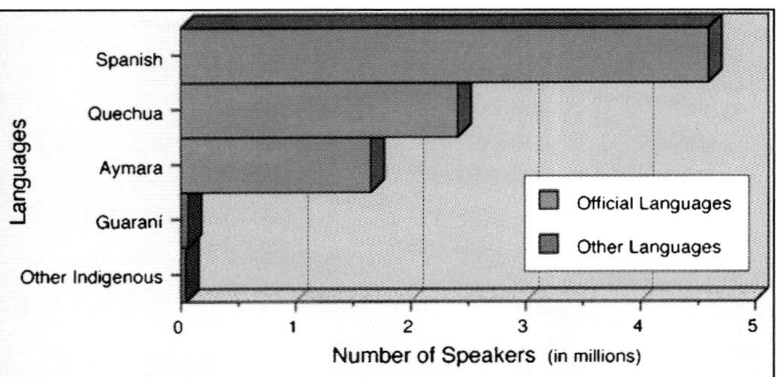

Languages spoken in Bolivia, 1992 census. Note: Bilinguals are 'double-counted' in the above chart. (Source: CIPCA, 1995).

Brazil

Brazil has an estimated population of over 135.5 million people (1995), most of whom live in the densely populated areas of eastern Brazil. The official language is Portuguese. Brazil is the largest Portuguese-speaking nation in the world, and the majority of the population speak the language, with the exception of some 35,000 American Indians living in isolated groups in the interior of the country. Other Brazilians who do not speak Portuguese include recent in-migrant groups to the country, such as the Japanese.

Over the centuries, there has been a great deal of migration to Brazil. European languages were brought by the colonialists, and African languages with slave traffic. There are a number of in-migrant languages currently in Brazil. These include German, Italian, Polish, Ukrainian and Japanese, being found especially in the cities and tropical regions in the south of Brazil. In 1994, an estimated 800,000 German speakers were living in Brazil, mostly Protestant Mennonites from Russia and North America, who have migrated to Brazil since the Second World War. The Mennonite communities use German mainly for religious and informal purposes, and most speak Portuguese as well. In many in-migrant communities there has been a shift to Portuguese as the main language, and this led to the disappearance of some older in-migrant languages, mainly African.

Languages such as Portuguese have over the centuries also been in contact with the numerous indigenous languages. There are currently between 150 and 170 different Amerindian languages spoken in Brazil. These are related to five main language families, Tupi-Guarani, Carib, Arawak, Ge and Pano. One of the largest languages in the Tupi-Guarani family is Kaiwá, with between 12,000 and 14,000 speakers.

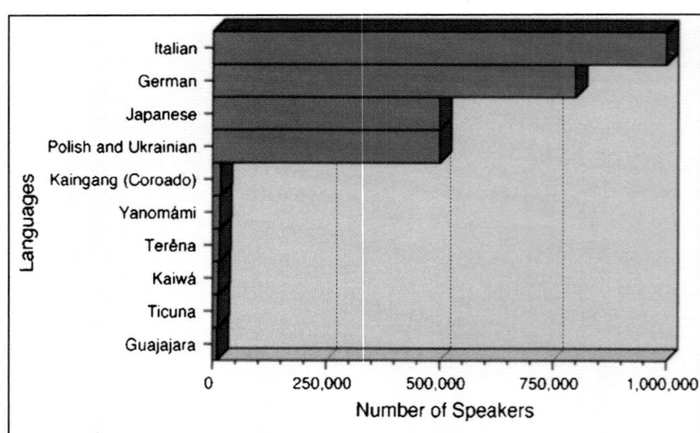

Languages spoken in Brazil. The official language, Portuguese, not shown on chart, has 150 million speakers.

Chile

The official language of Chile is Spanish. In 1995, the population was estimated to be 14 million, and over 90 percent spoke Spanish as their first language. Spanish is the dominant language throughout the country and is the language of education and the media. Most of the population of Chile are mestizos, of mixed American Indian and European ancestry. Around five percent of the population are pure Indian.

Although Spanish is widely used throughout the country, some of the original American Indians still speak their indigenous languages. One such group are the Araucanians, or Mapuche. They live mainly in the Bio-Bio and Araucania regions in the south of Chile. There are between 200,000 and 400,000 speakers of Araucano (Mapudungun). The majority of the Araucanians are bilingual in Spanish and their mother tongue.

In the northernmost regions of Chile bordering Peru and Bolivia, there are a few thousand speakers of Aymara and Quechua. These two Amerindian languages have large numbers of speakers in both Peru and Bolivia. Easter Island (Rapa Nue), a territory of Chile lying some 4000 kilometres off the west coast, is inhabited by two thousand speakers of a Polynesian language, Rapa Nue. Speakers of Rapa Nue also speak Spanish.

Colombia

The estimated population of Colombia in 1995 was over 36 million. Most of the Colombians are mestizos, of mixed Spanish, American Indian or Black African descent. American Indians constitute around one percent of the population.

The official language in Colombia is Spanish, and this is the language spoken by most of the population. It is the language used in government and in education. Many of the speakers of Amerindian languages also speak Spanish, although the degree of bilingualism can vary widely throughout the country.

It is estimated that there are around 80 languages present in Colombia. After Spanish, the largest language group is the Guajiro. This Arawakan language is spoken by over 80,000 people, mainly in the La Guajira region of the country, a peninsula on the Caribbean coast. Páez, the second largest indigenous language group, has around 40,000 speakers. These, and other minority language groups, are distributed throughout Colombia.

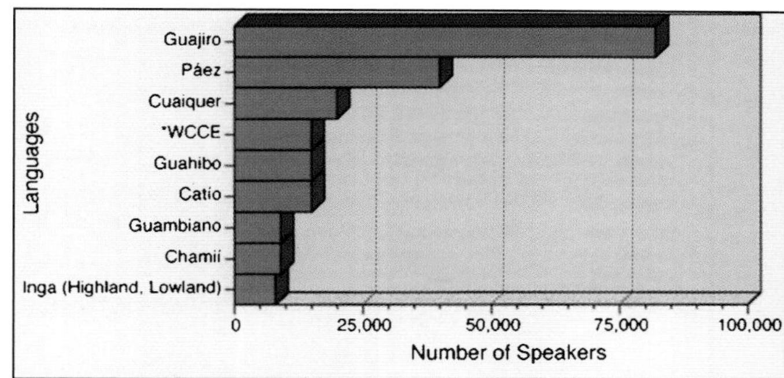

*Main languages spoken in Columbia. The official language, Spanish, not shown on chart, has over 26 million speakers. Note * WCCE = Western Caribbean Creole English.*

Western Caribbean Creole English is spoken on the islands of San Andrés and Providencia by some 15,000 inhabitants, mainly of Black African descent, but is not widely spoken on the mainland of Colombia. Varieties of this English-based creole, which developed as a contact language on British colonial plantations, are spoken in Belize, Jamaica and Guyana.

Ecuador

The Republic of Ecuador lies on the northern Pacific coast of South America. It includes the Galapagos Islands off the Pacific coast, and is bordered by both Colombia and Peru. In the 1982 Census, Ecuador had a population of 8,050,630. In 1995, the estimated population was almost 11 million. Forty percent of the population are American Indian, and 40 percent are mestizos, (those of mixed Indian and European descent). The remaining percentage of the population are of European or African descent.

The official language of Ecuador is Spanish, spoken as a first or second language by most of the population, along with Quichua, the language of the American Indians. In Ecuador, between 10 and 20 percent of the population speak the Indian language Quichua, a variety of Quechua. The speakers of Quichua are mostly those from the original, indigenous population. The highest concentration of Quichua speakers are found in the province of Chimborazo. Quichua speakers can also be located in considerable numbers in other provinces. Although Spanish is the main language of the cities and the Costa region of the country, urban migration has led to the use of Quichua in the cities.

Quichua is not the only Amerindian language spoken in Ecuador. The second largest Amerindian language is Shuar, or Jívaro, which has around 30,000 speakers concentrated mainly in the south-east of the country.

Languages of Ecuador	Speakers
Spanish (official language)	7,000,000
Quechua (Quichua)	1,459,000
Shuar (Jívaro)	30,000
Chachi	5,000
Achuar-Shiwiar	2,000
Colorado	1,800

French Guiana

In 1995, the estimated population of French Guiana was about 145,000. People of mixed European and African descent account for some 66 percent, while the American Indians constitute 12 percent of the population. There are also small minorities of Chinese, Laotians and Europeans, mostly French.

As the official language, French is used in both education and administration. However, it is not used by the whole population. In the remote interior of French Guiana, Amerindian languages are spoken by descendants of the Arawak, Carib and Tupi-Guaraní groups. Also spoken throughout the country is French Guiana Creole. It is the mother tongue of some 50,000 (34 percent) of the population, but this figure is decreasing with a shift to French.

Guyana

In 1993, Guyana had a population of 730,000, Guyana is a former British colony, and became independent in 1966. English is the official language, but the first language of 85 percent of the population is Guyanese Creole English, or Creolese. A diglossic situation exists in Guyana. Creole is the language of informal situations, folk songs and popular culture, with Standard English used in the media, education and for official purposes.

There are a number of different ethnic groups living in Guyana, the largest of which are the East Indians who constitute 50 percent of the population. The ancestors of these people migrated to the country from the Indian subcontinent,, and although many of their original languages have disappeared, Hindi and Urdu are still used by the East Indians for religious purposes. There are few monolingual Hindi or Urdu speakers in Guyana.

The second largest ethnic group are the Africans, who make up 35 percent of the population. These are people descended from slaves, imported to work in the sugar plantations. None of the original African languages is still in use today. Most of the Black Guyanese are concentrated in the capital of the country, Georgetown, and in other urban centers, and speak Guyanese Creole English. Eight percent of the population are of mixed racial origin, five percent are American Indians, with Europeans and Chinese both constituting one percent of the country's population.

A number of American Indian languages are spoken in Guyana, including Arawak, Wapishana, Akawaio and Patamona. These languages have been preserved, mostly due to the remoteness and inaccessibility of the areas in which the American Indians live. However, the American Indian cultures and languages are not encouraged. There are no more than a few thousand speakers of these languages, with the number of monolingual speakers decreasing.

Languages in Guyana	Speakers
Guyanese (Creole English)	650,000
Wapishanas	9,000
Akawaio	3,000 to 4,000
Patamona	3,000 to 4,000
Arawak	1,500

Paraguay

Paraguay has an estimated population of five million people (1995), and has two official languages, Spanish and Guaraní. Guaraní is an Amerindian language, and is spoken by around 90 percent of the population.

A large percentage of the population are bilingual in Spanish and Guaraní. Over two million people are bilingual in these languages, with a further 1.6 million people being monolingual Guaraní speakers. Those who are bilingual tend to use Spanish in formal situations, turning to Guaraní in less formal domains. Guaraní is the language most used throughout the Amazon region.

Ninety one percent of Paraguayans are mestizos, that is of mixed American Indian and Spanish descent. A number of European minority groups live in Paraguay, the most prominent of which is the German community. There are between 20,000 and 40,000 speakers of German, most of them Mennonites, members of a

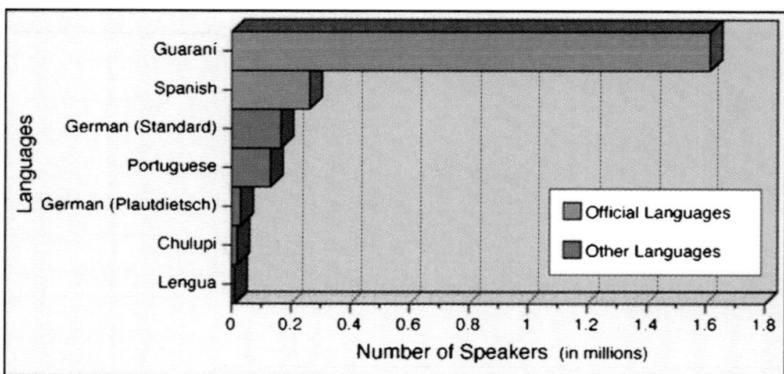

Languages spoken in Paraguay.

Protestant evangelical religious group, which originated in Switzerland and Germany. Communities of Mennonites have migrated to both North and South America since the 18th century. Older communities still speak an archaic form of German, known as Plautdietsch, or Mennonite German, but more recent inmigrants speak modern Standard German. Most of these German communities are found in the Chaco region of Paraguay, a sparsely populated region in the west of the country.

Some of the larger indigenous language minority communities live in the Chaco region. These include the Chulupe and Lengua languages, which are two of the minority indigenous languages which have over 10,000 speakers. Many of the indigenous peoples from this region use Guaraní as their main language. European minority groups also include descendants of Italian, Dutch and Portuguese settlers.

Peru

Peru lies on the western coast of South America, and had an estimated population of over 24 million in 1995. There are two official languages in Peru, Spanish and Quechua. Spanish had been the sole official language, but in 1975, Quechua was given the same status by the Peruvian Government. Spanish is the dominant spoken language, and the main language of the media and education. The highest concentrations of Spanish speakers live in the coastal lowlands. These are the urbanized areas of Peru which have few speakers of Amerindian languages. In recent years urban migration has resulted in small communities of minority language speakers, especially Quechua, being present in the larger cities, such as the capital Lima.

Most of the speakers of Quechua are to be found in the south of Peru. The 1981 Census showed that 16 percent of the population were bilingual in Quechua and Spanish, while another 11 percent were monolingual in Quechua. Quechua is a language which has many different varieties, some of which are not mutually intelligible. In 1975, when the language was given official status, the government produced dictionaries and grammars for six of the dialects. Many Quechua speakers are bilingual in Spanish, except for a minority who live in the most rural and isolated areas. Although Spanish is the main language of education, in the areas where Quechua, and other indigenous languages such as Aymara, are important, bilingual education is provided.

The second largest indigenous language in Peru is Aymara. Although this language does not have official status, since 1975 it has been given limited official recognition. As with Quechua, most Aymara speakers are found in the south of the country which borders Bolivia. Around 300,000 people use this language.

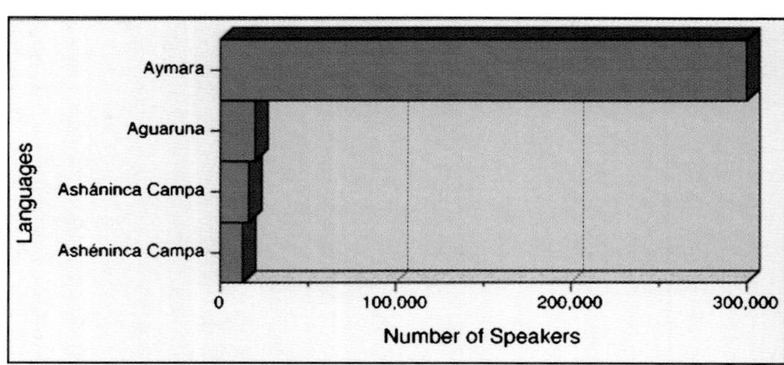

Languages spoken in Peru. The official language, Spanish, not shown on chart, had 13.2 and 4.9 million speakers respectively (1981 census). In 1981 the total population was 18.3 million. (Source: Gleich & Suny, 1994).

Suriname

Suriname, formerly Dutch Guiana, is a republic in north-eastern South America. In 1995, the estimated population was 429,000. Suriname is a former Dutch colony, and gained its independence in 1975. Before the arrival of Dutch colonists, the country was inhabited by groups of Arawak, Carib and Warrau Indians. The official language of Suriname is Dutch. There are a few thousand Surinamese who speak Dutch as their first language, with around 100,000 second language speakers. Dutch is the main language of instruction in schools, with both English and Spanish taught as foreign languages.

The largest ethnic group in Suriname are Asian Indians (Hindus), who constitute 37 percent of the population. The language spoken by most Asian Indians is Caribbean Hindi, or Sarnami Hindi. This language is based on the Indian languages Bhojpuri, Awakhi and Hindi. There are some monolingual speakers, but most use Dutch as their second language.

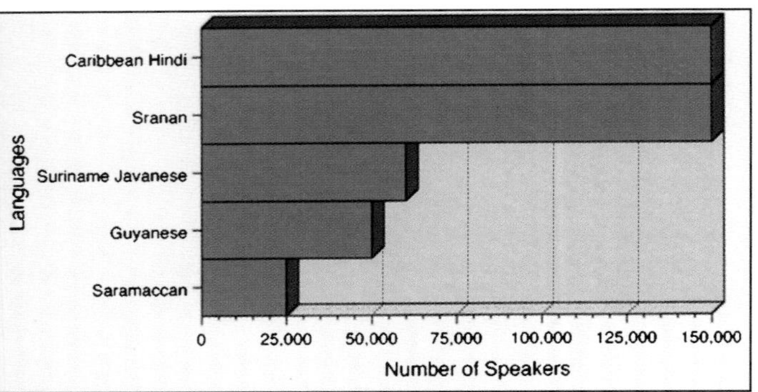

Languages spoken in Suriname. The official language, Dutch, not shown on chart, has around one thousand speakers.

A further 15 percent of the Suriname population are Indonesians. Both the Indonesians and Asian Indians were brought into Suriname to replace Black African slaves after emancipation in 1863. Most Indonesians in Suriname speak Suriname Javanese, a variant of Javanese, as their first language.

Three main Amerindian languages are spoken in Suriname by American Indians, who constitute ten percent of the population. These are Trio, Wayana, and Kalinha. Approximately 2500 American Indians speak Kalinha, six hundred speak Wayana, and eight hundred speak Trio.

Sranan, known also as Suriname Creole English or Taki-Taki, is spoken by some 80 percent of the population as a second language. It is the lingua franca for Hindustanis, Javanese, American Indians, and the Bush Negroes (descendants of Black African slaves). It is also the mother tongue for around 150,000 Surinamese.

The Falkland Islands (Islas Malvinas)

The Falkland Islands (called Islas Malvinas by neighboring Argentines) consist of approximately 200 islands in the Atlantic Ocean, north-east of the southern tip of South America. The islands are a dependent territory of the United Kingdom. The population of 2317 (1995) are English-speaking of British descent. The official language and the language used on the islands is English. The Falkland Islands were taken by the British from the Argentinians in 1833, and since then, Argentina has laid claim to the islands. This dispute gave rise to the Falkland War in 1981.

Uruguay

Uruguay is the second smallest nation in South America, and in 1995 had an estimated population of 3.2 million. The original inhabitants of Uruguay were Charrua Indians. In the 17th century, the Spanish first established a colony in Uruguay. The official language of the country is Spanish, and this is the language spoken by most of the population.

Eighty five percent of Uruguay's population are of European descent, mainly Spanish and Italian. A small part of the population migrated to Uruguay from other South American countries, such as neighboring Brazil and Argentina. Around five percent to ten percent of the country's population are mestizos, of mixed European and American Indian ancestry. The original small indigenous population has long since been absorbed by those migrating to the country.

Near the Brazilian border, there is a considerable degree of bilingualism in Spanish and Portuguese. A mixture of Portuguese and Spanish is also spoken in this area, and known as Brazilero. Foreign languages (mainly English) are often taught in schools.

Venezuela

Venezuela lies on the northern coast of South America, with Columbia to the west, and Brazil to the south. In the 1992 Census, the country had a population of 20.5 million, most of whom speak Spanish, the official language. About 70 percent of the population are mestizos, those of mixed American Indian and European descent. Approximately 20 percent of Venezuelans are of European descent, and are concentrated in the larger cities. Black people count for around 8.5 percent, living mainly along the Caribbean. Many are descendants of Black Africans brought by the slave trade. The indigenous American Indians form a small proportion of the population. The 1992 Census showed that 315,815

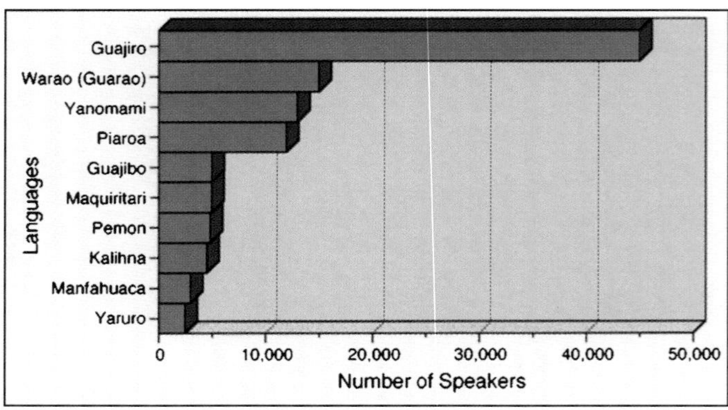

Languages spoken in Venezuela. The official language, Spanish, not shown on chart, is spoken by over 14 million. (Source: Censo Indigena de Venezuela, 1992).

ethnic Indians lived in Venezuela, forming 1.54 percent of the population.

Some 37 indigenous languages are found in Venezuela, some spoken by only a handful of people. Other languages number in the thousands. Eighty percent of the American Indian population speak at least one Amerindian language. The 1992 Census showed that there were 28 different ethnic groups living in Venezuela. The largest ethnic group are the Wayuu, who make up 54.5 percent of the American Indian population. They live mainly in the Zulia region of Venezuela, with over 127,000 living in neighboring Colombia. Most of the Wayuu speak the language of their own ethnic group more than Spanish, but there is a high degree of bilingualism. Most of the American Indians are bilingual, with 75 percent able to speak Spanish and their mother tongue.

Languages Spoken by Members of the Original Indigenous Population, Five Years and Over

Census of Venezuela, 1992

Language Spoken	Number
Spanish	50,692
Indigenous Language	49,286
Indigenous Language and Spanish	153,100
Indigenous, Spanish and Other	1,251
Indigenous and Other	292
Other	20
TOTAL	254,641

Languages Spoken by the Wayuu Ethnic Group Over Five Years of Age

Census 1992

Language Spoken	Number
Spanish	19,822
Indigenous Language	13,602
Indigenous Language and Spanish	106,194
Indigenous and Other	0
Other	0
TOTAL	139,618

SECTION FOUR

BILINGUAL EDUCATION

'Language is the amber in which a thousand precious and subtle thoughts have been safely embedded and preserved. It has arrested ten thousand lightning flashes of genius, which, unless thus fixed and arrested, might have been as bright, but would have also been as quickly passing and perishing, as the lightning.'

Richard Chevenix Trench, Irish ecclesiastic and Archbishop of Dublin (1807–1886)

The Aims of Bilingual Education

1: The Nature and Aims of Bilingual Education

Bilingual education would seem to describe a situation where two languages are used in a school. However, 'bilingual education' is a simple label for a complex phenomenon. This is reflected in the following questions:

- Are both languages used in the classroom?
- For how long are the languages being used in school?
- Are two languages used by all or some students?
- Are two languages used by the teachers or just by the students?
- Is the aim to teach a second language or to teach through a second language?
- Is the aim to support the home language or to move to an alternative majority language?

Eight important aspects of the international structure of bilingual education will be presented to help unravel the complexity of bilingual education:

1. Bilingual children in monolingual or bilingual education.
2. Second language teaching and bilingual education.
3. Public and private bilingual education.
4. Bilingual education as existing in 'weak' and 'strong' forms.
5. Bilingual education for different age groups.
6. The concept extending to trilingual and multilingual education.
7. Bilingual schooling as distinct from bilingual education.
8. The language minority background of the child.

A school in Bombay, India. One aim of Indian education is for children to become competent in their native language, plus Hindi and English.

One important distinction is between a school where there are bilingual children and a school that promotes bilingualism. In many schools of the world, there are bilingual and multilingual children. Yet the aim of the school may be to ensure that children develop in one language only. For example, a child may come to school speaking Spanish fluently and English a little. The school may aim to make that child fluent and literate in the English language only. The integration and assimilation of that child into mainstream society is regarded by the teachers as their most important language aim.

In other types of schools, the aim may be to teach the children two languages and through the medium of two languages, so that they may develop full bilingualism and biliteracy. For example, in heritage language schools, children may receive much of their instruction in the home language, with the majority language of the nation being used to transmit 20 percent to 50 percent of the curriculum.

Alternatively, a child from a majority language background may go to an Immersion school or a mainstream bilingual school and learn a second majority (or minority) language. For example, in Canada, an English-speaking child may go to a French Immersion school where much of the curriculum will be taught through the medium of French.

The second aspect of bilingual education is the distinction between schools that teach a second language and schools that teach through the medium of a second language. Many schools throughout the world include foreign language or second language teaching as subjects within the curriculum. For example, English as a second language or French as a second language means that the language will be taught as a subject in the classroom, just like Social Studies, Mathematics and Science. The aim of second and foreign language teaching can range from giving the children 'survival skills' or basic competency in the target language, to enabling them to achieve near fluency.

Second language-medium teaching is different from second language teaching. Here a child may be taught other

Ten Aims of Bilingual Education

Ferguson, Houghton and Wells (1977) provide ten examples of the varying aims of bilingual education:

1. To assimilate individuals or groups into the mainstream of society; to socialize people for full participation in the community.
2. To unify a multilingual society; to bring unity to a multiethnic or multinational linguistically diverse state.
3. To enable people to communicate with the outside world.
4. To provide language skills which are marketable, aiding employment and status.
5. To preserve ethnic and religious identity.
6. To reconcile and mediate between different linguistic and political communities.
7. To spread the use of a colonializing language, socializing an entire population to a colonial existence.
8. To strengthen elite groups and preserve their position in society.
9. To give equal status in law to languages of unequal status in daily life.
10. To deepen understanding of language and culture.

This list shows that bilingual education does not necessarily concern merely the balanced use of two languages in the classroom. Behind bilingual education are varying and conflicting philosophies of the purpose of education. Sociocultural, political and economic issues are ever present in the debate over the provision of bilingual education.

Girls playing in a school in Khartoum, in Northern Sudan. Over a hundred languages are spoken in the Sudan, including Colloquial Sudanese Arabic, the first language of over half the population. At school, all children in the north learn Modern Standard Arabic, which is the official language of the country.

Students at St George College, a Greek Orthodox bilingual college in South Australia. The school is mainly attended by students from Greek in-migrant families. The major portion of the curriculum is delivered in English, but the study of modern Greek to a high level is an important aspect of the curriculum. Greek traditions, foods, customs and festivals are part of the school experience and great emphasis is placed on the teaching and observance of the Greek Orthodox faith. In the words of the school brochure, 'Students benefit fully from education when the language and culture of the home are respected and affirmed'.

Some schools wish children to move from their home language to the dominant language of the country. Other schools help children maintain their home language.

subjects through the medium of that second language. For example, in the European schools movement, children in the middle years of secondary education may learn History, Geography and Social Sciences through a second language. In Canadian Immersion schools, children in elementary years learn much of the curriculum through their second language, French. If there is a useful demarcation, then bilingual education may be said to start when more than one language is used to teach content (e.g. Science, Mathematics, Social Sciences or Humanities) rather than just being taught as a subject by itself. When language learning moves on from being a subject by itself to being used to teach content in other areas of the curriculum, then bilingual education may be an appropriate term. However, as we will see later, many programs are called bilingual education when there are merely two languages taught, or when the students are bilingual and the medium of schooling is monolingual.

Third, bilingual education tends to be aligned with public-funded education (although there are exceptions considered later, e.g. International Schools). In Canada, Wales, Luxembourg, Malaysia, Kuwait, United States and Australasia, the tendency is to think of bilingual education as part of the state system. The governments of these countries fund bilingual education to maintain and develop bilingualism in the official or widely spoken languages of the countries. Yet there is also a solid tradition of bilingual education in private educational establishments. For example, the elites of various countries of the world go to select Swiss Finishing Schools. The International Schools movement is another example of fee paying schools where bilingualism flourishes in many countries of the world. Private establishments of this kind aim to maintain or develop individual bilingualism for the purpose of work, travel, living abroad or personal enrichment.

A fourth dimension in the structure of bilingual education is an important difference between 'weak' and 'strong' forms of bilingual education. 'Weak' forms of bilingual education are where schools aim to transfer language minority children to using the majority language almost solely in their schooling. Such schools are said to be bilingual because they contain bilingual children, and not because they foster bilingualism. 'Weak' forms of bilingual education are basically assimilationist. The aim is usually for a transition from the home culture and language to the majority culture and language.

In contrast, 'strong' forms of bilingual education aim to give children full bilingualism and biliteracy, where two languages and two cultures are seen as mutually enriching. The aim is for children to maintain their mother tongues, their minority languages and become culturally pluralist. Maintenance and enhancement of language, literacy and cultural skills are a major part of the school's ambitions. This aspect of bilingual education is crucial to understanding debates, policies and practices of bilingual education. (See Types of Bilingual Education, page 469.)

The Ranking of Bilingual Aims, Goals and Objectives

Sally Tilley (1982) of the University of New Orleans carried out research on the ranking of bilingual goals and objectives among a random sample of directors of bilingual project centers in the United States. She asked her respondents to rate 57 bilingual goals and objectives. It is interesting for us to speculate what research would find with different samples of people from differing geographical areas (e.g. parents, administrators, mainstream teachers, politicians, different language minorities). The order is unlikely to be the same as Tilley's (1982). A score of ten represents 'a most desirable' goal; a score of zero represents 'a least desirable' goal. The resulting order from Tilley's (1982) research, from more to less important, is presented below.

Goals and Objectives	Rank Score
To develop and maintain child's self-esteem in both cultures	10.0
To establish co-operation between school and home of bilingual child	8.0
To prevent students' retardation in school performance	8.0
To develop measurements for evaluation of bilingual programs	7.5
To instruct children in their cultural heritage	7 5
To counteract high drop-out rates resulting from language handicaps	7.5
To teach all subject matter in two languages	7.0
To return to schools those individuals unable to attend because of language handicaps	7.0
To increase number of non-English dominant children receiving high-school diplomas	7.0
To develop a bilingual staff for a self-supporting district program	7.0
To provide in-service training for all levels of bilingual personnel	7.0
To help students overcome educational handicap from minority group isolation	7.0
To teach all skills in two languages: reading, writing, listening, speaking	6.5
To teach native language skills so child will perform at or above grade level	6.5
To teach English skills so child will perform at or above grade level	6.5
To offer English classes to parents of bilingual children	6.0
To upgrade English ability for better vocational and career opportunities	6.0
To teach the language and culture of child's native country or community	6.0
To maintain instruction in two languages in Kindergarten to Grade 12	5.5
To develop teaching personnel from bilingual non-Anglo groups	5.5
To develop instructional materials from a locally based source	5.5
To eliminate minority group segregation among students and faculty	5.5
To make bilingual child aware of the process of acculturation	5.0
To develop functional bilinguals among native English-speaking population	5.0
To promote understanding between privileged and deprived groups	5.0
To gain an economic advantage for minority groups	5.0
To encourage bilingual children to participate in extracurricular activities	5.0
To provide bilingual counselors and job placement personnel in schools	5.0
To develop in-service field experience for teacher certification	5.0
To develop demonstration programs for replication in other areas	5.0
To develop demonstration programs for replication in other areas	5.0
To develop teaching personnel from bilingual Anglo groups	5.0
To make majority culture aware of the process of acculturation	4.5
To make minority parents aware of the process of acculturation	4.5
To give two cultures present in a society a more equal prominence	4.5
To teach only selected skills in two languages	4.0
To teach two languages for future employment in bilingual positions	4.0
To develop bilingualism in the United States to ensure national survival	4.0
To introduce English-speaking monolinguals to foreign cultures via language	4.0
To absorb individuals or groups into mainstream society	4.0
To act in compensatory fashion for pre-school children	4.0
To act as clearinghouse for materials imported from abroad	4.0
To develop teaching personnel from monolingual non-Anglo groups	4.0
To develop teaching personnel from monolingual Anglo groups	4.0
To teach elementary English-speaking children another language and culture	3.5
To teach secondary English-speaking children another language and culture	3.5
To enable Americans to communicate with other nations	3.5
To break the monolingual pattern of a majority society	3.0
To urge the learning of language for its own sake	2.5
To reconcile different political or socially separate communities	2.5
To preserve ethnic or religious ties	2.5
To teach English skills only	2.0
To develop measurements for evaluation of bilingual child's performance	2.0
To teach child's native language skills only	2.0
To maintain status quo of the non-English-speaking child in his own culture	1.5
To embellish or strengthen the education of social elites	0.5
To teach the language and culture of Spain and France	0.0

REFERENCE: TILLEY, 1982

Fifth, bilingual education spans all age groups. Bilingual nursery schools exist in many countries of the world. For example, young children may attend a nursery school to learn a second or local language, or to socialize in their mother tongue. Internationally, bilingual education mostly exists at primary school level. However, in Canada, Wales, Catalonia and elsewhere there are numerous examples of bilingual education in its strong form at the secondary school level as well.

Bilingual education is also found at the further and higher educational levels. Increasingly in Europe, students are moving around from one country to another to experience higher education. Through schemes such as Erasmus (funded by the European Commission), students take part of their higher education in other countries. In Wales, students can take arts and humanities subjects through the medium of Welsh to undergraduate and postgraduate degree level. Courses in Music, Sociology, History, Education, Geography, Communication Studies, Environmental Studies, Drama, and Religious Studies can all be taken partly or sometimes wholly through the medium of Welsh.

Bilingual education continues beyond statutory schooling. In language learning classes for adults, in universities, colleges and other institutes of further and higher education, bilingual education can still take place. A person may learn a new language, be taught in two languages, and use curriculum resources in more than one language (e.g. English on the computer, Internet and computer assisted learning while all writing on paper is in Spanish).

Sixth, bilingual education is an umbrella term that includes not only 'weak' and 'strong' forms but also trilingual or multilingual education, where three or more languages are used in the school (e.g. in the European Schools Movement, or Luxembourgish/German/French education in Luxembourg, or Hebrew/English/French in Canada).

Seventh, bilingual education is a more expansive term than bilingual schooling. Too often, bilingual education is formal, state-funded education for children approximately between the ages of 5 and 16. Bilingual education encompasses the informal aspects of schooling that can be present from cradle to grave. From birth onwards, parents may be bilingually educating their children in the home. When mother reads to the child in one language and father in the other, then bilingual education is occurring. Education involves processes such as enculturation, socialization, imparting of knowledge, skills, attitudes and beliefs, and thus is carried out in the home as well as the school.

Eighth, there are other 'contextual' factors that need including when analyzing the aims of bilingual education. We must ask what kind of language background a child comes from? Is it from a language minority or a language majority background? If the child is from a language minority background, is that minority language prestigious (e.g. Welsh and Catalan) within the region, or does the language lack status (e.g. Spanish in many parts of the United States, or Turkish, Greek, Urdu and Bengali in schools of the UK)? This suggests that it is difficult to understand bilingual education except through the status, power and politics of languages within a region. This factor and others are included in a typology of bilingual education in the accompanying table and examined elsewhere (see pages 469 and 473).

To conclude. Bilingual education is a wide, 'umbrella' term, encompassing a number of dimensions:

- high status and low status forms of education;
- all age groups;
- public or private education;
- where two languages are both used to teach the curriculum;
- where language learning begins to merge with content teaching;
- trilingual education;
- nursery schools, primary schools, secondary schools as well as in further and higher education;
- schools where there is no bilingual policy in the school but bilingual children, as well as schools with a strong policy of bilingualism;
- schools that wish to assimilate children into the majority language and culture, and those that foster cultural pluralism.

Further Reading

CUMMINS, J., 1986, Empowering Minority Students: A Framework for Intervention. *Harvard Educational Review*, 56 (1), 18-36.

DELPIT, L. D., 1988, The Silenced Dialogue: Power & Pedagogy in Educating Other People's Children. *Harvard Educational Review*, 58 (3), 280-298.

GARCÍA, O., 1996, Bilingual Education. In F. COULMAS (ed.), *The Handbook of Sociolinguistics*. Oxford: Blackwell.

GARCÍA, O. (ed.), 1991, *Bilingual Education: Focusschrift in Honor of Joshua A. Fishman*. Amsterdam/Philadelphia: John Benjamins.

GARCÍA, O. & BAKER, C. (eds), 1995, *Policy and Practice in Bilingual Education. A Reader Extending the Foundations*. Clevedon: Multilingual Matters Ltd.

2: Types of Bilingual Education

Ten different types of bilingual education are proposed in the accompanying table. Each of these is considered in more detail in separate topics. Six of these types represent 'weak' forms of education for bilingualism. The other four represent 'strong' forms of education for bilingualism and biliteracy. The idea of a weak form is generally that the program will contain bilingual children. However, the aim of schooling is often to produce monolingualism or limited bilingualism rather than full bilingualism. In contrast, a strong form of bilingual education will aim to produce students who are proficient in two languages and biliterate as well.

In other topics, submersion and Transitional Bilingual education, for example, are discussed. Each is a weak form of bilingual education where the societal educational aim is basically assimilationist. The aim of such bilingual education is for a transition from the minority language to the majority language, as well as a transition from the home culture to the culture of those with most power and status. A weak form of bilingual education will often seek to assimilate language minority children within the language majority society. For example, Spanish-speaking children in the United States may undergo submersion or transitional bilingual education which aims to make them thoroughly competent in English without attending to equal proficiency in their home language. The aim of such education is often to integrate children into mainstream society, aiming to provide equality of opportunity in schooling and employment. The language of the classroom in weak forms of bilingual education would tend to be the majority language. The minority language may be used for a short period. However, this is a temporary period of acclimatization to school for the child. The child is expected to be able to operate in the curriculum in the majority language as soon as possible.

In strong forms of bilingual education, the language of the classroom will often be varied. For example, early on in the school the emphasis may be on one language with a movement towards a more equal use of languages as the child proceeds. The aim of strong forms of bilingual education is generally to make children bilingual and biliterate, but also to maintain a language minority, and to create cultural pluralism and multiculturalism within the child and the child's society.

The differences between weak and strong forms of bilingual education reflect differences between a monolingual and a bilingual view of the world. There are also differences in beliefs about societies; one about the need to assimilate language minorities into mainstream majorities; the other about the importance of multiculturalism and language diversity in an increasingly global village.

The ten different types of program have many subvarieties, as Mackey's (1970) 90 varieties of bilingual education indicate. One of the intrinsic limitations of typologies is that not all real-life examples will fit easily into the classification. For example, elite 'Finishing Schools' in Switzerland, and classrooms in Wales where first language Welsh speakers are taught alongside 'Immersion' English first language speakers make classification essentially simplistic, although necessary for discussion and understanding. This typology is extended in García (1997).

Lesotho schoolgirls. In Lesotho, a former British colony, English and Sesotho are both official languages. The first four years of primary education are through the medium of Sesotho, with a gradual transition to English thereafter.

WEAK FORMS OF EDUCATION FOR BILINGUALISM

Type of Program	Typical Type of Child	Language of the Classroom	Societal and Educational Aim	Aim in Language Outcome
1. SUBMERSION (Structured Immersion)	Language Minority	Majority Language	Assimilation	Monolingualism
2. SUBMERSION (Withdrawal Classes/ Sheltered English)	Language Minority	Majority Language with 'pull-out' lessons	Assimilation	Monolingualism
3. SEGREGATIONIST	Language Minority	Minority Language (forced, no choice)	Apartheid	Monolingualism
4. TRANSITIONAL	Language Minority	Moves from minority to majority language	Assimilation	Relative Monolingualism
5. MAINSTREAM with Foreign Language Teaching	Language Majority	Majority Language with L2/FL lessons	Limited Enrichment	Limited Bilingualism
6. SEPARATIST	Language Minority	Minority Language (out of choice)	Detachment/ Autonomy	Limited Bilingualism
STRONG FORMS OF EDUCATION FOR BILINGUALISM AND BILITERACY				
7. IMMERSION	Language Majority	Bilingual with initial emphasis on L2	Pluralism & Enrichment	Bilingualism & Biliteracy
8. MAINTENANCE/ HERITAGE LANGUAGE	Language Minority	Bilingual with emphasis on L1	Maintenance, Pluralism & Enrichment	Bilingualism & Biliteracy
9. TWO-WAY/ DUAL LANGUAGE	Mixed Language Minority & Majority	Minority & Majority	Maintenance, Pluralism & Enrichment	Bilingualism & Biliteracy
10. MAINSTREAM BILINGUAL	Language Majority	Two Majority Languages	Maintenance, Pluralism & Enrichment	Bilingualism & Biliteracy

Transitional and Maintenance Bilingual Education

A child from a Chinese in-migrant family in a British primary school learns to write in Chinese. In some multi-ethnic areas of Britain there is provision for the maintenance and development of community languages at primary level.

One early and very detailed classification of bilingual education is by William Mackey (1970). His account of 90 different patterns of bilingual schooling considers: the languages of the home; the languages of the curriculum; the languages of the community in which the school is located and the international and regional status of the languages. A different approach to categorizing types of bilingual education is to examine the aims of such education. A frequent distinction is between transitional and maintenance bilingual education.

Transitional Bilingual education aims to shift the child from the home, minority language to the dominant, majority language. Social and cultural assimilation into the language majority is the underlying aim. Maintenance bilingual education attempts to foster the minority language in the child, strengthening a sense of cultural identity and affirming the rights of an ethnic minority group in a nation. Otheguy & Otto (1980) make the distinction between the different aims of static maintenance and developmental maintenance. Static maintenance aims to maintain language skills at the level of the child entering a school. Developmental maintenance seeks to develop a student's home language skills to full proficiency and full biliteracy or literacy. This is often referred to as enrichment bilingual education. Static maintenance attempts to prevent home language loss but not increase skills in that first language. Developmental maintenance has a 'goal of proficiency and literacy in the home language equal to English' (Otheguy & Otto, 1980, page 351). Enrichment bilingual education aims to go beyond static maintenance to extending the individual and group use of minority languages, leading to cultural pluralism and to the social autonomy of an ethnic group.

Bilingual Education in the South Pacific Islands

Countries in the Pacific Region have colonial histories and such history has tended to leave an effect on languages in education. Thus almost all Pacific children are educated in a world language such as English or French (or Spanish in Rapa Nui – Easter Island, which is an overseas territory of Chile). The language education policy varies from island to island in the Pacific, with a presence of submersion, transitional and occasionally heritage bilingual education.

Where there is submersion education, for example in the Melanesian countries, children are often expected to use English from their first day of schooling. The submersion model is found particularly in Pacific countries where children come from heterogeneous language backgrounds (e.g. the Solomon Islands). Where there is the transitional model, children are initially educated in basic literacy and numeracy skills in their mother tongue, with a transition to working through English after a few years of basic primary schooling. Often by Grade 4, children are required to switch from their mother tongue to using English as the medium of education. This only tends to be practical when the teacher and children share the same mother tongue or the teacher is a fluent second-language speaker of the home language.

In the Melanesian countries of the Solomon Islands and Vanuatu, there is no attempt at mother tongue literacy. Rather children are placed in a submersion situation as soon as they enter school. This is partly defended by there being over a thousand languages in the Melanesian countries of the Pacific. Therefore common languages are chosen, usually former colonial languages. In Vanuatu, (which was jointly administered by France and the United Kingdom until 1980), submersion education can be in French or English.

English is regarded as an important language in the Pacific region particularly for its economic, employment and status value. Students' prospects of success in school and outside school tend to be adversely affected if their competence in English is poor. Another argument for the use of English in education is that in Vanuatu, the Solomon Islands and Fiji, there are many languages in existence. Thus English becomes a 'common denominator' language. The outcome is a wide variety of language provision in education, ranging from submersion, through to a mixture of submersion and language maintenance education, to some programs which are highly supportive of the mother tongue.

One of the problems is that many primary school teachers do not have sufficient competence in English, and often lack confidence in their oral English. Therefore, mother tongues are used to explain to children, although literacy is through English-only. Such a submersion experience in the Solomon Islands and Vanuatu means that children learn to read and write in a language that is generally not present in the community, that they do not hear before coming to school or out of school, and receive limited 'proficient speaker' contact with a teacher inside a classroom. While English is high status and equated with educational success and high prestige jobs, learning English does not provide a continuation of home and community learning. This large gap between school learning and community learning tends to devalue mother tongues and decreases the opportunity for community participation in children's literacy development. Also, many children do not become fluent in English.

Bilingual Education in Kenya

Some 30 native languages are spoken in Kenya of which few have any written form. Swahili (Kiswahili), which is the native language of a small coastal group, has long been a vehicle for intergroup communication. With economic development and increased mobility, more and more people speak it. British colonial rule in Kenya ended in 1963, when Kenya became an independent African state, but English is still the official language of Kenya. It is also the main language of education. This reflects the status of English as a major international language, the availability of textbooks and other resources in English, and the use of English in science and technology throughout the world. English is also a neutral language, being the first language of only a small number of Kenyans, and thus does not reinforce the superiority of any one language group over the others.

The Kenyan government sponsors a national, standardized system of primary education, between the ages of 6 and 14. English is the official language of instruction from the fourth grade onwards and Swahili is taught as a subject. The first three grades may be taught in a combination of three languages, the local vernacular, Swahili and English, depending on the location of the school and the linguistic composition of the class.

In rural schools where the students usually share the same native language, instruction is often through the medium of that language, and it continues to be used as a support in higher grades. In urban schools English may be the dominant language from the first grade onwards, with Swahili, and sometimes the main local language, being used as well. Teachers codeswitch frequently in lessons, often for explanation and clarification, or when speaking to individual students.

Multilingualism is a fact of life in modern Kenya. Although the first three years of school are based on a system of bilingual education, this does not usually have a detrimental effect on the students, for a number of reasons.

- The Kenyan educational system prepares children for life in a diglossic or triglossic society, where different languages are used in different contexts, and for different purposes. The local language is used for communication with family, friends and people in the same locality, Swahili is used for informal communication between members of different language groups. English is used in official life, in higher education, in prestigious jobs. The learning of English does not detract from the child's use of the other languages.
- Very few children in Kenya know any English on first arrival at school, so learners do not have to compete with native speakers in the class.
- Instruction in English usually precedes the teaching of content through English.
- The class teachers speak the children's native languages and frequently codeswitch to help the children.

Language Education in Israel

In the early years after the creation of the State of Israel in 1948, there was considerable pressure to promote and secure the Hebrew language as the official language and to assimilate linguistically the flood of in-migrants (see page 195). Languages other than Hebrew were generally not supported in the school curriculum. Now that the position of Hebrew is relatively secure, a more multilingual position has become possible. Also, the great influx of Russian speakers into Israel since 1989 has led the government to review its language education policy.

In 1995, the Israeli Ministry of Education formulated a policy for language education in Israel which was revised in 1996. This policy covers mother tongue teaching, second and foreign language education. The policy for language in education in Israel places a high store by languages. Its major features may be summarized as follows:

1. For those whose mother tongue is Hebrew or Arabic, such children should become literate in their mother tongue.

2. Provision is made for the language maintenance of in-migrants, particularly those who speak Russian as their mother tongue.

3. Hebrew is to be taught to all in-migrants, and literacy is to be developed in Hebrew.

4. Within the Arabic education sector, there is to be provision for the teaching of Hebrew optionally in the first grade and compulsorily from the second grade to the twelfth grade, (i.e. the end of secondary education).

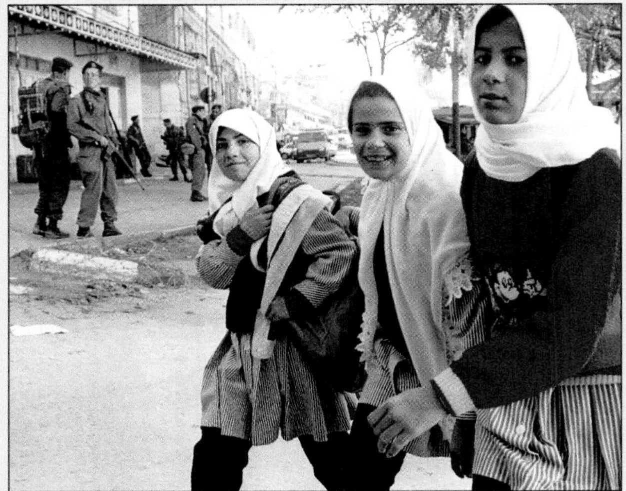

Palestinian girls in the West Bank walk home from school.

5. For speakers of Hebrew, Arabic is a required subject from the seventh to the tenth grade and is optional in the fifth, sixth, eleventh and twelfth grade. Schools may choose to offer French instead of Arabic, and new in-migrants are exempted from this requirement.

6. English is to be considered the first foreign language and is optional in the third and fourth grade and compulsory through the rest of the grade system.

7. French is recognized as an important language for cultural, political, economic and community reasons. It can be taught optionally from the fifth to the twelfth grade.

8. Russian is offered as an optional language for new in-migrants, and as an alternative to Arabic or French throughout the grade system.

10. Yiddish can be used as a language of instruction and taught in the independent Orthodox schools.

11. The policy encourages the development of special language schools and encourages the use of Ladino, Spanish, German and Japanese in the system.

In practice, all schools in the Arabic education sector use Arabic as their language of instruction, teach Hebrew as a second language and English as a foreign language. In Jewish state schools, Hebrew is the language of instruction and all students learn English, with many schools starting English lessons before the third grade. About half of such Jewish students learn Arabic for the required three years. A significant number of students also learn French, Russian and Yiddish.

The new language education policy moves significantly towards a multilingual curriculum. There appears to be an increasing realization of the language capacity, and the value of a multiplicity of languages in Israel. The new policy acknowledges the unfortunate loss of the potential of early in-migrant languages (e.g. French). Fostering a variety of languages means that Israel has the potential for strong trade links and access to international markets in the future. The future relationship between Hebrew and Arabic is an unknown, as is the effect of an increasing accent on English.

REFERENCE: SPOLSKY ,1996

3: A Bilingual Education Model

To understand bilingual education, we need to relate and integrate four main factors, namely inputs, outputs, contexts and process. A four-part model gives an organizing framework for thinking about bilingual education (Baker, 1985; Stern, 1983a). Bilingual education has inputs, outputs, contexts and process over and above that of 'normal' schooling as detailed by Dunkin & Biddle (1974). First, we will consider, in an overview, the nature of the whole model.

There are inputs, or human ingredients, into the classroom which are formed from varying student (and teacher) characteristics. Research examines how different inputs (e.g. teacher qualities, student language ability, motivation) influence outputs. Outputs or outcomes may be short-term (e.g. test attainment) or longer-term (e.g. attitude to language learning). The relationship between inputs and outputs can be modified by the context or environment in which schooling occurs. At a macro level, context could be, for example, ethnic group or local community effects on education. Context could also refer to the wider societal and governmental level. At a micro level, context may refer to the classroom environment (e.g. a classroom poor or rich in dual language resource material). The final part of the model is process, where the second by second life of actual classroom practice may be examined. The model is illustrated on page 474 and then explained in more detail.

The linguistic and cultural knowledge of bilingual teachers, their competency to operate in two languages and transmit two or more cultures are examples of teacher inputs. Student inputs include aptitude and skill in the two languages, their attitudes and motivations. Outputs could be many and are likely to be contentious, but are likely to include proficiency in the two languages, biliteracy, attitudes towards the languages and cultures, initial and subsequent integration into linguistically and culturally different groups and self-esteem.

Five overlapping categories of context can be defined:

1. Society: particularly differing political aims and ideologies. Assimilationist and integrationist, pluralist and separatist viewpoints may variously affect language minorities. The relationship between the dominant and the dominated, the empowered and the powerless, the enabled and the 'disabled' is crucial in understanding the nature, aims and outcomes of bilingual education, in whatever form.

2. Community: the extent to which a community is bilingual, bicultural, positive, negative or ambivalent towards bilingual education and bilingualism.

3. School: e.g. Immersion, Transitional Bilingual, a bilingual unit within a mainstream school, a school using a minority language within a majority language area.

4. Classroom: e.g. the language balance of the classroom (e.g. early Immersion where students are at the same level in the second language, compared with some United States 'submersion' schools where minority language children are expected to learn English alongside English first language speakers).

5. Curriculum material: the kind of curriculum resources used to achieve progress in bilingualism and biculturalism, the use of audio-visual techniques, formal grammar lessons, technological aids (e.g. Computer Assisted Language Learning (CALL) on microcomputers) and creative activity.

Finally, the process concerns inspection and analysis of topics such as teacher's reinforcement and reward systems when students use their first and second language, criticism for using the first language, teacher's explaining

Input – Context – Process – Output Model of Bilingual Education

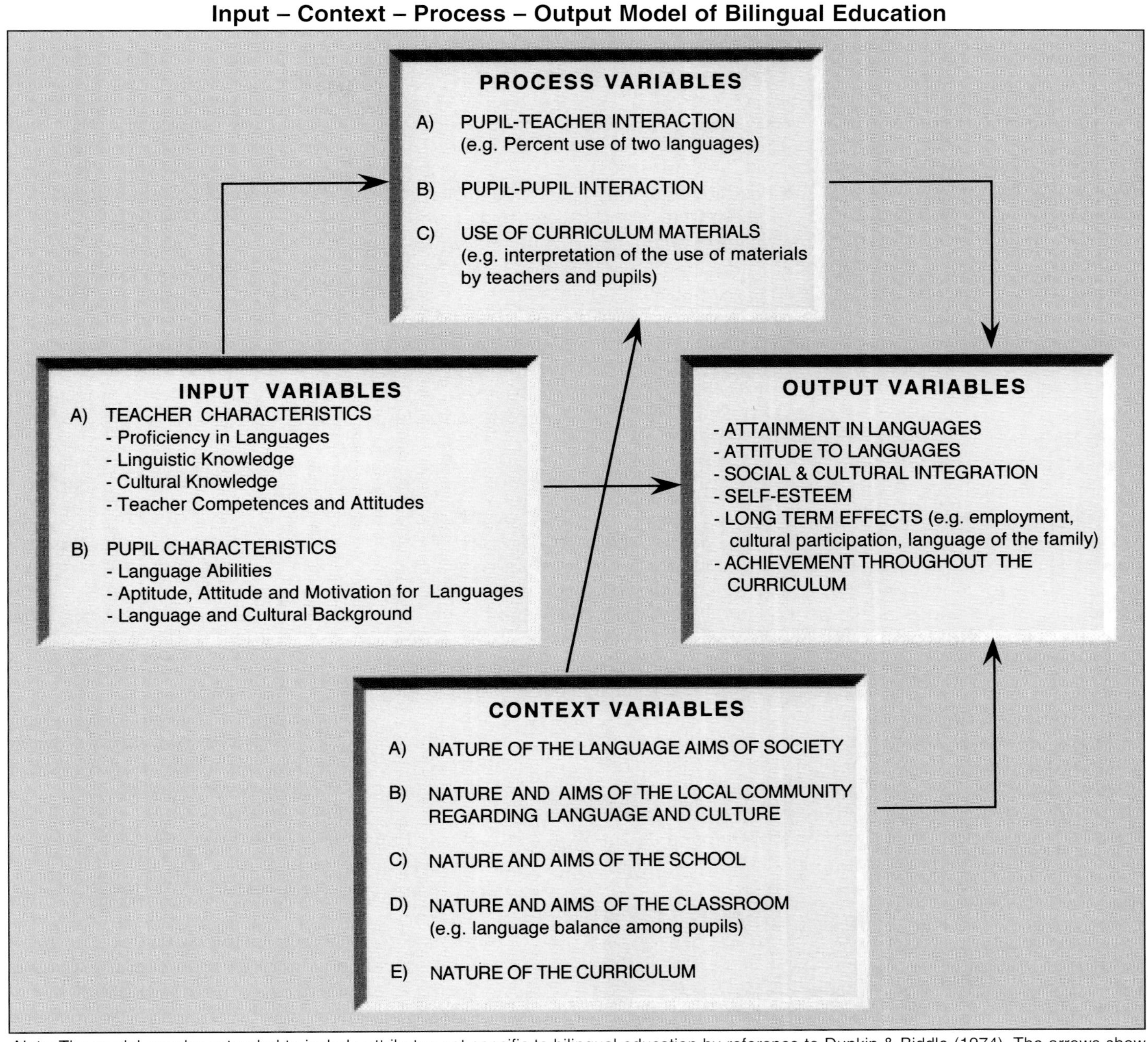

PROCESS VARIABLES
A) PUPIL-TEACHER INTERACTION
(e.g. Percent use of two languages)
B) PUPIL-PUPIL INTERACTION
C) USE OF CURRICULUM MATERIALS
(e.g. interpretation of the use of materials by teachers and pupils)
INPUT VARIABLES
A) TEACHER CHARACTERISTICS
- Proficiency in Languages
- Linguistic Knowledge
- Cultural Knowledge
- Teacher Competences and Attitudes
B) PUPIL CHARACTERISTICS
- Language Abilities
- Aptitude, Attitude and Motivation for Languages
- Language and Cultural Background
OUTPUT VARIABLES
- ATTAINMENT IN LANGUAGES
- ATTITUDE TO LANGUAGES
- SOCIAL & CULTURAL INTEGRATION
- SELF-ESTEEM
- LONG TERM EFFECTS (e.g. employment, cultural participation, language of the family)
- ACHIEVEMENT THROUGHOUT THE CURRICULUM
CONTEXT VARIABLES
A) NATURE OF THE LANGUAGE AIMS OF SOCIETY
B) NATURE AND AIMS OF THE LOCAL COMMUNITY REGARDING LANGUAGE AND CULTURE
C) NATURE AND AIMS OF THE SCHOOL
D) NATURE AND AIMS OF THE CLASSROOM (e.g. language balance among pupils)
E) NATURE OF THE CURRICULUM

Note: The model may be extended to include attributes not specific to bilingual education by reference to Dunkin & Biddle (1974). The arrows show the most typical connections made by research in relating the elements of the model.

systems when using either language, language error correction, language lesson patterns and structures, language teaching styles, students' work involvement rate in their two languages, and teacher's use of two languages, in a qualitative and quantitative sense, in the classroom.

Such an 'organizing' bilingual education model pinpoints some important issues:

1. Generalization of a research finding to a variety of contexts can be dangerous. Immersion education appears to work well in Canada. This does not mean it can be imported into other international contexts without changes. As contexts, student characteristics and teacher attributes change, so may the success of Immersion education. Different ingredients produce different meals. Occasionally the change of just one ingredient can change the taste of the whole product. Recipes for success need testing in a variety of contexts to assess their generalization potential. Research on bilingual education needs to be replicated in as many different social and educational contexts as

possible, both across and inside countries. Such research also needs replication with the inputs varied. For example, using different socioeconomic groups of children, or schools where teachers have varying levels of commitment to bilingual education. Recipes for success are likely to be varied, complex and not necessarily stable over time.

2. Outputs from bilingual education need to be thought of in a relative, contentious and pluralistic manner. Different interest groups expect different outcomes from bilingual schooling. Some research has narrowly focused on traditional skills which can be quantitatively measured by achievement tests. There may be alternative outcomes of bilingual education, sometimes debated, difficult to define and measure, which need investigating (e.g. self-esteem, open-mindedness, responsibility, independence, initiative, tolerance, curiosity, originality, perseverance, honesty, reliability, vocational success and social adjustment). Paulston (1992b) suggests that employment rates for school leavers, drug-addiction and alcoholism statistics, suicide rates, personality disorders and drop-out rates are more important indicators of the success of bilingual education than standardized test scores. Bilingual education needs to be evaluated in terms of social justice and not just school scores. Has too much emphasis been placed on end of year, end of school outcomes? Are the more important effects of bilingual schooling longer-term? For example, attitude to both languages and cultures after schooling, commitment and participation in the two languages and cultures, raising children in the minority language or not, and sending such children to bilingual schools are all researchable long-term effects. Does bilingual education have a short-term effect that dies after leaving school? Does bilingual schooling have long-term, cumulative effects that are beneficial or otherwise to society?

3. The process issues are most important in successful bilingual education. The way teachers and students behave and interact, think, feel, talk, write, move and relate to one another are vital issues for teachers, parents and school administrators. Bilingual classrooms are different from mainstream classrooms and therefore particularly need research on classroom processes.

'Weak' Forms of Bilingual Education

1: Submersion Education

Definition

Submersion education, sometimes called submersion bilingual education, represents the 'weakest' form of bilingual education. It concerns children from language minority homes who are taught immediately through the majority language. For example, children from US Spanish-speaking homes are placed in a school where all the instruction, from the first day onwards, is through the medium of English. The aim of submersion is to enable children to be fluent and literate in English as soon as possible so they can work alongside majority language children. No schools are actually called submersion schools. Such submersion occurs in mainstream schools where ethnic minority children represent anything from a small numerical minority to a significant majority (e.g. in schools in inner-city areas attracting recent in-migrants).

In the United States, one form of Submersion education is called Structured Immersion. In Structured Immersion, the teacher is expected to use a simplified form of the majority language (i.e. English) for a short while. Just as a mother simplifies her language with a very young child, or Spanish speakers will simplify their Spanish when talking to a Spanish learner, so the Structured Immersion teacher reduces the complexity of her English. Such a teacher may also accept contributions from children in their home language for a short while. However the aim is still to switch a child to using only the majority language in the classroom as soon as possible.

In some British primary schools there is a large proportion of students from in-migrant families, speaking a variety of languages at home. Bilingual staff provide some in-class support but the general aim of education in most schools is for children to learn English as soon as possible.

The concept of submersion is allied to the idea of getting children to swim quickly by throwing them into the deep end. A child is submerged in, for example, English and expected to survive in English as quickly as possible. Supporters of submersion believe that if a child is surrounded constantly by the majority language, he or she will quickly learn that language. Their belief is that allowing a child to use the home language only delays the development of the majority language. Since the teacher and majority language students inside the same classrooms act as role models, the belief is that language minority children will quickly acquire fluency in the

Submersion among Indigenous Students

A submersion experience is not only experienced by in-migrant children. Indigenous language minority children may also experience the suppression of their home language and the single-minded advancement of the majority language. The Maoris in New Zealand and the Aborigines in Australia are two examples of peoples whose native languages have been historically endangered by the imposition of English-only submersion school experiences.

In Wales, in the second half of the 19th century, children were forbidden to speak Welsh in the classroom and playground. To eradicate Welsh in school, the 'Welsh Not' or 'Welsh Stick' was used. This was a small piece of wood with 'Welsh Not' or 'Welsh Stick' carved on it. Attached to the wood was string so that it could be placed around the neck of any child heard speaking Welsh. The child could transfer the 'Welsh Not' to any other child heard speaking Welsh. At the end of the morning, afternoon, day or week, whoever was wearing the 'Welsh Not' was punished with a flogging from a birch rod or a cane. This act has come to symbolize in Wales the educational oppression of English-only submersion schooling. Similar approaches were used in other countries (e.g. Kenya, Japan, Brittany and New Zealand) to discourage the use of minority languages in schools.

In the former British colony of Zimbabwe, English is the mother tongue of only one percent of the population, but is the main language of government, business, the mass media, training and education. Most of the population speak either Shona or Ndebele as their native language, but many schools educate only through English from the beginning.

majority language. Such students are thus placed in mainstream schools, and may either linguistically sink, struggle or learn to swim.

Aims

The basic aim of Submersion education is not only about language shift. It also concerns politics. In the United States, for example, with the large immigration that has taken place this century, Submersion education has been valued as a way of assimilating language minority speakers into mainstream US society. Given the vast mix of different ethnic groups and different languages, it was felt that the schools should become a melting pot to help create common social, political and economic ideals. The melting pot, assimilationist preference meant that language diversity was often discouraged in the United States in the 20th century. Submersion education became the perceived means of producing a harmonious, economically healthy and homogeneous society within America. A common language would provide, it was thought, common attitudes, aims and values. A common language and culture would cement society. An English-speaking America was preferable to the threat of Babel.

A parallel movement has occurred in the United Kingdom. In-migration from the 1950s to the present has led to children whose first language is, for example, Panjabi, Urdu, Bengali, Hindi, Greek, Italian, Cantonese or Gujarati, being placed in mainstream, English-only classrooms. Some language help has been available in reception centers, withdrawal classes and lessons, and recently through bilingual assistants working alongside mainstream classroom teachers. Generally, the British preference has been for a submersion approach in almost all the urban areas where such language minority children are educated. Among politicians and administrators, there is a widespread assumption that submersion is the most effective route to the children speaking standard English, acquiring English culture and becoming assimilated into a homogenized British society.

Outcomes

Some children do cope with the Submersion education experience. Some become proficient in the four language skills (speaking, listening, reading and writing) and become successful in society. For many others, the Submersion education experience is stressful and problematic. Students may understand little of what the teacher or language majority students are talking about in the classroom. With little or no English, for example, students may learn little content. What they may learn is that their language is not valued, nor are they, nor their parents or their ethnic group. The child, the parents, the home language and culture each appear to be discouraged and disparaged, rejected and rebuffed.

Listening to a new language demands high concentration. It is often tiring to try to decode what the teacher and other students are saying in a strange tongue. The child may have difficulty in understanding the words, let alone the content of the subject being taught. The child has to try to take in information from different curriculum areas, each with their own special language, and learn a language at the same time. While some children do succeed in Submersion education, there appear to be many children who fail to achieve to their potential. Such failure may be academic, dropping out from High School without graduation. Other effects may be in terms of physical and mental health. A child may have a lack of self-confidence, low self-esteem, may learn to opt out physically, academically and emotionally from the school. School disaffection and alienation also occur as outcomes.

While submersion may logically be regarded as the quickest way to ensure a child learns the majority language,

A Student's Experience

McKay (1988, page 341) quotes from a student in a Submersion classroom:

'School was a nightmare. I dreaded going to school and facing my classmates and teacher. Every activity the class engaged in meant another exhibition of my incompetence. Each activity was another incidence for my peers to laugh and ridicule me with and for my teacher to stare hopelessly disappointed at me. My self-image was a serious inferiority complex. I became frustrated at not being able to do anything right. I felt like giving up the entire mess'.

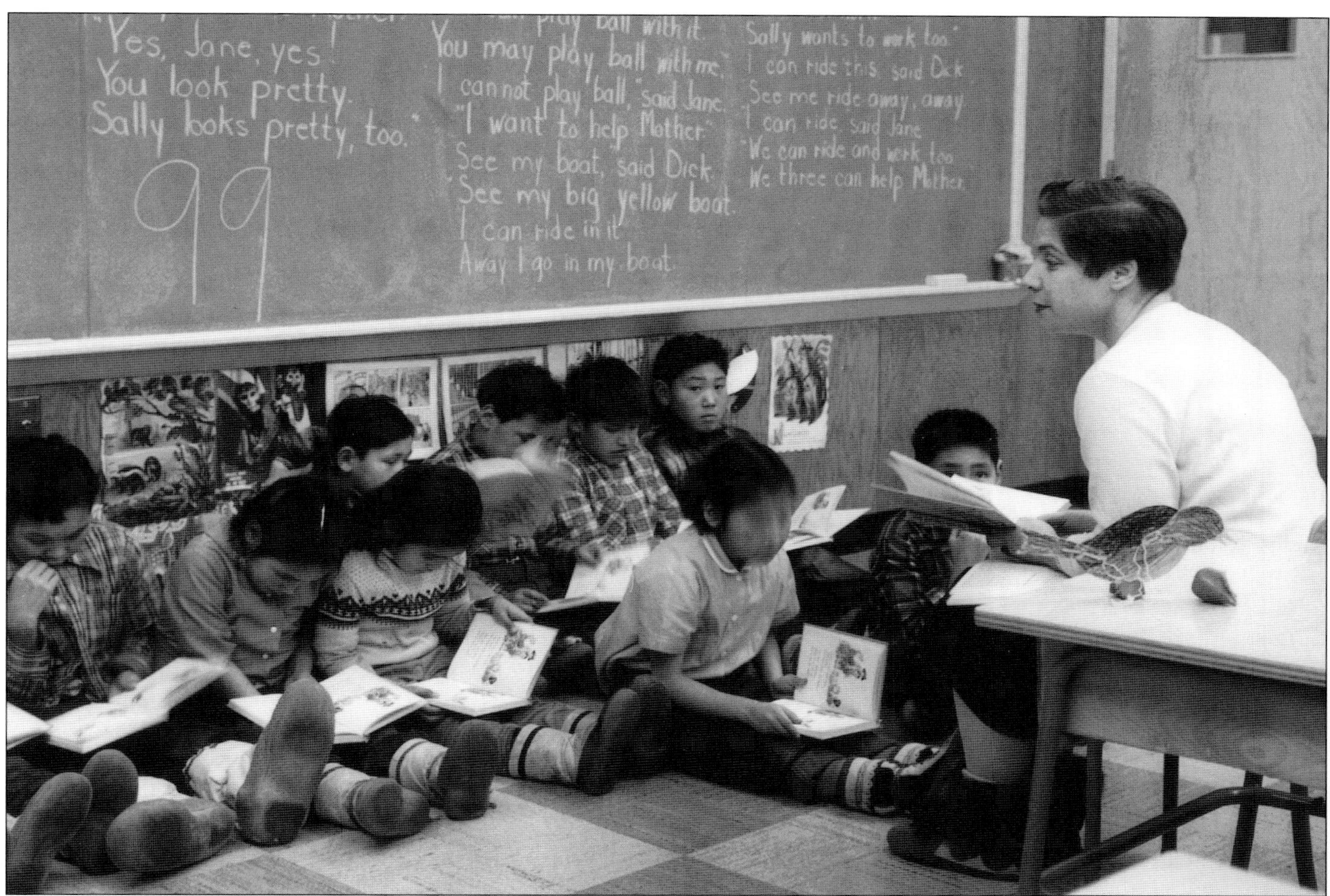

Inuit and other children from indigenous language groups learn English in a school in Inuvik in the North West Territories of Canada in 1959. Canadian educational policy was initially harsh towards indigenous language groups, educating them entirely in English or French, sometimes in boarding schools away from their families.

and learns through that language, research (see the section on Effectiveness of Bilingual Education, page 550) suggests that submersion is not the most efficient way of second language learning. It also tends to result in underperformance in the curriculum, with consequent negative outcomes in terms of personality and social development. A rejection of a child's language means a rejection of the child.

Among academics, submersion has come to be regarded as not the best alternative for children from language minority backgrounds. The support for Submersion education is mostly political and is also present in large sections of the US populace. Those concerned with assimilating language minorities into mainstream society, with the melting pot, and with a homogeneous national culture, tend to support Submersion education.

'There is no such thing as "the Queen's English." The property has gone into the hands of a joint stock company and we own the bulk of the shares!'

Mark Twain, US author (1835-1910).

Further Reading

BAKER, C., 1996, *Foundations of Bilingual Education and Bilingualism* (Second edition). Clevedon: Multilingual Matters Ltd.

GARCÍA, O. (ed.), 1991, *Bilingual Education: Focusschrift in Honor of Joshua A. Fishman*. Amsterdam/Philadelphia: John Benjamins.

GARCÍA, O. & BAKER, C. (eds), 1995, *Policy and Practice in Bilingual Education*. Clevedon: Multilingual Matters Ltd.

2: Transitional Bilingual Education

Introduction

Transitional Bilingual education allows a child to use the home language for two or three, and sometimes more years in the elementary school. However, the aim is for that child to move as rapidly as possible into using, and working through, the majority language (e.g. English in the United States). After approximately two years, students are expected to be sufficiently proficient in the majority language to cope in mainstream classrooms. After a few years of being allowed to use their home language in the classroom, such students are expected to make the transition to majority language content classes.

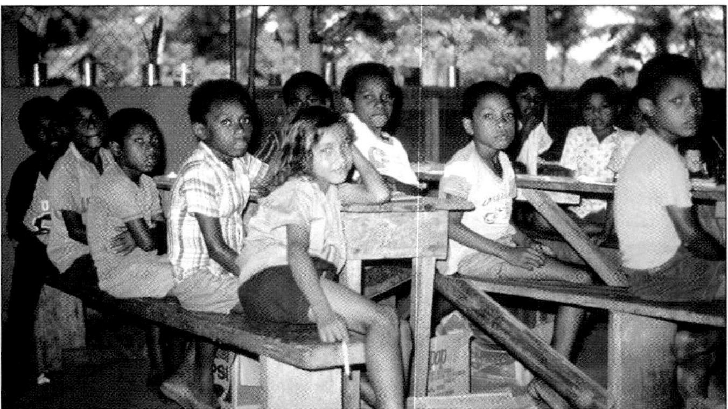

Seven to nine year olds in a rural classroom in Papua New Guinea. Over 700 language varieties are spoken in Papua New Guinea. A recent government language policy has encouraged the use of local vernaculars for the first years of primary education with a transition to English thereafter.

Students in Transitional Bilingual Education Programs

Students in Transitional Bilingual education (often shortened to TBE) programs come from language minority backgrounds. For example in the United States, such students may be recent in-migrants, or from second or third generation language minority communities. Such students will be placed in a program within the mainstream school. Such programs occur in both US elementary and high schools. In high schools, Transitional Bilingual education programs will be particularly for recent in-migrants to the United States.

Aims of Transitional Bilingual Education

The central aim of Transitional Bilingual education is not to produce bilingual, biliterate or bicultural students, but for children to function as quickly and as confidently as possible in the majority language. When such basic proficiency, for example in English, appears to be present, students will be rapidly transferred to mainstream classrooms where English is the sole medium of instruction.
To use a swimming pool analogy, Transitional Bilingual education is like a brief, temporary swim in the home language while being taught the four majority language skills (listening, speaking, reading and writing) to enable transfer to the mainstream school as quickly as possible. While bilingual teachers in the first grade will allow children to use their home language in the classroom, the aim is to increase the use of the majority language while proportionally decreasing use of the home language.

Political Aims

The political aim of Transitional Bilingual education is integrative and assimilationist. The goal is to assimilate in-migrant and language minority children into the host society, to provide them with equal access to employment and wealth. While some children do succeed and meet these aims, others find that Transitional Bilingual education results in a gradual loss of their native language and culture but without integration into mainstream society. Because of limitations in majority language fluency, or underachievement in school, or because of race and color, full integration into mainstream society is often denied.

Because Transitional Bilingual Education is a 'weak' form of bilingual education, not supporting the home language and culture, it attempts to discourage children's acceptance of the cultural and linguistic norms of their ethnic group. At the same time, the early-exiting of children into the mainstream classroom tends to result in a relative lack of full linguistic, cultural and educational accomplishments. This will be examined in detail later in this subsection. It may also result in disaffection with schooling for some students. Thus equality of access to employment and wealth tends to be denied by the very form of education that aims to provide such access.

Types of Transitional Bilingual Education

Transitional Bilingual education can be split into two major types: Early-exit and Late-exit. Early-exit Transitional Bilingual education usually allows children around two years' use of their home language before transition to mainstream classes. Late-exit Transitional Bilingual education allows, for example, around 40 percent of the classroom teaching to be in the mother tongue until the sixth grade.

Research has shown that a distinction between Early- and Late-exit Transitional Bilingual education is important. Children tend to succeed in the curriculum (e.g. Mathematics, English language and English reading) more in Late-exit than in Early-exit Transitional Bilingual education. Ramirez & Merino (1990) found in schools in New York, New Jersey, Florida, Texas and California that by the end of the third grade, there was little difference in the curriculum performance of children in submersion, Early-exit or Late-exit Bilingual education. By the sixth grade, Late-exit Transitional Bilingual education students were out-performing their peers in other types of education. It was concluded that Spanish-speaking students could be taught through their home language for substantial amounts of time without impeding their acquisition of English.

At a political level, submersion and Early-exit Transitional Bilingual education have often been supported by both politicians and much of the public, with Late-exit and 'strong' forms of bilingual education much less supported. Since recent research results show little difference between Early-exit Transitional Bilingual education and Submersion education, opponents of bilingual education have argued for submersion rather than Early-exit. Since submersion is administratively more easy and less expensive than Transitional Bilingual education, submersion may be favored by politicians and many professionals.

Language Approach

Bilingual teachers will initially allow children to use their mother tongue. Teachers will use the mother tongue of the children to explain curriculum content and organizational instructions. The mother tongue will also be used to introduce the majority language, and this becomes a major focus of a Transitional Bilingual education program. Progressively, particularly in an Early-exit program, teachers will use the majority language while decreasingly using the home language. The home language is only valued to the extent that it allows gradual rather than sudden instruction in, and through the medium of English. Often, after two or more years, (or when students are regarded as sufficiently proficient in English), they exit into mainstream majority language classrooms within the same school.

In United States Late-exit Transitional Bilingual education, the movement from the home language to the English language will be slower and more gradual. Late-exit programs may have approximately three-quarters of teaching through the medium of Spanish in the first grade, lowering to around 40 percent in the fifth and sixth grades. In comparison, in the first and second grades of US Early-exit programs, English will be used for approximately two-thirds of the time and one-third may be in the language of the home.

In Transitional Bilingual education, there will be lessons specifically on the English language, on its structure, rules and vocabulary. There will not often be formal lessons in the home language, although sometimes there are language arts sessions. While curriculum content in other areas (e.g. Mathematics, Social Studies) will be partly in the home language, the switch to using English is a dominant US aim. The cultural element of the curriculum will usually be about the host nation, rather than about an ethnic group's history, geography and culture. However, there are some programs (e.g. for Haitian in New York) where an element of heritage culture will be considered.

Teachers

Transitional Bilingual education programs require teachers who are bilingual and are able to teach through the majority language and the home language of the child. Such bilingual teachers, who can switch from one language to another, may ostensibly be more sympathetic to the language and home background of the child. This has some value and benefits. The use of bilingual teachers provides employment for recent and established immigrant communities.

In the United States, an English monolingual teacher will therefore not be imposed on language minority children; the conversion from, for example, Spanish to English is achieved by a bilingual. The bilingual teacher provides a role model for the child. The transition from home to school language, cultural integration and assimilation is seen to occur within the child's own cultural or ethnic group. A bilingual teacher may be in touch with the needs and wishes of the local language community.

However, bilingual teachers in Transitional Bilingual education programs may be compromised. The aim of such a US program is for the child to become dominantly English-speaking, at least in schooling. While language communities may want their children to speak English, they may not want their child to lose the home language. Thus, the US Transitional Bilingual education teacher may be caught 'in the middle', between a language community that wants to preserve the native language and culture, and an administration, inside and outside school, whose concern is with increasing proficiency in the English language and assimilation into North American culture. Bilingual teachers in such programs may become unwitting allies in portraying English as the only prestigious language, and Spanish or another minority language as the stigmatized language.

In most US schools with Transitional Bilingual education programs, the people with status and power (e.g. principals, assistant principals and department leaders) are often English language monolinguals. The people with the lowest status and power in the school (the cook, the janitor, the office staff) may be speakers of the minority language. English may be the language of communication across the loudspeaker and in letters to parents. Thus English becomes the language of power and status, and the minority language used by those who serve and are subservient. A United States Transitional Bilingual education program may therefore have a hidden curriculum. The child may learn that one language is prestigious, the other is the stigmatized language of the underclass and the less successful in society. The latent message of the school may be quickly picked up by students. They may not want to be seen as speakers of a minority language, nor do they want to be bilingual. The students may simply want to be regarded as speakers of English with its connotations of status, power and success.

In Transitional Bilingual classrooms, the bilingual teacher will normally use the two languages interchangeably. There will be little or no compartmentalization or boundaries between the languages. No specific roles or functions will be assigned to the two languages. This allows the higher status language to grow, and the lower status language to decline in usage. Such switching between languages and lack of separation tends to work against bilingualism and biliteracy.

For bilingualism to flourish, it can be a help to separate the times and places where the two languages are used. For example, one language may be used for one particular curriculum area (e.g. Mathematics and Science), while the other language may be used for Social Studies, Music and Physical education/Games. Sometimes, one language is spoken in one classroom. When children switch to a different classroom, a different language is used. Here, language belongs to a particular territory. In Transitional Bilingual education, there is no such separation of languages via different classrooms, use of different teachers, or in different curriculum areas. This pattern tends to work against the minority language because, for example, it does not allow the development of the minority language in its spoken or a written form, nor give it status or a specific use.

Teachers within United States Transitional Bilingual education programs will usually be eager to show success, create effective classrooms and raise their personal promotion potential. For such a bilingual teacher to be effective, she must show secure progress in English in her children. Thus the bilingual teacher becomes the unwitting agent in the promotion of the majority language, often at the expense of development of the minority language.

Outcomes from Transitional Bilingual Education

One outcome of Transitional Bilingual education is the many children who have both limited bilingualism and limited success in the curriculum. There are many exceptions, with many students becoming highly proficient in English, succeeding throughout the curriculum and moving through to higher education and prestigious employment. However, is such success despite rather than

'Limited English Proficient' Students in the United States

An official United States term for those for whom English is an additional language is 'Limited English Proficient'. Classifications of 'Limited English Proficient' students are variously based on language proficiency tests, home language surveys, teacher observation, information from parents, achievement tests, student school records, teacher interviews or referrals. Such students may be in submersion language education (see page 476), Transitional Bilingual education (see page 479) or developmental (maintenance) bilingual education (see page 508). Unfortunately, the term 'Limited English Proficient' students tends to emphasize students limitations in English rather than their potential as bilinguals, a deficiency rather than a developing proficiency.

Over 3,200,000 'Limited English Proficient' students are present in US schools of whom some 98.35 percent are enrolled in public schools. These students represent approximately seven percent of the all US students between Kindergarten and Grade 12. From 1990-1991 to 1994–1995, the reported number of 'Limited English Proficient' students increased by 44.8 percent. States with the largest populations and school enrollments tend to be the states with the largest number of 'Limited English Proficient' students (e.g. 1994-1995 figures show California with 1,262,982 students, followed by Texas (457,437), New York (236,356), Florida (153,841), and Illinois (107,084). Approximately 80 percent of 'Limited English Proficient' students are in some form of special educational provision.

REFERENCE: MACÍAS & KELLY, 1996

because of Transitional Bilingual education? Particularly with United States Early-exit Transitional Bilingual education, a student's achievement in English and across the curriculum may be lower than those in Late-exit, dual language and developmental maintenance situations.

Since there is only support for the home language in the early grades, bilingualism, biliteracy and biculturalism is neither the aim nor the outcome of this form of education. Because majority language skills may have insufficiently developed, this lack of proficiency may, in itself, cause a lowering of achievement among students. When children exit from Transitional Bilingual education, they may neither have the language skills sufficient to cope in mainstream classrooms, nor the cognitive development to allow them to cope with the level of concepts being introduced in mainstream classrooms.

According to Jim Cummins (1984b), for such children to succeed, their majority language needs to be at the level of being able to cope in the relatively cognitive demanding academic setting. Conversational skills in the English language may not be at the level required to cope in the more complex language of a mainstream classroom. Such children may be mainstreamed into English-only classes before they have the linguistic skills to cope with cognitively demanding academic tasks. Two or three years of English language instruction may be insufficient time for development of linguistic skills to participate and compete in English-only classrooms, especially with peers for whom English is the mother tongue (see page 561 on Collier & Thomas).

Thus Transitional Bilingual education may lead to many language minority children failing. Such failure may not only be in the majority language and the curriculum. There may be other detrimental consequences: lack of self-esteem, negative stereotyping and stigmatization. When Transitional Bilingual education is seen to fail, the perception of students and teachers may be affected. The language minority and culture that a child represents may be seen as imperfect or inferior compared with mainstream culture. When such Transitional Bilingual education students show inferior use and understanding of English, when their academic performance is poorer, racist attitudes and stereotypes may be born or reinforced.

As one extreme outcome, Transitional Bilingual education may be creating a caste-like minority, an underclass. When there is failure, the victim is blamed. That the underclass have to bear a greater share of hardship, poverty and unemployment is blamed on their inability to speak English and having not taken advantage of such Transitional Bilingual education.

The segregation of in-migrant communities, different ethnic groups and language groups, is thus reinforced by the education system. The education system may inadvertently play a role in creating a pool of language minority adults who become the economically exploited, unemployed or underemployed members of society. Those members of society most in need of high quality education are the impoverished and underemployed ethnic, racial and language minorities. Such minorities tend to be confronted by the dominant majority in society who are less and less willing to pay for 'strong' forms of bilingual education and tend to be more in support of submersion and Early-exit Transitional Bilingual education programs.

Further Reading

ARIAS, B. & CASANOVA, U. (eds), 1993, *Bilingual Education: Politics, Research and Practice*. Berkeley, CA: McCutchan.

BAKER, K. A. & de KANTER, A. A., 1983, *Bilingual Education*. Lexington, MA: Lexington Books.

CRAWFORD, J.,1995, *Bilingual Education: History, Politics, Theory and Practice* (Third edition). Los Angeles: Bilingual Educational Services.

RAMIREZ, J. D. & MERINO, B. J., 1990, Classroom Talk in English Immersion, Early-exit & Late-exit Transitional Bilingual Education Programs. In R. JACOBSON & C. FALTIS (eds), *Language Distribution Issues in Bilingual Schooling*. Clevedon: Multilingual Matters Ltd.

RAMIREZ, J. D., YUEN, S. D. & RAMEY, D. R., 1991, *Final Report: Longitudinal Study of Structured English Immersion Strategy, Early-exit & Late-exit Programs for Language-Minority Children*. Report Submitted to the US Department of Education, San Mateo, California: Aguirre International.

3: Withdrawal Classes

Introduction

When children are in regular classes or a mainstream school and their language proficiency is not as well developed as others within the school, withdrawal classes may be established. Compensatory lessons may be provided to enable children with insufficient competence in the majority language to catch up with their peers. Such classes may last from a few weeks to a few years. A number of alternative terms are used for withdrawal classes. In the United States, it is common to speak of Submersion education with withdrawal classes. Other terms are 'pull out' classes, compensatory language education and special ESL (English as a Second Language) classes.

Withdrawal classes are different from Structured Immersion. Structured Immersion uses a simplified form of the majority language and may initially accept contributions from children in their home language. Withdrawal classes are also different from Sheltered English. In Sheltered English, minority language students are taught the curriculum with a simplified vocabulary, purpose-made curriculum materials, and defined strategies of learning (e.g. small group, cooperative learning). In Sheltered English, the language of the classroom must be English-only using an 'English as a first language' methodology. Withdrawal classes, in contrast, tend to follow an 'English as a second language' methodology, (that is, a language approach drawn from ESL traditions), plus no input in the mother tongue.

While in most cases the students in withdrawal classes will be minority language students requiring extra tuition in the majority language, there are international examples of majority language children requiring withdrawal classes. For example, if a school operates almost totally through the medium of the minority language, a language majority child may receive lessons in the minority language to enable that child to have sufficient proficiency in the minority language to cope in the curriculum. Examples of different types of withdrawal classes will now be given.

The United Kingdom

In the United Kingdom, there is a mosaic of in-migrant community languages similar to the United States. The community languages of the United Kingdom include Arabic, Bengali, Cantonese, Gujarati, Greek, Hindi, Italian, Panjabi, Polish, Portuguese, Spanish, Turkish, Ukrainian and Urdu. In the 1950s, when the recent in-migrant trend started, children were either placed immediately in submersion classrooms without extra English language help, or in separate units set up for in-migrants.

During the 1960s, withdrawal classes in English as a second language were instituted alongside reception centers for such in-migrant children. In such withdrawal classes, students were taken out of their regular classrooms and given a few hours' instruction in English in a separate class alongside other ethnic minority children. Withdrawal lessons posed the danger of associating bilingual children with a language deficiency.

There was a movement away from withdrawal classes in the United Kingdom (in centers or in mainstream schools) towards the use of language support teachers (known as resource teachers in Canada) working in partnership with class and subject teachers. However, most of these initial language support teachers in the UK were monolingual English speakers, and not bilinguals. The reasons for a movement away from withdrawal classes was: (1) the English language interaction was with the teacher only. There were no peers to act as first language language models. Thus the language experience could be limited. (2) The opportunities for 'authentic' English language communication, for lively and enriching verbal exchanges, might only occur in withdrawal classes. (3) Children in such withdrawal classes did not have full access to the curriculum, having a limited amount of

content input. This served to ignore their cognitive capability when operating in the home language, and delay their progress in many curriculum areas.

During the 1970s and 1980s, it was felt preferable (in the more progressive schools) not to stigmatize children by extracting them from regular lessons. Instead, they were given extra help inside their regular classrooms by bilingual support teachers. Such bilingual support teachers undertook three main duties: individual support for students in the class; translating the language in displays, making audio tapes and interpreting for students; and either leading the class (e.g. story reading) or working in partnership with the teacher (Bourne, 1989a).

Such help aided the child's transition from the home language to working solely in English. Such language support teachers also provided a multicultural dimension to the classroom by their cultural knowledge and ethnic identity. Also, fully qualified bilingual teachers have increasingly become available (although there is still a shortage), providing a model of help for community language children in UK schools.

In the 1970s and 1980s, some schools attempted to go further to celebrate the linguistic diversity of their children. The new languages of Britain were given some attention and status in such progressive schools. By colorful wall displays, cultural ceremonies and exhibitions, bringing in parents and language community leaders, monolingual English-speaking children were also introduced to the value of bilingualism and multiculturalism while language minority children were encouraged to take pride in their linguistic and cultural heritage. However, schools have often found it difficult to promote bilingualism. This is partly due to dominant central politics that are assimilationist, to a National Curriculum that has fostered standard English and not second and foreign languages, and to National Curriculum assessment that accentuates English language competence. Another factor in the UK that has slowed the development of bilingualism through schooling has been the difficulty of recruiting teachers from community language groups (Bourne, 1989b).

However, even in the dark valley there are rays of hope. A 'dual language' education (Panjabi and English) experiment in Bradford found that children's English language achievement was not hindered (compared with children in submersion schooling) by dual language education (Fitzpatrick, 1987). In particular urban areas of the UK (e.g. Bradford, Leeds, London, Midlands) some 'flagship' schools have fostered valuable community links, developed a vigorous anti-racist and multicultural curriculum, increasingly with community languages on the secondary school timetable, and with rising entries in community language examinations at the age of 16.

United States

In the United States, withdrawal classes to teach English as a second language (ESL) are a way of keeping language minority children within mainstream schools. For administrators and budget managers, this is often regarded as preferable to setting up a special Transitional Bilingual education program within the school or a separate school.

The United States and British experiences are similar. There may be a stigma when children are withdrawn from the mainstream classroom. Such children may be seen by their peers as remedial, disabled, and not proficient in English. By being withdrawn from their regular classrooms, such language minority children are also in danger of falling behind on regular curriculum content delivered to others not in the withdrawal classes.

Wales

A different kind of withdrawal class exists in Wales. Welsh-medium elementary schools, where Welsh is the main language used in delivering the curriculum, exist in both predominantly English-speaking and predominantly Welsh-speaking areas. In largely Anglicized areas, where the majority of the school intake consists of monolingual English children, the early years of elementary school represent an Immersion experience for the students. (See Immersion Bilingual Education, page 496). When young English language monolingual children wish to enter Welsh-medium elementary schools in largely Welsh-speaking areas, where the majority of the students are native speakers, they are usually offered withdrawal classes to help them master the Welsh language. Older monolingual English newcomers are invited to attend withdrawal classes in a specially set up reception center. Reception centers in the United Kingdom became heavily criticized because they were ghettos for in-migrant children. Such reception centers in the United Kingdom were for language minority children only, different in race, color and creed. In Wales, a reception center is for language majority children (i.e. English language monolingual children) and therefore they do not become stigmatized. Rather, such reception centers are perceived as being highly successful, although the research evidence is minimal on the issue.

Such reception centers contain highly skilled language teachers, who teach Welsh in a vivacious, enjoyable, varied and entertaining manner. The Welsh language is

learnt through playing language games, action songs and dances, humorous interactions between students and teacher, highly motivating pair-work and group-work, projects and activities involving co-operation between students and with the teacher, in such a way that language is the medium but not the focus of the activity. Welsh is acquired informally as a young child acquires a first language rather than through formal language lessons. Ideally, within one semester (about 14 weeks) a child may have sufficient Welsh to join peers in the mainstream heritage language school. Monolingual English-speaking children who attend withdrawal classes, whether within school, or at reception centers, are not stigmatized because they speak a highly prestigious majority language. English is taught as a subject in Welsh-medium elementary schools and is also used to deliver a small proportion of the curriculum in higher classes. All teachers are bilingual in Welsh and English, and can switch to English to help English first language speakers with their work. Thus the native language and culture of English speakers is not devalued.

European Schools

Another example of withdrawal classes comes from the European Schools. In European schools, children are able to study through the native language and also study part of the curriculum through a second language (see page 527). In such European schools, two types of special support are provided for children who arrive during the middle of a school year or from a monolingual program at another school. Students with no knowledge of a second language are sent to 'catching up classes' (*'cours de rattrapage'* in French). Such 'catching up classes' operate when other students are receiving second language instruction. In these 'catching up classes', teachers will try to bring new arrivals up to class norms by intensive language teaching. These lessons may be supplemented by extra lessons outside the normal school timetable.

The second type of special provision for late arrivals with an inadequate proficiency in the second language is known as 'support classes' (*'cours de soutien'* in French). Such support classes occur in the secondary school program and provide help with handling subjects that are taught through the second language (e.g. History and Geography). Such support classes do not tend to be regarded as compensatory or to solve a deficiency. Because the child is already proficient in the majority language, stigmatization does not tend to occur. There is a special team of teachers whose function it is to provide such support lessons.

Conclusion

Where withdrawal classes are purely for language minority children, there may be problems. Majority language children may develop negative attitudes towards those who are withdrawn. Those language minority children in withdrawal classes may suffer in terms of self-esteem and regard themselves as inferior and deficient. The segregation of withdrawal classes may be linguistically defensible, but can have negative social and emotional effects. Therefore, in-class help may be preferable, where this is feasible.

When language majority children are placed in such withdrawal classes, there is less danger of prejudice, rejection or attributions of deficiency. Already owning a prestigious language means that learning a minority language is additive rather than subtractive for such children.

A central aim of withdrawal classes for minority language children is to promote competence in the majority language so that minority language children may cope effectively in a monolingual majority language classroom. The aim is not to maintain or develop competence in the minority language. Thus withdrawal classes for minority language children, like Submersion education and Transitional Bilingual education, are 'weak' forms of bilingual education. They encourage assimilation and majority language monolingualism, rather than bilingualism and cultural pluralism. However when majority language children attend withdrawal classes to promote competence in a minority language, this does not tend to have a detrimental effect on their confidence or on their command of the prestigious majority language. Thus withdrawal classes for language majority children can form part of a 'strong' bilingual education program.

Further Reading

BOURNE, J., 1989, *Moving into the Mainstream: LEA Provision for Bilingual Pupils*. Windsor: NFER/Nelson.

EDWARDS, V. & REDFERN, V., 1992, *The World in a Classroom. Language in Education in Britain and Canada*. Clevedon: Multilingual Matters Ltd.

GARCÍA, O., & BAKER, C. (eds), 1995, *Policy and Practice in Bilingual Education*. Clevedon: Multilingual Matters Ltd.

GEACH, J., 1996, Community Languages. In E. HAWKINS (ed.), *30 Years of Language Teaching*. London: Centre for Information on Language Teaching and Research (CILT).

'Strong' Forms of Bilingual Education

1: Bilingual Nursery Education

Introduction

The family and home have traditionally been the center of the young child's world, and the site of the young child's earliest learning experiences. However, during recent decades in Western Europe and North America, some form of organized, professional, educational provision has gradually been encroaching upon the traditionally family domain of early childhood. There have been various reasons for this.

- In some cases, nursery education was originally established to provide for socially deprived children.
- In many Western countries, it has become increasingly common for both parents to go out to work, necessitating some kind of nursery provision.
- Because of the increasing geographical mobility of Western society, the extended family living nearby and a stable local population are less common. Some have argued that the relatively isolated nuclear family does not provide a sufficiently rich and varied environment for a young child.
- In recent years, educationalists have recognized the importance of the early years of life for a child's cognitive, social and linguistic development. They have stressed the importance of a stimulating environment to give a child the best possible start in life. The development of language and languages is part of this.

Types of Nursery Education

Nursery education is an umbrella term that covers any organized provision for pre-school children from birth until the beginning of compulsory formal education at the age of five, six or seven years. It includes crèches, nurseries and day-care for infants under two to three years. However, the term is generally used to refer to provision for children from the age of two or three onwards.

Nursery education has an enormous variety of dimensions. It may be privately run or be state-funded. It may be for a few hours a week to full-time. It may be an informal play group, where children have the opportunity to socialize with their peers and engage in free, unstructured play. On the other hand, it may be a more formal nursery school, with a structured program of activities and specific educational aims. In private, informal playgroups, teachers or helpers may not need formal qualifications. In state-run nursery schools, teachers may be required to have appropriate qualifications. In many countries, there is only voluntary and private provision for children under the age of compulsory schooling. In other countries there is statutory pre-school or kindergarten provision which is integrated into the total educational system.

The aims of nursery education tend to include the following overlapping areas.

- **Social integration**
  The children learn to interact with adults outside the family and to socialize with their peers.
- **Cultural integration**
  The children learn about their local culture and community, which may be a minority or a majority culture.
- **Physical development**
  The children have the opportunity to run, climb, ride tricycles, dance to music and go for walks.
- **Cognitive development**
  By means of games, activities and discussions, the children develop spatial awareness, understanding of mathematical concepts and logical reasoning.
- **Readiness for literacy**
  The children learn to follow a story in a book, to recognize symbols and individual words, to make patterns with a pencil.
- **Oral language development**
  This is a most crucial and fundamental factor in a child's total development. Through activities, stories, songs and interaction with the teacher or helper, the child is exposed to a linguistically rich environment.

In largely monolingual countries, the nursery school usually supports and reinforces the home language of the

children. Through the medium of the nursery school, the child gains further competence in the home language in preparation for formal education. However, the nursery school can be a means of fostering and developing bilingualism in a child. The bilingual language development of children through nursery education is the focus of this topic.

Types of Bilingual Nursery Education

The term 'bilingual nursery education' can be interpreted in three ways. Firstly, it can refer to types of nursery education which include bilingual children (or children who are monolingual in a minority language) but where only one language, the majority language, is used with the children. The linguistic goal of this type of education is to promote competence in the majority language in preparation for schooling through the majority language. The home language of minority language children is not maintained or fostered. Secondly, it can refer to pre-school education where two languages are used with the children. Thirdly, it can refer to nursery education where only a second language is used with the children, but where the eventual goal or outcome for the child is bilingualism. These three types will be considered in turn.

Monolingual majority language nursery education

In some cases, there is no educational provision in the minority language, either at pre-school level or at the level of compulsory schooling. Children from minority language homes are encouraged to attend monolingual majority language nursery schools. It is considered advantageous for such children to learn the majority language as early as possible, in order to 'succeed' at school. However, the result of this early exposure to the majority language is often that the majority language supplants the minority language. The child is unable to build on the linguistic skills acquired at home, and learn and develop through the medium of the home language. This is not beneficial to the child's linguistic development and cognitive development. The child may also feel that his or her home, family, ethnic identity and language community are not being accepted. In denying the child's home language, the child may feel that his or her identity is being denied. A loss of self-esteem may result. A pattern of failure may result, both academic failure and social problems. (See Language Shift among Pre-school Language Minority Children in the US, page 493.)

Nursery education in two languages.

When two languages are used at a kindergarten or nursery school, one of these is usually the first language of the children. This may be a minority language or a majority language of the country. The second language will also be a minority language or a majority language of the country, or a prestigious international language. Nursery education in two languages is often carefully planned and structured. The two languages are kept separate, and are used at different times, often by different teachers and in different classrooms. If native speakers of both languages are present in a dual language nursery school, careful consideration is given to the balance of languages within the school. This ensures that native speakers of one language do not swamp native speakers of the other language. Thus, the status, usage and development of both languages is assured.

Young children learn a language through play and structured activities.

Nursery education in two languages is often the first step in a complete program of bilingual education. In dual language schools in the United States, for instance, children in the kindergarten section have separate sessions in Spanish and English. Spanish-speaking children and English-speaking children learn the basics of one another's languages in preparation for formal education through the medium of both languages.

In some international schools, native speakers of majority languages such as English, Japanese, French or Arabic may enter a dual language kindergarten section. They spend half of each day in activities in the mother tongue, and the other half with a teacher who speaks a second majority language to them. After a year or two in kindergarten, the children enter the primary section where the curriculum is delivered in both languages. The goal is competency and fluency in both languages. The children do not learn another language at the expense of their native language. Both languages are developed.

Pre-school Education in Alsace

The region of Alsace is situated in the north-east of France, bordering on the German Federal Republic and Switzerland. As in the rest of France, the sole official language of the area is French. However, two-thirds of the adult population are able to speak the Alsatian dialect, which is closely related to German. Among children, however, use of the dialect is dwindling rapidly. According to 1989 figures, only 34.5 percent of 14–17 year olds could speak Alsatian, and only a quarter of nursery age children (two to six years). Furthermore, the dialect is heavily influenced by French vocabulary and syntax. Standard German is little used in Alsace but 80 percent of heads of household claim to be able to speak it. Many people watch German and Swiss television regularly and listen to German radio.

Alsace shares the same educational system as the rest of France. Compulsory schooling begins at the age of six, but pre-school provision between the ages of two and six is an integral part of the system and comes under the control of the Ministry of Education. The language of instruction is French and, until the early 1980s, the use of regional languages within the school system was banned. However, two ministerial circulars on 'The Teaching of Regional Cultures and Languages' (1982 and 1983) legalized the limited use of regional languages in schools. Within the context of pre-school education, it was recognized that the use of a child's home language could help the child settle in school, and develop his or her full potential, including linguistic potential. In Alsace, this meant that the use of the Alsatian dialect was permitted and even encouraged at nursery level. On a practical level, teachers had always made unofficial use of the Alsatian dialect to help the younger children settle in school. They continued to do this, but they found it difficult to adapt their style of teaching to give the dialect a more positive role in schools. After all, the dominant aim was still for the children to achieve fluency in French as soon as possible, in preparation for primary education. Thus the role of Alsatian in school continued to be one of aiding a transition to French.

Given time, use of the dialect in Alsatian schools might have increased. However, in 1985, a new initiative was launched, the teaching of Standard German to pre-school and primary children. This came about as a result of the new European emphasis on learning the major languages of the European Union, mainly for reasons of trade, employment and cultural and social integration. Dual language units within monolingual French schools have been established, where classes work through the medium of French and German alternately, with different teachers. At pre-school level, this means that children have activity sessions in French and German alternately, usually half a day in each language. The eventual goal is to establish a system of dual language education up to the end of compulsory education. Given the geographical proximity of Alsace to Germany, Switzerland, Luxembourg and Austria, it is believed that fluency in two languages will help children to gain employment and aid the economic prosperity of the region. The initiative is strongly supported by many middle class parents.

The question is, what is the position of the Alsatian dialect within this new bilingual initiative? In publicity pamphlets for dual language education, the close relationship between Alsatian and Standard German is stressed, and parents are encouraged to speak the dialect to their children. In dual language programs where the majority of the children are native speakers of Alsatian, the use of the dialect is encouraged to ease the transition to Standard German. The aim is not to maintain and enrich the children's ability in their native dialect, but, rather, to use it as a temporary measure on the road to competence in Standard German. For speakers of Alsatian, German is a foreign language, albeit a familiar one and relatively easy to learn. It is unlikely that the promotion of Standard German in schools will increase the use of Alsatian among children.

The issue of Alsatian and Standard German in education in the Alsace region is not an easy one. The supporters of Standard German have utilitarian arguments. German is a prestigious, widely spoken language which is useful for employment, study and travel in many countries. The supporters of Alsatian argue, on the other hand, that the use of Alsatian respects the child's identity, background and culture and develops the whole person. It seems likely, in view of the strong government support for the dual language initiative, that Standard German will continue to be promoted as the new second language of Alsace, at the expense of Alsatian.

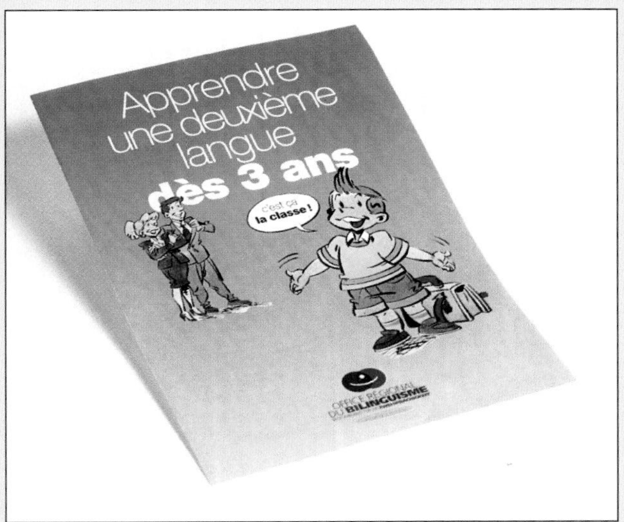

A publicity leaflet for the bilingual pre-school education in Alsace. The slogan reads 'Learn a second language from the age of three'.

Alternatively, two languages may be used informally in the nursery school. One language may be the official language of the nursery school, and also the official language of formal education. However some of the children attending the nursery school may have as their mother tongue a regional or minority language. The teacher or assistant may also know this language and may use it with the children, to greet them, to give instructions, to comfort and admonish. The deficiency with this type of bilingualism is that there is no policy or aim to preserve and promote the minority language. The aim is to use the minority language temporarily to ease the transition to the official or majority language in preparation for formal schooling. (See Pre-school Education in Alsace, page 488.)

Monolingual nursery education that develops bilingualism

Bilingual nursery education can also include a second category of schools, where only one language is used, but where the outcome or stated aim is the development of bilingualism within the children. This is often the case in regions where minority language speech communities exist.

In monolingual minority language nursery schools, children from minority language homes have the opportunity to consolidate and strengthen their language skills in a wider context before coming into contact with the majority language at school. In monolingual minority language nursery schools, the child is shielded from the overpowering, all-pervasive influence of the majority language. The child's first language skills are given a chance to develop further, and also the child's cognitive skills are allowed to develop through the medium of the first language. Seeing the home language in a position of status and respect may also give the child confidence and an enhanced self-image.

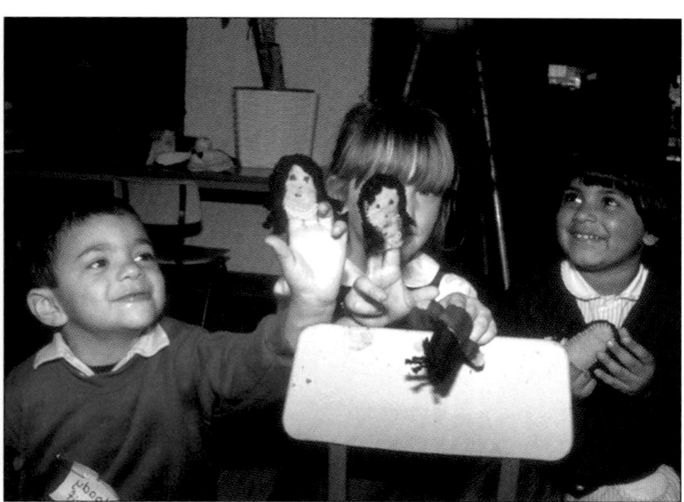

Monolingual minority language nursery schools ideally exist as a precursor to a complete program of bilingual or heritage language education. However, where there is no statutory provision for minority language education, minority language activists may initiate a nursery school movement as a first step towards a complete bilingual educational system. This has happened in Brittany for instance, with the *Diwan* movement. *Diwan* originally started as an independent Breton language pre-school movement for children aged between two and six. As the first group of *Diwan* children began primary education, *Diwan* primary schools were established wherever funds and parental support permitted. The first *Diwan* secondary school has now been established in the city of Brest.

Nursery education may also be a way of developing bilingualism in children who are monolingual in the majority language of a country. Parents who do not speak a minority language, or a second majority language, may wish their children to learn it, for economic, social, cultural or ideological reasons.

In Canada, since 1965, many anglophone parents have sent their children to special French language Immersion schools from kindergarten onwards. The beginning of the Canadian 'early total Immersion' movement is discussed in detail in the topic on 'Immersion bilingual education' (see page 496). Briefly, in 'early total Immersion', English-speaking children are educated entirely in French in kindergarten and the first or second year of primary education. From the second or third year of primary onwards, English is gradually introduced.

Canadian Immersion education has provided a model for other countries seeking to introduce majority language children to a minority language at an early age. In New Zealand, Maori language nursery schools and primary schools (*kohanga reo* and *kura kaupapa*) and in Wales, *Mudiad Ysgolion Meithrin* (Welsh language Nursery Schools Movement) and Welsh-medium primary schools in Anglicized areas, have benefited from the Canadian experience.

Characteristics and Language Aims of Effective or 'Strong' Bilingual Nursery Education

As we have seen, types of bilingual pre-school provision can be divided into two main groups. The first group contains majority language schools that make no use, or only limited and temporary use, of the first language of minority language children. This group can be described as a 'weak' form of bilingual education. The second

Mudiad Ysgolion Meithrin – The Welsh Language Nursery Schools Movement

In the small country of Wales, in the United Kingdom, the ancient Celtic language of Welsh is still spoken by approximately a fifth of the population of two and a half million. Since the late 1940s, the growing use of Welsh in education has strengthened the position of the language in its struggle against the influence of English. At that time, the first designated Welsh-medium primary schools were established in Anglicized areas. In the early 1960s, the first designated Welsh-medium secondary school was opened near Cardiff. During this period there was also a growing use of Welsh as a medium of education in primary and secondary schools serving Welsh-speaking communities. Alongside the development of Welsh-medium education, there was a recognition of the need to encourage the learning and use of Welsh among pre-school children, to prepare them for bilingual education. It was felt that Welsh-speaking children would benefit from the opportunity to socialize with other Welsh speakers and from the use of their language in a wider context. For Welsh learners, it would be advantageous to acquire the basics of Welsh as early as possible, in preparation for Welsh-medium education.

By 1970 over 60 *cylchoedd meithrin* ('nursery circles') had been established, catering for children aged between two and a half and school age. In September 1971, *Mudiad Ysgolion Meithrin* (The Welsh language Nursery Schools Movement) was officially established in Aberystwyth, Wales. The aims of the Movement were twofold: firstly, to establish and support Welsh-medium nursery education and secondly, to support and promote Welsh education. It was recognized that nursery education through the medium of Welsh could only be valuable within the context of a complete system of Welsh-medium education.

The goal of the *cylch meithrin* is to promote the education of pre-school children by providing the opportunity for children to develop physically, mentally, emotionally and socially through various forms of play and structured activities. All activities are carried out through the medium of Welsh. These might include free play with equipment such as tricycles, tractors and climbing frames, painting, coloring or craft work, doing puzzles and jigsaws, building with bricks or threading beads, singing, dancing, playing shop, telling stories and having discussions. Sessions normally last for two to two and a half hours, either in the morning or the afternoon, and children normally attend between two and four sessions per week.

Mudiad Ysgolion Meithrin tries to attract trained nursery or primary teachers to run its local groups. Comprehensive training courses that include studies of child development and language acquisition are held in every county. In Anglicized areas, where a high proportion of the children attending the *cylch meithrin* are English speakers, the teachers use Immersion techniques to introduce the language to children. In largely Welsh-speaking areas, peripatetic second language teachers visit local groups to advise teachers on the needs of Welsh learners. They also hold sessions with Welsh learners to improve their basic language skills by means of various activities.

Between 1987 and 1991, the organization produced a range of pre-school material for Immersion teaching through playgroups, including a handbook for teachers, teaching aids and audio-cassettes.

During the 1980s, *Mudiad Ysgolion Meithrin* began to target an even younger group of children, those too young to attend a *cylch meithrin*. Many *cylchoedd meithrin* now have an affiliated mother and toddler group, called *Cylch Ti a Fi* (literally 'You and I Circle'). This extends the opportunity to socialize in Welsh to an even younger group of Welsh-speaking children, and gives children from English-speaking homes, and their parents, the chance to learn a little Welsh, and to prepare for the *cylch meithrin*.

Since the 1970s, *Mudiad Ysgolion Meithrin* has received a yearly government grant, partly in recognition of its pioneering work in bilingualism. However, this is not sufficient to finance the work entirely. Local circles still rely largely on children's fees (these are deliberately kept low to give access to children from all socioeconomic backgrounds) and fund-raising activities. Teachers' salaries are relatively low and this makes it difficult to attract trained teachers of suitable caliber. Many group leaders create a rich linguistic environment for the children, that facilitates first language development and second language acquisition. However, due to a lack of money, it is not always possible to hold sufficient sessions, and thus children's contact hours with Welsh are limited.

In Anglicized areas of Wales, it has often been difficult to find Welsh speakers to lead *cylchoedd meithrin*. One imaginative solution to this problem has been the establishment of a Link Course at the University of Glamorgan, near Cardiff. The course gives non-Welsh-speaking parents the opportunity to learn Welsh for four mornings a week and to follow a training course for *cylchoedd meithrin* teachers on the fifth morning. The Link Course lasts for a year, and has been a successful means of ensuring that there are sufficient teachers for *cylchoedd meithrin* in Cardiff and the surrounding area.

Mudiad Ysgolion Meithrin has overcome a variety of practical problems and has grown in strength and professionalism over the last decades, ensuring that many thousands of Welsh children are well prepared for Welsh-medium education.

group contains those nursery schools, whether bilingual or monolingual in a minority language, that aim to develop and promote children's bilingualism. This group can be described as a 'strong', or effective form of bilingual nursery education. Strong bilingual nursery education has two main language aims.

1. It aims to strengthen and consolidate the mother tongue of children from minority language homes, often as a first step in bilingual or heritage language education.

2. It aims to help children from majority language homes to acquire the fundamentals of a minority language or a second majority language, often as a first step in bilingual or Immersion education.

Consolidation and reinforcement of the mother tongue

Some children from minority language homes have a less stimulating language experience than children from monolingual majority language homes in the same region. Minority language children (e.g. in-migrants, refugees, children of guest workers) do not always experience their language in a rich variety of contexts, in the shops, in different social situations, in the media. Minority language parents may occasionally be illiterate in their language, or may not have easy access to children's books in the minority language. In some minority language homes, the majority language may have encroached upon many of the functions of the minority language. This is where an effective nursery school can play an important role.

In an effective minority language nursery school or playgroup, the teacher will be a fluent and articulate speaker of the minority language. He or she will aim to provide a rich and diverse linguistic and cultural experience for the children. Games, songs, stories, discussions, cookery, crafts, birthday celebrations, cultural festivals and excursions into the community: all these can be a means of enriching the child's language.

It is crucial for the child who speaks a minority language to see that the minority language is given status and importance outside the home. The child improves language competencies and develops cognitive skills through the medium of the home language.

Second language acquisition by children from majority language homes

It is a common belief that young children learn languages easily. Adults who have struggled for years in school lessons or at night classes to gain competence in a foreign language are often envious at the way small children seem to 'pick up' a first, second or even third language with relative ease.

However, research has suggested the relationship between language learning and age is not so simple. Studies have shown that, because of their superior ability to analyze and process information, older children and adults often learn language more efficiently than young children. (See the topic on Age and Bilingualism, page 658.) However, for adults, lack of motivation and lack of time can be a problem. Psychological factors such as shyness, self-consciousness or negative attitudes towards the target language can hinder or obstruct learning. Older children and adults are used to expressing complex thoughts and abstract concepts in their first language. They are often frustrated at their inability to achieve this in the target language. If second language learning takes place in a classroom environment, it is not always easy for a second language teacher to present the target language in a way that is relevant and authentic.

For these reasons, there is increasing awareness of the value of introducing second and third languages to children at an early age. The world of a small child is simple and concrete. The child's language needs are simple and are linked to everyday activities, familiar people and objects, and happenings that affect the child directly. A second language can also be acquired quite naturally and incidentally during day-to-day activities and in interaction with other people. An effective way of teaching a second language to a child is to use the language with the child in daily living, while eating, drinking, playing with toys, singing, telling stories, painting, gardening, cooking, shopping and so on. Motivation is not a problem because such interesting activities are intrinsically motivating. The level of language required is not high, and comprehension is not a problem because the language is used in concrete and familiar contexts, with plenty of visual stimuli. This is the principle underlying the methods of French 'early Immersion' teaching in Canada, that have been emulated in many other countries. The basic principles of Immersion teaching are discussed more fully in the section on Immersion Education (see page 496), and are summarized below.

1. The teacher always uses the target language with the children, but uses simplified, repetitive speech, making use of gestures, mime and intonation. The teacher reiterates vocabulary and structures in different contexts. (The teacher may make some use of the students' first language during the early months, but generally in tandem with a translation into the target language).

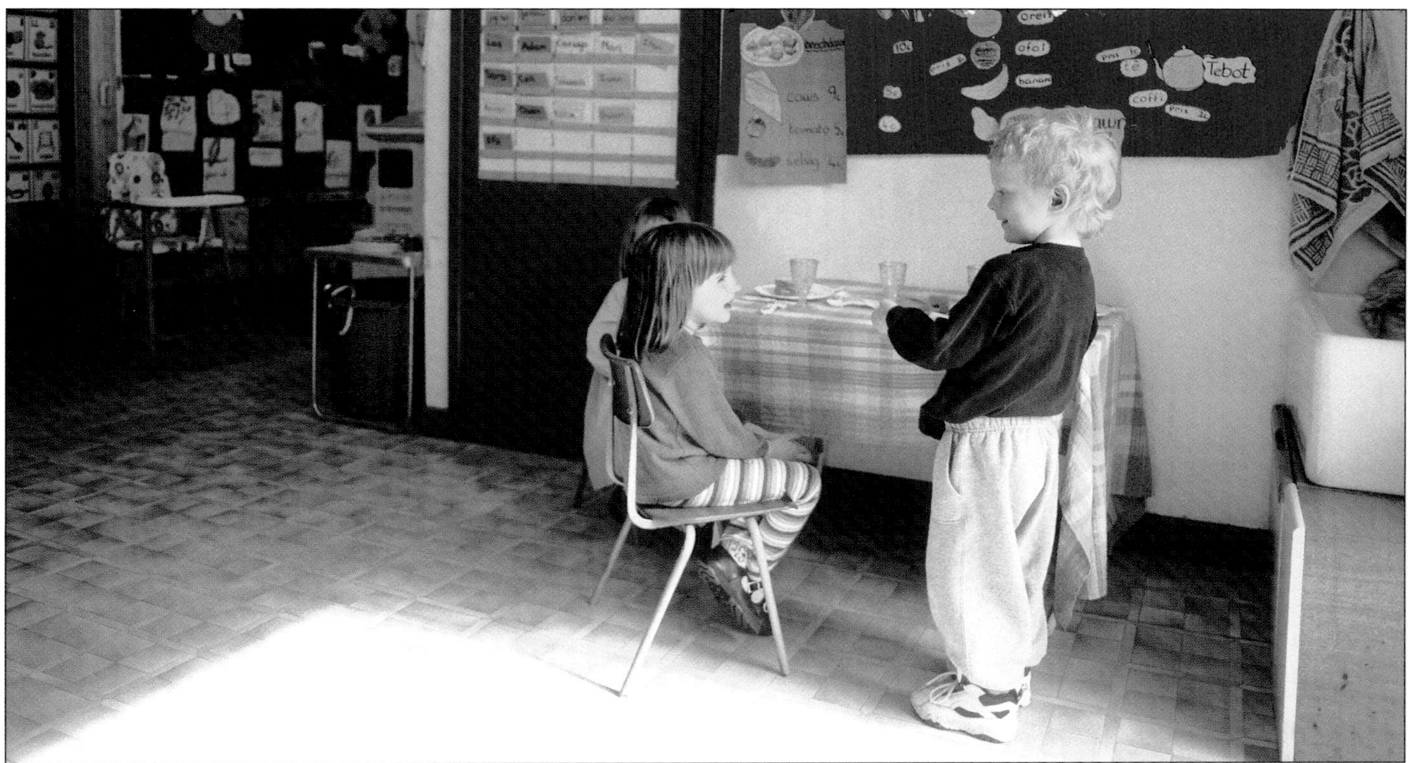

A private Welsh nursery school in Caernarfon, North Wales, attended by Welsh speakers and Welsh learners.

2. The teacher makes use of visual aids and other objects and materials to aid comprehension.

3. Children learn the target language, not by studying the language as a subject, but by playing and engaging in interesting activities through the medium of the language.

Other places with second language programs for preschool and primary children, such as Wales, New Zealand, Brittany and the Basque country, use a similar approach to Canadian 'early Immersion' learning. Many dual language schools and international schools use these methods to introduce a second language to their children at kindergarten or nursery level.

Linguistically mixed classes

A kindergarten class often does not consist solely of native speakers of a language or second language learners, but a mixture of the two. It is important, in such situations, that there are adequate resources to cater for the linguistic needs of both groups of children. This means, in practical terms, sufficient trained staff to work with the children in a structured program of activities, sometimes in separate groups and sometimes together.

When a large proportion of the class are second language learners from majority-language homes, the language of play and peer interaction naturally tends to be the majority language. This situation tends to exist in Immersion education, and is a limitation of the system. In a linguistically mixed class it is important that native speakers of the minority language are not overwhelmed by majority language speakers. There is a need for dynamic, imaginative teachers, adequate staffing and a carefully structured program to ensure that the native speakers have sufficient input in the minority language. This might involve some separate activities in a smaller group, at a higher language level, and sufficient one-to-one interaction in the minority language. Where the majority of the class are native speakers, there might be group work for the learners, learning colors, numbers or basic phrases through simple games and activities.

Where nursery schools operate in two languages, there is often a deliberate policy to admit reasonably equal numbers of native speakers of both languages. This ensures that one language does not swamp the other. Teachers in the kindergarten sections of dual language schools and international schools are usually well trained in the teaching of both native speakers and learners. First and second language speakers are often taught in separate groups in kindergarten, coming together for some activities. Thus, the children's language needs are not met at the expense of integration.

Language Shift Among Pre-school Language Minority Children in the US

In recent years, there has been concern amongst educators, the government and much of the public in the US about what has been perceived as the problem of non-English-speaking in-migrant families to the country. It has been acknowledged that it is necessary for the children of these in-migrants to learn English to participate in education and employment. There has been concern about the low attainment of many in-migrant children in English, that seems to affect their performance across the curriculum. Consequently many of these children drop out early from school and fail to graduate from high school.

One perceived solution to this problem is that such children should be taught English as early as possible, preferably in pre-school programs. The argument is that early childhood is an advantageous time to learn a second language. The expectation is that such children will have gained competence in English by the time they enter elementary education and will not be disadvantaged.

Academics, however, have been increasingly concerned at the possible negative consequences of introducing English to in-migrant children at too young an age. During the 1990 conference of the National Association for Bilingual Education, a group of experts initiated a national survey to document the negative consequences of English-medium pre-school education for language minority children. Over 1000 families were interviewed, whose languages included Spanish, Korean, Japanese, Chinese, Khmer and Vietnamese.

Allowing for a number of variables (e.g. length of residence in the US, ages of children in the family), a clear pattern emerged in the survey. It was evident that, in families where children received their pre-school education exclusively or partly through the medium of English, there was a greater shift to using English, by children speaking to adults, by children speaking to one another, and by adults speaking to children, than in families where pre-school children were educated exclusively through their mother tongue. This had a number of worrying consequences.

The home language of the children tends to decline

Pre-school children aged three or four years old have not obtained complete competence in their mother tongue. They are consequently very vulnerable to the influence of English at nursery school, and tend to shift to using English quite quickly, speaking it not only at school but also in the home. The development of their home language is impaired. The children are also vulnerable to the high social status and predominance of English. They hear the language not only at nursery school, but on television, in the cinema and in the community. They wish to assimilate into the community, consequently they choose to speak English. They make less and less use of their home language, which becomes atrophied and is sometimes totally lost.

The children's English may not develop properly

In many schools with large numbers of in-migrant children learning a majority language, the children have insufficient contact with good models of the target, majority language. Thus, they tend to speak an imperfect version of the majority language to one another which becomes the norm. In addition, pre-school language minority children being educated in the majority language often opt to speak the majority language at home, before they have become fully competent in it. Their parents may have a very poor command of English, but they may try to speak it to the children. This may be because the children are no longer able to speak or understand the minority language with any degree of competence. It may also happen because the parents themselves are aware of the importance of English, and mistakenly believe that they are helping the children by switching from the minority language, which they speak fluently, to English, of which they have little knowledge. Misinformed teachers may also encourage in-migrant parents (who may have little competence in English), to speak English to their children in the home. Thus both children and adults are speaking a language in which they have little competence, and an imperfect and inadequate model of English is perpetuated.

There may be negative consequences for the child's educational development across the curriculum

If the child enters primary school with neither the home language nor English sufficiently developed to cope with the demands of the curriculum, this can create an immediate pattern of failure that may continue throughout the child's school career. Early experiences of failure may become expectations of failure that become self-fulfilling.

Problems can be created in family relationships

If adults in a US language minority family have little English, and if the children fail to develop an adequate command of the native language, then communication problems and interpersonal problems can result. Parents and other adults in a caretaker role may find it difficult to discuss problems with their children, give advice and convey their own personal, cultural and religious values to the next generation. This can have serious consequences for parent-child relationships, for the stability of the family and for the development of the child as a whole person.

In Lily Wong Fillmore's report (1991a) on the conclusions of the survey, she tells a tragic story of fractured family relationships within a Korean in-migrant family in the US. The Korean language requires the marking of many levels of deference in ordinary speech. Choice of vocabulary and grammatical structures depend on the relationship of the speaker to the person addressed. In this particular family the children had stopped speaking Korean, although the parents spoke little English. Communication between parents and children was not easy, but there were no outward conflicts, until the children's grandfather came to stay from Korea. Since he spoke no English, the children tried to speak Korean with him. Unfortunately, they had forgotten many aspects of the language, including the complex ways of expressing courtesy and respect for an honored elder relative. The grandfather was shocked at what the children's apparent rudeness and scolded his son - the children's father- for not bringing them up properly. The children's father did what he felt was his duty. He took a stick and beat the children for their rudeness and lack of respect. The children's bruises were noticed in school and they were taken into protective custody. Lily Wong Fillmore (1991a) remarks: 'What was sad was that no one seemed to realize the role language played in this family drama' (page 344).

Lily Wong Fillmore (1991a) addresses the question of the best time for language minority children to learn English: 'Does this suggest that we should abandon English in programs for language-minority children? Not at all. The problem is timing, not English. The children have to learn English, but they should not be required to do so until their native languages are stable enough to handle the inevitable encounter with English and all it means. Even then, teachers and parents must work together to try to mitigate the harm that can be done to children when they discover that differences are not welcome in the social world represented by the school. Parents need to be warned of the consequences of not insisting that their children speak to them in the language of the home. Teachers should be aware of the harm they can do when they tell parents that they should encourage their children to speak English at home, and that they themselves should try to use English when they talk to their children.' (pages 345-6).

Pre-Primary Education in the Lesser Used Languages of Europe

In recent years, two important studies have been published on the situation of pre-primary education in regional or minority languages in Europe. The first, commissioned by the European Commission and conducted by Helen Ó Murchú, was published in 1987 under the title *Pre-primary Education in Some Lesser Used Languages.* The report contains information about pre-primary education in 29 language communities in 11 member states. A more recent report was conducted by Mercator-Education and published in 1994, under the title *Pre-Primary Education – An Inventory of the Current Position of Lesser Used Languages in Pre-Primary Education in Some Member States of the European Union* (Van der Groot *et al.*, 1994a, 1994b). It contains data on the situation of pre-school provision in 17 regional languages in five countries of the European Union.

The conclusions of both reports are similar and can be summarized briefly as follows:

Regional autonomy is an important factor in the effectiveness of minority language pre-school provision. If a region is given the power to make decisions concerning language policy and if the legal status of the minority language is assured, then it is easier to establish appropriate pre-school provision and to finance it adequately. In the Spanish province of Catalonia, where 68 percent of the population speak Catalan, as well as Castilian Spanish, the Generalitat or provincial government has autonomy over education. An effective system of bilingual education has been established, starting at kindergarten between the ages of three and six. Children receive their pre-school and primary education in Catalan, although children from Spanish-speaking homes can opt to be taught in Spanish by an individual teacher within the classroom. Few children take up this option, and there is an effective program of linguistic immersion in Catalan for children whose first language is Spanish.

The most appropriate form of pre-school education for minority language communities is monolingual minority language education. This is the best way of safeguarding the language development of language minority children and of teaching the minority language to language majority children. In a monolingual minority language nursery school, the status, prestige and development of the language is safeguarded from the influence of the dominant majority language. Bilingual minority/majority language nursery education does not tend to be so effective in the maintenance of the minority language because the influence of the dominant language is so strong.

Monolingual minority language education tends to have wider effects than the maintenance and development of the language among children. Within the minority language community, it can lead to an increased awareness of the value of the minority language and a greater commitment to its maintenance, both within the family and in public life. Within the wider (majority language) community it can lead to a reaction of hostility, but also, in many cases, to a new respect for the minority language and an awareness of others' linguistic rights. The linguistic objectives of monolingual minority language education are clear, and this makes more impact on the wider community. This may lead to policy changes and to greater public status for the minority language.

Monolingual minority language pre-school education can only be fully effective if it forms part of a complete program of minority language/bilingual education. If a child progresses from minority language pre-school education to majority language primary education, the development of the minority language is arrested and the child from a minority language home is expected to 'sink or swim' in a majority language classroom. According to a Mercator-Education report, this abrupt discontinuity can have serious effects on the language development of children (Van der Groot *et al.,* 1994a).

Helen Ó Murchú

Helen Ó Murchú was educated in Rathkeale, County Limerick in Ireland, and later at the University College, Cork and Trinity College, Dublin. She was a founder member of the European Bureau for Lesser Used Languages, serving as its first Honorary Secretary, and then as President from 1992 to 1995. As a driving force for the status and maintenance of lesser used languages in Europe, Helen Ó Murchú has made an important contribution in Europe through her writing and political activity. She is expert on the changing European political relationships between state and voluntary activity to support language minorities. Apart from teaching at the elementary, secondary and higher education levels, she has worked with the Irish language planning statutory body *Bord na Gaeilge*, the Congress of Voluntary Organizations for Irish, the Council of Europe and the World Organization for Early Childhood Education.

Helen Ó Murchú is well-known for a monograph entitled *Pre-Primary Education in Some European Lesser Used Languages* which was published in 1987 by the Commission of the European Communities through the European Bureau for Lesser Used Languages. This provided a well researched, detailed and influential examination of language reproduction through pre-primary education, and raised the status and importance of this activity in the field of language maintenance. She also researched and co-authored the *Notional-Functional Syllabus for Adult Learners of Irish* and an accompanying volume for school learners.

Factors Affecting the Success of Bilingual Nursery Education

Bilingual nursery education should not introduce a second language at the expense of a child's home language

Where a child's home, minority language is only used sporadically and incidentally in nursery education, or not at all, and is supplanted by an official majority language, bilingualism is not being fostered. This is a subtractive bilingual situation, where one language develops at the expense of another.

Bilingual nursery education should aim to create an additive bilingual situation, where a second language does not develop at the cost of the home, native language. For instance, where majority language children attend kindergarten 'total Immersion' programs, the development of the home, majority language is not endangered, because of its high social value and influence. Similarly, minority language children should have the opportunity to consolidate their home language in nursery education, without encountering the majority language too soon. This is the best way of assuring the satisfactory development of both languages in the long term.

Ideally, bilingual, second language or minority language nursery education should exist as part of a structured program of bilingual education

A child who speaks a minority language has the opportunity to strengthen competence, and confidence in the home language. This child is thus better equipped to enter formal education, where teaching will take place in both minority and majority languages. A child who speaks a majority language at home has the chance to learn the basics of a second (minority or majority) language, as the first step in an Immersion or dual language program.

The effectiveness of bilingual nursery education depends to an extent on adequate material provision, funding and legislation. For instance, many minority language nursery schools are privately run and financed largely by voluntary contributions and children's fees. This may create problems of finding adequate premises and equipment. Teachers' salaries can also be meager and employment is usually part-time so it is not always easy to attract trained and well-motivated staff. Where there is no legislation for bilingual pre-school education, local provision may depend on the commitment of language activists and parents to set up, run and provide students for nursery groups.

Where there is adequate funding and legislation, on the other hand, free bilingual nursery schools for all children in the appropriate age group can be provided. These will usually include suitable premises and equipment and well-trained staff. However, meager material conditions may still allow effective bilingual nursery provision if teacher skills and the enthusiasm of committed parents and administrators are high.

Children learning a second language in nursery school will develop varying degrees of competence in that language, according to the quantity and quality of the provision

Parents who send their children to a nursery school to learn a second language are often disappointed that their children seem to make little apparent progress. However, proficiency in a second language demands many contact hours with that language. For instance, if a child spends eight hours a week between the ages of two and four in a minority language nursery group, before going on to bilingual elementary education, that child might not speak the language fluently. What the child will probably have acquired, however, is a good passive competence in the language (i.e. the ability to understand a second language). If the child proceeds to full-time bilingual or Immersion education, this passive competence will soon transform into active speaking ability. On the other hand, if a child spends a year or two in a full-time kindergarten total Immersion program, that child will probably speak the second language quite well upon entry to primary school. It may take several years of full-time Immersion education for a child to develop fluency that approximates to that of native speakers.

The quality of the provision is also a factor in children's language development. The competence of staff in the language, the ratio of staff to children, the ability of the staff to interact with the children, the variety of interesting and attractive activities available, staff training in techniques of language presentation both to first language and second language speakers: all these factors will affect the rate of children's language development in the nursery school.

Further Reading

ARNBERG, L., 1987, *Raising Children Bilingually: The Pre-school Years*. Clevedon: Multilingual Matters Ltd.

BAKER, C., 1995, *A Parents' and Teachers' Guide to Bilingualism*. Clevedon: Multilingual Matters Ltd.

Ó MURCHÚ, H., 1987, *Overview and Synthesis of Dossiers Established on Some Forms of Current Pre-primary Provision in Lesser Used Languages in EC Member States* (Commission of the European Communities). Dublin: European Bureau of Lesser Used Languages, Dublin.

WONG FILLMORE L., 1991, When Learning a Second Language Means Losing the First. *Early Childhood Research Quarterly*, 6, 323-346.

2: Immersion Bilingual Education

Introduction

Submersion, Withdrawal Classes and Transitional approaches are often given the title of bilingual education. This is because such schemes contain bilingual children. This can be described as a 'weak' form of bilingual education because bilingualism is not fostered in school. Such education does not by aim, content or structure have bilingualism as a defined outcome. The types of bilingual education discussed in this subsection all have bilingualism as an intended outcome, and therefore represent 'strong' forms of bilingual education.

Immersion bilingual education derives from Canadian educational experiments. The Immersion movement started in St. Lambert, Montreal, in 1965. Some disgruntled English-speaking, middle class parents persuaded school district administrators to set up an experimental kindergarten class of 26 children. The aims were for students (1) to become competent to speak, read and write in French; (2) to reach normal achievement levels throughout the curriculum including the English language; (3) to appreciate the traditions and culture of French-speaking Canadians as well as English-speaking Canadians. In short, the aims were for children to become bilingual and bicultural without loss of achievement.

The St. Lambert experiment suggested that the aims were met. Attitudes and achievement were not hindered by the Immersion experience. Tucker & d'Anglejan (1972, page 19) summarized the outcomes as follows:

> 'the experimental students appear to be able to read, write, speak, understand, and use English as well as youngsters instructed in English in the conventional manner. In addition and at no cost they can also read, write, speak and understand French in a way that English students who follow a traditional program of French as a second language never do.'

Types of Immersion Bilingual Education

Immersion education is an umbrella term. Within the concept of Immersion experience are various Canadian programs differing in terms of the following:

Age at which a child commences the experience. This may be at the kindergarten or infant stage (**early** Immersion); at nine to ten years old (delayed or **middle** Immersion), or at secondary level (**late** Immersion).

Amount of **time** spent in Immersion in a day. **Total** Immersion usually commences with 100 percent immersion in the second language, after two or three years reducing to 80 percent for the next three or four years, finishing junior schooling with approximately 50 percent immersion. **Partial** Immersion provides close to 50 percent immersion in the second language throughout infant and junior schooling. **Early Total Immersion** is the most popular entry level program, followed by late and then partial Immersion (Canadian Education Association, 1992). The histograms on the following page illustrate several possibilities, with many other variations around these.

The Success of Immersion Education

Since 1965, Immersion bilingual education has spread rapidly in Canada. There are currently around 300,000 English-speaking Canadian children in some 2000 French Immersion schools. This represents some six percent of the total school population in Canada. What are the essential reasons for this speedy educational growth?

First, Immersion in Canada aims at bilingualism in two prestigious, majority languages (French and English). This relates to an additive bilingual situation. Students acquire French at no cost to their home language and culture. Such enrichment may be contrasted with subtractive bilingual situations (see page 154) where the home minority language is replaced by the second, majority language (e.g. Spanish-speaking children in the US who attend monolingual English schools). In such a subtractive, assimilationist environment, negative rather than positive effects may occur in school performance and self-esteem. Although such an approach has been termed 'Immersion' or 'Structured Immersion', 'submersion' is a more appropriate term.

Second, Immersion bilingual education in Canada has been optional, not compulsory. Parents choose to send

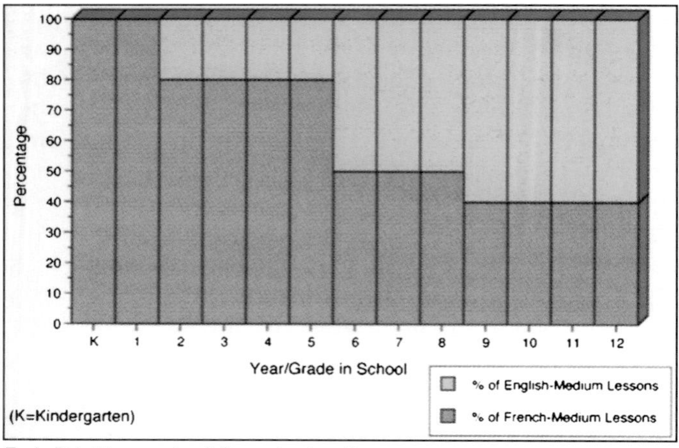

Early Total Immersion bilingual education.

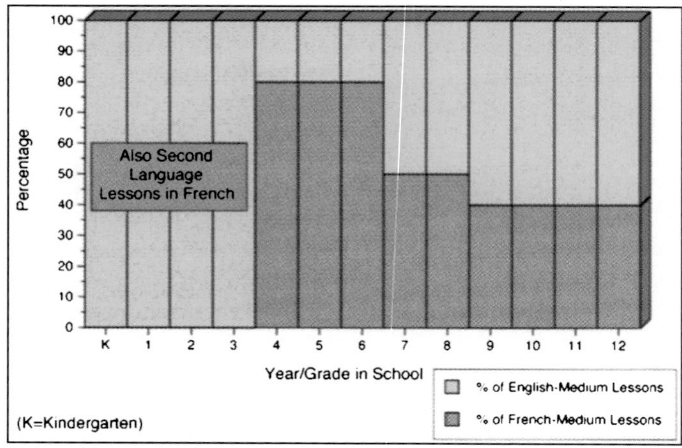

Delayed Immersion bilingual education.

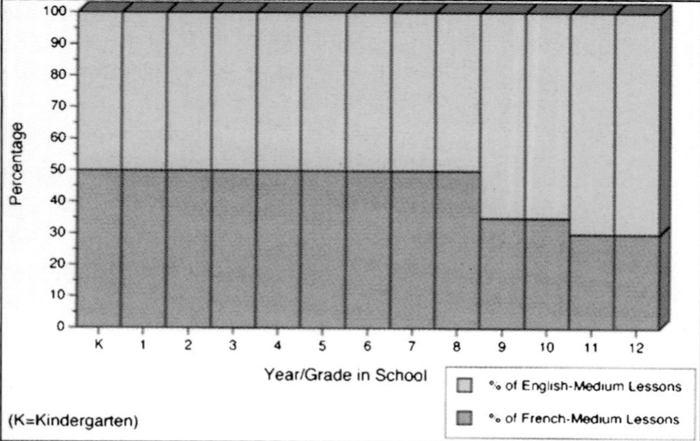

Early Partial Immersion bilingual education.

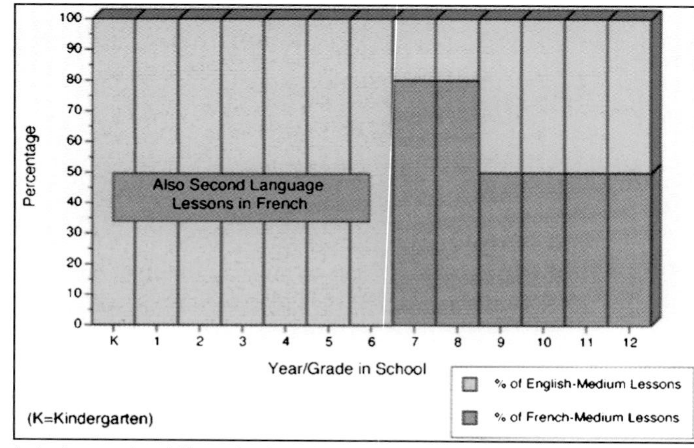

Late Immersion bilingual education.

their children to such schools. The convictions of parents plus the commitment and enthusiasm of the teachers may aid the motivation of students. French Immersion parents tend to be middle class, involved in school-teacher-parent committees, and take a sustained interest in their children's progress. Immersion education in Canada has, from its beginnings in Montreal in 1965 to the present, been powerfully promoted by parents. Most Immersion teachers are enthusiastically committed to bilingual education and to developing bilingualism in society. Roberts (1985) suggests the importance of teacher commitment in minority language medium education.

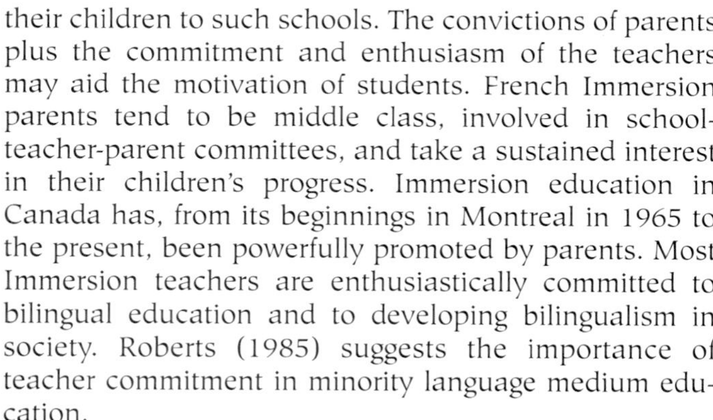

Third, children in early Immersion are often allowed to use their home language for up to one and a half years for classroom communication. There is no compulsion to speak French in the playground or dining hall. The child's home language is appreciated and not belittled.

Fourth, the teachers are competent bilinguals, with native or native-like proficiency in both French and English. They speak to the children almost entirely in French but are able to understand the children speaking in their home language. Teachers are thus important language models through their status and power, identifying French with something of value.

Fifth, most of the students are monolingual and start Immersion education with a similar lack of experience of the second language. Students commencing schooling with relatively homogeneous language skills not only simplify the teacher's task, they also reduce the risk to their self-esteem and classroom motivation that may arise from other students being linguistically more expert.

Sixth, students in Immersion education experience the same curriculum as mainstream 'core' students.

Research on the Success of Immersion Bilingual Education

The various reviews of Canadian Immersion tend to paint a relatively uniform picture. The overviews of

Swain & Lapkin (1982), the California State Department of Education (1984), and Genesee (1983, 1984b,1987) highlight four major outcomes of Canadian Immersion bilingual education.

Second language (French) learning

It is easy to predict that Immersion students will surpass those in mainstream (core) programs who are given 'drip-feed' French lessons for 30 minutes a day. Most students in early total Immersion programs approach native-like performance in French at around 11 years old in receptive language skills (listening and reading). Such levels are not so well attained in the productive skills of speaking and writing (Lapkin, Swain & Shapson, 1990).

First language (English) learning

Research has shown consistently that achievement in French is not reached at the cost of attainment in English.

For the first four years of early total Immersion, students tend not to progress in English as do monolingual English students in mainstream classes. Reading, spelling and punctuation, for example, are not so well advanced. Since such children are usually not given English language instruction for one, two or three years after starting school, these results are to be expected. However, the initial pattern does not last. After approximately six years of schooling, early total Immersion children have caught up with their monolingual peers in English language skills. By the end of elementary schooling, the early total Immersion experience has generally not affected first language speaking and writing development. Parents of Immersion children tend to perceive the same positive effects in their children.

Indeed, when differences in English language achievement between Immersion and mainstream children have been located by research, it is often in favor of Immersion students (Swain & Lapkin, 1982; Swain & Lapkin, 1991a). This finding links with the topic on Bilingualism and Intelligence that discussed the possible cognitive advantages consequential from bilingualism. If bilingualism permits increased linguistic awareness, more flexibility in thought, more internal inspection of language, such cognitive advantages may help to explain the favorable English progress of early Immersion students.

Early partial Immersion students also tend to lag behind for three or four years in their English language skills. Their performance is little different from that of total early Immersion students, which is surprising since early partial Immersion education has more English language content. By the end of elementary schooling, early partial Immersion children catch up with mainstream peers in English language attainment. Unlike early total Immersion students, partial Immersion children do not tend to surpass mainstream comparison groups in English language achievement. Similarly, late Immersion has no detrimental effect on English language skills (Genesee, 1983).

The evidence suggests that Immersion children learn French at no cost to their English. Indeed, not only is there the gain of a second language, there is also evidence to suggest that Immersion results in possible extra benefits in English proficiency.

Other curriculum areas

If Immersion education results in children becoming bilingual in French and English, the question is whether this is at the cost of achievement in other curriculum areas, such as Mathematics and Science, History and Geography? The reviews of research suggest that early total Immersion students generally perform as well in these subjects as do mainstream children. That is, achievement in the curriculum is typically not adversely affected by early total Immersion bilingual education.

The evaluations of early partial Immersion education are not quite so positive. When children in early partial Immersion learn Mathematics and Science through the

Fred Genesee

Fred Genesee is a Canadian scholar, educated at the University of Western Ontario and McGill University in Montreal, Quebec. A prolific author of articles, chapters, reviews and books, he is widely acknowledged as an expert on second language immersion programs as well as on the psychological and neuro-psychological aspects of bilingualism and second language learning. One of his most distinguished books is entitled *Learning Through Two Languages: Studies of Immersion and Bilingual Education.* This provides a wide-ranging study of immersion in Canada and the United States, covering educational, psychological, sociocultural and political aspects of immersion bilingual education.

The First Immersion Teacher

Canadian Immersion schooling came into being in 1965, as the result of a determined campaign by a group of English-speaking parents in the town of Saint Lambert in Quebec, Canada. These parents all wished their children to be educated bilingually, and in 1963 they formed a pressure group 'Saint Lambert Parents for Bilingual Education'. For two years, they waged a struggle with the Chambly County School Board for permission to experiment with a kindergarten Immersion class, where English-speaking children could be taught through the medium of French. School board members were concerned that this would have an adverse effect on the development of the children's competence in English. The parents brought in language specialists to support their case. The famous Montreal neurosurgeon Wilder Penfield and McGill University psychologists gave evidence in favor of Immersion.

In 1965, the battle was won and permission was granted to establish the first kindergarten Immersion class. The first teacher was appointed, a young French woman, Mme. Evelyne Billey-Lichon. Mme. Billey-Lichon was born in Saint-Germain-des-Bois in France in 1938. She began her teaching career in France in 1957. In 1961 she came to live in Canada, in Pointe-aux-Trembles, Quebec. For a year (1964–1965) she taught Saturday Art courses in French for English-speaking children, before being appointed as the teacher of the first Immersion class.

Mme. Billey-Lichon had three splendid qualifications for the post – an excellent command of French, some years' teaching experience, and very limited English. The parents obviously did not want her to translate into English for the children.

The first Immersion class was held in the Margaret Pendlebury school at Saint Lambert. Mme. Billey-Lichon has happy recollections of that first year. Because the class was a new experiment, the parents told her not to worry if half the class dropped out during the year. 'It turned out very well', she recalls. 'No one at all wanted to drop out. I have the most wonderful memories of it!'

After the first year, more teachers were hired to meet the growing demand for French Immersion education. Soon it became fashionable, with the majority of parents in Saint Lambert opting for Immersion education for their children, and with Immersion classes being established in other localities. During those first years, there was a spirit of pioneering zeal, and many, many visitors from other countries came to observe the revolutionary new experiment. One year, 165 people visited the classes.

Madame Billey-Lichon taught for six years, and then became pedagogical assistant for Immersion classes for the local School Board. Between 1973 and 1981, she was Assistant Principal at two French Immersion schools. She then expressed a wish to spend the final years of her career as a class teacher again. In 1986 she was assigned to a second grade Immersion class which she taught until her retirement in 1993.

Parents of the first Immersion students still remember and pay tribute to Mme. Billey-Lichon's superb teaching abilities. She was a pioneer in a teaching experiment that represented a milestone in bilingual education and that has provided a rationale for other developments in bilingual and second language education throughout the world.

Evelyne Billey-Lichon.

The first Immersion school at Saint Lambert.

medium of French, they tend to lag behind comparable mainstream children, at least initially. This may be because their French skills are insufficiently developed to be able to think mathematically and scientifically in their second language.

The results for late Immersion are similar. The important factor appears to be whether second language skills (French) are sufficiently developed to cope with reasonably complex curriculum material. Johnson and Swain (1994) argue that there is a gap in second language proficiency that needs bridging when students move from learning a language as a subject to learning through that second language. The more demanding the curriculum area, the higher the level of learning expected, and the later the switch to learning through a second language, the more important it is to provide 'bridging' programs. Such bridging programs ease the discrepancy between second language proficiency and the language proficiency required to understand the curriculum. A bridging program may require a language teacher and a content teacher (e.g. of Mathematics) to operate together.

The results overall suggest that bilingual education by an Immersion experience need not have negative effects on curriculum performance, particularly in early total Immersion programs. Indeed, most children gain a second language without cost to their performance in the curriculum. However, the key factor seems to be whether their language skills have evolved sufficiently in order to work in the curriculum in their second language.

Attitudes and social adjustment

Apart from performance throughout the curriculum, evaluations of Immersion education have examined whether immersion has positive or negative effects on students' motivation, attitude and study skills. The most positive results in this area have been found with early total Immersion students. Parents of such students tend to express satisfaction with their children's learning as well as their personal and social behavior. Early Immersion students also tend to have more positive attitudes towards themselves, their education and to French Canadians in comparison, for example, with late Immersion students. However the danger here is attributing the positive attitudes to schooling. The cause may alternatively be parental values and beliefs, home culture and environment.

Language Strategies in Immersion Classrooms

Immersion education is based on the idea that a first language is acquired relatively unconsciously. Children are unaware that they are learning a language in the home. Immersion attempts to replicate this process in the early years of schooling. The focus is on the content and not the form of the language. It is the task at hand that is central, not conscious language learning. In the early stages, there are no formal language learning classes, although simple elements of grammar such as verb endings may be taught informally. In the latter years of elementary schooling, formal consideration may be given to the rules of the language (e.g. grammar and syntax). The early stages of Immersion tend to mirror the unconscious acquisition of learning of the first language. Only later will a child be made conscious of language as a system, to reinforce and promote communication.

Immersion also tends to assume that the earlier a language is taught the better. While research has shown that teenagers and adults may learn a second language more efficiently, the evidence tends to suggest that young children acquire authentic pronunciation better than adults. Young children also seem to acquire a second language in a more painless, trouble-free manner, by means of play and activities. (This is discussed more fully in Age and Bilingualism, page 658). Thus, the argument for Immersion schooling tends to be, 'the earlier the better'.

At the beginning of Early French Immersion, the teacher concentrates on listening comprehension skills. Students are not made to speak French with their teacher or with their peers in the initial stages. Early insistence on French may inhibit children and cause them to develop negative attitudes to the French language and to education in general. Over the first two years, Immersion children develop an understanding of French and then begin to speak it, particularly to the teacher. 'Oral skills are given more importance in kindergarten to Grade 3; reading and writing skills, even though started as early as Grade 1, are stressed in Grades 4 to 6' (Canadian Education Association, 1992).

In these initial stages of Early French Immersion, it is crucial that the teacher is comprehensible to the children. The teacher needs to be sympathetically aware of the level of a child's vocabulary and grammar, to deliver in French at a level the child can understand, and simultaneously, be constantly pushing forward a child's competence in French. The teacher will be aiming to enlarge the frontiers of a child's French by ensuring that messages are both comprehensible and are slightly ahead of the learner's current level of competence in the language.

The language used to communicate with the child at these early stages is called caretaker speech. For the first year or two in French Immersion, the vocabulary will be deliberately limited. There will be a simplified presenta-

Immersion Education Throughout the World

With over a thousand research studies, Canadian Immersion bilingual education has been an educational experiment of unusual success and growth. It has influenced bilingual education in Europe and beyond. For example, with variations to suit regional and national contexts, the *Catalans* and *Basques* (Artigal, 1991, 1993, 1996; Bel, 1993) *Finnish* (Helle, 1994; Laurén, 1994; Manzer, 1993), *Japanese* (Hideo Oka, 1994; Kiyoshi Aihara, 1996; D. Thomas, 1996), *Australians* (Berthold, 1992; Caldwell & Berthold, 1995), the Gaelic speakers in *Scotland* (MacNeil, 1994), *Swiss* (Stotz & Andres, 1990), the *Welsh* and *Irish* (Baker, 1988 & 1993) and the *Maori* in New Zealand have emulated the experiment with similar success. In Catalonia, research indicates that Spanish-speaking children who follow an Immersion program not only become fluent in Catalan, but also their Spanish does not suffer. Throughout the curriculum, such Catalan Immersion children 'perform as well and sometimes better than their Hispanophone peers who do not' [follow an Immersion program] (Artigal, 1993, page 40-41). Similarly, the EIFE studies in the Basque Country show that their Model B Immersion program (50 percent Basque and 50 percent Spanish) has successful outcomes in bilingual proficiency (Sierra & Olaziregi, 1989).

When Immersion education is generalized to other countries, there are certain conditions that need keeping in mind.

Immersion bilingual education as practiced in Canada is optional not enforced. The convictions of teachers and parents and of the children themselves affect the ethos of the school and the motivation and achievement of the children. Immersion education will work best when there is conviction and not enforced conformity.

Immersion education in Canada starts with children who are at a similar level in their language skills. Such a homogeneous grouping of children may make the language classroom more efficient. Where there are wide variations in ability in a second language, teachers may have problems in providing an efficient and well-structured curriculum with equality of provision and opportunity. In Wales and Ireland, for instance, classes often contain a mixture of children whose home language is the minority language, and others whose home language is English, but whose parents are keen for them to be educated through the minority language. Some of the latter group may arrive in school having had a grounding in the minority language at nursery school. Others may start school monolingual in English. Such a heterogeneous situation can provide a considerable challenge for the teacher who seeks to meet the needs of native speakers and also to present the minority language to those with no knowledge of it.

The Irish and Welsh experience tend to suggest that most children whose home language is English will cope successfully in minority language Immersion classrooms. For such children, the language context is additive rather than subtractive. The danger is that the majority language of English, being the common denominator, will be the language used between students in the classroom, in the playground and certainly out of school. According to Lindholm (1990) 'To maintain an environment of educational and linguistic equity in the classroom, and to promote interactions among native and non-native English speakers, the most desirable ratio is 50 percent English speakers to 50 percent non-native English speakers' (page 100). However, Lindholm (1990) admits that little research has been conducted to determine the optimal classroom composition for successful bilingual education. The Irish and Welsh experience suggest that a greater proportion of minority language speakers may be essential to ensure that the 'common denominator' majority language does not always dominate in informal classroom and playground talk.

The Canadian Immersion experience ensures there is respect for the child's home language and culture. This relates to the additive bilingual situation. Parents have generally been seen as partners in the Immersion movement and some dialogue has existed with administrators, teachers and researchers.

Immersion teachers in Canada tend to be committed to Immersion education. Research in Wales has also pointed to the crucial importance of teacher commitment to bilingual education in enhancing achievement in school (Roberts, 1985).

Immersion Bilingual Education in Australia

In Australia, English is the only official language. As in the UK and the United States, much value is placed on English by the community, educationalists and politicians, and English is centrally regarded as sufficient for all practical purposes, and for education and employment in particular.

Despite such a strong English orientation, bilingual education in Australia has a history and a tradition. In the 19th century, for example, Lutheran church schools taught various subjects in German as well as English. Prior to the First World War, there were 49 bilingual German-English schools in south Australia and another ten such schools in Victoria. Bilingual education for aboriginal students commenced in the mid 1930s.

Bilingual education did not progress until the 1970s and 1980s. This was partly due to the xenophobia created by two world wars – a fear of foreigners, foreign influence and foreign culture, including foreign languages. Also, foreign languages were perceived as part of the enculturation of cultural elites. There was little concern prior to the 1970s for foreign languages for communicative purposes. In the 1970s, the growing popularity of 'Multiculturalism for all' and an increased interest in ethnic revivals produced a changed climate of opinion more favorable to bilingual education. However, the dominant viewpoint has often been that English is all that is needed for communication and employment in Australia, and in communication with other countries.

The Benowa experiment

In 1985, a nationally innovative education experiment in language teaching began in Australia. Based in Queensland at the Benowa State High School on the Gold Coast, a late partial Immersion program was begun. The program differs from Canadian late Immersion in that the children have no background in French (either at primary school level or in the community). From the success of this innovation, other Immersion schools in Australia grew: three schools in the Brisbane area developed programs in French, German and Indonesian, and another French Immersion program was started in the early 1990s on the Gold Coast. This innovation is well documented in a book edited by Michael Berthold (1995b) *Rising to the Bilingual Challenge: Ten Years of Queensland Secondary School Immersion.*

The first secondary Immersion program was initiated in 1985 at Benowa State High School in Queensland. Frustrated by low levels of language competence among their students, even after five years of language study, the staff of the school were keen for some kind of Immersion experience. Students studied approximately 60 percent of their school program through the medium of French. Initially, Science and Maths, plus Music were taught through the medium of French. Twenty-two students were recruited from primary schools to begin this innovation. The students tended to be of average and above average academic ability, and were told that they needed to be hard-working to survive in an intensive Immersion program.

At the end of the first semester in the first year of the program, the Mathematics department set a test for those in the English language classes and those in the Immersion class. There was immediate success. The Immersion class's average mark in Mathematics equaled that of the best English-only class. In subsequent semesters during that first year of operation, the Immersion Mathematics class significantly out-performed all of the other thirteen classes in their first year of secondary schooling.

An acorn had been sown and immediately began to grow. The parents of the Immersion students requested an extension of the program to cover the first three years of secondary schooling. The school agreed. Subjects currently taught through French at Benowa are Mathematics, Science, Social Sciences, History, Physical Education as well as French itself. French content teaching comprises around 60 percent of the timetable in Immersion classes.

The students in this Immersion program have won success both inside and outside Benowa High School. Although having studied Mathematics entirely through the medium of French, in 1985, three members of the first Immersion class came second in a state-wide Mathematics competition. In 1989, students from the Immersion class out performed francophone students in a local high school competition in French verse speaking. When the first cohort of Immersion students graduated, five were placed in the highest rank possible in the entrance tests to the next level of education.

The local community and the students' parents also viewed the Benowa experiment as a great success. By 1992, there were so many applicants for the late partial Immersion class in the school, that it had to be expanded to two classes.

Apart from the Benowa experiment, there have been other Australian bilingual programs in English and one of the following languages: Hebrew, Japanese, German, French, Italian and Indonesian. Immersion teachers are aided by the Australian Association of Language Immersion Teachers (AALIT) which has biennial conferences, a journal and other publications. AALIT has a valuable video entitled *Immersion Teaching Practices* (1995).

References: BERTHOLD, 1992; 1995a; 1995b; 1995

tion of grammar and syntax. The teacher may be repetitive in the words used and the ideas presented, with the same idea presented in two or more different ways. The teacher will deliberately speak slowly, giving the child more time to process the language input and understand the meaning. This tends to parallel the talk of mother to child (motherese) and foreigner talk (a person deliberately simplifying and slowing the language so a foreigner can understand). During this caretaker stage, the teacher may be constantly questioning the child to ensure that understanding has occurred.

A teacher may also present the language to be used before a lesson topic is presented. When new words and new concepts are being introduced into a lesson, the teacher may spend some time in introducing the words and clarifying the concepts so that the language learner is prepared. Such teachers may also be sensitive to nonverbal feedback from students: glazed or questioning looks, lack of attention. A student may be encouraged to question the teacher for clarification and simplification when understanding has not occurred.

Such Immersion classrooms need to have a particular view about language errors. Language errors are a normal and important part of the language learning process. Errors are not a symptom of failure. They are a natural part of learning. Therefore, Immersion teachers are discouraged from over-correcting children's attempts to speak French. Language accuracy tends to develop over time and with experience. Constant correction of error disrupts communication and content learning in the classroom and hinders language learning. When a child or several children constantly make the same errors, then appropriate and positive intervention may be of value.

In the early stages of Immersion, there will be a natural interlanguage among children. A child may change round the correct order in a sentence yet produce a perfectly comprehensible message. For example, faulty syntax may occur due to the influence of the first language on the second language. A child may put the pronoun or a preposition in the wrong order: as in 'go you and get it'. Interlanguage is not to be seen as error. Rather it indicates the linguistic creativity of students who are using their latent understanding of the first language to construct meaningful communication in the second language. Interlanguage is thus an intermediate, approximate system. It is a worthwhile attempt to communicate and therefore needs encouragement. Seen as a halfway stage in-between monolingualism and being proficient in a second language, interlanguage becomes part of the journey and not a permanent rest point.

For the Immersion teacher, an assumption is that proficiency in the first language will contribute to proficiency in the second language. Concepts attached to words in the first language will easily be transferred into the second language. The acquisition of literacy skills in the first language tends to facilitate the acquisition of literacy skills in the second language. However, not all aspects of a language will transfer. Rules of syntax and spelling may not lend themselves to transfer. The closer a language structure is to the second language structure, the greater the transfer there is likely to be between the two languages. For example, the transfer between English and Spanish is likely to be more than Arabic to English due to differences in syntax, symbols and direction of writing. However, the system of meanings, the conceptual map and skills that a person owns, may be readily transferable between languages.

The focus of Immersion classrooms is very much on tasks and curriculum content. However, there is also a place for an analytical approach to the second and the first language in the classroom. An Immersion classroom will not just enable children to acquire the second language in an unconscious, almost incidental manner. Towards the end of elementary education, the experiential approach may be joined by a meaning based focus on the form of language. Children may at this point be encouraged to analyze their vocabulary and grammar. At this later stage, some lessons may have progress in the second language as their sole aim. After early sheltering with language, the development of vocabulary and grammar may be dealt with in a direct and systematic manner.

The Problems and Limitations of Canadian Immersion Programs

Various authors have recently highlighted possible limitations in Immersion education that were not present in the early evaluations. First, Immersion students do not always become grammatically accurate in their French. Immersion students also tend to lack the social and stylistic sense of appropriate language use which the native speaker possesses. One solution is to locate problematic areas of vocabulary and grammar and provide increased opportunities for receptive and particularly productive language in such weak areas.

Second, surveys of graduates of Immersion programs tend to find that relatively few students make much use of French outside school and after leaving school (Harley, 1994; Wesche, 1993). This partly reflects a lack of opportunity to use French, partly a lack of confidence in their competence in speaking French, and partly a preference for English use. Ability in French is not frequently translated into use of French outside school, except, for example, where employment and personal

Teaching Strategies in Late Immersion Classrooms

The Australian experiment has suggested that a partial Immersion program in secondary school can have excellent results. However, the nature of the curriculum at secondary level means that a successful Immersion program requires not only hard work by well motivated students, but a great deal of competence on the part of teachers. Because the content of the curriculum is much more cognitively and conceptually demanding at this stage, teachers must use well formulated language strategies to ensure that curriculum delivery is not beyond the level of the students' language abilities. These are similar to the language strategies used in early Immersion classrooms, but in many ways demand even more skill and preparation at secondary level.

Comprehensible language input

An important aspect of Immersion teaching is the emphasis on a comprehensible level of language so that the student understands easily. To ensure comprehensible language input at secondary level, while at the same time conveying curriculum content effectively and extending students' language and cognitive abilities, teachers may make use of several strategies.

A feature of Immersion classrooms is the use of concrete and visual support materials to bridge the gap in understanding caused by students' limited language. When students are educated through their first language at secondary level, the accent tends to be on written materials and 'teacher talk'. Secondary Immersion teachers need to make extensive use of support materials such as diagrams, models, sketches, pictures and maps to convey information.

The demands of the secondary curriculum mean that new vocabulary is introduced almost daily. When a new word or phrase is used, the teacher may attempt find a way to make the meaning clear without using the majority language. Strategies might include rephrasing, mime, gestures, sketches or photographs, and asking the students to guess the meaning.

An important aspect of late partial Immersion programs is a dual focus approach. One early criticism of Immersion programs was that children were expected to acquire language structures naturally and incidentally through ad hoc exposure to the language, just as they had acquired their first language. The argument was that the exposure to the second language in an Immersion program, although extensive, is still limited compared to the exposure to a first language in a natural environment. Thus, provision must be made for a deliberate and planned focus on language while teaching other curriculum areas. This is particularly important at secondary level, where the language required to deliver the curriculum is inevitably more complex. This dual focus approach, language and content, may involve using content to teach an aspect of language as well as the other way around. For instance, a discussion of laboratory equipment in a French-medium science lesson may provide an opportunity to teach the expression 'On utilise... pour...' 'You use... (a thermometer, a Bunsen Burner) ... for... (measuring temperature, heating) ...'.

The emphasis in Immersion programs is on letting students' language develop naturally, without correcting errors. However, if a teacher feels that a student is making a repeated error, or if several members of a class are making the same error, this may provide an opportunity for constructive correction and a brief explanation or drill. By secondary level, students are more aware of the structure of language and may benefit from explanation and analysis. Some attention to the structure of language may be a more efficient means of language development than relying on unplanned exposure.

A supportive environment

Another priority in late Immersion programs is creating a supportive environment for students. Most students in late Immersion have made a conscious choice to enter the program. It has been a major commitment on their part, involving the prospect of a great deal of effort and hard work. They have taken the risk of choosing to study a large proportion of the curriculum through the second language at a crucial stage in their school careers and at a time in their lives when lack of confidence, shyness and inhibitions may be problems for some. Late Immersion students need much support from their teachers. Their school work and especially their second language output needs to be praised and valued. At secondary level there is a tendency for lessons to be teacher-centered, with students as passive, silent participants. In Immersion programs lessons need to be student-centered, with the students being encouraged to contribute, to ask questions, to participate in discussions, to interact with their peers, to extend their language abilities and take risks in the second language. Such students need to find immediate and continued success in their efforts so that motivation will remain high.

A late Immersion program is not an easy option for teachers or students. However, with hard work and dedication on the part of both groups, it can be an enriching experience, encouraging bilingualism while maintaining or even enhancing curriculum performance.

An astronomy presentation in a French Immersion classroom.

economics become a focus. Stern (1984) argued that the Immersion programs were strong on language, but weak on widening students' cultural horizons and weak on sensitizing them to francophone culture and values. This points to a lack of research on the outcomes of Immersion schooling, after students have left school. What effects has Immersion education had on Canadian society? What paths have Immersion students followed subsequently, and how much, or how little influence has Immersion had on post-school work, social and cultural lifestyles?

Third, the discourse of school lessons is different from that of the street, shop and disco. Hence, the danger is that Immersion students are initiated into a discourse at school that is inappropriate for out-of-school communication. The language of the curriculum is often specialized, formal, intricate and expansive. The language of the street is often very different, such that Immersion students have not been socialized into an appropriate everyday vernacular.

Fourth, there is difficulty in pinpointing the crucial interacting factors that create an effective Immersion experience. Teaching techniques may be one factor. Genesee (1983) argued that individualized, activity-based teaching techniques may be more effective than traditional whole class techniques. Genesee (1983) also argued that the intensity of language learning, for example, how many hours per day, is likely to be more important than the number of years of second language learning. (This is connected with the finding that older students tend to learn a second language more quickly than younger learners). Is it Immersion as a system that leads to relatively successful outcomes or, or as well as, factors such as 'student motivation, teachers' preparation, home culture, parental attitude, ethnolinguistic vitality, amount of time studying different curricula' (Carey, 1991a, page 953).

Fifth, Immersion programs can have effects on mainstream schools. For example, effects may include: a redistribution of classroom teachers and leaders, a change in the linguistic and ability profile of mainstream classes, discrepancies in class size with increasing numbers of mixed age classes.

Sixth, Heller (1994) has argued that Immersion schools in Canada provide anglophones with the linguistic and cultural capital for increased social and economic mobility and for political power. Immersion education is thus, in this perspective, about ulterior motives and vested interests. Such education is about gaining advantages in Canadian society: educational, cultural, linguistic, social, power, wealth and dominance advantages. Hence, Immersion education may produce conflict with the minority francophone community (e.g. in Ontario) rather than the harmonious unity and 'bridge building' that bilingualism aims to achieve in Canadian society.

Seventh, there is a danger in generalizing from the Canadian experience to elsewhere in the world. In Canada, Immersion concerns two major high status international languages: French and English. In many countries where bilingualism is present or fostered, the situation is different. Often the context is one of a majority and a minority language (or languages) co-existing. Canada is regarded as an additive bilingual context. Many countries across the five continents contain subtractive bilingual contexts.

Eighth, most Immersion teachers have to 'wear two hats': promoting achievement throughout the curriculum and ensuring second language proficiency. Such a dual task requires Immersion teacher training. Lack of suitable training tends to be a weakness in countries using the Immersion approach or a version of it. Both at the pre-service and in-service levels of education of teachers, the special needs of Immersion teachers need addressing. Methods in Immersion classroom require an induction into skills and techniques beyond those required in ordinary mainstream classrooms. Immersion teaching (and teacher training) methods are still developing and are at a relatively early stage.

Conclusion

It is important not to view Immersion education in Canada in purely educational terms. Behind Immersion education are political, social and cultural ideologies. Immersion education is not just immersion in a second language (French). Such bilingual education has aims and assumptions, beliefs and values that sometimes differ from, other times are additional to, mainstream education. It is important to see Immersion education not just as a means to promote bilingualism, but also as a move to a different kind of society. By promoting bilingualism in English speakers, Immersion education in Canada may support French language communities, increase the opportunities for francophones outside Quebec and help promote bilingualism in the public sector (and debatably in the private sector). However, Immersion education is seen as a Trojan horse of further English assimilation by some francophones. 'Francophones question whether an increase in bilingual anglophones will simply act to deprive them of their historical advantage in occupying bilingual jobs' (Lapkin, Swain & Shapson, 1990, page 649). This is linked to the finding that children from higher socio-

Immersion Techniques

Snow (1990) provides a list of ten specific techniques that tend to be used by experienced and effective Immersion teachers. This is a useful summary of the discussion in this topic.

1. Providing plenty of contextual support for the language being used (e.g. by body language – plenty of gestures, facial expressions and acting).

2. Deliberately giving more classroom directions and organizational advice to Immersion students. For example, signaling the start and the end of different routines, more explicit directions with homework and assignments.

3. Understanding where a child is at, thereby connecting the unfamiliar with the familiar, the known with the unknown. New material is linked directly and explicitly with the child's present knowledge and understanding.

4. Extensive use of visual material. Using concrete objects to illustrate lessons, using pictures and audio-visual aids, giving the child plenty of hands-on manipulative activities to ensure all senses are used in the educational experience.

5. Obtaining constant feedback as to the level of a student's understanding. Diagnosing the level of a student's language.

6. Using plenty of repetition, summaries, restatement to ensure that students understand the directions of the teacher.

7. The teacher being a role model for language emulation by the student.

8. Indirect error correction rather than constantly faulting students. Teachers ensure that the corrections are built in to their language to make a quick and immediate impact.

9. Using plenty of variety in both general learning tasks and in language learning tasks.

10. Using frequent and varied methods to check the understanding level of the children.

REFERENCE: SNOW, 1990

Concrete, hands-on activities are a good way to learn a language.

Singing, miming and role-play are frequently used in Immersion classrooms.

Stimulating teacher-student interaction is important for second language development.

economic backgrounds tend to be over-represented in Immersion programs. Thus Immersion education may act to reproduce elite groups, giving anglophone children with bilingual abilities an advantage in the jobs market (Heller, 1994).

Further Reading

GENESEE, F., 1987, *Learning Through Two Languages*. Cambridge, MA: Newbury House.

HELLER, M., 1994, *Crosswords. Language, Education and Ethnicity in French Ontario*. Berlin and New York: Mouton de Gruyter.

REBUFFOT, J., 1993, *Le Point sur L'Immersion au Canada*. Anjou, Québec: Centre Educatif et Culturel.

SWAIN, M. & LAPKIN, S., 1982, *Evaluating Bilingual Education: A Canadian Case Study*. Clevedon: Multilingual Matters Ltd.

Language learning can continue during play times.

Language Teaching and Learning in the Immersion Classroom

What are the main classroom features of successful Immersion programs in Canada?

First, there is a distinction between learning a language and learning through a language. Language acquisition in the Canadian Immersion program is mainly through the second language being used as a medium of instruction in 50 percent to 100 percent of the curriculum. All subject areas, from Music to Mathematics, Science to Sport, contribute to the growth of a child's language competence.

Second, the minimum time the second language needs to be used as a medium to ensure 'receptive' (listening and reading) second language proficiency is regarded as a minimum of four to six years. Around the end of elementary schooling, Immersion students show equal or higher performance in the curriculum compared with their mainstream peers.

Third, the curriculum tends to be the same for Immersion children as for their mainstream peers. Thus, Immersion children can easily be compared with mainstream children for levels of achievement. Immersion students compared with Core French Second Language students are neither more advantaged nor more disadvantaged by studying a common (sometimes called a 'core') curriculum.

Fourth, studies of bilingual education indicate that it may be preferable to separate languages in instruction rather than to mix them during a single lesson. It tends to be regarded as preferable that one language is used for one set of subjects; the other language for a separate set. When there is language mixing inside a lesson, students may wait for the explanation in their stronger language. Such students may simply switch off when transmission is in their weaker language. Sustained periods of monolingual instruction will require students to attend to the language of instruction, thus both improving their language competencies and acquiring subject matter simultaneously.

Fifth, there is the question of how much time should be devoted to the two languages within the curriculum. The typical recommendation is that a minimum of 50 percent of instruction should be in the second language. Thus, in French Immersion, French-medium teaching and learning may occur from 50 percent to 100 percent of the school week. As the graphs showed, the amount of instruction in the English language may increase as children become older. One factor in such a decision can be the amount of exposure to English a child receives outside school. Where a child's environment, home and street, media and community are English-medium, such saturation may imply that a smaller proportion of time needs to be spent on English in the school. At the same time, the public will normally require bilingual schools to show that children's first majority language skills, particularly literacy, are not affected but rather are monitored and promoted by bilingual education.

Sixth, teachers in Canadian Immersion classrooms are competent bilinguals, with native or native-like proficiency in French. Teachers are language models for the child, providing a variety of language experiences and models of different language usage.

Seventh, the French Immersion approach allows a relatively homogeneous language classroom. For example, in early total Immersion, children will start from the same point. All are beginners without French proficiency. This makes the task of the teacher relatively easy. Children can grow in the French language under a shared teaching and learning approach. Initially, there will be no disparity of status due to some children being more proficient than others in French.

3: Language Maintenance Bilingual Education

Definition

Language maintenance (also called heritage language) bilingual education occurs where language minority children use their native, home or heritage language in school as a major medium of instruction. The goal of such education is full bilingualism, biculturalism and biliteracy. The heritage language is usually the medium of instruction for between 50 percent to 90 percent of curriculum time. Thus a language maintenance bilingual program is not a transitional program (see page 479). A heritage language bilingual program does not aim to develop a majority language at the expense of the minority language.

Language maintenance bilingual education is an umbrella term which incorporates many different international examples of education under different names. For example, language maintenance bilingual education includes 'maintenance bilingual education' and 'developmental maintenance bilingual education' in the United States.

Examples of language maintenance bilingual education include:

- Navajo and English; Spanish and English in the United States.
- Catalan and Spanish in Spain.
- Ukrainian and English in Canada.
- Gaelic and English in Scotland.
- Irish and English in Ireland.
- Finnish and Swedish in Sweden.
- Welsh and English in Wales.
- Maori and English in New Zealand.

Students

Not all children in language maintenance bilingual education come from language minority homes. Take the example of Wales, where approximately 20 percent of the population of 2.9 million speak Welsh, and the province of Catalonia, in North East Spain, where 68 percent of the inhabitants are bilingual in Spanish and Catalan. In state schools in some rural areas of Wales and Catalonia, where there is a high density of language minority speakers, it is possible that most or all of the children within the school will be native speakers of the minority language. The language of the school simply reflects the native language of that area.

Other schools may contain a mixture of language minority children and language majority children. In other parts of Catalonia and Wales, language majority children (Spanish in Catalonia; English in Wales) may be newcomers or in-migrants to the area. Their parents may wish them to have a bilingual education. Language maintenance programs may thus include children from majority language backgrounds.

Alternatively, parents may have lost the native language despite living in the area and wish their children to revive that heritage language. In urban areas of Wales and Catalonia, where use of the minority language has declined, parents who have not had the opportunity to learn the language may send their children to schools where the minority language is the medium of education. The hope is to revive the language in their offspring. In such schools, majority language children often vastly outnumber children from minority language homes. Maori schools in New Zealand also fall into this category.

Language maintenance schools may be established where a language minority exists in an area as a result of immigration. Private ethnic schools in the United States and state-run heritage language schools in Canada are in this category. These schools may be composed entirely of children who are native speakers of the minority language, or of majority language children whose parents have lost the minority language and wish them to revive it.

All children in language maintenance education will follow much or most of the curriculum through the native or heritage language. For children from language minority backgrounds, this is education through their first language. For children from majority language backgrounds, this will be an Immersion experience, being taught through a second language.

Parents will often have the choice of sending their children to monolingual mainstream schools or to language maintenance education. In Canada, for example, Ukrainian and Jewish heritage language programs have

The Notion of a Heritage Language

Questions are often raised about the definition of a heritage language and heritage language education. Should the heritage language in Catalonia be seen as Spanish or Catalan or both? In Canada, should the heritage language of permanent, established immigrants be English or French or their ancestral language or both? For native North Americans in Canada and the United States, their native language may be the ancestral language, with English being seen as imported. In the United States, should Spanish speakers come to see their heritage language as being English increasingly and Spanish decreasingly?

The heritage language may be seen by an individual as an indigenous language (e.g. Navajo in the US) or as an ancestral language (e.g. Spanish among Latinos in the US). Both Navajo and Spanish speakers in the United States have heritage languages depending on their perception (as different from society's perception) of what constitutes their heritage language. A Navajo or a Spanish speaker in the United States may alternatively wish to regard their heritage language as being English following assimilation.

The use of the term 'heritage language' has been confined mainly to Canada, although recently it has become less favored (as there are pejorative connotations) with 'international language' being preferred. The danger of the term 'heritage' is that, relative to powerful majority languages, it points more to the past and less to the future, to traditions rather than the contemporary. The danger is that the heritage language becomes associated with ancient culture, past traditions and more 'primitive' times. This is also true of the terms 'ethnic' (used in the US) and 'ancestral'. These terms may fail to give the impression of a modern, international language that is of value in a technological society.

In some other countries, more neutral terms have tended to be used. One British term is 'community language' and 'community language schools'. In Wales, schools which serve rural communities where there are high densities of Welsh speakers are called 'natural Welsh schools'. In areas where Welsh speakers are in the minority, and where parents can choose between Welsh-medium and English-medium schools, the term used is 'designated Welsh schools'. In New Zealand, the term 'Immersion schools' tends to be used for Maori language primary schools, since the majority of Maori children do not speak the Maori language, and thus are taught by Immersion methods. However, no terms are neutral. Over time, meanings develop, and what is politically correct in one decade becomes pejorative in the next decade.

Languages in Australian Education

In 1996, almost 400,000 Australian dollars was granted to 30 schools or projects supporting bilingual education among Aboriginal students in Australia. Current statistics suggest that there are 20 schools with accredited bilingual programs supporting 34 Aboriginal languages and dialects. The students in such bilingual education speak an Aboriginal language as their mother tongue and learn English as an additional language. Such bilingual education aims to foster proficiency in school work through the use of the Aboriginal languages; to develop competency in literacy in English and Aboriginal languages; and to support and to promote Aboriginal languages and culture under the guidance of their communities. It is regarded as important that there is ownership of such programs, and involvement in such programs by communities, rather than bilingual education being imposed from without. To support this, Aboriginal teachers are being trained and encouraged to work in such bilingual programs.

The cultural content to preserve Aboriginal community traditions includes: personal name systems, the kinship system, groups and clans, totems, family history, traditions of discipline and social responsibility determined by family grouping, knowledge of bush foods and bush medicines, environmental knowledge, traditional ceremonial life as well as an understanding of the variety and value of Aboriginal languages. Such bilingual schools are particularly found in the following regions: Alice Springs, Barkly, Darwin and Palm, East Arnhem and Katherine.

In the Northern Territory, the development of skills in Aboriginal languages and literacy amongst students has impacted on other areas apart from education. For example, such development in Aboriginal languages has also affected literacy and cultural practices, tourism, local government, art, music and whole community development.

One model of bilingual education for Aboriginal students has the following pattern:

School Grade	Percent of Instruction through Aboriginal language	Percent of Instruction through English
Pre-school	95%	5%
Transition	90%	10%
Grade 1	80%	20%
Grade 2	70%	30%
Grade 3	60%	40%
Grade 4	50%	50%
Grade 5	20%	80%
Grade 6	20%	80%
Grade 7	20%	80%
Secondary School	20%	80%

REFERENCE: Northern Territory Department of Education, 1996

A Language Maintenance Program: Navajo Community Schools

The Rock Point Community School is situated on Highway 191, Rock Point, Arizona in the United States. The school has been famous since the early 1970s for its role in attempting to maintain the Native American language of Navajo. A fascinating history of this school is given by Holm and Holm (1990). Containing 99 percent Navajo children, the languages used in this Kindergarten to Grade 12 bilingual education program are Navajo and English. By 1994 there were 18 classes with around 470 students.

The three program aims are defined as:

1. Students will become proficient speakers, readers, and writers of the Navajo and English languages.
2. Students will acquire cultural knowledge of at least two cultures: Navajo and Anglo-American.
3. Students will develop critical thinking skills in Navajo and English.

In Kindergarten to Grade 5, Navajo is used for 50 percent of class time; in Grade 6 for 25 percent, and in grades 7 to 12 for 15 percent of total class time. In Kindergarten to Grade 5, Reading, Language Arts, Math, Science, Social Studies, Health are taught through both Navajo and English, with separation of languages by differing blocks of time.

In Grades 6 to 12, teaching through Navajo occurs for Literacy, Social Science, Electives and Science (one semester in Grade 6) with teaching in English for Reading, Language Arts, Math, Science, Social Studies, Health, Home Economics and PE. The language of initial reading instruction for Navajo speakers is Navajo and for English speakers it is English. All program teachers are proficient in both languages. Over 90 percent of the teaching staff are members of the Navajo ethnic group and provide bilingual role models.

Another Navajo school, about 40 miles north-west of Rock Point, is Rough Rock school, the first American Indian-controlled school founded in 1966.

REFERENCES: HOLM & HOLM, 1990; ROSIER & HOLM, 1980

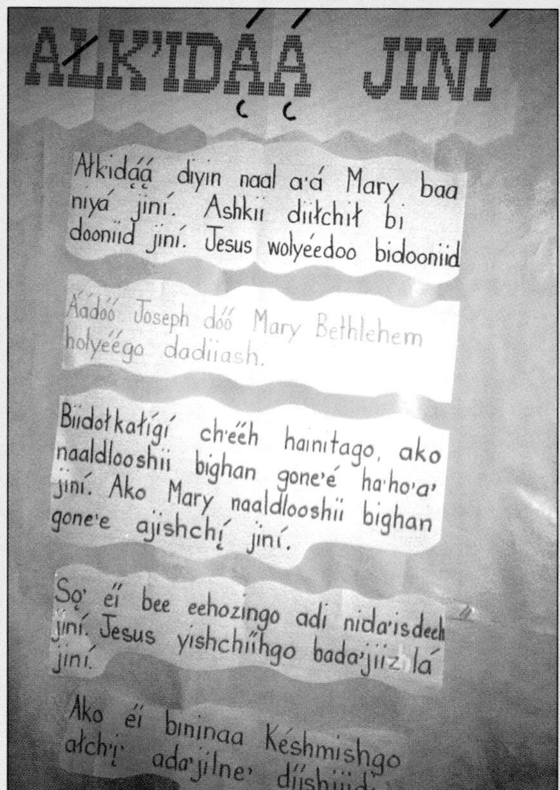

The Christmas Story in Navajo by elementary students and their teacher at Rough Rock Community school, Arizona, the first Native American-controlled school founded in 1966.

A Navajo language lesson at Rough Rock Community School.

Creative writing in Navajo and English at Rough Rock Community School.

given parents freedom of choice in selecting monolingual English or heritage language education.

Aims

The aim of language maintenance bilingual education is to ensure full bilingualism, biculturalism and biliteracy. While much of the curriculum may be taught through the minority language, the aim is normally to achieve language and literacy skills in both the majority and minority language. The child's native language is protected and developed alongside development in the majority, international language.

Such language maintenance schools will not only have bilingualism and biliteracy as their aims. They are often competing against monolingual mainstream schools. Therefore their overall educational performance needs to be comparable to such mainstream schools. Given that the minority language may have less status, power and support in the nation at large and internationally, it is often imperative that language maintenance schools show achievement on a par or better than mainstream schools. Language maintenance bilingual schools will normally strive to ensure that performance throughout all areas of the curriculum is comparable (or superior) to local norms.

To promote, extend and maintain such schools, publicity regarding their success is important. The commitment of parents, teachers and students themselves towards maintaining the minority language will often translate into the extra motivation that creates effective schools and acceptable curriculum performance.

The Language Approach in Language Maintenance Bilingual Education

The minority language will usually be used for at least half of curriculum time. For example, Ukrainian programs in Alberta and Manitoba have created a 50/50 split between Ukrainian and English. Mathematics and Science are taught in English; Music, Art and Social Studies in Ukrainian. There is a tendency in language maintenance bilingual education to use the minority language for the Arts and Humanities subjects (e.g. Music, Art and Craft, History, Geography, Social Science and also Games), and to teach Mathematics, Physics, Chemistry, Biology, Technology and Computer Studies through the majority language, particularly English.

This may initially appear to be a logical distribution of each language across the curriculum. In subjects such as History and Geography, there are cultural attachments that may be more appropriately relayed in the heritage language. Where religious instruction is given, the ancestral language may be the most suitable medium. Prayer and devotions which are part of the inner self may feel more appropriate in the heritage language. Since information about Science and Technology, Computers and Chemistry is often in the majority language, it may feel natural for such subjects to be taught through the majority language.

However there is a problem with the allocation of the minority language to Humanities and Arts, and the majority language to Science and Technology. The minority language may be seen to be part of ancient culture, the modern language part of modernity. Does the minority language therefore lose status because of this? If the minority language is not used for Science or Technology or Computers, is it perceived by students as old-fashioned, of lower prestige and status, not part of employment and affluence?

This is one reason amongst others that some language maintenance education programs use the minority language for much more than 50 percent of the curriculum.

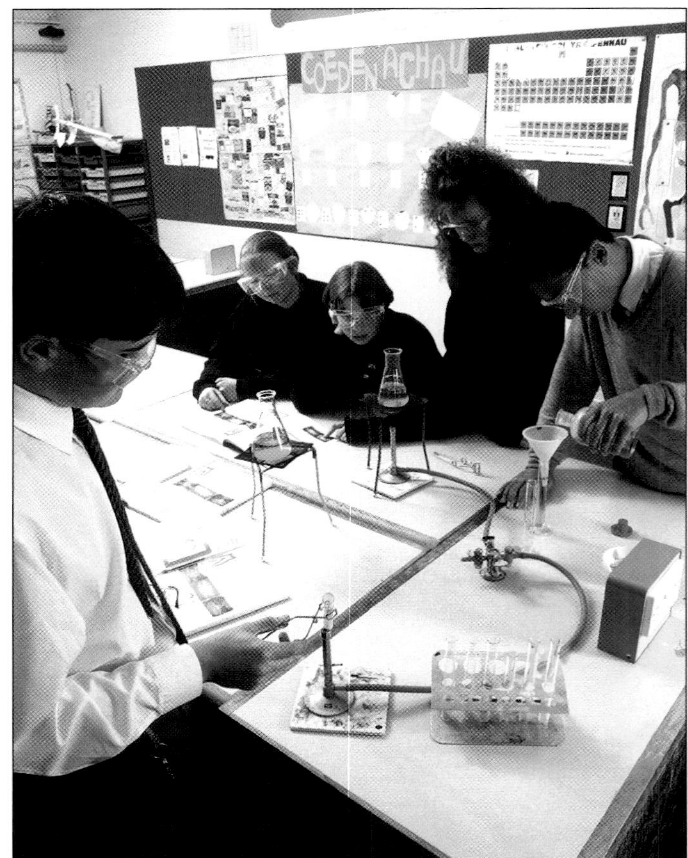

A science lesson in a bilingual Welsh-English school. Science is increasingly taught bilingually or through the medium of Welsh in bilingual schools in Wales.

In Wales, for example, the minority language of Welsh is used in such programs for between 80 percent to almost 100 percent of curriculum time. In this case, Science is increasingly taught bilingually or through the medium of Welsh. Computer programs are translated and created, and are available through the medium of Welsh. Children are therefore latently taught that their minority language can be used for all the functions of modern society.

The relatively greater use of the minority language to teach the curriculum is also justified by arguing that children easily transfer ideas, concepts, skills, attitudes and knowledge into the majority language. Having taught a child multiplication in Spanish, this mathematical concept does not have to be retaught in English. If a child is taught how to use the library in Spanish, they do not have to be retaught in the English language. Classroom concepts and content transfer relatively easily between languages so long as such languages are sufficiently well developed to cope with them.

A further justification for a high proportion of curriculum time in the minority language is that the minority language is more easily lost; the majority language is more easily acquired and developed. Language minority children tend to be surrounded by the majority language. Where there are plenty of majority language speakers in the playground, in the street or in the shops, minority language speakers will tend to switch to the majority language, that is, the common denominator. Television, videos, compact disks, the Internet and cinema tend to be persuasive purveyors of the majority language. Adverts on trains and buses, shops and signposts, visits to neighboring areas and leisure centers, often ensure plentiful occasions where the majority language is practiced.

Language maintenance supporters will therefore tend to argue that balanced bilingualism can be achieved by a relative concentration on the minority language at school. Given that out of school experiences promote the majority language increasingly, they will often argue that full biliteracy and bilingualism is most possible by a concentration on that minority language at school.

However, there are arguments to the contrary. Some experts oppose the teaching of scientific and technical subjects through the medium of the minority language, particularly at secondary or high school level, because of practical difficulties. Minority languages often lack status and official and financial support. It has not been easy for some language minorities to develop the vast plethora of scientific and technical terms needed to teach some curricular areas successfully. This does not reflect any inherent deficiency in the minority language, but rather a lack of money and government backing which would finance the expertise needed to develop the resources of the language. (This is discussed more fully in the topic entitled 'Language Standardization', see page 210.) Lack of money also creates problems for the writing/translation and publication of textbooks and other curriculum materials in the minority language. Even when terms and textbooks are available, there are still difficulties to be overcome if effective teaching and learning through the minority language is to be ensured. Teachers have often studied their subjects in the majority language and may find it difficult to switch.

Because of the majority language influence, students may be familiar with terms in the majority language (e.g. in computing) and may find it hard to adjust to using the minority language. If students proceed to higher education, these types of courses are not often available in the minority language, and students may find it difficult to switch to using the majority language for technical and scientific discussions. In these areas, hopes and aspirations for the maintenance and development of the minority language must be balanced by pragmatic considerations.

One partial solution to these practical difficulties has been to develop a bilingual teaching strategy, so that subject competence may be developed through the medium of both the majority and the minority languages. (See Language Allocation in Bilingual Methodology, page 586.) Another helpful solution has been to borrow and adapt international terminology for many specialized academic terms. This has provided a bridge between languages and made the task of achieving bilingual competence in individual subject areas easier for many students. (See Foreign Borrowings page 164.)

Minority language education should not be at the cost of literacy and communicative competence in the majority language. The perceived effectiveness and prestige of such heritage language schools often depends on examination success or graduation with majority language oracy and literacy being under the spotlight.

> When the mother tongue is used in school, Guiora suggests that there are:
>
> '...cognitive and affective benefits for the reason that the mother tongue is the very lifeblood of human self-awareness, the carrier of identity, the safe repository of a vast array of affective and cognitive templates making up the total web of personality'.
>
> Reference: GUIORA, 1984

Bilingual Education in Mexico

Educational policy has been the responsibility of the federal government in Mexico since 1917. At this time, there was generally a low level of educational achievement among Mexican citizens, relatively low rates of literacy and a lack of schools, particularly in rural areas. There were also more than 50 indigenous Indian linguistic groups in Mexico (see page 396).

After 1917, education became a main element in the government's desire to increase standards of living throughout Mexico. In the early years, this meant the spread of primary schooling to rural areas where many language minority populations lived. However, an aim of education for language minority groups was assimilation and Hispanization. This is because Mexico has had an official language policy, with Spanish as the national language. Nevertheless, there has been a debate in Mexico regarding the policy of educating the indigenous populations to become Spanish-speaking or, through bilingual education, to retain their indigenous language. Over time, policies have changed, as will now be considered.

In the 1920s and the 1930s, education was by immersion in Spanish. No instruction was provided in minority languages. Staying as a Mexican Indian was seen as an obstacle to progress and civilization throughout the country. The aim was to integrate indigenous groups into the larger society. In those years, communicating in the minority language in school was forbidden. Teachers were expected to inculcate in children a feeling of guilt about belonging to native cultures. Clever students were sometimes removed from their communities and sent to schools in urban areas.

In the 1940s, small changes occurred, with minority language groups requesting respect for their local language and culture. Some bilingual education pilot projects were started, and this spawned debates that commenced in the 1950s through to the 1970s about the most efficient means to educate linguistic minorities.

Between the 1950s and the 1970s, some educators and politicians argued that Spanish immersion was the most efficient method to enable high performance and high literacy in Mexico. Others argued for bilingual education in the indigenous language and Spanish, with a bilingual and a bicultural outcome. However, even in bilingual education programs, literacy in the minority language was conceived of as an intermediate step to learning Spanish.

In the 1960s, a combination of academic instruction in the indigenous language and the teaching of Spanish as the second language became official policy. However, the dominant ideology was more about transition into using the majority language of Spanish, particularly if education was available after the primary stage.

In the 1990s, while there are still debates, the tendency is towards bilingual education for indigenous minorities with a more bilingual and bicultural view. Programs of bilingual and bicultural education for language minority children are provided in areas where 60 percent or more of the population does not speak Spanish. There is also central government training for indigenous teachers and 'cultural promotion workers' to live among their own groups and communities.

Generally, it has been found that students achieve Spanish literacy more effectively when the basic skills are first taught in their heritage language. Also, oracy and literacy in an indigenous language does not hinder the development of Spanish speaking, reading or writing skills. However, the use of the native language in school is gradually replaced by Spanish, often around Grade 5 or Grade 6. Having acquired reading and writing skills in their indigenous language, and once familiar with oral Spanish, students increasingly read and write in Spanish.

Text books are provided in indigenous languages, and since 1984, official primary school text books have been produced and distributed, at no cost to schools, by the central government.

While bilingual programs in Mexico attempt to be both bicultural and bilingual, there is an increasing loss of indigenous language speakers in many areas, as the higher prestige, more economically valuable Spanish language permeates the indigenous communities. For example, with the Otomi language, it has been found that Spanish displaces this indigenous language geographically, functionally and in its linguistic structure. Thus bilingualism provides the opportunity to move out of the minority language into an increasing use of Spanish. Bilingual education does not guarantee the permanence or maintenance of indigenous minority languages.

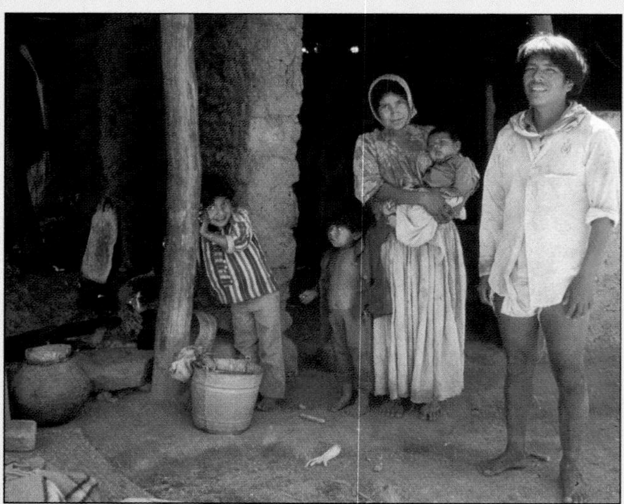

A Tarahumara Indian family from the north-west of Mexico.

There is a tendency in language maintenance schools for the minority language to be used decreasingly as the years and grades go by. Children in the kindergarten and elementary school may have most or even all of their education through the medium of the minority language. Towards the end of the elementary school and into secondary education, there may be increasing use of the majority language. Often, language maintenance education is a primary school phenomenon, with little or no provision at the secondary and tertiary/higher education level. This need not be the case. In Catalonia for example, it is possible for students to receive their education almost totally through the medium of Catalan from elementary school through to university. Such students are still fully bilingual and biliterate.

Teachers

Teachers in language maintenance bilingual programs need to be thoroughly bilingual and biliterate. Usually, they will be very committed to maintaining the culture surrounding the heritage language. Such teachers will tend to be strong and loyal supporters of their minority language culture, and they may even be seen by some as language activists.

While capable of teaching in both languages, most of their teaching will be in the minority language. Where curriculum materials are only partly available in the minority language, such teachers will often be expected to adapt and produce their own materials. The training, in-service education and supply of language minority teachers is sometimes a problem. In some ethnic communities, becoming a teacher is not an expectation or a tradition. This trend can occur among both men and women – but for different reasons (e.g. attitudes to the role of women in childcare, tendency to expect to gravitate towards lower status employment).

Outcomes from Language Maintenance Bilingual Education

Major reviews of language maintenance education are provided by Cummins (1983a) and Cummins & Danesi (1990). Apart from looking at individual international educational interventions, the reviews also examine the pattern that can be found in the results of evaluations of language maintenance education, thus attempting to derive international generalizations.

The results of such evaluations, particularly in Canada, suggest that language maintenance programs can be effective in four different ways.

First, the students maintain their home language. This is especially in comparison with language minority children who are placed in mainstream (i.e. monolingual/majority education) or transitional education. Such mainstreamed children tend partly to lose and sometimes avoid using their heritage language.

Second, such children tend to perform as well as comparable mainstream children in curriculum areas such as Mathematics, Science, History and Geography. That is, there is no loss in curriculum performance for such children taking their education in their home language. Indeed the evaluations suggest that they perform better than comparable children in mainstream education.

To illustrate: take two 'equal' children from a language minority background. One attends a mainstream program, the other attends language maintenance education. The chances are that the child in language maintenance education will achieve more highly, all other factors being equal. One 'cognitive' explanation is that heritage language education commences at the level of linguistic-cognitive competence reached on entry into school. In comparison, mainstreaming such language minority students has negative cognitive implications. It seemingly rejects a child's level of cognitive competence. It entails redeveloping sufficient language capability in order for them to cope with the curriculum. If the analogy will stand, it is like someone with a basic level of skill in salmon fishing with a rod who is made to learn big game sea fishing instead. The instructor ignores skills already attained with a rod. The student is made to practice casting on dry land, instead of building on existing skills with the fishing rod.

Third, studies suggest that children's attitudes are positive when placed in language maintenance education. When the home language is used in school, there is the

A Quote from Samuel Betances

'Not only must these newcomers learn English, it might be good if we didn't move in too quickly and tell them to forget Spanish or Vietnamese or Chamorro, or Togalo. Maybe we can come of age and realize that we cannot, in the name of turning out good Americans limit the freedom of speech of those new to our shores and/or tell people to forget what they know. In the name of education we cannot argue that it is better to know less than more. Bilingual education enriches our best hopes for a democratic society, making it safe for differences as well – powerful, practical reasons why we need it today even though such programs did not exist for yesterday's arrivals.'

REFERENCE: BETANCES, 1985

Maori Immersion Education

The Maori language, culture and way of life has been under threat since the arrival of European settlers in New Zealand and the establishment of British sovereignty in the mid-19th century, During the 20th century the Maori language has declined rapidly owing partly to urbanization and industrialization, involving migration from rural areas to find work. English-medium education has been another major factor in the decline of the Maori language, and also the low social and economic status of the Maori people. Since the late 1960s there has been some provision in New Zealand schools for teaching the Maori language and culture. There have also been bilingual programs since the late 1970s in which part of the curriculum has been delivered through the medium of Maori. However, these programs have tended to be transitional in nature. They have tended to increase knowledge rather than use of the Maori language among young people, and have not been viewed as sufficient to reverse the tide of language shift among the younger generation.

It was felt among the Maori community that there were two main requirements for education that would contribute to the reinvigorating of the Maori language. Firstly, education should be conducted entirely through the medium of Maori, with an Immersion-type approach for the majority of students whose home language was English. Secondly, education should respect and incorporate the Maori culture and lifestyle. Children should learn to be Maori as well as to speak Maori.

Maori children playing at a kohanga reo or Maori language pre-school at a settlement in Rotorua, North Island, New Zealand.

In 1981, the first *kohanga reo* ('language nests') or Maori Immersion nursery schools were opened, as a Maori initiative, followed by Maori Immersion primary schools, *kura kaupapa maori*. Important features of these schools are that they not only operate through the medium of the Maori language, but that they operate within a framework based on Maori cultural and social practices, Maori philosophy and spiritual and metaphysical beliefs. The aim of these schools is not just to teach children the Maori language but to enable them to access their cultural and spiritual heritage. The *kohanga reo* and *kura kaupapa* are initiated and administered by parents and other members of the local Maori community, and this grass roots involvement and high level of community participation has the result that the community itself is strengthened and invigorated by the school activities, and the school children feel themselves to be an integral part of the community. In rural areas, the community is the *iwi* or local ethnic group. In urban areas, the community may consist of members of many ethnic groups.

Many *kohanga reo* or *kura kaupapa* are based on the *whanau* or family group, the smallest unit of the *iwi*. Schools are small (a maximum of 60 in the *kura kaupapa*) and children often work in mixed age groups, with the development of family-type relationships within the group. Maori learning styles are used, which emphasize learning from others in the group. Learning is not confined to the classroom: the children learn in other environments, including the *marae* (the space designated for formal ceremonies), the bush and the seaside. Neither is the learning experience restricted to conventional school hours. In one *kura* the children sleep at the school overnight once every two weeks and get up in the early hours of the morning, the time viewed by Maori as the best time for learning. *karakia* (prayers) are important, as a preparation for the learning of the day. Traditional Maori art and craftwork are taught and displayed while traditional Maori ceremonies and social practices are observed. For instance, Spolsky (1989) describes how visitors to the schools may be welcomed with the formal *powhiri* or welcome ceremony, with songs and speeches, denoting a welcome from the whole community, and the importance of the school within the community.

REFERENCES: MAY, 1994b, 1996; SPOLSKY, 1989; TE PUNI KOKIRI, 1993

The Canadian Experience

In Canada, there has been a distinction between heritage language lessons and heritage language bilingual education. There are heritage language lessons, sometimes called heritage language programs, which aim to give around two and a half hours per week of language teaching in the heritage language to students. Around 60 ethnic languages have been supported by such programs with around a 100,000 students being enrolled per year. These lessons aim to maintain the ancestral language of such children with lessons during lunch breaks, after school and at weekends. In provinces such as Manitoba, British Columbia, Saskatchewan and Alberta, there are also heritage language bilingual education programs. The heritage language is the medium of instruction for around 50 percent of the day. For example, there have been programs where Ukrainian, Italian, German, Hebrew, Yiddish, Mandarin Chinese, Arabic and Polish have been utilized as the medium of instruction alongside English.

While evaluations of heritage language education are positive, the Canadian population are divided on the issue. Official Canadian policy has been supportive of multiculturalism, especially of French language and English language cultures. Extending multiculturalism to other heritage languages has provoked more contention. Ethnocultural communities (e.g. Ukrainian, German, Hebrew, Yiddish, Mandarin Chinese, Arabic and Polish) tend to support heritage language education. Anglophone and francophone Canadians tend to have a tolerance and good-will towards such communities. Lukewarm support for heritage language communities tends to stop short if public monies are to be used to support heritage language education. However, in Toronto, for instance, if sufficient parents have requested classes, they have been funded.

The anxieties of sections of public opinion and of government include: the disruption of mainstream schools (e.g. falling rolls), problems of staffing, minimal communication between heritage language teachers and mainstream teachers, segregation of school communities, financial burdens of the absorption of in-migrants into the education system, loss of time for core curriculum subjects, social tensions, and effects on the integration and stability of Canadian society .

Such anxieties have increased with the high levels of Canadian in-migrants since the mid 1980s onwards. Due to low birth rates and a rapidly aging population in Canada, the population has been increased by in-migration policies. Hence language diversity in Canada has increased. In Toronto and Vancouver, for example, more than half the school population comes from a non-English-speaking background. With increased in-migration and hence increased linguistic and cultural diversity, how does a government respond? What is the consensus of public opinion in Canada about fostering language diversity and multiculturalism?

Cummins (1992a, page 285) portrays the debate about the nature of Canadian identity, the debate about multiculturalism and the self-interest of public opinion thus:

> 'While the dominant Anglophone and Francophone groups generally are strongly in favor of learning the other official language, they see few benefits to promoting heritage languages for themselves, for Canadian society as a whole, or for children from ethnocultural backgrounds. The educational focus for such children should be on acquiring English and becoming Canadian rather than on erecting linguistic and cultural barriers between them and their Canadian peers. In short, whereas advocates of heritage language teaching stress the value of bilingual and multilingual skills for the individual and society as a whole, opponents see heritage languages as socially divisive, excessively costly, and educationally retrograde in view of minority children's need to succeed academically in the school language.'

If the focus switches from public political opinion to the educational opinion of teachers, parents and students, there is general satisfaction with Canadian heritage language programs. While such programs may present administrative challenges (e.g. shortage of teachers, availability of pre-service and in-service teacher education and a lack of curriculum materials), the advantages may be summarized as follows (Canadian Education Association, 1991):

- positive self-concept and pride in one's background;
- better integration of child into school and society;
- more tolerance of other people and different cultures;
- increased cognitive, social and emotional development;
- ease in learning new languages;
- increased probability of employment;
- fostering stronger relationships between home and school;
- responding to the needs and wishes of community.

Language Maintenance Schools in the United States

One particular case in the United States is that of the 'ethnic community mother tongue schools.' Numbering over five thousand and located in almost every state of the United States, these are schools which use a native language, ethnic language or ancestral language of minorities within a community. The following ethnic and language minority groups, among others, are represented by these schools: Arab, African, Asian, French, Jewish, Polish, Russian, Latin American, Dutch, Bulgarian, Romanian, Serbian and Turkish. Maintained by communities who have lost or are in danger of losing their native language, the schools aim to ensure bilingualism, biculturalism and biliteracy plus retaining in their students a feeling of roots and ethnic identity. Such students will be expected to become North Americans as well as having a sense of identity with a particular ethnic group (e.g. US Jews). 'These schools must be recognized as filling an important identity-forming and identity-providing function for millions of Americans'

REFERENCE: FISHMAN, 1989

possibility that a child's self-esteem and self-concept will be enhanced. The child may perceive that the home language, the home and community culture, parents and relations are accepted by the school when the home language is used. In comparison, a language minority child who is mainstreamed is vulnerable to a loss of self-esteem and status. The home language and culture may seem to be disparaged. The school system and the teachers may seem latently or manifestly to be rejecting the child's home language and values. This may affect the child's motivation and interest in school work and thereby affect performance. A student whose skills are recognized and valued may feel encouraged and motivated; a student whose skills are ignored may feel discouraged and rejected.

The fourth finding of language maintenance evaluations is perhaps the most unexpected. Indeed, it tends to go against 'common sense'. When testing children's majority language performance, it is generally comparable with mainstreamed children particularly when children have developed literacy in their home language. To explain this, take the previous example of two children from identical heritage language backgrounds with the same 'intelligence', socioeconomic class and age. One is placed in language maintenance education, the other in mainstream schooling. It might be expected that the child placed in mainstream English language education would perform far better in English language tests than the child in a language maintenance education program. The prediction might be that the greater the exposure to English in mainstream education, the higher the English language test performance. Evaluations of language maintenance education suggest something different. The child in language maintenance education is likely to perform at least as well as the child in mainstream education. The explanation seems to be that self-esteem is enhanced, and language and intellectual skills better promoted by education in the home language. Such skills appear to transfer easily into second language (majority language) areas.

The overall conclusions from Cummins' (1983a) and Cummins and Danesi's (1990) review of language maintenance education is that such education is not likely to have detrimental effects on a child's performance throughout the curriculum. Indeed, the indication from research is that language minority children tend to prosper more in such education than when placed in mainstream education. They maintain and enrich their home language and culture. Their performance throughout the curriculum does not suffer. This notably includes performance in the second language (majority language). Cognitive enhancement can also occur (Danesi, 1991).

Further Reading

CUMMINS, J., 1992a, Heritage Language Teaching in Canadian Schools. *Journal of Curriculum Studies*, 24 (3), 281-286.

CUMMINS, J. & DANESI, M., 1990, *Heritage Languages. The Development and Denial of Canada's Linguistic Resources*. Toronto: Our Schools/Ourselves Education Foundation & Garamond Press.

EDWARDS, V. & REDFERN, A., 1992, *The World in a Classroom: Language in Education in Britain and Canada*. Clevedon: Multilingual Matters Ltd.

GARCÍA, O., 1997, Bilingual Education. In F. COULMAS (ed.), *The Handbook of Sociolinguistics*. Oxford: Blackwell.

OUDIN, A-S., 1996, *Immersion and Multilingual Education in the European Union. Inventory of Educational Systems in which Teaching is Provided Partly or Entirely Through the Medium of a Regional or Minority Language*. Dublin & Brussels: The European Bureau for Lesser Used Languages.

4: Dual Language Schools

Definition

Dual language schools contain a balance of language majority and language minority children. Such schools use two languages approximately equally in the curriculum so that children become bilingual and biliterate. Mostly found among United States elementary schools, such institutions have bilingual teachers who aim to keep the two languages separate in their classrooms.

There are a variety of terms used to describe such schools: Two-Way Schools, Two-Way Immersion, Two-Way Bilingual Education, Developmental Bilingual Education, Dual Language Education, Double Immersion and Interlocking Education.

The Language Balance of Students in Dual Language Schools

Dual language classrooms contain a mixture of language majority and language minority students. For example, half the children may come from Spanish-speaking homes; the other half from English language backgrounds. A language balance is sometimes attempted among an intake of students. If one language becomes dominant (e.g. due to much larger numbers of one language group), the aim of bilingualism and biliteracy may be at risk. However, many such schools have a preponderance of minority language children and successfully nurture both languages among students.

A substantial imbalance between the two languages among students may result in one language being used to the exclusion of the other (e.g. Spanish-speaking children having to switch to English to work cooperatively). Alternatively, one language group may become sidelined (e.g. Spanish speakers become excluded from English-speaking groups). Segregation rather than integration may occur. In the creation of a Dual Language school or classroom, careful student selection decisions have to be made to ensure a reasonable language balance.

If an imbalance does exist, it may be preferable to have more language minority children. Where there is a preponderance of language majority children, the tendency is for language minority children to switch to the higher status, majority language. In most (but not all) language contexts, the majority language is well represented outside school (e.g. in the media and for employment). Therefore, the balance towards the majority language outside the school can be complemented by a slight balance towards the minority language in school (among student intake and in curriculum delivery). However, if the school contains a particularly high number of language minority children, the prestige of the school may sometimes suffer (both among language majority and language minority parents).

Magnet schools exist in the US at both elementary and secondary level. Such schools teach the whole curriculum, but specialize in a certain field e.g. language arts, technology, or science. Where dual language Magnet schools exist, students may be drawn from a wide catchment area. For example, if a Magnet school focuses on environmental arts and sciences, parents throughout a district may be eager to gain a place for their children. Ensuring a language balance in each classroom then becomes a key selection feature.

There are situations where attracting language majority students to a Dual Language school is difficult. Where the monolingual mainstream school is as (or more) attractive to prospective parents, recruitment to Dual Language schools may be a challenge. For parents, allocation of their children to such dual language bilingual programs will be voluntary and not enforced. Hence, the good reputation, perceived effectiveness and curriculum success of such Dual Language schools becomes crucial to their continuation. Evidence from the US suggests that

'The best setting for educating linguistic minority pupils- and one of the best for educating any pupil – is a school in which two languages are used without apology and where becoming proficient in both is considered a significant intellectual and cultural achievement.'

REFERENCE: GLENN, 1990.

language minority parents may be supportive of such a program (e.g. Hornberger, 1991). Majority language parents may need more persuading. Community backing and involvement in the school may also be important in long-term success.

The development of Dual Language schools often starts with the creation of a dual language kindergarten class rather than an implementation throughout a school. As the kindergarten students move through the grades, a new dual language class is created each year. Apart from elementary Dual Language schools, there is also dual language secondary education in the US and, with different names, in many other countries of the world (e.g. Wales, Spain, India). A Dual Language school may be a whole school in itself. Also, there may be dual language classrooms within a 'mainstream' school. For example, there may be one dual language classroom in each grade.

Aims of Dual Language Schools

The aim of a Dual Language school is not just to produce bilingual and biliterate children. To gain status and to flourish, such a school needs to show success throughout the curriculum. On standardized tests, on attainment compared with other schools in the locality, and in specialisms (e.g. Music, Sport, Science), a Dual Language school will strive to show relative success. A narrow focus on proficiency in two languages will be insufficient in aim.

The aims of Dual Language schools may be couched in terms such as 'equality of educational opportunity for children from different language backgrounds', 'child-centered education building on the child's existing language competence', 'a community dedicated to the integration of all its children', 'enrichment not compensatory education', 'a family-like experience to produce multicultural children', and 'supporting Bilingual Proficiency not Limited English Proficiency'. Such Dual Language schools thus have a diversity of aims. These essentially include achievement throughout the curriculum, positive cross-cultural attitudes, social integration of children in the school and community, a positive self-image in each child, and attempting equality of access to opportunity among all students. Such equality of opportunity is offered to recent or established in-migrants, to those living in language minority or language majority homes.

Language Aims of Dual Language Schools

One of the special aims of Dual Language schools (e.g. compared with mainstream schools) is to produce thoroughly bilingual, biliterate and multicultural children. Language minority students are expected to become literate in their native language as well as in the majority language. Language majority students are expected to develop language and literacy skills in a second language. At the same time, majority language students must make normal progress in their first language. To achieve these aims, a variety of practices are implemented in Dual Language schools.

- The two languages of the school (e.g. Spanish and English, Chinese and English, Korean and English) have equal status. Both languages will be used as a medium of instruction. Math, Science and Social Studies, for example, may be taught in both languages.

- The school ethos will be bilingual. Such an ethos is created by classroom and corridor displays, notice boards, curriculum resources, cultural events, lunch break and extra curricula activity using both languages in a relatively balanced way. Announcements across the school address system will be bilingual. Letters to parents will also be in two languages. While playground conversations and student to student talk in the classroom is difficult to influence or manipulate, the school environment aims to be transparently bilingual.

- In some Dual Language schools, the two languages are taught as languages (sometimes called Language Arts instruction). Here, aspects of spelling, grammar, metaphors and communicative skills may be directly taught. In other Dual Language schools, use of both languages as media of instruction is regarded as sufficient to ensure bilingual development. In such schools, children are expected to acquire proficiency in language informally throughout the curriculum and through interaction with children who are effective first language role models. In both cases, reading and writing in both languages are likely to receive direct attention in the curriculum. Biliteracy is as much an aim as full bilingualism. Literacy will be acquired in both languages either simultaneously or with an initial emphasis on native language literacy.

- Staff in the dual language classrooms are often bilingual. Such teachers use both languages on different occasions with their students. Where this is difficult (e.g. due to teacher supply or selection), teachers may be paired and work together closely as a team. A teacher's aide, paraprofessionals, secretaries, custodial staff, parents offering or invited to help the teacher may also be bilingual. Language minority parents can be valuable 'teacher auxiliaries' in the classroom. For example, when a wide variety of Spanish cultures from many regions is brought to the classroom, parents and grandparents may describe and provide the most authentic stories, dances, recipes, folklore and festivals. This underlines the impor-

tance of the cultural heritage of language minorities being shared in the classroom to create an additive bilingual and multicultural environment.

• The length of the dual language program needs to be longer rather than shorter. Such a program for two or three grades is insufficient. A minimum of four years extending through the grades as far as possible is more defensible. Length of experience of a dual language program is important to ensure a fuller and deeper development of language skills and biliteracy. Where a US dual language program exists across more years, there is a tendency for the curriculum to be increasingly taught in the majority language – English. In some schools, the curriculum is initially taught for around 90 percent of time through the minority language. In later grades in the elementary school, this percentage is decreased until it reaches approximately 50 percent. In these programs, majority language students have an Immersion experience in a second language (e.g. Spanish), while minority language students initially receive most of their education in their home language.

Language Separation

A central idea in Dual Language schools is language separation and compartmentalization. In each period of instruction, only one language is used. Language boundaries are established in terms of time, curriculum content and teaching. These will each be considered.

First, a decision is made about when to teach through each language. One frequent preference is for each language to be used on alternate days. On the door of the classroom may be a message about which language is to be used that day. For example, Spanish is used one day, English the next, in a strict sequence. Alternately, different lessons may use different languages with a regular change over to ensure both languages are used in all curricular areas. For example, Spanish may be used to teach Mathematics on Monday and Wednesday and Friday; English to teach Mathematics on Tuesday and Thursday. During the next week, the languages are reversed, with Mathematics taught in Spanish on Tuesday and Thursday.

There are other possibilities. The division of time may be in half-days, alternate weeks, alternate half-semesters. The essential element is the distribution of time to achieve bilingual and biliterate students.

The amount of time spent learning through each language varies from school to school. Sometimes, a 50/50 balance in use of languages is attempted in early and later grades. In other classrooms, the minority language will be given more time (60 percent, 75 percent, 80 percent and 90 percent is not uncommon), especially in the first two or three years. In the middle and secondary years of schooling, there is sometimes a preference for a 50/50 balance, or more accent on the majority language (e.g. 70 percent through English; 30 percent through Spanish).

Whatever the division of time, instruction in a Dual Language school will keep boundaries between the languages. Switching languages within a lesson is not considered helpful. If language mixing by the teacher occurs, students may wait until there is delivery in their stronger language, and become uninvolved at other times. When there is clear separation, the Spanish speakers, for example, may help the English speakers on Spanish days, and the English speakers help the Spanish speakers on English days. Interdependence may stimulate co-operation and friendship, as well as learning and achievement. The potential problems of segregation and racial hostility may thus be considerably reduced.

However, the two languages will sometimes be switched or mixed in the classroom (e.g. in private conversations, in further explanations by a teacher, and internal use of the dominant language). Use of languages by children, especially when young, is not usually consciously controlled. Switching language can be as natural as smiling and using a particular accent.

> 'Emerging results of studies of two-way bilingual programs point to their effectiveness in educating non-native English-speaking students, their promise of expanding our nation's language resources by conserving the native language skills of minority students and developing second language skills in English-speaking students, and their hope of improving relationships between majority and minority groups by enhancing cross-cultural understanding and appreciation.'
>
> REFERENCE: CHRISTIAN, 1994

There is an important paradox in Dual Language schools. Boundaries are kept between languages so that separation does not occur between children. English and non-English speakers are integrated in lessons through language segregation.

Second, bilingual teachers ensure they do not switch languages. Children hear them using one language (during a lesson period or during a whole day) and are expected to respond in that same language. When, as in many forms of 'strong' bilingual education, there is a shortage of bilingual teachers, a pairing of teachers may ensure language separation. A teacher using Spanish only will work in close association with a teacher who only uses English with the same class. Such teamwork requires teachers to be committed to bilingualism and multiculturalism as important educational aims.

Third, language boundaries may be established in the curriculum. This may occur according to which 'language day' it is. Alternatively, in some schools, different parts of the curriculum are taught in different languages. For

The Origins of Dual Language Schools

Dual language schools in the US date from 1963 in Dade County, Florida, and were developed by the US Cuban community in that area (see Lindholm 1987; García & Otheguy, 1985; García & Otheguy, 1988).

Background
The first Cuban in-migrants in the early 1960s were mostly middle class, white, entrepreneurial professionals. Many were easily accepted by white power groups. By the end of the 1970s, Cubans owned around 40 percent of Miami's construction companies and 20 percent of its banks. Yet many Cubans retained loyalty to the Spanish language and ethnic culture. From 1973 to 1989, Dade County was officially bilingual in English and Spanish. This promoted tourism and investment from Latin America.

Beginnings
The modern movement in support of bilingual education in the US possibly dates from September 1963. In this month, the Coral Way Elementary School started a bilingual program that embraced both Spanish and English-speaking students. During the 1960s, another 14 such bilingual schools were set up in Dade County. This is related to the fact that many Cubans expected to return to Cuba, believing the Castro regime wouldn't survive. Local people supported the maintenance of Spanish among the soon-to-leave Cubans.

Local English-speaking children from middle class families were enrolled in the school. This reflected a wish among parents for foreign language instruction following Russia's triumph over the US in the space race. (In 1958, Sputnik was launched.) It was subsequently felt that the US needed to be less isolated from other countries. One way of achieving this was to encourage foreign language learning.

Changes
The Castro regime continued. The social and racial mix of Cuban in-migrants changed. The law changed and favored funding of Transitional Bilingual education programs. Hence, many Dade County public schools moved away from a strong form of bilingual education. Private ethnic schools in Miami continued to use Spanish as the teaching medium and produced bilingual and biliterate students. One major aim of such schools was to preserve traditional Cuban values and behavior.

Coral Way Dual Language School.

Young students at Coral Way Dual Language School

The Distribution of Dual Language Bilingual Programs in the United States

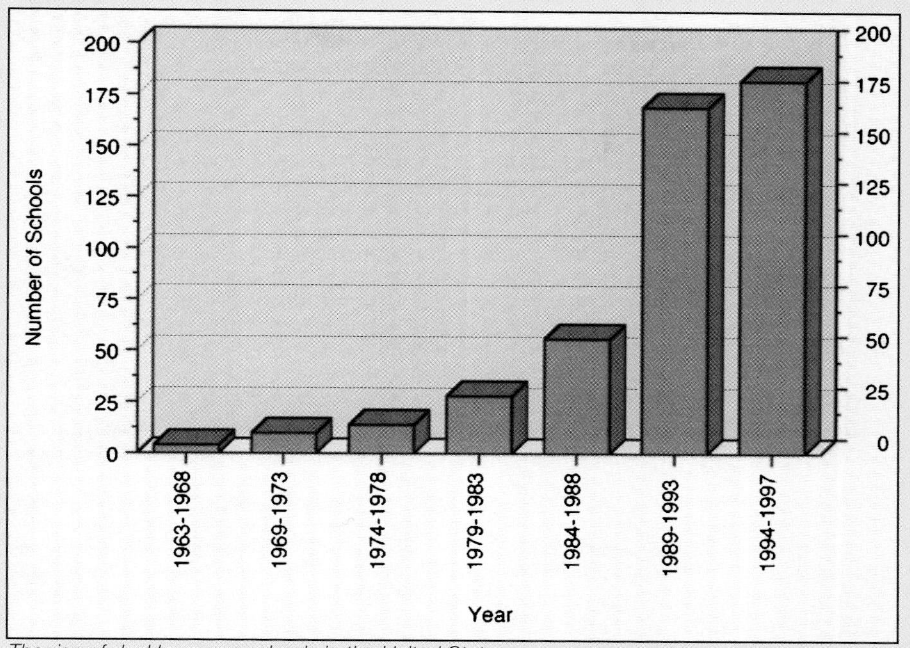

The rise of dual language schools in the United States.

The Number of Dual Language Programs in the United States

Alaska	1
Arizona	8
California	58
Colorado	5
Connecticut	3
District of Columbia	1
Florida	6
Illinois	12
Massachusetts	13
Michigan	2
Minnesota	1
New Jersey	2
New Mexico	1
New York	49
Oregon	3
Pennsylvania	1
Texas	9
Virginia	6
Wisconsin	1

NOTE: Some programs have more than one school in their program.

Languages of Learning in Dual Language Programs in the United States

Number of Schools

Spanish/English	167
Korean/English	4
Cantonese/English	3
French/English	2
Navajo/English	2
Arabic/English	1
Japanese/English	1
Portuguese/English	1
Russian/English	1

Grade Levels of Dual Language Programs in the United States

Grade	Number of Programs
Kindergarten only	8
Kindergarten to Grade 5/6	141
Kindergarten to Grade 7/8	11
Kindergarten to Grade 10/12	2
Grade 3/4 to 5/6/7	3
Grade 6 to 9	16
Grade 9 to 12	1

SOURCES : CHRISTIAN, 1994; CHRISTIAN & MAHRER, 1993, 1994.
Also on the World-Wide Web at: http://www.cal.org/cal/db/2way/

A Washington (DC) Dual Language School

In Washington DC, the James F. Oyster Bilingual Elementary School has a two-way program that commenced in 1971. The initiative was taken by the local community among parents and local politicians to produce a school that crossed language, cultural, ethnic and social class lines. Parents are still active in the running of the school. With students from kindergarten to 6th Grade, there is a ethnic mix from 25 countries (1993): 58 percent Hispanic, 26 percent Anglo; 12 percent African American and 4 percent Asian. Around two in every five children come from low-income families.

The program is distinctive because it has two teachers in each classroom: one teacher speaks only Spanish to the students; the other speaks only English. The students experience Spanish and English-medium instruction for approximately equal amounts of time. A strong multicultural dimension pervades the curriculum, with the contributions of different children encouraged and respected. The notion of equality permeates the ethos of the school. This is reflected in the 1988 mission statement below:

> 'Oyster Bilingual School's focus is on the development of bilingualism, biliteracy, and biculturalism for every student through the mastery of academic skills, the acquisition of language and communicative fluency, the appreciation of differences in racial and ethnic backgrounds, and the building of a positive self-concept and pride in one's heritage'.

REFERENCE: FREEMAN, 1995

example, Social Studies and Environmental Studies may be taught in Spanish, Science and Math in English. Such a policy establishes separate occasions where each language is to be used, and keeps the two languages apart. However, one danger is that the majority language becomes aligned with modern technology and science, while the minority language becomes associated with tradition and culture. This may affect the status of the language in the eyes of the child, parents and society. The relationship of languages to employment prospects, economic advantage and power thus need to be considered.

Comparisons with other Bilingual Schools

Such Dual Language schools differ from Transitional Bilingual education and Submersion/Mainstream/ESL approaches by teaching through the medium of two languages over four or more grades. United States Transitional Bilingual education essentially aims to move children into English-only instruction within two or three years. In contrast, Dual Language schools aim to enable the child to achieve increasing proficiency in two languages (e.g. Spanish and English in the US). Dual language schools differ from Immersion bilingual education in the language backgrounds of the students. Immersion schools normally contain only language majority children learning much or part of the curriculum through a second language (e.g. English-speaking children learning through the medium of French in Canadian schools). Dual language schools contain a balanced mixture of children from two (or more) different language backgrounds (e.g. from Spanish-speaking and English-speaking homes in the US) .

Further Reading

CHRISTIAN, D., 1994, *Two-Way Bilingual Education: Students Learning Through Two Languages.* University of California at Santa Cruz: National Center for Research on Cultural Diversity and Second Language Learning.

LINDHOLM, K. J., 1990, Bilingual Immersion Education: Criteria for Program Development. In A. M. PADILLA, H. H. FAIRCHILD & C. M. VALADEZ (eds), *Bilingual Education: Issues & Strategies.* London: Sage.

MORISON, S. H., 1990, A Spanish-English Dual Language Program in New York City. In C. B. CAZDEN & C. E. SNOW (eds), *The Annals of the American Academy of Political & Social Science.* Volume 508, 160-169. London: Sage.

Public School 84 – A Spanish-English Dual Language School in New York

Public School 84 is one of thousands of public schools in New York, yet is well known in bilingual education circles. Situated on West 92nd Street, it has gained a reputation as a model dual language school. Part of its fame was gained from a celebrated article by its Principal, Sidney H. Morison, published in the Annals of the American Academy of Political and Social Science, March 1990.

A rainbow-colorful student-made sign at the entrance to the school reads 'Welcome' and *'Bienvenidos'*. This immediately announces the equal status of Spanish and English in the school. Notices, announcements and displays are also thoroughly bilingual. Children, teachers, paraprofessionals, custodial staff and others all use both Spanish and English.

On the door of each classroom, there is a small colorful picture and a notice that indicates what day it is. The day does not refer to the day of the week, but rather to whether it is a Spanish-speaking or an English-speaking day. Inside the colorful classrooms, the posters, children's work and teacher exhibitions are all in Spanish and English. While in practice the language is not rigidly Spanish or English according to the day, the teachers and older students are aware of the need for separation of languages. Younger children naturally switch in and out of Spanish and English with their teacher and class peers according to different needs and situations. However, teachers attempt to implement the policy of language separation wherever feasible.

After visits to two or three classes, it becomes clear that Spanish enjoys equal status with English as a language of instruction, for interaction between children and in the administrative and management life of the school. Since the Dual Language school was first established in 1984, the children are mixed in terms of Latino and non-Latino origins and home language. Approximately half the children are Spanish first language speakers.

Within the class there is no obvious grouping by language. Rather teachers arrange mixed groups of Spanish-speaking and English-speaking children for both social and educational activities. However, teachers take care that Spanish as a language of instruction is fully promoted and does not fall into disuse because it is a minority language in the US and has lower prestige than English.

In the early grades, there are alternating Spanish and English-speaking days in the children's own classroom. In the middle grades, a different model is used. Each teacher has her own room and speaks one language to the children. So on Monday, a class may go to the English-speaking teacher and her room for the day, switching to the Spanish-speaking teacher and her room on Tuesday, with an alternating schedule operating continuously. The curriculum is shared between the two teachers of the middle grade children in a carefully conceived strategy. Each teacher may teach to her strengths and interests, with no topics or subject content being repeated in the other language.

For example, Mathematics may be taught in English by one teacher, Social Studies in Spanish by the other teacher. Thus, language is used in a complementary rather than a repetitious way in the classroom.

Sidney Morison (1990) suggests that 'Strict separation, with no switching, is really the lynchpin of the program, providing necessary support for Spanish, the minority language, while adding to its status as a language of instruction.' While strict separation between the two languages with no switching is the necessary theory of the dual language program, in practice young children naturally switch their languages on occasions to ensure their communication is efficient and understood. The result of such dual language education tends to be thoroughly bilingual and biliterate children. The school has a very successful record of academic achievement not only in languages, but throughout the curriculum.

Officially, the dual language program at Public School 84 was inaugurated in the Autumn of 1984. However, the first bilingual classes were present in 1970. The dual language nature of the school was only achieved through considerable political effort. A political movement of parents, supported by enthusiastic teachers, was instrumental in this 'grass roots' pressure to establish a Dual Language school. Academic experts such as Professor Ricardo Otheguy of City College of New York, were important in providing a basic language philosophy, policy and practice for the school.

REFERENCE: MORISON, 1990

A Spanish-English Dual Language School in New York.

5: Dual Majority Language Bilingual Education

In some countries of the world, two majority languages co-exist inside a school. In dual majority language bilingual education, two majority languages are used for curriculum delivery within a school. The languages are not necessarily used in equal proportions. However, both languages are not only taught as a language, but are also used to transmit the curriculum. Some international cases will illustrate the concept of such dual majority language bilingual education.

In Kuwait and Saudi Arabia, the joint use of Arabic and English in some schools represents dual majority language bilingual education. Such dual language usage in school reflects out-of-school Arabic in the home, wider society and in Islam, while English is used inside each country for its international trade and communication value. In Kuwait, both Arabic and English have relatively high prestige, particularly among students studying the sciences.

Other continents show similar situations. In Brunei, for example, Malaysian (Bahasa Melayu) and English co-exist in schools as majority languages, both with high status and value. In Malaysia, Bahasa Melayu and English are both prestigious languages. Bahasa Melayu and Tamil, and Bahasa Melayu and Chinese, create dual majority language situations, with some representation in schools at the primary level. Neighboring countries have similar dual majority language bilingual education practices. The use of Japanese and English in schools in Japan is a growing phenomenon. In Africa and India, there are also schools where a majority regional language and an international language such as French and English co-exist as the schools' teaching media. Enabling children to be bilingual and biliterate in both their regional majority language and an international language is the aim and outcome of such education. In Brunei and Taiwan, the dominant indigenous language is used in school along with a second international language to form an enrichment bilingual education program.

The students in many of these schools tend to come from the middle classes and there is a tendency to produce elites. However, in countries where linguistic diversity is thoroughly embodied in tradition and demography, the combination of languages such as Tamil or Chinese and Bahasa Melayu may be for many rather than for the few. The aim of such education is to produce students who are bilingual, biliterate and bicultural. Such students may be expected to help in harmonizing and integrating diverse ethnic groups and cultures within the country. In other contexts, such students are expected to spearhead that country's desire to expand trade, foster international relationships and aid economic prosperity. Developing a country is seen partly through its developing languages. A developing nation becomes a bilingual nation.

In many international cases, the second language is introduced in the primary school. It is often introduced as a language first of all, and then when developing, is used to transmit other areas of the curriculum. There is sometimes a tendency to teach science subjects (e.g. Physics, Chemistry, Biology, Engineering, Mathematics, Computing, Medicine) in an international second language (e.g. English). The teaching staff are often a mixture of native speakers of English from the United States and Britain for example, plus teachers educated within their home country who have also taken part of their education abroad.

While little evidence of the effectiveness of dual majority language bilingual education exists at the moment, it is likely that this will be an area for future research. From generalizations that could possibly be made from other international contexts, there is no reason why full bilingualism, biliteracy, biculturalism and achievement across the curriculum should not be possible within such dual majority language bilingual education.

One particular example of dual majority language bilingual education is the European School movement. Another example is certain schools in the International Schools movement. These are detailed in separate topics.

Further Reading

GARCÍA, O., 1997, Bilingual Education. In F. COULMAS (ed.), *The Handbook of Sociolinguistics*. Oxford: Blackwell.

GARCÍA, O. & BAKER, C. (eds), 1995, *Policy and Practice in Bilingual Education*. Clevedon: Multilingual Matters Ltd.

Trilingual Education in Luxembourg

The Grand Duchy of Luxembourg has been an independent European state since 1839. It is a small country, less than 1000 square miles, and can be crossed in less than an hour by car. It is bordered on the north and west by Belgium, on the east by Germany, and on the south by France.

Approximately 75 percent of the population of approximately 385,000 are Luxembourgians and native speakers of Luxembourgish (known to its own speakers as Letzeburgesch, also spelt Lëtzebuergesch), a language closely related to German. (Luxembourg also has a large population of in-migrant workers.) However, the reality of life demands that the citizens of this small country become fluent in French and German for employment, trade and professional careers. The two official languages of Luxembourg are German and French. Thus a triglossic situation exists in Luxembourg. Luxembourgish is the daily spoken language of the vast majority of the population, but written documents, street signs and public notices, for example, are sometimes in German or more often French. French is the official language of administration, parliament and courts, whereas German is the language of popular publishing and some levels of discussion. Luxembourgish has the status of national language, decreed by the law of February 24, 1984. Its use as a written language has begun to increase slightly.

Most people will need to use German and French in their working life, and, since only first year university education exists in Luxembourg, students wishing to study for a degree will need to go to another country. Thus, one of the main aims of compulsory education in Luxembourg (for those between six and 15 years old) is to produce young people who are fluent in Luxembourgish, German and French. English is of less importance in language teaching than these three languages.

The first stage of education in Luxembourg is the *jardin d'enfants* or *spillschoul* for children between four and six. The language of the *spillschoul* is Luxembourgish. Twenty seven percent of the population of the country are in-migrant workers and their families, often from countries like Portugal and Italy, and it is considered important that their children learn Luxembourgish, which is the main spoken language of the country. Compulsory education begins in the second year of kindergarten, but parents who do not speak Luxembourgish at home are strongly advised to send their children to the *spillschoul* at four.

At the age of six children begin their primary education, German is soon introduced as a written language and as a working language through which subjects are studied. Because Luxembourgish and German are similar, the children do not usually have much difficulty in learning to read and write in German, and later doing other subjects through the medium of German. Children who are not native speakers of Luxembourgish may experience a little more difficulty.

French is introduced as a subject halfway through the second year of primary school. The emphasis is initially on oral work. Then the children learn to read and write the language. During the primary school years, there is a gradual shift towards French, and by the first years of secondary school, the children are studying all their subjects through the medium of French. German is still studied as a subject. English or Latin is introduced after the age of 12. In addition the children receive an hour's teaching in Luxembourgish every week up to the age of 12. The accent is usually on oral work or reading, with discussions on personal matters and current affairs.

The educational system in Luxembourg is remarkable because of the accent placed on fluency in three languages. In primary and secondary schools, nearly half the weekly timetable is based on language learning in one form or another. The hours devoted to teaching Luxembourgish, French and German in Luxembourg schools is in particular contrast to the drip-feed hour-on-hour language teaching that occurs in the United States and the United Kingdom. In Luxembourg, German is taught as a subject for eight hours a week in the first two years of primary school, and for five hours in the remaining four years of primary education, as well as being the medium of instruction for most subjects in the primary school. French is taught for three hours a week from age seven and for seven hours a week for most of the remainder of primary education.

At the secondary level, German is timetabled for around four hours per week at the start of secondary schooling and for three hours during the latter stages. French language teaching occurs for six hours per week in the first two years and for slightly less afterwards. There is also the hour of Luxembourgish which is dropped during the second year of secondary education, when six hours a week of English or Latin is added. There is a special Immersion program for late incomers to Luxembourg where they spend 15 hours a week out of a total of 30, studying French.

Children in Luxembourg seem to cope well with what might appear to be the difficult task of gaining competence in, and being educated, through the medium of two foreign languages. By the end of compulsory secondary education, most children have an excellent command of both languages.

A number of factors appear to contribute to this successful model of trilingual education. Firstly, all school teachers in Luxembourg are required to be fluent in Luxembourgish as well as French and German, and all language teachers at the secondary level must have acquired higher education qualifications outside Luxembourg. Thus they can help the children with communication in any language. The medium of informal communication between teachers and students is Luxembourgish, and during the early school years, teachers switch frequently to Luxembourgish in class to help understanding. Secondly, although Luxembourgish is the everyday language of the majority of the population, French and German are seen and heard widely, on radio and television, in print and on signs and public notices. Thus the children receive some exposure to these languages out of school. Thirdly, the children are highly motivated to learn French and German because they will need them for employment and higher education.

Children in Luxembourg spend more hours per week in class than their counterparts in some other countries (30 hours in secondary school compared with about 24 hours in the UK, for instance). This allows more time, compared to many schools (e.g. in the US and UK) for language learning.

The 'strong' language policy in Luxembourg is based on the idea that languages should be acquired and taught in school from a very young age; that language education should continue as a compulsory element until the end of secondary schooling; and that subjects in the curriculum should and can be taught through second and third languages. The motivation for such a strong language policy in the schools tends to be for commercial and economic reasons. The high level of success of Luxembourg children in achieving trilingualism suggests that, in the economy of Europe of the future, they stand a fine chance of success.

Reference:
LEBRUN & BAETENS BEARDSMORE, 1993

6: European Schools

Definition

European Schools aim to produce children who are bilingual and biliterate in at least two languages of the European Union. There are nine such schools, located in various countries in Europe. Children learn through their home language and a second language. They are also taught a third language. Classroom time is allocated for activities to integrate children of diverse language backgrounds.

The Students

The first European School was established in the Grand Duchy of Luxembourg following a parental initiative, and received official recognition in 1958. Schools were later opened in Belgium, Italy, Germany, the Netherlands and England. The schools were originally designed to provide education for the children of European Union workers. The children of European Union employees such as civil servants, translators, technicians and domestic workers have priority of access. Spare places are made available to other children within the locality, particularly to balance the language mix of the school. Education is free, although non-European Union parents pay a small contribution to the costs of running the school. Fees can be waived or reduced if families are unable to meet the cost of fees. The schools are multilingual in character and cater for some 15,000 children from a wide variety of different European Union nations. The students study for the European Baccalaureate.

Students at the European School at Culham England stand on a map of Europe.

Young European school students holding balloons bearing the symbol of the European Union. Each star represents a country in the European Union.

Bulwer (1995) has shown that the original intention of the European schools was for relatively open access to children of different nationalities who were not necessarily members of European Union officials. Bulwer (1995) found that 40 percent of children in European schools were not children of scientists, technicians or administrators working for the EU. However, this varied from school to school. The Brussels II school contained 12 percent of non-EU workers' students, and the Luxembourg school 20 percent of such children. In comparison, at least five in every six children in schools at Bergen, Karlsruhe and Mol were not from EU worker homes. There are no entry 'ability' selection tests, and although non-EU workers pay fees, there are hardship funds to reduce fees.

The Languages of the School

The eleven official languages of the European Union have equal status within the schools. Therefore, each school may have up to eleven subsections reflecting the first language of the children (this may increase in the future as further countries join the European Union). One central aim of the school is to support and extend the child's first language. Thus, in the primary years, much of a child's instruction is through their native language. Children become thoroughly literate in their native language and are taught its attendant culture. Such schools promote bilingualism for all. Biliteracy is also thoroughly developed. The schools deliberately

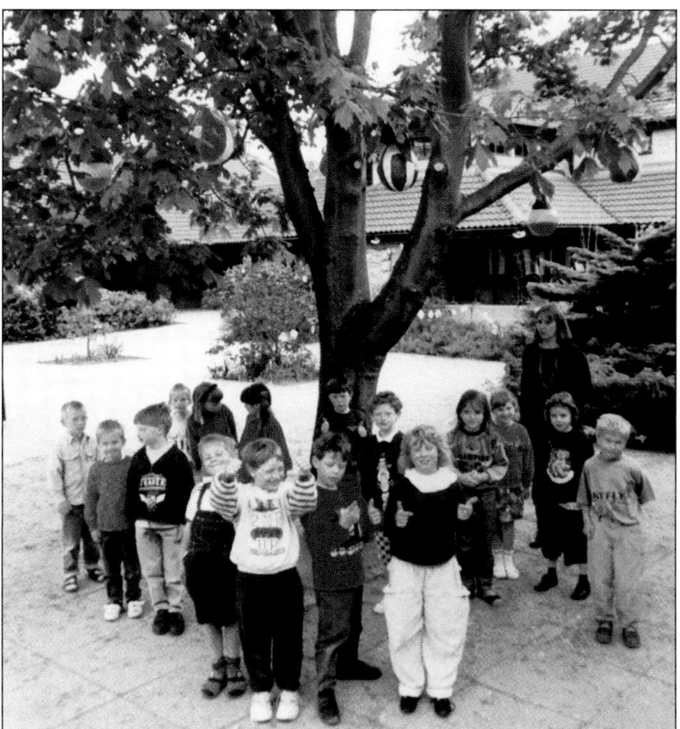

Young European School students under a tree bearing balloons representing the flags of the various native countries of the students.

engineer the integration between children from different regions.

All children are taught a second language from the beginning of the primary school. The language is taught by native speakers and not the class teacher, to ensure excellent role models. Native speakers of the vehicular language may also be present in the schools. In European Schools this second language is called a working language.

In the first and second grades, the second language will only be taught as a subject. In these grades, no curriculum subjects will be taught through the second language. In the third, fourth and fifth grades, such language teaching continues. Physical education may also be taught through the second language. By the end of primary education, approximately 25 percent of the curriculum is taught through the second language.

This proportion increases as the child goes through secondary education. In Grades 6 though 8 in the secondary school program, the second language will be taught as a subject and the following subjects can also be taught through that second language: Design Technology, Music, Physical Education and complementary activities. From the third year onwards, Grades 9 through 12, History, Geography and options such as Economics and Social Sciences will be taught through the second language.

The charts show which subjects are taught, and which languages are used to teach those subjects. For late arrivals to the school, there are 'catching up classes' and support classes to increase proficiency in the second language. In addition, all students are taught a third language for a minimum of 360 hours, beginning in the second class of secondary school. Any language available in the school may be chosen. Some children opt to learn a fourth language, beginning in the fourth class of secondary school.

European Hours

European Schools ensure the development of the child's first language and cultural identity. They also aim to promote a sense of European identity. Many centuries of rivalry and conflict in Europe have meant that national differences rather than a shared European identity are still common. An English, French or German person tends to take great pride in national identity, with the concept of European identity being new and sometimes strange. With a considerable mix of different nationalities within a European School, teachers are on guard against prejudice and rivalry. European schools have become a laboratory for testing whether integration and harmony can be promoted within an educational setting.

One form of integration is through communal lessons. The more the child progresses through the grades, the more lessons are taught to mixed language groups. In the primary school, these communal lessons are known as European Hours. Starting in the third year of primary education, there are three such lessons a week lasting a total of 2 hours and 15 minutes.

The primary aim is for children from different language sections to work and play together. As the lessons develop, children should become more aware of their similarities rather than differences, of their common European heritage, and of the importance of living peacefully and harmoniously together. In classes of 20 to 25 students, co-operative activities such as cooking, or constructing objects (e.g. making puppets) are used to integrate children. Teachers are given freedom of choice of activity so long as such activity engages co-operation between children. All elementary school teachers are involved in the European Hours. However, teachers change classes during the school year to reinforce the multicultural and multilingual aspects of European Hours.

The classroom atmosphere and ethos of European Hours is regarded as essential. Enjoyable, motivating projects are used, with satisfying and attainable goals. Small multilingual groups work together to attain a goal. Co-operation is essential for a successful outcome. The results of

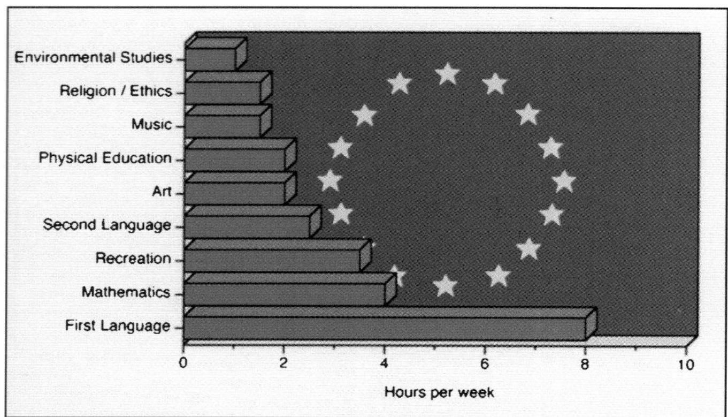

The European School curriculum in Grades 1 and 2.

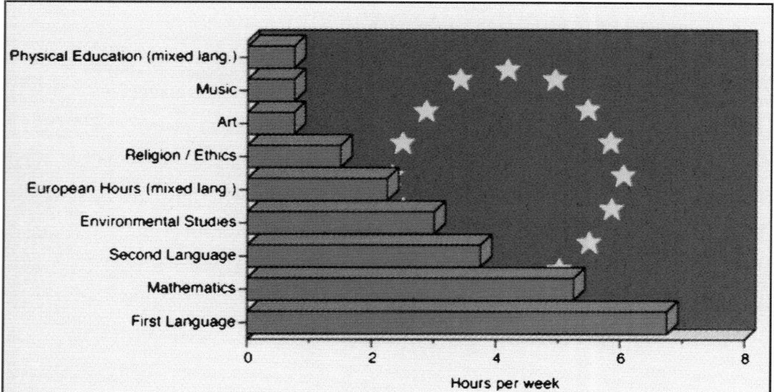

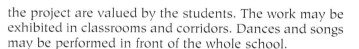

The European School curriculum in Grades 3 to 5.

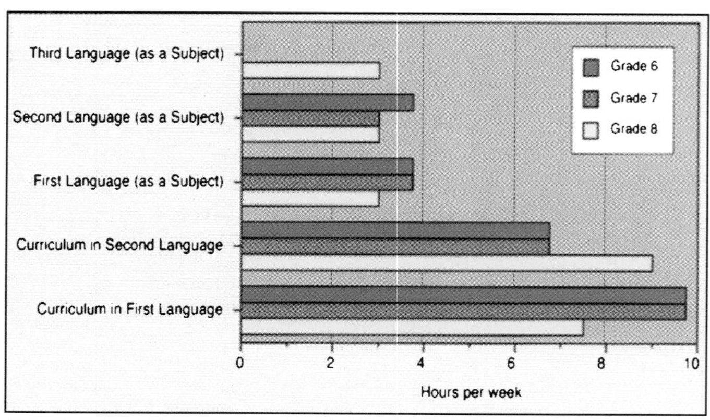

The European School curriculum in Grades 6 to 8.

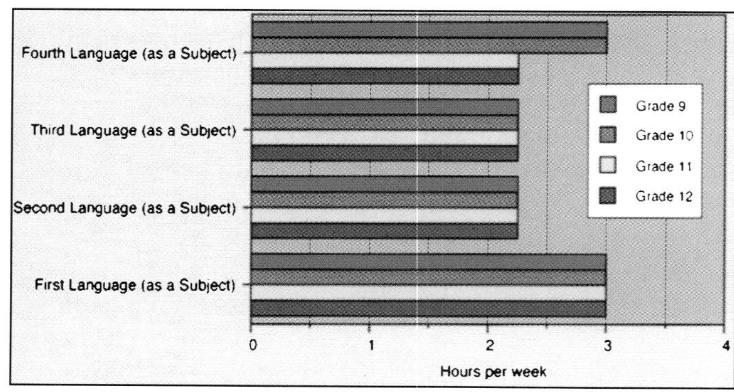

The European School curriculum (languages only) in Grades 9 to 12.

the project are valued by the students. The work may be exhibited in classrooms and corridors. Dances and songs may be performed in front of the whole school.

Given that five or six different languages may co-exist among students within the European Hours classroom, children act as translators for the teacher. If the instructions are given in French and the teacher cannot speak German, children who can speak in French and German act as informal interpreters.

Two European Hours lessons per week are conducted in the classroom. The third European Hours lesson is a games activity conducted outside, but with the same aims and processes. No child is forced to use a particular language in European Hours. The hidden message to the child is of the importance of co-operation between languages, of accepting multilingualism as natural and workable.

The demands of using a second or a third language are lessened for the child. The nature of the European Hours project is cognitively less demanding than other subjects. The project also tends to be 'context-embedded'. That is, the activity does not depend on language alone, but actions (non-verbal communication) can relay a lot of information between children. This teaches the child that harmony and co-operation can occur with relative ease and that languages are not barriers to co-operation.

In the secondary school, classes in Art, Music and Sport are composed of mixed nationalities. In addition, everyday interaction between students outside classes encourages the acquisition of other languages, and friendships between children of different nationalities and language backgrounds.

Does it work? In one research study, it was found that in the latter stages of secondary schooling, the majority of students had best friends in a language section other than their own (Housen & Baetens Beardsmore, 1987).

Teachers

Teachers are recruited from different European education systems. All teachers are native speakers of a school language. They must also be bilingual or multilingual. No special teacher training or certification is required to work in a European School. Only a National Teachers' Certificate is needed from that person's native country. There is currently almost no training in Europe for working in a multilingual or multicultural school such as a

European School. Therefore, teachers learn 'on the job'. New teachers normally spend two or three weeks in observation before starting teaching. New teachers are placed in the care of an experienced 'mentor' teacher.

Within European Schools, there are in-service training sessions for its teachers. This covers both refreshing and updating on language and subject content. Other professionals in the school look after the library, science and technology laboratories, and have responsibility for particular grades.

Parents

Communication with parents is multilingual. Meetings with parents are normally for that parent's language group only. When a large meeting of parents needs to take place, interpretation facilities will sometimes be available. Parents who send their children to such European Schools are often bilingual or multilingual themselves. Therefore, their children start with an extra interest and familiarity with bilingual or multilingual settings. Many students come from literacy-oriented, middle class homes, with a positive view of bilingualism.

Research

Research on the effectiveness of European Schools suggests that there appear to be no detrimental effects on academic achievement stemming from the bilingual and multilingual policies. Students tend to succeed in the European Baccalaureate Examination and many go to university. While the schools provide a fine example of the production of bilingual and biliterate children, they produce relatively privileged European School children. European Schools produce children secure in their own national culture and having a supranational European identity. However, there is the issue of whether they produce an educational and cultural elite, not by intention but by outcome. The Schools may be reproducing families who already have a considerable bilingual advantage.

Comparisons with other Bilingual Schools

European Schools differ from heritage language schools. A heritage language school is mostly populated by language minority students. The minority language is the main medium of instruction. European Schools tend to recruit children from majority language backgrounds who are taught through two majority languages.

European Schools have many similarities with Immersion bilingual education. Both forms of bilingual education tend to recruit from the middle classes and offer education through two majority languages. A major difference between the European Schools Movement and the Canadian Immersion program is that the second language is taught as a subject in the European Schools before being used as a medium of instruction. In Canadian Immersion programs, the second language is used as a medium of instruction from the beginning. In European Schools, there is also relatively more emphasis on the second language being taught as a subject in itself.

A Quote from Jacques Delors, Former President of the European Community

'To be able to foster European ideals within young people and, most of all, to do this in a way which they will be able to translate into moment by moment living, is, without a doubt, the most beautiful and the most certain route towards a lasting peace, the sole guarantee of Europe, which people have dreamt of so much in the past, and which we have the opportunity to build'.

Further Reading

BAETENS BEARDSMORE, H., 1993, The European School Model. In H. BAETENS BEARDSMORE (ed.), *European Models of Bilingual Education*. Clevedon: Multilingual Matters Ltd.

BAETENS BEARDSMORE, H., & SWAIN, M., 1985, Designing Bilingual Education: Aspects of Immersion and 'European School' Models. *Journal of Multilingual and Multicultural Development*, 6 (1), 1-15.

BULWER, J., 1995, European Schools: Languages For All? *Journal of Multilingual and Multicultural Development*, 16 (6), 459-475.

CENTRAL OFFICE OF THE REPRESENTATIVE OF THE BOARD OF GOVERNORS OF THE EUROPEAN SCHOOLS, 1994, *The European Schools*. Brussels, Belgium.

Some Facts about the European Schools

- In 1952, six European countries came together to establish the European Coal and Steel Community, the forerunner of the European Economic Community.
- These countries were Germany, Belgium, France, Italy, Luxembourg, Netherlands.
- The headquarters of the community were in Luxembourg.
- The first European School opened in Luxembourg on October 4th, 1953, to provide an education for children of European Community workers. It was not originally called a European School.
- The school catered for the five years of primary education. There were 70 students, and six teachers, one from each of the member states of the Community.
- Education was initially provided in the four official languages of the community, Italian, French, German and Dutch.
- The present day European Union has 15 member states: Austria, Belgium, Denmark, Finland, France, Germany, Greece, Ireland, Italy, Luxembourg, Portugal, The Netherlands, Spain, Sweden and the United Kingdom.
- There are eleven official languages of the European Union: Danish, Dutch, English, Finnish, French, German, Greek, Italian, Portuguese, Spanish and Swedish.
- There are currently nine European schools, one in Luxembourg, three in Belgium, two in Germany, one in Italy, one in the United Kingdom and one in the Netherlands. A tenth will soon be opened in Belgium.
- In the school year 1992-3, 15,000 students were receiving their education in European schools.

The Schools are:

European School of Luxembourg (established 1953)
Boulevard Konrad Adenauer
L-1115 Luxembourg/Kirchberg, Luxembourg

European School of Brussels I/Uccle (established 1958)
Avenue du Vert Chasseur 46
B-1180 Brussels, Belgium

European School of Mol/Geel (established 1960)
Europawijk
B-2400 Mol, Belgium

European School of Varese/Ispra (established 1960)
Via Montello 118
I-21100 Varese, Italy

European School of Karlsruhe (established 1962)
Albert Schweitzer Strasse 1
D-7500 Karlsruhe 1, Germany

European School of Bergen N.H./Petten (established 1963)
Molenweidtje 5
NL-1862 BC Bergen N.H., The Netherlands

European School of Brussels II/Woluwe (established 1974)
Avenue Oscar Jespers 75
B-1200 Brussels, Belgium

European School of Munich (established 1977)
Elise-Aulinger Strasse 21
D-8000 Munchen 83, Germany

European School of Culham (established 1978)
Culham, Abingdon
Oxfordshire
OX14 3DZ, United Kingdom

The co-ordinating institution is: The Central Office of the Representative of the Board of Governors of the European Schools, Rue de la Loi 200, Batiment Beliar 5-7, B-1049 Brussels, Belgium.

European Schools and the Spirit of Europe

The French statesman, Jean Monnet, the first president of the European Coal and Steel Community, uttered the following words. They express the essential aims of the European Schools and have been sealed, in parchment, into the foundation stones of all the Schools:

'Educated side by side, untroubled from infancy by divisive prejudices, acquainted with all that is great and good in the different cultures, it will be borne in upon them as they mature that they belong together. Without ceasing to look to their own lands with love and pride, they will become in mind Europeans, schooled and ready to complete and consolidate the work of their fathers before them, to bring into being a united and thriving Europe.'

The 'Working Language' or '*Langue Vehiculaire*'

'Teaching through the medium of the working language constitutes one of the corner stones of the European schools. How did it come into being? Where does the idea come from? Was it the result of a scholarly pedagogical study conducted by 'experts' in an office? Not at all. During the first years, History and Geography, for example, were only taught in German and French for financial reasons. The German and French speaking pupils followed these courses in their mother tongue, the Italian and Dutch speaking pupils had to choose between French and German. Italian and Dutch speaking teachers, parents and pupils were quick to protest against the injustice of the system: some studied History and Geography in their mother tongue, others were forced to study these subjects in a foreign language. If economies were necessary, at least these sacrifices should be the same for everyone. In this spirit of equality, it was decided that the Germans would study these subjects in French, the French speakers in German, and the others would choose between French and German. Teaching through the medium of the working language had come into being!

As experience grew, a formula (which was considered at the beginning as a necessary evil) revealed such positive aspects that it became one of the basic tenets of the European Schools. Teaching through the working language considerably reinforces the knowledge of the first foreign language. It brings together teachers and pupils of different nationalities and it compels the teacher to rethink the teaching of History and Geography, to distance it from its purely national dimension, because it is addressed to an international audience.'

Translated from a French language article by Yvon Heumann (Director of the European School of Munich): *'L'École européenne: une contribution à la construction d'une Europe unie'.* Schola Europa, Bruxelles, 1993.

The Stated Objectives of the European Schools Movement

- to give students confidence in their own cultural identity – the bedrock for their development as European citizens;
- to give a sound education, based on a broad range of subjects, from nursery level to university entrance;
- to develop high standards in speaking and writing both the mother tongue and two or more foreign languages;
- to develop mathematical and scientific skills throughout the whole period of schooling;
- to encourage a European and global perspective in the study of history and geography, rather than a narrower, nationalistic one;
- to encourage creativity in music and the plastic arts and an appreciation of all that is best in a common European artistic heritage;
- to develop physical skills and instill in students an appreciation of the need for healthy living through participation in sporting and recreational activities;
- to offer students professional guidance in their choice of subjects and in career/university decisions in the later years of the secondary school;
- to foster tolerance, co-operation, communication and concern for others throughout the school community;
- to provide high quality teaching through the recruitment of well qualified and experienced staff by the respective countries' Ministries of Education.

REFERENCE: CENTRAL OFFICE OF THE REPRESENTATIVE OF THE BOARD OF GOVERNORS OF THE EUROPEAN SCHOOLS, 1994

7: International Schools

International Schools are a diverse collection of schools throughout the world. Numbering over 850 schools, they are found in over 80 countries of the world, mostly in large cities. Mainly for the affluent, parents pay fees for mostly private, selective, independent education. Children in these schools often have parents in the diplomatic service, multinational organizations, or in international businesses and who are geographically and vocationally mobile. Other children in an International School come from the locality, and have parents who want their children to have an internationally flavored education.

International Schools represent an excellent example of dual majority language education. One language (sometimes the main language) of the school is usually English. Such schools are bilingual because a national or another international language is incorporated in the curriculum. Sometimes, the second language (taught for up to 12 years) is only taught as a language. In other schools, the second language is used as a medium to teach part of the curriculum. In schools where the national language co-exists with an international language like English, and where a good proportion of the students are native speakers of the national language, both languages will be used in school administration, extracurricular activities, and informally amongst the students and staff. Some schools enable their students to acquire third and fourth languages. Generally, the languages of International Schools are majority languages with international prestige. Minority languages are rarely found in such schools.

The primary and secondary curriculum tends to reflect a United States or British as well as the local curriculum tradition. The teachers are from various countries, usually with a plentiful supply of British- and American-trained staff. Most International Schools prepare children for the International Baccalaureate, United States tests or British examinations, and for universities in Europe and North America.

Some Brief Examples of International Schools

An added flavor of the varied nature of International Schools is portrayed in further brief examples given below. A book listing and describing such schools in every part of the world is: *The ECIS International Schools Directory,* published annually by the European Council of International Schools.

Ecole Active Bilingue Jeannine Manuel
Situated in Paris, France. Age range: 3 to 19; 150 students. The teachers come from ten nationalities. The school aims to 'develop bilingualism and biculturalism' in French and English. Japanese is begun at primary level and continued through the secondary school. Science and Humanities are available in French or English. United States university and college exams and tests (e.g. SAT, Achievement Tests, PSAT), the French Baccalaureate, and the International Baccalaureate can be taken.

John F. Kennedy School
Situated in Berlin. Age range: 5 to 19; 1280 students from 23 nationalities. Half the teachers are from the United States and the other half from Germany. The school is bilingual, binational and bicultural in German and English. Instruction is 'conducted in both languages continuously'. Tuition is free.

International School of London
Situated in London. Age range: 4 to 18; 170 students from 36 nationalities. Teachers come from 12 nationalities. The school offers: Arabic, French, Italian, Japanese, German, Portuguese and Spanish native language instruction. Language instruction in 20 languages can be arranged.

Chinese International School
Situated in Hong Kong. Age range: 4 to 18; 1045 students from 23 nationalities. Teachers come from eight nationalities. The school is 'dedicated to providing an education in the language and culture of both the Chinese and Western worlds'. Chinese (Mandarin) and English are taught. Children come from diverse ethnic, religious and linguistic backgrounds. Most students are of United States, British and Chinese origin, but students also derive from seven other countries.

Aloha College
Situated in Marbella, Spain. Age range: 3 to 18; 440 students from 33 nationalities. Teachers are graduates from Spain or the UK. Up to 40 percent of the curriculum is taught in Spanish; the remainder in English. French, German, Swedish and Arabic are also available. The students are 45 percent Spanish, 25 percent British and 10 percent Scandinavian and go on to college or university in Europe or North America.

International School of Berne
Situated in Switzerland. Age range: 4 to 19; 174 students from 33 nationalities. Teachers come from 10 nationalities. 'Tolerance of racial, religious, cultural and political differences is stressed. The school aims to foster an appreciation and understanding of diverse cultures and to promote open communication, open-mindedness, fairness, and respect for the particular backgrounds of its students.' The languages of instruction are English, French and German.

Al Mawakeb School
Situated in Dubai, United Arab Emirates. Age range: 3 to 18; 1846 students from 40 nationalities. Teachers come from 16 nationalities. Trilingual education is provided in Arabic, French and English which are regarded as core subjects in the curriculum. Science, Mathematics and Economics are taught in English.

United Nations International School
Situated in New York. Age range: 5 to 18; 1442 students from 102 nationalities. Teachers come from 46 nationalities. There are two campuses: one in Manhattan, the other in Queens. Languages include: English, French, Spanish, Arabic, Chinese, Dutch, German, Italian, Japanese, Russian and Swedish.

Atlanta International School

One example of an International School is Atlanta International School (AIS), situated in Atlanta, Georgia, USA. The school was founded in 1985 by a group of international educators and members of the business community whose aim was to provide the Atlanta area with similar international educational opportunities to those found in other major cities throughout the world.

Atlanta International School is an independent, fee-paying school. High academic standards are required and students are tested before admission. By September, 1994, there were almost 600 students on the school roll. More than half came from other countries, with over 50 nationalities being represented in the school. Twenty-six percent were non-white. Sixty percent came from homes where English was the only language spoken. Twenty percent came from bilingual families.

From first year kindergarten (age four) to the fifth grade, the school operates a bilingual program. Parents can choose one of three tracks for their children: English-German, English-French or English-Spanish. Each class has two classrooms and two sets of teachers. Teaching time is divided equally between the two languages. A class in the English-French track, for instance, might spend a Monday morning in the English-medium classroom and the afternoon in the French-medium classroom. On Tuesday, the class would be taught in French in the morning and then switch to English in the afternoon. In this way, over a two week cycle, the class spend an equal amount of time in each of their two languages.

The majority of the children at the school are native speakers of English, but there are special ENNS (English for non-native speakers) classes at all levels. The Spanish, German and French classes comprise a mixture of non-native speakers, who learn the language by a process of immersion, and native speakers, who are helped to increase their language skills. During the second year of kindergarten (age five), children begin to read and write in English. Reading and writing in the second language begins slightly later, usually in the first grade. Mathematics and other subjects are taught in both languages by specialist teachers, with careful co-operation ensuring the whole syllabus is covered. Morning assemblies in the primary section are conducted in four languages, English, Spanish, French and German.

From the sixth grade onwards, students are educated through the medium of English. In Grades 6, 7 and 8, they can opt to study Social Studies through the medium of French, German, Spanish or English. They also study language and literature through the medium of the appropriate language, and at the level corresponding to their ability in the language. Intensive courses in all languages, including English for beginners, are also offered. In the sixth and seventh grades the students are obliged to study Latin. In the eighth grade they can choose between Latin and another modern language. The students prepare for the International Baccalaureate, as well as the US university entrance examinations.

English is naturally the language used most outside the classroom, but French and Spanish are also widely used by native speakers of those languages.

AIS is fully accredited by the European Council of International Schools and the International Baccalaureate Association, as well as the appropriate educational authority within the United States. The school's elementary bilingual program is also recognized by educational authorities in France and Germany.

The Atlanta International School has realistic language aims. Its Kindergarten Handbook states that, in its bilingual program,

> 'some students will achieve bilingualism, all students will vary in their linguistic ability as much as students all over the world vary in all academic areas, including those who are 'monolingual.' Our students do not learn two languages, they learn *in* two languages.'

The school aims to foster a harmonious multicultural and multiracial community. To include students from all social backgrounds, the school offers help with fees if the student's circumstances warrant this.

Bayan Bilingual School

Bayan Bilingual School is a day school which provides an education in both Arabic and English for students from the ages of 3 to 18. The Arabic program is supervised by the Ministry of Education in Kuwait while the school follows an American style of program for the English-medium curriculum. Bayan was one of the first bilingual schools in the Arabian Gulf and remains the only bilingual school in the State of Kuwait. The school was first established in 1977 and recommenced in September 1991 following the liberation of Kuwait from the Iraqi invasion. In the 1994-5 school year, there were almost 900 students at the school. The school is fully accredited by the European Council of International Schools (UK), the New England Association of Schools and Colleges (US) and the Kuwait Ministry of Education.

In the pre-school program, the children spend approximately equal time with thematic studies in either language. At elementary level, students study through the medium of Arabic for approximately 50 percent of their day. The subjects studied in Arabic are the Arabic language, Religion, Civics, Mathematics, Music and Computer Studies. The students study English, Science, Art, PE and Computer Studies through the medium of English. The students alternate languages throughout the day, a lesson through the medium of Arabic being followed by a lesson through the medium of English. Throughout the school, Computer Studies are taught in both languages, as all subjects make use of computer technology.

At the Intermediate Stage (Grades 5 through 8) and in the high school (Grades 9 through 12), more subjects are taught through the medium of English: English Language and Literature, Mathematics, Science, Art, Music, Computer Studies, PE and electives in History and Psychology, while Arabic, Social Studies, Religion and Computer Studies are taught in Arabic. In the Intermediate Stage, students spend approximately 45 percent of their time studying through the medium of Arabic and about 30 to 40 percent of their time at high school level. This compares favorably with bilingual schools in other Arabic countries where, on average, only 10 to 20 percent of the time throughout the school is allocated to Arabic.

At Grades 11 and 12, students choose one of two streams (international and science). The International Branch Diploma is based upon the American Secondary School Diploma. It prepares students for entry into American style universities and is acceptable in many European and Arabic countries including Kuwait University. Students are required to study Islamic Education and the Arabic language, and may select from other courses in English, Mathematics, US History, Psychology, Computer Studies, Art or Physical Education.

The Science Branch Diploma consists of the following required courses: Islamic Education, Arabic Language, Advanced Physics, Chemistry, Advanced Mathematics. Students may choose further courses from a number of options. This branch is designed for students who wish to study Science, Mathematics, Medicine or Engineering at university.

Bayan Bilingual School has a demanding academic program and aims to develop fluency in both English and Arabic by the time a student reaches graduation. To gain admission to the school, students must fulfill certain criteria. Students should normally have one Arab parent, although pre-school age children of non-Arab parents may be considered where the parents are clearly committed to bilingual education. The child must pass detailed assessment tests in English, Arabic and Math. Parents must demonstrate at the interview an understanding of, and a commitment to, the aims of the school and to a bilingual education.

The school places the command of Arabic, the mother tongue of the majority of the students, as a central goal. The school believes that the priority is to ground students firmly in their own language, culture and religion, so that they may be worthy and useful citizens of their own community, before they make a contribution in an international sphere.

Bayan Bilingual School is a school for the relatively privileged in Kuwait. The fees and rigorous academic standards mean that only children of high academic ability and of relatively rich parents can be admitted. The school expects the children to develop not just conversational ability in both Arabic and English, but sufficient proficiency to cope with a demanding curriculum in both languages. Arabic and English are dissimilar languages, belonging to different language families, with different orthographical systems. This provides an added challenge for the child. The school requires a high degree of commitment from both students and parents. The school's aim is to help young Kuwaiti men and women, and students of other nationalities living in Kuwait, to make an effective contribution to the development of Kuwait and to the international world. The school's motto is 'The Best of Two Worlds!'

Nishimachi International School, Tokyo, Japan

Nishimachi is a private day school founded in 1949 to provide children with an education in Japanese and English. The school seeks to develop an international perspective and understanding. The school believes that the development of ability in a second language provides an opportunity to grow beyond a single culture. The program extends from kindergarten to Grade 9. The school tries to maintain a balance of boys and girls, of native speakers of English and native speakers of Japanese, as well as a variety of nationalities which gives the school a wider perspective. Of the 381 students on the school roll in June, 1994, approximately 40 percent were children of US citizens, 20 percent were Japanese, 20 percent had one parent who is Japanese, and 20 percent were of other nationalities. Many of the non-Japanese students have a bilingual home background in languages other than Japanese.

The school is accredited by the Western Association of Schools and Colleges and by the European Council of International Schools. It is recognized by the Metropolitan Government of Tokyo.

The school features a dual language program in English and Japanese. All students study Japanese, either as a first (F) or second (S) language. Usually Japanese (F) students have lived in Japan since birth or have a parent who is Japanese. At kindergarten level, the children are divided into (S) and (F) groups, but these groups are regularly combined so that the children can benefit from one another's cultural background and linguistic abilities. In the Japanese (S) group, Japanese is introduced by means of games, songs, stories, greetings and basic classroom conversation.

From the first grade onwards all subjects (with the exception of Japanese language and Japanese (F) Social Studies), are taught in English. Japanese (F) students also spend three weeks in the summer studying Mathematics, Science, Social Studies, Art and Drama in Japanese in preparation for the Japanese national achievement tests.

Second language students at each grade level study Japanese at a level appropriate to their degree of competence in the language. There is also a beginners' class at each grade level for newcomers to the school. Students study Japanese, as well as international history, civilization and culture. The school has no religious affiliation but both Japanese and Western festivals and culture are celebrated.

Educating Children Whose Thinking Embraces the World

The playground resounds with the shouts and laughter of children of many nationalities - blue-eyed, black-eyed, fair haired, brown-haired, pale-skinned, dark-skinned.

It is recess time at Nishimachi International School, where some 400 children from 30 nationalities, kindergarten through ninth grade, study, play, and learn to appreciate each other.

Founded in 1949 by Miss Tane Matsukata, Nishimachi International School provides its students a dual-language, multicultural education. As the only accredited international school in Japan that remains independent of any church or national affiliation, Nishimachi is unique. It requires all its students to study the Japanese language daily, the only school of its kind to do so. More than half of its students are bilingual. And while its course structure is basically American, supplementary texts from Britain, Canada, and Australia are used.

Nishimachi is recognized by the governments of Japan and the United States, and is accredited by the Western Association of Schools and Colleges. It is a private school, with operating funds generated by tuition as well as corporate and private donations. The officers of the School include seven Directors and fifteen Trustees.

The objective of Nishimachi is to provide the academic, cultural, linguistic and moral background required for future success in diplomacy, business and the arts.

Familylike Atmosphere Fosters Individual Attention

Small classes. Familylike atmosphere. Individual attention. These have been characteristic of the school from the start. It began with a student body of four in the home of Mrs. Yuri Murata, one of the school's founding parents. It continues to this day with its main office and Junior High located in the spacious Western-style mansion that used to be Miss Matsukata's parental home in a quiet, central residential area in Tokyo.

Intercultural activities and field trips are an integral part of the NIS curriculum. Each New Year, all students take part in the making and eating of mochi (Japanese rice cakes).

Sports day, which takes place every spring, is one of the school's most popular events. The whole Nishimachi Community: students, faculty, staff, family, alumni and friends; turns out for the fun-filled competition and festivities.

Teachers Blend Academics with Global Scholastic Goals

In class, Nishimachi teachers blend strong academic fundamentals with global scholastic goals, offering subjects required by institutions of higher education around the world.

The School's social studies program is an example of this in its offering a sequential world history, culture and geography program, beginning with the ancient civilizations and continuing through the twentieth century.

Japan, as a country and people, is studied as a separate subject. Beginning as a year's project in fourth grade, it continues in the sixth through ninth grade as a required class - Japanese Social Studies. Here, NIS students learn of Japan's history and geography, resulting in four years of specialized Japanese studies, offered in both English and Japanese.

Other standard courses include mathematics, Japanese, English literature and composition, science, music, art and physical education.

In addition, students develop skills which will be expected in the future, such as the use of computers.

Part of the Nishimachi school brochure.

Currently, the school is in the process of developing its Japanese language program. The goal is to expand the use of Japanese to other areas of the curriculum and to increase the integration of English and Japanese in all curricular areas. The school is examining ways of developing the Japanese language provision for three designated groups of students, (rather than the (F) and (S) groups hitherto defined). These are, firstly, students with native-like fluency, secondly, those with some degree of bilingualism in English and Japanese, and thirdly, those students, (usually short-stay), who arrive at the school with no knowledge of Japanese. An Immersion program was considered, but it was decided that this would not be suitable for the school since it would separate two groups of students. However, some aspects of Immersion teaching are being incorporated into the curriculum, (e.g. activity-based language lessons and fostering language learning through using the language for projects and as a teaching medium).

Bilingual Education and the Community

1: Home and School Relationships

Introduction

For many language minority children and their families, the relationship between school and parents is limited and often non-existent. Many parent-teacher relationships are marked by non-co-operation, a lack of understanding, alienation and even antagonism between home and school cultures. Understanding the reasons for this helps explain why many language minority children fail in the system, have high drop-out rates and exhibit relatively low achievement.

Such language minority families may be socially and educationally isolated from the school. There is a knowledge gap between such families and the school that needs bridging. If language minority parents are unable to speak the majority language of the teachers in the school, there may be an increased sense of helplessness and isolation. Such parents are reluctant or unable to discuss their children's progress with the teacher, unable or unwilling to go to parent-teacher meetings and other school events.

While such parents may discuss problems about their children's schooling with one another, the issues and worries do not become resolved because there is a chasm between school and the home. Some parents may be intimidated by high status schools or feel that schools know best and should act unilaterally in dealing with their children.

A Study of Parental Empowerment

In a case study of what can be constructively accomplished to empower such parents and resolve this problem, Delgado-Gaitán (1990) explains via an ethnographic study how parents were encouraged to organize themselves into a leadership group, and teach one another how to communicate with schools. Through building awareness, followed by mobilization, motivation, and commitment, the attitudes and actions of a group of parents were changed.

Over time, parents became convinced that they had the right, responsibility and power to deal with their children's academic and social concerns, and to foster strong relationships with the school for their children's greater achievement. Individual parents also began to realize that they had something to offer other parents, their children and the school. As parents became more involved, they felt more in control of their lives. They became empowered.

Parents involved in their children's education.

> 'Feelings of incompetence create isolation for parents. Those feelings must be replaced with a recognition of the ability to collaborate with others before active participation can occur' (Delgado-Gaitán, 1990, page 158).

In this research study, the pre-school teacher included Mexican family activities in the classroom, and taught parents to be more conscious of their own interactions with their children. This teacher organized a parent committee that involved parents in decision-making activities in the kindergarten. She also incorporated the students' culture into the daily school curriculum. Therefore, she produced a culturally and educationally congruent education experience between the home and the school. Such a teacher became an important advocate of the power of parent-teacher co-operation.

However, there are occasions when parents are a highly conservative, even a reactionary voice. For example some parents may narrowly insist on skills achievement in the core curriculum and wish to ignore the advances

of progressive education in the 20th century. It is also important for conflicts between parents and teachers to be avoided, and co-operation sought for the benefit of the children. Teachers' professionalism and expertise need to be respected, as do parents' rights and interests in their children's socialization.

Parents as Partners in Literacy

'Parents as partners' is as possible in the writing process as in reading. For example, parents may help compose books in their heritage language for use in the classroom. Children, teachers and parents may collaborate together to produce a multilingual book (e.g. starting school in different countries and cultures). Personal meaning, home and community culture, and classroom activity are joined in the promotion of biliteracy.

As Hornberger (1990b) has shown, there can be different effective classroom strategies to make literacy tasks congruent with the community culture and values of the children. Use of first and second language texts, using students' community-based prior knowledge enables 'connect and transfer' to promote literacy and biliteracy. A danger occurs when the school naïvely imposes its literacy practices on the home. With the best of intentions in promoting school-type reading practices in the home, the worst of outcomes may result. Parents may be educated by the school about 'good reading habits' in their children, mirroring school literacy practices and school culture. This assumes a deficit in family literacy practices that may be unwarranted.

Marginalized language minority parents may be highly motivated towards literacy in their children. Literacy may be highly valued as a key to vocational and economic mobility. Plenty of books may be present in the home with plenty of encouragement and help given by parents within the traditions of their culture. Delgado-Gaitán (1990) argues that there is a great need for parents to become involved in their children's literacy development. She reports three models of parental involvement in children's education.

The first, the **Family Influence Model** involves families attempting to provide the type of home learning environment most suited to cognitive and emotional development. Such parents believe that there is a body of information that children need to acquire for life skills. Teachers know this and teach it, and therefore parents need also to be partners in imparting such knowledge. Parents assume that there is a correct and right way to rear children (including literacy development) that can be learnt from books or child psychology experts, and that parents who apply this information will be successful as parents. Turning the situation round, the Family Influence Model also contains the idea of the school attempting to influence and change family life so that it fits the values and strategies of learning used by the school. The family is seen as a direct recipient of the school's influence, and the school-family collaboration establishes maximally effective environments for learning.

Parents can be encouraged to help at home with minority language literacy.

The **School Reform Model** operates where parents take more than an interest in the schooling of their children. Parents within this model try to change schools and make them more responsive to parents. Parents may place pressure on the schools to ensure that their values and standards are transmitted by the schools. Such parents know how to pressure and interact with schools, getting schools to change to being more responsive to student needs as perceived by parents. The assumption is that the school will accommodate parents' suggestions and influence. Such parents will attempt to become part of the power structure of the school by being on advisory committees, school governing committees or parent-teacher committees.

The **Cooperative Systems Model** moves one step further. Rather than collaboration as in the first model, and influence as in the second model, parents within the third model attempt to participate directly in school activities. For example parents may attend workshops in

Funds of Knowledge

One traditional view of language minority homes is that they do not provide the social, cultural and intellectual stimulation and resources to enable children to progress well at school. Thus, teachers of children from language minorities may have low expectations about such children's performance in school, particularly if they come from working class or materially disadvantaged backgrounds.

Another tradition is that effective teachers make home visits to discuss with parents particular problems the child has, to enlist parents' help in, for example, the teaching of reading, and to request parents to help children with their homework. This traditional view assumes that the school knows best, and parents are valuable to the extent to which they encourage their children to adopt the norms and values of the school.

A radically different viewpoint about such language minority homes is that there exists among parents and communities important 'funds of knowledge'. 'Funds of knowledge' refers to historically developed and accumulated knowledge (e.g. skills, abilities, strategies, ideals, ideas, practices and cultural events) that are regarded as important within a household and community to their functioning and well-being. For example, where parents are farmers or building construction workers, there are prized skills, knowledge and cultural practices that are valued, and worth sharing in the classroom.

If parents, community leaders, workers and artists are included in the learning experiences of children, 'indigenous' and home notions of culture are valued, celebrated and represented. Different forms of worthwhile knowledge, experience and expertise are shared in the classroom, raising the self-esteem of a child, the language minority group and the community. Hidden talents, oral histories, household skills and latent abilities are discovered and shared in the classroom. The social, cultural and intellectual resources that are available in families and communities are made an important element of the curriculum.

Reference: MOLL *et al.*, 1992

Community Language Education

In countries where there has been an assimilationist pressure on in-migrants (e.g. United Kingdom), language, cultural and religious education sometimes occurs outside of formal schooling. In countries such as Australia, Canada and the United States, no provision may be made in schools for in-migrant languages such as Italian, Panjabi or Hebrew. When the school does not support in-migrant languages, reproduction of those languages in the family may be not enough for language maintenance. Therefore, local community groups have developed extra schooling for their children on, for example, Friday evenings, vacation periods and particularly in Saturday schools.

Jewish communities using a local synagogue are often enthusiastic for Hebrew to be taught to their children to maintain a Jewish identity and for religious observance. Muslims have often been keen for Qur'anic Arabic to be transmitted for worship in the mosque, just as *gurdwaras* have been instrumental in the acquisition of Panjabi. The Roman Catholic Church also has promoted the community language teaching of Polish, Ukrainian and Lithuanian. In the United Kingdom, there has been community language teaching in Italian, Spanish, Portuguese, Greek, Turkish, Urdu, Panjabi and Bengali, for example. In the case of such European languages, High Commissions and Embassies in London have often lent support. Sometimes using local schools or community centers, sometimes rooms in religious buildings, such extra schooling not only may attempt to preserve a community language but also be designed for cultural and religious continuity.

In the UK, despite indifferent, privately antagonistic and sometimes openly hostile attitudes of education officials, administrators and politicians, pressure from multilingual communities has risen. This reflects a concern to combat the racism that poisons British society and a philosophy of child-centered education on the part of a few leaders of education, and a growing sense of empowerment, vitality and sense of injustice among many language communities. Such language communities are also often concerned that children were drifting away from the traditional values of their ethnic, cultural and religious groups. This has been linked to a growing realization that the communities themselves, and not just individual families and schools can be depended on to deliver such continuity in values, beliefs and traditions. At the moment, the development of bilingualism and bilingual education is more likely through the efforts of such communities, particularly when there is a sympathetic local education authority, than through central administration and central political change. Central UK policy remains predominantly assimilationist.

References: EDWARDS, 1984, 1995; EDWARDS & REDFERN, 1992; GHUMAN, 1994

A Saturday school at a Sikh Gurdwara (temple) in London, England. Religious institutions can help maintain a language within a community

the school, help the teachers in the classroom, and become like paraprofessionals. Such parents see the home, school and community as interrelated and functioning as a whole. Parents play the roles of volunteer, paid employee, teacher at home, adult learner and collaborator.

Further explication of processes in teacher-parent relationships is given by Moll (1992a). Luis Moll and his colleagues at the University of Arizona have used ethnographic studies of student communities to identify skills, knowledge, expertise and interests that Mexican households own, that can be used for the benefit of all in the classroom.

Moll shows how parents and other community members have much to give children in Latino classrooms. Such people can supplement the teacher, providing what Moll calls 'funds of knowledge' that are 'cultural practices and bodies of knowledge and information that households use to survive, to get ahead or to thrive' (Moll, 1992a, page 21). Examples of funds of knowledge that could be used by schools include information about flowers, plants and trees, seeds, agriculture, water distribution and management, animal care and veterinary medicine, ranch economy, car and bike mechanics, carpentry, masonry, electrical wiring and appliances, fencing, folk remedies, herbal cures and natural medicines, midwifery, archaeology, biology and mathematics.

Further Reading

AUERBACH, E. R., 1989, Toward a Social-Contextual Approach to Family Literacy. *Harvard Educational Review*, 59 (2), 165-181.

DELGADO-GAITÁN, C., 1990, *Literacy for Empowerment: The Role of Parents in Children's Education*. New York: Falmer.

DELGADO-GAITÁN, C., 1991, Relating Experience and Text: Socially Constituted Reading Activity. In M. E. MCGROARTY & C. J. FALTIS (eds), *Languages in School and Society*. Berlin/New York: Mouton de Gruyter.

HORNBERGER, N. H., 1990b, Creating Successful Learning Contexts for Bilingual Literacy. *Teachers College Record*, 92 (2), 212-229.

MOLL, L. C., 1992a, Bilingual Classroom Studies and Community Analysis. *Educational Researcher*, 21 (2), 20-24.

MULTILINGUAL RESOURCES FOR CHILDREN PROJECT, 1995, *Building Bridges: Multilingual Resources for Children*. Clevedon: Multilingual Matters Ltd.

2: A Framework for Language Minority Student Empowerment

A theoretical framework proposed by Cummins (1986b, 1996) concerns the empowerment or disablement of minority students. There are three fundamental statements to Cummins' theory.

First, 'language minority students instructed through the minority language (for example, Spanish) for all or part of the school day perform as well in English academic skills as comparable students instructed totally through English' (Cummins, 1986b, page 20). Teaching children through a second or minority language usually leads to the satisfactory development of English academic skills.

The second statement is the 'interdependence hypothesis'. This proposes that 'to the extent that instruction through a minority language is effective in developing academic proficiency in the minority language, transfer of this proficiency to the majority language will occur given adequate exposure and motivation to learn the language' (Cummins, 1986b, page 20). Underlying the surface characteristics of both languages is one common core of developed ability or 'academic proficiency'. Beneath the two protrusions above the surface lies the one iceberg.

The third statement concerns context. Community and school liaison, power and status relationships all need to be considered in a proper bilingual education theory. Cummins' (1986b) theory suggests that minority language students are 'empowered' or 'disabled' by four major characteristics of schools.

The extent to which minority language students' home language and culture are incorporated into the school curriculum

If minority language children's home language and culture are excluded, minimized or quickly reduced in school, the likelihood exists of that child becoming academically 'disabled'. Where the school incorporates, encourages and gives status to the minority language, the chances of empowerment are increased. Apart from potential positive and negative cognitive effects, the inclusion of minority language and culture into the curriculum may have effects on personality (e.g. self-esteem), attitudes, social and emotional well being.

This point is important because it raises a question about why bilingual education which emphasizes the minority language is successful. Is it due to such education fostering cognitive and academic proficiency, as the interdependence hypothesis suggests? Or is it also due, or more due to students' cultural identity being secured and reinforced, thus enhancing self confidence and self-esteem?

The extent to which minority communities are encouraged to participate in their children's education

Where parents are given power and status in the partial determination of their children's schooling, the empowerment of minority communities and children may result. When such communities and parents are kept relatively powerless, inferiority and lack of school progress may result. The growth of paired reading schemes is evidence of the power of a parent-teacher partnership. Parents listening to their children reading on a systematic basis tend to be effective agents of increased literacy. As an illustration of the importance of community participation, Cummins (1986b) cites the Haringey Project in London. Parental involvement in children's reading, even when parents were non-English-speaking and non-literate, had an important effect on children's reading progress.

Teachers are seen as leaning towards being either collaborative or exclusionary. Teachers at the collaborative end encourage parents of minority languages to participate in their children's academic progress through home activities or the involvement of parents in the classroom. Teachers at the exclusionary end maintain tight boundaries between themselves and parents.

Collaboration with parents may be seen as irrelevant, unnecessary, unprofessional, even detrimental to children's progress.

The extent to which education promotes the inner desire for children to become active seekers of knowledge and not just passive receptacles

Learning can be active, independent, internally motivated or passive, dependent and requiring external pulls and pushes. The transmission model of teaching views children as buckets into which knowledge is willingly or unwillingly poured. The teacher controls the nature of the fluid being poured and the speed of pouring. The hidden curriculum of the transmission model may reinforce and symbolize the powerlessness of language minority students. There are those in control and those controlled.

The alternative model, reciprocal interaction,

> 'requires a genuine dialogue between student and teacher in both oral and written modalities, guidance and facilitation rather than control of student learning by the teacher, and the encouragement of student/student talk in a collaborative learning context. This model emphasizes the development of higher level cognitive skills rather than just factual recall, and

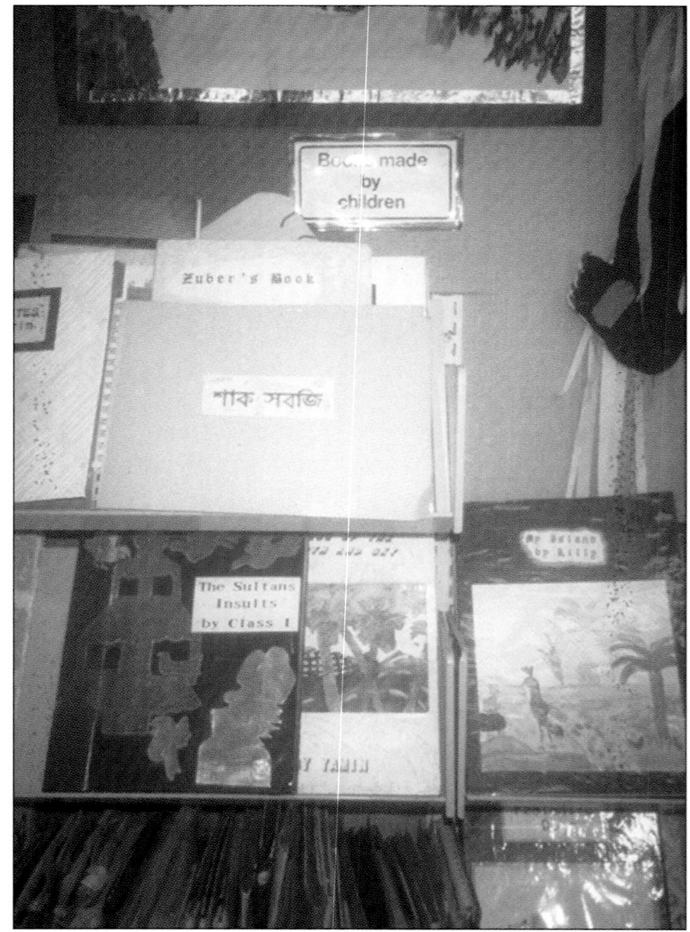

The extent to which the home language is used and respected at school may affect not only the cognitive development but also the social development of the children.

> meaningful language use by students rather than the correction of surface forms. Language use and development are consciously integrated with all curricular content rather than taught as isolated subjects, and tasks are presented to students in ways that generate intrinsic rather than extrinsic motivation' (Cummins, 1986b, page 28).

If the transmission model is allied to the disablement of minority language students, then the reciprocal interaction model is related to the empowerment of students. This latter model aims to give students more control over their own learning, with consequent potential positive effects for self-esteem, co-operation and motivation.

The extent to which the assessment of minority language students avoids locating problems in the student and seeks to find the root of the problem in the social and educational system or curriculum wherever possible

Psychological and educational tests tend by their very nature to locate problems in the individual student (e.g. low IQ, low motivation, backwardness in reading). At worst, educational psychologists and teachers may test and observe a child until a problem can be found in that child to explain poor academic attainment. Such a testing ideology and procedure may fail to locate the root of the problem in the social, economic or educational system. The subtractive nature of Transitional Bilingual education, the transmission model used in the curriculum, the exclusionary orientation of the teacher towards parents and the community and the relative economic deprivation of minority children could each or jointly be the real origin of a minority language child's problem. Therefore assessment and diagnostic activity need to be 'Advocacy' rather than 'Legitimization' oriented. Advocacy means the assessor or diagnostician advocating for the child, by critically inspecting the social and educational context in which the child operates. This may involve comments about the power and status relationships between the dominant and dominated groups, at national, community, school and classroom level. Legitimization in testing a child points the cause of a problem as within the person rather than the system, with the system not being at fault. The system is thus not criticized, and the problem requires an individual rather than a societal solution.

Empowerment thus becomes an important concept in transforming the situations of many language minorities. For Cummins (1996), schools need actively to challenge historical patterns of disempowerment, and become potentially subversive towards existing language majority language minority power relationships. Power relationships are at the core of schooling for Cummins (1996), and such relationships exist in the classroom (e.g. between teachers and students) to either confirm powerlessness or evoke empowerment. Coercive power relations in the class will maintain a feeling of subordination and inferiority among students. Instead, Cummins (1996) argues that collaborative power relations between all classroom participants will generate achievement, self-confidence and motivation among students. They will also feel a sense of ownership of their education, their lives and their future. An aim of empowerment is thus to provide students with positive, valued and honored identities.

'Empowerment means the process of acquiring power, or the process of transition from lack of control to the acquisition of control over one's life and immediate environment' (Delgado-Gaitán & Trueba, 1991, page 138). Empowerment can be furthered by education, but also needs to be realized in legal, social, cultural and particularly economic and political events. Delgado-Gaitán & Trueba (1991) thus add the necessary sociocultural and political dimensions of empowerment to the possibilities of empowerment through education.

Empowerment and Pedagogy

When the focus is on the language minority group, and particularly when the focus is on the experience of individual bilinguals, differences in prosperity and economic opportunity, in power and pedagogic opportunity are evident. As a generalization, language minorities have less power and less chance of acquiring political power compared with language majorities. This powerlessness is enacted in the classroom (Delpit, 1988). If classrooms transmit and reinforce power relations and powerlessness, is this reversible? Is language minority powerlessness reproduced inside 'weak' forms of bilingual education? Can this be reversed by 'strong' forms of bilingual educa-

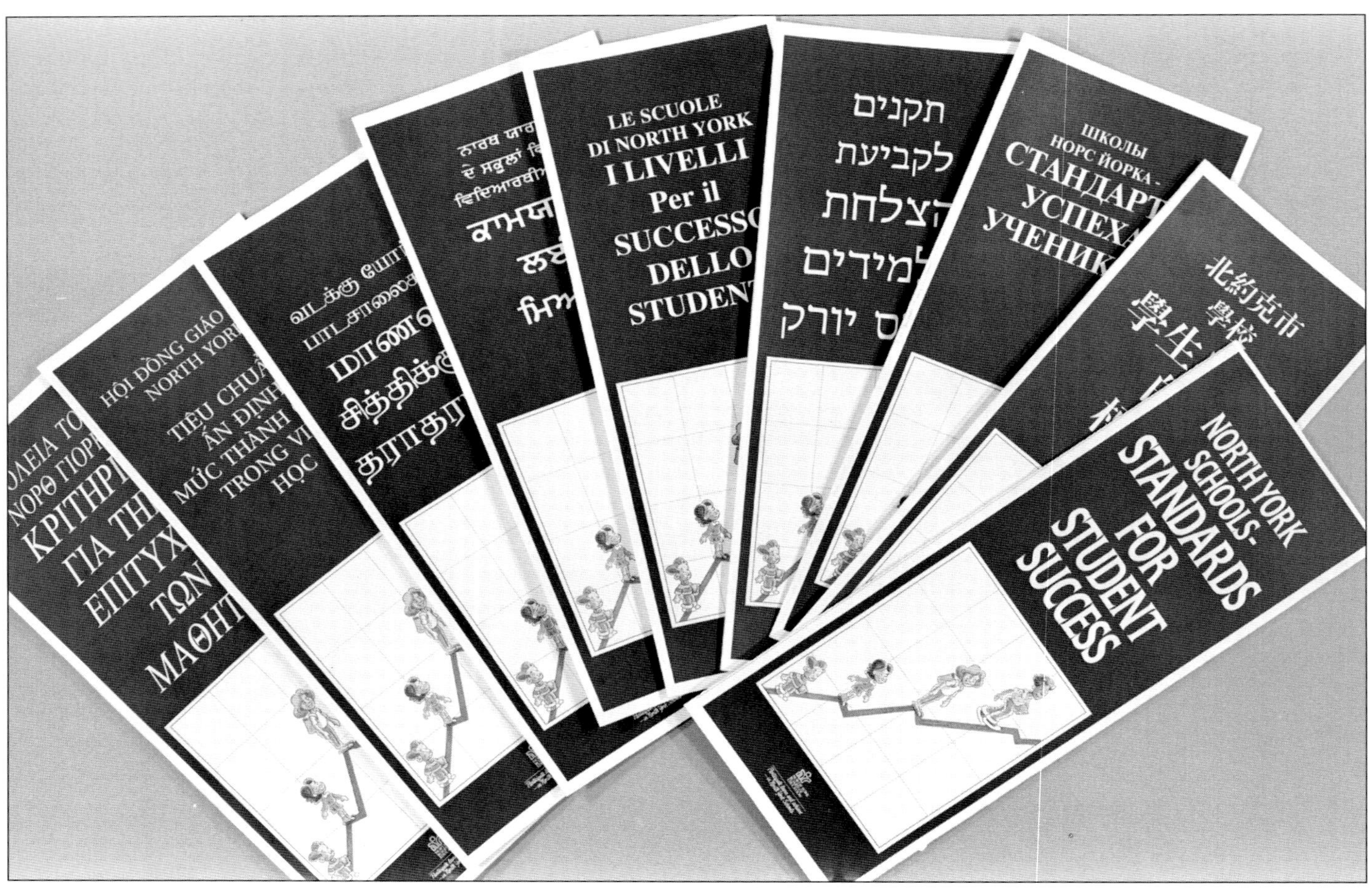

The theoretical framework can be summarized as follows:

	Empowered Minority Language Children	Disabled Minority Language Children
Dimension 1:	Additive: Incorporation of Home Language and Culture in the School	Subtractive: Home Language and Culture excluded from the School
Dimension 2:	Collaborative Community Participation	Exclusionary Community Non-participation
Dimension 3:	Reciprocal Interaction Curriculum	Transmission-Oriented Curriculum
Dimension 4:	Advocacy-Oriented Assessment and Diagnosis	Legitimization-Oriented Assessment and Diagnosis

tion? It is important to ask 'how' and 'why' language minority children are at a disadvantage in the classroom. Can there be attempted reversal and empowerment?

The danger is in expecting bilingual education to be the sole institution to right all wrongs. Empowerment of the disadvantaged has also to come from other agencies, other processes and other interventions. Yet bilingual education can help provide a student with the potential (e.g. literacy, knowledge, understandings, ideals) to become empowered. Delpit (1988) provides some ideas of how this can occur:

1. The 'Culture of Power' is enacted in the classroom by:
   - teachers having power over students;
   - the curriculum (e.g. via text books) determining a legitimate world view;
   - what is regarded as 'intelligent' behavior is defined in terms of the majority culture, to the detriment of minority students;
   - school leading to employment (or unemployment) and hence to economic status (or a lack of status).

2. The 'Culture of Power' is embedded in ways of talking and writing, ways of dressing, manners and ways of interacting (e.g. compare 'upper', ' middle' and 'lower' or 'working' class children).

3. Success in school and employment often requires acquiring or mimicking the culture of those in power. This is essentially upper and middle class culture. 'Children from other kinds of families operate within perfectly wonderful and viable cultures but not cultures that carry the codes or rules of power' (Delpit, 1988, page 283).

4. Those outside of the 'Culture of Power' should be taught explicitly the rules and nature of that culture in order to become empowered. If styles of interaction, discourse patterns, manners and forms of dress, for example, are explained to a child, does this lead to the language minority child being empowered, or does this move such a child towards cultural separation?

Conclusion

Cummins' (1986b) theoretical framework incorporates psychological functioning and educational attainment, and includes a focus on the social, economic and political background that is so often crucial to fully understanding bilingualism and bilingual education. The theory covers research on cognitive functioning, motivation, educational success or failure in different forms of bilingual education, and includes the context of education in terms of power relationships, culture, community and parental involvement.

Further Reading

CUMMINS, J., 1986, Empowering Minority Students: A Framework for Intervention. *Harvard Educational Review*, 56 (1), 18-36.

CUMMINS, J., 1996, *Negotiating Identities: Education for Empowerment in a Diverse Society*. Ontario, CA: California Association for Bilingual Education.

DELGADO-GAITÁN, C. & TRUEBA, H., 1991, *Crossing Cultural Borders: Education for Immigrant Families in America*. New York: Falmer.

DELPIT, L. D., 1988, The Silenced Dialogue: Power & Pedagogy in Educating Other People's Children. *Harvard Educational Review*, 58 (3), 280-298.

Bilingual Education in the United States

1: A Brief History of Bilingual Education in the United States

Introduction

Bilingual education in the United States has moved through four overlapping periods: permissive, restrictive, opportunist and dismissive. These periods are not neat in their divisions and, in each period, there are variations in different states in policies and practices. There are exceptions inside these broad historical periods. However, generally, there have been changes in the perspectives of politicians, administrators, educationalists and in school practice that indicate that discernible shifts in ideology, preference and practice have occurred.

The Permissive Period

Long before European in-migrants arrived in the United States, the land contained a variety of native (indigenous) languages. When the Italian, German, Dutch, French, Polish, Czech, Irish, Welsh and other in-migrant groups arrived, there already existed many mutually unintelligible languages in the United States (estimates vary from two to seven hundred). The in-migrants brought with them a wide variety of languages. In the 18th and 19th centuries in the United States, up until the First World War, linguistic diversity was generally accepted and the presence of different languages was encouraged. Language variety was accepted as the norm and encouraged through religion, newspapers in different languages, and in both private and public schools.

Examples of this permissive period in bilingual education in the United States are found in German-English schools. Set up by German communities in Ohio, Pennsylvania, Missouri, Minnesota, Dakota and Wisconsin, bilingual as well as monolingual German education was accepted. Norwegian and Dutch were also languages of instruction within ethnic-based schools. This openness to in-migrant languages in the latter half of the 19th century was partly motivated by competition for students between public and private schools. Other factors such as benevolent (or uninterested) school administrators, the isolation of schools in rural areas, and ethnic homogeneity within an area also enabled a permissive attitude to mother tongue and bilingual education during this period. In most large cities in the latter half of the 19th century, English monolingual education was the pattern. However, in cities such as Cincinnati, Baltimore, Denver and San Francisco, dual language education was present. In some schools in Cincinnati for example, half the day was spent learning through German and the other half of the curriculum was delivered through English.

A typical 19th-century one-roomed rural school in the United States. Many small rural schools in this period educated the children in the main language of the community, which might be German, Norwegian, Swedish or some other European language, while others were English-medium from their inception and were prime agents for linguistic assimilation.

At the turn of the 20th century, Italian and Jewish in-migrants were mostly placed in mainstream schools. However, examples of bilingual education existed and were permitted. For example, some Polish in-migrants in Chicago attended Catholic schools where a small amount of teaching was through the mother tongue. So long as policy was within the jurisdiction of local towns and districts, the language of instruction did not become an issue in educational provision.

The Restrictive Period

In the first two decades of the 20th century, a change in attitude to bilingualism and bilingual education occurred in the United States. A variety of factors are linked to this change and the subsequent restriction of bilingual education.

- The number of in-migrants increased dramatically around the turn of the century. Public schools filled their classrooms with in-migrants. This gave rise to fears of foreigners, and the call for integration, harmonization and assimilation of in-migrants, whose lack of English language and English literacy was seen as a source of social, political and economic concern. The call for Americanization was launched, with competence in English becoming associated with loyalty to the United States. The Nationality Act (1906) required in-migrants to speak English to become naturalized Americans. The call for child literacy in English rather than child labor, socialization into a unified America rather than ethnic separation, along with increased centralized control, led to a belief in a common language for compulsory schooling. By the turn of the century, California and New Mexico had 'English-only' instruction laws.
- In 1919, the Americanization Department of the United States Bureau of Education adopted a resolution recommending 'all states to prescribe that all schools, private and public, be conducted in the English language and that instruction in the elementary classes of all schools be in English'. By 1923, thirty-four states had decreed that English must be the sole language of instruction in all elementary schools, public and private.
- A major influence in the movement from permissiveness to repression in bilingualism and bilingual education in the United States came with the entry of the United States into the First World War in 1917. Anti-German feeling in the United States spread, with a consequent extra pressure for English monolingualism and a melting pot policy achieved through monolingual education. The German language was portrayed as posing a threat to the unity of Americanization. Linguistic diversity was replaced by linguistic intolerance. Schools became the tool for the assimilation and integration of diverse languages and cultures. Socialization into being American meant the elimination from schools of languages and cultures other than English. The interest in learning foreign languages declined.
- Mandatory attendance laws in public schools were established. Such legislation made the continuation of private schools difficult. Public funding for church-affiliated schools was eliminated.

Children of all ethnic backgrounds learn to respect the flag in this early 20th century US classroom.

This period was not totally restrictive as García (1992a) reveals. She speaks of a 'tolerant parenthesis' between 1923 and 1942. In 1923, the US Supreme Court declared that a Nebraska state law prohibiting the teaching of a foreign language to elementary school students was unconstitutional under the Fourteenth Amendment. This case, known as *Meyer* v. *Nebraska* concerned a case against a teacher convicted of teaching German literacy to a ten-year-old child. The original Nebraska ruling was that such mother tongue teaching cultivated ideas and affections foreign to the best interests of the country. The Supreme Court, in overturning the Nebraska ruling, found that proficiency in a foreign language was 'not injurious to the health, morals, or understanding of the ordinary child'.

Although a 'tolerant parenthesis', this Supreme Court finding did not support bilingualism or bilingual education. This is revealed in three ways: (1) the ruling included a requirement for English language instruction in all schools, (2) it commented that the desire of a state legislature to foster a homogeneous people was 'easy to appreciate' and (3) the finding is symbolic of a shift in attitude to non-English languages (García, 1992a). No longer were such languages 'ethnic' but 'foreign'. Such languages were no longer seen as spoken by ethnolinguistic minorities in the US, but by 'foreigners' (i.e. non-US or unnaturalized citizens).

This restrictive movement continued at least until the 1960s, and carried on being one major theme in US politics until the present.

The Period of Opportunity

In 1957, the Russians launched their Sputnik into space. For United States politicians and public, a period of soul-

searching led to debates about the quality of US education, US scientific creativity and US competence to compete in an increasingly international world. Doubts arose about the hitherto over-riding concern with English as the melting pot language, and a new consciousness emerged of the need for foreign language instruction. In 1958, the National Defense Education Act was passed, promoting foreign language learning in elementary schools, high schools and universities. This in turn helped to create a slightly more tolerant attitude to languages other than English spoken among ethnic groups in the US.

In the United States in the 1960s, various other factors allowed a few opportunities to bring back bilingual education, albeit in a disparate, semi-isolated manner. The 'opportunity' movement for bilingual schools to be re-established in the United States needs to be understood in the wider perspective of the Civil Rights movement, the concern for the rights of African Americans, and the need to establish equality of opportunity and equality of educational opportunity for all people, irrespective of race, color or creed. The 1964 Civil Rights Act prohibited discrimination on the basis of color, race or national origin, and led to the establishment of the Office of Civil Rights. This Act is an important marker that symbolizes the beginning of a change in a less negative attitude to ethnic groups, and possibilities for increased integration and tolerance of ethnic languages. However, the restoration of the practice of bilingual education in the US is often regarded as starting in 1963, in one school in Florida.

In 1963, Cuban exiles established a Dual Language school (Coral Way Elementary School) in Dade County

A Florida classroom in 1960. Cuban in-migrant children, newly arrived in the US after the Cuban revolution of 1959, learn English. However, the arrival of many Cuban refugees provided an impetus for the restoration of bilingual education in the US.

in Florida. Believing they were only in exile for a short period, the educated, middle class Cubans set up this dual language (Spanish-English) bilingual school. The need to maintain their mother tongue of Spanish was aided by having highly trained professional teachers ready to service such schools, the Cubans' plight as victims of a harsh Communist state, and their expected temporary stay in the United States. Their unquestioned loyalty to United States policies and democratic politics gained sympathy for the Cubans. Bilingual education in Dade County received both political support and funding. (Further details of this movement are found in the item on Dual Language Schools, page 518.)

While the re-establishment of bilingual schools in the US has benefited from the example and success of Coral Way Elementary School, an understanding of bilingual education in the United States requires a comprehension of legislation and lawsuits.

In 1967, a Texas Senator, Ralph Yarborough, introduced a Bilingual Education Act as an amendment of the 1965 Elementary and Secondary Education Act. The legislation was designed to help mother tongue Spanish speakers who were seen as failing in the school system. Enacted in 1968 as Title VII of the Elementary and Secondary Education Act, the Bilingual Education Act indicated that bilingual education programs were to be seen as part of federal educational policy. It authorized the use of federal funds for the education of speakers of languages other than English. It also undermined the English-only legislation still lawful in many states. However, the 1968 Bilingual Education Act allocated funds for such minority language speakers only as a temporary measure for students (i.e. while they shifted to working through English in the classroom). The underlying aim was a transition from a minority language (e.g. Spanish) to English, rather than support for the mother tongue.

A landmark in United States' bilingual education was a lawsuit. A court-case was brought on behalf of Chinese students against the San Francisco School District in 1970. The case concerned whether or not non-English-speaking students received equal educational opportunities when instructed in a language they could not understand. The failure to provide bilingual education was alleged to violate both the equal protection clause of the 14th Amendment and Title VI of the Civil Rights Act of 1964. The case, known as *Lau* v. *Nichols*, was rejected by the federal district court and a court of appeals, but was accepted by the Supreme Court in 1974. The verdict outlawed English submersion programs for language minority children and resulted in nationwide 'Lau remedies'. The Lau remedies acknowledged that students not profi-

cient in English needed help. Such remedies included English as a Second Language classes, English tutoring and some form of bilingual education. The Lau remedies created some expansion in the temporary use of minority languages in schools. They rarely resulted in heritage language, enrichment or maintenance programs as the accent was still on a transitional use of the home language for English language learners. The Lau court case is symbolic of the dynamic and continuing contest to establish language rights in the US particularly through testing the law in the courtroom (see Casanova, 1991; Hakuta, 1986b; Lyons, 1990).

In this period of opportunity, the kind of bilingual education needed to achieve equality of educational opportunity for language minority children was not defined. However, the right to equal opportunity for language minorities was asserted. The means of achieving that right was not declared. During this period, there was a modest growth in developmental maintenance bilingual education and ethnic community mother tongue schools. (See the items on Heritage Language Bilingual Education and Dual Language Schools, pages 508 and 518.)

The Dismissive Period

While bilingual education has not disappeared in the United States in the last two decades, since the 1980s there have been central moves against an emergence of a strong version of bilingual education, a preference for submersion and Transitional Bilingual education, and the rise of pressure groups such as English First and US English that seek to establish English monolingualism and cultural assimilation.

To understand the current dismissive or repudiation period, it is helpful to examine the legislative changes with respect to bilingual education in the United States. We return to the 1968 Bilingual Education Act (Title VII and part of the Elementary and Secondary Education Act). This provided a 'poverty program' for the educationally disadvantaged among language minorities. It did not require schools to use a child's home language other than English. However, it did allow a few opportunists to bring 'home languages' into the classroom rather than exclude them. The 1974 amendments to this Bilingual Education Act (see the chronology table) required schools receiving grants to include teaching in a student's home language and culture so as to allow the child to progress effectively through the educational system. Effective progress in student achievement could occur via the home language or via English. However, this gave rise to fierce debates about how much a student's native language should be used in school. Some argued that it was essential to develop a child's speaking and literacy skills in their native language before English was introduced in a major way. Others argued that educational equality of opportunity could best be realized by teaching English as early

A Summary of Some of the Major United States Events in the Rights of Language Minorities

Year	United States Legislation/Litigation affecting Bilingual Education	Implication
1906	Nationality Act passed	First legislation requiring in-migrants to speak English to become naturalized.
1923	Supreme Court in *Meyer* v. *Nebraska*	Rules that state provision requiring English language instruction is permitted by the Constitution, but proficiency in a foreign language was also constitutional.
1950	Amendments to the Nationality Act	English literacy required for naturalization.
1954	*Brown* v. *Board of Education*	Segregated education based on race made unconstitutional.
1965	Elementary and Secondary Education Act (ESEA)	Funds granted to meet the needs of 'educationally deprived children'.
1968	Elementary and Secondary Education Act (ESEA) amendment: The Bilingual Education Act, Title VII	Provided funding to establish bilingual programs for students who did not speak English and who were economically poor.
1974	*Lau* v. *Nichols*	Established that language programs for language minorities not proficient in English were necessary to provide equal educational opportunities.
1974	Reauthorization of Bilingual Education Act Title VII of ESEA	Grants available to include native language instruction in schools to 'effect progress' of students not proficient in English. Bilingual Education was defined as transitional (TBE).
1978	Reauthorization of Bilingual Education Act Title VII of ESEA	Reauthorized funding for bilingual programs (transitional). Poverty criteria for eligibility was removed. The term 'Limited English Proficient' (LEP) introduced, replacing LES (Limited English Speaking).
1984	Reauthorization of Bilingual Education Act Title VII of ESEA	Extended the range of fundable bilingual education programs for students not proficient in English. Transitional (TBE) given 75 percent of funds. Developmental Bilingual Education (dual language) programs funded, as were Special Alternative Instructional programs (SAIP). SAIP provided funding for English-only 'submersion' classes with no instruction in the student's native language.
1988	Reauthorization of Bilingual Education Act Title VII of ESEA	Same as in 1984, but 25 percent of funding given for English-only SAIP.

as possible and assimilating language minority children into mainstream culture.

In 1978, the United States Congress re-authorized Transitional Bilingual education, allowing the native language to be used only to the extent necessary for a child to achieve competence in the English language. Title VII funds could not be used for Maintenance Bilingual Education programs. The 1984 and 1988 amendments allowed increasing percentages of the funds available to be allocated to programs where a students' first language was not used.

The Reagan administration was particularly hostile to bilingual education. In the New York Times on the 3rd March 1981, President Reagan is quoted as saying that 'It is absolutely wrong and against the American concept to have a bilingual education program that is now openly, admittedly, dedicated to preserving their native language and never getting them adequate in English so they can go out into the job market'. Reagan believed that preservation of the native language meant neglect of English language acquisition. Bilingual education programs were seen as serving to neglect English language competence in students. Reagan dismissed bilingual education in favor of submersion and transitional programs.

In 1985, William Bennett, the new Secretary of Education, suggested that there was no evidence that children from language minorities (whom the Bilingual Education Act had sought to help), had benefited from this Act. Some 25 percent of funds were made available for English monolingual, alternative instructional programs (e.g. Structured English programs; Sheltered English programs). This represented a further political dismissal of education through the minority language and a dismissal of 'strong' forms of bilingual education.

The Lau remedies were withdrawn by the Reagan government and do not have the force of law. The federal government left local politicians to create their own policies. For example, in New York, bilingual education was mandated following an out-of-court Aspira Consent Decree by the New York City Board of Education in 1974. Further changes in the rights to United States bilingual education are given in the table below. Legislation and litigation has often led to 'weak' forms of bilingual education (e.g. Transitional Bilingual education). Also, recent legislation has not tended to increase rights to a bilingual education. In the Reagan and Bush years in the United States Presidency, the accent was more on submersion and Transitional Bilingual education. The right to early education through a minority language failed to blossom in those years.

Conclusion

This topic has suggested that bilingual education in the United States has moved through four overlapping periods: permissive, restrictive, opportunist and dismissive. These broad historical trends contain plenty of exceptions and variations within each period.

Two conclusions. First, there is a common perception that educational policy is often static, always conservative and very slow to change. The history of bilingual education in the United States tends to falsify and contradict such beliefs. Such history shows that there is constant change, a constant movement in ideas, ideology and impetus. There is action and reaction, movement and contra-movement, assertion and response. One conclusion is that change will always occur in bilingual education policy and provision. Nothing is static. While there will be periods when bilingual education is criticized, forbidden and rejected, there will be reactions, with the possibility of more positive, accepting periods ahead. There is no certainty in the future history of bilingual education, only uncertainty and change. Yet uncertainty and change do provide occasional opportunities for bilingual education to progress.

Second, the conclusion must not be that the four overlapping periods (permissive, restrictive, opportunist and dismissive) will always operate in that sequence. The history of bilingual education in Wales follows a different sequence. In Wales, the last 200 years of bilingual education have witnessed a movement through the following five approximate periods: permissive, dismissive, suppressive, opportunist and progressive. From a time when Welsh was banned in the classroom (suppressive period), there is currently a widespread acceptance, and provision of bilingual education in Wales (progressive period). No universal patterns of change can or should be deduced from either the United States or the Welsh experience. Such unpredictability provides a challenge to bilingual educators.

Further Reading

CRAWFORD, J.,1995, *Bilingual Education: History, Politics, Theory and Practice* (Third edition). Los Angeles: Bilingual Educational Services.

LYONS, J. J., 1990, The Past and Future Directions of Federal Bilingual-Education Policy. In C. B. CAZDEN & C. E. SNOW, *Annals of the American Academy of Political & Social Science*, Volume 508, 119-134. London: Sage.

PERLMANN, J., 1990, Historical Legacies: 1840-1920. In C. B. CAZDEN & C. E. SNOW (eds), *English Plus: Issues in Bilingual Education*, London: Sage.

2: Research on the Effectiveness of Bilingual Education

The purpose of this subsection is to consider research on the major types of bilingual education. How effective are these major models for which children? What are the recorded successes and limitations? What makes a bilingual school more or less effective? These are the issues considered in this subsection.

From early research in the 1920s in Wales (Saer, 1922) and Malherbe's (1946) evaluation of bilingual education in South Africa, there has been a flood of evaluations of bilingual projects and experiments, programs and experiences.

It is possible to find support for most of the different forms of bilingual education by selecting and emphasizing a particular study. Some examples will illustrate. Criticism of Irish Immersion education for children from English-speaking homes was given by Macnamara (1966). He found such Immersion children to be 11 months behind mainstream children on mechanical arithmetic. He suggested that it is 'probable that the use of Irish in teaching problem arithmetic hinders the progress of English-speaking children' (Macnamara, 1966, page 103). In comparison, support for Immersion education comes from the Canadian research studies (e.g. Swain & Lapkin, 1982). Danoff *et al.* (1977, 1978) found submersion to be superior to Transitional Bilingual education with a large US sample of almost 9000 children. McConnell (1980) found US Transitional Bilingual education to be better than submersion, while Matthews (1979), also in the US, found no difference between these two 'weak' forms of bilingual education.

Heritage language education has been evaluated as successful in Canada by Keyser & Brown (1981) and in the UK by Fitzpatrick (1987). In contrast, early research in Wales (e.g. Smith, 1923) questioned educational outcomes from heritage language programs for Welsh bilinguals.

Whether research finds a consensus in favor of one or some of the types of bilingual education is examined later in this topic. For the moment, it is important to outline some reasons why studies vary in their findings.

The Sample of Children

The results of any one study in educational research are limited to that sample of children at the time of the study. Evaluations of bilingual education are usually based on small and unrepresentative samples. It is usually ethically questionable and practically impossible to allocate children randomly into experimental and control groups that contain perfect mirrors of a large population of school children.

Given the wide variety of samples of children used in bilingual education effectiveness research, it is not surprising that differences in findings emerge. Samples of children include urban and rural schools, various social class backgrounds, different ages and varying levels of motivation. The international research includes a mixture of bilingual groups: indigenous language minority groups, in-migrants, and majority language children in minority language education. Generalization of results from one group to another is not valid. Such children may be in a subtractive or additive environment (see page 154) at home, school, community and nation.

Interacting Factors

Various factors, other than the sample of children, may have a variable effect on bilingual education. Parental interest, parental involvement in their children's education and parental co-operation with teachers is one intervening factor. Another factor is likely to be the enthusiasm and commitment of teachers to the education program. With a novel experiment in bilingual education, there may be extra enthusiasm and interest. The level of material support (e.g. books, curriculum guidelines, computers, science equipment) may also produce variable outcomes.

There is likely to be as much variation in outcomes (e.g. achievement in different curriculum areas) inside a particular bilingual education program (e.g. transitional, immersion or heritage language) as between different types of program.

The crucial point is this. Language policy and language practice in schooling are only one element amongst many that make a school more or less successful. A recipe for success is unlikely to result from one ingredient (e.g. the language of the classroom). A great variety of factors act and interact to determine whether bilingual education is successful or not. As will be considered at

the end of the topic, it makes more sense to consider the wide variety of conditions which make bilingual education more or less successful. We need to specify all the ingredients in different recipes to fully understand the success or failure of forms of bilingual education. Bilingual education, whatever type or model, is no guarantee of effective schooling.

Measures of Success

An important question is: 'What tests or other sources of evidence are used to determine whether a form of bilingual education is successful?' Should the sole outcome be competence in one or two languages? What aspects of language should be assessed? Should science and social studies be included? Should the measure of success be performance across the whole curriculum? How important is it to include non-cognitive outcomes such as self-esteem, moral development, school attendance, social and emotional adjustment, integration into society and gaining employment? What are the long-term effects of bilingual schooling (e.g. students later becoming parents who raise their children in the minority language)? The questions indicate there will be debates and disputes over what are the valuable outcomes of schooling. Research on the effectiveness of bilingual education has varied in the choice of measures of outcome, as is illustrated later in the topic.

A particular problem is that measures of success tend to accent what is measurable. Quantitative outcomes (e.g. test scores) are often used; qualitative evidence is less often gathered, although recent US research has begun to correct this imbalance (e.g. studies from the National Research Center for Cultural Diversity). Can a play be judged only on an applause meter reading? Do a drama critic's notes add a vigorous, insightful interpretation to the performance? While critics will differ in their evaluations, they may add flesh and life to the statistical skeleton of educational tests.

The Researchers

Research on bilingual education is rarely neutral. Often the researchers have hypotheses which reflect their expectations. No educational research can be totally value-free, neutral or objective. The questions asked, the methodological tools chosen, decisions in analysis and manner of reporting usually reveal ideological preferences. Many researchers will be supporters of bilingual education, ethnic diversity, minority language rights and cultural pluralism. Other researchers derive their inspiration from in-migrant communities, political and cultural activism and affirmative action. This is not to argue that all evaluation research on bilingual education is invalid. Rather, it cannot be assumed that results are not affected by researchers, their beliefs, opinions and preferences.

Some of the research on bilingual education is committed, prescriptive in nature, with interests, idealism and ideology mixed with investigation and intelligent discussion. 'Bilingual education is not merely a disinterested exercise in the application of theory and research to real-life situations. It is also an exercise in social policy and ideology' (Edwards, 1981, page 27).

Reviews of Research

After a substantial number of different studies on bilingual education accumulated, various reviews and overviews appeared. A reviewer assembles as many individual studies as possible and attempts to find a systematic pattern and an orderliness in the findings. Is there a consensus in the findings? Is it possible to make some generalizations about the effectiveness of different forms of bilingual education? Rarely, if ever, will all the evaluations agree. Therefore the reviewer's task is to detect reasons for variations. For example, different age groups, different social class backgrounds and varying types of measurement device may explain variations in results.

Early reviews of bilingual education effectiveness were published in the 1960s and 1970s. For example, the two volumes of Anderson & Boyer (1970) entitled *Bilingual Schooling in the United States* became a classic text, examining definitions, models, historical developments and recommendations for bilingual education. Zappert & Cruz (1977), Troike (1978) and Dulay & Burt (1978, 1979) each concluded that bilingual education in the US effectively promoted bilingualism with language minority children and was preferable to monolingual English programs. That is, language minority students became skilled in both the majority and minority language. Since these early reviews, many individual studies have been added and more recent reviews have emerged (e.g. Baker & de Kanter, 1983; Collier, 1989; Collier, 1992; Lam, 1992; Thomas & Collier, 1995). The US debate on the effectiveness of bilingual education is considered in more detail later (see page 555).

Canadian Immersion education was evaluated in a number of important studies in the 1970s and 1980s. The major findings of the research were encouraging. It was found that students in Immersion programs tended to achieve age-appropriate levels of proficiency in French without detriment to their English language skills and at no cost to their levels of achievement across the curriculum. Limitations were that students did not attain the same command of grammar and the same stylistic range as native speakers, and also that their use of French out-

Increasing the Effectiveness of Bilingual Education

Bilingual education research has examined effectiveness at four different levels. First, there is the effectiveness at the level of the individual child. Within the same classroom, children may respond and perform differently. Second, there is effectiveness at the classroom level. Within the same school and type of bilingual education program, classrooms may vary considerably. It is important to analyze the factors connected with varying effectiveness at classroom level. Third, effectiveness is often analyzed at the school level. What makes some schools more effective than others even within the same type of bilingual education program and with similar student characteristics? Fourth, beyond the school level there can be aggregations of schools into different types of programs (e.g. transitional compared with heritage language programs) or into different geographical regions.

It is possible to look at effective bilingual education at each and all of these levels, and at the inter-relationship between these four levels. For example, at the individual level we need to know how bilingual education can best be effective for different social classes, and for children of different levels of 'intelligence' or ability. How do children with learning difficulties and specific language disorders fare in bilingual education? At the classroom level, we need to know what teaching methods and classroom characteristics create optimally effective bilingual education. At the school level, the characteristics of staffing, the size of groups and the language composition of the school all need to be taken into account to find out where and when bilingual education is more and less successful.

Apart from individual classroom and school characteristics, the effectiveness of bilingual education can take into account the social, political and cultural context in which such education is placed. For example, the differences between being in a subtractive or additive context may affect the outcomes of bilingual education. The willingness of teachers to involve parents, and good relationships between the school and its community may be important in effective bilingual education. (See The Input-Context-Process-Output Model of Bilingual Education, page 473.)

It is also important in bilingual education effectiveness research to examine a wide variety of outcomes from such education. Such variety may include examination results, tests of basic skills (e.g. oracy, literacy, numeracy), the broadest range of curriculum areas (e.g. Science and Technology, Humanities, Mathematics, Languages, Arts, physical, practical and theoretical pursuits, skills as well as knowledge). Non-cognitive outcomes are also important to include in an assessment of effectiveness. Such non-cognitive outcomes may include: attendance at school, attitudes, self-concept and self-esteem, social and emotional adjustment, employment and moral development.

The point behind such a comprehensive consideration of bilingual education is that effective bilingual education is not a simple or automatic consequence of using a child's home language in school (as in heritage language education) or a second language (as in Immersion bilingual education). Various home and parental, community, teacher, school and society effects may act and interact to make bilingual education more or less effective. The relative importance of different ingredients and processes in various school and cultural contexts needs investigating to build a comprehensive and wide-ranging theory of when, where, how and why bilingual education can be effective.

This approach to studying effectiveness of bilingual education not only considers the infrastructure of such education. It can also use the important studies from Britain and North America on what makes a school effective. For example, Mortimor *et al.* (1988) found that 12 factors were important in making a school effective. These may be listed as: purposeful leadership by the head teacher, involvement of the deputy head teacher, the degree of involvement of the teachers, consistency amongst teachers, having structured classroom sessions, providing intellectually challenging teaching, a work-centered environment, a limited focus within sessions, maximum communication between teachers and students, good record keeping, plenty of parental involvement and a positive classroom atmosphere.

Where the focus changes from school to teacher effectiveness when dealing with language minority students, certain elements appear important (Tikunoff, 1983; E. García, 1988; E. García, 1991a, 1991b). These include:

1. Teachers having high expectations of their students. Teachers being committed to the educational success of their students and serving as student advocates.
2. Teachers displaying a sense of confidence in their ability to be successful with language minority students.
3. Teachers communicating directions clearly, pacing lessons appropriately, involving students in decisions, monitoring students' progress and providing immediate feedback.
4. Teachers using students' native language for instruction; alternating between languages in a compartmentalized way to ensure clarity and understanding but without translating.
5. Teachers integrating aspects of a student's home culture and values into classroom activity to build trust and self-esteem as well as promoting cultural diversity and cultural pluralism. Teachers involving parents in their student's learning and activities in the classroom.
6. Teachers promoting a curriculum that has coherence, balance, breadth, relevance, progression and continuity.
7. Teachers organizing instruction to utilize collaborative instructional techniques. Students interacting with students in clearly explained, focused and meaningful activities.
8. Teachers placing no undue pressure on students to proceed from literacy in the home to the second language (e.g. Spanish to English literacy).

side school and after leaving school was limited. (See Immersion Education, page 496.)

Reviews of heritage language education and developmental maintenance education in the US and Canada found positive results for such programs. Positive outcomes were that students maintained their home language, that their performance across the curriculum matched or even surpassed that of comparable students in mainstream education, and that their English language performance was at least equal to that of comparable mainstream students. (See Heritage Language Education, page 508.)

Conclusion

This topic has examined the development of studies which have investigated whether bilingual education is more or less effective than monolingual education. It has also examined studies which look at the relative effectiveness of different forms of bilingual education. Having considered the historical origins and the nature of different forms of bilingual education, the topic has sought to portray how questions about the effectiveness of bilingual education have evolved. The initial studies examined individual programs and schools. A wide variety of different outcomes and conclusions resulted. Following this first stage, the second stage reviewed the voluminous research. This stage continues to the present. Reviews of Canadian Immersion education, heritage language education throughout the world, reviews of United States research by government officials and by meta-analysis have produced differing conclusions.

If there is a tentative overall pattern to the research, it would seem to be supportive of early total Immersion education for children whose first language is a majority language. The tentative conclusion also is that maintenance or heritage language education has advantages for language minority children. Public opinion on such matters tends to be divided revealing the political undertones of discussion about different forms of bilingual education.

However, one of the conclusions that comes from this discussion may be that simple questions give simplistic answers. We cannot expect a simple answer to the question of whether or not bilingual education is more or less effective than mainstream education. The question itself needs to become more refined. It needs to look at the different conditions under which different forms of bilingual education become more or less successful.

It has been suggested that the effectiveness of bilingual education needs to consider children, teachers, the community, the school itself and type of program. One particular factor cannot be isolated from another. A whole variety of ingredients need specifying, all of which make for a more or less successful recipe. Children have a wide variety of characteristics which need investigating. Children cannot be isolated from the classroom characteristics within which they work. Within the classroom there are a variety of factors which may make for a more or less effective education. Outside the classroom the different attributes of schools may in their turn interact with children and their classrooms to make education for language minority children more or less effective. Outside the school are the important effects of the community. The social, cultural milieu and political environment in which a school works will affect the education of language minority children at all levels.

The key issue becomes 'what are the optimal conditions for children who are either bilingual, becoming bilingual or wish to be bilingual?' Answers to 'optimal condition' questions may involve a complex set of answers. Rather than a simple black and white sketch, a complex multicolored canvas may need to be painted.

Further Reading

ARIAS, M. & CASANOVA, U. (eds), 1993, *Bilingual Education: Politics, Practice, Research.* Chicago: National Society for the Study of Education/University of Chicago Press.

BAETENS BEARDSMORE, H. (ed.), 1993, *European Models of Bilingual Education.* Clevedon: Multilingual Matters Ltd.

CAZDEN, C. B. & SNOW, C. E., 1990, English Plus: Issues in Bilingual Education. *The Annals of the American Academy of Political and Social Science,* Volume 508: March 1990. London: Sage.

CRAWFORD, J.,1995, *Bilingual Education: History, Politics, Theory and Practice* (Third edition). Los Angeles: Bilingual Educational Services.

CUMMINS, J. & DANESI, M., 1990, *Heritage Languages. The Development and Denial of Canada's Linguistic Resources.* Toronto: Our Schools/Ourselves Education Foundation & Garamond Press.

GARCÍA, O. (ed.), 1991, *Bilingual Education: Focusschrift in Honor of Joshua A. Fishman.* Amsterdam/Philadelphia: John Benjamins.

GARCÍA, O. & BAKER, C. (eds), 1995, *Policy and Practice in Bilingual Education: A Reader Extending the Foundations.* Clevedon: Multilingual Matters Ltd.

GENESEE, F., 1987, *Learning Through Two Languages.* Cambridge, MA: Newbury House.

HELLER, M., 1994, *Crosswords: Language, Education and Ethnicity in French.* Ontario & New York: Mouton de Gruyter.

SWAIN, M. & LAPKIN, S., 1982, *Evaluating Bilingual Education: A Canadian Case Study.* Clevedon: Multilingual Matters Ltd.

A Case Study of Effectiveness in Bilingual Education

An example of research into bilingual education effectiveness is a case study by Lucas, Henze & Donato (1990) in six schools in California and Arizona. This research revealed eight features seemingly important in promoting the success of language minority students.

Value and status were given to the language minority students' language and culture
While English literacy was a major goal, native language skills were celebrated, encouraged inside and outside the formal curriculum and advertised as an advantage rather than a liability.

High expectations of language minority students were prevalent
Apart from strategies to motivate students and recognize their achievement, individualized support of language minority students was available. The provision of counseling, co-operation with parents and the hiring of language minority staff in leadership positions to act as role models were some of the initiatives to raise expectations of success at school.

School leaders gave the education of language minority students a relatively high priority
This included good awareness of curriculum approaches to language minority children and communicating this to the staff. Strong leadership, the willingness to hire bilingual teachers and high expectations of such students were also part of the repertoire of such leaders.

Staff development was designed to help all the staff effectively serve language minority students
For example, the teachers were provided with staff development programs which sensitized them to students' language and cultural background, increased their knowledge of second language acquisition and of effective curriculum approaches in teaching language minority students.

A variety of courses for language minority students was offered
Such courses included English as a second language and first language courses. Small class sizes (e.g. 20 to 25) were created to maximize interaction.

A counseling program was available
Counselors were able to speak the students' home language, could give post-secondary opportunity advice and monitored the success of the language minority students.

Parents of language minority children were encouraged to become involved in their children's education
This included parents' meetings, contact with teachers and counselors, telephone contact and neighborhood meetings.

School staff were committed to the empowerment of language minority students through education
Such commitment was realized through extra curricular activities, participation in community activities, interest in developing their pedagogic skills and interest in the political process of improving the lot of language minority students.

REFERENCE: LUCAS, HENZE & DONATO, 1990

The Competencies Needed by Bilingual Teachers

Eleanor Thonis (1991) outlines many of the qualities and competencies that bilingual teachers require, especially when teaching language minority students. Many of these competencies are needed by all teachers; some are particular to teachers in bilingual education programs. The qualities and competencies she lists include the following:

- A genuine interest in youth
- An enthusiasm for learning
- An ability to express praise and liking for students
- A commitment to *all* students
- A respect for parents
- Organizational skills
- An openness for change
- An awareness of cultural differences
- A recognition of language diversity in the classroom
- A knowledge of second language methodology
- An understanding of students' lives outside the school
- A sensitivity to students' families and their values
- A knowledge of the history and heritage of a minority language group
- A recognition of the strengths and potential of all students
- A willingness to modify and adapt instruction and materials as needed to suit the students
- Knowledge of the sociocultural context of the school
- Managing several different groups within a single classroom
- Creating interest and enthusiasm for learning
- Monitoring students' progress
- A courtesy and consideration of others
- Fairness and justice applied equally to all
- The responsibilities and rights of different language groups
- Recognition of the similarities and differences between first and second language acquisition
- Knowledge of the nature of reading in the first and second language
- Organizing instruction to accommodate students' different stages of language development
- Understanding of the interdependence of the language skills of speaking, listening, reading and writing

REFERENCE: THONIS, 1991

Participants in the American Indian Language Development Institute (AILDI) at the University of Arizona, Tucson, devising language games and curricula for the teaching of indigenous North American languages.

3: The Debate in the United States over Bilingual Education

Introduction

While there are many research reports from the US evaluating bilingual education in its many different forms, the recent US debate starts with a Federal Government review of research published in the early 1980s.

The Baker and de Kanter Review of Bilingual Education (1983)

At the beginning of the 1980s, the United States Federal Government commissioned a major review of Transitional Bilingual education by Keith Baker & Adriana de Kanter (1983). While in the 1960s and 1970s bilingual education slowly evolved in the United States, in the late 1970s, 1980s and 1990s public support for bilingual education tended not to favor such evolution. One branch of public opinion in the United States saw bilingual education as failing to foster integration. Rather, such opinion saw bilingual education as leading to social and economic divisions in society along language grounds. Minority language groups were sometimes portrayed as using bilingual education for political and economic self interest, even separatism. Thus the Baker & de Kanter (1983) review needs viewing in its political context.

Baker & de Kanter (1983) posed two questions to focus their review. These two questions were:

1. Does Transitional Bilingual education lead to better performance in English?
2. Does Transitional Bilingual education lead to better performance in non language subject areas?

The review looked at bilingual education through 'transitional' eyes. It did not start from a neutral, comprehensive look at the various different forms of bilingual education. Notice also the narrow range of expected outcomes of bilingual education in the questions. Only English language and non-language subject areas were regarded as the desirable outcome of schooling. Other outcomes such as self-esteem, employment, preservation of minority languages, the value of different cultures were not considered. Nor were areas such as moral development, social adjustment and personality development considered.

At the outset of their investigation, Baker & de Kanter (1981, 1983) located 300 pieces of research from North America and the rest of the bilingual world. Of these 300, they rejected 261 studies. The 39 they considered in their review of bilingual education had to conform to six criteria. These may be listed as:

1. English and non-language subject area performance must have been measured in the research.

2. Comparisons between bilingual education and, for example, mainstream children must have ensured the groups were relatively matched at the outset. This means that initial differences between the two comparison groups must have been taken into account. If not, the results may be explained by such initial differences (e.g. different socioeconomic grouping) rather than the form of education in which children were placed.

3. Baker & de Kanter (1983) required the studies to be statistically valid. For example, appropriate statistical tests need to have been performed.

4. Some studies were rejected because they compared the rate of progress of a bilingual education sample with national averages for a particular subject area. Such a comparison is invalid as the comparison would be between bilinguals and monolingual English speakers, rather than two different groups of bilinguals in different forms of schooling.

5. It was insufficient for chosen studies to show that a group of students had progressed over the year. Rather 'gain scores' needed to involve comparisons between different forms of schooling. That is, relative gain (one form of bilingual education program compared with another) rather than absolute gain (how much progress made in a specified time) was required.

6. Studies were rejected which solely used grade equivalent scores. There are problems of comparability and compatibility between students, schools and states when US grade scores are used.

The conclusion of Baker & de Kanter's (1983) review is that no particular education program should be

legislated or preferred by the US Federal Government:

> 'The common sense observation that children should be taught in a language they understand does not necessarily lead to the conclusion they should be taught in their home language. They can be taught successfully in a second language if the teaching is done right. The key to successful teaching in the second language seems to be to ensure that the second language and subject matter are taught simultaneously so that subject content never gets ahead of language. Given the American setting, where the language-minority child must ultimately function in an English-speaking society, carefully conducted second language instruction in all subjects may well be preferable to bilingual methods'. (page 51)

The review therefore came out in support of the dominant government preference for English-only and Transitional Bilingual education. Functioning in the English language rather than bilingually was preferred. Assimilation and integration appear as the social and political preference that underlies the conclusions.

There has been considerable criticism of the Baker & de Kanter (1983) review (e.g. Willig, 1981/82; American Psychological Association, 1982). The main criticisms may be summarized as follows: a narrow range of outcome measures was considered, although this is often the fault of the original research rather than the review; focusing on Transitional Bilingual education implicitly valued assimilation and integration and devalued aims such as the preservation of a child's home language and culture; and the criteria used for selecting only 39 out of 300 studies were narrow and rigid.

While the studies included may be relatively more sophisticated, this still left studies with technical deficiencies (e.g. studies with small samples) included in the review. It also excluded well known and oft-quoted studies such as the Rock Point Navajo research (Rosier & Holm, 1980; see also Holm & Holm, 1990). The review therefore concentrated on a selective sample of technically superior research. It failed to look at patterns across the broadest range of research.

An alternative and more rule-bound strategy is to use meta-analysis. This is a methodological technique which quantitatively integrates empirical research studies. The technique mathematically examines the amount of effect or differences in the research studies. For example, how much difference is there in outcome between transitional and Immersion bilingual education? There is no need to exclude studies from the meta-analysis which the reviewer finds marginal or doubtful in terms of methodology. The quality of the evaluations is something that is examined in the meta-analysis and can be allowed for statistically. Meta-analysis may show consistency of finding where narrative reviewers tend to highlight variation and disagreement in findings.

Willig's (1985) Meta-Analysis

Willig (1985) adopted a statistical meta-analysis approach to reviewing bilingual education. She selected 23 studies from the Baker & de Kanter (1981, 1983) review. All of her 23 studies concerned United States bilingual education evaluations and deliberately excluded Canadian Immersion education evaluations. As a result of the meta-analysis, Willig (1985) concluded that bilingual education programs that supported the minority language were consistently superior in various outcomes. Bilingual education programs tend to produce higher performance in tests of achievement throughout the curriculum. Small to moderate advantages were found for bilingual education students in reading, language skills, mathematics and overall achievement when the tests were in the students' second language (English). Similar advantages were found for these curriculum areas and for writing, listening, social studies and self-concept when non-English language tests were used.

Willig's (1985) analysis also portrays the variety of bilingual education programs in existence that makes simple generalization difficult and dangerous. For example, the social and cultural ethos surrounding such programs is one major variation. Another variation is the nature of students in such programs and the variety of language intake. For example, some bilingual education programs start with children at a similar level of language skills. In other classrooms, there are various language and second language abilities, rendering classroom teaching more difficult.

Further Research

Major US research is now described to exemplify the problems of limited focus evaluations of bilingual education, as well as to exemplify some recent trends in research findings. An eight-year, congressionally mandated, four and a half million dollar longitudinal study of bilingual education in the US compared Structured English 'Immersion', Early-exit and Late-exit bilingual education programs (Ramirez, Yuen & Ramey, 1991; Ramirez, 1992). (The term 'Immersion' is not used in the original Canadian sense – English Submersion is more accurate.) Dual Language or other forms of 'strong' bilingual education were not evaluated. The focus was only on 'weak' forms of bilingual education. The programs compared 'have the same instructional goals, the

Opposition to Bilingual Education in the US

It has been suggested by Huddy & Sears (1995) that there are three theoretical explanations for opposition to bilingual education. First, realistic interest theory suggests that those in power wish to protect their own (and their group's) political and economic self-interests. Thus majority language groups may oppose bilingual education as such education does not benefit monolinguals (e.g. in the US) or majority language speakers. Indeed, language majority groups may be subsidizing such bilingual education. If there is a feeling of threat among the majority language group, the threat may not be based on 'reality' but narrowly subjective, constructed out of prejudice and stereotyping rather than realism.

Such majority language groups may endorse the principle of racial and ethnic equality and believe in the equality of all languages. However, a stronger motivation and priority is language majority self-interest and hence the best of intentions can be killed by the strongest of motives.

This phenomenon is not confined to the United States. There is a belief in many countries where one language is dominant that bilingual education takes away resources from monolingual, majority language schools. However, a stronger concern among those in power may be that minority language bilingual education programs threaten majority language economic interests and political ascendancy.

A second theoretical explanation as to why there is opposition to bilingual education according to Huddy & Sears (1995) is that those in bilingual education are perceived as undeserving of special treatment. For example, in the United States, Huddy & Sears (1995) suggest that there is Anglo prejudice towards Latinos who are viewed as 'lazy' and as 'violators of the work ethic'. A new form of racism produces stereotypes of non-Whites not in terms of color but as 'unwilling to work', 'complaining', with an 'ethnic chip on their shoulder'. Therefore, language majority members may see bilingual education as giving undeserved government assistance to those who are perceived as unwilling to work, unwilling to assimilate and likely to be politically subversive.

A third explanation for opposition to bilingual education derives from social identity theory. Language majority members may oppose bilingual education because they view it as a threat to national, cultural and personal identity. Bilingual education becomes equated with the spread of foreign customs, foreign influences, challenging a sense of pride in nationality, national image and integration. From a language majority viewpoint, both individual rights and national solidarity may seem to be threatened by bilingual education. Bilingual education is seen to promote diversity rather than unity.

REFERENCE: HUDDY & SEARS, 1995

The Need for Bilingual Teachers in the United States

In a survey of the demand and supply of teachers in the United States in 1993, Haselkorn & Calkins (1993) found that there was a relatively high demand for bilingual education teachers. Bilingual education teachers were in the shortage category alongside Physics, Chemistry, Mathematics and Computer Science. This shortage has changed little since 1989 and is apparent across the US but more problematic on the west and southwest coast and in Texas.

The chart shows bilingual education teacher demand in relation to 15 other curriculum areas.

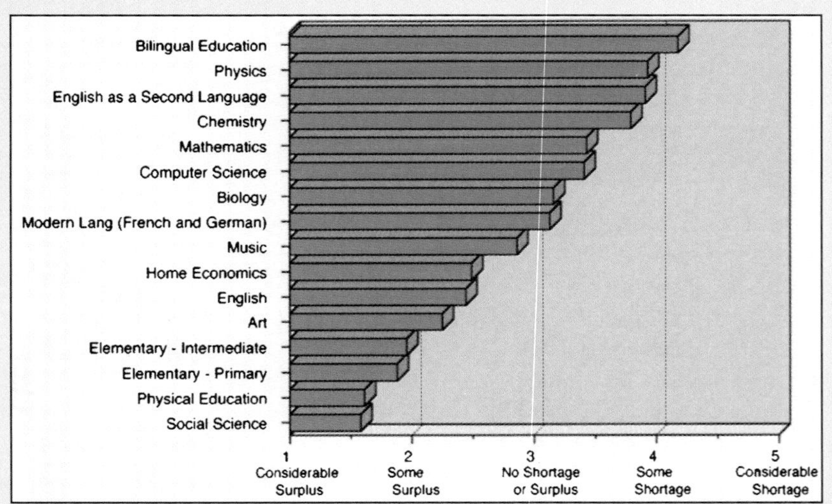

The need for bilingual teachers in the United States. (Source: Haselkorn & Calkins, 1993).

acquisition of English language skills so that the language-minority child can succeed in an English-only mainstream classroom' (Ramirez, Yuen & Ramey, 1991, page 1).

Over 2300 Spanish-speaking students from 554 kindergarten to sixth grade classrooms in New York, New Jersey, Florida, Texas and California were studied. Ramirez & Merino (1990) examined the processes of bilingual education classrooms. The language of the classrooms was radically different in Grades 1 and 2:

- 'Structured Immersion' (Submersion) contained almost 100 percent English language.
- Early-exit Transitional Bilingual education contained around two-thirds English and one-third Spanish.
- Late-exit Transitional Bilingual education moved from three-quarters Spanish in Grade 1 to a little over half Spanish in Grade 2.

As a generalization, the outcomes were different for the three types of bilingual education. By the end of Grade 3, Maths, Language and English reading skills were not particularly different between the three programs. By Grade 6, Late-exit Transitional Bilingual education students were performing higher at Mathematics, English Language and English reading than other programs. Parental involvement appears to be greatest in the Late-exit transitional programs. Although Spanish language achievement was measured in the research, these results were not included in the final statistical analyses.

One conclusion reached by Ramirez, Yuen & Ramey (1991) was that Spanish-speaking students can be provided with substantial amounts of primary language instruction without impeding their acquisition of English language and reading skills. When language minority students are given instruction in their home language, this:

> 'does not interfere with or delay their acquisition of English language skills, but helps them to "catch-up" to their English-speaking peers in English language arts, English reading and Mathematics. In contrast, providing LEP students with almost exclusive instruction in English does not accelerate their acquisition of English language arts, reading or Mathematics, i.e. they do not appear to be "catching-up". The data suggest that by Grade 6, students provided with English-only instruction may actually fall further behind their English-speaking peers. Data also document that learning a second language will take six or more years' (Ramirez, 1992, page 1).

This is evidence to support 'strong' forms of bilingual education and support for the use of the native language as a teaching medium. The results also showed little difference between Early-exit and the English Immersion (Submersion) students. Opponents of bilingual education have used this result to argue for the relative administrative ease and less expensive mainstreaming (Submersion) of language minority students and for the over-riding desirability of Transitional Bilingual education (e.g. Baker, K., 1992). Cziko (1992, page 12) neatly sums up the ambiguity of the conclusions, suggesting that the research: 'provides evidence both for and against bilingual education, or rather, against what bilingual education normally is and for what it could be'.

A series of reviews and criticisms of the Ramirez, Yuen & Ramey (1991) research then ensued (e.g. Cazden, 1992; Meyer & Fienberg, 1992; Thomas, 1992) with a particular emphasis on the following issues:

- The benefits of 'strong' forms of bilingual education programs are not considered (e.g. Two-Way bilingual education; Heritage Language education). This makes statements about bilingual education based on an incomplete range of possibilities. Mainstream classrooms with English Second Language (ESL) pull-out (withdrawal) classes – widely implemented in the US – were also not included in the study.

- The range of variables used to measure 'success' is narrow. For example, language minority parents may expect attitudinal, self-esteem, cultural and ethnic heritage goals to be examined as a measure of successful outcomes.

- The considerable differences that exist within bilingual education programs (let alone comparing differing types of bilingual education program) makes comparisons and conclusions most difficult. Also, the complexity of organization within a school, the ethos and varying classroom practices makes categorization of schools into watertight bilingual education programs formidable.

- The National Academy of Sciences reviewed this (and other) studies and concluded that the design of the study was ill-suited to answer key policy questions. More clarity in the aims and goals of bilingual education in the US is needed before research can be appropriately focused. Currently, the goals for bilingual education in the US are implicit and not defined.

- There is a lack of data to support the long-term benefits of Late-exit transitional programs over other programs.

Achievement in United States Bilingual Education Programs

Thomas & Collier (1995) show the pattern of language minority English language achievement in different types of bilingual education programs. This is summarized in the charts and in the text below.

In kindergarten through to Grade 2, there is little difference between language minority children in ESL 'pull-out', Transitional and Two-Way (Dual Language) programs in the United States. On a 'English language achievement' scale of 0 to 100 (with 50 as the average performance of native English language speakers), Language Minority children score around the 20 mark.

ESL 'Pull-out' children initially (Grades 1 & 2) progress faster in English language achievement than children in transitional and dual language programs. This might be expected as they have more intensive English-medium activity.

By Grade 6, students in dual language programs and Late-exit transitional programs are ahead on English language performance compared with Early-exit and ESL pull-out students. Dual language and Late-exit transitional students are achieving in English language tests close to that of native English speakers (i.e. around 50th percentile). Early-exit and ESL pull-out students tend to perform around the 30th percentile on such tests.

By Grade 11, the order of performance is:

1. Two-Way bilingual education
2. Late-exit Transitional Bilingual education
3. Early-exit Transitional Bilingual education
4. ESL Pull-out programs

By Grade 11, Two-Way bilingual education students are performing above the average levels of native English speakers on English language tests. On a 'English language achievement' scale of 0 to 100, Two-Way bilingual education students average around 60, Late-exit students about the same as native English speakers around 50, Early-exit students around 30 to 40, and ESL pull-out students around 20.

When ESL is acquired through content teaching, this provides higher English achievement than language learning.

REFERENCE: THOMAS & COLLIER, 1995

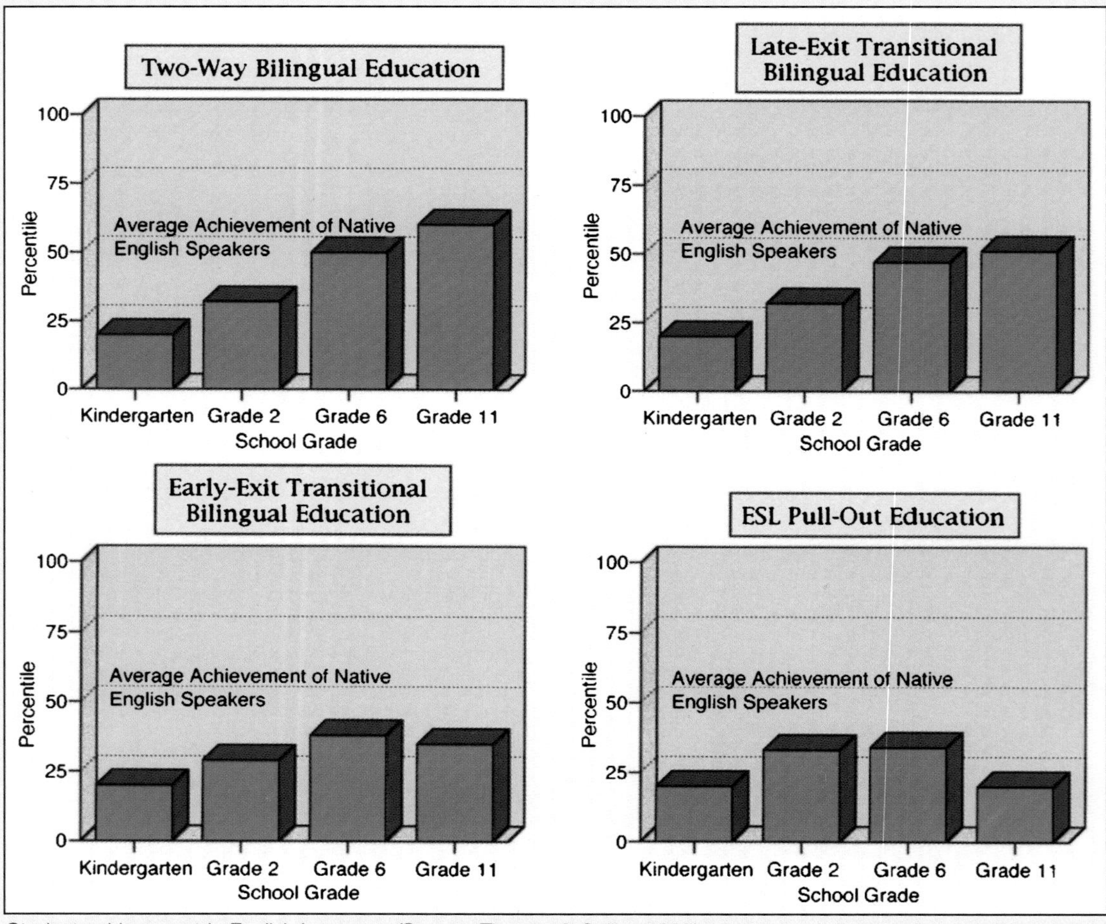

Student achievement in English language. (Source: Thomas & Collier, 1995).

Expert Overviews of the Effectiveness of Bilingual Education in the US

One inadequacy in bilingual education research is the relative absence of public opinion surveys. We lack the evidence for the amount of parental and public support that exists for different forms of bilingual education in various countries where bilingual education is a political and educational issue. Parents and children are rarely asked about their degree of satisfaction with bilingual education during or after the experience. There is a paucity of information about the democratic wishes of language minorities in the United States. What does the US public think about bilingual education? What are the varieties of opinion and viewpoint expressed? How do different forms of bilingual education in the eyes of clients and consumers satisfy their wants and wishes? Is the debate only between politicians and liberal academics? Are there Hispanics who prefer assimilation via bilingual education and are there US academics who have a reasoned argument against bilingual education? There is a danger that we deal with bilingual education controversies without reasonably or fully representing the varied viewpoints of public, politicians and policy makers. Rarely have the present or future clientele or the general public been asked their opinions on the aims and nature of bilingual education.

An exception is Huddy & Sears (1990) who 'telephone' interviewed a US national sample of 1170 in 1983. They found that while the majority tended to be favorable towards bilingual education, a substantial minority (around a quarter of respondents, depending on the specific question) who included well-informed respondents, opposed bilingual education, particularly on the integration issue.

While public opinion surveys are infrequent, expert opinion is more likely to be privately or publicly sought. After the various narrative reviews of research on bilingual education and Willig's (1985) meta-analysis, there followed an expert overview in the US. A United States House of Representatives subcommittee on Education and Labor asked the General Accounting Office (1987) to conduct a study on whether or not the research evidence on bilingual education supported the current government preference for assimilationist, Transitional Bilingual education. The General Accounting Office (1987) therefore decided to conduct a survey of experts on bilingual education. Ten experts were assembled, mostly professors of education, selected from prestigious institutions throughout the United States. Each expert was provided with a set of questions to answer in written form. The experts were asked to compare research findings with central political statements made about such research. The purpose was to verify the veracity of official statements.

In terms of learning English, eight out of ten experts favored using the native or heritage language in the classroom. They believed that progress in the native language aided children in learning English because it strengthened literacy skills which easily transferred to operating in the second language. With the learning of other subjects in the curriculum, six experts supported the use of heritage languages in such teaching. However, it was suggested that learning English is important in making academic progress (General Accounting Office, 1987).

That all the experts did not agree was to be expected. The group of ten had diverse research backgrounds and perspectives. Eight were knowledgeable about language learning and schooling for language minority children. Two were expert on social science accumulation and synthesis (meta-analysis). These ten people were also sent

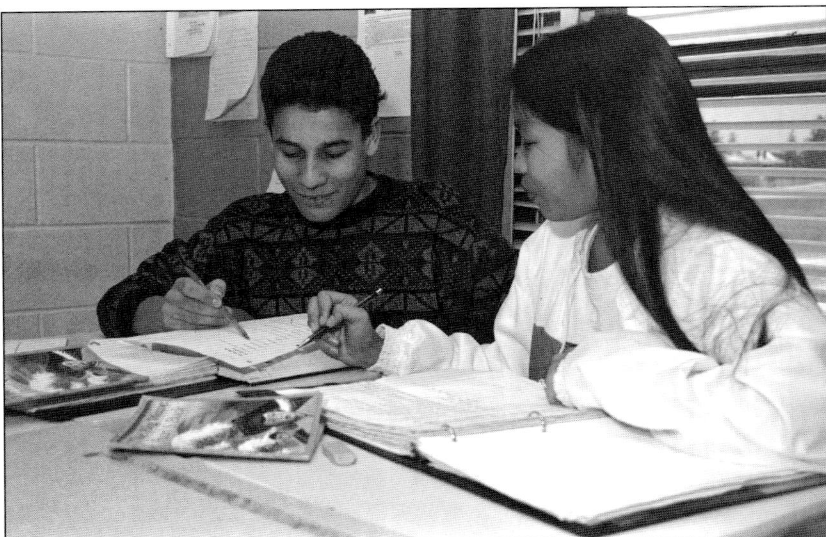

The importance of uninterrupted cognitive development.

Key Factors in Bilingual Schooling: The Findings of Collier and Thomas

Longitudinal studies by Virginia P. Collier and her co-researcher Wayne Thomas, have identified four particular factors that affect minority language students' success or failure in schooling in the United States. In particular, Collier & Thomas are concerned with the length of time it takes for such students to acquire a second language to compete in the curriculum on an equal footing with native speakers of that language.

Virginia Collier's (1995a) model for acquiring a second language for schooling has four major components: sociocultural, linguistic, academic and cognitive. These four factors are regarded as interdependent and interactive.

First, Collier (1995a) stresses the importance of sociocultural processes in acquiring a second language in school. The particular examples she has in mind are those students in the United States in Transitional Bilingual education or dual language education. The student may experience prejudice and discrimination, the subordinate status of their language minority group and assimilation forces. Such external influences may effect internal psychological workings such as self-esteem, anxiety, integration with peers and achievement in school. Thus Virginia Collier emphasizes the importance of a socioculturally supportive environment for language minority students.

Second, Collier (1995a) argues that academic success in the second language requires the student's first language to be developed to a high cognitive level. Her argument starts with the continuous development of the first language. She emphasizes that language development is a life-long process and cannot occur in a two-year period or even a five-year period. Throughout schooling, a child acquires more vocabulary, increased understanding of meaning, more complex syntax, more formal discourse patterns, increasingly complex aspects of pragmatics and subtle phonological distinctions in their first language. Children throughout schooling acquire increasingly complex skills in reading and writing, developing through to college when further vocabulary development and more complex writing skills are required. In adult life, our language use evolves as new and varied experiences occur. We develop new subtleties in meaning such that language acquisition is an unending process throughout a lifetime.

The argument then moves on to suggest that second language acquisition is an equally complex and evolving phenomena. If a child is required to work through a second language in school, a very deep level of language proficiency is required and this has to be developed throughout schooling and college.

How long does it take to develop academic second language proficiency? Collier argues that it is difficult for second language students to develop proficiency levels in their second language to compete with native speakers. One reason is that native speakers are not sitting around waiting for non-native speakers to catch up. During the school years, native speakers' first language development continues at a rapid rate, such that the goal of proficiency equal to a native speaker is a moving target for the language learner.

Collier's longitudinal studies suggests that, in United States schools where all the instruction is given through the second language (submersion schooling), second language speakers of English with no schooling in their first language take between seven and ten years or more to reach the language proficiency of native English-speaking peers. Some do not reach native levels of language proficiency at all. Where students have had two or three years of first language schooling in their home country before emigrating to the United States, they take between five and seven years to reach native speaker performance. Collier found this pattern among different home language groups, different ethnic groups and different socioeconomic groups of students.

The most significant variable in becoming proficient in the second language (English in the US) is the amount of formal schooling students have received in their first language. Those students who are schooled solely in their second language, particularly from the 4th grade onwards, when the academic and cognitive demands of the curriculum increase rapidly, tend to progress slowly and show relatively less academic achievement. Thus one essential feature for students to develop academic language proficiency is that there is strong development through the first language of academic-cognitive thinking skills. Thinking abilities, literacy development, concept formation, subject knowledge and learning strategies developed in the first language transfer to the second language. As students expand their vocabulary and literacy skills in their first language, they can increasingly demonstrate the knowledge that they have gained in the second language.

The third part of Collier's (1995a) model is academic development. With each succeeding grade in school, the curriculum requires an ever-expanding vocabulary, higher cognitive levels and a more complex form of discourse. It is most efficient to develop academic work through a student's first language, while progress in the second language occurs through teaching meaningful academic content. Postponing or interrupting academic development to promote the second language, tends to result in academic failure. Students cannot afford to lose time when the curriculum is both full and increasingly complex and demanding.

Thus Collier argues for the importance of uninterrupted cognitive development in primary and secondary schooling for second language children. The key to understanding the role of the first language in the academic development of the second language is to ensure that there is uninterrupted cognitive development which best occurs through education in the first language. When students have to use an undeveloped second language at school (as in submersion schooling), they will be functioning at a lower cognitive level. Thus, cognitive maturity fails to occur, or occurs relatively slowly.

The fourth factor in Collier's (1995a) model is cognitive development. She argues that the teaching of a second language should avoid simplified, structured and artificially sequenced language work. The danger is in breaking down language into cognitively simple tasks. Rather, cognitive development occurs when there is development of the first language as the foundation for both cognitive development and second language proficiency.

Collier goes on to argue that all four components, sociocultural, academic, cognitive and linguistic are interdependent. If one is developed at the neglect of the other, the student's overall growth and performance will suffer.

Collier's conclusion is that Two-way Bilingual education at the elementary school level is the optimal program for the long-term academic success of language minority students. Such students maintain their first language skills and cognitive/academic development while developing in a second language. In such a model, students develop deep academic proficiency and cognitive understanding through their first language to compete successfully with native speakers of the second language.

Reference: COLLIER, 1995a

ten literary reviews to examine with the detailed questionnaire. The experts worked individually; they were not brought together for an overall discussion to produce a consensus opinion. When the experts had submitted their written report, they were given an opportunity to clarify and correct the General Accounting Office's Report to Congress of their views. Also, an outside evaluation expert reviewed the written responses of the experts, as well as the draft text, to check on the accuracy of the representation of the experts' views.

The key question is whether a different group or groups of ten experts would produce different conclusions. Experts tend to disagree amongst themselves. This tends to reflect the developing nature of research in this area and the complexity and political nature of what makes a particular school or program work successfully or not. One problem is the effect of interacting factors with different types of bilingual education. For example, the characteristics of the student, the parents and the community each serve to make a program, school or child more or less successful. The degree of parental interest and involvement in bilingual education is sometimes seen as an important intervening variable. Also, the status of the heritage language in the community and the country may affect the success of a bilingual education program. If the analogy may stand, there are multitudinous ingredients that go in the educational recipe. Focusing purely on the language part of schooling (e.g. bilingual or monolingual education) only examines a narrow range of ingredients in the recipe. Complex reactions between ingredients mean that making simple statements about what works successfully or not is difficult.

One area on which seven out of the ten experts agreed was that evidence did not exist on the long-term effects of various forms of bilingual education. Seven out of the ten firmly rejected the idea that there was support for connecting bilingual education, either positively or negatively, to long-term outcomes. This reveals that research on the effectiveness of bilingual education is still low down in the evolutionary process. In the experts' survey, four out of ten experts agreed that the literature on language learning did not allow generalizations to be drawn at this stage.

Having considered overviews of research on bilingual education, it is important to note one basic factor. There is likely to be a divergence of opinion about the aims of education and bilingual education. This difference of viewpoint will exist in both the academic and the non-academic outcomes of schooling. Some may emphasize English language skills, some attainment throughout the curriculum, some the importance of second and even third language learning. Others may focus on the non-academic outcomes of education such as moral and social skills, employment, drop-out rates, absenteeism and self-esteem. At societal level, there will also be a variety of aims. For some pluralism, biculturalism and multilingualism are a desirable outcome. For others the assimilation of minority languages, the integration of minorities within overall society are the important outcomes. This suggests that a definitive statement that bilingual education is more or less successful than, for example, mainstream education is impossible due to the variety of underlying values and beliefs that different interest groups have about education and the kind of future society desired.

Trueba (1989, page 104) sums up the use of effectiveness studies by different interest groups for their own ends. 'It is unfortunate that bilingual education and other educational programs for minority students have become part of a political struggle between opposing groups. Educators and parents have been forced into political camps, and campaigned for or against these programs, without a thorough understanding of their instructional attributes and characteristics. Perhaps it would be easier to reach a consensus regarding the nature of sound pedagogical principles and practices rather than to continue to debate such politically loaded issues.'

Further Reading

ARIAS, B. & CASANOVA, U. (eds), 1993, *Bilingual Education: Politics, Research and Practice*. Berkeley, CA: McCutchan.

BAKER, K. A. & de KANTER, A. A., 1983, *Bilingual Education*. Lexington, MA: Lexington Books.

CAZDEN, C. B. & SNOW, C. E. (eds), 1990b, *English Plus: Issues in Bilingual Education. (The Annals of the American Academy of Political and Social Science*, Volume 508). London: Sage.

CRAWFORD, J., 1995, *Bilingual Education: History, Politics, Theory and Practice* (Third edition). Los Angeles: Bilingual Educational Services.

GARCÍA, O. & BAKER, C. (eds), 1995, *Policy and Practice in Bilingual Education. A Reader Extending the Foundations*. Clevedon: Multilingual Matters Ltd.

MEYER, M. M. & FIENBERG, S. (eds), 1992, *Assessing Evaluation Studies. The Case of Bilingual Education Strategies*. Washington, DC: National Academy Press.

RAMIREZ, J. D., 1992, Executive Summary. *Bilingual Research Journal*, 16 (1&2), 1-62.

WILLIG, A. C.,1985, A Meta-Analysis of Selected Studies on the Effectiveness of Bilingual Education. *Review of Educational Research*, 55 (3), 269-317.

WILLIG, A. C. & RAMIREZ, J. D., 1993, The Evaluation of Bilingual Education. In B. ARIAS & U. CASANOVA (eds), *Bilingual Education: Politics, Research and Practice*. Berkeley, CA: McCutchan.

Bilingual Education for Deaf and Hearing Impaired People

1: Deaf and Partially Hearing Bilingual People

There is a growing recognition that those people who are deaf or have partial hearing are already, or can become, bilinguals. There is a growing campaign for deaf people to become bilingual through learning to sign first of all, followed by literacy in the language of the non-deaf (e.g. English in the United States). There are other forms of deaf bilingualism: those who learn to speak from hearing parents, followed by learning to sign. Others learn to sign first and then learn an oral form of the hearing language. Others learn to communicate by different means, by signs, speaking and writing – a Total Communication approach. The path from signing to majority language literacy is discussed later in this topic.

For the moment, it is important to recognize that deaf people (like many hearing bilinguals) form relatively disadvantaged language minorities and have certain things in common with hearing, language minority individuals and groups. Like most hearing bilinguals, deaf people may use their two languages for different functions and purposes. For example, signing may be used to communicate with the deaf community, while a spoken language or literacy in a majority language is used to communicate with the hearing community. Deaf people will sometimes wish to identify with the deaf cultural community. At other times they will be assimilated into the hearing community. Deaf people have too often been placed in deficit types of education that submerge them in the language and culture of hearers rather than an enrichment model where signing is allowed as the primary language.

Two Viewpoints about Deaf People

The first viewpoint is the medical view of deafness. Here deafness is defined as a defect or a handicap that distinguishes 'abnormal' deaf people from 'normal' hearing persons. Deafness is seen as a condition that needs to be remedied or cured as much as possible. Viewed as a disability, hearing aids and other devices that enhance hearing or the understanding of speech are recommended. Deaf people are expected to become as 'normal' as possible by avoiding purely visual methods of communication such as sign language, and learning spoken language as much as is viable.

In the medical view of deafness, sign language is, at worst, perceived as a primitive, rudimentary, simple picture language in contrast to the subtlety and complexity of spoken languages. Thus a spoken language is seen as the natural language for all in the community, including

deaf people, and a central aim of their education therefore becomes a competence in spoken and eventually written language. Such education, and social pressures within the community, aim for the integration or assimilation of deaf people with hearing people into a homogeneous community. Deaf people existing in separate communities, miming to each other, and having a deaf culture is not entertained as wholesome or desirable. Thus such educators, professionals and policy makers see themselves as helping deaf people to overcome their 'handicap' and to live in the hearing world.

A second viewpoint is more in line with that increasingly expressed about hearing bilinguals: one of bilingualism, vitality as a linguistic and cultural minority community, and the need for an enriching dual language education. Such a viewpoint commences with the assertion that deaf people can do everything except hear. While there are differences between deaf and hearing people, these are natural cultural differences, not deviations from a hearing norm. Signing for deaf people is natural.

Thus, in this second viewpoint, deafness is regarded as a difference, a characteristic which distinguishes 'normal' deaf people from 'normal' hearing people. Deaf people are regarded as owning sign language which is a full language in itself, grammatically complex and capable of expressing as much as any spoken language. Deaf people are regarded as a linguistic and cultural minority that needs preservation, enrichment and celebration.

Instead of emphasizing the deficiencies of deaf people, their abilities are emphasized. A strong emphasis is placed on the use of vision as a positive, efficient and full communicative alternative to audible speaking and hearing. Sign language is thus used not only as equal to spoken language, but also as the most natural language for people who are born deaf.

In education, the focus is often on language development through signing, and later on bilingualism through literacy in the majority language. It is felt important that maximal language development occurs early on through signing. Early signing enables a focus on the subject matter of the curriculum (rather than learning to speak a majority language). Early use of signing in the classroom allows deaf children access to the curriculum.

In this viewpoint, deaf people should form, where possible, a cultural community of their own. Deaf people have a common language in signing, a culture and a set of needs that are distinct from the hearing community. The deaf community is seen as an important vehicle for the socialization of deaf and partially hearing people. Deaf adults can provide important role models for deaf children, either as teachers or in the community. Thus, this second viewpoint supports bilingualism, a deaf culture and the bilingual education of deaf people.

Differences in Bilingual Goals

It is important to recognize that, both among deaf people and among the hearing, there are not only different subgroupings but also differences of opinion about the appropriate language of deaf people, the education of deaf people and their integration into mainstream speaking society. Such differences will now be briefly represented.

Hagemeyer (1992) suggests that there are nine distinct subpopulations among deaf people in the United States. Such subdimensions refer to deaf culture and not to whether a person is also a member of Hispanic, Native American, Asian or any other ethnic group that exists alongside being deaf. The nine groupings are as follows:

1. Those who use sign language (e.g. American Sign Language – often represented as ASL) as their primary language.
2. Those who can communicate both in ASL and English.
3. Those mostly from the hearing impaired group who communicate primarily through speech.
4. Adults who became deaf later in life, who were not born deaf and may have acquired speech before deafness. Such people have the experience of hearing normally for a shorter or a longer period and may have speech patterns relatively well embedded before deafness occurred.
5. The elderly who became hearing impaired or deaf later in life as the result of the aging process.

A quote from Harvey Corson, Vice President of Gallaudet University

'From the days of antiquity to modern times, deaf people have existed and coped with a pressing human need to think and communicate. Over time, deaf people have developed signed languages, and have lived lives as self-sustaining and productive people. Nevertheless, we have been misunderstood, viewed as defective, and pitied for living in a world of silence. We have struggled to achieve equal rights, opportunities and full access to society, and to continue to struggle to the extent that our linguistic, educational, and cultural needs are still neither recognized nor understood.'

Reference: CORSON, 1993

Gallaudet University

Gallaudet University is based in Washington, District of Columbia in the United States. It is renowned as an undergraduate, graduate and research center for deaf and hard of hearing people from both the United States and around the world. Gallaudet University has eight extension centers, including Hawaii, Puerto Rico and Costa Rica. The following provides some of the features of this unique university.

- The University was started by Amos Kendall, a well-known journalist, politician and philanthropist who became interested in the welfare of five deaf children and set out to educate them. He donated two acres of his private estate in north-east Washington to establish a school for deaf and blind children. Kendall hired as his Superintendent the 20-year-old Edward Miner Gallaudet, who had a clear aim in life, a college for deaf students. In 1964, Congress responded favorably to this idea and allowed the institution to confer degrees in liberal arts and sciences. The College originally opened with just 13 male students, one professor and one assistant. In 1887, it opened its doors to women and six were accepted in a controversial two-year experiment. In 1894, the name of the college was changed from The National Deaf-Mute College to Gallaudet College in honor of its first Principal.

- There are currently over 1600 full-time students, 300 part-time students, 1400 full-time deaf students and around 200 part-time deaf students.

- Services provided on the campus include sign interpreters, volunteer note takers, amplified phones, group listening systems, and different technologies to help the deaf (e.g. computer systems).

- Communication in the university is by sign communication (with or without voice) in classrooms, meetings and between students.

- Hearing students are also admitted to graduate programs. Such programs include: MA and MSc degrees with specialist areas in Audiology, Counseling, Education, Education Technology, Interpreting, Linguistics, Psychology and Social Work programs. There are particular strengths in clinical psychology, deaf education and special education administration.

- Gallaudet University operates two national demonstration education programs. The Kendall Demonstration Elementary School and the Model Secondary School for the Deaf not only educate deaf students but also conduct research and developmental activities, providing a living demonstration of excellence for other schools and programs for deaf children.

- In 1988, the Board of Trustees announced the selection of Dr Elisabeth Zinser as the seventh President of Gallaudet University. Dr Zinser was not a deaf person. Students mounted a protest movement entitled 'Deaf President Now', as the appointment of a hearing person to a college for deaf students carried an apparent message about the lower status and capability of deaf people. This student-led movement united students, faculty, staff, alumni and members of deaf communities across the United States to support the selection of a deaf president for the University. This movement closed the University for a week and captured worldwide attention, creating considerable awareness about deafness, deaf people and their languages and cultures. Two days after her appointment, under pressure from the student protest, Zinser resigned and Gallaudet's eighth and first deaf president, Dr I. King Jordan was elected.

- The address for Gallaudet University is 800 Florida Avenue, N.E. Washington, DC 20002, US.

6. Those who do not know either ASL nor English, but communicate through gestures, mime and their own signing system. Such people may have been denied access to a deaf culture, to ASL and to education at an early age.
7. Those who have residual hearing, perhaps describing themselves as hard of hearing, and who can hear with the use of various aids.
8. Those people who are deaf and blind. An example is Helen Keller.
9. Those people who have normal hearing, but because their parents, children, or other members of the family are deaf, they understand signing, or are fully conversant with deaf culture and integrate with the deaf community.

Sign Language

Sign language is a fully developed, real language which allows its users to communicate the same, complete meaning as in spoken language. Sign language is not gesturing. Gesturing is relatively unsystematic, and is used in an *ad hoc* way to express a small number of basic expressions. We all use non-verbal communication to add emphasis to our speech. In contrast, signing is a very comprehensive, structurally complex, rule-bound, full means of communication. Sign language can perform the same range of functions as a spoken language, and can be used to teach any aspect of the curriculum.

There are a wide variety of sign systems in existence: to name but a few: American sign language, British sign language. Chinese sign language, Danish sign language, French sign language and Russian sign language, plus the artificial systems such as the Paget-Gorman sign system, and manual English.

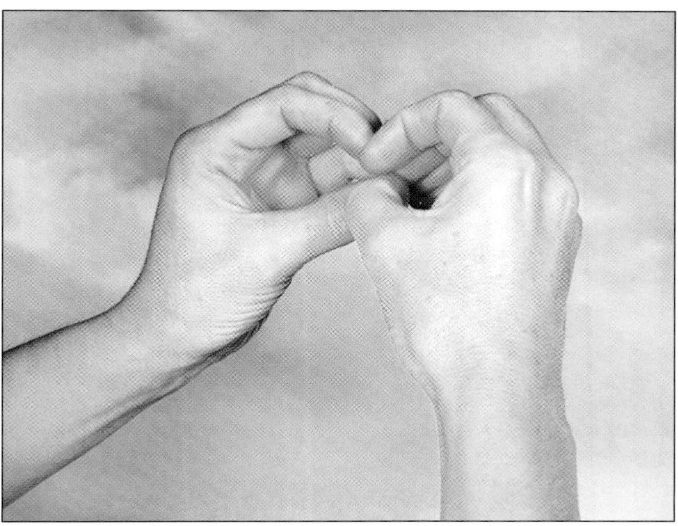

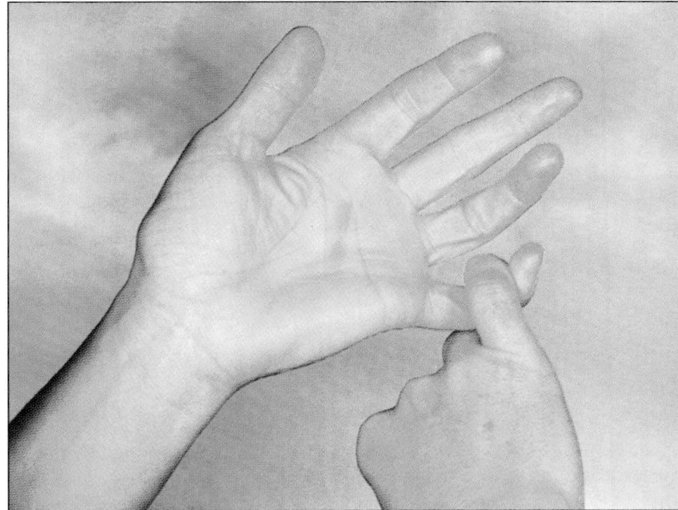

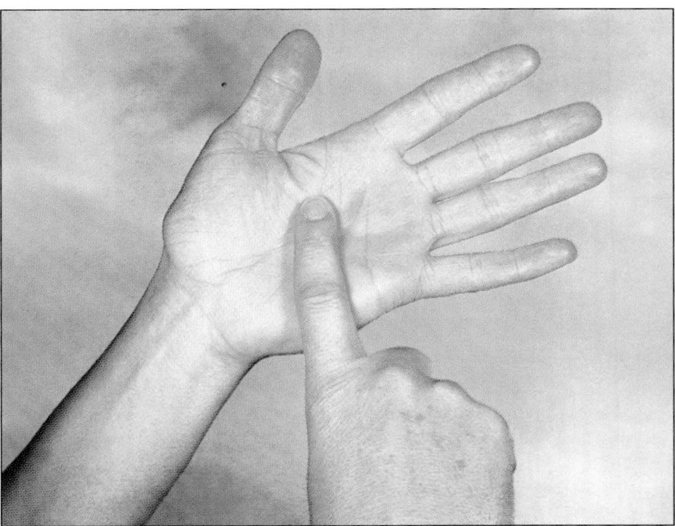

These three pictures show the use of 'finger spelling' i.e. the alphabet represented by signs rather than sounds. The signs represent the three letters B,S, and L.

Further Reading

KYLE, J. G. & WOLL, B., 1988, *Sign Language. The Study of Deaf People and their Language.* Cambridge: Cambridge University Press.

MAHSHIE, S. N., 1995, *Educating Deaf Children Bilingually.* Washington, DC: Gallaudet University.

McCRACKEN, W. & SUTHERLAND, H., 1991, *Deaf-ability–Not Disability: A Guide for the Parents of Hearing Impaired Children.* Clevedon: Multilingual Matters Ltd.

2: Deaf Students and Bilingual Education

There are differing approaches to the education of deaf students and those who are hearing impaired. These approaches range from minimal help to specially designed programs. At its worst, in mainstream 'hearing' education, deaf people may be regarded as having a serious mental as well as an auditory 'defect' and classified as remedial. In the history of schooling in most countries, there are plentiful examples of such insensitive and uncivilized treatment.

In contrast, there are special schools and units for deaf people where, for example, the children are taught to thoroughly learn signing first of all, are given a full curriculum mostly through signing, and develop written and sometimes oral skills in the majority spoken language.

There is considerable discussion, debate and development occurring in deaf education. There is not total agreement as to preferred methods of approach: for example, using signing and literacy in the spoken language, a Total Communication approach, using sign supported English, the kind of sign language to use, whether to develop oral and/or written skills in the spoken majority language, policies of integration with hearing children and the development of relatively segregated deaf communities.

One traditional approach (oralism) has been to develop any residual hearing with the assistance of hearing aids and to develop speech reading skills and speech production among deaf people and the hearing impaired. For most of this century until the 1970s, this was the approach that dominated the education of deaf children in North America and Europe. Such an approach was based on a belief:

- that deaf children should integrate into mainstream society;
- that the curriculum could not be taught through sign language but required majority language proficiency;
- that signing as a language was insufficient for full intellectual development;
- that sign language was only a temporary crutch for those for whom the majority spoken language was essential;
- that achievement in the curriculum requires oracy and literacy in the majority language (e.g. English).

A second approach developed since the 1970s has been

based on the philosophy of 'Total Communication'. All modes of communication are regarded as appropriate for those who are deaf or partially hearing. Simultaneous communication is used that combines auditory input plus visual information, for example, via the use of signed English.

The most recent development has been in terms of ten suggestions:

1. That natural sign language should be the first language of all deaf children and be regarded as their primary language.

2. That sign language should be used to teach curriculum subjects such as Science, Humanities, Social Studies and Mathematics.

3. Sign language can be used to teach English or another majority language as a second language. Usually this will be to teach reading and writing skills in English rather than English oracy.

4. The culture and language of the deaf community are recognized and validated, with children learning that they belong to the culture of deaf people. This

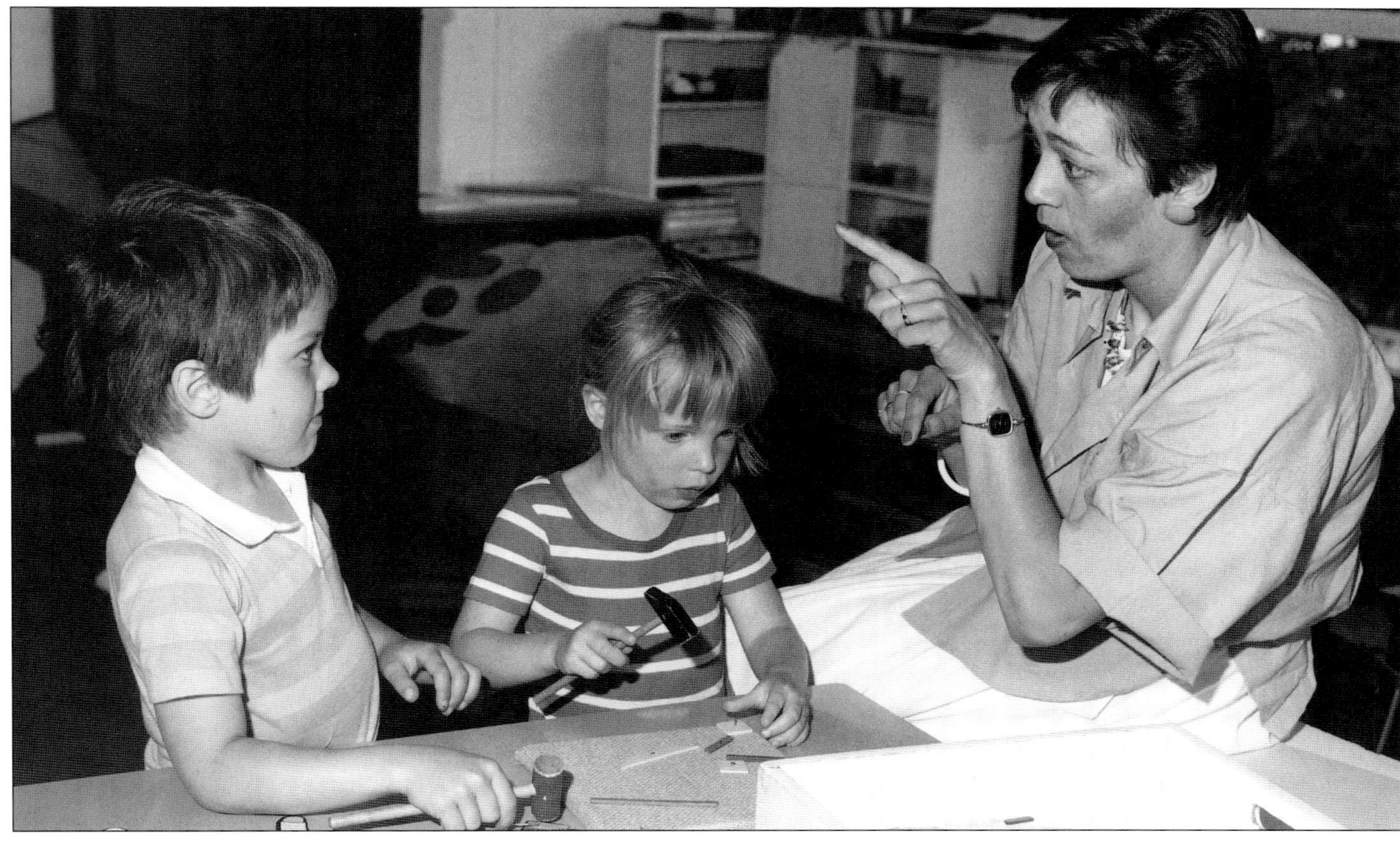

approach tends to be favored by most but not all the deaf community, but has not been favored by many politicians and education professionals who formulate policy and provision.

5. Such bilingual education for deaf people is partly based on the research and arguments for an enrichment form of bilingual education for hearing children:

   - bilingual education builds on a child's existing linguistic and intellectual resources;
   - concepts and knowledge developed in the first language transfer easily to the second language;
   - use of children's heritage language gives pride and confidence in their culture and community;
   - children's self-esteem and self-identity are boosted and not threatened by use of their first language;
   - school performance and curriculum attainment is raised when the first language is celebrated rather than devalued.
   - the lower achievement of minority language students and deaf students needs to be addressed by enrichment forms (or 'strong forms') of bilingual education.

6. Deaf children cannot acquire a spoken language easily or quickly because they have limited hearing abilities. If the curriculum is transmitted in the spoken language, they are being expected to learn the content of the curriculum using a level of language not yet acquired. This is analogous to minority language children being expected to operate in Submersion education in the language of the majority they have yet to conquer.

7. The acquisition of a sign language should begin as early as possible, ideally soon after birth. Current thinking among deaf people tends to suggest that early signing is preferable in most cases. This gives the deaf child the opportunity to develop age appropriate competence in a first language, i.e. sign language. Without the development of language, a child cannot form concepts or develop cognitive skills, nor can a child learn social and communicative skills through interaction with others.

   Where a deaf child has had the opportunity to develop adequate sign language during the pre-school years, that child arrives in school ready to cope with the curriculum and able to socialize with others. Children who have had early access to sign language appear to progress better in school. It is important to avoid language-delay in deaf children, as has been

found to occur when using auditory approaches and sometimes the Total Communication approach. Curriculum achievement will suffer if there is language-delay.

Where deaf children arrive in school with very little grasp of either sign language or hearing language, the priority must be sign language input. Children must learn to think and conceptualize before they can learn.

8. Ninety percent of deaf children are born to hearing parents, but with such parents being increasingly willing to sign and learn signing, the first language of such deaf children can be sign language. It is very important that hearing parents receive adequate support from sign language teachers and that there is good pre-school provision for deaf children. Parents of deaf children need to be aware of deaf communities, of bilingual education for deaf children, and to enhance their child's curriculum achievement, to expect signing as the medium of curriculum delivery plus literacy in the majority language.

   The parents of deaf children need considerable emotional support, information and guidance to help their children become bilingual. In order for cognitive, linguistic, social and emotional development to occur among deaf children, there needs to be a partnership between school and parents, and between school and community. While there is a considerable debate about the integration of deaf children into a hearing society, (and their first loyalty being to the deaf community), hearing parents of deaf children need considerable support and sensitivity.

9. The supply of trained personnel in deaf bilingual education, staff pre-service education programs, sign language teaching resources (e.g. signed stories on video), in-service education and certification and funding are often current challenges that are being faced by deaf educators. These are practical problems to be overcome rather than problems of principles that are insurmountable.

10. The teaching situation in a bilingual deaf education system may involve team-teaching. The deaf teacher may be a natural model for the acquisition of sign language with a hearing teacher acting as a model for the acquisition of proficiency in a majority language such as English or French. Ideally, both teachers should be bilingual models, being able to communicate in both sign language and the 'hearing' language. Also, both teachers in the team should have a knowledge of deaf culture, deaf differences and all the possibilities for deaf children and adults.

Conclusion

This topic has shown that there are many similarities between hearing bilinguals and deaf bilinguals. Many of the justifications for retaining a minority language child's first language and for a 'strong' form of bilingual education for such children also hold for deaf children. The argument that children from language minorities should become bicultural and culturally pluralistic also tends to hold for deaf bilinguals. Language minorities are often the poor, low power, low status, relations of majority language speakers. Even more so among deaf people. Deaf bilinguals are often the poor relations of language minority bilinguals. This particularly occurs when deaf people come from (spoken) language minority communities themselves. The examples of a Latino deaf person in the US, a deaf Turk in Germany and a deaf Bengali in the UK all represent individuals who are a minority within a minority. They are often the doubly underprivileged and the doubly despised. Where being a member of a (spoken) language minority is joined by being deaf, disempowerment, low status, discrimination and low self-esteem may be compounded. If many groups of bilinguals are underprivileged, even more so are deaf bilinguals

Further Reading

BARNUM, M., 1984, In Support of Bilingual/Bicultural Education for Deaf Children. *American Annals of the Deaf*, 129 (5), 404-08.

BOUVET, D., 1990, *The Path to Language. Bilingual Education for Deaf Children*. Clevedon: Multilingual Matters Ltd.

COLLEGE FOR CONTINUING EDUCATION, 1992, *Bilingual Considerations in the Education of Deaf Students: ASL and English*. Washington DC: Gallaudet University.

KNIGHT, P. & SWANWICK, R. (eds), 1996, *Bilingualism and the Education of Deaf Children: Advances in Practice*. Leeds, UK: ADEDC, School of Education, University of Leeds.

KYLE, J. (ed.), 1987, *Sign and School: Using Signs in Deaf Children's Development*. Clevedon: Multilingual Matters Ltd.

MAHSHIE, S. N., 1995, *Educating Deaf Children Bilingually*. Washington, DC: Gallaudet University.

MILLER-NOMELAND, M. & GILLESPIE, S., 1993, *Kendall Demonstration Elementary School: Deaf Studies Curriculum Guide*. Washington DC: Gallaudet University.

STRONG, M.,1995, A Review of Bilingual/Bicultural Programs for Deaf Children in North America. *American Annals of the Deaf*, 140 (2), 84-94.

Bilingual Education for Students with Special Needs

1: Explanations of Under-Achievement in Bilinguals

There are frequent occasions when language minorities are found to under-achieve (e.g. UK, US). Sometimes this is reported in research as differences between ethnic groups (e.g. Department of Education and Science, 1985; Figueroa, 1984; Tomlinson, 1986a, 1986b). It is also discussed by teachers, educational psychologists, speech therapists, parents and students themselves in 'single individual' terms.

When language minority children appear to exhibit underachievement in the classroom, what may be the explanation? When first, second or third generation inmigrant children appear to fail in the classroom, where is the 'blame' popularly placed? When guest workers' children, indigenous minorities and distinct ethnic groups are shown statistically to leave school earlier, achieve less in examinations and tests or receive lower grades and averages, what is the cause?

First, the blame may be attributed to the fact that the child is bilingual. Bilingualism itself is often popularly seen as causing cognitive confusion. The bilingual brain is depicted as two engines working at half throttle, while the monolingual has one well tuned engine at full throttle. Such an explanation is usually incorrect. Where two languages are well developed, then bilingualism is more likely to lead to cognitive advantages than disadvantages. Only when a child's two languages are both poorly developed can 'blame' be attributed to bilingualism itself. Even then, the blame should not be placed on the victim, but on the societal circumstances that create underdeveloped languages.

Second, where underachievement exists, the reason may be given as lack of exposure to the majority language. In the US and the UK, a typical explanation for the underachievement of certain language minorities is insufficient exposure to English. Failure or below average performance is attributed to students having insufficiently developed English language competence to cope with the curriculum. Those who use Spanish or Bengali at home and in the neighborhood are perceived to struggle at school due to a lack of competence in the dominant, mainstream language. Thus submersion and transitional forms of bilingual education attempt to ensure a fast conversion to the majority language (Cummins, 1980b).

However, a fast conversion to the majority language stands the chance of doing more harm than good. It denies the child's skills in the home language and even denies the identity and self-respect of the child itself. Instead of using existing language skills, the 'sink or swim' approach attempts to replace those skills. The level of English used in the curriculum may be too advanced for the child. Consequently, the child underachieves. The remedy proposed is then further English language lessons.

Underachievement in majority language education (e.g. submersion and Transitional Bilingual education) may be combated by providing education through the medium of the minority language (e.g. two-way, developmental maintenance, heritage language programs). When the language minority child is allowed to operate in the heritage language in the curriculum, the evidence suggests that success rather than failure results. Such success includes becoming fluent in the majority language (e.g. English). Thus lack of exposure to English is a popular but incorrect explanation of underachievement. This explanation fails to note the advantages of education in the minority language for achievement. It inappropriately seeks an answer in increased majority language tuition rather than increased minority language education.

Third, when bilingual children exhibit underachievement, the reason may sometimes be a mismatch between home and school. Such a mismatch may be not just about language differences but also about dissimilarities in culture, values and beliefs (Delgado-Gaitán & Trueba, 1991). As an extreme, this tends to reflect a majority viewpoint that is assimilationist, imperialist and even oppressive. (See Home-School Relationships, page 537). The child and family are expected to adjust to the system, rather than the system being pluralist and incorpo-

rating variety. For such an assimilationist viewpoint, the solution is in the home adjusting to mainstream language and culture to prepare the child for school. Past advice by some educational psychologists and speech therapists has been for language minority parents to raise their children in the majority, school language.

The alternative view is that, where practicable, the school system should be flexible enough to incorporate the home language and culture. A mismatch between home and school can be positively addressed by 'strong' forms of bilingual education for language minorities. By two-way, developmental maintenance and heritage language programs, by a multicultural approach in the classroom with respect for the child's value systems and cultural and religious beliefs, through the inclusion of parents in the running of the school, by involving parents as partners and participants in their child's education (e.g. paired reading schemes), the mismatch can become a merger.

Fourth, underachievement may be attributed to socioeconomic factors that surround a language minority group. Some typical circumstances are described by Trueba (1991). 'Many immigrant and refugee children have a life of poverty and rural isolation in crowded dwellings where they lack privacy, toilet and shower facilities, comfort, and basic medical attention. In some cases migrant life for children means abuse, malnutrition, poor health, ignorance and neglect. Uprooting a child from his/her land can lead to a life of stigma and low status.' (Trueba, 1991, page 53)

Socioeconomic status is a broad umbrella term that rightly points to a definite cause of language minority underachievement. It provides an example of the importance of not blaming the victim, but analyzing societal features that contribute to underachievement. Such features may be economic deprivation, material circumstances and living conditions as well as psychological and social features such as discrimination, racial prejudice, pessimism and immobilizing inferiority.

While socioeconomic factors are a proper partial explanation of language minority underachievement, two cautions must be sounded. Socioeconomic status does not explain why different language minorities of similar socioeconomic status may perform differently at school. In the item entitled 'Types of Language Minorities' (see page 99), the different ideologies or orientations that may vary between ethnic groups are discussed. Sociocultural factors within and between ethnic groups and not simply socioeconomic status need examining to begin to work out the equation of language minority achievement and underachievement.

This raises another issue. Underachievement cannot be simply related to one or several causes. The equation of underachievement is going to be complex, involving a number of factors. Those factors will interact together in complex ways and not be simple 'stand alone' effects. For example, umbrella labels such as socioeconomic status need decomposing into more definable predictors of underachievement (e.g. parents' attitude to education). Home factors will then interact with school factors providing an enormous number of different routes that may lead to varying school success and failure. The recipes of success and failure are many, with varying ingredients that interact together. However, socioeconomic and sociocultural features are important ingredients in most equations of underachievement.

Fifth, part of the language minority achievement and underachievement equation is the type of school a child attends. This topic has highlighted the different outcomes for language minority children in 'strong' compared with 'weak' forms of bilingual education. The same child will tend to attain more if placed in programs that use the heritage language as a medium of instruction than in programs which seek to replace the home language as quickly as possible. Therefore, when underachievement occurs in a language minority child or within a language minority group, the system of schooling needs scrutiny. A system that suppresses the home language is likely to be part of the explanation of individual and ethnic group underachievement where such problems exist.

Sixth, 'type of school' is a broad heading under which there can exist superior and inferior submersion schools, outstanding and mediocre dual language and heritage language schools. Where underachievement exists, it is sometimes too simple to blame the type of school rather than digging deeper and locating more specific causes. Baker (1996), Cummins (1984a) and Hornberger (1991) have listed some of the attributes that need to be examined to assess the quality of any educational system that serves language minority children (e.g. the supply, ethnic origins and bilingualism of teachers, balance of language minority and language majority students in the classroom, use and sequencing of the two languages across the curriculum over different grades, reward systems for enriching the minority language and culture).

Seventh, underachievement may be due to real learning difficulties and the need for some form of special education. It is important to make a distinction between real and apparent learning difficulties. Too often, bilingual children are labeled as having learning difficulties which are attributed to their bilingualism. As we have discussed in this topic, the causes of apparent learning problems may be much less in the child and much more in the

school or in the education system. The child is perceived as having learning difficulties when the problem may lie in the subtractive, assimilative system which itself creates negative attitudes and low motivation. In the 'sink or swim' approach, 'sinking' can be attributed to an unsympathetic system and to insensitive teaching methods rather than individual learning problems. Apart from system-generated and school-generated learning problems, there will be some children who are bilingual and have genuine learning difficulties (Cummins, 1984a). The essential beginning is to distinguish between real, individual learning difficulties and problems which are caused by factors outside of the individual.

Such a distinction between the real and the apparent, the system-generated and the remediable problems of the individual, highlights the alternatives. When underachievement exists, do we blame the victim, blame the teacher and the school, or blame the system? When assessment, tests and examinations occur and show relatively low performance of language minority individuals and groups, will prejudices about bilingual children and ethnic groups be confirmed? Or can we use such assessment to reveal deficiencies in the architecture of the school system and the design of the curriculum rather than blame the child? As this topic has revealed, underachievement tends to be blamed on the child and the language minority group. Often the explanation lies in factors outside of the individual.

Further Reading

CUMMINS, J., 1984, *Bilingualism & Special Education: Issues in Assessment and Pedagogy.* Clevedon: Multilingual Matters Ltd.

HARRY, B., 1992, *Cultural Diversity, Families and the Special Education System. Communication and Empowerment.* New York: Teachers College Press.

2: Bilingualism and Learning Difficulties

In the previous topic, it was shown that there was no link between bilingualism and underachievement in school. Rather, the failure of some language minority children to achieve in school was shown to be the result of a complex equation of factors, none of which was directly linked to bilingualism. These included an educational system that devalued the child's home language and culture and that did not build on the child's existing abilities in the home language. The social and economic difficulties that many indigenous and in-migrant minorities face were shown to be another possible cause of underachievement at school. In no way could bilingualism be blamed as a direct cause of underachievement.

Another unfair assumption that some people make is that bilingualism is the cause of specific learning difficulties. This topic aims to show how that assumption is usually false. Bilingualism is rarely a cause of learning difficulties.

A first important point is that bilingual children are often wrongly assessed as having learning difficulties. This can occur because basic mistakes in assessment and categorization are made. The child is often assessed in a weaker, second language, thereby inaccurately measuring both language development and general cognitive development. For example, in Britain and the United States, in-migrant children are sometimes still assessed through the medium of English and on their English proficiency. Their level of language competence in Spanish, Bengali, Cantonese, Turkish, Italian or Panjabi, for example, is ignored. (This is discussed more fully in Assessment and Bilingual Children, see page 575.)

The result is that such children are sometimes classed as having a 'language disability' and perhaps a 'learning disability'. Instead of being seen as developing bilinguals (i.e children with a good command of their first language who are in the process of acquiring a second, majority language), they may be classed as of 'limited English proficiency' (LEP in the United States), or even as having general difficulties with learning. Their below average test scores in the second language (e.g. English) are wrongly defined as a 'deficit' or 'disability' that can be remedied by some form of special education.

While learning difficulties occasionally occur within bilingual children, this does not indicate that bilingualism is the cause of their learning difficulties. Learning difficulties are caused by a variety of possibilities, almost none of them aligned to bilingualism. Six examples of causes follow, which are similar to the causes of general underachievement at school.

1. Poverty and deprivation, child-neglect and abuse, feelings of helplessness and desperation in the home, extended family and community may create personal-

ity, attitudinal and learning conditions that make assessment of learning difficulties more probable. Sometimes, such assessment will reflect prejudice, misjudgements and misperceptions about the child's home experiences.

The learning problem may thus be in a mismatch between the culture, attitudes, expectations about education and values of the home and school. Different beliefs, culture, knowledge and cognitive approaches may be devalued, with the child immediately labeled as of inferior intelligence, academically incompetent and of low potential.

2. The problem may be in the standard of education. A child may be struggling in the classroom due to poor teaching methods, a non-motivating, even hostile, classroom environment, a dearth of suitable teaching materials, or clashes with the teacher.

3. The school may be inhibiting or obstructing learning progress. If a child is being taught in a second language and the home language is ignored, then failure and perceived learning difficulties may result. One example is that of some Spanish-speaking children in the United States. Such children are often placed in English-only classrooms on entry to school. They must sink or swim in English. Some swim; others sink and may be deemed to have a deficiency. By being assessed in their weaker second language (English) – rather than in their stronger home language (Spanish), such children are labeled as in need of special or remedial education. Thus the monolingual school system is itself responsible for specific learning difficulties as well as general underachievement. A school that promoted bilingualism would be more likely to ensure learning success for the same child.

4. Another set of causes of learning difficulties are a lack of self-confidence, low self-esteem, a fear of failure and high anxiety in the classroom.

5. A fourth possibility is failure caused partly by interactions among children in the classroom. For example, where a group of children encourage each other to fool around, have a low motivation to succeed, or where there is bullying, hostility, social division, rather than cohesion among children in a classroom, the learning ethos may hinder the child's development.

6. Another case is where there is a mismatch between the gradient of learning expected and the ability level of the child. Some children learn to read more slowly than others, still learning to read well, but after a longer period of time. Less able children can learn two languages within the (unknowable) limits of their ability. Other children experience specific learning difficulties (for example, dyslexia, neurological dysfunction, 'short-term memory' problems, poor physical co-ordination, problems in attention span or motivation). None of these specific learning difficulties or other language disorders are caused by bilingualism. At the same time, bilingual children will not escape from being included in this group. Bilingual families are no less likely to be affected than other families.

This list, neither exhaustive or nor comprehensive, shows that bilingualism has almost nothing to do with these problems, either as a secondary or a primary cause. Bilingualism is unlikely to be a direct or indirect cause of a child's learning difficulties.

Almost the only occasion when a learning difficulty of a bilingual child is attached to bilingualism is when a child enters the classroom with neither language sufficiently developed to cope with the higher order language skills demanded by the curriculum. In the rare cases where a child has simple conversational skills in two languages but cannot cope in the curriculum in either language, language may be related to learning difficulties. In this case, the problem is not really with bilingualism but with insufficient language practice in the home, in the nursery

Language Disorder

According to Wei, Miller & Dodd (1997), around five percent of all children, bilingual or not, experience some form of language disorder. Bilingual children are no more or less likely to have a language disorder. Such language disorders include: late development of speech, a very slow development in language competences, speaking less often and less accurately, an inability to produce certain sounds, an inability to remember new words, and never achieving the same language competence as peers. However, such language disorders do not include: bilinguals being inaccurate when speaking a second language as they may be on the learning curve, and adding a sound to one language from the other language as this is often playful and creative.

If the child requires professional assessment and help (e.g. psychologist, speech therapist), the professional needs to understand the child's bilingual background, the nature of bilingualism in children, assess the child in both (or all) languages, and use tests normed on bilinguals and not compare bilinguals with monolinguals in phonology, vocabulary, syntax and fluency.

Reference: Wei, Miller & Dodd, 1997

Language-delay

A particular problem that illustrates the wrongly attributed link between bilingualism and developmental problems is 'language-delay'. Language-delay occurs when a child is very late in beginning to talk, or lags well behind peers in language development. Estimates of young children experiencing language-delay vary from five percent to 20 percent of the child population. Such varying estimates partly reflect that some delays are brief and hardly noticeable. Others are more severe.

Language-delay may have a variety of causes; for example, partial hearing, deafness, autism, severe subnormality, cerebral palsy, physical problems (e.g. cleft palate), psychological disturbance, emotional difficulties. However, in approximately two-thirds of all cases, the precise reason for language-delay is not known. Children who are medically normal, with no hearing loss, of normal IQ and memory, who are not socially deprived or emotionally disturbed, can be delayed in starting to speak, slow in development or have problems in expressing themselves well. In such cases, specialist, professional help is needed. Speech therapists, clinical psychologists, educational psychologists, counselors and doctors may give such advice and treatment.

Parents of bilingual children with such problems should not believe that bilingualism is the cause. Sometimes, well meaning professionals make this diagnosis. If the causes are unknown, bilingualism might seem a likely cause. Raising children bilingually is widely believed to produce language-delayed children. The evidence does not support this belief. Raising children bilingually does not increase or reduce the chance of language disorder or language-delay.

A key consideration for a parent is whether removal of one language will improve, worsen or have no effect on the child's language development. Given that the cause of the problem may be partially unknown, intuition and guesswork rather than 'science' often occurs. Research in this area is still in its infancy.

One issue is which language to concentrate on if there is a major diagnosed language-delay? The danger is that parents, teachers and other professionals will want to accent the perceived importance of the majority language. In the United States, the advice is often that the child should have a solid diet of English – the language of school and employment. The advice too frequently given is that the home, minority language should be replaced by the majority language. Such an overnight switch may well have painful outcomes for the child.

If someone who has loved, cared for and played with the child in one language (e.g. a minority language) suddenly only uses another language (e.g. the majority language), the emotional well-being of the child may well be negatively affected. The language used to express love and caring disappears. Simultaneously, and by association, the child may feel that the love and care is also not as before. Such a language change is often drastic with its own negative after-effects and consequences.

Even when parents and professionals accept that bilingualism is not the cause of a child's problem, moving from bilingualism to monolingualism is seen by some as a way to help improve the problem. The reasoning is usually that the 'extra demands' of bilingualism, if removed, will lighten the burden for the child. For example, if the child has a language-delay problem, for whatever cause, simplifying the language demands on the child may be seen as one way of solving or reducing the problem. The apparent complexity of a two language life is relieved by monolingualism. Is this right?

There are many occasions when changing from bilingualism to monolingualism will have no effect on the problem. For example, if the child seems slow to speak without an obvious cause or seems low in self-esteem, dropping one language is unlikely to have any effect. On the contrary, the sudden change in family life may exacerbate the problem. The stability of a child's language life is disrupted, with possible negative consequences. In most cases, it is inappropriate to move from bilingualism to monolingualism. However, it is dangerous to make this advice absolute and unequivocal.

To give only 'stick with bilingualism' advice is unwise and too simplistic. When there is language-delay, for example, there will be a few family situations where maximal experience in one language is preferable. For example, where one language of a child is much securer and more well developed than another, it may be sensible to concentrate on developing the stronger language. If, for example, the child only hears one language from one parent and that parent is away often, a short-term concentration on the stronger language may help in a language-delay period.

This does not mean that the chance of bilingualism is lost forever. If, or when, language-delay disappears, the other language can be reintroduced. If a child with emotional problems really detests using (or even being spoken to) in a particular language, as part of a solution, the family may sensibly decide to accede to the child's preference. Again, once problems have been resolved, the 'dropped' language may be reintroduced, so long as it is immediately associated with pleasurable experiences.

Any temporary move from bilingualism to monolingualism should not be seen as the only solution needed. A focus on such a language change as the sole remedy to the child's problem is naïve and dangerous. For example, emotional problems may require other rearrangements in the family's pattern of relationships (as discussed with a counselor or psychologist). Language-delay may require visits to a speech therapist for advice about language interaction between parents and child. Temporary monolingualism should only be seen as one component in a package of attempted changes to solve the child's language problem. However, it is important to reiterate that, in the great majority of cases, the problem of language-delay will not be exacerbated by retaining a bilingual approach.

Reference: WEI, MILLER & DODD, 1997

Ability Effects

Is it the case that less able bilingual children will experience cognitive advantages or would it be preferable for such children to be monolingual as far as thinking is concerned?

Research has centered on more able, middle class children of above average ability (see page 550). Rueda's (1983) research suggests that a 'cognitive advantages' link may be found in less able children. Using children of well below average IQ (51-69 IQ points, where a 100 IQ is average), Rueda (1983) compared bilinguals and monolinguals on three tests: a Meaning and Reference Task which examines the stability and meaning of words (e.g. an imaginary animal called a 'flump' who dies); the Arbitrariness of Language Task (could we call a 'cat' a 'dog'); and the Non-Physical Nature of Words Task (e.g. Does the word 'bird' have feathers?).

On each of the three tasks, the low IQ bilinguals tended to score significantly higher than the monolinguals.

Although Rueda (1983) found no difference on a Piagetian conservation test, this research hints that the bilingualism–cognitive advantages link may not be specific to high or average ability children.

Reference: RUEDA, 1983

school or in the outside world. Here we are talking not about bilingual deprivation, but about deprivation in any language. This is a great rarity but is the only reason bilingualism appears indirectly connected with learning difficulties.

If children have lower ability than most in the school, there is evidence to suggest that they can acquire two languages within the unknown limits of their abilities. While well-meaning friends, teachers and speech therapists sometimes suggest that one language only should be developed, Canadian research tends to show that less able bilingual children share some of the cognitive advantages of bilingualism. (An accompanying textbox provides details of the research.) Just as their mathematical ability, literacy and scientific development may occur at a slower pace, so the two languages will develop with less speed. The size of vocabulary and accuracy of grammar may be less in both languages than the average bilingual child. Nevertheless, such children acquiring two languages early, will usually be able to communicate in both languages, often as well as they would communicate in one language.

Further Reading

HARRY, B., 1992, *Cultural Diversity, Families and the Special Education System. Communication and Empowerment.* New York: Teachers College Press.

3: Assessment and Bilingual Children

Introduction

It is essential for any psychological and educational assessment of bilingual children to be fair, accurate and broad. Too often, tests given to bilingual children only serve to suggest their 'disabilities', supposed 'deficits' or lack of proficiency in a second language. Assessment can too easily legitimize the disabling of language minority students. Such students may come to be stigmatized by such tests, for example, because tests locate apparent weaknesses in the majority language and use monolingual scores as points of comparison. English language tests and IQ tests administered in the second language to US children are particular examples.

In the United States, there is legislation to govern appropriate processes of assessment of those for whom English is an additional language. For example, the 1973 Californian case of *Diana* v. *the State Board of Education* was based on nine Mexican-American parents who protested that their children (who were dominant in Spanish) were given an English language IQ test. The IQ test revealed 'normal' non-verbal IQ scores, but ludicrously low verbal IQ scores (as low as 30 for one child). As a result of this linguistically and culturally inappropriate IQ test, the Mexican-American children were placed in classes for the 'mentally retarded'. This case never went to court, but it established that testing should be conducted in a child's native language (and in English), and that non-verbal IQ tests were usually a fairer measurement of IQ than verbal tests (Valdés & Figueroa, 1994). As a result of this case, the collection of broader data on language minority children was required (rather than simple test data) to justify placement of such children in Special Education. This is examined in the section on Special Education and Bilinguals (see page 580).

In 1975, Public Law 94-142, *The Education for All Handicapped Children Act,* federally mandated that all testing and assessment procedures should be non-discriminatory. 'Non-discriminatory' means using tests that are culturally and linguistically appropriate. Such testing procedures were only to be used by trained members of a multidisciplinary team. Apart from tests, teacher recommendations, observations of a child and other relevant information should create a multisource file of evidence.

Yet for all the advice in legislation, all the discussions in academic literature and in research, bilinguals tend in many countries to be discriminated against in testing and assessment. Therefore, it is important to review the components of such bias, and more constructively, to suggest desirable practice. Ten overlapping and interacting issues in the assessment of bilingual children are now considered.

First, the temporary difficulties faced by bilinguals must be distinguished from more long-lasting difficulties that impede everyday functioning and learning. Brief language-delays, temporary adjustment problems of inmigrants and short-term stammering (stuttering) are examples of transient difficulties. Dyslexia, hearing loss and neuroticism are examples where longer-term problems may need treatment. This simple distinction hides different and complex dimensions. The means of distinguishing temporary and longer-term problems follows below.

Second, diagnosis needs to go beyond a few, simple tests and engage a wide diversity of measurement and observation devices. Diagnosis needs to be extended over a time period and to avoid an instant conclusion and instantaneous remedy. Observing the child in different contexts (and not just in the classroom) will provide a more valid profile (language and behavior) of that child. The family and educational history of the child needs assembling. Parents and teachers need consulting, sometimes doctors, counselors, speech therapists and social workers as well. Samples of a child's natural communication need gathering, with the child in different roles and different situations.

An awareness or basic knowledge of a child's ethnic, cultural and linguistic background is important in fair assessment, but it may not be enough. To interpret test scores and classifications meaningfully and wisely, and in particular, to make decisions on the basis of assessment, requires a highly sensitive and sympathetic understanding of a child's community, culture, family life and individual characteristics. Children come to school with very differing home experiences, where different kinds of ability are cultivated and stressed. Such abilities prized by parents may be different from the abilities learned at school.

For example, discovery learning and learning through play is not a part of all cultures. An investigative, questioning mode of thinking may not be encouraged within a culture. As reflected in parent-child relationships, adults provide authoritative knowledge that must be accepted and enacted by the child. Parents may teach literacy in a similar style, for example, in a religious context, where the child is expected to memorize much or all of the holy book and repeat it without comprehension. Such family and community socialization practices have implications (1) for the type of assessment that reveals the strengths and weaknesses of the child, (2) for the importance of acquiring evidence about the culture of the child, and (3) for the process of assessment by the teacher, psychologist, speech therapist, counselor or other professional.

Test scores (e.g. on educational and psychometric tests) tend to be decontextualized and attenuated. An analogy helps to illustrate this important point.

Test scores are like latitude and longitude. They provide a point of reference on a map of human characteristics. As a standard measurement usable on all maps, they provide initial, rapid and instantly comparable information. But imagine the most beautiful place you know (e.g. a flower-enfolded, azure-colored lake set amid tall, green-sloped, ice-capped mountains). Does the expression of the latitude and longitude of that scene do justice to characterizing the personality and distinctiveness of that location? The attempted precision of the sextant needs to be joined by the full empathic exploration and evaluation of the character and qualities of the child.

Authentic language and behavior needs assessing rather than trivial and decontextualized language skills. The levels of thinking and understanding of a child through both languages need assessing rather than superficial comprehension gleaned from a superficially 'scientific' test (e.g. with high test-retest reliability, and high correlations with similar tests). 'Unauthentic language' tests relate too often to a transmission-style curriculum where obtaining the correct answer and 'teaching to the test' dominates teacher thinking and classroom activity. Such tests do not capture the communication abilities of the child, as for example, occur in the playground, on the street, at the family meal-table and in internal conversations when alone.

Third, the choice of assessors for the child will affect the assessment. Whether the assessors are perceived to be from the same language group as the child will affect the child's performance (and possibly the diagnosis). The

perceived age, social class, powerfulness and gender of the assessor(s) will affect how the child responds and possibly the assessment outcomes. The assessment process is not neutral. Who assesses, using what devices, under what conditions, all contribute to the judgment being made. An inappropriate assessor creates an increased risk of making two common, opposite judgmental errors concerning bilingual children: (1) generating a 'false positive', that is, diagnosing a problem when none is present; (2) generating a 'false negative', that is, failing to locate a problem when one exists.

Fourth, children need assessing in their stronger language. Ideally children need assessing as bilinguals – in both their languages. The tests and assessment devices applied, and the language of communication used in assessment, should ideally be in the child's stronger language. An assessment based on tests of (and in) the child's weaker language may lead to a misdiagnosis, a false impression of the abilities of the child and a very partial and biased picture of the child. This sometimes occurs in the United Kingdom and the United States where language minority children are tested in English, partly because of the availability of well regarded psychometric tests.

Fifth, parents and educators need to make sure the language used in the test is appropriate to the child. For example, a translation of the test (e.g. from English to Spanish) may produce inappropriate, stilted language. Also, the different varieties of Spanish, for example, may not be that used by the student. Chicano Spanish-speaking parents will want the tests in Chicano Spanish rather than the Cuban, Puerto Rican or Castilian variety of Spanish. Once Spanish-speaking children have been in the United States for a time, their Spanish changes. English influences their way of speaking Spanish. So a test in 'standard' Spanish is inappropriate. A Spanish test may accept only one right answer, penalizing children for their bilingualism and their United States Spanish. A monolingual standard of Spanish is inappropriate to such bilingual children.

Since there are language problems with tests (as outlined above and continued below), it is important to distinguish between a child's language profile and performance profile. The performance profile is more important as it attempts to portray a child's underlying cognitive abilities rather than just language abilities. A performance profile seeks to understand the overall potential of the child, not just their language proficiency.

Cummins (1984a) has shown this distinction between a language profile and a performance profile on one frequently used IQ test in individual assessment – the Wechsler Intelligence Scale for Children – Revised (WISC-R). Language minority children tend to score significantly higher on the Performance than the Verbal subtests. As Cummins (1984a, page 30) suggests: 'The analysis of student performance on this test suggested that the majority of Verbal subtests were tapping ESL students' knowledge of the English language and North American culture in addition to, or instead of, verbal cognitive/academic ability'.

Sixth, there are times when a test or assessment device cannot be given in the child's stronger language. For example, appropriate language minority professionals may not be available to join the assessment team, tests may not be available in the child's home language, and translations of tests may make those tests invalid and unreliable.

Interpreters are sometimes necessary. Interpreters do have a valuable function. If trained in the linguistic, professional and rapport-making competencies needed, they can make assessment more fair and accurate. Interpreters can also bring a possible bias into the assessment (i.e. 'raising' or 'lowering' the assessment results through the interpretation they provide).

Seventh, there is a danger of focusing the assessment solely on the child. If the child is tested, the assumption is that the 'problem' lies within the child. At the same time, and sometimes instead, the focus needs to shift to causes outside the child. Is the problem in the school? Is the school failing the child by denying abilities in the first language and focusing on failures in the second (school) language? Is the school system denying a child's culture and ethnic character, thereby affecting the child's academic success and self-esteem? Is the curriculum delivered at a level that is beyond the child's comprehension or is culturally strange to the child? The remedy may be in a change to the school system and not to the child.

Eighth, the danger of assessment is that it will lead to the disablement rather than the empowerment of bilingual children (see page 541). If the assessment separates children from powerful, dominant, mainstream groups in society, the child may become disabled. The assessment may lead to categorization in an inferior group of society and marginalization. Instead, assessment should work in the best, long-term interests of the child. Best interests doesn't only mean short-term educational remedies, but also long-term employment and wealth sharing opportunities. The assessment should initiate advocacy for, and not against the child.

Ninth, it is important to use the understanding of a child's teachers who have observed that child in a variety of learning environments over time. What do the child's

teachers think is the root problem? What solutions and interventions do teachers suggest? Have the child's teachers a plan of action? A team of teachers, meeting regularly to discuss children with problems is a valuable first stage in assessment and support. Such a team can also be the school decision-maker for referral to other professionals (e.g. speech therapist, psychologist, counselor).

Tenth, norm-referenced tests are often used to assess the child (e.g. for entry into, or exit from a bilingual program). This means that the assessor can compare the child with other so called 'normal' children. The assessor can indicate how different the child is from the average. Many such tests are based on scores from 'native' language majority children. Thus, comparisons can be unfair for language minority children. For example, tests of English language proficiency may have norms (averages, and scores around the average) based on native speakers of English. This makes them biased against bilinguals and leads to the stereotyping of particular language and ethnic groups.

The testing of bilinguals has developed from the practice of testing monolinguals. Bilinguals are not the simple sum of two monolinguals but are a unique combination and integration of languages. The language configuration of bilinguals means that, for example, a bilingual's English language performance should not be compared with that of a monolinguals. A decathlete should not be compared with a 100-metre sprinter solely for speed of running. Monolingual norms are simply inappropriate for bilinguals. One example helps illustrate this point. Bilinguals use their languages in different contexts (domains). Thus they may have linguistic competence in varying curriculum areas, on different curriculum topics and on different language functions. Equal language facility in both languages is rare. Comparison on monolingual norms assumes such equal language facility across all domains, language functions and curriculum areas. This is unfair and inequitable.

Such norm-referenced tests are often written by white, middle class, Anglo test producers. The test items often reflect their language style and culture. For example, the words used such as 'tennis-racquet', 'snowman' and 'credit cards' may be unfamiliar to some in-migrants who have never seen a snowman, played or watched tennis, or discovered the culture of plastic money. Assessment items that reflect the unique learning experiences of language minority children will be excluded from a test for majority language or mainstream children. Such items will be highlighted by item analysis of an early draft of the test as 'unconnected' with the majority of the test items.

Such norm-referenced tests are often 'pencil and paper' tests, sometimes involving multiple choice answers (one answer is chosen from a set of given answers). Such tests do not measure all the different aspects of language, of 'intelligence' or any curriculum subject. Spoken, conversational language and financial intelligence, for example, cannot be adequately measured by a simple pencil and paper test.

Some norm-referenced tests report the results in percentiles (especially in the United States). Percentiles refer to the percentage of children above and below the child being tested. For example, being in the 40th percentile means that 39 percent of children score lower than the child being tested. Sixty percent of children of an age group score above the 40th percentile child. The child is in the 40th group from the bottom, all children being assumed to be divided into 100 equal-sized groups. Percentiles are often used for entry and exit of students into bilingual programs in the US. For example, a student may need to reach the 40th percentile on an English language test to exit to a mainstream class. Which 'percentile threshold' (e.g. 40th percentile) is used for entry or exit is essentially arbitrary, and liable to political rather than educationally derived decisions.

Norm-referenced tests essentially compare one person against others. Is this important? Isn't what a bilingual child can and cannot do in each curriculum subject the more important measurement? To say a child is in the 40th percentile in English doesn't tell the parent or the teacher what are a child's strengths and weaknesses, capabilities and needs in English. The alternative is assessment related directly to progress in each curriculum area.

Curriculum-based assessment is called criterion-referenced testing, and seeks to establish the relative competency of a child in a curriculum area. It seeks to establish what a child can do, and what is the next specific step of a curriculum area (e.g. an aspect of reading) where progression can be made. A diagnosis may also be made, not necessarily of a fundamental psychological or learning problem, but of weaknesses that need remedial treatment to enable conceptual understanding (e.g. if a child makes grapho-phonic miscues). Such criterion-referenced assessment of language minority students gives parents and teachers more usable and important information. It profiles for parents and teachers what a child can do in a subject (e.g. Mathematics) and where development, or accelerated learning, should occur next. Such assessment enables an individualized program to be set for the child.

However, the sequences of learning that underpin a criterion-referenced test may still reflect a cultural mismatch for the child. Criterion-referenced assessment (usually, but not necessarily) assumes there is a relatively linear, step-by-step progression in a curriculum area (e.g. in learning to read, in number skills, in science). Such a progression may be culturally relative and culturally determined. As Cline (1993, page 63) noted 'because of their different prior experiences, their learning hierarchy for a particular task may follow different steps or a different sequence (e.g. in relation to phonology and orthography in learning to read)'. Therefore, it is important to use curriculum assessment contexts and processes that are appropriate, comprehensible and meaningful to the bilingual child.

The Bilingual Oral Language Development Inventory

Mattes & Omark (1984) constructed a Bilingual Oral Language Development Inventory for elementary schoolchildren. This 20-item scale is used to record observations of bilingual children's performance in both the English language and their other language. The 20 dimensions on which to observe and rate children's performance are as follows, with some adaptations:

1. Comments on own actions. (Example: I'm doing well.)
2. Comments on other's actions. (Example: She kicks the ball very well.)
3. Describes experiences accurately.
4. Describes a sequence of events sequentially.
5. Listens appropriately to the person speaking.
6. Follows directions in a classroom setting.
7. Initiates conversations with classmates.
8. Takes turns as a speaker and a listener during conversations with friends.
9. Maintains a topic of discussion over a series of utterances during interactions with peers.
10. Responds appropriately to simple questions.
11. Uses language to seek the attention of others (e.g. the teacher).
12. Asks questions to attain information.
13. Uses language to direct the actions of others.
14. Requests clarification when statements are made by others that are not understood.
15. Uses language to inform others of personal needs.
16. Uses language to express feelings such as happiness, anxiety, anger and pain.
17. Describes plans for events that will take place in the future.
18. Expresses personal opinions and viewpoints and provides a basis for these opinions.
19. Describes solutions to simple problems.
20. Uses language to express imagination through drama or story telling or imitation.

REFERENCE: MATTES & OMARK, 1984

Solutions

Three solutions to the problems of testing bilinguals are provided by Valdés & Figueroa (1994). Their first solution is to attempt to minimize the potential harm of existing tests when given to bilingual individuals, by applying some of the guidelines given above. Their second solution is, temporarily, to ban all testing of bilinguals until more valid tests can be produced for bilingual populations. Their third alternative is that alternative approaches to testing and development be developed. This third option may be the one most favored by many teachers, educationalists and parents. It would, for example, bring in bilingual norms, more curriculum-based assessment and portfolio-type assessment, and a greater cultural and linguistic awareness of bilinguals.

However, this third solution is probably a new beginning but is not enough. A more radical solution places change in assessment within (and not separate from) a change in expectations about the nature and behavior of language minority students. This entails a shift in the politics and policy dimensions of the assessment of bilinguals. Merely changing tests may alleviate the symptoms of a problem, but not change the root cause. The root cause tends to be a bias against language minorities that is endemic in many societies and is substantiated by tests. By being biased against bilinguals in a cultural and linguistic form, and by a failure to incorporate an understanding of the cognitive constitution of bilinguals, assessment confirms and perpetuates various discriminatory perceptions about language minority children.

Assessment thus sometimes serves by its nature and purpose, its form, use and outcomes, to provide the evidence for discrimination and prejudice against language minorities (e.g in the US and Britain) to be perpetuated. Assessment results serve to marginalize and demotivate, to reveal underachievement and lower performance in language minority children. These results are often a reflection of the low status, inequitable treatment and poverty found among many language minorities. Assessment provides the data to make expectations about language minority students self-fulfilling and self-perpetuating. Changing assessment does not necessarily break into that cycle, unless it is a component of a wider reform movement.

Assessment must not in itself be blamed for bias against bilinguals. It is a conveyer and not a root cause of language minority discrimination and bias. Until

there is authentic and genuine acceptance of cultural pluralism in a nation, a more widespread assent for multiculturalism, a minimizing of racism and prejudice against ethnic minorities, minor modifications in the assessment of bilinguals stand the chance of merely confirming the lower status and perceived 'deficiencies' of language minority children.

Too often the focus in assessing bilinguals is on their language competence (or on their 'limited proficiencies' as in the test-designated 'Limited English Proficient' students in the United States via tests such as the English Language Assessment Battery (LAB)). Rarely does the assessment of bilinguals in the education system focus on other important competencies of a bilingual.

In the US, the 1991 Secretary's Commission on Achieving Necessary Skills (SCANS) recommended that attention be given in high schools to work-related competencies. For example, performance standards were called for in: interpersonal skills (e.g. working in a team, negotiating, working well with people from culturally diverse backgrounds), interpreting and communicating information, thinking creatively, taking responsibility, sociability, self-management and integrity. These important 'life-skills' are regarded as 'essential accomplishments' for employment, self-respect and building a better world.

On some of these attributes, there is evidence to suggest that bilinguals may have advantages over monolinguals (e.g. negotiating, working well with people from culturally diverse backgrounds, interpreting and communicating information, thinking creatively). If the assessment of bilinguals focused more on these 'outside world' attributes and less on classroom linguistic skills in the majority language, a more affirmative and favorable, productive and constructive view of bilinguals might be promoted.

Further Reading

CLINE, T., 1993, Educational Assessment of Bilingual Pupils: Getting the Context Right. *Educational and Child Psychology*, 10 (4), 59-68.

CUMMINS, J., 1984, *Bilingualism and Special Education: Issues in Assessment Pedagogy*. Clevedon: Multilingual Matters Ltd.

GENESEE, F. & UPSHUR, J. A., 1996, *Classroom-Based Evaluation in Second Language Education*. Cambridge: Cambridge University Press.

HAMAYAN, E. V. & DAMICO, J. S. (eds), 1991, *Limiting Bias in the Assessment of Bilingual Students*. Austin, TX: PRO. ED.

HERNANDEZ, R. D., 1994, Reducing Bias in the Assessment of Culturally and Linguistically Diverse Populations. *Journal of Educational Issues of Language Minority Students*, 14, 269-300.

SPOLSKY, B., 1995, *Measured Words: The Development of Objective Language Testing*. Oxford: Oxford University Press.

VALDÉS, G., & FIGUEROA, R. A., 1994, *Bilingualism and Testing: A Special Case of Bias*. Norwood, NJ: Ablex.

4: Bilingual Special Education

Introduction

It is initially important to define who are the children with special needs who may need Special Education provision. Categories of special need vary from country to country but are likely to include the following areas: visual impairment, hearing impairment, communication disorders, learning disabilities (e.g. dyslexia and developmental aphasia), severe subnormality in cognitive development, behavioral problems and physical handicaps. Some bilingual children will have special needs, and this includes children from 'elite' bilingual families (e.g. English-German) as well as from language minorities. In the United States, the Office of Special Education has estimated that nearly one million children from language minority backgrounds are in need of some form of special education. This immediately raises questions as to why language minority children may need special education.

1. Do language minority children experience special needs more frequently than other children due to their bilingualism and their communicative differences from monolingual children?

2. Are language minority children often wrongly assessed and categorized as having a 'disability' and, as such, incorrectly placed in special education?

These two questions will now be considered in turn.

Do language minority children experience special needs more frequently than other children due to their bilingualism and their communicative differences from monolingual children?

It seems very unlikely that bilingualism is a direct cause of, or linked to the following main categories of special need, namely visual impairment, hearing impairment, learning disabilities (e.g. dyslexia and developmental aphasia), severe subnormality in cognitive development, behavioral problems and physical handicaps. Being a member of a language minority may co-exist with such conditions, but is not connected (see Explanations of Underachievement, page 570).

There is some evidence in the United States (on a state by state analysis) that language minority children are over-represented among those in need of special education (Harry, 1992; Gersten & Woodward, 1994). Harry (1992) also suggests that the rate of placement of Latinos in special education rises as the number of these students in the school system increases. Any over-representation in the categories listed above is very unlikely to be a result of bilingualism by itself.

Are language minority children often wrongly assessed and categorized as having a 'disability' and, as such, incorrectly placed in special education?

When language minority children are assessed it is important that three different aspects of their development be kept distinct: (1) first language proficiency, (2) second language proficiency, and (3) the existence (or not) of a physical, learning or behavioral difficulty. This three-fold distinction enables a more accurate and fair assessment to be made with regard to special education. The child's level of functioning in a second language must not be seen as representing the child's level of language development. The child's development in the first language needs to be assessed (e.g. by observation if psychological and educational tests are not available) so as to paint a picture of proficiency rather than deficiency. The child's language proficiency is different from potential problems in an individual's capacities that require specialist treatment (e.g. hearing impairment, severely subnormal, specific learning difficulties). Neither the language and culture of the home, nor socioeconomic and ethnic differences should be considered as handicapping conditions in themselves. Social, cultural, family, educational and personal information needs to be collected to make a valid and reliable assessment and to make an accurate placement of the child in mainstream or special education. This was considered more fully in the previous chapter on Assessment and Bilingual Children (see page 575).

The Example of the United States

In the United States, Public Law (94-142) gives the right to assessment that is not culturally discriminatory, to tests in the child's native language, to multidimensional 'all areas' assessment for all 'handicapped' students. The misdiagnosis of language minority students for special education has led to court cases (see Assessment and Bilingual Children, page 575). Such court cases revealed how language minority students were wrongly assessed as in need of special education. In some cases, teachers were unsure how to cope with a child whose English was relatively 'weak'. On this basis only, the teacher wanted special education for the 'Limited English Proficient' child.

Such litigation has shown the importance of separating bilinguals with real learning difficulties from those bilinguals whose second language (e.g. English) proficiency is below a 'native' average. The latter group should not be assessed as having learning difficulties and therefore in need of special education. The litigation also showed the wrongs done to language minority students: misidentification, misplacement, misuse of tests and failure when allocated to special education.

Unfortunately, the fear of litigation by school districts can lead to an over-referral of language minority students with a real need of special education. In the early 1980s, the trend was (in California, for example), to assume that too many language minority students were in need of special education. When students did not appear to be benefiting from instruction in 'regular' classrooms, special education classes became the easy answer. Or if teachers were unsure how to deal with a behavioral or learning problem, transfer to special education provision became an instant solution.

Towards the end of the 1980s, this had been reversed. The tendency moved to underestimating the special needs of language minority children (Gersten & Woodward, 1994). Wrongful placement of children in special education (over-referral) made various administrators cautious of special education placement. A fear of legal action by parents and a realization that assessment devices often had low validity led administrators to be hesitant to place language minority children in special education.

Pendalar school in the town of Caernarfon in Gwynedd, North Wales, caters for children with special educational needs. In the county of Gwynedd, the majority of the population are bilingual in Welsh and English, and one aim of the county's educational policy is that every child should be fully bilingual and biliterate in Welsh and English by the time they leave school. The county's special schools also aim to enable their students to become bilingual according to their individual abilities. All Pendalar staff are bilingual and Welsh is the main language of school administration and school activities. Small group and one-to-one teaching means that students are generally taught in their home language, whether Welsh or English, but both languages are used in class. In Pendalar, bilingualism is seen not as an additional burden but as an enrichment for children with special needs, and as a valuable help to integration into the wider community.

The see-saw between over-estimation and under-referral of special education need makes accurate assessment very important. The chapter on Assessment and Bilingual Children (see page 575) raises the important issues about valid assessment of special need. However, accurate assessment and placement in different schools is not enough. The development of effective instruction strategies and an appropriate curriculum is crucial. So is the need to train teachers for bilingual students in special education. Educating the parents of special needs children is also a high priority.

Assessment will sometimes locate those who are bilingual and have a physical, neurological, learning, emotional, cognitive or behavioral difficulty. Such children may need some kind of special education or intervention. One estimate in the United States is that one in eight (approximately 12 percent) of language minority students will fit into this category. Similar figures are quoted in other countries. What form of Special Education should such children receive? Should such education be in their home language, where feasible, or in the majority language of the region? Or should such children be provided with education that uses both home and majority languages?

Special education bilingual children can be served by a variety of institutional arrangements (Cloud, 1994). These include: special education schools (resident and non-resident), hospital-based education, residential homes, special education units attached to mainstream schools, specially resourced classes in mainstream schools, withdrawal and pull-out programs (e.g. for extra speech and language help, behavioral management) and special help given by teachers, paraprofessionals or support staff in 'regular' classes. The extent to which such provision will be bilingual or monolingual will vary within and across such institutional arrangements. Such bilingual or monolingual provision will also depend on availability of provision (material and human), the type and degree of special education need or condition, proficiency in both languages, learning capacity, age, social and emotional maturity, degree of success in any previous education placements, and not least, the wishes of the parents and child.

When bilingual or language minority children have been accurately assessed as having special needs, many educators will argue that education solely in the dominant, majority language is needed. In the United States, the advice is sometimes given that Latino and other language minority children with special needs should be educated in monolingual, English language special schools. The argument is that such children are going to live in an English-speaking society. When there is very severe mental retardation, it seems sensible that a child should be educated monolingually, in the minority or majority language. Such a child develops very slowly in one language. However, this would only affect a very minute proportion of children with special needs.

Many special needs children will benefit considerably from bilingual special education rather than monolingual special education. One example is the recently arrived

in-migrant, special needs child. Placing such a child in a class where he or she doesn't speak the language of the classroom (e.g. English in the United States) will only increase failure and lower self-esteem. To be educated, the child preferably needs initial instruction mostly in the first language, with the chance to become as bilingual as possible. Most children with special needs are capable of developing in two languages. Many do not reach levels of proficiency in either language compared with peers in mainstream classrooms. Nevertheless, they reach satisfactory levels of proficiency in two languages according to their abilities. Becoming bilingual does not detract from achievement in other areas of the curriculum (e.g. Mathematics and the Creative Arts). Canadian research tends to show that less able bilingual children share some of the cognitive advantages of bilingualism (Rueda, 1983). Just as their Mathematics ability, literacy and scientific development may occur at a slower pace, so the two languages will develop with less speed. The size of vocabulary and accuracy of grammar may be less in both languages than the average bilingual child. Nevertheless, such children acquiring two languages early, will usually be able to communicate in both languages, often as well as they would communicate in one language.

The movement of a bilingual student into special education should occur after a conclusion is reached that the child's needs cannot be met by integration in a regular (i.e. non-special) school. This holds for those currently in bilingual education who may need special bilingual education because generally, integration is preferable to segregation. If children are placed in bilingual special education, it is important that they gain the benefits of those in other forms of bilingual education: dual language competence, biculturalism and multiculturalism, and other educational, cultural, self-identity and self-esteem benefits.

One example of children needing special attention is when they are failing in a mainstream school due to their language proficiency not being sufficient to operate in the curriculum. For example, in the United States, some Spanish-speaking children are in mainstream schools (a 'submersion' experience) and, although of normal ability, fail in the system (e.g. drop out of school, repeat grades, leave high school without a diploma) because their English proficiency is insufficiently developed to comprehend the increasingly complex curriculum.

This situation creates an apparent dilemma. By being placed in some form of special education, the child is possibly stigmatized as having a 'deficiency' and a 'language deficit'. Such special education may be a separate school (or a special unit within a larger school) that provides special ('remedial') education for bilingual children. Such schools and units may not foster bilingualism. Often, they will emphasize children becoming competent in the majority language (e.g. English in the United States). Such segregation may allow more attention to the second language but result in ghettoization of language minorities. While giving some sanctuary from sinking in second language submersion in a mainstream school, special education can be a retreat, marginalizing the child. Will children in such special education realize their potential across the curriculum? Will they have increased access to employment? Will their apparent failure be accepted and validated because they are associated with a remedial institution? Will there be decreased opportunities for success in school achievement, employment and self-enhancement?

The ideal for children in this dilemma is not mainstreaming or special education. It is education which allows them to start and continue learning in their first language. The second language is nurtured as well – to ensure the development of bilinguals who can operate in mainstream society. In such schools, both languages are developed and used in the curriculum. Such schools avoid the 'remedial' or 'compensatory' associations of special education. Such schools celebrate the cultural and linguistic diversity of their students. Yet bilingual education is sometimes in danger of being seen as a form of special education.

Further Reading

BACA, L. M. & CERVANTES, H. T., 1989, *The Bilingual Special Education Interface*. Columbus, OH: Merrill.

CARRASQUILLO, A. L., 1990, Bilingual Special Education: The Important Connection. In A. L. CARRASQUILLO & R. E. BAECHER (eds), *Teaching the Bilingual Special Education Student*. Norwood, NJ: Ablex.

CLOUD, N., 1994, Special Education Needs of Second Language Students. In F. GENESEE (ed.), *Educating Second Language Children*. Cambridge: Cambridge University Press.

GERSTEN, R. & WOODWARD, J., 1994, The Language Minority Student and Special Education: Issues, Trends and Paradoxes. *Exceptional Children*, 60 (4), 310-322.

HARRY, B., 1992, *Cultural Diversity, Families and the Special Education System*. New York: Teachers College Press.

MALDONADO, J. A., 1994, Bilingual Special Education: Specific Learning Disabilities in Language and Reading. *Journal of Educational Issues of Language Minority Students*, 14, 127-147.

5: Language and Speech Therapy in a Bilingual Context

Language and speech therapists (also called speech pathologists) work with people of all ages, from small children to old people. They work with infants who are born with physical disabilities, such as a cleft palate or deafness, or handicaps such as Down's Syndrome. They help older children who have been found to have problems acquiring, comprehending or producing speech. This might form part of a general learning disability or reflect a more specific language-related problem. Their work includes children with speech problems such as stuttering, or children who have acquired disabilities (e.g. brain damage) following an accident or serious illness. Language and speech therapists also work with adults with language and speech disabilities, as a result of strokes, head injuries, Parkinson's Disease, alcohol abuse and other causes. A speech therapist's job often includes not just speech, but many aspects of language, including reading and writing among certain adults.

A bilingual situation provides an extra dimension to the work of the language and speech therapists, since a proportion of their work must be carried out through different languages, and sometimes they must use both languages concurrently in their work.

One policy among language and speech therapists is to work with individuals in their first or preferred language. For children with language and speech difficulties, this will be the language their parents speak to them. For adults, this will be their first language or their present language of habitual use. This can present some interesting dimensions to the work. Many older adults, for instance, have spoken a minority language all their lives, and it is their dominant language and the language they use mainly in the home and community. Yet they have received most of their education through the medium of a majority language and have been accustomed to read and write mainly in that language.

Thus a language and speech therapist working with a stroke victim, for instance, may work with that person on speech and aural comprehension in their minority language, and yet may have to work on reading and writing skills in the majority language. The separation of languages can be so firm in the person's mind that the speech therapist may have to 'cue' the person orally in the minority language for that person to produce a written sentence in the majority language.

There have been many documented cases of bilingual or multilingual stroke victims in countries such as Switzerland who seemingly 'lose' one or more of their languages after a stroke, either temporarily or permanently, while retaining another or other languages. The language (or languages) retained is not necessarily the language learnt first by the patient. These are usually individuals who speak one language as a mother tongue and have learnt one or more other languages at a later age.

According to the Gwynedd (North Wales) Language and Speech Therapy team, this does not appear to happen with bilingual Welsh-English speakers, possibly because they have come into contact with English at a very early age. Most Welsh speakers in Gwynedd speak the language as their first language or mother tongue and for many of them, Welsh is still the language they use mainly, and is their dominant and preferred language. However, the majority of them have been exposed to English from early childhood, through education and the mass media. Possibly because both languages have taken root at a very early age, they do not appear to lose one at the expense of the other. However, there is often a mingling of languages following a stroke. A person may search for a word or phrase in one language and it may spring to mind in the other language. One language and speech therapist tells an interesting story of a stroke patient whose written English was progressing very well, except that he used Welsh orthography!

These kinds of experiences underline the importance of bilingual language and speech therapists. Both languages may need to be used in a single session. The reality of the bilingual situation may mean that different languages are used for different purposes and in different domains. This must be reflected in the help given by the language and speech therapists.

In the course of their work, language and speech therapists teams often come across many misconceptions about bilingualism. One of these is that learning two languages can prove an unacceptable burden for a child who is slow to acquire a first language. In fact, there is almost no truth in this belief.

When working with young children, many language and speech therapists work with the children in their first lan-

guage, or, in the case of children with no speech at all, their potential first language (i.e. the language their parents speak to them). When children have made progress in their first language, the work does not usually have to be repeated when the child encounters a second language at school. The language skills acquired in the first language (e.g. labeling objects, using verbs) typically transfer to the second language.

The experience of many language and speech therapists is that learning a second language does not pose any particular problems for a child with general learning disabilities, although the level achieved in both languages may be lower than that of the peer group. It would appear that the stimulus of learning a second language, with another label for objects and concepts, helps the child to make progress in both languages. Similarly, a child whose slower progress in the first language (e.g. English) is partly or wholly attributable to social deprivation, may benefit from learning a second language (e.g. French) in an Immersion situation. The careful grading of language by the teacher, the repetition of key phrases and vocabulary, the use of visual cues and stimuli to aid understanding, the emphasis on learning language through activities, may all enable such a child to make good progress in the second language alongside the peer group.

The only instance where a child may find it difficult to cope with a second language is when a child has a specific language-related disability (see page 572). A child who has difficulty 'tuning into' or processing language may find it difficult to cope with a class where the curriculum is delivered through the medium of a second language. The child may not find it easy to 'pick up' the second language and may be shut out of classroom interaction between the teacher and other students, and between the children and one another. A preferable option for such a child might be to attend a school where the curriculum is delivered mainly through the medium of the first language, and where the second language is presented in certain set periods.

One situation which language and speech therapists come across is when minority language parents decide to speak a majority language to their children. This can occur because the child has learning difficulties and the parents mistakenly believe that two languages would be an extra burden, and that the child should learn the useful majority language. Sometimes this can happen when a child has no particular problem, but when the parents have made the decision from the child's birth that it would be educationally advantageous for the child to learn the majority language first 'to get a good start in life'. The result is that the child is shut out from the interaction between the parents, and often between other family members and members of the surrounding community. The parents are not native majority language speakers, and sometimes the language model they offer to the child is impoverished and deficient. Thus the child grows up not advantaged, but linguistically deprived. A child with learning difficulties is further disadvantaged. It may be preferable, wherever possible, for parents to speak their own language to the child. If there are problems with acquiring the first language, language and speech therapy can help, and then the second language can be built on the strong foundations of the first language.

Occasionally language and speech therapists are called upon to help individuals whose native language is neither the local minority language nor the majority language. When helping adults or children whose daily language is an Asian or Chinese language (in the US), for instance, the speech pathologist relies on the collaboration of family members or other members of that minority language community. The speech pathologist relies on speakers of the language to translate cues or instructions for the individual concerned, and then depend on them to monitor the person's response, and relay it accurately to the speech therapist. When speech pathologists are themselves bilingual, they may be more aware of the difficulties of translation between languages, and the tendency that can occur for family members to change or 'improve' a person's response in translation, relaying what they think a person meant to say rather than what that person did say.

Many modern language and speech therapists now refute the suggestion that bilingualism is a burden or a problem, even for those individuals with congenital or acquired language disabilities. Bilingualism is simply a dimension in the life of an individual, family and community that can be taken into account when working with people with different kinds of language difficulties. The ability to speak two languages is also a privilege and a resource that should not be denied any individual.

Further Reading

BACA, L. M. & CERVANTES, H. T., 1989, *The Bilingual Special Education Interface*. Columbus, OH: Merrill.

The Bilingual Classroom

1: Language Allocation in Bilingual Methodology

Introduction

Apart from teaching the curriculum in the first language or, as in Submersion education, solely in the second language, there is a wide variety of possibilities in using two languages in the curriculum. One example is the Immersion strategy, for example in Canada, where majority language children are educated through the medium of their second language, but where their first language is gradually introduced into the curriculum.

The purpose of this topic is to look at different dimensions of 'how and when' two languages can be (1) separated and (2) integrated in bilingual methodology. The initial focus will be the separation of languages within the curriculum. For example, when two languages are assigned to different areas of the curriculum, the intention is usually to establish clear boundaries between the use of those languages. In the second part of this topic, an examination will be made of the more integrated or concurrent use of two languages. For example, a teacher may repeat an explanation in a different language. The concluding part of this topic will examine the problems and limitations of the concurrent use of two languages in the classroom.

A bilingual sign on the door of the kindergarten at PS 84, a Spanish-English dual language school in New York (see page 524). At PS 84, kindergarten children are taught in Spanish and English on different days.

There are different purposes in separating and possibly integrating languages in bilingual methodology. Such purposes are the foundation of such a methodology and provide the tools to evaluate the effectiveness of different strategies. First, a 'strong' form of bilingual education will enable students to develop competence in both languages, in oracy and in literacy. A bilingual methodology that results in more successful language development outcomes will usually be preferred. Such a methodology may hold that language development needs to develop throughout the curriculum, but also requires targeted development in language lessons. However, secondly, success throughout the curriculum may be as strong, if not a stronger preference among teachers and parents. If a strategic integration of languages in a class gives higher student performance in Science, Mathematics, Humanities and the Arts than language separation, the chosen methodology may be valued and disseminated.

Third, a bilingual methodology may be necessary or desirable in a mixed language school. Where there is a mixture of, for example, Spanish first language speakers and English first language speakers in two-way education, a clear policy and practice in language allocation is required. Fourth, where children in linguistically mixed classrooms have different levels of ability in two languages, as well as different levels of ability in tackling the curriculum, a bilingual methodology may be essential. In Wales, a class may contain children who are relative beginners in Welsh (e.g. recent in-migrants), those with some second language Welsh fluency, and native Welsh speakers. Some native Welsh speakers will be fluent in English, others may have more competence in Welsh than English. A school that aims to achieve a high standard of ability in both languages will need to implement a clear language allocation methodology. (See page 592.)

Language Separation

In the allocation of two languages in the classroom and in the curriculum, the need for distinct separation and clear boundaries between two languages has often been advocated. First, such separation has support from the sociolinguists who argue that, for a minority language to

survive, it must have separate and distinct uses in society. In the discussion of diglossia (see page 117), maintaining a relatively stable societal arrangement for the separate use of two languages was presented as important in minority language survival. Therefore, the argument has been in schools that, for a minority language to have purpose and strength, it must have a distinct language allocation in transmitting the curriculum.

Second, from child development research with bilinguals, it has often been argued that the 'one person, one language' situation is one of the most effective patterns enabling childhood bilingualism to occur. If the mother speaks one language and the father another language, there is a distinct separation of languages. The child will therefore learn to speak one language to one parent, another language to the other parent. Alternatively, one language may be spoken at home, and another in the neighborhood or school. Such separation tends to result in the successful development of both languages within the very young child because there are distinct boundaries between the languages and a separate reception and production of language. Thus, an argument is that effective bilingual schools should find ways of mirroring language separation in such 'one person, one language' homes by establishing boundaries between languages. What can constitute boundaries will be examined in detail later.

Third, a constant problem in many minority language situations is the development of an unstable codemixing among adults as well as children. Derogatory terms such as 'Spanglish' (for a mixture of Spanish and English) and 'Wenglish' (for a mixture of Welsh and English) highlight the concern of minority language preservationists about codemixing. The mixing of languages within sentences and across sentences can be a half-way house, indicating a movement away from a minority language towards the majority language. Therefore, educationalists have often argued for the importance of separation of languages within the school. This is particularly to strengthen and maintain the purity and integrity of a minority language.

Having established three bases for language separation in the classroom and curriculum, we will now consider how languages can be separated. There are eight non-independent dimensions along which the separation of languages can occur in school settings. These will now be considered in turn:

Subject or topic

In elementary schools and high schools, different curriculum areas may be taught in different languages. For example, Social Studies, Religious Education, Art, Music and Physical Education may be taught through the minority language (e.g. Spanish in the US). Math, Science, Technology and Computer Studies may be taught through the majority language (e.g. English). Certain curriculum areas are reserved for one language, other curriculum areas for the second language. In kindergartens and elementary schools, the allocation may be by topic rather than subject. For example, a project on 'Conservation' may be through the minority language, a project on 'Weather' through the majority language.

The examples given so far reveal 'content sensitive' issues. That is, there is sometimes a call for arts and humanities culture to be relayed through the minority language, with Science and Technology relayed in an international majority language. Curriculum areas such as History and Geography are often regarded as best reflecting the heritage and culture of a language group. In contrast, Science and Technology may be seen as international, and dominated by the English language. The danger is that the minority language becomes associated with tradition and history rather than with technology and science. The minority language is thereby allocated a lower status and seen as much less relevant to modern existence.

Person

The use of two languages in a school may be separated according to person. Just as in some homes there is the 'one person, one language' system, so different school staff may be identified with different languages. For example, there may be two teachers working in a team-teaching situation. One teacher communicates with the children through the majority language, the other teacher through the children's minority language. There is a clear language boundary established by person. Alternatively, teachers' assistants, parents helping in the classroom, auxiliaries and paraprofessionals may function in the classroom as an alternative but separate language source for the children.

Time

A frequently used strategy in language allocation in schools is for classes to operate at different times in different languages. For example, in some Dual Language schools, one day may be through Spanish, the next day through English. Other schools alternate by half days. The morning may be in Spanish, the afternoon in English, the next day reversing that situation. A third alternative is for different lessons to be allocated to different languages. This overlaps with the idea of separation by subject and topic.

The separation of time need not be solely in terms of days, half-days or lessons. It may be also in terms of

whole weeks, months or semesters. It also may valuably include a policy that varies by grade and age. For example, children may be taught through the minority language for the first two or three years of elementary education for 100 percent of time. Over Grades 3 to 7, an increasing amount of time may be allocated to the majority language inside the school.

Place

A lesser-used means of language separation in the classroom is via different physical locations for different languages. For example, if there are two Science laboratories in the school, one may be labeled as a Spanish-speaking laboratory, the other the English-speaking laboratory. The children are expected to speak the language of that laboratory when entering it. The assumption is that a physical location provides enough cues and clues to prompt the child to adhere to different languages in different places. In reality, the teacher and other students may be more crucial in influencing the choice of language. Location is however, a valuable 'extra' in encouraging language segregation.

A consideration of 'place' in language allocation needs to include all areas of the school. During morning and afternoon breaks, lunch-breaks, religious services and announcements, music and drama events, games and sports, the language balance of the school is affected. Sometimes teachers can allocate languages (e.g. in drama); other times, students have a dominant influence (e.g. in the playground). However, all informal events in the school create a language atmosphere, a language balance, and contribute to the creation of the overall language experience of the school.

Medium of activity

Another form of separation focuses on distinguishing between listening, speaking, reading and writing in the classroom. For example, the teacher may give an oral explanation of a concept in one language, with a follow-up discussion with the class in that same language. Then the teacher may ask the children to complete their written work in a second language. This sequence may be deliberately reversed in a second lesson. Another example would be when children read material through one language, and are then invited to write about it in the second language.

The aim of such a teaching strategy is to reinforce and strengthen the learning by children. What is initially assimilated in one language is transferred and reinterpreted in a second language. By re-processing the information in a different language, greater understanding may be achieved. However, this example shows that language separation soon links with a strategy to use both languages in the learning process. This idea of a rational, structured and sequenced use of two languages in learning is considered later – when the concurrent use of languages is examined.

One danger of 'different medium' separation is that one language may be used for oracy and another language for literacy. Where a minority language does not have a written script this may be a necessary boundary. Where a minority language has no or few written materials, the danger is that the minority language will be identified with oracy and the majority language with literacy. This has a potential effect of giving higher status and more functions to the majority language and its associated literacy. Hence, where this kind of 'medium separation tactic' is used, it is important for reversal to occur. For example, if oral explanations are given in one language with reading/writing in a different language, on the next day or next lesson, that situation can be reversed.

Curriculum material

There are a variety of ways in which written, audio-visual and information technology curriculum material can be delivered in two languages, ensuring clear separation and non-duplication. Textbooks and course materials may only be allocated in one language with the oral teaching in another language. For example, in Wales, the equivalent of some three million US dollars is allocated for producing curriculum material in Welsh for all ages and all ability levels. This is separation 'across' curriculum material; there is also separation possible 'within' such material. For example, in elementary schools, dual language books (e.g. with English one side of the page and Spanish on the other, sharing the same pictures) may be useful in the early stages of biliteracy. Consideration of dual language books is given later (see page 611).

In high schools, reading material in History or Science may be allocated by the teacher in both languages. However, duplication of information and ideas is not necessarily present. Rather, there can be a continuation and progression in themes and content. For example, a new topic may be introduced in one language by the student reading selected material. When a major subtopic occurs, the teacher may require students to conduct their reading in a different language. Use of both languages helps understanding of the content while separation is occurring. The child does not have the choice of reading the English or the Spanish text, but needs to read both to gain a full comprehension of the topic. Again, it will be seen that language separation does not necessarily mean using two languages in isolation (or repeating the same content). A concern for separation involves policy and

practice that includes more or less use of both languages. The outcome is a classroom paradox; languages that are separated by function but are connected in an overall, holistic language and educational development policy.

Such a 'curriculum material separation' strategy tends to be used when, and only when both the child's languages are relatively secure, competent and well developed. When this has occurred, the argument is that a child has to think more deeply about the material when moving between languages, comparing and contrasting, developing the theme of the material, assimilating and accommodating, transferring and sometimes translating in order to secure a concept and understanding.

Function

In schools and classes where there are bilingual children, there is often teaching in the majority language while the management of the classroom occurs in the minority language. For example, in US 'Transitional Bilingual education' schools with many Spanish speakers, the teacher may transmit the 'formal' subject matter in English, while conducting 'informal' episodes in Spanish. In this example, the stipulated curriculum is relayed in the majority language. However, when the teacher is organizing students, disciplining, informally talking with individual students or small groups, giving additional explanations, a switch to the minority language is made.

Student

The previous seven dimensions have suggested that a school or a teacher may develop a policy about language allocation in a bilingual classroom. However, there is the real situation where students themselves help define the language that is being used in a classroom. For example, if a pupil addresses the teacher, it may not be in the language that the teacher has used to deliver the curriculum. To explain something with clarity, and for ease of communication, the pupil may switch to his or her preferred language. Students influence when and where languages are used, and affect boundary making. Thus separate dual language use can occur in the classroom by varying circumstance, student influence, and the formality or informality of particular events (e.g. students may feel at ease talking to teachers in their minority language in private or in classroom conversations).

Concurrent Use of Languages in a Lesson

In many bilingual classrooms, the frequent switching between two or more languages is customary. The concurrent use of two languages in a bilingual classroom tends to be regular in practice, but rare as a predetermined teaching and learning strategy. Jacobson (1990) has argued that, on occasions, the integrated use of both languages rather than language separation can be of value in a lesson. Such a purposeful and structured use of both languages inside a lesson has certain problems that will be considered later. Four concurrent uses will now be considered (Jacobson,1990).

Randomly switching languages

Bilingual children may switch languages both within sentences and across sentences. In many minority language groups, this is frequent both in the home and street as it is in the school. It is relatively rare for such switching to be stable across time. More often it is a half-way house, a sign of movement towards the majority language. For minority languages to survive as relatively distinct and standardized languages, few would argue for such a random practice to be encouraged in a bilingual classroom.

Translating

In some bilingual classrooms, teachers will repeat in another language what they have previously said. For example, the teacher may explain a concept in Spanish, and then repeat the same explanation in English. Everything is said twice for the benefit of children who are dominant in different languages. The danger is that the pupil will opt out of listening when the teacher is transmitting in the weaker language. The students know that the same content will be given in their preferred language and wait for that to occur. Such duplication appears to result in less efficiency, less language maintenance value and less likely achievement in the curriculum.

Previewing and reviewing

One strategy in the concurrent use of languages in a classroom is to give the preview in the minority language and then the fuller review in the majority language. That is, a topic is introduced in the child's minority language, for example, to give an initial understanding. Then, the subject matter is considered in depth in the majority language. This may be reversed. While an extension and reinforcement of ideas occurs by moving from one language to another, there is sometimes also unnecessary duplication and a slow momentum.

Purposeful concurrent usage

In a variety of publications, Jacobson proposed the purposeful concurrent use of two languages (see Jacobson, 1990). The properties of what Jacobson calls the 'New Concurrent Approach' is that equal amounts of time are allocated to two languages, and teachers consciously initiate movement from one language to another. Such language movement inside a lesson occurs where there are discrete events and episodes with distinct goals for each

language There must be a conscious and planned movement from one language to another in a regular and rational manner. Jacobson (1990) proposes this to strengthen and develop both languages, and to reinforce taught concepts by being considered and processed in both languages. A use of both languages, it is suggested, contributes to a deeper understanding of the subject matter being studied.

Jacobson (1990) suggests a variety of cues that can trigger a switch from one language to another. Examples of such cues include:

- Reinforcement of concepts.
- Reviewing.
- Capturing (and re-capturing) student attention.
- Praising and reprimanding students.
- Change of topic.
- Change in the stimulus material.
- Change from formality to informality.
- To gain rapport.
- When there is fatigue.

The amount of time allocated to each language in the curriculum is important. Some kind of balance (e.g. 50/50 or 75/25) between languages is needed, but more important is the purpose, manner and method in which the two languages are used. All four language abilities may need fostering in both languages. To emphasize oracy in one language and literacy in another language may result in lopsided bilingualism.

As is discussed in the limitations given below, there are potential problems in the complexity of managing, allocating and organizing such a purposeful use of two languages. However, the value of the idea is that the teacher plans the strategic use of two languages in the classroom, thinks consciously about the use of the two languages, reflects and reviews what is happening, and attempts to cognitively stimulate students by a 'language provocative' and 'language diversified' lesson.

Issues and Limitations

In decisions about language separation and language allocation in a bilingual classroom, there are other ingredients and contexts that need to be taken into account before an effective dual language policy can be formulated.

First, the aims of the school in terms of language preservation and second language competence need to be examined carefully. School teachers are language planners, even if subconsciously. Where a minority language is to be preserved in the children, then separation may be a central part of the policy. Where teachers are more enthusiastic about competence in the majority language (a second language), then different practices and outcomes in terms of language allocation will be desired. Fewer language boundaries may be maintained. There may be a deliberate loosening of boundaries to ensure the development of the majority language.

Second, the nature of the students must be considered in any policy regarding language boundaries and concurrent use. Different policies and practices may be required according to the age and grade level of the children. If the children's language development is still at an early evolutionary stage, boundary setting will be more important. With older children, whose languages are relatively well developed, the concurrent use of two languages may be more viable and desirable. Older children may have more stability and separation in their language abilities.

Third, this suggests that a static policy with regard to boundaries and concurrent use within the school is less justifiable than a progressive policy that examines different uses across years and across grade levels. Early separation may be very important. Later on in high school, a more concurrent use may enable conceptual clarity, depth of understanding and possibly to accelerate cognitive development.

A progressive policy also needs to consider different types of communication in the classroom. For example, when the teacher is talking more informally and simply to the class, the weaker language may be appropriate. In practical activities, where there is 'context-embedded' help, the weaker language may also be valuably used. Where the cognitive level in transmitting the curriculum is higher (e.g. more complex, abstract ideas), either the stronger language or a bilingual approach may be needed. Different types of episode in the classroom (e.g. managerial, instruction, practical activity) constrain or allow comprehensible second language communication and concurrent usage.

Fourth, different dimensions of the school need different discussions about the separation and integration of languages (e.g. curriculum, whole school policies, classrooms, lessons). At what level of organization should separation occur? The discussion of language separation by curriculum material and medium of curriculum delivery showed how language separation is not a distinct issue from rational concurrent use. Language separation merges into a consideration of integrated use.

Fifth, the language balance of the class is often an important factor in a language separation decision. If all the children are native speakers of a minority (or majority)

language, there may be ease in determining a language allocation. However, classes may be mixed, with differing balances of majority and minority language native speakers. Who dominates numerically, linguistically and psychologically in the classroom? When the balance is tilted against language minority children, a clear separation with the curriculum balance towards the minority language may be desirable. Whether the children in a school are language minority children in a subtractive or additive situation will also impact on language allocation policies.

Sixth, where language minority children are in the numerical majority, a slow change rather than a sharp shift from language separation to concurrent use may be advisable. The minority language is often in danger of being perceived as less powerful, less useful and of less status as students become older. Therefore, the minority language needs protection and a constant high profile in the school.

Seventh, a school language policy needs to take into account 'out of school exposure' to the first and second language. Sometimes, an equal amount of time is advocated in the separation of two languages in the school, with half the curriculum in one language, the other half in a different language. If the child is surrounded by the majority language outside the school (e.g. street, screen and shop), then the 'separation' balance may need to be more towards the minority language in school. Such 'out of school exposure' may also make some teachers hesitant about concurrent usage.

Eighth, the replication and duplication of content is a danger in bilingual classroom methodology. Where the same subject matter is repeated in a different language, some pupils will not concentrate or will go 'off task'. However, in multilingual classrooms, repeating is sometimes pragmatically necessary. Where there is a considerable variety of different home and preferred languages in the classroom, for the sake of comprehension, a teacher (and her bilingual assistant) may need to repeat an instruction in different languages. For example, there are some multilingual classrooms (e.g. in New York, Toronto and London) with a considerable diversity of home languages among the children. Replication of teaching in two (or three) languages in the early grades may be essential for as many children as possible to comprehend. This makes debates about concurrent use and language boundaries all the more difficult. One solution is the possibility of individualized learning via small groups (as occurs in progressive British and North American primary school practice). This may allow some language boundaries to be established, with different children addressed (e.g. by teachers aides) in their preferred language.

Ninth, the use of bilingual materials, particularly when they are built in a non-repetitive, non-parallel, but incremental and well sequenced and structured manner, can be valuable, particularly in high schools. However, the production and availability of materials in many minority languages is difficult to achieve. Funding may be difficult to secure for such separate minority language materials.

Tenth, in a concurrent and purposeful use of two languages in the classroom as advocated by Jacobson (1990), there is a danger that teachers may be expected to manage an unnatural, artificial, and highly complex language situation demanded of teachers. Where teachers are expected to manage the concurrent use of two languages in a classroom, it assumes they have a very high level of management skill, monitoring and reflection. In reality, classrooms are busy, very fluid, often unpredictable places. Teachers have to react to the moment, to individual pupils who don't understand, with many situations being unplannable, unpredictable and spontaneous. Students themselves have an important influence on language use in the classroom, needing to communicate their understanding or lack of understanding in the most appropriate way. Classroom management of learning and behavior needs to be fluent, accepted by students and not abrupt and too unpredictable. Thus, language allocation in the classroom must fit naturally, predictably, fluently and flexibly into the complex management of the curriculum.

Further Reading

JACOBSON, R., 1990, Allocating Two Languages as a Key Feature of a Bilingual Methodology. In R. JACOBSON & C. FALTIS (ed.), *Language Distribution Issues in Bilingual Schooling*. Clevedon: Multilingual Matters Ltd.

WONG FILLMORE, L. & VALADEZ, C., 1986, Teaching Bilingual Learners. In M. C. WITTROCK (ed.), *Handbook of Research on Teaching* (3rd edition). New York: Macmillan.

2: Bilingual Methodology in Welsh Classrooms

Introduction

In North Wales, western districts (e.g. Gwynedd, Anglesey) generally have a strong bilingual education policy. In the old county of Gwynedd, such a policy was created in 1975 (and revised in 1986 and 1997). The 1986 policy declared that all children in the Gwynedd educational system should be fully bilingual in Welsh and English by the end of compulsory schooling at 16. This policy was implemented in various ways according to the linguistic nature of the catchment area of the school (i.e. according to whether there are more or fewer first language Welsh speakers in a community).

The current area of Gwynedd is one of the heartlands of the Welsh language, with over 60 percent of the population speaking Welsh according to the 1991 census figures. Many primary schools in Welsh-speaking areas have traditionally taught mainly in Welsh, and there is a strong Welsh component in the primary schools in more Anglicized areas. Special Welsh language immersion centers for primary age children were established where non-Welsh-speaking in-migrants can spend a term learning the language before entering primary school. Second language teachers visited primary schools to help Welsh learners with their language skills.

At secondary school level, advances have been made in extending Welsh-medium teaching to all areas of the curriculum, including Mathematics, Science and Computer Studies. Progress has also been made in the integration of native Welsh speakers and second language learners. Previously, Welsh learners, even those who had achieved a high standard in Welsh, tended to be segregated at secondary level and followed the majority of the curriculum in English. It was natural for them to speak English together, and their Welsh language skills tended to atrophy. The modern trend is to keep Welsh learners and native speakers together.

These new developments in bilingual education at secondary level have posed many challenges and some problems. These can be summarized as follows.

The unequal relationship between English and Welsh in the outside world

Although Welsh is still spoken by the majority of the inhabitants of Gwynedd, it is a minority language which must continually struggle for survival against the tremendous influence of English, a prestigious majority language used in all parts of the world. This means that the bias within schools must be towards Welsh to redress the balance. It also means that the tendency is to concentrate on improving the Welsh language skills of native speakers of English. However, there is a tendency to think that native speakers of Welsh will automatically be able to cope with the demands of the academic curriculum in English. In reality, both groups need help to develop their academic competence in both languages.

The necessity of teaching students of varying abilities in the two languages in the same class

This often means that both languages must be used, to fill in gaps in understanding and to explain more clearly.

The goal of developing ability in two languages across the curriculum

Bilingual education must involve more than the use of two languages across the curriculum. Ideally, there should be a structured plan to develop the four language skills in both languages, not just in language lessons, but in other curricular areas.

The Concurrent Use of Welsh and English in Schools in Gwynedd, North Wales

Cen Williams (1994) researched on the development of language skills across the secondary curriculum, and also on the use of concurrent methodologies in the bilingual classroom. His work is based on research carried out in Gwynedd secondary schools, but its conclusions are valuable for the development of bilingual education elsewhere in Wales and in other countries.

Cen Williams (1994) argues that the purposeful concurrent use of both languages in the classroom can be beneficial for the development of language skills in both languages, and also contribute towards a deeper understanding of the subject matter being studied. He maintains that it is not the amount of time allotted to each language in the lesson that is significant, but rather the use made and the activities allocated to each language. The aim should be to develop academic competence (CALP) in both languages, rather than just conversational competence (BICS) – see also page 93. Hearing a language spoken in a lesson is not enough, although it is important to use Welsh as the medium of communication inside

Cwestiynau

1 Dyluniwch gêm bysgota magnetig ar gyfer plant ifanc.
Gallech ddefnyddio magnet, clipiau papur, cerdyn, llinyn a ffon.
Gwnewch ddiagram a lluniwch reolau ar gyfer y gêm.

2 Dyluniwch boster i rybuddio plant ifanc rhag dringo peilonau trydan a mynd ar reilffyrdd trydanol.

3 Lluniwch ddiagram wedi ei labelu o fwlb golau.
Pa rannau sy'n; (a) ynysyddion? (b) ddargludyddion?

4 Yn y gylched a ddangosir yn y diagram, beth sy'n digwydd os:
(a) ceir swits A yn unig?
(b) ceir swits B yn unig?
(c) ceir switsys A a B?
(ch) A yw'r bylbiau mewn cyfres neu yn baralel?

5 (a) Mae llif trydan angen 2 swits er diogelwch.
Dyluniwch gylched fel bod rhaid i'r ddau swits fod ymlaen i gychwyn y llif, ond dim ond un swits sydd rhaid ei droi i ffwrdd i stopio'r llif.
(b) Mae banc angen system larwm lladron.
Dyluniwch gylched sydd â batri a chloch larwm y gellir ei switsio ymlaen gan ddau fotwm gwthio ar wahân.
(c) Pa un o'r cylchedau yma (a neu b) fyddech chi'n gallu ei ddefnyddio ar gyfer switsys clychau ar gyfer eich drws cefn a'r drws ffrynt?

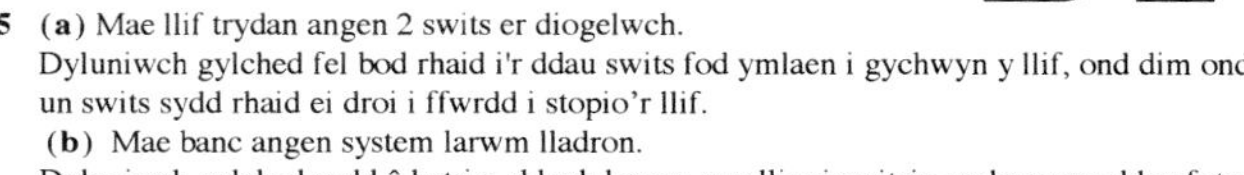

6 Mae'r diagram yn dangos un math o amedr.
Beth yw'r darlleniadau a, b, c ac ch?

7 Gwnewch ddiagram cylched i ddangos sut y gellir goleuo dau fwlb 6 folt yn ddisglair o ddau fatri 3 folt.

8 Mae pob un o'r darluniau isod yn dangos sefyllfa berylus. Ar gyfer pob un (i) ysgrifenwch frawddeg am beth sy'n anghywir (ii) dywedwch beth ddylid ei wneud i'w wneud yn ddiogel.

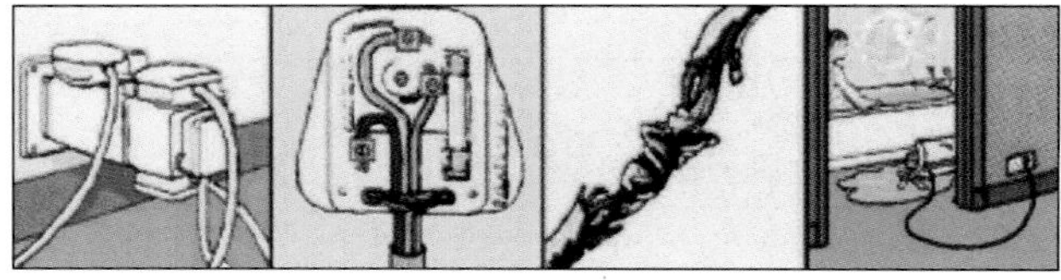

Questions

1 Design a 'magnetic fishing game' for young children. You could use a magnet, paper-clips, card, string and a stick. Draw a diagram and make a set of ruses for the game.

2 Design a poster to warn children against climbing electric pylons or going on to electric railway lines.

3 Draw a labelled diagram of a light bulb.
Which parts are: (a) insulators? (b) conductors?

4 In the circuit shown in the diagram, what happens if:
(a) switch A only is closed?
(b) switch B only is closed?
(c) A and B are closed?
(d) Are the bulbs in series or in parallel?

5 (a) An electric saw needs 2 switches for safety.
Design a circuit so that both switches must be 'on' to start the saw, but only one switch need be turned 'off' to stop the saw.
(b) A bank needs an alarm system. Design a circuit that has a battery and an alarm bell that can be switched on by 2 separate push-buttons.
(c) Which of these two circuits (a or b) could you use for door-bell switches at your front door and back door?

6 This diagram shows one kind of ammeter.
What are the readings a, b, c and d?

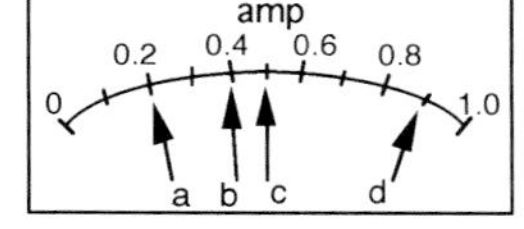

7 Draw a circuit diagram to show how two 6 volt bulbs can be lit brightly from two 3 volt batteries.

8 Each of the pictures below shows an unsafe situation. For each one:
(i) write a sentence about what is wrong (ii) say what sould be done to make it safe.

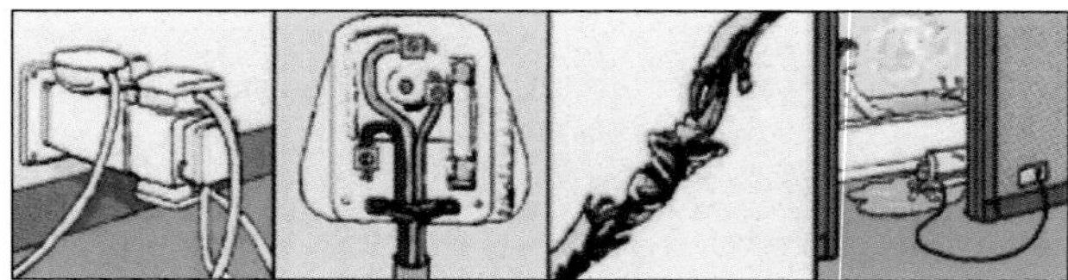

A bilingual (Welsh-English) Science work sheet.

and outside the class, and not just for academic activities. Thus, staff may use Welsh for personal conversations, class announcements, discussing the school trip, praise and censure. In addition, however, there must be a balanced program to develop the four language skills across the curriculum in both languages.

This means more than the random and unsystematized use of both languages. An example of the random use of both languages is as follows. A teacher might introduce a topic in English, making some remarks and giving some explanations in Welsh. Hand-outs and work sheets might be in English. Class activities e.g. discussions, experiments, might be carried out in the students' preferred language. The teacher would interact with small groups and individual students in a random mixture of Welsh and English. The students would complete the work sheet in English. This type of situation would not develop the students' competence in Welsh. To allow students to make progress in their language skills in both languages, there must be a variety of planned and made-to-measure activities to develop the four language skills of speaking, listening, reading and writing.

Williams (1994) describes some real instances of dual language use observed during his research that are also not helpful.

(a) Some forms of codeswitching by the teacher. This might include switching from one language to another in the middle of an explanation or presentation, to highlight or reiterate a point. It also includes instances where the teacher codeswitches in response to students, but where this upsets the language balance of the lesson. For instance, a teacher might be discussing a topic with the whole class in Welsh. When the teacher asks questions, some students answer in English. The teacher switches to English in response to the cue from these students. By the end of the discussion, the teacher is speaking entirely in English.

(b) Simple translation. This can be tedious and time consuming and does not aid the development of the students' weaker language since students tend to screen out the weaker language. Another danger of translation is that it can take the place of explanation. For instance, a student in a science class might ask *'Be' ydy ystyr anweddu?'*

(What is the meaning of *'anweddu'?'*) The teacher might reply 'evaporate'. The student might be more familiar with the English term, but would still have no real understanding of the scientific process of evaporation.

Beneficial methods include:

(a) Purposeful codeswitching by the teacher. This might occur during a class discussion, where the teacher switches languages to give a fuller explanation in a student's stronger language. It might happen during group work, or in one-to-one interaction, where the teacher might choose to address the student in his or her preferred language. Alternatively, where a pair or group of students has switched to their stronger language during a discussion or activity, a teacher might intervene using the weaker language, as a subtle way of persuading students to switch back to that language.

(b) *'Trawsieithu'* (literally: 'translanguaging'). This term describes the hearing or reading of a lesson, a passage in a book or a section of work in one language and the development of the work (i.e. by discussion, writing a passage, completing a work sheet, conducting an experiment) in the other language.

'Translanguaging' is a more specific term than the general umbrella term 'concurrent use of two languages'. In 'translanguaging', the input (reading or hearing) tends to be in one language, and the output (speaking or writing) in the other language.

For instance, a science work sheet in English might be read by the students. The teacher might initiate a discussion on the subject matter in Welsh, switching to English to elucidate a point for Welsh learners. The students might then have to do written work in Welsh.

Translanguaging has two potential advantages. Firstly, it may promote a deeper and fuller understanding of the subject matter. It is possible, in a monolingual teaching situation, for students to answer questions or write an essay about a subject without fully understanding it. Whole sentences or paragraphs can be copied or adapted out of a text book without really understanding them. It is less easy to do this in a bilingual situation. To read and discuss a topic in one language, and then to write about it in another language, means that the subject matter has to be properly 'digested'.

Secondly, 'translanguaging' may help students develop skills in their weaker language. Students might attempt the main part of the work in their stronger language and then undertake less challenging, related tasks in their weaker language. In a class mainly composed of Welsh learners, a topic might be introduced and discussed in English. An information sheet consisting of articles on the topic in both English and Welsh would be read. The Welsh articles would be shorter and written in a simple and straightforward fashion. The articles might be discussed in groups, with the teacher circulating the groups, and initiating discussion in both languages. Finally, a series of simple, written questions in Welsh might be set. This format would give the students the chance to work on their reading and writing skills in Welsh, and attempt to express the ideas they had absorbed in their stronger language.

Another example of 'translanguaging' might be a lesson delivered in Welsh, with the students taking notes in their preferred language, whether Welsh or English.

(c) Bilingual lesson notes and hand-outs. These are valuable if used in conjunction with a methodology that aims to develop and use both languages in the curriculum. If teaching in two languages means nothing more than translation, and if students are allowed to work solely in their stronger language, then students will tend to use one half only of bilingual lesson notes. However, if students are used to working in both languages, then bilingual lesson notes can be a valuable tool, with the student checking meanings by reference to both versions.

If the teacher switches languages for another activity during the lesson, bilingual lesson notes or hand-outs ensure that the relevant vocabulary is at hand in both languages.

Bilingual lesson notes can also facilitate home-school cooperation. They can be a valuable help to monolingual parents who wish to support their children in their school work.

(d) In some schools, subjects are taught on a modular or unit basis, with modules or units being taught alternately in English and Welsh. This approach officially encourages the separation of languages: in practice, both languages are often used concurrently in lessons (e.g. if a module is taught in English and the students' preferred language is Welsh, Welsh may be used by both students and teacher in discussions and practical work). If the course is well-structured, the main points of the syllabus can be covered in both languages and the basic technical and subject-specific vocabulary can be learnt in both English and Welsh. Thus the concurrent use of both languages is facilitated. This structured approach is particularly valuable with subjects that require a cumulative understanding, such as Science and Mathematics. As the headteacher of one Gwynedd secondary school commented, 'If the students have understood it in two languages, they've really understood it'.

(e) Bilingual examination papers. Up until the present time, bilingual teaching strategies have only been an option for the first three years in secondary school. At the beginning of the fourth year, students must opt to study

their subjects either entirely in Welsh or entirely in English, in preparation for the national examinations held at the end of the fifth year. So far, the Welsh Joint Education Committee, the body responsible for setting examination papers for the majority of Welsh schools, has been unwilling to set bilingual examination papers (with some exceptions), or give students the option of answering in more than one language. Its decision is based on the argument that the examination system should be fair and unbiased to all students. It argues that seeing and using both languages in an examination would give bilingual students an unfair advantage. Williams (1994) maintains that bilingual examination papers would give students in the fourth and fifth years of secondary school the option to continue to study in both languages, and to develop their ability in both languages.

(f) The integration of fluent Welsh speakers and Welsh learners of various levels of attainment. If the two groups are segregated, the tendency is for learners to be taught mainly in English, and to use only English with their peers in class. If they are integrated with Welsh speakers, and if strategic use is made of both languages in class, then the Welsh learners can develop their second language ability without detracting from the language balance of the lesson. Both groups can improve their language skills in their weaker language. This can be achieved in various ways.

Use of a methodology that is both teacher-centered and student-centered. The teacher decides on the format and language balance of the lesson, teaches from the front and initiates discussions and whole class work. However, there is opportunity for the students to work independently and in small groups, using both languages, according to their level of attainment.

Integration of native speakers and recent Welsh learners for practical lessons such as Physical Education and Technology. Since so much of the teaching is supported by visual cues and clues, comprehension is easier. It is possible for the teacher to introduce the topic or task in Welsh, and for Welsh learners to take notes in English. During the part of the lesson where the students take part in practical activities, the teacher has the opportunity to interact with them in small groups, or one-to-one. The teacher may choose to interact with individual students in their preferred language, or to initiate a discussion with learners in simple Welsh. Some schools also teach Personal Education and Pastoral Care through the medium of Welsh to Welsh learners, since the subject content deals with topics close to the students' personal experience, such as friendships, bullying and family problems.

The careful selection of the type of oral and written language used with the students. If a large proportion of the class are Welsh learners, oral presentation should be simple and straightforward, avoiding too much colloquial and idiomatic usage. Lesson notes should be simple, avoiding literary forms such as the short form of the passive, (e.g. *gwnaethpwyd* – it was done), which may not be familiar to the students, using instead the familiar periphrastic construction (e.g. *cafodd ei wneud*). Conversely, the teacher should ensure that the language input is sufficiently stimulating for the students, that it extends their abilities, and that the register of language used is appropriate for the task involved. It is important to ensure that the language does not become a burden and a barrier between the child and the subject matter.

The opportunity to develop the four language skills, speaking, listening, reading and writing through the medium of both English and Welsh. Students' spoken language can be subtly corrected, by the teacher repeating a statement with the correct form. Students can be encouraged to use their weaker language to make notes and to write essays, using terms and expressions from their stronger language if necessary. They can be helped to redraft for a final version.

Co-operation between the Welsh and English departments and other subject departments to establish the attainment level of individual students in either language. This will help other subject teachers to organize work in a way that will stimulate and develop students' abilities in both languages. Most specifically, it will avoid the situation where students who have attained a fair degree of competence in Welsh in the primary school are put in a class of Welsh learners on their arrival in secondary school. They follow most or all of the curriculum in English, speak English to their peers, and their Welsh language skills atrophy.

Williams (1994) acknowledges that many academics have maintained that the separation of two languages in the curriculum gives students the best chance to develop their language abilities. However, his research valuably shows how the concurrent use of two languages in the classroom arises inevitably in response to the reality of a bilingual school situation. He suggests how it can be used positively to deepen the students' understanding of curriculum material and also to facilitate the development of their competence in both languages. His research is a valuable contribution to the continuing debate.

Further Reading

WILLIAMS, C., 1994, Arfarniad o Ddulliau Dysgu ac Addysgu yng Nghyd-destun Addysg Uwchradd Ddwyieithog. Unpublished PhD thesis. Bangor: University of Wales.

WILLIAMS, C., 1996, Secondary Education: Teaching in the Bilingual Situation. In C. WILLIAMS, G. LEWIS & C. BAKER (eds), *The Language Policy: Taking Stock*. Llangefni (Wales): CAI.

3: Literacy among Bilingual Students

Introduction

In education systems throughout the world, reading and writing are usually regarded as central in the curriculum. In developed and developing countries, literacy is often associated with progress, civilization, social mobility and economic advancement. A classic, if much disputed claim, is by Anderson (1966) who suggests that any society requires a 40 percent literacy rate for economic 'take off', a belief which is embedded in many literacy programs.

Irrespective of whether bilingual students are found in highly literate societies (e.g the United States and much of Europe), or whether children come from less literate societies, the ability to read and write is often regarded as essential for personal survival, security and status. Literacy impacts on people's daily lives in innumerable ways. Where language minority members are relatively powerless and underprivileged, literacy is often regarded as a major key to self advancement as well as empowerment. If this is so, it is important to consider the needs or uses for literacy in students and adults in bilingual and multicultural societies.

In considering such needs and uses, it is important to note that literacy education for language minority students is often in a majority language (e.g. English language literacy in the United Kingdom and the United States; English or French in parts of Africa as an 'official' or international language). However, where language minorities have access to bilingual education, literacy may be introduced in the home/minority language. This issue is considered in the latter part of this section.

Minority language literacy can be crucial for the survival, revival or enhancement of a minority language. At both the individual and the group level, minority language literacy gives that language increased functions and usage. A minority language has a greater chance of survival when bureaucracy and books, newspapers and magazines, adverts and signposts are in that language. This may help to avoid the colonial situation where the majority language is used for all literacy purposes and the vernacular language is used purely for oral communication. Where oral communication is in the minority language and literacy is in the majority language, that minority language may have less chance of survival. The survival of a minority language depends on it having a function or

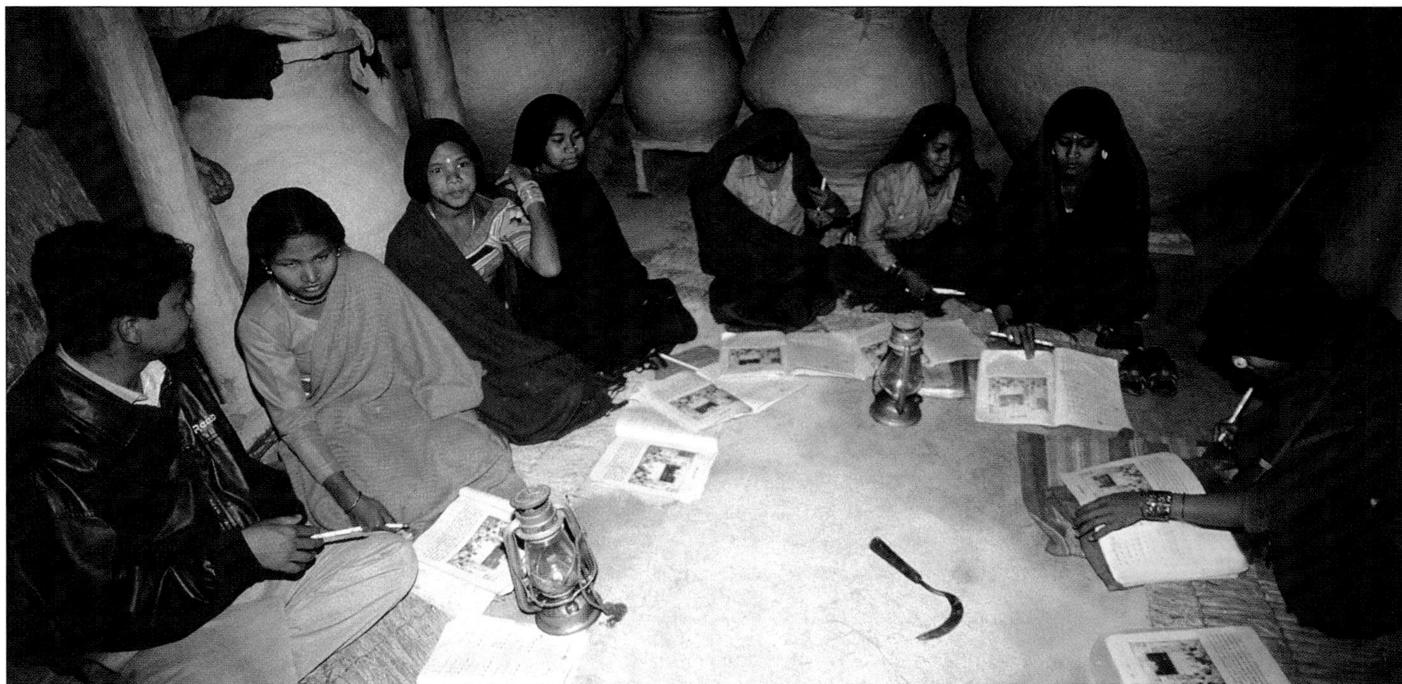

Adult literacy classes in Tulsipur, Nepal.

Informal outdoor education in India.

role in a great number of domains, and also on its public profile and status. If speakers of a minority language are not literate in that language, this restricts the number of domains in which it can be used, and tends to confine it to a domestic, low profile role.

The importance and usefulness of literacy for language minorities is revealed in public perceptions of those who are illiterate. Being unable to read and write is often regarded as shameful, embarrassing, a symbol of low or marginal status, and in need of remedying in school or in adult classes. Reducing illiteracy is regarded as a key priority in UNESCO's aims, irrespective of country, continent, culture or caste.

Reading literature in the minority language may be both for education and recreation, for instruction and for enjoyment. Whether literature is regarded as aiding moral teaching, of value as an art form, or as a form of vicarious experience, literacy is both an emancipator and an educator.

Literacy in the minority language also enables the attendant culture to be accessed and reproduced. Literacy in the minority language is of value because it recreates the past in the present. It may both reinforce and extend the oral transmission of a minority culture. Minority language oracy without literacy can disempower the student. Literacy in the minority language not only provides a greater chance of survival at an individual and group level for that language. It also may encourage rootedness, self-esteem, the vision and world-view of one's heritage culture, self-identity and intellectual empathy. Literacy enables access to language minority stories that not only shape and develop thinking. Children develop concepts through stories (oral and written). Stories are a strong means of making sense of the world and hence affect the structure of human cognition. Biliteracy gives access to different and varied social and cultural worlds. Does this in turn lead to more diversified cognitive abilities, an increased ability to process and manipulate ideas and symbols? The research of Swain & Lapkin (1991a) points to first language literacy and then biliteracy as a strong source of cognitive and curriculum advantage for bilinguals.

The Uses of Literacy in Bilingual and Multicultural Societies

The idea that literacy and, preferably, biliteracy is desirable for language minorities and for bilingual societies may seem self-evident. But it is not simple to define precisely what is meant by literacy, and what kind of literacy might be a desirable goal for a language minority community, for instance.

There are many possible uses for literacy in modern society. Literacy can be essential for day-to-day survival (e.g. reading road signs and food labels). It is essential for education, for citizenship and for personal empowerment (e.g. participating in local or regional government, reading newspapers or political pamphlets). It is needed for personal contact (e.g. writing letters) and for personal pleasure and creativity (e.g. reading magazines and novels). It is required for many kinds of higher status and higher paid employment. Lastly, literacy is needed to

Functional and Critical Literacy in the Classroom

The functional view of literacy compared with the critical view of literacy is paralleled by two stereotypes of literacy classrooms. In one style, there is much teacher talk, much student listening, closed and factual questions rather than open and stimulating questions, with silence and control very evident. The hidden curriculum is that teachers are implicitly teaching dependence upon authority, correct and convergent thinking, social control, passive involvement, neutral thinking and passive learning. Knowledge is posed as static, correct and inert, to be internalized and reproduced when necessary. The critical literacy concept is that children should learn to search out differing authorities often with differing viewpoints, to depend on their own judgement, to think divergently and creatively, to work cooperatively and sociably, to avoid accepting knowledge and to question its source and motive, to be actively involved in learning, and, if necessary, to be critical of social, economic and political issues in their own and their community's lives. Knowledge is seen as dynamic, ever changing, always relative, a catalyst for further inquiry and a catalyst for action. Cummins (1994a) sums this up as follows:

Transmission-style

Language is decomposed; knowledge is inert; learning is hierarchical, by internalization, moving from the simple to the complex. This may be connected to a social control orientation where curriculum topics are neutralized in respect to societal power relations and students are expected to be compliant and uncritical.

Critical approach

Language is meaningful; knowledge is catalytic, and there is a joint interactive construction of knowledge through critical enquiry within a student's zone of proximal development. This may be connected to a social transformation orientation where curriculum topics are focused on issues relevant to power relationships and students are enabled to become critical and empowered.

The literacy that is developed in classrooms varies considerably in reality and escapes neat classification into transmission and critical literacy orientations. However the stereotyped positing of two opposites, while simple and sometimes extreme, reflects a key debate in literacy development in language minority children. The following lists some of the practical characteristics of the functional literacy and critical literacy classrooms.

Functional literacy/transmission classrooms

1. Literacy is getting the correct answers on worksheets, filling in blanks, circling appropriate answers.
2. Literacy is answering closed questions having read a story.
3. Literacy is reading words, sometimes without understanding their meaning.
4. Literacy is reading aloud to the teacher and the rest of the class, being perfect in pronunciation, intonation and accent.
5. Literacy is spelling words correctly, and writing in correct grammar.
6. Literacy is mechanically going through exercises, practicing skills, and giving correct answers on tests.
7. Literacy is learning to do but not necessarily to think.

Critical literacy classrooms

1. Literacy is seeing oneself as an active reader and writer.
2. Literacy involves enjoying reading, developing independent thoughts and judgments about reading and writing.
3. Literacy is sharing ideas, reflections, experiences and reactions with others in the classroom, both peers and teachers.
4. Literacy is gaining insights into oneself, one's life in the family and the community, into social and political control, the use of print and other mass media to inform, persuade and influence so as to maintain the status quo.
5. Literacy is about understanding the power relationships that lie behind reading and writing.
6. Literacy is about constructing and reconstructing meaning, critically examining the range of meanings in the story and outside the story.
7. Literacy is active writing for various purposes and audiences, often to influence and assert.
8. Literacy is about developing consciousness, increased self-reflection, increased reflection about status, power, wealth and privilege in society.
9. Literacy is about developing critical thinking habits, creative imagination, and posing alternatives, some of which may be radical.
10. Literacy is about learning and interpreting the world, explaining, analyzing, arguing about and acting upon the world in which a person lives.

Amerindian children reading with their mother in Ecuador.

empower the mind. Wells & Chang-Wells (1992) suggest that literate thinking is 'the building up, metaphorically speaking, of a set of mental muscles that enable one effectively to tackle intellectual tasks that would otherwise be beyond one's powers' (page 122). Literacy is seen as a mode of thinking, as a means of reasoning, reflecting and interacting with oneself. This links with the idea of the empowerment of individuals, and having a public voice.

Whether language minority children should first become literate in the majority language or in their minority language will be discussed later in this section. Also considered later will be whether majority language monoliteracy or biliteracy should be attempted. Before engaging such discussions, it is important to explore the kind of literacy that language minority students and adults require.

Definitions of Literacy

The list of needs for literacy given above has already hinted that literacy plays different roles for different people and for different cultures. While for some cultures literacy is about promoting abstract thought, rationality, critical thinking, balanced and detached awareness, empathy and sensitivity, for other cultures literacy is about memorization, transmission of life stories revealing the heritage, values and morality, and centrally in certain religions, for the transmission of rules of religious and moral behavior. Orthodox Jews learn classical Hebrew to read the Torah. Muslims become literate in classical Arabic to study the Qur'ān. In some cultures, the mother is expected to read to her children and help them develop literacy skills, but is not expected to read national newspapers or complete bureaucratic forms herself. The concept of literacy is therefore not single but plural, relative to a culture and not universal. The concept of literacy held by a nation or culture will affect the approach to literacy.

Approaches to Literacy

The skills approach

In 1962, UNESCO published a definition of a literate person as someone who 'has acquired the essential knowledge and skills which enable him to engage in all those activities in which literacy is required for effective functioning in his group and whose attainments in reading, writing and arithmetic make it possible for him to continue to use those skills towards his own and the community's developments' (cited in Oxenham, 1980, page 87).

The concept of functional literacy, as in the UNESCO definition, appears to assume that literacy is primarily a technical skill, neutral in its aims and universal across languages. The skills of reading and writing can be categorized into vocabulary, grammar and composition. Teaching sounds and letters, phonics and standard language may be the important focus. Errors in reading and writing will also incur keen attention, alongside a concern with achieving scores on tests of reading and writing. Such tests tend to assess fragmented and decontextualized language skills, eliciting superficial comprehension rather than deeper language thinking and understanding.

Underlying the skills approach to literacy there tends to be a belief that children need functional or 'useful' literacy only. Effective functioning implies that the student or adult will contribute in a collaborative, constructive and non-critical manner to the smooth running of the local community. Functional literacy is perceived as recognizing the status quo, understanding and accepting one's place in society, and being a 'good citizen'.

While there are various types of literacy, it is important not to forget the amount of illiteracy and low levels of literacy in many countries. Functional literacy does not mean reading print in 'quality' newspapers and books. Functional literacy is at a lower level: being able to read labels on tins and road signs, finding a number in a telephone directory. Functional literacy may not be enough in advanced, technological societies. The populace constantly faces bureaucratic forms and written instructions which demand more advanced literacy skills. Functional literacy is unlikely to be enough to cope with such complex tasks

The Whole Language approach

The Whole Language approach to literacy is diametrically opposed to reading and writing as decoding and a series of separate skills. The Whole Language approach emphasizes learning to read and write naturally, for real purposes, for meaningful communication and for inherent pleasure. Writing means reflecting on one's ideas and

sharing meaning with others. Writing can be in partnership with others, involving drafting and redrafting.

In the Whole Language approach, reading and writing involve real and natural events, not artificial stories, artificial sequences, rules of grammar and spelling, or stories that are not relevant to student's experiences. Reading and writing need to be interesting, relevant, allowing choice by the learner, giving students power and understanding of their world. In reality, a Whole Language approach and attention to the skills of literacy are combined eclectically by many practicing teachers.

The Whole Language approach also has features that overlap with functional literacy. The child can be viewed by the Whole Language approach as a relatively non-critical, monocultural, assimilated being. Literacy can be about socialization into customary, normative values and beliefs. In such an approach to literacy, the meaning of text can be decoded because it has a definite, autonomous meaning. Reading therefore is detecting the meaning of the author; writing is conveying meaning to readers. Thus, the Whole Language approach can still result in an uncritical, accepting attitude by the child. For language minority students, in stigmatized, racist and prejudiced contexts, this may not be seen as empowering.

The construction of meaning approach

A recent consideration of literacy (partly connected to the Whole Language approach) emphasizes that readers bring their own meanings to text, that reading and writing is essentially a construction and reconstruction of meaning. Part of this consideration is that the meaning individuals give to a text depends on their culture, personal experiences and histories, personal understandings of the themes and tone of text, and the particular social context where reading occurs. As will be revealed later, this idea has implications for language minority children and adults.

Readers bring meaning with them to texts. They make sense of a text from previously acquired knowledge. Without relevant background knowledge, readers may fail to construct any meaning at all. To help construct meaning, we need to know what kind of text it is, is it a folk story or a real event, or is it an advertisement that seeks to persuade? It helps to know who has written the text, what are their background and persuasion. A reader's current knowledge, family background, social and economic lifestyle, and political orientation will all affect how the reader constructs meaning from the text.

Different students of varying backgrounds will make different meanings from the text. When there is a mismatch between the reader's knowledge and that which is assumed by the writer, the construction of meaning will be difficult. This is the 'vicious circle' situation faced by many illiterate adults. They are denied access to certain kinds of knowledge and understanding of the world because they cannot read. Because they do not understand what is being taken for granted by writers of adult material, becoming literate as an adult is made difficult. Language minority groups in particular can be caught in this 'vicious circle' situation. Trying to make sense out of texts from a different culture, with different cultural assumptions, makes predicting the storyline and understanding the text more difficult.

To help children construct meaning from text, teachers need to be aware that literacy in classrooms exists in a social context, guided by culturally-bound ways of thinking. In classrooms, there are adult and educational criteria of relevant and appropriate ways of responding, reading and writing. Students have to learn about the rules of behavior for the different literacy events that teachers create. A typical teacher-student interaction is an initiation by the teacher, response by the student, followed by evaluation by the teacher. This signals expectancies and rules not only of classroom behavior, but also of literacy. There are rights and wrongs, authoritative knowledge and culturally inappropriate responses. The power relationships of the classroom shape language and literacy use. The social roles of students and teachers are taught and embedded in literacy events of the classroom. As will be argued later in this topic, to promote literacy, teachers need to expand rather than limit students' roles so that literacy needs can be fully met. Children need to be empowered through celebrating the different uses of literacy, including critical literacy.

The further reading and writing develops, the more text becomes socially and culturally embedded. The reading process within is shaped by the social forces from without. Dyson (1989) and Graves (1983) have shown how young writers develop and change in the midst of social influences from peers, teachers and influences from out-

United States Minority Groups and Preparation for School Literacy

Research from the United States from Shirley Brice Heath (1986) showed how Chinese United States families, for example tend towards parent-controlled conversations that closely mirror the type of language behavior expected in many formal classrooms. The parents asked children factual questions, evaluated their language, and gave verbal correction and elaboration. Thus a certain form of literacy behavior and literacy use was established. Chinese United States families saw their role as complementing that of the school in literacy. Such parents saw themselves as active agents in their children's literacy development.

In contrast, Mexican United States parents often expected the extended family to share some of the responsibility for child-rearing. Such parents seldom expected conversations with their children while they were working. They relatively rarely asked questions of the children to assess their knowledge, understanding or attitudes. Older children within such families were expected to entertain the younger children. Younger children rarely interacted with just one adult, often being surrounded by a larger number of adults and children. However, young children grew up in a rich language environment, and although little conversation was directed specifically at them, they experienced the constant flow of language between adults, and between adults and other children. Children were taught to be respectful of adults, and usually not to initiate social conversations with them. This cultural behavior is directly related to literacy expectations and uses. That is, literacy is not a separate cultural event, but mirrors in its form and function general socialization practices. This tends to vary from the expectations of school language use where interaction with the teacher in formal classrooms is expected. In such formal classrooms, it is not expected that children should interact only with other children. Thus a mismatch may occur between patterns of language and literacy in the home and that expected in schools. For different cultural and ethnic groups, this may make school a more frightening, difficult and strange experience. The transition from the language and literacy of home to school may be more difficult for some language communities than for others. The differences between language minorities, as well as between such minorities and the language majority may affect the acquisition of literacy in school.

In Shirley Brice Heath's (1982) research, certain preschool children gained experience of books with their parents in a manner which paralleled that of teachers in elementary schools. The initiation-reply-evaluation sequence so often used by teachers was used by a particular group of parents. Such students were therefore prepared for the literacy culture of teachers in classrooms and had also learnt to build book knowledge on to their own experience of the world and use it to frame and express that experience. These students had implicitly learnt that literacy provides new dimensions of experience. Such 'school-prepared' children had also been taught by their parents to 'listen and wait'. They had grown accustomed to listening to adults reading stories and waiting to the end before asking questions. Thus they became used to using books in a way that they would experience for most of their schooling.

Shirley Brice Heath (1982, 1983) also described two communities in the United States who had different literacy practices, important in themselves, but which did not match school-oriented literacy practices. Roadville children were members of working class, committed Christian parents who used literacy for Biblical and moral instruction. Fictional writing was rejected in favor of reading about real events that contained a moral message. The reading of a book in this community was a performance, rather than an interactive event. Books were used to inform and instruct a passive audience. 'Roadville adults do not extend either the context or the habits of literacy events beyond book reading. They do not, upon seeing an item or event in the real world, remind children of a similar event in a book and launch a running commentary on similarities and differences.' (Shirley Brice Heath 1982, page 61).

Thus Roadville children regarded a story as a real event containing accurate facts and as a lesson about being a good Christian. Fictional accounts of real events were regarded as lying. Reality and the truth were needed, not fiction. Roadville children were socialized into a particular world view, a particular series of norms and beliefs, and specific beliefs about the uses (and uses 'to be avoided') of literacy. Such children were encouraged and rewarded for telling stories that derived a moral message from real experience. While some may see such families as failing to prepare the children for the literacy events of the school, another view is that the school fails to respond to the preferred literacy style of this type of community. A third view is that all children need to be exposed to the widest variety of 'cultures of literacy' and know what alternative functions exist for literacy. Shirley Brice Heath (1982) concludes that literacy can only be understood and interpreted 'in relation to the larger sociocultural patterns which they may exemplify or reflect. For example, ethnography must describe literacy events in their sociocultural context, so we may come to understand how such patterns as time and space usage, care giving roles, and age and sex segregation are interdependent with the types and features of literacy events a community develops.' (page 7).

side school such as the local community, political movements and ideological forces.

Similarly, writing is not just a technical process of putting words down on paper with correct spellings and correct grammatical structure. Writing is sharing meaning. When students and adults write, they have an interpersonal purpose. They write in order to be read by an audience, to inform, persuade, influence or purely delight readers. In writing, there is an anticipation of a response or reaction from the audience. We write with some kind of understanding of the background, knowledge and culture of our readers. We use language in different ways to meet particular purposes. Newspaper editorials sometimes try to persuade. Cookery books try to inform and explain. Poets try to give deeper and fresh meanings. The effectiveness of writing depends on the writer being familiar with the conventions expected by readers. This all suggests that literacy is a social event and not a private, personal event. We often discuss our reading and writing with other people, making the social dimension of literacy even more prominent.

This leads to an argument that literacy is not just about information gathering and giving. It is also about developing thinking that is appropriate within a culture. Thus Wells & Chang-Wells (1992) conceive of literacy as 'a mode of thinking that deliberately makes use of language, whether spoken or written, as an instrument for its own development' (page 123).

The sociocultural literacy approach

A related and overlapping approach to the construction of meaning approach spotlights the enculturation aspect of literacy. For example, a language minority literacy program may be enthusiastic to ensure the child is fully socialized and enlightened in the heritage culture.

Sociocultural literacy is the ability to construct appropriate cultural meaning when reading. In theory, a person can be functionally literate but culturally illiterate (e.g. reading without meaning). In reading and writing, we bring not only previous experience, but also our values and beliefs enabling us to create meaning from what we read and insert understanding into what we write. Reading and writing are acts of construction by the individual. The cultural heritage is discovered and internalized in reading. While reading and writing have certain overt, testable skills, there is an information processing activity ensuring enculturation. Beyond the observable skills of reading and writing is cultural literacy. For some people, such cultural literacy may lead to assimilation and integration (e.g. accenting the values embedded in English classics). Assimilationists may argue for a common literacy, transmitting the majority language culture to ensure assimilation of minority groups within the wider society.

In contrast, a cultural pluralist viewpoint will argue that national unity is not sacrificed by cultural literacy in the minority language or multicultural literacy. Multicultural literacy is likely to give a wider view of the world, a more extensive view of human history and custom, and a less narrow view of science and society.

Discussion of the social and cultural context of literacy raises the importance of literacy in the mother tongue. While the educational feasibility of this is discussed later, for the moment the educational argument is that literacy is most easily and most effectively learnt in the home language. The cultural argument is that mother tongue literacy gives access to the wealth of local and ethnic heritage contained in the literature. However, mother tongue literacy, while often culturally advantageous, is sometimes not without practical problems and objections. Some native languages do not yet have a formal grammar or a writing system, have few educational materials for teaching purposes, a shortage of teachers and teacher training. Political objections include native language literacy being an impediment to national unity and in-migrant assimilation and the cost of maintaining a variety of indigenous and 'in-migrant' languages in a region. Preservationists may wish to preserve literacy in the mother tongue in order to resist change.

Where there is much variety of language cultures within a region, support for local literacies may be found. Local literacies are literacy practices identified with local and regional cultures (as different from national culture). Such local literacies may be forgotten by international and national literacy campaigns or there may be tensions between local and national/international literacy practice. Local literacies (for examples, see Street, 1994), avoid the impoverishment of uniformity in literacy that is created by the dominance of English. They make literacy relevant to people's lives, their local culture and community relationships.

The social and cultural context of literacy importantly includes the relationship between an ethnic community and literacy acquisition. What counts as reading differs between cultures, subcultures and ethnic groups. As Gregory (1993, 1994) demonstrates in a study of British Bangladeshi and Chinese families, the purposes of reading, the resources provided by the home and the process of parents helping their children to read may vary with the school. Indeed, the varying expectations of home and school may produce a mismatch or a conflict that leads to uncertainty in the child, low achievement and even failure. She contrasts the school and language minority

Developing Critical Literacy in the Classroom

At school level, the critical literacy approach is that learners should not just be invited to retell a story. They should be encouraged to offer their own interpretation of text. From the beginning, children should be encouraged to interpret and evaluate who is the writer, what is their perspective and bias, what kind of moral interpretation is made? What alternative interpretations and viewpoints are possible? Children will be encouraged not just to find the right answer to such questions, but to look critically at multiple viewpoints. Multicultural and multilingual children may be given diverse pieces of writing that reflect different cultural knowledge and attitudes. Differences in interpretation, and differences in experience and knowledge children bring to the text can be contrasted and compared. This involves a change in teacher and student roles in the classroom. Teachers become facilitators rather than transmitters of authoritative knowledge. Literacy development becomes a joint developmental and co-operative event rather than duplicating the dominant-subservient relationship that often occurs in classrooms and which mirrors political domination and subservience.

For example, rather than children being solely taught that Columbus discovered America and that Columbus was a hero whose arrival brought civilization and salvation to the indigenous population, teachers may broaden out and invite students to search out other views about Columbus. Having read that Columbus initiated the slave trade, cut off the hands of any indigenous people who failed to bring him gold, and that the indigenous population suffered when Spanish rule was established, students would be asked to write their own critical versions of not only the life and contribution of Columbus, but also the way that Columbus is treated in many historical texts. Students will be encouraged by discovery methods to find that historical facts about Columbus have been selectively treated and interpreted by historians. More than one viewpoint is possible. One single viewpoint is both dangerous and biased, even if it is politically desirable and comfortable.

A statue of Christopher Columbus at La Paz, Bolivia. Columbus is commonly portrayed as a brave and worthy pioneer, but he was also cruel, callous and greedy.

The Role of Creative Imagination

One dimension that is missing from the dualism of transmission and critical literacy approaches is the idea of the importance of extending a child's imagination and sheer enjoyment in reading. Much of what children and adults read is for leisure and pleasure, and while not politically neutral or morally objective, novels, magazines, comics and some poetry are designed to satisfy and stir the imagination. The importance of developing aesthetic appreciation, interpersonal sensitivity, and enjoyment is one part of another dualism: between the use of reading books and real books in classrooms. This dualism is now discussed, particularly because it brings out ideas about stimulating the creative imagination through literacy.

Reading books, sometimes called basal readers, or graded reading books, are written primarily to teach reading. They aim to provide instruction in the skills of reading and writing, being firmly sequenced and written so that vocabulary and grammar is tightly controlled in a theoretically ever increasing incline of difficulty. The learning of technical skills of reading are the prime aim of these books. Such graded series of readers move from smaller to larger skill elements, in a carefully controlled sequence of learning.

Such basal reading books tend to promote the ability to recognize rather than to comprehend. The child may be able to read out loud to the teacher yet not understand the meaning and inner meanings of the stories.

One alternative is the reading of 'real books'. 'Real books' is a term used to describe books that entertain, sometimes inform, often have a point and an aim that is much more than purely 'reading skills improvement' in children. While reading books are written primarily to teach reading, 'real books' will be written by people who describe themselves as authors. While too often these books in secondary and high schools are subverted for purposes similar to those that typify the use of basal readers, emphasizing comprehension and the drawing of inferences, such books are originally intended for recreation, enjoyment and to stir the imagination.

'Real books' should, but do not always, avoid the overwhelming 'white', middle class, male perspectives that are manifestly and latently present in so much of children's literature, where boys are often given the leading roles, with girls the more passive supporting roles.

'Robert climbed the tree and looked down the valley. "Let's go down the valley and search for gold" said Robert, while Ruth stood in the shade of the tree and agreed. Robert bravely led the way and Ruth followed in his tracks'.

Books which fit into a critical literacy tradition need to challenge stereotypes. These include stereotyped gender roles, traditional roles ascribed to mothers and fathers, the absence of African and Asian people and ethnic minorities or their portrayal as subservient or inferior.

While reality has to be portrayed, understood and criticized by students, they also need informing about alternatives. Reading needs to reflect and challenge contemporary reality, and pose different life styles and values. Ethnic minorities need to be presented, not in restricted stereotyped social contexts, but outside their stereotypes so as to challenge the status quo.

parents' differing viewpoints and practices. The school teaches reading for recreation and enjoyment; the family wants literacy for utilitarian purposes (e.g. avoiding unemployment and poverty, for trading and business transactions). The school literacy policy aims for a child-centered, individualized approach, with teacher as facilitator, partner and guide, allowing a wide choice of colorful attractive books. An ethnic group may in contrast provide literacy classes in Saturday schools, at the Mosque or Temple, with large-class tuition, the teacher as an authority and director, with learning the will of Allah, for example, the valued outcome. A treasured Bible, the Qur'ān or other holy or highly valued book may be the focus of reading.

Gregory (1993, 1994) further compares the style of literacy teaching. In school, the child is socialized gently into the 'literary club' via 'playing' with books in a relaxed atmosphere with little correction of mistakes. In ethnic Saturday schools, for example, children learn by rote, repeating letters, syllables and phrases until perfect. There is continuous practice, testing and correction of mistakes in a reasonably strict and disciplined regime, with an expectation that the child will succeed.

The mismatch of school and ethnic group literacy expectations and practices may be tragic for the child. The child is caught between two literacy worlds, two versions of appropriate literacy behavior, and in the middle of a clash between home and school concepts of literacy. Despondency, learning paralysis, low motivation and disaffection with school may result for the child. However, other children successfully negotiate a path between two literacy worlds. Some teachers are particularly successful in engineering such a successful rapprochement, particularly when there is collaboration and dialogue with parents.

The critical literacy approach

Literacy can work to maintain the status quo, to ensure that those with power and dominance in society influence and even control what the masses read and think. Propaganda, political pamphlets, newspapers and books, formal and informal education can all be used to attempt to control the thinking and minds of the masses.

Thus, those in power maintain control over those who could be subversive to social order, or democratically challenge their power base. Literacy can be used to instill certain preferred attitudes, beliefs and thoughts. Similarly, some religious traditions deliberately use literacy to ensure that their members are influenced, at the least, by texts, at the worst, by brainwashing. Careful selection by religious leaders and parents over what their children read, is an attempt to use literacy to control and contain the mind.

Graff (1979) has shown that in 19th-century Canada, literacy was used for normative, controlling purposes. Illiterates were conceived as dangerous to the social stability, as alien to the dominant culture, representing a threat to the established order. Thus, an effort to increase literacy was a political move to maintain and further the position of the ruling elite. Since the elite realized that literacy could also lead to radical beliefs and ideas antagonistic to those in power, the teaching of literacy was carefully controlled.

Graff (1979) also attempted to show that literacy did not necessarily improve a person's chances of acquiring employment, wealth or power. Certain ethnic groups were disadvantaged, whatever their literacy rates, while others disproportionately obtained employment despite their relatively high illiteracy rates. For example, Irish Catholics in Canada did badly, irrespective of being literate or illiterate. In comparison, English Protestants fared better. Similarly, literate North African Americans did relatively less well than other literate people. Whether literacy was an advantage or disadvantage depended on ethnicity. Being unemployed or in the worst paid jobs was a function more of ethnic background than of illiteracy.

Those with power and dominance in society also maintain their position by their view of what is 'correct language'. Ethnic minorities with little political and economic power are often taught that their very patterns of speech and writing are inferior, and are connected with their economic deprivation. Such groups are expected to adopt standard majority language use (e.g. to speak 'proper' or 'correct' English).

Some forms of literacy education in schools and adult classes pose literacy as a technical skill. The emphasis is on reading skills rather than comprehension, on being able to say the words and copy down words from a blackboard, with less emphasis on meaning and understanding. Students are not allowed to ask questions. Rather they are expected to read aloud large chunks of text that are subsequently corrected for pronunciation, stress and fluency. This restricted form of literacy is still present in many schools in all continents of the world.

The functional view of literacy, as evidenced in the UNESCO definition given earlier, can be used to maintain the status quo, a stable political structure, to avert subversion or activism among the masses. National literacy may promote integration of the masses and different ethnic groups. National literacy may attempt to promote

unification and standardization of both language and culture. Literacy education always has ideological roots (Street, 1984).

At its worst, this restricted, functional literacy can maintain oppression, a distance between elites and the subservient, and not focus on the empowering and 'critical consciousness' possibilities of literacy.

In colonization and 'missionary' movements, a different kind of cultural standardization was sometimes attempted. For example, when literacy was brought by the missionaries to non-Christian areas of the world in the 19th century, the aim was to spread the Christian gospel, control the thinking, and affect the moral behavior of those who were assumed to be 'primitive' and 'heathen'. In literacy projects in developing countries in the 20th century, literacy has often been promoted for economic development. A literate workforce was considered essential for economic growth. Yet such programs were also used, consciously or subconsciously, to shore up the established order in a social system founded on injustice and inequality. Literacy in such programs has sometimes been used to condition the masses, to consolidate existing divisions of labor.

There is an alternative to using literacy as a way of showing people how to work co-operatively within a system from the perspective of people in power. Literacy can be a tool of oppression; it can also be a liberator (Hornberger, 1994b). It can be bar to opportunity; or a means of opening a door to empowerment. One way of attempting to empower people is through critical literacy. Freire (1970, 1973, 1985) and Freire & Macedo (1987) have argued for a literacy that makes oppressed communities socially and politically conscious of their subservient role and lowly status in society. The argument is that literacy must go well beyond the skills of reading and writing. It must make people aware of their sociocultural context and their political environment. This may occur through mother tongue literacy, multilingual literacy (and local/national/international 'multiple' literacies of value in differing contexts) and local literacies.

For language minority speakers, literacy for empowerment can be about literacy stimulating language activism, the demand for language rights, self determination and an equitable share of power. Freire's literacy education in Brazil's peasant communities and with other oppressed groups around the world first teaches such people that they must become conscious about their subordinate role and inferior position in their community and society. People afterwards become empowered to change their own lives, own situations and communities.

An Assimilationist Approach to Cultural Literacy

A well known example of a majority assimilationist approach to cultural literacy is Hirsch's book (1988) *Cultural Literacy: What Every American Needs To Know.* In the Appendix to the book, Hirsch (1988) provides a list of 5000 items of what 'literate Americans know', or should know by the end of high school. The entry below lists the letter 'j' entries to provide a flavor of the entries. Such a list is intended as a 'reliable index of American literate culture' for 'effective national communication' and to 'insure domestic tranquility' (pages xi and xii). Yet, it mainly reflects North American, 'white', middle class, Christian and classical culture. It is the culture of those in power and fails to represent adequately Latino, Asian or native Indian culture.

Jack and Jill (rhyme), *Jack and the Beanstalk* (title), Jack be Nimble (text), Jack Frost, jack-of-all-trades – master-of-none, Andrew Jackson, Jesse Jackson, Stonewall Jackson, Jacksonian democracy, Jacksonville, Jack Sprat (text), Jacob and Esau, Jacobin, Jacob's Ladder (song,) Jakarta, Jamaica, Henry James, Jesse James, William James, Jamestown settlement, Janus, jargon, Jason and the Golden Fleece, Java, jazz, Thomas Jefferson, Jehovah, Jehovah's Witnesses, *Dr Jekyll and Mr Hyde* (title), *je ne sais quoi*, Jeremiah, Battle of Jericho, Jersey City, Jerusalem, Jesuits, Jesus Christ, jet stream, Jew, Jezebel, *jihad*, Jim Crow, jingoism, Joan of Arc, The Book of Job, Johannesburg, Gospel according to Saint John, John Birch Society, John Brown's Body (song), John Bull, John Doe, John Henry (song), Pope John Paul II, Andrew Johnson, Lyndon B. Johnson, Samuel Johnson, John the Baptist, Pope John XXIII, *joie de vivre*, Joint Chiefs of Staff, joint resolution, Jolly Roger, Jonah and the whale, John Paul Jones, Scott Joplin, Jordan, River Jordan, Joseph and his brothers, Chief Joseph, Saint Joseph, Joshua, Joshua Fit the Battle of Jericho (song), journeyman, James Joyce, Judaism, Judas Iscariot, Judge not that ye be not judged, Judgment Day, Judgment of Paris, judicial branch, judicial review, *Julius Caesar* (title), Carl Jung, Juno (Hera), junta, Jupiter (planet), Jupiter (Zeus), justification by faith, justify the ways of God to men, juvenilia.

Through literacy, one can understand political power and activity, leading to collectively working together to change society, operating appropriately, able to challenge and complain, to assert natural rights, and to demand equality of access, opportunity and treatment. Through critical reflection on texts, information and propaganda, people will have a growing consciousness, an influence over their own lives and the institutions which serve them, and strive for more equal status in society.

Freire argued that people acquiring literacy must have their consciousness raised, enabling them to analyze the historical and social conditions which gave rise to their particular status, position and low power-base in society. Thus literacy teaching can become a direct political challenge to the hegemony of ruling capitalist states. Many adult literacy programs have been influenced by this 'critical literacy' ideology .

In radical adult literacy programs, students create their own learning material rather than passively reading information and books that propagate a centralist, dominant perspective. Through creating their own books, (and the binding and distributing of them – for example poetry books), what it is to be literate is radically changed. Rather than reading becoming a passive exercise, literacy is seen as a production of ideas that need to be spread into the community. Students who had previously believed themselves to be failures in learning to read and write may come to recognize that it was the system that had failed them. Their illiteracy was seen not as a personal problem but as a condition imposed or allowed by those in power.

Such a radical viewpoint about literacy needs to be seen in contrast to the celebrated modern idea of the Whole Language approach in literacy development. Delpit (1988) argues that books within the Whole Language approach can be an uncritical celebration of stories and a transmission of accepted information. As such, the Whole Language movement may neglect issues of power and social justice, and maintain the status quo.

Conclusion

This topic has revealed that literacy in bilingual and multicultural societies is neither a simple nor a straightforward concept. While reading and writing initially seem easily understandable events, the different uses and definitions of literacy immediately spotlight complexity and controversy. The five different approaches to literacy discussed in this topic highlight variations and contrasts to literacy education. Each approach has different expectations about bilingual children that pervade literacy policies, provision and practices. One recent contrast is literacy in a majority language (e.g. English) or an accent on local, regional literacies perhaps leading to 'multiple literacies' with different uses of literacy in different contexts.

One expectation is that children should have skills so they can function as 'good citizens' in a stable society. A contrasting expectation is that children should become empowered, even politically activated by becoming literate. Language minority children, for example, need to be able to read to understand propaganda, and to write to defend their community's interests or protest about injustice, discrimination and racism. A different view is that reading and writing are for sheer pleasure and enjoyment, to celebrate, create and self-cultivate. Biliteracy may be particularly valuable for both empowerment and enjoyment approaches.

The importance of the six approaches lies in their varying proposals for the role, status and self-enhancement of bilingual children and adults. Does literacy produce cogs that aid the smooth running of a well oiled system? Does literacy produce students who are activated into asserting their rights to equality of power, purse and opportunity? The fundamental issue of literacy and biliteracy is thus political. When clarity is achieved in defining the intended uses of literacy for bilingual students, educational considerations such as approaches, methods and strategies become more rational.

Further Reading

EDELSKY, C., 1996, *With Literacy and Justice for All: Rethinking the Social in Language and Education* (Second edition). London: Falmer.

HORNBERGER, N. H., 1989, Continua of Biliteracy. *Review of Educational Research*, 59 (3), 271-296.

MCKAY, S L., 1996 Literacy and Literacies. In S. L. MCKAY & N. H. HORNBERGER (eds), *Sociolinguistics and Language Teaching*. Cambridge: Cambridge University Press.

MCLAREN, P., 1988, Culture or Canon? Critical Pedagogy and the Politics of Literacy. *Harvard Educational Review*, 58, 211-234.

PEREZ, B., & TORRES-GUZMAN, M. E., 1996, *Learning in Two Worlds: An Integrated Spanish/English Biliteracy Approach* (Second edition). New York: Longman.

STREET, B. V., 1993, *Literacy in Theory and Practice*. Cambridge: Cambridge University Press.

STREET, B. V., 1995, *Social Literacies: Critical Approaches to Literacy in Development., Ethnography and Education*. London: Longman.

WELLS, G. & CHANG-WELLS, G. L., 1992, *Constructing Knowledge Together: Classrooms as Centers of Inquiry and Literacy*. Portsmouth, NH: Heinemann.

4: The Development of Biliteracy

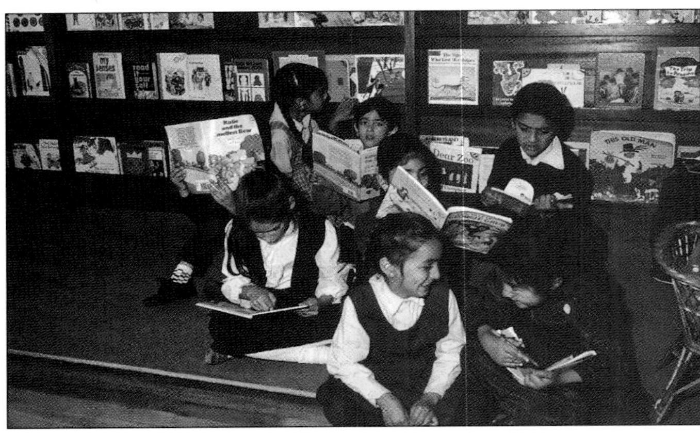
Asian children in British schools learn to read in English.

Given that literacy emancipates, enculturates, educates and can be an inherently enjoyable activity, there seems to be a strong argument for biliteracy. Pragmatically, most students from a minority language need to function in the minority and majority language society. This requires biliteracy rather than literacy only in the minority language.

In different minority language situations, the same question is often asked by parents and teachers. Is it better to be thoroughly literate in one language rather than attempt to be literate (or semi-literate) in two languages? Does literacy in one language interfere with becoming literate in a second language? Questions typically tend to be phrased in this negative way. The positive questions must also be asked. Does literacy in one language aid rather than impede literacy in a second language? Do the skills learnt in reading and writing one language transfer to reading and writing in a second language?

From recent reviews (Hornberger, 1989; Williams & Snipper, 1990) and research (e.g. Lanauze & Snow, 1989; Torres, 1991; Hornberger, 1990b; Calero-Breckheimer & Goetz, 1993), the evidence tends to reflect the positive rather than the negative questions. Research has suggested that academic and linguistic skills in a minority language transfer relatively easily to the second language. Simply stated, a child who learns to read in Spanish at home or in school, does not have to start from the beginning when learning to read in English. Both in learning to read and in learning to write, 'language skills acquired in a first language can, at least if developed beyond a certain point in L1, be recruited at relatively early stages of L2 acquisition for relatively skilled performance in L2, thus shortcutting the normal developmental progression in L2' (Lanauze & Snow, 1989, page 337).

When biliteracy is encouraged in minority language children, literacy skills and strategies learnt first in one language appear to transfer to the other language. This happens more easily if both languages use a similar writing system. For instance, a bilingual child learning to read and write first in French and then English has the advantage that they are both written in the Roman alphabet and that many of the consonants and vowels have similar values. A child becoming literate in French and then Russian has the added difficulty that the Russian is written in the Cyrillic alphabet. A child moving from a Western language to an Eastern language such as

Many bilingual children first learn to read their home minority language, and then transfer their reading skills to the majority language.

It is generally preferable for minority language children to establish literacy in their home language first.

Hebrew or Arabic will have to adjust to very different orthographical conventions and a different direction of writing. However, even when the vocabulary, grammar and orthography are very different, generalizable skills in decoding and reading strategies may easily transfer from first language literacy to second language literacy. Concepts and strategies (e.g. scanning, skimming, contextual guessing of words, skipping unknown words, tolerating ambiguity, reading for meaning, making inferences, monitoring, recognizing the structure of text, using previous learning, and using background knowledge about the text) readily and easily transfer from first to second language literacy (Calero-Breckheimer & Goetz, 1993; Jiménez, García & Pearson, 1995). This is the idea found in the Common Underlying Proficiency or Dual Iceberg idea of Cummins and his Interdependence principle (see page 81).

Reading ability in a second language is partly promoted by the degree of proficiency in that second language. However, the view that reading ability in a second language is mainly a function of proficiency in that second language is not generally supported by research (Calero-Breckheimer & Goetz, 1993). While the sounds of letters and decoding of words have a separation in learning to read in each language, the higher cognitive abilities and strategies required in making meaning from text are common to both languages. Overall reading competence in two languages thus does not operate separately.

This 'transfer' rather than 'separation' viewpoint has implications for the teaching of reading among language minority students. A 'separation' view is that reading in the second language (e.g. English for language minority students in the United States) depends on the level of proficiency in the second language and not on first language reading ability. Therefore, students should be swiftly moved to education through to second language; maximal exposure is needed to literacy in the second (majority) language. Time spent reading in the minority language is time lost in learning to read in the majority language. In contrast, a 'transfer' view argues for initial command of literacy in the minority language so that the cognitive skills and strategies needed for reading can be fully developed. Once well developed, these literacy skills and strategies transfer easily and readily to the second language.

An important factor is the context in which such language and literacy acquisition occurs. In Canadian Immersion programs, for example, the context is additive. That is, the child's home language of English is not being replaced but is being added to by the acquisition of French. Evaluations of Immersion programs (see Immersion Education, page 496) show that literacy in French is acquired at no cost to literacy in English. In this additive, majority language context, a child may acquire literacy through the second language at no cost to literacy in the first language. In contrast, in a subtractive environment, where the status and maintenance of the minority language is threatened by the powerful majority language, the transfer of literacy skills between the two languages may be impeded. In such subtractive situations, literacy may more efficiently be acquired through the home, heritage, minority language. Literacy can be built up via the higher level of language skills in the home language rather than through the weaker majority language. When literacy is attempted first through the second, majority language, the child's oracy skills in English may be insufficiently developed for such literacy acquisition to occur.

For teachers, this leaves the question of when to encourage biliteracy, given that there is some degree of literacy in one language. One model will be the simultaneous acquisition of biliteracy as well as bilingualism. Some bilingual children simultaneously learn to read and write in both languages. Other children will learn to read and write in their second language before they learn to read

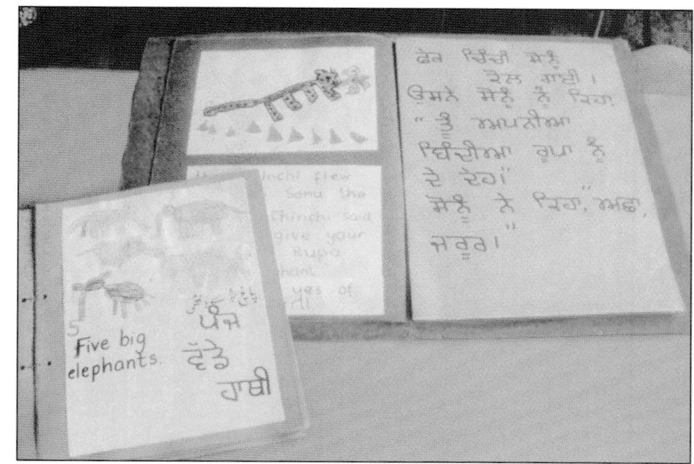

Literacy and Bilingual Education in Peru

In the country of Peru in South America, the majority language is Spanish while about one in three of the population (approximately six million people) are native speakers of Quechua (see page 152). Quechua has official status alongside Spanish. Also, nearly half a million residents speak Aymara (see page 460).

Bilingual education in Peru, particularly for Quechua speakers, has grown in the last three decades (Hornberger and King, 1996). Beginning from some experimental projects in the 1960s and 1970s, Quechua-Spanish bilingual education spread geographically in Peru particularly in the latter part of the 1980s. As Hornberger (1994c) indicates, 'research on the experimental efforts realized thus far points to positive outcomes for Quechua-Spanish bilingual education with respect to more active participation of learners in the classroom, new opportunities for educational success for hitherto disadvantaged students, improved reading comprehension and logical reasoning, improved oral and written Spanish use, and improved oral and written mother tongue use' (page 74).

Not without struggle or dispute, one of the successes of bilingual education in Peru has been the introduction of Quechua and Aymara reading material for all six grades at primary school level. Such texts provide a support for mother tongue instruction, a recognition of the status and worth of these languages and a means by which such languages are accepted for functions where Spanish has hitherto been dominant. Written Quechua has become a new instrument to express an individual's culture, heritage and origins, thus strengthening ethnic identity and potentially increasing social participation through the mother tongue.

However, the spread of bilingual education and literacy through the mother tongue among Quechua and Aymara peoples has not been without conflict. For some parents, Spanish is regarded as the language of civilization, employment, social mobility and perceived empowerment. Other people have argued that mother tongue written materials contain the Quechua language but not their culture. Indeed, some have suggested that the curriculum of bilingual schools tends not to reflect nor respect the cultural practices of the Quechua and Aymara people. The oral traditions, mythology, communal rituals and funds of knowledge that have traditionally been transmitted in a community are sometimes perceived as absent in translations of National Curriculum material.

For example, Aikman (1995) suggests that, among the Shipibo people, 'if mother tongue literacy is to contribute in any way to the maintenance and regeneration of indigenous culture, then it must be used as a part of existing cultural practices rather than introduced from outside according to very different cultural traditions and as mirror-images of successful projects with other indigenous peoples.' (page 420)

As May (1994a) has shown among the Maori in New Zealand and Hornberger (1988) in the Quechua community in Peru, the autonomy of local language communities to decide for themselves about the functions of languages and the use of literacy in schools is important in empowering such peoples. Where bilingual education for minority language communities and literacy in the mother tongue is concerned, success can be generated when there is ownership by such language communities, when there is local conviction rather than conformity to central desires, and where there is full participation and a sense of control over their own educational, cultural and linguistic destinies.

Nancy Hornberger

Nancy Hornberger is currently the Goldie Anna Professor in the Graduate School of Education at the University of Pennsylvania. She graduated from Harvard University, followed by a Masters at New York University and a PhD at the University of Wisconsin-Madison. Well-known internationally for her work on biliteracy (particularly among language minorities), Nancy Hornberger is renowned for a book published in 1988 entitled *Bilingual Education and Language Maintenance: A Southern Peruvian Quechua Case*. This book has come to be regarded as a classic ethnomethodological study. Her understanding of language minorities in South America as well as research on biliteracy in the United States has provided new insights into relationships between language minority maintenance, language shift, local literacies and bilingual education.

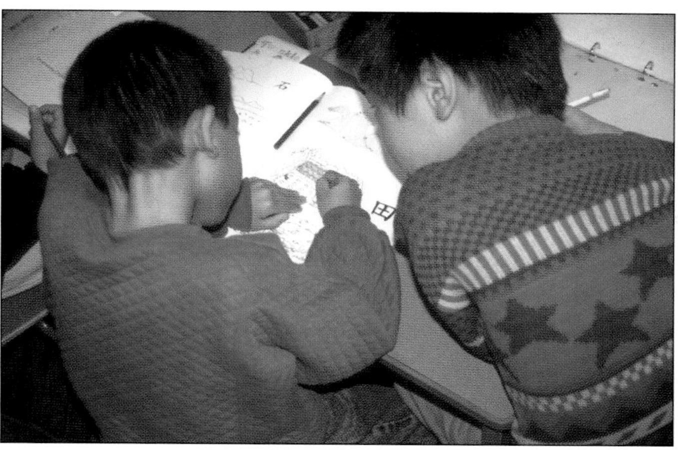

in their first (majority) language e.g. in Immersion education in Canada. Both these approaches will tend to result in successful biliteracy.

The third approach is where children acquire literacy in their first language, a minority language, and then later, develop literacy skills in the majority language. This can be a successful route to biliteracy if the minority language continues to play a strong role in the school curriculum after literacy in the majority language is achieved. However, in some circumstances, minority (first) language literacy may be simply regarded as a convenient path to majority language literacy, rather than as being valuable in itself. This tends to happen in Transitional Bilingual education, where education and the development of literacy skills in the minority language is a temporary measure, gradually phased out in favor of monolingual education in the majority language. The result is monoliteracy in the majority language. However, in Maintenance, Two-Way/Dual Language and Heritage Language education, this third approach tends to be additive, promoting literacy in both languages.

Simple answers about when to promote literacy in the second language are made difficult by other factors such as the educational and societal context and the age and ability of the child. Contrast the six year old just beginning to acquire pre-reading and pre-writing skills in the first language with an 18-year-old student, fluent in a first language. In the first case, biliteracy may best be delayed. In the latter case, oracy and literacy in the second language may be mutually reinforcing. Contexts will also vary. When a language minority child is constantly bombarded with majority language written material, from adverts to comics, computers to supermarkets, biliteracy may occur relatively easily. The accent in school can be on ensuring that first language literacy is relatively well established before introducing literacy in the second (majority) language. Such introduction may come in the middle years of elementary schooling (e.g. from seven years of age to 12 years of age depending on the level of literacy achieved in the first language).

Further Reading

DELGADO-GAITÁN, C., 1990, *Literacy for Empowerment: The Role of Parents in Children's Education*. New York: Falmer Press.

EDELSKY, C., 1996, *With Literacy and Justice for All: Rethinking the Social in Language and Education*. (Second edition). London: Falmer.

EDWARDS, V. (ed.), 1995, *Building Bridges: Multilingual Resources for Children*. Clevedon: Multilingual Matters Ltd.

PEREZ, B., & TORRES-GUZMAN, M. E., 1996, *Learning in Two Worlds: An Integrated Spanish/English Biliteracy Approach* (Second edition). New York: Longman.

Multilingual Classroom Resources

As far as possible, the language resources of the classroom need to be multilingual partly to reflect the mother tongues of the children in the classroom, but also for the multilingual awareness of all children. Sometimes it is difficult to find the quantity, quality and variety of reading materials in the mother tongues of children in bilingual classrooms. There are often problems importing books from other countries and problems in purchasing expensive books. Yet some schools do manage to collect excellent libraries of books in different languages (and multicultural books via help from language communities, parents of children in the school and using minority language organizations who have contacts and a commitment to literacy development in children's mother tongues.

REFERENCE: EDWARDS, 1995

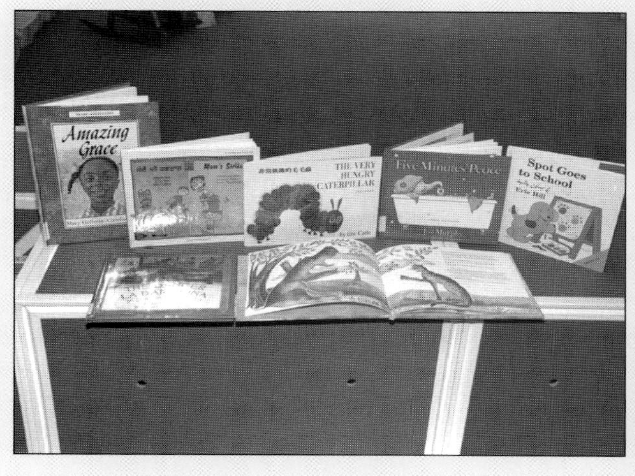

Dual Language Books

Dual language books contain a story, folk tale, myth or information in two languages. Such languages may have a similar script (as in French and English, or Spanish and English) or different scripts (for example Chinese and English, Urdu and English, Bengali and English). Often the two languages are on the same page or on opposite sides of the page, sharing the same pictures.

The origins of dual language books are many. (1) Some books have resulted from funded projects. (2) Other dual language books have been created by 'smaller' publishers (e.g. ethnic minority presses). Professionally produced and published books usually have high quality text and colorful illustrations. Locally produced materials may be in black and white, sometimes word processed or occasionally handwritten. (3) When teachers work with children to produce dual language texts, it is often the children themselves or their parents who produce the story lines. The final books are handwritten or word processed with group produced collages or the children's own drawings. (4) Monolingual teachers who did not want to use books in children's home languages that they themselves did not understand also instigated the production of dual language books. In this respect, dual language books offered a valuable alternative, giving teachers and learners some equality of access to understanding the storyline.

There are a variety of different aims in dual language books.

Simply to make all children, both bilinguals and monolinguals, aware that other languages exist and have the same value and functions. Such books can be a valuable part of a multicultural approach in the curriculum. As Feuerverger (1994, page 136) suggests:

> 'Students learn to admire and respect those who come from other backgrounds and languages, rather than to be prejudiced against them. I believe that this is such an important part of multicultural teaching'.

For children whose first language is not the majority language of the country, dual language books may serve as a bridge to literacy in English. Such children will read the story in Greek or Turkish, Bengali or Urdu first of all. Subsequently, they may read the other language (e.g. English version) and, having already understood the storyline, be able to make sense of English words.

Dual language books act as an important bridge between parents and children, and between the home and the school. Parents and other members of the extended family may be able to read to their children in their home language. At the same time, the child will be able to read a book in the majority language of the school, such as English.

Dual language books can enable small groups or pairs of children to work collaboratively on the book. If one child can read in Bengali and the other in English, they can work together, discuss the story and complete activities set by the teacher around that story.

Teachers may use such books with smaller or larger groups of children. For example, the story may be read by the teacher in one language first, and then in the other language. The teacher may be able to point out similarities and differences in script, in the use of language, and in the meaning of words in the different languages.

Dual language books are not without controversy. Firstly, some teachers and parents argue that children only read one language in the book, and ignore the other. Having understood the story in one language, it may be tiresome and pointless reading the story in another language. Children may thus concentrate on just one half of the book.

Secondly, teachers and children sometimes observe that the presence of the majority language such as English tends to remove the desire to read in the home, minority language. The different status of the two languages may mean that the child will only wish to read in the higher status language.

In a detailed and balanced discussion of dual language books by Viv Edwards (*The Multilingual Resources for Children Project,* 1995), further problems of dual language texts are analyzed. In the typography, one script often takes precedence, or has higher status than the other. For example, in the size of the print, the spacing between lines and the boldness of the print, there may be differences between the two languages. One script may be of higher quality than the other, this occurring particularly when a Latin and a non-Latin alphabet are used – indicating that equal status is not given to the two languages. The way the two languages are placed on a page, whether one is printed and the other typewritten or handwritten, and the order in which the languages appear, may each reflect different status accorded to the two languages.

There is also sometimes a practical problem in translation. Not only does the storyline have to be authentically conveyed in both languages, but also the style of language, the difficulty level of the text and the culturally relevant use of vocabulary may each affect the status accorded to each language. It is also important that the cultural 'message' is not lost in translation, this being very much a part of the multicultural aim of dual language books.

REFERENCE: EDWARDS, 1995

Viv Edwards

Viv Edwards is Professor of Education at Reading University in England. A prolific author of books and curriculum materials, Viv Edwards is an authority on the many Community Languages of the UK and also has lectured internationally. Currently Director of the Reading and Language Information Centre at the University of Reading, her publications include: *Language in Multilingual Classrooms* (1983), *Multilingualism in the British Isles* (co-edited, 1990), *The World in a Classroom* (with Angela Redfern, 1992), *Building Bridges: Multilingual Resources for Children* (1995) and *Classroom Materials for Speaking and Listening, Reading and Writing in Multilingual Classrooms* (1995). Viv Edwards is also co-editor of a journal entitled *Language and Education*, and on the editorial board of many other journals.

Bilingualism and Biliteracy in Poetry

Biliteracy exists in a variety of different written forms. Apart from dual language children's reading books, there are, for example, bilingual and multilingual Bibles, multilingual prayer books, bilingual editions of famous literary classics and bilingual poetry.

Bilingual poetry provides a varied example of biliteracy. To illustrate: some bilingual poetry places the original and a translation side by side, as in Olga Sedakova's (1994) Russian/English *'The Silk of Time'*. Other poetry is mixed in language inside the poem – codeswitching inside the poem to add richness, creativity, color and deeper meaning (e.g. Firmat's (1995) *'Bilingual Blues'* and Carlson's (1994) *'Cool Salsa: Bilingual Poems on Growing Up Latino in the United States'*). The codeswitching in the following poem reflects issues of mixed identity in the poet's psyche:

'I have mixed feelings about everything.
Soy un ajiaco de contradicciones.
Vexed, hexed, complexed,
hyphenated, oxygenated, illegally alienated,
psycho soy, cantando voy;'

(From Firmat's (1995) *'Bilingual Blues'*, page 28)

Other poetry reflects the bilingual or multilingual and multicultural experience of the poet. For example, the poet Lori Carlson (1994) reflects (in a translation from Spanish):

Life
to understand me
you have to know Spanish
feel it in the blood of your soul.

If I speak another language
and use different words
for feelings that will always stay the same
I don't know
if I'll continue being
the same person.

Yet Carlson (1994, page xii) also speaks positively of bilingualism. 'Speaking more than one language, I have found, enriches life, broadens perspective, extends horizons of opportunity, and makes us more sensitive to nuance, difference, contrast'. There is more than a correspondence here between the experiences of the poet and the experiments of the psychologist (e.g. see page 54 on Sensitivity in Communication and page 71 on Metalinguistic Awareness).

REFERENCES: CARLSON, 1994; FIRMAT, 1995

Biliteracy in History

Bilingualism and biliteracy has been part of learned activity throughout history. Indeed, biliteracy was present from the earliest days of the invention of writing in Ancient Mesopotamia.

Ancient Mesopotamia (present day Iraq) was a multilingual, multicultural and multiethnic society. Writing was invented in Mesopotamia (Uruk, Southern Babylon) around 3100 BC. While many early texts are monolingual, the diversity of peoples and cultures in Mesopotamia led to bilingual texts, bilingual glossaries and translations at an early stage in the development of writing systems. Ancient Mesopotamia included the Sumerians, who invented cuneiform writing, and also large numbers of speakers of Semitic languages. Semitic speakers soon wished to adopt the Sumerian writing system. Bilingual and trilingual cuneiform tablets were produced, containing Sumerian writing and often translation into Semitic Akkadian (Cooper, 1993). One example is a multicolumn bilingual word list from Ebia in Syria dated at around 2400 BC. A Sumerian word is followed by its Semitic equivalent. Thus biliteracy was present almost from the beginning of writing.

For many centuries, scholarly activity necessitated bilingualism. Latin writers such as Seneca, Virgil, Ovid, Horace and the two Plinys were not native speakers of Latin. They were bilingual at least. Medieval scholars wrote in more than one European language (e.g. Chaucer wrote in Italian and English, and was fluent in French and Latin as well). John Milton in the Renaissance period wrote sonnets in Italian and English, and was competent in Latin, Greek and Hebrew.

Up to the 17th century, many Western writers were biliterate (Mackey, 1993). The Classical tradition in education required literacy in Greek and Latin, and sometimes literacy in the mother tongue. By the middle of the 19th century, such biliteracy (and bilingualism) was no longer in vogue, or even tolerated in Europe. A tendency towards monolingualism and monoliteracy was associated with the rise of Nationalism during the Romantic Period (see page 327). Nationalism bred linguistic allegiance: one people, one nation, one unifying language. The national tongue was the soul and symbol of the nation. Love of the national language was a mark of a love of the nation. Nationalism meant writing in the national language as a sign of solidarity with the nation, and as a way of enriching and educating readers' commitment to citizenship. Bilingual writers had to choose where their literary allegiance lay, and in which language to write.

As nationalism is moving towards supranationalism (e.g. Europeanization), Mackey (1993) predicts that literary bilingualism may flourish again. The great movement of guest workers, refugees and displaced persons and many other in-migrants to new countries, plus the ease of communication and travel across the world, may open the door to increased biliteracy.

Bilingualism in Modern Literature

Many modern writers possess more than one linguistic and sometimes ethnic identity. This may be reflected in various ways in their work. One example is the Russian American writer, Vladimir Nabokov, who was born in 1899 in St Petersburg, Russia, to a prominent aristocratic family. Like many other children of the Russian aristocracy, he learnt French and English at an early age, as well as his native Russian. He began to write in Russian during his teens. Following the Russian revolution, Nabokov's family fled to England, where he studied at Cambridge University. Later he lived in Berlin for 17 years and France for three years, during which time he published nine novels in Russian under the pseudonym V.Sirin, as well as many plays, poems and short stories. However, he had already begun to write in English by the time he moved to America in 1940. He wrote seven novels in English, as well as translating his own Russian novels into English. Nabokov's novels in both languages show humor, inventiveness, playfulness, parody, aestheticism, lyricism and brilliance of style. He treated fiction partly as a game and avoided social and moral messages. In 1959 he moved to Switzerland, where he died in 1977.

Another famous multilingual writer was Elias Canetti, born in 1905 in Rutschuk, Bulgaria to a family of Sephardic Jews. His father was Turkish and his mother of Spanish descent. He was educated in Manchester, Vienna, Zurich and Frankfurt. He lived in Austria, Switzerland and Germany and finally moved to England in 1938, when the Nazis came to power in Austria. He wrote both novels and plays in German, and was awarded the Nobel prize for literature in 1981. His most famous novel, *Crowds and Power*, was written in London and published in 1960. It deals with the relationship of power and totalitarianism to mass movements, and reflects Canetti's perspective, as a Jew, on Naziism and the holocaust. He died in 1994.

Many African writers have chosen to write in a language other than their mother tongue, for instance in a colonial language. This may be because they have been educated in a language other than their mother tongue, or because they wish to reach a wider audience than would be possible through their local native language. Another reason may be that a language such as English has been nativized or Africanized to such an extent that African writers can express their own local identity through it without compromise, and also give voice to a wider national or pan-African identity.

One famous African writer is the Nigerian Wole Soyinka, born in 1934 near Abeokuta, Nigeria. His native language is Yoruba but he has written mostly in English. He studied in Nigeria and England and has written plays, novels and poetry. He won the Nobel prize for literature in 1986. He lives and works in Nigeria but has traveled widely and taught in many British and American universities and produced his own plays abroad. Although his works are written mostly in English, he draws on the myths, symbolism and traditions of the Yoruba ethnic group.

One particularly interesting example of a writer who possesses more than one linguistic and possibly ethnic identity is that of the Israeli Arab, Anton Shammas, who was born in Fassuta, an Arab village in the Upper Galilee, in 1950. He lived in Jerusalem for 20 years before moving to the United States. He has written poetry in both Hebrew and Arabic and a novel in Hebrew, *Arabesques,* published in 1986. The novel tells the story of an Arab in the Galilee, and is written in an intricate style and with consummate skill. Shammas describes Hebrew as his 'stepmother tongue' and the fact that an Israeli Arab can write Hebrew with such ease, complexity and brilliance has challenged Israeli Jews to rethink their image of modern Hebrew as the sole possession of the Israeli Jewish people and only able to express Israeli Jewish culture and life perspectives. The novel *Arabesques* brings together history, myth, memory and experience, the past and the present in one seamless whole. This bringing together of opposing perspectives characterizes Shammas' poetry as well as his prose and is perhaps the result of his dual linguistic identity and thus identification with two world views.

REFERENCES: COOPER, 1993

Multiculturalism in Education

1: Multicultural Education

Introduction

Wherever bilingual people live, there also exist important issues related to language. Bilinguals are often situated in areas where cultural diversity, racism and multiculturalism are topics of discussion, debate and action. Similarly, bilingual education does not concern languages only. Bilingual education often includes multiculturalism in different ways in the curriculum, and sometimes in the whole aims and infrastructure of the school. Just as language and culture are entwined, so bilingualism and multiculturalism are important partners in bilingual classrooms, as will be explored in this topic.

The recent movement in favor of multiculturalism and multicultural education occurred mostly after the Second World War. Various factors generated this movement. Many societies began to change through, for example, economic expansion, mass migration, refugees, and greater economic co-operation. Partly due to atrocities that occurred in the Second World War, there has also been increasing concern for international human rights (see page 286) to oppose racism and help promote equality of educational opportunity. There has been an increasing awareness of other cultures as portrayed in the mass media and through fast progress in international communications and global transport. Thus multicultural education has grown as an element in educational policy, provision and practice. Yet the meaning of 'multicultural education' is varied and diverse.

Lynch (1986) makes a distinction between five different but overlapping approaches under the umbrella heading of 'multiculturalism in education'.

Intercultural Education

This style, also termed citizenship education, has often been for in-migrants, and has focused on the competences and understandings needed by in-migrants to adapt to the host country while retaining their home language and culture in case they return to their country of origin. Such intercultural education is concerned with the human rights of such in-migrants and the avoidance of discrimination. The human rights accent in such education concerns equality, freedom and partnership, with the ideal of friendly intercommunication between different cultural and linguistic groups.

International and Multicultural Education

This style includes development education (the interdependence of different global communities), environmental education, human rights education, education about cultural diversity and peace education. The aims and ideals are to develop a sense of world citizenship in students, to cultivate students who are empathic towards others of a different culture and creed, and to instigate a concern for the welfare of all citizens of the world.

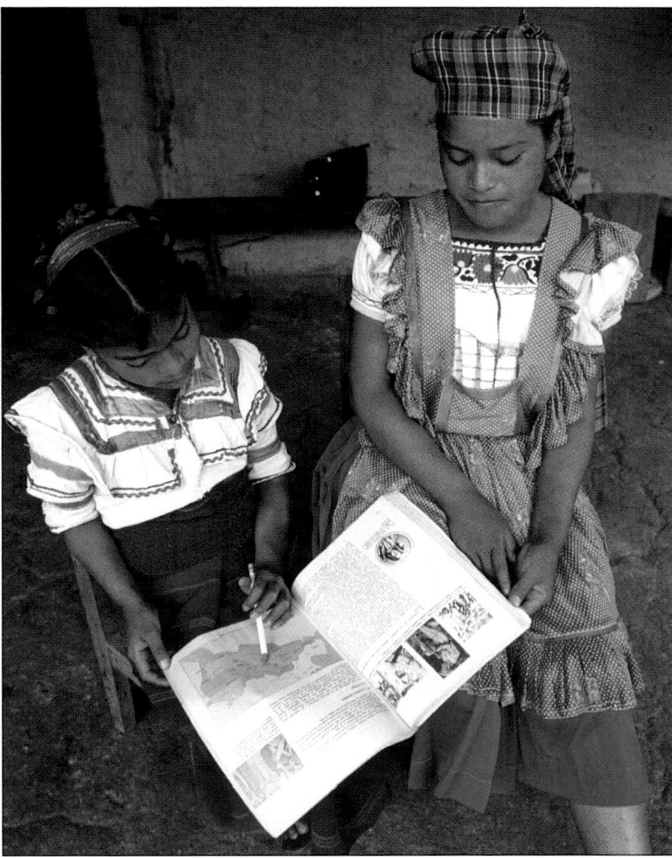

Tzeltal Mayan Indian girls in Amatenango, Mexico study the history of Europe, rather than their own history. Education may often reflect the dominant or colonial viewpoint.

Multicultural Education

Lynch (1986) regards multicultural education as engaging whole school policy and provision in improving race relations, ensuring all the curriculum includes a multicultural perspective, a study of other languages, cultures and religions, with a concern to ensure equality of educational opportunity, and respect for cultural differences. This is distinguished from multiethnic education.

Multiethnic Education

Multiethnic Education focuses more on 'ethnic minority studies' and the 'revitalization of ethnic minorities', but with a strong initiative to tackle all those elements of schooling to provide equality of opportunity for all racial and ethnic groups. In this approach, there is a concern for raising the expectations of ethnic minority children (e.g through curriculum, tracking, assessment, parent and community involvement), combating racism in school, encouraging the recruitment and promotion of staff who promote, or can act as role models for ethnic revitalization. The aim is for students to become acculturated citizens of their own cultural or ethnic communities while also becoming cohesive members of their nation and the global community.

Anti-Racist Education

The many visible signs of racism, the enduring and stubborn existence of racism despite combative measures, and racism being a rudimentary cause of an inequitable and unjust society, has led to racial prejudice and racial discrimination as the central focus of some 'multicultural' programs.

Doubts have been expressed about the capacity of multicultural education to combat racism in schools and wider society. Therefore, some educators have argued for a more specific focus than 'multiculturalism' to confront individual acts of racism and more covert institutional racist practices. While some multicultural education programs include racism as a topic, an anti-racist program goes further and deeper, sometimes becoming an alternative to multicultural education. Supporters of such anti-racist programs argue that multicultural education often derives from dominant social class members who evade central issues of inequality of power, of dominance and subordination in society, of marginalization and deprivation, and of internal colonialism, economic exploitation and linguistic and cultural assimilation (Bullivant, 1981; Nieto, 1996; May, 1994a).

The argument is that multicultural education is in danger of placing too much importance on cultural, linguistic and ethnic identity, and too little importance on righting wrongs and gaining social, economic and political equality for language and cultural minorities. Multicultural education is in danger of 'inserting' minorities into the dominant way of understanding and order. Instead, anti-racist educationalists argue, multicultural education needs to center on changing and challenging hierarchies, class disadvantages and racism. Such a multicultural program therefore has to engage life chances and not just life styles. An anti-racist (or prejudice-reduction) program thus aims to tackle basic power and status issues as well as racist behaviors among individuals, cultures and institutions.

The Aims of Multicultural Education

The aims and assumptions of multicultural education are underpinned by political and ideological aims. The assumptions of multicultural education therefore include the following:

- There is a fundamental equality of all individuals and all minority groups irrespective of language and culture.
- In a democracy, there should be equality of opportunity irrespective of ethnic, cultural or linguistic origin.
- Any manifest or latent form of discrimination by the dominant power group against minorities requires elimination.
- A culturally diverse society should avoid racism and ethnocentrism.
- While generalizations about cultural behavior may be a natural part of humans making sense of their world, cultural stereotypes are to be avoided.
- Minority cultural groups in particular need awareness of their culture as a precondition and foundation for building on intercultural awareness.
- In mainstream monocultural education, language minority parents tend to be excluded from participation in their children's education. In multicultural education, parents should become partners.
- A pluralist integration is established by interaction and not a mosaic, by intermingling and a discovery of others to improve mutual understanding, break down stereotypes and prejudice, while increasing self-knowledge and self-esteem.

Anti-Racism and Prejudice Reduction in School

The psychological roots of racial prejudice and racial hostility are separate from the philosophical basis of multicultural education. However, as will be considered later, anti-racism and prejudice reduction are often included in a 'strong' version of multicultural education. There are multicultural programs and materials that do not include a study of racism or anti-racism. One can learn, for example, about other cultures and ethnic groups without confronting the racism that exists in one's own (and other) ethnic groups. Thus such multicultural education has been accused of leaving unaltered the racist fabric of society and failing to see racism as a causal need for multicultural education. When a study of racism and anti-racism is absent from a multicultural program, such a program can become a tranquilizer of action against racism, diverting resistance and confrontation of racism into harmless channels. Instead a form of anti-racist multiculturalism is possible (Todd, 1991). Such a program needs to include an analysis of the structural reasons (e.g. the institutionalization of racism, social stratification, discriminatory practices by government) why racism is perpetuated, and not just viewed as an attitude of individuals. Its proponents argue that rather than just engendering sympathy for the victims of racism, some sympathy is needed for the struggle to defeat racism, even when this means confrontation and non-violent direct action.

Rarely, if ever, does language diversity, in itself, cause poor race relations. While color of skin, creed and language often become the symbols and badges of racism, the roots of racism tend to lie in fear and misunderstanding, and in the unequal distribution of power and economic rewards. If the school is a witting or unwitting agent in the reproduction of social and economic differences in society, then schools may be perpetrators of racism. Multicultural education in school is therefore sometimes seen as a way of raising consciousness of racism both in the aggressor and the victim.

Even when bilingual education exists, there is a danger that the focus is on two languages rather than on many cultures. Creating bilingual students may not be enough to reverse the inequalities and injustices in society. A bilingual child may still be the victim of racism and may still be confined to dominated status unless the school system as a whole works to redress rather than reproduce inequalities.

> 'The crucial element in reversing language minority students' school failure is not the language of instruction but the extent to which educators work to reverse – rather than perpetuate – the subtle, and often not so subtle, institutionalized racism of the society as a whole. In other words, bilingual education becomes effective only when it becomes anti-racist education. Strong promotion of students' primary language can be an important component in empowering language minority students but it is certainly not sufficient in itself'. (Cummins, 1986a, page 11)

It is a debated point as to the extent of the influence of school in combating racism and reducing prejudice. The preconceptions and attitudes of children and teachers, of politicians and policy makers, the message of the hidden curriculum and the material of the formal curriculum may make the winning of hearts and minds difficult. So widespread, brutal and ingrained is racism in the school and street, that some argue for skill training rather than liberal education. Explicit racism may be combated in liberal education by a careful and conscious selection of teaching resources, the language of teaching, school organization and grouping in the classroom. Increased knowledge and greater understanding are sought as outcomes. For some, a more direct confrontational style with regard to racism is required. For example, through role-play, 'white' individuals may be confronted with their own racism and its consequences on others. Such role-play will attempt to redress an inherent problem, in that some white skinned people can never fully understand racism because they do not experience it.

A different viewpoint, pessimistic but with an element of reality, is that schools can do little to reconstruct power and racial relationships within society. This belief stems from the idea that multicultural education is a token and patronizing exercise. An alternative, radical view is that non-violent political activity is required amongst the victims of racism in school and particularly through political activity outside school. Such activity will attempt to reconstruct the power, dominance and political relationships in society and to seek to eradicate prejudice and fear, victimization and racial violence.

Such a radical view indicates that multicultural and anti-racist education can be neither value-free nor politically neutral. It aims at promoting equality of educational opportunity, the eradication of racial and cultural discrimination, and erasing racial dominance. Its danger is in being only for minorities and not for the enlightenment of majorities. In Britain, multicultural education may be provided in areas where ethnic minority children reside. It has often been seen as irrelevant in most, but not every all-white English-only school.

Multicultural Education for Whom?

Multicultural education is relevant to the experience and needs of a wide variety of students, in a broad range of situations. Minority students in 'Submersion education', for instance, are educated solely through the medium of the majority language. The added danger is that only the majority culture will be transmitted in the classroom. This may make minority language children feel less confident of their cultural background, their language community, their home values and beliefs, even less confident of themselves. This is also true of students in Transitional Bilingual education, where the minority language is gradually superseded by the majority language in classroom teaching. Therefore, language minority students need, at the least, their heritage culture to be well represented in the curriculum.

Minority language children in 'strong' forms of bilingual education (e.g. Dual Language schools, heritage language schools), where the minority language has a permanent place and high status in the curriculum, also need the heritage culture to be strongly promoted in the classroom and in all the school activities. This is particularly valuable to encourage participation by children in their heritage culture. Language skills in the minority language are no guarantee of continued use of that language into teens and adulthood. Enculturation therefore becomes essential if that language is to be useful and used.

There is also a need for multicultural and anti-racist teaching for students belonging to the dominant, majority culture, to help them interact with in-migrants, refugees and guest workers, and feel comfortable and enriched when crossing national boundaries. If ethnically diverse populations are to co-exist within a nation, one essential educational activity should be to promote awareness of, and respect for cultural diversity. A classroom response has been to develop various programs to develop sensitivity and sympathy, understanding and awareness of diverse cultural groups. Such programs are often considered to be relevant solely for students attending multiracial or ethnically mixed schools. However, they are no less relevant for students living in areas where the majority culture predominates.

Types of Multicultural Program

In its 'weak' sense, multicultural programs in the classroom focus on the different beliefs, values, eating habits, cultural activities, dress and gestures (e.g. greetings and non-verbal reward systems) of varying ethnic groups. This form of 'cultural artifact' multicultural education attempts to extend the cultural vocabulary and cultural grammar of the individual child. One danger of such an approach is that it accents cultural differences, and emphasizes the colorful and bizarre. It may even reinforce and extend differences. A 'weak' form of multicultural education also tends to divorce language from culture, paying little or no attention to the home language of minority children. Since language and culture are inseparable, and since merely using a language is to impart its culture, a stronger form of multicultural education requires attention to the minority language that is part of the minority culture. This is sometimes attempted through Language Awareness programs. Such programs attempt to increase understanding, consciousness and sensitivity to the nature of language in everyday life. (Language Awareness is considered separately as a topic, see page 628).

The language aspects of multicultural education may be presented by vicarious experience of languages through videos, tape recordings and live performances where the language and the culture are both presented in an authentic, inseparable way. Just as there is a danger of teaching about cultural diversity with sparse or no reference to the attendant language, so there is a danger of teaching a second language without an immersion in the attendant culture.

In Europe, another variety or constituent of multicultural education is referred to as citizenship education. Citizenship education sometimes has curriculum content in common with the aims of multicultural and anti-racist education. However, it can also have assimilation aims. Butts (1980) suggested ten topics for citizenship education in the US: justice, freedom, equality, diversity, authority, privacy, due process, participation, personal obligation for the public good, and international human rights. Most of these concepts are part of multicultural aims (e.g. international understanding, equality, freedom and diversity). However, participation, authority and personal obligation for the public good could be taught to achieve assimilation.

A Classification of Objectives in Anti-Racist Education

1. Respect for Others

1.1 Cognitive (knowledge)

All students should know and understand:

- basic information on race and racial difference;
- the customs, values and beliefs and achievements of the different cultures in the local community, in their ethnic group, in their present country and in the world;
- why different groups have immigrated and emigrated in the past and how the local community has come to acquire its present ethnic composition;
- the interdependence of nations and cultures around the globe;
- the international and national context of human and civil rights.

1.2 Cognitive (skills)

All students should be able to:

- recognize racism and other forms of prejudice and discrimination;
- detect stereotyping and scapegoating in what they see, hear and read, and be able to devise appropriate counter strategies;
- evaluate their own and other cultures objectively against agreed and explicit criteria.

1.3 Affective (attitudes, values and emotional sets)

All students should be taught:

- the unique value of each individual human being;
- the underlying humanity and essential core values shared by all democratic societies;
- the principles of equal rights and justice for all, and the value of the achievements of other cultures and nations;
- 'strangeness' without feeling threatened;
- that multicultural societies have a long history, are a reality of the present, and a certainty for the future;
- that no culture is ever static, and that constant, mutual accommodation of all cultures, creating an evolving multicultural society, is customary;
- that prejudice and discrimination are as widespread as they are morally unacceptable, and that the historical, social, political and economic causes which have given rise to prejudice and discrimination should be examined;
- the damaging effect of prejudice and discrimination on all groups in society;
- the process of multiple acculturation in a multicultural society and the legitimacy and acceptability of multiple loyalties within democratic society.

2. Respect for Self

2.1 Cognitive (knowledge)

All students should know and understand:

- the history, values and achievements of their own culture and what is distinctive about that culture;
- the values of their local community;
- the common values of the wider society.

2.2 Cognitive (skills)

All students should be able to:

- communicate competently in their own mother tongue;
- communicate competently in the majority language, if the majority language is not their mother tongue;
- be aware of different languages in their community, their present country and the world;
- relate creatively to members of other cultures;
- master the basic skills necessary for success at school and when leaving school;
- formulate criteria for judgment and action, compatible with the values of a multicultural society;
- analyze alternative value positions of different cultural groups;
- contribute to conflict resolution by persuasion and rational discourse.

2.3 Affective (attitudes, values and emotional sets)

All students should have developed:

- a positive self-image;
- confidence in the sense of their own identity;
- a feeling of comfort with cultural diversity and a willingness and ability to learn from others.
- a feeling of ease and pleasure when with people of other ethnic groups

ADAPTED FROM: CLINE & FREDERICKSON, 1991

The aims of a 'stronger' form of a multicultural program have their basis partly in arousing awareness of, and sensitivity to, cultural diversity (Sleeter & Grant, 1987). The educational basis of a relatively 'strong' form of multicultural education is that all cultures are attempts to discover meaning. No one culture (including the umbrella idea of Western culture) has the monopoly of understanding. There is value in the meanings of those in a subordinate position (e.g. language minorities). The voices of the poor are as meaningful as the privileged; the understandings of the oppressed become as valid as those of the oppressor.

When the educational basis of a multicultural program is discussed, politics is not very far away. In the US, multicultural programs have been criticized for being governed and manipulated from within a conservative education profession and by textbook companies and local and state education authorities (Olneck, 1993). As such, multicultural education is perceived to be contained and controlled by those in power, posing little threat to the academic, cultural or bureaucratic establishments. Political activists in the US have regarded multiculturalism as a key battleground for a reordering of political relationships and power structures. Multiculturalism has therefore, sometimes become a call for the mobilization of those who wish to challenge ethnic inequalities and the established order. For conservatives, multiculturalism symbolizes contests about whose values and ideology should be dominant in the curriculum, whose traditions and perspectives should be transmitted in the enculturation of students. For such conservatives, the hidden agenda of multiculturalism is sometimes perceived as self determination and autonomy rather than unity; the destabilization and undermining of society rather than equality; tribalization and separation rather than plurality.

Multiculturalism Across the Curriculum

Multicultural education may require a reappraisal of the whole curriculum with an analysis of how seemingly neutral subjects like Science and Mathematics often solely use and perpetuate majority, dominant culture. In the pictures of textbooks and the prose of the teacher, in the 'real life' problems to be tackled, the majority dominant culture may be represented and minority cultures ignored.

While more subtle differences may exist in Mathematics, Science and Technology, the more common and obvious examples of monoculturalism appear in the teaching of History and Geography, Literature and Art, Music and Home Economics (e.g. Cookery), Social Studies and Health Education.

For example, in the past, Welsh children have been taught the history of England and Europe more than the history of Wales and the Celts. Mexican American children are taught US history, but not the history of Mexico, the annexation of Mexican territory or the role of Mexican Americans in US history. Not only do many Mexicans in the US not know the history of their country of origin, they are often not taught how their ethnic group has contributed to the development of the United States. The aim becomes assimilation rather than awareness; dominance rather than diversity. The fear and ignorance that tend to breed racism may unintentionally be perpetrated. Rather than celebrating ethnic identity and cultural diversity, a view of cultural inequality may latently be conveyed. As Olneck (1993, page 248) states: 'marginalized and subordinated groups are represented as voiceless objects, defined by their "apartness" and difference from, or by their inferior relationship to, those more central. In curricular representations, it is alleged, the perspectives from which history and experience occur, the actors deemed central, and the experiences, cultural expressions, and projects deemed valid and valuable are all those of dominant groups'.

One approach to multiculturalism in the curriculum is through content, showing that rationality is not the monopoly of any one culture, and that understanding requires an interdependence of peoples. The 'discovery' of North America can be taught from the perspective of native, indigenous peoples as well as the invaders; the Crusades from a Muslim and Christian perspective; and heresies from the viewpoint of heretics and 'orthodox believers'. In curriculum areas such as Music and Art, there can be a genuine celebration of diversity (e.g. African, Caribbean, Asian and different forms of Latino music; African art, Chinese and Japanese kites, Islamic and Egyptian calligraphy). In curriculum areas that systematically pursue a critical approach to understanding the world (e.g. nuclear physics), some cultures have been more fruitful than others in explaining the world. However, the methods and approaches of different cul-

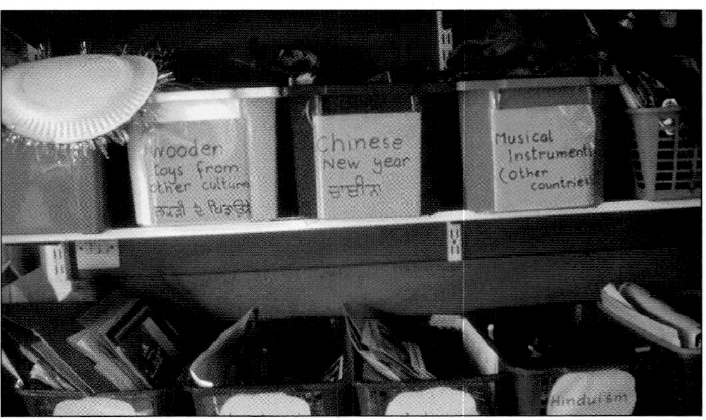

Heritage Cultural Awareness

Minority language communities not only encounter the dominant influence of the majority language, but also its accompanying culture. For minority language groups in Britain and North America, for instance, the majority language is English. From an early age, minority language children are exposed to prestigious Anglo-American culture, beliefs, history, political thought and ways of viewing the world. Such exposure often leads to minority language groups adopting and valuing the dominant language and its attendant culture and neglecting and devaluing their own language and culture.

Even in minority language communities where bilingual or heritage language education is available, it is essential to present the minority language within the context of its culture. A language divorced from its culture is like a body without a soul. Therefore, developing heritage cultural awareness alongside first language teaching is an important element in minority language education.

Classroom activities to foster minority culture awareness can include: performing cultural rituals and traditions using authentic visual and written materials, observing social conventions (e.g. ways of greeting visitors to the school), discussing cultural variations within a language (e.g. the colorful kaleidoscope of Spanish dances, festivals, customs and traditions from the many Spanish-speaking areas of the world), identifying the varying experiences and perspectives of the particular language variety (e.g. of French Canadians, of the French majority in France, of bilinguals in France (e.g. Breton, Provençal), and classroom visits by native speakers of the language for 'question and answer' sessions.

In Wales, developing a Welsh cultural awareness about Wales is contained in the concept of the 'Curriculum Cymreig' that endeavors to reflect the whole range of historical, social, cultural, political and environmental influences that have shaped contemporary Wales. This involves giving students a sense of place and heritage, of belonging to the local and a wider community with its own traditions, access to the literature of Wales, differences and traditions in use of the Welsh and English languages, the distinctive nature of Welsh music, arts, crafts, technology, religious beliefs and practices (ACAC, 1993). There is a clear emphasis on developing heritage cultural awareness in Mathematics, Science and Technology and not just in Humanities and Aesthetic areas. For example, students study William Jones (1675-1749), a mathematician from Llanfihangel Tre'r Beirdd who first used the 'pi' (π) symbol and Robert Recorde (died 1558) a mathematician from Tenby who devised the 'equals' (=) symbol. In Science, children discuss local soil samples and how they connect with local farming and agriculture, as well as coal and slate mining which have been important to the Welsh economy. Students make contact with local small industries, some of which operate from home via computer and communication networks. Some of this involves cross-curricular activity.

It is sometimes argued that a minority language must be fostered to preserve the attendant culture. The opposite is also tenable. The attendant culture must be fostered in the classroom to preserve the minority language. While separation of culture and language is false, minority language culture can be weakly or strongly represented in the classroom and in the whole ethos of the school. Such culture may be incidentally taught with little intent or rationale. Alternatively, such culture may be consciously included in language teaching and the overall physical and psychological environment of the school. This is particularly valuable to encourage participation by children in their heritage culture. Language skills in the minority language are no guarantee of continued use of that language into teens and adulthood. Enculturation therefore becomes essential if that language is to be useful and used.

Presenting the heritage culture is a most important facet of multicultural education for minority language children. However, it does not remove the need for a broader focus on multiculturalism. Minority language children are often keenly aware of the seeming insignificance of their heritage culture compared with the prestige and high profile of the majority culture. Learning about other languages, cultures and ethnic heritages can be a valuable way of redressing the balance, and of giving such children a fresh and more balanced perspective. Learning about other minority groups may give language minority children a renewed appreciation and pride in their own culture, and a determination to maintain it. Studying other majority cultures makes such children realize that the majority culture that surrounds them does not have the same prestige and influence in other countries.

To foster a minority language in school without fostering its attendant culture may be to fund a costly life-support machine attached to a dying organism. To promote the attendant culture alongside minority language teaching may be to give a life-preserving injection to that language and culture.

REFERENCE: ACAC, 1993

tures may all be worthwhile, as is competition between differing and opposing ideas. Different cultures have used science to develop different knowledge and belief systems as Young (1987, page 19) argues:

> 'Science is practice. There is no other science than the science that gets done. The science that exists is the record of the questions that it has occurred to scientists to ask, the proposals that get funded, the paths that get pursued and the results which lead . . . scientific journals and textbooks to publicize the work. . . . Nature "answers" only the questions that get asked and pursued long enough to lead to results that enter the public domain. Whether or not they get asked, how far they get pursued, are matters for a given society, its educational system, its patronage system and its funding bodies.'

Another danger in multicultural education is in stereotyping 'Third World' situations as rural and rudimentary, famished and inferior. An alternative is in profiling African and Asian scientists, learning about inventions from Africa and India, and discovering the rapid recent changes in horticulture and forestry, soil science and social science in developing countries.

Alternative perspectives should not be included as an appendix to a mainstream view, isolating different perspectives from each other, and presenting a sanitized or expurgated version of history. Instead, there is a need to present integrated multiple perspectives, with the distinctive contributions of different cultural groups justly represented, and the interdependence of different experience faithfully told. For a school, this means avoiding the presentation of isolationist ideas in the curriculum (e.g. only a North American or Eurocentric view of the world) and avoiding cultural supremacist viewpoints (e.g. apartheid). In religious education, isolationism is sometimes taught. For example, a particular Christian fundamentalist or extreme Muslim viewpoint may be taught with alternative viewpoints forbidden. Similarly, supremacist viewpoints need avoiding. An example is when Christianity or Islam is taught as superior to all other world religions.

Yet religion is a key element in multiculturalism. In Europe, religion has re-emerged as a key social issue in relationships between different ethnic and language groups. With the relatively permanent settlement in Europe of eight to nine million in-migrants from West and North West Africa, the Indian subcontinent and South East Asia, the mixing of Muslim (estimated at 6.5 million adherents in Europe), Buddhist, Hindu and Sikh with different Christian denominations has made religion a key element in debates about multiculturalism and multicultural education (Perotti, 1994).

In conclusion, this topic has revealed that attempts to provide multicultural education are varied and diverse in aim, ideology, style and delivery. The term 'multicultural education' is broad, ambiguous and diverse. It ranges from awareness programs for majority language children to the sharing of cultural experiences within a classroom containing a variety of ethnic groups. Multicultural education extends from the transmission of formal knowledge within a classroom, to the informal, hidden and pastoral curriculum, each working towards mutual understanding, and to fighting against prejudice and racism. Multicultural education can be about points of difference – dress and diet, language and religion. It may include lip-service to cultural diversity by a superficial 'saris, samosas, and steel bands' approach. At its worst, multicultural education may unintentionally serve to reinforce and extend differences. The range is from a timetabled, one lesson a week program to a radical reconstruction of both the whole curriculum and of relationships between schools and their communities (Davidman & Davidman, 1994; Nieto, 1996). Multicultural education ranges at one end from occasional, token multicultural lessons to a political movement to secure equality of opportunity, combating underachievement, a political awareness of rights, debates about the reconstruction of society and a redress for the domination of many language and cultural minorities.

Further Reading

DAVIDMAN, L. & DAVIDMAN, P. T., 1994, *Teaching with a Multicultural Perspective: A Practical Guide.* New York: Longman.

LYNCH, J., 1992, *Education for Citizenship in a Multicultural Society.* New York: Cassell.

MAY, S., 1994, *Making Multicultural Education Work.* Clevedon: Multilingual Matters Ltd.

NIETO, S., 1996, *Affirming Diversity: The Sociopolitical Context of Multicultural Education* (Second edition). New York: Longman.

OLNECK, M. R., 1993, Terms of Inclusion: Has Multiculturalism Redefined Equality in American Education. *American Journal of Education,* 101 (3), 234-260.

SLEETER, C. E., & GRANT, C. A., 1987, An Analysis of Multicultural Education in the United States, *Harvard Educational Review,* 57 (4), 421-444.

TODD, R., 1991, *Education in a Multicultural Society.* London: Cassell.

The Role of Schools with In-migrants and Refugee Children

Elizabeth Coelho (1994) provides some sensitive advice regarding the transition of in-migrant and refugee children into the classroom. A few of a wealth of procedures that she recommends for a smooth transition are listed below:

1. Create welcome signs in the languages of the in-migrant children.
2. Ensure that there is a person or team responsible for welcoming the child and family to the school.
3. Use an interpreter where possible to facilitate a transition period. Interview the parents with the interpreter present. This allows for the provision of basic information and the initiation of relationship with parents in a friendly and facilitative manner.
4. Provide children with a welcome booklet in their language, giving basic information about the day-to-day life of the school, special events, and the role of parents.
5. Encourage parents to continue to use the first language at home to promote the child's language development. Explain that development in the first language will help acquisition of the second, majority language.
6. Appoint friendly and sensitive children as official student ambassadors or student friends, to befriend newcomers and help them settle in the school.
7. Funds should be available in the school to assist refugee and in-migrant families with items such as gym clothing, money for field trips, school uniform, extra curriculum resources.
8. The newcomer should be introduced into the classroom in a positive way, showing other children with the aid of a world map where that child originates from, ensuring all children understand the spelling and pronunciation of the newcomer's name, and appreciate that the child speaks a different language at home and is learning the majority language (instead of the negative connotations of the phrase 'So-and-so doesn't speak English); putting a photograph of all children on the wall as a symbol that they all belong equally to the classroom; providing a resource corner for newcomers, and ensuring that the newcomer understands via translation or paralinguistic language the activities and announcements of the day. It is important to communicate positive attitudes about the linguistic and cultural diversity of the classroom.
9. A second (host) language program for adult learners in the school that encourages in-migrant parents to attend helps both the parent and the children. Such a second language program can also provide information about the locality and about survival and success in the new culture and employment system.
10. Hire teaching and non-teaching personnel who speak the major languages of the school: they act as role models for the children, linguistic and cultural interpreters, and inform staff about the cultural backgrounds of children.
11. Make announcements in the different languages of the school, to ensure the spread of information and to raise the status of community languages.
12. Select classroom and library materials with a multicultural and multiracial approach, as well as books in community languages.
13. Establish heritage language programs, either in or out of school hours. Such programs promote children's self-esteem and cultural identity as well as building on their first language skills.

Reference: COELHO, 1994

(Arabic)

Dear Parents,

A lot of attention, in the papers and on the television, has been given recently to childrens reading and language development. We, at Wellington recognize how important it is to develop these skills especially in the Nursery stages, so in the Spring term we would like to run a special language project.

We are planning a range of activities from story telling to making language games. We need your help, your hands and your language skills to make this work.

Please come to our open day on 16th January anytime between 9 and 3.30 p.m. There will be a book display and examples of some of the activities we hope to achieve. We'll be there to chat with you and explain our aims and hear what you have to say. Please do come, it is important and tea and coffee will be available

(English) Wellington Nursery Staff

If your child has lost anything in school, please look in the lost property box in room 7 on the bottom corridor, or ask Mrs. Johnson in the medical room upstairs.

Curriculum Adaptation with In-migrants and Refugee Students

Coelho (1994) makes suggestions about adapting the content and delivery of curriculum in the classroom, and also methods of assessment, to the experiences, viewpoints and value systems of children from a variety of ethnic backgrounds. Here are some of the wide variety of suggestions.

1. Curriculum content and materials should be modified to take students' backgrounds and experiences into account. If materials (e.g. reading books) include concepts, lifestyles, cultural values and habits that are unfamiliar to the students, this will detract from their ability to learn. It is important to introduce unfamiliar content gradually. The content should relate to the real life experiences of the students and depict people of all racial backgrounds and both genders in positive roles.

2. Differences and similarities between cultures should be highlighted and celebrated. Discussing and working on themes such as 'Birthdays', 'Getting Married', 'Coming of Age' help children to appreciate the differences and also the shared experiences of various cultures.

3. The teacher should be aware of children's expectations of the learning process. Newcomers from different cultures may be unfamiliar with an approach which emphasizes student initiative and individual or group projects. They may expect the teacher to guide every step of the way. Student-centered learning should be introduced gradually.

4. Classroom language should be simplified and modified to assist children not yet proficient in the language, especially when the content is new and unfamiliar. New content should not be introduced with new language.

5. Use should be made of group work and cooperative learning techniques. These promote interaction between students and enable them to practice the classroom language in a smaller, less threatening group.

6. Methods of assessment should take account of the fact that there are no tests that are equally appropriate for all cultures. If possible, tests should contain tasks and content with which the children are familiar.

Coelho (1994) concludes with the following:

> 'Immigrant and other language minority children come from many different backgrounds and bring with them a great variety of experience. They face a period of adjustment on entry to school systems where a new language is spoken; for some, this period is very stressful. During this period they need the support of their teachers and the acceptance of their peers. The school program itself is also required to change in order to reflect the presence of all the children in positive ways. Major initiatives in curriculum development, staff development, and community outreach have to be implemented in order to create an appropriate learning environment and home-school relationship.' (page 325).

REFERENCE: COELHO, 1994

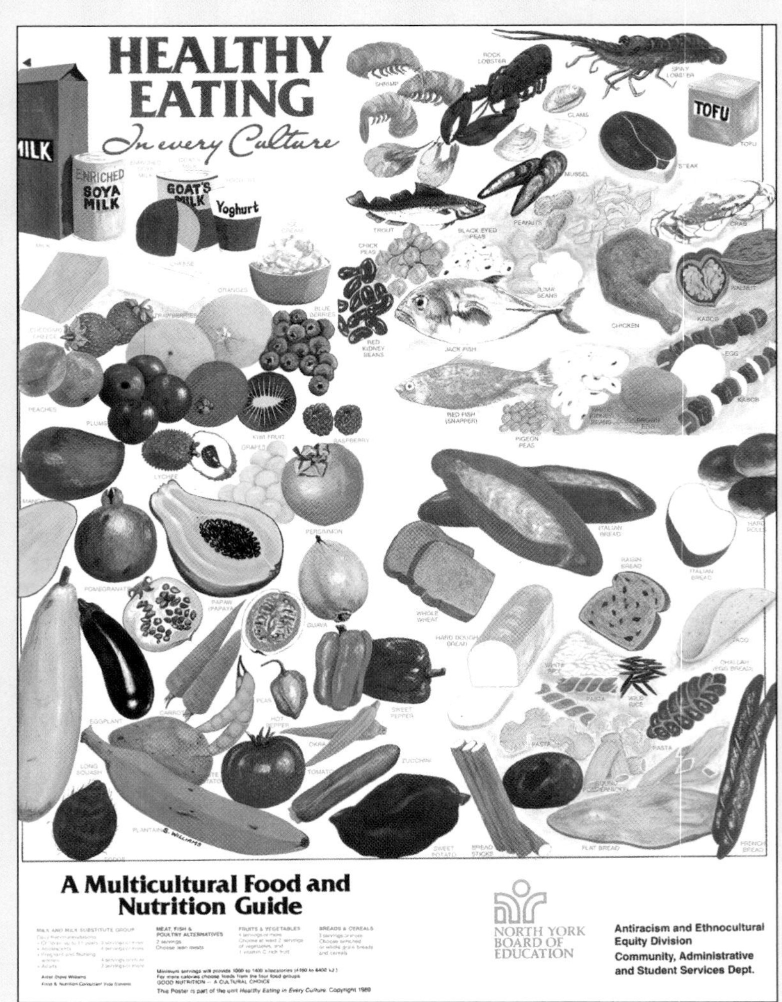

2: Visits and Exchanges to Other Countries and Cultures

Introduction

Since medieval times to the present, it has been customary for affluent parents to send their children abroad for further education and enculturation. In medieval times in Britain, the sons of the rich were sent to cultural centers of Europe such as Paris, Vienna, Florence, Berlin, Rome, Prague and Madrid. Since the 19th century in Europe, the daughters of the rich have often been sent to Swiss Finishing Schools (see Prestigious Bilingualism, page 15) to be refined by contact with other European cultures. In recent decades, many thousands of North Americans, Malaysians, Japanese and other nationalities have traveled abroad with one aim being to extend education and achieve some cultural polish. A refinement of character and a broadening of cultural horizons may be added by interaction with people from other countries. Another aim of visits abroad is for language experience and practice. Such visits may advance a person's bilingualism and biculturalism.

The Central Bureau for Educational Visits and Exchanges in London co-ordinates and promotes international contacts between schools and other types of educational exchange.

Visits

In the 20th century, a variety of 'official' or 'formal' visits and exchanges between individuals and groups from different countries have become common. Under a general heading of 'visits' go twinning links between different countries, where two towns or cities may be in a partnership together. The German expression for this is *'partnerschaft'* which indicates the partnership element. The North Americans often talk about 'sister cities', whereas the French talk about *'jumelage'* which is close to the British concept of twinning.

In a twinning or sister city relationship, the people of two communities attempt to acquire knowledge of each other's way of life and language, discuss mutual interests, and particularly exchange visits and develop friendships. The visits may include school exchanges or visits of special interest groups such as sports teams, choirs, chess clubs, brass bands, theater groups, churches and youth clubs.

School Exchanges

School exchanges, where the students from one school visit students from another school in a different country, have become popular. The visit is reciprocated at a later date. These may be arranged as part of a twinning link, or independently.

A student exchange tends to involve, firstly, some time in a school in the country being visited. Students may attend lessons with their hosts. Rather than just observe lessons, visiting students may participate in lessons, or engage in mutually valuable projects and activities that involve co-operation between students from different countries. Similarly, staff may share teaching roles.

Secondly, there will be excursions to places of interest and organized out-of-school activities so that students from different countries interact with each other. For example, there may be discos, a social evening, plus visits to sports events or museums. Thirdly, the visiting student will spend some time with a family and gain a taste of authentic family life, culture and language in another country. Such students will be introduced to new foods, new life styles, new daily routines and form new relationships by becoming part of a 'foreign' family. These three events (school, excursions and family experience) can provide a valuable language and cultural immersion experience, where language acquisition rather than formal language learning occurs.

The Aims and Nature of Exchanges and Visits Abroad

With the growing popularity of school exchanges and other types of exchanges in Europe, there has been an increasing realization that visits abroad involve more than an exercise in language competence.

Exchanges and links include the following overlapping aims and goals:

- To help students acquire an authentic multicultural, multilingual experience.
- To break down barriers of language and culture, reduce prejudice and increase understanding and awareness of peoples from other countries.
- To increase an awareness of the variety of histories, geographies, cultures, politics and economies in different areas of the world.
- To encourage an interest in, and improve competence in another language.
- To provide a first-hand experience of bilingualism and biculturalism and promote positive attitudes to bilingualism and biculturalism.

With the realization that a school exchange has a wider purpose than that of merely improving language competence, there have been new initiatives in arranging exchanges for a category of students who have traditionally not had access to school visits abroad i.e. students with special needs. These might include students with learning difficulties, emotional or behavioral problems or physical disabilities. In recent years, there have been initiatives in extending the teaching of modern languages to students with special needs. Courses have been devised or adapted with a very practical approach, the aim being to develop a basic language competence and an awareness and appreciation of other countries and cultures. There have been encouraging reports that students have benefited greatly from their modern language experience. Learning skills and social skills have been enhanced, and self-esteem, confidence and motivation have been promoted. (See Modern Languages for Students with Special Needs, page 685).

Some schools for children with special needs have taken a further step of organizing exchanges with special schools abroad. Considerable groundwork has been needed to prepare students for these trips, but the reaction of students to their experience has been mainly positive and enthusiastic. They have had the opportunity to practice basic language skills, have coped with the reality of an unfamiliar environment and culture, different food and new experiences. Their confidence is generally enhanced and their awareness and appreciation of differences in culture and language has been promoted.

School Linking

As school exchanges have become more popular, there has been an increasing emphasis on the value of linking with schools in other countries on a more permanent basis, for several reasons. First, it can provide a way of preparing the students for a school exchange. If students arrive in a foreign country unaware of the differences in culture, knowing little about social conventions and norms of politeness in the host country, unfamiliar with a different school routine and having had no previous contact with the host students or their families, then a school exchange can be a miserable, negative, confidence-sapping experience. A prior link with the exchange school can give students the opportunity to build friendships by letter, learn about the town or city they will be visiting, familiarize themselves with social conventions, (e.g. ways of greeting, handshakes, etc.), talk about the school routine, leisure activities, the food they will be eating and the lifestyle of their peers in the host country.

Second, school linking can be an alternative to a school exchange. A school exchange may not be possible because of financial constraints. Not all school students may be offered the chance to go on an exchange, because of a limited number of places. Elementary school students who are too young to travel abroad on a school exchange may take part in a linking project. School linking permits contact with schools at a great geographical distance. In Britain, for instance, the vast majority of school exchanges take place with schools in Western Europe, mainly France and Germany. School linking allows schools throughout the world to make contact with schools in geographically distant places.

International curriculum linking means that schools can be linked on a number of cross-curricular activities. Linking can involve contact by letter or parcel, but also the use of the latest technology, fax and electronic mail (e-mail). Overnight e-mail, where messages are sent one evening for arrival the next morning, has cut the cost for budget-conscious schools. Schools can exchange letters, poems, songs, stories, artwork and photographs. They can collaborate on environmental, scientific or mathematical projects. Videos of the school, students, neighborhood and places of interest can be made. Audio cassettes can be recorded by the students.

School linking can be a preparation for school exchanges, but is valuable in its own right. It can involve

Five European Programs

The ERASMUS Program

This program was adopted by the European Community in June 1987 to promote student mobility and co-operation between Higher Education institutions in 12 Member States. Over 100,000 European students per year are eligible to spend a fully recognized part of their course of study in another European country. Students are given a grant towards expenses involved in studying abroad (e.g. travel, language courses, extra costs of accommodation and living). Exemption is given from paying tuition fees to the host institution. The objectives of the ERASMUS program include:

- To increase staff and student mobility across higher education in Europe, for long-term study, short-term courses and visits.
- To promote broad and lasting inter-institutional co-operation.
- To develop the European dimension in higher education, including the learning of European languages and the incorporation into curricula of material on other Member States.
- To contribute to the economic and social development of Europe through the creation of a significant number of higher education graduates with direct experience of European co-operation.
- The development of comparable curricula, to facilitate recognition of academic qualifications between countries.

The LINGUA Program

This program was adopted in July 1989 to promote foreign language competence throughout the European Union. Mobility of language teachers was encouraged as well as innovative projects in initial and in-service training. Language teachers have been encouraged to improve their own communication skills, cultural knowledge and teaching competence. Support has been given for the preparation of language teaching materials, and for the use of new educational technologies, including distance learning.

The languages covered by LINGUA are Spanish, Danish, German, Greek, English, French, Irish, Italian, Luxembourgish, Dutch and Portuguese. An important priority of the program has been to support the teaching and learning of the 'least widely used and least taught' of these languages.

The SOCRATES program

In June 1994, the European Union adopted this program. Three areas of action are intended to cover 75 million young people. It aims to add a strong European dimension to young people's studies and their preparation for working life. The Program should help them 'benefit from the career opportunities of a truly open European employment market'.

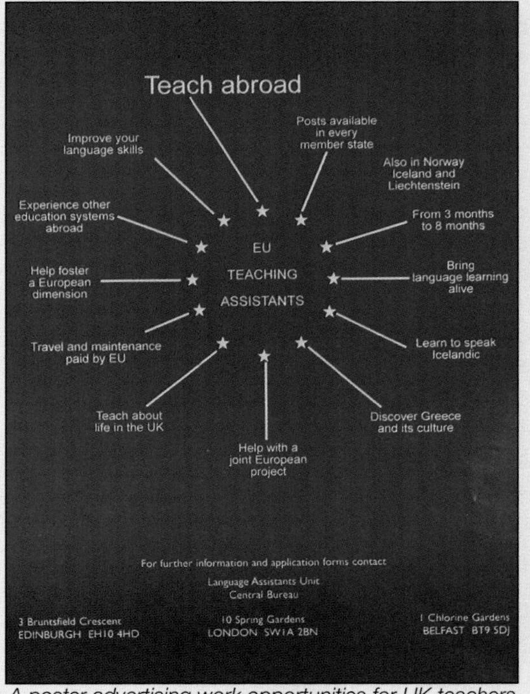

A poster advertising work opportunities for UK teachers in other EU countries under the Lingua Program.

First, under the SOCRATES program, the ERASMUS initiative is continued. Second, a COMENIUS initiative is directed at school education. One of the aims of COMENIUS is to create partnerships between schools in different Member States. The partnership would involve projects and activities with a European dimension, and exchange of information and teaching materials between schools. COMENIUS also supports equal educational opportunities for the children of migrant workers, occupational travelers and Gypsies. COMENIUS also promotes intercultural education for all children, and the improvement of the skills of educational staff.

Third, HORIZONTAL ACTIVITIES includes a continuation of the LINGUA program. It supports open learning and distance education, adult education, and the exchange of information and experience in education. An underlying language aim is captured in the following quote from the SOCRATES program:

> 'The promotion of language skills is a key factor in establishing an open European area for co-operation in education and for strengthening understanding and solidarity between the peoples of the European Union without sacrificing any of their linguistic and cultural diversity.'

KALEIDOSCOPE 1995

This European Community Program promotes cultural exchange and co-operation within Europe. Innovative cultural events are supported as is the European mobility and further training of creative and performing artists. Cultural networks in Europe are promoted to increase cultural co-operation in the European Community.

Not only are EC Member States engaged in the Program, but the partnership extends to Bulgaria, the Czech Republic, Hungary, Poland, Romania and Slovakia.

LEONARDO

This is a four year program (1995–1999) providing support for vocational training within the European Union. It supports transnational mobility and exchanges of expertise and experience, work placements and training courses abroad. The aims are:

- to improve vocational training systems by joint training actions and modules, work placements and international exchanges;
- to increase co-operation between the work force, companies and higher education (e.g. training for innovation and technology transfer);
- to develop the linguistic capabilities of those in vocational training;
- to promote the European dimension in vocational training.

every single student in a school, including those who may never participate in a school exchange.

Teacher Exchanges

Teacher exchanges may form part of a school exchange, or may be conducted separately. Language teachers may swap posts for a number of weeks (e.g. a teacher of French in England and an teacher of English in France may exchange jobs for two or three weeks). The students benefit from being taught the foreign language by a native speaker, and from having access to authentic and up to date materials from the target country. (The teacher of English may bring a selection of teenage magazines, English language pop or rock records, videos, CDs, British food, etc. for the students in France.) The teachers themselves benefit from the opportunity to brush up their language skills in an authentic environment, to have contact with contemporary school and cultural life in the target country, to collect materials for language lessons in their home school.

Teachers of other subjects benefit from study visits in other countries and the opportunity for first-hand observation of teaching methods, curriculum content and materials and teacher-student interaction. Teacher exchanges can be a step in initiating or promoting collaboration between schools in curricular projects.

Work Experience in Other Countries

There is an increasing interest in work experience in other countries arranged through different programs (e.g in the European Community). This provides language experience that is relevant, authentic and focused. Social and personal development is promoted, as well as professional or vocational education. Work exchanges promote cultural awareness and prepare students for life in an increasingly mobile workforce. Work placements may be in banks, schools, hotels, offices, factories and businesses, cafés and restaurants. To gain the maximum benefit from a work placement, students must be prepared for their duties, and for the specific language demands likely to be made on them. They must also be adequately supported and monitored in the placement. Direct work experience may not always be possible, e.g. because the duties of a certain position are beyond the student's professional or linguistic competence, or because local health and safety regulations may not permit it. As an alternative to work experience, visits may be arranged for work observation or work shadowing. Students make a visit of one or more days to a workplace where they accompany employees on their daily duties, observing their work and asking questions.

The Effectiveness of an Exchange

The value and effectiveness of an exchange depends on criteria such as (Hamnett, 1992):

- Does the exchange offer insights into the language and culture of a different community?
- Does the exchange encourage positive attitudes to languages and other cultures?
- Does the exchange promote cultural awareness?
- Does the exchange help to improve linguistic competence in an important way?
- Does the exchange contribute to the participants' knowledge of another culture and more sensitivity to others' experience and lifestyle?
- Does the exchange widen students' perspectives on different languages and cultures?
- Does the exchange enhance social contacts which are further developed over time?
- Does the exchange enable participants to reduce their own preconceptions, prejudices and reduce stereotypes of other countries and nations?

Further Reading

CENTRAL BUREAU FOR EDUCATIONAL VISITS AND EXCHANGES, 1994, *Home from Home: The Complete Guide to Homestays and Exchanges* (Third edition). London: Central Bureau for Educational Visits and Exchanges (also Cincinnati, OH: Seven Hills).

CENTRAL BUREAU FOR EDUCATIONAL VISITS AND EXCHANGES, 1996, *Making the Most of your Partner School Abroad*. London: Central Bureau for Educational Visits and Exchanges.

CENTRAL BUREAU FOR EDUCATIONAL VISITS AND EXCHANGES, 1996, *School Linking Across the World – A Directory of Agencies Supporting North-South Linking*. London: Central Bureau for Educational Visits and Exchanges.

3: Language Awareness: Knowledge About Language

Introduction

There is an important difference between language learning and language awareness. The traditional aim of language learning has been for learners to acquire an accurate knowledge of language, with the accent on correct grammar, spelling and pronunciation of a standard form of the language. Irrespective of whether the language is a first language, a second language or a foreign language, the accent in the school curriculum has been on accuracy and conformity to a standardized norm.

In the 1970s, language teachers adopted a different view of language to that of accuracy. They saw language, not as a pattern or structure, but as having different purposes or functions. A functional approach to the study of language emphasizes the importance of using appropriate communication in varying contexts. The language to be used depends on whom a person is speaking to, on what occasion, where, and particularly for what purpose. Differences in context require different uses of language. There is the language of the shop, of science lessons, of the street, and of story telling. Whether students were studying their first language or learning a second or foreign language, the emphasis was on using contextually appropriate language.

In conjunction with this, the idea that bilinguals use their languages in different contexts and domains (as in the concept of diglossia) became important. A child might use Gujarati at home, Arabic in the Mosque, English at school and learn French as foreign language. A bilingual's languages have different purposes and functions and are used in different contexts.

Language awareness is a relatively new topic – and one which is growing in popularity and power. Only recently has knowledge about language or language awareness been included in the curriculum. This can involve, for example, making students aware of different dialects and accents, and showing how the language varies with sociocultural class, age, race, creed, occupation and gender. The aim is to focus on an analysis of the language that is used. Language awareness involves reflection about languages, encouraging curiosity about language itself, an exploration of language, and the raising of implicit knowledge about language to a conscious, explicit level.

Definition

One definition is that 'Language Awareness is a person's sensitivity to and conscious awareness of the nature of language and its role in human life' (Donmall, 1985, page 7). Part of language awareness is to improve sensitivity to, and tolerance of linguistic diversity. Appreciation of bilinguals and bilingualism is one key element in language awareness. So too are awareness, insight and understanding of the variety of world languages, as well as tolerance and curiosity about the form and functions of languages. Defining 'Language Awareness' can be clarified and broadened by examining its aims.

The Aims and Goals of Language Awareness

The aims and goals of language awareness include the following:

1. To make explicit a student's implicit knowledge of their first language or languages.
2. To develop skills in studying languages.
3. To develop a perception and understanding of the structure, nature and functions of language.
4. To increase effectiveness in communication in the first, second and/or foreign languages.
5. To give insights into the language learning process and thereby to aid the learning of the first language, second language and foreign languages.
6. To develop an understanding among students of the richness of language variety within the class, school, community, region, nation and world. This may include discussing the variety of spoken and written forms of, for example, Spanish, Chinese, French, English, German throughout the world. This is to mitigate feelings of inferiority amongst those who speak a variety of a language (e.g. English as a second or third language).
7. To foster better relations between ethnic groups by arousing students' awareness of the origins and characteristics of their own language and its place in the world.

A Language Awareness Lesson at North Westminster Community School, London

The 20 twelve year olds were buzzing quietly while the register was called. There were only 20 because last night was the school play and some had leave to come in after the break. I passed a paper to my neighbor, a girl from Armenia, and asked her to write down for me the countries of origin of the pupils present. This was her list (some of her spellings amended): Bulgaria, Italy, Vietnam, Lebanon, Yemen, Egypt, Bangladesh, Portugal, North Africa, Iran, Scotland, England.

The lesson began briskly. ... [The teacher] referred to an earlier discussion about 'language families'. What was the evidence that languages belonged to families? Several pupils gave instances from counting in the Indo-European family.

Why did some languages spread far away from the places where they were first used? Why had English spread so far? How far?

Deftly, without losing the thread, the teacher produced and unfolded a large map of the world which she blue-tacked to the blackboard behind her. A chair was placed in front of the board and volunteers were invited to come out and find countries where English is spoken.

So directly to the main theme planned for the lesson: another great world language, Arabic. Where is Arabic spoken?

Pupils in the class who spoke Arabic came out in turn, got up on the chair and found their own country of origin on the map. So, one by one, the Lebanon, the Yemen, Iran and Algeria were located. Was Arabic spoken in countries so far apart? What about the countries in between? How many can you count? Let's look at it more closely.

Here the teacher produced a lesson hand-out, ready cyclostyled, showing in outline the Mediterranean and the Middle East and listing 18 Arabic-speaking countries. Later in the lesson pupils would work on the hand-out.

Before we do that, can anybody tell us why Arabic spread so widely? Was it like the spread of English, following trade and colonization?

The teacher mentioned the use of Arabic in Muslim prayers. She used the word 'liturgical' language and asked the class to remember the word. Some of the pupils looked unimpressed.

When did Arabic spread so widely? The date 622 AD was written on the board. The date of Mohammed's flight from Mecca to Medina.

So Muslims got a new calendar, different from the Christian calendar. Who else uses a different calendar from the Christian one? The Jews. And who else? Of course, the Chinese.

But back to our map of the Arabic language. Do Arabic speakers in all these 18 countries all speak the same form of Arabic?

Let's count to ten in Arabic. (This had been learnt in a previous lesson and many of the pupils could remember most of it.) Do all our Arabic-speaking pupils agree? No! The pupil from the Lebanon and the one from Algeria both disagreed with the teacher, but for different reasons. The pupil from the Yemen thought the teacher's Arabic numbers were OK. The teacher asked the class to compare the distance from Belfast to London. From her own experience she gave examples of differences between her own idiom, and accent, and London 'standard' forms.

Was it to be expected that over the much greater distances the forms of Arabic would differ? Again volunteers came out and identified on the map the countries referred to.

Let's go on with Arabic. When you come to a strange country what is the first thing you might want to say? 'Hello!' Practise this in Arabic. But first an interesting contrast with English. A different address and reply for girls and boys. Again the Arabic speakers volunteered their own experience and their versions.

In many of the Arabic-speaking countries a second language was also commonly used. Examples? Volunteers mentioned French and Spanish. Why was this? The spread of these languages. Why?

Now what about the written form of Arabic. Was this different in different countries? The teacher said the written form of Arabic was spread by the Koran and the Muslim prayers. (Again the word 'liturgical' was insisted on.) At this point there was a diversion. A pupil who had been given an individual project to work on in a previous lesson wished to report. He had consulted his parents and found out why certain parts of his country of origin, the Yemen, are densely populated and others desert. He read his report carefully and it was briefly discussed.

Time was running on and now the pupils had to turn to the written task planned for the lesson. They were asked to fill in the prepared outline on the hand-out.

The discussion had been two-way and purposeful. Despite the distraction of a lot of noise from heavy traffic outside the windows which sometimes made it hard to hear the teacher or the pupils, and the presence of several pupils with learning problems who might have been capable of upsetting a less professionally equipped teacher's plans, the lesson had proceeded throughout with businesslike concentration on the questions that the teacher had planned to raise with the class.

Her winning smile, her obvious rapport with the pupils and their respect for her, and her well-prepared materials, all made for an interesting and thought-provoking lesson. A marked feature was the way in which, at each stage in the discussion, the multilingual nature of the class, far from being a 'problem' to be overcome, was turned into an enrichment giving force and example, at the level that pupils could readily seize, to each step in the exploration. It was more like a seminar with 12 year olds taking part on level terms, than the conventional lesson.

But it was time to move next door, where a similar group of pupils, with an equally gifted teacher (like the first, a conventionally trained modern linguist who had acquired a knowledge of non-European languages partly with the help of pupils in the school) was engaged in a discussion of 'writing'. With the help of a hand-out she was exploring logographic systems, with special reference to Chinese, which the pupils were practicing writing, using felt-tip pens in various colors.

KNOWLEDGE ABOUT LANGUAGE
it's all around you...
PURPOSE
INITIALS ABBREVIATIONS
IDIOMS
LANGUAGE AND IDEOLOGY IDENTITY
PLACE NAMES
NATIONALITY
WORD STRUCTURE
PERSUASIVE LANGUAGE
CLICHES
JOKES
PUNS
BILINGUALISM
AUDIENCE
FOREIGN BORROWINGS
INVENTED SPELLING
ARCHAIC TERMS
FORM
READING REPERTOIRE
READING AND GENDER, AGE
LANGUAGE AND THE PRESS
AMBIGUITY
RHYME AND SPELLING
TEXT AND ILLUSTRATION
SIGNS
HEADLINES
ARCHAIC LANGUAGE
LANGUAGE AND RELIGION
PERSUASIVE LANGUAGE
A CUT ABOVE
WRAP N'SELL PARTY SUPPLIES "LET YOUR HAIR DOWN"
MOORE MOORE AND STILLMORE
PHARMACIST fferyllydd
KALORY KOUNT KAFE
PRUE'S NEWS
TOBACCONIST STATIONER'S
TROUBLE IN SLEEPING Don't count Sheep contact the SHEPHERD
PREPARE YE THE WAY OF THE LORD
ORGAN APPEAL
MARKET SQUARE
EYE LEVEL
L. Davies
Sick as a parrot? NO MORE PILLS PARROTS ATE 'EM ALL
HEDEX FOR HEADACHES
LINCTUS KALPOL
WAITRESS WANTED
NO DOGS ALLOWED
The Fokal Point
FREEHOUSE
WE SH BR W R'S
BAR MEALS AT YOUR LOKAL
CAN THE DOLLAR HAVE POSSIBLY FALLEN 17 POINTS ON THE DOW-JONES INDEX OVERNIGHT? ANOTHER BLACK MONDAY?
AT THIRTEEN HUNDRED HOURS I WAS PROCEEDING DOWN MARKET SQUARE...
JARGON
LANGUAGE AND OCCUPATION
THE SHAMBLES
CWMDU
CHURN WORKS
TUNSGATE
PENTRE FELIN
BUS STOP
(KEY) STAGE 2/3
IF I HADN'T PRANGED MY WHEELS - I WOULDN'T BE STUCK NEXT TO THIS OLD BIDDY
RWY NEWYDD FEDDWL AM RAP GRÊT I DDECHRAU'R GYMANFA.
JIW! JIW!, IN DADCU'S DAY WE 'AD A GAMBO TO GET FROM BY 'ERE TO BY THERE
NOW WHERE'S MY BUS PASS? I WOULDN'T HAVE NEEDED IT ON THE CHARABANC OR THE TRAM
MY PROF'S PROMISED TO GIVE ME A BIBLIOGRAPHY FOR MY DISSERTATION BEFORE THIS AFTERNOON'S SEMINAR. I HOPE SHE'S NOT LATE.
NOW MUMMY AND JOHNNY WILL GO FOR A NICE RIDE HOME ON THE BUS.
GOO, - GOO
ADAGIO, NOW, BACH! PUT YOUR CHOPIN IN HERE ALLEGRO, THE REST OF YOU LOOK VIVACE, NOT SO FORTE. WHAT A PERFORMANCE!
REGIONAL DIALECT
LANGUAGE & CULTURE
LANGUAGE CHANGE: OLD & NEW WORDS
DIALECT & AGE-LANGUAGE & GENDER
TERRITORY MARKING ANIMAL COMMUNICATION
I'M A BOW-LEGGED CHICKEN I'M A KNOCK-KNEED SPARROW MISSED MY BUS SO I WENT BY BARROW
LISZT
MOTHERESE
LANGUAGE ACQUISITION
AMBIGUITY
TECHNICAL TERMS
LANGUAGE & TOPIC
CHILDREN'S GAME LANGUAGE & RITUAL

Knowledge about Language Poster

The poster, on page 630 opposite, was produced by the Welsh Joint Education Committee in July 1991. Using some general and some specifically Welsh illustrations, the poster cleverly and imaginatively proclaims that language is all around us. The poster shows that language is not uniform and monochrome: there can be different styles of language. This diversity can be even richer in a bilingual situation, Some of the messages of the poster are now briefly listed.

- Language varies according to the context in which it is used (e.g. the persuasive language of advertisements; official language of police; the jargon of teenagers and students; mother-baby talk; stock market jargon; musical terminology).
- Different styles of language are used by different people. The speech of the people in the poster varies according to their age, occupation, social background and region of origin.
- Language is continuously changing with new words being invented. Other words become obsolete e.g. charabanc and tram. Words may be borrowed from other languages to express certain concepts e.g. the foreign foods listed on the café window, the musical terms used by the conductor. Language can also express continuity of tradition and culture over time, e.g. the children's hopscotch rhyme.
- The way people speak contains variations of dialect, accent, word borrowing, codeswitching, clichés, idioms, archaic terms, jargon and slang (e.g. pranged my wheels=smashed my car).
- Language can be manipulated creatively for effect, to attract, inform or sometimes merely to make a joke. The rhyme and alliteration in the shop names are one example of language used to gain attention. The musical bus conductor puns on the word 'Bach' which is the name of a composer and also means 'little one' in Welsh. The presence of an orchestral conductor instead of a bus conductor is itself a visually-expressed pun.
- In a bilingual situation, people may codeswitch from one language to another. In the bus queue, the old gentleman speaks English, but uses Welsh words from his childhood. (*Dadcu*=Grandfather: *Gambo*=Cart). The minister in front of him is speaking Welsh but borrows from contemporary English slang. (I've just thought of a great rap to start the hymn singing service.)

Typical Content of a Language Awareness Course

Animal communication
How bees, dolphins, birds, ants and whales communicate.

Non-verbal communication
The use of facial expressions, gestures, body language to communicate. For example, different greetings and gestures in the world may be enacted in pair work: hand shaking, bowing, the Hindu 'palms together to forehead' greeting, the kiss of peace, the European Continental kiss on each cheek.

Signs and symbols
For example, traffic signs, shop signs, advertisement signs and the Morse code may be studied.

Reading and scripts
The variety of text type (e.g. Greek, German, Arabic, English, Hebrew, Bengali).

World languages
Who speaks which language to whom and where. Language families of the world may be taught not so much for their geographical content but more for language awareness of the variety of languages around the globe, and the relationship between them.

Variations in dialect and accent
Variations according to sociocultural class, age, race, occupation, creed and gender.

How language changes
How new words such as megabyte, telefax, sweat-shirt, flyover, hovercraft came to be invented, how words change their meaning (e.g. in a version of the Eysenck Personality Test there used to be a statement 'Can you usually let yourself go and enjoy yourself at a gay party?' The word 'gay' has changed its meaning, from 'lively' in this sentence, to 'homosexual' in everyday talk.) Change also means the disappearance of 'old-fashioned' words in a language.

Bilingualism and language contact
Codeswitching and foreign borrowings (e.g. matador, croissant) as well as shared words (e.g. discotheque in English, French, Spanish) may be considered.

Language standardization and shift
How language shift occurs across decades and centuries. How calls for standardization are linked with a desire for unification in an ethnic group.

Language and power
How language varies according to purpose and audience. In this module, language for persuasion, assertion, information, deception, and power brokering may be studied. Examples of the relationship between language and power may include: (1) adverts on television and on the subway; (2) the language of religion to persuade and attract; (3) the psychology of television, radio and street adverts; (4) the use of language alongside images, humor, rhyme and music to persuade.

Language use
For example, the use of idioms, clichés, jokes, puns, jargon, motherese, interlanguage.

Gender and language
The use of sexist language; how gender is embedded in a language (e.g. in talking about God; the difference between grammatical gender and sexual gender).

8. To help students overcome any feeling of dislocation between the language of the home, the language of the school, of text books and employment.
9. To impart an understanding of the value of language as a crucial part of human life.
10. To develop an understanding of bilingualism and biculturalism in the world.

The aims and goals of language awareness do NOT usually include the following:

1. Language awareness is not a Trojan horse to return to grammar-translation methods in teaching a second or foreign language, even though such methods impart knowledge about language. However, learning about grammar and all other aspects of language structure can increase awareness about language and can be a part of a language awareness program.
2. Language awareness courses do not replace the learning of a second and/or foreign language. Language awareness is an add-on and not a replacement for language learning.
3. Language awareness courses are not for the less able students who seem to have less aptitude for second or foreign language learning. Language awareness courses are for every child, from primary school through secondary education to tertiary and higher education.

James & Garrett (1991) suggest that there are five domains of language awareness:

1. The affective domain refers to forming attitudes, awakening and developing attention, sensitivity, curiosity, interest and aesthetic responses from students.
2. The social domain aims to foster better relationships between all ethnic groups. Language awareness is seen as an instrument for social harmonization through an understanding of language diversity in the world.
3. The power domain is important in that it allows students to understand how language is used as an instrument of persuasion, manipulation as well as information. Students are encouraged to be sensitive to the purpose of language, as well as to give the student control over their language for communicative as well as achievement purposes.

   Language awareness in Brazil is called *conscientizacao*. Influenced by the work of Paulo Freire, language awareness explores political as well as educational uses. Social and political awareness can be achieved through increasing language proficiency. To read critically or to understand the message of a politician, analysis of the style and content of language is crucial. Students need to be made conscious of the polemic, power and persuasion qualities of language. Such conscious realization of the power of language becomes empowering. Hidden meanings, tacit assumptions and rhetorical traps in newspapers and on television, politicians' oratory from soap boxes can be perceived and understood by students. Governments, religious organizations, marketing companies and politicians, for example, all use language to persuade and occasionally deceive. Language awareness attempts to give a student the power of linguistic vigilance.
4. The cognitive domain aims at improving the intellectual functioning of students. This may be achieved through developing awareness of language pattern, contrast, system, categories, rules of language in use and the ability to reflect upon language. Enabling students, for example, to develop clarity of expression, to analyze and be sensitive to their own communication, may enable them to grow cognitively.
5. Finally, the performance domain attempts to improve efficiency and proficiency in an individual's language use. Competence in language use is encouraged in language awareness courses through a deeper understanding of how language is best learnt and how it works.

The description of five categories of language awareness helps to clarify and broaden a vision of language awareness. There is also an interaction between these domains as is visible in a consideration of types of language awareness course that exist.

Further Reading

DONMALL, B. G. (ed.) 1985, *Language Awareness*. London: Centre for Information on Language Teaching and Research (CILT).

FAIRCLOUGH, N. (ed.), 1992, *Critical Language Awareness*. London and New York: Longman.

HAWKINS, E., 1992, Awareness of Language/Knowledge About Language in the Curriculum in England and Wales: An Historical Note on Twenty Years of Curricular Debate. *Language Awareness*, 1 (1), 5-17.

JAMES, C. & GARRETT, P. (eds), 1991, *Language Awareness in the Classroom*. London: Longman.

4: A Critical Awareness of Language

In the previous topic, three aspects of language study were described, namely, accuracy, contextual appropriateness, and language awareness. First, there has traditionally been a view of language that stresses the importance of accuracy and conformity to a single, standard or literary language. According to this viewpoint, language can be either correct or incorrect. Dialectal forms, colloquial speech or street slang are usually deemed incorrect or inferior. This perspective makes value judgements about different types of language and deems that some are better than others. Instead, all languages or styles of language may be seen as 'linguistically equal', none linguistically superior to another, each able to convey meanings and ideas as well as any other language.

Second, a recent perspective on language has emerged, namely, that language should be contextually appropriate. No form of language is intrinsically better or more valuable than others, but different types or forms of language are appropriate in different contexts. People may use different styles or registers of language, or even different languages, in the boardroom or bar, in the shop or street, but one is not better than another. In bilingual or diglossic situations different languages may be appropriate in different contexts, without one being superior to another.

The third perspective on language has stressed the importance of an awareness of language. Language awareness courses also promote an 'egalitarian' view of language. Through discussions of different dialects and different languages, through looking at the way languages change and influence one another, students become aware that different languages and different registers or styles of language are equally effective as modes of communication. They learn tolerance of linguistic as well as cultural differences.

However, one aspect of language awareness that has become more evident in recent years is a critical awareness of language. This aspect of language awareness explores how languages or styles of language reflect and sustain differences in power and status. Critical awareness of language focuses on the status differences between varieties within the one language (e.g. the way English is spoken in different parts of US, Ireland and Britain). There is usually a standard variety (or standardized variety) and alongside that, dialects or styles of language that, implicitly and sometimes explicitly, are judged by those in power as deviations from the norm. Critical awareness also explores how the use of majority and minority languages mirrors the differences in power and status of their users.

For language learners, particularly for students from a language minority, there is danger in both the 'correctness/accuracy' and the 'contextual appropriateness' viewpoints of language. Both are normative. That is, in both these viewpoints, there are conventions of accuracy and appropriateness to which people must conform. Such viewpoints do not challenge how languages maintain inequality in power and status. Power relations, for example, affect how people speak to each other. Those groups with high status, much power and who are dominant in society are regarded as using the correct language accurately and appropriately. Language can exclude people. For example, a student who cannot use language in an academic way may be seen as having less knowledge, less intelligence and hence less value. In a majority/minority language situation, a person who is not proficient in the majority language may be perceived as being unintelligent or inferior (although that person may be a fluent and articulate speaker of the minority language).

There are power relations in everyday language. For example, when a person visits the doctor, the doctor asks questions and receives replies and content-appropriate questions from the patient. Given that the doctor has high medical status, the patient is usually perceived as inferior in status. Asking the doctor a string of inappropriate questions, thereby disrupting the status/power relationship, is usually regarded as unacceptable.

A critical view of language recognizes that there are prestigious social groups who symbolize and maintain their status and power through language forms. A critical view of language means an awareness that language can convey discrimination, superiority, inferiority, dominance and ascendancy. Such an awareness may allow the bilingual, for example, to challenge, as well as be aware of, how language reinforces and sometimes creates inferiority and superiority. Such awareness may include the idea that language is not fixed, not a natural right of any one power group. A critical awareness also assumes that perceptions of accuracy and appropriateness change over years, are not fixed but are socially constructed.

A List of Objectives for Critical Language Awareness

Critical awareness of the relationship between language and power

1. Recognize how people with power choose the language to describe people, things and events.
2. Understand how language, especially written language, has been shaped by the more prestigious social groups, and seems to exclude and sometimes devalue other lower status groups.
3. Understand how the relative status of people involved affects the way they use language.
4. Recognize that when power relations change, language changes too – both historically and between individuals.
5. Understand that language use can either reproduce or challenge existing power relations.

Critical awareness of language variety

1. Recognize the nature of prejudice about language minorities, different languages of the world, and varieties of English.
2. Understand why some languages or language varieties are valued more than others.
3. Understand how devaluing languages or language varieties devalues their users.
4. Value an individual's spoken language.
5. Recognize that speakers of languages and varieties other than standardized English also contain experts.

Turning awareness into action

1. Recognize how language can either be offensive or show respect. Become sensitive to choosing language accordingly.
2. Recognize what possibilities for change exist in current circumstances, and what are the constraints.
3. Learn how to understand and challenge different conventions of language practice in different circumstances.
4. Learn how to oppose conventional language practice.

ADAPTED FROM: IVANIC, 1990

From the 'critical awareness' perspective, languages are not all equal. Some are more prestigious than others, requiring a critical awareness of how, why, where and when different languages have different values placed upon them. Within a critical view of language, accuracy and appropriateness are not skills to be learnt. Rather they need to be questioned, criticized and understood. While people may want to conform to standards of language accuracy and appropriateness, they may also need to challenge such standards. A person living in Asia, for example, may learn English as a second language for a specific purpose such as employment and educational success. That person may need to be made aware that English does not have to be learnt at the cost of the mother tongue, nor does it have to conform to a British or US standard of English.

It may be important for people to become critically aware of their own values with regard to languages, any conflicts in those values, and importantly, to become aware that language used by higher status groups can be patronizing, demeaning, disrespectful, offensive and exclusive. Language minorities are labeled, patronized, excluded, distanced and devalued by language majority groups. Critical language awareness can give someone self-assurance in how, when, where and with whom they use their one, two or more languages. A bilingual may thus feel confident and safe enough to challenge the present power structures and differences in status that are marked by language. With critical language awareness, bilinguals may challenge the status quo by requesting certain information in a language other than the majority language, they may codeswitch without feeling guilty, and use non standardized forms of English for example when speaking and writing.

Further Reading

FAIRCLOUGH, N. (ed.), 1992, *Critical Language Awareness*. London and New York: Longman.

IVANIC, R., 1990, Critical Language Awareness in Action. In R. CARTER (ed.), *Knowledge about Language and the Curriculum*. London: Hodder & Stoughton.

WIDDOWSON, H. G., 1995, Discourse and Social Change. *Applied Linguistics*, 16 (4), 510-516.

Bilingualism and Second Language Acquisition

1: An Introduction to Second Language Acquisition

Introduction

This topic examines some key frameworks and theories of second language acquisition. The topic is a broad one, and is an important aspect of bilingualism. Apart from those bilinguals who learn two languages simultaneously from birth (see Development of Bilingualism in Childhood, page 36), people become bilinguals by acquiring a second language as children or adults. The topic also focuses on the main factors that might affect the degree, rate and success of second language acquisition (e.g. age, aptitude and motivation).

Some people become bilinguals by picking up a language informally in a natural environment e.g. small children picking up a second language in the community. Others become bilingual by studying a language formally in a classroom. Some researchers on second language acquisition make a useful distinction between informal acquisition of a language and formal learning. However, the distinction between acquisition and learning is not clear or absolute. Many people become bilingual through a combination of informal acquisition and formal learning (e.g. in-migrants gradually picking up a second language at work and with neighbors, and also studying the language at night classes). The accent these days in many second language classrooms is on acquiring language informally and incidentally while engaged in interesting communicative activities. Thus any distinction between 'acquisition' and 'learning' is a useful way of indicating in general terms how a person has gained competence in a second language, but is not meant to be a scientific description of the process. (See Krashen's Monitor Model, page 649.)

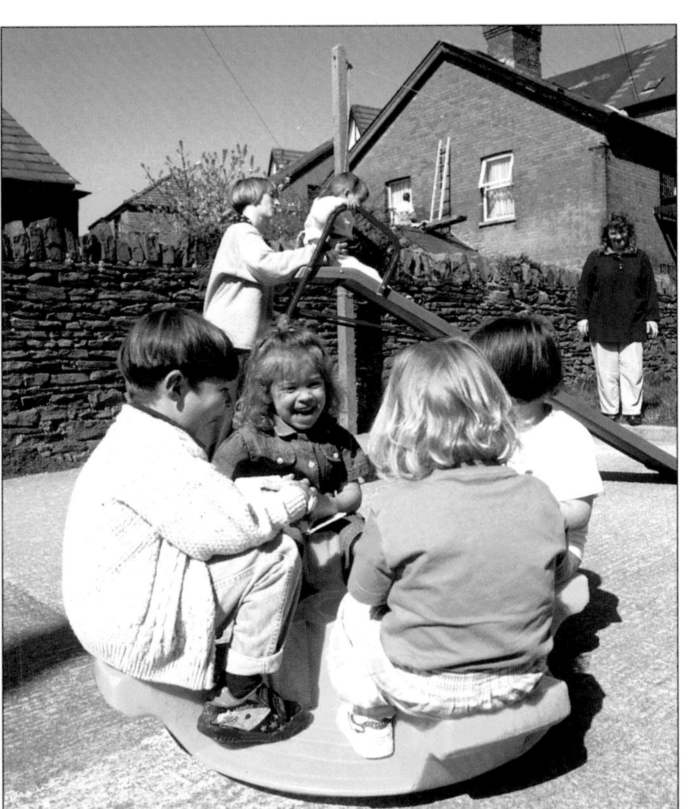

Language can be acquired informally, at play or in the neighborhood.

Central Issues

The important issues surrounding second language acquisition can be summarized in one question: 'Who learns how much of what language under what conditions?' Spolsky (1989c, page 3). Answers to this question form the substance of this topic.

The 'who learns' question raises a debate about individual differences. Who learns a second language more easily, more quickly and with better retention? What part do general ability, aptitude for learning a language, attitudes to a language, motives and personality play in second language learning? What is the size of each factor's contribution? How do these factors interrelate in a 'successful' second language acquisition equation? The word 'learns' accents the idea of a process, constantly changing and evolving.

The 'how much of what language' part of the question focuses on what is being learnt: oral skills, written skills, fluency for everyday communication, grammar for test and examination purposes? What is the yardstick for successful learning? What dialect of language has been

Students in Tokyo, Japan, study English. Language can be learned formally and consciously in the classroom.

learnt? Has another culture been acquired as part of language acquisition?

The 'under what conditions' phrase in the question highlights situation and context. What effect do different learning environments have on the acquisition of a second language: a formal teacher-directed classroom, flexible individual learning, adult classes (e.g. an Ulpan), acquisition in the street and community, correspondence courses, different forms of bilingual education (e.g. immersion and submersion)? What teaching strategies are more or less effective?

Distinctions and Definitions

Ellis (1985) makes a distinction between three parts of the development of a second language. First, there is the sequence in second language learning. This refers to the general stages through which children and adults move in learning a second language. Irrespective of the language and irrespective of whether that language is acquired naturally or formally in the classroom, there is a natural and almost invariant sequence of development. Moving from simple vocabulary to basic syntax, to the structure and shape of simple sentences, to complex sentences is a reasonably universal sequence in language acquisition.

Second, the order in which a language is learnt may be different from the sequence. The term 'order' in this respect refers to specific, detailed features of a language. For example, the order in which specific grammatical features or situation-specific vocabularies of a language are acquired may differ from person to person, classroom to classroom. Third, there is the rate of development of the second language and the level of proficiency achieved. While the sequence of second language development may be invariant, and while only minor variations in the order of development may occur, there may be major variations in the speed in which a second language is acquired and in the level of final proficiency achieved.

Situational factors (who is talking to whom, about what, where and when) considerably affect the rate of development of the second language. However, situational or contextual factors 'do not influence the sequence of development, and affect the order of development only in minor and temporary ways' (Ellis, 1985, page 278). Similarly differences in attitude, motivation, learning strategy and personality may affect the rate at which the second language is acquired and the level of final proficiency, but do not influence sequence nor the order of the development of the second language. The sequence of development is also not affected by the learner's first language. The first language, particularly concerning the degree to which it has developed, is likely to affect the order of development, the rate of development and the level of final proficiency.

In becoming functionally bilingual in the classroom and in the community, Cummins' interdependence theory (see page 81) suggests that second language acquisition is influenced considerably by the extent to which the first language has developed. When a first language has developed sufficiently well to cope with decontextualized classroom learning, a second language may be relatively easily acquired. When the first language is less well developed, or where there is attempted replacement of the first language by the second language (e.g. in the classroom), the development of the second language may be relatively impeded.

Further Reading

DICKERSON, P. & CUMMING, A., 1996, *Profiles of Language Education in 25 Countries*. Slough (UK): NFER.

ELLIS, R., 1985, *Understanding Second Language Acquisition*. Oxford: Oxford University Press.

KRASHEN, S. D., 1981, *Second Language Acquisition and Second Language Learning*. Oxford: Pergamon Press.

KRASHEN, S. D., 1982, *Principles and Practices of Second Language Acquisition*. Oxford: Pergamon Press.

SPOLSKY, B., 1989, *Conditions for Second Language Learning*. Oxford: Oxford University Press.

STERN, H. H., 1983, *Fundamental Concepts of Language Teaching*. Oxford: Oxford University Press.

Bernard Spolsky

Bernard Spolsky is Professor and Head of the Department of English at Bar-Ilan University in Ramat-Gan in Israel. He is also Director of the Language Policy Research Center in Israel. Bernard Spolsky was educated at the University of New Zealand and the University of Montreal and has held Professorships at McGill University, Indiana University, the University of New Mexico as well as Bar-Ilan University. His research and writing output is voluminous in terms of books, journal articles, conference papers and reports. One of his most famous books is entitled *Conditions for Second Language Learning.* Published in 1989, this book won both a Modern Language Association Book Prize and the British Association of Applied Linguistics Annual Book Prize. The book comprises a comprehensive and extensive model of second language learning at both the theoretical and the applied level.

2: A Framework of Second Language Acquisition

Ellis' (1985) summarizing framework of second language acquisition provides a useful overview of research and theory. Ellis suggests that there are five interrelated factors that govern the acquisition of a second language: situational factors, input, learner differences, learner processes and linguistic output.

Situational Factors

Situational factors have an important effect on language production. Situational factors refer to who is talking to whom, the environment of the interaction, whether it is in a classroom, formal situation or in a naturalistic setting (e.g. a shop, a café or a basketball game) and the topic of the conversation.

Linguistic Input

Linguistic input concerns the type of second language input received when listening or reading in a second language. For example, how do teachers or native speakers adjust their language to the level of second language learners to make it comprehensible? What kind of differences are there in the input from natural settings compared with formal classroom settings? In a behaviorist theory of language learning, precise and tight control of input from the teacher is regarded as very important. The second language has to be presented in small, highly sequenced doses with plenty of practice and reinforcement. Individual bricks need to be carefully laid in a precise sequence to build second language skills and habits. In contrast, Chomsky's mentalist view of language acquisition regards input as merely activating the learner's internal language acquisition device. Input from a teacher sets the wheels in motion rather than creating the wheels of language.

Current research and theory is between the behaviorist and the Chomskyan view point. Learning a language is not simply putting bricks in place nor pressing the button to start the machine. Efficient and effective second language learning does not occur purely by the building of stimulus-response links. Nor does second language learning occur by merely exposing a child or adult to the second language. Providing input which suits the stage of development of the second language learner becomes important. A second language learner and a native speaker work together to produce purposeful and efficient communication. There are strategies and tactics to make conversation appropriate and meaningful. For example, finding topics of conversation that can be mutually understood, speaking at a slow pace, repeating important phrases, stressing the key words in a sentence will help the input factor in second language acquisition. A learner will similarly give signals by verbal and non-verbal communication to indicate understanding, lack of understanding or to indicate the need to switch topics or level of language.

The input of language learning classrooms varies according to the type of second language learning occurring. Foreign language and second language classrooms have traditionally tended to focus more on the form of the language (e.g. grammar) rather than on meaning. In contrast, modern communicative approaches have placed the accent on communicating meaning. In genuinely bilingual classrooms, where the second language may be a medium of teaching in the curriculum, the focus may be more on meaning than on form. While the aim in both situations is to ensure the comprehensible input of the second language, input is different from intake. The learner receives input of the second language from 'outside'. Intake refers to the inner assimilation of that second language. Input does not always result in intake; only when there is intake does second language acquisition occur.

Individual Learner Differences

An important part of Ellis' (1985) framework is individual learner differences. It is popularly regarded that the level of proficiency a child attains in the second language is not only a factor of exposure to various contexts and to classroom teaching methodology, it is also due to individual differences. For example, the age at which somebody learns a second language, their aptitude for learning languages, cognitive style, motivation, attitude, previous knowledge, learning style, learning strategies and personality variables, such as anxiety, have variously been thought to influence second language acquisition.

It is important to distinguish between variables on which there are individual differences (e.g. anxiety level) and 'universal capabilities' which are basic, shared features of human beings. An example is Chomsky's (1965) idea of an innate, endowed capability for developing grammar. Available to all learners, universal capabilities are a necessary condition for learning. However, they need to be viewed as a 'prior assumption' that will not explain variations in second language learning among learners.

Variations among individual language learners create two different questions (Ellis, 1985). First, do individual differences in age and learning style, for example, result in children and adults following different routes in second language acquisition? Second, do individual differences affect the speed or rate at which second language acquisition occurs and the level of final proficiency achieved? People who research on individual differences in second language acquisition tend to emphasize the importance of individual differences (Wong Fillmore, 1979). Inbuilt into research designs is often the likelihood of finding significant differences between learners. On the other hand, second language acquisition theory and research that concentrate on situation, input and process tend to de-emphasize the role of individual differences.

While it is possible to list the factors which research has connected with more or less effective second language acquisition, what is unclear is the extent to which those factors affect both the route and the rate of second language acquisition. For example, there is some evidence to suggest that extroversion and reduced inhibition may be connected to second language acquisition. In both these cases, the research is not only methodologically weak (see Ellis, 1985) but also fails to examine, in an overall model, the relative influence of these factors against other individual differences, situational factors and language input variables.

It is possible to specify a list of factors that appear to be related to second language acquisition. Self-esteem and self-concept, competitiveness in the classroom, anxiety that may facilitate or hinder learning, field independence as a cognitive style and social skills have each and all been related by research to the degree of success in second language acquisition. On the other hand, the separate and interacting size of influence of each of these ingredients in the overall recipe is not clear.

Learner Processes

Another part of Ellis' (1985) framework is learner processes. It is clearly insufficient to consider second language acquisition by external input and by second language output. The input that second language learners receive is sifted, processed and organized. The teacher must have some insight into the processing strategies of the learner in order to give the learner comprehensible input. One three-fold typology of learner strategy is by Tarone (1980). First, there are learning strategies, that is ways in which the learner consciously and subconsciously processes second language input (e.g. memorization). Second, there are production strategies that comprise attempts to use second language knowledge in an efficient way. Third, a learner has communication strategies or the means of communicating with others in using the second language when there is a lack of linguistic proficiency.

An alternative way of peering into the black box of the mind is that of Chomsky (1965). Chomsky tends to depart from positing general cognitive strategy devices, claiming instead that there are mental mechanisms that are specifically linguistic. Chomsky describes this as the language acquisition device that contains an innate blueprint for a person to acquire a language. Chomsky thus proposed that between language input and language production is a linguistic process that involves the activation of universal principles of grammar with which the learner is endowed.

Second Language Outputs

The final part of Ellis' (1985) framework is second language outputs. The language proficiency of any learner at any one point of time is best seen as:

1. Evolutionary and not fixed. A language competence test as a measure of current language output should ideally reveal not just the current ceiling, but also the fittings and floors that need to be added and developed.

2. Variable according to the context where the learner is placed. A learner may appear relatively fluent in a restaurant or shop situation, yet much less fluent in a business or religious context.

An important contribution to the idea of language output is by Swain (1985, 1986). Swain argues that the opportunity to engage in meaningful oral exchanges (in the classroom or in the community) is a necessary component in second language acquisition. In conveying meaning, a person learns about the structure and form of a language.

A person may understand a language (passive, receptive skills) but, through lack of meaningful practice, speak that second language less than fluently. People learn to read by reading, and learn to write by writing. To speak, and to be understood when speaking, requires participation in meaningful and realistic conversations. We learn to speak a second language when given the opportunity to speak it. Such opportunities may be too infrequent in language classrooms.

The danger of the classroom is that students may learn to read and write a second language but not to understand and use the spoken form. The classroom emphasis has traditionally been on written correctness and not on spoken language skills. When a student has opportunities to use the spoken language outside the classroom (e.g. in the street), language skills (e.g. grammar, syntax and communication of meaning) may be considerably enhanced (Housen & Baetens Beardsmore, 1987; Baetens Beardsmore & Swain, 1985).

Further Reading

ELLIS, R., 1985, *Understanding Second Language Acquisition*. Oxford: Oxford University Press.

KRASHEN, S. D., 1981, *Second Language Acquisition and Second Language Learning*. Oxford: Pergamon Press.

KRASHEN, S. D., 1982, *Principles and Practices of Second Language Acquisition*. Oxford: Pergamon Press.

MCLAUGHLIN, B., 1987, *Theories of Second-Language Learning*. London: Edward Arnold.

SPOLSKY, B., 1989, *Conditions for Second Language Learning*. Oxford: Oxford University Press.

STERN, H. H., 1983, *Fundamental Concepts of Language Teaching*. Oxford: Oxford University Press.

SWAIN, M., 1986, Communicative Competence: Some Roles of Comprehensible Input and Comprehensible Output in its Development. In J. CUMMINS & M. SWAIN (eds), *Bilingualism in Education*. New York: Longman.

Rod Ellis

Rod Ellis has been a University Professor in the area of second language acquisition and applied linguistics in England, Japan and the United States. Currently at the Temple University in Philadelphia, his prolific writing in the area of second language acquisition has included major books which have been influential and internationally widely adopted. One thorough review of research in second language acquisition was published in a book entitled *Understanding Second Language Acquisition* in 1985. This was followed by *Instructive Second Language Acquisition* in 1990 and a further book in 1994 entitled *The Study of Second Language Acquisition.* Each book combines both depth of scholarship and width of treatment making a most learned and influential contribution to the study of second language acquisition.

Second Language Learning Strategies: 1

A student perspective

When students learn a second language, there are various strategies that are favored by some students and not others. The different strategies used by different students help explain differences in proficiency. Some students prefer lots of interaction with classmates. Other students like learning from a cassette tape, CD or video independent of other students. Some people use plenty of gestures to aid communication in a second language and are happy to take risks. Other people only use phrases they know are correct with little experimenting.

Early researchers tended to make lists of strategies that were the attributes of 'good language learners'. Rubin (1975) and Naiman, Frohlich & Todesco (1975) suggested that good second language learners are willing guessers, have a strong drive to communicate, are less anxious in trying out their second language, willing to make mistakes, look for patterns and analyze language, seek out chances to practice, and observe their own performance as well as the language of others.

Research, particularly from Rebecca Oxford and associates, has shown the importance of using such learning strategies and that successful language learners often use strategies in an orchestrated fashion (e.g. Oxford, 1989; Oxford, 1990b; Oxford, 1992; Oxford *et al.*, 1992; Oxford & Shearin, 1994). Successful language learners often select strategies that work well together. For example, translating, analyzing, planning and organizing strategies may be used in an integrated way. Particular strategies are used with particular tasks. For example, writing in a second language benefits from strategies of planning, self-monitoring, guessing and finding alternatives. Speaking in a second language is helped by risk-taking, summarizing and self-evaluation.

Factors considered to influence the choice of strategies used among students learning a second language include: motivation, gender, cultural background (e.g. preferred use of rote memory), attitudes, type of task, age, learning style, tolerance of ambiguity.

A consideration of learner strategies indicates the importance of understanding the social and affective aspects of learning along with the more cognitive aspects. Teachers thus need to use affective and social strategies, as well as intellectually related strategies, to promote effective second language learning. Helping individual students locate particular strategies most relevant to their learning styles, and developing orchestrated strategies can facilitate second language learning.

A teacher's perspective

Dörnyei (1994) provides a list of overlapping and interacting strategies for teachers to use to motivate their students:

Language

1. Include a sociocultural component in the syllabus (e.g. television programs, inviting native speakers).
2. Develop learners' cross-cultural awareness systematically, focusing on cross-cultural similarities rather than differences.
3. Promote student contact with second language speakers (e.g. exchange programs, pen pals, trips).
4. Develop learners' instrumental motivation by highlighting the usefulness of second language study.

Learner

1. Develop students' self-confidence in use of the language (e.g. realizable short-term goals, praise and encouragement, a regular experience of success, using confidence building tasks).
2. Promote students' self-efficacy with regard to achieving learning goals (e.g. teaching useful communication strategies, developing realistic expectations).
3. Promote favorable self-perceptions of competence in the second language (e.g. highlighting what students can do rather than what they cannot do, students not worrying about making mistakes).
4. Decrease student anxiety in learning a second language.
5. Promote motivation-enhancing attributions (e.g. students recognize the link between effort and outcome, attribute past failures to factors that can be changed).
6. Encourage students to set attainable subgoals for themselves (e.g. by a personal learning plan).

Second Language Learning Strategies: 2

Situational

1. Make the syllabus of the course relevant (e.g. based on a student 'needs analysis').
2. Increase the attractiveness of course content (e.g. use of more authentic materials, audio-visual aids, multimedia technology).
3. Discuss the choice of teaching materials with students (e.g. type of textbooks, computer assisted language learning programs).
4. Arouse and sustain curiosity and attention (e.g. introduce the unexpected and novel; break-up tedious or repetitious routines).
5. Increase students' interest and involvement in language learning tasks (e.g. selecting varied and challenging activities, including students interests, problem-solving, engaging students' emotions, personalizing tasks, using pair work and group activities).
6. Match the difficulty of the students' language learning tasks with students' abilities.
7. Increase student expectancy of task fulfillment (e.g. by creating realistic expectations, explanations of content and process, giving ongoing guidance about how to succeed, and making the criteria of success clear and transparent.
8. Facilitate student satisfaction (e.g. allowing students to complete tasks that they can display or perform, celebrating student success).

Teachers

1. Try to be empathic (sensitive to students' needs), congruent (behave in honest and true-to-self manner) and accepting of students' strengths and weaknesses.
2. Adopt the role of a facilitator rather than an authority figure.
3. Promote learner autonomy by allowing students real choices in learning, minimize external pressure, with students sharing tasks and responsibility for their own learning, using peer-teaching and project work.
4. Act as a role model, sharing personal interests and perspectives, transmits personal positive values about second language, sharing personal commitment to the second language.
5. Introduce language learning tasks to stimulate intrinsic motivation and help internalize extrinsic motivation, showing the purpose (and its integration into a whole) of each language learning task.
6. Use motivating feedback, giving feedback that is informative, and not over-reacting to errors.

Learning group

1. Establish goals that the group agree with and feel they own so as to establish a clear sense of direction.
2. From the beginning, promote the internalization of classroom norms of behavior.
3. Maintain classroom norms of acceptable behavior in a consistent manner, not letting violations going unnoticed, and maintaining unvarying professional standards of personal behavior.
4. Minimize any detrimental effects of assessment on intrinsic motivation by focusing on improvement and progress, avoiding comparison of one student with another, making student assessment private rather than public, not encouraging a focus on competition in achievement outcomes, with personal interviews to consider the individual assessment of language proficiency.
5. Promote the development of group cohesion and enhance inter-member relations by promoting friendships and effective working relationships, organizing outings and extra-curricula activities.
6. Use cooperative learning techniques by plenty of groupwork where the evaluation of success is appropriate to the group rather than a focus on individual success.

REFERENCES:
DÖRNYEI, 1994; OXFORD, 1990; OXFORD & SHEARIN,1994

3: Theories of Second Language Acquisition and Learning

The topics of bilingualism and second language acquisition are closely related. Becoming bilingual often involves second language acquisition, either achieved formally (e.g. in the classroom) or informally (naturally, for example, in the street and playground, via television and radio). At the same time, research into bilingualism feeds into the wide topic of second language acquisition. This topic outlines some of the key theories of second language acquisition. The essence of second language theories is to describe the individual and contextual conditions for efficient second language learning to occur. Major theories or models of second language acquisition will now be discussed, highlighting particularly important ideas in second language acquisition.

Lambert's Model of Second Language Learning

Lambert's (1974) model is valuable because it combines both the individual and societal elements of bilingualism and is presented in a diagram below. It is the important societal element of the model that is emphasized in the following discussion.

The model starts with an individual's attitudes and aptitude towards a language. Aptitude and attitude are regarded as two major and relatively separate influences on becoming bilingual. (See Aptitude and Becoming Bilingual and Attitudes to Languages, pages 174 and 655.) For example, aptitude in learning a second language may be an important factor in second language learning (Skehan, 1986). Similarly, the attitudes of a person towards a language may be important not only in learning that language but also in retaining the language. The next part of Lambert's (1974) model is motivation – the readiness to engage in language learning or language activity. These three preceding factors all contribute to the third part of the model which is a person's bilingual proficiency. Bilingual proficiency in its turn impacts upon a person's self-concept.

For Lambert (1974), becoming bilingual or being bilingual has effects on the self-esteem and the ego. Having gained competence in a second language and being able to interact with a different language group may change one's self-concept and self-esteem. An English monolingual who has learnt Spanish may develop new reference groups and engage in new cultural activities that affect the self-concept. This suggests that bilingualism usually involves enculturation. Someone who is bicultural or multicultural may have different aspirations, world views, values and beliefs because of being bilingual or multilingual.

Lambert's (1974) model finishes with two alternative outcomes: additive or subtractive bilingualism (see page 154). This outcome can be interpreted both in personal and societal ways. When a second language and culture

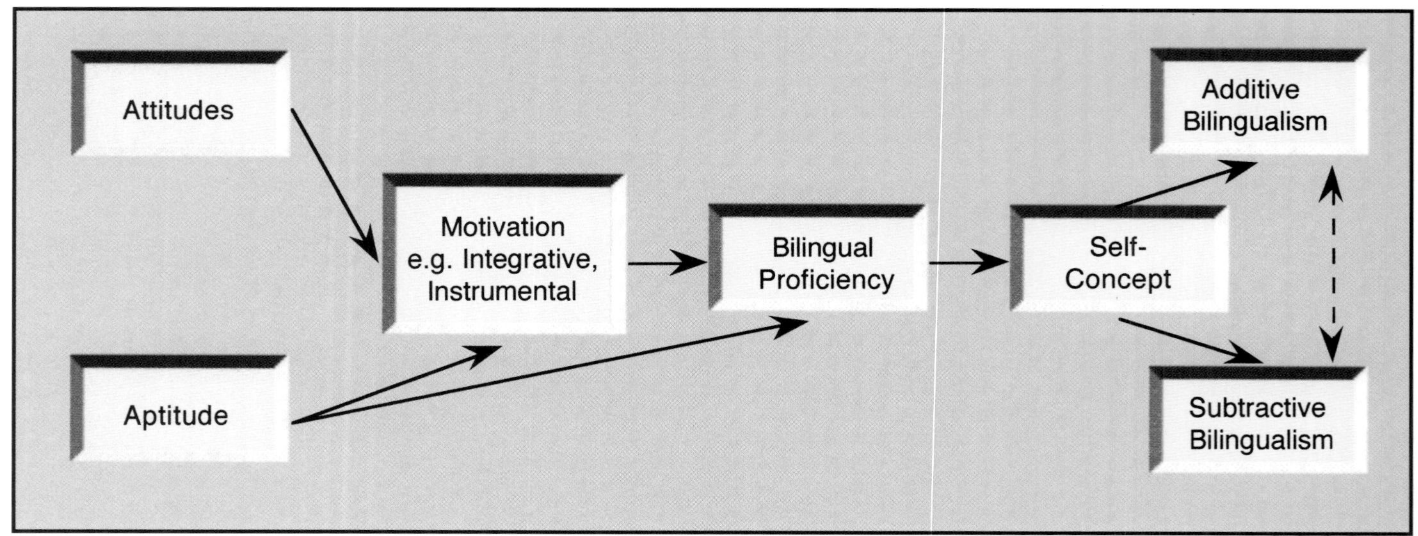

Wallace (Wally) Lambert

Wally Lambert was born in 1922 in Nova Scotia in Canada. He was educated at Brown University, Cambridge University, Colgate University and gained his PhD from the University of North Carolina. After brief teaching posts in the United States, Wally Lambert has been a Professor in the Department of Psychology at McGill University in Montreal since 1954. Wally Lambert has a reputation as a gifted teacher and this is reflected in the many publications that are co-authored with his research students.

He has been a visiting Professor at ten universities, served on many international committees, acted as a Consultant for many international organizations, has been awarded four honorary doctorates and has a publication record which stretches from 1952 to 1994. In 1991, an edited book entitled *Bilingualism, Multiculturalism, and Second Language Learning: The McGill Conference in Honour of Wallace E. Lambert* was published in recognition of the outstanding contribution made by Wally Lambert as a prolific researcher and writer of over 160 articles and eight books.

His research interests include: the social psychology of second language learning and immersion schooling, cross-cultural aspects of child rearing practices, and the cognitive and neuro-psychological characteristics of bilinguals. He has achieved a reputation as a scientist and a scholar, and as someone who combines both rigor and relevance in his research and writings.

His marriage to a French speaker, and a deep interest in breaking down barriers of culture and language, facilitated the raising of bilingual and bicultural children in Montreal. This 'breaking down barriers' theme underlies much of his work: human beings of all ethnic groups, races and social classes being able to move freely across the boundaries of different cultures and languages, integrating and co-participating to create a world where there is individual fulfillment and a harmonious and integrated society.

have been acquired with little or no pressure to replace or reduce the first language, an additive form of bilingualism may occur. Positive self-concept is likely to relate to additive bilingualism. When the second language and culture are acquired (e.g. in-migrants) with pressure to replace or demote the first language, a subtractive form of bilingualism may occur. This may relate to a less positive self-concept, loss of cultural identity, with possible alienation and assimilation.

Additive and subtractive bilingualism have become important concepts in the explanation of research. Lambert's (1974) distinction between additive and subtractive bilingualism has been used in two different ways. First, additive bilingualism is used to refer to positive cognitive and affective outcomes from being bilingual. Subtractive bilingualism hence refers to the negative affective and cognitive effects of bilingualism (e.g. where both languages are 'underdeveloped'). Landry, Allard & Théberge (1991) suggest this first use is too narrow, with a second use of additive and subtractive bilingualism being more appropriate. This wider use of additive and subtractive bilingualism relates to the enrichment or loss of minority language, culture and ethnolinguistic identity at a societal level. In an additive situation, language minority members are proficient (or becoming proficient) in both languages, have positive attitudes to the first and second language, with ethnolinguistic vitality in the minority language community.

Lambert's (1974) model contains the basic ingredients that help make up an explanation of individual and societal bilingualism. It suggests that both individual and sociocultural factors are important in the possession and passage of bilingualism. Like most models, it is static rather than dynamic. It tends to suggest that there is an easy, functional flow in relationships between the factors. What it may fail to do is to represent the dynamic, ever changing, often conflicting and politicized path of bilingualism at an individual and at a societal level.

Gardner's Socio-Educational Model of Second Language Acquisition

Gardner and his colleagues (see Gardner, 1985a) have presented a model of second language acquisition that developed from Lambert's (1974) model, and has been well researched and tested. Some of its key parts will be discussed first before the model is presented as a whole. We begin with ability and aptitude for languages: two concepts that are part of the popular 'common sense' explanation of why some learn languages quickly, some not.

Ability and aptitude

Second language learning in the classroom has often been connected to the general ability of a child ('intelligence') and to a specific language ability usually termed language aptitude. While the idea of a general academic ability or 'intelligence' has been criticized, it has been argued that the general factor of intelligence is allied to a global factor of language ability. At its simplest, this means that a more 'intelligent' person is likely to learn a second language more easily. An overview would suggest that general academic ability can be substantially related to the acquisition of second language in a formal classroom setting. General ability may positively correlate with test scores on the formal aspects of language learning, (e.g. grammar, translation, parsing verbs).

However, as Cummins (1984b) has discussed, basic everyday language skills may not be so closely related to general academic ability. That is, the skills required for picking up 'street' conversation may be less dependent on general academic ability than the skills required to learn language in an academic environment.

In a similar way, tests of language aptitude have been connected with second language learning. Aptitude tests can be used to predict the success of formal, traditional second language learning in the classroom rather than second language acquisition in naturalistic, communicative contexts.

The concept of aptitude tends to be a popular explanation for failure to acquire a second language. However, the concept of aptitude has recently come under attack. It is unclear how aptitude is different from general academic ability. Thus, it is difficult to know precisely what is being tested in modern language aptitude tests. (See Aptitude and Becoming Bilingual, page 655).

While aptitude may affect the speed of second language acquisition in the formal classroom environment, it would not seem to affect the sequence or order of second language acquisition. There is also no evidence to show that aptitude affects the sequence in second language acquisition.

Attitudes and motivation

Another popular explanation for failure to learn a second language (or of success in learning) is attitudes and motivation (Baker, 1992). What are the motives for learning a second language? Are the motives economic, cultural, social, vocational, integrative or for self-esteem and self-actualization? Reasons for learning a second (minority or majority) language tend to fall into two major groups:

1. *A wish to identify with or join another language group.* Learners sometimes want to affiliate with a different language community. Such learners wish to join in with the minority or majority language's cultural activities, find their roots, or form friendships. This is termed integrative motivation.

2. *Learning a language for useful purposes.* The second reason is utilitarian in nature. Learners may acquire a second language to obtain employment or promotion, or help their children's education. This can be termed instrumental motivation.

Considerable research on this area has been conducted by Gardner and associates (see Gardner, 1985a). Gardner argues that integrative and instrumental attitudes are independent of 'intelligence' and 'aptitude'.

Much of the research in this area, but not all, links integrative motivation rather than instrumental motivation with the greater likelihood of achieving proficiency in the second language. The reason would seem to be that personal relationships tend to be long-lasting, and sustain motivation better than, for instance, the temporary need to pass an examination or gain employment. However, such research tends to derive from relatively affluent Western countries. In parts of the world where there is relative material deprivation, instrumental motives (e.g. learning a language for employment) may play a more central role than integrative motives.

However, there may be occasions when the instrumental motive is stronger than the integrative motive in learning a language. There are other instances where the two types of motivation are integrated within the experience

Robert Gardner

Robert Gardner was educated at the University of Alberta and McGill University in Canada. Following a short time at Harvard University, he joined the Department of Psychology at the University of Western Ontario, becoming Lecturer, Assistant Professor, Associate Professor and full Professor in 1970. A Fellow of the Canadian Psychological Association, Robert Gardner is internationally famous for his socio-psychological approach to language learning. In 1972, he published a book with W. E. Lambert on *Attitudes and Motivation in Second Language Learning.* This book, and his sole author book in 1985 entitled *Social Psychology and Second Language Learning: The Role of Attitudes and Motivation* both became classics and have dominated the field of attitudes and motivation in second language learning ever since.

of an individual or group. It is clear that motivation is an important factor in second language acquisition, affecting the speed and final proficiency of the second language. It is unlikely to affect the sequence or order of acquisition. (This is discussed more fully on page 651.)

In summary, the research of Gardner and colleagues since the early 1970s suggests that attitudes to the second language and motivation to learn a second language are crucial additional ingredients into the language learning recipe. Having the ability and aptitude without the motivation and favorable attitude would tend to result in lower achievement than having both aptitude and motivation.

To represent in an integrated fashion his own and others' research on second language learning, Gardner (1979, 1983, 1985) offers a four-stage model. This is presented in the diagram below.

Gardner's model starts with the social and cultural background of language learning. (In this sense, Gardner starts where Lambert finishes.) Children may be influenced by the beliefs, values and culture of the community in which they are placed. For many people living in England, for example, the belief is that the 'universal' English language is all that is required; bilingualism is unnecessary. In other communities of Europe, bilingualism and biculturalism reflect the values of the community. In Gardner's model, social and cultural background refers not only to the wider community but also to the influence of the home, neighbors and friends. This influence is further explored in the model of Hamers & Blanc (1982, 1983) and Siguan & Mackey (1987).

The second stage of Gardner's model is termed individual differences. This comprises four major variables: intelligence, language aptitude, motivation and situational anxiety. Individual differences in attitudes and personality are thus included in this stage. Gardner suggests that the degree of intelligence of an individual, an aptitude or talent for language learning, instrumental and integrative motives and anxiety felt in language learning will all affect the outcomes of language learning.

The third stage of Gardner's model concerns the context or environment where language is acquired. He makes a distinction between formal and informal environments in language learning. An example of a formal context is the classroom that explicitly aims to teach a child a second language by a defined teaching method and various classroom materials and resources. A language laboratory, drill and practice, computer assisted language learning, audio visual methods and translations and grammar

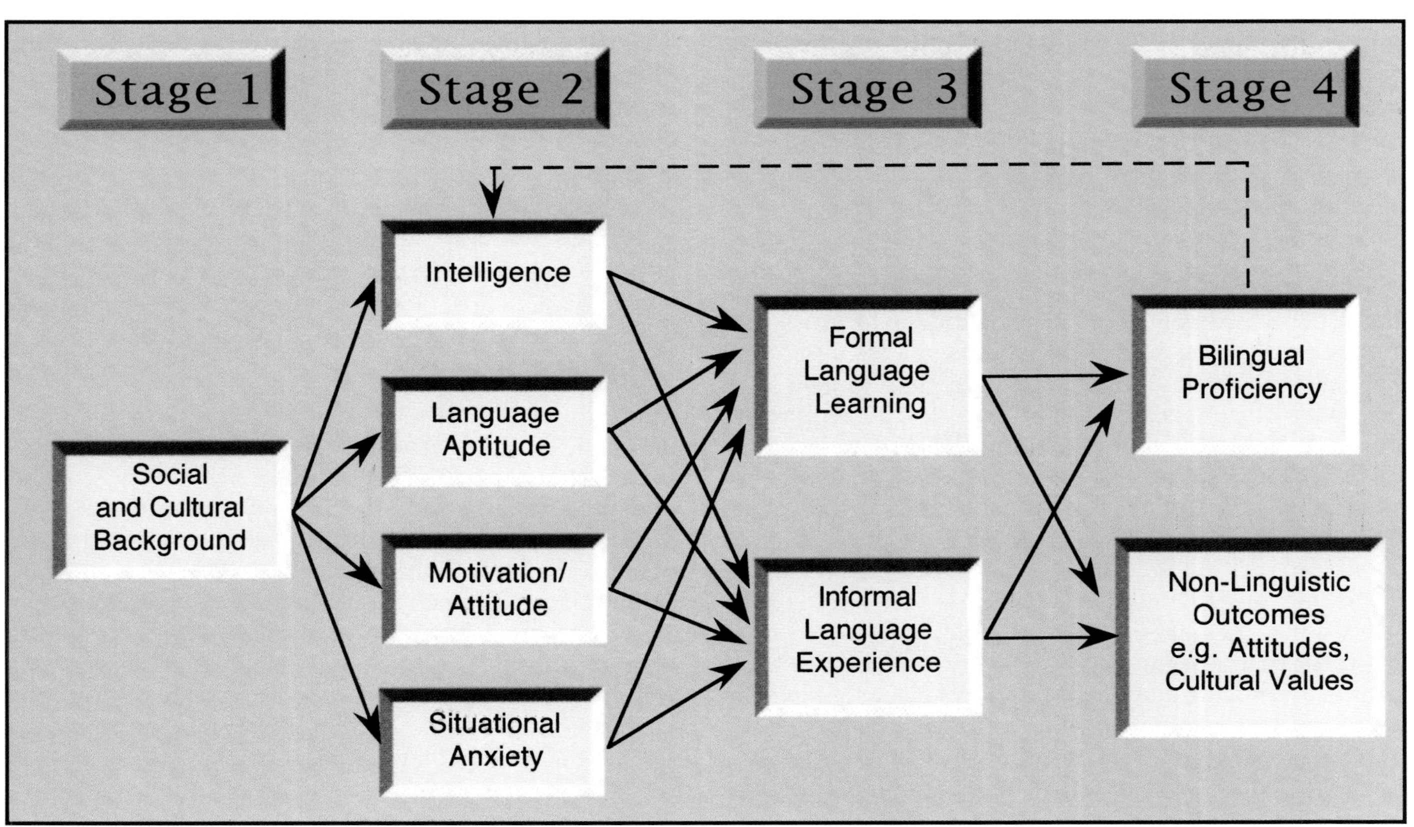

exercises are all examples of a formal and directed approach to language learning. An informal language learning context or experience is when language learning is more incidental, accidental or uncontrived. For example, a person might watch a Spanish film not primarily to widen vocabulary, but for the entertainment value of that film. In this instance, a person's Spanish vocabulary may be incidentally extended but that would be an unintended outcome.

The fourth and final stage of Gardner's model represents two expected outcomes of second language acquisition. One outcome refers to bilingual proficiency. The second involves non-linguistic outcomes such as change in attitudes, self-concept, cultural values and beliefs. The placing of attitudes in the second and the fourth stage suggests that the model should be conceived as something that is not static but cyclical. Attitudes are not only ingredients into the language learning situation. Attitudes are also products or outcomes of language learning. That is, the learning of a second language and the act of becoming bilingual, may change attitudes. As the diagram above indicates by the dotted arrow from bilingual proficiency to the second stage, competence in a second language may in turn positively affect intelligence, motivation and situational anxiety levels.

The value of Gardner's model is that it is not only a summary of existing research in the social psychology of language learning. It also has been directly and formally tested as a complete model (Gardner, 1983; Gardner, Lalonde & Pierson, 1983; Lalonde, 1982) and found to fit collected data. This is different from most theories of bilingualism where the theory attempts to summarize previous research but is not subsequently directly and rigorously tested.

One limitation of Gardner's model is that it does not include the sociopolitical dimension that often surrounds routes to bilingual proficiency. A full understanding of language acquisition, language change and bilingual education (at individual and societal levels) requires a political dimension. For example, the preference in a region for assimilation of minorities, integration or cultural pluralism, influences language policies, provision and practices surrounding bilinguals.

There are other limitations. Oxford & Shearin (1994) suggest that there are reasons for second language learning other than integrative and instrumental motives. For example, students may learn a new language for intellectual stimulation, for a personal challenge, to fulfill school or examination requirements, travel interests, to enjoy some symbols of elitism (e.g. when learning an international language of high status) or for cultural curiosity. These authors also argue that foreign language learning frequently has different motives than second language learning. For example, integrative motivation may be less relevant for foreign language learners who have relatively little interaction with, or experience of the foreign language community. Therefore, such learners may not have an interest in integrating with the foreign language community. Foreign language learners may have more instrumental orientations, such as learning a language for employment and status. In contrast, second language learners (e.g. English speakers learning French in Canada) may have relatively more integrative reasons for language learning. Dörnyei (1994) also provides a critique of Gardner's model from the perspective of a practicing teacher rather than from a social psychological perspective. Dörnyei provides an education-centered perspective (detailed on page 640) that is more pragmatic than Gardner's model and more action oriented.

Like all models, Gardner's model is valuable for summarizing and providing clarity but tends to imply descriptions rather than deep explanations. It suggests a straightforward, well functioning, clearly ordered system of actions and reactions, ingredients and events. An individual's internal conflicts, the complexity of competing multiple pressures and motives, the many and varied individual recipes of success and failure, the many individual exceptions, changing and interacting contexts, and effects of immediate and long-standing situations, are not represented in a model. Over time, there are changes in motivation, twists and turns in reasons for second language study, and an evolution of interests and involvement in the learning process. Student strategies in language learning and teacher strategies in language teaching are many, varied, complex and interacting (see page 640) and cannot all be included in a simple model.

The Acculturation Model of Second Language Learning

John Schumann (1978) proposed an acculturation model of second language acquisition whose essential element is the second language learner adapting to a new culture. The model starts with the idea that language is one aspect of culture, and the relationship between the language community of the learner and the second language community is significant in second language acquisition. The basic premise of the model is that 'the degree to which a learner acculturates to the target language group will control the degree to which he acquires the second language' (Schumann, 1978, p.34). Schumann portrays the various factors that are important in 'good' language learning. Expressed in group rather than individual terms, these facilitating social factors comprise:

1. The target language group and the second language learner group are self-perceived as relatively socially equal. The greater the equality distance (e.g. domination, subordination) the less the chance of language learning.

2. The target language and second language learner groups both desire assimilation of the learner's social group.

3. Both groups expect the second language group to share social facilities as operated by the target language group.

4. The second language learner group is small, not very cohesive and can be assimilated into the target language group.

5. The extent to which the second language learner group's culture is congruent and similar to that of the target language group thus assisting assimilation.

6. The extent to which both groups have positive attitudes and expectations of each other.

7. The extent to which the second language learner group expects to stay with the target language group for a longer rather than a short period (e.g. in-migrants).

These are the social factors that for Schumann (1978) determine the probability of a second language individual or group receiving the target language group. Schumann also lists psychological factors that are important in second language learning. These include: possible language confusion when using the second language (language shock); the feeling of stress, anxiety or disorientation because of the differences between the learner's culture and the target language culture (culture shock); the degree of motivation in learning a language, and the degree of inhibition, or self-consciousness adolescent learners particularly may have in language learning.

Schumann's factors provide dimensions that may determine the amount of contact a language learner will have with the target language. The amount of contact is defined both by social, external factors and by individual factors. When social and/or psychological distances are large, the learner may fail to progress very far in learning a second language. When the social and psychological factors are positive, second language acquisition may occur relatively painlessly. When psychological and social distances are great, then, at an individual and societal level, pidginization (the development of a simplified form of a language) may occur. Pidginization is regarded by Schumann as the characteristic of early second language acquisition. Also, when conditions of social and psychological distance are great, pidginization will occur at a societal level.

For Schumann (1978), language has three broad functions: a communicative function, an integrative function and an expressive function. That is, language aids the transmission of information, aids affiliation and belonging to a particular social group, and allows the display of individual feelings, ideas and personality. Schumann argues that second language learners will initially use their second language for communication, and then those who develop in that language will seek to use the language to affiliate to a social group. Some learners, but not all may achieve the expressive use of the second language.

Schumann's Acculturation model, extended by Andersen's (1983) Nativization model, is one way of understanding the politics and power of language in its societal contexts. It provides a valuable explanation of why some children with aptitude and ability fail to learn or use a second language. It does not specify how such language acquisition occurs via internalized learning processes. The information processing approach to second language learning is not included in this model. Absent from this account of second language learning is: the interaction between a particular, defined context and the learner; the changing, variable nature of attitudes and motivation; whether attitude is a cause of language learning or an outcome of language learning, or is both a cause and an effect; the shifting power relations and distance between groups; and the difficulty of testing the theory. The model may also be more appropriate to societal contexts where, for instance, in-migrant or other minority groups learn the majority language than it is to individualized language learning.

The Accommodation Theory of Second Language Acquisition

Accommodation theory derives from Giles and colleagues (e.g. Giles & Byrne, 1982). Like Schumann (1978), Giles & Byrne's theory seeks to explain second language acquisition in a group or intergroup situation. For Giles & Byrne (1982), the important factor is the perceived social difference between the ingroup (the language learner's social group) and the outgroup (the target language community). The relationships between the ingroup and outgroup are seen as both fluid and constantly negotiated. There is a tendency in Schumann's Acculturation model for social and psychological distances to be seen as static or changing relatively slowly over time. For Giles & Byrne (1982), relationships between ingroup and outgroup are dynamic and constantly changing. One way of portraying Giles &Byrne's (1982) model is to profile a person from a subordinate group (i.e. a language minority) who is likely to acquire the language of the dominant group.

The learner is likely to show the following characteristics (simplified from Giles & Coupland, 1991):

- Have a relatively weak identification with their own ethnic group. That is, such learners do not see themselves as purely a member of their minority language group separate from the dominant language group. Alternatively, their first language is not important to membership of their ethnic group.

- Do not regard their ethnic group as inferior to the dominant group. A good language learner makes 'quiescent' comparisons between their ethnic group and the dominant group, or is not concerned about a difference of status.

- Perceive their ethnic group as having low vitality compared with the dominant group. Giles and Byrne (1982) talk of a perception of ethnolinguistic vitality which includes: (1) the economic, historic, social, political and language status of the ethnic group; (2) size and distribution of an ethnic group, mixed marriages, amount of in-migration and out-migration; and (3) institutional support for the ethnic group (e.g. mass media, education, religion, industry, services, culture and government).

- See their ethnic group boundaries as 'soft and open' and not 'hard and closed'.

- Hold adequate status within their ethnic group (e.g. in terms of employment, gender, power and religion).

Thus for Giles & Byrne (1982), a person less likely to acquire a second language may have: a strong identification with their own group, makes 'insecure' comparisons with the outgroup; regard their own language community as having high vitality, good institutional support, being sizable and stable and of high status; perceive the boundaries between their own and the second language group as separate and rigid, and have inadequate status within their first language group. Further factors are considered in Giles & Coupland (1991).

Like the Acculturation Model, Accommodation Theory does not explain the internal mechanisms of how a child or adult acquires a second language. It is essentially a socio-psychological model rather than a cognitive-processing model of second language acquisition. Tollefson (1991) also criticizes Accommodation Theory for its ahistorical analysis and failure to account for domination and coercion in language shift.

Glyn Williams (1992) is critical of the apparent assumption that language development is gradual and cumulative, of a consensus nature, concerned with order and cohesion. He argues that this view tends to play down conflict and power, thereby not expressing the anger, discrimination and frustration felt by language minority groups and their members.

One strength of the theory is that it takes into account ethnic identity in language learning, an important determining factor for many children and adults in second language acquisition.

Further Reading

GARDNER, R. C., 1979, Social Psychological Aspects of Second Language Acquisition. In H. GILES & R. ST. CLAIR (eds), *Language and Social Psychology*. Oxford: Blackwell.

GARDNER, R. C., 1983, Learning Another Language: A True Social Psychological Experiment. *Journal of Language and Social Psychology*, 2, 219-239.

GARDNER, R. C., 1985a, *Social Psychology and Second Language Learning*. London: Edward Arnold.

GILES, H. & BYRNE, J. L., 1982, An Intergroup Approach to Second Language Acquisition. *Journal of Multilingual and Multicultural Development*, 3 (1), 17-40.

GILES, H. & COUPLAND, N., 1991, *Language: Contexts and Consequences*. Milton Keynes: Open University Press.

LAMBERT, W. E., 1974, Culture and Language as Factors in Learning and Education. In F. E. ABOUD & R. D. MEADE (eds), *Cultural Factors in Learning and Education*. Bellingham, WA: 5th Western Washington Symposium on Learning.

SCHUMANN, J. H., 1978, *The Pidginization Process: A Model for Second Language Acquisition*. Rowley, MA: Newbury House.

SCHUMANN, J. H., 1986, Research on the Acculturation Model for Second Language Acquisition. *Journal of Multilingual and Multicultural Development*, 7 (5), 379-392.

4: Krashen's Monitor Model

The Monitor Model of Stephen Krashen (1977, 1981a, 1982, 1985) is probably the most widely cited theory of second language acquisition and has often dominated education debate in this field. Krashen's Monitor Model comprises five central hypotheses plus other variables that need considering in second language acquisition. The five hypotheses are:

The Acquisition-Learning Hypothesis

According to Krashen, language is acquired, not learnt. Acquisition is a subconscious process that results from informal, natural communication between people where language is a means and not a focus nor an end in itself. Acquisition is the process by which young children develop a first language. Second language acquisition should attempt to parallel this process, by creating an environment in which language can be presented in authentic communicative situations.

Second language learning, on the other hand, is a conscious process that enables a learner to 'know about' the second language. With second language learning, the analysis and correction of errors is formally and explicitly addressed. Conscious language learning (as opposed to acquisition) can only act as a monitor that checks and corrects the utterances of the acquired system. Learning often occurs in a more formal situation where the overt properties of a language are taught (e.g. a classroom). Language learning has traditionally involved grammar, vocabulary learning and the teaching of other formal linguistic properties. However, acquisition and learning are not defined by 'where' a second language occurs. Formal learning can occur in the street when a person asks questions about correct grammar, mistakes and difficulties. Language acquisition can occur in the classroom, when opportunities for authentic communication occur.

The Monitor Hypothesis

The Monitor is an editing device that may operate before language performance. Utterances may be modified by being acted upon by the Monitor of learnt knowledge. Such editing may occur before the natural output of speech; it may occur after the output via a correcting device. Krashen suggests that monitoring occurs when there is sufficient time, when there is pressure to communicate correctly and not just convey meaning, and when the appropriate rules of speech are known. Examples include knowing the correct tense to use, when to use the third or first person and rules about plurals. This hypothesis has been criticized for being untestable and for a lack of supportive research evidence.

The Natural Order Hypothesis

This hypothesis suggests that grammatical structures are acquired in a predictable order for both children and adults, irrespective of the language being learnt. When a learner engages in natural communication, then the standard order will occur. This hypothesis has been criticized (e.g. McLaughlin, 1987). Research on morphemes and on the development of specific grammatical forms does not support a 'strong' version of the hypothesis. Variations between different people and a lack of supportive evidence suggest that only a 'weak' version of the natural order hypothesis is tenable.

The Input Hypothesis

Krashen proposes that language acquisition occurs when the student is exposed to sources of comprehensible input (oral or written) which are slightly above the level of the learner's current ability. (Krashen expresses this by means of the formula 1+1). Krashen emphasizes that 'acquisition' is the result of this comprehensible language input rather than of language production. Input is made comprehensible because of the help provided by the context. If the language student receives understandable input, language structures will be, according to Krashen, naturally acquired. For Krashen, the ability to communicate in a second language 'emerges' rather than is directly put in place by teaching.

The Affective Filter Hypothesis

Dulay & Burt (1977) proposed the idea of an Affective Filter, that determines how much a person learns in a formal or informal language setting. The filter comprises affective factors such as attitudes to language, motivation, self-confidence and anxiety. Thus learners with favorable attitudes and self-confidence may have 'a low filter' with consequent efficient second language learning. Those with unfavorable attitudes and/or high anxiety have 'high filters' and so the input of second language learning may be blocked or impeded. The Affective Filter

Stephen Krashen

Stephen Krashen is a Professor of Curriculum and Teaching at the School of Education, University of Southern California in Los Angeles and former Director of ESL at Queens College in New York. His expertise lies in the fields of second language acquisition, bilingual education and literacy, specializing particularly in theories of language acquisition and development. He is the author of many books, book chapters and articles on language acquisition, literacy development and bilingual education, including the influential *Second Language Acquisition and Second Language Learning* (1981) and *Principles and Practice in Second Language Acquisition* (1982). His other major publications include: *Writing: Research Theory and Application* (1984), *The Input Hypothesis* (1985), *Inquiries and Insights* (1985), *Fundamentals of Language Education* (1992) and *The Power of Reading* (1993). He is co-author of *Language Two* (1982), *The Natural Approach* (1983) and *On Course: Bilingual Education's Success in California* (1988). Few single authors in the 20th century have influenced second language methodology as much as Stephen Krashen.

hypothesis influences the rate of development in second language learning and the level of success in becoming bilingual. The Affective Filter hypothesis was adopted by Krashen as part of his Monitor Model.

Views about the Monitor Hypothesis

Stephen Krashen's Monitor Model has been popular and internationally disseminated. It has been favored and influential because of its relatively comprehensive nature and because that it moves from theory to classroom practice (see page 676). One line of criticism has been that the Acquisition-Learning hypothesis cannot be tested empirically. Because acquisition is more subconscious and learning is relatively more conscious, it is difficult or even impossible to test the hypothesis empirically and comprehensively. It can be argued that acquisition and learning are not separate. Acquired knowledge can become learnt knowledge. Once learnt knowledge is practiced it may reach a level of automatization that equates to acquired knowledge, being available in spontaneous 'unconscious' conversation. As Larsen-Freeman (1983) comments, the Monitor hypothesis does not explain the cognitive processes that underlie acquisition and learning. Thus the Monitor Model is a 'black box' theory of language acquisition. It does not specify what goes on in cognitive processes to explain second language acquisition.

Another line of criticism concerns the Monitor hypothesis. In reality, is there a distinction between rule application (as in the Monitoring device) and having a subconscious feel for what is right and wrong in a communication situation? Is there an underlying faculty that makes people aware of the correctness or incorrectness of their language communication? The theory needs extending to explain variability between individuals in language learning.

While other theories of second language acquisition have attracted research and become adopted as part of a psychological understanding of second language acquisition, Krashen's Monitor Model has also directly fed teaching practice, teacher training and classroom strategies. Its movement from theory to classroom practice (see page 676) is one major reason for its popularity.

Further Reading

KRASHEN, S. D., 1977, The Monitor Model for Second Language Performance. In M. BURT, H. DULAY & M. FINOCCHIAO (eds), *Viewpoints on English as a Second Language*. New York: Regents.

KRASHEN, S. D., 1981a, Bilingual Education and Second Language Acquisition Theory. In CALIFORNIA STATE DEPARTMENT OF EDUCATION (ed.), *Schooling and Language Minority Students. A Theoretical Framework*. Los Angeles, CA: Evaluation, Dissemination and Assessment Center.

KRASHEN, S. D., 1981c, *Second Language Acquisition and Second Language Learning*. Oxford: Pergamon Press.

KRASHEN, S. D., 1982, *Principles and Practices of Second Language Acquisition*. Oxford: Pergamon Press.

KRASHEN, S. D., 1985, *The Input Hypothesis: Issues and Implications*. London: Longman.

KRASHEN, S. D. & TERRELL, T., 1983, *The Natural Approach: Language Acquisition in the Classroom*. Oxford: Pergamon.

5: Instrumental and Integrative Motivation and Language Acquisition

In learning a second language, retaining the first or the second language, being committed to the maintenance and survival and spread of the minority language, motivation and attitudes may be important. For example, if we ask people why they are committed to retaining their minority language at a personal and societal level, different reasons may be found. Some want to preserve roots and traditions, others want to share in the language life of the community, for others it is an important badge of family life, religious activity or ethnic identity, others want to access particular aspects of culture in the minority language, others are concerned with seeking job opportunities and promotion.

Similarly, motivation is very important in language learning. Whether a language is acquired informally in the neighborhood or at work (e.g. in-migrants picking up the language of the host country) or learnt in formal language classes, motivation is an important factor. The type and degree of motivation has a direct effect on the success or otherwise of second language learning and retention.

Two major groupings of language motivation and language attitude have been located by research in the last two decades. Such motivations underlie success in second language learning as well as providing explanations of minority language survival and spread. Each will be considered in turn.

US Hispanic in-migrants in an English class, part of a bilingual outreach program in Arlington, Virginia. Their motivation for learning English includes the necessity to find employment, but also the need to integrate socially and help their children at school.

Instrumental Motivation

First, there are utilitarian motives for learning or maintaining a language. Some people will want to learn a second language or retain their minority language to gain social recognition and status, economic openings and advantages. Learners may acquire a second language to find a job or earn money, further career prospects, pass examinations, help fulfill the demands of their job, or assist their children in bilingual schooling. These kinds of motivations come under the broad heading of instrumental motivation. In Gardner's (1985b) attitude and motivation test battery, two instrumental items are as follows:

> Studying French can be important to me because I think it will someday be useful in getting a good job.
>
> Studying French can be important for me because it will make me a more knowledgeable person.

An instrumental motivation to acquire or preserve a language is mostly self-oriented, individualistic and often related to the need to achieve success. Personal self-enhancement, self-development or basic security and survival will be the utilitarian, pragmatic need of an individual.

Integrative Motivation

As a separate (but not necessarily as a distinct) category of motivation, are integrative motives or attitudes. An integrative motivation is about social or interpersonal reasons for second language learning or minority language activity. Integrative motives reflect a desire to be like, or identify with members of a particular language community.

Examples of integrative test items are as follows:

> Studying Spanish can be important for me because it will allow me to meet and converse with more and varied people.

> Studying Spanish can be important to me because other people will respect me more if I have knowledge of their language.

An integrative motivation may reflect the need to affiliate, be friendly with, attached to or to identify with people in a particular language group and their cultural activities. A person may wish to join, and be accepted within a particular language group.

Integrative and instrumental motives have been found to be important in language research. They provide a potent reason why some people learn a second language and retain that language (separate from their level of intelligence or aptitude for language learning). Some learners may be intelligent but not learn a second language. Their lack of instrumental or integrative motivation may explain this. Other people appear to have relatively less intelligence and aptitude for language learning, yet due to a high motivation (integrative and or instrumental), still manage to become proficient in a second language.

Gardner & Lambert (1972) originally considered that integrative motivation was more powerful in language learning than instrumental motivation. The argument is that integrative motivation concerns personal relationships which may be more long-lasting. Instrumental motivation, in comparison, may be more short-term. Once a particular examination has been passed or economic goal obtained, such instrumental motivation may decrease, even disappear. The relative endurance of personal relationships may be in contrast with short-term goals reflected in instrumental motives.

An individual's motives may be a subtle mix of instrumental and integrative motives, without necessarily a clear division between the two. In the research of Yatim (1988), the language motivations of student teachers in Malaysia appeared to combine instrumental and integrative motives into an integrated entity.

It is not the case that integrative motives are always stronger than instrumental motives. Lukmani (1972) found that Bombay female school students gave instrumental reasons rather than integrative reasons for learning English. The explanation lies in the functions that a second or minority language has in a particular society. Factors such as employment and career development can be stronger than the desire to affiliate to a group. The social context will be one determinant of which kind of motivation is more powerful. In certain contexts, both motivations may be equally and strongly operative.

While the normal preference is to see motives as affecting behavior (e.g. an integrative or instrumental motive as influencing someone to achieve bilingual proficiency), the chicken and egg question is raised. Which comes first? Becoming bilingual may change an individual's attitudes. As someone becomes more proficient in a minority language, so may the integrative attitudes and instrumental attitudes of that person become increasingly favorable towards the language. In this sense, there is a two-way relationship between language and motivation. One can be both the cause and the effect of the other. There is an interactive, cyclical process.

Many adults learn a second or foreign language for social or integrative reasons.

It is not always easy to distinguish an instrumental from integrative motivation, or to classify particular behavior in terms of its prior motivation. Is traveling abroad an instrumental or an integrative motive? Traveling abroad could represent an integrative attitude for one person or ethnic group, an instrumental attitude for another person or group.

Motivation in Language Classrooms

Instrumental and integrative motivations have been found as important explanations of classroom language learning. For example, Gliksman (1976, 1981) classified 14–16 year olds by their level of integrative motivation and then systematically observed the number of times the students:

- volunteered information by raising a hand;
- were asked by teachers without volunteering;
- answered correctly or incorrectly;
- asked questions;
- received positive, negative or no feedback from the teacher.

Motivation in the Successful Learning of English as a Foreign Language

Success in foreign language learning appears to depend to an extent on the students' native language and the language that is learnt. The relationship of the target language to the students' native language may affect students' motivation. If the target language has a high status in the eyes of the students, they will be more eager to learn it. If competence in the language opens up possibilities for educational and economic progress, then students' motivation will be higher. If the area where the target language is spoken is geographically close, students may see more point in learning it. It may be difficult to motivate students to learn the language of a country that they may never have an opportunity to visit.

This can be seen clearly if we consider the teaching of English as a foreign language. English is learnt successfully by many children and adults in Scandinavian countries, for example, because of the perceived usefulness of English as a major international language, in business, employment, travel and the media. Many younger people also have a desire to identify with and be part of Anglo-American culture.

In Kuwait, many students learn English successfully due to a variety of 'status', 'usefulness' and 'relevance' factors such as:

- identification with US and British people who aided them in the Gulf War;
- the need of science students to learn English for undergraduate and postgraduate studies;
- the desire of many Kuwaiti people to travel abroad – English being perceived as the most useful international language;
- interest in English language mass media.

In contrast, foreign language learning in countries where English is the first language of most children and adults tends to have a low success rate. The monolingual belief often appears to be that having one international language is all that is required. In such situations, the second language being learnt is of less perceived relevance, status and power. The first language is seen as internationally viable, creating little pressure to add a second language.

In such English-speaking majority situations, high cost investment in second language training often results in poor language outcomes. In France, a monolingual tradition also relates to a relatively weak performance in second language outcomes. Children do not succeed in second language learning because there is little opportunity or motivation to practice. Often more problematic is that the value and relevance (and hence motivation) of second language learning is not relayed to students. Few students become highly proficient in a second language partly because they are not aware of its purpose and worth. An important part of the teacher's role in such a situation is to increase student motivation. The teacher may focus on cultural aspects of the target language that are likely to appeal to the students and may arrange trips and exchange visits to the target country (integrative motivation). The teacher may also emphasize the relevance of the language for employment prospects (instrumental motivation).

The linguistic background of the students is another factor affecting their degree of motivation. If students are already multilingual or come from a multilingual background they may be more 'attuned' to the possibility of speaking different languages. Students from a monolingual background may have a less positive attitude to the learning of a second language. Studies have shown that students from a higher socioeconomic background may have more favorable attitudes to the learning of a foreign language. It may be that such students have a more positive attitude to education generally and that they see the learning of a foreign language as more relevant to their future employment and lifestyle.

Gliksman found that students with a higher integrative motivation volunteered information more frequently, gave correct answers and received more positive feedback from the teacher than did less integratively motivated students. The two groups did not differ significantly on the number of questions they asked in class. Gliksman found such differences were consistent across a whole term and were not sporadic or temporary.

Further Reading

BAKER, C., 1992, *Attitudes and Language*. Clevedon: Multilingual Matters Ltd.

GARDNER, R. C., 1985, *Social Psychology and Second Language Learning*. London: Edward Arnold.

GLIKSMAN, L., 1976, Second Language Acquisition: The Effects of Student Attitudes on Classroom Behaviour. Unpublished MA Thesis, University of Western Ontario.

GLIKSMAN, L., 1981, Improving the Prediction of Behaviours Associated with Second Language Acquisition. Unpublished PhD Thesis, University of Western Ontario.

A Scale to Measure Instrumental and Integrative Motivation

Here are some reasons for learning a second or foreign language. Indicate how important or unimportant these reasons are for you in the language you are learning. There are no right or wrong answers.

I am learning .... as a second or foreign language.

	IMPORTANT	FAIRLY IMPORTANT	FAIRLY UNIMPORTANT	UNIMPORTANT
1. To make friends	❑	❑	❑	❑
2. To earn plenty of money	❑	❑	❑	❑
3. Understand conversations	❑	❑	❑	❑
4. Read	❑	❑	❑	❑
5. Write	❑	❑	❑	❑
6. Watch TV/Videos	❑	❑	❑	❑
7. Get a job	❑	❑	❑	❑
8. Become cleverer	❑	❑	❑	❑
9. Be liked	❑	❑	❑	❑
10. Live in this region	❑	❑	❑	❑
11. Religious attendance	❑	❑	❑	❑
12. Sing (e.g. with others)	❑	❑	❑	❑
13. Play sport	❑	❑	❑	❑
14. Bring up children	❑	❑	❑	❑
15. Go shopping	❑	❑	❑	❑
16. Make phone calls	❑	❑	❑	❑
17. Pass exams	❑	❑	❑	❑
18. Be accepted in the community	❑	❑	❑	❑
19. Talk to friends	❑	❑	❑	❑
20. Talk to people generally	❑	❑	❑	❑

ADAPTED FROM: BAKER, 1992

6: Aptitude and Becoming Bilingual

Introduction

It is popularly believed that different people have different aptitudes for different things. Some people are said to have a musical aptitude. Such people appear to have a musical talent and can be spotted by musical aptitude tests as young as six to eight years old. It is popularly believed that some people have a knack for learning second languages quickly and easily. Other people appear to have little language learning aptitude. Despite being of reasonable intelligence and having sufficient motivation, such people are still slow at learning, although learning a language is still possible for all.

Aptitude has been distinguished from general ability (or general intelligence) and from motivation. Language aptitude has been regarded as a special bent for language learning. Some people appear to tune into language learning more easily than others, irrespective of their level of motivation and general ability. For example, some immigrants learn the host majority language with relative ease. Others are slow and may never become fluent.

It is dangerous totally to separate language aptitude from general ability. There is a large overlap between the two ideas. Those people with more academic ability may also be the ones who have a higher aptitude for learning a second language. This overlap between ability and aptitude will become apparent when considering tests of language aptitude.

Tests of Language Aptitude

Various tests can be used to measure a person's language aptitude: the Modern Languages Aptitude Test (MLAT), (Carroll & Sapon, 1959, revised in 1981); Pimsleur's Language Aptitude Battery (1966); and the York Language Aptitude Test (Green, 1975). Such Aptitude for Language tests measure components such as:

- the ability to perceive and memorize new sounds;
- sensitivity to the grammar and patterning of sentences;
- the ability to notice and identify similarities and differences in grammar and meaning in sentences;
- sound discrimination in listening to foreign language words, and
- the ability to relate sounds to symbols.

The Value of Language Aptitude Tests

An important question about such tests is what kind of success do they predict? Do they predict how well immigrants will pick up a language informally in shops and on the street? Do these tests of aptitude pick out children who will acquire a second language in the playground and in watching television? Do these tests only pick out children who will learn a second language through teaching and formal classroom situations?

Language Aptitude tests do predict success in the language classroom. Those students who score highly on such tests tend to become more proficient in a second language. From the examples given on page 657, it will be seen that language aptitude test items relate mainly to formal language learning in classrooms. The informal, incidental acquisition of a language outside school is much less represented in such language aptitude tests.

Such tests tend to assume that children and adults will learn words by heart (rote memorization of second language), and that grammar and structural patterns will be taught in a formal way in the classroom. They also assume that analyzing language will be part of the language teacher's approach. Such Language Aptitude tests tend to predict how well a student will do in a course that is based on grammar-translation methods or a formal, analytical approach.

The Limitations of Language Aptitude Tests

Two limitations of Language Aptitude tests need to be mentioned. First, they may not relate to the acquisition of language in informal, out of school situations. Such tests do not usually measure the ability to pick up a language in the street and via the mass media. Tests of attitudes and motivation for second language learning are more likely to gauge success in such informal acquisition situations. Secondly, such aptitude tests relate more to traditional, structurally based language classrooms. Recent developments in language teaching (e.g. the communicative approach), tend to place less emphasis on grammar, rote memorization and translation. These new approaches show less relationship to such aptitude tests. Nevertheless, second language learning is certainly helped by an ability to memorize vocabulary and by being sensitive to the grammar of a new language.

Language Aptitude tests reflect the linguistic rather than the communicative aspects of language learning. Therefore, they tend to be better predictors of whether somebody becomes proficient in the more academic aspects of a second language (e.g. correct grammar) rather than the kinds of skills of simple interpersonal communication that are required in the street and shops.

High scores on language aptitude tests may predict grade or examination success, and going on to college or university to study that second language further. Such Language Aptitude tests often pick out those in-migrants who will quickly pick up the majority language needed for success in school, but they may also pick out particular language minority children who may be slow to pick up the more abstract, academic language required to operate in classrooms.

Aptitude and Language Learning

The above discussion about tests of Language Aptitude raises a series of questions. If classrooms were different in the way a foreign or second language is taught, would language aptitude have less predictive value? When language is acquired informally and incidentally (e.g. by drama and activities), do current language aptitude tests have little predictive value? If such aptitude tests relate to formal language learning, what language approaches would be more suitable for children with lower aptitude scores? Does language aptitude play a minor role in the acquisition of basic interpersonal and communicative language skills?

The learning of a language by memorization, translating sentences and learning grammar may seem for some remote and irrelevant. Others accept it – these may be the ones who tend to have high scores on language aptitude tests. Thus language aptitude may be a combination of fundamental language skills coupled with an ability to cope with classroom procedures. Language aptitude may in part reflect the extent to which learners can make sense of the language learning situation they are in, and tune in to the organizational procedures and the routines of the teacher.

While aptitude may influence the rate at which someone learns a second language, it does not necessarily affect the level of proficiency finally reached. Aspects such as motivation may have a greater effect on ultimate success in second language acquisition. Language aptitude does not place limits on learning a language, but it appears to affect the speed of language learning in more formal language classes.

Language aptitude is a popular reason given for success and failure in second language acquisition, retention and loss in western and monolingual societies. This concept is rarely mentioned in regions where bilingualism and multilingualism are everyday occurrences. Where people use two or more languages daily, as in India, Pakistan, Papua New Guinea and Fiji, language aptitude is rarely a matter for discussion. In these countries, it is usually accepted that bilingualism or multilingualism is customary and as easy as learning to play sports. In western or monolingual societies, language aptitude is sometimes given as the reason for exceptional success. All too often, it is used as an excuse for failing to become proficient.

Where differences of language aptitude exist among students, a teacher or a school administrator should use this information wisely. In most educational situations, it would be unthinkable that some students be barred from learning a second language because of a low score on a Language Aptitude test. Equality of opportunity and open access to learning experiences may be the priority. This is particularly the case when Language Aptitude tests relate to traditional approaches (e.g. audiolingual, grammar-translation). A student with a low aptitude score may use the information to request opportunities to attend a course emphasizing a communicative approach. A low test score may indicate the need to accent informal acquisition rather than formal learning, or self-directed language learning.

Language Aptitude test scores have been used to stream (or set or track) students into different classes. Many second language teachers will argue that language learning requires tracking (streaming) rather than mixed ability classes. If aptitude can predict the speed students learn a second language, there may be pressure to select groups of children with similar proficiencies and aptitudes. However, tracking (streaming) may itself affect progress. Those placed in the higher tracks may speed ahead, those placed in the lower tracks may simply make the prophecies made about them self-fulfilling. Tracking produces expectations of children, who may behave in a way that fulfils the 'aptitude' expectations held of them.

One alternative is that children of different language aptitudes be given different teaching and learning environments. Different language contexts may suit different types of students in language learning. A student who fails to learn the language in one type of class may become gifted in a different one. For example, some students may speed ahead using formal structural approaches to language teaching. Other students may prefer more individualized, informal or self directed learning. Aptitude for different language learning routes is an important concept.

Further Reading

SKEHAN, P., 1986, Where Does Language Aptitude Come From? In P. MEARA (ed.), *Spoken Language: Papers from the Annual Meeting of the British Association for Applied Linguistics*. London: Centre for Information on Language Teaching and Research.

SKEHAN, P., 1989, *Individual Differences in Second-Language Learning*. London: Edward Arnold.

Examples of Language Aptitude Test Items

Example 1

Some language aptitude tests use a lesser-known foreign language to test the candidate's ability to perceive grammatical patterns in language. Here is one example.

In **English** most nouns form their plural by adding 's' (e.g. door – doors). There are some exceptions (e.g. man – men, child – children, mouse – mice).

In **Breton** there are several different ways of forming the **plural** of nouns, some of which are shown below. Read carefully through the tables and see if you can guess the missing words in the spaces.

butcher	*kiger*	butchers	*kigerien*
writer	*skrivagner*	writers	*skrivagnerien*
teacher	*kelenner*	teachers	*kelennerien*
singer	*kaner*	singers	....

ant	*merienenn*	ants	*merien*
wasp	*gwespedenn*	wasps	*gwesped*
spider	*kevnidenn*	spiders	*kevnid*
bee	*gwenanenn*	bees	....

Example 2

In **English**, we say 'I see', 'you see', 'he sees'. In **Breton**, people say the equivalent of 'See I do', 'See you do', 'See he does'.

Look at these **Breton** examples and guess the missing words.

I see	*gwelout a ran*	I eat	*debriñ a ran*
you see	*gwelout a rez*	you eat	*debriñ a rez*
he/she sees	*gwelout a ra*	he/she eats	....

7: Age and Becoming Bilingual

Introduction

There is a popular belief that it is better to learn a second language as early as possible. For both a majority language speaker learning a second language (e.g. an English-speaking person learning French) and a minority language speaker learning a majority language (e.g. English), many people believe that the second language should be acquired early. Many adults learning a language formally or picking up that language as an in-migrant may struggle to become proficient. Yet they see their young children picking up a second language in the street and in school with relative ease.

There is considerable research on language learning among children and adults. There is also much evidence on language learning early or later in school. While it would be helpful to find a simple conclusion, questions about when to begin acquiring a second language have few answers. Research has shown that this area is highly complex, with so many different ingredients making up a whole variety of relatively successful and less successful 'recipes' for second language proficiency. No simple statements can be made because so many different factors may be present or absent, and situations and circumstances are so different. There are so many exceptions, and no rules.

Popular Beliefs

The view that younger children learn a second language better is often based on the idea that young children have more flexible, plastic malleable brains so that learning a second language is natural to a child. Observation would seem to support this claim. Many children seem to acquire a second or third language as easily as learning to swim or ride a bicycle. Young children enjoy learning new skills and becoming competent in different areas. Young children seem able to pick up a second language early on as easily as they pick up their first language. Young children may adapt easily to new sound systems and different grammatical structures without having to learn them formally.

Young children appear to learn language effortlessly and naturally through play and activities. But according to research, they do not learn language more efficiently than older children and adults.

The popular 'negative' belief about older learners is that teenagers and adults have a more set and a less flexible brain. Too much is going on in the thinking quarters of an adult to allow second language learning to be efficient.

Research Findings

Such a popular view that it is better to learn a second language early, and that older learners are at a disadvantage, has little credibility among researchers (Singleton, 1989). Many teenagers and adults do learn a second language and become both proficient and accomplished in that second language. Older children and adults may learn a language more efficiently and quickly. For example, a 14 year old or 44 year old learning Spanish as a second language will have superior intellectual processing skills compared to a four year old learning Spanish. Less time is required in teenage and adult years to acquire a second language. Some adults have considerable motivation and a very positive attitude to learning a second language. Such adults would tend to learn a language well and speedily.

In Israel and Wales, New Zealand and Canada, the United States and many parts of Asia, the adult route to bilingualism has many success stories. In-migrants to Israel have learnt Hebrew. In the United States many adults have learnt English within a few years of in-migrancy. In Wales, there are adult learner classes for Welsh in almost every town and many villages throughout Wales. Adults learning a second language are often successful when certain situations exist: for example, the need for economic survival and prosperity, or wanting to be accepted within a community and wishing to

Learning a Language in Later Life – Den and Ann Rees

The county of Gwent in south-east Wales has been for generations one of the most Anglicized areas of Wales. By the time of the 1961 census, less than five percent of the population of the county spoke Welsh. Yet most people in the area still regard themselves as Welsh and during the last decade, there has been an upsurge of interest in learning Welsh. Several Welsh-medium primary schools and two secondary schools have been established, and every week over 150 Welsh classes for adults are held in various centers in the county.

Until 1984, Den and Ann Rees kept the local garage in the little village of Croesyceiliog near Newport in Gwent. Both are Welsh, Ann from Troed y rhiw, a little village about 20 miles north of Cardiff, and Den from Llanfrynach, a village near Brecon. Neither are from Welsh-speaking families, although Ann remembers that her grandparents were able to speak Welsh. Since Welsh is rarely heard in the Newport area, there was no need to use it in their business. In any case, their busy, seven-day, working week did not allow much spare time for language learning. However, like most non-Welsh-speaking Welsh people, they considered themselves Welsh. Den, particularly, always had the dream that one day he would learn Welsh. As a young man he had worked as a joiner. At one time he had two young Welsh-speaking apprentices and he still remembers his envy at their ability to speak Welsh.

In 1984 Den and Ann decided to sell the garage and enjoy an early retirement with the opportunity for more leisure time. One day late in 1990 they watched a television program for Welsh learners 'Now You're Talking' . At the same time they noticed an advertisement for an '*Wlpan*' or intensive Welsh course, starting in Newport after Christmas. The course would be held for three two-hour sessions each week. They decided to join. 'We thought we would learn Welsh in about six months' Ann remembers, 'and then go on to do something else!' They did not realize at the time that learning Welsh would take somewhat more than six months and that the language would become such an integral part of their lives.

From the beginning, Ann and Den were determined to practice their Welsh together. 'We didn't see the point of learning it if we didn't use it', Ann says. Over a period of months they progressed from simple requests like 'Would you like a cup of coffee?' and ' What time is it?' to using more and more Welsh together.

They also sought out opportunities to hear Welsh and to practice the language. They visited Welsh-speaking areas on holiday and mixed with Welsh speakers. On a visit to Lampeter in West Wales in the summer of 1991, they were invited out to dinner by their hosts and found themselves at the Annual Dinner of the Cardiganshire Society of Fishermen, surrounded by Welsh speakers and with a famous TV personality giving the after-dinner speech. They began to visit the National Eisteddfod every year, the greatest Welsh cultural festival, where Welsh is the only official language. During the 1992 Aberystwyth Eisteddfod, they began to speak only Welsh to one another.

Den and Ann have realized the importance of developing listening skills. They have listened constantly to Welsh radio and television and to conversations between Welsh speakers. Ann says ' I feel sometimes that I've done a degree course in listening'. They have also read widely in Welsh, beginning with simple books for learners and progressing to classic works.

Ann and Den disprove the myth that the ability to learn a language decreases after childhood. Today they both speak Welsh fluently and express themselves more articulately and with a wider vocabulary than many Welsh speakers. Like many bilingual people they are sometimes at a loss for a word in Welsh and sometimes in English, depending on the topic of conversation. They are fortunate that the one aspect of a second language which adults may find so difficult to acquire, an authentic accent, has not been a problem. Like many South Walians, they have a strong Welsh accent in English and this has transferred naturally to their Welsh.

Den and Ann have no background of higher education. They both left school at 16 and are proud to say that their certificates for Welsh examinations are their first ever academic qualifications. They had never studied grammar before learning Welsh and now discuss parts of speech more confidently in Welsh than in English.

Ann and Den's experience shows that age need not be a significant factor in second language learning. Other factors, such as motivation, commitment, perseverance and opportunities for practice count for much more. Personality is also an important factor. Ann and Den are friendly, extrovert, gregarious people who enjoy mixing and have never found it hard to approach Welsh speakers. They contend that learning Welsh has enriched and transformed their lives and opened a new network of relationships for them.

Age and the Use of Hebrew in Israel

In-migrants into Israel during this century have often learnt Hebrew in an attempt to be accepted by the community, to revive the ethnic, religious language and to belong to the centuries old Jewish tradition. From Israeli census data, it is possible to examine the extent to which older and younger adults who learn Hebrew go on to use Hebrew in everyday life. For example, do younger in-migrants who learn Hebrew as a second language tend to use that language more than older in-migrants?

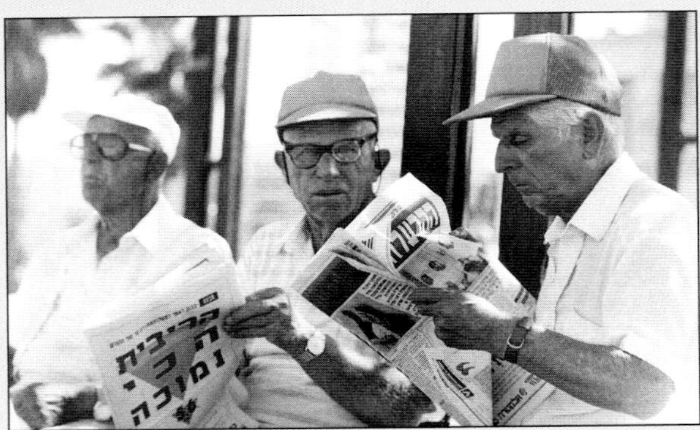

Older Israeli folk read a Hebrew newspaper, but often the use of the language is less among older Hebrew learners.

The chart below (adapted from Bachi's (1956) data) shows that the extent of everyday use of Hebrew compared with age of in-migration. The conclusion is straightforward. The younger the child, the more likely he or she will use Hebrew after learning it. Between 30 and 40 years of age, a notable drop in use of learnt Hebrew occurs. While the reasons for this may be multiple and complex (e.g. less exposure to Hebrew, less motivation, less social pressure to learn Hebrew, fewer chances to practice, possible loss in learning ability and memorization), the results show that use of a second language does vary with age. Whether the same patterns occur in other countries is waiting to be researched. A similar pattern is quite possible.

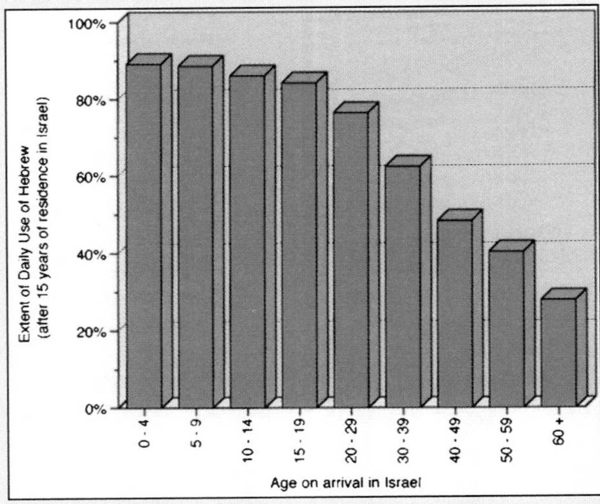

Age and use of Hebrew in Israel, from sample of 15,616 males. (Source: Bachi, 1956).

Critical Periods and Becoming Bilingual

The concept of a critical period comes from biology. The idea is that there is a particular phase in the development of a person during which language, for example, is best acquired. To give one example: baby ducks follow the first moving object they see and form an attachment to this object (e.g. mother, another bird, an ornithologist, a child). This has been interpreted as revealing a critical period in the development of attachment by ducks.

In bilingual development, a similar idea of a critical period among very young children was popularized in particular by Eric Lenneberg (1967). He believed that language could not begin to develop until a certain stage of maturation and growth had been attained. Between the ages of two and three years or between 21 and 36 months was regarded as the critical age of language acquisition. When puberty started, (e.g. around the age of 14), the brain was fully developed. At puberty, the plasticity of the brain that enabled language learning had considerably diminished. Thus, the period between 21 months and about 14 years of age was regarded as the critical period for the development of first and second languages.

An authoritative review is provided by Singleton (1989) showing that a critical period of language development is now discredited. Singleton concludes that language acquisition is a continuous process that begins at birth and continues throughout life. There is no absolute age limit beyond which it is impossible to become bilingual. First and second language acquisition will continue well into adulthood. The idea that language learning capacity peaks between the ages of two and 14 is not supported from international research. The development of the thinking processes, memorization, writing and reading skills that are all part of language acquisition, occur in older children and well into adulthood.

However, there are often advantageous periods. Research shows that, for reasons not yet fully understood, acquiring a language before puberty has advantages for pronunciation. After the age of about 12, it becomes more difficult to acquire authentic pronunciation. Developing a second language in the primary school is advantageous, giving an early foundation and many more years ahead for that language to mature. In the nursery, kindergarten and primary school years, a second language is acquired rather than learnt. So while there are no critical periods, there are advantageous periods. Such periods occur when there is a higher probability of language acquisition due to circumstances, time available, teaching resources and motivation.

REFERENCE: SINGLETON, 1989

share in neighborhood culture and to communicate with local people. One conclusion is that it is never too late to start to learn a second or a third language. Adults have successfully learnt language when over 60 or 70 years of age.

Research has found that, in practice, young children who have learnt a second language early on have a slightly higher probability of attaining proficiency in that second language. (However, this research is not without its critics). Young children seem able to adapt more easily to new sound systems. Research does show that younger language learners, before the age of puberty, seem to find it easier to pick up native-like pronunciation. After this age it may be more difficult. Very young children seem to find a natural enjoyment, an internal motivation, a desire for competency and the sheer excitement of having new skills. This all helps second language learning. Teenagers sometimes need persuading to learn a second language. The motivation and desire to learn a second language are not always strong in the teenage years. Older students in the secondary school may feel that learning a second language is an imposition.

Adults tend to have many home, work and leisure activities to think about, so that second language learning has great competition. They sometimes lack the social contexts and opportunities to practice their new language, and have set peer groups and reasonably fixed relationships with first language speakers. Adults learning a second language may face psychological hurdles such as shyness, inhibition, fear of failure, and inability to adapt to new ways of thinking, in this case, the different grammatical patterns and different expressions of a new language. People learning a second language later in life may not always have the motivation to continue to proficiency. Hence, younger learners seem to have the edge.

Younger learners also, in practice, have more potential years of language learning. Those who start in the nursery or kindergarten, and continue through elementary and secondary education, will have more years of language acquisition and language learning than those who start in mid-teens or later in life. Therefore, in practice, many second language speakers who start to learn early do have fine communication and fluency skills. While there are no critical periods of language learning, there are advantageous periods. Early childhood and school days are two advantageous periods. But many successful adult second language learners show that increasing age is not a disadvantage. Older learners will show a similar development sequence in learning a second language. They will also tend to learn quicker. Under sufficiently motivating circumstances, adults can learn as quickly, sometimes more quickly, than children.

When a person comes from a language minority home, there may be dangers in learning a majority language too early. For example, in the United States, Latino children are often pressured into learning English early in life. When young children still have an uncertain grasp of their own, native language and are constantly exposed to the language of the majority, there may be a risk to language development in either language. When children are very young, in a subtractive bilingual environment, priority needs to be given to the solid acquisition of the mother tongue. One example of this is in-migrants who are encouraged by politicians or teachers, speech therapists or educational psychologists to give their children as much practice as possible in the language of the area (e.g. English in the United States). When the second language is learnt at the expense of the first language, it may be better to leave second language learning to later.

Contexts

There is often a difference between the circumstances in which young children, older children and adults learn a second language. Such circumstances have nothing intrinsically to do with age. Nevertheless, such circumstances are often connected with certain ages.

Many young children learn a second language in a 'natural' environment, where language acquisition is coincidental. For example, a young child learns spontaneously in the home, in the street and neighborhood, school playground, or when with relatives. The language acquisition is through play, everyday activities and general interaction with other people. Learning a language is not the focus of the interaction. It is incidental. There are often many contact hours in such informal language acquisition contexts. Such contexts do not require a high level of language. The concrete contexts, plentiful use of body language and intrinsically motivating nature of such contexts aids language acquisition.

In comparison, many older children and adults learn a second language in a relatively more 'artificial' environment. Language classes in the secondary school, Saturday schools for language minority children, and adult learner classes during evenings and weekends are each examples of formal, manufactured language learning contexts. There are relatively fewer contact hours in such circumstances (e.g. half an hour a day language lessons). Because language learning is the main aim, interest and motivation may vary across time (e.g. wane as teenagers grow older) and across different people. Rapid progress is often expected of the teenager and adult in learning a second language, and this may be unrealistic. Such formal educational settings are now further considered.

Education

In schooling, teaching methods and curriculum materials need adapting to the needs and preferences of different age groups. Young children acquire language easily, almost accidentally, when doing drama and music, when playing, role-playing, in small group projects and activities. Younger children tend often to enjoy language learning in more informal, 'hands-on' situations.

Older children may expect second language practice to reflect secondary school methods and not the project work, simple simulations and role-play accepted by younger children. Adults and some teenagers expect more formal learning of language. The formal teaching of vocabulary and grammar may be expected, sometimes producing efficient learning, but not necessarily making language learning more enjoyable.

Adults are sometimes discouraged by simple and mechanical activities they are expected to complete. For adults, learning a second language through children's activities may be uncomfortable and unmotivating. However, when language learning is not necessarily the focus, but a by-product of enjoyable activities, motivation may be high for both teenagers and adults. Keep Fit sessions where the second language is constantly used, fun games around a table (e.g. Monopoly) using the second language, conversations over glasses of beer or cups of tea, and achieving a constant change of activity may be motivating for adults learning a language.

While for young children there is often an inherent pleasure of competency in a second language, for teenagers and adults, there needs to be an inherent enjoyment and positive attitude to language learning. The desire to integrate with, or affiliate to the target language group may produce some of the necessary enthusiasm to learn a second language amongst teenagers and adults. Instrumental reasons such as needing a second language for employment or promotion need to be harnessed. Pleasurable learning experiences are also needed to create a positive second language learning atmosphere for teenagers and adults.

One issue that has regularly arisen in this topic of 'age and becoming bilingual' is whether children should learn a second language in the elementary school or in the secondary school. The answer will tend to differ according to whether children come from a language minority or language majority home. With language minority children, there is a danger that they will learn the second language (and be taught through the second language) too early in school. Strong development of the first language seems more of a priority.

For the language majority child, there is considerable dispute whether it is preferable to learn a language in the elementary school or to leave it to the secondary school. Burstall *et al.* (1974) examined the value of introducing French as a second language to British students in elementary schools from the age of eight. Using over 17,000 children, Burstall compared children who began to learn French at eight years of age with those who began to learn French in their secondary school at the age of 11. By the age of 16, the two groups did not differ in their performance in speaking French, only on the listening to French test. Children who began to learn French in the secondary school tended to show superior scores on reading and writing in French.

Claire Burstall concluded that early and extra exposure to French did not have any long-term benefits. The results are disputed because: explanations are inconsistent; there were experimental and control students within the same classes; the tests used may also have been unfair to the early starters; the curriculum resources available for teaching French at an early age may have been inadequate; the competence of teachers in elementary schools to teach French well was in doubt. In many countries, the decision about when to teach a second language is often not an educational one. Where immigrants are concerned in particular, the decision may be political, administrative and economic.

Further Reading

DICKERSON, P. & CUMMING, A., 1996, *Profiles of Language Education in 25 Countries*. Slough (UK): NFER.

HARLEY, B., 1986, *Age in Second Language Acquisition*. Clevedon: Multilingual Matters Ltd.

SINGLETON, D., 1989, *Language Acquisition: The Age Factor*. Clevedon: Multilingual Matters Ltd.

8: Second Language Retention

The focus in this subsection has been on the factors affecting the speed, success and nature of second language acquisition. It has been shown that attitudes and motivation, situational factors, type of language input, aptitude and age all are ingredients in the complex recipe of informal and formal language acquisition.

Suppose, however, a certain degree of proficiency in a second language has been achieved, whether by informal acquisition or by formal language learning. How is that competence then maintained? How can loss or attrition of the second language be avoided?

The topic of second language retention has become a focus of attention in countries such as the Netherlands, Japan, US and particularly Canada. The growing popularity and success of Immersion schooling has meant that many students leave high school proficient in a second language. However, research has shown that a large proportion of these students do not retain proficiency in their second language. Rather, the second language shrivels.

Research in the Netherlands, Canada and Wales has suggested that second language retention is linked to interrelated factors such as use, proficiency, relevance, motivation and status. These will now be discussed.

To learn a second language, it must be used. A person learns to speak by speaking, and to write by writing. Similarly, to retain a second language, it must be used. For many Immersion students, the second language is primarily a classroom language. Even during the school years, many Immersion students tend to use the majority language with their peers outside lessons and outside school. There are few opportunities to use the second language beyond the school gates. In recent years supporters of Immersion schooling in Wales and Canada have recognized the need to create a network of opportunities for the informal use of the second language by Immersion students and graduates from Immersion schooling.

There must be encouragement for students to take their own initiatives and seek out opportunities to use their second language. For example, summer camps, cultural festivals, school exchanges, living for a few weeks, a term, or a year, with a family who regularly speaks that second language, travel opportunities, competitions and festivals in school, each create valuable second language environments. In Wales, for instance, most Welsh Immersion students come from non-Welsh-speaking homes and do not have easy access to the modern Welsh youth cultural scene. This culture and opportunities for socializing in Welsh need to be made available to them.

Students need to be furnished with pleasurable and meaningful opportunities for using the language. Part of second language learning and teaching may be to facilitate movement into using a language once formal learning has finished.

A factor linked with use is that of proficiency. The continuing popularity of Immersion schooling in Canada and Wales is based on the perception that Immersion students achieve native-like fluency in the second language. Research in both countries has suggested that this is not strictly true. Although Immersion students do achieve very high levels of fluency in their second language, they do not attain the same stylistic range and variation as native speakers. This may be linked to the fact that they use their language in a narrower range of contexts than native speakers. Although this lack of stylistic variation may not impede communication, it may mean that students who have graduated from Immersion education possibly lack the confidence to use their second language in out-of-school situations (e.g. social situations and employment.) The Welsh Language Board recently reported that very few of its advertised posts (for which Welsh is a requirement) attract applicants who are second language speakers and who have attended Welsh-medium schools.

A third factor is that of relevance. Students may use a second language at school, but if they do not perceive it as being relevant to their lives outside school and after they have graduated, they will not continue to use it. If use of the language is not relevant to their own needs and goals, retention may be a problem. While parents, schools and government may be keen for the second language to be used in school and afterwards, teenagers in particular often have other priorities. The social and individual needs of teenagers, in particular, have to be taken into account when encouraging second language retention in individuals.

Relevance is closely linked to motivation. Language retention occurs when there are positive attitudes within an individual, among parents, teachers and leaders who influence the attitudes of the child. When there is motivation to identify with those who speak the second language, or a motivation to learn a language for employment, retention is more likely to occur.

In countries where English is widely learnt and used as a second language, problems of retention are not so great. In Scandinavian countries, for instance, school students tend to learn English very successfully, and tend to retain their English after leaving school. The reason for this is that English is perceived to be useful and relevant for travel, employment and access to the prestigious Anglo-American culture.

The fifth factor affecting retention of the second language is status. Research has indicated that one factor in successful second language acquisition is that the target language is perceived to be of equal or superior status to the native language of the learner. Welsh and French are both minority languages in the areas of Wales and Canada where Immersion schooling occurs. Both have to compete against the prestige of the major international language of English. Students use the second, minority language at school, but see all around them the high status language of English.

The mass media plays both a 'language experience' and a symbolic 'status' role in aiding second language retention. In Scandinavia, for example, it is easy to find television channels with English and German language programs. Some films are dubbed, but many have subtitles, others are broadcast without translation. Therefore, there is plenty of opportunity to hear spoken English or German. Satellite television and global communications such as the Internet have extended the availability of language retention via the media.

Mass media also plays a symbolic 'status' role in language retention. A language well represented in the mass media (not only in television and information technology, but also in books, newspapers, radio, etc.) radiates a sense of modernity, high value, status and worth. The speaker or learner of a minority language may be influenced into retaining that language if it feels contemporary, useful and desirable. In Wales, as in a few other language minority situations (e.g. Catalonia), there is the provision of minority language television. This helps to increase the status of the language in the eyes of its users, and encourages them to use and retain it.

This brief discussion of the topic of language retention indicates that many of the factors that aid second language acquisition also facilitate second language retention. For a second language to be successfully learnt, and then retained, it must be perceived by the speaker to be useful, relevant, valuable and prestigious. In minority language situations where English is the majority language, this is not easily achieved. In such situations, the minority language may need to be 'marketed' effectively, to increase people's motivation to learn it and to retain it.

Further Reading

HARLEY, B., 1986, *Age in Second Language Acquisition*. Clevedon: Multilingual Matters Ltd.

SINGLETON, D., 1989, *Language Acquisition: The Age Factor*. Clevedon: Multilingual Matters Ltd.

Second Language Learning in Education

1: Ten Dimensions of Classroom Language Learning

Bilinguals and second language learners are not two discrete groups. The stock of bilinguals will include those who have learnt a second language in school, in language laboratories, in adult classes and through correspondence courses, for example. Second language learning enables the growth of bilingualism not only within an individual, but also within a language group. For example, the survival and spread of minority languages often depends not just on intergenerational transmission but also on schools, for example, introducing majority language speakers to minority languages. Thus, a comprehensive study of bilingualism must include a consideration of second language learning and second language acquisition.

Foreign and second language learning to achieve a degree of bilingualism occurs in a wide variety of contexts, and uses many different approaches. However, it is possible to identify ten basic issues around which different language teaching methods and approaches are based. The structure, organization and declared aims of any language course are not usually decided by individual teachers at classroom level. However, teachers' attitudes to these basic issues will influence their interpretation of the course and choice of classroom methods and techniques.

1. A language teacher will have an implicit or explicit theory of what constitutes a second language and what is its purpose. For some teachers, language is essentially about vocabulary, correct grammar and sentence structure. For other teachers, language concerns communication, sharing information, and personal and social interaction.

2. There is more than one theory of how children and adults best learn a language. If language is seen as a series of structures which have to be overcome, then the emphasis is likely to be on memorization, drill and practice in order to secure fluency and correctness. On the other hand, if language is seen as a means of communication, rather than an end in itself, then the focus shifts to meaningful tasks involving real communication, in order to acquire the skills of effective communication.

A language teacher leads the class in an action song. A teacher may assume the role of motivator and facilitator rather than controller.

3. Theories of language and of language learning will determine the aims of the class. Some teachers will define second language classroom goals as the accurate control of the four language abilities, of conscious second language learning and successful academic examination outcomes. For other teachers, the goal becomes social communication or communicating information, equipping the child with functional skills to communicate in an uninhibited and as intelligible a way as possible (but not necessarily correctly).

4. Goals in language learning have implications for a language syllabus. Some language courses introduce new vocabulary and structures in a carefully graded sequence, gradually increasing in complexity. Others introduce lists of everyday functions and tasks through which the student may acquire language (e.g. greetings, taking leave, thanking, apologizing).

5. The syllabus chosen will lead to classroom activities that may vary from translation and substitution, drill and practice, to role-play (e.g. in the market, having a meal, shopping) and problem-solving tasks (e.g. working out the route for a journey using maps and train timetables).

6. Such classroom activities have direct consequences for the role taken by the teacher. When classroom activities center round drill and practice, the teacher is in control, setting the pace and direction of the learning and correcting and testing progress. When students are working in pairs, or small groups, on meaningful tasks that reflect their own communicative needs, the teacher may take on a more informal role, as a facilitator and a participant.

7. The role taken by the teacher will determine the role taken by the learner. When teachers are controlling, students will be dependent and reactive. The students answer, imitate and hopefully internalize. When the teacher is the facilitator rather than the director, students take a more active role, deciding with the teacher and fellow students the nature of course content and how to complete a given task.

8. The nature of the course will determine the materials and facilities that exist inside and outside the classroom. A more structured, linguistic approach will tend to co-exist with graded text books, visual aids, graded exercises, language laboratories and computer assisted language learning programs. Curriculum materials will be tightly organized and carefully structured. A more communicative approach will tend to connect with an eclectic variety of materials, many of which will be authentic materials taken directly from the target language (e.g. advertisements, bus and train timetables, restaurant menus, excerpts from radio and video programs). Group work, pair work and a greater emphasis on learner initiative will lead to more flexibility and improvisation in the classroom. There may also be more emphasis on field trips and out-of-classroom planned experiences (e.g. short visits to the target language community, student exchanges, local contacts with 'native speakers', visits to plays, concerts, folk dances and festivals through the medium of the target language).

9. Different methods and approaches will relate to different forms of assessment of the outcomes of second language learning. The goal of some approaches is academic examination success, often accenting literacy as, much as, or more than, oracy, and emphasizing grammatical correctness. Other approaches may aim at the assessment of oral skills, where the student's ability to convey and negotiate meaning with the examiner is the important outcome. Where language learning is self-controlled, self-planned and self-responsible, then assessment can be informal and self-evaluatory.

10. Another variation tends to be the contexts of second language learning. Language teaching sometimes takes place with no reference to the culture of the target language. A student may become fluent in Chinese or German without learning very much about Chinese or German culture, and without feeling any affiliation or empathy with the target language community. Alternatively, the language and culture may be taught in an integrated way. This will be reflected in the ethos of the classroom. Sometimes, language learning takes place in bare classrooms and halls which are used for other purposes. At other times, creative teachers, working in rooms allocated for language teaching, surround students with appropriate language and cultural artifacts; colorful posters and postcards, books, tourist relics and objects (e.g. costumes and food packets). The student is provided with an appropriate atmosphere for learning the target language. When second language learning occurs in the Mosque, Temple, Synagogue, Church Hall or Language Community Center, the context may engender a feeling of becoming and belonging.

Further Reading

COOK, V. J., 1991, *Second Language Learning and Language Teaching*. London: Edward Arnold.

RICHARDS, J. C. & RODGERS, T. S., 1986, *Approaches and Methods in Language Teaching: A Description and Analysis*. Cambridge: Cambridge University Press.

STERN, H. H., 1992, *Issues and Options in Language Teaching*. Oxford: Oxford University Press.

2: Foreign and Second Language Learning

Introduction

Formal foreign and second language learning to achieve a level of bilingualism occurs when students learn a language as a subject in the classroom. This differs from acquiring a language in an informal environment (e.g. in the street or playground). When young children learn a first language at home they receive many thousands of hours' exposure to the language. They acquire language within real contexts and for real purposes (e.g. eating, playing, shopping, visiting the extended family). Many visual and contextual clues help them understand language. A tiny child, for instance, may soon learn to associate the appearance of pajamas, a bottle and a storybook with the utterance 'It's time for bed'. Older children or adults learning a second language in a 'naturalistic' situation (e.g. an in-migrant picking up the language of the host country at work or in the neighborhood) have the advantage that they are hearing and practicing the language in real situations and for real purposes.

Classroom foreign and second language learning has the potential disadvantage that it takes place within a formal, 'context-reduced' environment. It is harder to create opportunities for the language to be used for real purposes, and the learners have few contextual clues to help them with comprehension. In addition, teaching time is often limited. However, the classroom can have advantages as a learning environment for older children and adults. Adult learners can find it hard to cope with the bewildering complexity and variety of the language as used in the speech community. Native speakers of the target language do not usually know how to adjust or simplify their language when addressing language learners. Older children and adults learning a second language may feel ill at ease and disadvantaged in social situations.

Classroom foreign or second language learning also differs from a situation where children at a nursery school or school are taught through the medium of a second language (e.g. Immersion education). In Immersion education, for instance, children have many more contact hours with the second language than those learning the language as a subject in school. Some or all of the school curriculum is taught through the medium of the second language. School activities such as games, sports, concerts, plays, craft work, trips and fund raising activities may take place wholly or partly in the second language. The teachers interact naturally with the children outside the classroom in the second language. The child learns and uses the language in authentic contexts and for authentic purposes.

However there are often no clear lines of demarcation between classroom foreign and second language learning and other ways of acquiring a second language. A child learning a second language at school that is also a language widely used in the community will have opportunities to hear or speak that language outside the classroom. An in-migrant to a country may hear the new language at work, in shops and in social situations, but may also have the opportunity to attend formal classes. Learning will occur outside and inside the classroom. In some international schools a second language may be introduced as a subject and then other subjects in the curriculum may also be taught through the medium of that language. Also, community language teaching (see page 681) fits neither into a second language nor foreign language category but somewhere inbetween.

In recent years, there have been attempts to make second and foreign language learning more meaningful and purposeful by centering the teaching on activities based on the learners' communicative needs. (See the Communicative Approach, page 674). This has also involved taking learners out of the classroom environment, through trips to the target region or country, visits to language centers where students take part in tasks and role-play in a simulated foreign language environment, correspondence with pen pals and exchange visits.

Foreign Language and Second Language

The terms 'foreign language' and 'second language' are often used interchangeably, but a useful distinction can be made between them. The term 'foreign language' can be used to describe a language not commonly used in the student's country of residence. A student learning French in the United States is learning a foreign language. The term 'second language' can be used to describe a language more widely spoken in the student's country of residence. An English-speaking student learning French in Canada is learning a second language. However there are not always clear distinctions between second and foreign language learning. French is one of the two official languages of Canada, and thus is taught as a 'second' language to anglophone students. Students learning French in

Montreal where the language is widely used will feel that they are learning a 'second language' whereas students in a French class in Vancouver, far from the francophone region of Canada, may regard French more as a foreign language. Irrespective of how a language is officially classified, much will depend on the student's perception. In this topic the term 'second language' is taken to include 'foreign language'.

Languages in Education in Hungary

On the 23rd of October 1989, Hungary became a Republic for the fourth time in its history. The new independent, democratic state wished to establish a free market economy, and move away from being over-centralized, highly bureaucratic and merely a satellite country of the communist world. Therefore, the language needs and preferences of the country changed, particularly with regard to languages at school. Such a change needs placing in its historical context.

Between 1949 and 1989, Russian was a compulsory foreign language in all Hungarian schools, reflecting the subordinate and dependent relationship between Hungary and the USSR. Few learnt to communicate fluently in Russian, although Russian was the lingua franca of the Warsaw Pact countries. Before 1989, Hungarians did not linguistically or culturally identify with Russia. The current status of Russian in Hungary is associated with a defeated political order, something of the past and not the present.

The preference of Hungarians with regard to language learning was already being established by the late 1980s. Radnai (1994) suggests that 50 percent of registrations for language examinations were for English, 30 percent for German, only 15 percent for Russian and 16 percent for French. During the 1990s, a considerable growth has occurred in German language teaching. In the 1993/1994 school year, the distribution of languages offered in Hungarian schools was as follows: 27.4 percent English, 23 percent German, 14.2 percent French, and 9.7 percent Italian. Russian, Spanish, Dutch and Swedish were also being offered.

Alongside foreign language teaching (which often occurs from the beginning of primary education), there has been a concern since 1989 for national language minority rights and language usage. Language minority groups in Hungary form approximately ten percent of the total population of Hungary. The ethnic minorities of Hungary include Germans, Slovaks, Croats, Serbs, Slovenes, Romanians and Gypsies. There is a growing movement for bilingual education including Hungarian as the national language along with either a foreign or a minority language currently present in Hungary.

Languages other than English in the United States

- In the United States, there are around 60 Spanish television channels, 850 Spanish radio stations and 40 Spanish newspaper titles.
- There are approximately 190 Polish radio stations, 100 German radio stations, 80 Italian radio stations and 70 French radio stations.
- In the United States there were (in 1996) ten newspaper titles in German, eight in Polish, and five in Italian.
- Most tourists to the United States come from Canada (17 million), Mexico (10 million), Japan (3.5 million), United Kingdom (three million), Germany (two million) and France (one million).
- Tourists from the United States visit Mexico (16 million), Canada (12 million), England (three million), France (two million), Germany (two million) and Italy (one million).
- There is no official federal policy on the teaching of foreign languages. However, in 1994, *'Goals 2000: Educate America Act'* provided legislation that encourages student achievement by developing goals and standards in the core curriculum subjects, including foreign languages.
- All 50 states include foreign languages in their curricula. Forty states have laws requiring public school students to have a minimum of two years of foreign language study. The remaining 10 states require second language study at the secondary level, but only for those going on to further education.
- It is been estimated that 40 percent of students in Grades 9 to 12, 25 percent of those in Grades 7 to 8, and about five percent in Grades 1 to 6 are studying a foreign language.
- Spanish is the most popular language studied in school, followed by French, German, Russian, Italian and Japanese. The study of Japanese is on the increase, especially in primary schools.
- In Grades 9 to 12, approximately 25 percent of students study Spanish as a foreign language, 10 percent study French and three percent study German. Less than one percent study Japanese.
- There are approximately 80,000 foreign language teachers in the United States, forming approximately three percent of all teachers. Over 50 percent of these language teachers were working at the upper secondary school level.

A second language that is taught in a classroom is often called a target language, because to learn it is the aim or 'target' of the course. The community where it is spoken is called the 'target community'. Where languages are spoken in more than one community, the target community will usually be the community nearest to the language learners' community. For students learning French in Britain, France is the target community. For students learning French in the United States, Canada is the target community. This will affect the style of language used, and the cultural component of the course.

Reasons for Language Learning

An analysis of language teaching and learning commences from the implicit or explicit aims and philosophy of the educationalists. The way second languages are taught will be determined by different views of the value of second languages and foreign languages in the local and wider society, as well as varying ideas about learning and teaching in classrooms. What languages are taught, the provision of time and finances allotted, and the approaches and methods used, are not usually decided by individual learners or even course organizers and teachers, but at governmental level. Many underlying reasons influence decisions about what languages are taught, to whom, what approach is used and how resources are allocated. These may be clustered under three headings: ideological, international and individual.

Ideological Reasons

For language minority children, the aim of second language learning may be assimilationist. For example, the teaching of English as a second language in the United States and in England often aims at rapidly integrating minority language groups into mainstream society. In contrast, when children learn a minority language as their second language, maintenance and preservation of that minority language may be the societal aim (e.g. English-speaking children learning Irish in school in Ireland or Maori in New Zealand). This provides an additive situation: a second language is added at no cost to the first language. Such maintenance may not only exist in indigenous language 'territory'. Where first language English children in the US learn to speak Spanish as a second language, there may be an attempt to promote a language community within a particular area.

Second language learning is also promoted in some countries to increase harmony between language groups. In Canada, the teaching of English to French-speaking children, and the teaching of French to English-speaking children, is perceived as one method by which a dual language, integrated Canadian society may be attained.

International Reasons

Language learning is often encouraged or enforced for economic and trade reasons. With the growth of the free market economy, and world-wide trade competition, facility with languages may promote success in business.

The learning of a second language can be a valuable asset in travel across continents. For many mainland Europeans, for example, to speak two or three languages is not uncommon. Such language facility enables holidays to be spent in neighboring European countries or in North, Central or South America. In the planned unification of Europe, traveling, working and doing business across frontiers is becoming more common, encouraging a person to acquire a repertoire of languages.

Third, languages provide access to information. In the Information Society, access to information via satellite, computer, Internet or print, is often access to power. A larger repertoire of languages gives wider access to social, cultural, political, economic and educational information.

Individual Reasons

Language learning is often encouraged for the personal benefits that accrue to the individual. One benefit has traditionally been training of the mind. The study of foreign languages has been viewed as a way of sharpening the mind and developing the intellect. A second benefit is cultural sensitivity and awareness, which is seen as increasingly important as the world becomes more of a global village. A third benefit might be the social, moral and emotional development of the individual, increased self-awareness, self-confidence and the ability to create effective relationships with speakers of the target language.

A fourth reason for learning a language is for careers and employment. For language minority and language majority children, being able to speak a second or third or fourth language may mean escaping unemployment, opening up possibilities of a wider variety of careers or gaining promotion in a career.

Further Reading

COOK, V. J., 1991, *Second Language Learning and Language Teaching*. London: Edward Arnold.

RICHARDS, J. C. & RODGERS, T. S., 1986, *Approaches and Methods in Language Teaching: A Description and Analysis*. Cambridge: Cambridge University Press.

STERN, H. H., 1983a, *Fundamental Concepts of Language Teaching*. Oxford: Oxford University Press.

STERN, H. H., 1992, *Issues and Options in Language Teaching*. Oxford: Oxford University Press.

3: Foreign and Second Language Teaching Approaches

Introduction

Throughout the ages, foreign language learning has been part of the education of many people. In countries where a number of dialects or languages are spoken, a common language has been used traditionally as a medium for education, commerce or religion, usually a language of culture and prestige. In Medieval Europe, for instance, Latin was the language of religion and intellectual life and those who wished to enter the church, practice law or attend school or university, had to learn to read, write and speak it. In many African countries today the same situation exists. Many different ethnic languages are spoken while English, French or a major African language like Swahili, are used in education, commerce and official life.

During the 20th century, the teaching of foreign languages has become more widespread, for a number of reasons. The ease of travel and communication and the increase of trade between countries have made more people eager or obliged to learn a foreign language. Two World Wars have made governments more aware of the need to learn foreign languages for military and security reasons and to promote harmony and understanding between people. Many people from developing countries have been anxious to learn prestigious Western languages like English and French in order to improve their education and succeed in their careers. The standardization of languages and the spread of nationalism have made people more eager to promote indigenous languages, including minority languages, as a symbol of national and cultural identity. More people have been eager to learn a minority language to find their roots and to identify with a particular cultural or ethnic group.

The growing popularity of second and foreign language learning has also meant that new approaches and methods of teaching have evolved. A brief overview of some broad trends within foreign and second language learning in the 20th century will now be given.

The Grammar Translation Method

Foreign language teaching in 19th century Western Europe was dominated by the Grammar Translation Method. This derived from the method of teaching classical languages. During the Middle Ages in Western

A 1948 British classroom. The traditional grammar-based approach to foreign language learning emphasized study of the written literary language.

Europe, Latin was the dominant language in education, commerce and politics. It was gradually superseded as a language of written and spoken communication and its use declined. However, by the 19th century, it was still studied as a vehicle for literary and creative expression and as a training for the mind. Latin grammar was taught and analyzed. Students learnt to translate to and from Latin and to read the great Classical authors.

As modern languages began to enter the curriculum of European schools in the 18th century, they were taught according to the same method. Vocabulary was learnt by rote and the grammatical rules of the language were taught systematically. The student's native language was the medium of instruction. The focus was on the acquisition of reading and writing skills and there was little emphasis on the development of oral proficiency. Passages for translation were constructed to demonstrate and practice various points of grammar. There was no emphasis on authentic communication or on introducing the students to the society where the target language was spoken.

The Reform Movement

During the latter half of the 19th century, an increase in opportunities for travel and communication in Western Europe and America meant that more people were anxious to acquire oral proficiency in modern languages. In

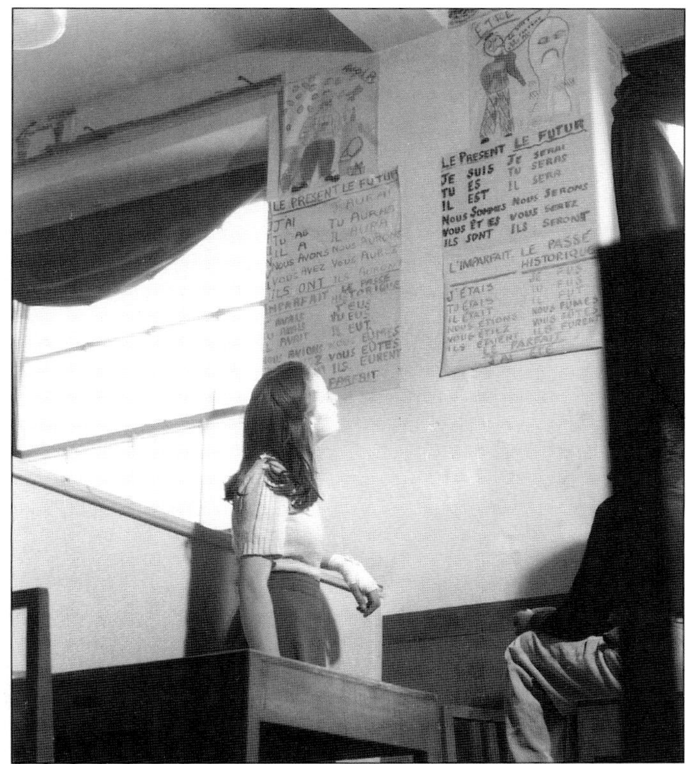

Rote learning of grammar did not necessarily lead to competence in speaking the language.

addition, developments in linguistics and phonetics meant that the spoken language received new attention. Linguists began to emphasize that speech, rather than the written word, was the primary form of language. Phonetics, the study of the sounds of the spoken language, was developing as a science, and in 1886, the International Phonetic Association was founded. In America and Europe, experts began to call for a reform in the teaching of languages. The spoken language should be emphasized and the language should be used for normal, everyday needs. The reformers believed:

1. The spoken language is the central form of language, and this should be reflected in teaching methods.
2. New developments in phonetics should be applied to teaching.
3. Learners should hear the language first before seeing it written down.
4. Words should be not be introduced in isolation, but in meaningful contexts.
5. The students should practice grammar points within the context of meaningful speech, before learning the rules of grammar.
6. Translation into the students' native language should be avoided. The native language should only be used to explain the meaning of words.

The 'Natural' or 'Direct' Method

The 'Natural' or 'Direct' Method tried to emulate the way in which young children acquire a second language. Teachers spoke only the target language in class and the accent was on speech rather than writing. This method had several weaknesses. Firstly, it presumed that second language skills were acquired in the same way as first language skills. It did not take into account the practical realities of the classroom. Older children and adults were expected to absorb in a couple of hours a week within the artificial environment of the classroom what small children take thousands of hours to learn within a 'naturalistic' environment.

Secondly, there was no careful grading of language. Students were exposed to a confusing range of language within the context-reduced environment of the classroom. Thirdly, the method required teachers who were native speakers or had native-like fluency and these were difficult to come by. Fourth, teachers were not allowed to use the the students' native language. Instead, they tended to use strategies like mime and gesture to aid comprehension when sometimes a brief explanation in the native language would have been easier. Because of these problems, the method was difficult to implement within the school system. Commercial language schools like the Berlitz schools (see page 692) tended to be more successful, because of the high level of motivation of the students and the fact that native speakers were always employed.

The 'Oral Approach' and 'Situational Language Teaching'

During the first half of the 20th century, approaches were developed in Britain and America that introduced vocabulary and grammatical structures in a carefully graded sequence. In Britain, the 'Oral Approach' or 'Situational Language Teaching' had its origins in the work of applied linguists in the 1920s and 1930s. Scholars such as Harold Palmer and A.S. Hornby viewed language as a system of structurally related elements. To gain competence in language, students must understand the basic structures. This would be accomplished by means of intensive and strictly controlled practice or reinforcement, using drills and repetition exercises. The main points of this method were as follows.

1. The emphasis on the spoken language. Material introduced orally before the written form is presented.
2. The target language used exclusively in the classroom.
3. New language points introduced and practiced by means of concrete objects or situations.
4. Vocabulary graded and introduced in sequence.

5. Items of grammar introduced in sequence, according to complexity.
6. Reading and writing introduced once a sufficient basis of vocabulary and grammar has been established.
7. No grammatical explanations given. Rules of grammar induced from the situation.

The Reading Method

In the United States, between the two World Wars, versions of the Direct Method continued to be used and also an approach based on reading. The Coleman Report (1929) concluded that the goal of teaching oral proficiency was impractical in view of the limited skills of teachers and the lack of time available for foreign language teaching in schools. The report recommended that a more realistic goal for a foreign language course would be a reading proficiency in the foreign language. This would be accomplished through the gradual introduction of vocabulary and grammatical structures in graded reading texts. As a result of this recommendation, reading became the goal of most foreign language programs in the United States until World War II.

Army Training Program

The entry of the United States into World War II after Pearl Harbor changed attitudes to foreign language teaching. The US Army needed personnel who were competent in a variety of different languages for work as interpreters, translators, and in occupation duty. Oral proficiency in these languages would be essential. The Government commissioned American universities to develop foreign language training programs for military personnel and the Army Specialized Training Program was set up in 1942. By the beginning of 1943, 55 US universities were involved in the program. The methodology for these courses came from the research of people like Leonard Bloomfield of Yale University, who had already developed training programs to help linguists and anthropologists learn Native American and other indigenous languages. These languages had no written form that could be studied. The technique used by Bloomfield and his colleagues was sometimes known as the Informant Method. A native speaker of the language provided the linguistic input in the form of phrases and vocabulary and was aided by a trained linguist.

Learners in the Army Specialized Training Program were taught in small groups by a qualified instructor and a native speaker of the language. The emphasis was on conversational competence and also on learning about the culture and customs of the country in which the target language was spoken. This was a new development. In spite of the aims of the early reformers, there had been little prior attempt to combine foreign language teaching with an introduction to the culture of the target language.

The students of the Army Specialized Training program had a high success rate because they had very high levels of instrumental motivation. The opportunity to learn a foreign language was important to their career and would help them to gain promotion. The Army Specialized Training Program lasted only two years but attracted considerable attention. Linguists became convinced of the value of an intensive oral-based approach to the learning of a foreign language.

Audiolingualism

During the period after the Second World War, the US was emerging as a major international power. Many thousands of foreign students entered the United States to study in colleges and universities, and needed to improve their English. The US Government was also anxious to improve the standard of foreign language teaching for the sake of international relations and influence.

During this period, the structural theory of language began to influence the way in which foreign languages were taught. Like their British counterparts, the American structural linguists viewed language as a structured system, combining phonological, grammatical and lexical elements. The goal of language learning was competence in the basic structures.

The methodology was quite similar to the British oral approach, but the American approach put an emphasis on contrastive analysis, comparing and contrasting the grammatical and phonological patterns of the native

The audiolingual approach. A 1966 language laboratory.

language and the target language in order to pinpoint the potential difficulties that learners might face. The new approach was called the 'Oral-aural' approach and then 'Audiolingualism'.

The basic characteristics of Audiolingualism are as follows:

1. The vocabulary and sentence patterns are carefully graded and introduced in a sequence.
2. The skills of listening and speaking are practiced first before reading and writing is introduced.
3. Emphasis is placed on accuracy of grammar and pronunciation. This is achieved by means of tightly controlled, repetitive practice known as drills.

This method made extensive use of drill and dialogue. The basic sentence patterns were taught by intensive oral drilling. Drill work involves the reiteration of words, phrases or sentences uttered by the teacher, by the students, either individually or as a group. This might take the form of simple repetition, for pronunciation practice, or a substitution for part of the original utterance, for grammatical or structural practice (e.g. plural noun for singular noun, past tense of the verb for the present tense, pronoun for noun, question for statement).

Dialogues were used to introduce new grammatical structures in a meaningful and cultural context. Dialogues were repeated and memorized. New items were presented in a tightly structured way to minimize the possibility of making mistakes.

The method was teacher-centered and teacher-dominated. The teacher controlled the speed and the direction of the learning process, supervising and correcting the students' language. This method made use of equipment such as tape recorders, audiovisual equipment and the language laboratory. The language laboratory provided the opportunity for controlled, error-free practice of basic structures.

The proponents of Audiolingualism were heavily influenced by the behaviorist theory of learning. B. F. Skinner, in his book *Verbal Behavior* (1957), argued that all learning is a process of habit formation in which a stimulus creates a response and is reinforced to become a habit. This school of thought argued that language learning is no different from any other learning, and that good results could be achieved by intensive drills and repetition.

The use of Audiolingualism declined for two main reasons. Firstly, the weaknesses of the system became apparent. Even students who had thoroughly gained language competence in audiolingual courses found it hard to transfer their skills to real-life situations. The demands of communication outside the classroom were much more complex than the structural style suggested.

Secondly, American linguistic theory changed in the 1960s. The linguist Noam Chomsky rejected the structuralist analysis of language as well as the behaviorist theory of language learning. His theory of transformational grammar proposed that all humans possess an innate linguistic system that enables them to organize, process and generate language. Chomsky proposed a new theory of language learning. Utterances are not learnt by imitation and repetition but are generated by the learner's underlying competence. Learners create new utterances from an underlying linguistic system.

Chomsky's criticism of behaviorist and structural theories of language and language learning had an influence on the British language teaching in the late 1960s. There was a realization that the functional and communicative potential of language was being neglected. This gave rise to the Communicative approach, which is discussed later in the next chapter.

Further Reading

COOK, V. J., 1991, *Second Language Learning and Language Teaching*. London: Edward Arnold.

RICHARDS, J. C. & RODGERS, T. S., 1986, *Approaches and Methods in Language Teaching: A Description and Analysis*. Cambridge: Cambridge University Press.

STERN, H. H., 1992, *Issues and Options in Language Teaching*. Oxford: Oxford University Press.

4: The Communicative Approach

Introduction

By the late 1960s, in America and Britain, Audiolingualism and the Oral Situational Language approach were becoming outdated. Second language teachers recognized the limitations of an approach based on tightly controlled structures, in that it did not prepare students for natural, authentic communication in the world outside the classroom. Also, the influential theories of Chomsky rejected the notion of language as a relatively rigid set of structures and viewed it rather as a dynamic system that allowed the creation of new and unique utterances. British applied linguists were also focusing on the need to emphasize the functional and communicative aspects of language.

The Council of Europe reports on communicative language learning.

In the early 1970s, another catalyst for a fresh approach to language teaching came from the goal of European economic co-operation. Closer links between European countries created an awareness of the need for effective teaching of the major languages of the European Common Market. The creation of a new European community would result in the breaking down of economic barriers and greater possibilities for travel and employment in other countries. The mass media and the 'communications explosion' meant that Europe, like the rest of the world, was becoming smaller. It was felt that there was a need to improve the second language skills of adults in the European community, especially in largely monolingual countries like Britain where the results of foreign language teaching had traditionally been so poor.

The Council of Europe Initiative

The Council of Europe, a regional organization for cultural and educational co-operation, put considerable effort into developing alternative methods of language teaching. It was felt that there was a need for a learner-centered approach that would focus on the specific communicative needs of individuals and groups.

In 1971 a Modern Languages Project Group was set up by the Council for Cultural co-operation of the Council of Europe. The aim of the group was to research new initiatives in adult second language learning. The group aimed to create an approach to language teaching which would reflect modern educational principles. One important principle was that education should enable individuals to realize their potential and to take responsibility in a democratic society. Thus the approach to language learning should be centered on the needs of learners, and should also aim to give learners control over the pace and direction of their learning. Rather than focusing on the grammar or structures of a language and on the methods of teaching, a new approach would concentrate on the communicative needs of learners. For what purposes and in what situations would they need to use a second language? What social and personal skills would they need to develop in order to communicate effectively with others in the second language?

The Functional-Notional Approach

The group began to discuss the possibility of developing language courses based on a series of units, each of which corresponded to a specific aspect of the communicative needs of learners. A system of communicative objectives was created, based on the research into the communicative needs of learners and this formed the basis of syllabuses for adult foreign and second language learners. In the communicative approach the language is introduced according to functions (asking, apologizing, greeting) and notions (time, place). Wilkins' (1976) Notional Syllabuses provided an analysis of the communicative meanings that a language learner needs to understand and express, notional categories (concepts such as time, location, frequency, quantity) and categories of communicative function (requests, greetings, agreements, complaints, apologies).

The Threshold Level

The 'Threshold Level' is an extensive and detailed framework for the learning of any language. The Threshold Level is a detailed specification of minimum language requirements, in any language, for people who want to learn a language for basic communicative and social reasons. This concept entailed a movement away from the form of the language (e.g. grammar teaching) to language use in real situations.

The Threshold Level Specifications (e.g. Van Ek & Alexander, 1977) had a strong influence on the design of communicative language programs and textbooks in Europe. The specifications include descriptions of the objectives of foreign language courses for European adults, the situations in which they might typically need to use a foreign language (e.g. travel, business), the topics they might need to talk about (e.g. personal identification, education, shopping), the functions they might need language for (describing something, requesting information, expressing agreement and disagreement), the notions made use of in communication (e.g. time, frequency, duration), as well as the vocabulary and grammar needed.

Basic threshold systems initially occurred for English language learning, followed by *Un Niveau Seuil* for French, *Kontaktschwelle* for German, and also systems for Dutch, Portuguese, Norwegian, Catalan, Basque and Welsh. Each threshold level is based on the use that is likely to be made of the target language in various situations. The threshold level for Catalan, for example, takes into account the needs of in-migrant workers in industry, rather than tourists. The threshold level for Welsh reflects the evident dominance of English in Wales, and is slanted towards the needs of adult learners in social and personal situations. The threshold level for Basque (*Atalaise Maile*) is based on the needs of adult learners from the indigenous population. *Threshold Level Swedish for Migrants* (1981) is orientated towards the needs of the many in-migrant workers in the country. A multimedia language learning package called *Follow Me* based on the Threshold Level is available (or shortly available) in: French, German, Spanish, Italian, Danish, Dutch, Swedish, Norwegian, Catalan, Basque, Portuguese, Welsh, Galician, Russian, Latvian, Estonian, Lithuanian, Maltese, Irish and Greek.

Communicative Competence

The main goal of communicative language teaching can be summed up in a term coined by Hymes (1972a), namely 'communicative competence'. The definition of this term is wider than Chomsky's theory of linguistic

In the Communicative approach, language is used for real purposes. A US Spanish teacher and students seek information from a map of South America.

Needs Analysis in Language Teaching and the Eclectic Approach

As the focus of language learning has shifted from the role of the teacher to the communicative needs of the learner, so the assessment of those needs has become more central in the preparation of courses. Instead of a blind belief that a certain approach or course will be suitable to teach any learner, the accent is currently on the tailoring of content and objectives to the perceived needs of the individual learner or, more often, to a specific group. A typical assessment will focus on the learners' present level of proficiency and on the language requirements of the group. This will precede any decisions about content and objectives. The needs of military personnel, business people, hospital staff, in-migrant factory workers, parents of young children will all be different, and the content and objectives of the course must be adjusted accordingly.

Similarly, teaching methods and classroom techniques may be adjusted or varied to meet the needs of a group of students. Many teachers use a combination of methods and materials with their classes. This is generally termed an 'eclectic approach'. Most language classrooms and language teachers tend to be eclectic in approach, combining in different ways and in a different balance the structural, functional and interactional methods. In real classrooms, there is often a combination of drills and pair work, task-based activity and teacher-directed transmission, correct habit formation and improvised dialogue between students with interlanguage allowed. It is important, however, that this be a carefully worked out strategy, rather than a careless mishmash of styles which the teacher has unconsciously adopted. At its worst, eclecticism is unselective, directionless, with shifting ground according to the most recent technological innovation, theory or jargon. At its best, eclecticism may lead to rational integration of 'classroom-wise' approaches.

The Natural Approach

Krashen (1982) and Krashen & Terrell (1983) have applied Krashen's Monitor Model (see Theories of Second Language Acquisition, page 649) to language teaching and classroom language learning. The classroom applications that follow from the Monitor Model are as follows.

First, Krashen & Terrell (1983) argue that the goal of language teaching must be to supply understandable input in order for the child or adult to acquire language easily. A good teacher therefore is someone who continuously delivers at a level understandable by the second language speaker. Just as father and mother talk (motherese) help the young child to acquire the first language by a simplified and comprehensible language (and non-verbal language), so an effective teacher is said to facilitate second language learning by ensuring a close match between the level of delivery and the level that is understandable.

Second, teaching must prepare the learner for real life communication situations. The classroom needs to provide conversational confidence so that, when in the outside world, the student can both linguistically cope and continue language learning.

Conversational competence also means communication strategies to get native speakers to explain their meaning when it is not initially apparent, devices for changing topics and for facilitating understandable communication with the native speaker.

Third, Krashen & Terrell (1983) suggest that teachers must ensure that learners do not become anxious or defensive in language learning. This relates to the Affective Filter hypothesis. The confidence of a language learner must be encouraged in a language acquisition process. When a learner is relaxed, confident and not anxious, then the input of the classroom situation will be more efficient and effective. If teachers insist on children conversing before they feel comfortable in doing so, or a teacher constantly corrects errors and makes negative remarks, the learner may feel inhibited in learning.

Fourth, formal grammar teaching is of limited value because it contributes to learning rather than acquisition. Only simple rules should be learnt. Complex rules will not be used consciously or unconsciously by the language learner. Therefore, little appears to be gained from formally teaching the rules of a second language. Fifth, errors should not be corrected when acquisition is occurring. They may be corrected when the goal is formal learning. Error correction is valuable when learning simple rules but may have negative effects in terms of anxiety and inhibition.

For Krashen & Terrell (1983), a 'Natural Approach' is required in language teaching. The Natural Approach is very different from traditional grammar teaching and language laboratory types of approach. Its main tenets are as follows: meaningful and authentic communication should be the aim of the good language classroom; the emphasis should be on selecting topics and subject matter that will be interesting and relevant for the students; comprehension of language should precede production (listening should precede speaking); speaking and then writing will emerge when the language learner is ready and should not be forced; acquisition rather than formal learning is central in good language learning; and the affective filter needs to be kept low (that is, favorable attitudes, positive motivation and low anxiety are important in language learning).

REFERENCE: KRASHEN & TERRELL 1983

Language Learning and Information Technology

During the past 30 years, computers have become an accepted tool in language learning. Increasingly sophisticated language programs have become available, enabling learners to develop reading, writing and comprehension skills. In addition, learners are given control over the speed and direction of learning. Computers can be used to access and co-ordinate language learning information. Increasing numbers of self-access (flexible learning) language centers have been established in recent years, some in further and higher education, others in industrial companies. At centers of this kind, information accessed from computers allows advisers and learners to decide together which language is to be learnt, for what purposes, and by what method. The learner is then directed to suitable materials indexed on computer, which might include books and worksheets, magazines, newspapers, cassettes, audiotapes, video tapes, CDs and computer disks. Learners work alone, with a personally appropriate schedule and at a pace convenient for them. The support of advisers is available, and facilities are available for language sessions with teachers and other learners.

Many commercial, multimedia courses have been marketed during the last decade, for personal and corporate use. These include text books, television and radio programs, video tapes, cassettes and CDs, and computer programs.

Students use a computer program to learn Spanish.

Young children at a South of England primary school learn the basics of French by role play and games.

competence, which deals primarily with abstract grammatical knowledge. Communicative competence deals with actual speech in actual situations, the ability to interact with others, to know what to say, to whom, when, where and how.

The main tenets of communicative language teaching are as follows:

1. Language is a system for conveying meaning.
2. The primary purpose of language is interaction and communication.
3. Language can be analyzed in terms of its grammatical structures, but also according to categories of meaning as used in speech events.

In communicative language teaching, activities are selected according to how well they engage the learner in meaningful and authentic language use (rather than merely mechanical practice of language patterns).

Communicative language teaching is an approach rather than a method or a teaching style. A 'weak' communicative approach combines different styles (e.g. audiolingual, grammatical, structural) with opportunities for the learners to engage in communicative activities. The purpose of the communicative activities is to practice the language already learnt.

The 'strong' communicative approach proposes that language is acquired through communication. Rather than using communicative techniques to reinforce language already learnt, language itself is learnt and developed through communication.

The communicative approach is learner-centered, rather than teacher-dominated. The teacher does not control the direction of the class but rather responds to the language needs of the students. Emphasis is placed on effectiveness of communication rather than accuracy of utterance. Students attempt to get their message across, even if this involves errors in grammar and pronunciation, and codeswitching to the student's native language.

Further Reading

CANALE, M. & SWAIN, M., 1980, Theoretical Bases of Communicative Approaches to Second Language Teaching and Testing. *Applied Linguistics*, 1, 1-47.

HYMES, D., 1972a, On Communicative Competence. In J. PRIDE & J. HOLMES (eds), *Sociolinguistics*. London: Penguin.

MITCHELL, R., 1988, *Communicative Language Teaching in Practice*. London: Centre for Language Teaching and Research.

NUNAN, D., 1988, *The Learner-Centered Curriculum*. Cambridge: Cambridge University Press.

NUNAN, D., 1991, Communicative Tasks and the Language Curriculum. *TESOL Quarterly*, 25 (2), 279-295.

PAULSTON, C. B., 1992a, *Linguistic and Communicative Competence*. Clevedon: Multilingual Matters Ltd.

VAN EK, J. A., 1986, *Objectives for Foreign Language Learning*. Volume I: Scope. Strasbourg: Council of Europe.

VAN EK, J. A., 1987, *Objectives for Foreign Language Learning*. Volume II: Levels. Strasbourg: Council of Europe.

VAN EK, J. A. & ALEXANDER, L. G., 1977, *The Threshold Level for Modern Language Learning in Schools*. London: Longman.

WILKINS, D. A., 1976, *Notional Syllabuses*. Oxford: Oxford University Press.

YALDEN, J., 1991, *Communicative Language Teaching: Principles and Practice*. Ontario: OISE Press.

Effective Foreign Language Learning

A checklist of effective and less effective foreign language learning has been offered by the California State Department of Education (1989).

1. Student-centered.
2. Meets the expectations and needs of students.
3. Features much communicative activity.
4. Aims for language comprehension before language production.
5. Uses a variety of activities, is well paced throughout.
6. Provides for a grouping of students that maximizes interaction.
7. Includes physical movement during communication interaction.
8. Presents the foreign language through content in authentic contexts.
9. Uses the foreign language as the medium of teaching.
10. Uses a variety of materials, including the use of computers and other technologies.
11. Students experience and enjoy fine examples of literature in the foreign language.
12. Class activities encourage creative, divergent thinking and negotiation.
13. Use of the language is non-threatening and supportive.
14. Encourages the students to use the language outside the classroom.
15. Increases students' awareness of multicultural, international considerations.
16. Is timetabled for a minimum of one hour per day.
17. Evaluates students' ability to use a foreign language for communicative purposes

Less Effective Learning

1. Teacher-centered.
2. Follows a set curriculum without regard to student needs and expectations.
3. Focuses on drill and grammar.
4. Students are expected to speak the language before they can understand it well enough.
5. Few activities in a classroom period.
6. Focuses on whole class activities.
7. Students are expected to be quiet and passive and not permitted to move around.
8. Emphasizes features of the language itself in unauthentic situations.
9. Uses the students' native language as a medium of teaching.
10. Depends on set text books.
11. Presents foreign language literature as a translation exercise.
12. Emphasizes one single, acceptable correct answer.
13. Emphasizes constant correction of mistakes.
14. Leads students to see the foreign language as another academic subject in school.
15. Focuses on language structure rather than its international value.
16. Is given minimal time within the curriculum or is only allocated as a short course.
17. Evaluates short-term command of discrete elements of the language, such as vocabulary and grammar.

REFERENCE: CALIFORNIA STATE DEPARTMENT OF EDUCATION, 1989

Meeting Consumer Needs in Language Learning Classrooms

A variety of methods, strategies and activities are often used in the same classroom. Many teachers 'pick and choose' their approach from a variety of possibilities. Many teachers will also be interested in, and responsive to the preferences of their students. Students come to language learning classes with their own preferred methods, strategies and activities. Ignorance of such preferences may relate to less progress, just as awareness of such preferences may accelerate achievement. Prior learning experiences are a crucial determinant of new learning. The knowledge and experiences that a student brings to language learning need taking into account in curricula planning. Prior experience is a major determinant of new knowledge which is constructed in the process of learning rather than imposed from outside the student. However, customer needs and preferences have to be balanced against a teacher's experience of effective practice.

The following questionnaire is an adaptation and extract from an investigation of the needs and preferences of Kuwaiti students learning English as a foreign language (Malallah, 1994). In her research on 409 University students enrolled in the College of Arts, the College of Science and the College of Sharia in the University of Kuwait, students taking English language (EFL) courses were asked about their preferences for language learning class activities (Malallah, 1994). The research showed that students' top preferences were for: activities that encouraged communication, using English in class as much as possible; playing games; trips outside the University to museums,exhibitions, and markets where they had to talk in English; and traveling abroad to learn English. The findings indicate that Kuwaiti students wanted authentic communicative activities, not traditional classroom exercises, with the accent on informal acquisition rather than formal learning. The desired method of second language acquisition was through pleasurable activities where language learning was part of intrinsically motivating events, but not the sole or even the primary focus of the activity.

Language Classroom Activities Questionnaire

How much, or how little, do you like the following language learning class activities:

	Like very much	Like a little	Neither like nor dislike	Dislike a little	Dislike a lot
1. Group work	❑	❑	❑	❑	❑
2. Pair work	❑	❑	❑	❑	❑
3. Working alone	❑	❑	❑	❑	❑
4. With the whole class	❑	❑	❑	❑	❑
5. Role-play	❑	❑	❑	❑	❑
6. Traveling abroad to learn the language	❑	❑	❑	❑	❑
7. Speaking the language in class	❑	❑	❑	❑	❑
8. Discussions	❑	❑	❑	❑	❑
9. Playing games	❑	❑	❑	❑	❑
10. Telling stories	❑	❑	❑	❑	❑
11. Reading poetry	❑	❑	❑	❑	❑
12. Writing a diary	❑	❑	❑	❑	❑
13. Making advertisements	❑	❑	❑	❑	❑
14. Writing newspapers articles (reports)	❑	❑	❑	❑	❑
15. Writing letters	❑	❑	❑	❑	❑
16. Making travel brochures	❑	❑	❑	❑	❑
17. Listening to songs	❑	❑	❑	❑	❑
18. Having trips outside the classroom to use the language	❑	❑	❑	❑	❑
19. Project work (e.g. creating a radio program in English)	❑	❑	❑	❑	❑
20. Tests and assessments	❑	❑	❑	❑	❑
21. Singing	❑	❑	❑	❑	❑
22. Videos	❑	❑	❑	❑	❑
23. Cassette tapes	❑	❑	❑	❑	❑
24. Using computers	❑	❑	❑	❑	❑
25. Problem-solving	❑	❑	❑	❑	❑
26. Studying grammar	❑	❑	❑	❑	❑

Communicative Activities in the Classroom

Typical activities in a communicative teaching situation would be simulation and role-play, personal real life discussions, problem-solving tasks and information gap activities, games and puzzles.

In simulation, learners act out imaginary situations that they might be likely to encounter (e.g. camping, meeting a pen-friend for the first time, shopping, visiting a family, finding the way). In role-play, learners act out assumed roles in a situation (e.g. waiters or waitresses and customers in a restaurant, a shopkeeper and customers).

Simulation and role-play both involve dialogue. However, there is a difference between communicative dialogue and the dialogues used in the audiolingual and structural approach. In the structural approach, the dialogue is scripted, and must be rehearsed and memorized by the students. Any improvisation must be based on the structures in the original dialogue, to ensure accuracy. In communicative dialogue there is more scope for improvisation and creativity.

Students read Spanish cartoons in class.

The communicative approach centers on the communicative needs of the individual learner. An important aspect of communicative teaching is the equipping of learners to talk about what is important to them, such as families, jobs, leisure activities, ambitions and beliefs. Sports, current affairs and local events might also be discussed. The teacher may collect or prepare materials to respond to the needs of the moment e.g. extracts from current newspapers and periodicals or excerpts from television or radio news.

Problem-solving tasks might include activities such as planning a journey (using maps and timetables) or shopping within a budget (using price lists in the target language). Information gap activities might also be used. One example of an information gap activity is when both members of a pair are given diaries for a week with different information on them. Their task is to arrange a convenient time to meet during the week. They accomplish this by trading information about their activities. An example of a whole class information gap activity might be a tape of a radio excerpt advertising the day's programs. Each member of the class is given a timetable of programs with some information missing (e.g. program times and titles, names of presenters and content). The class complete the information on their sheets by listening to the tape.

Games and puzzles might include number games (e.g. Bingo), mime and charades, guessing games (guessing a person's identity from a number of clues), crosswords and word searches, 'Call my Bluff' (guessing the meaning of obscure words from three or four definitions in the target language).

A student practices Spanish oral skills in a real-life context by using the phone.

5: Different Modern Language Teaching Approaches

The recent accent on communicative competence and on a student-centered approach to language teaching has given rise to a number of innovative teaching methods. Some of these are described below. They have not become widely popular, and they may appear rather odd, but they reflect the modern emphasis on student initiative and student autonomy in the learning process, and also the importance of an approach based on 'authentic' communication.

Community Language Learning

Community language learning was devised in the early 1970s by Charles A. Curran, a specialist in counseling and a Professor of Psychology at Loyola University, Chicago. Curran drew upon his experience of Rogerian counseling techniques, to apply these techniques to learning generally and specifically to language learning. In a counseling situation, the counselor tries to empathize with the client, giving advice, assistance and support for needs and problems. In Community Language Learning, this strategy is adapted for the classroom.

The teacher takes the role of counselor and attempts to respond to the expressed language needs of the learners as clients. The class functions as a 'community' and there is a sense of intimacy and commitment among the members. The language learning process is compared to the stages of human growth, from infancy and total dependence to maturity and independence.

A Community Language Learning course would not have a planned syllabus since the students would define the lesson content. A typical lesson might include utterances expressed by the students in the native language and translated or interpreted by the teacher into the target language. The lessons would include an opportunity for the students to discuss their feelings about language learning and about the lesson.

Total Physical Response

Total Physical Response is a language teaching method devised by James Asher, an American Professor of Psychology. It is based on the co-ordination of speech and action. It attempts to teach language through physical activity. Asher draws parallels between adult second language acquisition and child first language acquisition. These are the main attributes.

- Speech directed at small children consists mainly of commands, to which children respond with physical action. Total Physical Response attempts to reproduce this process in the classroom with adults. Command drills are the major classroom activity in Total Physical Response, the students typically responding to the commands with physical actions.
- When learning a language, comprehension abilities precede the production of speech. At this stage, the learner, whether a small child or an adult, may be creating a mental 'map' of the language that makes it possible to produce spoken language later. Once a foundation in listening comprehension has been established, speech should evolve naturally. Therefore, it is recommended that conversational dialogues are delayed until after about 120 hours of instruction. Learners are encouraged to speak when they feel ready.
- Emotional/affective factors play an important role in learning. Students learn more effectively if they are in a stress-free environment. A method that involves 'play' and that does not place too many demands on the student is likely to reduce learner anxiety and contribute to more effective learning.

Suggestopedia

This controversial method was developed in the 1970s by the Bulgarian psychiatrist-educator Georgi Lozanov. Suggestopedia is a specific set of learning recommendations derived from Suggestology, which Lozanov describes as a science, concerned with the systematic study of the non-rational and/or non-conscious influence to which human beings are consciously responding. Suggestopedia tries to direct these influences to achieve successful learning.

In Suggestopedia, the environment plays an important role. The classroom should be bright and cheerful, the chairs comfortable and arranged informally. Slow music with a steady beat is used to induce a relaxed but aware state, a 'pseudo-passive state', in the students. In this state, the students should be very suggestible and ready

Learning Language by Compact Disk (CD)

The learning of a second or foreign language is not an easy task for most people. One major difficulty is finding the opportunity to practice the new language in real life situations, to gain competence in pronunciation, and to be able to understand speech at a typical 'native talker' speed.

The potential of modern technology to aid the language learner by stimulating authentic foreign language situations has long been recognized. The use of language on records and tapes, language laboratories and computer assisted learning programs for a wide range of computers have all been heralded as providing a breakthrough in the slow process of acquiring a language.

The latest device is CD-ROMs that incorporate advanced speech recognition technology and graphics. They can act as a language conversation partner, correcting pronunciation and offering comments for improvements. Courses in French, German, Italian, Spanish, English, Dutch and Russian are available from a number of publishing houses. Often built around conversations from everyday life such as restaurants, shops, airports and playing games, the courses develop recognition routines to assess the quality of speech recorded by the student when responding to prompts from the CD-ROM. At each stage of the dialogue, a student must repeat a given phrase to the satisfaction of the computer before being allowed to progress to the next stage. Different responses are available so that the student can repeat the same conversation without following the same route each time.

Such programs are particularly aimed at increasing oral competence. With colorful moving graphics, excellent speech quality for imitation and modeling, and real-life scenes such as the Paris Metro, the CD-ROMs also include visual help with pronunciation. The use for the mouth and tongue and lip movements are visually demonstrated to enable correct pronunciation. While many of the courses available on CD-ROM are carefully graded and structured, this is not in a rigid sense. There are also tests and assessments to complete before proceeding to the next module. Such CD-ROMs are a major step beyond text books but a few steps behind 'virtual reality' language learning packages promised for the future.

to receive and retain the linguistic material offered them. The teacher should be authoritative and confident and the learners should acknowledge this authority and assume the role of eager and receptive children.

Suggestopedia has had a mixed reception in language teaching circles in the West, ranging from enthusiastic acclaim to those who dismiss it as pseudo-scientific gobbledygook.

The Silent Way

The Silent Way is the name of a method of language teaching devised by Caleb Gattegno in the early 1970s. Gattegno conceives of learning as a co-operative process between teacher and student, in which the student, aided by the teacher, learns by means of discovery and problem-solving.

Silent Way courses follow a basically structural syllabus, with lessons planned around grammatical items and related vocabulary. The method uses varied material such as color charts and colored cuisenaire rods. Language is separated from its social context and taught through artificial situations, usually represented by the rods. The rods can be used for naming colors, comparing sizes, to represent people and maps, for example. New structures and vocabulary are introduced and then practiced with the aid of the 'props'. They provide a focus for the students' attention and a stimulus to memory.

The method is remarkable for its emphasis on teacher silence. Typically the teacher will introduce a new word or sentence once and then allow the students to practice it together without correcting them. The method places great importance on the development of awareness and responsibility which themselves will increase the student's capacity to learn.

Further Reading

ASHER, J., 1977, *Learning Another Language Through Actions*. Los Gatos, CA: Sky Oaks.

CURRAN, C. A., 1972, *Counseling-Learning: A Whole-Person Model for Education*. New York: Grune & Stratton.

CURRAN, C. A., 1976, *Counseling-Learning in Second Languages*. Apple River, IL: Apple River Press.

GATTEGNO, C., 1972, *Teaching Foreign Languages in Schools: The Silent Way*. (Second Edition). New York: Educational Solutions.

GATTEGNO, C., 1976, *The Common Sense of Teaching Foreign Languages*. New York: Educational Solutions.

LOZANOV, G., 1978, *Suggestology and Outlines of Suggestopedy*. New York: Gordon & Breach.

RICHARDS, J. C. & RODGERS, T. S., 1986, *Approaches and Methods in Language Teaching: A Description and Analysis*. Cambridge: Cambridge University Press.

RICHARDS, J. C., PLATT, J. & PLATT, H., 1992, *Dictionary of Language Teaching and Applied Linguistics* (Second edition). Harlow, Essex: Longman.

6: The Cultural Syllabus and the Multidimensional Language Curriculum

Introduction

Foreign and second language teaching in the 19th century was often devoid of any explicit cultural content. The foreign language was taught as a process of skill acquisition and there was little attempt to place it in the context of the country or community where it was spoken. The language reformers of the late 19th century called for a reappraisal of language teaching in order to place language within the context of the culture and society of which it was a part.

In the first half of the 20th century, culture became a component of the second language syllabus in many countries. Culture was equivalent to high culture; the art, literature, architecture and great achievements of the country where the target language was spoken.

The Cultural Syllabus

Since the Second World War, the cultural syllabus has concentrated more on culture with a small 'c', sometimes called 'deep culture' – the study of the everyday life of the target country. Such study might include minutiae such as greeting or leave-taking behavior, table manners, birthday customs, as well as larger issues such as religious observance and school life. Classroom environments have come to reflect the culture of the target language, with posters, calendars, books, postcards, tourist items and products from the target country. Culture teaching gives life, meaning and relevance to the language. It can help learners integrate more successfully in the target language community and work against stereotypes.

The requirements of the cultural syllabus are likely to be different in the following situations: a foreign language learner on holiday in the target country, a business person needing the foreign language for practical and instrumental reasons, or a foreign diplomat anxious to observe the rules of etiquette and good behavior in the host country. In certain situations, a cultural element in the syllabus may not be appropriate (e.g. when a major international language like English is taught as a second language for the purposes of communication between different speech communities in developing countries such as India or Nigeria). Here the goal is not to integrate the learners into the Western culture of Britain or the United States but rather to teach the target language as a utilitarian means of communication, for economic and employment purposes.

A Multidimensional Language Curriculum

An attempt at integrating the different aims and goals of a second or foreign language approach stems particularly from the Boston Paper on Curriculum Materials (Lange, 1980). A group of second language learning experts proposed the idea of a multidimensional curriculum. This would comprise four types of syllabuses: (1) Linguistic, (2) Cultural, (3) Communicative, and (4) General Language Education. The Boston Paper argued that current syllabuses were too ambitious in their linguistic features. Too much time was spent in language classrooms in learning word lists and grammar. Too little time was spent on generating communicative competence in children. The Boston Paper suggested that a linguistic syllabus was important but it should be joined by a cultural syllabus that would accent the content of modern languages rather than just the form of the language. Children require an understanding of the cultural attributes of the language being learnt and this should be thoroughly integrated with the linguistic elements. Such a cultural syllabus needs to be assessed and examined in order to raise its status.

The Boston Paper (Lange, 1980) argued that a multidimensional curriculum would also involve a communicative syllabus. Here the focus would be on efficient communication rather than on accurate language. Language errors would be tolerated so that the accent could be on effective transmission of meaning. Authentic language needed to be encouraged. While simulation and role-playing may lead to a limited degree of communicative ability, contact with foreign language speakers, preferably in natural situations, was much to be desired. Encouragement should be given to students spending time in the homes and communities of second language speakers. Alongside immersion experience in the second language community, language camps, festivals, visits to language communities and the use of native speakers within the classroom is encouraged.

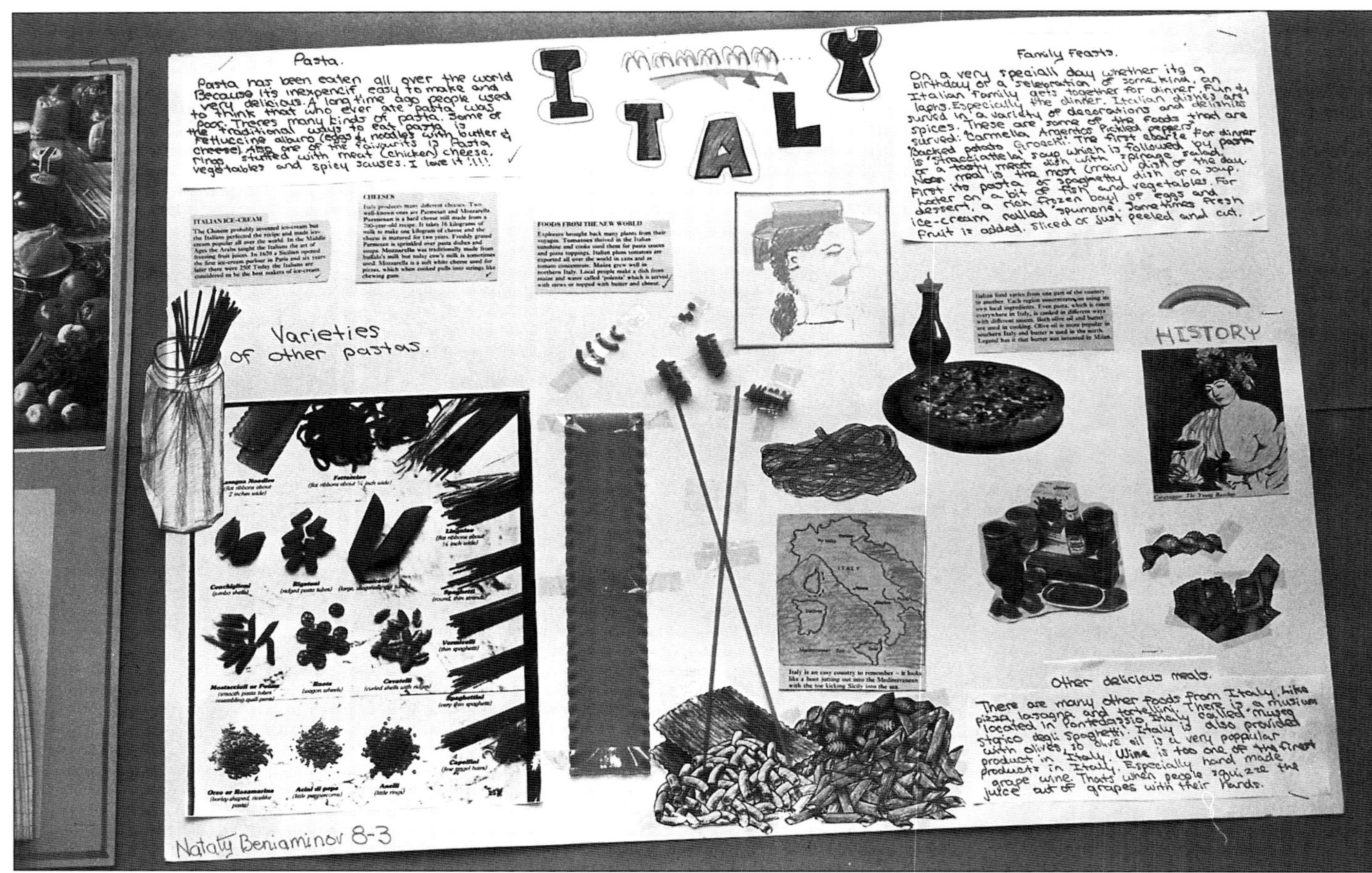

The final part of the Boston Paper (Lange, 1980) suggested that a multidimensional language curriculum include a general language education syllabus. In the syllabus, students would come to understand more about the nature and functions of language. Topics such as learning how to learn a language, language varieties, and language and culture would be considered.

The theoretical basis of a multidimensional foreign language curriculum was subsequently expanded and refined by Stern (1983b, 1992) and has been furthered by the Canadian National Core French Study (LeBlanc, 1990). A national study in Canada has suggested major developments in the teaching and learning of French as a second language in mainstream, core programs.

Canadian Core French programs have hitherto taught French for between 20 and 50 minutes a day. Sometimes starting at Grade 1, often at Grade 4, or later at Grade 7, a child may receive (e.g. in Ontario) around 1200 hours of instruction in French, with a target active vocabulary of 3000 to 5000 words and around 100 basic sentence patterns (Lapkin, Harley & Taylor, 1993). The suggested development of this Core program is through four integrated syllabuses.

A language teaching syllabus

This is structural and functional in approach. Both the form, the functions and the context of language learning are addressed. Grammatical 'consciousness raising' and an analytical approach to language learning is to be partnered by an experiential approach. Thus, communicative competence in a second language needs to be integrated with grammatical knowledge.

A communicative activities/experiential syllabus

This is designed to give the second language learner authentic experiences in communication and usable communication skills. Curriculum themes are to be motivating, interesting, relevant, and to enrich experience as well as give communicative competence.

A cultural syllabus

Such a syllabus presents the French culture as something to be observed and analyzed as well as experienced. It aims to develop sociocultural awareness and integrate French language learning with French culture. Focusing on contemporary culture, the syllabus is principally concerned with enabling students to communicate effectively first and foremost with French-Canadians, but with other francophones as well. Stern's (1992) vision extends the cultural syllabus to increased contact with the target language community, if possible. While cultural competence is essential for successful communicative skills, the cultural syllabus underlines the essential relationship between language and culture. The one stimulates and enriches the other in second language learning. The learning of a language gathers meaning and purpose when there is simultaneous enculturation.

A general language education syllabus

This explores languages and communication as intrinsically important topics. It aims to increase students' awareness of language and of the process of language learning via a three-pronged attack: language awareness, cultural awareness and strategic awareness. Topics might include: dialects and registers, languages across the world, the origins of languages, the language development of children, language prejudice, and correspondence (including across distance by electronic mail).

A mathematically imaginative answer is given to the question of how much time to allot to these four strands. 'An ideal distribution of time in the core French program might be: 75 percent communicative/experiential, 40 percent linguistic syllabus, 15 percent general language, and 25 percent culture. While this may seem to add up to 155 percent, in reality it adds up to an effective and efficient core French program. Providing that French is the language of communication in the classroom, and providing that teachers and students focus on learning a living second language for use in real life, each syllabus will compliment the others and be realized simultaneously. That is, integration will occur almost naturally and the time allocations will truly overlap' (LeBlanc & Courtel, 1990, page 91). The integration of the four syllabuses is crucial. Limited time for second language learning, and too demanding a schedule within available time makes integration a challenge for language educators.

Further Reading

LANGE, D. L. (ed.), 1980, *Proceedings of the National Conference on Professional Priorities, November 1980*. New York: ACTFL Materials Center.

LEBLANC, C. & COURTEL, C., 1990, Executive Summary: The Culture Syllabus. *Canadian Modern Language Review*, 47 (1), 82-92.

LEBLANC, R., 1990, Le curriculum multidimensionnel: Une synthèse, *Canadian Modern Language Review*, 47 (1), 32-42

STERN, H. H., 1992, *Issues and Options in Language Teaching*. Oxford: Oxford University Press.

7: Modern Language Learning and Special Educational Needs Students

Introduction

In recent years, there has been increasing emphasis on the rights of school students with special educational needs to participate in a wider variety of educational experiences, just like other students. There has also been a greater recognition of the potential for personal development which such educational experiences offer.

The phrase, 'special educational needs' includes students with physical and conceptual difficulties, mild and moderate learning difficulties, severe learning difficulties and emotional and behavioral difficulties. Until recently in the UK, many students with these kinds of problems did not have access to learning a foreign language

UK Initiatives

In 1991 the Centre for Information on Language Teaching and Research (CILT) in London, set up a project with support from the National Curriculum Council, focusing on foreign language learning for students with special needs. The project directors worked in collaboration with 20 local education authorities on the project, trialing teaching methods and materials with groups of 'special needs' students in a wide variety of schools.

The project showed that there were particular strategies that could help Special Educational Needs learners achieve success. These included a variety of interesting activities designed to build students' confidence and give them a feeling of success; clear, practical tasks; plenty of reinforcement and repetition; short-term goals to be achieved by small, easy steps; and illustrative materials to support language learning.

The project also indicated the importance of student-centered learning, tailored to the needs of individual students. There must be accurate assessment of the needs of students. Techniques that work for some students may not work for all. Some students may have difficulty with audio recall, and with discriminating between sounds, which makes comprehension and production of speech very difficult. Others have poor visual memories and have problems with interpreting and recalling visual stimuli. Some students have poor conceptual development and may have difficulty with sequencing, quantifying and qualifying. Other students may struggle with manual skills, and find writing and drawing a problem. Focusing on students' problems may seem a negative approach, but it allows teachers to work out positive strategies, to compensate for students' areas of particular difficulty.

Teaching Approaches

One answer is to employ a multisensory approach, where new material is introduced and reinforced by a variety of stimuli, hearing, seeing, touching, smelling, tasting. A

typical activity might involve learners being blindfolded and being allowed to taste and smell different bottles of syrup to identify the fruit flavor. *'Orange? Framboise? Fraise? Citron?'* In another activity, objects might be hidden in envelopes or parcels, to be felt, heard or smelt by the students, before the parcel is opened to discover what is inside.

Another answer is to foster independent and selective learning, allowing students access to individual learning materials. These allow learners of different abilities, and with different strengths and weaknesses, to access appropriate materials for self-study. They also allow for the breaks in learning which are more likely to occur in Special Educational Needs students, for reasons such as illness, hospitalization, truancy and therapy, as well as lapses in effort and concentration.

Computers may be used for different activities. Children can take turns filling in a database of personal details on a computer. Working in groups of three or four, one child may sit in front of the computer, interrogate the other children and fill in the details. This allows the exercise of speaking and listening skills, as well as reading and writing skills. Special Educational Needs learners may especially enjoy word processing on computers, allowing them to correct and improve their own work over a period of time. Students who have problems with handwriting and presentation of work may appreciate the chance to produce text that looks attractive and professional.

The use of role-play and drama can be valuable for students with Special Needs. Enacting a visit to the target country, for instance, can enhance cultural awareness, promote use of the target language and improve social skills. The use of props and other cultural items (e.g. foreign food) makes the activity interesting and meaningful and is a help to students with conceptual problems. Each student can participate according to his or her level of skills and development. In the non-threatening environment of 'play acting', students can make mistakes without losing confidence.

It is a common assumption that many students with Special Educational Needs can only cope with language set in familiar, concrete contexts, e.g. oneself, school, family, neighborhood, food, hobbies. Foreign language courses can avoid this in two-ways. Firstly, the cultural component of foreign language courses helps to make students more aware of other countries and peoples. Second, many Special Needs schools and departments engage in cross-curricular activities. Teaching a foreign language through music, art, drama and physical education provides an opportunity to use language in a different, wider context.

It is important for teachers to have realistic goals for students. Some students may be able to achieve the four attainment targets of speaking, understanding, reading and writing. Others may only be able to achieve one or two. For children with severe dyslexia, for example, speaking and comprehension may be more easily attainable targets than reading and writing.

Reports indicated that the majority of students enjoyed their experience of second language learning and made noticeable progress. The evidence suggested that students could operate in a foreign language at the same conceptual and linguistic level as in their own language and that the experience benefited their general linguistic and educational development. Examples of such development included improvement in pronunciation, progress in reading and listening skills, enhancement of general learning skills such as memory, attention span, problem-solving, and growing awareness of language in general.

The social development of the children was also enhanced. Through pair work and group activities, question and answer sessions and talking about themselves, they gained experience and confidence in interacting with others. There was an increase in self-esteem, and they showed better motivation.

The third area where progress was made was in cultural awareness. Through practical activities, the students came into contact with aspects of the culture of other countries. Some students were able to make a visit to the target country and this proved to be an experience that heightened their cultural awareness as well as benefiting their general self-confidence and social skills. (See Visits and Exchanges to Other Countries and Cultures, page 624.)

There is a growing opinion that learning a foreign language benefits students of all educational abilities. Introducing students with special educational needs to a foreign language is a challenge, but, provided that realistic goals are set and that appropriate teaching strategies are adopted, it is a feasible, and worthwhile task.

Further Reading

BOVAIR, K. & BOVAIR, M., 1992, *Modern Languages for All.* London: Kogan Page.

HOLMES, B. 1996, Special Educational Needs. In E. HAWKINS (ed.), *Thirty Years of Language Teaching.* London: Centre for Information on Language Teaching and Research (CILT).

LEE, B. & DICKSON, P., 1991, *Foreign Languages for Low Attaining Pupils.* Slough, Bucks: NFER.

MCLAGAN, P. (ed.), 1994, *Steps to Learning: Modern Languages for Pupils with Special Educational Needs.* London: Centre for Information on Language Teaching and Research.

8: Adult Language Learning

Introduction

Previous articles in this section have traced the spread and development of second and foreign language learning during the 20th century. There are numerous reasons for this development which have included: easier methods of travel and communication, mobility of populations, the mass media, increased trade between nations, the need for international co-operation and understanding after two World Wars, the rise of nationalism and a fresh desire for roots and identification with a particular ethnic group.

The 20th century emphasis on command of the spoken language and effective communication, rather than on the written or literary language and grammatical accuracy, has given rise to new innovations in language teaching. These have been been developed very largely in response to the needs of adult second language learners.

There is essentially no difference between the way children and adults learn a second language. It is widely believed that age is a negative factor in second language learning. It is claimed that adults do not learn languages as well as children and that older people do not learn as effectively as younger people. The chapter on Age and Becoming Bilingual (see page 658) shows that there is no evidence to support this belief. Adults can learn more swiftly and efficiently than children because of their superior cognitive abilities. Their greater experience of life gives them an advantage in a learning situation. A child learning language has to learn new concepts at the same time. An adult is already familiar with the concepts and only has to learn the linguistic symbols for them. However adults may be hindered in their language learning by other factors. Lack of time may be a problem and also lack of opportunity to practice the language outside the classroom. Personality and emotional factors may hinder progress: shyness, inhibition, inflexibility, unwillingness to accept new ideas. The language needed by a small child is simple and often related to concrete, everyday matters. The language used by adults is frequently complex and abstract. Thus, the teaching of second language to adults involves some particular and special considerations.

Particular Considerations in Adult Language Learning

The importance of sustained motivation

Small children in Dual Language schools, Immersion programs or other school situations where a second language is taught, tend to 'pick up' the language by means

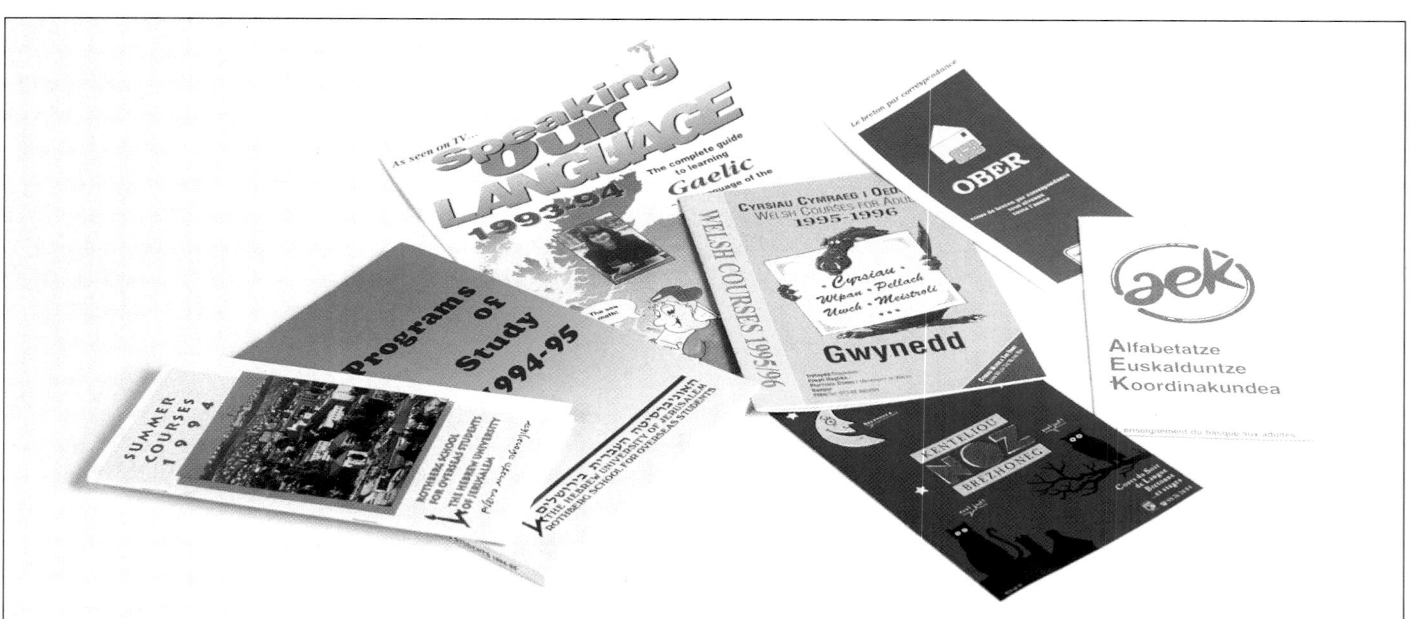

Pamphlets advertising adult language courses in Hebrew, Breton, Basque, Welsh and Gaelic.

of enjoyable, intrinsically motivating, 'hands-on' activities. During the teenage years, motivation becomes an important factor in effective language learning. However, for most students in Western secondary schools, second language learning forms part of the statutory curriculum. Motivation in the teenage years may be linked to the need to pass an examination or gain a credit rather than to a perception of the value of the second language.

In contrast, most adults choose to study a second language. Adult motivation for language learning tends to be linked to a perception of the worth or usefulness of the foreign language. The chapter on Instrumental and Integrative Motivation (see page 651) showed that motives for language learning may be usefully divided into two main categories. 'Instrumental motivation' is when a person learns a second language for a utilitarian purpose, to work in a foreign country, to get a certain job. 'Integrative motivation' is when a person learns a language to gain entry to a certain culture, to be accepted by a certain group of people, to identify with an ethnic minority. Many people's motives are a mixture of the two. Often, an instrumental motive is not totally separate or 'pure'. Rather, there are integrative strands to instrumental motives, as there are instrumental components to integrative motives. The dichotomy of integrative and instrumental motives is helpful but in danger of over-simplifying real life overlap and inter-connectedness.

With adult language learners, it is very important that motivation should be sustained over a long period. Current research suggests that an integrative attitude is the one which appears to sustain long-term motivation. Motivation is also sustained by success, and thus it is important for the teacher to provide appropriate course content and materials and allow the learners to work at a pace and in a direction that will ensure successful learning. Many adults simply do not have sufficient motivation to accomplish the marathon task of learning a second language. Others are initially motivated, but then become afraid that their own identity will be lost if they integrate fully with the target group of speakers. This is often the case with adults learning a minority language. The teacher has a crucial role to play in sustaining motivation and perseverance for the very demanding task of second language learning.

Motivation is a precursor to language learning, but may be increased or decreased by the act of language learning. It is important that the learning process takes a direction that is likely to augment favorable attitudes and positive motivation to gain competence in a second language. For instance, if a class of adult learners is motivated by a desire to integrate socially with the target language community, the course should aim to equip learners with the communication skills to interact socially with native speakers of the second language in the shop, pub or at the school gate. The course might also include, if possible, real out-of-class opportunities to interact with fluent speakers at social events. This leads to the next point.

The importance of courses and materials tailored to the communicative needs of adult learners

Because sustained motivation is so crucial to the adult language learner, it is vital that adult courses are relevant to the needs of adult learners. The chapter on The Communicative Approach (see page 674) shows how the Council of Europe initiated an approach based on research into the general communicative needs of adult second language learners. The topic showed how the Threshold Level was adapted to the likely needs of second language learners in various countries e.g. tourists, in-migrants, guest workers. This approach has led to an even more individual approach, whereby courses are tailored to the needs of a specific category of learners (e.g. doctors, business people, military personnel, parents of young children, workers in the tourist industry). Such courses may focus on a particular language skill or function e.g. a course for secretaries in a company may accent reading and writing skills more than oral and aural skills, to enable them to deal with correspondence.

The importance of teaching approaches and methods tailored to the requirements of adults

Current second language teaching practice in many parts of the world is in favor of an eclectic approach, geared to the needs and expectations of the students. For example, 'English for academic purposes' courses are run to help mature-age students, for example, to acquire a style of English needed for University study. Most adult language learners have some background of formal education and come to class with certain expectations of the teacher and of the learning process. Many adults, for instance, have studied languages at school according to a formal, grammatical method, and benefit from a cognitive approach which includes some explanation or study of the language itself. Most adult language learners are literate in their first language and are accustomed to learning by means of the written word. They benefit from an approach where oral material is backed up by reading or written work. All learners have expectations of learner-teacher relationships and classroom interaction based on their cultural background and educational experience. A learner-centered approach may not be appropriate in a culture where the teacher is respected as a figure of authority. An individualistic approach many not work in a society where co-operation and the importance of the group are paramount (e.g. Japan).

The Linguaphone Method

Since its establishment in 1924, the Linguaphone Institute has given many millions of people all over the world the opportunity to gain competence in a foreign language, for travel or professional purposes, or simply as a hobby. The Institute was set up by Jacques Roston, a translator and language teacher who emigrated from Poland at the beginning of the 20th century. A few years before founding the Institute, Roston had taken over the International Linguaphone Company, which had been established by a certain Mr Rees.

Mr Rees had devised the first Linguaphone courses as classroom aids for language teachers. The *Rees Linguaphone Records*, using the voices of authentic native speakers, could be used in conjunction with the illustrated texts of the *Rees Pictorial Language Books*. The books also incorporated grammatical notes. This group of materials was available in the most common languages-French, German, Italian and Spanish-and English for Spanish speakers. Jacques Roston acquired the *Rees Pictorial Language Books*, the *Rees Linguaphone* recordings and the International Linguaphone Company in around 1919-20.

New technological inventions at the end of the 19th century had opened up new possibilities for language teaching. In 1877, Edison invented the phonograph, using tinfoil and cylinders to reproduce sound. In 1888, Alexander Graham Bell developed wax cylinders, which gave a better sound quality. The *Rees Linguaphone Records* were recorded on wax cylinders. By the end of the 19th century Emile Berliner had perfected his flat records, or '*Berliners*', and the age of the gramophone had dawned.

Roston was swift to recognize the potential of these new developments for language teaching and to market his product effectively with a persuasive advertising campaign. Roston and his family acted as their own photographic models for the first Linguaphone brochure (1925). They posed around the gramophone in their sitting room, with the founder seated in an armchair, pipe in hand, listening to one of his own Linguaphone courses.

Roston had a keen interest in the latest developments in language teaching and believed in the primacy of the spoken language. An early advertisement for the Linguaphone Method shows that it was based on the 'direct method' favored by progressive language teachers of the 1920s and 1930s in Britain. The 'direct' or 'natural' method made exclusive use of the target language and aimed to imitate the language learning process of small children when learning a first language.

'A Linguaphone course is composed of a series of records dealing with everyday subjects, situations and needs. Whenever you have a moment to spare you slip one of these records on your gramophone and follow, in a special pictorial textbook, the speaking of a cultured native teacher. The textbook contains, side by side with the printed text, composite pictures illustrating the various persons, objects and actions described in the text. With the aid of these pictures you learn to associate the appearance of things with the appropriate word-sounds. This is the truly natural way of learning a language, the way you first, as a child, learned your own mother tongue. The results of this method are astonishing. Under this tireless tutor, mastery becomes easy. Quite soon you find yourself able to speak fluently, to understand others and also to read and write correctly. A course gives you a vocabulary of about 2500 words, and in two or three months you find you have acquired a sound practical knowledge of the language, with correct accent and pronunciation'.

Roston's early work involved re-writing and improving the Rees Linguaphone courses and also extending their range to encompass most of the world's major languages including many Oriental languages, such as Bengali, Hindustani and Urdu. Courses were soon available in several African languages, including Efik, Hausa, Luganda and Zulu.

In 1924 Roston founded the Linguaphone Institute. Foreign branches were soon established and, by 1927, Linguaphone courses were in use in 92 countries, with overseas branches in Australia, Belgium, France, Holland, Hungary, Norway, South Africa, Latvia and the US. Many handbooks were produced in languages ranging from Arabic to Vietnamese, enabling foreign students from all over the world to learn English and other languages using the Linguaphone method.

During World War II, Linguaphone London taught English and other languages to thousands of Allied soldiers, sailors and airmen of many nationalities. Immediately after the war, Linguaphone was called upon to assist the United Nations International Relief Organization in helping to prepare tens of thousands of displaced persons for resettlement in new countries. At its peak, 40,000 students a month were undergoing Linguaphone language training, using 1000 Linguaphone sets. This program needed 500 teachers drawn from the refugees themselves who were specially trained in group methods by Linguaphone. Since then there have been regular demands for this sort of language instruction, most recently to aid the Vietnamese boat people.

Linguaphone currently offers starter courses in 30 languages, including all major European languages and many other widely spoken ones, such as Mandarin Chinese, Arabic, Korean and Afrikaans, Latin American Spanish and American English. Advanced courses and business courses are available for a smaller range of languages. The course materials currently include text books and workbooks, audio cassettes, CDs and videos.

The Linguaphone Method

The Linguaphone method has kept abreast of the latest developments in language teaching. The original 'Direct Method' approach gave way to a structurally-based situational approach. The courses now reflect the learner-centered, functional-notional approach, initiated by the Council of Europe. The Linguaphone Courses currently focus on key language functions, which are taught within the context of common situations likely to be encountered by the learner on a trip to the target community. The Finnish starter course, for instance, deals with a trip to Helsinki, eating out and experiencing a sauna.

First you Listen then . . .

YOU FIND YOURSELF SPEAKING THE LANGUAGE

Listen to Linguaphone—to the living language of your choice, spoken by expert linguists. Then try the language yourself: follow the phrases one by one in the text book. There's no one to worry you or hold you up. Your teachers are always patient and encouraging and their perfect speech is always there on the record for you to pick up.

Then—success! A thrilling moment when you find yourself talking like a native. A lifetime to enjoy the advantages of a new language. A lifetime for the few weeks' learning that you'll enjoy so much.

TEST LINGUAPHONE FREE

A complete course is yours free of cost or obligation. Give it a thorough trial and make up your mind at leisure, as a million other people have done already. Whatever conclusion you may reach, you'll at least have *tried for yourself* the actual records, and acquired a first-hand knowledge of the famous Linguaphone method.

There is no obligation or cost whatever

SEND THIS CARD TO-DAY

PLEASE FILL IN YOUR NAME AND ADDRESS IN BLOCK CAPITALS

Name..........

Address..........

Please send me (post free) your 26-page book and details of Week's Free Trial as offered to readers of..........

I have a gramophone. I have no gramophone. (*Please strike out one of these*)

I am interested in the.......... language(s) for general purposes.

I am also specially interested in: (*Strike out whichever does not apply*)

FOREIGN TRAVEL BUSINESS WIRELESS LITERATURE AND THE ARTS EXAMINATIONS CHILDREN'S STUDY SCIENCE CONSULAR SERVICE

The Linguaphone Institute, Linguaphone House, 207/209, Regent St., London, W.1

COURSES IN:

French, Italian, Spanish, Polish, German, Swedish, Russian, Portuguese, Dutch, Afrikaans, Czech, Finnish, Irish, Chinese, English, Hindustani, Iranian, Modern Hebrew, Esperanto, Arabic

Linguaphone has been used by over a million adult students as well as in 11,000 colleges and schools throughout the world.

An early Linguaphone advertisement and a modern Linguaphone multimedia course.

Maximilian Berlitz and the Berlitz Schools of Languages

The Berlitz schools of language pioneered the conversational approach to language teaching. The first Berlitz school was founded in 1878 in Providence, Rhode Island, by Maximilian D. Berlitz (1852-1921). A native of Germany, Berlitz emigrated in 1872 prepared to teach Greek, Latin and six European languages, all by the grammar-translation method. A rather apocryphal story surrounds his adoption of the new method.

Needing an assistant to teach French, Berlitz advertised in a New York newspaper and hired a young Frenchman, Nicholas Joly, on the strength of the impeccable French of his letter of application. The new assistant arrived in Providence to find his employer ill from overwork. Berlitz did not feel any better when he discovered that his new assistant spoke no English! In desperation Berlitz suggested that Joly should try his best to teach the students, by pointing at objects and acting out verbs as well as he could. Berlitz was ill for six weeks and when he returned to his classroom he was worried that his students would be very angry. Instead, he found that his students had made excellent progress in his absence, and were having lively conversations with the teacher in French, with good accents. Berlitz quickly realized the possibilities of this novel method of teaching, which emphasized conversation and the use of the target language for real communication, instead of grammar analysis and rote learning. He made it the basis of his system of language teaching which is still used today in the Berlitz courses.

The precepts of the Berlitz system are:

1. Reading and writing are not taught until after the student has learned to speak, and practice in speaking precedes practice in reading and writing.
2. In class, the teacher asks questions that the student must answer with a complete sentence, not simply 'Yes' or 'No'.
3. Students participate actively, that is, by questioning their fellow students or responding to their questions, for example.
4. Only the target language is used, and no translations are offered.
5. Grammar is studied later when examples can be cited; no rules are memorized.
6. All instruction is directed to practical ends – ordering a restaurant meal, for instance – and is drawn from life, not literature.

More than 200 Berlitz schools now exist throughout the world, in 21 countries and five continents. Berlitz phrase books also have world-wide sales.

The importance of autonomy, responsibility and flexibility in adult language learning

Modern second language methodology aims to give learners control over the pace and direction of their learning, realizing their potential and fulfilling their needs. One aspect of this has been the increase in self-study centers for adult language learners, making use of the media and information technology. Many self-study centers have been established in Britain and Europe, some in universities and some others in industrial centers. Self-study centers offer an initial assessment by an adviser, focusing on the communicative needs of the learner, the time available, etc. The adviser then helps the learner to prepare a flexible program of self-study, using text books, cassettes and videos, language laboratories, computers. The learners study at their own pace, but have the option of regular counseling by the adviser, and opportunities for tutorials and conversation sessions with other learners.

In addition a wider choice of course formats are now on offer. In contrast to the traditional 'once a week' evening class, many learners now have a choice of full-time crash courses, lunch time courses, one day a week courses, and early morning or late afternoon courses for office and shift workers. This enables learners to integrate their language learning into their schedule in a convenient way.

The importance of an environment that facilitates learning

Classroom second language learning has several disadvantages compared to real life opportunities to acquire a second language. It is harder to create and sustain motivation in the artificial environment of the classroom. Opportunities for 'authentic' use of the target language must be engineered. Comprehension is more difficult without the contextual clues of the outside world. However, the classroom has advantages as a learning environment for adults. Adults often benefit from a more analytical approach to second language learning, organizing and reflecting upon new material. They may appreciate grammatical explanations and the chance to reinforce oral work with written work.

Also, although adults learn languages more efficiently than children, because of their superior processing skills and cognitive abilities, they may be hindered by psychological factors such as shyness, inhibitions, inflexibility and resistance to change. Adults learning a second language may feel uncomfortable and disadvantaged when encountering native speakers in real life situations. The classroom can provide a safe and reassuring environment for the adult language learner, provided that it is not totally isolated from the outside world. Modern adult language courses tend to accent real life, out-of-class activities using the second language, coffee evenings and pub nights, barn dances, work experience, trips to the target country or community, etc. These kind of authentic language opportunities are important to sustain motivation. After all, most adults learn a language because they want to use it.

Further Reading

ESCH, E. (ed.), 1994, *Self-Access and the Adult Language Learner.* London: Centre for Information on Language Teaching and Research.

PERDUE, C. (ed.), 1993, *Adult Language Acquisition: Cross-linguistic Perspectives.* Cambridge: Cambridge University Press.

RICHTERICH, R. & CHANCEREL, J., 1987, *Identifying the Needs of Adults Learning a Foreign Language.* New Jersey: Prentice Hall.

SIDWELL, D., 1987, *Modern Language Learning: Tutor's Handbook.* Leicester: National Institute of Adult Continuing Education.

SIDWELL, D. (ed.), 1987, *Teaching Languages to Adults.* London: Centre for Information on Language Teaching and Research.

TRIM, J. L. *et al.*, 1980, *Systems Development in Adult Language Learning : A European Unit/Credit System for Modern Language Learning by Adults* (Second edition). Oxford: Published for and on behalf of the Council of Europe by Pergamon Press.

VAN EK, J. A., 1980, *Threshold Level English in a European Unit/Credit System for Modern Language Learning by Adults* (Second edition). Oxford: Published for and on behalf of the Council of Europe by Pergamon Press.

9: The *Ulpan* Experience: From Israel to Wales and the Basque Country

Introduction

Perhaps the most notable example of a mass movement of adult language learning has been the case of Hebrew in Israel. Until the last quarter of the 19th century, Hebrew had not been the living language of a Jewish community for nearly 2000 years. Many Jews could read and understand Hebrew as the language of the synagogue, many learned works were written in Hebrew, some religious groups spoke Hebrew on the Sabbath, for instance, and it was a useful lingua franca between various Jewish groups of different languages. But for no Jewish individual was it the mother tongue or the sole means of communication. The 'revival' of Hebrew in Israel, engineered by Eliezer Ben Yehuda and others, succeeded because for many Jewish in-migrants to Israel, Hebrew had always been a symbol of their cultural and religious identity. Hebrew also had a utilitarian function. Jewish in-migrants from many countries spoke so many different languages that it was necessary to establish a common language for the homeland.

The Hebrew *Ulpan*

From the beginning the emphasis was on establishing and teaching Hebrew as a living, spoken language and as a vehicle for ordinary communicative needs, and this influenced the methods of teaching Hebrew to in-migrants.

As the use of the Hebrew language spread at the beginning of this century, teachers in schools used the 'natural' or 'direct' method to teach the language to children. Hebrew night classes were started for adults. However, after the establishment of the State of Israel in 1948 the steady flow of immigration became a flood. The in-migrants came from many different countries and many had experienced little formal education. Emergency measures were needed to teach Hebrew in a short time to large numbers of people. The idea of creating an intensive course was born. In September 1949 the first *Ulpan* course was begun. The word '*Ulpan*' is derived from an Aramaic root meaning 'custom, training, instruction, law'. There were 25 students in the class, and they met for six hours each day apart from the Sabbath. From the beginning, the emphasis was on equipping the learners for everyday communication in the spoken language. Cultural activities such as singing and field trips were part of the course.

Over the years many different kinds of *Ulpanim* have been established.

- Intensive courses for new in-migrants at the '*merkaz klita*' (residential absorption centers for new in-migrants). These are intensive courses, usually 30 hours a week for five months.

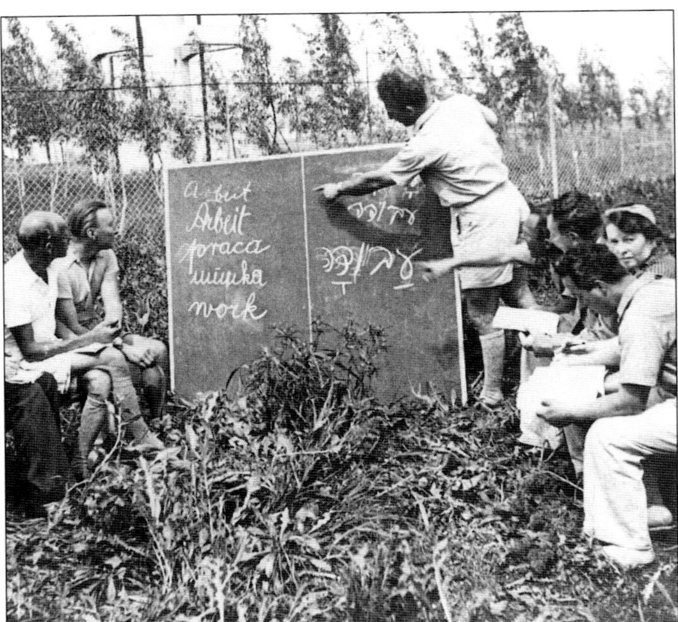

An early Ulpan in Israel. The word 'work' is written in several languages on the left, with the Hebrew equivalent on the right, indicating the various language backgrounds of the learners.

- Less intensive *ulpanim*, called *ulpaniyot*. These are non-residential *ulpanim*, held perhaps a couple of mornings or evenings a week, to fit in with the needs of professional people or those with home responsibilities.

- *Ulpanim* at Kibbutzim. The learners have lessons and also work on the kibbutz.

- Military *Ulpanim*. These are very intensive in order to bring the students' language to the very high level of Hebrew required by the Israeli military. These courses place emphasis on technical vocabulary and reading skills (maps, plans, written instructions etc.).

- Specialized courses for advanced learners in various vocational fields.

Modern *Ulpanim* courses have kept abreast of the latest trends in language teaching and continue to emphasize the spoken language and equipping learners to function in society. A typical *Ulpan* course for beginners will include drill and pronunciation practice, dialogues, pair work, emphasis on authentic communication. Reading and writing are also included in the course, in order to give the learners some proficiency in the intricacies of Hebrew orthography. Many courses include singing and other cultural activities, trips to places of interest and stays with Hebrew speaking families.

On the whole, *Ulpanim* courses have had high success rates. In-migrants to Israel usually have a high degree of instrumental and integrative motivation to learn Hebrew. Learning the language can help them gain employment and also integrate fully into Israeli society. However success depends on many factors. Studies have shown, for instance, that in-migrants from Eastern Europe were generally more successful in learning Hebrew than anglophone in-migrants. This was attributed to the fact that speakers of languages like Russian or Romanian have a greater need to learn Hebrew in order to become part of Israeli society. English, on the other hand, is one of the official languages of Israel and is understood and spoken by a great many Israelis, especially in the cities. Thus English speakers are not so strongly motivated to learn Hebrew. Age can also be a factor. Research has shown that the older age groups are less likely to use Hebrew on a daily basis than the younger age groups. However, this does not mean the older folk are less effective learners. Older folk may find it harder to learn a new language and to use it because of shyness, inhibition, resistance to change.

The Welsh '*Wlpan*'

Other countries have followed the example of the Hebrew *Ulpanim*, notably Wales. In 1973, a group of Welsh teachers went on a fact-finding mission to Israel. In September 1974 the first Welsh '*Wlpan*' began in the capital city of Wales, Cardiff, two hours a night and five nights a week for ten weeks. Since then '*Wlpanau*' have been held regularly in villages, towns and cities the length and breadth of Wales .

Like their models in Israel, the Welsh *Wlpanau* vary in intensity from five days a week courses to two mornings or two evenings a week. Some vocational courses are held, for teachers, hospital workers, administrators. Other courses have a bias towards the needs of particular groups like parents. Some courses are held in the mornings, at lunchtimes or after work to fit the needs of office workers. As in Israel, the emphasis in Wales is on developing competence in the spoken language. *Wlpanau* have been a successful route to language learning for many adults in Wales.

However the situation in the two countries is very different. In Wales only 20 percent of the total population of 2.9 million speak Welsh and English is spoken and understood by the entire population. In some parts of Wales Welsh is needed for jobs in teaching, local government and public services and this provides motivation for some adults to learn the language. However the majority of adult learners are motivated by the desire to integrate into Welsh-speaking society, to participate in Welsh culture and for those of Welsh parentage, to recover a lost heritage.

A modern Hebrew Ulpan.

Adult Language Learning in the Basque Country

During the last decade and a half innovations in adult language learning in the Basque country have been inspired by the example of Israel and Wales. The Basque people live in the westernmost part of the Pyreneean mountains and the surrounding regions. This area comprises four provinces in Spain and three in France. Known to the Spanish as *Vascos* and to the French as Basques, the Basques call themselves *Euskaldunak* and their homeland *Euskadi*. Their language bears no apparent relation to any other known language. The Basque people have endured much oppression during the last two centuries and their language has been disparaged and (in Spain) outlawed until recent years.

According to 1987 figures, Basque speakers number about 900,000 in Spain and 80,000 in France, only 23 percent of the total population in the area. Yet many more consider themselves to be Basque and the Basque language is a central symbol of their separate ethnic identity. There is a vigorous adult language learning movement, run chiefly by the government, through HABE (Institute for the Alphabetization and Re-Euskaldunization of Adults) and by the independent body AEK (Basque Language Learning Groups Organization). This movement reached its peak in the 1980s, with over 100,000 enrolled on courses in 1986-87. There are many weekly course (*gau eskola*), intensive courses (*iskaltaldi*), and also some residential courses (*barnetegi*).

The aims of the adult language learning organizations are not just to teach Basque to adults but to recreate a Basque-speaking country. To this end, the adult courses are based on the communicative approach. The learning of vocabulary and grammar and command over communicative functions is interwoven with contact with the outside world, with cultural societies, organizations and industry. A lesson involving the communicative function of expressing wishes and preferences might involve planning a holiday, contacting tourist organizations for information, and even complaining if they write back in Spanish! The aim is to enable the students to play a full part in Basque-speaking society. In addition, many cultural activities are organized, including music festivals. One of the best known of these is the '*korrika*', a 2000 km relay race organized by AEK in which over 3000 teams take part. The race lasts for ten days, and is accompanied by many other cultural activities. Basque-medium courses in other subjects, such as photography, music, geography and history are also run, so that the students learn Basque for authentic purposes.

The literacy rate among Bascophone adults is very low. HABE and AEK also run literacy courses to educate Basque-speaking adults in the reading and writing of their native tongue. Books and magazines are regularly published.

Further Reading

RICHTERICH, R. & CHANCEREL, J., 1987, *Identifying the Needs of Adults Learning a Foreign Language*. New Jersey: Prentice Hall.

SCHUCHAT, T., 1990, *Ulpan: How to Learn Hebrew in a Hurry!* Jerusalem and Woodmere, New York: Gefen Books.

SIDWELL, D., 1987, *Modern Language Learning: Tutor's Handbook*. Leicester: National Institute of Adult Continuing Education.

SIDWELL, D. (ed.), 1987, *Teaching Languages to Adults*. London: Centre for Information on Language Teaching and Research.

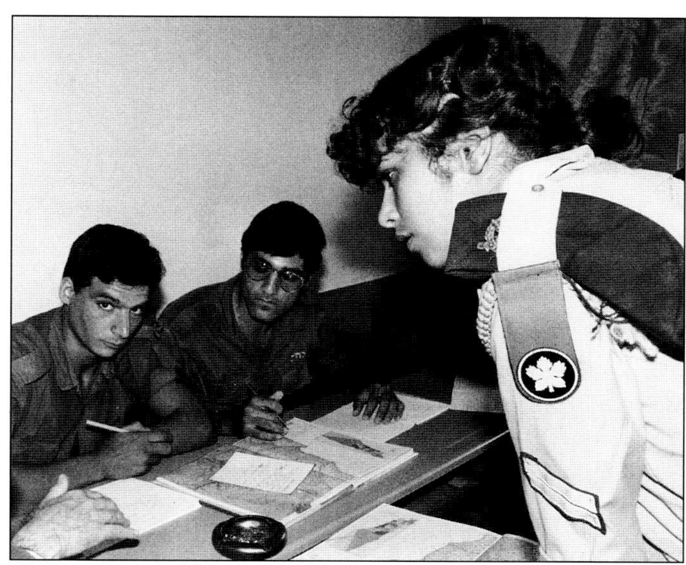

A specialist army Ulpan in Israel.

האוניברסיטה העברית בירושלים
THE HEBREW UNIVERSITY OF JERUSALEM
ROTHBERG SCHOOL FOR OVERSEAS STUDENTS
The Summer Ulpan 1994
Ministry of Education, Culture and Sport
Division of Adult Education, Hebrew Language Department
THE ULPAN FOR HEBREW LANGUAGE INSTRUCTION
aek
Alfabetatze
Euskalduntze
DENOK
Maite dugu gure herria
EUSKARAZ!
1993ko martxoaren 26tik apirilaren 4era
IRUÑEA - BILBO
As seen on TV...
Speaking Our LANGUAGE
1993-94
The complete guide to learning
Gaelic
- the language of the 90's
Study Packs
WHY CHOOSE WELSH
Census shows rise in Welsh speakers
People now regard the Welsh language as something they are proud to say they speak.
Plea for more Welsh Schools
MORE LEARN WELSH
KENTELIOÙ NOZ BREZHONEG
evel just!
WELSH COURSES
CYRSIAU CYMRAEG I OEDOLION
WELSH COURSES FOR ADULTS
1995-1996
Cyrsiau
Wlpan • Pellach
Uwch • Meistroli
Gwynedd
Trefnydd/Organiser:
Elwyn Hughes,
Prifysgol Cymru / University of Wales
Bangor.
Ffôn/Tel: 01248 382260

GLOSSARY
BIBLIOGRAPHY
PHOTOGRAPHIC CREDITS
INDEX

Glossary

A

Accent: People's pronunciation and intonation which may reveal which region, country or social class (for example) they come from.

Accommodation: Adapting speech to make oneself understood or accepted by others in a conversation.

Acculturation: The process by which an individual or group adapts to a new culture.

Achieved Bilingualism: The acquisition of bilingualism later than childhood. Also termed Successive Bilingualism.

Achievement Test: Usually a classroom-based test to measure how much someone has learnt as the result of a program of teaching and learning a second language.

Acrolect: See Decreolization.

Active Language: The production of language in speaking and writing. This is distinguished from passive language which refers to listening, understanding and reading. The distinction between **Productive** and **Receptive Language** is the same.

Active Vocabulary: This refers to the actual number of words that people use as opposed to a **passive vocabulary** which is words they understand. Native language speakers often have an active vocabulary of between 30,000 and 50,000 words. Their passive vocabulary may extend up to 100,000 words. In foreign language learning, reasonable proficiency is achieved when someone attains an active vocabulary of between 3000 and 5000 words with a passive vocabulary of up to 10,000 words.

Additive Bilingualism: A situation where a second language is learnt by an individual or a group without detracting from the maintenance and development of the first language. A situation where a second language adds to, rather than replaces the first language. This is the opposite of subtractive bilingualism.

Affective Dimension: Feelings and emotions.

Affective Filter: Associated with Krashen's Monitor Model of second language learning, the affective filter is a metaphor which describes a learner's attitudes that affect the relative success of second language acquisition. Negative feelings such as a lack of motivation, lack of self-confidence and learning anxiety are like a filter which hinders and obstructs language learning.

Agraphia: Difficulty in writing, connected with Aphasia.

Alexia: Difficulty in reading, connected with Aphasia.

Ambilingualism: The ability to function equally well in two or more languages across a wide variety of domains.

Anomie: A feeling of disorientation and rootlessness, for example in in-migrant groups. A feeling of uncertainty or dissatisfaction in relationships between an individual learning a language and the language group with which they are trying to integrate.

Aphasia: Damage to the brain which causes a loss of ability to use and understand language. This may be partial or total and affect spoken and/or written language.

Artificial Language: (1) A language invented as a means of international communication (e.g. Esperanto, Ido). (2) A system of communication created for a specific purpose (e.g. computer language).

Ascribed Bilingualism: The acquisition of bilingualism early in childhood.

Assimilation: The process by which a person or language group lose their own language and culture which are replaced by a different language and culture.

Attribution: Giving reasons why things happen. The allocation of intention and meaning to behavior.

Attrition: See Language Attrition.

Authentic Texts: Texts taken from newspapers, magazines, tapes of natural speech from radio and television. They are not created by the teacher but already exist in the world outside the classroom.

Autochthonous Languages: A term particularly used in Europe to describe indigenous languages or languages resident for a considerable length of time in a territory or region.

Autonomous Variety of Language: A standard language that has its own established norms, as opposed to a heteronomous variety. See Heteronomous Variety.

Auxiliary Language: (1) A language used as a means of communication between different language groups. See also Lingua Franca, Pidgin, Language of Wider Communication. (2) An artificial language invented as a means of communication between different language groups.

B

Back Translation: A translation is translated back into the original to assess the accuracy of the first translation.

Balanced Bilingualism: Approximately equal competence in two languages.

Barrios: Spanish for 'neighborhood'. Used in the United States for areas where many Latinos live.

Basal Readers: Reading texts that use simplified vocabulary and grammar, carefully graded and structured.

Basilect: See Decreolization.

BEA: Bilingual Education Act (United States legislation: part of ESEA – see below).

BICS: Basic Interpersonal Communicative Skills. Everyday, straightforward communication skills that are helped by contextual supports.

Bicultural: Identifying with the culture of two different language groups. To be bilingual is not necessarily the same as being bicultural.

Big Books: Used frequently in 'whole language classrooms'. They are teachers' books that are physically big so that students can read along with the teacher.

Biliteracy: Reading and writing in two languages.

Black English: The variety of English spoken by some black people in the United States, for example in cities such as New York, and Chicago. Black English is regarded as a language variety in its own right with its own structure and system. It is not regarded in any way as a second class variety of English.

Borrowing: A word or a phrase from one language that has become established in use in another language. When borrowing is a single word, it is often called a loan word.

BSM: Bilingual Syntax Measure (attempts to establish the dominant language of a bilingual).

C

CALL: Computer Assisted Language Learning.

CALP: Cognitive/Academic Language Proficiency. The level of language required to understand academically demanding subject matter in a classroom. Such language is often abstract, without contextual supports such as gestures and the viewing of objects.

Caretaker Speech: A simplified language used by parents to children to ensure understanding, also called Motherese. Caretaker Speech usually has short sentences, is grammatically simple, has few difficult words and much repetition with clear pronunciation. Caretaker speech is also used by teachers with children in Immersion classrooms.

Chicanos: Mexican-Americans.

Circumstantial Bilingual: Someone who, by force of circumstances, becomes a bilingual.

Classical Language: A standardized, written form of a language from a period in its history when it had high literary and cultural prestige (e.g. Greek).

Classroom Discourse: A special type of language used in the classroom. Such language is governed by the different roles that students and teachers assume and the kind of activities that occur in classrooms. The kind of 'open' (many different answers possible) or 'closed' questions (only one or a few correct answers possible) that teachers ask is one particular area of interest in Classroom Discourse.

Classroom Ethos: The atmosphere and feelings in the classroom that promote or detract from effective classroom learning.

Classroom Interaction: The interaction and relationships between teachers and students, and between students themselves both in terms of oral, written and non-verbal communication.

Cloze Procedure: A technique for measuring students' reading comprehension. In a Cloze test, words are removed from a reading passage at specific intervals, and students have to fill in the blanks. The missing words are guessed from the context.

Code: A neutral term used instead of language or speech or dialect.

Codemixing: The mixing of two languages within a sentence or across sentences.

Codeswitching: Moving from one language to another, inside a sentence or across sentences.

Codification: A systematic description of a variety of a language (e.g. vocabulary, grammar). This may occur when a language is being standardized, or when an oral language is being written down for the first time.

Cognate: A language or linguistic form, historically derived from the same source as another (e.g. French, Catalan and Spanish are cognate languages derived from Latin).

Cognition: The acquisition, storage, retrieval and use of knowledge. Mental processes of perception, memory, thinking, reasoning and language.

Cognitive/Academic Language Proficiency (CALP): The level of second language proficiency needed by students to perform the more abstract and cognitively demanding tasks of a classroom. Little support is offered in many classrooms from the context. CALP is distinguished from Basic Interpersonal Communication Skills (BICS), that are relatively undemanding cognitively and rely on the context to aid understanding.

Cognitive Style: The way in which different learners efficiently and effectively learn. Different students have different preferences, patterns and styles of learning.

Common Underlying Proficiency (CUP): Two languages working integratively in the thinking system. Each language serves one underlying, central thinking system.

Communal Lessons: Lessons in which students of different first languages are mixed for common activities, such as working on projects, doing art or physical education. The European Hours in the European Schools are Communal Lessons.

Communicative Approach: A second language teaching approach that accents the acquisition of a language by use in everyday communicative situations.

Communicative Competence: Proficiency in the use of a language in everyday conversations. This term accents being understood rather than being 'correct' in using a language. Not only knowing the grammar and vocabulary of a language, but also knowing the social and culturally appropriate uses of a language.

Community Language: A language used by a particular community or in a particular area, often referring to ethnic minority groups. The term has been used in Britain to refer to the language of Asian and European groups which are resident in particular areas.

Community Language Learning: A second language teaching methodology based on Rogerian counseling techniques and responding to the needs of the learner 'community'.

Compensatory Education: See Deficit Model.

Competence in Language: A person's ability to create and understand language. This goes further than an understanding of vocabulary and grammar requiring the listener to understand sentences not heard before. The term is often used in association with Chomsky's theory of transformational grammar, describing a person's internalized grammar of the language, which enables the person to create new sentences and interpret sentences never heard before. Competence is often used to describe an idealized speaker/hearer with a complete knowledge of the whole language, and is distinguished from performance which is the actual use of the language by individuals.

Compound Bilingualism: One language is learnt at the same time as another, often in the same contexts. Therefore, the representation in the brain was thought to be fused and interdependent.

Comprehensible Input: Language delivered at a level understood by a learner.

Concept: The idea or meaning associated with a word or symbol in a person's thinking system. All languages can express the same concepts, although different languages construct concepts in different ways (e.g. languages tend to distinguish colors on the color spectrum in different ways).

Consecutive Bilingualism: See Simultaneous Bilingualism

Consecutive Interpreting: See Interpreting.

Content-Based Instruction: A term particularly used in the United States. Such a program teaches students the language skills they will need in mainstream classrooms. The focus is on the language skills needed for content areas such as mathematics, geography, social studies and science.

Content Reading: The reading of books to learn particular curriculum areas as separate from reading for enjoyment only.

Context: The setting in which communication occurs, and which places possibilities and constraints on what is said, and how it is said. The context can refer to the physical setting or to the language context in which a word or utterance occurs.

Context-Embedded Language: Communication occurring in a context that offers help to comprehension (e.g. visual clues, gestures, expressions, specific location). Language where there are plenty of shared understandings and where meaning is relatively obvious due to help from the physical or social nature of the conversation.

Context-Reduced Language: Language where there are few clues as to the meaning of the communication apart from the words themselves. The language is likely to be abstract.

Contrastive Analysis: The comparison of the linguistic systems of two languages.

Co-ordinate Bilingualism : Two languages learnt in different and separate environments. The two languages were therefore thought to be independent (e.g. in representation in the brain).

Core Language Class: Teaching the language as a subject. Used mostly to describe foreign language instruction.

Core Subject: A subject that is of prime importance in the curriculum. In England, the three core subjects are Mathematics, English and Science. These are said to form the Core Curriculum.

Corpus Language Planning: Language planning which centers on linguistic aspects of language, vocabulary and grammar for example, to try and ensure a normative or standardized system of language within an area. (See also Language Planning).

Creole: A pidgin language which has been adopted as the native language in a region. A creole tends to be more complex in grammar with a wider range of vocabulary than a pidgin language. There are for example, English-based, French-based Creoles.

Creolization: The process by which a pidgin becomes a creole by the expansion of vocabulary and the development of a more complex linguistic structure.

Criterion-Referenced Testing: A form of educational assessment which compares students in terms of their mastery of a subject as opposed to a norm-referenced test where a student is compared with other students. A criterion-referenced test in language requires a clear specification of the structure of the language to be learnt.

Critical Period Hypothesis: A genetically determined period of child development when learning must take place, otherwise it will not be learned later. In language, this is a largely discredited theory that a child best learns a first or second language between birth and up to about 13 years of age.

Cultural Pluralism: The ownership of two or more sets of cultural beliefs, values and attitudes. Multicultural education is often designed to encourage cultural pluralism in children.

Culture: The set of meanings, beliefs, attitudes, customs, everyday behavior and social understandings of a particular group, community or society.

Culture Shock: Feelings of disorientation, anxiety or insecurity some people experience when entering a different culture. For example when people move to a foreign country there may be a period of culture shock until they become more familiar with their new culture.

CUP: See Common Underlying Proficiency.

D

Daughter Language: A language historically derived from another language called the 'parent' language.

DBE: Developmental Bilingual Education: Also known as Two-Way Dual Language Programs and Two-Way Bilingual/Immersion Programs. Two languages are used for approximately equal time in the curriculum.

Dead Language: (1) A form of language that is no longer used as a medium of communication in society. Its speakers have died or have shifted to using another language. (2) The term is used inaccurately to describe a language that has evolved into a distinct new variety or varieties. For example, through a process of historical change and development, Latin is described as a 'dead language', but it did not die but evolved into different Romance languages.

Decoding: In learning to read, decoding is the deciphering of the sounds and meanings of letters, combinations of letters, whole words and sentences of text. Sometimes decoding refers only to being able to read a text without necessarily understanding the meaning of that text.

Decreolization: The process by which a creole becomes closer in its form to the base language from which it derived much of its grammar and vocabulary. During this process, many varieties develop at various distances from the base language. Among the recognized varieties are the acrolect (closest to the standard, prestige variety), the basilect (furthest from the standard, base language) and the mesolect (intermediate between acrolect and basilect). These varieties form what is known as a post-creole continuum.

Deficit Model: The idea that some children have a deficiency in their language- in vocabulary, grammar or understanding, particularly in the classroom. The child has a perceived language 'deficit' that has to be compensated for by remedial schooling or compensatory education. The problem is seen to be located in the child rather than in the school system or society or in the ideology of the perceiver. The opposite is an enrichment model (see Enrichment Bilingual Education).

DES: Department of Education and Science (Britain).

Diagonal Bilingualism: Situations where a 'non-standard' language or a dialect co-exists with an unrelated 'standard' language.

Dialect: A language variety whose features identify the regional or social background of the user. The term is often used in relation to a standard variety of a language (e.g. a dialect of English).

Dialect Continuum: A chain of dialects spoken in a geographical area. Mutual intelligibility is often high between dialects in close proximity and low between geographically distant dialects.

Diglossia: Two languages or language varieties existing together in a society in a stable arrangement through different uses attached to each language.

Discourse: A term used to describe relatively large chunks of conversation or written text. Rather than highlighting vocabulary or grammar, discourse extends into understandings and meanings of conversation or written text.

Discourse Analysis: The study of spoken and written language particularly in terms of negotiated meanings between participants in speech, choice of linguistic forms, shared assumptions that underlie utterances, structures, strategies and symbolism in communicating, and the role relationships between participants.

Disembedded Thinking: Thinking that is not allied to a meaningful context but is treated as a separate, distinct task with little relevance in itself.

Distance Learning: Independent learning outside the classroom, by telephone, satellite, distance learning packages, for example.

Divergent Thinking: Thinking that is original, imaginative and creative. A preference for open-ended, multiple answers to questions.

DL: Dual Language (School).

Domain: Particular contexts where a certain language is used. For example, there is the family domain where a minority language may be used. In the work domain, the majority language may be used.

Dominant Language: The language which a person has greater proficiency in or uses more often.

Double Immersion: Schooling where subject content is taught through a second and third language (e.g. Hebrew and French for first language English speakers).

Dual Language Program: see Two-Way Programs.

Dyslexia: Problems in learning to read, word blindness where students may have difficulty in, for example, distinguishing different letter shapes and words.

E

Early-Exit/Late-Exit Bilingual Education Programs: Early-exit programs move children from bilingual classes in the first or second year of schooling. Late-exit programs provide bilingual classes for three or more years of elementary schooling. Both programs are found in Transitional Bilingual Education.

EC: European Community. A grouping of most European countries for mutual economic, social and cultural benefit.

Eclectic Method: Using a variety of methods in language teaching, preferably in a rational manner.

EEC: European Economic Community. A grouping of European countries, accenting economic cooperation. This term has largely been superseded by EU (European Union).

EFL: English as a Foreign Language.

Elective Bilingual: Someone who has chosen to become a bilingual (e.g. through taking second language classes).

ELL: English Language Learners. This is sometimes preferred to LEP (Limited English Proficiency) as it focuses on development rather than deficit.

ELT: English Language Teaching.

Empowerment: The means by which those those of low status, low influence and power are given the means to increase their chances of prosperity, power and prestige. Literacy and biliteracy are major means of empowering such individuals and groups.

English-Only: An umbrella term for federal and state legislation and organizations that aim to make English the official language of the US. This includes two national organizations: US English and English First.

English Plus: A US movement promoting the belief that all US residents should have the opportunity to become proficient in a language other than English.

Enrichment Bilingual Education: A form of bilingual education that seeks to develop additive bilingualism, thus enriching a person's cultural, social and personal education. Two languages and cultures are developed through education.

Equilingual: Someone who is approximately equally competent in two languages.

ERA: Education Reform Act (British).

ERASMUS: A European program for students to take part of their higher education at one or more European universities or colleges as well as their 'home' university or college.

ESEA: Elementary and Secondary Education Act (United States).

ESL: English as a Second Language. An ESL program (e.g. in the US) usually involves little or no use of the first language, and occurs for part of the school timetable.

ESOL: English for Speakers of Other Languages.

ESP: English for Special Purposes. For example, English may be taught for its use in the science and technology curriculum, or English for business, specific vocational needs and professions.

Ethnic Identity: Those aspects of an individual's thinking, feelings, perceptions, and behavior that are due to ethnic group membership, as well as a sense of belonging and pride in the ethnic group.

Ethnic Mosaic: In-migrants of different geographical origins co-existing in a country (e.g. United States) and retaining colorful constituents of their ethnicity.

Ethnocentrism: Discriminatory beliefs and behaviours based on ethnic differences. Evaluating other ethnic groups by criteria specific to one's own group.

Ethnographic Pedagogy: Teaching practices and learning strategies that are derived from ethnography (see below) and conducted in the classroom. An ethnographic researcher becomes involved in a classroom, observing, participating and helping transform teaching practices. Ethnographic pedagogy includes learning to read by harnessing students' prior cultural knowledge and experience, and encouraging peer interaction.

Ethnography: Research that describes and analyzes groups (e.g. ethnic, cultural) and is qualitative rather than quantitative in approach (e.g. engages in fieldwork, interviews and observation). Such research is often intensive and detailed, hence small-scale.

Ethnography of Communication: The study of the place of language in different groups and communities. Language is particularly studied for its social and cultural purposes.

Ethnolinguistic: A set of cultural, ethnic and linguistic features shared by a cultural, ethnic, or sub-cultural social group.

EU: European Union. A recent term to describe the grouping of European countries for mutual benefit.

Expanded Pidgin: See Pidgin.

F

Faux Amis: (false friends). Cognate words in different languages that have developed different meanings.

FEP: Fluent English Proficient.

Field Dependency: A learning style where the whole of the learning task is focused on, rather than component parts.

Field Independence: Field independence occurs when the learner is able to focus on particular components distinguished from the whole.

First Language: This term is used in different, overlapping ways, and can mean (a) the first language learnt (b) the stronger language (c) the 'mother tongue' (d) the language most used.

FLAP: The Foreign Language Assistance Program authorized under Title VII of the *Improving America's Schools Act of 1994*, that awards grants to US states and local educational agencies to promote programs that improve foreign language learning.

Flexible Learning: The provision of materials for learners to be used independently with minimal guidance and direction from a teacher.

Foreign Language: A language taught in school which is not normally used as a means of instruction in schools or as a language of communication within the country, in the community or in bureaucracy.

Foreigner Talk: The kind of speech used by native speakers when talking to foreigners who are not proficient in their language. Foreigner talk is often slower, with clear pronunciation, simplified vocabulary and grammar with some degree of repetition. This makes the speech easier for foreigners to understand.

G

GAO: General Accounting Office (United States).

Gastarbeiter: (German term) An in-migrant or guestworker.

Gemeinschaft: A society based on close community bonds, kinship, close family ties; an emphasis on tradition and heritage. Sometimes portrayed stereotypically as village life.

Geolinguistics: The study of language or dialects as spoken in different geographical areas and regions. Sometimes referred to as Areal Linguistics.

Gesellschaft: A society with less emphasis on tradition and more on rational goals; duty to organizations with many secondary relationships. Sometimes portrayed stereotypically as one type of urban existence.

Graded Objectives: Objectives in a language curriculum which describe levels of attainment at different stages. These provide short-term, immediate goals for learners who are required to gain mastery of these goals before moving on to higher objectives.

Graded Reader: A simplified book or set of children's books, carefully graded in terms of increasingly difficult vocabulary and complexity of grammar. Such books are written for first language learners, adult second language learners and students learning a second language. In order to control the linguistic features precisely, authenticity may be sacrificed on occasions.

Grammar: The structure of a language; the way in which elements are combined to make words and the way in which words and phrases are combined to produce sentences.

Graphology: The study of systems of writing and the way a language is written.

Guest Workers: People who are recruited to work in another society. Also known as Gastarbeiter.

H

Hegemony: Domination; the ascendance of one group over another. The dominant group expects compliance and subservience from the subordinate group.

Heteronomous Variety of a Language: A language variety (e.g. a dialect) that is perceived as dependent on an autonomous language or standard variety, and which gains its norms from that standard variety.

Heritage Language: The language a person regards as their native, home, ancestral language. This covers indigenous languages (e.g. Welsh in Wales) and in-migrant languages (e.g. Spanish in the United States).

Heterogeneous Grouping: The use of mixed ability and/or mixed language groups or classes. The opposite is 'homogeneous grouping' or tracking (see below).

Hispanics: Spanish speakers in the United States. The term is officially used in the United States Census.

Horizontal Bilingualism: Situations where two languages have similar or equal status.

I

Immersion Bilingual Education: Schooling where some or most subject content is taught through a second language. Pupils in immersion are usually native speakers of a majority language, and the teaching is carefully structured to their needs.

Incipient Bilingualism: The early stages of bilingualism where one language is not strongly developed. Beginning to acquire a second language.

Indigenous Language: A language relatively native to an area, contrasted with an in-migrant language.

Individualized Instruction: A curriculum which is carefully structured to allow for the different needs and pace of learning of different students. Individualized instruction tries to give learners more control over what is learned, the style of learning and the rate of progress.

In-Migrants: Encompasses immigrants, migrants, guest workers and refugees. The term in-migrant is used throughout the Encyclopedia to avoid the negative connotations of the term 'immigrant' and to avoid the imprecise and loaded distinctions between migrant workers, guest workers, short-stay, long-stay and relatively permanent in-migrants.

Input: A distinction is often made in second language learning between input and intake. Input is what the learner hears but which may not always be understood. In contrast, **Intake** is that which is assimilated by the learner.

Input Hypothesis: Language in the second language classroom should contain elements that are slightly beyond the learner's present level of understanding. Using contextual clues to understand, the learner will gradually increase in language competence.

Instrumental Motivation: Wanting to learn a language for utilitarian reasons (e.g. to get a better job).

Intake: See Input.

Integrated Approach: The integration of listening, speaking, reading and writing in language teaching and language assessment.

Integrative Motivation: Wanting to learn a language to belong to a social group (e.g. make friends).

Interactionism: A position which argues that language cannot be understood without reference to the social context in which language occurs.

Interference: Interference (or transfer) in second language learning is said to occur when vocabulary or syntax patterns transfer from a learner's first language to the second language, causing errors in second language performance. The term interference has been decreasingly used because of its negative and derogatory connotations. See Language Transfer.

Interlanguage: An intermediate form of language used by second language learners in the process of learning a language. Interlanguage contains some transfers or borrowing from the first language, and is an approximate system with regard to grammar and communicating meaning.

Interlocutors: Those who are actively engaged in a conversation as opposed to those who are silent participants.

International Language: A high prestige, majority language used as a means of communication between different countries speaking different languages (e.g. English, French).

Interpreting: The process of oral translation from one language to another. Consecutive interpreting occurs when an interpreter orally translates while a speaker pauses. Simultaneous translation occurs when the interpreter orally translates while the speaker continues to speak. For example, an interpreter sits in a sound-proof booth, receiving the speaker's words through headphones. The translation is relayed to listeners via a microphone linked to listeners' headphones.

Intranational Language: A high prestige language used as a medium of general communication between different language groups within a country (e.g. English in India).

Involuntary Minorities: Also known as 'caste-like minorities'. They differ from immigrants and 'voluntary minorities' in that they have not willingly migrated to the country.

Isolate: A language isolate is a language that has no apparent relationship to any other known language.

K

Koine: The spoken language of a region that has become a standard language or lingua franca.

L

L1/L2: First Language/Second Language.

Language Ability: An 'umbrella' term and therefore used ambiguously. Language ability is a general, latent disposition, a determinant of eventual language success. Language ability is also used to describe the outcome of language learning, in a similar but less specific way than language skills, providing an indication of current language level. Language ability measures what a person can currently do, as different from what they may be able to do in the future.

Language Achievement: Normally seen as the outcome of formal language instruction. Proficiency in a language due to what has been taught or learnt in a language classroom.

Language Acquisition: The process of acquiring a first or second language. Some linguists distinguish between language acquisition and 'language learning' of a second language, using the former to describe the informal development of a person's second language, and the latter to describe the process of formal study of a second language. Other linguists maintain that no clear distinction can be made between informal acquisition and formal learning.

Language Across the Curriculum: A curriculum approach to language learning that accents language development across all subjects of the curriculum. Language should be developed in all content areas of the curriculum and not just as a subject in its own right. Similar approaches are taken in writing across the curriculum and reading across the curriculum.

Language Approach: A term usually used in a broad sense to describe the theories and philosophies about the nature of language and how languages are learned, (e.g. aural/oral approach, communicative approach). The term 'method' is used to describe how languages are taught in the classroom, (e.g. audiolingual method), and the term 'techniques' is used to describe the activities involved (e.g. role playing, drill).

Language Aptitude: A particular ability to learn a language as separate from intelligence, motivation.

Language Arts: Those parts of the curriculum which focus on the development of language: reading, writing, spelling as well as oral communication.

Language Attitudes: The beliefs and values expressed by people towards different languages in terms of favorability and unfavourability.

Language Attrition: The loss of a language within a person or a language group, gradually over time.

Language Awareness: A comprehensive term used to describe knowledge about and appreciation of the attributes of a language, the way a language works and is used in society.

Language Change: Change in a language over time. All living languages are in a process of gradual change (e.g. in pronunciation, grammar, vocabulary).

Language Competence: A broad and general term, used particularly to describe an inner, mental representation of language, something latent rather than overt. Such competence refers usually to an underlying system inferred from language performance.

Language Contact: Contact between speakers of different languages, particularly when they are in the same region or in adjoining communities.

Language Death: Language death is said to occur when a declining language loses its last remaining speakers through their death or their shift to using another language. This language no longer exists as a medium of communication in any language domains.

Language Decline: See Language Loss.

Language Demographics: The distribution of the use of a language in a defined geographical area. Also called Geolinguistics.

Language Dominance: One language being the stronger or preferred language of an individual, or the more prestigious language within a particular region.

Language Family: A group of languages historically derived from a common ancestor.

Language Laboratory: A room with individual booths fitted with cassette recorders. Students listen to recorded tapes and practice speaking exercises which can be monitored by teachers.

Language Learning: The process by which a first or second language is internalized. Some authors restrict the use of the term to formal learning (e.g. in the classroom). Others include informal learning (e.g. acquisition in the home). See also Language Acquisition.

Language Loss: The process of losing the ability or use of a language within an individual or within a group. Language loss is particularly studied amongst in-migrants to a country where their mother tongue has little or no status, little economic value or use in education, and where language loss subsequently occurs. See also Language Decline.

Language Loyalty: The purposeful maintenance and retention of a language, when that language is viewed as being under threat. This is often a concern of language minorities in a region where another language is the dominant language.

Language Maintenance: The continued use of a language, particularly amongst language minorities (for example through bilingual education). The term is often used with reference to policies that protect and promote minority languages.

Language Minority: A language community (or person) whose first language is different from the dominant language of the country. A group who speaks a language of low prestige, or low in power, or with low numbers in a society.

Language of Wider Communication: A language used for communication within a region or country by different language groups.

Language Performance: A person's production of language particularly within a classroom or test situation. The outward evidence of language competence, but which is not necessarily an accurate measure of language competence.

Language Planning: The development of a deliberate policy to engineer the use of language varieties within a region or country on linguistic, political or social grounds. Language planning often involves Corpus Planning (the selection, codification and expansion of norms of language) and Status Planning (the choice of language varieties for different functions and purposes).

Language Proficiency: An 'umbrella' term, sometimes used synonymously with language competence; at other times as a specific, measurable outcome from language testing. Language proficiency is viewed as the product of a variety of mechanisms: formal learning, informal uncontrived language acquisition (e.g. on the street) and of individual characteristics such as 'intelligence'.

Language Retention: The opposite of Language Attrition. Language retention refers to an individual or a group who continue to use (or retain their ability) in a language.

Language Revitalization: The process of restoring language vitality by promoting the use of a language and its range of functions within the community.

Language Shift: A change from the use of one language to another language within an individual or a language community. This often involves a shift from the minority language to the dominant language of the country. Usually the term means 'downward' shift (i.e. loss of a language).

Language Skills: Language skills are usually said to comprise: listening, speaking, reading and writing. Each of these can be divided into subskills. Language skills refer to highly specific, observable, clearly definable components such as writing.

Language Transfer: The effect of one language on the learning of another. There can be both **negative transfer**, sometimes called **interference**, and more often **positive transfer**, particularly in understandings and meanings of concepts.

Language Use Survey: An investigation of which languages are spoken in different areas, the functions and uses of languages in different domains, and sometimes an assessment of the proficiency of different language groups in terms of their minority and the majority language.

Language Variety: A regionally or socially distinctive variety of language. A term used instead of 'dialect' because of the negative connotations of that term, and because 'dialect' is often used to indicate a hierarchical relationship with a standard form of a language.

Language Vitality: The extent to which a language minority vigorously maintains and extends its everyday use and range of functions. Language vitality is said to be enhanced by factors such as language status, institutional support, economic value and the number and distribution of its speakers.

Latinos: Spanish speakers of Latin American extraction. This Spanish term is now used in English, especially by US Spanish speakers themselves. Often preferred to 'Hispanics'.

Learning Log: Students record in a note book their personal experiences in and out of school, and often record their responses and reactions to their reading and other curriculum activity. Such logs may be shared with the teacher who responds with a non-judgemental written reply. Logs aim to encourage students through personalization, increased motivation and enjoyable dialogue.

LEP: Limited English Proficient (US term). Used to refer to students in the United States who are not native speakers of English and who have yet to reach 'desired' levels of competence in understanding, speaking, reading or writing English. Such students are deemed to have insufficient English to cope in English-only classrooms.

Lexical Competence: Competence in vocabulary.

Lexis/Lexicon: The vocabulary or word stock of a language, their sounds, spelling and meaning.

LINGUA: A European program to increase majority language learning across Europe. The program funds scholarships, student exchanges and teaching materials to improve language learning and teaching in the European (EU) countries.

Lingua Franca: A language used for communication between different language groups. A lingua franca may be a local, regional, national or international language. It may be the first language of one language group. Lingua francas are especially common in multilingual regions.

Linguicism: The use of ideologies, structures and practices to legitimize and reproduce unequal divisions of power and resources between language groups.

Linguistic Purism: A deliberate attempt to rid a language of perceived undesirable elements (e.g. dialect forms, slang, foreign loan words).

Linguistics: The study and analysis of language.

Literacy: The ability to read and write in a language.

Living Language: A language used as a medium of communication (at least for some functions) within a community.

LM: Language Minority.

LMP: Linguistic Minorities Project (Britain).

LMS: Language Minority Students.

Loan Word: An item of vocabulary borrowed by one language from another. A **loan blend** occurs when the meaning is borrowed but only part of the form is borrowed; **loan shift** when the form is nativized; and **loan translation** when the components of a word are translated (e.g. 'skyscraper' into '*gratte ciel*' in French).

M

Machine Translation: Translation from one language to another by computer.

Mainstreaming: Putting a student who has previously been in a special educational program into ordinary classes. Language mainstreaming occurs when children are no longer given special support (e.g. English as a Second Language classes) and take their subjects through the majority language.

Maintenance Bilingual Education: A program that uses both languages of students to teach curriculum content.

Majority Language: A high status language usually (but not always) spoken by a majority of the population of a country.

Marked Language: A minority language spoken by a minority of the population in a country (as distinct from a majority language), and therefore often not highly valued in society.

Meaningful Learning: Learning which becomes accommodated within a person's conceptual system. This has been distinguished from rote learning which is not necessarily integrated into existing conceptual understandings and may exist for a short, temporary period of time.

Media: A general term for television, radio, satellite, books, newspapers and other written media which spread information to large numbers of people.

Medium of Education: The language used to teach content. Also Medium of Instruction.

Medium of Instruction: The language used to transmit instructional material.

Melting Pot: Used mainly in the US to describe how a variety of in-migrant ethnic groups have blended together to create modern US society.

Mesolect: See Decreolization.

Message: The meaning of a communication which may be conveyed in verbal form but also by non-verbal communication such as eye contact, gestures and posture. A distinction is often made between the form of message and message content. The form refers to how communication occurs and the content as to the meaning conveyed.

Metacognition: Becoming aware of one's own mental processes.

Metalinguistic: Using language to describe language. Thinking about one's language.

Metalinguistic Knowledge: An understanding of the form and structure of language arrived at through reflection and analyzing one's own communication.

Minority Language: A language of low prestige and low in power. Also used to mean a language spoken by a minority of the population in a country.

Miscue Analysis: Analysis of errors and incorrect responses readers make in reading.

Monitor Hypothesis: A theory of second language developed by Krashen. According to this theory, language can only be acquired in a natural, unconscious manner. The consciously learned rules of language have the function of monitoring or editing communication. This involves monitoring one's own speech or writing, to ensure accuracy of form and meaning, making corrections where necessary.

Monogenesis: A theory that all the languages in the world derive historically from a single ancestor.

Monoglot: See Monolingual.

Monolingual: A person who knows and/or uses one language.

Morphology: The internal structure of words (a morpheme is the smallest unit of meaning).

Mother Tongue: The term is used ambiguously. It variously means (a) the language learnt from the mother (b) the first language learnt, irrespective of 'from whom' (c) the stronger language at any time of life (d) the 'mother tongue' of the area or country (e.g. Irish in Ireland) (e) the language most used by a person (f) the language to which a person has the more positive attitude and affection.

Motherese: A simplified language used by parents to children to ensure understanding. See Caretaker Speech.

Multilingual: A person who typically knows and/or uses three languages or more.

Mutual Intelligibility: A situation where speakers of two closely related or similar language varieties understand one another. The degree of mutual intelligibility depends on factors such as the proportion of shared vocabulary, similarity of pronunciation, accent and grammar, as well as non-linguistic factors such as the relative status of the languages, attitudes of speakers to the other language and extent of exposure to that other language.

N

NABE: The National Association for Bilingual Education (NABE) is a professional association of teachers, administrators, parents, policy makers and others concerned with securing educational equity for language minority students.

National Language: On the surface, this refers to a prestigious, authorized language of the nation, but the term has varying and debated meanings. Sometimes it is used interchangeably with 'official language'. However, in multilingual countries, an official language (or languages) may co-exist with one or more national languages. Such national languages are not so widely used in public and official use throughout the country, but carry symbolic status and prestige. Also, a national language may be formally recognized as such, or may be informally attributed as a national language.

Native Language: Language which a person acquires first in life, or identifies with as a member of an ethnic group.

NCBE: The National Clearinghouse for Bilingual Education is funded by the US Department of Education, Office of Bilingual Education and Minority Languages Affairs (OBEMLA) to collect, analyze, and disseminate information related to the education of linguistically and culturally diverse students.

Negative Transfer: See Transfer.

Negotiation: Negotiation occurs in a conversation so that successful and smooth communication occurs. The use of feedback, corrections, exemplification, repetition, elaboration and simplification may aid negotiation.

NEP: Non-English Proficient.

Network: A group of people within a community who are regularly in communication with each other and whose manner of communication is relatively stable and enduring. Analysis of a language network examines different status relationships within the network.

Non-Native Variety: A language variety not indigenous to a region, but imported by in-migrants.

Non-Verbal Communication: Communication without words; for example, via gestures, eye contact, position and posture when talking, body movements and contact, tone of voice.

O

OBEMLA: The Office of Bilingual Education and Minority Languages Affairs in the US Department of Education, established in 1974 by Congress to provide equal educational opportunities for Limited English Proficient students.

OCR: Office of Civil Rights (United States).

Official Language: The language used in a region or country for public, formal and official purposes (e.g. government, administration, education, media).

Orthography: Spelling.

P

Parallel Teaching: Where bilingual children are taught by two teachers working together as a team, each using a different language. For example, a second language teacher and the class teacher planning together but teaching independently.

Passive Bilingualism: Being able to understand (and sometimes read) in a second language without speaking or writing in that second language.

Passive Vocabulary: See Active Vocabulary.

Patois: A derogatory term used to describe a low status language or dialect.

Personality Principle: The right to use a language based on the history and character of the language. Such use reflects two languages existing together in a society in a stable arrangement through different uses attached to each language.

Phonetics: The study of speech sounds.

Phonics: A method of teaching reading based on recognizing the sounds of letters and combinations of letters.

Phonology: The sound system of a language.

Pidgin: A language that develops as a means of communication when different language groups are in regular contact with one another. A pidgin usually has a small vocabulary and a simplified grammatical structure. Pidgins do not usually have native speakers although there are expanded pidgins (for example, in Papua New Guinea) where a pidgin is the primary language of the community. If a pidgin language expands to become the native language of a group of speakers, with a larger vocabulary and a more complex structure, it is often called a creole.

Pidginization: (1) The evolution of a pidgin language. (2) In second and foreign language learning, the development of a simplified form of the target language (also called **Interlanguage**). This intermediate stage is usually temporary, but according to the pidginization hypothesis, it may become permanent when learners remain socially apart from native speakers, or when the target language is infrequently used.

Plurilingual: Someone competent in two or more languages.

Polyglot: Someone competent in two or more languages.

Post-Creole Continuum: See Decreolization.

Pragmatics: The study of the use of language in communication, with a particular emphasis on the contexts in which language is used.

Preferred Language: A self-assessment of the more proficient language of an individual.

Primary Bilingualism : Where two languages have been learnt 'naturally' (not via school teaching, for example).

Primary Language: The language in which bilingual/multilingual speakers are most fluent, or which they prefer to use. This is not necessarily the language learnt first in life.

Process Approach in Language Teaching: This is particularly used in teaching children to write where planning, drafting and revising are used to improve writing competence. The process rather than the product is regarded as the important learning experience.

Process Instruction: An emphasis on the 'activity' of a classroom rather than a creating a product. A focus on procedures and techniques rather than on learning outcomes, learning 'how to' through inquiry rather than learning through the transmission and memorization of knowledge.

Productive Bilingualism: Speaking and writing in the first and second language (as well as listening and reading).

Productive Language: Speaking and writing.

Project Work: Independent work by an individual student or a group of students often on an interdisciplinary theme. The process of planning, execution, discussion and dialogue, reviewing and reflecting, evaluating and monitoring is an important part of the process. Project work accents co-operative group work and authentic language situations.

Prosody: The study of the melody, loudness, speed and rhythm of spoken language; apart from intonation, it includes the transmission of meaning that can be understood from different emphases.

Psychometric Tests: Tests to measure an individual's characteristics. The best known psychological tests are IQ tests. Other dispositions are also measured (e.g. attitudes, creativity, skills, dyslexia, personality, needs and motives).

Pull-Out Program: Minority language students are taken out of regular, mainstream classrooms for special instruction in the majority language. Special language classes are provided to try to raise a child's level of language in the dominant language of the classroom or of the school.

Purism: See Linguistic Purism.

Pygmalion Effect: The self-fulfilling prophecy. A student is labeled (e.g. by a teacher as having 'limited English'). The label is internalized by the student who behaves in a way that later serves to confirm the label.

R

Racism: A system of privilege and penalty based on race. It is based on a belief in the inherent superiority of one race over others, and the maintenance or promotion of economic, social, political and educational differences based on such supposed superiority.

Readability: The level of difficulty in a written passage. Readability depends on factors such as length of words, length of sentences, grammatical complexity and word frequency.

Reception Classes/Centers: For newly arrived students in a country, to teach the language of the new country, and often the culture.

Receptive Bilingualism: Understanding and reading a second language without speaking or writing in that language.

Receptive Language: Listening/understanding and reading.

Register: (1) A variety of a language closely associated with different contexts in which the language is used (e.g. courtroom, classroom, church) and hence with different people (e.g. police, professor, priest). (2) A variety of a language used by an individual in a certain context.

Relexification Hypothesis: A hypothesis that all pidgin languages derive from the first widely-used pidgin which was based on Portuguese. Over time, this original pidgin developed differently in varying areas as the original vocabulary changed by substitution of words from other European languages.

Remedial Bilingual Education: Also known as Compensatory Bilingual Education. Uses the mother tongue only to 'correct' the students' presumed 'deficiency' in the majority language.

S

SAIP: Special Alternative Instructional Programs (USA).

Scaffolding Approach: Building on a child's existing repertoire of knowledge and understanding.

Secondary Bilingualism : The second language has been formally learnt (see also Primary Bilingualism).

Second Language: This term is used in different, overlapping ways, and can mean (1) the second language learnt (chronologically); (2) the weaker language; (3) a language that is not the 'mother tongue'; (4) the less used language. The term is sometimes used to cover third and further languages. The term can also be used to describe a language widely spoken in the country of the learner (as opposed to a foreign language).

Self-Fulfilling Prophecy: A student is labeled (e.g. by a teacher as having 'limited English'). The label is internalized by the student who behaves in a way that serves to confirm the label.

Semantics: The study of the meaning of language.

Semilingual: A controversial term used to describe people whose two languages are at a low level of development.

Separate Underlying Proficiency: The idea that two languages exist separately and work independently in the thinking system.

Sequential Bilingualism: Bilingualism achieved via learning a second language later than the first language. This is distinct from Simultaneous Bilingualism where two languages are acquired concurrently. When a second language is learnt after the age of three, sequential bilingualism is said to occur.

Sheltered English: Content (subject) classes that also include English language development. The curriculum is taught in English in the United States at a comprehensible level to minority language students. The goal of sheltered English is to help minority language students acquire proficiency in English while at the same time achieving well in content areas of the curriculum.

Sight Vocabulary: Words which a child can recognize in reading that require no decoding of letters or blends of letters. The instant recognition of basic words.

Sign Language: Languages used by many deaf people and by those people who communicate with deaf people that make use of non-verbal communication to communicate meaning. Sign languages are complete languages with their own grammatical systems. Various sign languages have developed in different parts of the world (e.g. American sign language; British sign language; French sign language).

Silent Way: A method of second language learning emphasizing independent student learning by means of discovery and problem solving.

Simultaneous Bilingualism: Bilingualism achieved via acquiring a first and a second language concurrently. This is distinct from Sequential Bilingualism where the two languages are acquired at different ages. When a second language is learnt before the age of three, simultaneous bilingualism is said to occur.

Simultaneous Intepreting/Translation: See Interpreting.

Sister Languages: Two or more languages historically derived from a common parent language.

Skills-Based Literacy: Where the emphasis is on the acquisition of phonics and other language forms, rather than on ways of using those forms.

SLT: Second Language Teaching.

Sociolinguistics: The study of language in relation to social groups, social class, ethnicity and other interpersonal factors in communication.

Speech Variety: A neutral term sometimes used instead of 'dialect' or 'language' where a distinction is difficult.

Standard Language: A prestigious variety of a language that has official, formal use (e.g. in government and schooling). A standard language usually has norms for orthography, spelling, grammar and vocabulary. The standard variety is often used in literature and other forms of media (e.g. radio, television), in school text books, in centralized policies of the curriculum.

Standardization: The attempt to establish a single standard form of a language particularly in its written form, for official purposes, literature, school curriculum etc.

Standard Variety: See Standard Language.

Status Planning: Language planning which centers on language use and prestige within a region and within particular language domains. See Language Planning.

Stereotyping: Classifying members of a group (e.g. a language minority) as if they were all the same. Treating individuals of that group as if no other characteristics of that group were important or existed.

Streaming: The use of homogeneous groups in teaching (also called tracking, setting, streaming, banding, ability grouping).

Submersion: The teaching of minority language pupils solely through the medium of a majority language, often alongside native speakers of the majority language. Minority language pupils are left to sink or swim in the mainstream curriculum.

Substrate Language: A language that has influenced the structure or use of a prestigious language. See Superstrate Language.

Subtractive Bilingualism: A situation in which a second language is learnt at the expense of the first language, and gradually replaces the first language (e.g. in-migrants to a country or minority language pupils in submersion education).

Successive Bilingualism: See Sequential Bilingualism.

Suggestopedia: A controversial language teaching methodology based on 'suggestology'. The method is concerned with subconscious and non-rational influences on the mind.

SUP: See Separate Underlying Proficiency.

Superstrate Language: (1) A prestigious language that has influenced less prestigious languages (e.g. minority languages), usually resulting in language shift. (2) The main source language, usually the language of the socially dominant group, for the lexicon and grammar of a pidgin or creole, which is also influenced by other languages known as substrate languages.

Syntax: The study of how words combine into sentences. Rules governing the ways words are combined and organized.

T

Target Language: A second or foreign language being learned or taught.

TBE: Transitional Bilingual Education. Temporary use of the child's home language in the classroom, leading to only the majority language being allowed in classroom instruction. (See Early-Exit/Late-Exit Bilingual Education Programs).

Teacher Talk: A variety of communication used by teachers in classrooms. Teacher talk is specific to the needs of instruction and classroom management, sometimes simplified as in Foreigner Talk.

TEFL: Teaching English as a Foreign Language.

Term Bank: A collection of technical terms, often on a computer database.

Terminology: The creation, selection and standardization of terms for use in specific (e.g. school curriculum) or technical (e.g. science, medicine, computing) contexts. See Corpus Planning/ Language Planning.

Territorial Principle: A claim to the right to a language within a territory. The right to use a language within a geographical area.

TESFL: Teaching English as a Second and a Foreign Language.

TESL: Teaching English as a Second Language.

TESOL: (1) Teachers of English to Speakers of Other Languages; (2) Teaching English as a Second or Other Language.

Text: This can refer both to spoken and written language.

Threshold Level: (1) A level of language competence a person has to reach to gain cognitive benefits from owning two languages. (2) The threshold level is used by the Council of Europe to define a minimal level of language proficiency needed to function in a foreign language. Various contexts are specified where languages are used and students are expected to reach specific objectives to attain the threshold level.

Title VII: The Bilingual Education Act: Title VII of the Elementary and Secondary Education Act of 1968, established US federal policy for bilingual education for language minority students. Reauthorized in 1994 as part of the Improving America's Schools Act, Title VII's new provisions increased the state role and aided applicants seeking to develop bilingual proficiency.

Total Communication: A method of teaching deaf and hearing impaired children based on the use of both sign language and spoken language.

TPR: Total Physical Response – a method of second language learning.

Tracking: The use of homogeneous ability groups in teaching (also called setting, streaming, banding, ability grouping).

Trade Language: A language that is adopted or evolves as a medium of communication in business or commerce between different language groups. Many pidgins evolved as trade languages in ports or centers of commerce.

Transfer: See Language Transfer.

Transitional Bilingual Education (TBE): The primary purpose of these US programs is to facilitate a student's transition to an all-English instructional environment while initially using the native language in the classroom. Transitional bilingual education programs vary in the amount of native language instruction provided and the duration of the program.

Transliteration: The notation of one language in the writing system of another language (e.g. Chinese or Russian place names written in Roman script).

Two-Way Programs: Also known as Developmental Bilingual Education, Two-Way Dual Language Programs and Two-Way Bilingual/Immersion Programs. Two languages are used for approximately equal time in the curriculum. Classrooms have a mixture of native speakers of each language.

U

UK: United Kingdom (England, Scotland, Northern Ireland and Wales).

UN: United Nations.

UNESCO: United Nations Educational, Scientific and Cultural Organization.

Unmarked Language: A majority language distinct from a minority language, and usually highly valued in society.

US: United States.

US English: An organization committed to making English the official language of the United States.

V

Vernacular: An indigenous or heritage language of an individual or community. A vernacular language is used to define a native language as opposed to (1) a classical language such as Latin and Greek, (2) an internationally used language such as English and French, (3) the official or national language of a country.

Vertical Bilingualism: Situations where two languages of different status (or a language and a dialect) co-exist, particularly within the individual.

W

Wanderarbeiter: A nomadic, seasonal worker, usually from a 'foreign' country. An itinerant worker in a 'foreign' country.

Whole Language Approach: An amorphous cluster of ideas about language development in the classroom. The approach is against Basal Readers (see above) and Phonics (see above) in learning to read. Generally the approach supports an holistic and integrated learning of reading, writing, spelling and oracy. The language used must have relevance and meaning to the child. Language development engages co-operative sharing and cultivates empowerment. The use of language for communication is stressed; the function rather than the form of language.

Withdrawal Classes: Also known as 'pull-out' classes. Children are taken out of an ordinary class for special instruction.

Writing Conference: The teacher and the student discuss the writing the student is to complete, the process of composing. The teacher plans regular discussions with individual students about their writing to promote personal awareness of their style, content, confidence and communication of ideas.

Z

Zone of Proximal Development: New areas of learning within a student's reach. Vygotsky saw the zone of proximal development as the distance between a student's level of development as revealed when problem solving without adult help, and the level of potential development as determined by a student problem solving in collaboration with peers or teachers. The zone of proximal development is where new understandings are possible through collaborative interaction and inquiry.

Bibliography

A

ABDULAZIZ, M. H., 1991, Language in Education: A Comparative Study of the Situation in Tanzania, Ethiopia and Somalia. In O. GARCÍA (ed.), *Bilingual Education: Focusschrift in Honor of Joshua A. Fishman*. Amsterdam/Philadelphia: John Benjamins.

ABUDARHAM, S. (ed.), 1987, *Bilingualism and the Bilingual. An Interdisciplinary Approach to Pedagogical and Remedial Issues*. Slough, United Kingdom: NFER-NELSON.

ABU-RABIA, S., 1996, Druze Minority Students Learning Hebrew in Israel. *Journal of Multilingual and Multicultural Development*, 17 (6), 415-426.

ACAC (previously Curriculum Council for Wales), 1993, *Developing a Curriculum Cymreig*. Cardiff: ACAC.

ADCOCK, J. C., 1987, Maori and English: New Zealand's Bilingual Problem. *Language Problems and Language Planning*, 11 (2), 208-213.

ADLER, M., 1977, *Collective and Individual Bilingualism*. Hamburg: Helmut Buske Verlag.

ADVISORY PLANNING COMMITTEE, 1986, *Irish and the Education System: An Analysis of Examination Results*. Dublin: Bord na Gaeilge.

AELLEN, C. & LAMBERT, W. E., 1969, Ethnic Identification and Personality Adjustments of Canadian Adolescents of Mixed English-French Parentage. *Canadian Journal of Behavioural Science*, 1 (2), 69-82.

AFOLAYAN, A., 1995, Aspects of Bilingual Education in Nigeria. In B. M. JONES & P. A. S. GHUMAN (eds), *Bilingualism, Education and Identity. Essays in Honour of Jac L. Williams*. Cardiff: University of Wales Press.

AGER, D., 1995, *'Francophonie' in the 1990s: Problems and Opportunities*. Clevedon: Multilingual Matters.

AGNEW, J. A., 1981, Language Shift and the Politics of Language: The Case of the Celtic Languages of the British Isles. *Language Problems and Language Planning*, 5 (1), 1-10.

AGUIRRE, A., 1992, The Sociolinguistic Basis for Code Switching in Bilingual Discourse and in Bilingual Instruction. In R. V. PADILLA & A. H. BENAVIDES (eds), *Critical Perspectives on Bilingual Education Research*. Tempe, AZ: Bilingual Press.

AIKMAN, S., 1995, Language, Literacy and Bilingual Education: An Amazon People's Strategies for Cultural Maintenance. *International Journal of Educational Development*, 15 (4), 411-422.

AITCHISON, J., 1991, *Language Change: Progress or Decay?* (2nd edition). Cambridge: Cambridge University Press.

AITCHISON, J., 1996, *The Seeds of Speech*. Cambridge: Cambridge University Press.

AITCHISON, J. & CARTER, H., 1994, *A Geography of the Welsh Language 1961-1991*. Cardiff: University of Wales Press.

AKUTAGAWA, M., 1987, A Linguistic Minority under the Protection of its Own Ethnic State: A Case Study in an Irish Gaeltacht. In G. MACEOIN *et al.* (eds), *Third International Conference on Minority Languages: Celtic Papers*. Clevedon: Multilingual Matters.

ALATIS, J. E. & STACZEK, J. J. (eds), 1985, *Perspectives on Bilingualism and Bilingual Education*. Washington, DC: Georgetown University Press.

ALBANESE, R., 1987, Three Rationales for Second-Language Study. *The Canadian Modern Language Review*, 43 (3), 461-470.

ALBÓ, X., 1995, *Bolivia Plurilingue: Guia para Planificadores y Educadores* (Three volumes). La Paz, Bolivia: UNICEF-CIPCA.

ALBÓ, X. & D'EMILO, L., 1990, Indigenous Languages and Intercultural Bilingual Education in Bolivia. *Prospects (UNESCO)*, 20 (3), 321-330.

ALDRIDGE, M. (ed.), 1995, *Child Language*. Clevedon: Multilingual Matters.

ALEXANDER, S. & BAKER, K., 1992, Some Ethical Issues in Applied Social Psychology: The Case of Bilingual Education and Self-Esteem. *Journal of Applied Social Psychology*, 22, 1741-1757.

ALEXANDER, S. & BAKER, K., 1995, A Marxist Analysis of the Bilingual Education Movement: The Emergence of an Elite in Language Minorities. *Sociological Spectrum*, 15 (2), 99-116.

ALFORD, M. R., 1987, Developing Facilitative Reading Programmes in Third World Countries. *Journal of Multilingual and Multicultural Development*, 8 (6), 493-511.

ALLADINA, S. & EDWARDS, V., 1991, *Multilingualism in the British Isles*. London: Longman.

ALLARD, R. & LANDRY, R., 1994, Subjective Ethnolinguistic Vitality: A Comparison of Two Measures. *International Journal of the Sociology of Language*, 108, 117-144.

ALLARDT, E., 1979, *Implications of the Ethnic Revival in Modern, Industrialized Society. A Comparative Study of the Linguistic Minorities in Western Europe*. Commentationes Scientiarum Socialium 12. Helsinki: Societas Scientiarum Fennica.

ALLARDT, E. & STARCK, C., 1981, *Sprakgranser och Samhallsstruktur*. Stockholm: Almquist and Wiksell.

ALLARDYCE, R., 1987, Planned Bilingualism: The Soviet Case. *Journal of Russian Studies*, 52, 3-16.

ALLEN, P. & CARROLL, S., 1987, Evaluation of Classroom Processes in a Canadian Core French Programme. *Evaluation and Research in Education*, 1 (2), 49-61.

ALLEN, P. *et al.*, 1989, Restoring the Balance: A Response to Hammerly. *The Canadian Modern Language Review*, 45 (4), 770-776.

ALLEYNE, M. C., Language and Society in St. Lucia. *Caribbean Studies*, 1 (1), 1-10.

ALVA, S. A. & PADILLA, A. M., 1991, Academic Invulnerability Among Mexican Americans: The Importance of Protective Resources and Appraisals. *Hispanic Journal of Behavioural Sciences*, 13 (1), 18-34.

ALVAREZ, L. P. & HAKUTA, K., 1992, Enriching Our Views of Bilingualism and Bilingual Education. *Educational Researcher*, 21 (2), 4-6.

AMADIO, M., 1990, Two Decades of Bilingual Education in Latin America 1970-90. *Prospects*, 20 (3), 305-310.

AMBROSE, J. E. & WILLIAMS, C. H., 1981, On the Spatial Definition of Minority. In E. HAUGEN, J. D. MCCLURE & D. THOMSON (eds), *Minority Languages Today*. Edinburgh: Edinburgh University Press.

AMERICAN PARK NETWORK, 1993, *Ellis Island and the Statue of Liberty: The Immigrant Journey* (Third edition). San Francisco, CA: American Park Network.

AMERICAN PSYCHOLOGICAL ASSOCIATION, 1982, *Review of Department of Education Report entitled 'Effectiveness of Bilingual Education: A Review of Literature'*. Letter to the Congressional Hispanic Caucus, April 22nd.

AMMON, U., 1991, The Status of German and Other Languages in the European Community. In F. COULMAS (ed.), *A Language Policy for the European Community*. Berlin/New York: Mouton de Gruyter.

AMMON, U. (ed.), 1992, Language Spread Policy. Languages of Former Colonial Powers and Former Colonies. *International Journal of the Sociology of Language*, 107.

AMOROSE, T., 1989, The Official-Language Movement in the United States: Contexts, Issues and Activities. *Language Problems and Language Planning*, 13 (3), 264-279.

ANDERSEN, R., 1983, Introduction: A Language Acquisition Interpretation of Pidginization and Creolization. In R. ANDERSEN (ed.), *Pidginization and Creolization as Language Acquisition*. Rowley, MA: Newbury House.

ANDERSON, A. B., 1990, Comparative Analysis of Language Minorities: A Sociopolitical Framework. *Journal of Multilingual and Multicultural Development*, 11 (1&2), 119-135.

ANDERSON, C. A., 1966, Literacy and Schooling on the Development Threshold. In C. A. ANDERSON & M. BOWMAN (eds), *Education and Economic Development*. London: Frank Cass.

ANDERSON, T. & BOYER, M., 1970, *Bilingual Schooling in the United States* (Two volumes). Austin, TX: Southwest Educational Laboratory.

ANDREASEN, A. R., 1994, Social Marketing: Its Definition and Domain. *Journal of Public Policy and Marketing*, 13 (1), 108-114.

ANDRES, F., 1990, Language Relations in Multilingual Switzerland. *Multilingual*, 9 (1), 11-45.

ANISFELD, E., 1964, *A Comparison of the Cognitive Functioning of Monolinguals and Bilinguals*. Unpublished Ph.D. thesis, McGill University.

ANNANDALE, E., 1985, French Teacher Training: Problems and Solutions: A Manitoba Perspective. *The Canadian Modern Language Review*, 41 (5), 910-916.

APLIN, T. R. W., CRAWSHAW, J. W., ROSELMAN, E. A. & WILLIAMS, A. L., 1985, *Introduction to Language* (Second edition). Sevenoaks, Kent: Hodder and Stoughton.

APPEL, R., 1988, The Language Education of Immigrant Workers' Children in The Netherlands. In T. SKUTNABB-KANGAS & J. CUMMINS (eds), *Minority Education: From Shame to Struggle*. Clevedon: Multilingual Matters, 71-77.

APPEL, R., 1989, Bilingualism and Cognitive-Linguistic Development: Evidence from a Word Association Task and a Sorting Task. *Journal of Multilingual and Multicultural Development*, 10 (3), 183-196.

APPEL, R. & MUYSKEN, P., 1987, *Language Contact and Bilingualism*. London: Edward Arnold.

ARENDS, J., MUYSKEN, P. & SMITH, N. (eds), 1995, *Pidgins and Creoles: An Introduction*. Amsterdam/Philadelphia: John Benjamins.

ARGUE, V. & HOWARD, J., 1990, *Teaching French in French Immersion: An Overview at Grades 6 to 8*. Ontario Modern Language Centre, Ontario Institute for Studies in Education.

ARIAS, B. & CASANOVA, U. (eds), 1993, *Bilingual Education: Politics, Research and Practice*. Berkeley, CA: McCutchan.

ARNBERG, L., 1981, *Bilingual Education of Young Children in England and Wales*. University of Linkoping, Sweden, Department of Education.

ARNBERG, L., 1987, *Raising Children Bilingually: The Pre-School Years*. Clevedon: Multilingual Matters.

ARTHUR, L. & HURD, S. (eds), 1992, *The Adult Language Learner: A Guide to Good Teaching Practice*. London: Centre for Information on Language Teaching and Research.

ARTIGAL, J. M., 1991, *The Catalan Immersion Program: A European Point of View*. Norwood, NJ: Ablex.

ARTIGAL, J. M., 1993, Catalan and Basque Immersion Programmes. In H. BAETENS BEARDSMORE (ed.), *European Models of Bilingual Education*. Clevedon: Multilingual Matters.

ARTIGAL, J. M., 1996, Plurilingual Education in Catalonia. In R. JOHNSON & M. SWAIN (eds), *Immersion Education: International Perspectives*. Cambridge: Cambridge University Press.

ASHER, J., 1977, *Learning Another Language Through Actions*. Los Gatos, CA: Sky Oaks.

ASHER, R. E. & SIMPSON, J. M. Y. (eds), 1994, *The Encyclopedia of Language and Linguistics* (Ten volumes). Oxford: Pergamon.

ATTINASI, J. J., 1994, Racism, Language Variety, and Urban US Minorities: Issues in Bilingualism and Bidialectalism. In S. GREGORY & R. SANJEK (eds), *Race*. New Jersey: Rutgers University Press.

AU, S. Y., 1984, *Social Psychological Variables in Second Language Learning*. Unpublished M.Phil. thesis, City University, London.

AU, S. Y., 1988, A Critical Appraisal of Gardner's Social-Psychological Theory of Second-Language (L2) Learning. *Language Learning*, 38 (1), 75-100.

AUERBACH, E. R., 1989, Toward a Social-Contextual Approach to Family Literacy. *Harvard Educational Review*, 59 (2), 165-181.

AWBERY, G. M., 1987, The Position of the Welsh Language in Wales. In G. MACEOIN *et al.* (eds), *Third International Conference on Minority Languages: Celtic Papers*. Clevedon: Multilingual Matters.

AZMITIA, M., COOPER, C. R., GARCÍA, E. E., ITTEL, A., JOHANSON, B., LOPEZ, E., MARTINA-CHAVEZ, R. & RIVERA, L., 1994, *Links Between Home and School among Low-Income Mexican-American and European-American Families*. United States Department of Education: National Centre for Research on Cultural Diversity and Second Language Learning.

B

BACA, L. & DE VALENZUELA, J. S., 1994, *Reconstructing the Bilingual Special Education Interface*. National Clearinghouse for Bilingual Education. Program Information Guide Series, 20.

BACHI, R., 1956, A Statistical Analysis of the Revival of Hebrew in Israel. *Scripta Hierosolymitana*, 3, 179-247.

BACHMAN, L. F., 1990, *Fundamental Considerations in Language Testing*. Oxford: Oxford University Press.

BADETS, J. & CHUI, T. W. L., 1994, *Focus on Canada: Canada's Changing Immigrant Population*. Ottawa: Statistics Canada.

BAETENS BEARDSMORE, H., 1986, *Bilingualism: Basic Principles*. Clevedon: Multilingual Matters.

BAETENS BEARDSMORE, H., 1993, The European School Model. In H. BAETENS BEARDSMORE (ed.), *European Models of Bilingual Education*. Clevedon: Multilingual Matters.

BAETENS BEARDSMORE, H., 1996, Reconciling Content Acquisition and Language Acquisition in Bilingual Classrooms. *Journal of Multilingual and Multicultural Development*, 17 (2-4), 114-122.

BAETENS BEARDSMORE, H. (ed.), 1993, *European Models of Bilingual Education*. Clevedon: Multilingual Matters.

BAETENS BEARDSMORE, H. & LEBRUN, N., 1991, Trilingual Education in the Grand Duchy of Luxembourg. In O. GARCÍA (ed.), *Bilingual Education: Focusschrift in Honor of Joshua A. Fishman*. Amsterdam/Philadelphia: John Benjamins.

BAETENS BEARDSMORE, H. & SWAIN, M., 1985, Designing Bilingual Education: Aspects of Immersion and 'European School' Models. *Journal of Multilingual and Multicultural Development*, 6 (1), 1-15.

BAETENS BEARDSMORE, H. & VAN BEECK, H., 1984, Multilingual Television Supply and Language Shift in Brussels. *International Journal of the Sociology of Language*, 48, 65-79.

BAHRICK, H. P. *et al.*, 1994, Fifty Years of Language Maintenance and Language Dominance in Bilingual Hispanic Immigrants. *Journal of Experimental Psychology*, 123 (3), 264-283.

BAIN, B., 1975, Toward an Integration of Piaget and Vygotsky: Bilingual Considerations. *Linguistics*, 160, 7-19.

BAIN, B. & YU, A., 1980, Cognitive Consequences of Raising Children Bilingually: 'One Parent, One Language'. *Canadian Journal of Psychology*, 34 (4), 304-313.

BAIN, B. & YU, A., 1984, The Development of the Body Percept among Working- and Middle-Class Unilinguals and Bilinguals. In M. PARADIS & Y. LEBRUN (eds), *Early Bilingualism and Child Development*. Lisse, Holland: Swets and Zeitlinger.

BAIN, B. & YU, A., 1987, *Issues in Second-Language Education in Canada, Contemporary Educational Issues*. Toronto: The Canadian Mosaic, Copp Clark Pitman Ltd.

BAINER, D. L., 1993, Essential Skills for Effective Minority Teacher Education. *Teacher Education Quarterly*, 19-29.

BAKER, C., 1984, Two Models for Curriculum Development in Minority Languages. In P. WILLIAMS (ed.), *Special Education in Minority Communities*. Milton Keynes: Open University Press.

BAKER, C., 1985, *Aspects of Bilingualism in Wales*. Clevedon: Multilingual Matters

BAKER, C., 1988a, *Key Issues in Bilingualism and Bilingual Education*. Clevedon: Multilingual Matters.

BAKER, C., 1988b, Normative Testing and Bilingual Populations. *Journal of Multilingual and Multicultural Development*, 9 (5), 399-409.

BAKER, C., 1991, The Effectiveness of Bilingual Education. *Journal of Multilingual and Multicultural Development*, 11 (4), 269-277.

BAKER, C., 1992, *Attitudes and Language*. Clevedon: Multilingual Matters.

BAKER, C., 1993, Bilingual Education in Wales. In H. BAETENS BEARDSMORE (ed.), *European Models of Bilingual Education*. Clevedon: Multilingual Matters.

BAKER, C., 1995a, *A Parents' and Teachers' Guide to Bilingualism*. Clevedon: Multilingual Matters.

BAKER, C., 1995b, Bilingual Education and Assessment. In B. M. JONES & P. A. S. GHUMAN (eds), *Bilingualism, Education and Identity. Essays in Honour of Jac L. Williams*. Cardiff: University of Wales Press.

BAKER, C., 1996a, *Foundations of Bilingual Education and Bilingualism* (Second edition). Clevedon: Multilingual Matters.

BAKER, C., 1996b, Educating for Bilingualism: Key Themes and Issues. In P. KNIGHT & R. SWANWICK (eds), *Bilingualism and the Education of Deaf Children: Advances in Practice*. Leeds, United Kingdom: ADEDC, School of Education, University of Leeds.

BAKER, C. & DAVIES, P., 1982, Factors Affecting the Guidance of Welsh as an Option Choice in the Comprehensive School. *The Counsellor*, 3 (6), 1-21.

BAKER, C. & GRIFFITH, C. L., 1983, Provision of Materials and Tests for Welsh Speaking Pupils with Learning Difficulties: A National Survey. *Educational Research*, 25 (1), 6-70.

BAKER, C. & HINDE, J., 1984, Language Background Classification. *Journal of Multilingual and Multicultural Development*, 5 (1), 43-56.

BAKER, K. A., 1987, Comment on Willig's 'A Meta Analysis of Selected Studies of Bilingual Education'. *Review of Educational Research*, 57 (3), 351-362.

BAKER, K. A. *et al.*, 1992, Misled by Bad Theory. *Bilingual Research Journal*, 16 (1&2), 63-89.

BAKER, K. A. & DE KANTER, A. A., 1981, *Effectiveness of Bilingual Education: A Review of Literature*. Washington, DC: Office of Planning, Budget and Evaluation, United States Department of Education.

BAKER, K. A. & DE KANTER, A. A., 1983, *Bilingual Education*. Lexington, MA: Lexington Books.

BAKER, K. A. & ROSSELL, C., 1987, An Implementation Problem: Specifying the Target Group for Bilingual Education. *Educational Policy*, 1 (2), 249-270.

BALKAN, L., 1970, *Les Effets du Bilingualisme Français: Anglais sur les Aptitudes Intellectuelles*. Brussels: Aimav.

BANKS, J., 1986a, Multicultural Education and Its Critics: Britain and the United States. In S. MODGIL, G. VERMA, K. MALLICK & C. MODGIL (eds), *Multicultural Education: The Interminable Debate*. Lewes: Falmer Press.

BANKS, J., 1986b, Multicultural Education: Development, Paradigms and Goals. In J. BANKS & J. LYNCH (eds), *Multicultural Education in Western Societies*. Eastbourne: Holt, Rinehart and Winston Ltd.

BANKS, J., 1988, *Multiethnic Education: Theory and Practice* (Second edition). Newton, MA: Allyn and Bacon.

BANKS, J. & LYNCH, J. (eds), 1986, *Multicultural Education in Western Societies*. Eastbourne: Holt, Rinehart and Winston.

BARBER, M. B., 1993, With Schools Becoming Towers of Babel, California Stumbles Along Without a State Bilingual Education Program. *California Journal*, 24 (6), 17-18.

BARBOUR, S., 1991, Language and Nationalism in the German-Speaking Countries. In P. MEARA & A. RYAN (eds), *Language and Nation*. London: Center for Information on Language Teaching and Research (CILT).

BARKE, E. M., 1933, A Study of the Comparative Intelligence of Children in Certain Bilingual and Monoglot Schools in South Wales. *British Journal of Educational Psychology*, 3, 237-250.

BARKE, E. M. & PARRY WILLIAMS, D. E., 1938, A Further Study of Comparative Intelligence of Children in Certain Bilingual and Monolingual Schools in South Wales. *British Journal of Educational Psychology*, 8, 63-67.

BARNUM, M., 1984, In Support of Bilingual/Bicultural Education for Deaf Children. *American Annals of the Deaf*, 129 (5), 404-08.

BARONA, M. S. DE & BARONA, A., 1992, Assessment of Bilingual Preschool Children. In R. V. PADILLA & A. H. BENAVIDES (eds), *Critical Perspectives on Bilingual Education Research*. Tempe, AZ: Bilingual Press.

BARRERA, R. B., 1983, Bilingual Reading in the Primary Grades: Some Questions About Questionable Views and Practices. In T. H. ESCOBEDO (ed.), *Early Childhood Bilingual Education*. New York/London: Teachers College Press.

BARRIK, H. C. & SWAIN, M., 1976, A Longitudinal Study of Bilingual and Cognitive Development. *International Journal of Psychology*, 11, 251-263.

BARTH, F., 1966, *Models of Social Organization* (Occasional Paper No. 23). London: Royal Anthropological Institute.

BARTSCH, R., 1987, *Norms of Language*. London: Longman.

BATIBO, H. M., 1995, The Growth of Kiswahili as Language of Education and Administration in Tanzania. In M. PUTZ (ed.), *Discrimination through Language in Africa? Perspectives on the Namibian Experience*. New York: Mouton de Gruyter.

BEATY, S., 1985, Post-Secondary Bilingual Education in British Columbia: To Be or Not To Be. *The Canadian Modern Language Review*, 41 (5), 816-818.

BEAUDOIN, M., CUMMINS, J., DUNLOP, H., GENESEE, F. & OBADIA, A., 1981, Bilingual Education: A Comparison of Welsh and Canadian Experiences. *The Canadian Modern Language Review*, 37, 498-509.

BEL, A., 1993, *Some Results of the Immersion Programme in Catalonia*. Notícies del SEDEC/Newsletter of the Servei d'Ensenyament del Catalonia 1993.

BELLIN, W., 1984, Welsh and English in Wales. In P. TRUDGILL (ed.), *Language in the British Isles*. Cambridge: Cambridge University Press.

BELLIN, W., 1989, Ethnicity and Welsh Bilingual Education. In G. DAY & G. REES (eds), *Contemporary Wales: An Annual Review of Economic and Social Research* (Vol. 3) Cardiff: University of Wales Press.

BELLIN, W., 1995, Psychology and Bilingual Education: Intelligence Tests and the Influence of Pedagogy. In B. M. JONES & P. A. S. GHUMAN (eds), *Bilingualism, Education and Identity. Essays in Honour of Jac L. Williams*. Cardiff: University of Wales Press.

BEN-ZEEV, S., 1977a, The Influence of Bilingualism on Cognitive Strategy and Cognitive Development. *Child Development*, 48, 1009-1018.

BEN-ZEEV, S., 1977b, The Effect of Bilingualism in Children from Spanish-English Low Economic Neighbourhoods on Cognitive Development and Cognitive Strategy. *Working Papers on Bilingualism*, 14, 83-122.

BEN-ZEEV, S., 1984, Bilingualism and Cognitive Development. In N. MILLER (ed.), *Bilingualism and Language Disability: Assessment and Remediation*. London: Croom Helm.

BENTAHILA, A., 1983, *Language Attitudes among Arabic-French Bilinguals in Morocco*. Clevedon: Multilingual Matters,

BENTAHILA, A., 1987, Morocco: Where Bilingualism is the Norm. *The Bilingual Family Newsletter*, March 1987, pages 1-2. Clevedon: Multilingual Matters.

BENTAHILA, A. & DAVIES, E. E., 1993, Language Revival: Restoration or Transformation? *Journal of Multilingual and Multicultural Development*, 14 (5), 355-374.

BENTON, R. A., 1986, Schools as Agents for Language Revival in Ireland and New Zealand. In B. SPOLSKY (ed.), *Language and Education in Multilingual Settings*. Clevedon: Multilingual Matters.

BENTON, R. A., 1988, The Maori Language in New Zealand Education. *Language, Culture and Curriculum*, 1 (2), 75-83.

BENTON, R. A., 1991, 'Tomorrow's Schools' and the Revitalization of Maori. In O. GARCÍA (ed.), *Bilingual Education: Focusschrift in Honor of Joshua A. Fishman*. Amsterdam/Philadelphia: John Benjamins.

BENYON, J. & TOOHEY, K., 1991, Heritage Language Education in British Columbia: Policy and Programs. *Canadian Modern Language Review*, 47 (4), 606-616.

BEREITER, C. & SCARDAMELIA, M., 1981, From Conversation to Composition: The Role of Instruction in a Development Process. In R. GLASER (ed.), *Advances in Instructional Psychology*, Volume 2. Hillsdale, NJ: Erlbaum.

BERLINER, D. C., 1988, Meta-Comments: A Discussion of Critiques of L. M. Dunn's Monograph 'Bilingual Hispanic Children on the United States Mainland'. *Hispanic Journal of Behavioural Sciences*, 10 (3), 273-300.

BERNHARDT, E. B., 1991, A Psycholinguistic Perspective on Second Language Literacy. In J. H. HULSTIJN & J. F. MATTER (eds), *Reading in Two Languages* (*AILA Review*, 8, 31-44).

BERNHARDT, E. B. & SCHRIER, L., 1992, The Development of Immersion Teachers. In E. B. BERNHARDT (ed.), *Life in Language Immersion Classrooms*. Clevedon: Multilingual Matters.

BERNSTEIN, D. K., 1989, Assessing Children with Limited English Proficiency: Current Perspectives. *Topics in Language Disorders*, 9 (3), 15-20.

BERRY, G. L. & MITCHELL-KERNAN, C., 1982, *Television and the Socialization of the Minority Child*. New York: Academic Press.

BERTHOLD, M., 1992, An Australian Experiment in French Immersion. *Canadian Modern Language Review*, 49 (1), 112-125.

BERTHOLD, M., 1995a, Multiplicité de Modeles en Australie. *Revue Internationale d'Education: Sevres No. 7*, 59-69. Sevres, France: Centre International d'Etudes Pedagogiques.

BERTHOLD, M. (ed.), 1995b, *Rising to the Bilingual Challenge. Ten Years of Queensland Secondary School Immersion*. Canberra: The National Languages and Literacy Institute of Australia.

BETANCES, S., 1985, 'My People Made it Without Bilingual Education – What's Wrong With Your People?' *Official Journal of the California School Boards Association*, 44, 7.

BETTS, C., 1976, *Culture in Crisis, The Future of the Welsh Language*. Wirral: Ffynnon Press.

BEYNON, J. & TOOHEY, K., 1991, Heritage Language: Education in British Columbia: Policy and Programs. *The Canadian Modern Language Review*, 47 (4), 606-616.

BHATIA, T. K. & RITCHIE, W. C., 1989, Introduction: Current Issues in 'Mixing' and 'Switching'. *World Englishes*, 8 (3), 261-264.

BIALYSTOK, E., 1981, The Role of Conscious Strategies in Second Language Proficiency. *Modern Language Journal*, 65, 24-35.

BIALYSTOK, E., 1987a, Influences of Bilingualism on Metalinguistic Development. *Second Language Research*, 3 (2), 154-166.

BIALYSTOK, E., 1987b, Words as Things: Development of Word Concept by Bilingual Children. *Studies in Second Language Learning*, 9, 133-140.

BIALYSTOK, E., 1988, Levels of Bilingualism and Levels of Linguistic Awareness. *Developmental Psychology*, 24 (4), 560-567.

BIALYSTOK, E. (ed.), 1991, *Language Processing in Bilingual Children*. Cambridge: Cambridge University Press.

BIALYSTOK, E. & RYAN, E. B., 1985, Toward a Definition of Metalinguistic Skill. *Merrill-Palmer Quarterly*, 31 (3), 229-251.

BICKERTON, D., 1980, Decreolisation and the Creole Continuum. In A. VALDMAN & A. HIGHFIELD (eds), *Theoretical Orientations in Creole Studies*. New York: Academic Press.

BICKERTON, D., 1981, *The Roots of Language*. Ann Arbor, MI: Keroma Publishing.

BICKERTON, D., 1984, The Language Bioprogram Hypothesis. *The Behavioral and Brain Sciences*, 7, 173-188.

BILD, E. & SWAIN, M., 1989, Minority Language Students in a French Immersion Programme: Their French Proficiency. *Journal of Multilingual and Multicultural Development*, 10 (3), 255-274.

BILINGUAL EDUCATION OFFICE, CALIFORNIA DEPARTMENT OF EDUCATION, 1990, *Bilingual Education Handbook: Designing Instruction for LEP Students*. Sacramento, CA: California Department of Education.

BILINGUAL EDUCATION OFFICE, CALIFORNIA DEPARTMENT OF EDUCATION, 1990, *Bilingual Immersion Education: A Program for the Year 2000 and Beyond*. Sacramento, CA: California State Department of Education.

BILINGUAL EDUCATION OFFICE, CALIFORNIA DEPARTMENT OF EDUCATION, 1994, *Assessing Students in Bilingual Contexts: Provisional Guidelines*. Sacramento, CA: California State Department of Education.

BIURA DO SPARAW MNIEJSZOSCI NARODOWYCH (Bulletin From the Office for Ethnic Minorities), 1993, *Mniejszosci narodowe w Polsce w 1993 roku*. Warsaw: Ministry of Arts and Culture Poland.

BLACKLEDGE, A. (ed.), 1994, *Teaching Bilingual Children*. Stoke-on-Trent: Trentham.

BLANCHE, P., 1992, Bilingual Crosscultural Education in Western Europe: An Overview. *RELC Journal*, 23 (2), 81-105.

BLOOMFIELD, L., 1933, *Language*. New York: Holt.

BLOOMFIELD, L., 1942, *Outline Guide for the Practical Study of Foreign Languages*. Baltimore: Linguistic Society of America.

BLOOR, T. & TAMRAT, W., 1996, Issues in Ethiopian Language Policy and Education. *Journal of Multilingual and Multicultural Development*, 17 (5), 321-338.

BOARD OF EDUCATION, 1927, *Welsh in Education and Life*. London: HMSO.

BOELENS, K. (original text), GORTER, D. & ZONDAG, K. (revised by), 1987, *The Frisian Language*. Leeuwarden: Information Service of the Province of Friesland.

BONYUN, R., 1985, The Ottawa High School Bilingual Program: Views of Two Groups of Graduates. *The Canadian Modern Language Review*, 41 (5), 842-864.

BOUNTROGIANNI, M., 1988, Bilingualism and Metaphor Comprehension. *European Journal of Psychology of Education*, 3 (1), 53-64.

BOURHIS, R. Y., 1984, *Conflict and Language Planning in Quebec*. Clevedon: Multilingual Matters.

BOURHIS, R. Y. & GILES, H., 1977, The Language of Intergroup Distinctiveness. In H. GILES (ed.), *Language, Ethnicity and Intergroup Relations*. London: Academic Press.

BOURHIS, R. Y., GILES, H. & TAJFEL, H., 1973, Language as a Determinant of Welsh Identity. *European Journal of Social Psychology*, 3, 447-460.

BOURNE, J., 1986, Towards An Alternative Model of Second Language Learning. In P. MEARA (ed.), *Spoken Language: Papers from the Annual Meeting of the British Association for Applied Linguistics*. London: Centre for Information on Language Teaching and Research.

BOURNE, J., 1989a, Bringing Bilingual Pupils into the Mainstream. *Topic: Practical Applications of Research in Education*, 27, 2-3.

BOURNE, J., 1989b, *Moving into the Mainstream: LEA Provision for Bilingual Pupils*. Windsor: NFER/Nelson.

BOURNE, J., 1990, Local Authority Provision for Bilingual Pupils: ESL, Bilingual Support and Community Languages Teaching. *Educational Research*, 32 (1), 3-13.

BOUVET, D., 1990, *The Path to Language. Bilingual Education for Deaf Children*. Clevedon: Multilingual Matters.

BOVAIR, K. & BOVAIR, M., 1992, *Modern Languages for All*. London: Kogan Page.

BOWEN, E. G., 1959, Le Pays de Galles. *Transactions of the Institute of British Geographers*, 26, 1-23.

BOWEN, E. G. & CARTER, H., 1974, Preliminary Observations on the Distribution of the Welsh Language at the 1971 Census. *Geographical Journal*, 140 (3), 432-440.

BOWEN, E. G. & CARTER, H., 1975, The Distribution of the Welsh Language in 1971: An Analysis. *Geography*, 60 (1), 1-15.

BOWIE, F., 1993, Wales from Within: Conflicting Interpretations of Welsh Identity. In S. MACDONALD (ed.), *Inside European Identities*. Oxford: Berg.

BOYER, J. & BOOTH, J., 1985, Preparation of Teachers of French at the University of Saskatchewan. *The Canadian Modern Language Review*, 41 (5), 917-930.

BOYLE, E. R., 1990, Is There a Bilingual Answer for Hong Kong? *Evaluation and Research in Education*, 4 (3), 117-127.

BRACE, J., 1982, The Educational State of Wales: The Debate Reviewed. *Education for Development*, 7 (2), 63-72.

BRAINE, M. D., 1987, Acquiring and Processing First and Second Languages. In P. HOMEL, M. PALIJ & D. AARONSON (eds), *Childhood Bilingualism: Aspects of Linguistic, Cognitive and Social Development*. Hillsdale, NJ: Lawrence Erlbaum.

BRENZINGER, M., 1997, Language Contact and Language Displacement. In F. COULMAS (ed.), *The Handbook of Sociolinguistics*. Oxford: Blackwell.

BRETON, R., 1991, The Handicaps of Language Planning in Africa. In D. F. MARSHALL (ed.), *Language Planning: Focusschrift in Honor of Joshua A. Fishman*. Amsterdam: John Benjamins.

BRIGHT, W. (ed.), 1992, *The International Encyclopedia of Linguistics*. Oxford: Oxford University Press.

BRIGHT, W., 1997, Social Factors in Language Change. In F. COULMAS (ed.), *The Handbook of Sociolinguistics*. Oxford: Blackwell.

BRITZMAN, D. P., 1993, The Ordeal of Knowledge: Rethinking the Possibilities of Multicultural Education. *The Review of Education*, 15 (2), 123-135.

BROOK, M. R. M., 1980, The 'Mother-Tongue' Issue in Britain: Cultural Diversity or Control? *British Journal of Sociology of Education*, 1 (3), 237-256.

BROUDIG, F., 1995, *La Pratique du Breton: de l'ancien Régime à nos Jours*. Rennes: Presses Universitaires de Rennes.

BROWN, D., 1997, *Education Policy and Language Learning for a Multilingual Society*. Durban: Education Policy Unit, University of Natal.

BROWN, H., 1980, *Principles of Language Learning and Teaching*. New Jersey: Englewood Cliffs.

BROWN, H., 1981, Affective Factors in Second Language Learning. In J. ALATIS, H. ALTMAN & P. ALATIS (eds), *The Second Language Classroom: Directions for the 1980's*. New York: Oxford University Press.

BRUCK, M., 1978, The Suitability of Early French Immersion Programs for the Language-Disabled Child. *Canadian Journal of Education*, 3, 51-72.

BRUCK, M., 1985, Predictors of Transfer out of Early French Immersion Programs. *Applied Psycholinguistics*, 6, 39-61.

BRUCK, M. & GENESEE, F., 1995, Phonological Awareness in Young Second Language Learners. *Journal of Child Language*, 22(2), 307-324.

BRUCK, M., LAMBERT, W. E. & TUCKER, G. R., 1976, *Cognitive Consequences of Bilingual Schooling: The St. Lambert Project Through Grade 6*. Unpublished manuscript. Department of Psychology, McGill University.

BRUMFIT, C., 1995, *Language Education in the National Curriculum*. Oxford: Blackwell.

BRUNER, J. S., 1975, Language as an Instrument of Thought. In A. DAVIES (ed.), *Problems of Language and Learning*. London: Heinemann.

BULL, B. L., FRUEHLING, R. T. & CHATTERGY, V., 1992, *The Ethics of Multicultural and Bilingual Education*. New York: Teachers College Press.

BULLIVANT, B. M., 1981, *The Pluralist*

Dilemma in Education: Six Case Studies. Sydney: Allen and Unwin.

BULLIVANT, B. M., 1984, *Pluralism: Cultural Maintenance and Evolution*. Clevedon: Multilingual Matters.

BULLIVANT, B. M., 1986, Towards Radical Multiculturalism: Resolving Tensions in Curriculum and Educational Planning. In S. MODGIL, G. VERMA, K. MALLICK & C. MODGIL (eds), *Multicultural Education: The Interminable Debate*. Lewes: Falmer Press.

BULLIVANT, B. M., 1994, Overtheorizing Versus Undertheorizing Plural Society and the Consequences. *International Journal of the Sociology of Language*, 110, 125-130.

BULLOCK REPORT (DEPARTMENT OF EDUCATION AND SCIENCE), 1975, *A Language for Life*. London: HMSO.

BULWER, J., 1995, European Schools: Languages For All? *Journal of Multilingual and Multicultural Development*, 16 (6), 459-475.

BUREAU OF THE CENSUS (United States), 1989, *200 Years of Census Taking: Population and Housing Questions: 1790–1990*. Washington, DC: Bureau of the Census.

BURNABY, B., 1980, *Languages and Their Roles in Educating Native Children*. Toronto: OISE Press.

BURNABY, B., 1987, Language for Native, Ethnic, or Recent Immigrant Groups: What's the Difference? *TESL Canada Journal*, 4 (2), 9-27.

BURNABY, B., 1988, Language in Native Education in Canada. In C. B. PAULSTON (ed.), *International Handbook of Bilingualism and Bilingual Education*. New York: Greenwood Press.

BURNS, G. E. & OLSON, C. P., 1989, Planning and Professionalizing Immersion and Other FSL Programs. *The Canadian Modern Language Review*, 45 (3), 502-516.

BURSTALL, C., JAMIESON, M., COHEN, S. & HARGREAVES, M., 1974, *Primary French in the Balance*. Windsor: NFER/Nelson.

BURTON, P., DYSON, K. K. & ARDENER, S. (eds), 1994, *Bilingual Women*. Oxford: Berg.

BUSH, E., 1979, *Bilingual Education in Gwent: Parental Attitudes and Aspirations*. Unpublished M.Ed. Thesis, University of Wales.

BUSH, E., ATKINSON, P. & READ, M., 1984, *A Minority Choice: Welsh Medium Education in an Anglicised Area: Parents' Characteristics and Motives*. Polyglot 5, Fiche 1 (April).

BUTTS, R. F., 1980, *The Revival of Civic Learning*. Bloomington, IN: Phi Delta Kappa.

BYRAM, M., 1994a, Authorities and People. *International Journal of the Sociology of Language*, 110, 131-136.

BYRAM, M. *et al.*, 1994b, *Teaching-and-Learning Language-and-Culture*. Clevedon: Multilingual Matters.

C

CACIOPPO, J. T. & PETTY, R. E., 1982, Language Variables, Attitudes and Persuasion. In E. B. RYAN & H. GILES (eds), *Attitudes Towards Language Variation*. London: Edward Arnold.

CALDWELL, G., 1988, Being English in a French Quebec: On the Denial of Culture and History in a Neo-Liberal State. *Language, Culture and Curriculum*, 1 (3), 187-196.

CALDWELL, J. A. & BERTHOLD, M. J., 1995, Aspects of Bilingual Education in Australia. In B. M. JONES & P. A. S. GHUMAN (eds), *Bilingualism, Education and Identity. Essays in Honour of Jac L. Williams*. Cardiff: University of Wales Press.

CALERO-BRECKHEIMER, A. & GOETZ, E. T., 1993, Reading Strategies of Biliterate Children for English and Spanish Texts. *Reading Psychology: An International Quarterly*, 14 (3), 177-204.

CALIFORNIA STATE DEPARTMENT OF EDUCATION, 1984, *Studies on Immersion Education. A Collection for United States Educators*. Sacramento, CA: California State Department of Education.

CALIFORNIA STATE DEPARTMENT OF EDUCATION, 1989, *Foreign Language Framework*. Sacramento, CA: California State Department of Education.

CALVET, L. J., 1994, Les politiques de diffusion des langues en Afrique francophone. *International Journal of the Sociology of Language*, 107, 67-76.

CAMPBELL, G. L., 1991, *Compendium of the World's Languages*. London and New York: Routledge.

CAMPOS, S. J. & KEATINGE, H. R., 1988, The Carpinteria Language Minority Student Experience: From Theory, To Practice, To Success. In T. SKUTNABB-KANGAS & J. CUMMINS (eds), *Minority Education: From Shame to Struggle*. Clevedon: Multilingual Matters.

CANADIAN EDUCATION ASSOCIATION, 1991, *Heritage Language Programs*. In Canadian School Boards. Toronto: Canadian Education Association.

CANADIAN EDUCATION ASSOCIATION, 1992, *French Immersion Today*. Toronto: Canadian Education Association.

CANALE, M., 1983, On Some Dimensions of Language Proficiency. In J. W. OLLER (ed.), *Issues in Language Testing Research*. Rowley, MA: Newbury House.

CANALE, M., 1984, On Some Theoretical Frameworks for Language Proficiency. In C. RIVERA (ed.), *Language Proficiency and Academic Achievement*. Clevedon: Multilingual Matters.

CANALE, M. & SWAIN, M., 1980, Theoretical Bases of Communicative Approaches to Second Language Teaching and Testing. *Applied Linguistics*, 1, 1-47.

CANTONI, G. (ed.), 1996, *Stabilizing Indigenous Languages*. Arizona: Northern Arizona University.

CAREY, S. T., 1984, Reflections on a Decade of French Immersion. *The Canadian Modern Language Review*, 41 (2), 246-259.

CAREY, S. T., 1985, Trends in Enrolment and Needs for French-Instructed Programs at the Post-Secondary Level. *The Canadian Modern Language Review*, 41 (5), 877-886.

CAREY, S. T., 1987a, *The Francophone School–Immersion School Debate in Western Canada. Contemporary Educational Issues*. Toronto: The Canadian Mosaic, Copp Clark Pitman Ltd.

CAREY, S. T., 1987b, Reading Comprehension in First and Second Languages of Immersion and Francophone Students. *Canadian Journal for Exceptional Children*, 3 (4), 103-108.

CAREY, S. T., 1991a, The Culture of Literacy in Majority and Minority Language Schools. *Canadian Modern Language Review*, 47, 5, 950-976.

CAREY, S. T., 1991b, Languages, Literacy and Education. *The Canadian Modern Language Review*, 4 (5), 839-842.

CAREY, S. T. & CUMMINS, J., 1983, Achievement, Behavioral Correlates and Teachers' Perceptions of Francophone and Anglophone Immersion Students. *The Alberta Journal of Educational Research*, 29 (3), 159-167.

CARLISLE, R. S., 1989, The Writing of Anglo and Hispanic Elementary School Students in Bilingual, Submersion and Regular Programs. *Studies in Second Language Acquisition*, 11 (3), 257-280.

CARLSON, L. M. (ed.), 1994, *Cool Salsa. Bilingual Poems on Growing Up Latino in the United States*. New York: Henry Holt.

CARPENTER-HUFFMAN, M. & SAMULON, M. K., 1983, Case Studies of Delivery and Cost of Bilingual Education. In K. A. BAKER & A. A. DEKANTER (eds), *Bilingual Education*. Lexington, MA: Lexington.

CARRASQUILLO, A. 1990, Bilingual Special Education: The Important Connection. In A. L. CARRASQUILLO and R. E. BAECHER (eds), *Teaching the Bilingual Special Education Student*. Norwood, NJ: Ablex.

CARRASQUILLO, A., 1991, *Hispanic Children and Youth in the United States. A Resource Guide*. New York: Garland Publishing Inc.

CARRASQUILLO, A. & HEDLEY, C. (eds), 1993, *Whole Language and the Bilingual Learner*. Norwood, NJ: Ablex.

CARRASQUILLO, A. & RODRIGUEZ, V., 1995, *Language Minority Students in the Mainstream Classroom*. Clevedon: Multilingual Matters.

CARRINGER, D. C., 1974, Creative Thinking Abilities of Mexican Youth. The Relationship of Bilingualism. *Journal of Cross-Cultural Psychology*, 5 (4), 492-504.

CARROLL, B., 1980, *Testing Communicative Performance*. Oxford: Pergamon Press.

CARROLL, J. B., 1968, The Psychology of Language Testing. In A. DAVIES (ed.), *Language Testing Symposium. A Psycholinguistic Perspective*. Oxford: Oxford University Press.

CARROLL, J. B. & SAPON, S. M., 1959, *The Modern Language Aptitude Test (MLAT)*. New York: The Psychological Corporation.

CARTER, R. (ed.), 1990, *Knowledge About Language and the Curriculum: The LINC Reader*. London: Hodder and Stoughton.

CARTER, T. P. & CHATFIELD, M. L., 1986, Effective Bilingual Schools: Implications for Policy and Practice. *American Journal of Education*, 95 (1), 200-232.

CARTWRIGHT, D., 1987, Accommodation Among the Anglophone Minority in Quebec to Official Policy: A Shift in Traditional Patterns of Language Contact. *Journal of Multilingual and Multicultural Development*, 8 (1&2), 187-212.

CARTWRIGHT, D., 1991, Bicultural Conflict in

the Context of the Core-Periphery Model. In C. H. WILLIAMS (ed.), *Linguistic Minorities, Society and Territory*. Clevedon: Multilingual Matters.

CASANOVA, U., 1991, Bilingual Education: Politics or Pedagogy? In O. GARCÍA (ed.), *Bilingual Education: Focusschrift in Honor of Joshua A. Fishman*. Amsterdam/Philadelphia: John Benjamins.

CASANOVA, U. & ARIAS, M. B., 1993, Contextualizing Bilingual Education. In B. ARIAS & U. CASANOVA (eds), *Bilingual Education: Politics, Research and Practice*. Berkeley, CA: McCutchan.

CASANOVA, U. & CHAVEZ, S., 1992, Sociopolitical Influences on Federal Government Funding of Gifted and Talented and Bilingual Education Programs. *Educational Foundations*, 6 (4), 45-73.

CASTONGUAY, C., 1987, The Anglicization of Canada, 1971–1981. *Language Planning and Language Problems*, 11 (1), 22-34.

CATTELL, R. B., 1971, *Abilities: Their Structure, Growth and Action*. Boston: Houghton Mifflin.

CAZABON, M., LAMBERT, W. E. & HALL, G., 1993, *Two-Way Bilingual Education: A Progress Report on the Amigos Program*. Santa Cruz, CA: National Center for Research on Cultural Diversity and Second Language Learning.

CAZDEN, C. B., 1992, *Language Minority Education in the United States: Implications of the Ramirez Report*. Santa Cruz, CA: National Center for Research on Cultural Diversity and Second Language Learning.

CAZDEN, C. B. & SNOW, C. E., 1990a, Preface. In C. B. CAZDEN & C. E. SNOW (eds), *English Plus: Issues in Bilingual Education*. London: Sage.

CAZDEN, C. B. & SNOW, C. E. (eds), 1990b, English Plus: Issues in Bilingual Education. *The Annals of the American Academy of Political and Social Science*, Volume 508. London: Sage.

CENOZ, J. & VALENCIA, J. F., 1994, Additive Trilingualism: Evidence from the Basque Country. *Applied Psycholinguistics*, 15 (2), 195-207.

CENSO 1992 (INE) y ALVARO DÍEZ ASTETE, JURGEN RIESTER, KATHY MIHOTEK *et al.*, 1995, *Mapa étnico, territorial y arqueológico de Bolivia*. Santa Cruz: CIMAR, Universidad Gabriel René Moreno.

CENSUS 1991 SCOTLAND, 1994, *The Gaelic Language*. Edinburgh: HMSO.

CENSUS AND STATISTICS DEPARTMENT, 1991, *Hong Kong Population Census, 1991*. Hong Kong: Census and Statistics Department.

CENTRAL BUREAU FOR EDUCATIONAL VISITS AND EXCHANGES, 1994, *Home From Home: The Complete Guide to Homestays and Exchanges* (Third edition). London: Central Bureau for Educational Visits and Exchanges (also Cincinnati, OH: Seven Hills).

CENTRAL BUREAU FOR EDUCATIONAL VISITS AND EXCHANGES, 1996a, *Making the Most of Your Partner School Abroad*. London: Central Bureau for Educational Visits and Exchanges.

CENTRAL BUREAU FOR EDUCATIONAL VISITS AND EXCHANGES, 1996b, *School Linking Across the World: A Directory of Agencies Supporting North–South Linking*. London: Central Bureau for Educational Visits and Exchanges.

CENTRAL DE ESTADÍSTICA E INFORMÁTICA (OCEI), 1993, *Censo Indígena de Venezuela*. Caracas: Central de Estadística e Informática.

CENTRAL INTELLIGENCE AGENCY, 1995, *The World Factbook*. Washington: Office of Public and Agency Information. Internet address: (http://www.odci.gov/cia/publications/95fact/pubinfo.html).

CENTRAL OFFICE OF THE REPRESENTATIVE OF THE BOARD OF GOVERNORS OF THE EUROPEAN SCHOOLS, 1994, *The European Schools*. Brussels, Belgium.

CENTRAL STATISTICS OFFICE, 1996, *Census 91, Irish Language*. Dublin: Stationery Office.

CHAMBERS, J. K. & TRUDGILL, P., 1980, *Dialectology*. Cambridge: Cambridge University Press.

CHAMOT, A. U., 1988, Bilingualism in Education and Bilingual Education: The State of the Art in the United States. *Journal of Multilingual and Multicultural Development*, 9 (1&2), 11-35.

CHAMOT, A. U. & KUPPER, L., 1989, Learning Strategies in Foreign Language Instruction. *Foreign Language Annals*, 22, 13-24.

CHAOMHANAIGH, D. N. & BUACHALLA, S. O., 1994, Factors Affecting the Acquisition of the Irish Language: Some Empirical Evidence. *Studies in Education*, 10 (1), 16-22.

CHAVEZ, L. C., 1980, Jean Piaget's Theory of Equilibration Applied to Dual Language Development. In R. V. PADILLA (ed.), *Ethnoperspectives. Bilingual Education Research, Volume II: Theory in Bilingual Education*. Michigan: Eastern Michigan University.

CHENG, L. & BUTLER, K., 1989, Code-Switching: A Natural Phenomenon vs Language 'Deficiency'. *World Englishes*, 8 (3), 293-309.

CHESHIRE, J. (ed.), 1991, *English Around the World*. Cambridge: Cambridge University Press.

CHIRO, G. & SMOLICZ, J. J., 1993, Is Italian Language a Core Value of Italian Culture in Australia? A Study of Second-Generation Italian-Australians. *Studi Emigrazione*, 30, No. 110, 311-344.

CHOMSKY, N., 1965, *Aspects of the Theory of Syntax*. Cambridge, MA: MIT Press.

CHRISTENSEN. K. M., 1989, A Bilingual Approach to Education of Children who are Deaf. *Teaching English to Deaf and Second Language Students*, 7 (2), 9-14.

CHRISTIAN, D., 1994, *Two-Way Bilingual Education: Students Learning Through Two Languages*. Santa Cruz, CA: National Center for Research on Cultural Diversity and Second Language Learning.

CHRISTIAN, D. & MAHRER, C., 1993, *'Two-Way Bilingual Programs in the United States*. Washington DC: Center for Applied Linguistics.

CHRISTIAN, D. & MAHRER, C., 1994, *'Two-Way Bilingual Programs in the United States: 1992–1993 Supplement*. Washington, DC: Center for Applied Linguistics.

CHRISTIAN, D., SPANDOS, G., CRANDALL, J., SIMICH-DUDGEON, C. & WILLETS, K., 1990, Combining Language and Content for Second-Language Students. In A. M. PADILLA & H. H. FAIRCHILD (eds), *Bilingual Education, Issues and Strategies*. London: Sage Publications.

CILAR (Committee on Irish Language Attitudes Research), 1975, *Report of the Committee on Irish Language Attitudes Research*. Dublin: Government Stationery Office.

CIPCA (Centro de Investigación y Promoción del Campesidado), 1995, *Bolivia Plurilingüe, Guia para Planifecadores y Educadores*. La Paz: UNICEF.

CLARK, R., FAIRCLOUGH, N., IVANIC, R., MCLEOD, N., THOMAS, J. & MEARA, P., 1990, *Language and Power*. Papers from the 22nd Annual Meeting of the British Association for Applied Linguistics Held at Lancaster University in September, 1989. London: Centre for Information on Language and Research (for the British Association for Applied Linguistics).

CLARK, R. P., 1984, *The Basque Insurgents: ETA 1952–1980*. Madison, WI: University of Wisconsin Press.

CLARKSON, P. C., 1992, Language and Mathematics: A Comparison of Bilingual and Monolingual Students of Mathematics. *Educational Studies in Mathematics*, 23, 417-429.

CLARKSON, P. C. & GALBRAITH, P., 1992, Bilingualism and Mathematics Learning: Another Perspective. *Journal for Research in Mathematics Education*, 23 (1), 34-44.

CLEMENT, R., GARDNER, R. C. & SMYTHE, P. C., 1977, Motivational Variables in Second Language Acquisition: A Study of Francophones Learning English. *Canadian Journal of Behavioural Science*, 9, 123-133.

CLEMENT, R., GARDNER, R. C. & SMYTHE, P. C., 1980, Social and Individual Factors in Second Language Acquisition. *Canadian Journal of Behavioural Science*, 12, 293-302.

CLINE, T., 1993, Educational Assessment of Bilingual Pupils: Getting the Context Right. *Education and Child Psychology*, 10 (4), 59-68.

CLINE, T. & FREDERICKSON, N., 1991, *Bilingual Pupils and the National Curriculum: Overcoming Difficulties in Teaching and Learning*. London: University College London.

CLINE, T. & FREDERICKSON, N. (eds), 1996, *Curriculum Related Assessment: Cummins and Bilingual Children*. Clevedon: Multilingual Matters.

CLOUD, N., 1994, Special Education Needs of Second Language Students. In F. GENESEE (ed.), *Educating Second Language Children: The Whole Child, the Whole Curriculum, the Whole Community*. Cambridge: Cambridge University Press.

CLYNE, M., 1988, Bilingual Education: What Can We Learn From the Past? *Australian Journal of Education*, 32 (1), 95-114.

CLYNE, M., 1991a, Bilingual Education For All. An Australian Pilot Study and its Implications. In O. GARCÍA (ed.), *Bilingual Education: Focusschrift in Honor of Joshua A. Fishman*. Amsterdam/Philadelphia: John Benjamins.

CLYNE, M., 1991b, *Community Languages: The Australian Experience*. Cambridge: Cambridge University Press.

CLYNE, M., 1992, *Pluricentric Languages: Differing Norms in Different Nations*. Berlin and New York: Mouton de Gruyter.

CLYNE, M., 1997, Multilingualism. In F. COULMAS (ed.), *The Handbook of Sociolinguistics*. Oxford: Blackwell.

COELHO, E., 1994, Social Integration of Immigrant and Refugee Children. In F. GENESEE (ed.), *Educating Second Language Children: The Whole Child, the Whole Curriculum, the Whole Community*. Cambridge: Cambridge University Press.

COHEN, A. D., 1976, The Case for Partial Total Immersion Education. In A. SIMOES (ed.), *The Bilingual Child*. New York: Academic Press.

COHEN, A. D., 1990, *Language Learning: Insights for Learners, Teachers and Researchers*. Boston: Heinle and Heinle.

COHEN, A. D., 1991, Testing Linguistic and Communicative Proficiency: The Case of Reading Comprehension. In M. E. MCGROARTY & C. J. FALTIS (eds), *Languages in School and Society*. Berlin/New York: Mouton de Gruyter.

COHEN. G., 1984, The Politics of Bilingual Education. *Oxford Review of Education*, 10 (2), 225-241.

COLEMAN, A., 1929, *The Teaching of Modern Foreign Languages in the United States*. New York: Macmillan.

COLEMAN, J. A., 1996, *Studying Languages: A Survey of British and European Students*. London: Centre for Information on Language Teaching and Research.

COLLEGE FOR CONTINUING EDUCATION, 1992, *Bilingual Considerations in the Education of Deaf Students: ASL and English*. Washington, DC: Gallaudet University.

COLLIER, V. P., 1989, How Long? A Synthesis of Research on Academic Achievement in a Second Language. *TESOL Quarterly*, 23 (3), 509-531.

COLLIER, V. P., 1992, A Synthesis of Studies Examining Long-Term Language Minority Student Data on Academic Achievement. *Bilingual Research Journal*, 16 (1&2), 187-212.

COLLIER, V. P., 1995a, Acquiring a Second Language for School. *Directions in Language and Education*, 1 (4), 1-8. National Clearinghouse for Bilingual Education.

COLLIER, V. P., 1995b, *Promoting Academic Success for ESL Students: Understanding Second Language Acquisition For School*. Elizabeth, NJ: New Jersey Teachers of English to Speakers of Other Languages-Bilingual Educators.

COLLINSON, V., 1989, Future Trends and Challenges in French Immersion. *The Canadian Modern Language Review*, 45 (3), 561-566.

COMMINS, N. L., 1989, Language and Affect: Bilingual Students at Home and at School. *Language Arts*, 66 (1), 29-43.

COMMINS, N. L. & MIRAMONTES, O. B., 1989, Perceived and Actual Linguistic Competence: A Descriptive Study of Four Low-Achieving Hispanic Bilingual Students. *American Educational Research Journal*, 26 (4), 443-472.

COMMISSION OF EUROPEAN COMMUNITIES, 1993, *The Outlook for Higher Education in the European Community*. Luxembourg: Office of Official Publications of the European Communities.

COMMITTEE ON EDUCATION AND LABOR, 1983, *Foreign Language Assistance for National Security Act of 1983 Report* (United States House of Representatives 98th Congress). Washington DC: GPO.

COMRIE, B., 1987, *The World's Major Languages*. London and New York: Routledge.

COMRIE, B. (ed.), 1991. *The World's Major Languages*. London and New York: Routledge.

CONKLIN, N. & LOURIE, M., 1983, *A Host of Tongues*. New York: The Free Press.

CONNOR, W., 1994, Maîtres Chez Nous. *International Journal of the Sociology of Language*, 110, 137-144.

CONSEIL REGIONAL ALSACE et CONSEIL GENERAL RESUSSIR LE HAUT-RHIN, 1994, *L'Enseignement Bilingue Précoce 1991–1994*. Colmar: Service Langue et Culture Régionales Conseil Général du Haut-Rhin.

CONVERY, A., EVANS, M., GREEN, S., MACARO, E. & MELLOR, J., 1997, An Investigative Study into Pupils' Perceptions of Europe. *Journal of Multilingual and Multicultural Development*, 18(1), 1-16.

COOK, V. J., 1991, *Second Language Learning and Language Teaching*. London: Edward Arnold.

COOK, V. J., 1992, Evidence for Multicompetence. *Language Learning*, 42 (4), 557-591.

COOPER, J., 1993, Bilingual Babel: Cuniform Texts in Two or More Languages from Ancient Mesopotamia and Beyond. In R. SARKONAK & R. HODGSON (eds), 1993, *Writing in Stereo: Bilingualism in the Text*. In *Visible Language*, 27 (1/2). Providence, RI: Rhode Island School of Design.

COOPER, R. L., 1969, Two Contextualized Measures of Degree of Bilingualism. *Modern Language Review*, 53, 166-172.

COOPER, R. L., 1989, *Language Planning and Social Change*. Cambridge: Cambridge University Press.

COOPER, R. L. (ed.), 1982, *A Framework for the Study of Language Spread. Studies in Diffusion and Social Change*. Washington, DC: Center for Applied Linguistics with Indiana University Press.

CORDER, S., 1967, The Significance of Learners' Errors. *International Review of Applied Linguistics*, 5, 161-170.

CORSON, D., 1985, *The Lexical Bar*. Oxford: Pergamon.

CORSON, D., 1990a, *Language Policy Across the Curriculum*. Clevedon: Multilingual Matters.

CORSON, D., 1990b, Three Curriculum and Organizational Responses to Cultural Pluralism in New Zealand Schooling. *Language, Culture and Curriculum*, 3 (3), 213-225.

CORSON, D., 1992, Bilingual Education Policy and Social Justice. *Journal of Education Policy*, 7 (1), 45-69.

CORSON, D., 1993, *Language, Minority Education and Gender: Linking Social Justice and Power*. Clevedon: Multilingual Matters.

CORSON, D., 1994, Minority Social Groups and Nonstandard Discourse: Towards a Just Language Policy. *The Canadian Modern Language Review*, 50 (2), 271-295.

CORSON, D., 1995, Norway's 'Sámi Language Act': Emancipatory Implications for the World's Aboriginal Peoples. *Language in Society*, 24, 493-514.

CORSON, H., 1993, Forword. In M. MILLER-NOMELAND & S. GILLESPIE, 1993, *Kendall Demonstration Elementary School: Deaf Studies Curriculum Guide*. Washington, DC: Gallaudet University.

COULMAS, F., 1991, European Integration and the Idea of the National Language.

In F. COULMAS (ed.), *A Language Policy for the European Community*. Berlin/New York: Mouton de Gruyter.

COULMAS, F., 1992, *Language and Economy*. Oxford: Blackwell.

COULMAS, F. (ed.), 1991, *A Language Policy for the European Community: Prospects and Quandaries*. Berlin, New York: Mouton de Gruyter.

COULMAS, F. (ed.), 1997, *The Handbook of Sociolinguistics*. Oxford: Blackwell.

COUNCIL FOR THE WELSH LANGUAGE, 1978, *A Future for the Welsh Language*. Cardiff: HMSO.

COUPLAND, N. & JAWORSKI, A. (eds), 1997, *Sociolinguistics: A Reader and Coursebook*. London: MacMillan Press.

COX, L., GAMMON, A. & PENFOLD, C. (eds), 1993, *Talking Maths, Talking Languages*. Derby: Association of Teachers of Mathematics.

CRAFT, M. (ed.), 1984, *Education and Cultural Pluralism. Contemporary Analysis in Education Series*. Sussex: The Falmer Press.

CRAIG, C. G., 1997, Language Contact and Language Degeneration. In F. COULMAS (ed.), *The Handbook of Sociolinguistics*. Oxford: Blackwell.

CRAWFORD, J., 1992, *Hold Your Tongue. Bilingualism and the Politics of 'English Only'*. Reading, MA: Addison-Wesley.

CRAWFORD, J., 1994, *Endangered Native American Languages: What Is To Be Done, and Why?* Washington, DC: National Clearinghouse for Bilingual Education.

CRAWFORD, J., 1995, *Bilingual Education: History, Politics, Theory and Practice* (Third edition). Los Angeles: Bilingual Educational Services.

CRAWFORD, J. (ed.), 1992, *Language Loyalties. A Source Book on the Official English Controversy*. Chicago: University of Chicago Press.

CROWLEY, T., 1994, Linguistic Demography: Interpreting the 1989 Census Results in Vanuatu. *Journal of Multilingual and Multicultural Development*, 15 (1), 1-16.

CRYSTAL, D., 1987a, *Child Language, Learning, and Linguistics: An Overview for the Teaching and Therapeutic Professions* (Second edition). London: E. Arnold.

CRYSTAL, D., 1987b, *The Cambridge Encyclopedia of Language*. Cambridge: Cambridge University Press.

CRYSTAL, D., 1992, *Introducing Linguistics*. London: Penguin.

CRYSTAL, D., 1993a, *Introduction to Language Pathology* (Third edition). London: Whurr.

CRYSTAL, D., 1993b, *The English Language*. Harmondsworth: Penguin.

CRYSTAL, D., 1994, *An Encyclopedic Dictionary of Language and Languages*. London: Penguin.

CRYSTAL, D., 1995, *The Cambridge Encyclopedia of the English Language*. Cambridge: Cambridge University Press.

CRYSTAL, D., 1997a, *English as a Global Language*. Cambridge: Cambridge University Press.

CRYSTAL, D., 1997b, *The Cambridge Encyclopedia of Language* (Second edition). Cambridge: Cambridge University Press.

CUMMINS, J., 1975, Cognitive Factors Associated with Intermediate Levels of Bilingual Skills (Unpublished Manuscript). Educational Research Centre, St. Patrick's College, Dublin.

CUMMINS, J., 1976, The Influence of Bilingualism on Cognitive Growth: A Synthesis of Research Findings and Explanatory Hypotheses. *Working Papers on Bilingualism*, 9, 1-43.

CUMMINS, J., 1977a, Cognitive Factors Associated with the Attainment of Intermediate Levels of Bilingual Skills. *Modern Language Journal*, 61, 3-12.

CUMMINS, J., 1977b, Immersion Education in Ireland: A Critical Review of Macnamara's Findings (with replies). *Working Papers in Bilingualism*, 1977, 13, 121-129.

CUMMINS, J., 1977c, A Comparison of Reading Achievement in Irish and English Medium Schools. In V. GREANEY (ed.), *Studies in Reading*. Dublin: Education Council of Ireland.

CUMMINS, J., 1978a, Bilingualism and the Development of Metalinguistic Awareness. *Journal of Cross Cultural Psychology*, 1978, 9, 131-149.

CUMMINS, J., 1978b, Metalinguistic Development of Children in Bilingual Education Programs: Data from Irish and Canadian Ukranian-English Programs. In M. PARADIS (ed.), *Aspects of Bilingualism*. Columbia: Hornbeam Press.

CUMMINS, J., 1978c, Immersion Programs: The Irish Experience. *International Review of Education*, 24, 273-282.

CUMMINS, J., 1978d, The Cognitive Development of Children in Immersion Programs. *Canadian Modern Language Review*, 34, 855-883.

CUMMINS, J., 1980a, The Construct of Language Proficiency in Bilingual Education. In J. E. ALATIS (ed.), *Georgetown University Round Table on Languages and Linguistics 1980*. Washington, DC: Georgetown University Press.

CUMMINS, J., 1980b, The Entry and Exit Fallacy in Bilingual Education. *NABE Journal*, 4 (3), 25-59.

CUMMINS, J., 1981a, *Bilingualism and Minority Language Children*. Ontario: Ontario Institute for Studies in Education.

CUMMINS, J., 1981b, The Role of Primary Language Development in Promoting Educational Success for Language Minority Students. In CALIFORNIA STATE DEPARTMENT OF EDUCATION (ed.), *Schooling and Language Minority Students. A Theoretical Framework*. Los Angeles: California State Department of Education.

CUMMINS, J., 1981c, Four Misconceptions About Language Proficiency in Bilingual Education. *NABE Journal*, 5 (3), 31-45.

CUMMINS, J., 1982, Reading Achievement in Irish and English Medium Schools. *Oideas*, 26, 21-26.

CUMMINS, J., 1983a, *Heritage Language Education. A Literature Review*. Ontario: Ministry of Education.

CUMMINS, J., 1983b, Language Proficiency, Biliteracy and French Immersion. *Canadian Journal of Education*, 8 (2), 117-138.

CUMMINS, J., 1984a, *Bilingualism and Special Education: Issues in Assessment and Pedagogy*. Clevedon: Multilingual Matters.

CUMMINS, J., 1984b, Bilingualism and Cognitive Functioning. In S. SHAPSON & V. D'OYLEY (eds), *Bilingual and Multicultural Education: Canadian Perspectives*. Clevedon: Multilingual Matters.

CUMMINS, J., 1984c, Wanted: A Theoretical Framework for Relating Language Proficiency to Academic Achievement Among Bilingual Students. In C. RIVERA (ed.), *Language Proficiency and Academic Achievement*. Clevedon: Multilingual Matters.

CUMMINS, J., 1984d, Implications of Bilingual Proficiency for the Education of Minority Language Students. In P. ALLEN & M. SWAIN (eds), *Language Issues and Education Policies*. Toronto: Pergamon.

CUMMINS, J., 1986a, Bilingual Education and Anti-Racist Education. *Interracial Books for Children Bulletin*, 17 (3&4), 9-12.

CUMMINS, J., 1986b, *Empowering Minority Students: A Framework for Intervention*. Harvard Educational Review, 56 (1), 18-36.

CUMMINS, J., 1987a, Bilingualism, Language Proficiency and Metalinguistic Development. In P. HOMEL, M. PALIJ & D. AARONSON (eds), *Childhood Bilingualism: Aspects of Linguistic Cognitive and Social Development*. Hillsdale, NJ: Erlbaum.

CUMMINS, J., 1987b, *Immersion Programs: Current Issues and Future Directions. Contemporary Educational Issues*. Toronto: Canadian Mosaic Press.

CUMMINS, J., 1988a, From Multicultural to Anti-Racist Education. An Analysis of Programmes and Policies in Ontario. In T. SKUTNABB-KANGAS & J. CUMMINS (eds), *Minority Education: From Shame to Struggle*. Clevedon: Multilingual Matters.

CUMMINS, J., 1988b, Position Paper: The Role and Use of Educational Theory in Formulating Language Policy. *TESL Canada Journal*, 5 (2), 11-19.

CUMMINS, J., 1988c, Teachers Are Not Miracle Workers: Lloyd Dunn's Call for Hispanic Activism. *Hispanic Journal of Behavioral Science*, 10 (3), 263-272.

CUMMINS, J., 1989a, Language and Literacy Acquisition. *Journal of Multilingual and Multicultural Development*, 10 (1), 17-31.

CUMMINS, J., 1989b, A Theoretical Framework for Bilingual Special Education. *Exceptional Children*, 56 (2), 111-119.

CUMMINS, J., 1991a, Conversational and Academic Language Proficiency in Bilingual Contexts. In J. H. HULSTIJN & J. F. MATTER (eds), *Reading in Two Languages* (*AILA Review* 8, 75-89).

CUMMINS, J., 1991b, The Politics of Paranoia: Reflections on the Bilingual Education Debate. In O. GARCÍA (ed.), *Bilingual Education: Focusschrift in Honor of Joshua A. Fishman* (Volume 1). Amsterdam/ Philadelphia: John Benjamins.

CUMMINS, J., 1991c, The Development of Bilingual Proficiency from Home to School: A Longitudinal Study of Portuguese Speaking Children. *Journal of Education*, 173 (2), 85-98.

CUMMINS, J., 1991d, Forked Tongue: The Politics of Bilingual Education: A Critique. *The Canadian Modern Language Review*, 47 (4), 786-793.

CUMMINS, J., 1991e, Introduction. *The Canadian Modern Language Review*, 47 (4), 601-605.

CUMMINS, J., 1992a, Heritage Language Teaching in Canadian Schools. *Journal of Curriculum Studies*, 24 (3), 281-286.

CUMMINS, J., 1992b, Bilingual Education and English Immersion: The Ramirez Report in Theoretical Perspective. *Bilingual Research Journal*, 16 (1&2), 91-104.

CUMMINS, J., 1994a, Knowledge, Power and Identity in Teaching English as a Second Language. In F. GENESEE (ed.), *Educating Second Language Children: The Whole Child, the Whole Curriculum, the Whole Community*. Cambridge: Cambridge University Press.

CUMMINS, J., 1994b, Lies We Live By: National Identity and Social Justice. *International Journal of the Sociology of Language*, 110, 145-154.

CUMMINS, J., 1996, *Negotiating Identities: Education for Empowerment in a Diverse Society*. Ontario, CA: California Association for Bilingual Education.

CUMMINS, J. & DANESI, M., 1990, *Heritage Languages. The Development and Denial of Canada's Linguistic Resources*. Toronto: Our Schools/Ourselves Education Foundation and Garamond Press.

CUMMINS, J. & GENESEE, F., 1985. Bilingual Education Programmes in Wales and Canada. In C. J. DODSON (ed.), *Bilingual Education: Evaluation, Assessment and Methodology*. Cardiff: University of Wales Press.

CUMMINS, J. & GULUTSAN, M., 1974, Some Effects of Bilingualism on Cognitive Functioning. In S. T. CAREY (ed.), *Bilingualism, Biculturalism and Education*. Edmonton: University of Alberta Press.

CUMMINS, J. & MULCAHY, R., 1978, Orientation to Language in Ukranian-English Bilingual Children. *Child Development*, 49, 1239-1242.

CUMMINS, J. & SAYERS, D., 1995, *Brave New Schools: Challenging Cultural Illiteracy through Global Learning Networks*. New York: St. Martin's Press.

CUMMINS, J. & SAYERS, D., 1996, Multicultural Education and Technology: Promise and Pitfalls. *Multicultural Education*, 3 (3), 4-10.

CUMMINS, J. & SWAIN, M., 1986, *Bilingualism in Education*. New York: Longman.

CUMMINS, P., 1988, Socioeconomic development and language maintenance in the Gaeltacht. *International Journal of the Sociology of Language*, 70, 11-28.

CURIEL, H., 1990, Bilingual Education and the American Dream: A Bridge or a Barrier? *Social Work in Education*, 13 (1), 7-21.

CURRAN, C. A., 1972, *Counseling-Learning: A Whole-Person Model for Education*. New York: Grune & Stratton.

CURRAN, C. A., 1976. *Counseling-Learning in Second Languages*. Apple River, IL: Apple River Press.

CURRICULUM AND EXAMINATIONS BOARD, 1985, *Language in the Curriculum. A Curriculum and Examinations Board Discussion Paper*. Dublin: The Curriculum and Examinations Board.

CURRICULUM COUNCIL FOR WALES, 1993, *Developing a Curriculum Cymreig*. Cardiff: Curriculum Council for Wales.

CZIKO, G. A., 1992, The Evaluation of Bilingual Education. From Necessity and Probability to Possibility. *Educational Researcher*, 21 (2), 10-15.

D

DA SILVA, F. G. & GUNNEWIEK, L. K., 1992, Portuguese and Brazilian Efforts to Spread Portuguese. *International Journal of the Sociology of Language*, 95, 71-92.

DAFIS, Ll. (ed.), 1992, *The Lesser Used Languages: Assimilating Newcomers*. Proceedings of the Conference held at Carmarthen, 1991. Carmarthen, Dyfed, Wales: Joint Working Party on Bilingualism in Dyfed.

DALLEY, P., 1992, Mes Langues, Mes Couleurs: Bilingualism in Conflict: Alberta Raconté et Re-Raconté. *Journal of Curriculum Studies*, 24 (6), 501-532,

DALPHINIS, M., 1988, Bilingualism, Dialect and Equal Opportunities in Education. *Language Issues*, 2 (1), 12-18.

DANESI, M., 1988, Mother-Tongue Training in School as a Determinant of Global Language Proficiency: A Belgian Case Study. *International Review of Education*, 34, 439-454.

DANESI. M., 1991, Revisiting the Research Findings on Heritage Language Learning: Three Interpretive Frames. *Canadian Modern Language Review*, 47 (4), 650-659.

DANESI, M., MCLEOD, K. A. & MORRIS, S. V. (eds), 1993, *Heritage Languages and Education: The Canadian Experience*. Oakville: Mosaic Press.

DANIEL, J. S. & BELANGER, C. H., 1988, Challenges of the Bilingual (Multilingual) University. Paper Presented at the 14th Quinquennial Congress of the Association of Commonwealth Universities, Perth, Australia February 1988.

DANOFF, M. N., COLES, G. J., MCLAUGHLIN, D. H. & REYNOLDS, D. J., 1977, *Evaluation of the Impact of ESEA Title VII Spanish/English Bilingual Education Programs, Volume 1*. Palo Alto, CA: American Institutes for Research.

DANOFF, M. N., COLES, G. J., MCLAUGHLIN, D. H. & REYNOLDS, D. J., 1978, *Evaluation of the Impact of ESEA Title VII Spanish/English Bilingual Education Programs, Volume 3*. Palo Alto, CA: American Institutes for Research.

DARCY, N. T., 1953, A Review of the Literature on the Effects of Bilingualism upon the Measurement of Intelligence. *Journal of Genetic Psychology*, 82, 21-57.

DAVIDMAN, L. & DAVIDMAN, P. T., 1994, *Teaching with a Multicultural Perspective. A Practical Guide*. New York: Longman.

DAVIES, A., 1996, Ironising the Myth of Linguicism. *Journal of Multilingual and Multicultural Development*, 17 (6), 485-496.

DAVIES, B. L., 1988, The Right to a Bilingual Education in Nineteenth Century Wales. *The Transactions of the Honourable Society of Cymmrodorion*, 133-151.

DAVIES, D. L., 1957, A Comparative Study of some of the Intellectual, Social and Emotional Characteristics of Bilingual and Monoglot Students at a Welsh University College. Unpublished M.A. Thesis, University of Wales.

DAVIES, J., 1993, *The Welsh Language*. Cardiff: University of Wales Press.

DAWE, L. C., 1982, The Influence of a Bilingual Child's First Language Competence on Reasoning in Mathematics. Unpublished Ph.D. Dissertation, University of Cambridge.

DAWE, L. C., 1983, Bilingualism and Mathematical Reasoning in English as a Second Language. *Educational Studies in Mathematics*, 14 (1), 325-353.

DAY, E. M. & SHAPSON, S. M., 1987, Assessment of Oral Communicative Skills in Early French Immersion Programmes. *Journal of Multilingual and Multicultural Development*, 8 (3), 237-260.

DAY, E. M. & SHAPSON, S. M., 1988, A Comparison Study of Early and Late French Immersion Programs in British Columbia. *Canadian Journal of Education*, 13 (2), 290-305.

DAY, R. R., 1982, Children's Attitudes Towards Language. In E. B. RYAN & H. GILES (eds), *Attitudes Towards Language Variation: Social and Applied Contexts*. London: Edward Arnold.

DE AVILA, E., 1987, Bilingualism, Cognitive Function and Language Minority Group Membership. In P. HOMEL, M. PALIJ & D. AARONSON (eds) *Childhood Bilingualism: Aspects of Linguistic Cognitive and Social Development*. Hillsdale, NJ: Erlbaum.

DE BHAL, P., 1994, The Irish Language and Education: A Review of Recent Research. *Studies in Education*, 10 (1), 37-46.

DE BOT, K. & CLYNE, M., 1994, A 16-Year Longitudinal Study of Language Attrition in Dutch Immigrants in Australia. *Journal of Multilingual and Multicultural Development*, 15 (1), 17-28.

DE GROOT, A. M. B., DANNENBURG, L. & VAN HELL, J. G., 1994, Forward and Backward Word Translation by Bilinguals. *Journal of Memory and Language*, 33 (5), 600-629.

DE HOUWER, A., 1995, Bilingual Language Acquisition. In P. FLETCHER & B. MACWHINNEY (eds), *The Handbook of Child Language*. Oxford: Blackwell.

DE JONG, J. H. A. L., 1992, Assessment of Language Proficiency in the Perspective of the 21st Century. In J. F. MATTER (ed.), *Language Teaching in the Twenty-First Century: Problems and Prospects (AILA Review*, 9, 21-38).

DE VRIES, J., 1984, Factors Affecting the Survival of Linguistic Minorities: A Preliminary Comparative Analysis of Data for Western Europe. *Journal of Multilingual and Multicultural Development*, 5 (3&4), 207-216.

DE VRIES, J., 1987, Problems of Measurement in the Study of Linguistic Minorities. *Journal of Multilingual and Multicultural Development*, 8 (1&2), 23-31.

DE ZULUETA, F., 1995, Bilingualism, Culture and Identity. Special Section: Identity and Cultures: Papers from the Bologna Symposium. *Group Analysis*, 28 (2), 179-190.

DEL VECCHIO, A. *et al.*, 1994, *Whole-School Bilingual Education Programs: Approaches For Sound Assessment. Program Information Guide Series, 18*. Washington, DC: National Clearinghouse for Bilingual Education.

DECHICCHIS J., 1995. The Current State of the Ainu Language. *Journal of Multilingual and Multicultural Development*, 16 (1&2), 103-124.

DELGADO-GAITAN, C., 1990, *Literacy for Empowerment: The Role of Parents in Children's Education*. New York: Falmer.

DELGADO-GAITAN, C., 1991, Relating Experience and Text: Socially Constituted Reading Activity. In M. E. MCGROARTY & C. J. FALTIS (eds), *Languages in School and Society*. Berlin/New York: Mouton de Gruyter.

DELGADO-GAITAN, C. & TRUEBA, H., 1991, *Crossing Cultural Borders: Education for Immigrant Families in America*. New York: Falmer.

DELPIT, L. D., 1988, The Silenced Dialogue: Power and Pedagogy in Educating Other People's Children. *Harvard Educational Review*, 58 (3), 280-298.

DENISON N., 1997, Language Change in Progress: Variation as it Happens. In F. COULMAS (ed.), *The Handbook of Sociolinguistics*. Oxford: Blackwell.

DENNICK, R., 1992, *Multicultural and Antiracist Science Education: Theory and Practice*. Nottingham: University of Nottingham.

DEPARTMENT FOR EDUCATION AND SCIENCE AND THE WELSH OFFICE, 1989, *English for Ages 5-11 (The Cox Report)*. London: HMSO.

DEPARTMENT OF EDUCATION AND SCIENCE, 1975, *A Language for Life (Bullock Report)*. London: HMSO.

DEPARTMENT OF EDUCATION AND SCIENCE, 1985, *Education for All (Swann Report)*. London: HMSO.

DEPARTMENT OF EDUCATION AND SCIENCE AND THE WELSH OFFICE, 1990, *English in the National Curriculum (No. 2)*. London: HMSO.

DEPARTMENT OF HEALTH AND SOCIAL SERVICES, 1993, *The Northern Ireland Census 1991*. Belfast: HMSO.

DEPARTMENT OF STATISTICS (SINGAPORE), 1990, *Census of Population, 1990*. Singapore: Ministry of Trade and Industry.

DESCOTES-GENON, C., EURIN, S., ROLLE-HAROLD, R. & SZILAGYI, 1992, *La Voyagerie: Pratique du Français du Tourisme*. Grenoble: Universitaires de Grenoble.

DESFORGES, M., 1982, The Assessment of Bilingual, Bicultural Children. *Association of Psychologists Journal*, 5 (10), 7-11.

DESFORGES, M., 1995, Assessment of Special Educational Needs in Bilingual Pupils. Changing Practice? *School Psychology International*, 16 (1), 5-17.

DEVILLAR, R. A., 1991, Co-operative Principles, Computers and Classroom Language. In M. E. MCGROARTY & C. J. FALTIS (eds), *Languages in School and Society: Policy and Pedagogy*. Berlin/New York: Mouton de Gruyter.

DEVILLAR, R. A., FALTIS, C. J. & CUMMINS, J. P. (eds), 1994, *Cultural Diversity in Schools: From Rhetoric to Practice*. New York: State University Press.

DI PIETRO, R., 1977, Code-Switching as a Verbal Strategy Among Bilinguals. In F. ECKMAN (ed.), *Current Themes in Linguistics*. Washington, DC: Hemisphere Publishing.

DIAZ, R. M., 1983, Thought and Two Languages: The Impact of Bilingualism on Cognitive Development. *Review of Research in Education*, 10, 23-54.

DIAZ, R. M., 1985, Bilingual Cognitive Development: Addressing Three Gaps in Current Research. *Child Development*, 56, 1376-1388.

DIAZ, R. M. & KLINGER, C., 1991, Towards an Explanatory Model of the Interaction between Bilingualism and Cognitive Development. In E. BIALYSTOK (ed.), *Language Processing in Bilingual Children*. Cambridge: Cambridge University Press.

DICKER, S. J., 1993a, 'Ethnic Irrelevance' and the Immigrant: Finding a Place for Minority Languages. *Educational Forum*, 57 (2), 120-133.

DICKER, S. J., 1993b, The Universal Second Language Requirement: An Inadequate Substitute For Bilingual Education (A Response to Aaron Wildavsky). *Journal of Policy Analysis and Management*, 12 (4), 779-785.

DICKER, S. J., 1996, *Languages in America: A Pluralist View*. Clevedon: Multilingual Matters.

DICKERSON, P. & CUMMING, A., 1996, *Profiles of Language Education in 25 Countries*. Slough, UK: NFER.

DICKS, J. E., 1992, Analytic and Experiential Features of Three French Immersion Programs: Early, Middle and Late. *The Canadian Modern Language Review*, 49 (1), 37-59.

DIEBOLD, A. R., 1964, Incipient Bilingualism. In D. HYMES *et al.* (eds), *Language in Culture and Society*. New York: Harper and Row.

DILLARD, J. L., 1992, *A History of American English*. New York: Longman.

DODSON, C. J., 1967, *Language Teaching and the Bilingual Method*. London: Pitman.

DODSON, C. J., 1978a, Evaluation Report. In *Bilingual Education in Wales, 5–11*. London: Evans/Methuen.

DODSON, C. J., 1978b, The Independent Evaluator's Report. In C. J. DODSON & E. PRICE (eds), *Bilingual Education in Wales, 5–11*. London: Evans/Methuen.

DODSON, C. J., 1981, A Reappraisal of Bilingual Development and Education: Some Theoretical and Practical Considerations. In H. BAETENS BEARDSMORE (ed.), *Elements of Bilingual Theory*. Brussels: Vrije Universiteit Brussel.

DODSON, C. J., 1983a, Bilingualism, Language Teaching and Learning. *British Journal of Language Teaching*, 21, 3-8.

DODSON, C. J., 1983b, Living with Two Languages. *Journal of Multilingual and Multicultural Development*, 4 (6), 401-414.

DODSON, C. J., 1985a, Second Language Acquisition and Bilingual Development: A Theoretical Framework. *Journal of Multilingual and Multicultural Development*, 6 (5), 325-346.

DODSON, C. J., 1985b, Schools Council Project on Bilingual Education (Secondary Schools) 1971-1978: Methodology. In C. J. DODSON (ed.), *Bilingual Education: Evaluation, Assessment and Methodology*. Cardiff: University of Wales Press.

DODSON, C. J., 1985c, Schools Council Bilingual Education Project (Primary Schools) 1968-1977: An Independent Evaluation. In C. J. DODSON (ed.), *Bilingual Education: Evaluation, Assessment and Methodology*. Cardiff: University of Wales Press.

DODSON, C. J., 1995, The Effects of Second-Language Education on First/Second Language Development. In B. M. JONES & P. A. S. GHUMAN (eds), *Bilingualism, Education and Identity*. Cardiff: University of Wales Press.

DODSON, C. J. (ed.), 1985, *Bilingual Education: Evaluation, Assessment and Methodology*. Cardiff: University of Wales Press.

DOLSON, D. P. & MAYER, J., 1992, Longitudinal Study of Three Program Models for Language-Minority Students: A Critical Examination of Reported Findings. *Bilingual Research Journal*, 16 (1&2), 105-157.

DONMALL, B. G., 1984, The Developing Role of Language Awareness in the UK as a Response to Problems posed by Linguistic Diversity. *European Journal of Education*, 19 (1), 25-37.

DONMALL, B. G., 1985, *Language Awareness. Report to the National Congress on Languages in Education*. London: Centre for Information on Language Teaching and Research (CILT).

DONMALL, B. G. (ed.), 1985, *Language Awareness*. London: Centre for Information on Language Teaching and Research (CILT).

DÖPKE, S., 1992, *One Parent One Language*. Amsterdam/Philadelphia: John Benjamins.

DORIAN, N. C., 1981, *Language Death: The Life Cycle of a Scottish Gaelic Dialect*. Philadelphia: University of Pennsylvania Press.

DORIAN, N. C., 1988, The Celtic Languages in the British Isles. In C. B. PAULSTON (ed.), *International Handbook of Bilingualism and Bilingual Education*. New York: Greenwood Press.

DORIAN, N. C., 1994, Choices and Values in Language Shift and Its Study. *International Journal of the Sociology of Language*, 110, 113-124.

DORIAN, N. C. (ed.), 1989, *Investigating Obsolescence. Studies in Language Contraction and Death*. Cambridge: Cambridge University Press.

DÖRNYEI, Z., 1994, Motivation and Motivating in the Second Language Classroom. *The Modern Language Journal*, 78 (3), 273-284.

DÖRNYEI, Z., 1994, Understanding L2 Motivation: On with the Challenge! *The Modern Language Journal*, 78 (4), 515-523.

DOSANJH, J. S. & GHUMAN, P. A., 1996, *Child-Rearing in Ethnic Minorities*. Clevedon: Multilingual Matters.

DOYLE, A., CHAMPAGNE, M. & SEGALOWITZ, N., 1978, Some Issues on the Assessment of Linguistic Consequences of Early Bilingualism. In M. PARADIS (ed.), *Aspects of Bilingualism*. Columbia: Hornbeam Press.

DRASGOW, E., 1993, Bilingual/Bicultural Deaf Education: An Overview. *Sign Language Studies*, 82, 243-265.

DUA, H. R., 1994, Hindi Language Spread Policy and its Implementation: Achievements and Prospects. *International Journal of the Sociology of Language*, 107, 115-143.

DUFF, P. A., 1991, Innovation in Foreign Language Education: An Evaluation of Three Hungarian-English Dual-Language Schools. *Journal of Multilingual and Multicultural Development*, 12 (6), 459-476.

DUFOUR, R. & KROLL, J. F., 1995, Matching Words to Concepts in Two Languages: A Test of the Concept Mediation Model of Bilingual Representation. *Memory and Cognition*, 23 (2), 166-180.

DUFOUR, R. *et al.*, 1995, Matching Words to Concepts in Two Languages: A Test of the Concept Mediation Model of Bilingual Representation. *Memory and Cognition*, 23 (2), 166-180.

DUHAMEL, R. J., 1985, French-Language Programs in Manitoba and Saskatchewan: Post-Secondary Education Challenges. *The Canadian Modern Language Review*, 41 (5), 819-826.

DULAY, H. C. & BURT, M. K., 1973, Should We Teach Children Syntax? *Language Learning*, 23, 245-258.

DULAY, H. C. & BURT, M. K., 1974, Errors and Strategies in Child Second Language Acquisition. *TESOL Quarterly*, 8, 129-136.

DULAY, H. C. & BURT, M. K., 1977, Remarks on Creativity in Language Acquisition. In M. BURT, H. DULAY & M. FINOCCHIARO (eds), *Viewpoints on English as a Second Language*. New York: Regents.

DULAY, H. C. & BURT, M. K., 1978, *Why Bilingual Education? A Summary of Research Findings* (Second edition). San Francisco: Bloomsbury West.

DULAY, H. C. & BURT, M. K., 1979, *Bilingual Education: A Close Look at its Effects*. Focus, No. 1.

DUNCAN, S. E. & DE AVILA, E. A., 1979, Bilingualism and Cognition: Some Recent Findings. *NABE Journal*, 4 (1), 15-50.

DUNKIN, M. & BIDDLE, B. J., 1974, *The Study of Teaching*. New York: Holt, Rinehart and Winston.

DURGUNOGLU, A. Y. & ROEDIGER, H. L., 1987, Test Differences in Accessing Bilingual Memory. *Journal of Memory and Language*, 26, 377-391.

DUTCHER, N., 1982, *The Use of First and Second Languages in Primary Education: Selected Case Studies*. Staff Working Paper No. 504. Washington, DC: World Bank.

DUTCHER, N., 1995, *Overview of Foreign Language Students in the United States.* National Clearinghouse for Bilingual Education. Resource Collection Series, 6. Washington, DC: Center for Applied Linguistics.

DYSON, A., 1989, *The Multiple Worlds of Child Writers: A Study of Friends Learning to Write.* New York: Teachers College Press.

E

EASTMAN, C. M., 1983, *Language Planning: An Introduction.* San Francisco: Chandler and Sharp.

EASTMAN, C. M., 1992, Codeswitching as an Urban Language, Contact Phenomenon. *Journal of Multilingual and Multicultural Development*, 13 (1&2), 1-17.

EASTMAN, C. M. & STEIN, R. F., 1993, Language Display: Authenticating Claims to Social Identity. *Journal of Multilingual and Multicultural Development*, 14 (3), 187-202.

ECHEVARRIA, J. & MCDONOUGH, R., 1993, *Instructional Conversations in Special Education Settings: Issues and Accommodations.* United States Department of Education: National Centre for Research on Cultural Diversity and Second Language Learning

EDELSKY, C., 1986, *Writing in a Bilingual Program.* Norwood, NJ: Ablex.

EDELSKY, C., 1996, *With Literacy and Justice for All: Rethinking the Social in Language and Education* (Second edition). London: Falmer.

EDELSKY, C. *et al.*, 1983, Semilingualism and Language Deficit. *Applied Linguistics*, 4 (1), 1-22.

EDUCATIEVE FACULTEIT, 1992, *Bilingualism in Education: A Local and International Perspective.* Ljouwert/Snits: Department of Education.

EDWARDS, D. G., 1984, Welsh-Medium Education. *Journal of Multilingual and Multicultural Development*, 5 (3&4), 249-257.

EDWARDS, D. G., 1986, Welsh-Medium Education. *Western European Education*, 18 (4), 86-97.

EDWARDS, H. P., FU, L., MCCARREY, H. & DOUTRIAUX, C., 1980, Partial French Immersion for English-Speaking Pupils in Elementary School: The Ottawa Roman Catholic Separate School Board Study in Grades One to Four. *Canadian Modern Language Review*, 38, 283-296.

EDWARDS, J. R., 1977, Students' Reactions to Irish Regional Accents. *Language and Speech*, 20, 280-286.

EDWARDS, J. R., 1980, Critics and Criticisms of Bilingual Education. *Modern Language Journal*, 64 (4), 409-415.

EDWARDS, J. R., 1981, The Context of Bilingual Education. *Journal of Multilingual and Multicultural Development*, 2 (1), 25-44.

EDWARDS, J. R., 1984a, The Social and Political Context of Bilingual Education. In R. J. SAMUDA, J. W. BERRY & M. LAFERRIERE (eds), *Multiculturalism in Canada: Social and Educational Perspectives.* London: Allyn and Bacon.

EDWARDS, J. R., 1984b, Irish: Planning and Preservation. *Journal of Multilingual and Multicultural Development*, 5 (3&4), 267-275.

EDWARDS, J. R., 1984c, Irish and English in Ireland. In P. TRUDGILL (ed.), *Language in the British Isles.* Cambridge: Cambridge University Press.

EDWARDS, J. R., 1985, *Language, Society and Identity.* Oxford: Blackwell.

EDWARDS, J. R., 1988, Bilingualism, Education and Identity. *Journal of Multilingual and Multicultural Development*, 9 (1&2), 203-210.

EDWARDS, J. R., 1994a, Canadian Update, and Rejoinder to the Comments. *International Journal of the Sociology of Language*, 110, 203-219.

EDWARDS, J. R., 1994b, Ethnolinguistic Pluralism and its Discontents: A Canadian Study, and Some General Observations. *International Journal of the Sociology of Language*, 110, 5-85.

EDWARDS, J. R., 1994c, *Multilingualism.* London/New York: Routledge.

EDWARDS, R. L. & CURIEL, H., 1989, Effects of the English-Only Movement on Bilingual Education. *Social Work In Education*, 12 (1), 53-66.

EDWARDS, V., 1984a, *Language Policy in Multicultural Britain.* London: Academic Press.

EDWARDS, V., 1994b, Edwards on Edwards: A Question of Relative Priorities. *International Journal of the Sociology of Language*, 110, 187-192.

EDWARDS, V., 1995a, Community Language Teaching in the UK: Ten Years On. *Child Language Teaching and Therapy*, 1995, 11 (1), 50-60.

EDWARDS, V., 1995b, *Reading in Multilingual Classrooms.* Reading: University of Reading.

EDWARDS, V., 1995c, *Speaking and Listening in Multilingual Classrooms.* Reading: University of Reading.

EDWARDS, V., 1995d, *Writing in Multilingual Classrooms.* Reading: University of Reading.

EDWARDS, V., 1996, *The Other Languages: A Guide to Multilingual Classrooms.* Reading: Reading and Language Information Centre.

EDWARDS, V. (ed.), 1995, *Building Bridges: Multilingual Resources for Children.* Clevedon: Multilingual Matters.

EDWARDS, V. & REDFERN, A., 1992, *The World in a Classroom: Language in Education in Britain and Canada.* Clevedon: Multilingual Matters.

EDWARDS, V. & REHORICK, S., 1990, Learning Environments in Immersion and Non-Immersion Classrooms: Are They Different? *The Canadian Modern Language Review*, 46 (3), 469-493.

EDWARDS, V. & WALKER, S., 1996, Some Status Issues in the Translation of Children's Books. *Journal of Multilingual and Multicultural Development*, 17 (5), 339-348.

EIFE, 1986, *Influence of Factors on the Learning of Basque.* Gasteiz, Spain: Universities and Research Secretariat for Language Policy, Department of Education.

EIFE, 1989, *Influence of Factors on the Learning of Basque. Study of the Models A, B and D in Fifth Year Basic General Education.* Gasteiz, Spain: Central Publications Service of the Basque Government.

EISEMAN, T. O., PROUTY, R. & SCHWILLE, J., 1989, What Language Should be Used for Teaching? Language Policy and School Reform in Burundi. *Journal of Multilingual and Multicultural Development*, 10 (6), 473-497.

EKSTRAND, L. H., 1989, The Relation Between Language, Affection and Cognition in Bilingualism. Paper Presented at the First European Congress of Psychology, Amsterdam, 2-7th July, 1989.

ELLIS, N., 1992, Linguistic Relativity Revisited: The Bilingual Word-Length Effect in Working Memory During Counting, Remembering Numbers and Mental Calculation. In R. J. HARRIS (ed.), *Cognitive Processing in Bilinguals.* Amsterdam: Elsevier Science Publishers.

ELLIS, R., 1984, *Classroom Second Language Development.* Oxford: Pergamon.

ELLIS, R., 1985, *Understanding Second Language Acquisition.* Oxford: Oxford University Press.

ELLIS, R., 1990, *Instructed Second Language Acquisition: Learning in the Classroom.* Oxford: Blackwell.

ESCH, E. (ed.), 1994, *Self-Access and the Adult Language Learner.* London: Centre for Information on Language Teaching and Research.

EUROPEAN BUREAU FOR LESSER USED LANGUAGES, 1993a, *Living Languages: The Sound of Europe.* Treforest, Wales: Zenith.

EUROPEAN BUREAU FOR LESSER USED LANGUAGES, 1993b, *Mini-Guide to the Lesser Used Languages of the EC.* Ireland: European Bureau for Lesser Used Languages.

EUROPEAN BUREAU FOR LESSER USED LANGUAGES, 1993c, *Select Bibliography on Lesser Used Languages in the European Community.* The European Bureau for Lesser Used Languages/Le Bureau Europeen pour les Langues Moins Repandues.

EUROPEAN BUREAU FOR LESSER USED LANGUAGES, 1994, *Vade Mecum: Guide to Legal Documents, Support Structures and Action Programmes Pertaining to the Lesser Used Languages of Europe.* Dublin: European Bureau for Lesser Used Languages.

EUROPEAN COMMISSION, 1994, *LINGUA Compendium 1993.* Brussels: European Commission.

EUROPEAN COMMISSION, 1996, *Euromosaic: The Production and Reproduction of the Minority Language Groups in the European Union.* Luxembourg: Office for Official Publications of the European Communities.

EUROPEAN COUNCIL OF INTERNATIONAL SCHOOLS, 1996, *The ECIS International Schools Directory.* London: Fieldwork Ltd.

EVANS, D. J., 1960, *Language Survey Report.* Dolgellau: Meirioneth Education Authority.

EVANS, E., 1972, Welsh as a Second Language in the Junior School. In M. CHAZAN (ed.), *Aspects of Primary Education.* Cardiff: University of Wales Press.

EXTRA, G. & VERHOEVEN, L., 1993, *Immigrant Languages in Europe.* Clevedon: Multilingual Matters.

F

FACT SHEETS ON HUNGARY, 1995, *The Republic of Hungary*. Budapest: Ministry of Foreign Affairs.

FACULTY OF EDUCATION, 1954, *A Welsh Linguistic Background Scale*. Pamphlet No. 2. Aberystwyth: University of Wales.

FACULTY OF EDUCATION, 1988, *Report on Secondary Education in Rural Wales*. Aberystwyth: University of Wales.

FACULTY OF EDUCATION, 1991, *Concept and Language Development in Children aged 5-7 (Welsh Office Project)*. Aberystwyth: University of Wales

FAHY, R. M., 1988, Irish in Education: A Study of Cognitive and Affective Aspects of Achievement in Irish Among Second-Level Learners. Ph.D. Thesis. Ireland: University College of Cork.

FAIRCHILD, H. H., 1990, Innovations in Bilingual Education: Contributions From Foreign Language Education. In A. M. PADILLA, H. H. FAIRCHILD & C. M. VALADEZ (eds), *Bilingual Education*. London/New Delhi: Sage.

FAIRCLOUGH, N. (ed.), 1992, *Critical Language Awareness*. London and New York: Longman.

FALTIS, C. J., 1993a, Critical Issues in the Use of Sheltered Content Teaching in High School Bilingual Programs. *Peabody Journal of Education*, 69 (1), 135-151.

FALTIS, C. J., 1993b, *Joinfostering: Adapting Teaching Strategies for the Multilingual Classroom*. New York: Macmillan.

FANTINI, A., 1985, *Language Acquisition of a Bilingual Child: A Sociolinguistic Perspective*. San Diego, CA: College Hill Press.

FASGOLD, R., 1984, *The Sociolinguistics of Society*. Oxford: Basil Blackwell.

FELDMAN, C. & SHEN, M., 1971, Some Language-Related Cognitive Advantages of Bilingual Five-Year-Olds. *Journal of Genetic Psychology*, 118, 235-244.

FELLMAN, J., 1973, *The Revival of a Classical Tongue, Eliezer Ben Yehudah and the Modern Hebrew Language*. The Hague: Mouton.

FERGUSON, C., 1959, Diglossia. *Word*, 15, 325-340.

FERGUSON, C., HOUGHTON, C. & WELLS, M., 1977, Bilingual Education: An International Perspective. In B. SPOLSKY & R. COOPER (eds), *Frontiers of Bilingual Education*. Rowley, MA: Newbury House.

FESTINGER, L., 1957, *A Theory of Cognitive Dissonance*. Stanford: Stanford University Press.

FEUERVERGER, G., 1989, Jewish-Canadian Ethnic Identity and Non-Native Language Learning: A Social-Psychological Study. *Journal of Multilingual and Multicultural Development*, 10 (4), 327-357.

FEUERVERGER, G., 1991, University Students' Perceptions of Heritage Language Learning and Ethnic Identity Maintenance. *The Canadian Modern Language Review*, 47 (4), 660-677.

FEUERVERGER, G., 1994, A Multilingual Literacy Intervention for Minority Language Students. *Language and Education*, 8 (3), 123-146.

FEUERVERGER, G., 1997, On the Edges of the Map: A Study of Heritage Language Teachers in Toronto. *Teacher and Teacher Education*, 13 (1), 39-53.

FIGUEROA, P., 1984, Minority Pupil Progress. In M. CRAFT (ed.), *Education and Cultural Pluralism*. London: Falmer Press.

FILLMORE, L. W. & VALADEZ, C., 1986, Teaching Bilingual Learners. In *Handbook of Research on Teaching* (Third edition). New York: MacMillan.

FINDLING, J., 1969, Bilingual Need Affiliation and Future Orientation in Extragroup and Intragroup Domains. *Modern Language Journal*, 53, 227-231.

FIRMAT, G. P., 1995, *Bilingual Blues*. Tempe, AZ: Bilingual Press.

FISHMAN, J. A., 1965, Who Speaks What Language to Whom and When? *La Linguistique*, 67-68.

FISHMAN J. A., 1971, The Sociology of Language. In J. FISHMAN (ed.), *Advances in the Sociology of Language, Volume 1*. The Hague: Mouton.

FISHMAN, J. A., 1972, *The Sociology of Language*. Rowley, MA: Newbury House.

FISHMAN, J. A., 1975, Review of CILAR. *Irish Times*, 15th August.

FISHMAN, J. A., 1976, *Bilingual Education: An International Sociological Perspective*. Rowley, MA: Newbury House.

FISHMAN, J. A., 1977, The Social Science Perspective. In CENTER FOR APPLIED LINGUISTICS (ed.), *Bilingual Education: Current Perspectives*. Arlington, VA: CAL.

FISHMAN, J. A., 1980a, Bilingualism and Biculturalism as Individual and as Societal Phenomena. *Journal of Multilingual and Multicultural Development*, 1, 3-15.

FISHMAN, J. A., 1980b, Ethnocultural Dimensions in the Acquisition and Retention of Biliteracy. *Basic Writing*, 3 (1), 48-61.

FISHMAN, J. A., 1984, Minority Mother Tongues in Education. *Prospects*, 14 (1), 52-61.

FISHMAN, J. A., 1989, *Language and Ethnicity in Minority Sociolinguistic Perspective*. Clevedon: Multilingual Matters.

FISHMAN, J. A., 1990, What is Reversing Language Shift (RLS) and How Can It Succeed? *Journal of Multilingual and Multicultural Development*, 11 (1&2), 5-34.

FISHMAN, J. A., 1991a, *Reversing Language Shift*. Clevedon: Multilingual Matters.

FISHMAN, J. A., 1991b, My Life Through My Work; My Work Through My Life. In K. KOERNER (ed.), *First Person Singular II* (Studies in the History of the Language Sciences, 61). Amsterdam: John Benjamins.

FISHMAN, J. A., 1993, Reversing Language Shift: Successes, Failures, Doubts and Dilemmas. In E. H. JAHR (ed.), *Language Conflict and Language Planning*. Berlin/New York: Mouton de Gruyter.

FISHMAN, J.A., 1996, *In Praise of the Beloved Language: A Comparative View of Positive Ethnolinguistic Consciousness*. Berlin: Mouton de Gruyter.

FISHMAN, J. A., 1997, Language and Ethnicity: The View from Within. In F. COULMAS (ed.), *The Handbook of Sociolinguistics*. Oxford: Blackwell.

FISHMAN, J. A. & RUBAL-LOPEZ, A., 1992, Cross-Polity Analysis of Factors Affecting English Language Spread: Predicting Three Criteria of Spread From a Large Pool of Independent Variables. *World Englishes*, 11 (2&3), 309-329.

FISHMAN, J. A., SOLANO, F. R. & MCCONNELL, 1991, A Methodological Check on Three Cross-Polity Studies of Linguistic Homogeneity/Heterogeneity. In E. M. MCGROARTY & C. J. FALTIS (eds), *Languages in School and Society. Policy and Pedagogy*. Berlin/New York: Mouton de Gruyter.

FITZGERALD, J., 1993, Views on Bilingualism in the United States: A Selective Historical Review. *Bilingual Research Journal*, 17 (1&2), 35-56.

FITZPATRICK, F., 1987, *The Open Door: The Bradford Bilingual Project*. Clevedon: Multilingual Matters.

FORTUNE, D. & FORTUNE, G., 1987, Karaja Literary Acquisition and Sociocultural Effects on a Rapidly Changing Culture. *Journal of Multilingual and Multicultural Development*, 8 (6), 469-49.

FRADD, S. H. & CORREA, V. I., 1989, Hispanic Students at Risk: Do We Abdicate or Advocate? *Exceptional Children*, 56 (2), 105-110.

FRADD, S. H. & TIKUNOFF, W. J. (eds), 1987, *Bilingual Education and Bilingual Special Education: A Guide for Administrators*. Boston: College-Hill Publication, Little, Brown and Company.

FRANKLIN, B. (ed.), 1995, *The Handbook of Children's Rights. Comparative Policy and Practice*. London and New York: Routledge.

FRASURE-SMITH, N., LAMBERT, W. E. & TAYLOR, D. M., 1975, Choosing The Language of Instruction For One's Children: A Quebec Study. *Journal of Cross-Cultural Psychology*, 6 (2), 131-155.

FREDERICKSON, N. & CLINE, T. (eds), 1990, *Curriculum Related Assessment with Bilingual Children. A Set of Working Papers*. London: University College, London.

FREEMAN, R., 1995a, An Alternative to Mainstream United States Educational Discourse: Implications for Minority Identity Development. In Georgetown University Round Table on Languages and Linguistics, *Educational Linguistics, Cross-Cultural Communication and Global Interdependence*. Washington, DC: Georgetown University Press.

FREEMAN, R., 1995b, Equal Educational Opportunity for Language Minority Students: From Policy to Practice at Oyster Bilingual School. *Issues in Applied Linguistics*, 6 (1), 39-63.

FREEMAN, R. & MCELHINNY, B., 1996, Language and Gender. In S. L. MCKAY & N. H. HORNBERGER (eds), *Sociolinguistics and Language Teaching*. Cambridge: Cambridge University Press.

FREIBEL, W. *et al.* (eds), 1996, *Education for European Citizenship: Theoretical and Practical Approaches*. Freiburg: Konzeption.

FREIRE, P., 1970, *Pedagogy of the Oppressed*. New York: Seabury Press/Continuum.

FREIRE, P., 1973, *Education for Critical Consciousness*. New York: Continuum.

FREIRE, P., 1985, *The Politics of Education*. South Hadley, MA: Bergin and Garvey.

FREIRE, P. & MACEDO, D., 1987, *Literacy: Reading the Word and the World*. South Hadley, MA: Bergin and Garvey.

FRENCK, C. & PYNTE, J., 1987, Semantic Representation and Surface Forms: A Look at Across-Language Priming in Bilinguals. *Journal of Psycholinguistic Research*, 16 (4), 383-396.

FROMM, E., 1970, Age Regression with Unexpected Reappearance of a Repressed Childhood Language. *International Journal of Clinical and Experimental Hypnosis*, 18, 79-88.

G

GAARDER, A. B., 1976, Linkages between Foreign Language Teaching and Bilingual Education. In J. E. ALATIS & K. TWADDELL (eds), *English as a Second Language in Bilingual Education*. Washington, DC: TESOL.

GAARDER, A. B., 1977, *Bilingual Schooling and the Survival of Spanish in the United States*. Rowley, MA: Newbury House.

GAGE, N. L., 1978, *The Scientific Basis of the Art of Teaching*. New York: Teachers College Press.

GAL, S., 1979, *Language Shift: Social Determinants of Linguistic Change in Bilingual Austria*. New York: Academic Press.

GALAMBOS, S. J. & GOLDIN-MEADOW, S., 1990, The Effects of Learning Two Languages on Levels of Metalinguistic Awareness. *Cognition*, 34 (1), 1-56.

GALAMBOS, S. J. & HAKUTA, K., 1988, Subject-Specific and Task-Specific Characteristics of Metalinguistic Awareness in Bilingual Children. *Applied Psycholinguistics*, 9 (2), 141-162.

GANDHI, M., 1929 (English edition 1949), *The Story of My Experiments with Truth*. London: Cape.

GARCÍA, E. E., 1986, Bilingual Development and the Education of Bilingual Children During Early Childhood. *American Journal of Education*, 95 (1), 96-121.

GARCÍA, E. E., 1988, Effective Schooling for Hispanics. *Urban Education Review*, 67 (2), 462-473.

GARCÍA, E. E., 1990, Educating Teachers for Language Minority Students. In W. R. HOUSTON, M. HABERMAN & J. SIKULA (eds), *Handbook of Research on Teacher Education*. New York: Macmillan.

GARCÍA, E. E., 1991a, *Education of Linguistically and Culturally Diverse Students: Effective Instructional Practices*. National Centre for Research on Cultural Diversity and Second Language Learning, United States Department of Education.

GARCÍA, E. E., 1991b, Effective Instruction for Language Minority Students: The Teacher. *Journal of Education*, 173 (2), 130-141.

GARCÍA, E. E., 1991c, The Politics of Bilingual Education. *The Review Of Education*, 13 (3&4), 192-194.

GARCÍA, E. E., 1993, Language, Culture and Education. *Review of Research in Education*, 19, 51-98.

GARCÍA, E. E. & HURTADO, A., 1995, Becoming American: A Review of Current Research on the Development of Racial and Ethnic Identity in Children. In W. D. HAWLEY & A. W. JACKSON (eds), *Toward a Common Destiny: Improving Race and Ethnic Relations in America*. San Francisco, CA: Jossey Bass Inc.

GARCÍA, E. E. & MCLAUGHLIN, B. (eds), 1995, *Meeting the Challenge of Linguistic and Cultural Diversity in Early Childhood Education*. New York: Teachers College Press.

GARCÍA, O., 1983, Sociolinguistics and Language Planning in Bilingual Education for Hispanics in the United States. *International Journal of the Sociology of Language*, 44, 43-54.

GARCÍA, O., 1988, The Education of Biliterate and Bicultural Children in Ethnic Schools in the United States. *Essays by Spencer Fellows of the National Academy of Education*, Volume 4, pp. 19-78.

GARCÍA, O., 1991a, Latinos and Bilingual Education in the United States: Their Role as Objects and Subjects. *New Language Planning Newsletter*, 6 (2), 3-5.

GARCÍA, O., 1991b, A Gathering of Voices, a 'Legion of Scholarly Decency' and Bilingual Education: Fishman's Biographemes as Introduction. In O. GARCÍA, (ed.), *Bilingual Education: Focusschrift in Honor of Joshua A. Fishman*. Amsterdam/Philadelphia: John Benjamins.

GARCÍA, O., 1992a, For It Is In Giving That We Receive: A History of Language Policy in the United States. Paper Presented to a Conference 'American Pluralism: Toward a History of the Discussion'. State University of New York at Stonybrook, June 7th, 1992.

GARCÍA, O., 1992b, Societal Multilingualism in a Multicultural World in Transition. In H. BYRNE (ed.), *Languages for a Multicultural World in Transition*. Illinois: National Textbook Company.

GARCÍA, O., 1994, Que Todo El Pluralismo Es Sueno, y Los Suenos, Vida Son: Ethnolinguistic Dreams and Reality. *International Journal of the Sociology of Language*, 110, 87-104.

GARCÍA, O., 1995, Spanish Language Loss as a Determinant of Income Among Latinos in the United States: Implications for Language Policy in Schools. In J. W. TOLLEFSON (ed.), *Power and Inequality in Language Education*. Cambridge: Cambridge University Press.

GARCÍA, O., 1997, Bilingual Education. In F. COULMAS (ed.), *The Handbook of Sociolinguistics*. Oxford: Blackwell.

GARCÍA, O. (ed.), 1991, *Bilingual Education: Focusschrift in Honor of Joshua A. Fishman*. Amsterdam/Philadelphia: John Benjamins.

GARCÍA, O. & BAKER, C. (eds), 1995, *Policy and Practice in Bilingual Education. A Reader Extending the Foundations*. Clevedon: Multilingual Matters.

GARCÍA, O. & FISHMAN, J.A. (eds), 1997, *The Multilingual Apple: Languages in New York City*. Berlin: Mouton de Gruyter.

GARCÍA, O. & OTHEGUY, R., 1985, The Masters of Survival Send Their Children to School: Bilingual Education in the Ethnic Schools of Miami. *Bilingual Review*, 12 (1&2), 3-19.

GARCÍA, O. & OTHEGUY, R., 1988, The Language Situation of Cuban Americans. In S. L. MCKAY & S. C. WONG (eds), *Language Diversity: Problem or Resource?* New York: Newbury House.

GARCÍA, O. & OTHEGUY, R., 1994, The Value of Speaking a LOTE in United States Business. *Annals of the American Academy of Political and Social Science*, 532, 99-122.

GARCÍA, O. & OTHEGUY, R. (eds), 1989, *English across Cultures. Cultures Across English*. Berlin: Mouton de Gruyter.

GARCÍA, R. & DIAZ, C. F., 1992, The Status and Use of Spanish and English among Hispanic Youth in Dade County (Miami) Florida: A Sociolinguistic Study. *Language and Education*, 6 (1), 13-32.

GARDNER, H., 1983, *Frames of Mind. The Theory of Multiple Intelligences*. New York: Basic Books.

GARDNER, R. C., 1979, Social Psychological Aspects of Second Language Acquisition. In H. GILES & R. ST. CLAIR (eds), *Language and Social Psychology*. Oxford: Blackwell.

GARDNER, R. C., 1981, Second Language Learning. In R. C. GARDNER & R. KALIN (eds), *A Canadian Social Psychology of Ethnic Relations*. London: Methuen.

GARDNER, R. C., 1982, Language Attitudes and Language Learning. In E. B. RYAN & H. GILES (eds), *Attitudes Towards Language Variation*. London: Edward Arnold.

GARDNER, R. C., 1983, Learning Another Language: A True Social Psychological Experiment. *Journal of Language and Social Psychology*, 2, 219-239.

GARDNER, R. C., 1985a, *Social Psychology and Second Language Learning*. London: Edward Arnold.

GARDNER, R. C., 1985b, *The Attitude/Motivation Test Battery*. Technical Report. Canada: University of Western Ontario.

GARDNER, R. C., 1988, The Socio-Educational Model of Second Language Learning: Assumptions, Findings and Issues. *Language Learning*, 38 (1), 101-126.

GARDNER, R. C., 1994, On Motivation, Research Agendas, and Theoretical Frameworks. *The Modern Language Journal*, 78 (3), 359-368.

GARDNER, R. C. & LAMBERT, W. E., 1959, Motivational Variables in Second Language Acquisition. *Canadian Journal of Psychology*, 13, 266-272.

GARDNER, R. C. & LAMBERT, W. E., 1972, *Attitudes and Motivation in Second Language Learning*. Rowley, MA: Newbury House.

GARDNER, R. C. & SMYTHE, P. C., 1975, *Second Language Acquisition: A Social Psychological Approach*. Research Bulletin 332, University of Western Ontario.

GARDNER, R. C. & SMYTHE, P. C., 1981, On the Development of the Attitude/Motivation Test Battery. *Canadian Modern Language Review*, 37, 510-525.

GARDNER, R. C., LALONDE, R. N. & MACPHERSON, J., 1986, Social Factors in Second Language Attrition. *Language Learning*, 35 (4), 519-540.

GARDNER, R. C., LALONDE, R. N. & MOORCROFT, R., 1987, Second Language Attrition: The Role of Motivation and Use. *Journal of Language and Social Psychology*, 6 (1), 29-47.

GARDNER, R. C., LALONDE, R. N. & PIERSON, R., 1983, The Socio-Educational Model of Second Language Acquisition: An Investigation Using LISREL Causal Modelling. *Journal of Language and Social Psychology*, 2, 51-65.

GARDNER R. C., MOORCROFT, R. & METFORD, J., 1989, Second Language Learning in an Immersion Programme: Factors Influencing Acquisition and Retention. *Journal of Language and Social Psychology*, 8 (5), 287-305.

GARIGUE, P., 1985, Bilingual University Education in Ontario. *The Canadian Modern Language Review*, 41 (5), 941-946.

GARMENDIA, KARMEN M. & AIZPURUA, X., 1990, A Demolinguistic Analysis of the Basque Autonomous Community Derived from the Census of 1986. In D. GORTER *et al.* (eds), *Fourth International Conference on Minority Languages, Vol. II: Western and Eastern European Papers*. Clevedon: Multilingual Matters.

GARRETT, P., GRIFFITHS, Y., JAMES, C. & SCHOLFIELD, P., 1992, Differences and Similarities Between and Within Bilingual Settings: Some British Data. *Language, Culture and Curriculum*, 5 (2), 99-115.

GATTEGNO, C., 1972, *Teaching Foreign Languages in Schools: The Silent Way* (Second edition). New York: Educational Solutions.

GATTEGNO, C., 1976, *The Common Sense of Teaching Foreign Languages*. New York: Educational Solutions.

GAUDART, H., 1987, A Typology of Bilingual Education in Malaysia. *Journal of Multilingual and Multicultural Development*, 8 (6), 529-552.

GAUDART, H., 1996, Some Malaysian Bilingual Student Teachers: A Profile. *Journal of Multilingual and Multicultural Development*, 17 (2-4), 169-189.

GEACH, J., 1996, Community Languages. In E. HAWKINS (ed.), *Thirty Years of Language Teaching*. London: Centre for Information on Language Teaching and Research (CILT).

GEACH, J. & BROADBENT, J. (eds), 1989, *Coherence in Diversity: Britain's Multilingual Classrooms*. London: Centre for Information on Language Teaching and Research.

GENERAL ACCOUNTING OFFICE, 1987, *Bilingual Education: A New Look at the Research Evidence*. Washington, DC: General Accounting Office.

GENESEE, F., 1976, The Role of Intelligence in Second Language Learning. *Language Learning*, 26, 267-280.

GENESEE, F., 1978, Second Language Learning and Language Attitudes. *Working Papers on Bilingualism*, 16, 19-42.

GENESEE, F., 1983, Bilingual Education of Majority-Language Children: The Immersion Experiments in Review. *Applied Psycholinguistics*, 4 (1), 1-46.

GENESEE, F., 1984a, Beyond Bilingualism: Social Psychological Studies of French Immersion Programs in Canada. *Canadian Journal of Behavioural Science*, 16 (4), 338-352.

GENESEE, F., 1984b, Historical and Theoretical Foundations of Immersion Education. In CALIFORNIA STATE DEPARTMENT OF EDUCATION (eds), *Studies on Immersion Education. A Collection for United States Educators*. California: California State Department of Education.

GENESEE, F., 1985, Second Language Learning Through Immersion: A Review of United States Programs. *Review of Educational Research*, 55 (4), 541-561.

GENESEE, F., 1986, The Baby and the Bathwater or What Immersion Has to Say About Bilingual Education: Teaching and Learning in Bilingual Education – Significant Immersion Instructional Features. *NABE Journal*, 10 (3), 227-254.

GENESEE, F., 1987, *Learning Through Two Languages*. Cambridge, MA: Newbury House.

GENESEE, F., 1988, The Canadian Second Language Immersion Program. In C. B. PAULSTON (ed.), *International Handbook of Bilingualism and Bilingual Education*. New York: Greenwood Press.

GENESEE, F., 1989, Early Bilingual Development: One Language or Two? *Journal of Child Language*, 16 (1), 161-179.

GENESEE, F., 1991, Second Language Learning in School Settings: Lessons from Immersion. In A. G. REYNOLDS (ed.), *Bilingualism, Multiculturalism and Second Language Learning*. Hillsdale, NJ: Lawrence Erlbaum.

GENESEE, F. (ed.), 1994, *Educating Second Language Children. The Whole Child, the Whole Curriculum, the Whole Community*. Cambridge: Cambridge University Press.

GENESEE, F., BOIVIN, I. & NICOLADIS, E., 1996, Talking with Strangers: A Study of Bilingual Children's Communicative Competence. *Applied Psycholinguistics*, 17 (4), 427-442.

GENESEE, F. & HAMAYAN, E., 1980 Individual Differences in Young Second Language Learners. *Applied Psycholinguistics*, 1, 95-110.

GENESEE, F. & HAMAYAN, E., 1994, Classroom-Based Assessment. In F. GENESEE (ed.), *Educating Second Language Children: The Whole Child, the Whole Curriculum, the Whole Community*. Cambridge: Cambridge University Press.

GENESEE, F., NICOLADIS, E. & PARADIS, J., 1995, Language Differentiation in Early Bilingual Development. *Journal of Child Language*, 22 (3), 611-63.

GENESEE, F., HOLOBOW, N. E., LAMBERT, W. E. & CHARTRAND, L., 1989, Three Elementary School Alternatives for Learning through a Second Language. *Modern Language Journal*, 73 (3), 250-263.

GENESEE, F., ROGERS, P. & HOLOBOW, N., 1983, The Social Psychology of Second Language Learning: Another Point of View. *Language Learning*, 33 (2), 209-224.

GENESEE, F., TUCKER, G. R. & LAMBERT, W. E., 1975, Communication Skills in Bilingual Children. *Child Development*, 46, 1010-1014.

GENESEE, F., TUCKER, G. R. & LAMBERT, W. E., 1978a, An Experiment in Trilingual Education. *Language Learning*, 28 (2), 343-366.

GENESEE, F. & UPSHUR, J. A., 1996, *Classroom-Based Evaluation in Second Language Education*. Cambridge: Cambridge University Press.

GERBER, S., 1994, Difficulties Involved with the Assessment of Bilingual Preschool Children: The Australian Context. *Australian Journal of Early Childhood*, 19 (2), 16-21.

GERSTEN, R., 1996, Literacy Instruction for Language-Minority Students: The Transition Years. *The Elementary School Journal*, 96 (3), 227-244.

GERSTEN, R. & WOODWARD, J., 1994, The Language-Minority Student and Special Education: Issues, Trends and Paradoxes. *Exceptional Children*, 60 (4), 310-322.

GERSTEN, R. & WOODWARD, J., 1995, A Longitudinal Study of Transitional and Immersion Bilingual Education Programs in One District. *The Elementary School Journal*, 95 (3), 223-239.

GHUMAN, P. A. S., 1991, Have They Passed the Cricket Test? A Qualitative Study of Asian Adolescents. *Journal of Multilingual and Multicultural Development*, 12 (5), 327-346.

GHUMAN, P. A. S., 1994, *Coping With Two Cultures: British Asian and Indo-Canadian Adolescents*. Clevedon: Multilingual Matters.

GHUMAN, P. A. S., 1995a, Acculturation, Ethnic Identity and Community Languages: A Study of Indo-Canadian Adolescents. In B. M. JONES & P. A. S. GHUMAN (eds), *Bilingualism, Education and Identity. Essays in Honour of Jac L. Williams*. Cardiff: University of Wales Press.

GHUMAN, P. A. S., 1995b, *Asian Teachers in British Schools: A Study of Two Generations*. Clevedon: Multilingual Matters.

GILES, H. & BYRNE, J. L., 1982, An Intergroup Approach to Second Language Acquisition. *Journal of Multilingual and Multicultural Development*, 3 (1), 17-40.

GILES, H. & COUPLAND, N., 1991, *Language: Contexts and Consequences*. Milton Keynes: Open University Press.

GILES, H. & SAINT-JACQUES, B. (eds), 1979, *Language and Ethnic Relations*. Oxford: Pergamon.

GILES, H., BOURHIS R. & TAYLOR, D., 1977, Towards a Theory of Language in Ethnic Group Relations. In H. GILES (ed.), *Language, Ethnicity and Intergroup Relations*. London: Academic Press.

GILES, H., HEWSTONE, M. & BALL, P., 1983. Language Attitudes in Multilingual Settings: Prologue with Priorities. *Journal of Multilingual and Multicultural Development*, 4 (2&3), 81-100.

GILES, H., LEETS, L. & COUPLAND, N., 1990, Minority Language Group Status: A Theoretical Conspexus. *Journal of Multilingual and Multicultural Development*, 11 (1&2), 37-55.

GILL, D., MAYOR, B. & BLAIR, M. (eds), 1992, *Racism and Education: Structures and Strategies*. London: Sage Publications in association with the Open University.

GILLETT, J. S., 1987, Ethnic Bilingual Education for Canada's Minority Groups. *The Canadian Modern Language Review*, 43 (2), 337-356.

GILLIES, W., 1987, Scottish Gaelic: The Present Situation. In G. MACEOIN *et al.* (eds), *Third International Conference on Minority Languages: Celtic Papers*. Clevedon: Multilingual Matters.

GIRARD, D., 1988, *Selection and Distribution of*

Contents in Language Syllabuses. Strasbourg: Council of Europe

GITTINS REPORT, 1967, *Primary Education in Wales. A Central Advisory Council Education Report*. Cardiff: HMSO.

GLENN, C. L., 1990, How to Integrate Bilingual Education Without Tracking. *Principal Magazine*, 47 (5), 28-31.

GLENN, C. L., 1992, Educating the Children of Immigrants. *Phi Delta Kappan*, 73, 404-408.

GLIKSMAN, L., 1976. Second Language Acquisition: The Effects of Student Attitudes on Classroom Behaviour. Unpublished M.A. Thesis, University of Western Ontario.

GLIKSMAN, L., 1981, Improving the Prediction of Behaviours Associated with Second Language Acquisition. Unpublished Ph.D. Thesis, University of Western Ontario.

GLINERT, L. H., 1995, Inside the Language Planner's Head: Tactical Responses to a Mass Immigration. *Journal of Multilingual and Multicultural Development*, 16 (5), 351-371.

GOLDENBERG, C., 1993, *The Home-School Connection in Bilingual Education, Bilingual Education: Politics, Practice and Research, Part II, Ninety-Second Yearbook of the National Society for the Study of Education*. Chicago: University of Chicago Press.

GOLDSTEIN, T., 1997, *Two Languages at Work: Bilingual Life on the Production Floor.* Berlin: Mouton de Gruyter.

GOMEZ-FERNANDEZ, D. E., SINEIRO-GARCIA, C., NOGUEIRA-GARCIA, A. & PULIDO-PICOUTO, M. T., 1990, The Differential Evaluation of Psycholinguistic Abilities of Bilingual Children. *Journal of Multilingual and Multicultural Development*, 11 (3), 191-197.

GONZALEZ, A. B., 1982, *Bilingual Schooling at De La Salle Grade School (Taft Avenue): A Case Study*. Manila, Philippines: De La Salle University.

GONZALEZ, A. B., 1991, *Managing Language and Literature Programs in the Philippine Setting*. Quezon City: Phoenix Publishing House.

GONZALEZ, A. B., 1992, Prospective Issues and Problems of Language Teaching in the Third World. In J. F. MATTER (ed.), *Language Teaching in the Twenty-First Century: Problems and Prospects* (*AILA Review*, 9, 55-62).

GONZALEZ, A. B., 1996, Using Two/Three Languages in Philippine Classrooms: Implications for Policies, Strategies and Practices. *Journal of Multilingual and Multicultural Development*, 17 (2-4), 210-219.

GONZALEZ, A. B. & BAUTISTA, M. L. S., 1986, *Language Surveys in the Philippines (1966–1984)*. Manila, Philippines: De La Salle University Press.

GONZALEZ, A. B. & SIBAYAN, B. P., 1988, *Evaluating Bilingual Education in the Philippines (1974–1985)*. Manila: Linguistic Society of the Philippines.

GONZALEZ, A. B., HALIM, A., ANGKAB, P. & NOSS, R. B., 1984, *An Overview of Language Issues in South-East Asia, 1950–1980*. New York: Oxford University Press.

GONZALEZ, G. & MAEZ, L. F., 1995, Advances in Research in Bilingual Education. *Directions in Language and Education*, 1 (5). Texas A. & M. University, Kingsville: National Clearinghouse for Bilingual Education.

GONZALEZ, J. M., 1979, Coming of Age in Bilingual/Bicultural Education: A Historical Perspective. In H. T. TRUEBA & C. BARNETT-MIZRAHI (eds), *Bilingual Multicultural Education and the Professional: From Theory to Practice*. Rowley, MA: Newbury House.

GONZALEZ, N., MOLL, L. C., FLOYD-TENNERY, M., RIVERA, A., RENDON, P., GONZALES, R. & AMANTI, C., 1993, *Teacher Research on Funds of Knowledge: Learning from Households*. National Centre for Research on Cultural Diversity and Second Language Learning, US Department of Education.

GOODMAN, K., GOODMAN, Y. & FLORES, B., 1979, *Reading in the Classroom: Literacy and Biliteracy*. Rosslyn, VA: National Clearing House for Bilingual Education.

GOODZ, N. S., 1989, Parental Language Mixing in Bilingual Families. *Infant Mental Health Journal*, 10 (1), 25-44.

GOODZ, N. S., 1994, Interactions Between Parents and Children in Bilingual Families. In F. GENESEE (ed.), *Educating Second Language Children: The Whole Child, the Whole Curriculum, the Whole Community*. Cambridge: Cambridge University Press.

GORDON, M. E., 1980, Attitudes and Motivation in Second Language Achievement. Unpublished Ph.D. Thesis, University of Toronto.

GORDON, M. M., 1964, *Assimilation in American Life: The Role of Race, Religion and National Origins*. New York: Oxford University Press.

GORRELL, J., 1987, Spatial Role-Taking Ability Among Bilingual and Monolingual Kindergarten Children. *Journal of Psycholinguistic Research*, 16 (2), 91-99.

GORTER, D., 1987, Aspects of Language Choice in the Frisian-Dutch Bilingual Context: Neutrality and Asymmetry. *Journal of Multilingual and Multicultural Development*, 8 (1&2), 121-132.

GORTER, D., 1994, A Malcontent from the Village: A Comment on John Edwards. *International Journal of the Sociology of Language*, 110, 105-112.

GOWAN, J. C. & TORRANCE, E. P., 1965, An Intercultural Study of Nonverbal Ideational Fluency. *Gifted Child Quarterly*, 9, 13-15.

GRABE, W. & KAPLAN, R. B., 1992, *Introduction to Applied Linguistics*. Reading, MA: Addison-Wesley.

GRABE, W. (ed.), 1993, *Issues in Second Language Teaching and Learning*. New York: Cambridge University Press.

GRADDOL, D. & THOMAS, S., 1995, *Language in a Changing Europe*. Clevedon: Multilingual Matters.

GRADDOL, D., THOMPSON, L. & BYRAM, M. (eds), 1993, *Language and Culture*. Clevedon: British Association of Applied Linguistics in association with Multilingual Matters Ltd.

GRAFF, H. J., 1979, *The Literacy Myth: Literacy and Social Structure in the 19th Century City*. New York: Academic Press.

GRANT, J. H., 1983, An Investigation into the Feasibility of Establishing Gaelic/English Bilingual Primary Schools on the Mainland of Scotland. Unpublished Master's thesis, University of Glasgow.

GRANT, N., 1984, Cultural Diversity and Education in Scotland. *European Journal of Education: Research, Development and Policies*, 19 (1), 53-64.

GRAVELLE, M., 1991, To Prove or Improve? Assessment Issues with Particular Reference to Bilingual Learners. *The Curriculum Journal*, 3 (2), 185-194.

GRAVES, D. H., 1983, *Writing: Teachers and Children at Work*. London: Heinemann.

GREEN, P. S., 1975, *Language Aptitude Test*. Language Teaching Centre: University of York.

GREENE, D., 1981, The Atlantic Group: Neo Celtic and Faroese. In E. HAUGEN, J. D. MCCLURE & D. THOMSON (eds), *Minority Languages Today*. Edinburgh: Edinburgh University Press.

GREGORY, E., 1993, Sweet and Sour: Learning to Read in a British and Chinese School. *English in Education*, 27 (3), 53-59.

GREGORY, E., 1994, Cultural Assumptions and Early Years' Pedagogy: The Effect of the Home Culture on Minority Children's Interpretation of Reading in School. *Language, Culture and Curriculum*, 7 (2), 111-124.

GREGORY, E., 1996, *Making Sense of a New World: Learning to Read in a Second Language*. London: Chapman.

GREGORY, S., 1996, Implications of Recent Research in the UK and Beyond. In P. KNIGHT & R. SWANWICK (eds), *Bilingualism and the Education of Deaf Children: Advances in Practice*. Leeds, United Kingdom: ADEDC, School of Education, University of Leeds.

GREGORY, S., WELLS, A. & SMITH, S., 1997, *Bilingual Education With Deaf Children*. Clevedon: Multilingual Matters.

GRIEGO-JONES, T., 1994, Assessing Students' Perceptions of Biliteracy in Two Way Bilingual Classrooms. *Journal of Educational Issues of Language Minority Students*, 13, 79-93.

GRIFFITHS, M., 1986, Introduction. In M. GRIFFITHS (ed.), *The Welsh Language in Education*. Cardiff: Welsh Joint Education Council.

GRILLO, R. D., 1989, *Dominant Languages. Language and Hierarchy in Britain and France*. Cambridge: Cambridge University Press.

GRIMES, B.F., 1996, *Ethnologue: Languages of the World* (Thirteenth edition). Texas: The Summer Institute of Linguistics. (http://www.sil.org/ethnologue/ethnologue.html)

GRIN, F., 1990, The Economic Approach to Minority Languages. *Journal of Multilingual and Multicultural Development*, 11 (1&2), 153-171.

GROSJEAN, F., 1982, *Life with Two Languages: An Introduction to Bilingualism*. Cambridge, MA: Harvard University Press.

GROSJEAN, F., 1985, The Bilingual as a Competent But Specific Speaker-Hearer. *Journal of Multilingual and Multicultural Development*, 6 (6), 467-477.

GROSJEAN, F., 1989, Neurolinguists, Beware! The Bilingual Is Not Two Monolinguals In One Person. *Brain and Language*, 36, 3-15.

GROSJEAN, F., 1992a, Another View of Bilingualism. *Cognitive Processing in Bilinguals*, 83, 51-62.

GROSJEAN, F., 1992b, The Bilingual and Bicultural Person in the Hearing and the Deaf World. *Sign Language Studies*, 77, 307-320.

GROSJEAN, F., 1994, Individual Bilingualism. In R. E. ASHER & J. M. SIMPSON (eds), *The Encyclopedia of Language and Linguistics, Volume 3*. Oxford: Pergamon.

GROSJEAN, F., 1995, A Psycholinguistic Approach to Code-Swtiching: The Recognition of Guest Words by Bilinguals. In L. MILROY & P. MUYSKEN (eds), *One Speaker, Two Languages*. Cambridge: Cambridge University Press.

GROSJEAN, F. & MILLER, J. L., 1994, Going In and Out of Languages: An Example of Bilingual Flexibility. *Psychological Science*, 5 (4), 201-206.

GROSSMAN, H., 1995, *Educating Hispanic Students: Implications for Instruction, Classroom Management, Counselling and Assessment* (Second edition). Springfield IL: Charles C. Thomas.

GROVER, M., 1993, Flowers in the Language Garden: The Story of Multilingual Matters. *Primary Teaching Studies*, 12-13.

GUBOGLO, M. N., 1986, Factors Affecting Bilingualism in National Languages and Russian in a Developed Socialist Society. In B. SPOLSKY (ed.), *Language and Education in Multilingual Settings*. Clevedon: Multilingual Matters.

GUILFORD, J. P., 1982, Cognitive Psychology's Ambiguities: Some Suggested Remedies. *Psychological Review*, 89, 48-59.

GUIMOND, S. & PALMER, D. L., 1993, Developmental Changes in Ingroup Favouritism among Bilingual and Unilingual Francophone and Anglophone Students. *Journal of Language and Social Psychology*, 12 (4), 318-351.

GUIORA, A., 1984, The Dialectic of Language Acquisition. *Language Learning*, 35, 3-12.

GUMPERZ, J. J. & HERNANDEZ-CHAVEZ, E., 1978, Bilingualism, Bidialectism and Classroom Interaction. In M. LOURIE & N. CLONKIN (eds), *A Pluralistic Nation*. Rowley, MA: Newbury House.

GUNTHER, W., 1990, Language Conservancy or Can the Anciently Established British Minority Languages Survive? In D. GORTER *et al.* (eds), *Fourth International Conference on Minority Languages. Vol. II: Western and Eastern European Papers*. Clevedon: Multilingual Matters.

GURDIAN, G. & SALAMANCA, D., 1990, Bilingual Education in Nicaragua. *Prospects (UNESCO)*, 20 (3), 357-364.

GUTIERREZ, K. D., 1992, A Comparison of Instructional Contexts in Writing Process Classrooms with Latino Children. *Education and Urban Society*, 24 (2), 244-262.

GUTIERREZ, P., 1994, A Preliminary Study of Deaf Educational Policy. *Bilingual Research Journal*, 18 (3&4), 85-113.

H

HAARMANN, H., 1986, *Language in Ethnicity*. The Hague: Mouton de Gruyter.

HAARMANN, H., 1991, Language Politics and the New European Identity. In F. COULMAS (ed.), *A Language Policy for the European Community*. Berlin/New York: Mouton de Gruyter.

HAARMANN, H., 1995, Multilingualism and Ideology: The Historical Experiment of Soviet Language Politics. *European Journal of Intercultural Studies*, 5 (3), 6-17.

HAAS, W. (ed.), 1982, *Standard Languages, Spoken and Written*. Manchester: Manchester University Press.

HABERLAND, H., 1991, Reflections about Minority Languages in the European Community. In F. COULMAS (ed.), *A Language Policy for the European Community*. Berlin/New York: Mouton de Gruyter.

HAGEMEYER, A., 1992, *The Red Notebook*. Silver Spring, MD: National Association of the Deaf.

HAGEN, S. (ed.), 1993, *Languages in European Business: A Regional Survey of Small and Medium-sized Companies*. London: Centre for Information on Language Teaching and Research (CILT).

HAKUTA, K., 1986a, *Cognitive Development of Bilingual Children*. University of California, LA: Center for Language Education and Research.

HAKUTA, K., 1986b, *Mirror of Language: The Debate on Bilingualism*. New York: Basic Books.

HAKUTA, K., 1987, Degree of Bilingualism and Cognitive Ability in Mainland Puerto Rican Children. *Child Development*, 58, 1372-1388.

HAKUTA, K., 1988, Why Bilinguals? In F. S. KESSEL (ed.), *The Development of Language and Language Researchers*. Hillsdale, NJ: Erlbaum.

HAKUTA, K., 1990a, Bilingualism and Bilingual Education: A Research Perspective. *Focus: Occasional Papers in Bilingual Education*, 1. Washington, DC: National Clearinghouse for Bilingual Education.

HAKUTA, K., 1990b, Language Cognition in Bilingual Children. In A. M. PADILLA, H. H. FAIRCHILD & C. M. VALADEZ (eds), *Bilingual Education: Issues and Strategies*. London/New Delhi: Sage.

HAKUTA, K. & DIAZ, R. M., 1985, The Relationship Between Degree of Bilingualism and Cognitive Ability: A Critical Discussion and Some New Longitudinal Data. In K. E. NELSON (ed.), *Children's Language, Volume 5*. Hillsdale, NJ and London: Erlbaum.

HAKUTA, K. & GARCÍA, E. E., 1989, Bilingualism and Education. *American Psychologist*, 44 (2), 374-379.

HAKUTA, K. & GOULD, L. J., 1987, Synthesis of Research on Bilingual Education. *Educational Leadership*, 44, 38-45.

HAKUTA, K. & PEASE-ALVAREZ, L., 1992, Enriching our Views of Bilingualism and Bilingual Education. *Educational Researcher*, 21 (2), 4-6.

HAKUTA, K. *et al.*, 1986, *Bilingualism and Cognitive Development: Three Perspectives and Methodological Implications*. Washington, DC: Office of Educational Research and Improvement.

HALL, D. D., 1995, *Assessing the Needs of Bilingual Pupils. Living in Two Languages*. London: David Fulton.

HALL, K., 1993, Process Writing in French Immersion. *The Canadian Modern Language Review*, 49 (2), 255-274.

HALLIDAY, M. A. K., 1973, *Explorations in the Functions of Language*. London: Edward Arnold.

HALLINGER, P. & MURPHY, J. F., 1986, The Social Context of Effective Schools. *American Journal of Education*, May, 328-355.

HALSALL, N., 1994, Attrition/Retention of Students in French Immersion with Particular Emphasis on Secondary School. *The Canadian Modern Language Review*, 50 (2), 313-333.

HALSALL, N. & WALL, C., 1992, Pedagogical Practices in French Immersion and Regular English Programs. *The Canadian Modern Language Review*, 49 (1), 61-79.

HAMAYAN, E. V. & DAMICO, J. S. (eds), 1991, *Limiting Bias in the Assessment of Bilingual Students*. Austin, TX: Pro-Ed.

HAMERS, J. F. & BLANC, M. H., 1982, Towards a Social-Psychological Model of Bilingual Development. *Journal of Language and Social Psychology*, 1 (1), 29-49.

HAMERS, J. F. & BLANC, M. H., 1983, Bilinguality in the Young Child: A Social Psychological Model. In P. H. NELDE (ed.), *Theory, Methods and Models of Contact Linguistics*. Bonn: Dummler.

HAMERS, J. F. & BLANC, M. H., 1989, *Bilinguality and Bilingualism*. Cambridge: Cambridge University Press.

HAMILTON, M., BARTON, D. & IVANIC, R. (eds), 1994, *Worlds of Literacy*. Clevedon: Multilingual Matters.

HAMMERLY, H., 1987, The Immersion Approach: Litmus Test of Second Language Acquisition through Classroom Communication. *Modern Language Journal*, 71 (4), 395-401.

HAMMERLY, H., 1988, French Immersion (Does It Work?) and the Development of the Bilingual Proficiency Report. *Canadian Modern Language Review*, 45 (3), 567-578.

HAMNETT, K., 1992, The Educational Benefits to be Derived from Twinning Links and Exchanges. Unpublished M.Ed. Thesis. Bangor: University of Wales.

HANSEGARD, N. E., 1975, *Tvasprakighet eller halvsprakighet?* Aldus, Series 253, Stockholm, Third edition.

HANSEN, S-E., 1987, Mother-Tongue Teaching and Identity: The Case of Finland-Swedes. *Journal of Multilingual and Multicultural Development*, 8 (1&2), 75-82.

HARDING, E. & RILEY, P., 1986, *The Bilingual Family: A Handbook for Parents*. Cambridge: Cambridge University Press.

HARLEY, B., 1986, *Age in Second Language Acquisition*. Clevedon: Multilingual Matters.

HARLEY, B., 1987, Developing and Evaluating Second Language Materials in Early French Immersion. *Evaluation and Research in Education*, 1 (2), 75-81.

HARLEY, B., 1991, Directions in Immersion Research. *Journal of Multilingual and Multicultural Development*, 12 (1&2), 9-19.

HARLEY, B., 1994, Maintaining French as a

Second Language in Adulthood. *Canadian Modern Language Review*, 50 (4), 688-713.

HARLEY, B. *et al.*, 1987, *The Development of Bilingual Proficiency*. Final Report (3 volumes). Toronto: Ontario Institute for Studies in Education.

HARLEY, B. *et al.*, 1990, *The Development of Second Language Proficiency*. Cambridge: Cambridge University Press.

HARLEY, B., HART, D. & LAPKIN, S., 1986, The Effects of Early Bilingual Schooling on First Language Skills. *Applied Psycholinguistics*, 7 (4), 295-321.

HARRIS, J., 1988, Spoken Irish in the Primary School System. *International Journal of the Sociology of Language*, 70, 69-88.

HARRIS, J. & MURTAGH, L., 1987, Irish and English in Gaeltacht Primary Schools. In G. MACEOIN *et al.* (eds), *Third International Conference on Minority Languages: Celtic Papers*. Clevedon: Multilingual Matters.

HARRIS, J. & MURTAGH, L., 1988, National Assessment of Irish-Language Speaking and Listening Skills in Primary School Children: Research Issues in the Evaluation of School-Based Heritage-Language Programmes. *Language, Culture and Curriculum*, 1 (2), 85-130.

HARRIS, J. G., CULLUM, C. M. & PUENTO, A. E., 1995, Effects of Bilingualism on Verbal Learning and Memory in Hispanic Adults. *Journal of the International Neuropsychological Society*, 1 (1), 10-16.

HARRIS, P. R. & MORAN, R. T., 1991, *Managing Cultural Differences: High Performance Strategies for a New World of Business*. Houston, TX: Gulf Publishing Company.

HARRISON, D. & MARMEN, L., 1994, *Languages in Canada*. Ottawa: Statistics Canada.

HARRISON, G., BELLIN, W. & PIETTE, B., 1981, *Bilingual Mothers in Wales and the Language of their Children*. Cardiff: University of Wales Press.

HARRIS, J., 1984, *Spoken Irish in Primary Schools: An Analysis of Achievement*. Dublin: Instituid Teangeolaiochta Eireann.

HARRY, B., 1992, *Cultural Diversity, Families and the Special Education System. Communication and Empowerment*. New York: Teachers College Press.

HARSCH, R., 1994/95, *Education in the Grand-Duchy of Luxembourg*. Luxembourg: Unité Nationale d'Eurydice.

HART, D., LAPKIN, S. & SWAIN, M., 1987, Communicative Language Tests: Perks and Perils. *Evaluation and Research in Education*, 1 (2), 83-94.

HARTMAN, D. & HENDERSON, J. (eds), 1994, *Aboriginal Languages in Education*. Alice Springs, Australia: IAD Press.

HARVEY, F., 1988, The Other Ethnic Groups in Quebec: The Stakes of the Linguistic Struggle. *Language, Culture and Curriculum*, 1 (3), 197-202.

HARWOOD, J. *et al.*, 1994, The Genesis of Vitality Theory: Historical Patterns and Discoursal Dimensions. *International Journal of the Sociology of Language*, 108, 167-206.

HASELKORN, D. & CALKINS, A., 1993, *Careers in Teaching Handbook*. Belmont, MA: Recruiting New Teachers Inc.

HATCH, E., 1978, Discourse Analysis and Second Language Acquisition. In E. HATCH (ed.), *Second Language Acquisition: A Book of Readings*. Rowley, MA: Newbury House.

HAUGEN, E., 1966, *Language Conflict and Language Planning: The Case of Modern Norwegian*. Cambridge, MA: Harvard University Press.

HAUGEN, E., 1967, *The Norwegians in America, 1825-1975*. Oslo: Royal Ministry of Foreign Affairs.

HAUGEN, E., 1969, *The Norwegian Language in America: A Study in Bilingual Behavior*. Bloomington, IN: Indiana University Press.

HAUGEN, E., 1972, *The Ecology of Language*. Stanford, CA: Stanford University Press.

HAUGEN, E., 1976, *The Scandinavian Languages*. London: Faber and Faber.

HAUGEN, E., 1981, *Language Conflict and Language Planning: The Case of Modern Norwegian*. Ann Arbor, MI: University Microfilms International.

HAUGEN, E., 1987, *Blessings of Babel: Bilingualism and Language Planning: Problems and Pleasures*. Berlin, New York: de Gruyter.

HAUGEN, E., MCCLURE, J. D. & THOMSON, D. (eds), 1981, *Minority Languages Today. A Selection from the Papers Read at the First International Conference on Minority Languages held at Glasgow University from 8 to 13 September 1980*. Edinburgh: Edinburgh University Press.

HAWKINS, E., 1981, *Modern Languages in the Curriculum*. Cambridge: Cambridge University Press.

HAWKINS, E., 1987, *Awareness of Language: An Introduction*. Cambridge: Cambridge University Press.

HAWKINS, E., 1992, Awareness of Language/Knowledge About Language in the Curriculum in England and Wales: An Historical Note on Twenty Years of Curricular Debate. *Language Awareness*, 1 (1), 5-17.

HAYES, J. L. *et al.*, 1991, The Bilingual/Bicultural Education of Deaf Individuals: A Vygotskian Perspective. *Teaching English to Deaf and Second Language Students*, 9 (2), 10-13.

HEARN, P. & BUTTON, D. (eds), 1994, *Language Industries Atlas*. Amsterdam/Oxford/Washington/Tokyo: IOS Press.

HEATH, S. B., 1982, What No Bedtime Story Means: Narrative Skills at Home and School. *Language in Society*, 11, 49-78.

HEATH, S. B., 1983, *Ways with Words: Language, Life and Work in Communities and Classrooms*. Cambridge: Cambridge University Press.

HEATH, S. B., 1986, Sociocultural Contexts of Language Development. OFFICE OF BILINGUAL AND BICULTURAL EDUCATION (eds), *Beyond Language: Social and Cultural Factors in Schooling Language Minority Students*. Los Angeles: California State University, Evaluation, Dissemination and Assessment Center.

HEATH, S. B., 1995, Race, Ethnicity, and the Defiance of Categories. In W. D. HAWLEY & A. W. JACKSON (eds), *Toward a Common Destiny: Improving Race and Ethnic Relations in America*. San Francisco: Jossey-Bass.

HELANDER, E., 1992, *The Sómi of Norway*. Oslo: Ministry of Foreign Affairs (NORINFORM).

HELLE, T., 1994, Directions in Bilingual Education: Finnish Comprehensive Schools in Perspective. *International Journal of Applied Linguistics*, 4 (2), 197-219.

HELLER, M., 1990, French Immersion in Canada: A Model for Switzerland? *Multilingua*, 9 (1), 67-85.

HELLER, M., 1994, *Crosswords. Language, Education and Ethnicity in French Ontario*. Berlin and New York: Mouton de Gruyter.

HELOT, C., 1988, Bringing Up Children in English, French and Irish: Two Case Studies. *Language, Culture and Curriculum*, 1 (3), 281-287.

HENZE, R. C. & VANETT, L., 1993, To Walk in Two Worlds – Or More? Challenging a Common Metaphor or Native Education. *Anthropology and Education Quarterly*, 24 (2), 116-134.

HER MAJESTY'S STATIONERY OFFICE, 1965, *Immigration from the Commonwealth*. London: HMSO.

HERMAN, S. R., 1968, Explorations in the Social Psychology of Language Choice. In J. A. FISHMAN (ed.), *Readings in the Sociology of Language*. The Hague: Mouton de Gruyter.

HERNANDEZ, R. D., 1994, Reducing Bias in the Assessment of Culturally and Linguistically Diverse Populations. *The Journal of Educational Issues of Language Minority Students*, 14, 269-300.

HERNANDEZ-CHAVEZ, E., 1984, The Inadequacy of English Immersion Education as an Educational Approach for Language Minority Students in the United States. In CALIFORNIA STATE DEPARTMENT OF EDUCATION (ed.), *Studies on Immersion Education. A Collection for United States Educators*. California: California State Department of Education.

HERNANDEZ-CHAVEZ, E., 1988, Language Policy and Language Rights in the United States: Issues in Bilingualism. In T. SKUTNABB-KANGAS & J. CUMMINS (eds), *Minority Education: From Shame to Struggle*. Clevedon/Philadelphia: Multilingual Matters.

HERNANDEZ-CHAVEZ, E., BURT, M. & DULAY, H., 1978, Language Dominance and Proficiency Testing: Some General Considerations. *NABE Journal*, 3 (1), 41-54.

HEUMANN, Y., 1993, *L'Ecole européenne: une contribution a la construction d'une Europe unie*. Schola Europa, Bruxelles.

HICKEY, T. and WILLIAMS, J. (eds), 1996, *Language, Education and Society in a Changing World*. Clevedon: Multilingual Matters.

HIGHAM, J., 1975, *Send These To Me*. New York: Athenaeum.

HIRSCH, E. D., 1988, *Cultural Literacy. What Every American Needs to Know*. New York: Vintage Books.

HIRSCH, E. D. (ed.), 1993, *What Your 6th Grader Needs to Know*. New York: Doubleday.

HOFFMAN, N., 1934, *The Measurement of Bilingual Background*. New York: Teachers College Press.

HOFFMANN, C., 1985, Language Acquisition in Two Trilingual Children. *Journal of Multilingual and Multicultural Development*, 6 (6), 479-495.

HOFFMANN, C., 1991a, *An Introduction to Bilingualism*. London: Longman.

HOFFMANN, C., 1991b, Language and Identity: The Case of German. In P. MEARA & A. RYAN (eds), *Language and Nation*. London: Center for Information on Language Teaching and Research.

HOFFMANN, C. (ed.), 1996, *Language, Culture and Communication in Contemporary Europe*. Clevedon: Multilingual Matters.

HOLM, A. & HOLM, W., 1990, Rock Point, A Navajo Way to go to School. In C. B. CAZDEN & C. E. SNOW (eds), *The Annals of the American Academy of Political and Social Science*, Volume 508, 170-184.

HOLMEN, A., HANSEN, E., GIMBEL, J. & JORGENSEN, J. N. (eds), 1988, *Bilingualism and the Individual*. Copenhagen Studies in Bilingualism, Volume 4. Clevedon/Philadelphia: Multilingual Matters.

HOLMES, B., 1996, Special Educational Needs. In E. HAWKINS (ed.), *Thirty Years of Language Teaching*. London: Centre for Information on Language Teaching and Research (CILT).

HOLMES, J., 1997, Keeping Tabs on Language Shift in New Zealand. *Journal of Multilingual and Multicultural Development*, 18(1), 17-39.

HOLOBOW, N. E., GENESEE, F., LAMBERT, W. E., GASTRIGHT, J. & MET, M., 1987, Effectiveness of Partial French Immersion for Children from Different Social Class and Ethnic Backgrounds. *Applied Psycholinguistics*, 8 (2), 137-151.

HOLT, D. D. (ed.), 1993, *Co-operative Learning: A Response to Linguistic and Cultural Diversity*. McHenry, IL: Delta Systems Inc.

HOMEL, P., PALIJ, M. & AARONSON, D. (eds), 1987, *Childhood Bilingualism: Aspects of Linguistic Cognitive and Social Development*. Hillsdale, NJ: Erlbaum.

HOPSTOCK, P. J. & BUCARO, B. J., 1993, *A Review and Analysis of Estimates of the LEP Student Population*. Arlington, VA: Special Issues Analysis Center.

HORNBERGER, N. H., 1988, *Bilingual Education and Language Maintenance: A Southern Peruvian Quechua Case*. Dordrecht, Holland: Foris.

HORNBERGER, N. H., 1989, Continua of Biliteracy. *Review of Educational Research*, 59 (3), 271-296.

HORNBERGER, N. H., 1990a, Teacher Quechua Use in Bilingual and Non-Bilingual Classrooms of Puno, Peru. In R. JACOBSON & C. FALTIS (eds), *Language Distribution Issues in Bilingual Schooling*. Clevedon: Multilingual Matters.

HORNBERGER, N. H., 1990b, Creating Successful Learning Contexts for Bilingual Literacy. *Teachers College Record*, 92 (2), 212-229.

HORNBERGER, N. H., 1991, Extending Enrichment Bilingual Education: Revisiting Typologies and Redirecting Policy. In O. GARCÍA (ed.), *Bilingual Education: Focusschrift in Honor of Joshua A. Fishman (Volume 1)*. Amsterdam/Philadelphia: John Benjamins.

HORNBERGER, N. H., 1992a, Biliteracy Contexts, Continua and Contrasts Policy and Curriculum for Cambodian and Puerto Rican Students in Philadelphia. *Education and Urban Society*, 24 (2), 196-211.

HORNBERGER, N. H., 1992b, Literacy in South America. *Annual Review of Applied Linguistics*, 12, 190-215.

HORNBERGER, N. H., 1992c, Presenting a Holistic and an Emic View: The Literacy in Two Languages Project. *Anthropology and Education Quarterly*, 23 (2), 160-165.

HORNBERGER, N. H., 1993, Language Policy and Planning in South America. *Annual Review of Applied Linguistics*, 14, 220-239.

HORNBERGER, N. H., 1994a, Continua of Biliteracy: Quechua Literacy and Empowerment in Peru. In L. VERHOEVEN (ed.), *Functional Literacy: Theoretical Issues and Educational Implications*. Amsterdam/Philadelphia: John Benjamins.

HORNBERGER, N. H., 1994b, Literacy and Language Planning. *Language and Education*, 8 (1&2), 75-86.

HORNBERGER, N. H., 1994c, Whither Bilingual Education in Peru? Quechua Literacy and Empowerment. In P. COLE, G. HERMON & M. D. MARTIN (eds), *Language in the Andes*. Newark, DE: University of Delaware.

HORNBERGER, N. H., 1996, Language and Education. In S. L. MCKAY & N. H. HORNBERGER (eds), *Sociolinguistics and Language*. Cambridge: Cambridge University Press.

HORNBERGER, N.H. (ed.), 1997, *Indigenous Literacies in the Americas*. Berlin: Mouton de Gruyter.

HORNBERGER, N. H. and KING, K. A., 1996, Language Revitalisation in the Andes: Can the Schools Reverse Language Shift? *Journal of Multilingual and Multicultural Development*, 17 (6), 427-441.

HORNBERGER, N. H. & MICHEAU, C., 1993, Getting Far Enough to Like It: Biliteracy in the Middle School. *Peabody Journal of Education*, 69 (1), 30-53.

HORVATH, B. M. & VAUGHAN, P., 1991, *Community Languages: A Handbook*. Clevedon: Multilingual Matters.

HOUGHTON, R. W., 1994, Habermas and Education. *Studies in Education*, 10 (1), 50-51.

HOULTON, D. & WILLEY, R., 1983, *Supporting Children's Bilingualism. Some Policy Issues for Primary Schools and Local Education Authorities*. York: Longman/ Schools Council.

HOUSEN, A. & BAETENS BEARDSMORE, H., 1987, Curricular and Extra-Curricular Factors in Multilingual Education. *Studies in Second Language Acquisition (SSLA)*, 9, 83-102.

HOUSTON, S. H., 1972, *A Survey of Psycholinguistics*. The Hague: Mouton.

HOWITT, D., 1982, *Mass Media and Social Problems*. Oxford: Pergamon.

HUANG, G. G., 1995, Self-Reported Biliteracy and Self-Esteem: A Study of Mexican American 8th Graders. *Applied Psycholinguistics*, 16, 271-291.

HUDDY, L. & SEARS, D. O., 1990, Qualified Public Support for Bilingual Education: Some Policy Implications. In C. B. CAZDEN & C. E. SNOW (eds), *The Annals of the American Academy of Political and Social Science*, Volume 508, 119-134.

HUDDY, L. & SEARS, D. O., 1995, Opposition to Bilingual Education: Prejudice or the Defense of Realistic Interests? *Social Psychology Quarterly*, 58 (2), 133-143.

HUDELSON, S., 1994, Literacy Development in Second Language Children. In F. GENESEE (ed.), *Educating Second Language Children: The Whole Child, the Whole Curriculum, the Whole Community*. Cambridge: Cambridge University Press.

HUDSON, L., 1966, *Contrary Imaginations. A Psychological Study of the English Schoolboy*. Harmondsworth, Middlesex: Penguin.

HUDSON, L., 1968, *Frames of Mind*. Harmondsworth, Middlesex: Penguin.

HUDSON, R. A., 1996, *Sociolinguistics* (Second edition). Cambridge: Cambridge University Press.

HUFFINES, M. L., 1991, Pennsylvania German: 'Do They Love It in Their Hearts?' In J. R. DOW (ed.), *Language and Ethnicity. Focusschrift in Honor of Joshua Fishman*. Amsterdam/Philadelphia: John Benjamins.

HUGHES, M., 1993, *Citizenship 2000. The Lesser Used European Languages*. The European Dimension in Education and Teacher Training, Citizenship 2000 Expert Group. Cardiff: University of Wales.

HULSTIJN, J. H., 1991, How is Reading in a Second Language Related to Reading in a First Language? In J. H. HULSTIJN & J. F. MATTER (eds), *Reading in Two Languages* (*AILA Review*, 8, 5-14).

HUMMEL, K. M., 1993, Bilingual Memory Research: From Storage to Processing Issues. *Applied Psycholinguistics*, 14, 267-284.

HUNTER, J. E., SCHMIDT, F. L. & JACKSON, G. B., 1982, *Meta-Analysis: Cumulating Research Findings Across Studies*. Beverly Hills, CA: Sage.

HUNTER-GRUNDIN, E., 1982, *Case Study on Parent Involvement in Education: A Multi-Ethnic Project in the London Borough of Harringay* (CDCC Project Number 7: The Education and Cultural Development of Migrants). Strasbourg: Council for Cultural Co-operation.

HURD, M., 1993, Minority Language Children and French Immersion: Additive Multilingualism or Subtractive Semi-Lingualism? *The Canadian Modern Language Review*, 49 (3), 514-525.

HUSBAND, C. & KHAN, V. S., 1982, The Viability of Ethnolinguistic Vitality: Some Creative Doubts. *Journal of Multilingual and Multicultural Development*, 3 (3), 193-205.

HUSEN, T. & OPPER, S. (eds), 1983, *Multicultural and Multilingual Education in Immigrant Countries*. Oxford: Pergamon Press.

HUSSEY, M., 1987, Bilingualism in a Day Nursery. *Primary Teaching Studies*, 2 (3), 205-210.

HUSS-KEELER, R. L., 1997, Teacher Perception of Ethnic and Linguistic Minority Parental Involvement and its Relationship to Children's Language and Literacy Learning: A Case Study. *Teacher and Teacher Education*, 13 (2), 171-182.

HYMES, D., 1972a, On Communicative Competence. In J. PRIDE & J. HOLMES (eds), *Sociolinguistics*. London: Penguin.

HYMES, D., 1972b, Models of Interaction of Language and Social Life. In J. J. GUMPERZ & D. HYMES (eds), *Directions in*

Sociolinguistics: The Ethnography of Communication. New York: Holt, Rinehart and Winston.

I

IANCO-WORRALL, A. D., 1972, Bilingualism and Cognitive Development. *Child Development*, 43, 1390-1400.

IMEDADZE, N., 1960, On the Psychological Nature of Early Bilingualism (in Russian). *Voprosy Psikhologii*, 6, 60-68.

IMOFF, G., 1990, The Position of United States English on Bilingual Education. In C. B. CAZDEN & C. E. SNOW (eds), *The Annals of the American Academy of Political and Social Science*, Volume 508, 48-61. London: Sage.

INNER LONDON EDUCATION AUTHORITY, 1979, *Report on the 1978 Census of those ILEA Pupils for whom English was not a First Language*. London: ILEA.

INNER LONDON EDUCATION AUTHORITY, 1982, *Bilingualism in the ILEA: The Educational Implications of the 1981 Language Census*. London: ILEA.

INSKO, C. A., 1965, Verbal Reinforcement of Attitudes. *Journal of Personality and Social Psychology*, 2, 621-623.

IRISH TOURIST BOARD, 1992, *The Irish Abroad*. Dublin: Irish Tourist Board.

ISAACS, E., 1976, *Greek Children in Sydney*. Canberra: Australian National University Press.

IVANIC, R., 1990, Critical Language Awareness in Action. In R. CARTER (ed.), *Knowledge about Language and the Curriculum*. London: Hodder and Stoughton.

J

JACOB, E. & MATTSON, B., 1990, Cooperative Learning: Instructing Limited-English-Proficient Students in Heterogeneous Classes. In A. M. PADILLA, H. H. FAIRCHILD & C. M. VALADEZ (eds), *Bilingual Education: Issues and Strategies*. Newbury Park, London: Sage.

JACOBSON, R., 1990, Allocating Two Languages as a Key Feature of a Bilingual Methodology. In R. JACOBSON & C. FALTIS (eds), *Language Distribution Issues in Bilingual Schooling*. Clevedon: Multilingual Matters.

JACOBSON, R. & FALTIS, C. (eds), 1990, *Language Distribution Issues in Bilingual Schooling*. Clevedon: Multilingual Matters.

JACQUES, K. & HAMLIN, J., 1992, PAT Scores of Children in Bilingual and Monolingual New Zealand Primary Classrooms. *Delta (NZ)*, 46, 21-30.

JAMES, C., 1977, Welsh Bilingualism: Fact and Friction. *Language Problems and Language Planning*, 1, 73-82.

JAMES, C., 1996, Mother Tongue Use in Bilingual/Bidialectal Education: Implications for Bruneian Dwibahasa. *Journal of Multilingual and Multicultural Development*, 17 (2-4), 248-257.

JAMES, C. & GARRETT, P. (eds), 1991, *Language Awareness in the Classroom*. London: Longman.

JAPHETH, J., 1983, Urdd Gobaith Cymru. *Education for Development*, 7 (4), 37-44.

JAROVINSKIJ, A., 1995, On Bilingual Socialization. In K. E. NELSON & Z. REGER (eds), *Children's Language*, Volume 8. Hillsdale, NJ: Erlbaum.

JARVIS, T., 1991, Science and Bilingual Children: Realising the Opportunities. *Education*, 3, 41-48.

JENKINS, G. H., 1986, The Welsh Language in Education: An Historical Survey. In M. GRIFFITHS (ed.), *The Welsh Language in Education*. Cardiff: Welsh Joint Education Committee.

JENKINS, J. R. G. (ed.), 1987, *Indigenous Minority Groups in Multinational Democracies in the Year 2000: Problems and Prospects*. Interdisciplinary Research Committee. Canada: Wilfred Laurier University, Waterloo.

JENSEN, J. V., 1962a, Effects of Childhood Bilingualism 1. *Elementary English*, 39, 132-143.

JENSEN, J. V., 1962b, Effects of Childhood Bilingualism 2. *Elementary English*, 39, 358-366.

JERNUDD, B. & SHAPIRO, M., 1989, *Politics of Language Purism*. Berlin: de Gruyter.

JIMENEZ, R. T., GARCÍA, G. E. & PEARSON, P. D., 1995, Three Children, Two Languages and Strategic Reading: Case Studies in Bilingual/Monolingual Reading. *American Educational Research Journal*, 32 (1), 67-97.

JOHNSON, D. M., 1994, Grouping Strategies for Second Language Learners. In F. GENESEE (ed.), *Educating Second Language Children: The Whole Child, the Whole Curriculum, the Whole Community*. Cambridge: Cambridge University Press.

JOHNSON, J., 1989, Factors Related to Cross-Language Transfer and Metaphor Interpretation in Bilingual Children. *Applied Psycholinguistics*, 10 (2), 157-177.

JOHNSON, J., 1990, What is the Project Saying About Assessment? *Oracy Issues*, Number 5, pages 1-4. (Based on the British National Oracy Project).

JOHNSON, R. K. & SWAIN, M., 1994, From Core to Content: Bridging the L2 Proficiency Gap in Late Immersion. *Language and Education*, 8, 211-229.

JOHNSTONE, R., 1994a, *Teaching Modern Languages at Primary School: Approaches and Implications*. Edinburgh: The Scottish Council for Research in Education.

JOHNSTONE, R., 1994b, *The Impact of Current Developments to Support the Gaelic Language. Review of Research*. Stirling: Scottish Centre for Information on Language Teaching and Research.

JONES, A. W., 1992, Marketing: A New Discipline for Language Planners. In Ll. DAFIS (ed.), *The Lesser Used Languages: Assimilating Newcomers*. Proceedings of the Conference held at Carmarthen, 1991. Carmarthen, Dyfed, Wales: Joint Working Party on Bilingualism in Dyfed.

JONES, A. W., 1993/94, Indigenous Cultures and Tourism. *Contact Bulletin*, 10 (3), 10-11.

JONES, B. L., 1981, Welsh: Linguistic Conservation and Shifting Bilingualism. In E. HAUGEN, J. D. MCCLURE & D. THOMSON (eds), *Minority Languages Today*. Edinburgh: Edinburgh University Press.

JONES, B. M., 1995, Schools and Speech Communities in a Bilingual Setting. In B. M. JONES & P. A. S. GHUMAN (eds), *Bilingualism, Education and Identity*. Cardiff: University of Wales Press.

JONES, C. M., 1991, The Ulpan in Wales. *Journal of Multilingual and Multicultural Development*, 12 (3), 183-193.

JONES, D. G., 1979, The Welsh Language Movement. In M. STEPHENS (ed.), *The Welsh Language Today* (Second edition). Llandysul: Gomer Press.

JONES, E. & GRIFFITHS, I. L., 1963, A Linguistic Map of Wales: 1961. *Geographical Journal*, 129 (2), 192-196.

JONES, E. P., 1982, A Study of Some of the Factors Which Determine the Degree of Bilingualism of a Welsh Child Between 10 and 13 Years of Age. Unpublished Ph.D. Thesis, University of Wales.

JONES, G. E., 1982, *Controls and Conflicts in Welsh Secondary Education, 1889–1944*. Cardiff: University of Wales Press.

JONES, G. M., 1996, Bilingual Education and Syllabus Design: Towards a Workable Blueprint. *Journal of Multilingual and Multicultural Development*, 17 (2-4), 280-293.

JONES, G. M. & OZOG, C. K. (eds), 1993, *Bilingualism and National Development*. Clevedon: Multilingual Matters.

JONES, G. W., 1993, *Agweddau ar Ddysgu Iaith*. Llangefni: Canolfan Astudiaethau Iaith.

JONES, G. W., 1995, *Llunyddiaeth*. Llangefni: Canolfan Astudiaethau Iaith.

JONES, K., KING, G., PICTON, B. & VASEY, C., 1988, The Assessment of Bilingual Pupils: A Way Forward? *Educational Psychology in Practice*, 4 (2), 69-74.

JONES, M. G., 1994a, Modern Languages in Wales: National Curriculum Review. *Language Learning Journal*, 10, 81-82.

JONES, M. G., 1994b, Teaching Subjects Through the Medium of a Second or Foreign Language in England and Wales. *Triangle 13, Proceedings of a Conference, Subject Learning and Teaching in a Foreign Language*. Paris: Didier Erudition.

JONES, M. G., 1994c, Tower of Babel or English Unlimited? *Language Learning Journal*, 10, 28-31.

JONES, M. G. & BORDAS, I., 1993, Students' Attitudes to Europe: An Investigative Study. In M. MONTANÉ & I. BORDAS (eds), *The European Dimension in Secondary Education for Teachers and Teacher Educators*. Network of Teacher Training Institutions (RIF) Subnetwork 6. Barcelona: Collegi de Doctors i Lliceniats de Catalunya.

JONES, M. G. & MORRIS, D., 1995, Lessons from Luxembourg. *Links*, 13, 10-12.

JONES, M. G. & NORMAN, N., 1997, Bilingual Teaching in Secondary Education and the Problem of Teacher Supply. *Language Learning Journal*, 15, 60-67.

JONES, R. T., 1979, The Welsh Language and Religion. In M. STEPHENS (ed.), *The Welsh Language Today* (Second edition). Llandysul: Gomer Press.

JONES, T. P., 1987, Thirty Years of Progress. A Brief Outline of the Development of Welsh Language Teaching Materials. *Education for Development*, 10 (3), 24-39.

JONES, T. P., 1990, Migrant Pupils: Welsh

Linguistic Implications. In D. GORTER *et al.* (eds), *Fourth International Conference on Minority Languages. Volume II: Western and Eastern European Papers.* Clevedon: Multilingual Matters.

JONES, W. R., 1933, Tests for the Examination of the Effect of Bilingualism on Intelligence. Unpublished M.A. Thesis, University of Wales.

JONES, W. R., 1949, Attitude Towards Welsh as a Second Language. A Preliminary Investigation. *British Journal of Educational Psychology*, 19 (1), 44-52.

JONES, W. R., 1950, Attitude Towards Welsh as a Second Language. A Further Investigation. *British Journal of Educational Psychology*, 20 (2), 117-132.

JONES, W. R., 1953, The Influence of Reading Ability in English on Intelligence Test Scores of Welsh-speaking Children. *British Journal of Educational Psychology*, 23, 114-120.

JONES, W. R., 1955, *Bilingualism and Reading Ability in English*. Cardiff: University of Wales Press.

JONES, W. R., 1959, *Bilingualism and Intelligence*. Cardiff: University of Wales Press.

JONES, W. R., 1960a, Replies to Comments by J. L. Williams. *British Journal of Educational Psychology*, 30, 272-273.

JONES, W. R., 1960b, *Ymchwil Addysgol yng Nghymru. Y Faner, May 12th. 1966, Bilingualism in Welsh Education.* Cardiff: University of Wales Press.

JONES, W. R., 1966, *Bilingualism in Welsh Education*. Cardiff: University of Wales Press.

JONES, W. R., MORRISON, J. R., ROGERS, J. & SAER, H., 1957, *The Educational Attainment of Bilingual Children in Relation to their Intelligence and Linguistic Background.* Cardiff: University of Wales Press.

JONG, E. de, 1986, *The Bilingual Experience: A Book for Parents*. New York: Cambridge University Press.

JORGENSEN, J. N., HANSEN, E., HOLMEN, A. & GIMBEL, J. (eds), 1988, *Bilingualism in Society and School.* Copenhagen Studies in Bilingualism, Volume 5. Clevedon: Multilingual Matters.

JUNG, U. O. H., 1992, Technology and Language Education in the 21st Century. In J. F. MATTER (ed.), *Language Teaching in the Twenty-First Century: Problems and Prospects* (*AILA Review*, 9, 21-38).

K

KACHRU, B. B. & NELSON, C. L., 1996, World Englishes. In S. L. MCKAY & N. H. HORNBERGER (eds), *Sociolinguistics and Language Teaching*. Cambridge: Cambridge University Press.

KALANTZIS, M., COPE, B. & SLADE, D., 1989, *Minority Languages and Dominant Culture: Issues of Education, Assessment and Social Equity*. London, New York, Philadelphia: Falmer Press.

KAPLAN, R. B., 1993, The Hegemony of English in Science and Technology. *Journal of Multlingual and Multicultural Development*, 14 (1&2), 151-172.

KARDASH, C. A., *et al.*, 1988, Bilingual Referents in Cognitive Processing. *Contemporary Educational Psychology*, 13, 45-57.

KARNIOL, R., 1992, Stuttering Out of Bilingualism. *First Language*, 12 (3), 255-283.

KATZNER, K., 1995, *The Languages of the World*. London and New York: Routledge.

KAUR, S. & MILLS, R., 1993, Children as Interpreters. In R. W. MILLS & J. MILLS, 1993, *Bilingualism in the Primary School. A Handbook for Teachers*. London: Routledge.

KEANE, M. J., GRIFFITH, B. & DUNN, J. W., 1993, Regional Development and Language Maintenance. *Environment and Planning*, 25, 399-408.

KEATING, N., 1989, The Summer Language Bursary Program: A Canadian Success Story. *The Canadian Modern Language Review*, 45 (3), 457-463.

KEGL, J., 1975, Some Observations on Bilingualism: A Look at Some Data From Slovene-English Bilinguals. Unpublished Master's Thesis, Brown University.

KELLER, G. D. & VAN HOOFT, K., 1982, A Chronology of Bilingualism and Bilingual Education in the United States. In J. A. FISHMAN & G. D. KELLER (eds), *Bilingual Education for Hispanic Students in the United States*. New York/London: Teachers College.

KELLER, P., 1990, Legal Aspects of Language Choice in Schools: Possibilities and Limits for Language Immersion in Switzerland. *Multilingua*, 9 (1), 105-112.

KENDALL, J. R., LAJEUNESSE, G., CHMILAR, P., SHAPSON, L. R. & SHAPSON, S. M., 1987, English Reading Skills of French Immersion Students in Kindergarten and Grades 1 and 2. *Reading Research Quarterly*, 22 (2), 135-159.

KERR, T. & DESFORGES, M., 1988, Developing Bilingual Children's English in School. In G. K. VERMA & P. PUMFREY (eds), *Educational Attainments: Issues and Outcomes in Multicultural Education*. London: Falmer Press.

KESSLER, C. & QUINN, M. E., 1982, Cognitive Development in Bilingual Environments. In B. HARTFORD, A. VALDMAN & C. R. FOSTER (eds), *Issues in International Bilingual Education. The Role of the Vernacular*. New York: Plenum Press.

KESSLER, C. & QUINN, M. E., 1985, Positive Effects of Bilingualism on Science Problem-Solving Abilities. In J. E. ALATIS & J. J. STACEK, *Perspectives on Bilingualism and Bilingual Education*. Washington, DC: Georgetown University Press.

KESSLER, C. & QUINN, M. E., 1987, Language Minority Children's Linguistic and Cognitive Creativity. *Journal of Multilingual and Multicultural Development*, 8 (1&2), 173-186.

KEYSER, R. & BROWN, J., 1981, *Heritage Language Survey Results*. Toronto, Canada: Research Department, Metropolitan Separate School Board.

KHAN, V., 1978, *Mother Tongue Teaching and the Asian Community*. SCOPE Communications, Occasional Paper 2. Southall, Middlesex: SCOPE.

KHLEIF, B. B., 1980, *Language, Ethnicity and Education in Wales*. New York: Mouton.

KHOO, R., KREHER, U. & WONG, R. (eds), 1994, *Towards Global Multilingualism: European Models and Asian Realities*. Clevedon: Multilingual Matters.

KING, A., 1975, Sections Bilingues in Somerset. *System*, 2 (1), 63-69.

KIYOSHI AIHARA, 1996, 'Immersed' in Bilingual Education Success. *Daily Yomiuri (Japan)*, Page 14(a), 29th July.

KJOLSETH, R., 1983, Cultural Politics of Bilingualism. *Sociolinguistics Today*, 20 (4), 40-48.

KLEIN, D., MILNER, B., ZATORRE, R., MEYER, E. & EVANS, A. C., 1995, The Neural Substrates Underlying Word Generation: A Bilingual Functional-Imaging Study. *Proceedings of the National Academy of Sciences of the United States of America*, 92 (7), 2899-2903.

KLEIN, D., ZATORRE, R. J., MILNER, B., MEYER, E. & EVANS, A. C., 1994, Left Putaminal Activation when Speaking a Second Language: Evidence from PET. *Neuro Report*, 5 (17), 2295-2297.

KLINCK, P. A., 1985, French Teacher Training: A Proposal for a New Pedagogy. *The Canadian Modern Language Review*, 41 (5), 887-891.

KLOSS, H., 1977, *The American Bilingual Tradition*. Rowley, MA: Newbury House.

KNIGHT, P., 1996, Deaf Children in a BSL Nursery: Who is Doing What? In P. KNIGHT & R. SWANWICK (eds), *Bilingualism and the Education of Deaf Children: Advances in Practice*. Leeds, United Kingdom: ADEDC, School of Education, University of Leeds.

KOLERS, P., 1963, Interlingual Word Association. *Journal of Verbal Learning and Verbal Behaviour*, 2, 291-300.

KRASHEN, S. D., 1977, The Monitor Model for Second Language Performance. In M. BURT, H. DULAY & M. FINOCCHIAO (eds), *Viewpoints on English as a Second Language*. New York: Regents.

KRASHEN, S. D., 1978, Is the 'Natural Order' an Artifact of the Bilingual Syntax Measure? *Language Learning*, 28 (1), 187-191.

KRASHEN, S. D., 1981a, Bilingual Education and Second Language Acquisition Theory. In CALIFORNIA STATE DEPARTMENT OF EDUCATION (ed.), *Schooling and Language Minority Students. A Theoretical Framework*. Los Angeles, CA: Evaluation, Dissemination and Assessment Center.

KRASHEN, S. D., 1981b, The 'Fundamental Pedagogical Principle' in Second Language Teaching. *Studia Linguistica*, 35, 50-70.

KRASHEN, S. D., 1981c, *Second Language Acquisition and Second Language Learning*. Oxford: Pergamon Press.

KRASHEN, S. D., 1982, *Principles and Practices of Second Language Acquisition*. Oxford: Pergamon Press.

KRASHEN, S. D., 1985, *The Input Hypothesis: Issues and Implications*. London: Longman.

KRASHEN, S. D., 1991, Bilingual Education: A Focus on Current Research. *Focus, Occasional Papers in Education*, 3. Washington, DC: National Clearing House for Bilingual Education.

KRASHEN, S. D., 1994, An Answer to the Literacy Crisis: Free Voluntary Reading. *School Library Media Annual (SLMA)*, 12, 113-122.

KRASHEN, S. D., 1995, Immersion: Why Not Try Free Voluntary Reading? *Mosaic*, 3 (1), 3-4.

KRASHEN, S. D. & TERRELL, T., 1983, *The Natural Approach: Language Acquisition in the Classroom*. Oxford: Pergamon.

KRASHEN, S. D. *et al.*, 1979, Age, Rate and Eventual Attainment in Second Language Acquisition. *TESOL Quarterly*, 13 (4), 573-582.

KRAUSHAAR, B. & LAMBERT, S., 1987, Shadowing Proficiency According to Ear of Input and Type of Bilinguality. *Bulletin Canadian Association of Applied Linguistics*, 9 (1), 17-31.

KRAUSS, M., 1992, The World's Languages in Crisis. *Language*, 68, 6-10.

KRAUSS, M. 1995, Language Loss in Alaska, the United States and the World. Frame of Reference. *Alaska Humanities Forum*, 6 (1), 2-5.

KROLL, J. F. & CURLEY, J., 1981, Lexical Memory in Novice Bilinguals: The Role of Concepts in Retrieving Second Language Words. In M. M. GRUNEBERG, P. E. MORRIS & R. N. SYKES (eds), *Practical Aspects of Memory: Current Research and Issues, Volume 2. Clinical and Educational Implications*. New York: J. Wiley and Sons.

KYLE, J. G. (ed.), 1987, *Sign and School: Using Signs in Deaf Children's Development*. Clevedon: Multilingual Matters.

KYLE, J. G. & WOLL, B., 1988, *Sign Language. The Study of Deaf People and their Language*. Cambridge: Cambridge University Press.

KYUCHUKOV, H., 1995, Bilingualism and Bilingual Education in Bulgaria. *European Journal of Intercultural Studies*, 6 (1), 46-55.

L

LADD, P., 1991, The British Sign Language Community. In S. ALLADINA & V. EDWARDS, *Multilingualism in the British Isles: The Older Mother Tongues and Europe*. London: Longman.

LADO, R., 1961, *Language Testing*. London: Longman.

LADO, R., 1964, *Language Teaching: A Scientific Approach*. New York: McGraw-Hill.

LAING, D., 1988, A Comparative Study of the Writing Abilities of English-Speaking Grade 8 Students in French-Speaking Schools. *Canadian Journal of Education*, 13 (2), 306-324.

LAITIN, D. D., 1996, Language Planning in the Former Soviet Union: The Case of Estonia. *International Journal of the Sociology of Language*, Number 118, 43-61.

LALONDE, R. N., 1982, Second Language Acquisition: A Causal Analysis. Unpublished M.A. Thesis, University of Western Ontario.

LAM, T. C. M., 1992, Review of Practices and Problems in the Evaluation of Bilingual Education. *Review of Educational Research*, 62 (2), 181-203.

LAMBERT, W. E., 1974, Culture and Language as Factors in Learning and Education. In F. E. ABOUD & R. D. MEADE (eds), *Cultural Factors in Learning and Education*. Bellingham, WA: 5th Western Washington Symposium on Learning.

LAMBERT, W. E., 1977, Culture and Language as Factors in Learning and Education. In F. E. ECKMAN (ed.), *Current Themes in Linguistics: Bilingualism, Experimental Linguistics and Language Typologies*. New York: Wiley.

LAMBERT, W. E., 1980, The Social Psychology of Language. In H. GILES, W. P. ROBINSON & P. M. SMITH (eds), *Language: Social Psychological Perspectives*. Oxford: Pergamon.

LAMBERT, W. E., 1991, And Then Add Your Two Cents' Worth. In A. G. REYNOLDS (ed.), *Bilingualism, Multiculturalism and Second Language Learning*. Hillsdale, NJ: Lawrence Erlbaum.

LAMBERT, W. E. & ANISFELD, E., 1969, A Note on the Relationship of Bilingualism and Intelligence. *Canadian Journal of Behavioural Science*, 1 (2), 123-128.

LAMBERT, W. E. & CAZABON, M., 1994, *Students' Views on the Amigos Program*. Santa Cruz, CA: National Center for Research on Cultural Diversity and Second Language Learning.

LAMBERT, W. E. & TAYLOR, D. M., 1990, *Coping with Cultural and Racial Diversity in Urban America*. New York: Praeger.

LAMBERT, W. E. & TUCKER, R., 1972, *Bilingual Education of Children. The St. Lambert Experiment*. Rowley, MA: Newbury House.

LAMBERT, W. E., GENESEE F., HOLOBOW, N. & CHARTRAND, L., 1993, Bilingual Education for Majority English-Speaking Children. *European Journal of Psychology of Education*, 8 (1), 3-22.

LAMENDELLA, J., 1979, The Neurofunctional Basis of Pattern Practice. *TESOL Quarterly*, 13, 5-13.

LANAUZE, M. & SNOW, C., 1989, The Relation Between First and Second-Language Writing Skills: Evidence from Puerto Rican Elementary School Children in Bilingual Programs. *Linguistics and Education*, 1 (4), 323-339.

LANDRY, R. & ALLARD, R., 1994a, Diglossia, Ethnolinguistic Vitality, and Language Behavior. *International Journal of the Sociology of Language*, 108, 15-42.

LANDRY, R. & ALLARD, R., 1994b, Introduction. Ethnolinguistic Vitality: A Viable Construct. *International Journal of the Sociology of Language*, 108, 5-13.

LANDRY, R. & ALLARD, R. (eds), 1994, Ethnolinguistic Vitality. *International Journal of the Sociology of Language*, 108. Berlin: Mouton de Gruyter.

LANDRY, R. G., 1974, A Comparison of Second Language Learners and Monolinguals on Divergent Thinking Tasks at the Elementary School Level. *Modern Language Journal*, 58, 10-15.

LANDRY, R. G., 1987, Additive Bilingualism, Schooling and Special Education: A Minority Group Perspective. *Canadian Journal for Exceptional Children*, 3 (4), 109-114.

LANDRY, R. G., ALLARD, R. & HENRY, J., 1996, French in South Louisiana: Towards Language Loss. *Journal of Multilingual and Multicultural Development*, 17 (6), 442-468.

LANDRY, R. G., ALLARD, R. & THEBERGE, R., 1991, School and Family French Ambiance and the Bilingual Development of Francophone Western Canadians. *Canadian Modern Language Review*, 47 (5), 878-915.

LANGE, D. L. (ed.), 1980, <WO>*Proceedings of the National Conference on Professional Priorities, November 1980*. New York: ACTFL Materials Center.

LANGER, J. A., BARTOLOME, L., VASQUEZ, O. & LUCAS, T., 1990, Meaning Construction in School Literacy Tasks: A Study of Bilingual Students. *American Educational Research Journal*, 27 (3), 427-471.

LANGRAN, J. & PURCELL, S., 1994, *Netword 2: Teaching Languages to Adults, Language Games and Activities*. London: Centre for Information on Language Teaching and Research.

LANZA, E., 1992, Can Bilingual Two-Year Olds Code-Switch? *Journal of Child Language*, 19, 633-658.

LAPKIN, S. & CUMMINS, J., 1984, Canadian French Immersion Education: Current Administrative and Instructional Practices. In CALIFORNIA STATE DEPARTMENT OF EDUCATION (ed.), *Studies on Immersion Education: A Collection for United States Educators*. CA: California State Department of Education.

LAPKIN, S., HARLEY, B. & TAYLOR, S., 1993, Research Directions for Core French in Canada. *Canadian Modern Language Review*, 49 (3), 476-513.

LAPKIN, S., HART, D. & SWAIN, M., 1991, Early and Middle French Immersion Programs: French Language Outcomes. *The Canadian Modern Language Review*, 48 (1), 11-44.

LAPKIN, S., SWAIN, M., KAMIN, J. & HANNA, G., 1983, Late Immersion in Perspective: The Peel Study. *The Canadian Modern Language Review*, 39 (2), 182-206.

LAPKIN, S., SWAIN, M. & SHAPSON, S., 1990, French Immersion Research Agenda for the 90s. *Canadian Modern Language Review*, 46 (4), 638-674.

LAPONCE, J. A., 1984, The French Language in Canada: Tensions Between Geography and Politics. *Political Geography Quarterly*, 3 (2), 91-104.

LARKING, L., 1996, Bilingualism Through the Classroom Strategies and Practices in Brunei Darussalam. *Journal of Multilingual and Multicultural Development*, 17 (2-4), 296-311.

LARSEN-FREEMAN, D., 1983, Second Language Acquisition: Getting the Whole Picture. In K. BAILEY, M. LONG & S. PECK (eds), *Second Language Acquisition Research*. Rowley, MA: Newbury House.

LAUREN, C., 1994, *Cultural and Anthropological Aspects of Immersion. Second European Conference, Vaasa Finland, Issue 192*, 21-26.

LAUREN, U., 1987, The Linguistic Competence of Mono- and Bi-Lingual Pupils in Swedish in the Finland-Swedish School. *Journal of Multilingual and Multicultural Development*, 8 (1&2), 83-94.

LAURIE, S. S., 1890, *Lectures on Language and Linguistic Method in the School*. Cambridge: Cambridge University Press.

LAURIN, C., 1977, *Quebec's Policy in the French Language*. Quebec: Ministry of State for Cultural Development.

LAVER, J. & ROUKENS, J., 1996, The Global Information Society and Europe's Linguistic and Cultural Heritage. In C. HOFFMANN (ed.), *Language, Culture and Communication in Contemporary Europe*. Clevedon: Multilingual Matters.

LEBLANC, C. & COURTEL, C., 1990, Executive Summary: The Culture Syllabus. *Canadian Modern Language Review*, 47 (1), 82-92.

LEBLANC, R., 1990, Le curriculum multidimensionnel: Une synthèse. *Canadian Modern Language Review*, 47 (1), 32-42.

LEBLANC, R., 1992, Second Language Retention. *Language and Society*, 37, 35-36.

LEBRUN, N. & BAETENS BEARDSMORE, H., 1993, Trilingual Education in the Grand Duchy of Luxembourg. In H. BAETENS BEARDSMORE (ed.), *European Models of Bilingual Education*. Clevedon: Multilingual Matters.

LEE, B. & DICKSON, P., 1991, *Foreign Languages for Low Attaining Pupils*. Slough, Bucks: NFER.

LEE, W. O., 1993, Social Reactions Towards Education Proposals: Opting Against the Mother Tongue as the Medium of Instruction in Hong Kong. *Journal of Multilingual and Multicultural Development*, 14 (3), 203-216.

LEMMON, C. R. & GOGGIN, J. P., 1989, The Measurement of Bilingualism and its Relationship to Cognitive Ability. *Applied Psycholinguistics*, 10 (2), 133-155.

LENNEBERG, E., 1967, *Biological Foundations of Language*. New York: Wiley.

LEOPOLD, W. F., 1939-1949, *Speech Development of a Bilingual Child. A Linguist's Record* (4 volumes). Evanston, IL: Northwestern University Press.

LEPRETRE, M., 1992, *The Catalan Language Today*. Barcelona: Generalitat de Catalunya, Departament de Cultura.

LESSOW-HURLEY, J., 1996, *The Foundations of Dual Language Instruction* (Second edition). New York: Longman.

LEUNG, C. & FRANSON, C., 1989, The Multilingual Classroom: The Case for Minority Language Pupils. *Journal of Multilingual and Multicultural Development*, 10 (6), 461-472.

LEWIS, C. & SHAPSON, S. M., 1989, Secondary French Immersion: A Study of Students Who Leave the Program. *The Canadian Modern Language Review*, 45 (3), 540-548.

LEWIS, D. G., 1959, Bilingualism and Non-Verbal Intelligence: A Further Study of Test Results. *British Journal of Educational Psychology*, 29, 17-22.

LEWIS, D. G., 1960, Differences in Attainment Between Primary Schools in Mixed-Language Areas. *British Journal of Educational Psychology*, 30, 63-70.

LEWIS, E. G., 1975, Attitude to Language among Bilingual Children and Adults in Wales. *International Journal of the Sociology of Language*, 4, 103-121.

LEWIS, E. G., 1977, Bilingualism and Bilingual Education: The Ancient World of the Renaissance. In B. SPOLSKY & R. L. COOPER (eds), *Frontiers of Bilingual Education*. Rowley, MA: Newbury House.

LEWIS, E. G., 1978, Review of Culture in Crisis. *Language Planning Newsletter*, 4 (3), 2-3.

LEWIS, E. G., 1981, *Bilingualism and Bilingual Education*. Oxford: Pergamon.

LEWIS, E. G., 1983, Modernization and Language Maintenance. In G. WILLIAMS (ed.), *Crisis of Economy and Ideology*. Bangor: UCNW.

LEWIS, R., RADO, M. & FOSTER, L., 1982, Secondary School Students' Attitudes Towards Bilingual Learning in Schools. *Australian Journal of Education*, 26 (3), 292-304.

LI WEI, MILLER, N. & DODD, B., 1997, Distinguishing Communicative Difference from Language Disorder in Bilingual Children. *Bilingual Family Newsletter*, 14 (1), 3-4. Clevedon: Multilingual Matters.

LI WEI, MILROY L. & PON SIN CHING, 1992, A Two-Step Sociolinguistic Analysis of Code-Switching and Language Choice: The Example of a Bilingual Chinese Community in Britain. *International Journal of Applied Linguistics*, 2, 1, 63-86.

LIEBERT, R. M., SPRAFKIN, J. N. & DAVIDSON, E. S., 1982, *The Early Window. Effects of Television on Children and Youth*. Oxford: Pergamon.

LIEBKIND, K., 1995, Bilingual Identity. *European Education*, 27 (3), 80-87.

LIEDTKE, W. W. & NELSON, L. D., 1968, Concept Formation and Bilingualism. *Alberta Journal of Educational Research*, 14 (4), 225-232.

LIEW, E. M., 1996, Developmental Interdependence Hypothesis Revisted in the Brunei Classroom. *Journal of Multilingual and Multicultural Development*, 17 (2&4), 195-204.

LINDE, S. G. & LOFGREN, H., 1988, The Relationship Between Medium of Instruction and School Achievement for Finnish-Speaking Students in Sweden. *Language, Culture and Curriculum*, 1 (2), 131-145.

LINDHOLM, K. J., 1987, *Directory of Bilingual Education Programs* Monograph No. 8). Los Angeles: University of Southern California, Center for Language Education and Research.

LINDHOLM, K. J., 1990, Bilingual Immersion Education: Criteria for Program Development. In A. M. PADILLA, H. H. FAIRCHILD & C. M. VALADEZ (eds), *Bilingual Education: Issues and Strategies*. London: Sage.

LINDHOLM, K. J., 1991, Theoretical Assumptions and Empirical Evidence for Academic Achievement in Two Languages. *Hispanic Journal of Behavioural Science*, 13 (1), 3-17.

LINDHOLM, K. J., 1992, Two-Way Bilingual/Immersion Education: Theory, Conceptual Issues and Pedagogical Implications. In R. V. PADILLA & H. BENAVIDES (eds), *Critical Perspectives on Bilingual Education Research*. Tempe, AZ: Bilingual Press.

LINDHOLM, K. J., 1994, Promoting Positive Cross-Cultural Attitudes and Perceived Competence in Culturally and Linguistically Diverse Classrooms. In R. A. DEVILLAR, C. FALTIS & J. CUMMINS (eds), *Cultural Diversity in Schools: From Rhetoric to Practice*. Albany, NY: State University of New York Press.

LINDHOLM, K. J. & ACLAN, Z., 1991, Bilingual Proficiency as a Bridge to Academic Achievement: Results from Bilingual/ Immersion Programs. *Journal of Education*, 173 (2), 99-113.

LINDHOLM, K. J. & FAIRCHILD, H. H., 1990, Evaluation of an Elementary School Bilingual Immersion Program. In A. M. PADILLA, H. H. FAIRCHILD & C. VALADEZ (eds), *Bilingual Education, Issues and Strategies*. London: Sage.

LINDSAY, C. F., 1993, Welsh and English in the City of Bangor: A Study in Functional Differentiation. *Language in Society*, 22, 1-17.

LINGUISTIC MINORITIES PROJECT, 1983, *A Short Report on the Linguistic Minorities Project/Pupil Questionnaire*. London: University of London Institute of Education.

LINGUISTIC MINORITIES PROJECT, 1984, Linguistic Minorities in England: A Short Report on the Linguistic Minorities Project. *Journal of Multilingual and Multicultural Development*, 5 (5), 351-366.

LINGUISTIC MINORITIES PROJECT, 1985, *The Other Languages of England*. London: Routledge and Kegan Paul.

LLOYD, D. T., 1979, The Welsh Language in Journalism. In M. STEPHENS (ed.), *The Welsh Language Today*. Llandysul: Gomer.

LO BIANCO, J., 1987, *National Policy on Languages*. Canberra: Australian Government Publishing Service.

LONG, M., 1985, Input and Second Language Acquisition Theory. In S. GASS & C. MADDEN (eds), *Input in Second Language Acquisition*. Rowley, MA: Newbury House.

LÓPEZ, L. E., 1990, Development of Human Resources in and for Intercultural Bilingual Education in Latin America. *Prospects (UNESCO)*, 20 (3), 311-320.

LOTHERINGTON, H., 1996, A Consideration of the Portability and Supportability of Immersion Education. *Journal of Multilingual and Multicultural Development*, 17 (5), 349-359.

LOWE, P., 1983, The Oral Interview: Origins, Applications, Pitfalls and Implications. *Die Unterrichtspraxis*, 16, 230-244.

LOZANOV, G., 1978, *Suggestology and Outlines of Suggestopedy*. New York: Gordon and Breach.

LUCAS, T., 1993, *Secondary Schooling for Students Becoming Bilingual, Bilingual Education: Politics, Practice and Research, Part II, Ninety-second Yearbook of the National Society for the Study of Education*. Chicago: University of Chicago Press.

LUCAS, T., HENZE, R. & DONATO, R., 1990, Promoting the Success of Latino Language-Minority Students: An Exploratory Study of Six High Schools. *Harvard Educational Review*, 60 (3), 315-340.

LUKMANI, Y. M., 1972, Motivation to Learn and Learning Proficiency. *Language Learning*, 22, 261-273.

LUYKEN, G. M., HERBST, T., LANGHAM-BROWN, J., REID, H. & SPINHOF, H., 1991, *Overcoming Language Barriers in Television: Dubbing and Subtitling for the European Audience*. Media Monograph No. 13. Manchester: European Institute for the Media.

LYNCH, J., 1986a, *Multicultural Education: Approaches and Paradigms*. Nottingham: University of Nottingham School of Education.

LYNCH, J., 1986b, Multicultural Education: Agenda for Change. In J. BANKS & J. LYNCH (eds), *Multicultural Education in Western Societies*. Eastbourne: Holt, Rinehart and Winston Ltd.

LYNCH, J., 1987, *Prejudice Reduction and the Schools*. London: Cassell.

LYNCH, J., 1992, *Education for Citizenship in a Multicultural Society*. New York: Cassell.

LYNCH, J., 1995, Youth, Interethnic Relations, and Education in Europe. In W. D. HAWLEY & A. W. JACKSON (eds), *Toward a Common Destiny: Improving Race and Ethnic Relations in America*. San Francisco: Jossey-Bass.

LYON, J., 1996, *Becoming Bilingual: Language Acquisition in a Bilingual Community*. Clevedon: Multilingual Matters.

LYON, J. & ELLIS, N., 1991, Parental Attitudes Towards the Welsh Language. *Journal of Multilingual and Multicultural Development*, 12 (4), 239-251.

LYONS, J. J., 1990, The Past and Future Directions of Federal Bilingual-Education Policy. In C. B. CAZDEN & C. E. SNOW, *Annals of the American Academy of Political and Social Science*, Volume 508, 119-134. London: Sage.

LYSTER, R., 1987, Speaking Immersion. *The Canadian Modern Language Review*, 43 (4), 701-717.

M

MAC AOGAIN, E., 1990, *Teaching Irish in the Schools: Towards a Language Policy for 1992*. Dublin: The Linguistics Institute of Ireland.

MACAULAY, D. (ed.), 1992, *The Celtic Languages*. Cambridge: Cambridge University Press.

MACCLANCY, J., 1993, At Play with Identity in the Basque Arena. In S. MACDONALD (ed.), *Inside European Identities*. Oxford: Berg.

MACDONALD, B., ADELMAN, C., KUSHNER, S. & WALKER, R., 1982, *Bread and Dreams. A Case Study of Bilingual Schooling in the USA*. Norwich: CARE Occasional Publications, No. 12.

MACDONALD, S., 1993, Identity Complexes in Western Europe: Social Anthropological Perspectives. In S. MACDONALD (ed.), *Inside European Identities*. Oxford: Berg.

MACEDO, D., 1991, English Only: The Tongue-Tying of America. *Journal of Education*, 173 (2), 9-20.

MACÍAS, R. F., 1993, Language and Ethnic Classification of Language Minorities: Chicano and Latino Students in the 1990s. *Hispanic Journal of Behavioral Sciences*, 15 (2), 230-257.

MACÍAS, R. F. & KELLY, C., 1996, *Summary Report of the Survey of the States' Limited English Proficient Students and Available Educational Programs and Services 1994–1995*. California: University of California Linguistic Minority Research Institute.

MACÍAS, R. F. & RAMOS, R. R. G., 1995, *Changing Schools for Changing Students: An Anthology of Research on Language Minorities, Schools and Society*. California: University of California Linguistic Minority Research Institute.

MACKEY, W. F., 1962, The Description of Bilingualism. *Canadian Journal of Linguistics*, 7, 51-85.

MACKEY, W. F., 1965, *Language Teaching Analysis*. London: Longman.

MACKEY, W. F., 1970, A Typology of Bilingual Education. *Foreign Language Annuals*, 3, 596-603.

MACKEY, W. F., 1972, *Bibliographie internationale sur le Bilingualisme*. Préparée au CIRB sous la direction de W. F. MACKEY. Quebec: Les Presses de l'Université Laval.

MACKEY, W. F., 1977a, *Irish Language Promotion: Potentials and Constraints*. Instituid Teangeolafochta Eireann, Dublin.

MACKEY, W. F., 1977b, The Evaluation of Bilingual Education. In B. SPOLSKY & R. COOPER (eds), *Frontiers of Bilingual Education*. Rowley, MA: Newbury House.

MACKEY, W. F., 1978, The Importation of Bilingual Education Models. In J. ALATIS (ed.), *Georgetown University Roundtable: International Dimensions of Education*. Washington, DC: Georgetown University Press.

MACKEY, W. F., 1982, *Bibliographie internationale sur le Bilingualisme* (Second edition). Préparée au CIRB sous la direction de W. F. MACKEY. Quebec: Les Presses de l'Université Laval.

MACKEY, W. F., 1991, Language Diversity, Language Policy and the Sovereign State. *History of European Ideas*, 13, 51-61.

MACKEY, W. F., 1993, Literary Diglossia, Biculturalism and Cosmopolitanism in Literature. In R. SARKONA & R. HODGSON (eds), 1993, *Writing in Stereo: Bilingualism in the Text*. In *Visible Language*, 27 (1/2). Providence, RI: Rhode Island School of Design.

MACKINNON, K., 1981, *Scottish Opinion on Gaelic. A Report on a National Attitude Survey for An Comunn Gaidhealach*. Hatfield Polytechnic, Social Science Research Publication No. 5514.

MACKINNON, K., 1984a, Power at the Periphery: The Language Dimension and the Case of Gaelic Scotland. *Journal of Multilingual and Multicultural Development*, 5 (6), 491-510.

MACKINNON, K., 1984b, Scottish Gaelic and English in the Highlands. In P. TRUDGILL (ed.), *Language in the British Isles*. Cambridge: Cambridge University Press.

MACKINNON, K., 1986, *Gaelic Language Regeneration Amongst Young People in Scotland 1971–1981 From Census Data*. Social Sciences Reports Series, No. SSR 15, School of Social Sciences, The Hatfield Polytechnic.

MACKINNON, K., 1987a, Gender, Occupational and Educational Factors in Gaelic Language-Shift and Regeneration. In G. MACEOIN *et al.* (eds), *Third International Conference on Minority Languages: Celtic Papers*. Clevedon: Multilingual Matters.

MACKINNON, K., 1987b, Language-Retreat and Regeneration in the Present-Day Scottish Gaidhealtachd. Paper Presented at the First International Seminar on Geolinguistics, North Staffs Polytechnic, Stoke-on-Trent, 13–15th May.

MACKINNON, K., 1990, Language-Maintenance and Viability in the Contemporary Scottish Gaelic Speech-Community: Some Social and Demographic Factors. In D. GORTER *et al.* (eds), *Fourth International Conference on Minority Languages. Volume II: Western and Eastern European Papers*. Clevedon: Multilingual Matters.

MACKINNON, K., 1994, *Gaelic in 1994. Report to EU Euromosaic Project. Language Group Correspondent Questionnaire: Scottish Gaelic*. University of Hertfordshire, Hatfield, United Kingdom.

MACNAB, G. L., 1979, Cognition and Bilingualism: A Reanalysis of Studies. *Linguistics*, 17, 231-255.

MACNAMARA, J., 1966, *Bilingualism and Primary Education: A Study of Irish Experience*. Edinburgh: Edinburgh University Press.

MACNAMARA, J., 1969, How Can One Measure the Extent of a Person's Bilingual Proficiency? In L. G. KELLY (ed.), *Description and Measurement of Bilingualism*. Toronto: University of Toronto Press.

MACNAMARA, J., 1970, Bilingualism and Thought. In J. E. ALATIS (ed.), *Report of the Twenty-First Annual Round Table Meeting on Linguistics and Language Studies*. Georgetown: Georgetown University Press.

MACNEIL, M. M., 1994, Immersion Programmes Employed in Gaelic-Medium Units in Scotland. *Journal of Multilingual and Multicultural Development*, 15 (2&3), 245-252.

MAGUIRE, G., 1987, Language Revival in an Urban Neo-Gaeltacht. In G. MACEOIN *et al.* (eds), *Third International Conference on Minority Languages: Celtic Papers*. Clevedon: Multilingual Matters.

MAHER, J. C. & YASHIRO, K. (eds), 1995, *Multilingual Japan*. Clevedon: Multilingual Matters.

MAHSHIE, S. N., 1995, *Educating Deaf Children Bilingually*. Washington, DC: Gallaudet University.

MAJHANOVICH, S., 1990, Challenge for the 90s: The Problem of Finding Qualified Staff for French Core and Immersion Programs. *Canadian Modern Language Review*, 46 (3), 452-463.

MALAKOFF, M., 1988, The Effect of Language of Instruction on Reasoning in Bilingual Children. *Applied Psycholinguistics*, 9 (1), 17-38.

MALAKOFF, M. & HAKUTA, K., 1990, History of Language Minority Education in the United States. In A. M. PADILLA, H. H. FAIRCHILD & C. M. VALADEZ (eds), *Bilingual Education: Issues and Strategies*. London: Sage.

MALALLAH, S., 1994, A Study in Some Aspects of Foreign Language Learning at Kuwait University with Special Reference to Computer Assisted Language Learning. Unpublished Ph.D. Thesis, University of Wales, Bangor.

MALDONADO, J. A., 1994, Bilingual Special Education: Specific Learning Disabilities in Language and Reading. *Journal of Educational Issues of Language Minority Students*, 14, 127-148.

MALHERBE, E. C., 1946, *The Bilingual School*. London: Longman.

MALICKY, G. V., FAGAN, W. T. & NORMAN, C. A., 1988, Reading Processes of French Immersion Children Reading in French and English. *Canadian Journal of Education*, 13 (2), 277-289.

MANSOUR, G., 1980, The Dynamics of Multilingualism. *Journal of Multilingual and Multicultural Development*, 1 (4), 273-293.

MANSOUR, G., 1993, *Multilingualism and Nation Building*. Clevedon: Multilingual Matters.

MANZER, K., 1993, Canadian Immersion: Alive and Working Well in Finland. *Language and Society*, 44, 16-17.

MAR-MOLINERO, C., 1987, The Teaching of Catalan in Catalonia. *Journal of Multilingual and Multicultural Development*, 10 (4), 307-326.

MARLAND, M., 1985, A New Approach to Language Study and Language Awareness in a Multilingual School, at North Westminster Community School, London. In B. G. DONMALL (ed.), *Language Awareness. National Congress on Languages in Education Reports 6*. London: Centre for Information on Language Teaching and Research (CILT).

MARLAND, M., 1986, Towards a Curriculum Policy for a Multilingual World. *British Journal of Language Teaching*, 24 (3), 123-138.

MARSHALL, D. F., 1996, A Politics of Language: Language as a Symbol in the Dissolution of the Soviet Union and its Aftermath. *International Journal of the Sociology of Education*, 118, 7-41.

MARTIN, P. W., 1996, Code-Switching in the Primary Classroom: One Response to the Planned and the Unplanned Language Environment in Brunei. *Journal of Multilingual and Multicultural Development*, 17 (2-4), 128-144.

MARTIN-JONES, M., 1984a, The Newer Minorities: Literacy and Educational Issues. In P. TRUDGILL (ed.), *Language in the British Isles*. Cambridge: Cambridge University Press.

MARTIN-JONES, M., 1984b, *The Sociolinguistic Status of Minority Languages in England* (in collaboration with the Linguistic Minorities Project research team – *Working Paper Number 5*). University of London: Institute of Education.

MARTIN-JONES, M., 1991, Sociolinguistic Surveys as a Source of Evidence in the Study of Bilingualism: A Critical Assessment of Survey Work Conducted Among Linguistic Minorities in Three British Cities. *International Journal of the Sociology of Languages*, 90, 37-55.

MARTIN-JONES, M. & ROMAINE, S., 1986, Semilingualism: A Half Baked Theory of Communicative Competence. *Applied Linguistics*, 7 (1), 26-38.

MARTÍNEZ, P. P., 1990, Towards Standardization of Language for Teaching in the Andean Countries. *Prospects (UNESCO)*, 20 (3), 377-386.

MARTÍNEZ-ARBELAIZ, A., 1996, The Language Requirement Outside the Academic Setting: The Case of the Basque Administration. *Journal of Multilingual and Multicultural Development*, 17 (5), 360-372.

MATSUMORI A., 1995, Ryukyuan: Past, Present and Future. *Journal of Multilingual and Multicultural Development*, 16 (1&2), 19-44.

MATTES, L. J. & OMARK, D. R., 1984, *Speech and Language Assessment for the Bilingual Handicapped*. San Diego, CA: College-Hill Press.

MATTHEWS, P., 1994, Science Education: Principles and Practice. *Studies in Education*, 10 (1), 59-63.

MATTHEWS, T., 1979, *An Investigation into the Effects of Background Characteristics and Special Language Services on the Reading Achievement and English Fluency of Bilingual Students*. Seattle, WA: Seattle Public Schools, Department of Planning.

MAY, S., 1992a, The Relational School: Fostering Pluralism and Empowerment Through a 'Language Policy Across the Curriculum'. *New Zealand Journal of Educational Studies*, 27, 35-51.

MAY, S., 1992b, Establishing Multicultural Education at the School Level: The Need for Structural Change. *Journal of Educational Administration and Foundations*, 7, 11-29.

MAY, S., 1993, Redeeming Multicultural Education. *Language Arts*, 70, 364-372.

MAY, S., 1994a, *Making Multicultural Education Work*. Clevedon: Multilingual Matters.

MAY, S., 1994b, School-Based Language Policy Reform: A New Zealand Example. In A. BLACKLEDGE (ed.), *Teaching Bilingual Children*. London: Trentham Press.

MAY, S., 1996, Indigenous Language Rights and Education. In C. MODGIL, S. MODGIL & J. LYNCH (eds), *Education and Development: Tradition and Innovation, Volume 1*. London: Cassell.

MAZRUI, A. A., 1996, Language Planning and the Foundations of Democracy: An African Perspective. *International Journal of the Sociology of Education*, 118, 107-124.

McARTHUR, T., 1992, *The Oxford Companion to the English Language*. Oxford: Oxford University Press.

McCARTHY, M. M., 1986, The Changing Federal Role in Bilingual Education. *Journal of Educational Equity and Leadership*, 6 (1), 73-79.

McCOLLUM, P. A. & WALKER, C. L., 1992, Minorities in America 2000. *Education and Urban Society*, 24 (2), 178-195.

McCONNELL, B., 1980, Effectiveness of Individualized Bilingual Instruction for Migrant Students. Unpublished Ph.D. Dissertation, Washington State University.

McCRACKEN, W. & SUTHERLAND, H., 1991, *Deaf-ability – Not Disability: A Guide for the Parents of Hearing Impaired Children*. Clevedon: Multilingual Matters.

McDONALD, M., 1993, The Construction of Difference: An Anthropological Approach to Stereotypes. In S. MACDONALD (ed.), *Inside European Identities*. Oxford: Berg.

McEACHERN, W., 1980, Parental Decision for French Immersion: A Look at Some Influencing Factors. *Canadian Modern Language Review*, 38, 238-246.

McGROARTY, M., 1991, What Do We Know About Effective Second Language Teaching? In M. E. McGROARTY & C. J. FALTIS (eds), *Languages in School and Society: Policy and Pedagogy*. Berlin/New York: Mouton de Gruyter.

McGROARTY, M., 1992, The Societal Context of Bilingual Education. *Educational Researcher*, 21 (2), 7-9.

McGROARTY, M., 1996, Language Attitudes, Motivation and Standards. In S. L. McKAY & N. H. HORNBERGER (eds), *Sociolinguistics and Language Teaching*. Cambridge: Cambridge University Press.

McGROARTY, M. & FALTIS, C. J. (eds), 1991, *Languages in School and Society. Policy and Pedagogy*. New York: Mouton de Gruyter.

McGUIRE, W. J., 1981, The Probabilogical Model of Cognitive Structure and Attitude Change. In R. E. PETTY, T. M. OSTROM & T. C. BROCK (eds), *Cognitive Responses in Persuasion*. Hillsdale, NJ: Erlbaum.

McGUIRE, W. J., 1985, Attitudes and Attitude Change. In G. LINDZEY & E. ARONSON (eds), *Handbook of Social Psychology Volume 3* (Second edition). New York: Random House.

McINTYRE, D. & MITCHELL, R., 1987, *Summary of the Report of an Independent Evaluation of the Western Isles Bilingual Education Project: Centre for Language and Education*. Southampton: University of Southampton.

McKAY, S. L., 1988, Weighing Educational Alternatives. In S. L. McKAY & S. C. WONG (eds), *Language Diversity: Problem or Resource?* New York: Newbury House.

McKAY, S. L., 1996 Literacy and Literacies. In S. L. McKAY & N. H. HORNBERGER (eds), *Sociolinguistics and Language Teaching*. Cambridge: Cambridge University Press.

McKAY, S. L. & FREEDMAN, S. W., 1990, Language Minority Education in Great Britain: A Challenge to Current United States Policy. *TESOL Quarterly*, 24 (3), 385-405.

McKAY, S. L. & HORNBERGER, N. H. (eds), 1996, *Sociolinguistics and Language Teaching*. Cambridge: Cambridge University Press.

McKAY, S. L. & WEINSTEIN-SHR, G., 1993, English Literacy in the United States: National Policies, Personal Consequences. *TESOL Quarterly*, 27 (3).

McKAY, S. L. & WONG S. C. (eds), 1988, *Language Diversity: Problem or Resource?* New York: Newbury House.

McLAGAN, P. (ed.), 1994, *Steps to Learning: Modern Languages for Pupils with Special Educational Needs*. London: Centre for Information on Language Teaching and Research.

McLAREN, P., 1988, Culture or Canon? Critical Pedagogy and the Politics of Literacy. *Harvard Educational Review*, 58, 211-234

McLAUGHLIN, B., 1978, The Monitor Model: Some Methodological Considerations. *Language Learning*, 28, 309-332.

McLAUGHLIN, B., 1984a, Are Immersion Programs the Answer for Bilingual Education in the United States. *Bilingual Review*, 11 (1), 3-11.

McLAUGHLIN, B., 1984b, Early Bilingualism: Methodological and Theoretical Issues. In M. PARADIS & Y. LEBRUN (eds), *Early Bilingualism and Child Development*. Lisse, Holland: Swets and Zeitlinger.

McLAUGHLIN, B., 1984c, *Second-Language Acquisition in Childhood. Volume 1: Preschool Children.* Hillsdale, NJ: Lawrence Erlbaum.
McLAUGHLIN, B., 1985, *Second Language Acquisition in Childhood. Volume 2: School Age Children.* Hillsdale, NJ: Lawrence Erlbaum.
McLAUGHLIN, B., 1987, *Theories of Second-Language Learning.* London: Edward Arnold.
McLAUGHLIN, B., 1992, *Myths and Misconceptions about Second Language Learning: What Every Teacher Needs to Unlearn.* Santa Cruz, CA: National Center for Research on Cultural Diversity and Second Language Learning.
McLAUGHLIN, B. & GRAF, P., 1985, Bilingual Education in West Germany: Recent Developments. *Comparative Education,* 21 (3), 241-255.
McLAUGHLIN, B., BLANCHARD, A. G. & OSANAI, Y., 1995, *Assessing Language Development in Bilingual Preschool Children.* Program Information Guide Series, 22. Washington, DC: National Clearinghouse for Bilingual Education.
McLEOD, K. A., 1984, Multiculturalism and Multicultural Education: Policy and Practice. In R. J. SAMUDA *et al.* (eds), *Multiculturalism in Canada: Social and Education Perspectives.* London: Allyn and Bacon.
McMAHON, A. M., 1994, *Understanding Language Change.* Cambridge: Cambridge University Press.
MEARS, P. & RYAN, A. (eds), 1991, *Language and Nation. Papers from the Annual Meeting of the British Association for Applied Linguistics Held at University College, Swansea, September 1990.* London: British Association for Applied Linguistics in Association with Centre for Information on Language Teaching and Research, London.
MEDINA, M. & ESCAMILLA, K., 1992, *Evaluation of Transitional and Maintenance Bilingual Programs: Urban Education.* London: Sage.
MEDRANO, M. F., 1986, Evaluating the Long-Term Effects of a Bilingual Education Program: A Study of Mexican American Students. *Journal of Educational Equity and Leadership,* 6 (2), 129-138.
MEHAN, H., 1992, *Sociological Foundations Supporting the Study of Cultural Diversity.* National Centre for Research on Cultural Diversity and Second Language Learning. Washington, DC: United States Department of Education.
MEKACHA, R. D. K., 1993, Is Tanzania Diglossic? The Status and Role of Ethnic Community Languages. *Journal of Multilingual and Multicultural Development,* 14 (4), 307-320.
MERCADO, C. & ROMERO, M., 1993, *Assessment of Students in Bilingual Education, Bilingual Education: Politics, Practice and Research, Part II. Ninety-Second Yearbook of the National Society for the Study of Education.* Chicago: University of Chicago Press.
MERCER, J., 1978/1979, Test 'Validity', 'Bias' and 'Fairness': An Analysis from the Perspective of the Sociology of Knowledge. *Interchange,* 9 (1), 1-16.
MERCER, J., 1988, Ethnic Differences in IQ Scores: What Do They Mean? *Hispanic Journal of Behavioral Sciences,* 10 (3), 199-218.
MERINO, B. J. & FALTIS, C. J., 1993, *Language and Culture in the Preparation of Bilingual Education, Bilingual Education: Politics, Practice and* Research, Part II. Ninety-Second Yearbook of the National Society for the Study of Education. Chicago: University of Chicago Press.
MESTRE, J. P., 1986, Teaching Problem-Solving Strategies to Bilingual Students: What Do Research Results Tell Us? *International Journal of Mathematics, Science and Technology,* 17 (4), 393-401.
MET, M., 1994, Teaching Content Through a Second Language. In F. GENESEE (ed.), *Educating Second Language Children: The Whole Child, the Whole Curriculum, the Whole Community.* Cambridge: Cambridge University Press.
MEY, J. L., 1989, 'Saying It Don't Make It So': The 'Una Grande Libre' of Language Politics. *Multilingua,* 8 (4), 333-355.
MEYER, M. M. & FIENBERG, S. (eds), 1992, *Assessing Evaluation Studies: The Case of Bilingual Education Strategies.* Washington, DC: National Academy Press.
MIKES, M., 1986, Towards a Typology of Languages of Instruction in Multilingual Societies. In B. SPOLSKY (ed.), *Language and Education in Multilingual Settings.* Clevedon: Multilingual Matters.
MILK, R. D., 1991, Preparing Teachers for Effective Bilingual Instruction. In M. E. McGROARTY & C. J. FALTIS (eds), *Languages in School and Society: Policy and Pedagogy.* Berlin/New York: Mouton de Gruyter.
MILK, R. D., 1993, *Bilingual Education and English as a Second Language: The Elementary School, Bilingual Education: Politics, Practice and Research, Part II. Ninety-Second Yearbook of the National Society for the Study of Education.* Chicago: University of Chicago Press.
MILLER, G. A., 1991, *The Science of Words.* New York: Freeman.
MILLER, J., 1983, *Many Voices: Bilingualism Culture and Education.* London: Routledge and Kegan Paul.
MILLER, N. (ed.), 1984, *Bilingualism and Language Disability: Assessment and Remediation.* London: Croom Helm.
MILLER-NOMELAND, M. & GILLESPIE, S., 1993, *Kendall Demonstration Elementary School: Deaf Studies Curriculum Guide.* Washington, DC: Gallaudet University.
MILLS, R. W. & MILLS, J., 1993, *Bilingualism in the Primary School. A Handbook for Teachers.* London: Routledge.
MILROY, J. & MILROY, L., 1991, *Investigating Language Prescription and Standardization.* London: Routledge.
MILROY, J. & MILROY, L., 1997, Varieties and Variation. In F. COULMAS (ed.), *The Handbook of Sociolinguistics.* Oxford: Blackwell.
MINAMI, M. & KENNEDY, B. P. (eds), 1991, Language Issues in Literacy and Bilingual/Multilingual Education. *Harvard Educational Review.* (Reprint Series No. 22).
MINISTERE DE L'EDUCATION NATIONALE LUXEMBOURG, 1993, *Eis Spillschoul: Brochure d'Information sur L'Education Préscolaire.* Luxembourg: Courrier de l'Education Nationale.
MINISTERE DE L'EDUCATION NATIONALE LUXEMBOURG, 1995, *Education in the Grand-Duchy of Luxembourg 1994/95.* Luxembourg: Unité Nationale d'Eurydice.
MINISTRY FOR EDUCATION, 1963, *English for Immigrants.* Pamphlet No. 43. London: HMSO.
MINISTRY OF EDUCATION, 1953, *The Place of Welsh and English in the Schools of Wales.* London: HMSO.
MINISTRY OF EDUCATION, 1994, *The Ulpan for Hebrew Language Instruction.* Jerusalem, Israel: Ministry of Education.
MIRAMONTES, O. B., 1993, Language and Learning: Exploring Schooling Issues that Impact Linguistically Diverse Students. National Reading Conference, 1992, San Antonio, Texas. *National Reading Conference Yearbook,* Number 42, 25-39.
MITCHELL, R., 1988, *Communicative Language Teaching in Practice.* London: Centre for Language Teaching and Research.
MITCHELL, R., BRUMFIT, C. & HOOPER, J., 1994, Knowledge about Language: Policy, Rationales and Practices. *Research Papers in Education,* 9 (2), 183-205.
MITCHELL, R., McINTYRE, D., MACDONALD, M. & McLENNAN, S., 1987, *Report of an Independent Evaluation of the Western Isles' Bilingual Education Project.* Southampton: University of Southampton.
MITCHELL, W. L., 1994, Pragmatic Literacy and Empowerment: An Aymara Example. Theme Issue: Alternative Visions of Schooling: Success Stories in Minority Settings. *Anthropology and Education Quarterly,* 25 (3), 226-235.
MODGIL, S., VERMA, G., MALLICK, K. & MODGIL, C. (eds), 1986, *Multicultural Education: The Interminable Debate.* Lewes: Falmer Press.
MOLL, L. C., 1992, Bilingual Classroom Studies and Community Analysis. *Educational Researcher,* 21 (2), 20-24.
MOLL, L. C. *et al.,* 1992, Funds of Knowledge for Teaching: Using a Qualitative Approach to Connect Homes and Classrooms. *Theory Into Practice,* 31 (2), 132-141.
MONTERO-SIEBURTH, M. & PEREZ, M., 1987, Echar Pa'lante, Moving Onward: The Dilemmas and Strategies of a Bilingual Teacher. *Anthropology and Education Quarterly,* 18 (3), 180-189.
MORA, M. T., 1995, Bilingual Education: Lessons to be Learned. In G. E. THOMAS (ed.), *Race and Ethnicity in America: Meeting the Challenge in the 21st Century.* Washington, DC: Taylor and Francis.
MORALES, F., 1991, The Role of Spanish Language Varieties in the Bilingual Classroom. In M. E. McGROARTY & C. J. FALTIS (eds), *Languages in School and Society: Policy and Pedagogy.* Berlin/New York: Mouton de Gruyter.
MORALES, R. & BONILLA, F., 1993, *Latinos in a Changing United States Economy.* London: Sage.
MORGAN, E. R., 1955, A Comparative Study of

the Effect of Varying Degrees of Bilingualism. Unpublished M.A. Thesis, University of Wales.

MORGAN, S., 1979, Roparz Hemon and the Breton Cultural Movement in the Twentieth century. Unpublished D.Phil. Thesis, University of Oxford.

MORISON, S. H., 1990, A Spanish-English Dual-Language Program in New York City. In C. B. CAZDEN & C. E. SNOW (eds), *The Annals of the American Academy of Political and Social Science*, Volume 508, 160-169. London: Sage.

MORRIS, D., 1992, The Effects of Economic Changes on Gwynedd Society. In Ll. DAFIS (ed.), *Lesser Used Languages: Assimilating Newcomers*. Carmarthen, Wales: Joint Working Party on Bilingualism in Dyfed.

MORRIS, D., 1995, Language and Class Fractioning in a Peripheral Economy. *Journal of Multilingual and Multicultural Development*, 16 (5), 373-387.

MORRIS, N., 1996, Language and Identity in Twentieth Century Puerto Rico. *Journal of Multilingual and Multicultural Development*, 17 (1), 17-32.

MORRISON, D. & LOW, G., 1983, Monitoring and the Second Language Learner. In J. RICHARDS & R. SCHMIDT (eds), *Language and Communication*. London: Longman.

MORRISON, J. R., 1958, Bilingualism: Some Psychological Aspects. *The Advancement of Science*, 56, 287-290.

MORTIMORE, P. *et al.*, 1988, *School Matters: The Junior Years*. Wells, Somerset: Open Books.

MOSELEY, C. & ASHER, R. E., 1994, *Atlas of the World's Languages*. London and New York: Routledge.

MOTET (Mother Tongue and English Teaching Project), 1981, *Summary of the Reports* (2 volumes). Bradford: School of Education, University of Bradford.

MOYA, R., 1990, A Decade of Bilingual Education and Indigenous Participation in Ecuador. *Prospects (UNESCO)*, 20 (3), 331-344.

MOYS, A. & TOWNSEND, R., 1991, *Pathfinder 8: Making the Case for Languages*. London: Centre for Information on Language Teaching and Research.

MULTILINGUAL RESOURCES FOR CHILDREN PROJECT, 1995, *Literacy and Learning in Multilingual Classrooms*. Clevedon: Multilingual Matters.

MURPHY, D., 1994, Education in Eastern Europe. *Studies in Education*, 10 (1), 52-55.

MURPHY, D. G., 1990, Comparison of Scores of Bilingual Urban and Monolingual Suburban Elementary School Children for Two Measures of Intelligence. *Psychological Reports*, 67 (3), 1375-1378.

MURRAY, J. & MORRISON, C., 1984, *Bilingual Primary Education in the Western Isles, Scotland*. Stornoway, Isle of Lewis: Acair.

MYDLARSKI, D. & WEST, A., 1985, Introduction. *Canadian Modern Language Review*, 41 (5), 810-815.

MYERS-SCOTTON, C., 1972, *Choosing a Lingua Franca in an African Capital*. Edmonton, Champaign, IL: Linguistic Research.

MYERS-SCOTTON, C., 1983, The Negotiation of Identities in Conversation: A Theory of Markedness and Code Choice. *International Journal of the Sociology of Language*, 44, 115-136.

MYERS-SCOTTON, C., 1991, Making Ethnicity Salient in Codeswitching. In J. R. DOW (ed.), *Language and Ethnicity. Focusschrift in Honor of Joshua Fishman*. Amsterdam/Philadelphia: John Benjamins.

MYERS-SCOTTON, C., 1992, Comparing Codeswitching and Borrowing. *Journal of Multilingual and Multicultural Development*, 13 (1&2), 19-39.

MYERS-SCOTTON, C., 1993a, *Duelling Languages: Grammatical Structure in Codeswitching*. Oxford, New York: Oxford University Press.

MYERS-SCOTTON, C., 1993b, *Social Motivations for Codeswitching: Evidence from Africa*. Oxford: Clarendon Press.

MYERS-SCOTTON, C., 1997, Code-Switching. In F. COULMAS (ed.), *The Handbook of Sociolinguistics*. Oxford: Blackwell.

MYERS-SCOTTON, C. & URY, W., 1977, Bilingual Strategies: The Social Functions of Code-Switching. *Linguistics*, 193, 5-20.

N

NAGY, P. & KLAIMAN, R., 1988, Attitudes to and Impact of French Immersion. *Canadian Journal of Education*, 13 (2), 263-276.

NAIMAN, N., FROHLICH, M. & TODESCO, A., 1975, The Good Second Language Learner. *TESL Talk*, 6, 58-75.

NAIMAN, N., FROHLICH, M., STERN, H. H. & TODESCO, A., 1978, *The Good Language Learner*. Research in Education Series No. 7. Ontario: Ontario Institute for Studies in Education.

NANEZ, J. E., PADILLA, R. V. & MAEZ, B. L., 1992, Bilinguality, Intelligence and Cognitive Information Processing. In R. V. PADILLA & A. H. BENAVIDES (eds), *Critical Perspectives on Bilingual Education Research*. Tempe, AZ: Bilingual Press.

NATION, R. & McLAUGHLIN, B., 1986, Novices and Experts: An Information Processing Approach to the 'Good Language Learner' Problem. *Applied Psycholinguistics*, 7 (1), 41-56.

NATIONAL COUNCIL FOR MOTHER TONGUE TEACHING, 1985, The Swann Report: Education For All?, *Journal of Multilingual and Multicultural Development*, 6 (6), 497-508.

NATIONAL CURRICULUM COUNCIL, 1993, *Modern Foreign Languages and Special Educational Needs: A New Commitment*. York: National Curriculum Council.

NATIONAL LANGUAGES FOR EXPORT CAMPAIGN, 1994a, *Business Language Strategies*. London: Department of Trade and Industry.

NATIONAL LANGUAGES FOR EXPORT CAMPAIGN, 1994b, *Business Language Training: Guide 4*. London: Department of Trade and Industry.

NATIONAL LANGUAGES FOR EXPORT CAMPAIGN, 1994c, *Trading Across Cultures*. London: Department of Trade and Industry.

NATIONAL OFFICE OF POPULATION (ETHIOPIA), 1993, *National Report on Population and Development*. Addis Ababa: National Office of Population.

NEHR, M., 1990, The Acquisition of Literacy in Bilingual Education: Turkish Schoolchildren in West Germany. *Multilingua*, 9 (1), 87-103.

NELDE, P. H., 1986, Language Contact Versus Language Conflict: The Fergusonian Impact. In J. A. FISHMAN, A. TABOURET-KELLER, M. CLYNE, B. H. KRISHNAMURTI & M. ABDULAZIZ, *Sociolinguistics and the Sociology of Language. Volume 2*. Berlin, New York and Amsterdam: Mouton de Gruyter.

NELDE, P. H., 1987, Language Contact Means Language Conflict. *Journal of Multilingual and Multicultural Development*, 8 (1&2), 33-42.

NELDE, P. H., 1991, Language Conflicts in Multilingual Europe: Prospects for 1993. In F. COULMAS (ed.), *A Language Policy for the European Community*. Berlin/New York: Mouton de Gruyter.

NELDE, P. H., 1997, Language Conflict. In F. COULMAS (ed.), *The Handbook of Sociolinguistics*. Oxford: Blackwell.

NELDE, P. H. (ed.), 1983, *Theory, Methods and Models of Contact Linguistics*. Bonn: Dummler Publishers.

NETTEN, J. E. & SPAIN, W. H., 1989, Student-Teacher Interaction Patterns in the French Immersion Classroom: Implications for Levels of Achievement in French Language Proficiency. *The Canadian Modern Language Review*, 45 (3), 485-501.

NEUFELD, G. G., 1974, A Theoretical Perspective on the Relationship of Bilingualism and Thought: Revisited. *Working Papers on Bilingualism*, Number 2, 125-129.

NEWMARK, P., 1981, *Approaches to Translation*. Oxford: Pergamon Press.

NEWMARK, P., 1993, *About Translation*. Clevedon: Multilingual Matters.

NEWTON, G., 1996, *Luxembourg and Lëtzebuergesch*. Oxford: Clarendon Press.

NG, SEOK MOI, 1996, Innovation, Survival and Processes of Change in the Bilingual Classroom in Brunei Darussalam. *Journal of Multilingual and Multicultural Development*, 17 (2-4), 149-162.

NICHOLS, P. C., 1996, Pidgins and Creoles. In S. L. McKAY & N. H. HORNBERGER (eds), *Sociolinguistics and Language Teaching*. Cambridge: Cambridge University Press.

NICHOLSON, R. & GARLAND, R., 1991, New Zealanders' Attitudes to the Revitalisation of the Maori Language. *Journal of Multilingual and Multicultural Development*, 12 (5), 393-410.

NICOLADIS, E. & GENESEE, F., 1996, A Longitudinal Study of Pragmatic Differentiation in Young Bilingual Children. *Language Learning*, 46 (3) 439-464.

NIETO, S., 1996, *Affirming Diversity. The Sociopolitical Context of Multicultural Education* (Second edition). New York, London: Longman.

NIXON, J., 1984, Multicultural Education as a Curriculum Category. *New Community*, 12, 22-30.

NOBLE, G. & DALTON, G., 1976, Some Cognitive Implications of Bilingualism. *Oideas*, 16, 42-52.

NOBUYUKI, H., 1995, English in Japanese

Society: Language within Language. *Journal of Multilingual and Multicultural Development*, 16 (1&2), 45-62.

NORTHERN TERRITORY DEPARTMENT OF EDUCATION, 1996, *Aboriginal Languages and Bilingual Education Newsletter, Number 96, Part 1*. Darwin: Northern Territory Department of Education.

NOVAK-LUKANOVIC, S., 1988, Bilingual Education in Yugoslavia. *Journal of Multilingual and Multicultural Development*, 9 (1&2), 169-176.

NUNAN, D., 1988, *The Learner-Centred Curriculum: A Study in Second Language Teaching*. Cambridge: Cambridge University Press.

NUNAN, D., 1991, Communicative Tasks and the Language Curriculum. *TESOL Quarterly*, 25 (2), 279-295.

NYALUGWE, M., 1994, Education in the South. *Studies in Education*, 10 (1), 56-58.

O

Ó BUACHALLA, S., 1984, Educational Policy and the role of the Irish Language from 1831 to 1981. *European Journal of Education: Research, Development and Policies*, 19 (1), 75-92.

Ó BUACHALLA, S., 1994, Structural Inequalities and the State's Policy on the Irish Language in the Education System. *Studies in Education*, 10 (1), 1-6.

Ó GLIASAIN, M., 1988, Bilingual Secondary Schools in Dublin 1960–1980. *International Journal of Sociological Language*, 70, 89-108.

Ó GLIASAIN, M., 1996, *The Language Question in the Census of the Population*. Dublin: Linguistics Institute of Ireland.

Ó MURCHU, H., 1987a, *Overview and Synthesis of Dossiers Established on Some Forms of Current Pre-Primary Provision in Lesser Used Languages in EC Member States*. (Commission of the European Communities). Dublin: European Bureau of Lesser Used Languages, Dublin.

Ó MURCHU, H., 1987b, *Pre-Primary Education in Some European Lesser Used Languages*. Dublin: European Bureau for Lesser Used Languages.

Ó MURCHU, M., 1988, Diglossia and Interlanguage Contact in Ireland. *Language, Culture and Curriculum*, 1 (3), 243-249.

Ó MURCHU, H. & MURCHU, M. W., 1988, *Aspects of Bilingual Education: The Italian and Irish Experience*. Dublin: Bord na Gaeilge.

Ó RIAGAIN, P., 1988, Bilingualism in Ireland 1973–1983: An Overview of National Sociolinguistic Surveys. *International Journal of the Sociology of Language*, 70, 29-52.

Ó RIAGAIN, P., 1991, National and International Dimensions of Language Policy When the Minority Language is a National Language: The Case of Irish in Ireland. In F. COULMAS (ed.), *A Language Policy for the European Community*. Berlin/New York: Mouton de Gruyter.

Ó RIAGAIN, P., 1992, *Language Maintenance and Language Shift as Strategies of Social Reproduction: Irish in the Corca Dhuibhne Gaeltacht: 1926–1986*. Dublin: Linguistics Institute.

Ó RIAGAIN, P., 1994, Public Attitudes to the Irish Language and Policies for Irish in Schools. *Studies in Education*, 10 (1), 7-15.

Ó RIAGAIN, P. & Ó GLIASAIN, M., 1984, *The Irish Language in the Republic of Ireland 1983: Preliminary Report of a National Survey*. Dublin: Instituid Teangeolaiochta Eireann.

O'CINNEIDE, M. S. & KEANE, M. J., 1992, *Summary of Report Entitled: Local Socioeconomic Impacts Associated with the Galway Gaeltacht, Social Sciences Research Centre*. Ireland: University College, Galway.

O'CIOSAIN, S., 1988, Language Planning and Irish: 1965–1974. *Language, Culture and Curriculum*, 1 (3), 263-279.

O'DOHERTY, E. F., 1958a, Bilingualism: Educational Aspects. *Advancement of Science* 56, 282-290.

O'DOHERTY, E. F., 1958b, Bilingual School Policy. *Studies*, 47, 259-268.

O'DONOGHUE, T. A., 1988, Bilingual Education in Ireland in the Late-Nineteenth and Early-Twentieth Centuries. *History of Education*, 17 (3), 209-220.

O'FLAHERTY, P., 1994, Freire's' Pedagogy of Hope. *Studies in Education*, 10 (1), 47-49.

O'GADHRA, N., 1988, Irish Government Policy and Political Development of the Gaeltacht. *Language, Culture and Curriculum*, 1 (3), 251-261.

O'HAGAN, M., 1996, *The Coming Industry of Teletranslation*. Clevedon: Multilingual Matters.

O'MALLEY, J. M. & CHAMOT, A. U., 1990. *Learning Strategies in Second Language Acquisition*. Cambridge: Cambridge University Press.

OBLER, L., 1983, Knowledge in Neurolinguistics: The Case of Bilingualism. *Language Learning*, 33 (5), 159-191.

OCHS, T., 1993, 'Why Can't We Speak Tagalog?' The Problematic Status of Multilingualism in the International School. *Journal of Multilingual and Multicultural Development*, 14 (6), 447-462.

OFFICE FOR STANDARDS IN EDUCATION, 1996, *Raising Achievement of Bilingual Pupils 1995–96*. London: Office of Her Majesty's Chief Inspector of Schools.

OGBU, J., 1978, *Minority Education and Caste: The American System in Cross-Cultural Perspective*. New York: Academic Press.

OGBU, J., 1983, Minority Status and Schooling in Plural Societies. *Comparative Education Review*, 27 (2), 168-190.

OGBU, J., 1987, Variability in Minority School Performance: A Problem in Search of an Explanation. *Anthropology and Education Quarterly*, 18, 312-334.

OGWEN, E., 1980, Learning to Read in a Bilingual Situation in Wales. *Journal of Multilingual and Multicultural Development*, 1 (4), 313-320.

OKA, HIDEO, 1994, Studies on Bilingualism and their Implication in Japan. In R. M. BOSTWICK (ed.), *Immersion Education International Symposium Report on Second Language Acquisition Through Content Based Study: An Introduction to Immersion Education*. Numazu, Japan: Katoh Gakuen.

OLLER, J. W., 1979, *Language Tests at School*. London: Longman.

OLLER, J. W., 1981, Research on the Measurement of Affective Variables. In R. ANDERSON (ed.), *New Dimensions in L2 Acquisition Research*. Rowley, MA: Newbury House.

OLLER, J. W., 1982, Evaluation and Testing. In B. HARTFORD, A. VALDMAN & C. FOSTER (eds), *Issues in International Bilingual Education*. New York: Plenum Press.

OLLER, J. W. & PERKINS, K., 1978, A Further Comment on Language Proficiency as a Source of Variance in Certain Affective Measures. *Language Learning*, 28, 417-423.

OLLER, J. W. & PERKINS, K., 1980, *Research in Language Testing*. Rowley, MA: Newbury House.

OLLER, J. W., HUDSON, A. & LIU, P., 1977, Attitudes and Attained Proficiency in ESL: A Sociolinguistic Study of Native Speakers of Chinese in the United States. *Language Learning*, 27, 1-27.

OLLER, J. W., PERKINS, K. & MURAKAMI, M., 1980, Seven Types of Learner Variables in Relation to ESL Learning. In J. W. OLLER & K. PERKINS (eds), *Research in Language Testing*. Rowley, MA: Newbury House.

OLMEDO, I. M., 1992, Teacher Expectations and The Bilingual Child. *Action in Teacher Education*, 14 (2), 1-8.

OLNECK, M. R., 1990, The Recurring Dream: Symbolism and Ideology in Intercultural and Multicultural Education. *American Journal of Education*, 98, 147-183.

OLNECK, M. R., 1993, Terms of Inclusion: Has Multiculturalism Redefined Equality in American Education? *American Journal of Education*, 10 (3), 234-260.

OLSON, D. R., 1994, *The World on Paper*. Cambridge: Cambridge University Press.

OLSON, P. & BURNS, G., 1983, Politics, Class and Happenstance: French Immersion in a Canadian Context. *Interchange*, 14, 1-16.

OPCS, 1992, *The 1991 Census of Great Britain*. London: HMSO.

OPCS, 1994, *Cyfrifiad 1991, Cymraeg/1991 Census, Welsh Language*. HMSO: London.

ORANGE, C., 1987, *The Treaty of Waitangi*. Wellington: Allen and Unwin.

ORELLANA, M. F., 1993, Struggling for the 'Bi' in Bilingual Education. *The Review of Education*, 15 (2), 203-206.

ORNSTEIN-GALICIA, J. L. & PENFIELD, J., 1981, A Problem-Solving Model for Integrating Science and Language. In *Bilingual/Bicultural Education. Bilingual Education Paper Series*. Evaluation, Dissemination and Assessment Center, California State University, Los Angeles.

OTHEGUY, R., 1982, Thinking about Bilingual Education: A Critical Appraisal. *Harvard Educational Review*, 52 (3), 301-314.

OTHEGUY, R. & OTTO, R., 1980, The Myth of Static Maintenance in Bilingual Education. *Modern Language Journal*, 64 (3), 350-356.

OUDIN, A-S., 1996, *Immersion and Multilingual Education in the European Union. Inventory of Educational Systems in Which Teaching is Provided Partly or Entirely Through the Medium of a Regional or Minority Language*. Dublin and Brussels: The European Bureau for Lesser Used Languages.

OVANDO, C. J., 1990, Essay Review: Politics and Pedagogy: The Case of Bilingual

Education. *Harvard Educational Review*, 60 (3), 341-356.

OVANDO, C. J. & COLLIER, V. P., 1987, *Bilingual and ESL Classrooms. Teaching in Multicultural Contexts.* New York: McGraw-Hill.

OWEN, D., 1995, *Ethnic Minorities in Great Britain, Patterns of Population Change, 1981–91.* University of Warwick, United Kingdom: Centre for Research in Ethnic Relations.

OWEN, P., 1985, *Welsh Language Exploratory Survey (For School Curriculum Development Committee).* Cardiff: University of Wales Press.

OXENHAM, J., 1980, *Literacy: Writing, Reading and Social Organization.* London: Routledge and Kegan Paul.

OXFORD, R. L., 1989 Use of Language Learning Strategies: A Synthesis of Studies with Implications for Strategy Training. *System*, 17, 235-247.

OXFORD, R. L., 1990a, Language Learning Strategies and Beyond: A Look at Strategies in the Context of Styles. In S. S. MAGNAN (ed.), *Shifting the Instructional Focus to the Learner.* Middlebury, VT: Northeast Conference on the Teaching of Foreign Languages.

OXFORD, R. L., 1990b, *Language Learning Strategies: What Every Teacher Should Know.* Boston: Heinle and Heinle.

OXFORD, R. L., 1992, Research on Second Language Learning Strategies: Linguistics. *Annual Review of Applied Linguistics*, 13, 175-187.

OXFORD, R. L., 1993, Individual Differences Among Your Students: Why a Single Method Can't Work. *Journal of Intensive English Studies*, 7, 27-42.

OXFORD, R. L., 1994, *Language Learning Strategies: An Update.* ERIC Digest. Washington, DC: ERIC Clearinghouse on Languages and Linguistics.

OXFORD, R. L. *et al.*, 1992, Language Learning Styles: Research and Practical Considerations for Teaching in the Multicultural Tertiary ESL/FL Classroom. *System*, 20, 439-456.

OXFORD, R. L. *et al.*, 1993, Learning a Language by Satellite Television: What Influences Student Achievement? *System*, 21, 31-48.

OXFORD, R. L. & BURRY-STOCK, J. A., 1995, Assessing the Use of Language Learning Strategies Worldwide with the ESL/EFL Version of the Strategy Inventory for Language Learning SILL. *System*, 23 (1), 1-23.

OXFORD, R. L. & COHEN, A. D., 1992, Language Learning Strategies: Crucial Issues of Concept and Classification. *Applied Language Learning*, 3, 1-35.

OXFORD, R. L. & CROOKALL, D., 1989, Research on Language Learning Strategies: Methods, Findings and Instructional Issues. *Modern Language Journal*, 73, 404-419.

OXFORD, R. L. & EHRMAN, M. E., 1992, Second Language Research on Individual Differences. *Annual Review of Applied Linguistics*, 13, 188-205.

OXFORD, R. L. & EHRMAN, M. E., 1995, Adults' Language Learning Strategies in an Intensive Foreign Language Program in the United States. *System*, 23 (3), 359-386.

OXFORD, R. L. & SHEARIN, J., 1994, Language Learning Motivation: Expanding the Theoretical Framework. *Modern Language Journal*, 78, 12-28.

OXFORD, R. L., PARK-OH, Y., ITO, S. & SUMRALL, M., 1993, Learning Japanese by Satellite: What Influences Student Achievement? *System*, 21, 31-48.

OYETADE, S. O., 1996, Bilingualism and Ethnic Identity in a Nupe-Yoruba Border Town in Nigeria. *Journal of Multilingual and Multicultural Development*, 17 (5), 373-384.

P

PADILLA, A. M., 1982, Bilingual Schools: Gateways to Integration or Roads to Separation. In J. A. FISHMAN & G. D. KELLER (eds), *Bilingual Education for Hispanic Students in the United States.* New York/London: Teachers College.

PADILLA, A. M., 1990, Bilingual Education: Issues and Perspectives. In A. M. PADILLA, H. H. FAIRCHILD & C. M. VALADEZ (eds), *Bilingual Education.* London/New Delhi: Sage.

PADILLA, A. M., 1991, English Only vs. Bilingual Education: Ensuring a Language-Competent Society. *Journal of Education*, 173 (2), 38-51.

PADILLA, A. M. (ed.), 1995, *Hispanic Psychology. Critical Issues in Theory and Research.* London: Sage.

PADILLA, R. V. & BENAVIDES, A. H. (eds), 1992, *Critical Perspectives on Bilingual Education Research.* Tempe, AZ: Bilingual Press.

PADILLA, R. V. & SUNG, H., 1992, A Theoretical and Pedagogical Framework for Bilingual Education Based on Principles from Cognitive Psychology. In R. V. PADILLA & A. H. BENAVIDES (eds), *Critical Perspectives on Bilingual Education Research.* Tempe, AZ: Bilingual Press.

PAIVIO, A., 1986, *Mental Representations: A Dual Coding Approach.* Oxford: University Press.

PAIVIO, A., 1991, Mental Representations in Bilinguals. In A. G. REYNOLDS (ed.), *Bilingualism, Multiculturalism and Second Language Learning.* Hillsdale, NJ: Lawrence Erlbaum.

PAIVIO, A. & DESROCHERS, A., 1980, A Dual-Coding Approach to Bilingual Memory. *Canadian Journal of Psychology*, 34, 390-401.

PALIJ, M. & HOMEL, P., 1987, The Relationship of Bilingualism to Cognitive Development: Historical, Methodological and Theoretical Considerations. In P. HOMEL, M. PALIJ & D. AARONSON (eds), *Childhood Bilingualism: Aspects of Linguistic Cognitive and Social Development.* Hillsdale, NJ: Lawrence Erlbaum.

PARADIS, M., 1990, Language Lateralization in Bilinguals: Enough Already! *Brain Lang (B5H)*, 39 (4), 576-86.

PARADIS, M., 1992, The Loch Ness Monster Approach to Bilingual Language Lateralization: A Response to Berquier and Ashton. *Brain Lang (B5H)*, 43 (3), 534-7.

PARADIS, M., 1995, Another Sighting of Differential Language Laterality in Multilinguals, This Time in Loch Tok Pisin: Comments on Wuillemin, Richardson and Lynch. *Brain Lang (B5H)*, 49 (2), 173-86.

PARADIS, J. & GENESEE, F., 1996, Syntactic Acquisition in Bilingual Children: Autonomous or Interdependent? *Studies in Second Language Acquisition*, 18 (1), 1-25.

PAREKH, B., 1986a, Bilingualism and Educational Investment. *New Community*, 13 (2), 185-194.

PAREKH, B., 1986b, The Concept of Multi-Cultural Education. In S. MODGIL, G. VERMA, K. MALLICK & C. MODGIL (eds), *Multicultural Education: The Interminable Debate.* Lewes: Falmer Press.

PARKE, T., 1993, Bilingualism, Language Awareness and the Resource Question. *Language Awareness*, 2 (2), 77-83.

PARKER, D. H. & BELANGER, C. H., 1987, A Challenge for Canadian Universities: Bilingual Students. *The Canadian Modern Language Review*, 43 (3), 538-547.

PARKER, G. & REUBEN, C. (eds), 1994, *Languages for the International Scientist.* London: Centre for Information on Language Teaching and Research.

PARRILLO, V. N., 1994, *Strangers to these Shores* (Fourth edition). New York: Macmillan.

PARRILLO, V. N., 1996, *Diversity in America.* Thousand Oaks, CA: Pine Forge Press.

PATTANAYAK, D. P., 1986, Language, Politics, Region Formation and Regional Planning. In E. E. ANNAMALAI, B. JERNUDD & J. RUBIN (eds), *Language Planning. Proceedings of an Institute.* Mysore: Central Institute of Indian Languages.

PATTANAYAK, D. P., 1988, Monolingual Myopia and the Petals of the Indian Lotus. In T. SKUTNABB-KANGAS & J. CUMMINS (eds), *Minority Education: From Shame to Struggle.* Clevedon: Multilingual Matters.

PAULSTON, C. B., 1980, *Bilingual Education. Theories and Issues.* Rowley, MA: Newbury House.

PAULSTON, C. B., 1986, *Social Factors in Language Maintenance and Language Shift: The Fergusonian Impact.* In J. A. FISHMAN, A. TABOURET-KELLER, M. CLYNE, B. H. KRISHNAMURTI & M. ABDULAZIZ (eds) *Sociolinguistics and the Sociology of Language. Volume 2.* New York: Mouton de Gruyter.

PAULSTON, C. B., 1992a, *Linguistic and Communicative Competence.* Clevedon: Multilingual Matters.

PAULSTON, C. B., 1992b, *Sociolinguistic Perspectives on Bilingual Education.* Clevedon: Multilingual Matters.

PAULSTON, C. B., 1994, *Linguistic Minorities in Multilingual Settings.* Amsterdam/Philadelphia: John Benjamins.

PAULSTON, C. B. (ed.), 1988, *International Handbook of Bilingualism and Bilingual Education.* New York: Greenwood.

PAULSTON, C. B., CHEN, P. C. & CONNERTY, M. C., 1993, Language Regenesis: A Conceptual Overview of Language Revival, Revitalisation and Reversal. *Journal of Multilingual and Multicultural Development*, 14 (4), 275-286.

PAWLEY, C., 1985, How Bilingual are French

Immersion Students? *Canadian Modern Language Review*, 41 (5), 865-876.

PEAL, E. & LAMBERT, W. E., 1962, The Relationship of Bilingualism to Intelligence. *Psychological Monographs*, 76 (27), 1-23.

PEASE-ALVAREZ, C. & VASQUEZ, O., 1994, Language Socialization in Ethnic Minority Communities. In F. GENESEE (ed.), *Educating Second Language Children: The Whole Child, the Whole Curriculum, the Whole Community*. Cambridge: Cambridge University Press.

PEASE-ALVAREZ, L., 1991, The Experience of Two Mexican-American Preschoolers. In M. E. McGROARTY & C. J. FALTIS (eds), *Languages in School and Society*. Berlin/New York: Mouton de Gruyter.

PEASE-ALVAREZ, L., 1993, *Moving In and Out of Bilingualism: Investigating Native Language Maintenance and Shift in Mexican-Descent Children*. National Center for Research on Cultural Diversity and Second Language Learning, United States Department of Education.

PEASE-ALVAREZ, L. & HAKUTA, K., 1992, Enriching Our Views of Bilingualism and Bilingual Education. *Educational Researcher*, 21 (2), 4-9.

PECCEI, J. S., 1994, *Child Language*. London and New York: Routledge.

PEDERSEN, R. N., 1992, *One Europe: 100 Nations*. Clevedon: Channel View Books.

PEDERSEN, R. N. & SHAW, J. W., 1993, *Gaelic Tourism Concepts*. Scotland: Highlands and Islands Enterprise.

PENNYCOOK, A., 1994, *The Cultural Politics of English as an International Language*. New York: Longman.

PERDUE, C. (ed.), 1993, *Adult Language Acquisition: Cross-Linguistic Perspectives*. Cambridge: Cambridge University Press.

PEREZ, B., 1994, Spanish Literacy Development: A Descriptive Study of Four Bilingual Whole Language Classrooms. *Journal of Reading Behaviour*, 26 (1), 75-94.

PEREZ, B., 1995, Language and Literacy Issues Related to Mexican American Secondary Students. Special Issue: The Mexican American Educational Experience. *High School Journal*, 78 (4), 236-243.

PEREZ, B. & TORRES-GUZMÁN, M. E., 1996, *Learning in Two Worlds. An Integrated Spanish/English Biliteracy Approach* (Second edition). New York: Longman.

PERLMANN, J., 1990, Historical Legacies: 1840/English Biliteracy Approach Secondary Stud*English Plus: Issues in Bilingual Education*. London: Sage.

PEROTTI, A., 1994, *The Case for Intercultural Education*. Strasbourg: Council for Europe Press.

PETHERBRIDGE-HERNANDEZ, P., 1990, Teacher Preparation in a Bilingual Setting: In-Service Training for Teachers in Catalonia. *Journal of Multilingual and Multicultural Development*, 11 (3), 215-226.

PETTERS, Y. J. D. & WILLIAMS, C. H., 1993, *The Cartographic Representation of Linguistic Data*. Discussion Papers in Geolinguistics Nos. 19-21. Department of Geography, Staffordshire University, United Kingdom.

PHADRAIG, M. N. G., 1994, The Status of Irish as a 'Mother-Tongue' or Primary Language. *Studies in Education*, 10 (1), 23-36.

PHAM, L., 1994, Infant Dual Language Acquisition Revisited. *Journal of Educational Issues of Language Minority Students*, 14, 185-210.

PHILLIPS, D. (ed.), 1989, *Which Language? Diversification and the National Curriculum*. London, Sydney, Auckland, Toronto: Hodder and Stoughton.

PHILLIPSON, R., 1992, *Linguistic Imperialism*. Oxford: Oxford University Press.

PIAGET, J., 1955, *The Language and Thought of the Child*. New York: World Press.

PICKEN, C., 1983, *The Translator's Handbook*. London: Aslib.

PIERSON, H. D., 1994, Ethnolinguistic Vitality During a Period of Decolonization Without Independence: Perceived Vitality in Hong Kong. *International Journal of the Sociology of Language*, 108, 43-62.

PIMSLEUR, P., 1966, *Language Aptitude Battery*. New York: Harcourt, Brace and World.

PINKER, S., 1994, *The Language Instinct*. London: Penguin.

PINTNER, R. & ARSENIAN, S., 1937, The Relation of Bilingualism to Verbal Intelligence and School Adjustment. *Journal of Educational Research*, 31, 255-263.

PLATT, J., WEBER, H. & HO, M. L., 1984, *The New Englishes*. London: Routledge.

POHL, J., 1965, Bilingualismes. *Revue Roumaine de Linguistique*, 10, 343-349.

PORTER, R. P., 1990, *Forked Tongue: The Politics of Bilingual Education*. New York: Basic Books.

PORTER, R. P., 1991, Language Choice for Latino Students. *Public Interest*, 105, 48-60.

POSNER, R., 1991, Society, Civilization, Mentality: Prolegomena to a Language Policy for Europe. In F. COULMAS (ed.), *A Language Policy for the European Community*. Berlin/New York: Mouton de Gruyter.

PRATOR, C. H., 1956, *Language Teaching in the Philippines: A Report*. Manila, Philippines: United States Educational Foundation in the Philippines.

PRESS AND INFORMATION OFFICE OF CYPRUS, 1994, *The Republic of Cyprus, An Overview*. Nicosia: Press and Information Office of Cyprus.

PRICE, D. & BAKER, C., 1993, Bilingualism and Information Technology. In H. BAETENS BEARDSMORE (ed.), *European Models of Bilingual Education*. Clevedon: Multilingual Matters.

PRICE, E., 1978, Report. In C. J. DODSON & E. PRICE (eds), *Bilingual Education in Wales 5 –11*. London: Evans/Methuen.

PRICE, E., 1983, Assessing the Listening and Speaking Skills of Welsh Learners: Lessons for Syllabus Design. In P. H. NELDE (ed.), *Theory, Methods and Models of Contact Linguistics*. Bonn: Dummler.

PRICE, E., 1985, Schools Council Bilingual Education Project (Primary Schools) 1968–1977: An Assessment. In C. J. DODSON (ed.) *Bilingual Education: Evaluation, Assessment and Methodology*. Cardiff: University of Wales Press.

PRICE, E. & POWELL, R., 1983, *Listening, Understanding and Speaking*. Cardiff: Welsh Office.

PRICE, E. *et al.*, 1984, *Survey of Writing Among 10–11 Year Old First Language Welsh Pupils*. Cardiff: Welsh Office.

PRICE, E., POWELL, R. & JONES, A., 1981, *Report on the Survey of Speaking Skills among 10–11 Year Old Welsh Learners*. Cardiff: Welsh Office.

PRICE, G., 1984, *The Languages of Britain*. London: Edward Arnold.

PURKEY, S. C. & SMITH, M. S., 1983, Effective Schools: A Review. *Elementary School Journal*, 86 (4), 427-452.

PUTZ, M. (ed.), 1994, *Language Contact and Language Conflict*. Amsterdam/Philadelphia: John Benjamins.

PUTZ, M. (ed.), 1995, *Discrimination Through Language in Africa? Perspectives on the Namibian Experience*. Berlin/New York: Mouton de Gruyter.

Q

QUAY, S., 1994, Language Choice in Early Bilingual Development. Unpublished Ph.D. Thesis, University of Cambridge.

QUINTERO, E. & HUERTA-MACIAS, A., 1990, All in the Family: Bilingualism and Biliteracy. *The Reading Teacher*, 44 (4), 306-312.

R

RADNAI, Z., 1994, The Educational Effects of Language Policy. *Current Issues in Language and Society*, 1 (1), 65-87.

RAJABU, R. & NGONNYANI, D., 1994, Language Policy in Tanzania and the Hidden Agenda. In C. M. RUBAGUMYA (ed.), *Teaching and Researching Language in African Classrooms*. Clevedon: Multilingual Matters.

RAMAGE, K., 1990, Motivational Factors and Persistence in Foreign Language Study. *Language Learning*, 40 (2), 189-219.

RAMIREZ, A. G., 1985, *Bilingualism Through Schooling: Cross Cultural Education for Minority and Majority Students*. Albany: State University of New York Press.

RAMIREZ, A. G., 1986, Language Learning Strategies Used by Adolescents Studying French in New York Schools. *Foreign Language Annals*, 19, 131-141.

RAMIREZ, A. G., 1991, Discourse Processes in the Second Language Classroom. In M. E. McGROARTY & C. J. FALTIS (eds), *Languages in School and Society: Policy and Pedagogy*. Berlin/New York: Mouton de Gruyter.

RAMIREZ, A. G., 1992, Language Proficiency and Bilingualism. In R. V. PADILLA & A. H. BENAVIDES (eds), *Critical Perspectives on Bilingual Education Research*. Tempe, AZ: Bilingual Press.

RAMIREZ, C. M., 1987, Developmental Linguistic Interdependence and Bilingual Education: Cummins and Beyond. *International Journal of the Sociology of Language*, 63, 81-98.

RAMIREZ, J. D., 1986, Comparing Structured English Immersion and Bilingual Education: First-Year Results of a National Study. *American Journal of Education*, 95 (1), 122-148.

RAMIREZ, J. D., 1992, Executive Summary. *Bilingual Research Journal*, 16 (1&2), 1-62.

RAMIREZ, J. D. & MERINO, B. J., 1990, Classroom Talk in English Immersion, Early-Exit and Late-Exit Transitional Bilingual Education Programs. In R. JACOBSON & C. FALTIS (eds), *Language Distribution Issues in Bilingual Schooling*. Clevedon: Multilingual Matters.

RAMIREZ, J. D., YUEN, S. D. & RAMEY, D. R., 1991, *Final Report: Longitudinal Study of Structured English Immersion Strategy, Early-Exit and Late-Exit Programs for Language-minority Children*. Report Submitted to the United States Department of Education. San Mateo, CA: Aguirre International.

RAMPTON, B., 1990, Some Unofficial Perspectives on Bilingualism and Education for All. *Language Issues*, 3 (2), 27-32.

RANNUT, M., 1994, Beyond Linguistic Policy: The Soviet Union versus Estonia. In T. SKUTNABB-KANGAS, R. PHILLIPSON & M. RANNUT (eds) *Linguistic Human Rights: Overcoming Linguistic Discrimination*. Berlin/New York: Mouton de Gruyter.

RANSDELL, S. E. & FISCHLER, I., 1987, Memory in a Monolingual Mode: When are Bilinguals at a Disadvantage. *Journal of Memory and Language*, 26, 392-405.

RANSDELL, S. E. & FISCHLER, I., 1989, Effects of Concreteness and Task Context on Recall of Prose among Bilingual and Monolingual Speakers. *Journal of Memory and Language*, 28 (3), 278-291.

RAWKINS, P. M., 1979, *The Implementation of Language Policy in the Schools of Wales*. Centre for the Study of Public Policy, University of Strathclyde.

RAWKINS, P. M., 1987, The Politics of Benign Neglect: Education, Public Policy and the Mediation of Linguistic Conflict in Wales. *International Journal of the Sociology of Language*, 66, 27-48.

READ, J., 1996, Recent Developments in Australian Late Immersion Language Education. *Journal of Multilingual and Multicultural Development*, 17 (6), 469-484.

REBUFFOT, J., 1993, *Le Point sur L'Immersion au Canada*. Anjou, Québec: Centre Educatif et Culturel.

REES. A. D., 1979, The Welsh Language in Broadcasting. In M. STEPHENS (ed.), *The Welsh Language Today*. Llandysul: Gomer.

REES. M. E., 1954, *A Welsh Linguistic Background Scale*. Pamphlet No. 2. Aberystwyth: Faculty of Education, University College of Wales.

REID, E., 1988, Linguistic Minorities and Language Education: The English Experience. *Journal of Multilingual and Multicultural Development*, 9 (1&2), 181-191.

REID, M. I., BARNETT, B. R. & ROSENBERG, H. A., 1974, *A Matter of Choice*. Slough: NFER.

REID, S., 1993, *Lament for a Notion: The Life and Death of Canada's Bilingual Dream*. Vancouver, Canada: Arsenal Pulp Press.

REISS, M. A., 1985. The Good Language Learners: Another Look. *Canadian Modern Language Review*, 41, 511-23.

RENKEMA, W. J. T., 1995, *Understanding the Position of Lesser Used Languages in European Educational Systems*. Netherlands: Mercator-Education.

RENNIE. J., 1993, *ESL and Bilingual Program Models*. An ERIC Digest. Washington, DC: ERIC Clearinghouse on Languages and Linguistics.

RESNICK, M. C., 1993, ESL and Language Planning in Puerto Rican Education. *TESOL Quarterly*, 27 (2), 259-275.

REYES, M. DE LA LUZ, 1991, A Process Approach to Literacy Using Dialogue: Journals and Literature Logs with Second Language Learners. *Research in the Teaching of English*, 25 (3), 291-313.

REYES, M. DE LA LUZ, 1992, Challenging Venerable Assumptions: Literacy Instruction for Linguistically Different Students. *Harvard Educational Review*, 62 (4), 427-446.

REYES, M. DE LA LUZ & McCOLLUM, P. A., 1992, Language, Literacy and Educational Reform. *Education and Urban Society*, 24 (2), 171-177.

REYES, M. DE LA LUZ, LALIBERTY, E. A. & ORBANOSKY, J. M., 1993, Emerging Biliteracy and Cross-Cultural Sensitivity in a Language Arts Classroom. *Language Arts*, 70 (8), 659-668.

REYNOLDS, A. G., 1991, The Cognitive Consequences of Bilingualism. In A. G. REYNOLDS (ed.), *Bilingualism, Multiculturalism and Second Language Learning*. Hillsdale, NJ: Lawrence Erlbaum.

REYNOLDS, D., 1982, A State of Ignorance? *Education for Development*, 7 (2), 4-35.

RICCIARDELLI, L. A., 1993, Two Components of Metalinguistic Awareness. *Applied Psycholinguistics*, 14 (3), 349-367.

RICHARDS, J. C. & RODGERS, T. S., 1986, *Approaches and Methods in Language Teaching: A Description and Analysis*. Cambridge: Cambridge University Press.

RICHARDS, J. C., PLATT, J. & PLATT, H., 1992, *Dictionary of Language Teaching and Applied Linguistics* (Second edition). Harlow, Essex: Longman.

RICHTERICH, R. & CHANCEREL, J., 1987, *Identifying the Needs of Adults Learning a Foreign Language*. New Jersey: Prentice Hall.

RICKFORD J. R. & McWHORTER, J., 1997, Language Contact and Language Generation: Pidgins and Creoles. In F. COULMAS (ed.), *The Handbook of Sociolinguistics*. Oxford: Blackwell.

RINGBOM, H., 1990, Effects of Transfer in Foreign Language Learning. In H. W. DCHERT (ed.), *Current Trends in European Second Language Acquisition Research*. Clevedon: Multilingual Matters.

RIPPBERGER, S. J., 1993, Ideological Shifts in Bilingual Education: Mexico and the United States. *Comparative Education Review*, 37 (1), 50-61.

RIVERA, C. (ed.), 1984, *Language Proficiency and Academic Achievement*. Clevedon: Multilingual Matters.

RIVERA, C. & ZEHLER, A. M., 1991, Assuring the Academic Success of Language Minority Students: Collaboration in Teaching and Learning. *Journal of Education*, 173 (2), 52-77.

ROBERTS, A., 1991, Parental Attitudes to Gaelic-Medium Education in the Western Isles of Scotland. *Journal of Multilingual and Multicultural Development*, 12 (4), 253-269.

ROBERTS, C., 1983, The Sociology of Education and Wales. In G. WILLIAMS (ed.), *Crisis of Economy and Ideology: Essays on Welsh Society 1840–1980*. Bangor: UCNW.

ROBERTS, C., 1985, Teaching and Learning Commitment in Bilingual Schools. Unpublished Ph.D. Thesis, University of Wales.

ROBERTS, C., 1987, Political Conflict over Bilingual Initiatives: A Case Study. *Journal of Multilingual and Multicultural Development*, 8 (4), 311-322.

ROBERTS, C. & STREET, B., 1997, Spoken and Written Language. In F. COULMAS (ed.), *The Handbook of Sociolinguistics*. Oxford: Blackwell.

ROBERTS, G. W., 1994, Nurse/Patient Communication Within a Bilingual Health Care Setting. *British Journal of Nursing*, 3 (2), 60-67.

ROBERTS, P. A., 1994, Integrating Creole into Caribbean Classrooms. *Journal of Multilingual and Multicultural Development*, 15 (1), 47-62.

ROBINS, R. H. & UHLENBECK, E. M. (eds), 1991, *Endangered Languages*. Oxford/New York: Berg.

ROBINSON, C. D. W., 1996, *Language Use in Rural Development: An African Perspective*. Berlin/New York: Mouton de Gruyter.

ROCA, A. & LIPSKI, J. M. (eds), 1993, *Spanish in the United States: Linguistic Contact and Diversity*. Berlin/New York: Mouton de Gruyter.

RODGERS, M. A., 1995, Language, Culture and Society: Bilingual Education in the United States. In G. E. Thomas (ed.), *Race and Ethnicity in America: Meeting the Challenge in the 21st Century*. Washington, DC: Taylor and Francis.

ROFFE, I., 1995, Teaching, Learning and Assessment Strategies for Interlingual Subtitling. *Journal of Multilingual and Multicultural Development*, 16 (3), 215-225.

ROMAINE, S., 1988, *Pidgin and Creole Languages*. New York: Longman.

ROMAINE, S., 1994a, From the Fish's Point of View. *International Journal of the Sociology of Language*, 110, 177-186.

ROMAINE, S., 1994b, *Language in Society: An Introduction to Sociolinguistics*. Oxford: Oxford University Press.

ROMAINE, S., 1995, *Bilingualism* (Second edition). Oxford: Basil Blackwell.

ROMERO, M. & PARRINO, A., 1994, Planned Alternation of Languages (PAL): Language Use and Distribution in Bilingual Classrooms. *Journal of Educational Issues of Language Minority Students*, 13, 137-161.

ROMNEY, J. C., ROMNEY, D. M. & BRAUN, C., 1988, The Effects of Reading Aloud in French to Immersion Children on Second Language Acquisition. *Canadian Modern Language Review*, 45 (3), 530-538.

RONJAT, J., 1913, *Le développement du langage observe chez un enfant bilingue*. Paris: Champion.

ROS, M. *et al.*, 1994, Ethnolinguistic Vitality and Social Identity: Their Impact on Ingroup Bias and Social Attribution. *International Journal of the Sociology of Language*, 108, 145-166.

ROSE, P. (ed.), 1993, *Interminority Affairs in the United States: Pluralism at the Crossroads*. The

Annals of the American Academy of Political and Social Sciences. London: Sage Periodicals Press.

ROSEBERY, A., WARREN, B. & CONANT, F. R., 1992, *Appropriating Scientific Discourse: Findings from Language Minority Classrooms*. National Centre for Research on Cultural Diversity and Second Language Learning, United States Department of Education.

ROSEN, H. & BURGESS, T., 1980, *Languages and Dialects of London Schoolchildren: An Investigation*. London: Ward Lock.

ROSENBERG, S., 1986, Bilingual Students and Tests in English/Communications. *Language Issues*, 39-41.

ROSENTHAL, J., 1995, *Teaching Science to Language Minority Students: Theory and Practice*. Clevedon: Multilingual Matters.

ROSENTHAL, R., 1966, *Experimenter Effects in Behavioural Research*. New York: Appleton-Century-Crofts.

ROSIER, P. & HOLM, W., 1980, *The Rock Point Experience: A Longitudinal Study of a Navajo School Program*. Washington, DC: Center for Applied Linguistics.

ROSSELL, C. & BAKER, K., 1988, Selecting and Exiting Students in Bilingual Education Programs. *Journal of Law and Education*, 17 (4), 589-623.

ROSSELL, C. H., 1992, Nothing Matters? A Critique of the Ramirez, *et al.* Longitudinal Study of Instruction Programs for Language-minority Children. *Bilingual Research Journal*, 16 (1&2), 159-186.

ROSSELL, C. H. & ROSS, J. M., 1986, The Social Science Evidence on Bilingual Education. *Journal of Law and Education*, 15 (4), 385-419.

ROSSIER, R. E., 1994, Bilingual Education. *California Political Review*, 5 (1), 18-22.

RUBAGUMYA, C. M., 1990, *Language in Education in Africa*. Clevedon: Multilingual Matters.

RUBAGUMYA, C. M., 1994, Epilogue: Towards Critical Language Awareness in Africa. In C. M. RUBAGUMYA (ed.), *Teaching and Researching Language in African Classrooms*. Clevedon: Multilingual Matters.

RUBAGUMYA, C. M. (ed.), 1994, *Teaching and Researching Language in African Classrooms*. Clevedon: Multilingual Matters.

RUBIN, H. & TURNER, A., 1989, Linguistic Awareness Skills in Grade One Children in a French Immersion Setting. *Reading and Writing: An Interdisciplinary Journal*, 1 (1), 73-86.

RUBIN, J., 1975. What the Good Language Learner Can Teach Us. *TESOL Quarterly*, 9, 41-51.

RUBIN, J., 1977, Attitudes Toward Language Planning. In C. C. ELERT *et al.* (eds), *Dialectology and Sociolinguistics*. Umea: Umea Studies in the Humanities 12.

RUDIN, R., 1988, English-Speaking Quebec and the Canadian Constitution: 1867–1988. *Language, Culture and Curriculum*, 1 (3), 215-232.

RUEDA, R., 1983, Metalinguistic Awareness in Monolingual and Bilingual Mildly Retarded Children. *NABE Journal*, 8, 55-68.

RUEDA, R. & GARCÍA, E., 1994, *Teachers' Beliefs about Reading Assessment with Latino Language Minority Students*. National Center for Research on Cultural Diversity and Second Language Learning, United States Department of Education.

RUEST, P. R., 1985, A Model for French Language Post-Secondary Education. *Canadian Modern Language Review*, 41 (5), 835-841.

RUHLEN, M., 1991, *A Guide to the World's Languages*. London: Edward Arnold.

RUIZ, N. T., 1995, Bilingual Special Education Teachers' Shifting Paradigms: Complex Responses to Educational Reform. *Journal of Learning Disabilities*, 28 (10), 622-635.

RUIZ, N. T., FIGUEROA, R. A., RUEDA, R. S. & BEAUMONT, C., 1992, History and Status of Bilingual Special Education for Hispanic Handicapped Students. In R. V. PADILLA & A. H. BENAVIDES (eds), *Critical Perspectives on Bilingual Education Research*. Tempe, AZ: Bilingual Press.

RUIZ, R., 1984, Orientations in Language Planning. *NABE Journal*, 8 (2), 15-34.

RUTTER, M. *et al.*, 1979, *Fifteen Thousand Hours*. London: Open Books.

RYAN, E. B., 1979, Why Do Low-Prestige Language Varieties Persist? In H. GILES & R. N. ST. CLAIR (eds), *Language and Social Psychology*. Oxford: Blackwell.

RYAN, E. B. & GILES, H. (eds), 1982, *Attitudes towards Language Variation*. London: Edward Arnold.

S

SAER, D. J., 1922, An Inquiry into the Effect of Bilingualism upon the Intelligence of Young Children. *Journal of Experimental Pedagogy*, 6, 232-240 and 266-274.

SAER, D. J., 1923, The Effects of Bilingualism on Intelligence. *British Journal of Psychology*, 14, 25-38.

SAER, D. J., SMITH, F. & HUGHES, J., 1924, *The Bilingual Problem*. Wrexham: Hughes and Son.

SAFTY, A., 1988, French Immersion and the Making of a Bilingual Society: A Critical Review and Discussion. *Canadian Journal of Education*, 13 (2), 243-261.

SAFTY, A., 1989, Some Reflections on a Decade in the French Immersion Classroom. *Canadian Modern Language Review*, 45 (3), 550-560.

SAFTY, A., 1990, Second Language Acquisition in French Immersion in Canada: Characteristics and Implications. *Language, Culture and Curriculum*, 3 (3), 179-197.

SAFTY, A., 1992a, Effectiveness and French Immersion: A Socio-Political Analysis. *Canadian Journal of Education*, 17 (1), 23-32.

SAFTY, A., 1992b, French Immersion: Bilingual Education and Unilingual Administration. *Interchange*, 24 (4), 389-405.

SAMUDA, R. J., BERRY, J. W. & LAFERRIERE, M., 1984, *Multiculturalism in Canada. Social and Educational Perspectives*. London: Allyn and Bacon.

SAMUELSSON-BROWN, G., 1993, *A Practical Guide for Translators*. Clevedon: Multilingual Matters.

SANCHEZ, A., 1992, Política de Difusión del Español. *International Journal of the Sociology of Language*, 95, 51-69.

SANKOFF, D. & POPLACK S., 1981, A Formal Grammar of Code-Switching. *Centro de Estudios Puertorriqueños Working Papers*, 8, 1-55.

SANKOFF, G., 1972, Language Use in Multilingual Societies. In J. B. PRIDE & J. HOLMES (eds), *Sociolinguistics: Selected Readings*. Harmondsworth: Penguin.

SARKONAK, R. & HODGSON, R. (eds), 1993, *Writing in Stereo: Bilingualism in the Text*. In *Visible Language*, 27 (1/2). Providence, RI: Rhode Island School of Design.

SAUNDERS, G., 1982, *Bilingual Children: Guidance for the Family*. Clevedon: Multilingual Matters.

SAUNDERS, G., 1988, *Bilingual Children: From Birth to Teens*. Clevedon: Multilingual Matters.

SAVILLE-TROIKE, M., 1984, What Really Matters in Second Language Learning for Academic Achievement? *TESOL Quarterly*, 18 (2), 199-219.

SAVILLE-TROIKE, M., 1996, The Ethnography of Communication. In S. L. McKAY & N. H. HORNBERGER (eds), *Sociolinguistics and Language Teaching*. Cambridge: Cambridge University Press.

SAYERS, D., 1991, Cross-Cultural Exchanges between Students from the Same Culture: A Portrait of an Emerging Relationship Mediated by Technology. *Canadian Modern Language Review*, 47 (4), 678-696.

SAYERS, D., 1995, Educational Equity Issues in an Information Age. *Teachers College Record*, 96 (4), 767-774.

SAYERS, D. & BROWN, K., 1987, Bilingual Education and Telecommunications: A Perfect Fit. *Computing Teacher*, 14 (7), 23-24.

SCARCELLA, R. & CHIN K., 1993, *Literacy Practices in Two Korean-American Communities*. National Center for Research on Cultural Diversity and Second Language Learning, United States Department of Education.

SCHERMERHORN, R. A., 1970, *Comparative Ethnic Relations*. New York: Random House.

SCHIFFMAN, H. F., 1987, Losing the Battle for Balanced Bilingualism: The German-American Case. *Language Planning and Language Problems*, 11 (1), 66-81.

SCHIFFMAN, H. F., 1997, Diglossia as a Sociolinguistic Situation. In F. COULMAS (ed.), *The Handbook of Sociolinguistics*. Oxford: Blackwell.

SCHINKE-LLANO, L., 1989, Early Childhood Bilingualism: In Search of Explanation. *Studies in Second Language Acquisition (SSLA)*, 11 (3), 223-240.

SCHLOSSMAN, S., 1983, Is There an American Tradition of Bilingual Education? *American Journal of Education*, 91, 139-186.

SCHOOL OF ORIENTAL AND AFRICAN STUDIES, 1993, *The Logosphere Programme*. London: School of Oriental and African Studies.

SCHOOLS COUNCIL COMMITTEE FOR WALES, 1983, *Small Schools in Concert*. Cardiff: Schools Council.

SCHUCHAT, T., 1990, *Ulpan: How to Learn Hebrew in a Hurry*. Jerusalem and Woodmere, NY: Gefen Books.

SCHUMANN, J. H., 1978, *The Pidginization Process: A Model for Second Language Acquisition*. Rowley, MA: Newbury House.

SCHUMANN, J. H., 1983, Art and Science in Second Language Acquisition Research. *Language Learning*, 33 (5), 49-75.

SCHUMANN, J. H., 1986, Research on the Acculturation Model for Second Language Acquisition. *Journal of Multilingual and Multicultural Development*, 7 (5), 379-392.

SCOTT, S., 1973, The Relation of Divergent Thinking to Bilingualism: Cause or Effect? Unpublished Research Report, McGill University.

SEARS, D. O. & HUDDY, L., 1993, The Symbolic Politics of Opposition to Bilingual Education. In S. WORCHEL & J. A. SIMPSON (eds), *Conflict Between People and Groups: Causes, Processes and Resolutions* (Nelson Hall Series in Psychology). Chicago, IL: Nelson Hall.

SECADA, W. G., 1991, Degree of Bilingualism and Arithmetic Problem Solving in Hispanic First Graders. *Elementary School Journal*, 92 (2), 213-231.

SECADA, W. G., 1993, The Political Context of Bilingual Education in the United States. In B. ARIAS & U. CASANOVA (eds), *Bilingual Education: Politics, Research and Practice*. Berkeley, CA: McCutchan.

SECADA, W. G. & LIGHTFOOT, T., 1993, *Symbols and the Political Context of Bilingual Education in the United States. Bilingual Education: Politics, Practice and Research, Part II, Ninety-Second Yearbook of the National Society for the Study of Education*. Chicago: University of Chicago Press.

SEDAKOVA, O., 1994, *The Silk of Time. Bilingual Selected Poems*. Keele, Staffordshire, United Kingdom: Ryburn Publishing/Keele University Press.

SEGALOWITZ, N., 1977, Psychological Perspectives on Bilingual Education. In B. SPOLSKY & R. COOPER (eds), *Frontiers of Bilingual Education*. Rowley, MA: Newbury House.

SELINKER, L., SWAIN, M. & DUMAS, G., 1975, The Interlanguage Hypothesis Extended to Children. *Language Learning*, 25, 139-152.

SHAFER, S. M., 1986, Persistent Issues in Bilingual Education. *Compare*, 16 (2), 189-197.

SHAKLE, C., 1994, Pakistan: Language Situation. In R. E. ASHER and J. M. Y. SIMPSON (eds) *The Encyclopedia of Language and Linguistics, Volume 6*. Oxford: Pergamon.

SHAMES, G. H., 1989, Stuttering: An RFP for a Cultural Perspective. *Discord*, 14, 67-77.

SHAMSHUR, O. V., 1994, Current Ethnic and Migration Issues in the Former USSR. *Current Issues in Language and Society*, 1 (1), 7-27.

SHAMSHUR, O. V. & IZHEVSKA, T., 1994, Multilingual Education as a Factor of Inter-Ethnic Relations: The Case of the Ukraine. *Current Issues in Language and Society*, 1 (1), 29-39.

SHANNON, S. M., 1990, Transition from Bilingual Programs to All-English Programs: Issues About and Beyond Language. *Linguistics and Education*, 2 (4), 323-343.

SHAPSON, S., 1985, Post-Secondary Bilingual Education: Identifying and Adapting to the Shift in Second-Language Demands. *Canadian Modern Language Review*, 41 (5), 827-834.

SHARP, D., 1973, *Language in Bilingual Communities*. London: Edward Arnold.

SHARP, D., BENNETT, G. & TREHARNE, C., 1977, *English in Wales*. London: Schools Council.

SHARP, D., THOMAS, B., PRICE, E., FRANCIS, G. & DAVIES, I., 1973, *Attitudes to Welsh and English in the Schools of Wales*. Basingstoke/Cardiff: MacMillan/University of Wales Press.

SHEILS, J., 1988, *Communication in the Modern Languages Curriculum*. Strasbourg: Council for Cultural Cooperation, Council of Europe.

SHENNAN, M., 1991, *Teaching About Europe*. London: Cassell.

SHIBATINI, M., 1994, *The Languages of Japan* (Cambridge Language Surveys). Cambridge: Cambridge University Press.

SHOHAMY, E., 1983, The Stability of the Oral Proficiency Trait on the Oral Interview Speaking Test. *Language Learning*, 33,527-540.

SHOHAMY, E., 1988, A Proposed Framework for Testing the Oral Language of Second/Foreign Language Learners. *Studies in Second Language Acquisition*, 10 (2), 165-179.

SHOHAMY, E., 1990, Discourse Analysis in Language Testing. *Annual Review of Applied Linguistics*, 11, 115-131.

SHOHAMY, E., 1990, Language Testing Priorities: A Different Perspective. *Foreign Language Annals*, 23 (5), 385-394.

SHOHAMY, E., 1993, *The Power of Tests: The Impact of Language Tests on Teaching and Learning*. Washington, DC: National Foreign Language Center.

SHOHAMY, E., 1994. Issues of Language Planning in Israel: Language and Ideology. In RICHARD LAMBERT (ed.) *Language Planning around the World: Contexts and Systemic Change*. Washington, DC: National Foreign Language Center.

SHOHAMY, E., 1995, Performance Assessment in Language Testing. *Annual Review of Applied Linguistics*, 15, 188-211.

SHOHAMY, E., 1997, Critical Language Testing and Beyond. Plenary Paper presented at the American Association of Applied Linguistics (AAAL), Orlando, March 1997.

SHORT, D., 1991, *Integrating Language and Content Instruction: Strategies and Techniques*. Program Information Guide Series, 7. Washington, DC: National Clearinghouse for Bilingual Education.

SIACHITEMA, A. K., 1994, The Social Significance of Language Use and Language Choice in a Zambia Urban Setting. In J. CHESHIRE (ed.), *English Around the World: Sociolinguistic Perspectives*. Cambridge: Cambridge University Press.

SIDIROPOULOS, E. *et al.*, 1995, *Race Relations Survey 1994/95*. Johannesburg: South African Institute of Race Relations.

SIDWELL, D., 1987, *Modern Language Learning: Tutor's Handbook*. Leicester: National Institute of Adult Continuing Education.

SIDWELL, D. (ed.), 1987, *Teaching Languages to Adults*. London: Centre for Information on Language Teaching and Research.

SIERRA, J. & OLAZIREGI, I., 1989, *EIFE 2: Influence of Factors on the Learning of Basque*. Gasteiz, Spain: Central Publications Service of the Basque Government.

SIGUÁN, M., 1993, *Multilingual Spain*. Amsterdam: Swets and Zeitlinger.

SIGUÁN, M. & MACKEY, W. F., 1987, *Education and Bilingualism*. London: Kogan Page.

SIKMA, J. & GORTER, D., 1991, *European Lesser Used Languages in Primary Education*. Ljouwert/Leeuwarden: Fryske Academy/ Mercator.

SILBERT, J., CARNINE, D. & ALVAREZ, R. Jr., 1994, Beginning Reading For Bilingual Students. *Educational Leadership*, 51 (5), 90-91.

SIMOES, A., 1995, A Suggested Paradigm to Evaluate a Bilingual Program. *Journal of Educational Issue of Language Minority Students*, 15.

SIMOES, A. (ed.), 1976, *The Bilingual Child: Research and Analysis of Existing Educational Themes*. New York: Academic Press.

SIMONS, H., 1979, *Mother Tongue and Culture in Bedfordshire. First External Evaluation Report*. Cambridge: Cambridge Institute of Education.

SINGH, R., 1986, Immersion: Problems and Principles. *Canadian Modern Language Review*, 42 (3), 559-571.

SINGLETON, D., 1989, *Language Acquisition: The Age Factor*. Clevedon: Multilingual Matters.

SINGLETON, D., 1992, Second Language Instruction: The When and How. In J. F. MATTER (ed.), *Language Teaching in the Twenty-first Century: Problems and Prospects* (*AILA Review*, 9, 46-54).

SINGLETON, D. & LENGYEL, Z. (eds), 1995, *The Age Factor in Second Language Acquisition: A Critical Look at the Critical Period Hypothesis*. Clevedon: Multilingual Matters.

SKEHAN, P., 1986, Where Does Language Aptitude Come From? In P. MEARA (ed.), *Spoken Language: Papers from the Annual Meeting of the British Association for Applied Linguistics*. London: Centre for Information on Language Teaching and Research.

SKEHAN, P., 1988, Language Testing. *Language Teaching*, 21 (January), 1-13 and (October), 211-22.

SKEHAN, P., 1989, *Individual Differences in Second-Language Learning*. London: Edward Arnold.

SKINNER, B. F., 1957, *Verbal Behavior*. New York, Appleton-Century-Crofts.

SKINNER, D. C., 1985, Access to Meaning: The Anatomy of the Language/Learning Connection. *Journal of Multilingual and Multicultural Development*, 6 (2), 97-116.

SKUTNABB-KANGAS, T., 1977, Language in the Process of Cultural Assimilation and Structural Incorporation of Linguistic Minorities. In C. C. ELERT *et al.* (eds), *Dialectology and Sociolinguistics*. Umea: Umea Studies in the Humanities.

SKUTNABB-KANGAS, T., 1981, *Bilingualism or Not: The Education of Minorities*. Clevedon: Multilingual Matters.

SKUTNABB-KANGAS, T., 1984, Why Aren't Children in the Nordic Countries Bilingual. *Journal of Multilingual and Multicultural Development*, 5 (3&4), 301-315.

SKUTNABB-KANGAS, T., 1991, Swedish Strategies to Prevent Integration and

National Ethnic Minorities. In O. GARCÍA (ed.), *Bilingual Education:* Focusschrift in Honor of Joshua A. Fishman. Amsterdam/Philadelphia: John Benjamins.

SKUTNABB-KANGAS, T. & CUMMINS, J. (eds), 1988, *Minority Education: From Shame to Struggle.* Clevedon: Multilingual Matters.

SKUTNABB-KANGAS, T. & PHILLIPSON, R., 1989, 'Mother Tongue': The Theoretical and Sociopolitical Construction of a Concept. In U. AMMON (ed.), *Status and Function of Languages and Language Varieties.* New York: Mouton de Gruyter.

SKUTNABB-KANGAS, T. & PHILLIPSON, R., 1994, Linguistic Human Rights, Past and Present. In T. SKUTNABB-KANGAS, R. PHILLIPSON & M. RANNUT (eds), *Linguistic Human Rights: Overcoming Linguistic Discrimination.* New York: Mouton de Gruyter.

SKUTNABB-KANGAS, T. & TOUKOMAA, P., 1976, *Teaching Migrant Children Mother Tongue and Learning the Language of the Host Country in the Context of the Socio-Cultural Situation of the Migrants Family.* Tampere, Finland: Tukimuksia Research Reports.

SKUTNABB-KANGAS, T., PHILLIPSON, R. & RANNUT, M. (eds), 1994, *Linguistic Human Rights: Overcoming Linguistic Discrimination.* New York: Mouton de Gruyter.

SLADE, D. & GIBBONS, J., 1987, Testing Bilingual Proficiency in Australia: Issues, Methods, Findings. *Evaluation and Research in Education*, 1 (2), 95-106.

SLEETER, C. E. & GRANT, C. A., 1987, An Analysis of Multicultural Education in the United State. *Harvard Educational Review*, 57 (4), 421-444.

SLOAN, T., 1992, Second-Language Retention. *Language and Society*, 37, 35-36.

SMITH, D. J. & TOMLINSON, S., 1989, *The School Effect: A Study of Multi-racial Comprehensives.* London: Policy Studies Institute.

SMITH, F., 1923, Bilingualism and Mental Development. *British Journal of Psychology*, 13, 271-282.

SMITH, J. F., 1980, *Language and Language Attitudes in a Bilingual Community.* Leeuwarden: Fryske Akademy.

SMITH, S., 1996, Adult–Children Interaction in a BSL Nursery: Getting Their Attention. In P. KNIGHT & R. SWANWICK (eds), *Bilingualism and the Education of Deaf Children: Advances in Practice.* Leeds, United Kingdom: ADEDC, School of Education, University of Leeds.

SMOLICZ, J. J., 1974, The Concept of Tradition: A Humanistic Interpretation. *The Australian and New Zealand Journal of Sociology*, 10 (2), 75-83.

SMOLICZ, J. J., 1981, Core Values and Cultural Identity. *Ethnic and Racial Studies*, 4 (1), 75-90.

SMOLICZ, J. J., 1984a, Minority Languages and the Core Values of Culture: Changing Policies and Ethnic Responses in Australia. *Journal of Multilingual and Multicultural Development*, 5 (1), 11-24.

SMOLICZ, J. J., 1984b, Multiculturalism and an Overarching Framework of Values: Some Educational Responses for Ethnically Plural Societies. *European Journal of Education*, 19 (1), 11-24.

SMOLICZ, J. J., 1985, Greek Australians: A Question of Survival in a Multicultural Australia. *Journal of Multilingual and Multicultural Development*, 6 (1), 7-29.

SMOLICZ, J. J., 1988, Tradition, Core Values and Intercultural Development. *Ethnic and Racial Studies*, 11 (4), 382-410.

SMOLICZ, J. J., 1989, Types of Language Activation and Evaluation in an Ethnically Plural Society. In U. AMMON (ed.), *Status and Function of Languages and Language Varieties.* Berlin/New York: de Gruyter.

SMOLICZ, J. J., 1990, The Monoethnic Tradition and the Education of Minority Youth in Germany from an Australian Multicultural Perspective. *Comparative Education*, 26 (1), 27-44.

SMOLICZ, J. J., 1991a, Language Core Values in a Multicultural Setting: An Australian Experience. *International Review of Education*, 37 (1), 33-52.

SMOLICZ, J. J., 1991b, Who is an Australian? Identity, Core Values and the Resilience of Culture. In C. A. PRICE (ed.), *Australian National Identity.* Canberra: Academy of the Social Sciences in Australia.

SMOLICZ, J. J., 1992, Minority Languages as Core Values of Ethnic Cultures. In W. FASE, K. JASPAERT & S. KROON (eds), *Maintenance and Loss of Minority Languages.* Amsterdam: John Benjamins.

SMOLICZ, J. J., 1994a, Australia's Language Policies and Minority Rights: A Core Value Perspective. In T. SKUTNABB-KANGAS, R. PHILLIPSON & M. RANNUT, *Linguistic Human Rights: Overcoming Linguistic Discrimination.* Berlin/New York: Mouton de Gruyter.

SMOLICZ, J. J., 1994b, *Australian Diversity* (Second edition). University of Adelaide: Centre for Intercultural Studies and Multicultural Education.

SMOLICZ, J. J., 1995, Language: A Bridge or a Barrier? Languages in Education in Australia From an Intercultural Perspective. *Multilingua*, 14 (2), 151-182.

SMOLICZ, J. J. & SECOMBE, M. J., 1987, Polish Culture and Education in Australia. *Zeszyty Naukowe Uniwersytetu Jagiellonskiego*, DCCCX, 113-151.

SMOLICZ, J. J. & SECOMBE, M. J., 1989, Types of Language Activation and Evaluation in an Ethnically Plural Society. In U. AMMON (ed.), *Status and Function of Languages and Language Varieties.* Berlin/New York: Mouton de Gruyter.

SMOLICZ, J. J. & SECOMBE, M. J., 1991, *Australian Schools Through Children's Eyes.* Melbourne: Melbourne University Press.

SMOLICZ, J. J., LEE, L., MURUGAIAN, M. & SECOMBE, M. J., 1990. Language as a Core Value of Culture among Tertiary Students of Chinese and Indian Origin in Australia. *Journal of Asian Pacific Communications*, 1 (1), 229-246.

SMOLLE, K. & BREATHNACH, D., 1995, More Lesser Used Languages Enter the European Union. *Contact Bulletin: The European Bureau for Lesser Used Languages.* Volume 12, Number 2.

SNOW, C. E., 1990, Rationales for Native Language Instruction: Evidence from Research In A. M. PADILLA, H. H. FAIRCHILD & C. M. VALADEZ (eds), *Bilingual Education. Issues and Strategies.* London: Sage.

SNOW, C. E., 1991a, *A New Environmentalism for Child Language Acquisition.* Cambridge, MA: Harvard Graduate School of Education.

SNOW, C. E., 1991b, The Theoretical Basis for Relationships between Language and Literacy in Development. *Journal of Research in Childhood Education*, 6 (1), 5-10.

SNOW, C. E., 1992, Perspectives on Second-Language Development: Implications for Bilingual Education. *Educational Researcher*, 21 (2), 16-19.

SNOW, C. E., 1993, Families as Social Contexts for Literacy Development. *New Directions for Child Development*, 61, 11-24.

SNOW, C. E. & HOEFNAGEL-HOHLE, M., 1978, The Critical Period for Language Acquisition: Evidence from Second Language Learning. *Child Development*, 49, 1114-1128.

SNOW, C. E. *et al.*, 1995, SHELL: Oral Language and Early Literacy Skills in Kindergarten and First-Grade Children. *Journal of Research in Childhood Education*, 10 (1), 37-48.

SNOW, M. A., 1990, Instructional Methodology in Immersion Foreign Language Education. In A. M. PADILLA, H. H. FAIRCHILD & C. M. VALADEZ (eds), *Foreign Language Education: Issues and Strategies.* London: Sage.

SONNTAG, S. K. & POOL, J., 1987, Linguistic Denial and Linguistic Self-Denial: American Ideologies of Language. *Language Problems and Language Planning*, 11 (1), 46-65.

SOUTHALL, J. E., 1895, *The Welsh Language Census of 1891.* Newport: Southall.

SPENCE, A. G., MISHRA, S. P. & GHOZEIL, S., 1971, Home Language and Performance on Standardized Tests. *Elementary School Journal*, 71, 309-313.

SPENER, D., 1988, Transitional Bilingual Education and the Socialization of Immigrants. *Harvard Educational Review*, 58 (2), 133-153.

SPINA, J. M., 1979, Adolescent Attachment to Canada and Commitment to Bilingualism. *International Journal of the Sociology of Language*, 20, 75-88.

SPOLSKY, B., 1978, A Model for the Evaluation of Bilingual Education. *International Review of Education*, 24 (3), 347-360.

SPOLSKY, B., 1981, Bilingualism and Biliteracy. *Canadian Modern Language Review*, 37 (3), 475-485.

SPOLSKY, B., 1989a, Maori Bilingual Education and Language Revitalization. *Journal of Multilingual and Multicultural Development*, 10 (2), 89-106.

SPOLSKY, B., 1989b, Review of 'Key Issues in Bilingualism and Bilingual Education'. *Applied Linguistics*, 10 (4), 449-451

SPOLSKY, B., 1989c, *Conditions for Second Language Learning.* Oxford: Oxford University Press.

SPOLSKY, B., 1995a, *Measured Words: The Development of Objective Language Testing.* Oxford: Oxford University Press.

SPOLSKY, B., 1995b, Conditions for Language Revitalisation: A Comparison of the Cases of Hebrew and Maori. *Current Issues in Language and Society*, 2 (3), 177-201.

SPOLSKY, B., 1996, Prologomena to an Israeli

Language Policy. In T. HICKEY & J. WILLIAMS (eds), *Language, Education and Society in a Changing World*. Clevedon: Multilingual Matters.

SPOLSKY, B. & COOPER, R. (eds), 1977, *Frontiers of Bilingual Education*. Rowley, MA: Newbury House.

SPOLSKY, B., GREEN, J. B. & READ, J., 1974, *A Model for the Description, Analysis and Perhaps Evaluation of Bilingual Education*. University of New Mexico: Navajo Reading Study Progress (Report No. 23).

SPROULL, A., 1993, *The Economics of Gaelic Language Development*. Glasgow: Glasgow Caledonian University.

SRIDHAR, K. K., 1991, Bilingual Education in India. In O. GARCÍA (ed.), *Bilingual Education: Focusschrift in Honor of Joshua A. Fishman*. Amsterdam/Philadelphia: John Benjamins.

SRIDHAR, K. K., 1996, Societal Multilingualism. In S. L. McKAY & N. H. HORNBERGER (eds), *Sociolinguistics and Language Teaching*. Cambridge: Cambridge University Press.

STAATS, A. & STAATS, C., 1958, Attitudes Established by Classical Conditioning. *Journal of Abnormal and Social Psychology*, 57, 37-40.

STAIRS, A., 1994, Indigenous Ways To Go To School: Exploring Many Visions. *Journal of Multilingual and Multicultural Development*, 15 (1), 63-76.

STANTON, P. J. & LEE, J., 1995, Australian Cultural Diversity and Export Growth. *Journal of Multilingual and Multicultural Development*, 16 (6), 497-511.

STEADMAN, S., PARSONS, C., LILLAS, K. & SALTER, B. (eds), 1981, *The Schools Council: Its Take-Up in Schools and General Impact. Final Report*. London: Schools Council.

STEBBINS, L. B., ST. PIERRE, R. G., PROPER, E. C., ERSON, R. B. & CERVA, T. R., 1977, *Education as Experimentation: A Planned Variation Model*. Cambridge, MA: ABT Associates.

STEIN, C. B., 1986, *Sink or Swim. The Politics of Bilingual Education*. New York: Praeger.

STEIN, R. F., 1990, Closing The 'Achievement Gap' of Mexican Americans: A Question of Language, Learning Style, or Economics? *Journal of Multilingual and Multicultural Development*, 11 (5), 405-419.

STEINER-KHAMSI, G., 1990, Community Languages and Anti-Racist Education: The Open Battlefield. *Educational Studies*, 16 (1), 33-47.

STEPHENS, M., 1976, *Linguistic Minorities in Western Europe*. Llandysul: Gomer Press.

STERN, H. H., 1983a, *Fundamental Concepts of Language Teaching*. Oxford: Oxford University Press

STERN, H. H., 1983b, Toward a Multidimensional Foreign Language Curriculum. In R. G. MEAD (ed.), *Northeast Conference on the Teaching of Foreign Languages. Foreign Languages: Key Links in the Chain of Learning*. Middlebury, VT: Northeast Conference.

STERN, H. H., 1984, A Quiet Language Revolution: Second Language Teaching in Canadian Contexts: Achievements and New Directions. *Canadian Modern Language Review*, 40 (5), 506-524.

STERN, H. H., 1992, *Issues and Options in Language Teaching*. Oxford: Oxford University Press.

STERNBERG, R. J., 1983, How Much Gall Is Too Much Gall? A Review of Frames of Mind: The Theory of Multiple Intelligences. *Contemporary Education Review*, 2 (3), 215-224.

STERNBERG, R. J., 1985a, *Beyond IQ: A Triarchic Theory of Human Intelligence*. Cambridge: Cambridge University Press.

STERNBERG, R. J., 1985b, *Human Abilities. An Information-Processing Approach*. New York: Freeman.

STERNBERG, R. J., 1988, *The Triarchic Mind: A New Theory of Human Intelligence*. New York: Viking.

STEVENS, A. (ed.), 1991, *Languages for the World of Work*. London: Centre for Information on Language Teaching and Research.

STEWIN, L. L. & McCANN S. J. H. (eds), 1987, *Contemporary Educational Issues*. Toronto: The Canadian Mosaic, Copp Clark Pitman Ltd.

STOTZ, D. & ANDRES, F., 1990, Problems in Developing Bilingual Education Programs in Switzerland. *Multilingua*, 9 (1), 113-136.

STREET, B. V., 1984, *Literacy in Theory and Practice*. Cambridge: Cambridge University Press.

STREET, B. V., 1993, *Literacy in Theory and Practice*. Cambridge: Cambridge University Press.

STREET, B. V., 1994, What is Meant by Local Literacies? *Language and Education*, 8 (1&2), 9-17.

STREET, B. V., 1995, *Social Literacies: Critical Approaches to Literacy in Development*. London: Longman.

STRONG, M., 1984, Integrative Motivation: Cause or Result of Successful Second Language Acquisition? *Language Learning*, 34 (3), 1-14.

STRONG, M., 1995, A Review of Bilingual/Bicultural Programs for Deaf Children in North America. *American Annals of the Deaf*, 140 (2), 84-94.

STRONG, M. *et al.*, 1987, Simultaneous Communication: Are Teachers Attempting an Impossible Task? *American Annals of the Deaf*, 132, 367-382.

STRUBELL, M., 1996, Language Planning and Bilingual Education in Catalonia. *Journal of Multilingual and Multicultural Development*, 17 (2-4), 262-275.

STUBBS, M., 1991, Educational Language Planning in England and Wales: Multicultural Rhetoric and Assimilationist Assumptions. In F. COULMAS (ed.), *A Language Policy for the European Community*. Berlin/New York: Mouton de Gruyter.

SUTTER, W., 1989. *Strategies and Styles*. Aalborg, Denmark: Danish Refugee Council.

SVANES, B., 1987, Motivation and Cultural Distance in Second-Language Acquisition. *Language Learning*, 37 (3), 341-359.

SWAIN, M., 1972, Bilingualism as a First Language. Unpublished Ph.D. Dissertation, University of California, Irvine.

SWAIN, M., 1981a, Bilingual Education for Majority and Minority Language Children. *Studia Linguistica*, 35 (1&2), 15-32.

SWAIN, M., 1981b, Core, Extended and Immersion Programs. *Canadian Modern Language Review*, 37 (3), 486-497.

SWAIN, M., 1984, *A Review of Immersion Education in Canada: Research and Evaluation Studies* (Studies of Immersion Education: A Collection for United States Educators). Sacramento: California State Department of Education.

SWAIN, M., 1985, Communicative Competence: Some Roles of Comprehensible Input and Comprehensible Output in its Development. In S. GASS & C. MADDEN (eds), *Input in Second Language Acquisition*. Rowley, MA: Newbury House.

SWAIN, M., 1986, Communicative Competence: Some Roles of Comprehensible Input and Comprehensible Output in its Development. In J. CUMMINS & M. SWAIN (eds), *Bilingualism in Education*. New York: Longman.

SWAIN, M., 1996, Discovering Successful Second Language Teaching Strategies and Practices: From Program Evaluation to Classroom Experimentation. *Journal of Multilingual and Multicultural Development*, 17 (2-4), 89-104.

SWAIN, M. (ed.), 1972, *Bilingual Schooling. Some Experiences in Canada and the United States*. Ontario: Ontario Institute for Studies in Education.

SWAIN, M. & CUMMINS, J., 1979, Bilingualism, Cognitive Functioning and Education. *Language Teaching and Linguistics Abstracts*, 12 (1), 4-18.

SWAIN, M. & LAPKIN, S., 1982, *Evaluating Bilingual Education: A Canadian Case Study*. Clevedon: Multilingual Matters.

SWAIN, M. & LAPKIN, S., 1986, Immersion French in Secondary Schools: 'The Goods' and 'The Bads'. *Contact*, 5 (3), 2-9.

SWAIN, M. & LAPKIN, S., 1991a, Additive Bilingualism and French Immersion Education: The Roles of Language Proficiency and Literacy. In A. G. REYNOLDS (ed.), *Bilingualism, Multiculturalism and Second Language Learning*. Hillsdale, NJ: Lawrence Erlbaum.

SWAIN, M. & LAPKIN, S., 1991b, Heritage Language Children in an English-French Bilingual Program. *Canadian Modern Languages Review*, 47 (4), 635-641.

SWANWICK, R., 1996, Deaf Children's Strategies for Learning English: How Do They Do It? In P. KNIGHT & R. SWANWICK (eds), *Bilingualism and the Education of Deaf Children: Advances in Practice*. Leeds, United Kingdom: ADEDC, School of Education, University of Leeds.

SWIGART, L., 1992, Two Codes or One? The Insiders' View and the Description of Codeswitching in Dakar. *Journal of Multilingual and Multicultural Development*, 13 (1&2), 83-102.

SWISS FEDERAL STATISTICAL OFFICE, 1994, *The 1990 Population Census, Switzerland in Profile*. Berne: Swiss Federal Statistical Office, Switzerland.

SZEPE, G., 1994, Central and Eastern European Language Policies in Transition (With Special Reference to Hungary). *Current Issues in Language and Society*, 1 (1), 41-59.

T

TABORS, P. O. & SNOW, C. E., 1994, English as a Second Language in Preschool Programs. In F. GENESEE (ed.), *Educating Second Language Children: The Whole Child, the Whole Curriculum, the Whole Community*. Cambridge: Cambridge University Press.

TABOURET-KELLER, A., 1997, Language and Identity. In F. COULMAS (ed.), *The Handbook of Sociolinguistics*. Oxford: Blackwell.

TAHMASIAN, L. T., 1986, Interaction in the Bilingual Child: An Overview. *Early Child Development and Care*, 25 (1), 11-24.

TAKAKI, R., 1993, Multiculturalism: Battleground or Meeting Ground? *Annals of the American Academy of Political and Social Science*, 530, 109-121.

TAKAKI, R. (ed.), 1994, *From Different Shores: Perspectives on Race and Ethnicity in America* (Second edition). New York: Oxford University Press.

TANSLEY, P. & CRAFT, A., 1984, Mother Tongue Teaching and Support: A Schools Council Enquiry. *Journal of Multilingual and Multicultural Development*, 5 (5), 367-384.

TARONE, E., 1980, Communication Strategies, Foreigner Talk and Repair in Interlanguage. *Language Learning*, 30, 417-431.

TARONE, E., 1983, Some Thoughts on the Notion of Communication Strategy. In C. FAERCH & G. KASPER (eds), *Strategies in Interlanguage Communication*. London: Longman.

TARONE, E., 1986, The Arm of the Chair Is Where You Use For To Write. In P. MEARA (ed.), *Spoken Language: Papers from the Annual Meeting of the British Association for Applied Linguistics*. London: Centre for Information on Language Teaching and Research.

TAYLOR, D. M., 1991, The Social Psychology of Racial and Cultural Diversity. In A. G. REYNOLDS (ed.), *Bilingualism, Multiculturalism and Second Language Learning*. Hillsdale, NJ: Lawrence Erlbaum.

TAYLOR, D. M., CRAGO, M. B. & McALPINE, L., 1993, Education in Aboriginal Communities: Dilemmas Around Empowerment. *Canadian Journal of Native Education*, 20 (1), 176-183.

TAYLOR, M. J., 1987, *Chinese Pupils in Britain. A Review of Research into the Education of Pupils of Chinese Origin*. Windsor, Berkshire: NFER-NELSON.

TAYLOR, M. J., 1988, *Worlds Apart?* Windsor, Berkshire: NFER-NELSON.

TE PUNI KOKIRI (Ministry of Maori Development), 1993, *The Benefits of Kura Kaupapa Maori*. Wellington, New Zealand: Te Puni Kokiri.

TEITELBAUM, H. & HILLER, R. J., 1979, Bilingual Education: The Legal Mandate. In H. T. TRUEBA & C. BARNETT-MIZRAHI (eds), *Bilingual Multicultural Education and the Professional. From Theory to Practice*. Rowley, MA: Newbury House.

THOMAS, B., 1986, Schools in Ethnic Minorities: Wales. *Journal of Multilingual and Multicultural Development*, 7 (2&3), 169-186.

THOMAS, B., 1987, Accounting for Language Maintenance and Shift: Socio-historical Evidence from a Mining Community in Wales. In G. MACEOIN *et al.* (eds), *Third International Conference on Minority Languages: Celtic Papers*. Clevedon: Multilingual Matters.

THOMAS, C. J. & WILLIAMS, C. H., 1977, A Behavioural Approach to the Study of Linguistic Decline and Nationalist Resurgence: A Case Study of the Attitudes of Sixth Formers in Wales. *Cambria*, 4 (2), 152-173.

THOMAS, C. J. & WILLIAMS, C. H., 1978, Linguistic Decline and Nationalist Resurgence in Wales. In G. WILLIAMS (ed.), *Social and Cultural Change in Contemporary Wales*. London: Routledge and Kegan Paul.

THOMAS, D., 1996, Early English Immersion in Japan. *Australian Association of Language Immersion Teachers Journal*, 4, 14-17.

THOMAS, G., 1991, *Linguistic Purism*. New York: Longman.

THOMAS, G. E. (ed.), 1995, *Race and Ethnicity in America: Meeting the Challenge in the 21st Century*. Washington, DC: Taylor and Francis.

THOMAS, J. G., 1956, The Geographical Distribution of the Welsh Language. *Geographical Journal*, 122, 71-79.

THOMAS, N., 1991, *The Welsh Extremist* (Second edition). Talybont, Wales: Y Lolfa.

THOMAS, W. I. & ZNANIECKI, F., 1918, *The Polish Peasant in Europe and America*. Chicago: University of Chicago Press.

THOMAS, W. P., 1992, An Analysis of the Research Methodology of the Ramirez Study. *Bilingual Research Journal*, 16 (1&2), 213-245.

THOMAS, W. P. & COLLIER, V. P., 1995, *Language Minority Student Achievement and Program Effectiveness. Research Summary*. Fairfax, VA: George Mason University.

THOMAS, W. P., COLLIER, V. P. & ABBOTT, M., 1993, Academic Achievement Through Japanese, Spanish, or French: The First Two Years of Partial Immersion. *Modern Language Journal*, 77 (2), 170-179.

THOMPSON, G. G., 1952, *Child Psychology: Growth Trends in Psychological Adjustment*. New York: Houghton.

THOMPSON, L., 1993, The Myth of the Asian in Britain. *Primary Teaching Studies: United Kingdom*, 14-16.

THONIS, E. W., 1991, Competencies for Teachers of Language Minority Students. In M. E. McGROARTY & C. J. FALTIS (eds), *Languages in School and Society: Policy and Pedagogy*. Berlin/New York: Mouton de Gruyter.

THORNTON, G., 1986, *APU Language Testing 1979–1983. An Independent Appraisal of the Findings*. London: Department of Education and Science.

TICKOO, M. L., 1996, English in Asian Bilingual Education: From Hatred to Harmony. *Journal of Multilingual and Multicultural Development*, 17 (2-4), 225-240.

TIKUNOFF, W. J., 1983, *Compatibility of the SBIF Features with Other Research Instruction of LEP Students*. San Francisco: Far West Laboratory.

TILLEY, S. D., 1982, A Rank Ordering and Analysis of the Goals and Objectives of Bilingual Education. In J. A. FISHMAN & G. D. KELLER (eds), *Bilingual Education for Hispanic Students in the United States*. New York/London: Teachers College Press.

TITONE, R., 1983, Psycholinguistic Variables of Child Bilingualism: Cognition and Personality Development. *Canadian Modern Language Review*, 39 (2), 171-181.

TITONE, R., 1986, Early Bilingual Reading: Psycholinguistic Theory and Research. *AILA Review*, 3, 24-36.

TITONE, R., 1990, Early Bilingual Growth as an Objective of Basic Education. *Canadian Modern Language Review*, 46 (4), 675-688.

TITONE, R., 1994, From Communicative Competence Through Bilingualism to Metalinguistic Development: Some Theoretical Pointers and Research Perspectives. *Perspectives*, 20 (1), 17-29.

TJEERDSMA, R. S., 1990, *Mercator Guide to Organizations*. Ljouwert/Leeuwarden: Fryske Akademy.

TJEERDSMA, R. S. & SIKMA, J. A., 1994, *Provision of Learning Materials for Primary and Pre-Primary Education*. Ljouwert/ Leeuwarden: Fryske Akademy/Mercator-Educaton.

TJEERDSMA, R. S. & STUIJT, M. B., 1996, *Bilingualism and Education: A Bibliography on European Regional or Minority Languages*. Ljouwert/Leeuwarden: Fryske Akademy/ Mercator.

TODD, R., 1991, *Education in a Multicultural Society*. London: Cassell.

TOLLEFSON, J. W., 1991, *Planning Language, Planning Inequality*. London: Longman.

TOLLEFSON, J. W. (ed.), 1995, *Power and Inequality in Language Education*. Cambridge: Cambridge University Press.

TOMLINSON, S., 1986a, Ethnicity and Educational Achievement. In S. MODGIL, G. VERMA, K. MALLICK & C. MODGIL (eds), *Multicultural Education: The Interminable Debate*. London: Falmer.

TOMLINSON, S., 1986b, *Ethnic Minority Achievement and Equality of Opportunity*. Nottingham: University of Nottingham School of Education.

TOMLINSON, S., 1989, Asian Pupils and Special Issues. *British Journal of Special Education (NCSE)*, 16 (3), 119-122.

TOMLINSON, T. & LAPKIN, S., 1989, Post-Secondary Education and the Development of Bilingual Canadians: Historical and Future Perspectives. *Canadian Journal of Higher Education*, 19 (3), 1-8.

TORRANCE, E. P., 1974a, *Torrance Tests of Creative Thinking: Directions Manual and Scoring Guide*. Lexington, MA: Ginn.

TORRANCE, E. P., 1974b, *Torrance Tests of Creative Thinking: Norms-Technical Manual*. Lexington, MA: Ginn.

TORRANCE, E. P., GOWAN, J. C., WU, J. J. & ALIOTTI, N. C., 1970, Creative Functioning of Monolingual and Bilingual Children in Singapore. *Journal of Educational Psychology*, 61, 72-75.

TORRES, G., 1991, Active Teaching and Learning in the Bilingual Classroom: The Child as an Active Subject in Learning to Write. In O. GARCÍA (ed.), *Bilingual Education: Focusschrift in Honor of Joshua A. Fishman*. Amsterdam/Philadelphia: John Benjamins.

TORRES, L., 1992, Code-Mixing as a Narrative Strategy in a Bilingual Community. *World Englishes*, 11 (2&3), 183-193.

TORRES-GUZMÁN, M. E., 1991, Recasting Frames: Latino Parent Involvement. In M. E. McGROARTY & C. J. FALTIS (eds), *Languages in School and Society*. Berlin/New York: Mouton de Gruyter.

TOSI, A., 1984, *Immigration and Bilingual Education*. Oxford: Pergamon.

TOSI, A., 1988, The Jewel in the Crown of the Modern Prince. The New Approach to Bilingualism in Multicultural Education in England. In T. SKUTNABB-KANGAS & J. CUMMINS (eds), *Minority Education: From Shame to Struggle*. Clevedon: Multilingual Matters.

TOSI, A., 1991, High-Status and Low-Status Bilingualism in Europe. *Journal of Education*, 173 (2), 21-37.

TOUKOMAA, P. & SKUTNABB-KANGAS, T., 1977, *The Intensive Teaching of the Mother Tongue to Migrant Children at Pre-School Age* (Research Report No. 26). Department of Sociology and Social Psychology, University of Tampere.

TOVEY, H., 1985, Local Community: In Defence of a Much-Criticized Concept. *Social Studies (now the Irish Journal of Sociology)*, 8 (3&4), 149-163.

TOVEY, H., 1988, The State and the Irish Language: The Role of Bord na Gaeilge. *International Journal of the Sociology of Language*, 70, 53-68.

TOWELL, R. & HAWKINS, R., 1994, *Approaches to Second Language Acquisition*. Clevedon: Multilingual Matters.

TOWNSEND, D. R., 1976, Bilingual Interaction Analysis: Development and Status. In A. SIMOES (ed.), *The Bilingual Child*. New York: Academic Press.

TREFFERS-DALLER, J., 1992, French-Dutch Codeswitching in Brussels: Social Factors Explaining its Disappearance. *Journal of Multilingual and Multicultural Development*, 13 (1&2), 143-156.

TREFFERS-DALLER, J., 1994, *Mixing Two Languages: French-Dutch Contact in a Comparative Perspective*. Berlin/New York: Mouton de Gruyter.

TREMBLAY, R., 1992, Developments in the Teaching and Evaluation of English and French as Second Official Languages. *Dialogue*, 7 (1), 1-12.

TREMBLAY, R. *et al.*, 1989, *Se lancer en affaires avec un jeu*. Winnipeg: Canadian Association of Second Language Teachers.

TRIANDIS, H. C., 1980, A Theoretical Framework for the Study of Bilingual-Bicultural Adaptation. *International Review of Applied Psychology*, 29 (1&2), 7-15.

TRIM, J. L., 1992, Language Teaching in the Perspective of the Predictable Requirements of the Twenty-First Century. In J. F. MATTER (ed.), *Language Teaching in the Twenty-First Century: Problems and Prospects* (*AILA Review*, 9, 7-20).

TRIM, J. L. *et al.*, 1980, *Systems Development in Adult Language Learning: A European Unit/Credit System for Modern Language Learning by Adults* (Second edition). Oxford: Published for and on behalf of the Council of Europe by Pergamon Press.

TRITES, R. L., 1981, *Primary French Immersion: Disabilities and Prediction of Success*. Ontario: Ministry of Education.

TROIKE, R. C., 1978, Research Evidence for the Effectiveness of Bilingual Education. *NABE Journal*, 3 (1), 13-24.

TROIKE, R. C., 1984, SCALP: Social and Cultural Aspects of Language Proficiency. In C. RIVERA (ed.), *Language Proficiency and Academic Achievement*. Clevedon: Multilingual Matters.

TROIKE, R. C. & SAVILLE-TROIKE, M., 1982, Teacher Training for Bilingual Education: An International Perspective. In B. HARTFORD, A. VALDMAN & C. FOSTER (eds), *Issues in International Bilingual Education*. New York: Plenum.

TRUDGILL, P., 1983, *On Dialect Social and Geographical Perspectives*. Oxford: Blackwell.

TRUDGILL, P. & HANNAH, J., 1982, *International English*. London: Edward Arnold.

TRUEBA, H. T., 1979, Bilingual Education Models: Types and Designs. In H. T. TRUEBA & C. BARNETT-MIZRAHI (eds), *Bilingual Multicultural Education and the Professional: From Theory to Practice*. Rowley, MA: Newbury House.

TRUEBA, H. T., 1988, Culturally Based Explanations of Minority Students' Academic Achievement. *Anthropology and Education Quarterly*, 19, 270-287.

TRUEBA, H. T., 1989, *Raising Silent Voices: Educating the Linguistic Minorities for the 21st Century*. New York: Newbury House.

TRUEBA, H. T., 1991, The Role of Culture in Bilingual Instruction. In O. GARCÍA (ed.), *Bilingual Education: Focusschrift in Honor of Joshua A. Fishman, Volume 1*. Amsterdam/Philadelphia: John Benjamins.

TSUSHIMA, W. T. & HOGAN, T. P., 1975, Verbal Ability and School Achievement of Bilingual and Monolingual Children of Different Ages. *Journal of Educational Research*, 68, 349-353.

TUCKER, G. R., 1984, A Language-Competent American Society. *International Journal of the Sociology of Language*, 45, 153-160.

TUCKER, G. R., 1986, *Implications of Canadian Research for Promoting a Language Competent American Society: The Fergusonian Impact*. In J. A. FISHMAN, A. TABOURET-KELLER, M. CLYNE, B. H. KRISHNAMURTI & M. ABDULAZIZ, *Sociolinguistics and the Sociology of Language. Volume 2*. New York: Mouton de Gruyter.

TUCKER, G. R., 1996, Some Thoughts Concerning Innovative Language Education Programmes. *Journal of Multilingual and Multicultural Development*, 17 (2-4), 315-320.

TUCKER, G. R. & D'ANGLEJAN, A., 1972, An Approach to Bilingual Education: The St. Lambert Experiment. In M. SWAIN (ed.), *Bilingual Schooling: Some Experiences in Canada and the United States*. Ontario: Ontario Institute for Studies in Education Symposium Series 1.

TUNMER, W. E. & HERRIMAN, M. L., 1984, The Development of Metalinguistic Awareness: A Conceptual Overview. In W. E. TUNMER, C. PRATT & M. L. HERRIMAN (eds), *Metalinguistic Awareness in Children*. Berlin: Springer-Verlag.

TUNMER, W. E. & MYHILL, M. E., 1984, Metalinguistic Awareness and Bilingualism. In W. E. TUNMER, C. PRATT & M. L. HERRIMAN (eds), *Metalinguistic Awareness in Children*. Berlin: Springer-Verlag.

TUNMER, W. E., PRATT, C. & HARRIMAN, M. L. (eds), 1984, *Metalinguistic Awareness in Children: Theory, Research and Implications*. Berlin: Springer-Verlag.

TYACK, D., 1995, Schooling and Social Diversity: Historical Reflections. In W. D. HAWLEY & A. W. JACKSON (eds), *Toward a Common Destiny: Improving Race and Ethnic Relations in America*. San Francisco: Jossey-Bass.

U

ULLMANN, R. & GEVA, E., 1984, *Approaches to Observation in Second Language Classes. Language Issues and Education Policies*. Toronto: Pergamon Press.

UMBEL, V. M., PEARSON, B. Z., FERNANDEZ, M. C. & OLLER, D. K., 1992, Measuring Bilingual Children's Receptive Vocabularies. *Child Development*, 63, 1012-1020.

UNITED NATIONS EDUCATIONAL, SCIENTIFIC AND CULTURAL ORGANIZATION (UNESCO), 1992a, *Number of Speakers of the World's Principal Languages in 1989. (Summary Prepared by the Section of Statistics on Culture and Communication, Division of Statistics)*. Paris: UNESCO.

UNITED NATIONS EDUCATIONAL, SCIENTIFIC AND CULTURAL ORGANIZATION (UNESCO), 1992b, *Number of Speakers of the World's Principal Languages in 1989. (Summary Prepared by the Section of Statistics on Culture and Communication, Division of Statistics)*. Paris: UNESCO.

UNITED NATIONS EDUCATIONAL, SCIENTIFIC AND CULTURAL ORGANIZATION (UNESCO), 1995a, *World Education Report 1996*. Paris: UNESCO.

UNITED NATIONS EDUCATIONAL, SCIENTIFIC AND CULTURAL ORGANIZATION (UNESCO), 1995b, *World Education Report 1995*. Paris: United Nations.

UNITED STATES BUREAU OF THE CENSUS, 1992, *Population Projections of the United States, by Age, Sex, Race and Hispanic Origin: 1992 to 2050*. Washington, DC: United States Government Printing Office.

UNITED STATES BUREAU OF THE CENSUS, 1996, *The Official Statistics; IDB Data Access – Display Mode*. Washington, DC: United States Government Printing Office. Internet address: http://www.census.gov/ftp/pub/ipc/www/idbprint.html.

UNITED STATES DEPARTMENT OF EDUCATION. OFFICE OF THE SECRETARY, 1992, *The Condition of Bilingual Education in the Nation. A Report to the Congress and the President*. Washington, DC: Department of Education.

US NEWS AND WORLD REPORT, 1995, *One Nation, One Language?* 25th September, pages 39-48.

V

VAID, J. & GENESEE, F., 1980, Neuropsychological Approaches to Bilingualism: A Critical Review. *Canadian Journal of Psychology*, 34 (4), 417-445.

VAID, J. & HALL, D. G., 1991, Neuropsychological Perspectives on Bilingualism: Right, Left and Center. In A. G. REYNOLDS (ed.), *Bilingualism, Multiculturalism and Second Language Learning*. Hillsdale, NJ: Lawrence Erlbaum.

VALADEZ, C. M. & GREGOIRE, C. P., 1990, Development of a Bilingual Education Plan. In A. M. PADILLA, H. H. FAIRCHILD & C. M. VALADEZ (eds), *Bilingual Issues and Strategies*. London: Sage.

VALDÉS, G.,1980a, Is Code-switching Interference, Integration or Neither? In E. BLANSITT (ed.), *Festschrift for Jacob Ornstein*. Rowley, MA: Newbury House.

VALDÉS, G.,1980b, Teaching Ethnic Languages in the United States: Implications for Curriculum and Faculty Development. *ADFL Bulletin (Bulletin of the Association of Departments of Foreign Languages)*, 11 (3), 31-35.

VALDÉS, G.,1988, The Language Situation of Mexican Americans. In S. L. McKAY & S. C. WONG (eds), *Language Diversity: Problem or Resource*. New York: Newbury House.

VALDÉS, G.,1989a, Teaching Spanish to Hispanic Bilinguals: A Look at Oral Proficiency Testing and the Proficiency Movement. *Hispania*, 72 (2), 392-401.

VALDÉS, G., 1989b, Testing Bilingual Proficiency for Specialised Occupations: Issues and Implications. In B. R. GIFFORD (ed.), *Test Policy and Test Performance: Education, Language, and Culture*. Boston: Kluwer.

VALDÉS, G., 1992a, Bilingual Minorities and Language Issues in Writing: Toward Professionwide Responses to a New Challenge. *Written Communication*, 9 (1), 85-136.

VALDÉS, G.,1992b, The Role of the Foreign Language Teaching Profession in Maintaining Non-English Languages in the United States. In H. BYRNES (ed.), *Language for a Multicultural World in Transition*. Lincolnwood, IL: National Textbook Company.

VALDÉS, G., 1995, The Teaching of Minority Languages as Academic Subjects: Pedagogical and Theoretical Challenges. *Modern Language Journal*, 79 (3), 299-328.

VALDÉS, G., 1996, *Con Respeto. Bridging the Distances between Culturally Diverse Families and Schools. An Ethnographic Portrait*. New York: Teachers College Press.

VALDÉS, G. *et al.* 1988, The Development of a Listening Skills Comprehension-Based Program: What Levels of Proficiency Can Learners Reach? *Modern Language Journal* , 72 (4), 415-425.

VALDÉS, G. *et al.* 1992, The Development of Writing Abilities in a Foreign Language: Contributions Toward a General Theory of L2 Writing. *Modern Language Journal*, 76 (3), 333-352.

VALDÉS-FALLIS, G., 1976, Social Interaction and Code-Switching Patterns: A Case Study of Spanish/English Alternation. In G. KELLER *et al.* (eds), *Bilingualism in the Bicentennial and Beyond*. New York: Bilingual Press.

VALDÉS-FALLIS, G., 1978, A Comprehensive Approach to the Teaching of Spanish to Bilingual Spanish-Speaking Students. *Modern Language Journal*, 62 (3), 102-110.

VALDÉS, G. & FIGUEROA, R. A., 1994, *Bilingualism and Testing: A Special Case of Bias*. Norwood, NJ: Ablex.

VALDÉS, G., LOZANO, A.G. & GARCIA-MOYA, R., 1981, *Teaching Spanish to the Hispanic Bilingual: Issues, Aims and Methods*. New York: Teachers College Press.

VALDMAN, A., 1991, On Teaching and Testing Learner Proficiency in the Case of Foreign Languages Used in a Diglossic Situation. In M. E. McGROARTY & C. J. FALTIS (eds), *Languages in School and Society*. Berlin/New York: Mouton de Gruyter.

VALENCIA, A. A., 1980-81, Cognitive Styles and Related Determinants: A Reference for Bilingual Education Teachers. *NABE Journal*, 5 (2), 57-68.

VALLEN, T. & STIJNEN, S., 1987, Language and Educational Success of Indigenous and Non-Indigenous Minority Students in the Netherlands. *Language and Education*, 1 (2), 109-124.

VAN DEN BERGHE, P. L., 1967, *Race and Racism: A Comparative Perspective*. New York: Wiley.

VAN DER GOOT, A. S., 1994, *Education and Lesser-Used Languages in the European Union: Data Collection by Mercator-Education*. Ljouwert/Leeuwarden: Fryske Academy/Mercator Education.

VAN DER GROOT, A. S., RENKEMA, W. J. T. & STUIJT, M. B. (eds), 1994a, *Pre-Primary Education, Volume 1*. Ljouwert/Leeuwarden: Fryske Academy/Mercator.

VAN DER GROOT, A. S., RENKEMA, W. J. T. & STUIJT, M. B. (eds), 1994b, *Pre-Primary Education, Volume 2*. Ljouwert/Leeuwarden: Fryske Academy/Mercator.

VAN EK, J. A., 1980, *Threshold Level English in a European Unit/Credit System for Modern Language Learning by Adults* (Second edition). Oxford: Published for and on behalf of the Council of Europe by Pergamon Press.

VAN EK, J. A., 1986, *Objectives for Foreign Language Learning. Volume I: Scope*. Strasbourg: Council of Europe.

VAN EK, J. A., 1987, *Objectives for Foreign Language Learning. Volume II: Levels*. Strasbourg: Council of Europe.

VAN EK, J. A. & ALEXANDER, L. G., 1977, *The Threshold Level for Modern Language Learning in Schools*. London: Longman

VANIKAR, R. & DALAL, K. P., 1986, Bilingual Education: Education for All? *Journal of Multilingual and Multicultural Development*, 7 (5), 423-427.

VARESE, S., 1990, Challenge and Prospects for Indian Education in Mexico. *Prospects (UNESCO)*, 20 (3), 345-356.

VÁSQUEZ, O. A., 1993, A Look at Language as a Resource: Lessons from La Clase Mágica. In M. B. ARIAS & U. CASANOVA (eds), *Bilingual Education: Politics, Practice and Research*. Chicago: University of Chicago Press.

VECHTER, A., LAPKIN, S. & ARGUE, V., 1988, *Second-Language Retention: A Summary of the Issues*. Toronto: Modern Language Centre, Ontario Institute for Studies in Education.

VEDDER, P., BOUWER, E. & PELS, T., 1996, *Multicultural Child Care*. Clevedon: Multilingual Matters.

VELTMAN, C., 1991, Theory and Method in the Study of Language Shift. In J. R. DOW (ed.), *Language and Ethnicity. Focusschrift in Honor of Joshua Fishman*. Amsterdam/Philadelphia: John Benjamins.

VERDOODT, A. F., 1997, The Demography of Language. In F. COULMAS (ed.), *The Handbook of Sociolinguistics*. Oxford: Blackwell.

VERHOEVEN, L., 1991, Acquisition of Biliteracy. In J. H. HULSTIJN & J. F. MATTER (eds), *Reading in Two Languages (AILA Review*, 8, 61-74).

VERHOEVEN, L., 1994, Transfer in Bilingual Development: The Linguistic Interdependence Hypothesis Revisited. *Language Learning*, 44 (3), 381-415.

VERHOEVEN, L., 1997, Sociolinguistics and Education. In F. COULMAS (ed.), *The Handbook of Sociolinguistics*. Oxford: Blackwell.

VERHOEVEN, L. & DE JONG, J. H. (eds), 1992, *The Construct of Language Proficiency*. Amsterdam/Philadelphia: John Benjamins.

VERMA, G. K. (ed.), 1989, *Education For All: A Landmark in Pluralism*. London: Falmer.

VERMA, M. K., CORRIGAN, K. P. & FIRTH, S. (eds), 1995, *Working With Bilingual Children*. Clevedon: Multilingual Matters.

VERNEZ, G. & ABRAHAMSE, A., 1996, *How Immigrants Fare in United States Education*. Santa Monica, CA: Rand.

VIDAL, A. B., 1994, La politique de diffusion du Catalan. *International Journal of the Sociology of Language*, 107, 41-66.

VOGHT, G. M. & SCHAUB, R., 1992, *Foreign Languages and International Business*. An ERIC Digest. Washington, DC: ERIC Clearinghouse on Languages and Linguistics.

VOLLMER, H. J. & SANG, F., 1983, Competing Hypotheses About Second Language Ability: A Plea for Caution. In J. W. OLLER (ed.), *Issues in Language Testing Research*. Rowley, MA: Newbury House.

VOLTERRA, V. & TAESCHNER, T., 1978, The Acquisition and Development of Language by Bilingual Children. *Journal of Child Language*, 5, 311-326.

VON GLEICH, U., 1994, Language Spread Policy: The Case of Quechua in the Andean Republics of Bolivia, Ecuador and Peru. *International Journal of the Sociology of Language*, 107, 77-113.

VON GLEICH, U. & SUNY, W. W., 1994, Changes in Language Use and Attitudes of Quechua-Spanish Bilingual in Peru. In P. COLE, G. HERMON & M. D. MARTIN (eds), *Language in the Andes*. Newark, DE: University of Delaware.

VON GLEICH, U. and WÖLCK, W., 1994, Changes in Language Use and Attitudes of Quechua-Spanish Bilinguals in Peru. In P. COLE, G. HERMAN and M. D. MARTIN (eds) *Language in the Andes*. Newark, DE: University of Delaware.

VYGOTSKY, L. S., 1962, *Thought and Language*. Cambridge, MA: MIT Press.

W

WA THIONG'O, NGUGI, 1985, The Language of African Literature. *New Left Review*, April-June, 109-127.

WAGGONER, D., 1988, Language Minorities in the United States in the 1980s. In S. L. McKAY & S. C. WONG (eds), *Language Diversity: Problem or Resource?* New York: Newbury House.

WAGNER, D. A., 1980, Cognitive Perspectives on Bilingualism in Children. *International Review of Applied Psychology*, 29 (1&2), 31-41.

WAGNER, S. T., 1980, The Historical Background of Bilingualism and Biculturalism in the United States. In M. RIDGE (ed.), *The New Bilingualism*. Los Angeles: University of Southern California Press.

WALDMAN, L., 1994, Bilingual Administrative Support Personnel in United States Corporations. *Modern Language Journal*, 78 (3), 327-338.

WALKER, A., 1993, An Educational Project Promoting Bilingualism and Biculturalism in Two North Frisian Communities. In K. ZONDAG (ed.), *Bilingual Education in Friesland: Facts and Prospects*. Ljouwert/Leeuwarden: Fryske Akademy.

WALLACE, C., 1988, *Learning to Read in a Multicultural Society: The Social Context of Second Language Literacy*. London: Prentice Hall.

WARDHAUGH, R., 1992, *An Introduction to Sociolinguistics* (Second edition). Oxford: Blackwell.

WATSON, K., 1984, Training Teachers in the United Kingdom for a Multicultural Society: The Rhetoric and the Reality. *Journal of Multilingual and Multicultural Development*, 5 (5), 385-399.

WATTS, R. J., 1991, Linguistic Minorities and Language Conflict in Europe: Learning from the Swiss Experience. In F. COULMAS (ed.), *A Language Policy for the European Community*. Berlin/New York: Mouton de Gruyter.

WEBB, V., 1996, Language Planning and Politics in South Africa. *International Journal of the Sociology of Education*, 118, 139-162.

WEBER, D. D., 1994, Mother-Tongue Education for Speakers of Quechua. In P. COLE, G. HERMON & M. D. MARTIN (eds), *Language in the Andes*. Newark, DE: University of Delaware.

WEBER, S. & TARDIF, C., 1990, Assessing L2 Competency in Early Immersion Classrooms. *Canadian Modern Language Review*, 47 (5), 916-932.

WEBSTER, J. R., 1982, Education in Wales. In L. COHEN, J. THOMAS & L. MANION (eds), *Educational Research and Development in Britain 1970–1980*. Slough: NFER-Nelson.

WEINREICH, U., 1968, *Languages in Contact: Findings and Problems*. The Hague: Mouton.

WELLER, G., 1978, *Measurement of the Degree of Bilingualism and Biculturalism*. Sociolinguistic Working Paper 48. Texas: South West Educational Development Laboratory.

WELLS, G., 1986, *The Meaning Makers: Children Learning Language and Using Language to Learn*. London: Heinemann.

WELLS, G. & CHANG-WELLS, G. L., 1992, *Constructing Knowledge Together: Classrooms as Centers of Inquiry and Literacy*. Portsmouth, NH: Heinemann.

WELSH EDUCATION OFFICE, 1977, *Welsh in the Primary Schools of Gwynedd, Powys and Dyfed*. Survey No. 5. Cardiff: Welsh Education Office.

WELSH LANGUAGE BOARD, 1996, *A Guide to Bilingual Design*. Cardiff: Welsh Language Board.

WELSH OFFICE, 1983, *Welsh in the Secondary Schools of Wales*. Cardiff: Welsh Office.

WELSH OFFICE, 1984, *The Teaching of Welsh as a Second Language to Adults*. Cardiff: Welsh Office/Her Majesty's Stationery Office.

WESCHE, M. B., 1985a, Immersion and the Universities. *Canadian Modern Language Review*, 41 (5), 931-940.

WESCHE, M. B., 1985b, What Can the Universities Offer to the Bilingual Student? *Canadian Modern Language Review*, 41 (5), 956-961.

WESCHE, M. B., 1993, French Immersion Graduates at University and Beyond: What Difference Has It Made? In J. M. ALATIS (ed.), *The Georgetown Roundtable on Languages and Linguistics 1992*. Washington, DC: Georgetown University Press.

WESCHE, M. B., MORRISON, F., READY, D. & PAWLEY, C., 1990, French Immersion: Post-Secondary Consequences for Individuals and Universities. *Canadian Modern Language Review*, 46 (3), 430-451.

WEST, A. A., 1985, Post-Secondary Bilingual Education at the University of Calgary. *Canadian Modern Language Review*, 41 (5), 947-955.

WHITMORE, K. F. & CROWELL, C. G., 1994, *Inventing a Classroom: Life in a Bilingual, Whole Language, Learning Community*. York, ME: Stenhouse.

WIDDOWSON, H., 1978, *Teaching Language as Communication*. Oxford: Oxford University Press.

WIDDOWSON, H. G., 1995, Discourse and Social Change. *Applied Linguistics*, 16 (4), 510-516.

WIJNSTRA, J. M., 1980a, Attainment in English in the Schools of Wales. *International Review of Applied Psychology*, 29, 61-74.

WIJNSTRA, J. M., 1980b, Education of Children with Frisian Home Language. *International Review of Applied Psychology*, 29 (1&2), 43-60.

WILEY, T. G., 1996, English-Only and Standard English Ideologies in the US. *TESOL Quarterly*, 30 (3), 511-533.

WILEY, T. G., 1996, Language Planning and Policy. In S. L. McKAY & N. H. HORNBERGER (eds), *Sociolinguistics and Language Teaching*. Cambridge: Cambridge University Press.

WILEY, T. G., 1996, *Literacy and Language Diversity in the United States*. McHenry, IL: Center for Applied Linguistics and Delta Systems Co. Inc.

WILKINS, D. A., 1976, *Notional Syllabuses*. Oxford: Oxford University Press.

WILLETTS, K. & CHRISTIAN, D., 1990, Material Needed for Bilingual Immersion Programs. In A. M. PADILLA, H. H. FAIRCHILD & C. M. VALADEZ (eds), *Bilingual Education, Issues and Strategies*. London: Sage.

WILLIAMS, CEN, 1994, Arfarniad o ddulliau dysgu ac addysgu yng nghyd-destun addysg uwchradd ddwyieithog. Unpublished Ph.D. Thesis, University of Wales, Bangor.

WILLIAMS, CEN, 1996, Secondary Education: Teaching in the Bilingual Situation. In C. WILLIAMS, G. LEWIS & C. BAKER (eds), *The Language Policy: Taking Stock*. Llangefni: CAI.

WILLIAMS, CEN, LEWIS, G. & BAKER, C., 1996, *The Language Police: Taking Stock. Interpreting and Appraising Gwynedd's Language Police in Education*. Llangefni: CAI.

WILLIAMS, C. H., 1978, Some Spatial Considerations in Welsh Language Planning. *Cambria*, 5 (2), 173-181.

WILLIAMS, C. H., 1979, An Ecological and Behavioural Analysis of Ethnolinguistic Change in Wales. In H. GILES & B. SAINT-JACQUES (eds), *Language and Ethnic Relations*. Oxford: Pergamon.

WILLIAMS, C. H., 1981, The Territorial Dimension in Language Planning: An Evaluation of its Potential in Contemporary Wales. *Language Problems and Language Planning*, 5 (1), 57-73.

WILLIAMS, C. H., 1982, The Spatial Analysis of Welsh Culture. *Etudes Celtiques*, 19, 283-322.

WILLIAMS, C. H., 1984, Ideology and the Interpretation of Minority Cultures. *Political Geography Quarterly*, 3 (2), 105-125.

WILLIAMS, C. H., 1986, Bilingual Education as an Agent in Cultural Reproduction: Spatial Variations in Wales. *Cambria*, 13 (1), 111-129.

WILLIAMS, C. H., 1987, Location and Context in Welsh Language Reproduction. *International Journal of the Sociology of Language*, 66, 61-83.

WILLIAMS, C. H., 1988, *Language in Geographic Context*. Clevedon: Multilingual Matters.

WILLIAMS, C. H., 1991a, Language Planning and Social Change: Ecological Speculations. In D. F. MARSHALL (ed.), *Language Planning, Volume III*. Philadelphia: John Benjamins.

WILLIAMS, C. H., 1991b, *The Cultural Rights of Minorities: Recognition and Implementation* (Discussion Papers in Geolinguistics No. 18). Staffordshire: Staffordshire Polytechnic.

WILLIAMS, C. H., 1994a, *Called Unto Liberty! On Language and Nationalism*. Clevedon: Multilingual Matters.

WILLIAMS, C. H., 1994b, Global Language Divisions. In T. UNWIN (ed.), *Atlas of World Development*. London: John Wiley.

WILLIAMS, C. H., 1994c, Development, Dependency and the Democratic Deficit. *Journal of Multilingual and Multicultural Development*, 15 (2&3), 101-127.

WILLIAMS, C. H., 1995a, Questions Concerning the Development of Bilingual Wales. In B. M. JONES & P. A. S. GHUMAN (eds), *Bilingualism, Education and Identity. Essays in Honour of Jac L. Williams*. Cardiff: University of Wales Press.

WILLIAMS, C. H., 1995b, Global Language Divisions. In T. UNWIN (ed.), *Atlas of World Development*. London: Wiley.

WILLIAMS, C. H., 1996a, Citizenship and Minority Cultures: Virile Participants or Dependent Supplicants? In A. LAPIERRE, P. SMART & P. SAVARD (eds), *Language, Culture and Values in Canada at the Dawn of the 21st Century*. Ottawa: International

Council for Canadian Studies, Carleton University Press.

WILLIAMS, C. H., 1996b, Ethnic Identity and Language Issues in Development. In D. DWYER & D. DRAKAKIS-SMITH (eds), *Ethnicity and Development: Geographical Perspectives*. London: Wiley.

WILLIAMS, C. H., 1996c, Geography and Contact Linguistics. In H. GOEBL, P. H. NELDE, Z. STARY & W. WOLCK (eds), *Contact Linguistics: An International Handbook of Contemporary Research*. Berlin/New York: de Gruyter.

WILLIAMS, C. H. (ed.), 1982, *National Separatism*. Cardiff: University of Wales Press.

WILLIAMS, C. H. (ed.), 1991, *Linguistic Minorities, Society and Territory*. Clevedon: Multilingual Matters.

WILLIAMS, C. H. & VAN DER MENEW, I., 1996, Mapping the Multilingual City: A Research Agenda for Urban Geolinguistic. *Journal of Multilingual and Multicultural Development*, 17 (1), 49-66.

WILLIAMS, D. T., 1937, A Linguistic Map of Wales. *Geographical Journal*, 89 (2), 146-157.

WILLIAMS, D. T., 1953, The Distribution of the Welsh Language, 1931–1951. *Geographical Journal*, 119, 331-335.

WILLIAMS, G., 1987, Bilingualism, Class Dialect and Social Reproduction. *International Journal of the Sociology of Language*, 66, 85-98.

WILLIAMS, G., 1992, *Sociolinguistics: A Sociological Critique*. London: Routledge.

WILLIAMS, G., 1996, Language Planning as a Discourse. In R. SINGH (ed.), *Towards a Critical Sociolinguistics*. Amsterdam/ Philadelphia: John Benjamins.

WILLIAMS, G. & ROBERTS, C., 1983, Language, Education and Reproduction in Wales. In B. BAIN (ed.), *The Sociogenesis of Language and Human Conduct*. London: Plenum.

WILLIAMS, G., ROBERTS, E. & ISAAC, R., 1978, Language and Aspirations for Upward Social Mobility. In G. WILLIAMS (ed.), *Social and Cultural Change in Contemporary Wales*. London: Routledge and Kegan Paul.

WILLIAMS, I. W., 1987, Mathematics and Science: The Final Frontier for Bilingual Education. *Education for Development*, 10 (3), 40-54.

WILLIAMS, J. D. & SNIPPER, G. C., 1990, *Literacy and Bilingualism*. New York: Longman.

WILLIAMS, J. G., 1915, *Mother-Tongue and Other-Tongue. A Study in Bilingual Teaching*. Bangor: Jarvis and Foster.

WILLIAMS, V., 1971, The Construction of Standardized Tests for Welsh Speaking Children. *Educational Research*, 14 (1), 29-34.

WILLIG, A. C., 1981/1982, The Effectiveness of Bilingual Education: Review of a Report. *NABE Journal*, 6 (2&3), 1-19.

WILLIG, A. C., 1985, A Meta-Analysis of Selected Studies on the Effectiveness of Bilingual Education. *Review of Educational Research*, 55 (3), 269-317.

WILLIG, A. C., 1988, A Case of Blaming the Victim: The Dunn Monograph on Bilingual Hispanic Children on the United States Mainland. *Hispanic Journal of Behavioral Sciences*, 10 (3), 219-236.

WILLIG, A. C. & RAMIREZ, J. D., 1993, The Evaluation of Bilingual Education. In B. ARIAS & U. CASANOVA (eds), *Bilingual Education: Politics, Research and Practice*. Berkeley, CA: McCutchan.

WILLLIAMS, J. L., 1960, Comments on Articles by Mr. D. G. Lewis and Mr. W. R. Jones. *British Journal of Educational Psychology*, 30, 271-272.

WILLLIAMS, J. L., 1974, Bilingualism in Wales. *System*, 2 (3), 60-66.

WILTS, O. & FORT, M. C., 1996, *North Frisia and Saterland: Frisian between Marsh and Moor*. Brussels: European Bureau for Lesser Used Languages.

WINK, J., 1994, Transformation: One School – One Answer. *Journal of Educational Issues of Language Minority Students*, 13, 223-238.

WISS, C., 1987, Issues in the Assessment of Learning Problems in Children from French Immersion Programs: A Case Study Illustration in Support of Cummins. *Canadian Modern Language Review*, 43 (2), 302-313.

WISS, C., 1989, Early French Immersion Programs may not be Suitable for Every Child. *Canadian Modern Language Review*, 45 (3), 517-529.

WITHERS, C. W. J., 1984, *Gaelic in Scotland 1698–1981: The Geographical History of a Language*. Edinburgh: John Donald.

WITKIN, H. A., DYK, R. *et al.*, 1962, *Psychological Differentiation*. New York: John Wiley.

WITKIN, H. A., OLTMAN, P. K. *et al.*, 1971, *A Manual for the Embedded Figures Tests*. Palo Alto, CA: Consulting Psychologists Press.

WITTEK, F., NIJDAM, M. & KROEGER, P., 1993, Cultural and Linguistic Diversity in the Education Systems of the European Community. *European Journal of Intercultural Studies*, 4 (2), 7-17.

WÖLCK, W., 1973, Attitudes Towards Spanish and Quechua in Bilingual Peru. In R. W. SHUY & R. W. FASOLD (eds), *Language Attitudes: Current Trends and Prospects*. Washington: Georgetown University Press.

WÖLCK, W., 1976, Community Profiles: An Alternative to Linguistic Informant Selection. *International Journal of the Sociology of Language*, 9, 43-57.

WÖLCK, W., 1985, Beyond Community Profiles: A Three-Level Approach to Sociolinguistic Sampling. In P. H. NELDE (ed.), *Methoden der Kontaktlinguistik*. Bonn: Duemmler.

WÖLCK, W., 1987, Types of Natural Bilingual Behavior. *Bilingual Review*, 14, 3-16.

WONG FILLMORE, L., 1979, Individual Differences in Second Language Acquisition. In C. FILLMORE, D. KEMPLER & W. WANG (eds), *Individual Differences in Language Ability and Language Behaviour*. New York: Academic Press.

WONG FILLMORE, L., 1982, Instructional Language as Linguistic Input: Second Language Learning in Classrooms. In L. WILKINSON (ed.), *Communicating in the Classroom*. New York: Academic Press.

WONG FILLMORE, L., 1991a, When Learning a Second Language Means Losing the First. *Early Childhood Research Quarterly*, 6, 323-346.

WONG FILLMORE, L., 1991b, Second-Language Learning in Children: A Model of Language Learning in Social Context. In E. BIALYSTOK (ed.), *Language Processing in Bilingual Children*. Cambridge: Cambridge University Press.

WONG FILLMORE, L. & VALADEZ, C., 1986, Teaching Bilingual Learners. In M. C. WITTROCK (ed.), *Handbook of Research on Teaching* (Third edition). New York: Macmillan.

WONG L. Y. F., 1992, *Education of Chinese Children in Britain and the USA*. Clevedon: Multilingual Matters.

WORCHEL, S. & SIMPSON, J. A. (eds), 1993, *Conflict Between People and Groups: Causes, Processes and Resolutions*. Chicago: Nelson-Hall.

WORLD BANK, 1988, *Education in Sub-Saharan Africa: Policies for Adjustment, Revitalization, and Expansion*. Washington, DC: World Bank.

WRIGHT, S. & AGER, D., 1995, 'Major' and 'Minor' Languages in Europe: The Evolution of Practice and Policy in the European Union. *The European Journal of Intercultural Studies*, 5 (3), 44-53.

WURM, S. A. (ed.), 1996, *Atlas of the World's Languages in Danger of Disappearing*. Paris: UNESCO.

Y

YALDEN, J., 1991, *Communicative Language Teaching: Principles and Practice*. Ontario: OISE Press.

YATIM, A. M., 1988, Some Factors Affecting Bilingualism amongst Trainee Teachers in Malaysia. Unpublished Ph.D. Thesis, University of Wales.

YELLAND, G. W., POLLARD, J. & MERCURI, A., 1993, The Metalinguistic Benefits of Limited Contact with a Second Language. *Applied Psycholinguistics*, 14, 423-444.

YITSMA, J. *et al.*, 1994, Ethnolinguistic Vitality and Ethnic Identity: Some Catalan and Frisian Data. *International Journal of the Sociology of Language*, 108, 63-78.

YOUNG, A., 1996, Family and Adjustment to a Deaf Child in a Bilingual Bicultural Framework. Unpublished Ph.D. Thesis, University of Bristol, UK.

YOUNG, R., 1996, *Intercultural Communication: Pragmatics, Genealogy, Deconstruction*. Clevedon: Multilingual Matters.

YOUNG, R. M., 1987, Interpreting the Production of Science. In D. GILL & L. LEVIDOV (eds), *Anti-Racist Science Teaching*. London: Free Association Books.

YTSMA, J., 1986, *The Frisian Language in Primary Education Friesland*. Ljouwert/ Leeuwarden The Netherlands: Fryske Akademy/EMU-Projekt.

YU, V. W. S. & ATKINSON, P. A., 1988, An Investigation of the Language Difficulties Experienced by Hong Kong Secondary School Students in English-Medium Schools: 11 Some Casual Factors. *Journal of Multilingual and Multicultural Development*, 9 (4), 307-322.

Z

ZAPPERT, L. T. & CRUZ, B. R., 1977, *Bilingual Education: An Appraisal of Empirical Research*. Berkeley, CA: Bay Area Bilingual Education League.

ZEHLER, A. M. *et al.*, 1994, *An Examination of Assessment of Limited English Proficient Students*. Special Issues Analysis Center, Task Order Report. Arlington, VA: Special Issues Analysis Center.

ZENTELLA, A. C., 1988, The Language Situation of the Puerto Ricans. In S. L. McKAY & S. C. WONG (eds), *Language Diversity: Problem or Recourse*. New York: Newbury House.

ZENTELLA, A. C., 1994, Ethnolinguistic Pluralism as Scapegoat: The Lessons of the Canadian Experience for US Latinos. *International Journal of the Sociology of Language*, 110, 155-168.

ZONDAG, K., 1991, Bilingual Education in Friesland from the Innovator's Point of View. In O. GARCÍA (ed.), *Bilingual Education: Focusschrift in Honor of Joshua A. Fishman*. Amsterdam/Philadelphia: John Benjamins.

ZONDAG, K. (ed.), 1993, *Bilingual Education in Friesland: Facts and Prospects*. Ljouwert/Leeuwarden: Gemeens chappelijk Centrum voor Onderwijsbegeleiding.

ZUNIGA, M., 1990, Educational Policies and Experiments Among Indigenous Populations in Peru. *Prospects (UNESCO)*, 20 (3), 365-376.

Photographic Credits

The authors would like to acknowledge the following for kindly supplying and granting permission to use the photographs that appear throughout this Encyclopedia. They are listed in the order in which the photographs appear in the book, using the page number and the following key to indicate position where necessary: L = left; R = right; T = top; B = bottom; M = middle. Every effort has been made to obtain permission to use copyright materials; the publishers apologise for any omissions and would welcome these being brought to their attention.

SECTION 1: INDIVIDUAL BILINGUALISM

2. Matt Bryant/Andes Press Agency
3. G. Harrison/Telegraph Colour Library
4T. Yale University
4B. Hugo Baetens Beardsmore
5. Alan Veldenzer/Telegraph Colour Library
6. Skjold Photographs
7T. Peter Sanders
7B. Carlos Reyes-Manzo/Andes Press Agency
10. John and Penny Hubley
11T. François Grosjean
11B. John Dorricott
12. Welsh Language Board
13. Carlos Reyes-Manzo/Andes Press Agency
15. Peter Sanders
16. John Dorricott
17. John and Penny Hubley
18. Skjold Photographs
19. Peter Sanders
20T. Casmir Rubagumya
20B. Mr and Mrs Farzand Ali
21. Alonso Rojas/Andes Press Agency
22T. Armando Gallo/Retna
22B. Tropix/J. Schmid
24T. Al Weinberg, Special Events and Media Productions, the North York Board of Education
24B. Photofusion
27. Joseph Sohm/ChromoSohm Inc./Corbis
28. Carlos Reyes-Manzo/Andes Press Agency
31. Annette Davis
32. Christine Helot
34. Elisabeth Mossler-Lundberg
35. Myers-Halling family
36. C. Stadtler/Photofusion
37. Janine Wiedel
40T. Al Weinberg, Special Events and Media Productions, the North York Board of Education
40B. Tropix/M. Auckland
41T. Alison Wright/Corbis
41B. Charlotte Hoffmann
42. Tropix/R. Cansdale
45. Hideo and Waltraud Oka
46. Tropix/M. & V. Birley
48. Janine Wiedel
50. Tove Skuttnab-Kangas
53. T. Jepson
56. Prifysgol Cymru Bangor
58. Carlos Reyes-Manzo/Andes Press Agency
62. Marian Delyth
68. Valmet, Finland
70. S. Prys Jones
72. Marian Delyth
75. Tropix/D. Davis
77. Al Weinberg, Special Events and Media Productions, the North York Board of Education
82. Jim Cummins
85. Don Williams, Bangor
91. Tony Arruza/Corbis
93. Welsh Language Board

SECTION 2: LANGUAGES IN SOCIETY

96. Corel Corporation
97. Lois Ioan
98T. Douglas Dickins
98B. John Edwards
100. Carlos Reyes-Manzo/Andes Press Agency
102T. George Wharton James, courtesy of the Head Museum, Phoenix, Arizona
102B. State Historical Society of Wisconsin WHi(X3)48856
103L. Associated Press
103R. Denis Hughes Gilbey
104. Corel Corporation
105T. Carlos Reyes-Manzo/Andes Press Agency
105B. Brown Brothers
106. Adastra/Telegraph Colour Library
109. Brown Brothers
111T. State Historical Society of Wisconsin WHi(X3)17708
111B. State Historical Society of Wisconsin WHi(x3)47140/WHi(X3)29241
112. Carlos Reyes-Manzo/Andes Press Agency
113. Carlos Reyes-Manzo/Andes Press Agency
115. Tropix/G. Barnish
116. Alex Gillespie/Edinburgh Photographic Library
119. Brown Brothers
121T. Associated Press
121B. Peter Sanders
122. Tropix/M. & V. Birley
123. John and Penny Hubley
125. Tropix/D. Davis
126. Douglas Dickins
132. Brown Brothers
133. State Historical Society of Wisconsin WHi(X3)25456
134T. Peter Sanders
134B. Tropix/M. & V. Birley
135. Denis Hughes-Gilbey
136. Orde Eliason/Link
137. S. Prys Jones
139L. Philip Schedler/Link
139R. Orde Eliason/Link
141. Associated Press
142. John and Penny Hubley
143. Library of Congress
145. Library of Congress
147. Tropix/M. & V. Birley
149. Suzanne Romaine
151. James Young/The Edinburgh Photographic Library
152. John Curtis/Andes Press Agency
154. State Historical Society of Wisconsin WHi(X3)40142
155. Nancy Dorian
156. George Wharton James, courtesy of the Head Museum, Phoenix, Arizona
157. Douglas Dickins
159. John Dorricott
160. Brown Brothers
161T. Camilla Haugen Cai
161B. St Pol-de-Léon Parish Council
163. Corel Corporation
170. Douglas Dickins
171. Tropix/M. Auckland
172. Marian Delyth
181. Welsh Language Board
183. John Noble/Corbis
184. Tropix/D. Charlwood
185. R. Lunney/National Archives of Canada/ PA–111382
187. Welsh Language Board
189. Joshua A. Fishman
193. Colin Williams
194. Christina Bratt Paulston
196. Paul Souders/Corbis
197. Paul Souders/Corbis
199. Carlos Reyes-Manzo/Andes Press Agency
200L. C. Baker
200R. Israeli Press and Photo Agency
201. Central Zionist Archives
203. Orde Eliason/Link
204. Ofelia García
205. Corel Corporation
212. Denis Hughes Gilbey
215. Wolfgang Kaehler/Corbis
219. Enrico Ferorelli/Telegraph Colour Library
221. John Dorricott, by permission of the Welsh Joint Education Authority
228T. Carlos Reyes-Manzo/Andes Press Agency
228B. Reading and Language Information Centre, University of Reading
229. London Educational Technology Support Service
231. Tropix/M. & V. Birley
242. Welsh Language Board
243. John Dorricott

245. Carlos Reyes-Manzo/Andes Press Agency
246L. Carlos Reyes-Manzo/Andes Press Agency
246R. Superstock Fine Art
247. Carlos Reyes-Manzo/Andes Press Agency
248. John Dorricott/Pater Noster Church, Jerusalem
249. Brown Brothers
250. Fujifotos/Andes Press Agency
251. Tropix: M. & V. Birley
252. Skjold Photographs
253. Carlos Reyes-Manzo/Andes Press Agency
255. Historical Association of Southern Florida, Miami News Collection
258. John Dorricott
262. John Dorricott
263. Carlos Reyes-Manzo/Andes Press Agency
264. Welsh Language Board
265. Welsh Language Board
269. V.C.L./Telegraph Colour Library
270T. Tropix/B. Coulter
270B. John and Penny Hubley
273. John Dorricott
274. Charles and Josette Lenars/Corbis
275T. St. John Pope/Telegraph Colour Library
275B. Alex Gillespie/The Edinburgh Photographic Library
276. M. Grover
278. Carlos Reyes-Manzo/Andes Press Agency
287. Brown Brothers
288. James Crawford
289. Brown Brothers
292. Michael Grecco/Telegraph Colour Library
293. Associated Press
294. John Egan/The Hutchinson Library, London
295. Nick Owen/The Hutchinson Library, London
296. Michael Yamashita/Telegraph Colour Library
299. Matt Bryant/Andes Press Agency
300. Historical Association of Southern Florida, Miami News Collection
303. Tropix/D. Charlwood
304. Tropix: A. & S. Higgins
305T. Tropix: M. & V. Birley
305B. Tropix/M. & V. Birley
306L. Jocasta Shakespeare/The Hutchinson Library, London
306R. Associated Press
310T. Danny Lehman/Corbis
310B. Joseph Sohm/ChromoSohm Inc./Corbis
312. Carlos Reyes-Manzo, Andes Press Agency
314. Roger Coles/Link
316. Orde Eliason/Link
317. Val Baker/Andes Press Agency
319. John and Penny Hubley
320T. Carlos Reyes-Manzo/Andes Press Agency
320B. R. Lunney/National Archives of Canada/PA-166310
321T. Tropix
321B. Tropix/M. & V. Birley
322. Associated Press
323. Dave and Ceri Hill/Andes Press Agency
324T. Tropix/P. Davies
324B. Sean Sprague/Mexicolore
325. Associated Press
326L. Emile Salmanov/The Hutchinson Library, London
326R. Tropix/M. & V. Birley
328. Tropix/J. Lee
329. James Young/The Edinburgh Photographic Library
331. National Archives of Canada/PA-117474
334L. Associated Press
334R. Trevor Page/The Hutchinson Library, London
336. Associated Press
337. Marian Delyth
338. Associated Press
340. John Dorricott
341. Associated Press

SECTION 3: LANGUAGES IN CONTACT IN THE WORLD

352. W.F. Mackey

SECTION 4: BILINGUAL EDUCATION

464. Carlos Reyes-Manzo/Andes Press Agency
465T. Peter Sanders
465B. St George's College, South Australia
466. Reading and Language Information Centre, University of Reading
469. John and Penny Hubley
470. Reading and Language Information Centre, University of Reading
472. Associated Press
473. Al Weinberg, Special Events and Media Productions, the North York Board of Education
475. Al Weinberg, Special Events and Media Productions, the North York Board of Education
476. Carlos Reyes-Manzo/Andes Press Agency
477. John and Penny Hubley
478. National Archives of Canada/PA-111777
479. Tropix/M. & V. Birley
483. Reading and Language Information Centre, University of Reading
487. Welsh Language Board
488. John Dorricott
489. Reading and Language Information Centre, University of Reading
492. John Dorricott, by permission of Mrs Rhian Williams, Meithrian, Caernarfon
494. Helen Ó Murchu
498. Fred Genesee
499L. Evelyne Billey-Lichon
499R. Evelyn Billey-Lichon
504. Andre Obadia
506T. Andre Obadia
506M. Andre Obadia
506B. Welsh Language Board
507. Andre Obadia
510. Teresa L. McCarty
511. Welsh Language Board
513. Sean Sprague/Mexicolore
515. Paul Souders/Corbis
521. Coral Way Dual Language School
524. C. Baker
527T. European School, Culham
527B. European School, Culham
528. European School, Culham
536. Nishimachi International School
537. Reading and Language Information Centre, University of Reading
538. Reading and Language Information Centre, University of Reading
539. Carlos Reyes-Manzo/Andes Press Agency
541. Reading and Language Information Centre, University of Reading
542. Reading and Language Information Centre, University of Reading
543. Al Weinberg, Special Events and Media Productions, the North York Board of Education
545. Brown Brothers
546. Brown Brothers
547. Historical Association of Southern Florida, Miami News Collection
554. AILDI, University of Arizona, Tucson, Arizona
560L. Reading and Language Information Centre, University of Reading
560R. Al Weinberg, Special Events and Media Productions, the North York Board of Education
563T. British Deaf Association
563B. British Deaf Association
564. British Deaf Association
566. British Deaf Association
567. The National Deaf Children's Society
568. The National Deaf Children's Society
582. John Dorricott
586. C. Baker
593. Dr Cen Williams
596. Carlos Reyes-Manzo/Andes Press Agency
597. Carlos Reyes-Manzo/Andes Press Agency
599. Steve Smith/Andes Press Agency
600. Reading and Language Information Centre, University of Reading
603. Carlos Reyes-Manzo/Andes Press Agency
607T. Christa Stadtler/Photofusion
607BL. S. Prys Jones
607BR. Reading and Language Information Centre, University of Reading
608T. Reading and Language Information Centre, University of Reading
608B. Reading and Language Information Centre, University of Reading
609. Nancy Hornberger
610T. Reading and Language Information Centre, University of Reading
610B. Al Weinberg, Special Events and Media Productions, the North York Board of Education
611. John Dorricott
612. Viv Edwards
614. Matt Bryant/Andes Press Agency
617. Reading and Language Information Centre, University of Reading
619. Reading and Language Information Centre, University of Reading
622. Reading and Language Information Centre, University of Reading

623. Al Weinberg, Special Events and Media Productions, the North York Board of Education
624. John Dorricott
626. John Dorricott, by permission of Lingua
630. John Dorricott, by permission of the Welsh Joint Education Authority
635. Welsh Language Board
636. Fujifotos/Andes Press Agency
637. Bernard Spolsky
639. Rod Ellis
643. Wallace Lambert
644. Robert Gardner
650. Stephen Krashen
651. David Wells/Corbis
652. Marian Delyth
658. Welsh Language Board
660. Israeli Press and Photo Agency
665. Skjold Photographs
670. Hulton Getty Picture Library
671. Hulton Getty Picture Library
672. Hulton Getty Picture Library
674. John Dorricott
675. Skjold Photographs
676. Skjold Photographs
677. St Robert Southwell R.C. School
680T. Skjold Photographs
680B. Skjold Photographs
684. Al Weinberg, Special Events and Media Productions, the North York Board of Education
686T. Alderman Jackson School, Kings Lynn, Norfolk
686B. Alderman Jackson School, Kings Lynn, Norfolk
688. John Dorricott
691. Linguaphone
694. Central Zionist Archives
695T. Israeli Press and Photo Agency
695B. Israeli Press and Photo Agency

Index

Author Index

A

B

C

D

U

V

W

Y

Z

Subject Index

A

B

C

D

E

F

G

H

I

J

K

L

M

N

O

P

Q

R

S

T

U

V

W

Y

Z